D0081601

Child Psychology

Child Psychology

Fourth Edition

Ross Vasta
State University of New York at Brockport

Scott A. Miller
University of Florida

Shari Ellis
University of Florida

WILEY

John Wiley & Sons, Inc.

Executive Editor	Ryan Flahive
Assistant Editor	Lili DeGrasse
Editorial Assistant	Aliyah Vinikoor
Developmental Editor	Beverly Peavler
Marketing Manager	Kate Stewart
Production Editor	Sandra Dumas
Senior Designer	Karin Kincheloe
Production Management Services	mb editorial services
Illustration Editor	Anna Melhorn
Senior Photo Editor	Sara Wight
Photo Researcher	MaryAnn Price
Cover Photo	Elyse Lewin/The Image Bank/Getty Images
Text/Cover Designer	Delgado Design, Inc.

This book was typeset in 10.5/12.5 Adobe Caslon Regular by Progressive Information Technologies and printed and bound by Von Hoffmann Corporation. The cover was printed by Von Hoffmann Corporation.

The paper in this book was manufactured by a mill whose forest management programs include sustained yield harvesting of its timberlands. Sustained yield harvesting principles ensure that the number of trees cut each year does not exceed the amount of new growth.

This book is printed on acid-free paper. ∞

Copyright © 2004 by John Wiley & Sons, Inc. All rights reserved.

No part of this publication may be reproduced, stored in a retrieval system or transmitted in any form or by any means, electronic, mechanical, photocopying, recording, scanning or otherwise, except as permitted under Sections 107 or 108 of the 1976 United States Copyright Act, without either the prior written permission of the Publisher or authorization through payment of the appropriate per-copy fee to the Copyright Clearance Center, 222 Rosewood Drive, Danvers, MA 01923, (978) 750-8400, fax (978) 750-4470. Requests to the Publisher for permission should be addressed to the Permissions Department, John Wiley & Sons, Inc., 111 River Street, Hoboken, NJ 07030, (201) 748-6011, fax (201) 748-6008, E-mail permreq@wiley.com. To order books or for customer service call 1-800-CALL-WILEY (225-5945).

Library of Congress Cataloguing in Publication Data:
Vasta, Ross, Scott, Miller, A., Ellis, Shari
Child Psychology, Fourth Edition

ISBN 0-471-14995-0
ISBN 0-471-44892-3 (WIE)

Printed in the United States of America

10 9 8 7 6 5 4 3 2 1

Dedication

Ross Vasta was a wonderful friend as well as a valued colleague. He was also by far the most important contributor to the first three editions of this book—the person who initiated the project, who made the major decisions about its form, and who continually did all the things necessary to bring it to successful completion. We have tried in this edition to continue and to build upon the vision that Ross had for the text and for the discipline of child psychology. We dedicate this book to his memory. The enthusiasm and genuineness that he brought to his writings and teachings will touch many for years to come.

Preface

The major goals of the first three editions of *Child Psychology* were to serve instructors' needs, to maximize student learning, and to reflect accurately and comprehensively the discipline of child psychology as it exists today. These goals have remained central as we prepared the fourth edition. We also, however, have expanded and reworked the coverage in ways that make this edition a truly new version of the textbook, one that captures the excitement and relevance of child psychology as the discipline enters the 21st century.

- We have added a fourth theoretical model—the sociocultural perspective—to the cognitive-developmental, environmental/learning, and ethological/evolutionary perspectives. In addition, we have broadened our coverage of evolutionary developmental psychology. As in previous editions, we discuss these perspectives early in the book to provide an overarching structure and also use the perspectives to help frame discussions in later chapters, providing an integrated view of theory, research, and applications.

- A new chapter, "Cognitive Development: The Sociocultural Approach," introduces interesting and important findings not covered in previous editions and consolidates related material previously scattered throughout the book, giving students a clearer picture of the contributions of this important point of view, as well as providing a theoretical framework for extended coverage of cultural research.

- We have increased and consolidated coverage of development in the context of schools and the family so that readers can focus more explicitly on these areas. School is now included with intelligence testing in the chapter "Intelligence and Schooling," and families are included in the book's final chapter, "Families and Peers." At the same time, we discuss the influence of school, family, and peers throughout the book as appropriate.

- In addition to these broad organizational changes, we have expanded coverage of numerous topics, including genetic bases for development, reading and reading difficulties, theory of mind, connectionism, rule-based and analogical reasoning, creativity and giftedness, peer problem solving, academic motivation, evolutionary bases for sex differences, cultural variations in child-rearing, and divorce.

- Finally, in updating the pedagogical features for the fourth edition, we have added "For Thought and Discussion" questions to foster critical thinking.

MAJOR FEATURES OF *CHILD PSYCHOLOGY*

Several important features have characterized *Child Psychology* throughout each of its editions: an emphasis on a contextualist view of human development, a concern with cultural context and cultural diversity, provision of a balanced theoretical framework for interpretation of findings, and an emphasis on psychology as a science and on the methods through which knowledge is obtained. In addition, *Child Psychology* has always featured topical organization, state-of-the art coverage, and a focus on readability and accessibility to students. The changes made in this edition are intended to maintain and to strengthen these features.

A Contextualist Approach

The most important and distinctive feature of *Child Psychology* remains its emphasis on the contextualist view of human development. Inspired by Urie Bronfenbrenner's seminal work and fueled by the rediscovery of Lev Vygotsky's writings, modern child psychology has increasingly adopted a contextualist perspective. The child is not viewed as a passive recipient of environmental influences but as an active producer of those influences. From the very beginning, the infant engages in a transactional "dance" with the caregiver, each regulating the behavior of the other. As the child grows, development interacts in critical ways with the social contexts in which it occurs, the most important being the family system, the peer group, the school, and the cultural environment.

As in previous editions, *Child Psychology* integrates relevant contextual material throughout the text. Thus, in addition to discussing the effects of schools, families, and peers in separate chapters, we consider such effects for each of the topics for which they are relevant. For example, Chapter 12 examines the contribution of maternal caregiving to the development of attachment, Chapter 13 discusses the ways in which schools can affect self-esteem, and Chapter 14 considers effects of both parents and peers on moral development. This approach allows the course to move from one area of development to another in a topical manner, while including the broad tapestry of variables that affect each area.

We have made three major changes to the present edition that we believe result in an even stronger presentation of contextual forces. First, we have greatly expanded our coverage of the theoretical tradition that is most concerned with contextual forces—the sociocultural perspective as exemplified in the writings of Vygotsky and Bronfenbrenner. We have made the sociocultural perspective one of the guiding theoretical positions that run throughout the book, and we have also added a chapter devoted solely to this perspective. Second, we have reworked the "Intelligence Test" chapter of the previous editions into an "Intelligence and Schooling" chapter. This chapter still provides a basic coverage of the IQ approach, but it adds fuller and more concentrated coverage of schooling than was true in the previous editions. Finally, we have reworked the former "Peer Relations" chapter to create a "Families and Peers" chapter. As is true for schooling, discussions of family influences still occur in the relevant contexts in earlier chapters (indeed, in virtually every chapter of the book). The new organization, however, permits a fuller consideration of general issues in the study of the family (e.g., parenting styles, the family as a system). It also reflects the prevailing view that parents and peers are interacting spheres of influence on children's development.

Cultural Diversity

Each edition of this book has seen expanded coverage of research in diverse communities in North America and in cultures around the world. This remains true for the fourth edition. Discussions of development in different cultures are woven throughout the text. For example, we describe how different cultures foster different approaches to language learning (Chapter 11), we discuss different conceptions of the self and morality across different cultures (Chapters 13 and 14), and we consider cultural variations in child-rearing practices (Chapter 16).

In addition, the inclusion of the sociocultural approach as a fourth guiding perspective has allowed us to provide a conceptual framework within which students can interpret such work. We believe that this change makes our treatment of development in cultural context exceptionally strong.

Balanced Theoretical Presentation

Rather than emphasizing any single theoretical orientation, *Child Psychology* has consistently examined child psychology from the perspectives of the principal theoretical traditions that characterize the discipline. In previous editions three such traditions were emphasized: the cognitive-developmental approach, the environmental/learning approach, and the ethological/evolutionary approach. In this edition we have added the sociocultural approach as a fourth general theoretical perspective. As noted, the writings of sociocultural theorists, in particular Vygotsky and Bronfenbrenner, have always been important to this text. Our new organization, however, allows us to give even greater prominence to such work, and it also provides a more satisfactory picture of distinctions among theories and the current influence of different theoretical positions.

The fundamental tenets of the four general approaches are first presented in Chapter 1. Many of the remaining chapters begin by examining what the four traditions have to say about that topic area and go on to consider relevant research findings and applications. As a consequence, the student can approach the substantive material in these chapters with a conceptual structure that facilitates interpretation, comparison, and critical analysis. For example, the introduction to Chapter 12, on early social development, includes an account of Bowlby's influential evolutionary model, and the subsequent discussion of attachment then considers the evidence in support of this position. Similarly, Chapter 14, on moral development, begins by outlining the theoretical models of Piaget, Kohlberg, and Turiel, each of which is returned to in the later discussion of research on moral reasoning.

Scientific Orientation

In this text we treat child psychology as a natural science and present it in a way that reflects its scientific underpinnings. In addition to providing a full chapter on research methods (Chapter 2), we discuss specific methodological issues frequently throughout the book, such as comparing research designs for examining genetic influences on development in Chapter 3, discussing methods of studying infant perception in Chapter 6, describing computer simulations in Chapter 8, and considering contrasting approaches to assessing infant–caregiver attachment in Chapter 12.

Topical Organization

We have chosen to organize the book topically. By considering each topic area in a single chapter, we believe we can most effectively present and critique the full body of research and theorizing relevant to that area. The 16 chapters can be grouped into four general parts:

- Chapters 1 and 2 provide the foundation of the discipline, covering history, theory, and research methods. In keeping with the scientific orientation of the text, both theories and research methods are presented in some detail.
- Chapters 3–5 focus on biological and physical development, including genetics, prenatal development, birth, growth, and motor development.
- Chapters 6–11 cover sensory and perceptual development; three approaches to cognitive development; intelligence and schooling; and language.
- Chapters 12–16 describe social and personality development, including emotional development, attachment, the self-system, moral reasoning, prosocial and antisocial behavior, gender-role development, family relations, and peer relations.

Although the overall organization is topical, the internal presentation of Chapters 6–16 is developmental. The topic area—be it language, gender roles, or whatever—begins with the newborn and describes development through adolescence. This approach helps the student to appreciate the continuity of growth within each area and also to understand the ongoing interactions between biological processes and contextual influences.

State-of-the-Art Coverage

Information is being generated in child psychology at a staggering rate. To prepare a textbook of manageable proportions, authors must make some tough decisions. We have chosen to present a state-of-the-art treatment of child psychology that focuses on the very latest issues and findings. To this end, this edition incorporates hundreds of new references published in just the last 3 or 4 years.

In addition to such general updating, some chapters include boxed sections titled "On the Cutting Edge." These sections permit a fuller discussion of some especially interesting recent research developments (see Pedagogical Features). Although our focus is on current work, we recognize that some truly classic studies should be known by every student of human development. In such cases, the material is presented in boxed sections titled "Classics of Research" (see Pedagogical Features).

Readability and Accessibility

We have worked hard to make our text above all interesting and accessible to the student reader. We believe that the text's comfortable writing style and the clarity with which concepts are introduced, discussed, and interrelated will enable students to read and understand a rigorous treatment of the issues. Users of previous editions have consistently praised the text's accessibility.

In addition, rather than presenting long tedious discussions of research findings that are likely to overwhelm students, we first decided what concepts and principles we wished readers to come away with and then carefully selected research findings and real-world examples to illustrate and support this material. As a consequence, we believe that we have produced a text that communicates the essence and excitement of child psychology simply and efficiently.

PEDAGOGICAL FEATURES

In our effort to be complete and up to date, we have not forgotten that this is a textbook whose audience includes college sophomores. We have designed into the book a number of features to maximize the likelihood that students will learn the material.

Chapter-Opening Vignettes

Each of the chapters begins with a brief story or anecdote designed to capture the student's interest and to introduce the topic under consideration. In Chapter 3, for example, we open with the story of Carbon Copy, the cloned kitten, and we consider some of the intriguing ethical questions posed by the research. In Chapter 9 we preview the discussion of cultural bases for cognitive development by telling the story of an 8-year-old boy who used various cultural supports to help deliver a baby sister.

"On the Cutting Edge" Boxes

We use boxes selectively in this text. The "On the Cutting Edge" boxes are designed to make students aware of recent and exciting research findings. Among the topics singled out for such coverage are the Human Genome Project (Chapter 3), theory of mind in infancy (Chapter 7), stereotype threat (Chapter 10), and sibling influences on gender-role development (Chapter 15).

"Classics of Research" Boxes

The "Classics of Research" boxes present studies of enduring historical value. Examples include Arnold Gesell's research on motor development in twins (Chapter 5), Harry Harlow's work with attachment in infant monkeys (Chapter 12), and Diana Baumrind's initial studies of parenting styles (Chapter 16).

"Applications" Boxes

These sections present examples of research programs and findings that have been applied to the solution of practical problems in schools, homes, hospitals, and other real-world settings. Examples include prevention of SIDS in infancy (Chapter 5), children's eyewitness testimony (Chapter 9), and methods of promoting literacy (Chapter 10).

"To Recap" Sections

At the end of each major section in a chapter, a brief summary of the material is presented. This organization encourages students to pause and reflect on what they have just read and helps set the stage for the sections that follow. Feedback from the previous editions indicated that students found these sections very helpful.

Visual Summaries

Each chapter ends with a summary of the major points and issues. Using a visual layout, much like a flow chart, these summaries help students organize and review the chapter's material.

Running Glossary

Boldfaced glossary items in the text highlight terms of continuing importance to students. These items are defined in the margin on the same page, as well as at the end of the book, providing a convenient guide for reviewing the material.

"For Thought and Discussion" Questions

Included at the end of each chapter are a set of questions designed to foster critical thinking. Each question notes a finding or principle from the chapter and asks the student to apply it to an issue of scientific, real-world, or personal relevance.

Illustration Program

We reworked many of the figures and drawings from the previous edition to create new, effective illustrations in a full-color format. We also carefully selected many color photos that depict situations and events described in the text, along with some that illustrate laboratory techniques and other research methods.

SUPPLEMENTARY MATERIALS

Accompanying the text is a full package of materials to support student learning and classroom teaching. The package includes the following.

Student Study Guide

The study guide for students contains chapter outlines, learning objectives, key terms, application exercises, critical thinking exercises, self-test questions, and practice exams. This guide was prepared by Alastair Younger of the University of Ottawa.

Instructor's Resource Manual

The Instructor's Resource Manual contains guidelines for the first-time instructor, chapter outlines, learning objectives, key terms, lecture topics, discussion questions, in-class and out-of-class activities, supplemental readings, video guide, and media materials. The guide is prepared by Meg Clark of the California State Polytechnic University, Pomona, and is available on-line at www.wiley.com/college/vasta.

Test Bank

The test bank provides approximately 120 questions for each chapter, keyed to the text in multiple-choice and essay formats. Each question notes the text page on which the answer can be found, and whether the question is factual or conceptual. The test bank is prepared by Susan Siaw of the California State Polytechnic University, Pomona, and is available on-line at www.wiley.com/college/vasta

PowerPoint Files

A set of files with accompanying lecture notes is available on-line at www.wiley.com/college/vasta for instructor use.

Video Library

Instructors can choose from a variety of videos and clips for class presentation from the Child Psychology Video Library. Please contact your local Wiley representative for more details about the different video options.

Web Site

Using the Vasta Web site, located at http://www.wiley.com/college/vasta, students can take practice quizzes for each chapter, and instructors can download the text supplements directly to their computers.

Acknowledgments

A project of this size requires the participation of many people. We are grateful to several researchers for sharing prepublication work with us: Barbara Rogoff, Janette Benson, Kevin Crowley, and Lynn Liben. We thank M. Jeffery Farrer for his input on Chapter 11 and Rachel Stewart Johnson for her assistance with several of the social development chapters. We are grateful to Alastair Younger for his contributions to the third edition of the text. Finally, we would like to make a special acknowledgment of the many contributions of Marshall Haith, who was a coauthor of the earlier editions of the book.

This book is about children, and we never would have entered the field of child psychology—let alone have pursued its study with such pleasure—without the inspiration of wonderful children of our own. They always have our deepest gratitude.

We owe special thanks to our Developmental Editor, Beverly Peavler. This book could not have been completed without her assistance, and incredible patience, at every step in the process.

We would also like to acknowledge the contributions of the many colleagues who have provided reviews or suggestions that have helped to strengthen the various editions of this text. The following individuals served as reviewers or provided other forms of input for the current edition.

Mary Beth Ahlum
Nebraska Wesleyan University

Daisuke Akiba
Queens College of the City University of New York

Dana Albright
Clovis Community College

Maria Bravo
Central Texas College

Nancy Budwig
Clark University

Bruce Carter
Syracuse University

Juan F. Casas
University of Nebraska, Omaha

Dionne Clabaugh
Gavilon College

Robert Cohen
University of Memphis

Donna Couchenour
Shippensburg University of Pennsylvania

Bill Curry
Wesleyan College

Shawn E. Davis
University of Houston–Downtown

Melanie Deckert-Pelton
University of West Florida

John Dilworth
Kellogg Community College

Janet DiPietro
Johns Hopkins University

Rosanne K. Dlugosz
Scottsdale Community College

Ken Dobush
Bridgewater State College

Gina Annunziato Dow
Denisen University

Jerome B. Dusek
Syracuse University

Anne O. Eisbach
Quinnipiac University

Khaya Novick Eisenberg
University of Detroit–Mercy

David Estell
Indiana University

S. A. Fenwick
Augustana College

Donna Fisher-Thompson
Niagara University

William Franklin
California State University

Harvey J. Ginsburg
Southwest Texas State University

Dennis M. Goff
Randolph-Macon Woman's College

Allen Gottfried
California State University

Elizabeth K. Gray
North Park University

Joelle K. Greene
Pomona College

Jiansheng Guo
California State University

Rob Guttentag
University of North Carolina – Greensboro

Dorathea Halpert
Brooklyn College – City University of New York

Steven J. Hayduk
Southern Wesleyan University

Beth Hentges
University of Houston – Clear Lake

Jennifer M. Hill
City University of New York Graduate Center

Jeffrey A. Howard
Eckerd College

Margaret Hellie Huyck
Illinois Institute of Technology

Marsha Ironsmith
East Carolina University

Elaine M. Justice
Old Dominion University

Kathleen N. Kannass
University of Kansas

Kevin Keating
Broward Community College – North

Cheri L. Kittrell
University of Tampa

Paul Klaczynski
Pennsylvania State University

Kathy F. Kufskie
Florissant Valley Community College

Lloyd Lorin La Rouge
The University of Wisconsin – Whitewater

Lana Larsen
University of Maryland, University College

Cynthia Legin-Bucell
Edinboro University of Pennsylvania

Angeline Lillard
University of Virginia

Wendy M. Little
Westmont College

Glenn Lowery
Springfield College

Arlene R. Lundquist
Utica College

Saramma T. Mathew
Troy State University

Jessica Miller
Mesa State College

Terry C. Miller
Wilmington College of Ohio

Mary Mindess
Lesley University

Elizabeth A. Mosco
University of Nevada, Reno

Ron Mulson
Hudson Valley Community College

Robin Musselman
Lehigh Carbon Community College

Jeffrey Nagelbush
Ferris State University

Dawn Niedner
Purdue University Calumet

Sonia Nieves
Broward Community College

Claire Novosad
Southern Connecticut State University

Alan Y. Oda
Azusa Pacific University

Rose R. Oliver
Amherst College

Leanne Olson
Wisconsin Lutheran College

Robert Pasternak
George Mason University

Margarita Pérez
Worcester State College

Wayne J. Robinson
Monroe Community College

Stephanie Rowley
University of Michigan

Claire Rubman
Suffolk County Community College

Larissa Samuelson
University of Iowa

Nicholas R. Santilli
John Carroll University

Pamela Braverman Schmidt
Salem State College

Billy M. Seay
Louisiana State University

Tam Spitzer
St. John Fisher College

Richard A. Sprott
California State University–Hayward

Ric Steele
University of Kansas

Mary Steir
University of Hartford

Margaret Szweczyk
University of Illinois, Urbana–Champaign

Francis Terrell
University of North Texas

David G. Thomas
Oklahoma State University

Lesa Rae Vartanian
Indiana Purdue University, Fort Wayne

Amy Wagenfeld
Lasell College

Alida Westman
Eastern Michigan University

Matthew Westra
Longview Community College

Colin William
Columbus State Community College

Herkie Lee Williams
Compton Community College

Laurie A. Wolfe
Raritan Valley Community College

Gretchen Miller Wrobel
Bethel College

We are also grateful to colleagues who provided reviews of the earlier editions of the book.

Brian P. Ackerman
University of Delaware

Linda Baker
University of Maryland, Baltimore County

Marie T. Balaban
Eastern Oregon University

Byron Barrington
University of Wisconsin-Marathon County

Karen Bauer
University of Delaware

Dan Bellack
College of Charleston

Sarah Bengston
Augustana College

Cynthia Berg
University of Utah

Rebecca Bigler
University of Texas, Austin

Dana Birnbaum
University of Maine

Fredda Blanchard-Fields
Georgia Institute of Technology

Cathryn L. Booth
University of Washington

Theodore Bosack
Providence College

Michelle Boyer-Pennington
Middle Tennessee State University

Kristine Brady
Rider University

Gordon F. Brown
Pasadena City College

Harriet Budd

Roger V. Burton
SUNY at Buffalo

Bruce D. Carter
Syracuse University

Stephen J. Ceci
Cornell University

Xinyin Chen
University of Western Ontario

Stewart Cohen
University of Rhode Island

Jodi Compton
Framingham State University

Ed Cornell
University of Alberta

James Dannemiller
University of Wisconsin–Madison

K. Laurie Dickson
Northern Arizona University

Janet DiPietro
Johns Hopkins University

Shelly Drazen
SUNY Albany

Beverly D. Eckhardt
Albuquerque Vocational-Technical Institute

Melissa Faber
University of Toledo

Beverly I. Fagot
University of Oregon

Shirlee Fenwick
Augustana College

Mary Ann Fischer
Indiana University–Northwest

William Franklin
California State University, Los Angeles

Barry Ghoulson
University of Memphis

Katherine W. Gibbs
University of California, Riverside

Gail S. Goodman
University of California, Davis

Allen Gottfried
California State University, Fullerton

Terry R. Greene
Franklin & Marshall College

Vernon Hall
Syracuse University

William S. Hall
University of Maryland at College Park

Yolanda Harper
University of Tulsa

Yvette R. Harris
Miami University

Vernon Haynes
Youngstown University

Melissa Heston
University of Northern Iowa

Erika Hoff
Florida Atlantic University

Kenneth I. Hoving
University of Oklahoma

Marsha Ironsmith
East Carolina University

Jane Jakoubek
Luther College

Boaz Kahana
Cleveland State University

Kenneth Kallio
SUNY Geneseo

Christine Kenitzer
Texas Tech University

Janice Kennedy
Georgia Southern University

Wallace Kennedy
Florida State University

Marguerite D. Kermis
Canisius College

Katherine Kipp
University of Georgia

Paul Klaczynski
Pennsylvania State University

Gerald Larson
Kent State University

Elizabeth Lemerise
Western Kentucky University

Gary Levy
University of Utah

Angeline Lillard
University of Virginia

Pamela Ludeman
Framingham State University

Kevin MacDonald
California State University, Long Beach

Barbara Manning
University of Nebraska-Omaha

Tammy A. Marche
St. Thomas More College

John C. Masters
Vanderbilt University

Robert G. McGinnis
Ancilla College

Patricia McKane
Augustana College

Margie McMahan
Cameron University

Carolyn Mebert
University of New Hampshire

Morton J. Mendelson
McGill University

Richard Metzger
University of Tennessee at Chattanooga

Barbara Moely
Tulane University

Ernst L. Moerk
California State University, Fresno

Derek Montgomery
Bradley University

Lisa Oakes
University of Iowa

Cynthia O'Dell
Indiana University–Northwest

Lynn Okagaki
Purdue University

Jeff Parker
Pennsylvania State University

Vicky Phares
University of South Florida

Harvey A. Pines
Canisius College

Catherine Raeff
Indiana University of Pennsylvania

Dina Raval
Towson State University

D. Dean Richards
University of California, Los Angeles

William L. Roberts
York University

Marite Rodriguez-Haynes
Clarion University

Karl Rosengren
University of Illinois

Jane Rysberg
California State University, Chico

Nicholas R. Santilli
John Carroll University

Ellin Scholnick
University of Maryland

Frederick M. Schwantes
Northern Illinois University

Gayle Scroggs
Cayuga Community College

Kathleen Sexton-Radek
Elmhurst College

Harriet Shaklee
University of Iowa

Cecilia Shore
Miami University

Susan Siaw
California Polytechnic State University

Robert S. Siegler
Carnegie Mellon University

Gregory Simpson
University of Kansas

Frank J. Sinkavich
York College of Pennsylvania

Rita Smith
Millersville University of Pennsylvania

Thomas R. Sommerkamp
Central Missouri State University

Kathy Stansbury
Mount Holyoke College

Debra Cowart Steckler
Mary Washington University

Ric G. Steele
University of Kansas

Margaret Szewczyk
University of Illinois at Urbana-Champaign

Francis Terrell
University of North Texas

David G. Thomas
Oklahoma State University

Laura Thompson
New Mexico State University

Katherin Van Giffen
California State University, Long Beach

Lesa Rae Vartanian
Indiana Purdue University, Fort Wayne

Diane N. Villwock
Moorehead State University

Leonard Volenski
Seton Hall University

Amye Warren
University of Tennessee at Chattanooga

Beth Wildman
Kent State University

Nanci Stewart Woods
Austin Peay State University

Alastair Younger
University of Ottawa

Martha Zlokovich
Southeast Missouri State University

About the Authors

Ross Vasta

Before his death in 2000, Ross Vasta was Distinguished Professor of Psychology at the State University of New York at Brockport. He received his undergraduate degree from Dartmouth College in 1969 and his Ph.D. in clinical and developmental psychology from the State University of New York at Stony Brook in 1974. He was a Fellow in the American Psychological Society and the American Psychological Association (Division 7). In 1987 he was awarded the SUNY Chancellor's Award for Excellence in Teaching. His previous books include *Studying Children: An Introduction to Research Methods*, *Strategies and Techniques of Child Study*, and *Six Theories of Child Development*. He also edited the annual series *Annals of Child Development*.

Scott A. Miller

Scott Miller is Professor of Psychology at the University of Florida. After completing his undergraduate work at Stanford University in 1966, he entered the Institute of Child Development at the University of Minnesota, where he earned his Ph.D. in 1971. His initial appointment was at the University of Michigan. He is a Fellow in the American Psychological Association (Division 7). He has previously authored *Developmental Research Methods*, second edition, and coauthored (with John Flavell and Patricia Miller) *Cognitive Development*, fourth edition. His research has been in the cognitive area, focusing on Piaget's work, children's understanding of logical necessity, theory of mind, and parents' beliefs about children.

Shari Ellis

Shari Ellis earned her Ph.D. in Developmental and Cross-Cultural Psychology from the University of Utah in 1987. During graduate training, she spent 2 years on the Navajo Reservation in northern Arizona. From 1991 through 1994, she did postdoctoral work at Carnegie Mellon University. She has held teaching positions at Williams College, Virginia Commonwealth University, and the University of Florida. She was awarded a University of Florida University Teaching Award in 1997 for excellence in teaching. Her research interests include parent-child interaction, peer relations, and the development of mathematical and scientific reasoning in school and informal settings. She is currently an Affiliate Assistant Professor of Psychology at the University of Florida and a Post-Doctoral Associate at the Florida Museum of Natural History.

Brief Contents

Contents

Chapter 3 GENETICS: THE BIOLOGICAL CONTEXT OF DEVELOPMENT 71

Chapter 4 PRENATAL DEVELOPMENT 99

Chapter 5 PHYSICAL DEVELOPMENT: BIRTH, MOTOR SKILLS, AND GROWTH 129

Chapter 8   **COGNITIVE DEVELOPMENT: THE INFORMATION-PROCESSING APPROACH**   257

Chapter 11 LANGUAGE DEVELOPMENT 393

Chapter 12   EARLY SOCIAL AND EMOTIONAL DEVELOPMENT   435

1

Background and Theories

*H*ave you ever wondered why children are treated so specially? Have you thought about why we have laws designed to protect children from dangerous toys, dangerous activities, dangerous substances, and even dangerous parents? Why we consider it important that all children receive a free public education—and why they must remain in school until they reach a certain age?

Likely, you have taken these matters for granted. It may seem obvious that children need special attention, care, and protection. The value of educating children, too, may seem self-evident. But these attitudes reflect a certain understanding of childhood and of how children develop. You might be surprised to learn that this understanding is a relatively recent development in Western culture.

Consider, for example, the status of children in the Greek and Roman civilizations, which extended from about 600 B.C.E. to about 400 C.E. Although such great Greek thinkers as Plato and Aristotle wrote of the importance of education, they also defended practices that today would seem unthinkable. *Infanticide,* the killing of newborns, was routine and viewed as an appropriate way to deal with babies who were illegitimate, unhealthy, or simply unwanted. Severe punishment and exploitation of children were neither uncommon nor considered wrong or cruel. The Romans, for example, bought and sold children for various purposes, including domestic work and service in brothels for the sexual pleasure of adults.

Following the collapse of the Roman Empire, the Catholic church attempted to improve the lives of children by promoting an image of them as pure and innocent. The church took a strong stand against infanticide and offered parents of unwanted children the alternative of shipping them away to convents and monasteries—an arrangement that benefited both parties.

Although educational training during this period reached one of its lowest levels in recorded history, the church did provide simple reading and writing instruction to children involved in religious studies. Unfortunately, however, the abuse and exploitation of children remained commonplace throughout the Middle Ages.

The Renaissance began early in the 14th century and extended into the 17th. This era brought increased concern for the welfare of children. In Florence, Italy—generally considered the birthplace of the Renaissance—charitable institutions known as foundling homes were set up by wealthy individuals to take in sick, lost, and unwanted children. Foundling homes, which eventually spread throughout Western Europe, were significant in that they represented a new and growing belief that society had some responsibility for the care and protection of its youngsters.

The Renaissance also saw the reemergence of scientific investigation in such fields as astronomy, medicine, and physics. The science of psychology did not yet exist, however, so the study of human development was primarily the concern of philosophers and religious scholars. As you will see in this chapter, the science of child psychology emerged around the turn of the 20th century. But before that, philosophers discussed and debated various ideas about human nature and human development. We find the roots of our modern scientific understanding of child development in these debates, and we discuss in this chapter important early theorists who contributed to this understanding, as well as pioneers in the science of psychology. ■

DEVELOPMENTAL PSYCHOLOGY AND ITS ROOTS

This book presents the modern science of child psychology. In it, we trace the growing child's development from the embryo's earliest beginnings in the mother's womb to the child's eventual ascent into adolescence. We describe the many factors that affect children's development, as well as how researchers go about the work of identifying them.

Attempts to explain children's development go as far back as history can trace. But child psychology as a science is only a little more than 100 years old. What distinguishes our efforts during this past century is psychologists' use of the scientific method. This approach involves rules that specify, for example, how research evidence should be gathered, how it may be analyzed, and what sorts of conclusions researchers may draw from their findings. Scientists have used this method to study an endless number of phenomena, from stars to starfish. In this book, we examine how they use it to study children.

At first glance, understanding child development may not appear to be very difficult. Certainly the typical behaviors of infants and young children—including their physical abilities, their interactions with others, and even the ways they think—are simpler than those same behaviors in adults. But it is a mistake to conclude that the processes involved are simple. Psychologists have learned that human development is a complex and intricate puzzle, and unraveling its mysteries has proved to be a major challenge. Since the methods of science were first applied to the study of children 100 years ago, we have learned a great deal. Yet the more we learn, the more apparent it becomes that we have only scratched the surface.

What Is Developmental Psychology?

To begin, it is important to understand exactly what psychology is and what psychologists study. Psychology is the scientific study of behavior. The behavior that most psychologists study is human behavior. But any species—from mice to mynah birds to monkeys—can be examined legitimately from a psychological (and developmental) perspective.

Developmental psychology, one of the largest of psychology's many subfields, is concerned with *the changes in behavior and abilities that occur as development proceeds.* Developmental researchers examine what the changes are and why they occur. To put it another way, developmental research has two basic goals. One is *description*—to identify children's behavior at each point in their development. This involves such questions as these: When do babies begin to detect colors? What do 5-year-olds understand about the mind? How do adolescents usually resolve conflicts with their peers? The second goal is *explanation*—determining the causes and processes that produce changes in behavior from one point to the next. This involves examining the effects of such factors as the genes children inherit from their parents, the biological characteristics of the human brain, the physical and social environment in which children live, and the types of experiences they encounter.

Developmental psychologists study behavior changes at all phases of the life cycle. Most, though, have focused on the childhood period, ending at adolescence. For this reason, *developmental psychology* and *child psychology* have traditionally referred to the same body of scientific knowledge. That situation has changed somewhat in recent years as increasing research is being directed toward issues of adulthood and old age. This book, however, focuses on the traditional early period (and so we have chosen the title *Child Psychology*).

Developmental psychology
The branch of psychology devoted to the study of changes in behavior and abilities over the course of development.

Why Study Children?

If developmental psychologists can study any species of animal and any period in the life cycle, why has so much research traditionally concentrated on humans during the childhood years? We have at least five answers to this question.

Period of Rapid Development   Because developmental researchers are interested in studying change, it makes sense for them to focus on a period when much change occurs. During the first part of the life of most species, more developmental changes take place than during any other period. In humans, changes involving physical growth, social interactions, the acquisition of language, memory abilities, and virtually all other areas of development are greatest during childhood.

Long-Term Influences   Another important reason for studying children is that the events and experiences of the early years strongly affect an individual's later development. As the poet William Wordsworth once noted (and many psychologists have since reiterated), "The child is father to the man." Almost all psychological theories suggest that who we are today depends very much on our development and experiences as children.

Insight into Complex Adult Processes   Not all psychologists are primarily concerned with early development. But even researchers who attempt to understand complex adult behaviors often find it useful to examine those behaviors during periods when they are not so complex. For example, humans are capable of sophisticated communication because languages follow systems of rules. Determining what these rules are, however, has proved very difficult.

One approach to this problem is to study our language system as it is being acquired. Thus, in language development, as well as in many other areas, the growing child is a showcase of developing skills and abilities, and researchers interested in different aspects of human development have taken advantage of this fact to help them understand adult behavior.

Real-World Applications   Developmental psychologists often conduct their research in laboratory settings, where they investigate theoretical questions regarding basic psychological processes. Nevertheless, the products of this research benefit children with real-world problems, such as poverty, illiteracy, drugs, and crime. Legislators and other policy makers often turn to psychologists to provide them with usable knowledge regarding the effects of these problems on children and possible ways to treat them (McCall & Groark, 2000; Zigler & Finn-Stevenson, 1999). Developmental research also touches such areas as the effects of day care, classroom teaching methods, and parental disciplinary techniques, among others. Simply put, one reason we study children is to make their lives better.

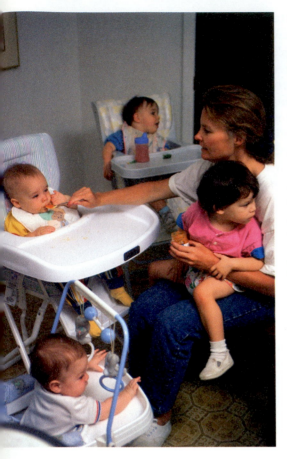

Research in child psychology often addresses issues of applied importance. One such issue is possible effects of infant day care on children's development.

Interesting Subject Matter   A final and important reason so many developmental psychologists have directed their efforts toward understanding children is that the human child is an intriguing and wondrous creature. When we consider that children have attracted attention from artists, writers, and scholars in many other fields of study, it is perhaps not surprising that psychologists, too, have found this subject matter appealing. Our own interest in pursuing this area of science reflects our personal love of children and our fascination with their behavior and development.

Early Theorists

Before there was a field called child psychology, children were topics of interest for philosophers and scientists. Four early scholars—John Locke, Jean-Jacques Rousseau, Johann Gottfried von Herder, and Charles Darwin—offered theories of human behavior that are the direct ancestors of the major theoretical traditions found in child psychology today. These modern traditions include one model that focuses on the influence of the child's environment, a second that emphasizes the role of the child's cognitive development, a third that argues that development is shaped by and embedded in a sociocultural context, and a fourth that is most concerned with the evolutionary origins of behavior.

John Locke, a 17th-century British philosopher, foreshadowed later environmentalists by proposing that a newborn's mind was like a blank sheet of paper on which environment and experiences wrote the script of the child's life.

Tabula rasa
Latin phrase meaning "blank slate," used to describe the newborn's mind as entirely empty of innate abilities, interests, or ideas.

John Locke (1632–1704)   The most famous of early English philosophers was John Locke, a physician as well as a leading political figure of the time. Locke espoused the belief that all men are created equal in the eyes of the law. This principle eventually became the cornerstone of the new government developed by the colonists in America. It also found its way into Locke's views regarding human development.

According to Locke's theory, all children are created (born) equal, and the mind of a newborn infant is like a piece of white paper—a **tabula rasa** ("blank slate"). All knowledge comes to the child only through experience and learning. Children are therefore neither innately good nor innately evil; they are simply the products of their environment and upbringing. This environmentalist point of view also means that any child theoretically is capable of becoming anything—a surgeon, an actor, a skilled artisan—if given the proper rearing and training. Similarly, the wrong environment can produce a scoundrel.

Locke's writings were not all scholarly. He also offered advice to parents on the best methods for rearing their children. Although he stressed the use of rewards and punishments, Locke did not favor material rewards (e.g., candy and toys) or physical punishment. Discipline, he believed, should involve praise for appropriate behaviors and scolding for inappropriate behaviors. Locke also discussed the importance of stimulating children to begin learning at a very early age. Locke's ideas gained wide acceptance among British and European scholars as well as the general public. But within less than a century, this strong environmentalist model was replaced by a very different conception of the child.

Jean-Jacques Rousseau (1712–1778)

Jean-Jacques Rousseau spent most of his life in France, where he became the leading philosopher of his day. He is considered the father of French romanticism, a movement that emphasized themes of sentimentality, naturalness, and innocence. These ideas were reflected in Rousseau's conception of the child.

Rousseau's views on development are presented in his novel *Émile* (1762), in which he describes the care and tutoring of a male child from infancy to young adulthood. Using this literary vehicle, Rousseau outlined his views of human development and offered suggestions on the most appropriate methods of child rearing and education (Mitzenheim, 1985).

In contrast to Locke, Rousseau believed that children are born with knowledge and ideas, which unfold naturally with age. In this view, development follows a predictable series of stages that are guided by an inborn timetable. Rousseau also believed that whatever knowledge the child does not possess innately is acquired gradually from interactions with the environment, guided by the child's own interests and level of development. Thus, the wisest approach to child rearing is not to instruct children formally but to have them learn through exploration and discovery. By emphasizing innate processes as the driving forces in human development, Rousseau's theory contrasted with the environmentalism of Locke and would today be referred to as **nativism.**

Rousseau's ideas had a major impact in Europe, and his nativistic view of development was hailed by both scientific and political writers. As we will see, they reappeared some 200 years later in the work of another Swiss theorist, Jean Piaget.

Johann Gottfried von Herder (1744–1803)

Another thinker whose writings anticipate modern ideas about development was Johann Gottfried von Herder, a leader in German romanticism. Herder's theory of development is essentially an account of socialization into a group or community (Jahoda, 1993). According to Herder, everyone is born into a specific cultural community with a shared language and historical traditions. These shared practices in turn shape the minds of the community's members. Herder was perhaps most revolutionary in his appreciation for cultural diversity; he opposed attempts to impose one culture's values on another. Instead, he argued for **cultural relativism,** the idea that each culture must be examined and evaluated on its own terms.

Herder placed special emphasis on language, the means by which cultural practices and values are transmitted from generation to generation, and argued that studying the diversity of the world's languages offers insights into the history of humankind. He also emphasized the dynamic nature of both language and culture. He believed that language and culture are not passively absorbed by children but are continually reinterpreted and changed by the members of the community: "We live in a world we create."

As we will see, Herder's views on the relationship between thought and language, the dynamic nature of culture, and the importance of a historical perspective foreshadow those of the Russian theorist Lev Vygotsky and modern adherents to the sociocultural approach.

Jean Jacques Rousseau, an 18th-century French philosopher, described his nativistic views of human development in *Émile,* a novel about the growth and upbringing of a young French boy.

Nativism
The theory that human development results principally from inborn processes that guide the emergence of behaviors in a predictable manner.

Johann Gottfried von Herder, a leader of German romanticism during the 18th century, developed ideas regarding culture and socialization that are the forerunner of the modern sociocultural approach.

Cultural relativism
The belief that each culture should be examined and evaluated on its own terms.

Charles Darwin's theory of evolution, developed in the mid-19th century, was quickly adopted by the early developmental psychologists and laid the foundation for the modern fields of ethology and sociobiology.

Natural selection
An evolutionary process proposed by Charles Darwin in which characteristics of an individual that increase its chances of survival are more likely to be passed along to future generations.

Recapitulation
An early biological notion, later adopted by psychologist G. Stanley Hall, that the development of the individual repeats the development of the species.

Baby biography
Method of study in which a parent studies the development of his or her own child.

Charles Darwin (1809–1882) A fourth major ancestor of modern developmental thought was the English biologist Charles Darwin. His theory of evolution, presented in *The Origin of Species* (1859), is the forerunner of the modern ethological approach. More generally, Darwin's ideas have had some influence on almost every major theory of development (Dixon & Lerner, 1999).

Darwin's evolutionary theory begins with the assumption that individual members of a species vary in many characteristics, so that some are faster, some are stronger, some weigh less, and so on. A further assumption is that some of this variation is biological in origin; that is, it results from inborn, hereditary differences rather than from differences in experience. It can thus be passed on from parent to offspring. A third assumption is that most species produce more offspring than their environment can support, which means that the individual members must compete for survival. Depending on the environment, some variations may increase the chances for survival, such as providing better ways of avoiding danger or acquiring food. If so, individuals possessing these traits are more likely to survive and so pass the traits along to future generations. Through this process, which Darwin called **natural selection,** the species evolves to more adaptive forms. The evolutionary model thus suggests that some of the present-day behaviors of humans (or any other organism) had their origins countless years ago, when they somehow contributed to the survival of an earlier form of our species.

Darwin's theory of evolution did not directly address the issue of child development, but his views led other biologists of the time to propose the principle of **recapitulation** (Haeckel, 1906/1977). According to this notion, the development of the individual proceeds through stages that parallel the development of the entire species. As applied to our species, it means that human development follows a progression similar to that which evolved through the various prehuman species (Wertheimer, 1985).

Although the recapitulation theory is no longer scientifically supported, the idea that the child's development repeats that of the species had great appeal for some early developmentalists. Furthermore, by providing a theory that both explained the developing behaviors observed by Rousseau and others and served as a framework for future research on human development, Darwin's writings helped launch the scientific study of the child (Charlesworth, 1992).

Darwin was also a keen observer of child development. Indeed, his detailed record of the growth and behavior of his infant son, "Doddy," was one of the first developmental studies (Darwin, 1877). The intensive study of one's own child's development—a method known as the **baby biography** approach—was an important early method in the attempt to develop a scientific approach to the study of childhood.

Pioneers of Child Psychology

The belief that the development of the child is related to the evolution of the species gave birth to the science of developmental psychology. But the evolutionary perspective was soon joined by other theoretical models as child development quickly became the focus of increasing scientific debate and research. Only a few of the individuals who contributed to the rise of this movement are discussed here. Our purpose is not to provide a detailed history of child study but to point out the origins of some important ideas and controversies that remain a part of modern developmental science.

G. Stanley Hall (1846–1924) Referred to as the father of child psychology, G. Stanley Hall is credited with founding the field of developmental psychology (Appley, 1986). He conducted and published the first systematic studies of children in the United States. Although neither his research nor his theoretical ideas, which favored the theory of recapitulation, ultimately had much impact, Hall did make lasting contributions to the field (Hilgard, 1987; Ross, 1972). As an educator at Clark University in Worcester, Massachusetts, Hall trained the first generation of developmental researchers. He also established several scientific journals for reporting the findings of child development research, and he founded and became the first president of the American Psychological Association. Finally, a more indirect contribution was his invitation to Sigmund Freud to present a series of lectures in the United States—an event that, as we will see later, led to the introduction of psychoanalytic theory into American psychology.

John B. Watson (1878–1958)

The theoretical idea that is generally shared by the scientists of a given period is referred to as its **zeitgeist**—a German term meaning "the spirit of the times." When a science is very young, the zeitgeist can change dramatically from one time to the next. Major shifts in thinking regarding one of the most basic issues of human development—what causes changes in behavior in growing children—had already occurred several times in the centuries before the science of developmental psychology emerged in the mid-1800s. We saw that the zeitgeist of the 17th century was Locke's environmentalist view of human development. This model was replaced first by Rousseau's nativistic explanation and then by the evolutionary theories of Darwin and Hall. As the 20th century dawned, the pendulum began to swing away from biological interpretations of development and back toward the environmentalist position.

John B. Watson was the first major psychologist to adopt Locke's belief that human behavior can be understood principally in terms of experiences and learning. His new approach, which he called **behaviorism,** also differed radically regarding what psychologists should study and which methods of investigation they should use (Horowitz, 1992).

Watson's early career was devoted to the study of animal psychology. Psychologists then (as now) were divided in what they studied and how they studied it. Some, like Watson, concentrated on the physiological workings of the body. But many were exclusively concerned with the psychological functioning of the human mind and, in particular, with consciousness and such issues as how individual perceptions are combined to form ideas and thoughts. The most common research method was *introspection*, which involved engaging research participants in a task and then having them try to look inward and report on the processes occurring in their minds.

Watson found this approach unsatisfactory for a number of reasons. First, little agreement was ever found across participants' descriptions of their internal experiences.

Zeitgeist
The spirit of the times, or the ideas shared by most scientists during a given period.

Behaviorism
A theory of psychology, first advanced by John B. Watson, that human development results primarily from conditioning and learning processes.

Some of the pioneers of psychology invited by G. Stanley Hall to Clark University in 1909. Hall is seated front center, and Sigmund Freud is seated front left.

Further, Watson felt strongly that psychology should follow the example of the other natural sciences and deal only with objective, observable subject matter—in this case, observable behavior. Finally, his interest in animal psychology led him to reject any method that could not also be used to study other species. These ideas were radical for the time, but Watson's persuasiveness soon propelled behaviorism into the forefront of psychological theory (Cohen, 1979).

The basic tenet of behaviorism is that changes in behavior result primarily from conditioning processes. Watson argued that learning occurs through the process of association, as described in the work of the Russian physiologist Ivan Pavlov (1849–1936). Pavlov had shown that any simple reflex can be conditioned to many different stimuli—for example, he conditioned dogs to salivate at the sound of a bell.

Watson believed that this simple conditioning process explained how human behavior changes over time. All human behavior, he argued, begins as simple reflexes. Then, through an association process like the one Pavlov described, various combinations of simple behaviors become conditioned to many stimuli in the environment. Language ("verbal behavior," to Watson), for example, begins as simple infant sounds that grow in complexity as they continue to be conditioned to objects and events in the surrounding environment. Furthermore, as speech grows more sophisticated, it gradually develops a silent form, which we know as thinking, reasoning, and problem solving. Watson therefore believed that it was crucial for psychologists to study infants and young children—not simply to observe early physical changes but to study the first steps in the conditioning process that produces complex human behavior.

The Pavlovian conditioning process that formed the core of Watson's behavioristic theory was straightforward and easy to understand. It was this simplicity, along with Watson's demand for strict experimental methods, that led American psychologists of the time to embrace behaviorism as a major advance in scientific thinking. By the second decade of the 20th century, a new zeitgeist had emerged.

Today, Watson's strict environmentalist views and the major role he assigned to conditioned reflexes are no longer taken very seriously. His contributions to psychology were nevertheless significant. His call for objective methods of study, in particular, brought early experimental psychology in line with the other natural sciences. Virtually all modern experimental psychology is based on the methods Watson espoused, including precise specification of experimental procedures and emphasis on observable and measurable behaviors.

Arnold Gesell (1880–1961)   Just as scientists begin to accept a particular way of looking at things, someone seems to come along with an important criticism of that view or with new evidence that supports some earlier position. So when the zeitgeist swings back toward a prior point of view, it is usually because of new research findings or a more complete theoretical explanation of the facts. Accordingly, developmentalists began returning to the biological model of child development in the 1930s, but it was not because they once again accepted recapitulation theory. Rather, they were persuaded to reconsider the nativistic viewpoint by the research and ideas of one of G. Stanley Hall's most successful students, Arnold Gesell.

Gesell established the Yale Clinic of Child Development in 1911 and spent almost 50 years there studying and describing the development of the typical child. Although Gesell did not agree that human development mirrors the evolution of the species, he did believe that development is guided primarily by biological processes. He therefore felt that growth and the emergence of motor skills (crawling and sitting, for example) should follow very predictable patterns. In his scheme, the environment plays only a minor role, perhaps affecting the age at which certain skills appear but never affecting the sequence or pattern of development. The complex of biological mechanisms that guide development Gesell described simply as **maturation.** The resulting patterns of growth and development were as yet unknown, and Gesell set about to identify them.

Maturation
The biological processes assumed by some theorists to be primarily responsible for human development.

Among Arnold Gesell's most important contributions to developmental psychology were his innovative research techniques, including an observation dome that permitted photographing the child unobtrusively from any angle.

Using observational methods and hundreds of children of many different ages as research participants, Gesell conducted the first large-scale study to examine children's behavior in great detail. This research revealed a high degree of uniformity in children's development. They did not all develop at the same rate—some walked earlier and others later—but the pattern of development was very consistent. For example, almost all children walked before they ran, ran before they skipped, and skipped before they hopped. From his work, Gesell established statistical **norms**—a sort of developmental timetable that describes the usual order in which children display various early behaviors and the age range within which each behavior normally appears (Gesell & Thompson, 1938). These norms proved very valuable to physicians and parents as general guidelines for evaluating developmental progress—so much so that they continue to be revised and used today.

In acquiring this sort of descriptive information, Gesell did not rely on the outdated research methods of the past. In fact, the sophisticated research techniques he developed for observing and recording children's behavior are among his most important contributions to psychology (Thelen & Adolph, 1992). Gesell pioneered the use of film cameras to record children's behavior. He also developed one-way viewing screens, and he constructed a photographic dome that allowed observations from all angles without disturbing the child under study.

Gesell's innovative methods of study and his establishment of developmental norms greatly expanded our knowledge of children's everyday skills and behavior. But his strongly biological philosophy, like most extreme viewpoints, was an oversimplification, because it largely neglected the crucial role of environmental factors. His emphasis on patterns of unfolding behavior and his focus on similarities in children's development, however, may have helped prepare American psychologists to accept the more influential views of another of Rousseau's theoretical descendants, Jean Piaget, whose work we discuss throughout the book.

Norms
A timetable of age ranges indicating when normal growth and developmental milestones are typically reached.

Sigmund Freud (1856–1939)   We backtrack now to 1909, when, as Watson was introducing behaviorism to the scientific world, another important event took place. G. Stanley Hall invited some of the most eminent psychologists of the day, including Sigmund Freud of Vienna, to Clark University to celebrate the institution's 20th anniversary (Hall and Freud are seen seated together on page 7). It was on this occasion that Freud first outlined his grand theory of psychological development. American psychologists were not immediately receptive to Freud's model, and it proved to be no obstacle to Watson's emerging behavioral movement. But the seeds of psychoanalytic thought had been planted in U.S. soil, and in time Freud's views would attract a good deal of attention both inside and outside psychology.

Freud made two major contributions to psychology. His greatest impact was in the area of clinical psychology, where his model of personality and techniques of psychoanalysis continue to represent a major school of thought in psychotherapy. His contribution to developmental psychology was his stage theory of psychosexual development. Although he spent little time observing children directly, he used his patients' and his own recollections of childhood experiences to construct a comprehensive model of child development.

The central theme of Freudian developmental theory is that each child is born with a certain amount of sexual energy, called *libido,* which is biologically guided to certain locations on the body, called the *erogenous zones,* as the child grows. "Sexual energy," in this model, refers simply to the ability to experience physical pleasure. The arrival of the libido at each location marks a new stage in the child's psychosexual development, and during that stage the child receives the greatest physical pleasure in that erogenous zone. Freud identified five stages, beginning at birth and ending in late adolescence (see Table 1.1). Successful movement from stage to stage requires that children receive the proper amount of physical pleasure from each erogenous zone.

Freud's theory of child development is actually a theory of personality formation. It assumes that many aspects of the adult personality result from events during the childhood psychosexual stages. If the child's experiences during a stage are not what they should be, some portion of the libido will remain *fixated* in that erogenous zone, rather than moving on to the next one. For example, if a child is not given the appropriate amount of oral gratification during the first stage, the libido will remain partially fixated

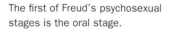
The first of Freud's psychosexual stages is the oral stage.

| Table 1.1 | **Stages of Development: Erikson and Freud** |

	ERIKSON'S PSYCHOSOCIAL STAGES		FREUD'S PSYCHOSEXUAL STAGES	
Ages (yrs)	**Name**	**Characteristics**	**Name**	**Characteristics**
Birth–1.5	Basic Trust vs. Mistrust	Infants must form trusting relationships with caregivers. If care is inadequate, mistrust develops instead.	Oral	Libido is located at the mouth; principal source of physical pleasure is sucking.
1.5–3	Autonomy vs. Shame	As they master various skills—walking, toileting, and so forth—children begin to develop feelings of autonomy and self-control. Failure to meet expectations can lead to shame and doubt.	Anal	Child attains physical pleasure first from having bowel movements and later from withholding them.
3–6	Initiative vs. Guilt	Children take more initiative in dealing with their environments but may experience guilt as a result of conflicts with caregivers.	Phallic	Libido moves to the genital area. Children become sexually attracted to the parent of the opposite sex but experience conflict as they realize the same-sex parent is a powerful rival. Resolving this conflict involves forcing the libido into the unconscious and trying to adopt the characteristics of the same-sex parent.
6–12	Industry vs. Inferiority	School-age children develop industry by successfully dealing with demands to learn new skills; failure leads to feelings of inferiority.	Latency	Libido remains repressed and inactive.
12–18	Identity vs. Role Confusion	Teenagers must develop a sense of identity in various areas, such as occupation and gender, or risk role confusion in adulthood.	Genital	Libido reemerges in the genital area; child again develops attraction toward opposite sex—this time directed toward peers.
Young adult	Intimacy vs. Isolation	Young adults must form intimate relationships or suffer from loneliness and isolation.		
Adult	Generativity vs. Stagnation	Adults must find ways to support future generations, through child rearing or other productive activities, or come to a standstill in their lives.		
Older adult	Ego Integrity vs. Despair	Older adults must come to feel a sense of fulfillment in life or experience despair as they face death.		

at the mouth. Later in life, this fixation will be manifested in the adult's continually seeking physical pleasure in this erogenous zone—perhaps by smoking, chewing on pencils, or having an unusual interest in kissing.

The most complex of the psychosexual stages is the phallic stage. During this stage, according to Freud, children become sexually attracted to the parent of the opposite sex, a situation referred to as the *Oedipus complex*. But they soon experience feelings of conflict as they realize that the same-sex parent is a powerful rival. Children presumably resolve this conflict in two ways. First, they force their desires into the unconscious, a process called **repression**, which also wipes out their memory of these feelings. Then, they compensate for this loss by making a determined effort to adopt the characteristics of the same-sex parent, a process called **identification**.

Although Freud's theory had some influence on American developmentalists, they never fully accepted it, for several reasons. First, it is vague, and its key elements cannot be scientifically verified or disproved. Furthermore, Freud's heavy reliance on unobservable mechanisms, such as unconscious motives, is not consistent with American psychology's belief that science should be based on measurable and verifiable observations.

Repression
Freud's term for the process through which desires or motivations are driven into the unconscious, as typically occurs during the phallic stage.

Identification
The Freudian process through which the child adopts the characteristics of the same-sex parent during the phallic stage.

In spite of its failings, though, Freud's theory of child development includes two fundamental concepts that are generally accepted today. The first is the rejection of both a purely nativistic and a strictly environmentalist explanation of human behavior. Freud was the first major developmentalist to argue for an **interactionist perspective,** which views both inborn processes and environmental factors as significant contributors to the child's development. Today almost all child psychologists subscribe to an interactionist position. The second fundamental concept is Freud's suggestion that early experiences can have important effects on behavior in later life. Most contemporary developmentalists agree with this idea, although few would explain these effects in terms of unresolved childhood conflicts hidden in the adult's unconscious (Beier, 1991; Emde, 1992).

Perhaps a third positive outcome of Freud's theory is that it inspired a number of related models of development that have achieved somewhat greater acceptance in developmental psychology. One of these, proposed by Erik Erikson, is described next.

Erik Erikson (1902–1994)

Erik Erikson grew up in Germany just after the turn of the century but practiced primarily in the United States. His comprehensive model of human development continues to be of interest to many psychologists today.

Erikson's model, although based on Freud's theory, differed from it in some major ways. For one, he believed that development continues throughout life. He thus replaced Freud's five stages of development with an eight-stage model that continues into old age. Erikson also believed that we cannot understand personality development without considering the environment in which it occurs. After studying a number of diverse cultures—including Native American tribes in California and South Dakota, inner-city youth, and the people of India—Erikson developed a psycho*social* model (in contrast to Freud's psycho*sexual* model) of personality that included a major role for social and cultural influences. Finally, Erikson's model was based on the study of normal individuals and emphasized the positive, healthy aspects of personality, whereas Freud's drew heavily on his work with patients in psychoanalysis.

Like Freud, Erikson believed that all children progress through a predictable series of stages. This progression, he argued, is not random but follows a blueprint or timetable built into our genes. According to Erikson, each individual's ultimate goal is the quest for **identity,** which develops gradually across the eight stages. But at each stage, a positive personality characteristic associated with the search for identity conflicts with a negative one resulting from interaction with the social world. For example, in Erikson's second stage, a toddler's newfound physical abilities—such as walking and controlling bladder and bowel functions—lead to the positive feelings of *autonomy* as the child begins to exert more control over his or her life. But these new abilities also tend to cause conflict in the child's social world—with parents, for instance—leading to feelings of *shame* and *doubt*. According to Erikson, the best resolution of these conflicts would have the child leaving the stage with a strong sense of the positive personality characteristic but also with a small degree of the negative characteristic. The eight stages are presented in Table 1.1, which includes a comparison with the stages proposed by Freud.

Erikson's theory is thus also interactionist, combining inborn and environmental factors. Each person is guided through the psychosocial stages by genetic processes, but the individual's social and cultural surroundings help determine how the conflicts are resolved at each stage and so also contribute heavily to personality development.

Interactionist perspective
The theory that human development results from the combination of inborn processes and environmental factors.

Identity
In Erikson's theory, the component of personality that develops across the eight stages of life and that motivates progress through the stages.

To Recap . . .

Developmental psychologists use the scientific method to study changes in behavior and abilities. The two basic goals of their research are to describe behaviors at each point in development and to explain the changes that occur from one point to the next.

Even before psychology emerged as a discipline, four early scholars presented important models of human development. John Locke based his approach on the strict environmentalist position that all knowledge is acquired through experience. Jean-Jacques Rousseau proposed a nativistic model in which development unfolds according to inborn processes. Johann Gottfried von Herder argued that shared cultural symbol systems and practices shape development. Charles Darwin's theory of evolution suggested that many human behaviors have their origins in the past, when they were valuable for our ancestors' survival.

The scientific study of children began with the research of G. Stanley Hall. John B. Watson helped make child psychology a natural science by introducing objective research methods based on observable and measurable behaviors. His behavioristic theory of development held that the conditioned reflex was the fundamental unit of development. Arnold Gesell's research with children renewed interest in the biological perspective by offering evidence that inborn maturational processes account for developmental changes. His observational studies produced age-related norms of behavior. Both Sigmund Freud and Erik Erikson proposed stage theories of child development that took an interactionist view. Whereas Freud's psychosexual stages found little favor with American developmentalists, Erikson's psychosocial stages continue to be of interest to many psychologists today.

ISSUES IN DEVELOPMENTAL PSYCHOLOGY

As we described the views of some of the pioneers of developmental psychology, a number of issues arose repeatedly. Three issues in particular have run through scientific thinking about development almost from the very beginning, and they remain a source of debate today. These issues revolve around the questions of nature versus nurture, continuity versus discontinuity, and normative versus idiographic development.

Nature versus Nurture

The most basic and long-standing issue in child psychology (and perhaps in all of psychology) involves the relative influence of inborn, biological **nature** factors and environmental, experiential **nurture** factors. This debate has existed at least since Locke and Rousseau first proposed their rather pure environmental and nativistic models of child development. The nurture view was later taken up by Watson and other learning theorists, whereas the nature position formed the basis of the theories of Hall and Gesell. The modern debate, however, is far more complex than it was in these early days of psychology (Elman et al., 1996; Rutter, 2002; Spelke & Newport, 1998).

We noted earlier that virtually all child researchers today subscribe to some form of interactionist position, in which both nature and nurture are assumed to contribute to human development. Nevertheless, the nature-nurture debate has not ended. Most psychologists continue to emphasize the importance of either nature or nurture in their accounts of development. For example, when a child demonstrates an unusual gift for chess or athletics, some psychologists believe the talent is due to a fortuitous combination of genes from parents who are probably pretty gifted in similar ways. Others point to environmental factors, such as the opportunities children are provided to acquire and practice the necessary skills and the rewards they receive for high levels of achievement.

Another example can be found in the development of aggressive behavior. Some psychologists explain aggressive behavior in terms of environmental factors, such as exposure to violent models or ineffective parenting that rewards aggression. Others might offer a biological account that focuses on an inherited disposition that makes it difficult for the child to regulate his or her emotions or perhaps neurological problems that interfere with the processing of social cues.

In reality, of course, both high levels of achievement and aggressive behavior are best understood in terms of a combination of biological and experiential factors. Children who excel in chess or in sports probably are born with a unique combination of

Nature versus nurture debate
The scientific controversy regarding whether the primary source of developmental change rests in biological (nature) factors or in environmental and experiential (nurture) factors.

Alexandra Nachita is a child artist prodigy. Her accomplishments are a result of both nature (the favorable genes with which she was born) and nurture (the supportive environment in which she has developed).

Continuity versus discontinuity debate
The scientific controversy regarding whether development is constant and connected (continuous) or uneven and disconnected (discontinuous).

Normative versus idiographic development
The question of whether research should focus on identifying common-alities in human development (normative development) or on the causes of individual differences (idiographic development).

characteristics that increases their likelihood of success in those domains. In turn, their early success often leads to increased opportunities and rewards. Similarly, some antisocial children may well have a biologically based propensity to respond with aggression to frustrating situations. Nonetheless, the fact that they act on their aggressive impulses is the result of learning.

The processes by which biological and environmental factors work together over the course of development are as yet far from understood. Recent advances in the fields of behavioral genetics and the brain sciences suggest that these processes may be even more complex than psychologists initially believed. We now know, for example, that biological entities such as genes and basic brain chemistry once thought to be unchanging are themselves responsive to environmental influence (Plomin & Rutter, 1998; Shonkoff & Phillips, 2000). Several theoretical models describing how our genes and environment may work together to guide our behavior are discussed in Chapter 3.

Nature-versus-nurture questions arise in almost every topic considered in this text. At times, however, they appear under different labels, such as heredity versus environment, maturation versus learning, or emergent abilities versus acquired skills. Whatever the name, these debates tend to involve the same fundamental issue.

Continuity versus Discontinuity

A second long-standing issue in child psychology is whether development displays **continuity** or **discontinuity.** This debate actually has two components (Emde & Harmon, 1984). One involves the pattern of development. Is development smooth and stable, with new abilities, skills, and knowledge gradually added at a relatively uniform pace (continuous)? Or does development occur at different rates, alternating between periods of little change and periods of abrupt, rapid change (discontinuous)? The second component involves the connectedness of development. Continuity theorists contend that many of the behaviors and abilities we see in adolescents and adults can be traced directly back to development early in life. Discontinuity theorists, in contrast, suggest that some aspects of development emerge relatively independently of what has come before and cannot be predicted from the child's previous behavior (Clarke & Clarke, 1976).

The continuity model is often associated with the belief that human behavior consists of many individual skills that are added one at a time, usually through learning and experience. As children acquire more and more of these skills, they combine and recombine them to produce increasingly complex abilities. This approach emphasizes quantitative change—the simpler elements are essentially added together to produce the more advanced capabilities—and tends to characterize environmentalist models of development. In contrast, psychologists who favor the discontinuity model usually hold that development is guided primarily by internal biological factors. Stage theorists, for example, argue that the unevenness of children's development—relatively stable periods followed by abrupt changes—reflects the discontinuous nature of the changes taking place in the underlying structures of the body and brain. Thus, development is thought to involve qualitative changes in previous abilities or behaviors.

Like the nature-versus-nurture issue, the question of continuity versus discontinuity is not all-or-nothing. Psychologists on both sides of the debate agree that some developmental processes are more accurately described by one model and others by the competing model (Bjorklund, 1997; Rutter, 1987).

Normative versus Idiographic Development

A third issue that commonly arises in child psychology is not a matter of debate so much as it is a description of a researcher's focus of study. Some psychologists are concerned with **normative** development, meaning what children have in common or how development is similar for all children. Others focus on **idiographic** development, meaning the differences in development from one child to the next.

Normative research attempts to identify commonalities among children, whereas idiographic research is concerned with why one child is different from the next.

Normative research focuses on the "average" child, with the primary goal of identifying and describing how normal development proceeds from step to step. A related issue involves the search for **universals of development**—behaviors or patterns of development that characterize all children everywhere. Idiographic research, in contrast, centers on the individual child and the factors that produce human diversity.

Research on language development illustrates these two approaches. Researchers interested in normative development search for common patterns of linguistic development both in children who speak the same language and in children who speak different languages. Theorists who adopt an idiographic perspective are more concerned with identifying and explaining the individual differences that are evident as children master language. Such differences might result from differences in experience, such as the type of speech adults use when talking with children, or from biological factors, such as brain trauma or inheritance of a particular genetic disorder.

Historically, the normative approach was associated with biological theories of development, such as Gesell's, whereas the idiographic approach was associated with researchers who emphasized environmental and experiential processes. This distinction is no longer tenable, however. Today, it is clear that individual differences in development can be due to biological factors and universals of development can be due to common experiences.

Universals of development
Aspects of development or behavior that are common to children everywhere.

 To Recap . . .

Three issues arise frequently in child psychology research. The nature-versus-nurture issue focuses on whether the primary source of developmental change is inborn and biological or environmental and experiential. The continuity-versus-discontinuity issue concerns whether the pattern of development is constant or uneven and whether development shows connectedness between early and later characteristics. The normative-versus-idiographic issue involves the researcher's preference for focusing either on the commonalities of children's development and the search for universals or on the factors that produce individual differences among children, such as cultural influences.

THEORIES OF DEVELOPMENT: COGNITIVE-DEVELOPMENTAL APPROACHES

Most psychologists characterize themselves in terms of a particular theoretical orientation—that is, their view of how development occurs and which factors are most responsible for changes in children's behavior. Today, the majority of child psychologists identify themselves with one of four general theoretical views: the cognitive-developmental approach, the sociocultural approach, the environmental/learning approach, or the evolutionary approach. In the remainder of this chapter, we outline the principal ideas and underlying assumptions of these four theories. Then, as we discuss various topics throughout the rest of the book, we will compare and contrast the approaches taken by each of the theories, including the types of questions they ask and the research methods they prefer.

We begin with the cognitive-developmental approach. As we have seen, the roots of this tradition lie in the 18th-century writings of Rousseau. The modern version of the approach includes several related theories. For years, it was most closely associated with the work of Jean Piaget. Since the 1970s, however, several other cognitively oriented models have become popular among psychologists.

An important characteristic of this approach is its emphasis on cognition. According to these theories, the changes we witness in children's behaviors and abilities arise largely from changes in their knowledge and intellectual skills. The major goals for psychologists of this tradition, therefore, are to specify what children know, how this knowledge is organized, and how it changes or develops.

Piaget's Theory

If we had to select one psychologist whose work has had the greatest influence on the study of child development, we would have to consider Jean Piaget (1896–1980) a very strong candidate. His ideas have inspired more research than those of any other theorist, and his conception of human development revolutionized thinking about children and their behavior.

Piaget was born and raised in Switzerland. From boyhood, he was interested in science, particularly biology and animal behavior. Although he eventually left this area of study, his background in biology is reflected in his theory of child development. Piaget had always been drawn to the study of psychology, and after earning his doctorate in 1918, he moved from Switzerland to Paris, where he became involved in the development of intelligence tests for children.

Intelligence testing was a new field at this time, and two of its founders, Alfred Binet and Theodore Simon, were attempting to develop tests that could predict children's success in school. Piaget was hired by Simon to administer the tests, which gave him his first real experience with developmental work. But unlike his employers, Piaget was less interested in the number of test items children answered correctly than in the reasons for their incorrect responses. Children of different ages, he observed, not only knew different amounts of information but also looked at the world in very different ways. Their answers revealed *qualitative* (style-related) differences in thinking beyond the *quantitative* (amount-related) differences in factual information.

After two years in Paris, Piaget returned to Switzerland and began his own research on the development of children's knowledge. Piaget called his area of interest **genetic epistemology,** by which he meant the study of the nature of knowledge in young children and how it changes as they grow older. Piaget was interested not in the precise knowledge and facts that children possess—for example, *what* children know when they enter school—but rather in how they go about acquiring and using that knowledge— that is, *how* children think.

To find support for his theory, Piaget developed his own research technique. Whereas Gesell's methods involved observing children without interfering with them, Piaget challenged children with simple tasks and verbal problems that required solutions and explanations. His technique, known as the **clinical method,** involved a loosely structured interview in which he asked a question or posed a problem and then, depending on the child's response, followed up with other questions that might reveal the child's reasoning or problem-solving approach.

Piaget's research initially attracted some attention in the United States during the 1920s and 1930s. But his writings were difficult for American scholars to understand because they contained many terms and concepts that differed from the scientific language Americans were using. Piaget's somewhat informal methods of investigation

Jean Piaget is one pioneer of child psychology whose early ideas remain largely accepted today by many researchers.

Genetic epistemology

Piaget's term for the study of children's knowledge and how it changes with development.

Clinical method

Piaget's principal research method, which involved a semistructured interview with questions designed to probe children's understanding of various concepts.

were also viewed as a problem by more rigorous experimental researchers. During the 1940s and 1950s, American child psychology once again turned toward environmental and conditioning models, and interest in Piaget's theory disappeared.

Beginning in the late 1950s, however, American psychologists began to rediscover Piaget's work. His theoretical writings were translated into more familiar concepts, and his studies were replicated under controlled experimental conditions (Flavell, 1963). In addition, his theory generated many new questions that psychologists felt could and should be investigated, such as questions about children's understanding of time, logic, and causality. Piaget's many books on child psychology remain the greatest contribution to the field by a single scholar (Beilin, 1992).

According to Piaget's theory, human development can be described in terms of *functions* and *cognitive structures.* The functions are inborn biological processes that are the same for everyone and remain unchanged throughout our lives. Their purpose is to construct internal cognitive structures. The structures, in contrast, change repeatedly as the child grows.

Cognitive Structures
The most fundamental aspect of Piaget's theory, and often the most difficult to understand, is the belief that intelligence is a process—not something that a child *has* but something that a child *does.* Piaget's child does not possess knowledge passively but understands the world by acting or operating on it.

For example, Piaget would describe an infant's knowledge of a ball in terms of the various actions the infant can perform with it—pushing the ball, throwing it, mouthing it, and so on. These actions are a reflection of the cognitive structures of infancy, which are called **schemes.** Note that a scheme involves two elements: an object in the environment (such as a ball), and the child's reactions to the object. A scheme is therefore not a physical structure but a psychological one. Early on, the infant has comparatively few of these schemes, and they are related to one another in very simple ways. As development proceeds, however, schemes increase in both number and complexity of organization. These two characteristics of children's cognitive structures—number and complexity—define the child's intelligence at any point in development.

Schemes and other cognitive structures also display certain flexibilities. An infant does not perform exactly the same behavior with every ball she encounters—some may produce more squeezing, others more rolling—nor are the infant's reactions the same with every object. The way a ball is grasped may be somewhat different from the way a rattle is grasped, and the way either of these objects is sucked may be different from the way a nipple is sucked. Cognitive structures are flexible in another sense—they change over time. A particular scheme, such as grasping, reflects more and more skill as the infant applies it to more and more objects. In this way, schemes eventually become more individualized, or *differentiated,* so that a ball becomes primarily an object to be thrown, a rattle primarily an object to be shaken, and a nipple primarily an object to be sucked.

Schemes
Piaget's term for the cognitive structures of infancy. A scheme consists of a set of skilled, flexible action patterns through which the child understands the world.

In Piaget's theory, children act upon the world at every stage of development. The schemes with which they do so, however, change as the child develops.

Beyond these simple schemes of infancy, new and higher-level cognitive structures gradually emerge. An 8-year-old confronted with a ball, for example, still has all the earlier schemes available (although sucking is not a very likely response), but the older child can also understand a ball by acting on it using mental operations, such as assigning it certain properties (color, size), actions (bouncing, hitting), or capabilities (being a member of the class "round things").

For Piaget, *development* referred to this continual reorganization of knowledge into new and more complex structures. Much of our discussion in Chapter 7 concerns what these structures are and how they change with development.

Functions   The functions that guide cognitive development are also central to Piaget's theory. Piaget stressed two general functions, both of which reflect his training in biology. One is **organization.** Because an individual's cognitive structures are interrelated, any new knowledge must be fitted into the existing system. According to Piaget, it is this need for integrating new information, rather than simply adding it on, that forces our cognitive structures to become ever more elaborately organized.

The second function is **adaptation,** which in general terms refers to an organism's attempt to fit with its environment in ways that promote survival. In Piaget's model, cognitive adaptation involves two processes. **Assimilation** entails trying to make sense of new experiences in terms of our existing cognitive structures. The infant who brings everything to his mouth to suck is demonstrating assimilation, as is the toddler who calls all men "Daddy." Note that assimilation may require some distortion of the new information to make it fit into the child's existing schemes. But trying to fit new things into what we already know is a necessary part of adapting to the world.

When new information is too different or too complex, **accommodation** occurs. Here, our cognitive structures change in order to integrate the new experiences. For example, the infant eventually learns that not all objects are to be sucked, just as the toddler learns that different labels or names need to be applied to different men. It is primarily through accommodation that the number and complexity of children's cognitive structures increase—that is, that intelligence grows.

Piaget assumed that assimilation and accommodation operate closely together. A growing child is continually making slight distortions of information to assimilate it into existing structures while also making slight modifications in these structures to accommodate new objects or events. The interplay of these two functions illustrates another important aspect of Piaget's theory, the concept of **constructivism.** Children's knowledge of events in their environment is not an exact reproduction of those events—it is not like a perfect photograph of what they have seen or a precise recording of what they have heard. Children take information from the environment and bend, shape, or distort it until it fits comfortably into their existing cognitive organization. As we said earlier, they *operate* on it. Even when they accommodate structures to allow for new experiences, the accommodation is seldom complete, and some distortion of the information remains. Thus, when children 6, 8, and 10 years old watch a movie or hear a lecture, they come away with somewhat different messages, even though they may have seen or heard the same input. Each child acts on the information somewhat differently, fitting it into his or her own existing set of structures. In this sense, the child constructs knowledge about the world, rather than simply receiving it.

The processes of assimilation, accommodation, and construction make the child's cognitive system increasingly more powerful and adaptive. However, these processes produce only small-scale changes. At certain points in development, Piaget argued, more major adjustments are required. At these points, the cognitive system, because of both biological maturation and past experiences, has completely mastered one level of functioning and is ready for new, qualitatively different challenges—challenges that go beyond what the current set of structures can handle. At such points, the child moves to a new stage of development.

Organization
The tendency to integrate knowledge into interrelated cognitive structures. One of the two biologically based functions stressed in Piaget's theory.

Adaptation
The tendency to fit with the environment in ways that promote survival. One of the two biologically based functions stressed in Piaget's theory.

Assimilation
Interpreting new experiences in terms of existing cognitive structures. One of the two components of adaptation in Piaget's theory.

Accommodation
Changing existing cognitive structures to fit with new experiences. One of the two components of adaptation in Piaget's theory.

Constructivism
Piaget's belief that children actively create knowledge rather than passively receive it from the environment.

An important accomplishment of the preoperational period is the ability to use symbols to represent the world.

Stages of Development   Piaget was a stage theorist. In his view, all children move through the same stages of cognitive development in the same order. At each stage, the child's cognitive functioning is qualitatively different and affects the child's performance in a wide range of situations.

There are four such general stages, or **periods,** in Piaget's model.

- The **sensorimotor** period represents the first 2 years of life. The infant's initial schemes are simple reflexes, and knowledge of the world is limited to physical interactions with people and objects.

- During the **preoperational** period, from roughly 2 to 6 years, the child begins to use symbols, such as words and numbers, to represent the world cognitively.

- The period of **concrete operations** lasts approximately from age 6 to age 11. Children in this stage are able to perform mental operations on the pieces of knowledge they possess, permitting a kind of logical problem solving that was not possible during the preoperational period.

- The final stage, the period of **formal operations,** extends from about age 12 through adulthood. This period includes all the higher-level abstract operations, enabling the child to deal with events or relations that are only possible, as opposed to those that actually exist.

The accuracy of Piaget's theory has been studied extensively over the years. In Chapter 7 we consider the four stages in detail and describe the evidence psychologists have gathered that both supports and questions various aspects of this theory.

Information-Processing Models

A second type of cognitive-developmental model is the information-processing approach, which we describe in detail in Chapter 8. Information-processing theorists view cognition as a system composed of three parts.

1. Information in the world provides the input to the system. Stimulation enters our senses in the form of sights, sounds, tastes, and so on.

2. Processes in the brain act on and transform the information in a variety of ways, including encoding it into symbolic forms, comparing it with previously acquired information, storing it in memory, and retrieving it when necessary. Most

Periods
Piaget's term for the four general stages into which his theory divides development. Each period is a qualitatively distinct form of functioning that characterizes a wide range of cognitive activities.

Sensorimotor
Form of intelligence in which knowledge is based on physical interactions with people and objects. The first of Piaget's periods, extending from birth to about 2 years.

Preoperational
Form of intelligence in which symbols and mental actions begin to replace objects and overt behaviors. The second of Piaget's periods, extending from about 2 to about 6 years old.

Concrete operations
Form of intelligence in which mental operations make logical problem solving with concrete objects possible. The third of Piaget's periods, extending from about 6 to 11 years of age.

Formal operations
Form of intelligence in which higher-level mental operations make possible logical reasoning with respect to abstract and hypothetical events and not merely concrete objects. The fourth of Piaget's periods, beginning at about 12 years of age.

psychologists working in the information-processing tradition have concentrated on this middle part of the system, designing their experiments to reveal the nature of these internal processes and how they interact with one another.

3. The third part of the system is the output, which is our behavior—speech, social interactions, writing, and so on.

As you have probably noticed, there is an inescapable connection between the information-processing approach to cognition and the operation of a computer. Some psychologists make this connection very strongly. Their goal is to construct computer programs that simulate human behavior, so that ultimately we will be able to specify our cognitive processes in precise mathematical and logical terms. More often, however, researchers use the *computer analogy* simply as a way of thinking about information flowing through a system, where it is processed, and then reemerging in a different form. This approach has been useful in guiding psychological research on children's problem solving, memory, reading, and other cognitive processes (Kail & Bisanz, 1992; Klahr & MacWhinney, 1998).

In recent years, the information-processing view has emerged as one of the leading approaches to the study of human cognition. Its popularity reflects in part the growing interest in *cognitive science,* an interdisciplinary field in which researchers in biology, mathematics, philosophy, and neuroscience, among other disciplines, are attempting to understand the workings of the human mind (e.g., Keil, 1998; Osherson, 1990).

Not all information-processing research has been concerned with children, and much of it has not been directed toward developmental issues. Nevertheless, the approach has infused many areas of child psychology, and it will turn up throughout the text in topics as diverse as perception, language, gender roles, and aggression.

 To Recap . . .

The cognitive-developmental approach is based on the belief that cognitive abilities are fundamental and that they guide children's behavior. The key to understanding changes in behavior across development, then, lies in understanding how children's knowledge is structured at any given time.

Piaget described human development in terms of inborn functions and changing cognitive structures. With development, the structures increase in number and complexity. Changes in structures are guided by two functions—organization and adaptation. Adaptation, in turn, consists of assimilation and accommodation. These processes reflect Piaget's constructivist view of development—the belief that children construct their understanding of the world rather than passively receive it from the environment. As children do this, they pass through four stages, or periods, of development: the sensorimotor period, the preoperational period, the period of concrete operations, and the period of formal operations.

Information-processing models conceptualize cognition as a computerlike system with three parts. Stimulation from the outside world makes up input, the first part; mental processes act on that information and represent the second part; and behavior of various sorts makes up the output of the system, the third part.

THEORIES OF DEVELOPMENT: THE SOCIOCULTURAL APPROACH

The theories discussed in the preceding section differ in important ways. Nevertheless, they share a focus on the child functioning largely on his or her own. Cognitive-developmental researchers typically investigate children's thinking by asking them to reason about problems alone, in settings far removed from the daily situations in which children usually apply their cognitive skills. Furthermore, cognitive-developmental theories locate the sources of cognitive change—be it reorganization of cognitive structures, faster processing of information, or growth in general knowledge—primarily in the heads of individual children.

The sociocultural approach offers a very different perspective. As von Herder observed nearly 200 years ago, development occurs in a social, cultural, and historical context. This context includes other people, such as parents and teachers, who support and guide children's cognitive activities. It also includes cultural tools and traditions that shape mental processes. Defining features of the sociocultural approach, then, include an emphasis on social processes, cultural practices, and the everyday contexts of development.

Vygotsky's Theory

The most influential contemporary theory in the sociocultural tradition is that of Soviet psychologist Lev Vygotsky. Vygotsky was born in Russia in the same year as Piaget, and their early work occupied the same period. Their backgrounds were very different, however. For example, Vygotsky was trained not in science, like Piaget, but in law, literature, and linguistics. The differences between these two contemporary theorists are reflected in the contrasting models of human development they constructed (Glassman, 1994; Kozulin, 1990).

A similarity between the two scholars, however, is that both received little attention from Western scientists until the 1960s, when their work was translated into English and their theories began to be tested experimentally. Piaget was still active at this time and continued to contribute to the scientific advances brought about by his theory. Vygotsky, however, had died at age 37 and never saw his ideas pursued by other researchers. Initially, his writings were misunderstood, and they were banned in the former Soviet Union for over 20 years. Thus, his work remained unknown even to many of his contemporary Soviet psychologists.

To understand Vygotsky's theory, it is important to appreciate the political environment of the time. Vygotsky began working in psychology shortly after the Russian Revolution, which replaced the rule of the czar with Marxism. The new philosophy stressed socialism and collectivism; individuals were expected to sacrifice their personal goals and achievements for the betterment of the larger society. Sharing and cooperation were encouraged, and the success of any individual was seen as reflecting the success of the culture. Marxists also placed a heavy emphasis on history, believing that any culture could be understood only through examination of the ideas and events that shaped it.

Vygotsky's model of human development incorporated these elements—hence the label *sociocultural* approach. The model holds that the individual's development is a product of his or her culture. In this theory, *development* refers largely to mental development, such as thought, language, and reasoning processes. Vygotsky assumed that these abilities develop through social interactions with others (especially parents) and thus represent the shared knowledge of the culture. Whereas Piaget believed that all children's cognitive development follows a very similar pattern of stages, Vygotsky saw intellectual abilities as much more specific to the culture in which the child was reared.

Vygotsky's theory emphasizes a number of related elements (Kozulin, 1990; Wertsch & Tulviste, 1992). Most important, it holds that culture is a major determinant of individual development. Humans are the only species that has created cultures, and every human child develops in the context of a culture. Culture makes two sorts of contributions to the child's intellectual development.

1. Children acquire much of the content of their thinking—that is, their knowledge—from the culture around them.

2. Children acquire their thinking and reasoning processes—what Vygotskians call the **tools of intellectual adaptation**—from their culture.

In short, culture teaches children both what to think and how to think.

How does culture exert its influences? Vygotsky believed that cognitive development results from a **dialectical process** in which the child learns through shared problem-solving experiences with someone else, usually a parent or teacher (Rogoff, 1998). Initially, the adult assumes most of the responsibility for guiding the problem solving.

Lev Vygotsky's sociocultural theory of cognitive development, originally published more than 70 years ago, has generated great interest in modern developmentalists.

Tools of intellectual adaptation
Vygotsky's term for the techniques of thinking and problem solving that children internalize from their culture.

Dialectical process
The process in Vygotsky's theory whereby children learn through problem-solving experiences shared with others.

Vygotsky believed that children acquire cognition through shared experiences with others in their culture who are more knowledgeable.

Gradually, however, the responsibility shifts partly and then completely to the child. Language plays a central role in this process in two ways. First, it describes and transmits to children the rich body of knowledge that exists in the culture. Second, it provides the means, or method, of problem solving, which is demonstrated by the adult and then adopted by the child.

Internalization

Vygotsky's term for the child's incorporation, primarily through language, of bodies of knowledge and tools of thought from the culture.

This transfer of control from adult to child reflects a final Vygotskian theme, development as a process of **internalization** (Cox & Lightfoot, 1997). Bodies of knowledge and thinking tools at first exist outside the child, in the surrounding culture. Development, according to Vygotsky, consists of gradually internalizing them. This is what Vygotskians mean when they say that children's cognitive abilities grow directly out of their cultural experiences.

Bronfenbrenner's Ecological Model

Vygotsky's theorizing is not the only basis for the modern sociocultural approach. Another important contributor is the **ecological perspective,** developed most fully by Urie Bronfenbrenner (1979, 1992; Bronfenbrenner & Morris, 1998).

Ecological perspective

An approach to studying development that focuses on individuals within their environmental contexts.

The ecological perspective is not really a new theoretical model but instead represents a different way of thinking about and studying human development (Moen, Elder, & Luscher, 1995). Traditionally, scientific research on children's development has taken place in laboratory settings. There are good reasons for this. The most important is that scientific investigation demands careful experimental control and, until recently, the laboratory has afforded the only setting in which such control could be achieved.

The starting point for the ecological perspective is an obvious fact: Children's development does not generally take place in laboratories. It takes place at home, with the family; at school, with classmates and teachers; in the park, with neighbors and peers; and, more generally, within a larger social and cultural environment. In short, *development always occurs in a context.* More important, the context often influences the course of that development.

The ecological approach is based on the notion that to understand development completely we must consider how the unique characteristics of a child interact with that child's surroundings. The child possesses a variety of personal characteristics. The most important of these are described by Bronfenbrenner as *developmentally generative—* capable of influencing other people in ways that are important to the child — and *developmentally disruptive*—capable of causing problems in the environment with corresponding negative effects on the child.

By instigating various responses and reactions from others, children in a sense become "producers" of their own environments—a concept we will come across again at various points. Examples of these characteristics include personality traits that are positive (sociability, cooperativeness, curiosity) or negative (impulsiveness, explosiveness, distractibility), physical appearance, and intellectual abilities.

Bronfenbrenner contends that the child and the environment continually influence one another in a bidirectional, or **transactional,** manner. For example, suppose a child has the developmentally generative characteristics of being bright and articulate. These may affect the child's environment by resulting in the parents' sending her to a better school, which in turn may influence the child by resulting in improved academic skills, which again may affect her environment by attracting friends who have high career aspirations, and so forth, in an ongoing cycle of interaction and development. These sorts of interactions, Bronfenbrenner argues, are very difficult to study if the child is removed from the natural environment in which they occur.

Figure 1.1 shows Bronfenbrenner's ecological model of development. At the center is the child and his or her physical and personal attributes. Around the child is the environment, viewed as a series of interrelated layers, with those closest to the child having the most direct impact and those farther away influencing the child more indirectly.

Nearest the child is the **microsystem,** which for most children includes the family, the school, the church, the playground, and so forth, along with the relationships that the child forms within these settings. The microsystem possesses physical characteristics, such as the size of the child's house, the amount of nearby playground equipment, and the number of books in the child's day care center. It also consists of people, including family members, the other children on the block, the child's teacher, and so on. These people, in turn, possess characteristics that may be relevant to the child's development, such as the socioeconomic status of the peer group, the educational background of

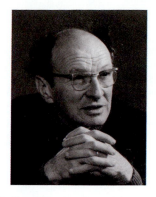

Urie Bronfenbrenner's work has revitalized interest in the ecological approach to studying human development.

Transactional influence

A bidirectional, or reciprocal, relationship in which individuals influence one another's behaviors.

Microsystem

The environmental system closest to the child, such as the family or school. The first of Bronfenbrenner's layers of context.

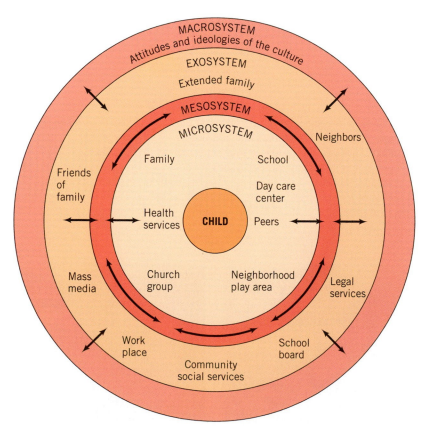

Figure 1.1

Bronfenbrenner's ecological model of the environment. U. Bronfenbrenner, from C. Kopp/Krakow, *The Child: Development in a Social Context* (figure 12.1), © 1982 by Addison-Wesley Publishing Co., Inc. Reprinted with permission of Addison Wesley Longman.

the parents, and the political attitudes of the teacher. The microsystem is not constant but changes as the child grows.

The **mesosystem** refers to the system of relationships among the child's microsystems. This might include the parents' relationship with the child's teacher and the relationship between the child's siblings and neighborhood friends. In general, the more interconnected these systems are, the more the child's development is likely to be supported in a clear and consistent way.

The **exosystem** refers to social settings that can affect the child but in which the child does not participate directly. Some examples are the local government, which decides how strictly air pollution standards will be enforced or which families will be eligible for welfare payments; the school board, which sets teachers' salaries and recommends the budget for new textbooks and equipment; and the parents' places of employment, which determine work hours and health care benefits.

Finally, there is the **macrosystem,** which involves the culture and subculture in which the child lives. The macrosystem affects the child through its beliefs, attitudes, and traditions. Children living in the United States may be influenced, for example, by beliefs regarding democracy and equality and perhaps the virtues of capitalism and free enterprise. In certain parts of the country, children may also be affected by regional attitudes regarding, say, the importance of rugged individualism. If a child lives in an ethnic or racially concentrated neighborhood, the values and cultural traditions of that group may add yet another source of influence. The macrosystem is generally more stable than the other systems, but it, too, can change as a society evolves—for example, from a liberal political era to a conservative one, from economic prosperity to depression, or from peace to war (Elder & Caspi, 1988).

Not shown in the diagram is an additional factor that must be considered when studying human development: the passage of time. The interactions that take place among the various systems in the child's world gradually change over time and as the child grows. This source of influence, which Bronfenbrenner terms the **chronosystem,** adds even more complexity and richness to the challenge of analyzing children's development.

Along with his conceptual model for studying development in context, Bronfenbrenner also proposed a theoretical account of how genes and environment operate together to guide human development. We will discuss that theory in Chapter 3, along with several other models of gene–environment interaction.

Mesosystem
The interrelationships among the child's microsystems. The second of Bronfenbrenner's layers of context.

Exosystem
Social systems that can affect children but in which they do not participate directly. Bronfenbrenner's third layer of context.

Macrosystem
The culture or subculture in which the child lives. Bronfenbrenner's fourth layer of context.

Chronosystem
Bronfenbrenner's term for the passage of time as a context for studying human development.

 To Recap . . .

Psychologists favoring a sociocultural approach contend that social processes are crucial in the development of children's cognitive abilities. Vygotsky's theory stresses the role of culture. Development involves the child's gradual internalization of bodies of knowledge and tools of thought, primarily through shared experiences with parents and teachers. Bronfenbrenner's ecological model focuses on the contexts in which development occurs. The model includes a series of four contextual layers: the microsystem, which is closest to the child; the mesosystem; the exosystem; and the macrosystem.

In Bronfenbrenner's ecological systems theory, development may vary depending on the context in which it occurs.

THEORIES OF DEVELOPMENT: ENVIRONMENTAL/LEARNING APPROACHES

Just as Rousseau was the ancestor of the cognitive-developmental approach, so Locke was the great-grandfather of the learning tradition. Locke's belief that environment and experiences are the keys to understanding human behavior—a view that Watson translated into behaviorism early in the 20th century—continues to be the guiding principle for many child psychologists today.

The essence of the environmental/learning view is that a great deal of human behavior, especially social behavior, is acquired rather than inborn. Of course, modern behavioral psychologists, like all contemporary psychologists, are interactionists. They accept that biological and cognitive factors make important contributions to human development. But they do not share the belief that biology and evolutionary history largely dictate human development (a view discussed later in this chapter). Nor do they accept the idea that cognition is the fundamental process in psychological development and that changes in behavior always reflect or require advances in cognitive abilities.

Defining Learning

Behavioral psychologists believe that the changes in behavior that occur as children develop often are *learned*, meaning they result from conditioning and learning principles. When psychologists use the term **learning,** they are not referring simply to what goes on in a classroom (although, one hopes, a good deal of it takes place there, too). Instead, they view learning much more generally, defining it as a relatively permanent change in behavior that results from practice or experience. This definition has three distinct elements.

Learning
A relatively permanent change in behavior that results from practice or experience.

1. The first part of the definition, "relatively permanent," distinguishes learned changes in behavior from changes that are only temporary and that often reflect physiological processes—such as when behavior changes as a result of sleep, illness, or fatigue.

2. The second part, "change in behavior," means that learning must always be demonstrated through changes in observable behavior. If a psychologist were interested in determining whether a child had learned a list of words, for example, the child would need to demonstrate this learning through some aspect of behavior, such as writing, reciting, or recognizing the words.

3. The final part of the definition, "results from practice or experience," is meant to separate learned changes in behavior from changes caused by more general biological processes, such as growth, pregnancy, or even death.

B. F. Skinner

We saw earlier that Watson attempted to build a comprehensive theory of child development based on the conditioning of reflexes. His attempt failed in part because human behavior was too complex to be explained by Pavlovian conditioning. Except in very young infants, reflexes account for only a small part of human behavior. How, then, can a learning theory attempt to explain the whole range of typical child behaviors? One answer emerged in the work of another pioneer of behaviorism, B. F. Skinner (Gewirtz & Pelaez-Nogueras, 1992).

Skinner accepted the role of Pavlovian conditioning of reflexes, but he added to learning theory a second type of behavior and, correspondingly, a second type of learning. According to his model, all behavior falls into one of two categories: It is either *respondent behavior* or *operant behavior*.

The first category of behavior involves reflexes. A **reflex** is composed of a stimulus that reliably elicits a response. This relation is biological and inborn. The salivation

B. F. Skinner's revision of Watson's early behavioristic views introduced principles of operant conditioning.

Reflex
A biological relation in which a specific stimulus reliably elicits a specific response.

Respondent behaviors

Responses based on reflexes, which are controlled by specific eliciting stimuli. The smaller category of human behaviors.

Operant behaviors

Voluntary behavior controlled by its consequences. The larger category of human behaviors.

Habituation

The decline or disappearance of a response as a result of repeated presentation of the eliciting stimulus. The simplest type of learning.

Habituation is a simple learning process that explains why babies can sleep in noisy surroundings.

response of Pavlov's dogs is an example. Skinner called these responses **respondent behaviors.** The most important characteristic of a respondent behavior is that it is completely controlled by the stimulus that elicits it; quite simply, the response occurs when the stimulus is present and does not occur when the stimulus is absent. In humans, respondent behaviors are particularly obvious during infancy and include such reflexive behaviors as sucking in response to a nipple's being placed in the mouth and grasping in response to an object's touching the palm of the hand. Older children and adults also display a few respondent behaviors, usually in the form of simple physiological responses (blinking and sneezing) and emotional responses (some aspects of fear, anger, and sexual arousal).

Operant behaviors are very different. We can think of them roughly as voluntary responses, and they include the vast majority of all human behaviors. Operant behaviors are controlled by their effects—that is, by the consequences they produce. In general, pleasant consequences make the behaviors more likely to occur again, whereas unpleasant consequences have the opposite result (Skinner, 1953).

Types of Learning

To understand environmental/learning accounts of child development, we must consider the various types of conditioning and learning that operate on the child. In this section, we examine three forms of learning: habituation, classical conditioning, and operant learning.

Habituation   You may have observed how infants can learn to sleep through routine household noises. If given enough exposure, babies very quickly get used to slamming doors, ringing phones, and similar sounds that might otherwise wake them. Unfortunately, many parents, unaware of this fact, try to keep everyone very quiet during nap times. The absence of typical household sounds, however, may prevent the infant from becoming accustomed to them and make her more likely to awaken at the first bark of the family dog.

The infant's change in behavior in this example illustrates the simplest form of learning, called **habituation.** Imagine that we clap our hands loudly near an infant. Initially, the infant will display a full-body startle reflex. If we continue to clap our hands at

frequent intervals (say, every 15 seconds), the size of the startle response will decrease steadily until it may be difficult to detect at all. This simple change in behavior caused by repeatedly presenting a stimulus illustrates learning through habituation.

How do we know that habituation really represents some form of learning? Maybe the infant's muscles have simply become too fatigued to produce the response any longer—a change in behavior that, according to our earlier definition, we could not consider to be learned. To demonstrate that fatigue is not the reason for the decreased response, we need only change the stimulus. Assume, for instance, that the repeated hand clapping has reduced the startle to a very low level. Now, after waiting 15 seconds, we sound a loud buzzer instead of clapping our hands. With great reliability, the startle response will reappear at the same high level it showed when we first clapped our hands. The recovery of a habituated response that occurs as a result of a change in the eliciting stimulus is known as **dishabituation.**

Although habituation does not account for a great deal of children's development, psychologists have discovered that it can be a very useful technique for studying infants' perceptual and cognitive abilities. We examine how this works in later chapters.

Classical Conditioning

Classical conditioning—sometimes called **respondent conditioning**—was developed by Pavlov. It involves reflexes or respondent behaviors. In this type of learning, the stimulus is termed the **unconditioned stimulus (UCS)** and the elicited response is called the **unconditioned response (UCR).** Classical conditioning involves having another stimulus, which previously did not elicit the UCR, acquire the power to do so. The neutral (new) stimulus is paired or associated with the UCS. After a number of such pairings, it elicits the UCR (or a response very similar to it), at which point the previously neutral stimulus is termed a **conditioned stimulus (CS).**

We can illustrate this process with an example involving children's emotional responses, the aspect of human development in which classical conditioning plays its largest role. Fear responses, for instance, can be naturally elicited by a number of stimuli, a very common one being pain. Suppose a child visits the dentist for the first time. The stimuli in that environment—the dentist, the office, the instruments, and so forth—are neutral to the child and so have no particular emotional effect on his behavior. During the visit, however, suppose that the child experiences pain (UCS), which elicits fear (UCR). The various neutral stimuli become associated with the UCS, because they are paired with it, and thus may become conditioned stimuli (CS) for the fear response. After that, the sight of the dentist or sound of the drill, for example, will also elicit the fear response. In the same way, many common fears of childhood can be learned responses to places or objects that previously were not frightening. (See Box 1.1 for a classic demonstration of the conditioning of fear.)

Classical conditioning often produces **stimulus generalization,** which means that stimuli similar to the CS also become conditioned. In our example, the child may come to fear not only his own dentist but all dentists, or perhaps anyone wearing a white medical coat. Fortunately, the conditioned association also can be unlearned, a process called **extinction.** Suppose the child in our example returns to the dentist often without experiencing any more pain. The dentist and other conditioned stimuli in the situation will then gradually cease to elicit fear and return to being neutral.

Operant Learning

A third type of learning is called **operant learning.** Unlike habituation and classical conditioning, operant learning is assumed by learning theorists to be very important for understanding the typical behavior of children.

Operant behaviors are influenced by their effects, and many of the everyday behaviors of children occur simply because they resulted in desirable consequences in the past. Any consequence that makes a response more likely to occur again is called a *reinforcer.* Consider the following examples. The same child may (1) share her toys with a friend because doing so often produces similar sharing by the other child, (2) throw a temper tantrum in the supermarket because this usually results in getting candy from her

Dishabituation
The recovery of a habituated response that results from a change in the eliciting stimulus.

Classical (respondent) conditioning
A form of learning, involving reflexes, in which a neutral stimulus acquires the power to elicit a reflexive response (UCR) as a result of being associated (paired) with the naturally eliciting stimulus (UCS). The neutral stimulus then becomes a conditioned stimulus (CS).

Unconditioned stimulus (UCS)
The stimulus portion of a reflex, which reliably elicits a respondent behavior (UCR).

Unconditioned response (UCR)
The response portion of a reflex, which is reliably elicited by a stimulus (UCS).

Conditioned stimulus (CS)
A neutral stimulus that comes to elicit a response through a conditioning process in which it is consistently paired with another stimulus (UCS) that naturally evokes the response.

Stimulus generalization
A process related to classical conditioning in which stimuli that are similar to the conditioned stimulus (CS) also acquire the power to elicit the response.

Extinction
A process related to classical conditioning in which the conditioned stimulus (CS) gradually loses its power to elicit the response as a result of no longer being paired with the unconditioned stimulus (UCS).

Operant learning
A form of learning in which the likelihood of an operant behavior changes as a result of its reinforcing or punishing consequences.

Little Albert and Little Peter: Conditioning and Counterconditioning Fear

Perhaps the most famous research conducted by John B. Watson involved the conditioning of a fear response in an 11-month-old child named Albert B. (Watson & Rayner, 1920). The study was designed to show that fear is an unconditioned response that can be easily conditioned to a variety of common stimuli.

Watson believed that children fear dogs, dentists, and the like because they associate these objects or persons with an unconditioned stimulus for fear, such as pain or a sudden loud noise. To illustrate this process, Watson first exposed Albert to a tame white laboratory rat, which produced only mild interest in the child. On several later occasions, Watson presented the rat to Albert and then made a loud noise (UCS) behind Albert. The noise elicited a pronounced fear response (UCR) in the form of crying and trembling. Very soon, the sight of the rat alone was enough to make Albert cry in fear—it had become a conditioned stimulus (CS) for that response. Watson demonstrated stimulus generalization by showing that objects similar to the rat, such as cotton or a white fur coat, also elicited the fear response.

A few years later, Watson and an associate named Mary Cover Jones applied the fear-conditioning process in reverse (Jones, 1924). A 3-year-old named Peter was brought to them with an intense fear of rabbits and other furry creatures. The researchers reasoned that if this fear had been learned (conditioned), it could be unlearned. They called their method for eliminating the fear response to the rabbit *counterconditioning.* It involved presenting the conditioned stimulus in such a way that it would not elicit the fear response but would instead elicit a competing emotional response—in this case, pleasure derived from eating.

On the first day of treatment, Peter was placed in a high chair and fed his lunch. At the same time, a caged rabbit was displayed on the other side of the room, far enough away so that the fear response did not occur. Each day, while Peter ate, the rabbit was moved slightly closer. In the end, Peter was not at all disturbed at having the rabbit sit next to him while he ate his lunch. The rabbit was no longer a conditioned stimulus for fear and had instead become associated with pleasure.

An experiment of the sort conducted with Little Albert, of course, would not be permitted today, because psychologists now have strict ethical guidelines for research that prohibit a child's being exposed to this type of fear experience (see Chapter 2). The experiment with Little Peter, however, is very similar to the type of fear-reduction therapy used today by clinical psychologists and would be considered a form of behavior modification.

BOX 1.1

Classics of
Research

Children may become fearful when they encounter stimuli that remind them of painful past experiences. This illustrates the principle of stimulus generalization.

parent, (3) twist and shake the knob of the playroom door because this behavior is effective in getting it open, (4) work hard at skating lessons because the coach praises her when she performs well, and (5) put a pillow over her head when her baby brother is crying because this behavior helps reduce the unpleasant sound.

It should be obvious from this list that reinforcers can take many forms. Nevertheless, they all fall into one of two categories: Those that involve getting something good are called **positive reinforcers,** and those that involve getting rid of something bad are called **negative reinforcers.**

It should also be apparent from our list of examples that the reinforcement process does not work only on desirable or beneficial responses. Reinforcement increases the likelihood of any behavior that leads to a pleasant consequence, whether we would typically view that behavior as appropriate (sharing toys), inappropriate (throwing a tantrum in a supermarket), or neutral (opening a door).

Not all consequences are reinforcing, however. Behavior sometimes produces effects that are unpleasant, and these *reduce* the likelihood that the behavior will occur again. Such consequences are called **punishers.** We usually think of punishment as something that is delivered by parents or teachers for misbehavior, but the principle of punishment, like the principle of reinforcement, is simply part of nature's learning process. Punishment teaches organisms which responses are wise to repeat and which are better to avoid. Punishment, too, can entail either getting something bad (such as a spanking, a failing grade, or a scraped knee) or losing something good (such as a baseball, a chance to sit by a friend at lunch, or TV privileges for a week). Either way, behaviors that lead to punishing consequences become less likely to occur again.

Social-Learning Theory

Over the years, the environmental/learning tradition has grown more like the other major theoretical traditions. In this section, we consider a second approach within the behavioral tradition, **social-learning theory.**

The leading spokesperson for the social-learning viewpoint has been Albert Bandura (1986, 1992, 2001). Like other behavioral psychologists, Bandura believes that cognitive development alone does not explain childhood changes in behavior and that learning processes are responsible for much of children's development. But some learning processes, he feels, are affected by the child's cognitive abilities. This is especially true for the more complex types of learning that Bandura believes are involved in children's development beyond the infant years. We turn next to one of these types, observational learning.

Observational Learning   Skinner's addition of operant learning to Watson's Pavlovian conditioning greatly expanded learning theory's ability to explain children's behavior. Nevertheless, some problems remained. One was that children sometimes acquire new behaviors simply by seeing someone else perform them. A second was that children sometimes become more or less likely to perform a behavior after seeing another person experience reinforcing or punishing consequences for that behavior. Neither of these facts is easily explained by a type of learning in which changes in behavior occur only when children experience direct consequences for their actions.

Bandura solved this problem by proposing that as children grow, their development is increasingly based on a fourth type of learning—**observational learning.** Learning by observation occurs when the behavior of an observer is affected by witnessing the behavior of a model (and often the consequences of this behavior). In developmental psychology, the observers are children, and the models include parents, teachers, siblings, classmates, sports celebrities, TV personalities, and even cartoon characters—in short, just about anyone in the child's world.

Positive reinforcer
A consequence that makes the behavior it follows more likely through the presentation of something pleasant.

Negative reinforcer
A consequence that makes the behavior it follows more likely through the removal of something unpleasant.

Punisher
A consequence that makes the behavior it follows less likely, either through the presentation of something unpleasant or the removal of something desirable.

Social-learning theory
A form of environmental/learning theory that adds observational learning to classical and operant learning as a process through which children's behavior changes.

Observational learning
A form of learning in which an observer's behavior changes as a result of observing a model.

Bandura and other researchers have studied three important questions regarding the modeling process:

1. Which models are most likely to influence a child's behavior?

2. Under what circumstances is this influence most likely to occur?

3. How does the child's behavior change as a result of observational learning?

The simple answer to the first question is that a model who possesses a characteristic that the child finds attractive or desirable—such as talent, intelligence, power, good looks, or popularity—is most likely to be imitated. Other issues can sometimes come into play, however, including the child's level of development and the types of behaviors being modeled.

The circumstances under which modeling is most effective also can vary, but one of the most important factors is whether the model receives reinforcing or punishing consequences for the behavior. One of Bandura's most significant contributions to social-learning theory was his demonstration that consequences of a model's behavior can affect the behavior of an observer. When a child sees a model receive reinforcement for a response, the child receives **vicarious reinforcement** and, like the model, becomes more likely to produce that same response. The opposite is true when the child receives **vicarious punishment** as a result of witnessing a model being punished. In some sense, then, observational learning is the same as operant learning, except that the child experiences the consequences vicariously rather than directly.

The most obvious and perhaps the most important result of modeling is **imitation,** which occurs when children copy what they have seen. Imitation can take such varied forms as adopting the clothing style of a popular professional athlete, climbing on a chair to steal a cookie from the shelf after seeing an older brother do it, or copying the problems a teacher writes on the chalkboard.

A second result of modeling occurs when the observer becomes less likely to perform a behavior that has just been modeled. This effect, known as **response inhibition,** is a common result of vicarious punishment. The teacher who publicly disciplines an unruly child to set an example for the rest of the class is counting on observational learning to inhibit similar behaviors in the other children.

Vicarious reinforcement
Reinforcing consequences experienced when viewing a model that affect an observer similarly.

Vicarious punishment
Punishing consequences experienced when viewing a model that affect an observer similarly.

Imitation
Behavior of an observer that results from and is similar to the behavior of a model.

Response inhibition
The absence of a particular response that has just been modeled; often the result of vicarious punishment.

Imitation is an important process by which children acquire new skills and behaviors.

Albert Bandura's early research showed that children exposed to filmed violence were capable of very accurately imitating the model's aggressive acts when given the opportunity to reproduce them.

Children do not always immediately display behavior learned from models. A striking illustration of this point occurred in one of Bandura's early studies, in which one group of youngsters observed a model rewarded for displaying new aggressive behaviors toward an inflated toy clown, and a second group saw those same behaviors punished. When given an opportunity to play with the doll themselves, the children who witnessed the reinforcement imitated many of the model's aggressive acts toward the doll, whereas the group who observed punishment did not. But when later offered rewards for reproducing the aggressive behaviors, both groups were able to perform them quite accurately (Bandura, 1965). Obviously, all of the children had acquired (learned) the new behaviors, even though the vicariously experienced punishment had inhibited some children from performing them. This distinction between acquisition and performance has been of particular interest to researchers studying the potential effects of viewing television violence on children's aggressive behavior, which we discuss in Chapter 14.

The acquisition–performance distinction is evident in Bandura's theoretical formulation of observational learning, depicted in Figure 1.2. Bandura believes that learning by observation involves four separate processes. The first two account for the acquisition,

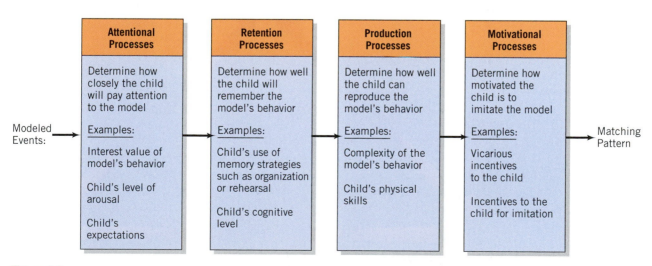

Figure 1.2

Bandura's model of observational learning. Adapted from Albert Bandura, *Social Learning Theory,* © 1977, p. 23. Reprinted by permission of Prentice-Hall, Inc., Upper Saddle River, New Jersey.

or learning, of a model's behavior, and the other two control the performance, or production, of these behaviors (Bandura, 1977).

- *Attentional processes* determine how closely the child pays attention to what the model is doing.
- *Retention processes* refer to how well the child can store the modeled information in memory for later use.
- *Production processes* control how well the child can reproduce the model's responses.
- *Motivational processes* determine who and what a child chooses to imitate.

Bandura's theory thus suggests four important reasons why, in everyday life, children do not imitate everything they see. A child may fail to imitate an observed behavior because he did not pay attention to what the model was doing, does not recall the model's responses, does not possess the physical skills to repeat the model's behavior, or simply feels little motivation to do what the model did.

Reciprocal Determinism   Bandura's social-learning analysis is truly interactionist. It is based on his view that human development reflects the interaction of the person (P), the person's behavior (B), and the environment (E). Bandura describes this process of interaction as **reciprocal determinism** (Bandura, 1978).

As illustrated in Figure 1.3, the reciprocal determinism model forms a triangle of interactions. The person includes the child's cognitive abilities, physical characteristics, personality, beliefs, attitudes, and so on, which influence both the child's behavior and the child's environment. Children choose not only what they want to do (P → B) but also where and with whom to do it (P → E). These influences are reciprocal, however. Children's behavior (and the reactions it engenders) can affect their feelings about themselves and their attitudes and beliefs about other things (B → P). Likewise, much of children's knowledge about the world and other people results from information they receive from TV, parents, textbooks, and other environmental sources (E → P).

Environment also affects behavior. The consequences of children's behavior and the models they observe can powerfully influence what they do (E → B). But children's behavior also contributes to creating their environment. A child who shares and cooperates with classmates is likely to attract many friends, whereas the opposite may be the case for a child who behaves selfishly or aggressively (B → E).

Reciprocal determinism
Bandura's proposed process describing the interaction of a person's characteristics and abilities (P), behavior (B), and environment (E).

Figure 1.3

Bandura's model of reciprocal determinism. Adapted from "Self System in Reciprocal Determinism" by Albert Bandura, 1978, *American Psychologist, 33,* p. 345. Copyright © 1978 by the American Psychological Association. Adapted by permission.

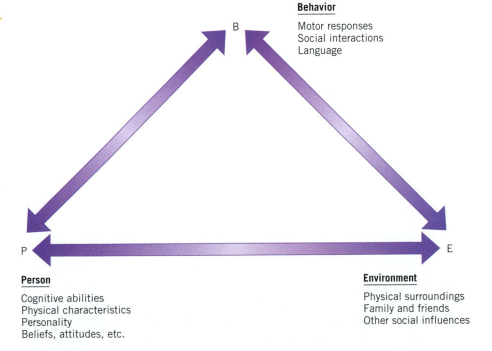

Behavior
B
Motor responses
Social interactions
Language

Person
P
Cognitive abilities
Physical characteristics
Personality
Beliefs, attitudes, etc.

Environment
E
Physical surroundings
Family and friends
Other social influences

Bandura's addition of observational learning to the environmental/learning tradition, along with his willingness to incorporate cognitive aspects of development, has greatly increased the explanatory power of social-learning theory and has made it the most important learning-based approach. We consider the role of this model in many aspects of children's development throughout this text.

To Recap . . .

Environmental/learning theories begin with the assumption that much of children's typical behavior is acquired through conditioning and learning principles. Learned behaviors are distinguished from behaviors that are temporary, unobservable, or based solely on biological processes.

Three types of conditioning and learning are stressed in traditional learning accounts: habituation (and dishabituation), classical conditioning, and operant learning. Habituation involves a decline in response to a repeated stimulus. In classical conditioning an originally reflexive response comes under the control of a new stimulus. Operant learning is controlled by the consequences of behavior. Consequences that make behavior more probable are called reinforcers; those that make behavior less probable are called punishers.

Social-learning theory, based largely on the ideas of Bandura, proposes a greater role for cognitive factors than did earlier learning models. According to this theory, observational learning occurs when an observer's behavior changes as a result of viewing the behavior of a model and perhaps the consequences of that behavior. The most important result of modeling is imitation. Conversely, response inhibition occurs when imitation of an observed behavior becomes less likely—usually because the model has received punishment for it. Acquisition of a modeled behavior is determined by the observer's attentional and retentional processes, whereas performance of the behavior is controlled by the observer's production and motivational processes.

Bandura's theoretical model, reciprocal determinism, holds that human development results from the complex interaction of characteristics of the person, the person's behavior, and the environment.

THEORIES OF DEVELOPMENT: EVOLUTIONARY AND BIOLOGICAL APPROACHES

The fourth major theoretical approach in modern child psychology is the evolutionary/biological approach. The historical roots of this tradition can be traced to the work of Darwin. The modern version of the approach begins with a discipline referred to as **ethology**: the study of development from an evolutionary perspective.

Ethology
The study of development from an evolutionary perspective.

Behavior and Evolution

When trying to understand the ethological approach, it is important to keep in mind that from an evolutionary perspective, our species is the product of millions of years of change. What we are today represents a small part of an enormous process. Human beings are only one of the 5 million or so species that presently inhabit the earth, and ethology considers human development within the context of the entire animal kingdom. It should not be surprising, then, that much of the research conducted within this tradition involves nonhuman species.

Like the other theoretical models, ethology attempts to explain the changes in behavior that occur across development. According to ethological theorists, these changes have two kinds of determinants, or causes—immediate and evolutionary. The immediate determinants are the more obvious and include the environment in which the behavior occurs, the animal's recent experiences, and the state or condition of the animal—whether it is hungry, tired, or angry, for example. The evolutionary determinants of behavior are less clear. Not all present-day behaviors or characteristics were necessarily selected for in evolution. Some, however, are presumed to have contributed to the animal's chances of survival and thus to have been passed along to future generations through the natural selection process. To explain such behaviors as hunting for prey or constructing a dam, then, ethologists consider both the immediate circumstances, such as the availability of prey or of appropriate building materials, and factors in the animal's evolutionary past, such as the climate and terrain in which the behaviors evolved.

Classical Ethology

Ethology first gained scientific recognition in the 1930s with the work of two pioneers in animal study, Konrad Lorenz and Niko Tinbergen. Both men were zoologists by training, and their early investigations focused exclusively on nonhuman animals. Nevertheless, their research laid the groundwork for the growing trend toward the application of ethological principles to child development, and in 1973 they were jointly awarded a Nobel Prize for their pioneering research.

Innate Mechanisms   Ethologists have identified four qualities that characterize virtually all innate, or inborn, behaviors (Eibl-Eibesfeldt, 1989).

1. They are *universal* to all members of the species.

2. Because they are usually biologically programmed responses to very specific stimuli, they *require no learning or experience.*

3. They are normally *stereotyped*, meaning that they occur in precisely the same way every time they are displayed.

4. They are only *minimally affected by environmental influences* (in the short run, that is; natural selection pressures affect them across generations).

Countless examples of such behaviors have been identified in virtually every known species, ranging from the nest-building behaviors of ants to the pecking responses of chickens to the herding behaviors of antelope.

In humans, such innate behaviors are most evident during infancy. An inborn response such as sucking, for example, is found in all babies, does not need to be learned, occurs in a stereotyped pattern, and is influenced very little by the environment (at least during the first weeks of life).

The idea of a stimulus that elicits a simple, reflexive, biological response, such as sucking, is neither new nor of interest only to ethologists (as the work of Pavlov and Watson clearly demonstrates). But ethologists have typically been interested in more complex sequences of innate behaviors, which they call **modal action patterns**. These are the chains of responses that we see, for example, when spiders spin webs, birds build nests, or bears care for newborn cubs. A modal action pattern is triggered by a specific stimulus in the animal's environment, what Lorenz called an **innate releasing mechanism**. A classic example of such a mechanism was demonstrated by Tinbergen (1973) in his work with the stickleback.

The stickleback is a freshwater fish with three sharp spines. In winter, the males stay in schools and are relatively inactive. In spring, the rising water temperature sets off a distinctive pattern of mating behaviors. Each stickleback leaves the school and builds a tunnel-like nest in the sand, which he defends as his own territory against other males. When a female approaches the area above the nest, the male begins his courtship by stabbing her with one of his spines. He then swims down to the nest in an unusual zigzag pattern. The stabbing and swimming motion apparently excite the female, who follows him to his nest. When she enters it, the male places his face against her tail and begins to quiver. This stimulates the female to release her eggs, which the male fertilizes by releasing his sperm. He then chases her away and waits for another female to approach. This ritual continues until five or so females have released eggs in the nest. The male subsequently cares for the developing eggs, driving away intruders and fanning the water with his tail to provide the eggs with sufficient oxygen.

In addition to observing this mating process in the wild, Tinbergen studied sticklebacks in the laboratory. There he exposed the fish to wooden models of other

---

Modal action pattern
A sequence of behaviors elicited by a specific stimulus.

Innate releasing mechanism
A stimulus that triggers an innate sequence or pattern of behaviors.

sticklebacks of various colors and shapes to determine experimentally which stimuli are necessary to trigger and maintain the chain of behaviors. The details of these experiments are not crucial for our purposes, but the work does raise several important issues.

One issue concerns the relevance of these sorts of modal action patterns for human development. Although the mating rituals of humans are (fortunately) very different from those of sticklebacks, ethologists believe that many response patterns in humans are triggered by very specific stimuli. These may include, for example, maternal responses to newborn babies or certain forms of aggression. A related issue concerns the nature versus nurture question. The stickleback does not need to learn the complex courtship responses; they are elicited biologically by stimuli in the environment. This does not mean, however, that other aspects of the stickleback's behavior do not change in response to experiences or consequences. From the opposite perspective, even though many aspects of human behavior clearly result from learning processes, ethologists contend that this does not rule out the possibility that other aspects of human behavior—perhaps even complex behavior patterns—are controlled by innate evolutionary processes. Thus, modern ethologists, too, are interactionists, assuming important roles for both nature and nurture processes.

Tinbergen's research strategy also illustrates how ethologists combine naturalistic and laboratory methods. The great majority of their investigations involve the observation of behaviors in the natural settings where they evolved. In this way, the researcher can examine how an animal's responses typically occur. But the behaviors are also studied in more structured settings, where the researcher can control the conditions under which events take place and can subject an animal's rituals and routines to various experimental tests.

Sensitive Periods

Sensitive Periods   An important issue in psychology concerns how an animal's genetic or biological makeup can influence the learning process—that is, how nature and nurture work together to change behavior. Ethologists argue that animals are biologically programmed so that some things are learned most easily during certain periods of development. A dramatic example of this is illustrated by Lorenz's research on **imprinting**, the process by which newborns of some species form an emotional bond with their mothers.

In many bird species whose young can walk almost immediately after hatching, baby birds soon begin to follow the mother as she moves about. Lorenz guessed that this simple act of following was responsible for the strong social bond that developed between the newborn and the parent. To confirm his suspicion, Lorenz removed just-hatched goslings from their mother and had them follow another animal, or various nonliving objects that he pulled along, or even himself. As he predicted, the young birds quickly imprinted to whatever they followed and thereafter treated it as their mother (Lorenz, 1937).

Lorenz further discovered that one of the most important influences on imprinting was the age of the chicks. If the act of following occurred during a period that began several hours after birth and lasted until sometime the next day, the attachment bond reliably developed. When the following occurred only before or after this period, however, little or no imprinting resulted. Ethologists now use the term **sensitive periods** to describe points in development when learning is much easier than it is at earlier or later points. Sensitive periods are not restricted to imprinting or even to the area of mother-infant attachment. Child researchers have applied the concept to areas as diverse as language acquisition (Newport, 1991) and gender-role development (Money & Annecillo, 1987), as we will see in later chapters.

Applications to Human Development

Our main interest in ethological theory is its application to child development, and modern researchers are finding many areas of development in which evolutionary processes may be important (Archer, 1992; Geary & Bjorklund, 2000; Scarr, 1993).

Imprinting
A biological process of some species in which the young acquire an emotional attachment to the mother through following.

Sensitive period
A period of development during which certain behaviors are more easily learned.

Konrad Lorenz found that newly hatched goslings, when permitted to follow him around for a short time, would imprint to him and thereafter treat him as their mother.

John Bowlby's Work

As early as the 1940s, Lorenz suggested that physical characteristics of babies, such as the shapes of their heads and the sounds of their cries, might serve as stimuli to trigger caregiving by mothers (Lorenz, 1950). Developmental psychologists likewise interpreted infants' early reflexive behaviors in terms of their evolutionary value to the species. Nevertheless, the scientific application of the ethological model to child development is usually considered to have begun in 1969, when John Bowlby published the first of his three volumes on the subject (Bowlby, 1969/1982, 1973, 1980).

Bowlby, an English physician and psychoanalyst, was the first to attract child psychologists to an evolutionary interpretation of human development. As a clinician, Bowlby had witnessed the emotional problems of children who had been reared in institutions. Such children often have difficulty forming and maintaining close relationships. Bowlby attributed this problem to the children's lack of a strong attachment to their mothers during infancy. His interest in this area eventually led him to an ethological explanation of how and why the mother–infant bond is established (Bretherton, 1995).

Bowlby's theory is an interesting mix of ethology and Freudian theory (Holmes, 1995; Sroufe, 1986). As did Freud, Bowlby believes that the quality of the early relationship (between baby and mother) is critical to later development and that these first experiences are carried forward by processes in the unconscious. Bowlby's theory also reflects a fundamental principle of classical ethology: that a close mother-infant bond is crucial in humans (and in most higher-level species) for the survival of the young. Infants who remain near the mother can be fed, protected, trained, and transported more effectively than can infants who stray from her side. The behaviors used by the mother and infant to keep the pair in close contact must therefore be innate and controlled by a variety of releasing stimuli (we discuss these behaviors in Chapter 12). Bowlby further maintains that the attachment bond develops easily during a sensitive period, but after this time it may become impossible for the child ever to achieve a truly intimate emotional relationship (Bowlby, 1988).

Bowlby's work has encouraged a great deal of additional research on attachment and bonding processes in humans. More important for this tradition, it began a general movement toward examining other aspects of child development within an evolutionary context. Psychologists have since investigated children's aggression, peer interactions, cognitive development, and many other topics.

Ethologists have also influenced developmental research methods. Observational methods have always been used by child researchers, but there has been a renewed interest in studying children in their natural environments. Increasingly, observational techniques that do not influence or intrude on children's normal social interactions are being added to more experimental approaches to studying these behaviors.

Sociobiology

One offshoot of classical ethology involves an attempt to apply evolutionary principles to human social behavior. This area of research began rather dramatically in 1975 with the publication of a book by Harvard biologist E. O. Wilson titled *Sociobiology: The New Synthesis*. According to Wilson's radical and somewhat controversial theory, genes are very selfish structures whose only interest is to ensure their own survival from generation to generation.

Many specific physical characteristics (color of fur, size of ears, and so on) are carried in an animal's genes. When a characteristic is valuable for survival or reproduction, the genes that produce it are more likely to be passed along to the next generation—Darwin's natural selection process. Sociobiologists believe that genes influence not only physical traits but also social behaviors. Social behaviors that are more adaptive for survival thus are assumed to undergo the same natural selection process as physical traits.

The sociobiological view can be illustrated by a frequently cited example. Consider a mother who risks her life to save her child from danger. According to the traditional ethological model, this response by the mother should not have an evolutionary basis, because natural selection would not favor behaviors that reduce an individual's chances of survival. Sociobiologists, however, contend that the mother's genes have in some way programmed her to do whatever she can to ensure that her genes are passed on to future generations. Because her child carries many of those same genes, and because he would have many reproductive years ahead, evolutionary mechanisms drive the mother to sacrifice her life to save that of her child (Dawkins, 1976).

Wilson suggests that genetic effects on social behavior are better understood at the level of the culture or society, rather than of the individual. He claims, for example, that many cultural practices, such as taboos against incest and laws against murder, reflect an evolutionary process that favors individuals whose social behaviors are in line with what is best for the survival of the species. This theory has been both praised and criticized (Lerner & von Eye, 1992). But it has sparked a great deal of debate and has drawn additional attention to the evolutionary perspective.

Evolutionary Developmental Psychology

A more recent development is the emergence of **evolutionary developmental psychology** (Bjorklund & Pellegrini, 2000, 2002), a subdivision of *evolutionary psychology* (Buss, 1999). Evolutionary developmental psychology shares the general ethological emphases on evolution and the selection of adaptive behavior, as well as the sociobiologists' specific concern with explaining the origins of human behavior patterns. Its scope, however, is broader than that of sociobiology; in particular, it encompasses the evolutionary origins of contemporary cognitive abilities as well as those that underlie social relations and social interactions. This emphasis is reflected in the titles or subtitles of several recent books devoted to the approach: *The Evolution of Cognition* (Heyes & Huber, 2000), *The Adapted Mind* (Barkow, Cosmides, & Tooby, 1992), and *The New Science of the Mind* (Buss, 1999).

Two themes can help characterize evolutionary developmental psychology. One concerns the fit between the adaptational challenges faced by our ancestors, across the millennia during which our present characteristics were selected, and those that confront contemporary humans. In some instances, the challenges are similar, and thus

Sociobiology
A branch of biology that attempts to discover the evolutionary origins of social behavior.

Evolutionary developmental psychology
A branch of evolutionary psychology that encompasses the evolutionary origins of contemporary cognitive abilities as well as those that underlie social relations and social interactions.

characteristics that evolved thousands of years ago still serve us well today. The formation of an attachment bond in infancy is one example; mastery of the culture's language system is another. In other instances, however, new challenges have arisen since the last significant evolutionary change in our species; learning to read is an example in this category, as are many of the other skills transmitted in school. Evolutionary psychologists predict that skills such as reading, which evolution has not prepared us for, will be more difficult to attain and more variable across children than are developments like attachment or language—and this, as we will see, is in fact the case.

A second theme is central to the *developmental* part of evolutionary developmental psychology. It is the argument that the attributes that are adaptive and promote survival will vary with the developmental level of the organism. Discussions of natural selection tend to stress the characteristics of adults that lead to successful mate selection and reproduction. Such characteristics are important; they can operate, however, only for individuals who also possess the characteristics that allowed them to survive infancy and childhood. Thus, this approach provides an evolutionary framework for making sense of the attributes and developmental tasks that characterize different phases of childhood.

As we saw, Lorenz provided an early version of this argument with his contention that certain characteristics of babies promote caregiving and thus survival. Bjorklund and Pellegrini (2002) offer another example. They suggest that the rough-and-tumble play that is common among boys may help boys learn forms of social signaling that will be beneficial for later social behavior, as well as provide exercise that is important for skeletal and muscular development.

To Recap . . .

Ethology is based on the principles of evolution as first proposed by Darwin. Ethologists believe that behaviors have both immediate and evolutionary determinants. These scientists are primarily concerned with innate behaviors, and they attempt to explain complex response patterns in terms of their survival value for the species.

Lorenz and Tinbergen, two founders of the ethological movement, identified four characteristics of innate behavior: It is universal; it is stereotyped; it requires no learning; and it is minimally affected by the environment. Ethologists have described how complex sequences of inherited responses (modal action patterns) are triggered by stimuli in the environment and how innate mechanisms, such as imprinting, influence the learning process.

Human ethology emerged largely as a result of Bowlby's research on the attachment process. Sociobiology is a recent attempt to explain social behavior in terms of an evolutionary model in which the survival of the genes supersedes any other goal. This mechanism is believed to be principally expressed in cultural and social structures. Evolutionary developmental psychology emphasizes the fit between our evolutionary history and our current adaptational challenges, as well as the variation in adaptive qualities across different phases of development.

CONCLUSION

Although child study is still young compared with other physical and biological sciences, our understanding of developmental processes is progressing so rapidly that it is difficult to keep up with the information that is being generated by researchers. The remainder of this text, therefore, focuses on the current state of the field rather than on historical issues and research. Yet as we proceed from topic to topic, you may be struck by how familiar some of the recurring controversies sound, reminiscent of the fundamental differences that arose between Locke and Rousseau or Watson and Gesell.

It may seem, indeed, that ideas regarding child development have not changed very much in the past few hundred years. Locke, Rousseau, and Darwin offered explanations of human behavior that are, in essence, still with us today. Modern theories of development, however, are different from these early models in several important ways.

The first is that today's viewpoints are much less extreme. There are no longer pure nature or nurture theories, for example. Thus, although each of the major developmental theories described in this chapter has its own ideas, philosophy, and methods, each also accepts many of the ideas of the other models. As psychologists continue to add to our knowledge of child development, the overlap among the approaches will undoubtedly grow.

A second difference is that today's psychologists no longer attempt to explain human development with only a few principles or processes. We have come to realize that behavior has many causes and that the mechanisms through which they operate are intricate and often interrelated. Modern theoretical explanations reflect this increasing complexity, and this trend, too, is likely to continue.

The final difference is that today's models are based on a great deal of scientific data. Early theories of human development were mostly the products of philosophical debates and logical deductions. Modern explanations, in contrast, have grown out of research findings, and they are continually being modified and revised in response to new observations and experimental data. A particular child psychologist may prefer one theoretical approach over another. In the final analysis, however, the evidence provided by research will determine which theories will survive and which will be abandoned.

FOR THOUGHT AND DISCUSSION

1. We suggest five reasons why developmental psychologists have traditionally focused their work on children. *Can you think of any others? What are some behaviors that can only be studied in children? What behaviors or aspects of children's development are you particularly interested in learning about in this course?*

2. One theme that has preoccupied philosophers and psychologists involves whether children are born with a tendency to be good, evil, or neither. *What do you think? Do you think this is a question that scientists should study?*

3. Some aspects of development are believed to be continuous from early childhood, whereas others are thought to be discontinuous. *Which aspects of your own personality have remained the same since you were a young child? Which have changed? Relate this stability and change to nature factors.*

4. This chapter described four major traditions of modern child psychology. *Which approach to explaining human development—cognitive, sociocultural, environmental, or evolutionary—fits best with your own thinking regarding how we develop? Why?*

5. Information-processing theorists conceptualize the mind in terms of computer operations. *What do you think are some advantages to this approach? Do you feel that viewing the mind as a machine makes it impossible for these theorists to investigate the more emotional aspects of human behavior? Why or why not?*

6. One aspect of both Bandura's concept of reciprocal determinism and Bronfenbrenner's ecological model is that to some degree people produce their own environment? *Can you think of some ways in which you have produced some of the desirable aspects of your environment? Have you produced any negative aspects? What could you do to change them?*

VISUAL SUMMARY FOR CHAPTER 1
Background and Theories

Developmental Psychology

Two Basic Goals of Developmental Research

1. To describe children's behavior at each point in development.
2. To explain developmental changes that occur from one point to the next.

Why Study Children?
Five reasons why developmental psychology has traditionally involved children

Period of rapid development

More developmental changes take place in childhood than at any other time.

Long-term influences

Experiences of early years may affect the individual's later development.

Insight into complex adult processes

Complex processes are easier to understand as they are forming.

Real-world applications

Knowledge of basic process can be used to help solve some of children's problems.

Interesting subject matter

Children are inherently interesting to study.

Early Theorists

John Locke

Based his approach on the strict environmentalist position that all knowledge is acquired through experience.

Jean-Jacques Rousseau

Proposed a nativistic model in which development unfolds according to inborn processes.

Charles Darwin

His theory of evolution suggested that some human behaviors may have had their origins in the past, when they were valuable to our ancestors' survival.

Pioneers of Child Psychology

G. Stanley Hall	Credited with founding the field of developmental psychology.
John B Watson	Proposed a behaviorist theory of development that held that the conditioned reflex was the fundamental unit of development and that experiential factors were primarily responsible for changes in behavior.
Arnold Gesell	Proposed a biological perspective that stressed inborn maturational processes. Produced valuable age-related norms of development.
Sigmund Freud	Proposed a 5-stage psychosexual theory of development that emphasized the combined importance of early experiences and inborn processes.
Erik Erikson	Developed an 8-stage theory that differed from Freud's in that it extended through adulthood, assigned a major role to social factors, and focused on the healthy aspects of personality.

Issues in Developmental Psychology

Nature versus Nurture	This issue focuses on whether the primary source of developmental change is inborn and biological or environmental and experiential.
Continuity versus Discontinuity	This issue focuses on whether the pattern of development is constant or uneven, and whether there is a connectedness between early and later characteristics.
Normative versus Idiographic	This issue relates to the researcher's preference for focusing on the commonalities of child development or on factors that produce individual differences among children.

Cognitive-Developmental Approaches

Cognitive abilities are fundamental and guide children's behavior. The key to understanding children's behavior lies in how their knowledge is structured at any given time and how it changes as they grow.

Major Approaches   **Key Assumptions**

Piaget's Theory	Development can be described in terms of functions and cognitive structures. Changes in structures are guided by two functions: organization and adaptation. Adaptation consists of assimilation and accommodation. Development consists of movement through four stages. sensorimotor, preoperational, concrete operations, and formal operations.
Information-Processing Models	Cognition is viewed in terms of a computerlike system with three parts: input from the senses, internal processes that act on and transform the information, output from the system in the form of behavior.

The Sociocultural Approach

Social processes are crucial in the development of a child's cognitive abilities.

Major Approaches **Key Assumptions**

Vygotsky's Theory

> Development involves the child's gradual internationalization of bodies of knowledge and tools of thought, primarily through shared experiences with parents and teachers. Culture thus teaches a child what to think and how to think.

Bronfenbrenner's Ecological Model

> Bronfenbrenner's model focuses on the contexts in which development occurs. The model includes four contextual layers: the microsystem, the mesosystem, the exosystem, and the macrosystem. Child and environment continually influence one another in a transactional manner.

Environmental/Learning Approaches

Much of children's typical behavior is acquired through conditioning and learning principles.

Major Approaches **Key Assumptions**

Behavior Analysis

> Three types of conditioning and learning are assumed to operate on children: habituation, respondent conditioning, and operant learning. Habituation and respondent conditioning involve reflexes, whereas operant learning is controlled by the consequences of behavior. Reinforces are consequences that make behavior more probable; punishers are consequences that make behavior less probable.

Social-Learning Theory

> Bandura's theory stresses the role of observational learning. Vicarious reinforcement and vicarious punishment can affect the behavior of an observer. The distinction is made between the acquisition of a modeled response and its performance. Reciprocal determinism holds that human development results from the interaction of characteristics of the person, the person's behavior, and the environment.

Evolutionary and Biological Approaches

Ethology is based on the principles of evolution. Ethologists are primarily concerned with innate behaviors, and they attempt to explain complex response patterns in terms of their survival value for the species.

Major Approaches   **Key Assumptions**

Classical Ethology

Lorenz and Tinbergen identified four charateristics of innate behavior: It is universal, it is stereo-typed, it rquires no learning, and it is minimally affected by the environment. Ethologists view com-lex sequences of inherited responses as modal action patterns that are triggered by innate releasing mechanisms in the organism's environment.

Sociobiology

Sociobiology is a recent attempt to explain social behavior in terms of an evolutionary model in which the survival of the genes supersedes any other goal.

Human Ethology

Human ethology emerged largely from the results of Bowlby's research on the attachment process. Many aspects of child development now are being studied from an ethological perspective.

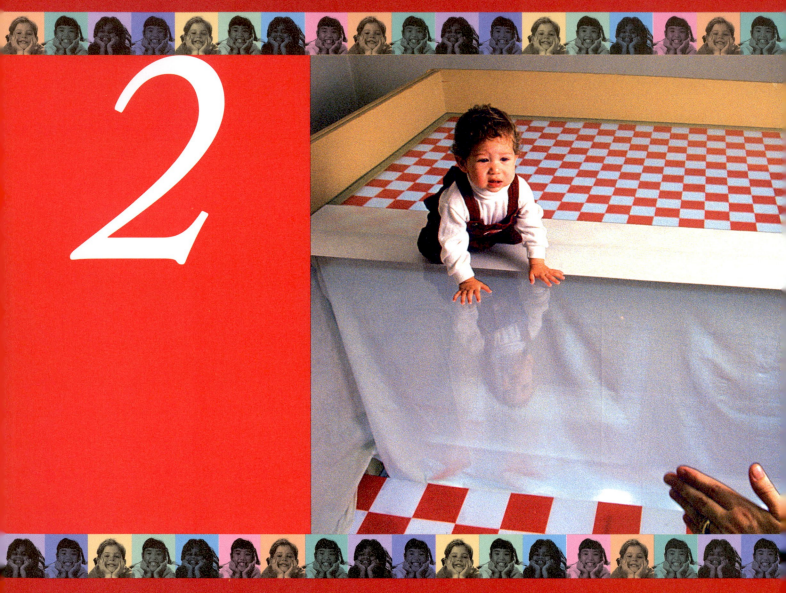

2

Research Methods

*S*ometimes things that we all know to be true turn out not to be true — or at least not true in any simple or automatic way.

Consider the effects of rewards on children's behavior. Long before there was a science of psychology to verify the phenomenon, parents and teachers knew that

they could promote desirable behavior in children by providing positive consequences for the behavior. And indeed, the principle of reinforcement is one of the most solidly established findings in psychology.

But are rewards always a good way to promote desired behavior? The following study suggests that they are not.

Preschool children were first given a chance to draw with colored markers during the free-play portion of the school day. This "baseline" period indicated to researchers how interested each child was in the activity. Then each child participated individually in an experimental session, during which he or she was asked to produce marker drawings for an adult "who's come to the nursery school for a few days to see what kinds of pictures boys and girls like to draw." For some of the children, these were the only instructions. Some children, however, were also promised an attractive reward for producing the drawings: a "Good Player Award" with a gold star and red ribbon and a place for the child's name.

The reward had an immediate positive effect: The children who had been promised the award churned out a large number of drawings. The surprising result occurred across the following days, when the children were again back in the classroom and had a choice of whether to play with the markers. The children who had been rewarded for drawing spent considerably less time drawing with the markers than did the other children — and

considerably less time than they themselves had spent during the baseline period. The reward, the researchers argued, had undercut the children's intrinsic interest in the activity. Drawing had become something to do in order to get a prize. When the prize was no longer there, drawing was no longer very attractive.

Note the message that this finding carries for parents. Using strong rewards to elicit desired behavior, or strong threats to discourage undesired behavior, may well be effective in the short term — at the cost, however, of making children believe that they are responding only for the reward or punishment. Long-term compliance with parental wishes might be better fostered by techniques that help children to value certain actions in themselves and not simply as a way to get something good or avoid something bad.

To some people, research in psychology — including child psychology — serves simply to support the folk wisdom that we all have about human behavior. And sometimes, research does verify what we already "know" (though this does not make the research valueless). But that is by no means always the case. Even for a topic as familiar as children, well-designed and original studies can produce a number of surprises and unexpected discoveries. The marker study provides one example, and we will see numerous other examples as we move through the book. In this chapter, we consider the research methods that make such discoveries possible. ■

The developing child may seem quite different from atoms fusing to produce nuclear energy or leaf cells using light and carbon dioxide to make food. Yet the research methods used by developmental psychologists to study children are essentially the same as those used by physicists, biologists, and other researchers in the natural sciences. In this chapter, we examine some of these methods and the ways child researchers can use them to unlock the mysteries of human development.

We saw in Chapter 1 that the study of the child became scientific in the 19th century, when G. Stanley Hall and other pioneers attempted the first systematic studies of child development. Since then, the research methods used by child psychologists have advanced in many ways. These advances have contributed importantly to the enormous growth in our knowledge and understanding of developmental processes (Miller, 1998).

We begin by outlining some of the ideas and concepts that are basic to all scientific research. We then consider the principal research methods used in developmental psychology. Last, we discuss the sometimes thorny issue of research ethics.

SCIENTIFIC RESEARCH

The approach scientists use to study any problem or issue is known as the **scientific method.** The method is really a system of rules that scientists use to design and conduct their research, evaluate their results, and communicate their findings to other scientists. These rules have evolved over hundreds of years, and they can be applied to the study of virtually anything.

Scientific method
The system of rules used by scientists to conduct and evaluate their research.

The Role of Theory

In Chapter 1, we presented four major theories, but we did not actually define that term. In psychology, a **theory** is a set of statements describing the relation between behavior and the factors that influence it. A specific statement that is well supported by research evidence is called a **law** or **principle**—the principle of reinforcement is a good example. A statement that simply postulates, or proposes, a relation is called a **hypothesis.** Any individual study is usually designed to test a researcher's hypothesis regarding how some aspect of children's behavior is affected by some factor in their world.

Theories have two important roles in scientific research. The first is to *organize research findings.* As investigators acquire knowledge, they use theories to fit the information together into a coherent explanation of the behaviors and processes being studied. Once the knowledge is organized, it is sometimes obvious that certain questions remain to be answered or that specific relations probably exist even though they do not yet have substantial supporting evidence. A second role of theories, then, is to *guide new research* by indicating to investigators which hypotheses should be tested next.

Psychologists do not investigate children's development by randomly studying any question that pops into their heads. Research is typically guided by an underlying theory and theoretical orientation. Thus, cognitive-developmentalists tend to investigate characteristics of children's knowledge, whereas environmental/learning theorists are more likely to study ways in which behavior is acquired through experience. Similarly, sociocultural theorists focus on the social and cultural bases for development, whereas ethologists are more likely to search for various innate patterns of response.

Theory
A broad set of statements describing the relation between a phenomenon and the factors assumed to affect it.

Law (principle)
A predicted relation between a phenomenon and a factor assumed to affect it that is supported by a good deal of scientific evidence.

Hypothesis
A predicted relation between a phenomenon and a factor assumed to affect it that is not yet supported by a great deal of evidence. Hypotheses are tested in experimental investigations.

Objectivity and Measurement

Children are not of interest only to psychologists, of course. Scholars in literature, music, and art, for example, have devoted much attention to the developing child. But in these fields, the emphasis frequently is on individual tastes, personal opinions, and other subjective judgments. In psychology and the other natural sciences, the emphasis is on **objectivity.**

Objective methods of study have as their primary goal the opportunity for any other scientist, at least in principle, to conduct the same research in the same manner (and presumably arrive at the same results). In addition, objectivity helps reduce potential sources of bias that may enter into the research, such as the experimenter's personal beliefs or preferences regarding what the results should be. These goals are achieved in a number of ways.

One is through a focus on *observable* behaviors. Recall that in child psychology our two primary goals—to describe children's behavior at each point in their development and to identify the causes and processes that produce changes in behavior from one point to the next—center on behavior. Even developmentalists who are concerned primarily with cognition observe the effects of internal cognitive processes on some aspect

Objectivity
A characteristic of scientific research; it requires that the procedures and subject matter of investigations should be formulated so that they could, in principle, be agreed on by everyone.

of behavior. For example, we study assimilation and accommodation by observing a child's reactions to new experiences; we study intelligence by calculating a child's performance on an IQ test; and we study social skills by examining how a child interacts with peers.

A second requirement for ensuring objectivity is that the behaviors under study must be *measurable.* It is not enough that we can observe behavior; we must also feel confident as to when the behavior did or did not occur, when one behavior ended and the next one began, and so forth. Such confidence is achieved by defining and describing the behavior very precisely, so that independent observers would have no trouble agreeing on what happened in a given situation. For example, suppose we are interested in studying children's altruism—their willingness to help someone else. We might first define altruism in terms of sharing behaviors and then develop a procedure that entails observing the number of pennies just won in a game that a child donates to a charity. Or suppose that we want to investigate an infant's attachment to her mother. We could define attachment in terms of specific behaviors, such as crying, smiling, and searching, and then measure the amount of time that elapses before the infant displays each of these behaviors after the mother has left the room. In this way, abstract concepts such as "altruism" and "attachment" become measurable in an objective, scientific way.

A third way to achieve objectivity—and a further important aspect of measurement—is to make everything in the research study *quantifiable,* that is, able to be counted. The researcher must quantify not only the children's behaviors but also the factors that the researcher hypothesizes may be affecting the behaviors. Often such factors are physical. The number of children in a classroom, the length of time a child spends reading, or the amount of alcohol that a pregnant mother has consumed, for example, are relatively easy to define in this way. Factors that involve the behaviors of others—social approval, peer interactions, or modeling, for instance—are more difficult to deal with, but they, too, must be carefully defined so that they can be measured and counted.

Deciding how to define the constructs of interest is important, but it is just one step in the measurement process. The researcher must also decide how to collect the relevant data. Suppose, for example, that a researcher has decided to measure attachment in the

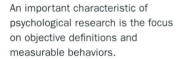

An important characteristic of psychological research is the focus on objective definitions and measurable behaviors.

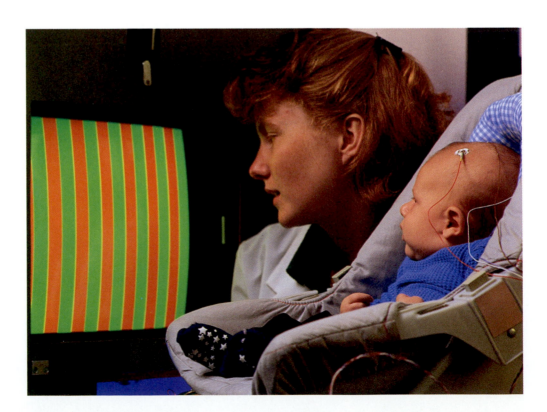

Table 2.1	Measurement Options in Psychological Research	
Source of Data	**Application to Attachment**	**General Strengths and Limitations**
Observation in the natural setting	Observers visit home on several occasions, recording behaviors relevant to attachment (e.g., response to separation from caregiver, reactions to stranger). Example: Strayer et al. (1995).	The only direct source of information for how children naturally behave in the natural setting. The presence of observers, however, may alter the setting and thus the behavior. Observers may not be able to record some behaviors accurately. Finally, some behaviors (e.g., perceptual processes) are difficult if not impossible to measure in the natural environment.
Measurement in a structured laboratory environment	The infant's behavior is recorded across a series of standardized situations designed to elicit behaviors relevant to attachment (e.g., separation from and reunion with mother, response to stranger). Example: Ainsworth et al. (1978).	The controlled laboratory environment ensures that the behaviors of interest will occur, and it maximizes both accuracy of measurements and comparability across participants. Furthermore, for some dependent variables (e.g., physiological changes) laboratory measurement is the only option. To the extent that the lab environment differs from the real-life settings of interest, however, behaviors measured in the lab may not be perfectly generalizable.
Verbal report of behavior (via interview or questionnaire) from some knowledgeable informant	An interview with the mother is used to elicit information about the infant's typical behaviors with familiar and unfamiliar people. Example: Ainsworth et al. (1978).	The scope of information provided is considerably greater with verbal reports than with any other method of study. As children develop, multiple sources become available, including peer reports and self-reports. Only some behaviors are accessible to verbal report, however. In addition, verbal reports are not direct measures of behavior, and for various reasons they may sometimes be inaccurate.

manner described, that is, through analysis of the behaviors that the infant shows on separation from the mother. How can the researcher determine which behaviors a particular baby in fact shows? There are three general possibilities: observe the behaviors in the natural setting, devise a laboratory situation to elicit the behaviors of interest, or gather the information from someone who is knowledgeable about the baby's typical behavior. Table 2.1 summarizes these three approaches as they apply to attachment. The table also discusses some of the strengths and weaknesses of each approach. It would be a good idea to revisit the table periodically—and to think through the strengths and weaknesses—as we discuss various topics throughout the book.

To Recap . . .

The scientific method consists of the rules that researchers use to conduct and describe their investigations. Scientific theories play two important roles in the research process. First, they help organize the information gathered from scientific studies. Second, they guide researchers to the important questions that need to be examined next.

   Scientific research requires objectivity, which in psychology leads to a focus on observable behaviors and a need for behaviors and their determining factors to be described so that they are measurable and quantifiable. The researcher who has decided to measure a particular behavior has three general measurement options: observing the behavior in the natural setting, eliciting the behavior in a laboratory setting, or obtaining reports of the behavior from some informed source.

TYPES OF RESEARCH

Research in psychology generally falls into one of three categories: descriptive, correlational, or experimental. Here we briefly discuss each of these approaches as they apply to the study of children.

Descriptive Research

Descriptive research
Research based solely on observations, with no attempt to determine systematic relations among the variables.

The oldest form of psychological research is the purely descriptive approach. When applied to children, **descriptive research** consists of simply observing or interviewing children or their parents and recording information of interest. The psychologist makes no formal attempt to identify relations among the children's behaviors and any other factors. Early baby biographies, such as those in which Darwin and others kept daily records of the behaviors of their infants, provided the first systematic descriptive data on human development. Gesell's norms, which described the typical skills and abilities of children of various ages, also used the descriptive method.

More recently, psychologists have used descriptive research to document the amount of time children of different ages devote to TV viewing and other leisure activities, the content of children's disputes with friends and family, and how adolescents distribute their time among friends, family, and peers. Today, descriptive research is typically only a first step in a research plan that will go on to use more sophisticated methods of investigation. It is of particular value when we know little about the topic under study.

Correlational Research

Variable
Any factor that can take on different values along a dimension.

The step beyond observing and describing behaviors is identifying any systematic relations in the observations. Specifically, researchers attempt to identify correlations among variables. A **variable** is any factor that can take on different values along some dimension. Common examples include human physical characteristics—height, weight, age, and so on—and aspects of the environment—temperature, room size, distance to the nearest library, and number of people in a family, for instance. Human behaviors, if properly defined, can also be variables and can vary along several dimensions—for example, how many times a child asks the teacher for help (*frequency*), how loudly a baby cries (*intensity*), or how long a child practices the piano (*duration*).

Correlation
The relation between two variables, described in terms of direction and strength.

A **correlation** is a statement that describes how two variables are related. Perhaps a psychologist would like to know whether children's ages are correlated with—systematically related to—their heights. The researcher might observe and record the heights of 100 children, aged 2 to 12, and examine whether changes in the one variable correspond to changes in the other. In this case, the psychologist could expect to find a clear relation between the variables of age and height—that is, as children increase in age, they generally increase in height as well. This type of relation, in which two variables change in the same direction, is described as a **positive correlation.**

Positive correlation
A correlation in which two variables change in the same direction.

What about the relation between a child's age and the number of hours each day that the child spends at home? Here we would also discover a systematic relation, but the variables involved would move in opposite directions—as a child's age increases, the amount of time the child spends at home generally decreases. This sort of relation is called a **negative correlation.**

Negative correlation
A correlation in which two variables change in opposite directions.

Finally, we might investigate the relation between a child's height and the number of children in the child's classroom. In this case, we would likely find that the two variables are not related to one another at all and so have no correlation.

Correlations can be described not only in terms of their direction (positive or negative) but also in terms of their strength. A strong correlation means that two variables are closely related. In such cases, knowing the value of one gives us a good indication of the value of the second. As a correlation grows weaker, the amount of predictability between the two variables decreases. When the variables become completely unrelated, knowledge of the value of one gives us no clue as to the value of the other.

Correlation coefficient (r)
A number between +1.00 and −1.00 that indicates the direction and strength of a correlation between two variables.

The direction of a correlation is indicated by a plus or minus sign, and its strength is indicated by a numerical value that can be calculated from a simple statistical formula. The result is called the **correlation coefficient (r),** which can range between +1.00 and −1.00. A correlation coefficient of +.86 indicates a strong positive correlation, and

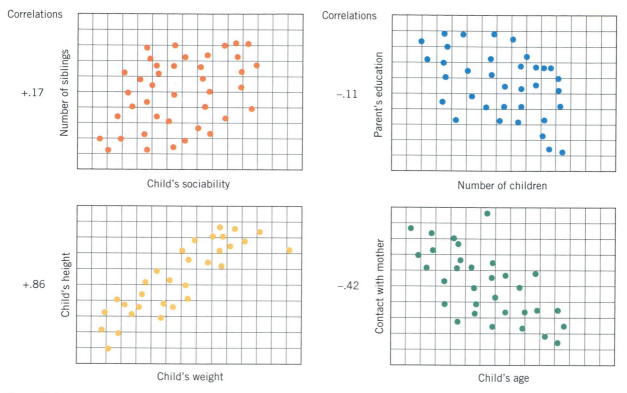

Figure 2.1

Scatter diagrams illustrating correlations between two variables. Each dot represents one child and shows the child's values for the two variables. One value is plotted from the vertical axis and the other from the horizontal axis. The left two graphs show positive correlations, and the right two graphs show negative correlations.

+.17 indicates a weak positive correlation. Similarly, −.93, −.41, and −.08 denote, respectively, a strong, moderate, and weak negative correlation. A coefficient of 0 means that there is absolutely no correlation between two variables. Correlations can also be presented visually with a **scatter diagram,** some examples of which are shown in Figure 2.1.

To illustrate both the usefulness and the limitations of correlational research, let us consider a hypothetical example. Suppose a research team is interested in learning whether a relation exists between the amount of time children watch the educational TV program *Sesame Street* and their readiness to learn to read. To begin, the researchers randomly select a number of children and measure each child's values on the reading-ability variable (perhaps by giving the children a reading readiness test on which they can score between 0 and 100) and on the viewing variable (perhaps by having parents record the number of hours each week that the child watches *Sesame Street*). Then the researchers calculate the correlation between the two sets of scores and discover that the variables have a correlation coefficient of +.78, as shown in Figure 2.2. What can the research team conclude from these findings?

Because the two variables display a strong positive correlation, we know that as one increases the other increases and also that knowing a child's value on one of the variables allows us to predict the child's value on the other variable fairly well. We therefore might be tempted to believe that the study shows that viewing *Sesame Street* promotes the skills children need to learn to read, or, in more general terms, that a change in one of the variables causes change in the other. Herein lies a major limitation of correlational research—*a correlation cannot be used to show causality between the variables*. The correlation in the example may accurately reveal the pattern and strength of the reading-viewing relation, but it cannot reveal cause and effect between the variables. Why not?

Scatter diagram
A graphic illustration of a correlation between two variables.

Figure 2.2

A scatter diagram of a hypothetical correlation between children's viewing of *Sesame Street* and their reading level. The correlation coefficient (*r*) shows a strong positive relation between the two variables.

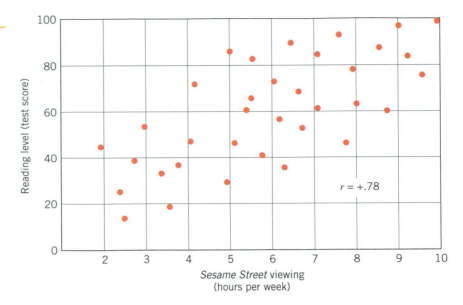

If we think carefully about the findings, we realize that some other conclusions cannot be ruled out. For example, rather than TV viewing having an effect on reading readiness, the reverse is equally plausible. That is, children whose prereading skills are relatively advanced may watch *Sesame Street* more often than do children whose skills are less advanced (possibly because they enjoy it more). Another possibility is that the two variables are both influenced by some third variable that we have not measured. For instance, both might be affected by the educational background of the child's parents. Indeed, there is a good chance that the better educated a child's parents are, the more likely they are to engage in other activities that promote prereading skills, such as reading books with their children, as well as encourage their children to view educational television. Thus, although correlational research is a valuable tool for identifying and measuring systematic relations, it cannot be used to explain them. Explanation requires a more powerful research method—the experimental approach.

Nevertheless, correlational research can play an important role in the scientific research process. Like descriptive research, correlational studies sometimes raise interesting and provocative questions. These questions may be formed into specific research hypotheses that investigators can examine using more rigorous methods of research.

Experimental Research

The most powerful type of research in developmental psychology is the experiment. A simple experiment often involves investigating the relation between just two variables, but, unlike correlational research, experimentation permits us to draw cause-and-effect conclusions about the variables.

The most important difference between a correlational study and an experimental study lies in how the information is gathered. Correlational research is based on measurement alone. The two variables of interest are observed and recorded without any intrusion or interference by the researcher. In an experiment, however, the researcher systematically *manipulates*—changes—one variable and then looks for any effects (changes) in the second variable. The variable that is systematically manipulated is called the **independent variable.** The variable affected (at least potentially) by the manipulation is called the **dependent variable.** In psychological research, the dependent variable is typically some aspect of behavior, whereas the independent variable is a factor the researcher suspects may influence that behavior.

Independent variable

The variable in an experiment that is systematically manipulated.

Dependent variable

The variable that is predicted to be affected by an experimental manipulation. In psychology, usually some aspect of behavior.

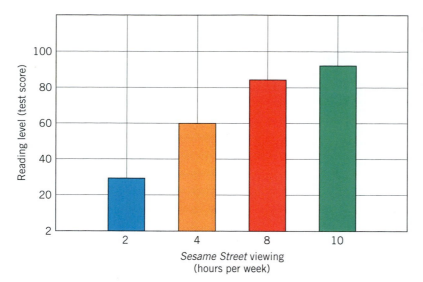

Figure 2.3

A bar graph illustrating an experimental test of the hypothesis that viewing *Sesame Street* improves reading test performance. Each bar shows the average test score for all the children in that experimental group.

Group Studies   Most experimental research conducted by developmental psychologists involves comparing the behavior of groups of research participants exposed to different manipulations of an independent variable.

Let us return to the previous example and consider how researchers might use the experimental method to address the question of whether watching *Sesame Street* affects reading level. First, the researchers need a hypothesis that clearly identifies the independent and dependent variables. If the hypothesis is that viewing the program causes improvements in reading ability, then the independent variable is the amount of viewing and the dependent variable is the child's reading level. The next step involves systematically manipulating the independent variable. As in the correlational approach, the researchers select a number of children, but in this case they randomly divide the children into, say, four groups. The first group is required to watch 2 hours of *Sesame Street* each week; the second group, 4 hours; the third group, 8 hours; and the fourth group, 10 hours. After perhaps 6 months, the researchers administer the reading test to all the children and examine how the different groups perform. Possible results are shown in Figure 2.3. If the differences in performance among groups are sufficiently large (as determined by the appropriate statistical tests), not only can the researchers conclude that the two variables are systematically related but they can also make the causal statement that viewing *Sesame Street* improves children's reading ability. That is, the psychologists' hypothesis now has been supported by experimental data.

Reversal-Replication Studies   Although experimental research most often involves exposing groups of participants to different values of an independent variable, there is an alternative called the **reversal-replication design** (or sometimes the **ABAB design**). In this method, the independent variable is systematically presented and removed and effects on the dependent variable are noted. The main advantage of this design is that fewer participants are needed; for instance, it can be used in an experiment involving a single child. Consider how we might use this method to test the hypothesis that the presence of the mother causes infants to smile more often. In this experiment, the independent variable would be the presence or absence of the mother, and the dependent variable would be the amount the infant smiles. As Figure 2.4 indicates, the basic procedure of the experiment involves counting the number of times the infant smiles per minute during a 20-minute daily session in which the mother is either present or absent.

To conduct the experiment, the researcher must first determine the *baseline,* or initial level of the behavior being observed. In this example, the baseline is the number of

Reversal-replication (ABAB) design

An experimental design in which the independent variable is systematically presented and removed several times. Can be used in studies involving very few research participants.

Figure 2.4

A reversal-replication design showing a causal relation between the presence of the mother (the independent variable) and the amount an infant smiles (the dependent variable). The third and fourth phases replicate the procedures and results of the first two phases.

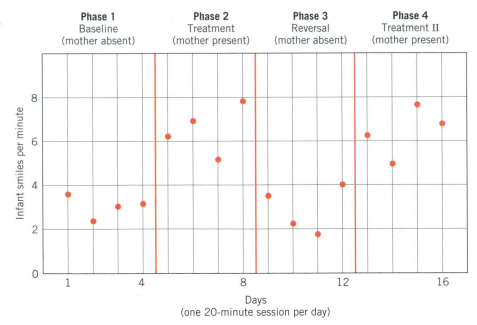

Phase 1
Baseline
(mother absent)

Phase 2
Treatment
(mother present)

Phase 3
Reversal
(mother absent)

Phase 4
Treatment II
(mother present)

Infant smiles per minute

Days
(one 20-minute session per day)

times the infant smiles when alone. In the second, or *treatment,* phase of the experiment, the independent variable is introduced. As shown in Figure 2.4, there is a clear increase in smiling when the mother is present. The change in the infant's behavior supports the researcher's hypothesis, but it is premature to conclude that a causal relation exists between the presence of the mother and the baby's smiling. Why? The change in the infant's behavior might have resulted from other factors—such as a better overall mood—that only coincidentally occurred when the mother was present.

To determine whether the change in behavior was only accidentally related to the change in the independent variable, the researcher attempts to *replicate* the procedure and results. In the next step, then, the independent variable is again removed. This is called the *reversal,* or withdrawal, phase. In our example, we can see that the infant's behavior returns to its baseline level. Finally, the independent variable is presented once more in a second treatment phase. If the subsequent change in behavior is the same as during the first treatment phase, then the researcher has enough evidence to infer a causal relation between the independent and dependent variables. Because the amount the infant smiles does indeed increase once again, the researcher can reasonably conclude that the baby's smiling is affected by the mother's presence.

Additional Considerations   Experimental research is a powerful scientific tool, not only because it can reveal cause-and-effect relations but also because it can be applied to a wide variety of problems and settings. Much of the experimentation conducted by child psychologists takes place in laboratories, where researchers can exert considerable control over testing conditions. But consistent with an ecological approach, experimental studies can also be conducted in field settings—playgrounds, classrooms, or children's homes, for example—where the child's behavior is studied under more natural conditions.

The experimental approach is of paramount importance in the study of child development, and examples of experiments are described frequently in the pages that follow. We have outlined here the most basic concepts involved in this method, but many detailed procedures not discussed must be followed before we can be confident that an experiment is scientifically sound. These involve such matters as how the research participants are selected and assigned to groups, under what conditions the data are gathered, which statistical tests are conducted, and so forth. Furthermore, experimental studies—as well as correlational studies—are typically more complex than we have indicated. For one thing, a single study often involves a number of variables rather than just two, and sometimes several hypotheses are tested at once.

Finally, perhaps the major caution with respect to conclusions from experimental research concerns generalizability. The imposition of experimental control, whether in the laboratory or in the natural environment, can sometimes create situations that are fairly far removed from the real-life situations to which we hope to generalize; if so, the researcher must be cautious in concluding that the effects demonstrated would hold under more natural circumstances. As we will detail, the issue of experimental control is a particular challenge for psychologists interested in studying child development in diverse cultures. Discussions of generalizability, as well as the other issues that we have just briefly mentioned, can be found in chapters and texts devoted to methodology in developmental psychology (e.g., Cozby et al., 1998; Hartmann & George, 1999; Miller, 1998; Vasta, 1982).

To Recap . . .

The three major research methods used by child psychologists are descriptive research, correlational research, and experimentation. The descriptive approach involves simple observation and is used today primarily as a first step in exploring areas about which little is known. Correlational studies are used to identify relations between variables and to describe them in terms of their direction and strength. This method does not permit conclusions regarding cause and effect. The experimental approach involves testing hypotheses by systematically manipulating the independent variable and examining its effects on the dependent variable. Experimental studies may involve groups of participants exposed to different values of an independent variable. They may also involve only a few participants, who are exposed to the repeated presentation and removal of an independent variable in a reversal-replication design. Experimental studies, in contrast to correlational studies, do permit cause-and-effect conclusions; their chief limitation is that effects demonstrated under experimental control may not always generalize to other settings.

STUDYING DEVELOPMENT

Development, as we have seen, involves changes in behavior over time. Many of the issues of interest to developmental researchers therefore focus on how children's behavior at one age differs from their behavior at another age. Sometimes these issues are mainly descriptive, such as how a child's speech progresses from the one-word utterances of the toddler to the ill-formed sentences of the preschooler to the reasonably accurate sentences of the preadolescent. At other times the issues concern the causes of behavior, such as the possible effects of day care programs on children's later social adjustment to school. For either type of question, however, the psychologist needs a research method that will allow the comparison of behaviors at different ages. Four methods are available for this purpose: the longitudinal study, the cross-sectional study, a method that combines the two, and the microgenetic technique.

Longitudinal Research

One approach to studying children's behavior at different ages is the **longitudinal design.** The logic of this approach is quite simple. The behaviors of interest are first measured at some early point in development and then measured again at various intervals as the child grows. The main advantage of this method is that it allows the researcher to study directly how each behavior changes as the child gets older (Menard, 1991).

The number of years required for a longitudinal study can vary considerably. Some questions can be explored within a relatively brief time frame. For example, determining whether different techniques of caring for premature infants have different effects on

Longitudinal design
A research method in which the same individuals are studied repeatedly over time.

In longitudinal research, the same individuals are studied over a period of time, sometimes many years.

the age at which the babies begin to walk and talk should take only about 18 months to 2 years of observation. Other questions, such as whether a child's early disciplinary experiences influence his or her own use of punishment as a parent, may need to extend over decades.

Longitudinal studies can be either correlational or experimental. If we measure behaviors at one age and then again at a later age, we can determine the consistency of the behaviors by calculating the correlation between the two sets of measurements. Experimental longitudinal studies usually involve introducing a manipulation at one point in development and then examining its effects on the dependent variables of interest at some later point or points in development.

Two types of research questions are particularly well suited to the longitudinal approach (Magnusson et al., 1994). Both are forms of the continuity-discontinuity issue introduced in Chapter 1. The first concerns the *stability*, or persistence, of behaviors. For instance, if we wish to determine the extent to which a child's temperament (an aspect of personality) remains constant throughout life, the best approach is to measure this characteristic in the same children periodically and examine the correlations among the sets of scores.

The second type of question that works well with the longitudinal method involves the *effects of early experiences* on later behavior. If we wish to determine whether certain events or conditions that occur during a child's early years—divorce, an infant stimulation program, or the quality of diet, for instance—produce long-term effects, the clearest answers will be obtained with an experimental longitudinal approach. For example, we might identify children who have participated in an early stimulation program and children who have not and then follow both groups for a number of years to see whether differences emerge in their success in school.

Despite the obvious value of the longitudinal approach, the method does have certain disadvantages. One is the problem of *attrition*, the loss of individuals under study, which can occur for a variety of reasons. Families may move away, children may become ill or develop other problems that interfere with participation in the study, or parents may simply lose interest and withdraw from the project. Other problems may develop because of the repeated testing. For example, a study concerned with the stability of a child's intelligence requires that IQ tests be administered at regular intervals. But repeated experience with tests itself may make a child test wise to the types of responses that are expected and may thus artificially improve the child's performance.

A third disadvantage relates directly to the fact that longitudinal studies are often designed to last for many years. There is a very real possibility that the issues involved or the instruments used at the beginning of the study may become outdated. For example, the experimental questions posed at the outset of the project may become less important as the years pass and other research findings are published. Similarly, the tests and instruments used may become obsolete. Finally, there is a major practical disadvantage.

Terman's Studies of Genius

The first major longitudinal study in developmental psychology was Lewis Terman's investigation of intellectually gifted children. This classic research remains especially noteworthy because it followed a very large group of individuals for almost their entire lives and generated some fascinating findings (Cravens, 1992).

Terman was a psychologist at Stanford University and is best known for having developed one of the first IQ tests, the Stanford-Binet (which we will describe when we discuss intelligence testing in Chapter 10). In the course of administering his new test, Terman became interested in the children who scored at the very highest levels. In 1921 he selected approximately 1,400 extremely intelligent 11-year-olds in California to participate in a longitudinal project, which he titled *Genetic Studies of Genius* (Terman, 1925).

Terman was not interested only in the intelligence of these children. He also collected a great deal of information on their families, schools, physical characteristics, mental and medical health, personality traits, and more. At intervals of about 10 years, Terman readministered many of the same tests and measures to find out whether gifted children develop differently from their peers of normal intelligence.

The participants in this study, who became known as Termites, proved to be quite different from what would have been predicted by the conventional wisdom of the time. They did not support the stereotype that genius children are sickly, meek, and social misfits. As they grew up, they were found to be healthier, wealthier, more successful professionally, and even happier than most of their peers in society.

Two of Terman's initial findings have been somewhat controversial. He reported that the gifted children came from wealthier, better-educated families and that many more males than females had high IQ scores. Both of these findings today are regarded skeptically by psychologists and may have resulted from flaws or biases in the way in which Terman selected his research participants (Shurkin, 1992).

Terman died in 1957, but his research was continued by others, including Robert Sears, a Termite who became a developmental psychologist. In 1972, when the participants had reached their 60s, they were asked to describe what aspects of their lives they had found most satisfying or rewarding. Interestingly, the majority of them pointed to their families—not their wealth, social status, or professional success—as having been their greatest source of happiness (Sears, 1977).

Although most of the Termites have now died, the vast amount of information collected by Terman's research team is still being studied, and scientists continue to generate new questions and better ways to look at the data (Friedman et al., 1995). Giftedness is also the subject of some exciting contemporary theorizing and research. We return to the topic in Chapter 10.

BOX 2.1

Classics of
Research

Because it often requires a large research staff and many hours of observation or testing, longitudinal research can be very expensive. (An early longitudinal study is presented in Box 2.1.)

Cross-Sectional Research

An alternative to longitudinal research is the **cross-sectional design,** which allows researchers to examine developmental differences in behavior by studying children of different ages at the same point in time. In this type of experiment, the age of the children becomes an independent variable in the research design. The major advantage of this approach is that it is much less time-consuming than the longitudinal method. Rather than waiting 5 years to determine, say, how memory processes in 3-year-olds differ from memory processes in 8-year-olds, we can simply study a group of 3-year-olds and a group of 8-year-olds at the same time. The relatively short time required also means that such experiments are rarely plagued by the problems of attrition, repeated testing, outdated issues and instruments, and high cost.

Still, the cross-sectional approach has two significant disadvantages. First, this method cannot be used to investigate questions of behavior stability and early experience, as it is impossible to determine persistence of an early trait or the impact of an early event by examining those behaviors in *different* older children.

Second is a problem known as the **cohort effect,** which occurs because certain aspects of people's behavior are influenced by the unique events and conditions experienced by their particular generation or cohort. For example, suppose we were

Cross-sectional design
A research method in which people of different ages are studied simultaneously to examine the effects of age on some aspect of behavior.

Cohort effect
A problem sometimes found in cross-sectional research in which people of a given age are affected by factors unique to their generation.

People of a given age may be affected by factors unique to their generation, such as growing up during the Great Depression.

investigating the cognitive skills of individuals at ages 40, 50, and 70 and found that the 50-year-olds performed better on our various reasoning and problem-solving tests than did the younger or older groups. Would these results allow us to conclude that cognitive development improves across part of the adult age span and then declines as people grow older?

Such an interpretation is certainly consistent with our data, but another explanation arises when we consider the educational backgrounds of the three groups of participants. The 70-year-olds were raised during the Great Depression, when many youngsters were forced to leave school early and find jobs. The 40-year-olds were raised during the late 1960s, when much greater emphasis was being placed on children's social and emotional development. But the 50-year-olds began attending school shortly after the launching of the Soviet satellite *Sputnik,* which stimulated a major U.S. effort to improve scientific and mathematical training. The point is that our research participants are members of three cohorts, or peer groups, which had different educational experiences. The performance differences we observe may not reflect the differences in their ages so much as their different life experiences.

It is worth noting that cohort can also be important in a longitudinal study. Most longitudinal studies examine a single cohort—that is, individuals who are the same age at the start of the study and thus were born at about the same time. It is possible, therefore, that whatever patterns we find across different ages reflect experiences specific to the particular cohort and not age effects per se. Imagine, for example, that we were to carry out a longitudinal study with people born in 1920. We are interested in stability or change as our sample progresses through various phases in the developmental span. All we know for certain, however, is what happens for a sample who experienced a Great Depression in childhood and adolescence, a world war in young adulthood, another war shortly thereafter, and so forth.

Combining Longitudinal and Cross-Sectional Research

Cross-sequential design
A research method combining longitudinal and cross-sectional designs.

To obtain the best features of the longitudinal and cross-sectional designs, researchers sometimes combine the two methods into a **cross-sequential design.** The combined approach begins with a simple cross-sectional investigation, during which groups of children of different ages are studied simultaneously. The same groups are then studied again at one or more later times to provide a longitudinal perspective on the question.

For instance, an investigator might begin by measuring the amount of competitiveness displayed by 4-year-olds, 7-year-olds, and 10-year-olds playing a game. Three years later, the investigator retests the children, who are now 7, 10, and 13. This procedure makes a number of data comparisons possible. For example, cross-sectional comparisons among the children can be made at both the initial testing and the later testing to see whether children at the different ages show different levels of competitiveness. In addition, the stability of each child's competitiveness can be examined by a comparison of the child's scores at the two ages.

The combined design also permits the investigator to check directly for two of the common problems associated with the individual designs. If the data for the groups at ages 7 and 10 during the first testing differ from the data for these groups during the second testing, then these differences are very likely the result of either a cohort effect (a cross-sectional design problem) or a repeated-testing effect (a longitudinal design problem). In either case, the investigator will need to exercise caution in drawing conclusions regarding age-related differences in competitiveness or the stability of the behavior over time. But if the data from these corresponding groups are very similar, the researcher can have considerable confidence in the results of the study.

Although combined designs are potentially very informative, they also are time-consuming and costly, and their use has therefore been limited. To date, their main applications have been in research on aging (Schaie, 1996).

Microgenetic Studies

A different approach to the study of developmental change involves the intensive study of a small number of children over a brief period of time. The purpose of this **microgenetic method** is to investigate changes in important developmental processes as they are occurring (Kuhn, 1995; Siegler, 1995).

Recall from Chapter 1 that some aspects of human development are thought to be discontinuous—they are relatively stable for a period of time but then move abruptly to a higher level. Investigators attempting to understand the nature of such changes have used the microgenetic approach in the hope of examining the particular developmental process as it goes from one level to the next. Much of the research using this approach has been concerned with children's cognitive abilities, probably because the concept of discontinuous change is consistent with the view of development held by Piaget and many other cognitive-developmental psychologists.

A microgenetic study begins with several children who are about the age at which a developmental change is expected to occur. The behavior of interest is observed and measured repeatedly in these children. For example, if the experiment is concerned with the children's use of a particular cognitive strategy for solving a certain type of problem (a common focus of such research), the children may be asked to complete many such problems over a period of weeks. In such an experiment, the researcher not only notes the correctness of the children's solutions but also examines precisely how they approach each problem, perhaps by asking them to describe what they are doing. In this way, the investigator attempts to identify when a child moves from the use of a simpler cognitive strategy to a more sophisticated one. By examining this process very carefully, the researcher may acquire a better understanding of exactly how it works.

Although the microgenetic method can yield a great deal of new information about a developmental process, it, too, has drawbacks (Miller & Coyle, 1999; Pressley, 1992). One practical problem is that making many observations over a compressed period of time can be expensive. Another consideration is that great care must be taken to ensure that the repeated assessment of the child's abilities does not itself cause changes in the behavior of interest.

Microgenetic method
A research method in which a small number of individuals are observed repeatedly in order to study an expected change in a developmental process.

Meta-Analysis: Making Sense of Groups of Studies

Not all articles in psychology are reports of individual studies. A helpful complement to reports of original research are review articles—that is, articles whose purpose is to summarize the body of research literature on a given topic. In recent years a form of review labeled **meta-analysis** has assumed increasing importance in the field (Hunt, 1997; Rosenthal & DiMatteo, 2001).

It is easiest to introduce meta-analysis through contrast with traditional methods of reviewing research. In a traditional, or "narrative" review, an author might begin by identifying the general topic to be considered—say, gender differences in aggression—as well as the specific questions and theoretical positions that will be the focus of the review. The subsequent review will then include descriptions of particular studies and illustrative findings, as well as general conclusions about the effects of the variables of interest. The review might conclude with an overall assessment of the current state of knowledge, coupled perhaps with suggestions for future research.

The goals of description and summary remain important in a meta-analysis. What is added to them is a set of *quantitative* rules for analyzing and interpreting the body of data on a particular topic. These rules parallel the statistical procedures that guide the analysis of individual studies. In the case of gender differences in aggression, for example, a basic question is whether there is a statistically significant difference in aggression between boys and girls. A meta-analysis of all relevant studies will answer this question; in contrast to an individual study, however, the answer will be

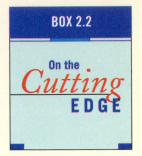

BOX 2.2

On the
Cutting
E D G E

based on hundreds of studies rather than just one and on several thousand research participants rather than just a few dozen. Assuming that there is some significant effect, the meta-analysis can also indicate the size of the effect—that is, by just how much do boys and girls differ? Again, the conclusion will be based on data from thousands of participants and on well-established statistical procedures for drawing quantitative and not just qualitative conclusions about research.

In addition to establishing the existence and size of an effect, meta-analyses can examine the variations across studies that potentially influence what is found. We might ask, for example, whether the effect varies with the age of the participants, or with the method of collecting the data, or with the gender of the principal investigator, or with the time period during which the data were collected. Note that the last two of these factors are not variables that could be examined in individual studies; it is easy, however, to incorporate them in a meta-analysis.

Although we will not always indicate explicitly that we are doing so, we will draw from the results of meta-analyses at various points throughout the book. Perhaps the content area for which such analyses have proved most informative is the one used as an example here: the issue of gender differences in behavior. Possible differences in aggression are just one of the topics for which meta-analysis has proved informative; others that we will encounter in Chapter 15 include empathy, prosocial behavior, and verbal and mathematical ability.

To Recap . . .

Meta-analysis
A method of reviewing the research literature on a given topic that uses statistical procedures to establish the existence and the size of effects.

Many developmental issues require comparisons of children's behavior at different ages. The longitudinal method assesses the behavior of the same children over a period of time. It is particularly useful for addressing the effects of early experience on later behavior and the stability of behavior. The longitudinal method commonly suffers from problems with attrition, the effects of repeated testing, and the fact that issues and instruments may become outdated. Cross-sectional research is less time-consuming than longitudinal research because it involves simultaneously studying children of different ages. However, it is sometimes plagued by the cohort effect. The longitudinal and cross-sectional approaches can be combined into the cross-sequential design, which offers some of the advantages of both methods. The microgenetic method is used to study emerging developmental changes by intensive assessment of the behavior of a small number of children over a brief period of time.

OTHER RESEARCH TACTICS

Many additional research methods are used by developmental psychologists. In this section we describe the case study, cultural research, and comparative research, three popular approaches to investigating various developmental issues.

Case Studies

Sometimes research involves only a single individual who becomes the subject of a **case study**. Often these studies are concerned with clinical issues, such as when a child displays a rare disorder or when a new treatment approach is applied to a developmental problem. Occasionally, a child has encountered experiences so unusual as to attract the interest of psychologists for theoretical reasons.

Case study research can involve several different methods. At times it is purely descriptive, as with the early baby biographies described in Chapter 1. But experimental research can also be conducted with only one child. We saw earlier, for example, that the reversal-replication design can be used in this way. At times case studies also represent natural experiments in the sense that a child has been exposed to a particular set of circumstances that could not have been otherwise arranged—usually for ethical reasons—but that offer researchers the opportunity to note the effects of these circumstances (independent variable) on one or more aspects of the child's behavior (dependent variable).

A dramatic example of such a situation is the case of "Genie," a child who was kept isolated by her parents and never spoken to until she was 13 years old (Curtiss, 1977; Rymer, 1994). Genie presented language researchers with a unique opportunity to investigate whether being deprived of exposure to language early on can affect a child's ability to acquire verbal skills at an advanced age. Such a question, of course, could never have been studied in any conventional experimental way.

The major limitation of using only a single research participant is that the researcher must be very cautious about drawing conclusions from the case. Genie, for example, was not only deprived of language but also experienced an extremely harsh and unusual childhood because of her parents. Whether the data regarding her language abilities can be generalized to other children thus remains unclear.

Despite limitations, case studies can be valuable in the research process. They may raise new questions or issues that can be studied using more carefully controlled research methods.

Case study
A research method that involves only a single individual, often with a focus on a clinical issue.

Cultural Research

We saw in Chapter 1 that an emphasis on the social and cultural contexts for development is a defining feature of the sociocultural approach to children's development. How can we determine the role culture plays in a particular aspect of behavior or development?

The most common approach is to study the same behavior in different cultures. In **cross-cultural studies,** researchers use culture as an independent variable and examine its effects on the dependent variable(s) of interest. Though we often associate the terms *independent variable* and *dependent variable* with carefully controlled manipulations, it would be a mistake to assume that all cross-cultural research involves standardized psychological procedures. Cross-cultural psychologists actually use a variety of methods, including interviews, observations of everyday activities, and archived reports of early travelers and anthropologists, as well as laboratory tasks and psychological tests.

One important use of cross-cultural studies is to test the universality of a phenomenon. Motor development serves as a good example. Although there are significant individual differences in the ages at which infants acquire motor skills, such as crawling and walking, differences between cultures are far smaller than one might expect given the large variations in the amount of time and encouragement children are given to practice those skills from culture to culture. Cross-cultural studies are also useful for documenting variations in child development across cultures. As we will see throughout this text, cross-cultural studies have revealed impressive variability across a wide range of behaviors and abilities including parenting, moral reasoning, mathematical reasoning, and memory (Berry et al., 1997).

Cross-cultural studies
Research designed to determine the influence of culture on some aspect of development and in which culture typically serves as an independent variable.

Cross-cultural studies can sometimes help determine whether patterns of behavior are universal to humans or result from factors specific to a particular culture.

Cross-cultural psychologists face a number of methodological challenges. One in particular bears mentioning here. This is the difficulty of devising experiments that measure the "same" behavior in different cultural contexts. Experimental tasks and situations that are common or sensible in one culture often seem strange to children living elsewhere. When experimental procedures differ markedly from a child's everyday experience, it is hard to know whether psychologists are tapping into the same behavior observed under conditions that more closely resemble the child's daily life.

A second approach to the study of culture and development has emerged, partly in response to the methodological problems of cross-cultural research. This approach, known as **cultural psychology,** favors studying a single or small number of cultures in depth. The aim of this approach is to understand as fully as possible the different aspects of culture and how they are interrelated (Cole, 1996; Jessor, Colby, & Shweder, 1996). The starting point, therefore, is not some set of measures developed by Western researchers (as is true in most cross-cultural research) but rather lengthy immersion in the culture or cultures of interest. The researcher might live for months or even years as a member of a culture, during which time he or she will use various **ethnographic methods** (observations, informal conversations, structured interviews) to gather as much information as possible about cultural practices and values. Cultural psychologists may use standardized psychological instruments, but they derive these procedures from practices in the cultures under study instead of importing established instruments from outside.

Cultural psychologists sometimes do compare cultures. In fact, cultural psychologists study many of the same issues as cross-cultural psychologists, including child rearing, reasoning, and basic cognitive processes. However, both their methods and their goals differ from researchers who employ traditional cross-cultural techniques. Specifically, cross-cultural psychologists make a concerted effort to test all groups under similar conditions, ideally using identical tasks and procedures. Cultural psychologists, in contrast, may vary their methods from culture to culture, adapting their methods to existing cultural practices. Cultural psychologists believe this approach is best suited to understanding development within cultural context. Cross-cultural psychologists have a different goal—to integrate the results of studies from a variety of cultures to create a more universal theory of human development.

Cultural psychology
Study of a single culture from the perspective of members of that culture, the goal being to identify the values and practices important to the culture.

Ethnographic methods
Methods of study employed in cultural psychology, in which the researcher lives as a member of a culture and gathers information about the culture through various techniques (e.g., observations, interviews) over an extended period of time.

Comparative research investigates similar behaviors across different species.

Comparative Research

Psychologists also study behaviors across species. Although **comparative research** of this sort has served many different purposes, developmentalists typically perform animal experiments for one of two reasons. First, researchers of the ethological tradition study animal behavior for clues to the evolutionary origins of similar human behaviors. For instance, determining how the imprinting process causes newborn birds to develop social attachments to their mothers may help child researchers understand the mechanisms involved in the development of attachment between human infants and their mothers. Similarly, studying the play fighting that commonly occurs among pups of many species may provide insights into the rough-and-tumble social interactions of young children.

More frequently, however, comparative research permits developmental psychologists to conduct studies that would be prohibited with humans for ethical reasons. What happens, for instance, to an infant who is reared for 6 months without a mother? Does the visual system develop normally in an infant raised in total darkness? Do high levels of stress early in life shape brain structure and function, and do such changes increase the risk for emotional disturbance? These, as well as many other questions, would be impossible to address experimentally with humans. Using other species, however, researchers have studied each of these issues in the laboratory.

Comparative research
Research conducted with nonhuman species to provide information relevant to human development.

✔ *To Recap . . .*

Case studies involve a single individual and often are concerned with clinical issues. The generalizability of the findings is limited, but the results sometimes prompt more rigorous research on an issue. Cross-cultural research is useful for studying the role that culture plays in development and for probing the universality or variability of various developmental outcomes. Researchers who adopt the cultural psychology perspective are less interested in comparing cultures than in understanding a single culture as fully as possible. Comparative research is conducted by ethologists to identify similarities in behavior processes of humans and nonhuman species. It also provides a way of experimentally addressing questions that would be unethical to investigate with humans.

ETHICAL ISSUES

No one would question the fact that psychological research often produces findings that benefit children, adults, and society as a whole. Nevertheless, almost any research involving humans can pose a variety of risks. Investigators have an obligation to determine exactly what potentially negative effects may result from their experiments and to consider whether these risks outweigh the potential value of the research findings (Fisher & Tryon, 1990; Thompson, 1990).

Concern over ethical issues has not always been as great as it is today. Early investigators had few restrictions on their research, as evidenced by such questionable experiments as Watson's conditioning of 11-month-old Little Albert. Today, however, attention is increasingly focused on safeguarding children's rights and well-being (Sieber, 1992).

Potential Risks

An obvious concern in any experiment is the possibility of physical injury to the child, although this problem is relatively rare in developmental research. A more common, and often more subtle, issue involves potential psychological harm to the child. Some experimental hypotheses may require, for example, observing how children respond when they cannot solve a problem, are prohibited from playing with an attractive toy, or are exposed to violent behavior. These procedures may produce various negative emotions, such as feelings of failure, frustration, or stress. The concern is that the children may continue to experience these emotions for some time after leaving the experimental situation.

A less obvious category of problems involves violations of privacy. If a researcher secretly gains access to a child's school records, if observations are conducted without a child's knowledge, or if data regarding a child or a family become public knowledge, the legal and ethical rights of these individuals may be violated.

Safeguards

The concern for ethical research practices has led to the development of safeguards designed to avoid or eliminate potential risks. These safeguards have become a routine part of modern research procedures. In addition, professional scientific organizations have developed codes of ethical standards to guide their members. *Ethical Principles of Psychologists and Code of Conduct* (2002), published by the American Psychological Association, and *SRCD Ethical Standards for Research with Children* (Committee for Ethical Conduct in Child Development Research, 1990), published by the Society for Research in Child Development and reproduced in part in Table 2.2, are two important examples.

Perhaps the most important measure used to ensure that research is conducted ethically is *peer review*. Before beginning a research study, investigators are encouraged (and in many situations required) to submit the research plan to others for comments and approval. This practice permits an objective examination of the procedures by knowledgeable individuals, including both scientists and community laypeople, who are not

Researchers who study children are required to ensure that neither physical nor psychological harm to the child is likely to result from their procedures.

| **Table 2.2** | **Ethical Standards for Research with Children, Society for Research in Child Development** |

Children as research participants present ethical problems for the investigator that are different from those presented by adult participants. Children are more vulnerable to stress than adults and, having less experience and knowledge than adults, are less able to evaluate the social value of the research and less able to comprehend the meaning of the research procedures themselves. In all cases, therefore, the child's consent or assent to participate in the research, as well as the consent of the child's parents or guardians, must be obtained.

In general, no matter how young children are, they have rights that supersede the rights of the investigator. The investigator is therefore obligated to evaluate each proposed research operation in terms of these rights, and before proceeding with the investigation, should obtain the approval of an appropriate Institutional Review Board.

The principles listed below are to be subscribed to by all members of the Society for Research in Child Development. These principles are not intended to infringe on the right and obligation of researchers to conduct scientific research.

Principle 1. Nonharmful Procedures
The investigator should use no research operation that may harm the child either physically or psychologically. The investigator is also obligated at all times to use the least stressful research operation whenever possible. Psychological harm in particular instances may be difficult to define; nevertheless its definition and means for reducing or eliminating it remain the responsibility of the investigator. When the investigator is in doubt about the possible harmful effects of the research operations, consultation should be sought from others. When harm seems inevitable, the investigator is obligated to find other means of obtaining the information or to abandon the research.

Principle 2. Informed Consent
Before seeking consent or assent from the child, the investigator should inform the child of all features of the research that may affect his or her willingness to participate and should answer the child's questions in terms appropriate to the child's comprehension. The investigator should respect the child's freedom to choose to participate in the research or not by giving the child the opportunity to give or not give assent to participation as well as to choose to discontinue participation at any time. Assent means that the child shows some form of agreement to participate without necessarily comprehending the full significance of the research necessary to give informed consent. Investigators working with infants should take special effort to explain the research procedures to the parents and be especially sensitive to any indicators of discomfort in the infant.

In spite of the paramount importance of obtaining consent, instances can arise in which consent or any kind of contact with the participant would make the research impossible to carry out. Nonintrusive field research is a common example. Conceivably, such research can be carried out ethically if it is conducted in public places, participants' anonymity is totally protected, and there are no foreseeable negative consequences to the participant.

Principle 3. Parental Consent
The informed consent of parents, legal guardians or those who act in loco parentis (e.g., teachers, superintendents of institutions) similarly should be obtained, preferably in writing. Informed consent requires that parents or other responsible adults be informed of all the features of the research that may affect their willingness to allow the child to participate. Not only should the right of the responsible adults to refuse consent be respected, but they should be informed that they may refuse to participate without incurring any penalty to them or to the child.

Principle 4. Additional Consent
The informed consent of any persons, such as school teachers for example, whose interaction with the child is the subject of the study, should also be obtained. As with the child and parents or guardians, informed consent requires that the persons interacting with the child during the study be informed of all features of the research which may affect their willingness to participate.

Principle 5. Incentives
Incentives to participate in a research project must be fair and must not unduly exceed the range of incentives that the child normally experiences. Whatever incentives are used, the investigator should always keep in mind that the greater the possible effects of the investigation on the child, the greater is the obligation to protect the child's welfare and freedom.

Principle 6. Deception
Although full disclosure of information during the procedure of obtaining consent is the ethical ideal, a particular study may necessitate withholding certain information or deception. Whenever withholding information or deception is judged to be essential to the conduct of the study, the investigator should satisfy research colleagues that such judgment is correct. If withholding information or deception is practiced, and there is reason to believe that the research participants will be negatively affected by it, adequate measures should be taken after the study to ensure the participant's understanding of the reasons for the deception.

Principle 7. Anonymity
To gain access to institutional records, the investigator should obtain permission from responsible authorities in charge of records. Anonymity of the information should be preserved and no information used other than that for which permission was obtained.

Principle 8. Mutual Responsibilities
From the beginning of each research investigation, there should be clear agreement between the investigator and the parents, guardians or those who act in loco parentis, and the child, when appropriate, that defines the responsibilities of each. The investigator has the obligation to honor all promises and commitments of the agreement.

Principle 9. Jeopardy
When, in the course of research, information comes to the investigator's attention that may jeopardize the child's well-being, the investigator has a responsibility to discuss the information with the parents or guardians and with those expert in the field in order that they may arrange the necessary assistance for the child.

(Continued)

| **Table 2.2** | **(Continued)** |

Principle 10. Unforeseen Consequences

When research procedures result in undesirable consequences for the participant that were previously unforeseen, the investigator should immediately employ appropriate measures to correct these consequences, and should redesign the procedures if they are to be included in subsequent studies.

Principle 11. Confidentiality

The investigator should keep in confidence all information obtained about research participants. The participants' identities should be concealed in written and verbal reports of the results, as well as in informal discussion with students and colleagues.

Principle 12. Informing Participants

Immediately after the data are collected, the investigator should clarify for the research participant any misconceptions that may have arisen. The investigator also recognizes a duty to report general findings to participants in terms appropriate to their understanding.

Principle 13. Reporting Results

Because the investigator's words may carry unintended weight with parents and children, caution should be exercised in reporting results, making evaluative statements, or giving advice.

Principle 14. Implications of Findings

Investigators should be mindful of the social, political and human implications of their research and should be especially careful in the presentation of findings from the research. This principle, however, in no way denies investigators the right to pursue any area of research or the right to observe proper standards of scientific reporting.

SOURCE: Excerpted from "SRCD Ethical Standards for Research with Children," 1990, *SRCD Newsletter,* Winter, pp. 5–6.

personally involved in the research. Peer review committees weigh the possible value of the research findings against potential risks. Sometimes they offer suggestions as to how negative effects might be prevented or minimized. Almost all research carried out at colleges and universities or funded by government organizations is subject to peer review.

Another basic measure for protecting children's rights is the requirement that researchers obtain the *informed consent* of the participants in the study. When children are the participants, researchers must first obtain the written permission of the child's parents. In addition, each child must be made aware of the general procedures of the study. Most important, the child has the right to refuse to participate or to withdraw from the study at any time, even though the parents have given their permission. Assuring that children understand their rights as research participants can be an especially challenging task (Abramovitch et al., 1991; Hurley & Underwood, 2002).

If the research procedures may produce negative feelings in the child, the investigator must provide some means of reducing those feelings before the child leaves. For example, if a child is participating in an experiment in which he or she experiences failure, the investigator might end the research session by having the child perform a relatively easy task that will ensure success. Also, to whatever extent seems reasonable, the investigator should at some point explain to the child the purpose of the study and the child's role in it, a procedure called *debriefing.*

Maintaining *confidentiality* is also a crucial aspect of ethical research. Whenever possible, the identities of the participants and information about their individual performance should be concealed from anyone not directly connected with the research. Anonymity is often achieved through the practice of assigning numbers to the participants and then using these numbers instead of names during the analysis of the data.

Finally, all research psychologists have some ethical responsibilities that go beyond the protection of the individuals participating in the research. For example, scientists who report data that may be controversial or that may affect social-policy decisions have an obligation to describe the limitations and degree of confidence they have in their findings. In addition, investigators should normally provide their research participants with some general information about the final results of the research, as an acknowledgment of the importance of their contribution to the overall research process.

To Recap . . .

Research with humans always involves a balance between the potential value of the findings and any risks that may be involved. The most common categories of risk include physical and psychological harm to the child and violations of privacy. Certain safeguards are now routinely used. They include prior review of research plans by other scientists; obtaining the informed consent of parents, teachers, and children involved in a research study; elimination of any experimentally produced negative feelings through extra procedures; debriefing as to the purpose of the research; and strict maintenance of confidentiality. Additional ethical requirements include taking some responsibility for the social ramifications of research findings and providing feedback to participants about the outcome of the research project.

CONCLUSION

Our purpose in devoting an entire chapter to research methods is to emphasize the fact that effective methods are crucial for advancing scientific knowledge. Unlocking the secrets of child development requires several elements. It begins, of course, with the perceptive insights of an astute researcher. Even the brightest researcher, however, cannot answer important theoretical questions without the necessary research techniques. For example, researchers suspected the existence of atoms and genes many years ago. But it was not until the advent of the particle accelerator and the electron microscope that scientists could confirm these suspicions. In the same way, psychologists have long debated the capabilities of the newborn. Only since the 1960s, however, have research techniques been developed that permit many related questions to be studied scientifically.

Another reason for including this chapter is that the remainder of the text presents a good deal of research evidence regarding developmental progress and processes. This evidence, for the most part, has been gathered through the methods described here, so it is helpful to approach it with an understanding of the differences between the correlational and experimental designs, longitudinal and cross-sectional experiments, and so on. These basics will also pave the way for the many more specific techniques and procedures used in various areas, which we describe as they come into play.

FOR THOUGHT AND DISCUSSION

1. Psychologists study children using methods that are objective and quantifiable. *Can you think of ways children are studied by other kinds of scholars that do not display these characteristics? What do you think are some advantages of each approach?*

2. We gave an example of a study that showed that children's reading level and their viewing of *Sesame Street* were correlated but that could not indicate whether one variable influenced the other. *Suggest some aspects of children's behavior that might correlate with their viewing of violence on TV. What are some possible explanations for these correlations?*

3. Studies of the life course indicate that major historical or political events can affect the development of an entire generation. *Can you think of any major events of this sort that have affected the life course of people your age? How might your life have been different had they not occurred?*

4. Comparative developmental research involves the use of nonhuman species. One ethical requirement of research with humans is that subjects' participation is voluntary. *Does research with animals violate the spirit of this requirement? Do you think 3-year-olds can give informed consent for research participation?*

VISUAL SUMMARY FOR CHAPTER 2
Research Methods

Scientific Research

Two roles of theory	1. To organize research findings. 2. To guide new research.
Ways in which researchers ensure objectivity	Focus on observable behaviors. Ensure that the behaviors to be studied are measurable and quantifiable.

Types of Research

Method	Characteristics
Descriptive Approach	Involves simple observation. Used primarily as a first step in exploring areas about which little is known.
Correlational Studies	Used to identify relations between variables and to describe them in terms of their direction and strength. Cannot produce conclusions regarding cause and effect.
Experimental Approach	Involves systematically manipulating the independent variable and examining the effects produced on the dependent variable. Allows researchers to draw conclusions regarding cause and effect.

Studying Development

Method	Characteristics
Longitudinal Research	Assesses the behavior of the same children over a period of time. Useful for looking at questions concerning the long-term effects of early experience and the stability of behavior. *Disadvantages:* Subject attrition, effects of repeated testing, issues and instruments may become outdated, time-consuming and expensive.
Cross-Sectional Research	Involves simultaneously studying children of different ages. Less time-consuming than longitudinal research. *Disadvantages:* Cohort effects.
Cross-Sequential Design	A combination of longitudinal and cross-sectional research offering some of the advantages of both methods.
Microgenetic Method	Used to study emerging developmental changes by intensively assessing the behavior of small number of children over a brief period of time.

Other Research Tactics

Method	Characteristics
Case Study	The study of a single individual, often focusing on clinical issues. Caution must be exercised in generalizing the findings to other individuals.
Cross-Cultural Research	Designed to determine the influence of culture on some aspect of development. Can also address some nature-nurture issues.
Comparative Research	Research conducted with nonhuman species to provide information relevant to human development.

Ethical Issues

Safeguards commonly used to reduce the risk of physical or psychological harm to the child and violations of privacy.

Peer review	Informed consent	Debriefing	Confidentiality
Have research plans reviewed by other individuals not personally involved in the research.	Obtain the informed consent of children, parents, and teachers involved in a study.	Explain to the child the purpose of the study and eliminate any experimentally produced negative feelings.	Conceal identities of participants and details of their individual performance.

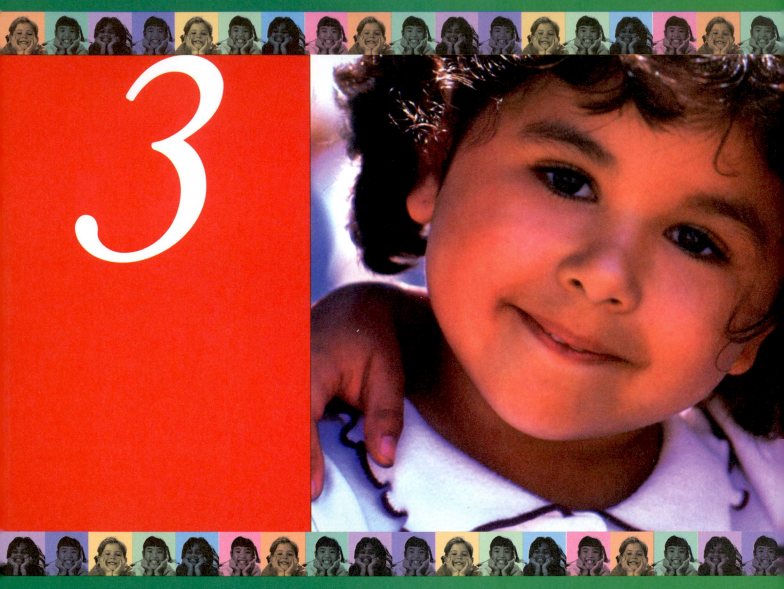

3

Genetics: The Biological Context of Development

71

"*C*opy cat" *aptly describes the calico kitten peering out from the photo. The kitten is the result of the first-ever cloning of a household pet, according to researchers at Texas A&M University, where she was born in December 2001. Scientists at the university performed the cloning*

procedure by inserting the nucleus of a cell from a genetic donor cat, Rainbow, into an egg cell in another cat, Allie. Because the kitten grew from this nucleus, her genetic makeup is identical to the genetic makeup of the donor. In contrast, a kitten produced in the ordinary way would receive half its genes from the mother and half from the father.

Successful cloning of mammals dates back to February 1997, when scientists in Scotland announced the birth of Dolly, a cloned lamb. Since then, researchers have produced sheep, cattle, goats, pigs, and mice through cloning, and efforts are reportedly under way to clone humans. Needless to say, this research has generated a great deal of controversy, both for practical reasons (the success rate is low, and cloned animals are often sickly) and for ethical reasons (many say life shouldn't be created in a laboratory). In fact, the U.S. Congress has considered banning human cloning experiments.

Amid the controversy, it's useful to think more closely about what cloning is. Is a clone a sort of photocopy, identical in every way to the original? That's what we might expect based on the identical genetic makeup of the clone and the donor. But according to Dr. Duane Kraemer, one of the Texas

A&M researchers, the cloning of Rainbow the cat "is a reproduction, not a resurrection."

For one thing, of course, Rainbow has had unique life experiences—and learning and experience are not inherited. What the new kitten learns as she develops may make her different from Rainbow in many ways.

That's not all. Take another look at the photo of the kitten—whose name is "cc," for "carbon copy"—and then look at Rainbow, the donor, shown in the photo. You can see that, in spite of her name, cc's coloration isn't exactly like Rainbow's. "The pattern of pigmentation in multi-colored animals is the result of genetic factors as well as developmental factors that are not controlled by genotype," explains Dr. Mark Westhusin, the lead investigator in the cloning project. As the embryo of a calico cat develops, chromosomes that determine fur color are randomly turned on or off in millions of cells. Even identical genes will not necessarily produce identical results. The basic elements—a mix of black, brown, and orange—will be present, but the pattern is unpredictable. Interestingly, environment plays a role in the switching on and switching off of chromosomes. ■

Despite the fact that she is her clone, Copy Cat, or cc, does not look exactly like Rainbow.

We saw in Chapter 1 that one of the enduring issues in developmental psychology concerns the relative importance of biological (nature) factors and environmental (nurture) factors. We saw, too, that most child researchers today favor an interactionist perspective. Environmental effects played out at the chromosomal level offer an insight into how complex and subtle these interactions can be. In this chapter, we delve more deeply into the fascinating world of genetics.

Now that we have presented some history, theory, and methodology of child development, it is time to turn to the development of the individual child. Where do we begin? People often think of birth as the beginning of life. We will see in the next chapter, however, that by the time a baby comes into the world, a good deal of development has already taken place inside the mother's womb. Perhaps, then, we should consider that development begins when the father's sperm fertilizes the mother's egg at conception. But even this event is a continuation, rather than the start, of the developmental process. To understand the development of the child, we must begin with genetic processes inside the child's parents that determine how they pass their heredity on to the next generation.

But this starting point is just that. Our genes guide, regulate, and influence development throughout our lives. Precisely how they do so, and exactly how much of our behavior is affected by our genes, are two exciting and controversial issues in modern child psychology.

Unlike most of the other topics in this book, genetics will take us briefly into the fields of biology and biochemistry. Our primary emphasis, however, will remain on the psychological perspective and how behavior is influenced by genetic processes. First, we discuss the basic concepts surrounding genes and their functions. Then we consider genetic disorders and why they occur. Next we examine the methods psychologists use to study gene-environment interactions and some of what they have learned. Finally, we present several models that attempt to explain how genes and environment interact to produce behavior.

MECHANISMS OF INHERITANCE

How does a baby inherit the characteristics of his or her parents—black or white skin, red or brown hair? How does a fertilized human egg know to develop into a person rather than a chimpanzee? How does a single cell give rise to trillions of other cells that become different parts of the body—the fingers, the heart, the brain, and so on? Such questions lie at the heart of the puzzle of inheritance, a mystery that scientists are now slowly beginning to solve.

Cell Division

All living things are composed of cells. Adult humans, on average, possess about 10 trillion of them. Cells have three major subdivisions: the nucleus; the cytoplasm, which surrounds the nucleus; and the cell membrane, which encases the cell.

Inside the nucleus lies the body's genetic material, DNA, which is organized into chemical strands called **chromosomes.** In humans, each cell nucleus contains 23 pairs of chromosomes, 46 in all. For each pair, one chromosome came from the father, the other from the mother. Twenty-two of the pairs are called **autosomes.** The members of these pairs are similar to one another and carry the same genes in the same locations. The 23rd pair makes up the **sex chromosomes,** which come in two varieties. The X chromosome is of about average size and carries a good deal of genetic material, whereas the Y chromosome is much smaller and has many fewer genes. When the pair consists of two X chromosomes (XX), the person is female; when it comprises one of each type (XY), the person is male.

Although there are many specialized cells, they can be divided into two broad types—*body cells* and *germ cells*. These cells are distinguished principally by how they reproduce and the roles they play in hereditary transmission.

Chromosomes
Chemical strands in the cell nucleus that contain the genes. The nucleus of each human cell has 46 chromosomes, with the exception of the gametes, which have 23.

Autosomes
The 22 pairs of human chromosomes, other than the sex chromosomes.

Sex chromosomes
The pair of human chromosomes that determines one's sex. Females have two X chromosomes; males have an X and a Y.

Cells constantly reproduce; their reproduction is probably the most fundamental genetic process that takes place in our bodies. In the time it takes you to read this sentence, more than 100 million cells in your body will have reproduced. Body cells, by far the larger category, reproduce by a process called mitosis, whereas germ cells reproduce by a process called meiosis.

In **mitosis,** diagramed on the left-hand side of Figure 3.1 (with only two pairs of chromosomes for simplicity), each parent cell produces two identical child cells through a series of three phases. In the first phase (Figure 3.1a), each of the 46 chromosomes in the cell duplicates itself, producing two identical strands connected near their centers, like an X. Next, these joined strands line up at the cell's midline (Figure 3.1b). Each X splits and the two identical chromosomal strands move to opposite sides of the cell, a nucleus forms around each set of chromosomes, and the cell itself divides in two (Figure 3.1c). With mitosis complete, each new cell contains 46 chromosomes and is genetically identical to the parent cell.

In **meiosis,** the process by which germ cells reproduce, four child cells are produced that are all different from one another and that contain only 23 chromosomes each. These child cells, called *gametes,* are the sperm or the ova that will combine at conception to form a new individual with the full complement of 46 chromosomes. Meiosis, diagramed on the right side of Figure 3.1, requires several additional phases. The 46

Mitosis
The process by which body cells reproduce, resulting in two identical cells.

Meiosis
The process by which germ cells produce four gametes (sperm or ova), each with half the number of chromosomes of the parent cell.

Figure 3.1

Mitosis and meiosis. Mitosis results in two cells identical with the parent cell and with each other. Meiosis results in four cells different from the parent cell and from each other. Adapted from *Biology: Exploring Life* (p. 152) by G. D. Brum & L. K. McKane, 1989, New York: John Wiley & Sons. Adapted by permission of the authors.

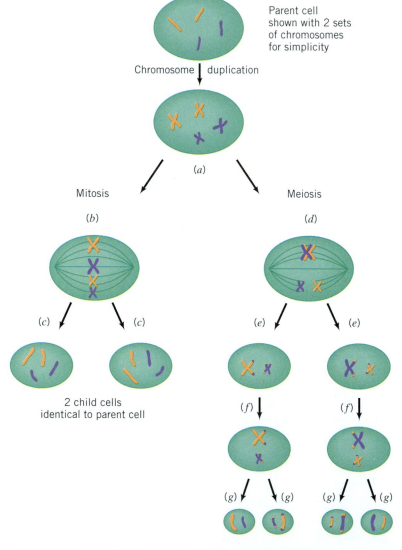

Parent cell shown with 2 sets of chromosomes for simplicity

Chromosome | duplication

(a)

Mitosis

(b)

(c) (c)

2 child cells identical to parent cell

Meiosis

(d)

(e) (e)

(f) (f)

(g) (g) (g) (g)

4 child cells with half the number of chromosomes as parent cell

chromosomes of the cell similarly duplicate themselves into two identical strands that remain attached like an X (Figure 3.1a). Then an important new process occurs. The X-shaped chromosomes pair up with their partners (remember, the 46 chromosomes are arranged in 23 pairs) and the strands of one X exchange pieces with the strands of the partner X (Figure 3.1d). This process, called **crossing over,** means that the two strands that form each X are no longer identical. (Figure 3.2 offers a greatly simplified representation of such an exchange.) The X's then line up at the midline of the cell. One X from each pair moves to one end of the cell, a nucleus forms around each half, and the cell divides (Figure 3.1e). This process is then repeated (Figures 3.1f and 3.1g). Thus, when meiosis is complete, the resulting four gametes possess 23 chromosomes each and are genetically unique.

If we consider that every one of the 23 chromosomes in a gamete now represents a one-of-a-kind combination of genetic material and that these 23 chromosomes must combine with another set of original chromosomes from a gamete of the other parent, it should become clear why people come in so many sizes, colors, and shapes. Crossing over virtually assures that no two people (except identical twins, produced from the same fertilized egg) will ever have exactly the same genes.

Inside the Chromosome

The idea that inheritance must involve genes on the chromosomes was generally accepted by the early 1940s, although no one had yet seen a **gene** or had any idea how it worked. The big breakthrough came in 1953, when James Watson and Francis Crick reported that they had uncovered the structure of a long and complicated molecule called **deoxyribonucleic acid (DNA)** that was the carrier of genetic information (Watson & Crick, 1953). The tale of their discovery is one of the most exciting detective stories in modern science (Watson, 1968), and the discovery itself earned them the Nobel Prize in 1962. Most important, their findings opened the door for an understanding of the basis of life itself.

Watson and Crick found that the DNA molecule has the structure of a double helix, much like the sides of a spiral staircase joined by rungs, as shown at the top of Figure 3.3. These rungs are composed of four bases: adenine (A), thymine (T), guanine (G), and cytosine (C). Each rung, called a *nucleotide,* consists of a pair of these bases linked together. Only two types of pairings occur, A–T and G–C. The sequence of these base pairs (rungs) determines the coded information carried by the gene.

Because each nucleotide base can link to only one other base, each half-rung of the DNA molecule can serve as a blueprint for the other half. Thus, during cell division, the chromosome "unzips" down the length of the staircase, breaking the links that connect the bases at the middle of each rung. The half-rungs then pair, base by base, with new material to form two new, identical copies of the original DNA sequence, as shown at the bottom of Figure 3.3.

What, then, is a gene? A gene is just a section of the DNA strand containing some set of these nucleotide rungs. On average, a gene contains about 1,000 nucleotides,

Crossing over
The exchange of genetic material between pairs of chromosomes during meiosis.

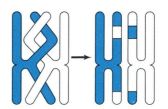

Figure 3.2

Crossing over results in the exchange of genetic material. After the crossover, all four strands are different. Adapted from *Biology: Exploring Life* (p. 44) by G. D. Brum and L. K. McKane, 1989, New York: John Wiley & Sons. Adapted by permission of the authors.

Gene
A segment of DNA on the chromosome that codes for the production of proteins. The basic unit of inheritance.

Deoxyribonucleic acid (DNA)
A stairlike, double-helix molecule that carries genetic information on chromosomes.

James Watson received the Nobel Prize with Francis Crick for discovering the structure of the DNA molecule.

Frank and Ernest

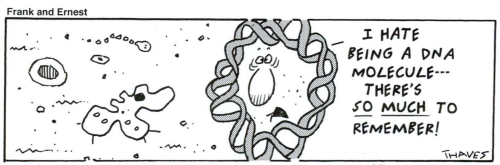

I HATE BEING A DNA MOLECULE--- THERE'S SO MUCH TO REMEMBER!

© Thaves 2001 / Dist. by NEA Inc.

Figure 3.3

Structure and replication of DNA.

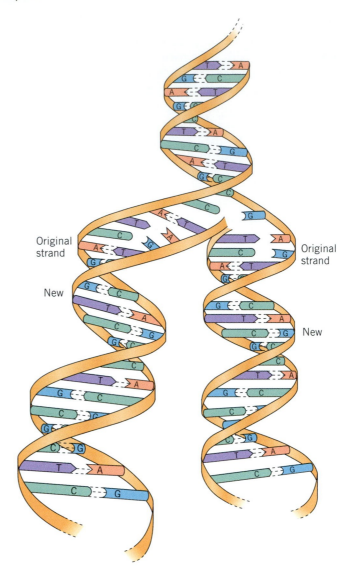

Original strand

New

Original strand

New

Alleles

Genes for the same trait located in the same place on a pair of chromosomes.

although some contain as many as 2 million. Again, when we consider that the chromosomes in a human body cell together contain about 30,000 or 40,000 genes, and that each chromosome underwent the crossing-over process during meiosis, it is easy to understand why each individual person is truly unique.

The number and precise sequence of nucleotides in the genes answers the question posed earlier about how the cell knows to develop into a human rather than a chimpanzee. The sequence is especially critical here because approximately 98% of human DNA is also found in the DNA of the chimpanzee ("Biological Systems," 1988).

The location of genes on the chromosome is likewise very important. For each pair of chromosomes, the genes for the same trait (e.g., eye color or nose shape) are in the same locations and are called **alleles.** We will see shortly that both genes are involved in how the trait is expressed but because the two alleles are not always the same, many different combinations of characteristics can result. In recent years scientists have made remarkable progress in mapping the precise locations of various genes on the human chromosomes, which will give them a clearer picture of the human genome (see Box 3.1) as well as make it possible to alter a person's hereditary code through genetic engineering (discussed in Chapter 4).

How do genes affect behavior? The answer to this question is complex and not yet entirely understood. It begins with the fact that there are two kinds of genes—structural genes and regulator genes. The job of the *structural genes* is to guide the

The Human Genome Project

If scientists knew where each of the genes was on the 46 human chromosomes, they would be in a better position to learn what each of these genes does. The potential benefits would be enormous. Health scientists, for example, would possess the tools to identify defective genes that produce many inherited diseases. In some cases, these defects could be detected even before people showed their effects, and preventive treatment might be possible. Locating the genes on the chromosomes is referred to as *mapping the genome.*

But such mapping is only one step toward understanding. If scientists knew the exact sequence of nucleotides in each gene, they would be able to specify how the gene is defective. This knowledge might, in turn, make it possible to correct the defective sequence. Identifying the sequence of the 3 billion nucleotides in the DNA molecule is called *sequencing the genome.*

In 1989 the United States launched the Human Genome Project, headed by James Watson, one of the discoverers of the DNA molecule (Cooper, 1994). The purpose of the research is to map and sequence human DNA. This project has been likened to the Manhattan Project, which produced the atomic bomb, or the Apollo program, which placed the first human being on the moon (Watson, 1990). One official exclaimed: "It's going to tell us everything. Evolution, disease, everything will be based on what's in that magnificent tape called DNA" (Jaroff, 1989, p. 63).

The task is not only exciting but of daunting magnitude. By 1997—and thus about halfway through the project's intended 15-year span—only 2% of the sequence had been completed. At this rate, it would have taken several thousand years to sequence the whole genome.

Two developments, however, have resulted in a remarkable scientific success story. One is that the publicly funded effort was joined by work in private laboratories, most notably Celera Genomics. The second was the development of new technologies for sequencing large amounts of DNA rapidly and automatically. The result is that a "working draft" of the genome, approximately 90% complete, was published in February 2001 (Genome International Sequencing Consortium, 2001; Human Genome Project, 2001). The expectation is that the complete sequence will be achieved by 2003, 2 years ahead of the original schedule.

The Human Genome Project is already yielding benefits with regard to the treatment and prevention of genetically related problems. It also is yielding some surprises for scientists. Perhaps the most surprising finding is that we have far fewer genes than was once believed—perhaps only 30,000 to 35,000, in contrast to previous estimates of as many as 140,000. This number is about the same as that for the mouse, and only about twice that for the fruit fly.

Clearly, it is not the sheer number of genes that defines a species, but rather their specific nature and specific combination. It is for this reason that comparative work is central to the Human Genome Project—that is, the attempt to map not only the human genome but those of other organisms as well. We noted that humans share approximately 98% of their DNA with chimpanzees. This means that there are roughly 45 genes that separate chimps and humans (Konner, 2002). Discovering what these are will tell us something about what it means to be human.

BOX 3.1

On the Cutting EDGE

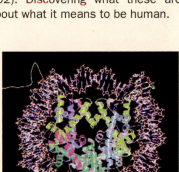

Figure 3.4

An image from the Human Genome project. The photo shows the molecular structure of the nucleosome core complex, the chromosome's basic building block.

---

production of proteins, which serve many different functions in various parts of the body. Indeed, one researcher has written that "the human cell can be viewed as a protein factory" (Brown, 1999, p. 37). The job of the *regulator genes* is to control the activities of the structural genes. The regulator genes thus can selectively suppress the production of protein so that the cells in a particular organ, such as the heart, liver, or brain, produce only proteins that are appropriate for that organ. The regulator genes also turn structural genes on and off at different points in development—for example, initiating and controlling the many changes that take place during puberty. They apparently do

The pioneering work of Gregor Mendel with pea plants paved the way for the modern science of genetics.

Phenotype
The characteristic of a trait that is expressed or observable. The phenotype results from an interaction of genotype and environment.

Genotype
The arrangement of genes underlying a trait.

Dominant gene
A relatively powerful allele whose characteristics are expressed in the phenotype regardless of the allele with which it is paired.

Recessive gene
A relatively weak allele whose characteristics are expressed in the phenotype only when it is paired with another recessive gene.

this in response to what is going on in their environment—meaning the cells around them—demonstrating that even at this molecular level, nature and nurture always operate together.

Through these as yet incompletely understood processes, our genes can affect our sensory abilities, our nervous system, our muscles and bones, and so on, thus influencing our behavior and development in a reasonably direct manner. Later in the chapter, we will see how genes also appear to affect human behavior through more indirect processes.

Mendel's Studies

Scientists' knowledge of genetic processes has relied in recent years on the development of advanced research techniques and powerful laboratory instruments. Yet some of the fundamental principles of heredity have been understood since the mid-1800s, when they were discovered and described by an Austrian monk named Gregor Mendel (1822–1884). Working alone in his garden, Mendel used pea plants, careful observations, and brilliant logic to develop a theory of inheritance that remains largely correct today.

Mendel was intrigued by the process of hereditary transmission. He wondered how pea plants passed on such characteristics as flower color to the next generation. To study this process, Mendel mated purple-flowered and white-flowered plants. People believed at the time that when a mother and father had different traits, the traits blend in the child. But Mendel believed that the process must work in some other way. He knew that parent plants with purple and white flowers did not produce offspring with lavender flowers. In fact, all the offspring of the purple- and white-flowered plants that he mated had purple flowers. Had the white trait disappeared entirely? Apparently not, because when Mendel next mated the new purple-flowered plants with each other, one out of every four of the second-generation offspring was white.

Through many experiments involving color and other characteristics, Mendel developed a theory to account for his observations. He correctly deduced that each observable trait, such as color, requires two elements, which we now know are a pair of genes (alleles), one inherited from each parent. Today, we call the expressed or observable trait the **phenotype** and call the underlying genes the **genotype.**

Principles of Genetic Transmission Mendel's theory involved several new principles, the most important of which was the *principle of dominance:* The alleles of a trait (purple-flower gene and white-flower gene) are not equal, and one usually dominates the other. As it turns out, in pea plants the gene for purple flowers is a **dominant gene** and the gene for white flowers is a **recessive gene.** Mendel discovered that when either gene is dominant, that characteristic is expressed; only when both genes are recessive is the other characteristic expressed. For example, if we think of the color trait in the pea plant as involving purple (P) or white (w) genes, then plants with the genotype PP, Pw,

Table 3.1	Some Common Dominant and Recessive Traits
Dominant	Recessive
Brown eyes	Blue, gray, or green eyes
Normal hair	Baldness (in men)
Dark hair	Blond hair
Normal color vision	Color blindness
Freckles	No freckles
Dimples	No dimples
Free earlobes	Attached earlobes
Double-jointed thumbs	Tight thumb ligaments

or wP will have purple flowers, and only those with the genotype ww will have white flowers. Plants thus can have the same phenotype (purple flowers) with different genotypes (PP, Pw, or wP).

Mendel's theory included several other principles. The *principle of segregation* states that each inheritable trait is passed on to the offspring as a separate unit (the alleles that produce flower color are separate from one another and passed on that way, which is why the blending idea was incorrect). The *principle of independent assortment* asserts that traits are passed on independently of one another (for example, which flower-color trait is passed on has no bearing on which stem-length trait is passed on).

Mendel's principles have proved to be surprisingly accurate, not just for pea plants but throughout the huge variety of life forms. Indeed, his discovery of dominant and recessive traits applies to many human characteristics, as shown in Table 3.1. One commonly cited example is eye color; the gene for brown eye color is dominant, and that for blue eye color is recessive. Thus, a mother and father who both possess brown–blue gene combinations for eye color have brown eyes themselves and are three times as likely to produce a brown-eyed child as a blue-eyed child.

Revisions of Mendel's Principles   Years of research have supported Mendel's basic ideas but have also uncovered other processes involved in hereditary transmission. For instance, single traits are often the product of more than one pair of genes—a process known as **polygenic inheritance.** In humans, height, weight, and skin color are all the product of polygenic inheritance. More critically for our purposes, most behavioral traits of interest—for example, temperament and intelligence—are also affected by multiple genes.

Polygenic inheritance
The case in which a trait is determined by a number of genes.

A second modification is that some traits result from genes that display **incomplete dominance,** that is, they are neither entirely dominant nor entirely recessive. For example, sickle-cell anemia is passed on through a recessive gene. However, the blood of people who have this recessive gene along with a dominant normal gene will show some mild characteristics of the disease (this differs from the early idea of blending, however, because the two genes remain separate and are passed on that way to future generations).

Incomplete dominance
The case in which a dominant gene does not completely suppress the effect of a recessive gene, which is then somewhat expressed in the phenotype.

A third addition to Mendel's principles involves **codominance,** in which both genes of a trait are dominant and so both characteristics are expressed completely. For example, the genes for A and B blood types are codominant, so a person who inherits one from each parent will have blood type AB.

Codominance
The case in which both alleles are dominant and each is completely expressed in the phenotype.

The impetus for a fourth and relatively recent revision was a puzzling finding. In some instances a trait does not follow any of the usual laws of inheritance; rather, it matters whether the mother or father provides a particular gene. For example, diabetes is more likely to be inherited from the father, whereas the mother is a more likely source of asthma. What occurs in such cases is **genomic imprinting:** The relevant alleles are biochemically marked such that one of them is "imprinted" or silenced (for example, the allele for diabetes in the mother) and only the other allele finds expression in the phenotype. It is estimated that the human genome contains between 100 and 200 imprinted genes (Davies, Isles, & Wilkinson, 2001).

Genomic imprinting
The case in which the allele from one parent is biochemically silenced and only the allele from the other parent affects the phenotype.

Mendel's principles must also be revised in one more important way. Scientists now know that the environment can play a crucial role in the expression of genes. One example is that the fur color of the Arctic fox changes with temperature from white in winter to brown in summer. In this way, the fox is camouflaged in both the winter snow and the brown underbrush of summer. A human example is that medical students taking exams show reduced activity of messenger RNA (the molecules responsible for protein synthesis) in the immune system, and thus a modification of the activity of the genes in response to environmental stress. Genes operate always within an environmental context, and the immediate context can affect the way in which they are expressed (Gottlieb, 1998).

To Recap . . .

Genes carry hereditary information from one generation to the next and direct and regulate development throughout life.

Cell reproduction occurs by mitosis in body cells and by meiosis in germ cells. Mitosis results in two identical cells with 46 chromosomes apiece, whereas meiosis produces four different gametes, each with 23 chromosomes. Gametes are the sperm and ova that combine to form a new cell with the full 46 chromosomes.

The basis of life is DNA, a double-helix-shaped molecule in the cell nucleus that contains billions of nucleotides. The nucleotides on a chromosome are subdivided into genes. Alleles are pairs of genes on the chromosomes that determine a trait. The precise order of nucleotides is important in the gene's functioning. The fixed location of genes on the chromosomes permits the crossing-over process and also has prompted scientists' attempts to map the human genome.

Structural genes direct the production of protein. Regulator genes control the activity of the structural genes and also turn them on and off as required across development.

Mendel's research with pea plants led to the first scientific theory of inheritance, based on the concept of dominant and recessive genes. His principles of segregation and independent assortment are generally accepted today, although several other processes have been added: Single traits may be affected by more than one gene; genes may be neither completely dominant nor completely recessive; the genes for some traits are both dominant; in some instances only the gene from one parent is activated; and the environment may influence the operation of the genes.

GENETIC DISORDERS

Given the billions of sperm cells generated by the male and the 2 million or so ova generated by the female, we should not be surprised that genetic imperfections sometimes occur. These variations, or *mutations,* are the driving force behind evolution.

| Table 3.2 | Examples of Genetic Disorders |

Disorder	Cause	Incidence (U.S.)	Description
Huntington's disease	Dominant gene on chromosome 4	1 in 18,000 to 25,000	Deterioration of the nervous system, uncontrollable muscular movements, disordered brain function, death
Neurofibromatosis (Type 1)	Dominant gene on chromosome 17	1 in 3,000	Discoloration and tumors of the skin, heightened probability of learning difficulties and mild retardation
Tay-Sachs disease	Recessive genes on chromosome 15	1 in 3,600 for Ashkenazik Jews	Nervous system deterioration, blindness, paralysis, early death
Phenylketoneuria	Recessive genes on chromosome 12	1 in 10,000	If untreated, severe mental retardation, hyperactivity, convulsions
Sickle-cell anemia	Recessive genes on chromosome 11	1 in 600 for African Americans	Oxygen deprivation, severe pain, tissue damage, early death
Cystic fibrosis	Recessive genes on chromosome 7	1 in 2,500	Breathing and digestive problems, infection of lungs, early death
Down syndrome	Extra chromosome at pair 21	1 in 1,000	Moderate to severe mental retardation, distinctive physical features, immune deficiencies, heart defects
Fragile X syndrome	Gene on X chromosome	1 in 1,000	Mental retardation, language difficulties, distinctive physical features
Turner's syndrome	Absence of one of the X chromosomes	1 in 2,500 for females	Short stature, incomplete development of sex characteristics, below-average spatial intelligence
Klinefelter's syndrome	Extra X chromosome	1 in 750 male births	Somewhat feminine appearance, incomplete development of sex characteristics, below-average verbal intelligence

When the "errors" turn out to be adaptive, they result in improvements in the species or the creation of a new species. The overwhelming majority of mutations, however, are maladaptive. Through a natural screening process in humans, about 90% of all genetic abnormalities result in miscarriage rather than live births. So although more than 10,000 single-gene disorders have been identified in humans (McKusick, 1998), only about 1% of all babies have detectable chromosomal abnormalities. The problems that we consider now are therefore the exception to the general rule.

Some human disorders are entirely hereditary and are passed along according to the same principles of inheritance that determine eye color and nose shape. Other genetic disorders are not inherited but may result from errors during cell division in meiosis. Chromosomes and the genes they carry can also be made abnormal by radiation, drugs, viruses, chemicals, and perhaps even the aging process. In this section, we examine the various kinds of genetic disorders and discuss some examples of each. Table 3.2 summarizes both the disorders discussed in the text and several other important examples.

Hereditary Disorders

Just as a child may inherit genes for brown or blue eyes, abnormal genes can be passed along to offspring according to Mendel's principles. Whether defective genes are expressed in the phenotype depends on whether they are dominant or recessive. If a defective gene inherited from one parent is recessive, the dominant (and usually normal) allele from the other parent can prevent the problem. Of course, the problem gene still exists in the genotype and will be passed on to half the person's offspring. Most of the offspring will themselves be unaffected; those who receive the defective gene from both parents, however, will develop the disorder.

Dominant Traits   Dominant genes that cause severe problems typically disappear from the species, because the affected people usually do not live to reproduce. In a few cases, however, severely disabling dominant genes are passed on because they do not become active until relatively late in life. People with these genes may reproduce before they know that they have inherited the disease.

An example is *Huntington's disease*. The age of onset of this disease varies, but it typically strikes people between about 30 and 40 years of age. Quite suddenly, the nervous system begins to deteriorate, resulting in uncontrollable muscular movements and disordered brain function. The disease became well known to many Americans when it took the life of folk singer Woody Guthrie.

Until recently, the children of a person stricken with Huntington's had no way of knowing whether they also carried the gene and could pass it on to their offspring. Late in 1983, scientists discovered which chromosome carries the gene for Huntington's, and, 10 years later, they located the exact gene responsible for the disease and learned how to tell whether a person has inherited it (Morell, 1993).

Recessive Traits   Like Mendel's purple flowers, which did not reveal the white-flower gene they carried, parents can carry problem recessive genes that have no effect on them. If both parents carry such a gene, they can combine in the offspring to produce the disorder (just as two brown-eyed parents can produce a blue-eyed child). It has been estimated that on average, each of us carries four potentially lethal genes as recessive traits (Scarr & Kidd, 1983), but because most of these dangerous genes are rare, it is unlikely that we will mate with someone who has a matching recessive gene. Even then, the probability of a child's receiving both recessive genes is only one in four.

Some diseases carried by recessive genes produce errors of metabolism, which cause the body to mismanage sugars, fats, proteins, or carbohydrates. With *Tay-Sachs disease,* the nervous system disintegrates because of the lack of an enzyme that breaks down fats in brain cells. The fatty deposits swell, and the brain cells die. Tay-Sachs disease is rare in the general population, occurring in only 1 in 300,000 births. However, among

Ashkenazic Jews, who account for more than 90% of the Jewish population of the United States, it occurs in 1 in every 3,600 births. Infants afflicted with the disease appear normal at birth and through their first half-year. Then, at about 8 months of age, they usually become extremely listless, and often by the end of their first year, they are blind. Most stricken children die by the age of 4. At present, there is no treatment for the disorder.

A more encouraging story is that of *phenylketonuria* (PKU), a problem involving the body's management of protein. This disease occurs when the body fails to produce an enzyme that breaks down phenylalanine, an amino acid. As a result, abnormal amounts of the substance accumulate in the blood and harm the developing brain cells. Infants with PKU are typically healthy at birth but, if untreated, begin to deteriorate after a few months of life as the blood's phenylalanine level mounts. Periodic convulsions and seizures may occur, and the victims usually become severely retarded.

Our understanding of how PKU disrupts normal metabolism has resulted in one of the early victories of science over genetic abnormalities. Discovery of the mechanism of the disease led to the development of special diets, which are low in phenylalanine and thus prevent its accumulation in the bloodstream. Children placed on these special diets shortly after birth remain at risk for some cognitive deficits (Diamond et al., 1997); most, however, achieve at least close to normal intellectual functioning, in marked contrast to the devastating effects in the absence of treatment. Because of the dramatic results of timely intervention in this disease, newborn babies are now routinely tested for PKU through a simple blood-test procedure. The lesson in the PKU story is that genes are not necessarily destiny—how or whether a gene's influence is played out can depend on interactions with the environment.

A recessive genetic abnormality that does not involve metabolism is *sickle-cell anemia* (SCA). People who have inherited a gene for this recessive trait from both parents have red blood cells that do not contain normal hemoglobin, a protein that carries oxygen throughout the body. Instead, abnormal hemoglobin causes their red blood cells to become sickled, as shown in Figure 3.5. These sickled cells tend to clog small blood vessels instead of easily passing through them as normal cells do, thus preventing blood from reaching parts of the body. An unusual oxygen demand, such as brought on by physical exertion, may cause the sufferer to experience severe pain, tissue damage, and even death because of the inadequate supply of oxygen.

About 8% of African Americans carry the recessive gene for SCA. Among the Bamba, a tribe in Africa, the incidence has been reported to be as high as 39%. Such a high rate of occurrence seems surprising from a Darwinian perspective, by which non-adaptive traits are weeded out through natural selection, because individuals who have two genes for SCA frequently die young and produce few children. How, then, could such a characteristic be preserved through evolution? The answer reveals a rare instance in which a gene is maladaptive for one purpose but adaptive for another.

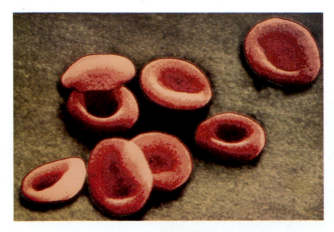

Figure 3.5

Scanning electron micrographs of red blood cells from normal individuals (left) and individuals with sickle-cell anemia (right).

Scientists have noted that the Bamba live in areas where the incidence of malaria is high, but Bamba children who carry the SCA gene are about half as likely to have malarial parasites as those who do not. Although it is unclear how this gene offers resistance to malaria, its presence appears to permit more carriers to grow up and have children, even though one in four will have SCA. Apparently, the negative effects of malarial parasites on reproduction are greater than the effects of carrying the SCA gene.

It is clear that many new findings are on the horizon of genetic research. Within the last few years, investigators have discovered the gene for a type of Alzheimer's disease that runs in families. They also have located the genes for cystic fibrosis and for amytrophic lateral sclerosis (ALS), also known as Lou Gehrig's disease. The genetic locus of many other diseases may soon be discovered as part of the Human Genome Project, discussed in Box 3.1.

Structural Defects in the Chromosome

The genetic abnormalities we have discussed thus far are all passed along according to the regular principles of inheritance. But genetically based problems may also result from physical changes in chromosomes. These changes can occur during meiosis in one of the parents, and they can involve any of the 22 autosomes or the sex chromosome. As mentioned, environmental hazards can also damage chromosomes.

Autosomal Disorders   One of the most frequently observed effects of structural abnormality is *Down syndrome,* named after John Langdon H. Down, the physician who first described it. In Down syndrome, one of the pairs of chromosomes has a third member. Children born with this disorder typically have cheerful dispositions and are friendly and outgoing. They also, however, are moderately to severely retarded; they tend to have poor muscle tone and problems with expressive language; and they have a distinctive appearance that includes a flattened face and folded eyelids. The cause of Down syndrome was identified in 1957, marking the first time a human disease had been directly linked to a chromosomal disorder.

The likelihood that a couple will produce a child with Down syndrome increases dramatically with the age of the mother. Fewer than 1 in 1,000 babies of mothers under age 30 have Down syndrome, whereas the incidence is 74 times greater for women between the ages of 45 and 49. Still, only a small proportion of births to these older mothers involve Down syndrome. In addition, the mother is not always the source of the problem; in 20 to 30% of the cases, it is the father who contributes the extra chromosome (Behrman, Kliegman, & Jenson, 2000).

Serious problems can also be caused when part of a chromosome is missing. For example, the deletion of a small amount of genetic material from one chromosome produces *cri du chat,* "cry of the cat," syndrome. Affected infants, who have a catlike cry, have mental retardation and neuromuscular problems.

Disorders of the Sex Chromosomes   Earlier we described the process through which children receive either two X chromosomes or one X and one Y. Occasionally, this process does not work as it should. When this happens, the embryo may have an unusual arrangement of sex chromosomes.

One such abnormality occurs when an ovum is fertilized by a sperm that carries no sex chromosome at all or when the sperm provides an X and the ovum has no sex chromosome. In either case, the resulting embryo has only an X and is designated 45,XO. Most of these embryos fail to develop in the uterus and are aborted by the mother's body without her even being aware that conception had occurred. But in the few cases in which the fetus develops completely, the child displays a variety of abnormalities referred to as *Turner's syndrome.* At birth, the baby is female in appearance, but the ovaries have already disappeared and do not produce the hormones necessary for the sex differentiation process to continue.

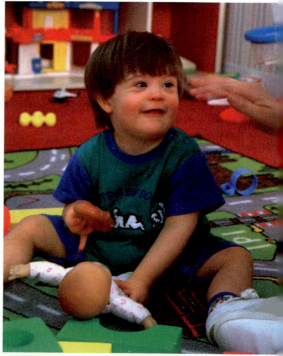

Children with Down syndrome have distinctive facial features.

As a result, women with Turner's syndrome do not develop breasts or menstruate unless they are given hormone therapy. Physically, they typically are short and have an unusual neck and chest structure. Behaviorally, they demonstrate deficiencies in spatial skills, and they have been described as having ultrafeminine personalities (El Abd, Turk, & Hill, 1995; Ross, Zinn, & McCauley, 2000).

Another chromosomal problem occurs when an egg carrying two X chromosomes is fertilized by a sperm carrying a Y chromosome. In this case, a 47,XXY child is produced, with characteristics referred to as *Klinefelter's syndrome*. The presence of the Y chromosome causes the child to have a male appearance, but he is somewhat feminized, because his male hormone levels are low. Men with Klinefelter's syndrome have long arms, very little body hair, an underdeveloped penis, and sometimes overdeveloped breasts. They often are somewhat timid and unassertive in their interpersonal interactions (Mandoki et al., 1991).

A third chromosomal abnormality occurs when the sperm provides two Y chromosomes. The 47,XYY males produced when this occurs are perhaps the opposite of the 45,XO females in that they have large body builds and masculine personality characteristics (Owen, 1979). It was once thought that these men were more likely than others to become criminals or to display antisocial behavior; more recent research, however, has not supported this contention (Ike, 2000).

The most common disorder of the sex chromosomes is *fragile X syndrome*, a condition caused by an abnormal gene on the X chromosome (Hagerman, 1996). Fragile X syndrome is second only to Down syndrome as a genetically based cause of mental retardation. Boys are more likely to be affected than are girls. The large majority of males who inherit the gene display retardation and a variety of other physical and behavioral symptoms; in contrast, only about 30% of girls who carry the gene on one of their X chromosomes show clear evidence of the syndrome.

One important application of our rapidly accumulating knowledge about genetic disorders involves genetic counseling for couples and prospective parents. We discuss this topic in Chapter 4.

 To Recap . . .

Certain disorders are transmitted genetically on the autosomes according to Mendelian principles. Huntington's disease is caused by a dominant gene that is expressed in all carriers, whereas Tay-Sachs disease, phenylketonuria, and sickle-cell anemia are caused by recessive genes expressed only when the individual inherits the defective gene from both parents. Other genetic diseases are caused by structural defects in chromosomes, which may occur during meiosis in one of the parents. Some, such as Down syndrome, result from defects in one of the autosomes, whereas others result from abnormalities of the sex chromosomes.

STUDYING THE EFFECTS OF GENES ON BEHAVIOR

How do researchers study the influences of genes on behavior? People are not pea plants, and scientists are not free to mate humans of their choice to see how the offspring will turn out. Researchers have to rely on observation, experiments of nature, and careful analyses of their data. Fortunately, scientists' statistical methods and their access to large populations of research participants have come a long way since Mendel's time (Lemery & Goldsmith, 1999; Pennington, 2001).

The effects of genes on human behavior and development have been studied extensively over the years in three principal areas: intellectual abilities, psychiatric disorders (including children's behavior problems), and aspects of personality (including infant temperament). In this section we present some of what psychologists have learned about genetic contributions to these areas as we examine the four major methods that have been used in their investigation: family studies, adoption studies, twin studies, and combinations of these approaches.

Family Studies

Children inherit 50% of their genes from each parent. Siblings, on average, share 50% of their genes. Grandparent and grandchild share 25%, as do aunts and uncles with their nieces and nephews. The family-study approach asks whether the phenotypic similarity on some trait follows from the genotypic similarity among the people being compared. If it does, then you should be more similar to your parents or siblings than you are to an uncle or cousin, and more similar to the uncle or cousin than you are to people with whom you share no genes.

One of the earliest family studies demonstrates both the potential and the limitations of this approach. In 1912 Henry Goddard published a report that claimed to demonstrate a genetic basis for intelligence. The subject of Goddard's study was the Kallikak family. During the American Revolution, a soldier whom Goddard called Martin Kallikak (a pseudonym) had an illegitimate son by a retarded tavern maid. Later, Kallikak married a woman of normal intelligence from a respected family.

Goddard traced five generations of Kallikak's offspring from these two lines. Of the 480 or so descendants of the tavern maid, he identified many as criminal, alcoholic, or "immoral," and 25% as retarded. In contrast, the 496 descendants from Kallikak's marriage were all intellectually normal, according to Goddard, and most occupied respected positions in their communities. Because Kallikak was the father to both family lines, Goddard concluded that the differences between them must be due to the genetic differences between his two mates. Of course, this conclusion ignored the vastly different environments and upbringing of the two lines of descendants. Distinguishing between hereditary and environmental influences is a major limitation of the family-study method. As scientists have pointed out, lots of things run in families—names, photo albums, and cake recipes, for example. Not all of these are determined by our genes.

Family studies can be of value, however. Sometimes they point up characteristics that might have a genetic component and so encourage more definitive research using one of the more rigorous methods that we discuss next. For example, family studies have shown that a number of traits, including measures of intelligence, *do* follow the pattern that we would expect if genes are important—that is, close relatives are most similar, and the degree of similarity drops off as the degree of genetic overlap drops. Similarly, family studies have shown that children of mothers who have schizophrenia are about 13 times as likely as children of normal mothers to develop the disorder, and children who have siblings with schizophrenia are 9 times as likely as children in general (Plomin et al., 1997a). Do findings such as these indicate an important role for the genes? Research using more sophisticated methods has been providing some answers.

Adoption Studies

As we have just seen, the difficulty in interpreting family studies is that either genes or environment could account for the patterns we find. The adoption-study method is designed to address this issue. Children who are living in adoptive homes are compared with their biological parents (who share their genes but not their environments) and with their adoptive parents (who share their environments but not their genes). If the correlation with one set of parents is stronger than that with the other, we have a good idea of which factor makes a greater contribution to individual differences in the trait we are measuring.

Sometimes the method includes siblings, because many adoptive families go on to adopt a second child. These two children share a similar environment but none of the same genes. Their similarity on whatever behaviors we choose to study can thus be compared with the similarity of biological siblings in families used for comparison. Again, differences in the correlations between the two sets of siblings could shed light on whether environment or heredity has more influence on the behaviors of interest.

A major study that employed this approach is the Colorado Adoption Project. This research, begun in 1975, is a longitudinal study of about 250 families with adopted children and, for comparison, 250 families with biological children. The children were first studied when they were infants and preschoolers, and they have been followed and studied ever since (Alarcon et al., 1999; DeFries, Plomin, & Fulker, 1994).

One focus of this project has been intelligence (we discuss methods of studying intelligence again in Chapter 10). The children have been tested using a variety of different instruments and on both general intellectual ability and specific cognitive skills (such as memory, vocabulary, spatial relations, and reading). The findings clearly support a role for genetic processes. Stronger correlations have been found between the scores of biological siblings than between those of adoptive siblings and between the adoptive children and their biological parents than between the children and their adoptive parents. These findings indicate that at least to some degree, children inherit their intellectual abilities (Cardon, 1994; Cherny & Cardon, 1994; Wadsworth et al., 2001).

Adoption studies also provide evidence about the origins of problems in development. For example, one study sought to explain the hostile and antisocial behaviors of a group of adolescents who had been adopted at birth (Ge et al., 1996). The hypothesis was that these behaviors could be connected to both the biological and the adoptive parents, but that both connections involved the children's genes. The researchers first showed that these adolescents were more likely to have biological parents with psychiatric disorders than were a comparison group of adopted adolescents who showed no such problems. This finding suggests, as had much other research, that some problem behaviors can be inherited (Rutter & Caesar, 1991). The researchers next showed that the troubled adolescents also were more likely to have adoptive parents who used harsh and inconsistent punishment. This apparent environmental influence also has been found many times before (Patterson, Reid, & Dishion, 1992).

What makes the study important is a third finding: a positive relation between the adoptive parents' disciplinary practices and the biological parents' history of psychiatric problem. Thus, children of parents with psychiatric problems were more likely to encounter harsh discipline from their adoptive parents. It is worth thinking for a moment about how this relation could come about. The two sets of parents, after all, had never met; why, then, should the behaviors of one group be related to the psychological characteristics of the other? The critical link, the researchers hypothesized, was the child. Specifically, the researchers speculated that:

1. The children initially inherited their behavior problems from their biological parents.

2. These problems then evoked responses (harsh discipline) from their adoptive parents.

3. The parents' disciplinary practices then served to maintain the children's problem behaviors.

Adoption studies have also addressed the issue of schizophrenia, described earlier. Children of schizophrenic mothers who are placed in adoptive homes are around 10 times as likely to develop schizophrenia as are either the biological children of the adoptive parents or adopted children of normal mothers (Plomin et al., 1997b). This finding suggests a major role for heredity in the development of the disease and is consistent with other research showing that psychological disorders can be inherited (Rutter et al., 1990).

Identical (monozygotic [MZ]) twins
Twins who develop from a single fertilized ovum and thus inherit identical genetic material.

Fraternal (dizygotic [DZ]) twins
Twins who develop from separately fertilized ova and who thus are no more genetically similar than are other siblings.

Twin Studies

Approximately 1 of every 85 births yields twins, providing investigators with an interesting opportunity to study the role of genetic similarity. Twins come in two varieties. **Identical twins** develop from the same fertilized egg and are called **monozygotic twins (MZ)** (mono, "one"; zygote, "fertilized egg"). They have exactly the same genes. **Fraternal twins** develop from two different eggs and are called **dizygotic twins (DZ)** (di, "two"). Their genetic makeup is no more similar than that of any two children who have the same parents; on average, 50% of the genes of dizygotic twins are the same.

Table 3.3	Average Correlations of Various Abilities from Several Twin Studies

	AVERAGE CORRELATION		
	Number of Studies	Identical Twins	Fraternal Twins
Ability			
General intelligence	30	.82	.59
Verbal comprehension	27	.78	.59
Number and mathematics	27	.78	.59
Spatial visualization	31	.65	.41
Memory	16	.52	.36
Reasoning	16	.74	.50
Clerical speed and accuracy	15	.70	.47
Verbal fluency	12	.67	.52
Divergent thinking	10	.61	.50
Language achievement	28	.81	.58
Social studies achievement	7	.85	.61
Natural science achievement	14	.79	.64
All abilities	211	.74	.54

SOURCE: Adapted from "Heredity and Environment: Major Findings from Twin Studies of Ability, Personality and Interests" by R. C. Nichols, 1978, *Homo,* 29, Table 1, p. 163.

The logic of the twin-study approach begins with the assumption that fraternal twins share an environment that is as similar as the environment shared by identical twins. Researchers then look at a particular trait or behavior displayed by the sets of twins. If the trait is more similar in the identical twins than in the fraternal twins, we should be able to conclude that the greater similarity results from the greater similarity of their genes.

Many twin studies have specifically targeted intelligence and its heritability. As shown in Table 3.3, hundreds of studies have been conducted, with virtually every one finding higher correlations between the IQ scores of MZ twins than between those of DZ twins (Bouchard & McGue, 1981; McGue et al., 1993). Clearly, intelligence—at least when measured by IQ tests—has a genetic component. In recent work with infants, whose intelligence is assessed using instruments that rely less on language and verbal abilities and more on simple motor and perceptual responses, MZ twins also showed higher correlations than did DZ twins (Cherny et al., 1994b; Wilson et al., 2001).

Twin studies have also been used to address a variety of personality issues. Many such studies have been conducted with adults and have produced some unusual findings. For example, if one identical twin experiences divorce, the chance that the other twin will experience divorce is six times that of the general population; the likelihood falls to two times the population average for a fraternal twin. Of course, there is no such thing as a divorce gene; the increase in risk for divorce is probably related to personality characteristics affected by genetic inheritance (McGue & Lykken, 1992).

An important personality area in children involves their *temperament.* Babies come into the world with a particular style of responding. Some are irritable and cry frequently; some are easygoing and smile a lot; some are active; some are cuddly; and so forth. Aspects of temperament sometimes persist well into the early school years and may eventually form the basis for adult personality. (We take up this subject again in Chapter 12.) Do genes influence temperament? Apparently they do, at least to some extent. As early as 3 months of age, and throughout the first years of life, identical twins are more similar than fraternal twins on a variety of measures, including attention, activity, and involvement in testing (Braungart et al., 1992; Emde et al., 1992; Manke, Saudino, & Grant, 2001). One study looked at the trait of shyness, testing twin babies at 14 and 20 months in both the laboratory and at home. Genes were found to be strongly involved in this aspect of temperament at both ages and in both locations (Cherny et al., 1994a).

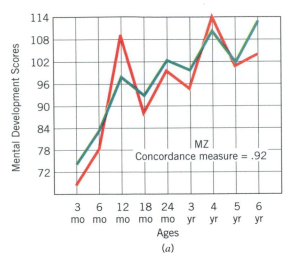

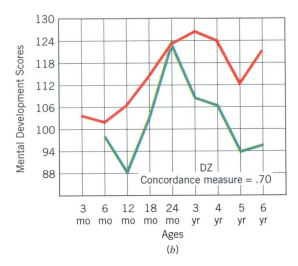

Figure 3.6

Concordance in IQ changes in (a) identical, or monozygotic (MZ), twins and (b) fraternal, or dizygotic (DZ), twins from 3 months to 6 years of age. The scales are different to accommodate different ranges of scores. The important point is that changes in performance are more similar for monozygotic twins. Adapted from "The Louisville Twin Study: Developmental Synchronies in Behavior" by R. S. Wilson, 1983, *Child Development, 54*, p. 301. Copyright © 1983 by The Society for Research in Child Development, Inc. Adapted by permission.

Developmental pacing
The rate at which spurts and plateaus occur in an individual's physical and mental development.

Finally, behavior geneticists have used twins to examine whether genetic influences underlie certain changes we see in children's development and behavior. Physical development (such as height and weight) tends to occur in spurts and plateaus. The rhythm of these life events is called **developmental pacing.** Psychologists assume that developmental pacing is guided by the regulator genes, which turn the structural genes on and off at different points in development and thus control protein production. But what about similar sorts of changes in behavioral traits, such as intellectual abilities? Are they also controlled by genes? One way to address this question is to see whether identical twins show more concordance (similarity) in these changes than do fraternal twins. The evidence suggests that they do. Figure 3.6 shows the results of a study comparing the intellectual development of almost 500 pairs of identical and fraternal twins, followed from the ages of 3 months to 15 years. The MZ twins clearly showed greater concordance in their shifts in performance than did the DZ twins, supporting the notion that genes direct the pacing of these abilities (Wilson, 1983, 1986).

Combined Twin-Study and Adoption-Study Approaches

There is one major problem with the twin-study approach: How do we know that a family treats a set of fraternal twins as similarly as a set of identical twins? Because identical twins look more alike, and perhaps because they know they are identical, parents and others may expect them to act the same. These expectations may influence how people behave toward the children and, as a result, may affect how the children themselves behave. A method that avoids these problems involves twins who are separated early in life and raised in different adoptive homes. If genes play a role in creating individual differences in behavior, then identical twins raised apart should still be more alike than are fraternal twins raised apart. Although this combined approach is the most desirable, it also is the most difficult to use, because so few twins are raised apart.

The best-known research project of this type is the Minnesota Study of Twins Reared Apart (Bouchard, 1997; Bouchard et al., 1990; Segal, 1999). The study involves 135 pairs of twins who are currently in their 50s. As with the handful of separated-twin studies that preceded it, the Minnesota Study provides strong evidence for a genetic contribution to differences in IQ. Even when reared apart, identical twins correlate

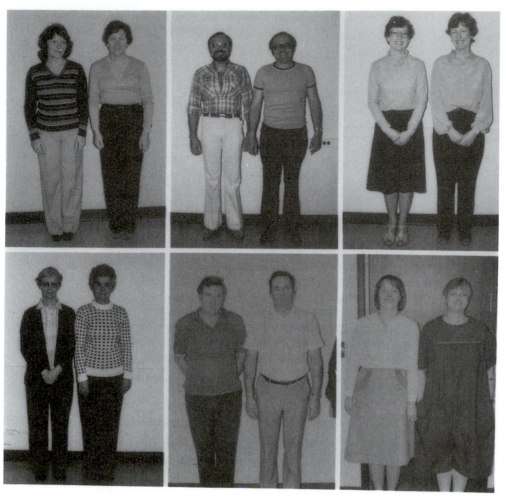

Figure 3.7

Twins reared apart on their first assessment day as participants in the Minnesota Study of Twins Reared Apart. The top row includes three pairs of identical twins and the bottom role includes three pairs of fraternal twins. These unposed photographs suggest genetic influence on body posture because the identical twins are standing in more similar positions than are the fraternal twins. Courtesy: Dr. Thomas J. Bouchard, Jr.

substantially in IQ—in fact, their average similarity is greater than that for fraternal twins growing up in the same home.

Identical twins who have been reared apart are also similar on a variety of personality characteristics, such as extraversion and neuroticism (Loehlin, 1992). Indeed, their similarity extends to some outcomes (for example, religious attitudes and beliefs) that we might have thought were unlikely to be affected by the genes (Waller et al., 1990). (Figure 3.7 shows some of the twin pairs from the Minnesota Study.)

To Recap . . .

Psychologists have used four research strategies to study the influence of heredity on behavior: family studies, adoption studies, twin studies, and a combination of the twin study and the adoption study. In three areas in particular—intellectual performance, personality, and psychiatric disorders—genetic processes have been shown to play a significant (although never all-important) role. The relevant evidence includes the similarity of adoptive children to their biological parents and the strong similarity between pairs of identical twins, even when the twins have been separated and reared in different environments.

MODELS OF GENE–ENVIRONMENT INTERACTION

When thinking about the role of genes in development, we must keep in mind an important distinction that we first discussed in Chapter 1. Recall that some psychologists focus on normative development—they are concerned with the ways in which humans are alike. Other psychologists are more interested in idiographic processes—they focus on what makes us different from one another. We can look at this issue in another way. Humans are different from other species, which are in turn different from one another. What gives a species its identity are the characteristics that all members *share*, that is, how they are alike. There is no doubt that genes are responsible for making each species unique. Psychologists who study normative development thus are really trying to learn about humans as a species. But humans (and all other animals) also differ among themselves—not just in physical characteristics but in behavior and development as well. These are the individual differences of interest to psychologists who take an idiographic approach. How much of a role do genes play in these sorts of differences? This is the main question being asked today by researchers in the field of **behavior genetics.**

All contemporary psychologists believe that genes (nature) and environment (nurture) interact to determine human behavior, but they differ as to which factor they feel has more influence. A related and perhaps even more useful question concerns *how* genes and environment exert their effects—that is, by what processes do these factors operate and how do they interact with one another?

In this section we examine four theoretical models that attempt to explain how genes and environment work together to determine any child's behavior and development. Because the models are complex, we will present only their fundamental ideas. But they illustrate the increasing role that psychologists are ascribing to genetic processes as this area is becoming better understood.

Gottesman's Limit-Setting Model

An early model proposed by Irving Gottesman (1974) suggested that genes interact with the environment by setting the upper and lower limits of our development. Our environment and experiences then determine where in this **reaction range** we end up.

Figure 3.8 illustrates this model by showing the ranges of possible basketball skills that might exist for groups of children born with different genotypes representing different heights. Group A consists of children who carry a gene that makes them unusually short. Groups B and C represent typical girls and boys, respectively, who are of average height for their gender. Group D represents children who have inherited genes

Behavior genetics

The field of study that explores the role of genes in producing individual differences in behavior and development.

Reaction range

In Gottesman's model, the term for the range of ability or skill that is set by the genes. The value achieved within this range is determined by the environment.

Figure 3.8

The reaction range concept, showing the simultaneous influences of genes and environment. Adapted from "Developmental Genetics and Ontogenetic Psychology: Overdue Détente and Propositions from a Matchmaker" by I. I. Gottesman, 1974. In A. D. Pick (Ed.), *Minnesota Symposia on Child Psychology,* vol. 8, p. 60. Copyright © 1974 by the University of Minnesota Press. Adapted by permission.

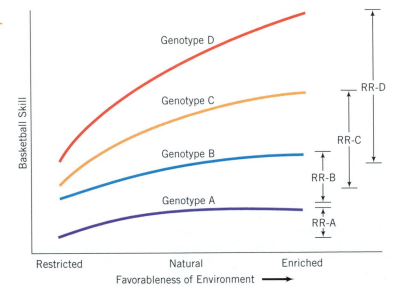

that make them unusually tall. Note that the reaction range (RR) of the groups varies, with the tallest individuals having the widest potential range of basketball abilities, and the shortest having the narrowest. The graph also includes three levels of environment: restricted (where perhaps the child has no exposure to basketball at all), natural (the environment of a youngster growing up in a typical U.S. town), and enriched (such as when the child's father is a basketball coach).

Note how genes and environment interact in this model. The genes have set the limits on potential basketball skills such that very short children (Group A) will not become proficient at these skills regardless of their environment, whereas very tall children (Group D) have the greatest opportunity to benefit from a more supportive environment. But it is important to note also that the reaction ranges overlap. This means that either poor genes or a poor environment can be overcome somewhat by strength in the other. This model, of course, could be applied to many other behaviors and abilities, such as mathematics performance, musical ability, or any number of traits or skills.

Scarr's Niche-Picking Model

In the model offered by Sandra Scarr, genes play a much more active role in development than simply setting limits within which the environment can operate (Scarr, 1992, 1993; Scarr & McCartney, 1983). In Scarr's model, the genes are one determinant of the kind of environment the child experiences.

The traditional view in psychology has been that different family environments cause children to develop in different ways. For example, we know that children whose parents provide books, educational activities, and encouragement to succeed tend to perform well in school, and children whose parents are harsh and punitive are more likely to be aggressive and to display various other behavior problems. The child's developmental outcome therefore was assumed to be rather directly determined by the child's family environment.

Scarr disagrees with this view. Her model invokes an important idea discussed in Chapter 1, namely, that children play a role in producing their own environments. This, she proposes, occurs through the genes. (Figure 3.9 provides a schematic summary of the model.) Consider the family example again. Although parents do provide children with their family environment, they also provide them with their genes. The child's genes, in turn, operate to produce a correlation between the child's genotype and the child's environment—that is, they ensure that both genes and environment push development in the same direction. They do so in three different ways, which Scarr believes change in relative importance as the child grows from infancy to adolescence.

During infancy, genes exert their influence principally through a **passive gene–environment correlation.** The baby's environment is almost entirely dictated by the parents, but because the parents and child share so many of the same genes, the environment they create is usually very consistent with, and supportive of, the child's genotype. For example, musically inclined parents are likely both to give birth to musically inclined children and to provide a musical home environment for them.

As children get older, their genes become more likely to produce an **evocative gene–environment correlation.** Children now do things that evoke certain responses from the parents and others (recall Bronfenbrenner's notion of developmentally generative and developmentally disruptive behaviors, presented in Chapter 1). For example, a

Passive gene–environment correlation
Situation in which genes and environment affect development similarly because the genes the child receives from the parents are compatible with the environment the parents provide.

Evocative gene–environment correlation
Situation in which genes and environment affect development similarly because genetically set predispositions of the child elicit compatible experiences from the environment.

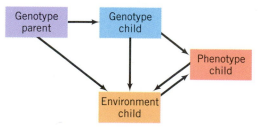

Figure 3.9

Scarr's model of the reciprocal influences between environments and genes. The child's genotype is important not only as a direct contributor to the child's phenotype; it is also one determinant of the enviroment the child experiences. Adapted from "How People Make Their Own Environments: A Theory of Genotype-Environment Effects" by S. Scarr & K. McCartney, *Child Development, 54,* p. 425. Copyright © 1983 by the Society for Research in Child Development. Adapted by permission.

According to Scarr and McCartney's model, niche-picking occurs when children choose environments that reflect and support their genetic predispositions.

child who speaks and reads early—behaviors that likely have some genetic basis—may prompt parents to provide a rich language environment, including books, storytelling, and educational games. In this way, the child's genes help create an environment that is compatible with the child's genetically set predispositions.

Finally, as children gain more independence, their genes can operate through a more **active gene–environment correlation** to produce environments that suit them. Children, on their own, can seek out the particular environments, or *niches*, that best fit their interests and talents—such as the library, gym, or rock concert.

Scarr's model of gene–environment interaction does not ignore the importance of the child's family environment, but it views the environment less as a direct cause of the child's development and more as a vehicle that enables the genes to guide the child along a particular developmental path. Scarr contends that genetic influences actually grow stronger with age, as children become better able actively to recruit the environments their genes bias them toward. This prediction runs counter to the traditional view that genes start us off in a particular direction and then our environment more or less takes over. As we will see shortly, there is some striking evidence in support of Scarr's prediction.

Plomin's Environmental Genetics Model

A third model of gene–environment interaction has been presented by Robert Plomin (1994, 1995, 2000a, 2000b). His approach shares many of the same ideas as Scarr's model. He believes that children's developmental outcomes are related to their family environments for two reasons:

1. Children share many genes with their parents, who in turn provide the environment for their children.

2. Children evoke from their parents the sorts of responses and surroundings that suit their genes.

Plomin has gone so far as to refer to his work as *environmental genetics,* which means the study of how our genes influence our environments. Further, his model is not limited to parent–child interactions but also extends to other family members (Plomin et al., 1994).

The most important addition in Plomin's model is the concept of **nonshared environment** (Hetherington, Reiss, & Plomin, 1994; Reiss et al., 2000). This idea is most easily understood in terms of siblings. We know that children reared in the same family have many similarities. Psychologists have not been surprised to find that intelligence, physical abilities, personality, and other characteristics are generally more similar between brothers and sisters than they are between unrelated children. These similarities have always been assumed to result from siblings' sharing both many of the same genes (50%) and the same family environment. Given these two major sources of similarity, a

Active gene–environment correlation
Situation in which genes and environment affect development similarly because children seek out experiences that are compatible with their genetic predispositions.

Nonshared environment
A concept used in behavior genetics to refer to presumed aspects of the environment that children experience differently.

more interesting question becomes why many siblings behave and develop so differently from one another.

Plomin's answer is that although these children live in the same family, they do not necessarily experience the same environments. Rather, parents often treat children differently from one another, and children frequently react to the same family events and experiences in different ways. Moreover, the source of both these differences, Plomin believes, is genetic. His argument is that although 50% of siblings' genes are the same, 50% are also different. These different genes, Plomin contends, lead siblings to evoke different treatment from their parents and to respond in different ways to the same events. In short, the aspects of the family environment that they experience differently—the nonshared aspects—are what make siblings different from one another.

What about siblings' similarities? Perhaps the most controversial aspect of this model is that, like Scarr and other behavior geneticists, Plomin believes that the similarities we see in siblings result mostly from their genetic similarity (the 50% of the genes they share). Their common family environment, by contrast, is thought to contribute very little to explaining why they are alike.

What sort of evidence might support such a position? Two findings from adoption studies provide the strongest support (Turkheimer & Waldron, 2000). First, adoptive siblings (that is, unrelated children growing up in the same home) are considerably less similar across a range of measures than are biologically related siblings. This finding suggests that sharing a common environment is not enough to make siblings alike; rather, the typical similarity between siblings apparently results from their shared genes. Second, adoptive siblings are more similar to one another in early childhood than they are by the time they reach adolescence, even though by adolescence they have had many more years of living together in the same home. Thus, the family environment apparently operates to make siblings different, not the same.

A further finding from adoption studies is relevant to both Scarr's and Plomin's models. With age, the psychological characteristics of an adopted child become increasingly similar to those of the biological mother and less similar to those of the adoptive mother. We might, of course, have expected the reverse: that the influence of the adoptive mother would grow with the years that she and the child spend together. Instead, it is the genes that grow in importance as children get older. This finding does not mean that the environment has become unimportant. Rather, the pattern presumably occurs because parents generally control children's environments at younger ages, but as children grow older they are increasingly able to choose their own environments and experiences—Scarr's "niche picking"—thus permitting their genes to operate in a more active way to influence their development (Plomin et al., 1997b).

Bronfenbrenner and Ceci's Bioecological Model

The most recent and perhaps most complex of the models we will consider is that of Urie Bronfenbrenner and Stephen Ceci (Bronfenbrenner, 1999; Bronfenbrenner & Ceci, 1994; Bronfenbrenner & Morris, 1998). This model derives from Bronfenbrenner's ecological approach, described in Chapter 1. We will see shortly why they call it a *bioecological model*.

Bronfenbrenner and Ceci assign much more importance to the environment than do many behavior geneticists. They agree with the idea that children's genes influence their development and that they do so, to some degree, by steering the environment in the right direction. But the bioecological model adds to this picture a more explicit description of how and when this occurs.

According to this analysis, genes can only exert their influence when certain experiences activate them. These experiences, called **proximal processes,** are interactions between the child and the child's direct-contact (microsystem) world—parents, siblings, toys, books, pets, and anything else of significance in the child's immediate environment—that have a positive effect on the child's psychological functioning. Such interactions may involve, for

Proximal processes
Bronfenbrenner and Ceci's term for interactions between the child and aspects of the microsystem that have positive effects on psychological functioning and that help maximize expression of the child's genetic potential.

example, play with siblings, social activities with friends, reading and problem solving with parents, and other sorts of stimulating experiences. An additional requirement is that these interactions must take place fairly regularly and must continue for some time. When these requirements hold, the child's genes are able to use the experiences to achieve their ends, and, as a result, the child reaches his or her maximum genetic potential. But if proximal processes are weak or missing in the child's life, the genes cannot fully express themselves, and so the child's development will remain below what it could have been.

Bronfenbrenner and Ceci also believe that proximal processes are valuable to the child in both high- and lower-quality environments, but in different ways. When the environment is stable and rich with resources—as is the case in many middle-income households—these interactions have the best opportunity to help children develop their fullest abilities (such as the example of musical talent described earlier). When the child's environment is disorganized and disadvantaged—as in many poor neighborhoods—proximal processes can help prevent undesirable outcomes that might otherwise have occurred (such as aggression, violence, or other problem behaviors to which genes may have predisposed the child).

Note how the child's biology (genes) and ecology (immediate environment) contribute more equally and in greater interaction in this model than in either the more strongly genetic or strongly environmental approaches. Perhaps for this reason, Bronfenbrenner and Ceci use the term *bioecological* to describe it.

To Recap . . .

Four models attempt to explain how genes and environment interact to produce human development. In Gottesman's limit-setting model, genes play a passive role by setting the limits, or reaction range, within which environmental effects can be observed. Genes play a more active role in Scarr's niche-picking model, affecting the child's environment through processes that move from passive (infancy) to evocative (early childhood) to active (later childhood). Plomin's model adds the concept of nonshared environment, whereby differences in the behavior of siblings are assumed to result from those aspects of the environment that they experience differently. Bronfenbrenner and Ceci's bioecological model proposes that genes exert their influence on the environment through proximal processes—stimulating interactions between the child and aspects of the microsystem.

CONCLUSION

There is probably no topic in this book for which the recent gains in knowledge have been as great as for genetics. Much of what we have presented in this chapter is very new. There seems little doubt that many additional discoveries will soon be forthcoming. What conclusions can be taken away from all this work?

A first conclusion is that genetic processes reach into many more areas of development than we once believed. One researcher summarizes this conclusion succinctly: "Everything is heritable" (Turkheimer, 2000, p. 160). This does not mean, of course, that any human psychological trait is totally genetic in origin. But it does mean that genes have been shown to play some role for virtually every psychological outcome of interest that has been the subject of behavior genetics research—whether the domain be cognitive abilities, personality attributes, or psychiatric problems.

A second conclusion concerns the question of greatest interest to the psychologist: *How* do genes exert their effects? Until recently, knowledge of specific genes and specific genetic mechanisms was limited to the case of disorders—identifying the gene for Huntington's disease, for example, or the chromosomal abnormality in the case of Down syndrome. This is no longer the case. Recent years have seen reports of specific genes that contribute to a wide range of important outcomes in human development; a partial list would include intelligence, language, aggression, neuroticism, dyslexia, homosexuality, and sensation seeking. With the success of the Human Genome Project, knowledge of specific genes for specific outcomes seems certain to grow.

A third conclusion is perhaps the most important, and it is that genes will never be the whole story. The same data from behavior genetics studies that tell us that genes are important also tell us that genes are not all-important—at best, genes account for about half the variation in particular outcomes, meaning that environment accounts for at least half. Furthermore, a grounding in the genetics of disorders can be misleading when we think about how specific genes contribute to psychological outcomes. As Plomin (2000a, p. 235) puts it, "If you inherit the Huntington's disease allele, you will die from the disease regardless of your other genes or your environment." Outcomes such as language or aggression, however, are not determined by a single gene; rather, there are multiple genes (perhaps thousands in the case of a complex trait like intelligence) that are relevant. The effect of any gene depends on the genotype as a whole, and the expression of the genes depends on an environmental context. The eventual phenotype—whether it be height, weight, intelligence, or personality—always depends on the environment as well as the genes.

This last point can serve as a conclusion not just for the present chapter but for the book as a whole. If there is one message that you should take away from this course, it is this: At every point in development genes and environment work together to determine each and every aspect of our behavior.

FOR THOUGHT AND DISCUSSION

1. We mentioned that genes may play a larger role in some behaviors than in others and that this issue has sometimes been a source of scientific controversy. *Which do you think plays the larger role in the following behaviors, genes or environment? (1) musical ability, (2) athletic skill, and (3) interpersonal skills. What leads you to these conclusions? How could you explore this issue?*

2. As a result of *crossing over,* every sperm and ovum is genetically unique. *If this process did not occur, would children look more or less similar to their siblings and parents? Why?*

3. Research is continuing to identify the genes responsible for various disorders. This knowledge makes it possible to predict, in some instances, who is likely to display a certain disorder. *Who should have access to this sort of information about an individual? For example, should an insurance company be able to find out whether an individual is genetically likely to develop a certain disorder? Should the company be able to refuse to insure such a person? Should an employer be able to get this information? In general, who should control genetic information about individuals? To what uses should it be put? Should there be limits on the uses?*

4. The concept of *nonshared environment* relates to the fact that children in the same family do not necessarily share the same experiences. *Think about your own childhood. Can you identify ways in which you and your siblings experienced different environments? If you have children, can you identify differences in their environments? Can you speculate on how these different experiences led you and your siblings, or might lead your children, down different life paths?*

VISUAL SUMMARY FOR CHAPTER 3
Genetics: The Biological Context of Development

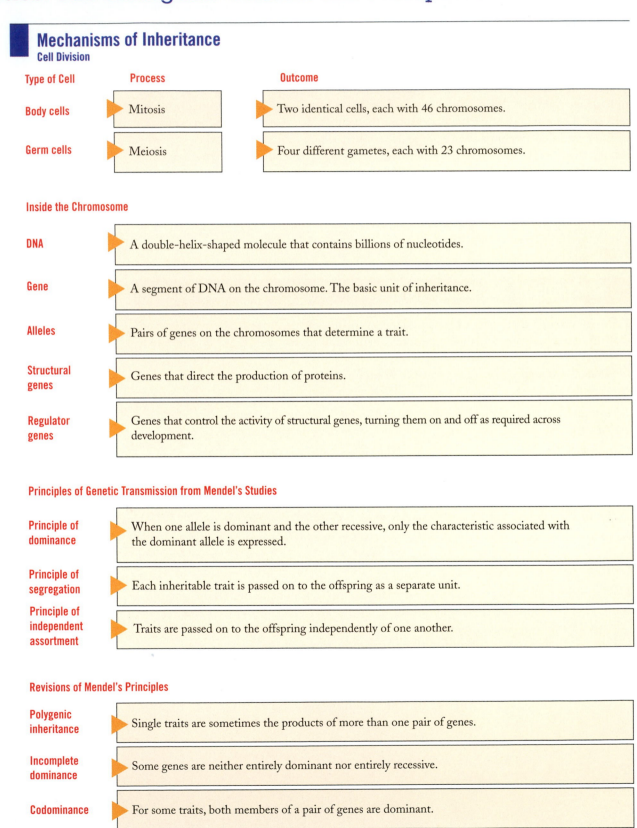

Mechanisms of Inheritance
Cell Division

Type of Cell	Process	Outcome
Body cells	Mitosis	Two identical cells, each with 46 chromosomes.
Germ cells	Meiosis	Four different gametes, each with 23 chromosomes.

Inside the Chromosome

DNA	A double-helix-shaped molecule that contains billions of nucleotides.
Gene	A segment of DNA on the chromosome. The basic unit of inheritance.
Alleles	Pairs of genes on the chromosomes that determine a trait.
Structural genes	Genes that direct the production of proteins.
Regulator genes	Genes that control the activity of structural genes, turning them on and off as required across development.

Principles of Genetic Transmission from Mendel's Studies

Principle of dominance	When one allele is dominant and the other recessive, only the characteristic associated with the dominant allele is expressed.
Principle of segregation	Each inheritable trait is passed on to the offspring as a separate unit.
Principle of independent assortment	Traits are passed on to the offspring independently of one another.

Revisions of Mendel's Principles

Polygenic inheritance	Single traits are sometimes the products of more than one pair of genes.
Incomplete dominance	Some genes are neither entirely dominant nor entirely recessive.
Codominance	For some traits, both members of a pair of genes are dominant.

Genetic Disorders

Cause of Disorder	Explanation	Examples
Domination traits	Caused by a dominant gene and therefore expressed in all carriers.	Huntington's disease
Recessive traits	Caused by a recessive gene and therefore expressed only when the defective gene is inherited from both parents.	Tay-Sachs disease, phenylketonuria, sickle-cell anemia
Chromosome defects	Caused by a structural defect in the chromosome that may have occurred during meiosis in one of the parents.	Down syndrome

Studying Gene Effects on Behavior

Type of Study	Description	Assumption
Family studies	Look for similarities over generations of a family in traits suspected to have a genetic basis.	Similarities among family members are assumed to be the result of heredity. Limitation: It can be very difficult to distinguish between heredity and environmental influences in family studies.
Adoption studies	Adopted children are compared both with their biological parents and with their adoptive parents; they may also be compared with siblings in the adoptive home.	If the correlation with biological parents is greater, genetic factors are assumed to play the stronger role; if the correlation with adoptive parents is greater, environmental factors play the stronger role.
Twin studies	Monozygotic twins and dizygotic twins are compared in terms of their similarity on traits suspected to have a genetic basis.	If the correlation is greater between MZ twins than between DZ twins, genetic factors are assumed to play the stronger role. Limitation: MZ twins may have a more similar environment than DZ twins.
Combined twin and adoption studies	Compares twins separated early in life and raised in different adoptive homes.	Controls for the similar-environment limitation of twin studies. If MZ twins are more similar than DZ twins, even when raised apart, the greater similarity is assumed to be the result of genetic factors.

Models of Gene–Environment Interaction

Model	Explanation
Gottesman's Limit-Setting Model	Genes set the upper and lower limits for developement; environmental influences determine development within this reaction range.
Scarr's Niche-Picking Model	Genes control the child's environment through processes that move from passive (infancy) to evocative (early childhood) to active (later childhood).
Plomin's Environmental Genetics Model	Differences in the behavior of siblings result from those aspects of the environment they experience differently (nonshared environment).
Brofenbrenner and Ceci's Bioecological Model	Genes exert their influence on the environment through proximal processes stimulating interactions between the child and aspects of the microsystem which must be frequent and continuing in the child's life.

4

Prenatal Development

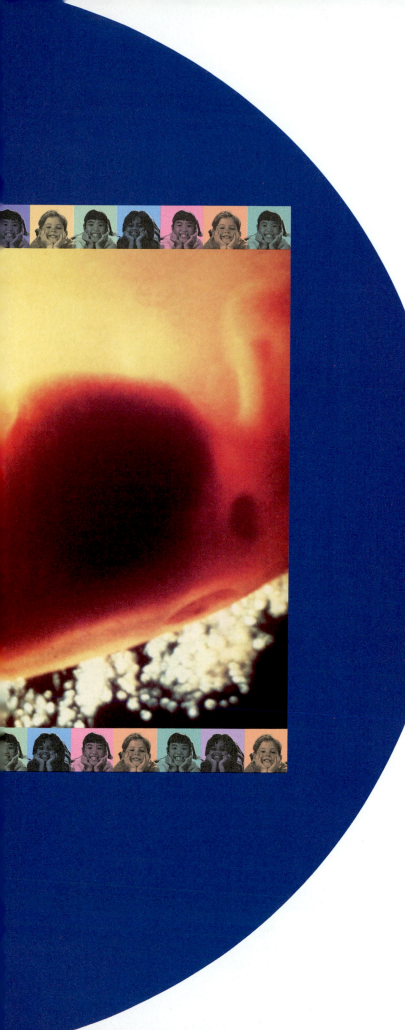

n 1989, Jennifer Johnson of Sanford, Florida, became the first woman to be convicted of dealing cocaine to her newborn baby—through the umbilical cord! The case represented a relatively new trend in the war on drugs. Because no state laws made it illegal for women to pass drugs to fetuses, prosecutors had

turned to laws aimed at dealers who sold drugs to minors. The case against Johnson, who had used cocaine during her pregnancy, essentially claimed that she had dealt drugs to her baby. A Florida appeals court upheld Johnson's conviction in 1991.

Law enforcement agencies in Florida and across the nation had good reason for concern about drug use among pregnant women. Experts had estimated that the number of babies born to women who used illegal drugs during their pregnancies had climbed to 375,000 a year. Some of these babies died; others had various medical and behavioral problems. Many were abandoned, becoming boarder babies in public hospitals. Prosecuting mothers, some said, was one way to get the mothers into treatment and thus protect their babies.

Many legal and medical professionals disagreed, however, arguing that pregnant women would be less—not more—likely to seek treatment if they feared prosecution. Legal experts also pointed out that drug-trafficking laws were never meant to be used to prosecute pregnant women. In 1992, the Florida Supreme Court struck down Johnson's conviction on precisely those grounds, holding that the Florida legislature had not intended state laws to be used in that way. In 2001, the U.S. Supreme Court ruled that hospitals could not forward the results of drug tests of pregnant women to the police.

The problem of how fetuses can be legally protected from their mothers' drug use has yet to be fully resolved. A central legal issue in this controversial area—and in the abortion controversy as well—is, What are a fetus's rights? However this question is eventually resolved in the U.S. legal system, one thing is certain: Women who use drugs during pregnancy place their children at risk.

In this chapter we examine the development of the child during the 9-month prenatal period. Drugs, we will see, are only one of many risk factors a fetus may face while growing in the mother's womb. ■

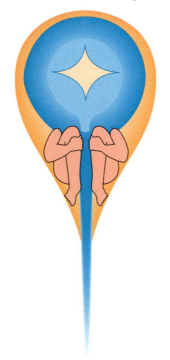

Figure 4.1

Copy of a 17th-century drawing of a sperm. The miniature human was thought to enlarge after entering the ovum.

When we consider the course of a child's life, the 9 months between conception and birth may be the most unappreciated period of development. This is probably because the events that occur during this time are largely hidden from view. Yet during these 9 months, what begins as a microscopic fertilized egg undergoes a series of dramatic changes and eventually emerges as a living, breathing baby.

You can probably imagine how people from ancient cultures must have struggled to explain how a fully formed creature could appear at birth. As late as the 18th century, some believed that people were completely formed even before conception. One theory, homunculism, proposed that each sperm cell contained a tiny individual, like the one shown in Figure 4.1, who would grow when deposited in a woman's womb. Another theory held that the fully formed baby resided instead in the ovum (Needham, 1959).

Just a bit more than 100 years ago, a Swiss zoologist peering through a microscope became the first person to see a sperm enter an egg, fertilize it, and produce the cell for a new embryo. Such discoveries led to our current understanding of fertilization and prenatal development (Touchette, 1990). This understanding also includes knowledge about factors that impair development, such as genetic defects, infections, drugs, and environmental poisons.

STAGES OF PRENATAL DEVELOPMENT

Even though it is the largest cell in the body, the ovum is no larger than the period at the end of this sentence, and the sperm cell that fertilizes it weighs less than 1/30,000 as much. This tiny genetic package nevertheless grows into a baby whose mass is billions of times greater in only 9 months.

Every stage of development along the journey from conception to birth represents a mix of the influences of nature and nurture. Even the genetic material that the mother and father contribute to the offspring can be affected by environmental factors, such as radiation. Other environmental factors, such as nutrition, infections, and drugs, can also influence development. In this section, we follow the baby's prenatal development through three stages, or periods—the period of the zygote, the period of the embryo, and the period of the fetus. First we consider the starting point of development—conception.

Conception

Prenatal development begins at **conception,** or fertilization, when a sperm unites with an ovum (egg) to form a single cell, called a **zygote.** The zygote receives 23 chromosomes from the mother and 23 from the father, to form a new and genetically unique person.

Once every 28 or so days, about halfway through a woman's menstrual cycle, an ovum is produced by either her left or right ovary (they alternate each month) and begins to travel through the fallopian tube toward the uterus, which at this point is only about the size of a plum. For the next 24 hours, the ovum is capable of being fertilized. Sperm from the male, which are deposited in the vagina, remain viable for 2 to 3 days. This time is crucial because their longer journey takes them through the cervix and the uterus before entering the fallopian tube, where the ovum is located. Of the several million sperm that are typically deposited, only 100 to 200 of the strongest and healthiest make it all the way to the ovum, and only one actually penetrates the wall to fertilize the ovum. Within about an hour of penetration, the genetic material from the sperm and the ovum have completely merged to form a zygote, and development of the baby begins.

The Period of the Zygote (Conception to Second Week)

The zygote multiplies rapidly as it continues its 4-day, 4-inch journey through the fallopian tube to the uterus. At first the zygote is a solid mass of cells, but it gradually changes into a hollow sphere as it prepares to implant into the wall of the uterus. Now the cells begin to specialize, some forming an inner cell mass, which will become the embryo, and some forming important structures that will support the embryo's development. Figure 4.2 diagrams the events of the first week of human development.

Implantation takes about a week. During this time, the zygote settles into the blood-enriched lining of the uterus, where it will remain attached for the duration of the pregnancy. The period of the zygote ends about 2 weeks after fertilization, which

Conception
The combining of the genetic material from a male gamete (sperm) and a female gamete (ovum); fertilization.

Zygote
A fertilized ovum.

Millions of sperm from the father enter the vagina of the mother, but only several hundred reach the ovum and only one actually fertilizes it.

Figure 4.2

Schematic representation of the events of the first week of human development.

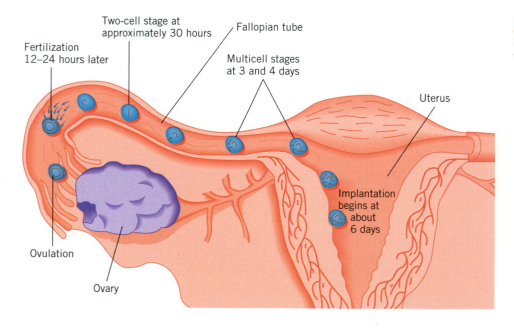

Two-cell stage at approximately 30 hours
Fallopian tube
Fertilization 12–24 hours later
Multicell stages at 3 and 4 days
Uterus
Implantation begins at about 6 days
Ovulation
Ovary

corresponds to the first missed menstrual period. By the time a woman suspects she may be pregnant, then, prenatal development is well under way.

The Period of the Embryo (Third to Eighth Week)

The period of the **embryo** begins when implantation is complete and lasts for around 6 weeks. Although the embryo at first is only the size of an apple seed, all major internal and external structures form during this period. For that reason, these weeks are the most delicate of the pregnancy and the time when the growing embryo is most vulnerable to threats from the internal and external environments (discussed shortly).

In the third week, the inner cell mass differentiates into three layers, from which all body structures will emerge. Two layers form first—the *endodermal* layer and the *ectodermal* layer. The endodermal cells will develop into internal organs and glands. The ectodermal cells become the parts of the body that maintain contact with the outside world—the nervous system; the sensory parts of the eyes, nose, and ears; skin; and hair. The third cell layer then appears between the endodermal and ectodermal layers. This is the *mesodermal* layer, which will give rise to muscles, cartilage, bone, sex organs, and the heart. The heart is beating by the end of the third week.

Around the beginning of the fourth week, the embryo looks something like a tiny tube. The shape of the embryo gradually changes, however, because cell multiplication is more rapid in some locations than in others. By the end of the fourth week, the embryo assumes a curved form, as shown in Figure 4.3. We can distinguish a bump below the head, which is the primitive heart, and the upper and lower limbs, which have just begun to form as tiny buds.

The embryo's body changes less in the fifth week, but the head and brain develop rapidly. The upper limbs form, and the lower limbs appear and look like small paddles. In the sixth week, the head continues to grow rapidly, and differentiation of the limbs occurs as elbows, fingers, and wrists become recognizable. It is now possible to discern the ears and eyes. The limbs develop rapidly in the seventh week, and stumps appear that will form fingers and toes.

By the end of the eighth week, the embryo has distinctly human features. Almost half of the embryo consists of the head. The eyes, ears, toes, and fingers are easily distinguishable. All internal and external structures have formed. Thus, in 8 weeks, a single, tiny, undifferentiated cell has proliferated into a remarkably complex organism consisting of millions of cells differentiated into heart, kidneys, eyes, ears, nervous system, brain, and other structures. Its mass has increased a staggering 2 million percent. Figure 4.4 gives some indication of the magnitude of this change.

The Prenatal Environment Just as the embryo's inner cell mass changes rapidly in the early weeks of development, so do its other cells. Three major structures arising from these cells develop by the end of the embryonic period: the amniotic sac, the placenta, and the umbilical cord, illustrated in Figure 4.5.

The **amniotic sac** is a watertight membrane filled with fluid. As the embryo grows, the amniotic sac surrounds it, cushioning and supporting it within the uterus and providing an environment with a constant temperature.

The **placenta,** formed from both the mother's tissue and the embryo's tissue, is a remarkable organ through which the mother and the embryo (later the fetus) exchange materials. Linking the embryo to the placenta is the **umbilical cord,** which houses the blood vessels that carry these materials.

The exchange of materials takes place in the placental villi. These ornate-looking structures (shown in Figure 4.5) are small blood vessels immersed in the mother's blood but separated from it by a very thin membrane. The membrane serves as a filter—nature's way of keeping many diseases, germs, and impurities in the mother's blood from reaching the baby. Unfortunately, as we will see shortly, it is not a perfect filter. Blood itself does not pass between the mother and the fetus (which is why the mother and baby

Embryo
The developing organism from the third week, when implantation is complete, through the eighth week after conception.

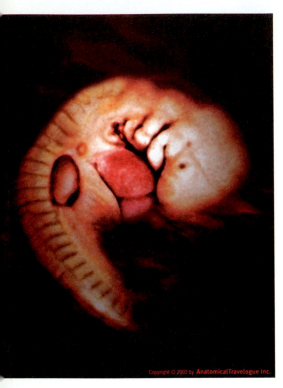

Figure 4.3

An embryo at 4 weeks.

Amniotic sac
A fluid-containing watertight membrane that surrounds and protects the embryo and fetus.

Placenta
An organ that forms where the embryo attaches to the uterus. This organ exchanges nutrients, oxygen, and wastes between the embryo or fetus and the mother through a very thin membrane that does not allow the passage of blood.

Umbilical cord
A soft cable of tissue and blood vessels that connects the fetus to the placenta.

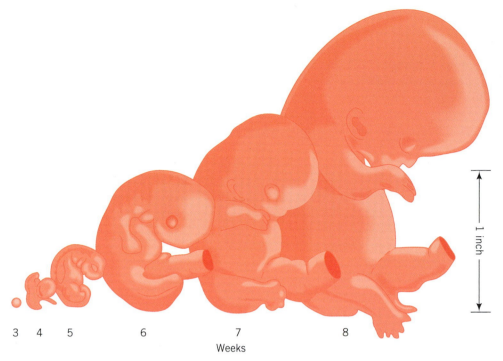

Figure 4.4

Human ova and embryos showing growth and body form from 3 to 8 weeks. Adapted from *Textbook of Embryology,* 5th ed. (p. 87), by H. E. Jordan and J. E. Kindred, 1948, New York: Appleton-Century-Crofts. Copyright © 1948 by Appleton-Century-Crofts. Adapted by permission.

can have different blood types); however, oxygen and nutrients do pass from the mother's blood through the placenta to the fetus, and waste products of the fetus pass into the mother's blood to be carried away and excreted.

The Period of the Fetus (9th to 38th Week)

At the end of the eighth week, the period of the **fetus** begins. The principal changes for the fetus are to develop further the already formed organ structures and increase in size and weight. Beginning its third month weighing less than an ounce and measuring 2 inches in length, the average fetus will be born 266 days after conception weighing about 7 to 8 lb. and measuring about 20 inches in length. Fetal growth begins to slow

Fetus

The developing organism from the 9th week to the 38th week after conception.

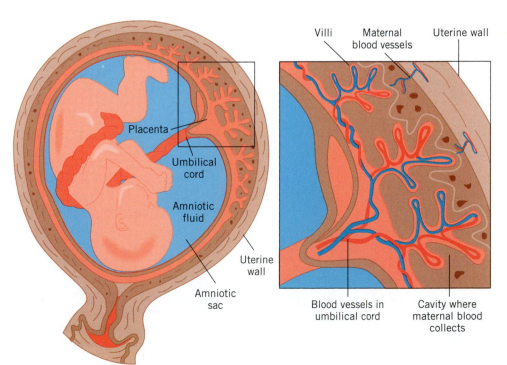

Figure 4.5

Maternal structures that support the embryo and fetus include the placental villi, amniotic sac, placenta, and umbilical cord.

around the eighth month—which is good for both the mother and the fetus because if it did not, the fetus would weigh 200 pounds at birth!

External Changes   During this period, the fetus's appearance changes drastically. The head grows less than do other parts of the body, so that its ratio decreases from 50% of the body mass at 12 weeks to 25% at birth. The skin, which has been transparent, begins to thicken during the third month. Facial features, which appeared almost extraterrestrial at 6 weeks, become more human looking as the eyes move from the sides of the head to the front.

The eyelids seal shut near the beginning of the third month and remain that way for the next 3 months. Nails appear on fingers and toes by the fourth month, and pads appear at the ends of the fingers that will uniquely identify the individual for life. Head hair also begins to grow. A bone structure begins to support a more erect posture by 6 months.

Growth of Internal Organs   Changes in external appearance are accompanied by equally striking internal changes. By 3 months, the brain has organized into functional subdivisions—seeing, hearing, thinking, and so on. Most of the 100 billion cells that make up the adult brain are already present in the fetus by the fifth month, but the 14 trillion connections they will make between themselves and incoming and outgoing nerve cells will not be completed until well after birth. Other nerve cells grow and establish connections throughout fetal development.

A major mystery facing scientists is how the single, undifferentiated zygote cell can give rise to billions of fibers that properly connect eyes, ears, touch sensors, muscles, and the parts of the brain. We discussed part of the answer to this question in Chapter 3: From the moment of conception, the subset of genes know as *regulator genes* direct the activity of other genes, causing some to form arms, some legs, and so forth. It is also clear, however, that environmental factors and interactions between nerve cells play a

A fetus at 12 weeks.

Copyright © 2002 by **AnatomicalTravelogue Inc.**

role, as no two brains are wired identically, not even those of identical twins, who have exactly the same genetic material (Edelman, 1993; Rakic, 1988).

Other internal organs continue to develop. Sexual development becomes apparent in males by the end of the third month with the appearance of external sexual organs. In females, the precursors of ova, or *oocytes,* form on the outer covering of the ovaries; all the oocytes the female will ever possess will be present at birth. The fallopian tubes, uterus, and vagina develop, and the external labia become discernible.

Early Signs of Behavior   Fetal activity begins in the third month, when the fetus is capable of forming a fist and wiggling toes; the mother, however, feels none of this. The fetus also appears to become sensitive to environmental stimulation, moving its whole body in response to a touch stimulus.

By the fourth month the eyes are sensitive to light through the lids, and by the fifth month a loud noise may activate the fetus. During this same month, the fetus swims effortlessly, a luxury gradually lost later as quarters become increasingly cramped. The fetus is now capable of kicking and turning and may begin to display rhythms of sleep and activity. By the seventh month, brain connections are sufficient for the fetus to exhibit a sucking reflex when the lips are touched.

Toward Independence   The later stages of prenatal development ready the fetus to live outside the mother's body. Although separate from the mother in many ways during development, the fetus is nevertheless completely dependent on her for survival during most of the prenatal period. Recall that the support system in the uterus provides oxygen, nutrients, waste disposal, and a constant temperature for the fetus. Although physicians have made marked progress in saving premature babies, they have been unable to lower the **age of viability** under around 23 to 24 weeks of fetal age.

The major obstacle to independent life for a fetus born prematurely is the immaturity of the air sacs of the lungs, which have to exchange carbon dioxide for oxygen. The fetus's inability to digest food or control body temperature is also a problem, and fat has not yet formed under the skin to assist in temperature regulation.

By 6 to 7 months of age, the fetus has a chance of survival outside the mother's body. The brain is sufficiently developed to provide at least partial regulation of breathing, swallowing, and body temperature. However, a baby born after only 7 months of development will need to be provided with extra oxygen, will have to take food in very small amounts, and will have to live for several weeks in an incubator for temperature control.

In the eighth month, fat appears under the skin, and although the digestive system is still too immature to extract nutrients from food adequately, the fetus begins to store maternal nutrients in its body. Even a baby born at 8 months, however, is susceptible to infection. Beginning in the eighth month, the mother's body contributes disease-fighting antibodies, which she has developed through her own exposure to foreign bodies, to the fetus. This process is not complete until 9 months of fetal age. It is an important process, because the antibodies help protect babies from infection until they are around 6 months of age, when they can produce their own antibodies in substantial amounts.

Some precursors of later individual differences among children become evident during the last weeks of prenatal life. Fetuses differ, for example, in how much they move around in the womb, and these differences show some relation to individual differences in both activity level and temperament at 2 years of age (DiPietro et al., 2002). Similarly, fetuses vary in their patterns of heart rate change, and these variations have been shown to correlate with some aspects of both temperament and cognitive development in early childhood (Bornstein et al., 2002; DiPietro et al., 1996). We hasten to add, however, that the relations that have been shown are modest, and that neither temperament nor anything else can be predicted with certainty from measures available during the prenatal period. Thus, parents should not anticipate a challenging toddler just because their fetus seems to kick more than the average baby.

Age of viability
The age (presently around 23 or 24 weeks) at which the infant has a chance to survive if born prematurely.

Families Created by Alternative Methods of Conception

Infertility can be a frustrating problem for couples hoping to start a family. Sometimes the difficulty involves the woman's eggs (or lack of them); other times the problem lies in the quantity or quality of the male sperm. Fortunately, medical science today offers couples several alternative methods for conceiving a child.

When the problem involves the male, the most common solution is *donor insemination,* in which sperm donated from another male is injected into the female, where it initiates a pregnancy. Another popular method is *in vitro fertilization* (IVF). In this process, an egg and sperm (donated from either a third party or from one or both members of the couple) are combined in a laboratory procedure; then the fertilized egg is implanted in the female's uterus where, if all goes well, it begins to develop. Presently, approximately 1% of children born in Western societies are conceived through IVF (Van Balen, 1998).

BOX 4.1

On the
Cutting
E D G E

These new reproductive technologies have effectively solved a long-standing problem of biology. But what are the psychological implications of these procedures? What impact do they have on the children who are products of this technology and on their parents?

One study investigated this issue by comparing families with a child conceived by each of these two methods with both families whose children were conceived naturally and families whose children were adopted (Golombok et al., 1995; Golombok, MacCallum, & Goodman, 2001). The focus of the study was social-emotional development and family functioning. Parents and children were interviewed, observed interacting with one another, and given a battery of tests. The first assessments were made when the children were between 4 and 8 years of age, and the sample was then followed up longitudinally when the children reached their 12th birthdays.

The researchers wondered whether families formed with the help of new technologies might experience more difficulties than the natural-conception families, for several possible reasons. For one, the child in most cases was genetically unrelated to one or both of the parents, but in only one family was the child informed of this. Would the nongenetic parent have difficulty relating to the child? Would the child feel deceived when eventually made aware of the situation? Would the absence of a biological connection among all family members interfere with the establishment of the normal social and emotional bonds? Among the other concerns

were whether the parents would feel unduly stressed by the unusual situation and whether the parents' relationship with one another would suffer if only one parent were genetically related to the child.

The results of the study are perhaps a little surprising. At the time of the first assessments, parents of children conceived by the two alternative reproductive methods were found to be similar to the adoptive parents and superior to parents in the natural-conception families in a number of areas. Mothers in these families were rated as warmer and more emotionally involved with their children, and both mothers and fathers were found to interact more with their children. By the time of the longitudinal follow-up the differences in parental involvement were no longer apparent. Importantly, at neither time period were there any differences among the children from the different family types. Thus, the children whose conception stemmed from the new reproductive technologies showed no ill effects of their unusual beginnings. Their feelings about themselves, their relations with their parents and with other children, and their overall psychological adjustment were no different from those of the children in the two comparison groups.

Other studies of IVF samples support these conclusions (Colpin, 2002; Hahn & DiPietro, 2001; Van Balen, 1998). Differences between IVF and natural-conception families are infrequent; and when they do occur, they tend to favor the parents or children in the IVF group. The one exception to this statement is that problems of pregnancy and birth (e.g., preterm birth, low birth weight) are greater with IVF conceptions. At present, however, it is not clear whether the problems result from the IVF procedure itself or from factors associated with the decision to use IVF conception—in particular, the relatively advanced age of many of the mothers in such samples.

Research on the new reproductive technologies is still very new, and any conclusions must therefore be tentative. To date, however, there is no evidence to suggest that the new technologies pose a serious threat to family functioning or harmony. It seems likely that parents who must seek special methods of conception will be heavily invested in the job of parenting. Genetic ties between parents and children may not be as important as the parents' strong commitment to parenthood.

✓ **To Recap . . .**

Prenatal development begins with conception and proceeds through the period of the zygote, the period of the embryo, and the period of the fetus. At conception, a sperm cell penetrates an egg cell to form a zygote. The zygote multiplies rapidly as it migrates toward the uterus, where it becomes fully implanted by the end of the second week.

Now an embryo, the cell mass rapidly differentiates into organs (heart, kidneys, eyes, ears, nervous system, and brain) and support structures (the amniotic sac, placenta, and umbilical cord). In the 6 weeks that make up the period of the embryo, a cluster of cells is transformed into a complex and differentiated organism.

At the end of the eighth week, the fetal period begins. The primary task for the fetus is growth and further development of organ systems. Behavior begins in the third month. The fetus grows toward increasing independence, but is unable to survive before about 23 to 24 weeks of fetal age. By 9 months following conception, the normal fetus is ready to face the external world.

TERATOLOGY

It is natural to think that prenatal development depends only on genes and that the environment begins to affect the baby only after birth. Yet although the uterus may not seem like an environment in the usual sense, it is the only home the embryo and fetus know. We will see that a number of factors affect the quality of this home and determine whether development is normal or abnormal—indeed, whether development can occur at all.

Approximately 3 to 5% of all live-born babies are identified as malformed at birth. Some malformations are difficult to detect at first, but become apparent with age. Thus, by the early school years, approximately 6 to 7% of children are identified as having congenital malformations—malformations that existed at birth. Many more babies would be born with malformations were it not for a natural prenatal process that results in miscarriage or spontaneous abortion. It is estimated that 90% of some kinds of malformations end in spontaneous abortions and that without this natural screening process, the observed incidence of congenital malformation would be 12% or higher (Shepard, 1986).

We have already seen that some abnormalities are caused by genetic defects. Malformations may also be caused by infectious diseases, drugs, and other environmental hazards. Nongenetic agents that can cause malformation in the embryo and fetus are referred to as **teratogens** (*tera* is a Latin base meaning "monster"). The term **teratology** refers to the study of the effect of teratogens on development.

Much of our discussion of teratogens will focus on their physical effects. Indeed, teratogens are defined in terms of their creation of physical malformations. However, psychologists have noted increasingly that teratogens can have psychological and behavioral effects as well. This realization has given rise to a new field, called *psychoteratology*. Researchers in this field use behavior rather than physical outcomes to study the potentially damaging effects of teratogens and have found that behavioral effects may show up even when physical effects do not. Thus, in many cases, behavioral measures may be more sensitive than physical measures.

Teratogen
An agent that can cause abnormal development in the fetus.

Teratology
The study of the effects of teratogens on development.

Historical Ideas

The field of teratology achieved scientific status only recently, but it has had an interesting history. The birth of malformed babies probably gave rise to at least some of the creatures of Greek mythology, such as the one-eyed cyclops and various creatures that are part human and part beast (Warkany, 1977). But although monsters were sometimes idolized in ancient times, people in the medieval period believed that the birth of malformed babies portended catastrophe, and malformed infants and children were often put to death. Some believed that these babies were produced through the mating of humans with animals, and it was not unusual for mothers and midwives who delivered malformed babies to be put on trial for witchcraft.

Such practices gradually gave way to the more benign belief that maternal fright, thoughts, and impressions could create a monster birth (Warkany, 1981). Running parallel to these theories were ancient beliefs that the food and drink a pregnant woman ingested could affect the fetus. In the Bible, an angel admonishes a man named Manoah that when his wife conceives a son, she should "drink no wine nor strong drink, and eat not any unclean thing" (Judges 13:4).

Despite the apparent fact that people of biblical times believed that maternal nourishment could affect the development of the fetus, a great deal of time elapsed before people fully realized the potential effects of the external world on the fetus. People generally believed that the embryo and fetus lived in a privileged environment, protected against harm by the placenta and its amniotic world.

By 1930, however, there was general recognition that X-rays could produce intrauterine growth retardation, microcephaly (an abnormally small head and brain), and small eyes. By the mid-1940s, it had become obvious that a pregnant mother who contracted rubella (German measles) during the early months of pregnancy had a relatively high chance of producing a baby with congenital abnormalities of the eye, ear, heart, and brain.

Still, these events were seen as exceptional. A major disaster finally shook people's faith in the privileged-environment belief, but only as recently as the early 1960s. A mild and seemingly harmless sedative, thalidomide, was marketed in the late 1950s, and many pregnant women took it for morning sickness. Physicians soon noticed a sharp increase in the number of babies born with defective limbs. Careful questioning of mothers, analysis of doctors' prescriptions, and epidemiological research implicated thalidomide as the culprit. The field of teratology experienced a dramatic surge as a result of this event and has been expanding rapidly ever since.

General Principles

Many teratogens have been identified as causing defects in humans. Evaluating an agent for teratogenic effects, however, is fraught with problems. For obvious reasons, animals must be the "guinea pigs" for substance testing, but the potential teratogen may not have the same effect on animal and human fetuses. Furthermore, people often take more than one drug, and a particular drug may do damage only in combination with another drug, with a disease, or with stress. Some common teratogens and their effects are listed in Table 4.1.

Several principles capture important features of how teratogens act (Hogge, 1990).

1. *A teratogen's effect depends on the genetic makeup of the organism exposed to it.* A prime example is thalidomide. The human fetus is extremely sensitive to this substance, but rabbits and rats are not. One reason thalidomide was not initially suspected to be a teratogen was that testing on these animals revealed no ill effects. The principle of genetic differences in sensitivity also applies to individuals within a species. Some babies are malformed because their mothers drank alcohol during pregnancy, but others are apparently not affected by this practice.

2. *The effect of a teratogen on development depends partly on timing.* Even before conception, teratogens can affect the formation of the parents' germ cells. Formation of female germ cells begins during fetal life, and formation of sperm can occur up to 64 days before the sperm are expelled. Thus, a fetus can be affected by drugs that the pregnant grandmother took decades earlier or by X-ray exposure that the father experienced many weeks before conception.

   For 2 to 3 weeks after conception, the zygote's fluids do not mix with those of the mother, so the zygote is relatively impervious to some teratogens. After the zygote has attached to the uterus, however, substances in the mother's bloodstream can pass through the placental barrier and mix with the blood of the embryo, and the embryo enters a particularly sensitive period. Teratogens can produce organ malformation from 2 to 8 weeks because this is a time when organs are forming. After the organs have formed, teratogens primarily produce growth retardation or tissue damage (Goldman, 1980).

   Which organ is affected by a teratogen depends in part on which organ is forming. Rubella is an example of how crucial timing can be. Rubella affects only 2 to 3% of the offspring of mothers infected within 2 weeks after their last period, whereas it affects 50% of offspring when infection occurs during the first month following conception, 22% when it occurs during the second month, and

6 to 8% when it occurs during the third month. The incidence falls to very low levels thereafter. Whether ear, eye, heart, or brain damage occurs depends on the stage of the formation of each organ when the mother is infected (Murata et al., 1992; Whitley & Goldenberg, 1990).

3. *The effect of a teratogen may be unique.* For example, thalidomide produces gross limb defects, whereas rubella primarily affects sensory and internal organs.

4. *The abnormal development caused by teratogens may be severe.* Teratogenic effects may include malformation of limbs or other parts of the body, growth retardation, functional and behavioral disorders, or even death.

Table 4.1	Some Teratogens and Conditions That May Harm the Fetus
Teratogen	**Potential Effect**
THERAPEUTIC DRUGS	
Aspirin	In large quantities, miscarriage, bleeding, newborn respiratory problems
Barbiturates	Newborn respiratory problems
Diethylstilbestrol (DES) (drug to prevent miscarriage)	Genital abnormalities in both sexes, vaginal and cervical cancer in adolescent females
Phenytoin (an anticonvulsant drug)	Threefold increase in likelihood of heart defects and growth retardation
Streptomycin	Hearing loss
Tetracycline	Most commonly, staining of teeth; can also affect bone growth
Thalidomide	Deformed limbs, sensory deficits, defects in internal organs, death
STREET DRUGS	
Cocaine and crack	Growth retardation, premature birth, irritableness in the newborn, withdrawal symptoms
Heroin and methadone	Growth retardation, premature birth, irritableness in the newborn, withdrawal symptoms, SIDS
LSD and marijuana	Probable cause of premature birth and growth retardation when used heavily; originally implicated in chromosomal breakage, but this effect is uncertain
ALCOHOL AND TOBACCO	
Alcohol use	Brain and heart damage, growth retardation, mental retardation, fetal alcohol syndrome
Smoking	Growth retardation, prematurity
INFECTIONS	
AIDS	Congenital malformations; leaves infant vulnerable to infections of all types
Cytomegalovirus	Deafness, blindness, abnormal head and brain growth, mental retardation
Herpes	Mental retardation, eye damage, death
Rubella	Mental retardation, eye damage, deafness, heart defects
Syphilis	Mental retardation, miscarriage, blindness, deafness, death
Toxoplasmosis	Abnormalities in brain and head growth, mental retardation
ENVIRONMENTAL HAZARDS	
Lead	Miscarriage, anemia, mental retardation
Mercury	Abnormal head and brain growth, motor incoordination, mental retardation
PCBs	Growth retardation
Radiation	Leukemia, abnormal brain and body growth, cancer, genetic alterations, miscarriage, stillbirth

5. *Teratogens differ in how they gain access to the fetus.* Radiation passes to the fetus directly through the mother's body, for example, whereas chemicals usually travel to the fetus through the blood and across the placental membrane. Physical blows are partially cushioned by the mother's body and the amniotic fluid. The mother's blood may be able to filter some potentially harmful chemicals to protect the fetus. The placenta serves as a filter, but not as a complete barrier; materials may be slowed by this filter, but will not necessarily be stopped. Some teratogens move past this filter faster than others.

6. *The likelihood and degree of abnormal development increase with the fetus's dosage of the harmful agent.* Depending on the amount of the teratogen to which the fetus is exposed, the outcome can range from no effect at all to death.

Types of Teratogens

As the examples that we have already mentioned suggest, teratogens can take several forms. They can be drugs—either prescription drugs, as was the case with thalidomide; or illegal drugs, such as heroin or cocaine; or even, as we will see, over-the-counter medications. They can be diseases contracted by the mother that cross the placental barrier and affect the fetus. Or they can be hazards from the external environment, such as radiation or mercury or lead poisoning. In what follows we discuss some of the most important instances within each category; other potential teratogens and their effects are indicated in Table 4.1.

Drugs "The desire to take medicine is, perhaps, the greatest feature which distinguishes us from animals." So said Sir William Osler, a medical historian (Finnegan & Fehr, 1980). People in our culture today consume chemicals not only as medicines to treat specific conditions but as means to induce various mental states. Many such substances—alcohol, caffeine, and nicotine—have become so much a part of daily life that we often do not think of them as drugs. A drug, however, can be defined as any substance other than food intended to affect the body. The average pregnant woman takes 4 to 10 drugs of some sort during pregnancy, and up to 80% of the drugs are not prescribed by a doctor.

We mentioned earlier that the effects of thalidomide dramatically increased awareness of the potential damage that chemicals can do to the fetus. The tragic consequences of the sedative became apparent in the early 1960s, soon after the drug appeared on the market. Depending on when a mother took the drug, her baby was born with malformations of the eyes and ears, deformation of the internal organs, or fused fingers and toes. Some babies were born with a rare defect called *phocomelia*, a condition in which the limbs are drastically shortened and the hands and feet are connected to the torso like flippers.

The teratogenic effects of thalidomide were especially surprising because doctors considered it a mild drug. The women who took it experienced no apparent side effects, and the drug produced no harmful effects in the offspring of pregnant animals on which it was tested. Clearly, we had a lot to learn about how chemicals affect the fetus, and we still do. This incomplete knowledge makes it all the more unwise for pregnant women to ingest drugs that they can avoid.

Street Drugs The increasing availability of powerful mood- and mind-altering illegal drugs since the 1960s has been a major health concern in the United States and, unfortunately, has provided substantial evidence about the dangers of drug intake by pregnant women, both to themselves and to their fetuses. Addictive drugs have attracted the most attention.

Heroin addicts, for example, are more likely to have medical complications during pregnancy and labor, and their newborn babies are likely to undergo drug-withdrawal symptoms (Sprauve, 1996). Frequently, addiction to heroin is compounded by poor nutrition and inadequate health care; almost 75% of addicts do not see a physician during pregnancy. Medical complications, including anemia, cardiac disease, hepatitis, tuberculosis, hypertension, and urinary infections, occur in 40 to 50% of heroin-dependent women who are observed during the prenatal period. These women are more likely to miscarry or to give birth prematurely. Their babies are usually lighter than normal and are more likely to have brain bleeding, low blood sugar, and jaundice. They are also more at risk for sudden infant death syndrome, or SIDS (in which the baby unexpectedly stops breathing and dies) (Hans, 1992; Rosen & Johnson, 1988).

Heroin-dependent expectant mothers may use methadone, a synthetic drug designed to help break the heroin habit. Methadone, however, is also addictive, and it too is associated with SIDS. Infants withdrawing from methadone may experience withdrawal symptoms even more severe than those associated with withdrawal from heroin (Chasnoff et al., 1984).

The story at the beginning of the chapter described the case of a pregnant woman passing cocaine to her fetus. Unfortunately, that case was not especially unusual. A conservative estimate is that at least 45,000 cocaine-exposed infants are born each year (Lester, Boukydis, & Twomey, 2000). The ready availability of cocaine, especially in the much cheaper form of crack, has increased use of the drug to epidemic proportions.

Cocaine affects the fetus indirectly through reduced maternal blood flow to the uterus, limiting the fetus's supply of nutrients and oxygen. Additionally, cocaine passes through the placenta and enters the fetus's bloodstream, where it gains direct access to the brain in as little as 3 minutes. In the brain, cocaine affects chemical nerve transmitters in addition to increasing heart rate and blood pressure.

Cocaine-exposed babies are more likely to be miscarried or stillborn. If they are born alive, they are more likely to be premature or to suffer retarded growth. They also are more likely to be difficult to arouse and irritable, and they may frequently be jittery and shaky. They may have difficulty regulating their level of alertness and with their sleep patterns and they may be hard to handle (DiPietro et al., 1995; Phillips et al., 1996).

Despite these problems, studies have turned up conflicting findings as to how babies exposed to cocaine turn out. Some studies have reported that exposed babies later are more impulsive than nonexposed babies and have greater difficulty regulating their attention. Other studies report few or no long-term effects that can be attributed to cocaine exposure alone. Cocaine research shares the same difficulties as research on many other teratogens. Mothers who use cocaine are more likely to use other drugs and to smoke and drink. They are also more likely to live in poverty and chaos, to be undernourished and in poor health, and to be depressed. Given this complex of factors, which often exist both before and after a child is born, it is difficult to pinpoint the role of

Newborn babies who have been exposed to cocaine as fetuses are more likely to be premature and irritable and to have disrupted sleep patterns.

prenatal cocaine exposure in the child's development (Lester, 2000; Mayes & Fahy, 2001; Stanwood & Levitt, 2001).

Investigators are becoming more sensitive to the effects of the postnatal environment on the cocaine-exposed child. Given an irritable baby who has difficulty falling into regular sleep patterns and a mother who is depressed, has few resources, and continues her drug habit, there is little likelihood that a healthy mother–infant interaction will develop. Many investigators believe that the quality of this relationship and the postnatal environment are the major determinants of the child's outcome (Hurt et al., 2001; Mayes, 1992).

The use of marijuana and hallucinogens accelerated rapidly in the 1960s and 1970s, and marijuana remains the most often used illicit drug. As with other drugs, the effects of marijuana are difficult to separate from other environmental and health-care practices. Research suggests that the heavy use of marijuana may cause newborns to be jittery and to habituate poorly to visual stimuli (Jones & Lopez, 1990; Levy & Koren, 1992). Research also suggests, however, that negative effects of marijuana are less likely if the users otherwise engage in good health practices (Fried, O'Connell, & Watkinson, 1992). To date, no long-term effects of prenatal marijuana exposure have been clearly established.

Therapeutic Drugs Many pregnant women take prescribed drugs as part of a continuing regimen of health care—for example, to treat diabetes or blood-clotting tendencies—or as treatments for health problems brought on by the pregnancy. Some of these drugs may increase the risk of fetal problems, creating the need to weigh the risk to the fetus from taking the drug against the risk to the mother from not taking it.

Anticoagulants, anticonvulsants (for epileptics), antibiotics, and even heavy use of aspirin have been implicated in increased likelihood of fetal growth retardation, fetal malformations, and fetal and newborn death, especially when taken during the first 3 months of pregnancy. The action of these drugs is often not straightforward. For example, aspirin, which is harmless at a particular dosage in rats, can be teratogenic if administered with benzoic acid, a widely used food preservative. However, it is important to keep in mind that the danger from these drugs is fairly low and that by far the majority of mothers taking them have healthy infants.

The effects of sex hormones are more clear. These hormones are sometimes used to treat breast cancer in women and to reduce the likelihood of miscarriage. The use of sex hormones in early pregnancy has been associated with central nervous system malformations in offspring and, more frequently, with masculinization of the external genitalia of females.

Some pregnant women took a particularly damaging synthetic hormone, diethylstilbestrol (DES), in the 1950s and early 1960s to reduce the likelihood of miscarriage. Much later, physicians discovered that a high percentage of the female children of these women developed vaginal and cervical problems when they reached adolescence, and some of these offspring developed cancer of the cervix (Giusti, Iwamoto, & Hatch, 1995). Recently, evidence has accumulated that the male offspring of mothers who took DES are more likely to develop testicular cancer and to have a lowered sperm count (Sharpe & Skakkebaek, 1993; Wilcox et al., 1995). The studies of sex hormones illustrate yet another problem in detecting teratogenic agents—the possible delay by many years of any observable effect.

Caffeine Caffeine, a substance present in coffee, tea, chocolate, and some soft drinks, is the drug most commonly consumed during pregnancy. Strangely, the possible effect of caffeine on the fetus has received relatively little attention. As is often the case, one of the difficulties in determining the effect of caffeine is separating its effects from the effects of other drugs, such as nicotine and alcohol. Some studies have associated caffeine use with miscarriage, premature birth, and lower birth weight (Eskanazi et al., 1999; Fernandes et al., 1998). The potential problems seem to become more likely as the amount of caffeine increases (Infante-Rivard et al., 1993).

Nicotine About one-fourth of the women of childbearing age in North America smoke. Although many quit at the time they become pregnant, 12% continue to smoke throughout pregnancy (Ebrahim et al., 2000).

The effects of nicotine and cigarette smoke on the fetus have been well investigated (Cornelius & Day, 2000). Smoking is known to impair the functioning of the placenta, especially oxygen exchange. The following are some risks to women who smoke while they are pregnant:

- On average, their babies are smaller.
- The likelihood of premature delivery and complications increases with the number of cigarettes they smoke per day (Cornelius et al., 1995).
- Their babies are 25 to 56% more likely to die at birth or soon thereafter (Murata et al., 1992).
- Their babies are as much as 50% more likely to develop cancer (Stjernfeldt et al., 1986).

As children, their babies are at heightened risk for social and behavioral problems (Day et al., 2000; Wasserman et al., 2001). They also are at heightened risk for relatively poor performance on measures of language and cognitive development (Cornelius et al., 2001; Fried et al., 1992).

Unfortunately, pregnant women cannot necessarily escape all of these consequences by refraining from smoking. Even passive exposure to others' smoke has been shown to affect the growth of the fetus (Dejin-Karlsson et al., 1998).

Alcohol In the United States, alcohol is the most widely used drug that is known to harm the fetus (Olson, 1994). It poses a major preventable health problem. Among the causes of birth defects in the United States, alcohol ranks third, just behind Down syndrome and spina bifida. It is the leading cause of congenital mental retardation in the Western world (Murata et al., 1992; Warren & Bast, 1988). Withdrawal effects in newborns of mothers who drink heavily can mimic those of drug addiction (Abel, 1980, 1981).

Although the effects of alcohol on the fetus were suspected in the 18th century, a clear picture of the consequences of chronic maternal alcoholism for the fetus did not emerge until 1973, when investigators described **fetal alcohol syndrome (FAS),** a unique set of features in the fetus caused by the mother's alcohol consumption (Jones et al., 1973). A photo of a child with this syndrome appears in Figure 4.6.

Limb and facial malformations, congenital heart disease, failure to thrive, anomalies of the external genitalia, growth retardation, mental retardation, and learning disabilities are associated with FAS. Behavior problems compound these difficulties, as infants with FAS are irritable, sleep less well, and are difficult to feed (Wekselman et al., 1995). By school age, these children are more likely to have difficulty sustaining effort and attention and to have language problems and motor-performance deficits (Larsson, Bohlin, & Tunell, 1985; Schonfeld et al., 2001; Streissguth & Connor, 2001). The incidence of fetal alcohol syndrome is 1 to 2 per 1,000 live births. Among samples of alcoholic women it rises to as high as 10% (Mayes & Fahy, 2001).

Some children who were exposed to alcohol during the prenatal period demonstrate some but not all of the characteristics of FAS. Such children are said to suffer from *fetal alcohol effects (FAE)*. FAEs are two to three times as common as is FAS (Streissguth & Connor, 2001).

Environmental Chemicals
The number and amount of chemicals in our environment have increased explosively since the beginning of the Industrial Revolution. Insecticides, herbicides, fungicides, solvents, detergents, food additives, and miscellaneous other chemicals have become common in our daily existence. Approximately 70,000 chemicals are presently in use (Bellinger & Adams, 2001). Only a small fraction of these chemicals have been tested as potential teratogens in pregnant laboratory animals.

Researchers often find that chemicals are potentially teratogenic in animals, but the doses that they use are typically quite large. People generally experience comparable

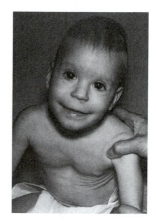

Figure 4.6

Infant born with fetal alcohol syndrome.

Fetal alcohol syndrome (FAS)
A set of features in the infant and child caused by the mother's use of alcohol during pregnancy; typically includes facial malformations and other physical and mental disabilities.

As research has furthered our knowledge of factors that can harm the fetus, agencies have become increasingly effective in alerting expectant mothers.

doses only in rare instances, such as industrial accidents or concentrated dumping (for example, in Love Canal, a former chemical dumping ground near Niagara Falls). The rates of defective births and spontaneous abortions are monitored routinely in many hospitals in the United States, providing a measure of protection against long-term chronic exposure of undiscovered teratogens. However, as we have seen, complex interactions among chemicals and delayed effects can often make detection difficult.

A clear example of the effects of environmental chemicals comes from Cubatão, a small town in an industrial valley in Brazil. Cubatão was slowly choking through pollution of its streams, air, and countryside. Thousands of tons of particulate matter were being discharged into the air from smokestacks, and huge amounts of organic matter and heavy metals were being dumped into the streams. Through an ambitious cleanup program the town reduced discharges of particulate matter by 72%, organic waste into rivers by 93%, and heavy metals by 97%. The infant mortality rate in Cubatão dropped to one-half the 1984 rate (Brooke, 1991).

Of the various chemicals present in the environment, metals have come under special scrutiny. Mercury and lead have been suspected teratogens for many years. A disaster comparable to that caused by thalidomide occurred in Japan between 1954 and 1960, when people ate fish from a bay that had been contaminated with mercury from industrial dumping. Soon after the contamination, the proportion of miscarriages and stillbirths rose to 43% (Bellinger & Adams, 2001). Many mothers who ate the fish gave birth to infants with mental retardation and neurological symptoms resembling cerebral palsy. Autopsies of those who died revealed severe brain damage (Dietrich, 1999).

Prenatal exposure to lead from automobile exhausts and lead-base paints has been implicated in miscarriages, neuromuscular problems, and mental retardation (Bellinger et al., 1986). Follow-ups of children who experienced high lead exposure as babies reveal negative effects even after 11 years on vocabulary, motor coordination, reading ability, and higher-level thinking (Needleman et al., 1990).

Another group of environmental chemicals that can harm fetuses consists of polychlorinated biphenyls (PCBs), widely used as lubricants, insulators, and ingredients in paints, varnishes, and waxes. Cooking oil used in Japan in 1968 and in Taiwan in 1979 was accidentally contaminated by PCBs, and pregnant women who used the oil were more likely to have stillborn infants and infants with darkly pigmented skin.

In the United States, PCB levels were relatively high in fish taken from Lake Michigan. Offspring of mothers who ate these fish were smaller at birth, had somewhat smaller heads, and were more likely to startle and be irritable. Babies who had detectable PCB levels in their blood at birth performed more poorly on various visual measures at both 7 months and 4 years of age (Jacobson & Jacobson, 1988; Jacobson et al., 1992). Partly for these reasons, PCBs are no longer produced in the United States.

Maternal Infectious Diseases   Several viral and bacterial infections in the mother can damage the fetus. We discuss some of the more common ones here.

Rubella   Rubella virus can damage the central nervous system of the fetus, resulting in blindness, deafness, and mental retardation. The heart, liver, and bone structure may also be damaged, depending on the timing of infection.

Herpes   Two viruses in the herpes group can produce central nervous system damage. Cytomegalovirus (CMV), the most common intrauterine viral infection, may cause abnormal brain and head growth, encephalitis, blindness, and mental retardation. An estimated 33,000 infants are born with CMV each year, but only 10% of them are seriously affected.

Because pregnant mothers are often unaware that they have been infected by CMV, doctors have made little progress in discovering the specific effects of fetal exposure at particular ages. CMV can be transmitted by sexual contact, blood transfusions, or mixing of body fluids (Behrman & Vaughan, 1987).

Another herpes virus, herpes virus type 2, infects the genitals of adults. This virus had reached epidemic levels in the United States by the early 1980s. In the infant, herpes 2 can cause encephalitis, central nervous system damage, and blood-clotting problems. Most herpes 2 infections of infants occur following direct contamination by the mother's infected birth canal (Murata et al., 1992; Whitley & Goldenberg, 1990).

HIV   Another virus that reached epidemic levels in the 1980s is the human immunodeficiency virus (HIV), which causes acquired immunodeficiency syndrome (AIDS). The virus is transmitted from one person to another exclusively through body fluids. It can be transmitted from mother to infant through breast milk following birth. It can also be transmitted from mother to fetus through the placenta prior to birth.

In addition to causing AIDS, HIV can act as a teratogen. Some infected babies are born with facial deformities—larger-than-normal eye separation, boxlike foreheads, flattened nose bridges, and misshapen eye openings. Until recently, approximately 25% of infants with HIV-infected mothers acquired the virus, and most died in early childhood. Fortunately, the development of new forms of drug treatment has substantially reduced the prenatal transmission of HIV, as well as lengthened the period before disease onset for children who are infected (Culhane et al., 1999; Hutton, 1996).

Syphilis and Gonorrhea   Syphilis and gonorrhea are sexually transmitted diseases. After declining for several years, the incidence of syphilis began to increase in the late 1980s. This disease is caused by a spirochete, a type of bacteria, which can infect the fetus and cause central nervous system damage, deformities of the teeth and skeleton, and even death. The fetus is relatively resistant to infection from the syphilis spirochete until the fourth or fifth month.

Gonorrhea is also caused by a bacterial agent. Its incidence has been reported to be as high as 30% in some populations. Premature birth, premature rupture of membranes, and spontaneous abortion are associated with gonorrhea. The fetus is affected in about 30% of cases. The most common problem is eye infection, which can lead to blindness if untreated. Fortunately, almost all newborns are treated with silver nitrate eyedrops at birth to prevent this problem (Murata et al., 1992; Whitley & Goldenberg, 1990).

To Recap . . .

Teratogens are agents that interfere with normal prenatal development, and teratology is the study of such agents. Psychoteratology focuses on the behavioral effects of teratogens. These effects may not always be obvious at birth and do not always include physical problems.

Six principles describe how teratogens act: (1) the effect depends on the genetic makeup of the organism; (2) the effect depends on timing; (3) the effect may be unique to the teratogen; (4) the effect may include serious disorders or death; (5) teratogens gain access to the fetus in different ways; and (6) the effect increases with the level of exposure.

Drugs are one category of teratogen. Street drugs, although illegal, have become increasingly available and can have highly negative effects on the fetus. Babies of drug-addicted mothers may be born addicted, and they are likely to have many developmental problems. Therapeutic drugs may also be harmful, as was the case with thalidomide.

Some substances are so common in our daily lives that we may fail to think of them as drugs. Caffeine, nicotine, and alcohol are examples. Smoking has consistently been shown to affect growth and to increase the risk of premature delivery and birth complications, and alcohol consumption can produce a range of physical malformations and intellectual consequences, including fetal alcohol syndrome.

Exposure to harmful chemicals can also occur when we take in the chemical by-products of industry through the food we eat and the air we breathe. Mercury and lead have been documented as particularly teratogenic, and PCBs also appear harmful.

Diseases contracted by a pregnant woman can also affect the fetus. Among the conditions that can be transmitted to the fetus and produce damage are rubella, herpes, and HIV, which is the cause of AIDS.

NATURAL CHALLENGES

Much current media attention focuses on potential teratogens that mothers voluntarily consume or to which mothers are exposed in the modern industrial environment. Yet mothers and fetuses have always faced natural challenges from the environment. The quality of the mother's nutrition is an important determinant of how the fetus develops. Parental age and even maternal experiences and stress may also have an effect.

Nutrition

The original fertilized egg must multiply into trillions of cells to form a fully developed fetus. During prenatal development, cells increase not only in number but also in size. As Table 4.2 illustrates, the baby and its accompanying support system will weigh 25 to 30 lb. by the ninth month of pregnancy, billions of times the weight of the fertilized egg.

Where does all of this mass come from? The answer is obvious—from the mother. Thinking about the issue this way brings home the importance of maternal nutrition. The quality of the fetus's cells can be no better than that of the nutrients the mother supplies through the placental circulation system. Oddly, this simple fact is often not fully appreciated. Earlier we said that, at least in the early stages of development, the functioning of cells depends on the environment they are in. The quality of the mother's nutrition is probably the most important environmental influence on the fetus and new-born baby (Morgane et al., 1993).

The prospective mother, then, must supply nutrients for the fetus and its support system. In part, her ability to do this depends on her nutrition during pregnancy. But it also depends to a great extent on her nutritional status *before* pregnancy. Both the mothers and their fetuses fare more poorly when the mother has had long-term malnutrition than when the mother has good prepregnancy nutrition (Rosso, 1990).

Maternal malnutrition can have devastating effects on the fetus. Autopsies of severely malnourished stillborn infants from developing countries reveal that their brains weighed up to one-third less than expected. Deficits in the size of major internal organs of between 6 and 25% have been found in the United States in infants born to urban poor families (Naeye, Diener, & Dellinger, 1969; Parekh et al., 1970). Malnutrition is associated with increased rates of spontaneous abortion, infant death, and congenital defects. Pregnant women who have inadequate diets are also more likely to have small and premature babies (Bauerfeld & Lachenmeyer, 1992). (Problems associated with low birth weight are discussed in Chapter 5.)

As is sometimes the case with teratogens, however, it can be difficult to isolate the effects of malnourishment from other factors. Malnutrition is often accompanied by inadequate housing and health care and inferior education and sanitation, as well as the daily stress of poverty. Catastrophes sometimes provide a means for separating out the influences of at least some of these factors. During World War II, for example, the

Table 4.2	**Weight Gain during Pregnancy**
Development	**Weight Gain (lb)**
Infant at birth	$7^{1/2}$
Placenta	$1^{1/2}$
Increase in blood supply to the placenta	4
Increase in mother's fluid volume	4
Increase in size of uterus and supporting muscles	2
Increase in breast size	2
Amniotic fluid	2
Mother's fat stores	7
Total	30

SOURCE: Reprinted by permission from page 507 *of Understanding Nutrition,* 9th edition, by E. N. Whitney and S. R. Rolfes. Copyright © 2002 by Wadsworth Publishing Co.

entire populations of many countries had severely limited food supplies not associated with the other factors. Food supplies in the Netherlands were especially scarce, and, in addition to a decline in conceptions, there was a substantial increase in miscarriages, stillbirths, and congenital malformations.

Food quantity is not the only issue in maternal nutrition. A pregnant woman and her fetus have special dietary needs. Proteins, vitamins, and minerals are especially important. Animal studies reveal that protein deficits produce damage to the kidneys and intestines and disrupt skeletal growth in the fetus. Low intake of certain vitamins can affect the eyes and internal organs and increase the number of malformations (Rosso, 1990).

Trace elements in the diet are also important. An absence of iron in the mother's blood can produce anemia in her baby. Diets lacking iodine are associated with an increased likelihood of cretinism, a severe thyroid deficiency that causes physical stunting and mental deficiency. Deficits of copper, manganese, and zinc produce central nervous system damage and other negative effects in rats, and zinc deficiency has been implicated in the occurrence of anencephaly (absence of the cortex of the brain). Deficits of folic acid in pregnant mothers have been associated with neural tube defects—anencephaly and nonclosure of the spinal cord (spina bifida)—in babies (Grantham-McGregor, Ani, & Fernald, 2001; Rosso, 1990).

What are the intellectual abilities of babies who are malnourished during fetal life? The outcome depends, to a large extent, on their childhood environments. Children who were malnourished as fetuses because of World War II but had adequate diet and stimulation as infants and children showed no long-term intellectual deficit. Many Korean children suffered malnutrition during the Korean War but were later adopted by families who provided them with good nutrition and education. These children later performed as well on intellectual and achievement tests as children who had not suffered early malnutrition. The general conclusion is that an enriched home environment may compensate for many of the effects of early malnutrition, but the outcome also depends on when during pregnancy the malnutrition occurred and how severe it was (Morgane et al., 1993; Vietze & Vaughan, 1988; Zeskind & Ramey, 1981).

On the other hand, babies who are malnourished both as fetuses and after birth are more likely to show delayed motor and social development. They become relatively inattentive, unresponsive, and apathetic (Bauerfeld & Lachenmeyer, 1992). Health organizations worldwide have recognized the lasting consequences of early nutritional deficits and have initiated attempts to supplement the diets of pregnant women and infants. Babies with supplemented diets are more advanced in motor development and more socially interactive and energetic, an encouraging sign that the consequences of bad nutrition may be avoided (Grantham-McGregor et al., 2001; Joos et al., 1983).

Excesses of nutrients can also be damaging. For example, recall from Chapter 3 that people with the disease phenylketonuria are unable to break down the amino acid phenylalanine. Mothers who have phenylketonuria, even though they have protected themselves through early dietary restrictions, still have excesses of phenylalanine circulating in their blood. The fetus, even if genetically normal, may suffer brain damage from intrauterine exposure to this excess product. Pregnant women can protect the fetus by maintaining a restricted diet during pregnancy (NIH, 2000).

Excesses of the sugar galactose in diabetic mothers may cause cataracts and other physical problems, even death, in fetuses; the babies at birth are more likely to have passive muscle tone and to be less attentive (Langer, 1990). Just as deficits in iodine can cause problems, excess iodine can have a detrimental effect on thyroid function. Excesses of vitamin A can cause damage to the eyes, brain, and spinal cord of the developing fetus (Ogle & Mazzullo, 2002).

Maternal Experiences and Stress

Of all the factors that might influence the fetus, none has generated more speculation than that of the mother's own experiences. The belief that the mother's mental impressions could affect the fetus is quite old. We may chuckle when we hear that a pregnant woman's child will favor classical music if the mother listens to Beethoven. Yet surveys in modern times in the United States and Europe reveal that many people still believe that birthmarks are caused by maternal frights or unsatisfied food cravings; for example, an unsatisfied craving for strawberries may produce a strawberry-colored birthmark (Ferriera, 1969).

Modern investigators have dismissed beliefs in magical influences on the fetus and have focused on psychological factors that have fairly well-documented influences on the body. For example, psychological stress increases the activity of the adrenal glands. The secretions from these glands enter the mother's blood and can be transmitted to the fetus through the placenta. Additionally, hormones released during stress can reduce the blood flow and oxygen available to the fetus. Thus, identifiable physical pathways exist by which maternal emotional states could affect the fetus.

Research reveals that there are in fact relations between maternal anxiety during pregnancy and some later child outcomes. High levels of anxiety have been associated, for example, with newborn irritability, with feeding and sleep problems during infancy, and with behavioral problems at age 4 (O'Connor et al., 2002; Van Den Bergh, 1992). They have also been associated with a heightened probability of congenital physical anomalies, such as heart defects and cleft palate (Carmichael & Shaw, 2000).

As with many of the other factors we have discussed in this chapter, there are problems in interpreting these relations because of limitations in researchers' ability to control all the potentially important variables. Often mothers' reports of anxiety were obtained after their babies were born. These reports of anxiety might have been influenced by the babies' malformation or irritability rather than the other way around—the cause-and-effect problem mentioned in Chapter 2. Further, there is often no way to separate prenatal and postnatal influences on the infant. A mother who has reported a great deal of prenatal anxiety may handle her infant differently, for example, and it may be this handling that makes her baby irritable. Finally, the genetic relation between the mother and her baby, rather than the prenatal experience, may be the operative factor. A mother who is genetically predisposed to anxiety, which might reflect abnormal hormonal activity, could pass this genetic predisposition on to her fetus.

Although factors such as these probably contribute to the predictive power of prenatal anxiety, it is unlikely that they account for all the effects. One kind of evidence in support of this conclusion is the fact that some effects of maternal stress are evident during the prenatal period and at birth—and thus before postnatal influences or characteristics of the child could be playing a role. For example, high levels of prenatal stress increase the probability of preterm birth, as well as low birth weight and problems during delivery (Lobel, Dunkel-Schetter, & Scrimshaw, 1992; Paarlberg et al., 1995). We should add, however, that the negative effects are by no means inevitable. An important determinant is the degree of social support available to the mother during pregnancy. When support is available—for example, a supportive spouse or readily available family members—then negative outcomes are a good deal less likely (Dunkel-Schetter et al., 1996; Feldman et al., 2000).

Parental Age

Traditionally, the optimal time for childbearing has been thought to fall between the ages of 20 and 34, with ages 25 to 29 as the best time within this optimal range. There has been concern, therefore, with departures in either direction from this supposed optimal period—births to mothers who are age 35 or older, and births to mothers who are still in their teens.

The typical age at which a woman gives birth to her first child has risen dramatically in the United States since the 1970s. Between 1978 and 2000 the rate of births to mothers between the ages of 35 and 39 rose by more than 100%, and the increase for mothers 40 or older was almost as great (Martin et al., 2002). In contrast, births to teenagers have declined in recent years. From 1991 to 2001 the rate of births to teenage mothers in the United States dropped by 26%, reaching an all-time low in 2001

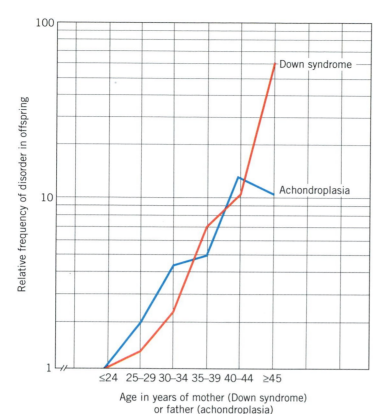

Figure 4.7

Relative frequency of Down syndrome and achondroplasia in the offspring of mothers (Down syndrome) and fathers (achondroplasia) of various ages. From "Paternal Age Effect" by J. M. Friedman. Reprinted with permission from the American College of Obstetricians and Gynecologists (*Obstetrics and Gynecology, 57,* 1981, p. 746).

(Martin, Park, & Sutton, 2002). Neverthless, almost 500,000 teenagers give birth in the United States each year.

We have already discussed one risk of motherhood at a relatively advanced age. As we saw in Chapter 3, increased maternal age is associated with an increased likelihood of giving birth to a baby with Down syndrome. The father's age also carries a risk for the fetus, because the relative frequency of mutation in the father's sperm increases with age. A genetic disorder related to the father's age is *achondroplasia,* a mutation that becomes dominant in the child who inherits it and causes bone deformities. The most obvious characteristics are dwarfism and a large head with a prominent forehead and a depressed bridge of the nose. As shown in Figure 4.7, the relative likelihood that a child will inherit achondroplasia increases with the father's age much as the relative likelihood of Down syndrome increases with the mother's age (Friedman, 1981).

Genetic disorders are not the only risk that older parents face. In some samples, older mothers have been found to be more at risk for preterm birth, difficulties during delivery, and both infant and maternal mortality (Gilbert, Nesbitt, & Danielsen, 1999). Such problems, however, are less common in births to older women today than they were 20 or 30 years ago. Women who defer birth until a later age are better educated today than were their counterparts decades ago, and they are more likely to seek early prenatal care and to be in good health. When the mother's health is good, motherhood at a relatively advanced age appears to carry only minimal risks.

In general, babies who are born to mothers in their teens are also at greater than average risk. The risks include complications during pregnancy, preterm birth, and low birth weight (Moore & Brooks-Gunn, 2002). Here, too, however, factors associated with pregnancy during a particular age period appear to be more important than maternal age per se. In particular, teenage mothers are less likely than mothers in general to receive adequate prenatal care and more likely to engage in behaviors that pose risks for both their own and their fetuses' health, such as smoking or use of illegal drugs during pregnancy. When these factors are controlled, the problems associated with teenage pregnancy are greatly reduced.

To Recap . . .

There are a number of natural challenges to the health of the embryo and the fetus. Nutritional factors are important for normal fetal growth, so poor nutrition can be harmful. The ultimate effect of fetal malnutrition depends in part on postnatal nutrition and on the level of stimulation in the environment. Maternal stress during pregnancy has been shown to have some effect on both the development of the fetus and later child outcomes. Finally, parental age can also be a risk factor. As the age of the parents increases, there is increased risk of Down syndrome and achondroplasia. On average, both older mothers and teenage mothers are more likely to have problems of pregnancy or birth than are women in the optimal childbearing age range. In both cases, however, factors associated with age (e.g., the mother's health) appear to be more important than age per se.

PREVENTING, DETECTING, AND TREATING BIRTH DEFECTS

We noted earlier that spontaneous abortion ends fetal development in most cases in which the fetus has genetic abnormalities or a problem exists in the uterine environment. Although there are thousands of genetic abnormalities and challenges to the fetus, it is important to view these risks in perspective. More than 90% of infants are born healthy and normal, and the large majority of the remaining infants have minor problems that can be corrected or will be outgrown. Still, small percentages can translate to large numbers of people, and statistics provide little comfort to those affected. In a single year, approximately 120,000 babies are born with birth defects in the United States, and 15 million Americans have some kind of handicap caused by a birth defect.

Can anything be done to prevent birth defects? How can a mother be sure the baby she is carrying is healthy? And how can birth defects be treated?

Prevention

At present, not all birth defects can be prevented. The causes of some are not controllable; the causes of others are not even known. Certain steps, however, can significantly lower the risk from teratogens. For example, a woman planning to become pregnant can avoid drinking alcohol, smoking, and taking unnecessary drugs, and she can eat prudently. Prenatal care is very important both for assessing risk and for monitoring the woman's progress and the fetus's development. Some experts advise women to see a physician even before they conceive (Murata et al., 1992).

Rapid progress in the area of genetics has made it possible for people to exert some control over the incidence of genetic problems. **Genetic counseling** involves a range of activities focused on determining the likelihood that a couple will conceive a child with a genetic disorder. Couples who are contemplating pregnancy often want to know the chances that their baby will be normal. DNA analysis of their blood may determine whether they are carriers of a defective gene, as in the case of Tay-Sachs disease or cystic fibrosis. This information can then guide decisions about whether to attempt to conceive. In some instances the results may be dramatic. Widespread screening of potential carriers of Tay-Sachs resulted in a 65 to 75% reduction in the incidence of the disease within 10 years (Kaback, 1982).

The probability that parents who are carriers of a defective gene will have a baby with problems depends on the type of gene involved. If one parent is a carrier of a defective dominant gene that is autosomal, the chances are one in two that their baby will inherit the disorder. If both parents are carriers of the same defective recessive gene, the chances are one in four that their baby will be affected. Defective genes on the sex chromosome affect the chances differently, depending on whether the fetus is a male or female and whether the mother or father is the carrier.

Genetic counseling
The practice of advising prospective parents about genetic diseases and the likelihood that they might pass on defective genetic traits to their offspring.

Genetic testing of parents typically occurs prior to pregnancy. When couples are at risk and the woman has become pregnant, parents often consider procedures for testing the fetus.

Screening for Abnormalities

Significant progress has been made in detecting problems in newborn infants, which opens up the possibility for early treatment. Phenylketonuria (PKU) again serves as an example. Although scientists understood at the beginning of the 1960s what caused PKU and how to treat it through diet, they had no method for determining which newborn infants had PKU. By the time they discovered the defect in a child, irreversible damage had occurred. Then, in 1961, a blood test was developed to detect excess phenylalanine in the blood. Infants with PKU were put on a special diet until they were around 7 years of age to prevent the severe retardation, seizures, and skin lesions characteristic of untreated PKU. By the late 1960s, approximately 90% of all babies in the United States were being screened at birth. Today, PKU is no longer a major health problem.

Even more dramatic advances permit parents to learn about the status of the fetus as early as 9 to 11 weeks into a pregnancy and, as we shall see, sometimes in the first days following conception.

Ultrasound Imaging

Ultrasound imaging uses soundlike waves to provide a continuous picture of the fetus and its environment. The level of detail in this image permits an assessment of fetal age, as well as identification of the sex of the fetus by 16 to 20 weeks. The ultrasound image can also determine whether there is more than one fetus. Although many potential problems are not detectable with ultrasound, the procedure can reveal some disorders, including abnormal head growth; defects of the heart, bladder, and kidneys; some chromosomal anomalies; and neural tube defects (Anderson & Allison, 1990; Stoll et al., 1993). Ultrasound imaging is also helpful for diagnostic procedures that require collection of amniotic fluid or tissue, such as the methods we consider next: amniocentesis and chorionic villus sampling.

Ultrasound imaging
A noninvasive procedure for detecting physical defects in the fetus. A device that produces soundlike waves of energy is moved over the pregnant woman's abdomen, and reflections of these waves form an image of the fetus.

Amniocentesis

An especially important tool for assessment is **amniocentesis**, because it provides samples of both the amniotic fluid and the fetal cells in it. A needle is passed through the mother's abdomen and into the amniotic cavity to collect the fluid. Analysis of the fluid can reveal abnormalities. For example, alpha-feto protein (FEP), a substance the fetus produces, circulates in the amniotic fluid. Abnormally high levels of FEP occur when the fetus has certain types of damage to the brain, the central nervous system, or the liver and kidneys. Chromosomal analysis of the fetal cells can also detect problems.

Women over the age of 35 frequently opt to have amniocentesis because of their heightened risk of having babies with Down syndrome, a defect that shows up in a chromosomal cell analysis. Fetal cells can also be tested for genetic defects, such as sickle-cell anemia, cystic fibrosis, and Duchenne muscular dystrophy (Winston & Handyside, 1993). With the success of the Human Genome Project, the list of detectable diseases has grown dramatically in recent years.

The amniocentesis procedure does have its drawbacks. It produces a slight increase in the risks of infection and miscarriage (Cunningham, MacDonald, & Gant, 1989; Tongsong et al., 1998). Also, amniocentesis is most effective after the period during which abortion is safest for the mother. Chorionic villus sampling, a relatively new procedure, can make information about the fetus available much earlier.

Amniocentesis
A procedure for collecting cells that lie in the amniotic fluid surrounding the fetus. A needle is passed through the mother's abdominal wall into the amniotic sac to gather discarded fetal cells. These cells can be examined for chromosomal and genetic defects.

Chorionic Villus Sampling

In a procedure called **chorionic villus sampling (CVS)**, cells are collected from the chorion, a part of the placenta. A small tube is inserted through the cervix and into the fetal placenta to collect a sample of fetal cells.

Chorionic villus sampling (CVS)
A procedure for gathering fetal cells earlier in pregnancy than is possible through amniocentesis. A tube is passed through the vagina and cervix so that fetal cells can be gathered at the site of the developing placenta.

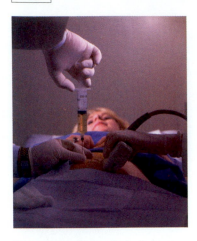

With modern diagnostic techniques, many potential problems can be detected prenatally. With amniocentesis, a needle is passed through the mother's abdomen to collect amniotic fluid and fetal cells.

These cells reveal large-scale defects of the chromosomes or more minute defects in the DNA. CVS is possible as early as 9 to 11 weeks but carries a slightly higher risk of miscarriage than amniocentesis, around 2% (Kuller, 1996).

Test-Tube Screening   Scientists have succeeded in screening embryos in the test tube before they are implanted in the mother's uterus. Egg cells are collected from the mother and then fertilized in a petri dish through in vitro fertilization. One cell is removed from each embryo when it reaches the eight-cell stage. From this one cell, the sex of the embryo can be determined, and, within a few hours, the DNA of the cell can be checked for suspected anomalies.

Chloe O'Brien, born in the United Kingdom in April 1992, was the first baby to be born after in vitro fertilization following DNA analysis before implantation. The parents were carriers of the cystic fibrosis gene. If they had conceived in the normal fashion and had discovered that their fetus had cystic fibrosis by the other techniques described, they would have faced a decision on abortion. By this technique, they were assured that the embryo that was implanted was free of this disease.

It is possible to detect several hundred disorders through various screening techniques. However, only a small minority of women who have at-risk pregnancies participate in prenatal screening. The risk of problem pregnancy is higher for a woman who (1) has a history of miscarriages or has had children with congenital disorders, (2) is outside the optimal childbearing age range, (3) has relatives (or is carrying a child whose biological father has relatives) with genetic abnormalities, (4) is poor and has inadequate medical supervision and nutrition, or (5) takes drugs during pregnancy.

Treatment

The growing sophistication of diagnostic procedures has made early detection of developmental abnormalities more likely. But what happens when a fetus is found to be developing abnormally? The parents may decide to terminate the pregnancy, but there may be treatment alternatives. Developments in the medical treatment of fetuses parallel the rapid advances in early diagnosis. Current approaches to prenatal treatment fall into three categories: medical therapy, surgery, and genetic manipulation.

Medical Therapy   Medical therapy is currently the most widely available of the three methods. An example is providing extra vitamins to the mother when enzyme deficiencies are discovered in the blood of the fetus. We discussed another example earlier in the chapter: Drug treatment of pregnant women with HIV has markedly reduced the incidence of babies who are born infected with the virus.

It is also possible to provide therapy directly to the fetus. One of the first such cases was reported in mid-1989. Parents in Lyons, France, whose first child had died in infancy of a hereditary disorder, learned that the fetus the mother was carrying had the same disorder, involving an immune deficiency that leaves the infant open to almost any infection. Doctors decided to try to treat the fetus in the womb. They injected immune cells from the thymus and liver of two aborted fetuses into the umbilical cord, the first time this had been done. After the baby was born, the injected cells multiplied, as the doctors had hoped (Elmer-DeWitt, 1994).

Surgery   The use of fetal surgery is illustrated by the experience of a pregnant woman who had earlier given birth to an infant with hydrocephaly, an abnormal accumulation of fluid inside the skull that results in brain damage. An ultrasound diagnosis indicated that the fetus was accumulating fluid on the brain and would likely suffer brain damage if treatment was delayed until birth. Surgeons at the University of Colorado Medical School, working through a long, hollow tube inserted through the mother's abdomen and the amniotic sac, inserted a small valve in the back of the fetus's head to permit the excess fluid to drain, thereby relieving pressure on the brain. The fetus survived the surgery and, at 16 months of age, appeared to be normal (Clewell et al., 1982).

Physicians are now able to carry out surgery on fetuses to address a variety of problems that are either life-threatening or that will result in severe damage if not corrected early in development. Among the conditions for which fetal surgery is an option are blockage of the urinary tract, congenital diaphragmatic hernia (a condition in which the diaphragm does not fully form, allowing organs to enter the chest cavity and affect lung growth), and spina bifida and other neural tube defects.

Genetic Engineering   Probably the greatest promise for prenatal treatment lies in the field of genetic engineering. Suppose we could detect, say, the lack of an enzyme in a fetus's blood and could identify the specific gene that caused the defect. Working in the laboratory with a blood sample from the fetus, we would clip out the defective gene and insert a synthetic gene. After producing many copies of the blood cells containing the repaired chromosome, we would inject them into the fetus, where they would survive and replicate and provide sufficient amounts of the enzyme for normal development.

In September 1990, scientists undertook the first federally approved attempt at human gene therapy of this kind. It involved a 4-year-old girl named Ashanti who suffered from ADA deficiency, a severe and incurable disease of the immune system. Cells were extracted from the girl, and harmless viruses were used to carry the needed ADA gene into the cells. The cells—a billion or so—were then reinjected into the child's bloodstream. The cells are producing the needed ADA, and Ashanti has now survived to adolescence. She does, however, need repeated treatments.

To date, applications of gene therapy have been limited—only about 600 clinical trials have been reported across the last dozen years (*Journal of Gene Medicine,* 2002). Applications of fetal gene therapy have been even more limited; rather, in most instances, as with Ashanti, the therapy has occurred in childhood or even adulthood. Finally, applications to date have been limited to the somatic or body cells and have not encompassed the germ cells (recall our discussion of these two types of cells in Chapter 3). In *germ-line therapy,* characteristics of the germ or sex cells are altered, which means that any changes affect not only the treated individual but also the genes that the individual passes on to his or her offspring. At present, germ-line therapy remains a prospect for the future.

Ashanti was the first recipient of human gene therapy. At age 15 she is still doing well.

Ethical Considerations

The ability to diagnose abnormal development raises innumerable ethical questions—questions that people may find difficult to answer. Today's fetal-screening techniques can detect the presence of sickle-cell anemia, Huntington's disease, Down syndrome, cystic fibrosis, and numerous other maladies. What are the consequences of this knowledge? If no treatment is possible, the options are to terminate the pregnancy or to bring a child with a serious disorder into the world. Should damaged fetuses be aborted? If so, how disabling must the genetic defect be? If a child is diagnosed as genetically damaged as a fetus, should insurance companies be able to deny the child insurance, given that the companies know that health expenses will be exorbitant compared with those of other children?

The treatment of disorders while babies are still in the womb also raises difficult ethical questions. Procedures such as fetal surgery and gene repair are expensive, and not all families have the resources to benefit from them. In addition, most such procedures are still in the experimental phase, and they carry risks for both the baby and the mother. Surgery for urinary tract defects, for example, results in fetal death in 5 to 10% of the cases (Yankowitz, 1996).

Still further issues arise when babies are born with severe disorders, as in the case of Baby Jane Doe. Baby Jane Doe was born with hydrocephalus, spina bifida, and microcephaly. Her parents had two options. They could approve two operations, after which it was likely that she would live past age 20 but be paralyzed, severely retarded, and in pain; or they could refuse to permit surgery, in which case she would likely die before the age of 3. They chose not to allow surgery. But others felt it was not the parents' choice to make alone. Most significantly, the U.S. Justice Department, for the first time, sued on behalf of the medical rights of an infant with a disability. Ultimately, the U.S. Supreme Court ruled against the government and with the parents' right to choose (Holden, 1986).

Decisions regarding the health and life of a fetus or infant are intensely emotional and deeply embedded in social, ethical, and moral convictions. They are also very personal. As new technologies are developed, the fine line that separates these personal beliefs and feelings on the one side, and the government's role in protecting the rights of fetuses and infants on the other, may become increasingly blurred.

To Recap . . .

We have progressed dramatically in our understanding of prenatal diseases and in the ability to diagnose and treat them. In some cases, the most useful approach is prevention, perhaps through genetic counseling.

During pregnancy, diagnostic procedures provide a window on prenatal development that was unknown only a few decades ago. Ultrasound imaging can detect growth anomalies, such as abnormal head growth. Amniocentesis and chorionic villus sampling provide fetal cells that can be analyzed for chromosomal defects and several genetic problems, as well as some other disorders. Screening has even been carried out on embryos in test tubes. When problems are detected, treatment can sometimes proceed even while the fetus is still in the uterus. Medical therapy is one possibility, as when there are chemical imbalances. Surgery is a second possibility. Increasingly, genetic engineering is becoming a third possibility.

As we become more skilled at understanding genetics, screening for and diagnosing problems, and developing treatment alternatives, however, individuals and society at large face a new array of ethical dilemmas.

CONCLUSION

We live in a time when knowledge and technology in many fields are expanding at a dizzying pace. Nowhere are the effects of progress more dramatic than in biology and health-related fields. The field of prenatal development has benefited enormously from these advances.

Only relatively recently have we developed an understanding of the processes of conception and embryological development. It has been especially important for us to learn that differentiation of body parts and limbs occurs in the first 8 weeks or so after conception. With this knowledge, we have been better able to understand why infections and certain drugs have more devastating effects on the organism during the early prenatal period than later.

Our awareness that the placenta does not always filter out chemicals and toxins from the mother's blood and that these substances thus enter the bloodstream of the fetus has had profound effects. Scientists actively look for causes of abnormal development that were previously ignored. Environmental pollutants, drugs, and other chemicals are suspect, and it is now routine to test new chemicals for toxic effects on the fetus. The new field of psychoteratology may provide even more sensitive indicators of harmful substances. Although we may not always know how or why these substances affect the fetus, at least we are learning when they do. Partly because of this knowledge, the ratio of stillbirths to live births in the United States has reached an all-time low.

An important message from this information is that the baby is in an environment from the moment of conception. By the time of birth, interactions between genes and the environment have been at play during the full 9 months of development.

One might come away from this chapter fearful about all the things that threaten a baby's prenatal development. Keep in mind, though, that the very large majority of babies are born healthy and whole. Fortunately, as we have learned about the dangers that the fetus faces, we have been increasingly able to take precautions that will increase the likelihood that the newborn will get a healthy start.

FOR THOUGHT AND DISCUSSION

1. The embryo stage is the most vulnerable time for the developing baby. But because this period occurs between 3 and 8 weeks after conception, many women do not realize that they are pregnant until after this point. *What ramifications might knowledge of this vulnerability have for college students and other young people who are sexually active? How would you suggest a young woman behave if she suspected she was pregnant?*

2. As we saw, many physical and behavioral problems of development result from inadequate prenatal care, such as failure to maintain an appropriate diet or exposure to teratogens of various kinds. *How might this knowledge affect one's beliefs regarding problems of development in impoverished areas or among disadvantaged people? What sorts of alternative explanations for these problems would it challenge?*

3. It is now clearly documented that exposing the developing fetus to large quantities of alcohol or drugs can cause serious developmental problems. *Under the circumstances, should pregnant mothers who knowingly ingest these teratogens be prosecuted for child abuse? Could this policy have any important drawbacks?*

4. Prenatal testing permits us to learn many things about the fetus before birth, including the baby's sex. *What are some potential advantages of learning whether the baby is male or female many months before birth? What are some possible problems with knowing? Would you want to know?*

5. We mentioned two diseases for which population screening has been undertaken or is being contemplated. Such screening is very expensive. *If you had to make the decision to approve such a project, what factors would you consider? What might be some potential dangers in implementing a policy to genetically screen people in a population?*

VISUAL SUMMARY FOR CHAPTER 4
Prenatal Development

Stages of Prenatal Development

Period	Duration	Major Events of the Period
Zygote	Conception to 2nd week	At conception a zygote is formed, combining the 23 chromosomes from the father with the 23 chromosomes from the mother. The zygote becomes fully implanted in the uterus by the end of the second week.
Embryo	3rd to 8th week	All major internal and external structures, as well as support structures needed for protection and growth, form during this period.
Fetus	9th to 38th week	Development of the organ structures formed in the embryonic period continues, and the fetus increases in size and weight. The age of viability is considered to be 23 to 24 weeks of age.

Teratology
Six Principles of How Teratogens Act

1. A teratogen's effect depends on the genetic makeup of the organism.

2. A teratogen's effect depends partly on timing.

3. The effect may be unique to the teratogen.

4. The effect may include death or serious disorders.

5. Teratogens gain access to the fetus in different ways.

6. The effect of a teratogen increases with the level of exposure to it.

Teratogen	Consequence
Street Drugs	Babies of drug-addicted mothers may be born addicted and are likely to have many developmental problems.
Therapeutic Drugs	Therapeutic drugs may also be harmful to the fetus, as was the case with thalidomide.
Caffeine	Some studies suggest risk associated with caffeine.
Nicotine	Can affect growth and can increase the risk of premature delivery and birth complications.

Alcohol	Can produce physical malformations and intellectual deficits, including fetal alcohol syndrome.
Environmental Chemicals	Mercury, lead, and PCBs appear to be harmful to the fetus.
Maternal Infectious Diseases	Diseases of the mother such as rubella, herpes, HIV, syphilis, and gonorrhea have the potential to harm a developing embryo or fetus.

Natural Challenges

Challenge	Effect
Nutrition	Maternal malnutrition may be associated with deficits in size of the brain and major internal organs in the fetus, small and premature babies, and increased rates of spontaneous abortion, infant death, and congenital defects.
Maternal Experiences and Stress	Maternal stress may be associated with abnormalities in the newborn, although more research is needed in this area.
Parental Age	Both the mother's and father's age are associated with increased risk for certain chromosomal or genetic abnormalities. Teenage mothers are also at higher risk for having premature or underweight babies, although the reasons may primarily involve socioeconomic factors.

Preventing, Detecting, and Treating Birth Defects

Prevention	Although not all birth defects can be prevented, women can lower the risk by avoiding risky behaviors. Genetic counseling can help couples determine if they are likely to conceive a child with a genetic disorder.

Methods of Screening for Abnormalities in the Fetus

Method	Description
Ultrasound Imaging	Uses soundlike waves to provide a continuous picture of the fetus and its environment. Can detect certain growth abnormalities.
Amniocentesis	Examines a sample of the amniotic fluid and the fetal cells contained in it. Can identify chromosomal defects and several genetic problems.
Chorionic Villus Sampling	Examines fetal cells collected from a sample of the chorion, a part of the placenta. Can identify chromosomal defects and several genetic problems.
Test-Tube Screening	Embryos that are the result of in vitro fertilization can be screened for DNA abnormalities before being implanted into the mother's uterus.

Treatment of Abnormalities in the Fetus

	Treatment of abnormalities in the fetus can involve in utero medical therapy or surgery. Genetic engineering holds promise as a treatment in the future.

5

Physical Development: Birth, Motor Skills, and Growth

ike most 8-year-old boys, Justin Lamar Washington loves to ride his bike, swim, and play with his friends. Justin has also just completed a second year as the March of Dimes National Ambassador. He was the first child to serve as ambassador for 2 years in a row.

By all indications, Justin is now a normal and healthy child. As his selection by the March of Dimes suggests, however, his childhood has by no means been typical or easy. Indeed, Justin has overcome obstacles that few children have ever had to face.

Because she had a history of miscarriages, Justin's mother took special precautions when she became pregnant with Justin, restricting her physical activity and seeing her doctor for weekly check-ups. Despite these precautions, she went into labor in her 5th month of pregnancy, and doctors were able to postpone the birth for only a brief period. Justin was born 4 months before the normal time period for birth. He weighed 1 pound, 8 ounces.

Until recently, babies as young and as tiny as Justin would not have survived. Justin's survival did not come easily. He spent the first 4 months of his life in the hospital, breathing with the aid of a ventilator for much of the time because his under-developed lungs could not function on their own. For 48 days he received intravenous feeding. He underwent intestinal, hernia, and laser eye surgery. He was treated for anemia of prematurity and temporary liver malfunction. When he finally went home at 4 months, much of the medical equipment went with him. It was only very slowly that Justin grew strong enough to be weaned away from the supports and to assume a normal developmental path.

Clearly, Justin's case is a triumph of modern medical science. It is also a testimony to the strengths that even the tiniest babies—and their families—can summon in the face of adversity.

We begin this chapter by examining the birth process, considering both the challenges that all newborns face and the special challenges that sometimes arise—and how medical science has learned to deal with the challenges. ■

This chapter focuses on the child's physical development, beginning at birth and continuing through adolescence. Physical development involves more than just growth, although that is certainly an important part of it. We will also see how a baby acquires the motor skills to manipulate objects and to explore the environment, skills that have enormous psychological impact on development. Psychological and physical growth depend crucially on the maturation of the brain, so we devote part of our discussion to how the brain develops and operates. Finally, we examine the physical changes during adolescence that prepare the body for reproduction but that also can affect the individual's self-image and identity.

BIRTH AND THE PERINATAL PERIOD

Perinatal period
The events and environment surrounding the birth process.

Our story starts with birth and its surrounding events—the **perinatal period.** Birth is truly a momentous event, as the child moves from a relatively sheltered and protected environment to the busy and much less predictable outside world, where the remainder of development will occur.

Typically, the birth process proceeds smoothly. In this technological age, we sometimes forget that humans have accomplished this feat over millions of years without hospitals, doctors, or elaborate equipment. Occasionally, however, modern technology is crucial for making the process work and even for saving the baby's life. After briefly describing the physical aspects of birth, we consider problems that can arise and the notion of infants at risk.

Labor and Delivery

Typically around 38 weeks after fertilization, a pregnant woman will go into labor, the first step in the birth process. Labor appears to be initiated by changes in the fetal brain

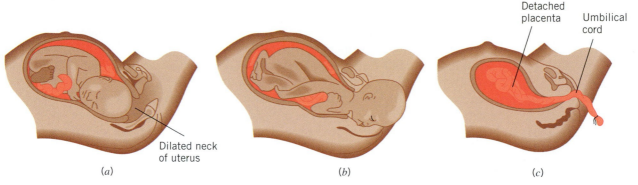

Detached placenta   Umbilical cord

Dilated neck of uterus

(a)   (b)   (c)

Figure 5.1

The three stages of labor: (a) the neck of the uterus dilates; (b) the baby is delivered; and (c) the placenta is expelled.

(Nathanielsz, 1995). Chemicals are released that signal the muscles of the mother's uterus to start contracting rhythmically, initially every 15 to 20 minutes and then at shorter intervals. The complete birth process requires, on average, about 8 to 16 hours for the first baby and about half as much time for later babies.

Labor consists of three stages, shown in Figure 5.1. The first and longest stage begins when the early contractions start to narrow the uterus and dilate (widen) the cervical opening through which the baby will pass. This stage ends when the cervix is fully dilated, usually about 10 cm. By the end of this stage, the contractions are very intense, occurring every 2–3 minutes. The second stage begins when the fetus starts to pass through the cervix and ends when the baby has been completely delivered into the world. During this stage, the contractions are long and closely spaced, and the mother is encouraged to assist the process by pushing with each contraction. The third stage, which often lasts only minutes, involves the delivery of the placenta and related other membranes, referred to as the *afterbirth*.

Technological advances permit the monitoring of the fetus's state during birth. Physicians can visualize the fetus, the umbilical cord, and the placenta by ultrasound to determine, for example, whether there is a danger that the umbilical cord will wrap around the fetus's neck (which can cause strangulation). They also can record electronically the heart rate and activity of the fetus through the mother's abdomen to determine whether there are signs of **fetal distress,** which would be indicated by an abnormally high or low heart rate (Anderson & Allison, 1990).

Sometimes birth cannot proceed according to nature's plan because, for example, the baby is lying in an unusual position in the uterus (such as sideways or buttocks down), delivery is proceeding too slowly, or the baby's head is too large to pass through the cervical opening. In such cases, the doctor often elects to perform a **cesarean section,** in which the baby is surgically removed directly from the uterus. The rate of cesarean deliveries has fluctuated markedly across the last several decades. In the United States the percentage of cesarean births skyrocketed from 5% in 1969 to an all-time high of 25% in 1988. Some critics were alarmed by this increase, charging that many of these procedures were performed for unjustifiable reasons, such as greater convenience for doctors or reduced risk of malpractice suits (Guillemin, 1993; Van Tuinen & Wolfe, 1993). Perhaps because of such criticisms, the rate of cesarean births declined across the first half of the 1990s, only to begin to move upward again in 1997. By 2000 the rate was again close to 25% (Menacker & Curtin, 2001).

Why might there be concern about a heightened rate of cesarean deliveries? Such deliveries pose greater risks of infection for the mother than do vaginal births, and they also expose the newborn to higher levels of pain-relieving medication (Trevathen, 1987). At present, however, there is no clear evidence that cesarean birth has any long-term negative effects on children's development.

Fetal distress
A condition of abnormal stress in the fetus, reflected during the birth process in an abnormal fetal heart rate.

Cesarean section
Surgical delivery of the fetus directly from the uterus; performed when normal delivery is prohibited.

Cultural Attitudes toward Birth

Although the stages of birth are the same in all cultures, there are many variations in how cultures think about and deal with birth.

It has been said that in most Western countries, pregnancy, labor, and delivery have typically been treated as if they were the symptoms of an illness. Pregnant women have been encouraged to visit the doctor regularly. Most have given birth in a hospital, lying down (some say for the convenience of the doctor) and having been given drugs to block pain. Often after the baby's birth, doctors and nurses, not the baby's mother, have taken over the baby's care, at least for a while.

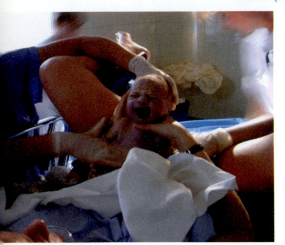

In Western societies, birth typically takes place in a hospital with the mother lying on her back.

Has Western civilization been unique in looking at pregnancy as a sort of disability and birth as a process requiring medical intervention? Not entirely. Among the Cuna Indians of Panama, for example, a pregnant woman must visit the medicine man daily for herbal medicines, and women are given medication throughout labor. Various interventions during labor are practiced in many cultures: The pregnant woman's abdomen may be massaged, perhaps with masticated roots or melted butter, or even constricted to help push out the baby. For difficult cases, midwives of Myanmar (formerly Burma) tread on the woman's abdomen with their feet.

Nevertheless, the attitude of the West is often contrasted with that of cultures in which birth is seen as an everyday occurrence. Among the Jarara of South America, for example, labor and birth are so much a part of daily life that a woman may give birth in a passageway or shelter in view of everyone. In many cultures, women give birth alone. And non-Western women often deliver in an upright position—kneeling, sitting, squatting, and even standing—rather than lying down.

Practices have changed fairly rapidly in the United States. For instance, as recently as 1972, only 27% of U.S. hospitals permitted fathers or other family members in the delivery room. By 1980, 80% of U.S. hospitals had an open policy; today very few do not. More generally, there has been a trend in the West toward making birth more "natural." An English obstetrician, Grantly Dick-Read, wrote a book called *Natural Childbirth* in 1933 and a second, called *Childbirth without Fear*, in 1944 to put forth the view that Western societies had created an association between childbirth and pain. Fear of pain, he said, actually created tension and muscle cramping that produced pain unnecessarily. These ideas were reinforced by Dr. F. Lamaze in *Painless Childbirth* (1970). Lamaze's popular method of preparation for childbirth is based on conditioning through breathing and muscle exercises and on educating the mother about pregnancy and labor.

Other, related obstetric practices have emerged in recent years. One involves having the father present during the birth process, sometimes serving as the mother's breathing coach. Another is a return to giving birth at home, often with the assistance of a trained midwife rather than a doctor. Although the number of home births in the United States has increased in recent years, the percentage remains low, about 1% (Curtin & Park, 1999). In many European countries, however, birth at home has long been a popular alternative to the hospital setting.

Is the naturalist trend right? Although more research is needed, to date no negative effects have been shown for practices that depart from the medicated, hospital-birth model that has been the norm in the United States. Maybe the truly remarkable fact is that mothers and newborns usually survive the birth process just fine, whatever the rituals with which their cultures surround them.

Culture also affects the likelihood that the mother will survive pregnancy and childbirth. In the United States, because of improved health care, maternal deaths per 100,000 pregnant women fell from approximately 660 in 1931 to approximately 7 today. In some African countries, however, the death rate is still as high as 1,300 per 100,000

Table 5.1	U.S. Infant Mortality Rates 1915–2000 (deaths in the first year per 1,000 live births)		
Year	African Americans	Whites	All Races
1915	150.4	92.8	95.7
1925	105.3	65.0	69.0
1935	80.1	49.2	53.2
1945	56.2	35.6	38.3
1955	43.1	23.6	26.4
1965	41.7	21.5	24.7
1975	26.2	14.2	16.1
1985	18.2	9.3	10.6
1995	15.1	6.3	7.6
2000	14.1	5.7	6.9

SOURCE: Based on information from U.S. Department of Health and Human Services, National Center for Health Statistics, Vital Statistics of the United States, 1995 and 2002.

pregnancies. Around the world even today, more than 500,000 women each year lose their lives from complications of pregnancy and labor (UNICEF, 2002).

Babies face hazards during the birth process as well, and some do not survive. Scientists and physicians have devoted enormous efforts to addressing these problems and are making good progress. As shown in Table 5.1, infant mortality rates in the United States have dropped substantially in recent years, although less so for African Americans than for Whites. Still, in 2000, 20 countries had newborn mortality rates lower than that of the United States (March of Dimes, 2001).

The Concept of Risk

Parents worry about whether their baby will be normal. In more than 9 of 10 cases, the baby is born on time and healthy. But some parents and their babies are not so fortunate. Approximately 3% of all babies born in the United States each year—120,000 or so infants—are born with major physical malformations.

Whereas some babies have immediately obvious physical problems, other babies are considered **at risk** for developmental delays and cognitive and social problems. Psychologists believe that the earlier they can identify these babies, the earlier they can intervene to help. Thus, over the past few decades, hundreds of studies have attempted to discover what factors put infants in the highest category of risk. Three indicators seem to be most important: maternal and family characteristics, the physical compromise of the newborn, and the performance of the newborn on behavioral assessments.

At risk
Describes babies who have a higher likelihood than other babies of experiencing developmental problems.

Maternal and Family Characteristics   A baby's chances of developing problems can be predicted in part from the family context in which the child is born. Around 85% of the risk of severe developmental problems can be attributed to what happens in the prenatal period. As mentioned in the preceding chapter, several maternal factors increase risk for the fetus, including the mother's use of drugs or alcohol, exposure to viral infections during pregnancy, smoking, and poor nutrition. A further contributor is the failure of the mother to seek prenatal care from a physician. In the United States, the proportion of women who receive timely prenatal care has increased by 10% over the past decade. Still, one woman in six receives no care at all during the first trimester of pregnancy, and approximately 4% receive no prenatal care at all (Martin et al., 2002).

Failure to see a doctor is in part attributable to lack of financial resources available to the mother. Living in conditions of poverty increases the probability of almost every early threat to the well-being of mother and child. Both preterm birth and low birth weight are almost twice as likely for low-income families as for the general population, and inadequate prenatal care is close to three times more common (Children's Defense Fund, 2002). Over time, babies born to families who have strained financial resources, poor social support, and little education are at greater risk for a number of negative outcomes than are those born to more advantaged families (Bradley & Corwyn, 2002).

Physical Compromise of the Newborn   A second general indicator of risk is evidence of physical problems in the newborn, most frequently, low birth weight. Around 6 to 7% of the babies born in the United States each year (around 250,000) have a low birth weight, below 2,500 g (about 5.5 lb). Low-birth-weight babies are about 40 times more likely to die in the first month of life than are babies with normal birth weight (Paneth, 1995). They also are at greater risk for many problems, large and small (Hack, Klein, & Taylor, 1995). Why is this so?

The newborn must make a number of adaptations to the outside world. Temperature control and nutrition are no longer provided by the mother's body, but these needs are rather easily met by the parents or other providers. Breathing, however, is a different story. After living in a water world for almost 9 months, the baby must draw the first breath of air within seconds after birth. Babies with low birth weight are more likely to have difficulty initiating or maintaining breathing. Failure to breathe prevents the delivery of oxygen to cells—a condition called **anoxia**—which can cause the cells to die. The brain cells are especially sensitive to oxygen deficits. Severe anoxia, for example, may damage the brain area that controls movement of the limbs, resulting in a spastic-type movement referred to as cerebral palsy (Behrman, Kliegman, & Jenson, 2000).

Low-birth-weight babies may be placed in two groups. One comprises babies whose birth weights are low because they were born **preterm,** meaning before the end of the normal 38 weeks of pregnancy. Preterm babies often have the breathing problems just described. In many, tiny blood vessels in the brain burst, causing bleeding and contributing to the infant's risk.

Even disregarding these physical challenges, development in a preterm baby may lag behind that in a full-term baby, at least for a time. Although we would expect the preterm infant, who is comparable to a fetus still in the womb, to be less advanced than the full-term baby, even when matched for the number of days following fertilization, the preterm infant usually has less mature brain patterns and is more disorganized and difficult to soothe (Als, Duffy, & McAnulty, 1988; Duffy, Als, & McAnulty, 1990). Longer term, these babies can be expected to have more frequent problems with growth and overall health issues (Saigal et al., 2000). They also are at greater risk for cognitive and behavioral problems in later childhood (Taylor et al., 2000).

The other group of babies born with a low birth weight are those whose fetal growth was retarded. These babies are considered **small for gestational age (SGA).** They may be born at the expected gestational age of 9 months, or they may be born earlier (and so be both SGA and preterm), but they are in this category because their weight places them among the bottom 10% of babies born at that particular gestational age. Although the cause is frequently unknown, several factors appear to increase the likelihood that a baby's prenatal growth will be delayed, including chromosomal abnormalities, infections, poor maternal nutrition, and maternal substance abuse.

SGA babies also face developmental risks (Goldenberg, 1995). For example, these infants do not arouse easily, and they tend to have poor muscle tone, appearing limp when held. They also are disadvantaged beyond the newborn period; for example, they

Anoxia
A deficit of oxygen to the cells, which can produce brain or other tissue damage.

Preterm
Describes babies born before the end of the normal gestation period.

Small for gestational age (SGA)
Describes babies born at a weight in the bottom 10% of babies of a particular gestational age.

show poorer recognition memory than do babies born at normal weight (Gotlieb, Baisini, & Bray, 1988). SGA babies who are preterm perform more poorly on verbal tests of IQ as preschoolers than do preterm babies whose weights were appropriate for their ages, although their eventual developmental course depends heavily on the quality of their postbirth environment (Dowling & Bendell, 1988; Gorman & Pollitt, 1992).

Steady improvement in technology has produced a dramatic decline in deaths resulting from low birth weight. Although a birth weight below 2,500 g (5.5 lb) is classified as low, babies weighing only 500 g (a little more than 1 lb) have at least a 25% chance of living, and the odds rise to more than 90% for babies who weigh at least 1,000 g (about 2.2 lb) (Minde, 1993). The tiniest babies, those who weigh less than 1,000 g, are 50 to 60 times more likely to survive today than was the case 35 years ago (Minde, 2000).

Much of this progress can be attributed to the development of neonatal intensive care units (NICUs). In these facilities, low-birth-weight babies receive various forms of stimulation—rocking, sound recordings of the mother's heartbeat, high-contrast mobiles, gentle massage, and the like—which appear to assist their early development (Field, 2001; Mueller, 1996). One consequence of these interventions is that very tiny babies who would once have died at birth are now kept alive. These babies, however, face strong challenges to life and well-being; the lighter the baby, the higher these risks.

Physical and Behavioral Assessment A third indicator of risk is poor performance on standard assessments. Perhaps as a sign of things to come, almost all babies born in the United States begin life with a test. Tests are used to screen babies for disorders, to determine whether a baby's nervous system is intact, and to characterize how a newborn responds to social and physical stimuli. Even though newborns are new to the external world, they possess a surprising range of behaviors and functions. Newborn tests can assess more than 85% of such behaviors and functions (Francis, Self, & Horowitz, 1987). Here we consider the two most often used tests: the Apgar exam and the Brazelton Neonatal Behavioral Assessment Scale.

In 1953, Dr. Virginia Apgar introduced a test that permitted obstetricians to record objectively the status of the newborn. This test has become the standard for the baby's first assessment. The **Apgar exam** focuses on five of the newborn's vital functions, which are measured by heart rate, respiration, muscle tone, response to a mildly painful stimulus, and skin color. The newborn receives a score from 0 to 2 on each of these items. For example, the baby earns a 2 for the heart-rate category if the heart beats 100–140 times per minute; a 1 if the rate is less than 100; and a 0 if no beat is detectable. Babies are typically assessed on the five categories almost immediately after birth and then again 5 minutes later. The highest possible score is 10. On average, about 77% of newborns receive a score of 8–10, 17% a score of 3–7, and 6% a score of 0–2 (Apgar, 1953).

Investigators use the Apgar test to identify babies who may need special monitoring and attention through early infancy. Several factors tend to lower the Apgar score, including maternal depression, anxiety, smoking, drinking, and labor medication. Psychologists have examined the relation between a newborn's Apgar score and intellectual functioning later in infancy and early childhood. The results have been mixed. Some investigators have reported a positive relation, but others report no relation when socioeconomic status, race, and gender are taken into consideration (Francis et al., 1987).

The Apgar exam assesses vital life processes and can be quickly administered, but the results provide only limited information. The newborn possesses a wealth of behavioral tools that cannot be captured in a brief exam that focuses on physiological functioning. Moreover, newborn babies differ substantially in how they behave, and these differences may affect how parents and others treat them. For these reasons, investigators have focused increasingly on tests of how well the newborn's behavior is organized. The **Brazelton Neonatal Behavioral Assessment Scale** (Brazelton & Nugent, 1995) is the most comprehensive of the newborn tests. The main idea underlying this scale is

Apgar exam
An exam administered immediately after birth that assesses vital functions, such as heart rate and respiration.

Brazelton Neonatal Behavioral Assessment Scale
The most comprehensive of newborn assessment instruments; assesses attention and social responsiveness, muscle tone and physical movement, control of alertness, and physiological response to stress.

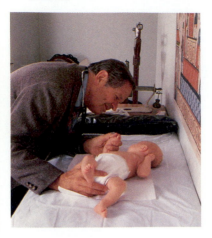

T. Berry Brazelton developed a widely used scale for assessing the newborn.

that the seemingly helpless newborn actually possesses organized behaviors for dealing with both attractive stimuli—such as pleasant sights, sounds, and tastes—and offensive stimuli—such as loud noises and pinpricks. Assessors observe the baby in a number of states, or levels of alertness, to obtain a sense of the baby's style and temperament. An important feature of the exam is that it evaluates the newborn's ability to habituate. Recall from Chapter 1 that habituation is a simple form of learning in which a reflex response to a stimulus declines or disappears when the stimulus repeatedly occurs.

The exam includes items in four categories: attention and social responsiveness; muscle tone and physical movement; control of alertness (habituation, irritability, and excitability); and physiological response to stress. The baby's performance on these measures provides indicators of well-being and risk. For example, a baby who is unable to habituate to a repeated stimulus or to remain alert may fall into a higher risk category. Table 5.2 provides some sample items from the Brazelton Scale.

The Brazelton Scale does a fairly good job of characterizing how a baby is doing in the early period. It is helpful, for example, in identifying problems in babies who have been subjected to conditions that put them at risk, such as low birth weight or prenatal drug exposure. It is not a good predictor, however, of development beyond the early infancy period (Lester & Tronick, 2001). The same conclusion applies to other early assessment instruments, as well as to each of the risk factors discussed when considered in isolation. This fact may seem surprising to anyone who has seen a very low-weight baby in the newborn intensive care nursery. A 2-lb baby, who is little more than tubes, able to breathe only with a respirator, and perhaps suffering internal brain bleeding, may seem to be on the verge of death. Amazingly, this baby is more than likely to turn out fine. The best predictor of developmental difficulties is the number of risk factors to which an infant is subjected. The greater the number, the more likely that the infant will have problems (Sameroff et al., 1993).

The Role of the Later Environment

Some babies who are born at risk have suffered brain or central nervous system damage that affects their functioning throughout life. However, in many cases, whether babies born at risk achieve normal development appears to depend largely on the context in which they are reared. Because most of the research supporting this finding has been carried out with preterm infants, we focus on that work, but many of these factors play a role in determining the outcome of any baby at risk.

One factor in a baby's developmental progress is the quality of the relationship that forms between the parents and the baby (Mangelsdorf et al., 1996). At-risk babies often pose special challenges to this relationship. For example, a preterm baby may spend weeks in a plastic enclosure in a special-care hospital nursery that affords the parents

Table 5.2	Examples of Items from the Brazelton Neonatal Behavioral Assessment Scale
Item	**Description**
Response decrement to light	While infant is asleep, shine light in eyes and observe response; after response disappears, wait 5 seconds and re-present; continue for either 10 trials or until habituation occurs.
Response decrement to rattle	While infant is asleep, shake rattle near ear and observe response; continue for either 10 trials or until habituation occurs.
Inanimate visual orientation	Slowly move a red ball across the infant's field of vision; record ability to track both horizontally and vertically.
Animate visual orientation	Have examiner slowly move his or her face across the infant's field of vision; record ability to track both horizontally and vertically.
Animate auditory orientation	While out of the infant's line of sight, have examiner speak softly into baby's ear; record ability to localize on each side.
Defensive movement	With infant in supine position, hold cloth over eyes for 30 seconds; record defensive responses (e.g., swipes at cloth).

SOURCE: Adapted from *Neonatal Behavioral Assessment Scale* (3rd ed.), by T. Berry Brazelton and J. K. Nugent, 1995. London: Mac Keith Press. Copyright © 1995 by Mac Keith Press. Adapted by permission.

little opportunity to hold and cuddle the baby. When finally at home, the baby is likely to have an irritating cry, be difficult to soothe, and have irregular patterns of sleep and wakefulness (Parmelee & Garbanati, 1987). Such babies also smile less when interacting with adults and are more likely to turn away and avoid eye-to-eye contact (Eckerman et al., 1999).

These real problems are aggravated by people's reactions to preterm babies. In one study, several sets of parents were shown a film of a 5-month-old baby after they had been told that the baby was either normal, difficult, or premature (a term the researchers used for both SGA and preterm babies). Those who were told that the baby was premature judged crying segments of the film as more negative than did other parents, and physiological measures indicated that they experienced the baby's cries as more stressful (Frodi et al., 1978).

Other investigators have observed that parents treat their preterm children differently even after apparent differences between them and full-term babies have disappeared (Barnard, Bee, & Hammond, 1984; Beckwith & Parmelee, 1986). The tendency to expect negative behavior from premature infants is referred to as *prematurity stereotyping* (Stern & Karraker, 1992). Such stereotypes increase the possibility that a negative cycle between parent and infant will be set in motion. Of course, the degree to which this occurs depends in part on the tolerance and flexibility of the caregivers, which is often related to their accurate understanding of the infant's needs (Benasich & Brooks-Gunn, 1996). The resources available to the family can also be important. By 2 to 3 years of age, children born preterm into families that have strong financial resources seem indistinguishable from children born at term. Conversely, the presence of financial and other stresses reduces the emotional availability of the parents, and makes it less likely that they will adapt successfully to the challenges of the preterm infant (Hoy, Bill, & Sykes, 1988).

A contributor to disruption of the parent−infant relationship in the past was the policy of hospitals not to permit the parents to hold or touch their infant in the special-care nursery because of the fear of infection. We can easily imagine how a mother's confidence in caring for her newborn might be jeopardized after being limited for 6 to 8 weeks to watching the baby through a transparent incubator shield. As investigators began to recognize the importance of the very earliest social interactions between mother and infant, the situation changed. A group at Stanford

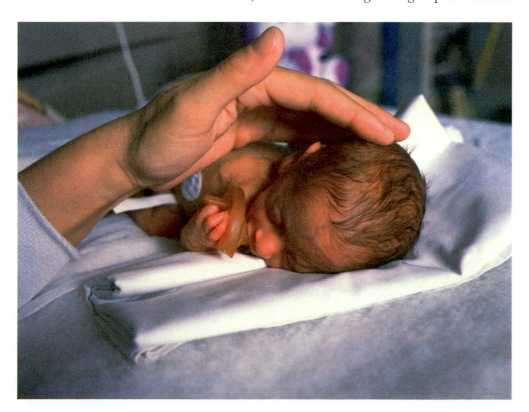

Modern hospital practice recognizes that the opportunity for parents to touch and to stimulate their preterm infants can be valuable—for both infant and parent.

University took the daring step of permitting parents to handle their infants in the special-care nursery and demonstrated that no increased danger of infection resulted (Barnett et al., 1970). Subsequent work demonstrated that handling enhanced mothers' self-confidence in responding to their babies (Leiderman & Seashore, 1975; Seashore et al., 1973).

A related factor is the lack of stimulation that infants often experience when they must spend time in the hospital. The temperature-controlled, patternless plastic chambers in which they are placed deprive them not only of human physical contact but of sensory input as well. As we have seen, intervention procedures introduced by NICUs have begun to address this problem.

There is concern, however, that for some premature babies added stimulation becomes overstimulation and has a negative rather than positive effect. One creative idea is to provide stimulation that the babies themselves can decide to experience or avoid. For example, one investigator placed a "breathing" teddy bear in the baby's bed, which the baby could either contact or avoid. Premature babies who had the breathing bear tended to stay near it more than those who had a nonbreathing bear, and they spent a longer amount of time in quiet sleep (Thoman, 1993).

To Recap . . .

Labor begins with regular contractions of the uterus and passes through three stages. Most births proceed normally, and technological advances have helped improve the outcomes of those that do not. Cultures vary considerably in their attitudes and practices regarding birth.

Psychologists have been particularly interested in identifying babies born at risk for developmental problems. One indicator of risk is maternal and family characteristics. A second indicator of risk is physical compromise of the newborn, most frequently identified by low birth weight. Low-birth-weight babies have more difficulties with breathing, which may lead to anoxia.

Babies have low birth weights for two reasons: Preterm babies were born before the end of the normal gestation period; SGA babies are small for their gestational age because of growth retardation in the womb. Whatever the cause of low birth weight, these babies show differences from normal-weight infants, and these differences may persist for several years.

A third indicator of risk is provided by newborn assessments. These tests include the Apgar exam, the most common and easiest to use, and the Brazelton Neonatal Behavioral Assessment Scale, the most comprehensive test. No single risk indicator predicts intelligence or personality especially well, but the number of risk factors seems to be a good predictor of developmental problems.

The long-term impact of early adversity also depends on the environment in which the child develops. Positive outcomes are most likely when financial resources are good and parents are sensitive to the child's capabilities and needs.

THE ORGANIZED NEWBORN

Look at a newborn baby and you will see that the baby's face, if he is awake, changes expression rapidly for no apparent reason and his legs and arms often flail around with no seeming purpose or pattern. A sleeping baby is less active, but her sleep is punctuated by twists, turns, startles, and grunts—a fairly unorganized picture. Seeing these behaviors, you can understand why, during most of the history of child psychology, people considered the newborn a passive and helpless creature whose activity was essentially random. Any organized behavior depended on external stimulation. Is it true that the newborn comes into the world with no organized patterns of behavior for sleeping, eating, getting the caregiver's attention, or even moving? Must caregivers teach the baby all these things?

Research on newborn behavior since the 1960s has drastically changed these views. Certainly the newborn is not as coordinated or predictable as the 2-year-old, but the behavior of the newborn is neither random nor disorganized. The newborn possesses natural rhythms of activity that generate patterns of sleeping and wakefulness, eating, and motion. Moreover, the newborn is equipped with many reflexive responses to external stimulation and a few organized behavioral patterns for investigating and controlling the environment through looking, sucking, and crying.

States of Alertness

Often the first question grandparents and friends ask the nurse about the new baby is, "Is the baby asleep or awake?" But there are other possibilities. Forty years ago, Peter Wolff, at the Harvard Medical School, carefully watched several newborn babies for many hours and was struck by how much their levels of alertness varied, yet how similar these levels were from one baby to another (Wolff, 1959, 1966). He captured these observations by defining six states of infant alertness: (1) quiet, or deep, sleep; (2) active, or light, sleep; (3) drowsiness; (4) alert inactivity; (5) alert activity; and (6) crying. These states are described in Table 5.3.

Several aspects of these states and how they change with age make them useful for understanding early development, for assessing the effects of various factors—such as teratogens—on development, and for comparing one infant with another. Recordings of brain activity by an **electroencephalograph (EEG)** reveal that states become increasingly distinct with age. Investigators believe this change reflects how the baby's brain matures (Colombo, 2001). Similar information can also be obtained by examining the ease with which babies move from one state to the next (Halpern, MacLean, & Baumeister, 1995).

The time distribution of sleep states changes rapidly with age (Groome et al., 1997). Whereas the fetus of 25 weeks gestational age engages almost exclusively in active sleep, the newborn spends only about half the time in active sleep and half in quiet sleep. By 3 months, quiet sleep occurs twice as much as active sleep (Berg & Berg, 1987). In active sleep, babies periodically move and breathe irregularly, but the most notable feature is that they frequently move their eyes back and forth with their eyelids closed (as do adults), so this sleep state is often called **rapid eye movement, or REM, sleep.**

The shift from dominantly active (REM) sleep to dominantly quiet sleep has aroused considerable speculation about the function of REM sleep. In the adult, REM sleep constitutes only about 20% of total sleep time and is associated with dreaming. Research suggests that the high rate of REM activity in early development reflects a kind of internal motor that keeps nerve pathways active until the baby receives enough stimulation from the external world (Kandel & O'Dell, 1992). Consistent with this idea is the finding that babies who have longer awake periods, which presumably provide needed stimulation, have shorter REM periods during sleep (Boismer, 1977; Denenberg & Thoman, 1981).

Because the organization of sleep states—how well they are differentiated and their time distribution—reflects brain maturation, we might expect at-risk babies to be less organized than other infants. Indeed, state organization is affected in babies of alcoholic

Electroencephalograph (EEG)
An instrument that measures brain activity by sensing minute electrical changes at the top of the skull.

Rapid eye movement (REM) sleep
A stage of light sleep in which the eyes move rapidly while the eyelids are closed.

Table 5.3	States of the Infant

State	Characteristics
Deep sleep	Regular breathing; eyes closed with no eye movements; no activity except for occasional jerky movements
Light sleep	Eyes closed but rapid eye movements can be observed; activity level low; movements are smoother than in deep sleep; breathing may be irregular
Drowsiness	Eyes may open and close but look dull when open; responses to stimulation are delayed, but stimulation may cause state to change; activity level varies
Alert inactivity	Eyes open and bright; attention focused on stimuli; activity level relatively low
Alert activity	Eyes open; activity level high; may show brief fussiness; reacts to stimulation with increases in startles and motor activity
Crying	Intense crying that is difficult to stop; high level of motor activity

Sudden Infant Death Syndrome

Each year in the United States approximately 3,000 babies go to sleep and never wake up. Such babies are victims of **sudden infant death syndrome**, or **SIDS,** which is defined as the sudden and unexpected death of an apparently healthy infant under the age of 1. In industrialized nations, SIDS is the most common cause of infant death beyond the neonatal period. The most vulnerable period is early in infancy, between about 2 and 4 months of age.

Despite decades of concerted research effort, the causes of SIDS are still not fully understood. Researchers have succeeded, however, in identifying a number of risk factors—that is, factors whose presence increases the likelihood of SIDS. Fortunately, many of these factors are conditions that are under the parents' control.

One clearly important factor is the positon in which the baby is placed for sleep. Sleeping in the prone, or on-the-stomach, position is associated with a heightened probability of SIDS (Simpson, 2001). Discovery of this association led to a "Back to Sleep" campaign in the United States, a campaign that encouraged parents to place babies on their backs rather than their stomachs. Within 5 years, the percentage of American babies who were placed on their stomachs had declined from 70% to 20%. The incidence of SIDS had declined by 42%. Comparable declines occurred in other countries in which similar campaigns were initiated (American Academy of Pediatrics, 2000).

Other aspects of the sleep environment may also be important. Soft bedding

BOX 5.1

Applications

is a risk factor, and so is overheating (Kleeman et al., 1999). It is perhaps natural for parents to bundle the baby up and keep the heat high during the winter months (the most common time period for SIDS); too much confinement and warmth, however, may be dangerous rather than beneficial.

Another risk factor that is clearly under parental control is maternal smoking. Both smoking while pregnant and smoking in the vicinity of the infant are associated with an increased probability of SIDS. The association with SIDS is hardly the only reason to stop the practice—parental smoking has been linked to a number of health problems in infancy (Mannino et al., 2001).

Some of the predictors of SIDS reside more in the infant than in the immediate environment. Babies who were born preterm or at low birth weight, who were exposed to drugs prenatally, or who had low Apgar scores are at heightened risk for SIDS. More immediately, babies who are suffering from respiratory infections are more vulnerable to SIDS. There is also evidence the some victims of SIDS may have abnormalities in the portion of the brain that controls breathing and waking from sleep (Panigrahy et al., 1997). Particularly when other risk factors are operating (e.g., overheating, a respiratory infection), these babies may simply be unable to rouse themselves from the sleep state.

Having noted these various risk factors, we should reiterate that scientists still do not fully understand the causes of SIDS, and at present there is no certain prescription for guarding against SIDS. Nevertheless, it clearly makes sense for parents to do all that is under their control to try to prevent this most heartbreaking of family tragedies.

Sudden Infant Death Syndrome (SIDS)
The sudden and unexpected death of an otherwise healthy infant under the age of 1.

and drug-addicted mothers, and babies who are unstable in their time distribution across various states between 2 and 5 weeks of life are more likely than are relatively stable babies to have later medical and behavioral problems (Halpern et al., 1995).

To this point, we have talked about infant states in terms of the internal processes they reflect. But states also play an important role in infants' interactions with the environment. When babies are in states of alertness—rather than crying, asleep, or drowsy—they are more receptive to stimuli and learn more readily (Berg & Berg, 1987; Thoman, 1990). Thus, states affect the impact of external events. External events, in turn, can affect an infant's state. For example, a crying baby will often shift to a quiet, alert state if picked up by an adult and gently rocked up and down on the adult's shoulder (Korner & Thoman, 1970; Pederson & Ter Vrugt, 1973).

Another external factor is where the baby sleeps. Although sleep and its various states have a strong biological basis, it is not clear where nature intended babies to sleep. In the United States, most middle-income families have babies sleep by themselves in their own beds. Among many lower-income families and some ethnic groups—such as African Americans—babies are more likely to sleep with their parents. The most common reason given by middle-income mothers for the separate sleeping arrangements is the desire to build the infant's independence. The most common reasons given by mothers who prefer sharing a bed are the desire to develop a closeness with the infant as

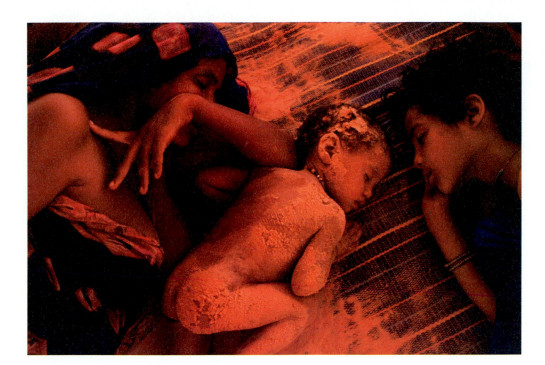

In many cultures, it is common for infants and young children to share the parents' bed.

well as the ease of feeding and caregiving (Kawasaki et al., 1994; Morelli et al., 1992). Having the infant share a bed or at least a room with the parents is a common practice across many of the world's cultures (Nelson, Schiefenhoevel, & Haimerl, 2000).

Rhythms

Most children and adults have regular patterns of daily activity. For the most part, they sleep at night, are awake during the day, and eat at fairly predictable times. We can say that their daily patterns obey a repeating rhythm. On the other hand, one need only look at the red, tired eyes of a new parent to know that the newborn baby's habits are not so regular. Can we conclude, then, that the baby enters the world with no rhythms at all and must be taught by the parents when to eat, when to sleep, and when to wake? Not at all. Newborn babies are rhythmic creatures. The newborn's biological clock just seems to tick at a different rate than ours, and it gradually shifts into synchrony with ours as the baby develops.

The newborn's states, like the adult's, occur as rhythms cycling within other rhythms. The baby engages in a cycle of active and quiet sleep that repeats each 50 to 60 minutes. This cycle is coordinated with a cycle of wakefulness that occurs once every 3 to 4 hours (Parmelee & Sigman, 1983). What produces this behavior? We might suspect that the sleep−wake cycle reflects a cycle of hunger or of external disruption by caregivers. However, the cycle seems to be internally controlled. Even before the first feeding and with external distractions held to a minimum, newborns still display roughly these same sleep−wake cycles (Emde, Swedberg, & Suzuki, 1975).

Much to the relief of their parents, infants gradually adapt to the 24-hour light−dark cycle. Sleep periods become longer at night, usually around 5 or 6 weeks of age, as awake periods lengthen during the day. By 12 to 16 weeks, the pattern of sleeping at night and being awake during the day is fairly well established, even though the baby still sleeps about the same amount as the newborn (Berg & Berg, 1987).

Although the rhythms of the newborn seem to be biologically programmed, they are not free from environmental influences. For example, newborn babies who stay in their mothers' rooms in the hospital begin to display day−night differences in their sleep cycles earlier than babies who stay in the hospital nursery. These rooming-in babies also spend more time in quiet sleep and less time crying than do babies in nursery

Table 5.4	Newborn Reflexes			
Name	**Testing Method**	**Response**	**Developmental Course**	**Significance**
Blink	Flash a light in infant's eyes	Closes both eyes	Permanent	Protects eyes from strong stimuli
Biceps reflex	Tap on the tendon of the biceps muscle	Contracts the biceps muscle	Brisker in the first few days than later	Absent in depressed infants or those with congenital muscular disease
Knee jerk or patellar tendon reflex	Tap on the tendon below the patella or kneecap	Quickly extends or kicks the knee	More pronounced in the first 2 days than later	Absent or difficult to obtain in depressed infants or infants with muscular disease; exaggerated in hyperexcitable infants
Babinski	Gently stroke the side of the infant's foot from heel to toes	Flexes the big toe dorsally; fans out the other toes; twists foot inward	Usually disappears near the end of the 1st year; replaced by plantar flexion of big toe in the normal adult	Absent in infants with defects of the lower spine; retention important in diagnosing poor myelination of motor tracts of the brainstem in older children and adults
Withdrawal reflex	Prick the sole of the infant's foot with a pin	Flexes leg	Constantly present during the first 10 days; present but less intense later	Absent with sciatic nerve damage
Plantar or toe grasp	Press finger against the ball of the infant's foot	Curls all toes under	Disappears between 8 and 12 months	Absent in infants with defects of the lower spinal cord
Tonic neck reflex	Lay baby down on back	Turns head to one side; baby assumes fencing position, extending arm and leg on this side, bending opposite limbs, and arching body away from direction faced	Found as early as 28th prenatal week; frequently present in first weeks, disappears by 3 or 4 months	Paves way for eye–hand coordination

groups (Keefe, 1987). Apparently, prenatal experience can also affect rhythmic activity. Newborns who have alcoholic or drug-dependent mothers have more difficulty synchronizing their various sleep–wake rhythms and adapting to the night–day cycle than do other babies (Parmelee & Sigman, 1983; Sander et al., 1977).

Reflexes

We have seen that the newborn baby has identifiable states of alertness and that these states fit into overall rhythms. Newborns are also equipped with a number of behaviors and behavior patterns. Some of these, called **reflexes,** are highly stereotyped and occur as brief responses to specific stimuli. As we discussed in Chapter 1, reflexes have evolved in humans over millions of years because they serve (or served at one time) an important survival function.

Reflexes are of interest not only to psychologists trying to understand early development; they can have applied value as well because their presence or absence provides information about the baby's brain and nervous system. For example, an infant should reflexively bend to the left side when the doctor runs a thumb along the left side of the baby's spinal column. If this reflex occurs on the left side but not on the right side, it may indicate damage to the nerves on the right side.

Some reflexes last throughout life, but the reflexes of most interest here are those that disappear in the first year of life, because their disappearance indicates the development

Reflex
An automatic and stereotyped response to a specific stimulus.

Table 5.4	(Continued)			

Name	Testing Method	Response	Developmental Course	Significance
Palmar or hand grasp	Press rod or finger against the infant's palm	Grasps the object with fingers; can suspend own weight for brief period of time	Increases during the 1st month and then gradually declines and is gone by 3 or 4 months	Weak or absent in depressed babies
Moro reflex (embracing reflex)	Make a sudden loud sound; let the baby's head drop back a few inches; or suspend baby horizontally, then lower hands rapidly about six inches and stop abruptly	Extends arms and legs and then brings arms toward each other in a convulsive manner; fans hands out at first, clenches them slightly	Begins to decline in 3rd month, generally gone by 5th month	Absent or constantly weak Moro indicates serious disturbance of the central nervous system; may have originated with primate clinging
Stepping or automatic walking reflex	Support baby in upright position with bare feet on flat surface; move the infant forward and tilt him slightly from side to side	Makes rhythmic stepping movements	Disappears in 2 to 3 months	Absent in depressed infants
Swimming reflex	Hold baby horizontally on stomach in water	Alternates arms and leg movements, exhaling through the mouth	Disappears at 6 months	Demonstrates coordination of arms and legs
Rooting reflex	Stroke cheek of infant lightly with finger or nipple	Turns head toward finger, opens mouth, and tries to suck finger	Disappears at approximately 3 to 4 months	Absent in depressed infants; appears in adults with severe cerebral palsy
Babkin or palmarmental reflex	Apply pressure on both of baby's palms when lying on back	Opens mouth, closes eyes, and turns head to midline	Disappears in 3 to 4 months	Inhibited by general depression on central nervous system

SOURCE: Excerpted from *Child Psychology: A Contemporary Viewpoint,* 2nd ed. (Table 4.1), by E. M. Hetherington and R. D. Parke, 1979, New York: McGraw-Hill. Copyright © 1979 by McGraw-Hill, Inc. Excerpted by permission of the McGraw-Hill Company.

of more advanced brain functions. Table 5.4 lists some of the more common reflexes as well as the stimuli that produce them and their developmental course. We discuss only a few of these reflexes here.

The *rooting reflex* is the first to appear. If we stroke a newborn's cheek next to the mouth, the baby will turn the head to that side and search with the mouth. This reflex is adaptive in an evolutionary sense because it helps the baby find the nipple of the mother's breast for feeding. This reflex appears as early as 2 to 3 months gestational age and represents the first indication that the fetus can respond to touch. Rooting generally disappears in infants around 3 to 4 months of age (Peiper, 1963).

The *palmar reflex* is elicited by pressure against the palm of a newborn's hand, such as with a finger, as shown in Figure 5.2a. The baby responds by grasping the finger tightly. Newborns are capable of supporting their own weight in this manner—a potentially important ability for babies of our evolutionary ancestors, who needed to cling tightly to the fur of their mothers as they moved along through the jungle. This reflex disappears at 3 to 4 months of age, and children will not again be able to support their own weight until around 4 or 5 years of age (McGraw, 1940).

The *Moro reflex* consists of a series of reactions to sudden sound or the loss of head support. The infant first thrusts her arms outward, opens her hands, arches her back, and stretches her legs outward, then she brings her arms inward in an embracing motion with fingers formed into fists. The absence of a Moro reflex is a sign of brain damage, and its failure to disappear after 6 or 7 months of age is also cause for concern. Moro,

Figure 5.2

Some newborn reflexes: (*a*) palmar and (*b*) stepping.

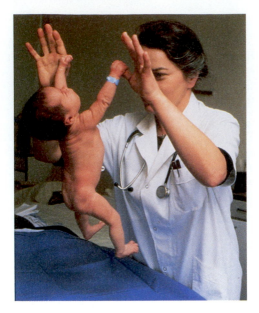

who first described the reflex (Moro, 1918), argued that it was a relic of an adaptive reaction by primates to grab for support while falling, but others have disputed this argument (e.g., Peiper, 1963). As with many newborn reflexes, the evolutionary roots of the Moro reflex are not certain.

When pressure is applied to the soles of the feet, the baby will flex her legs up and down in the *stepping reflex*, shown in Figure 5.2*b*. This reflex usually disappears by around 3 months of age. The disappearance of the reflex at this time seems to result from the increasing weight of the baby's legs. Research has shown that if the legs are supported in water, the reflex can be demonstrated in older infants (Thelen & Fisher, 1983). Similarly, if the reflex is practiced, it can become stronger (Zelazo et al., 1993).

Although there is an automatic quality to reflexes, environmental factors do affect them. For example, a baby who has just nursed may not show a rooting response, and most other reflexes are also somewhat sensitive to the baby's biological state. Still, reflexes are generally tied to specific stimuli and are rarely seen in their absence. This is not the case for the behaviors we refer to as congenitally organized behaviors.

Congenitally Organized Behaviors

Congenitally organized behaviors
Early behaviors of newborns that do not require specific external stimulation and that show more adaptability than simple reflexes.

Not all early behaviors are responses to stimulation. The newborn also initiates activities and is capable of sustaining them over considerable periods of time. Such activities are called **congenitally organized behaviors.** Specifically, looking, sucking, and crying are three well-organized behaviors that, unlike reflexes, are often not elicited by a discrete, identifiable stimulus. These behaviors provide infants with means to get nourishment and to control and explore their environments.

Looking   The newborn's looking behavior is often unexpected (Crouchman, 1985). New parents may be amazed when their baby, even in the first moments of life, will lie with eyes wide open, seemingly examining them and other objects in the room. In a room that is dimly lit, the light coming through the window may be an especially attractive target. And babies do not simply respond reflexively to light when they look. As early as 8 hours after birth, and in complete darkness, babies open their eyes wide and engage in frequent eye movements, as though they were searching for something to explore (Haith, 1991). We will say more about early perception in the next chapter. Our point now is that looking behavior shows that newborns possess tools for acting on their world, not just for reacting to it.

Sucking   In some respects, sucking seems to fit the definition of a reflex, because it is easily elicited by oral stimulation, at least when the newborn is hungry. In other respects, though, it is not reflexlike. Babies may suck spontaneously, even during sleep. The sucking act also is not stereotyped but adapts to a variety of conditions, such as how much fluid can be obtained with each suck. In addition, sucking is sensitive to sensory events. Babies who are sucking tend to stop when they see something start to move or when they hear a voice (Haith, 1966). These characteristics set sucking apart from simpler reflexes.

Sucking is a marvelously coordinated act. Babies suck one to two times each second, and each suck requires an orchestration of actions. Milk is extracted from the nipple both by suction (as with a straw) and by a squeezing action, and these actions must be coordinated with both breathing and swallowing. Some babies show excellent sucking coordination from birth, whereas others may require a week or so of practice (Peiper, 1963).

No other newborn behavior seems to serve quite as many purposes as sucking. It is, of course, a way to get nourishment, but it is also a primary means by which babies begin to explore the world. Even at birth, many babies suck their fingers and thumbs, and it appears that some newborns have even practiced this as fetuses. Later, they will continue to explore with their mouths as they become better able to grasp and find new objects (Rochat, 1989).

Sucking also seems to buffer the infant against pain and overstimulation. Agitated babies quiet when they suck on a pacifier, especially when it contains a sweet substance (Smith & Blass, 1996). One study found that crying during circumcision was reduced by about 40% when babies were permitted to suck on a pacifier (Gunnar, Fisch, & Malone, 1984). This finding confirms experimentally what civilizations have known for some time; for thousands of years, Jewish babies have been encouraged to suck on wine-soaked cotton during circumcision. Finally, sucking plays a social role in the process of emotional attachment between infant and mother (Bowlby, 1969).

Crying   A third organized behavior of the newborn is crying. Like sucking, crying coordinates various components of behavior, such as breathing, vocalizing, and muscular tensing, in a rhythmic pattern. Psychologists have been interested in crying both as a diagnostic tool and for its social role.

Wolff (1969) distinguished three types of cries in the very young infant: a hungry, or basic, cry; a mad, or angry, cry; and a pain cry. The first two are similar in pitch but different in that the mad cry forces more air through the vocal cords, producing more variation. The pain cry has a more sudden onset with a much longer initial burst and a longer period of breath holding between cries. Other researchers have identified the types as expressing hunger, fear, or pain (Wasz-Hockert, Michelsson, & Lind, 1985). Although it was once believed that parents could reliably distinguish among different types of cries, more recent research has called this idea into question (Gustafson, Wood, & Green, 2000). What seems clear is that parents—and adults in general—can distinguish among cries based on intensity and are more likely to respond as the cry becomes more intense. Contextual cues then aid in determining the meaning of the cry.

The crying of healthy, newborn infants is fairly characteristic in both pitch and rhythm. An unusual cry, therefore, can signal problems. Babies who are immature or brain damaged produce higher-frequency cries with abnormal timing patterns (Zeskind & Lester, 2001). Babies who show evidence of malnutrition at birth or who are preterm often also have higher-pitched cries. Infants who have genetic anomalies, such as cri du chat syndrome (in which the infant's cry sounds like that of a cat) and Down syndrome, have atypical cries as well.

Some investigators have speculated that babies influence early social relationships with their caregivers by the nature of their cries (Lester, 1984). Cries of at-risk babies are perceived as more grating, piercing, and aversive than the cries of other babies, and "difficult" babies seem to have more aversive cries than "easy" babies (Lounsbury & Bates, 1982). As noted earlier, cries experienced as aversive may set in motion a negative cycle between baby and caregiver.

More broadly, crying is a major factor in early social interaction because it is one of the infant's basic tools for getting the caregiver to come closer. Because adults dislike hearing babies cry, they typically do something to quiet the crying baby. Parents may try various techniques for soothing a baby who fusses for no apparent reason. Picking the baby up is an effective quieter; swaddling, or wrapping a baby snugly in a blanket, and pacifiers are also sometimes effective, as is continuous or rhythmic sound (Brackbill et al., 1966; Campos, 1989). Even in the first month of life, crying may be controlled by events other than food or pain relief; infants often stop crying if they have interesting things to watch or sounds to listen to (Wolff, 1969).

The three congenitally organized behaviors of looking, sucking, and crying are gradually fine-tuned by the infant to explore and control the physical and social world more effectively. Other skills, such as reaching, grasping, and walking, also play a role, and elaborate emotional behaviors, such as smiling and laughing, will enrich the social interactions of the developing infant. We will leave the more social components of early development to Chapter 12 and consider next some other physical accomplishments of the infant.

To Recap . . .

The activity of newborns is not random but is organized into states, rhythms, reflexes, and congenitally organized behaviors. The newborn's level of alertness is typically categorized according to six states, varying from quiet sleep to crying. Several aspects of these states change with age, providing information about early development. Although state organization is controlled primarily by internal factors, state can be affected by external stimulation. Conversely, the baby's response to stimulation is affected by the state the baby is in.

The newborn's states occur in rhythmic cycles. A basic rest–activity cycle is coordinated with a longer sleep–wake cycle. With age, the baby gradually adapts to the 24-hour light–dark cycle.

Other evidence for behavioral organization is found in reflexes. Although some reflexes last through life, others disappear during the first year. These reflexes and their developmental courses provide important information about the baby's central nervous system.

Congenitally organized behaviors, such as looking, crying, and sucking, are available at birth but, unlike reflexes, are not easily attributable to a particular stimulus. These are examples of inborn behaviors that the infant possesses for exploring and controlling the physical and social aspects of the world.

MOTOR DEVELOPMENT

Looking, crying, and sucking are limited in their ability to control the environment. Imagine for a moment that you cannot move around or grasp and manipulate objects so that you must depend on others to provide interesting things for you to inspect. This is the state of the newborn baby. Before long, however, these limitations disappear and the infant is a go-for-everything, grab-anything 9-month-old.

The acquisition of motor skills is a key feature of development in human infancy, in effect giving the baby power tools for acquiring knowledge and gaining a sense of competence and self-control. These skills continue to development well into the childhood years, when they play important roles in other aspects of development.

Motor development can be divided into two general categories. The first comprises **postural development** and **locomotion,** which involve control of the trunk of the body and coordination of the arms and legs for moving around. The second category is **prehension,** the ability to use the hands as tools for such purposes as eating, building, and exploring.

Principles and Sequences

The progression of motor skills tends to follow two general principles. The first principle is that development proceeds in a **proximodistal** direction—that is, body parts closest to the center of the body come under control before parts farther out.

The acquisition of early prehensile skills provides a good example. In the first weeks, the newborn can position himself toward an object but cannot reach it. Although

Postural development
The increasing ability of the baby to control parts of his or her body, especially the head and trunk.

Locomotion
The movement of a person through space, such as walking and crawling.

Prehension
The ability to grasp and manipulate objects with the hands.

Proximodistal
Literally, near to far. This principle of development refers to the tendency of body parts to develop in a trunk-to-extremities direction.

his arm movements seem random, the infant does direct some movements toward the object. In the second month of life, the baby sweeps his hand more deliberately near the object and begins to contact it more consistently. By 4 months of age, the infant can often grab at objects in a way that looks convincingly deliberate, but he uses the whole hand, with as yet little individual finger control. Gradually, the baby coordinates his fingers, so that at 6 months of age, he may reach with one hand for a cube with all fingers extended. Once the object is in hand, the baby may transfer the cube from hand to hand and rotate his wrist so as to see it from various perspectives. By 9 months, the baby can grasp a small pellet neatly between forefinger and thumb, and the 1-year-old can hold a crayon to make marks on paper.

The second principle is that control over the body develops in a **cephalocaudal,** or head-to-foot, direction. The progression of early postural and locomotor skills illustrates this principle.

The newborn who is placed on her stomach can move her head from side to side, although her head must be supported when she is lifted to someone's shoulder. A 3-month-old infant first holds her head erect and steady in the vertical position and then pushes off the mattress with her hands to lift her head and shoulders and look. At 6 months, the baby can pull herself to a sitting position and may even be able to drag herself around a bit by her arms (crawling). But only at around 8 months can the baby use her legs to move herself forward with her belly off the floor (creeping). By the time the infant is 1 year old, the parents are likely to find her standing in the crib, rattling the side bars and perhaps distressed by being unable to figure out how to sit down again! Typically, soon after her first birthday, the baby is able to control the legs sufficiently to begin walking without support.

The top portion of Figure 5.3 shows a typical baby's stages of progression toward self-produced locomotion. The cephalocaudal progression just described is clearly evident, with

Cephalocaudal
Literally, head to tail. This principle of development refers to the tendency of body parts to mature in a head-to-foot progression.

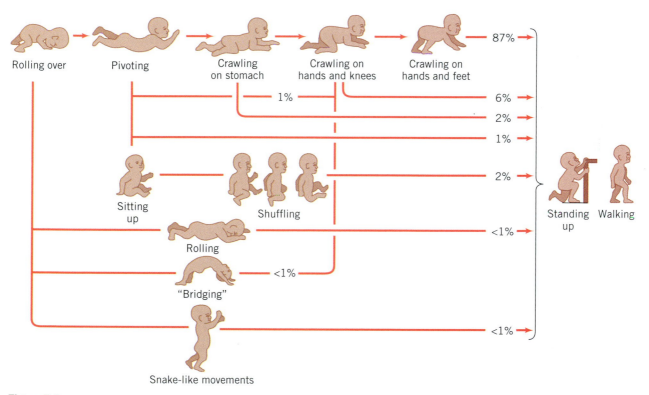

Figure 5.3

Most babies follow a fairly regular sequence in learning to walk, gradually transferring responsibility for movement from the arms to the feet. But some skip certain stages of crawling, and others never crawl at all. Adapted from "Early Development of Locomotion: Significance of Prematurity, Cerebral Palsy and Sex" by R. H. Largo, L. Molinari, M. Weber, L. C. Pinto, and G. Duc, 1985, *Developmental Medicine and Child Neurology, 27,* 183–191, figure 2. Copyright © 1985 by MacKeith Press. Adapted by permission.

Table 5.5	Motor Milestones	
Age in Months	**Locomotion and Postural Development**	**Prehension and Manipulative Skills**
0	Turns head to side when lying on stomach; poor head control when lifted; alternating movements of legs when on stomach as if to crawl	Reflex grasp—retains hold on ring
3	Head erect and steady when held vertically; when on stomach, elevates head and shoulders by arms or hands or elbows; sits with support; anticipates adjustment of lifting	Grasps rattle; reaches for objects with two hands
6	Sits alone momentarily; pulls self to sitting position with adult's hand as puller; rolls from back to stomach	Grasps cube with simultaneous flexion of fingers; reaches with one hand and rotates the wrist; transfers cube between hands
9	Sits alone; pulls self to sitting position in crib; makes forward progress in prone position toward toy; walks holding on to furniture	Opposes thumb and finger in seizing cube; picks up pellet with forefinger and thumb
12	Stands alone; lowers self to sitting from a standing position; walks with help; creeping perfected; into everything	Holds crayon adaptively to make a mark
18	Walks well (since about 15 months) and falls rarely; climbs stairs or chair	Throws balls into box; scribbles vigorously; builds tower of three or more blocks
24	Walks up and down stairs; walks backward; runs	Places square in form board; imitates folding of paper; piles tower of six blocks; puts blocks in a row to form a train

SOURCE: Based on information from *Manual for the Bayley Scales of Infant Development* by N. Bayley, 1969, New York: Psychological Corporation; and "The Denver Developmental Screening Test" by W. K. Frankenburg and J. Dodds, 1967, *Journal of Pediatrics, 71,* 181–191.

the hands most active early on and responsibility for movement gradually transferring down to the legs. The lower portion of Figure 5.3 illustrates how babies can reach the same goal by following different routes. Some babies, for example, never crawl before walking. Psychologists now know that infants do not all develop a given motor skill (such as walking or standing) in the same way—a point to which we return in a moment.

Table 5.5 presents some of the milestones of motor-skill acquisition; again, the proximodistal and cephalocaudal principles described earlier are apparent. The majority of babies follow these general sequences. It is important to note, however, that the ages given in the table are only approximate; some infants master these skills earlier, and others master them later. This variation in when motor skills are developed has taken on new significance since the recent discovery that infants also vary in how they develop specific skills. The result is that psychologists are now thinking about motor development very differently.

The Nature and Nurture of Motor-Skills Development

Motor skills appear in a fairly predictable sequence and at similar times from one infant to another. Does this mean that sitting, crawling, reaching, and so forth are genetically programmed and simply emerge according to a biological set of instructions within the child? More and more, psychologists are answering this question no.

Does Motor Development Depend on Practice or on Maturation?

BOX 5.2

Classics of
Research

The nature–nurture debate regarding motor development is very old. During the 1920s and 1930s, the zeitgeist in developmental psychology leaned heavily toward biological explanations of children's development. We saw in Chapter 1 that G. Stanley Hall's early evolutionary views were revised and resurrected during this period by his student Arnold Gesell at Yale University.

One major theoretical issue of the time concerned children's motor-skills acquisition. Learning-oriented psychologists, such as John B. Watson, argued that the crawling, climbing, and walking displayed by all normal infants represented reflexes conditioned through experience and practice. But Gesell and other biologically oriented theorists believed that these behaviors emerged according to a genetic timetable. Simple biological maturation, not conditioning and learning principles, guides their appearance.

To compare these two theories, Gesell developed a research method called the co-twin control, which used identical twins so that biological factors would be the same for the two infants. Gesell then selected one infant, whom he termed twin T, to receive training and extra practice each day at climbing stairs and related motor skills. The control infant, twin C, received no extra practice. After 6 weeks of training, twin T had become a very accomplished climber—but so had twin C. Gesell interpreted these findings to mean that the climbing skill must have been a result only of the children's biological development and not of their practice or experience (Gesell & Thompson, 1929). Studies of the same sort by other researchers appeared to confirm this conclusion (McGraw, 1935).

Later research, however, demonstrated that Gesell's conclusions had been a bit simplistic. Whereas extra training may not accelerate children's motor development, some amount of experience appears necessary for development to occur normally. Infants deprived of physical stimulation or the opportunity to move about were found to have delayed motor development (Dennis, 1960; Dennis & Najarian, 1957). When such infants were then given extra stimulation, their motor skills improved rapidly (Sayegh & Dennis, 1965).

The method of the co-twin control was a useful technique for comparing the effects of maturation and learning (which is, of course, a specific case of nature versus nurture). But as psychologists now agree, both of these processes are essential for normal motor development.

For one thing, different child-rearing experiences—often associated with different cultural practices—can clearly affect the timing of motor-skill development. For example, African infants generally sit, stand, and walk from 1 to several months earlier than do American infants (Konner, 1976; Super, 1981). But how the infants are dealt with, not heredity, seems to account for much of the difference.

One investigator reported that the Kipsigis in western Kenya believe their infants will not sit, stand, or walk without practice. Thus they energetically provide practice for their infants in these skills. For example, they dig a special hole in the ground using sand to reinforce their infants' sitting skills. In the development of skills that are not encouraged in this way, such as crawling and rolling over, Kenyan babies do not differ from American babies (Super, 1981). Mothers in Jamaica provide their babies with similar types of early physical stimulation, and these babies, too, develop motor skills earlier than do White infants in other cultures (Hopkins, 1991).

A glance back at Figure 5.3 shows a second reason that genetics cannot rigidly control motor development: Not all babies get to the same place by following the same path. Using the microgenetic method described in Chapter 2, researchers have carefully charted the development of motor skills in many individual infants. One study examined the development of reaching and grasping in four infants from ages 3 weeks to 1 year. Although all four eventually were able to reach out and grasp a toy, the manner in which they achieved this goal varied considerably from one child to the next (Thelen, Corbetta, & Spencer, 1996).

A Dynamic Systems Approach These sorts of findings have prompted researchers to think about motor development in a new way. The **dynamic systems approach** was developed within the science of physics, but in developmental psychology it has been applied to children's motor development most extensively by Esther Thelen (Thelen, 1995, 2000; Thelen & Smith, 1998).

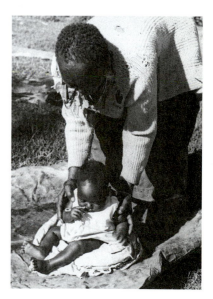

Kipsigis (in Kenya, Africa) believe that their infants need practice to learn certain postural skills, such as sitting. (Photo used by permission of Dr. Charles Super, Pennsylvania State University.)

Dynamic systems approach
Thelen's model of the development of motor skills, in which infants who are motivated to accomplish a task create a new motor behavior from their available physical abilities.

Thelen proposes that both nature and nurture contribute to the development of motor skills. Given that the emergence of these skills follows a predictable sequence for most babies, biological factors would seem to be strongly involved. Because practice and experience can affect motor-skills development and because children seem to acquire specific skills somewhat differently, environmental factors must be involved as well. Thelen argues that developmentalists need a model to help them understand the combined contributions of these two factors.

According to her dynamic systems analysis, the crucial element that unites the nature and nurture contributions and, more important, that stimulates the development of any particular skill is the infant's "task." As babies mature biologically and cognitively, they become motivated to accomplish more things in the world around them. They seek to reach things, to grasp things, to move or shake things, to move themselves closer to things, and so on. These are the tasks of infancy. To accomplish such tasks, babies learn that various motor behaviors—such as those involving the arms, fingers, head, shoulders, and so on—can be useful.

Sometimes, though, the task requires a behavior that the child does not possess, so the infant must create such a behavior. To do this, the infant draws on the physical responses and abilities already available to her—what the baby can already do with arms, legs, hands, and fingers; muscle strength; balance and coordination; and so on. These abilities, of course, depend largely on age and biological maturation, but they also depend on the abilities the baby has created up to that point. A 9-month-old, therefore, should have many more physical responses and abilities on which to draw than would, say, a 4-month-old. As a result, even when faced with the same task, the two children will likely create different new motor behaviors and so accomplish the task in different ways. Note that this is true not just for babies of different ages; any two children, even of the same age, will have different physical resources available to them as a result of both genetic differences and different experiences up to that point.

Thelen has found that as infants try to assemble a new motor behavior from the abilities currently available to them, they go through two stages. The first stage involves exploration, as the baby tries many different responses in a relatively random and uncoordinated fashion. In the second stage, selection, the baby learns exactly what works and what doesn't work and fine-tunes the many responses into an efficient package.

In short, the dynamic systems approach predicts that the motor skill a particular child develops at any given time will depend on (a) the task at hand, including how difficult it is and how motivated the child is to accomplish it, and (b) the physical abilities the child already possesses that form the starting point for creating the new behavior. The first of these (the task) is obviously very much influenced by the baby's environment and experiences; the second (the infant's physical abilities) is strongly influenced by the baby's biological maturation as well as prior experiences.

Research Examples Thelen demonstrated these principles in a clever laboratory study. Three-month-old infants were placed in cribs on their backs, where they could see a mobile suspended above them. The babies' feet were individually attached with cords to the mobile in such a way that either single kicks or alternating kicking movements were effective in making the mobile move. At first the babies explored different leg movements, but after a short while they learned to produce the necessary kicking behaviors, presumably because they were motivated to accomplish the task of moving the mobile. Thelen next tied each baby's feet loosely together, so that the motor behavior that would best move the mobile was a combined two-foot kick. Again the infants explored various leg movements before finally selecting a coordinated leg action that was effective in achieving their purpose (Thelen, 1994).

Another example involves locomotion. Researchers at the University of Denver videotaped the motions of babies' body parts as they learned to creep across the floor to reach an object. As shown in Figure 5.4, the babies wore black bodysuits that had small reflective markers (the kind bicyclists wear at night) at the shoulder, elbow, and other joints. Reflections from these markers were read by a computer and analyzed to determine the path, velocity, and timing of the children's movements.

The researchers found that once babies have the physical strength to move along with their bodies held above the floor, they begin to explore different patterns of arm-and-leg coordination and eventually settle on a diagonal pattern (right hand and left leg, then left hand and right leg) as the most efficient and stable way of locomotoring along and thus reaching the object (Benson, 1990; Freedland & Bertenthal, 1994).

The essence of the dynamic systems approach, then, is that an infant does not simply wake up one morning with a new motor skill that has emerged spontaneously from his or her genetic code. Instead, a new skill is developed only when the infant is motivated to accomplish a task and has sufficient physical abilities to assemble into the necessary motor behavior.

Why, then, do most babies follow the same general sequence of motor development? The answer is probably simply that the physical resources of infants at the same points in development are reasonably similar and infants' tasks in any given culture tend also to be reasonably similar. On the other hand, Thelen's dynamic systems analysis shows why it also should not be surprising that babies differ in the timing of their motor-skill development and in the manner in which they acquire these skills. Nature provides most of the raw material of motor development, but nurture determines the timing and direction development will take.

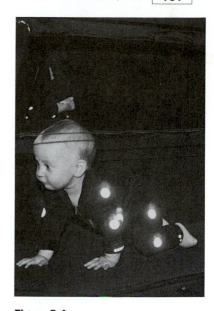

Figure 5.4

Scientists use computerized techniques to track light reflections on babies' joints to study how babies acquire skill in crawling. (Photo reproduced by permission of Dr. Janette Benson, University of Denver.)

The Psychological Implications of Motor Development

Learning to move around is not only a motor accomplishment for babies; it also helps them organize their world (Bertenthal, Campos, & Kermoian, 1994). For example, babies' self-produced locomotion seems to contribute to their spatial understanding (discussed in more detail in Chapter 6). In one study, a toy was hidden in one of two colored containers placed in front of an infant. Infants with crawling experience were better able to find the toy under a variety of conditions—such as when the babies were placed on the opposite side of the table (thereby reversing the left or right location of the toy from the baby's perspective)—than were babies of the same age who had not yet mastered crawling (Benson & Uzgiris, 1985).

A baby's control over body movement also helps her understand the meaning of distance and heights. Crawling seems to be related to infants' learning to fear heights (Campos, Bertenthal, & Kermoian, 1992). Later, when babies can control their distance from their mothers or other caregivers, they use their motor skills to venture off (when they feel safe) or to return for comfort (when they feel insecure), as we will see again in Chapter 12.

Motor Development in Childhood

Motor development has attracted the most attention from infant researchers, but motor skills continue to develop during the childhood years (Gallahue & Ozmun, 1995).

By the second birthday, most children have overcome their battle with gravity and balance and are able to move about and handle objects fairly efficiently. Their early abilities form the basis for skills that appear between 2 and 7 years of age. Three sets of fundamental movement skills emerge: locomotor movements, manipulative movements, and stability movements.

Locomotor movements include walking, running, jumping, hopping, skipping, and climbing. Manipulative movements include throwing, catching, kicking, striking, and dribbling. Stability movements involve body control relative to gravity and include bending, turning, swinging, rolling, head standing, and beam walking. These fundamental skills typically appear in all children and can be further refined by adolescents, who may develop exceptional skills as skaters, dancers, and gymnasts.

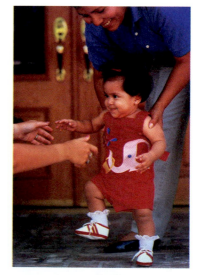

An infant's first steps are a major milestone of development.

The refinement of motor skills depends a great deal on the development of the muscles and the nerve pathways that control them, but other factors are important as well. Motor skills depend in part on sensory and perceptual skills, for example, and children acquire many of their motor skills in play, which involves social and physical interaction.

One important aspect of motor skills is reaction time—the time required for the external stimulus to trigger the ingoing nerve pathways, for the individual to make a decision, and for the brain to activate the muscles through the outgoing nerve pathways. Reaction time improves substantially through the preschool and elementary school years, even for simple motor movements (Bard, Hay, & Fleury, 1990; Dougherty & Haith, 1993).

✔ To Recap . . .

Motor development can be categorized as (1) locomotion and postural development or (2) prehension. In both, control over the body develops in a cephalocaudal and a proximodistal direction.

Infants' motor-skills development follows a reasonably predictable sequence, but differences in the timing and manner in which skills are acquired have led psychologists to doubt that motor development is rigidly genetically programmed.

Thelen's dynamic systems approach incorporates the contributions of both nature and nurture to motor development. The infant's task is viewed as the element that stimulates the development of new motor behaviors, as the baby attempts to accomplish the desired task by creating the necessary motor skill from the available physical resources. This process involves two stages: exploration and selection.

The infant's growing ability to act on the world has major psychological consequences. The infant gains knowledge of the environment, including spatial relations, height, and distance.

Motor development beyond infancy consists of increasing coordination of fundamental movement skills, including locomotor, manipulative, and stability movements.

Neuron
A nerve cell, consisting of a cell body, axon, and dendrites. Neurons transmit activity from one part of the nervous system to another.

Dendrite
One of a net of short fibers extending out from the cell body in a neuron; receives activity from nearby cells and conducts that activity to the cell body.

Axon
A long fiber extending from the cell body in a neuron; conducts activity from the cell.

Myelin
A sheath of fatty material that surrounds and insulates the axon, resulting in speedier transmission of neural activity.

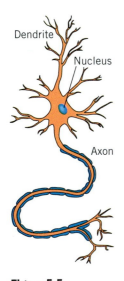

Figure 5.5
A nerve cell, or neuron.

THE HUMAN BRAIN

It is hardly necessary to say that the brain is central to every aspect of development and every sort of human function. Already we have mentioned connections between behavior and neurological maturity in newborns. In this section, we look more directly at the structure and development of the brain.

Structure of the Brain

The brain contains approximately 100 billion nerve cells, or **neurons;** each of these cells has around 3,000 connections with other cells, which adds up to several quadrillion message paths. No one completely understands how all these communication paths work, but we do know quite a bit.

Like every other cell, each neuron has a nucleus and a cell body. But neurons are unique among cells in that they develop extensions on opposite sides, as shown in Figure 5.5. On the incoming side, the extensions, called **dendrites,** often form a tangle of strands that look like the roots of plants. The outgoing extension, called an **axon,** is more like a single strand. Axons usually extend farther from the cell than do dendrites and may be quite long. They are often covered by a sheath of a fatty substance, **myelin,** which insulates them and speeds message transmission. Cells do not quite touch one another but are separated by fluid-filled gaps called **synapses.** Information is passed along a neuron as an electrical signal and crosses the synapse by the flow of chemicals called **neurotransmitters.**

The brain has three major parts. The **brain stem** includes the cerebellum, which controls balance and coordination. The **midbrain** serves as a relay station and controls breathing and swallowing. The **cerebrum,** the highest brain center, includes the left and right hemispheres and the bundle of nerves that connect them.

Of most interest to psychologists is the relatively thin shell of gray matter that covers the brain, called the **cerebral cortex.** This structure appears to be the most recently evolved part of the brain and is crucial for the functioning of the senses, language, memory, thought, and decision making, and the control of voluntary actions. Particular areas of the cerebral cortex have specific responsibilities, although some areas are more specialized than others. The cortex has more than 40 different functional areas. Some specialized tasks are identified in Figure 5.6.

Development of the Brain

Scientists only partially understand how the brain, in its amazing complexity, develops. It begins as a hollow tube. The neurons are generated along the inner walls of this tube and then travel to their proper locations (Kolb, 1989).

Scientists have identified three stages in this process. The first is *cell production.* Almost all of the neurons that we will ever have are produced between 10 and 26 weeks following conception—which means that the fetal brain generates these cells at a rate of 250,000 per minute! The brain actually overproduces neurons and then trims them back by as much as 50% (Barinaga, 1993).

Once the cells have been produced near the center of the brain, they must migrate outward to their proper locations. This *cell migration* is the second stage of early brain development. How do the neurons know where to go? That question has not been answered. It seems likely that there is a chemical attraction between the target location and the migrating neuron. Migration is complete by 7 months gestational age (Huttenlocher, 1990).

When the neuron has found its home, the third stage, *cell elaboration,* begins. In this process, axons and dendrites form synapses with other cells. Cell elaboration continues for years after birth and produces as many as 100% more synapses than will eventually exist in the adult. Thus, as they are being formed, synapses are also being cut back. Experience plays an important role in the eventual sculpting of the connections of the brain through this process. Neurons and their connections compete for survival, and the ones that are used appear to survive, whereas those that are not used disappear (Greenough & Black, 1999; Johnson, 2001). We return to the issue of selection and survival of neurons in Chapter 6.

The fetus's brain grows faster than any other organ (except perhaps the eye), and this pace continues in infancy. At birth, the baby's body weight is only 5% of adult

Synapse
The small space between neurons, across which neural activity is communicated from one cell to another.

Neurotransmitter
A chemical that transmits electrical activity from one neuron across the synapse to another neuron.

Brain stem
The lower part of the brain, closest to the spinal cord; includes the cerebellum, which is important for maintaining balance and coordination.

Midbrain
A part of the brain that lies above the brain stem; serves as a relay station and as a control area for breathing and swallowing and houses part of the auditory and visual systems.

Cerebrum
The highest brain center; includes both hemispheres of the brain and the interconnections between them.

Cerebral cortex
The thin sheet of gray matter that covers the brain.

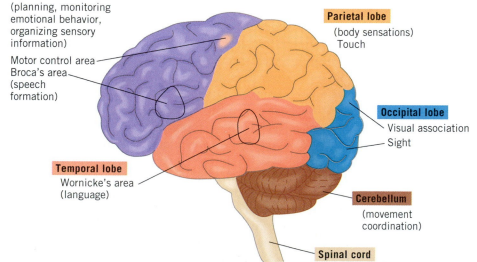

Frontal lobe
(planning, monitoring emotional behavior, organizing sensory information)
Motor control area
Broca's area
(speech formation)

Parietal lobe
(body sensations)
Touch

Occipital lobe
Visual association
Sight

Temporal lobe
Wornicke's area
(language)

Cerebellum
(movement coordination)

Spinal cord

Figure 5.6

Some areas of the cerebral cortex are specialized for particular functions; this diagram shows only a few.

weight, whereas the brain weighs 25% of its adult value. By 3 years of age, the brain has attained 80% of its ultimate weight, compared with 20% for body weight, and by 6 years it has reached 90% (Morgan & Gibson, 1991; Thatcher et al., 1996). However, the brain does not mature uniformly.

The first area to mature is the primary motor area. It may not be surprising to learn that within this area, the locations that control activity near the head mature first and maturation proceeds downward. This is the cephalocaudal direction in which motor control proceeds. Similarly, the areas that correspond to the arms mature earlier than those that control the fingers, which corresponds to the proximodistal principle.

Not far behind the motor area in maturity are the major sensory areas—touch, vision, and hearing, in that order. Myelin formation, or *myelination*, indicates how mature an area is. For example, the tracts that control fine-motor movement continue to myelinate until about age 4, whereas the areas concerned with attention and consciousness continue to myelinate up to puberty (Tanner, 1990).

Hemispheric Specialization

The two hemispheres of the brain are not perfectly symmetrical, but are *lateralized*—meaning that the left brain and the right brain are somewhat specialized. The left side of the brain is usually more specialized for language performance and the right side for spatial and mathematical tasks. Another way to think about this distinction is that the left side is more oriented to words and concepts, and the right side is more oriented to images. Pictures of the brain produced by a technique called *positron emission tomography (PET)* have confirmed that the left side of the brain is typically more active during language tasks and the right side more active during mathematical tasks. At the same time, however, these pictures show that most tasks, such as reading and listening, involve many areas of the brain (Corina, Vaid, & Bellugi, 1992; Posner et al., 1988).

Also, in some people, the right rather than the left side of the brain appears to be dominant for language, or there is mixed dominance. Left-handers more frequently fall into these categories than do right-handers. Problems with reading performance are sometimes associated with mixed or right-side dominance for language. Children who have dyslexia (reading difficulties), but with otherwise normal or superior intelligence, are more likely to lack strong left-brain dominance than are normal readers.

Hemispheric specialization appears quite early. For example, electrical brain recordings in newborn infants reveal more activity in response to speech sounds on the left than on the right side (Molfese & Molfese, 1979). In Chapter 15, we will see that hemispheric specialization may also play a role in certain gender differences in development.

Studying the Brain

Recent years have seen some exciting advances in techniques to study brain development and brain functioning (Johnson, 2002; Nelson & Luciano, 2001). In particular, various procedures for "imaging" brain composition and brain activity, such as the PET methodology mentioned above, have allowed scientists to literally look inside the brain in ways that were not possible before. Some of these techniques can reveal information not only about the anatomy of the brain but also about brain activity—that is, the changes that occur in the course of processing a stimulus or carrying out a task. Figure 5.7 shows an example from a technique labeled *functional magnetic resonance imaging (fMRI)*.

To date, use of imaging techniques with children, especially very young children, has been limited. Many of the techniques are sensitive to movement, which can be hard to control with young participants; in addition, the more invasive procedures (e.g., use of radioactive isotopes) carry too great a risk to be routinely used with children (Casey & de Haan, 2002). Nevertheless, it seems likely that our understanding of how the brain develops and how it works will grow greatly in the years to come.

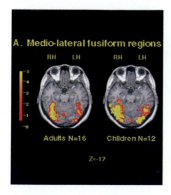
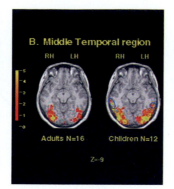
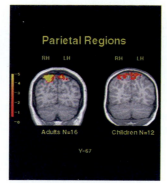

Figure 5.7

Examples of functional magnetic resonance imaging. Radio waves and a strong magnetic field are used to provide pictures of blood flow and chemical changes in the brain as different cognitive tasks are performed. In both children and adults, different regions of the brain are activated for different tasks. (*Note:* RH = right hemisphere and LH = left hemisphere.) From "The Development of Face and Location Processing: An FMRI Study" by A. M. Passarotti, B. M. Paul, J. R. Bussiere, R. B. Buxton, E. C. Wong, and J. Stiles, 2003, *Developmental Science, 6,* 108, 109. Copyright © 2003 by Blackwell Publishers. Reprinted by permission.

To Recap . . .

The brain operates through networks of communication that involve neurons and neuron pathways. Messages travel along neurons as electrical signals, which are picked up by the incoming dendrites and passed along by the outgoing axons. Neurotransmitters allow messages to travel across the synapses from cell to cell.

The brain has three major parts: the brain stem, the midbrain, and the cerebrum. Of most interest to psychologists is the cerebral cortex, which controls higher-level brain functions. Some areas of the cortex are specialized for various functions, including visual, auditory, and touch sensation.

Development of the fetal brain passes through three stages: cell production, cell migration, and cell elaboration. Although most neurons are present by around 26 weeks of fetal age, cell elaboration continues for years. Both neurons and synapses are overproduced and then cut back, and the cutting-back process continues into adolescence. Experience plays a role, affecting which neurons and synapses will die.

The left and right hemispheres of the brain are specialized to some extent. Evidence suggests that even at birth, the left side of the brain is usually prepared to control language functioning and the right side to control spatial and mathematical functioning.

PHYSICAL GROWTH

Growth is perhaps the most fundamental aspect of child development. It is continuous throughout childhood, but it does not happen uniformly. Rather, the overall rate of growth fluctuates during the growth years, with different body parts growing at different rates. In this section, we discuss the unfolding of whole-body growth, adolescent sex differentiation, and factors that affect physical growth and development.

Growth in Size

We saw in Chapter 4 that the fetus's growth rate is dramatically high, although it necessarily slows as birth approaches. This general slowing trend characterizes growth up to adolescence.

Figure 5.8 shows an average growth curve for males and females. Boys and girls are approximately the same height until around 10 years of age. A growth spurt typically

Figure 5.8

Typical male and female growth curves. Birth length doubles by around the 4th year, but growth slows, and length doubles again only around the 13th year. Adult height can be estimated by doubling the height of males at 24 months and of females at 18 months (Lowrey, 1978; Tanner, 1990). From "Standards for Growth and Growth Velocities" by J. M. Tanner, R. H. Whitehouse, and M. Takaishi, 1966, *Archives of Disease in Childhood, 41,* 467. Copyright © 1966 by Archives of Disease in Childhood. Reprinted by permission.

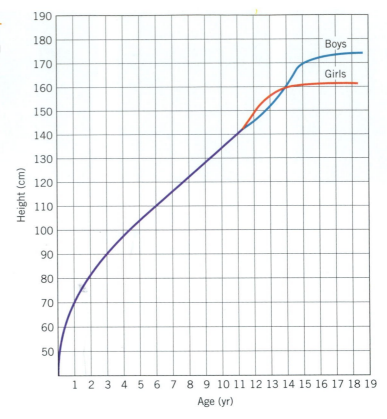

occurs between 10 and 12 years of age for girls and between 12 and 14 years of age for boys. This age difference accounts for the common observation that girls, on average, are taller than boys in grades 7 and 8, a relation that permanently reverses a few years later. In North America and northern and western Europe, where good records have been kept, we know that height increases are just about completed by 15.5 years of age in girls and 17.5 years in boys; less than 2% of growth is added afterward (Malina, 1990; Tanner, 1990).

There is evidence that growth rates have changed over recent history in some parts of the world. In Europe and North America after about 1900 the average height of 5- to 7-year-olds increased 1 to 2 cm per decade and the average height of 10- to 14-year-olds increased 2 to 3 cm per decade. Adult height, however, increased only 0.6 cm per decade between 1880 and 1960. Thus, the increase in children's heights apparently reflected a trend toward faster maturation more than a trend toward greater ultimate stature. Before this century it was fairly typical for people to grow until age 25 or so, whereas today growth usually continues only until about age 18 or 19.

Charts like the one in Figure 5.8 may give the impression that there is (or should be) a normal growth rate. But few children exactly fit the averages on these charts. Although it is obvious that individuals reach different ultimate heights and weights, it may be less apparent that their rates of growth may also differ. To illustrate, Figure 5.9 shows a growth curve for three girls. Girl B reached menarche, the onset of menstruation, before girls A and C. She was taller than both at age 12, but was ultimately shorter than girl A. Such differences in age of onset of the growth spurt are likely to accompany differences in age of puberty. They may also have long-term implications for personality development, a topic to which we return later.

Factors that may produce individual differences in growth rates include malnutrition and disease. For example, researchers recorded the growth rate of a child who suffered from two episodes of inadequate nutrition (Prader, Tanner, & von Harnack, 1963). The child's growth was severely affected. After the episodes were over, the

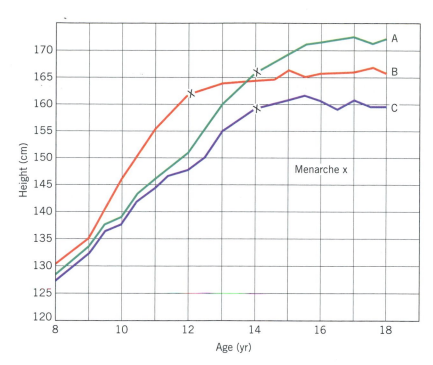

Figure 5.9

Curves showing the heights of three girls over time. Age of menarche is indicated by an X. Adapted from "Individual Patterns of Development" by N. Bayley, 1956, *Child Development, 27,* 52. Copyright © 1956 by The Society for Research in Child Development, Inc. Adapted by permission.

child did not simply return to his normal rate of growth. Rather, he experienced a remarkable acceleration in growth, which returned him to his expected growth path. This **catch-up growth** is relatively common as an aftermath of disease or limited malnutrition (Tanner, 1963).

How might we distinguish a child whose rate of maturation is slow from a child who is genetically targeted for a small adult stature? A technique for making this distinction uses the child's **skeletal maturity,** or **bone age,** which may differ from the child's chronological age. Bones develop from the center and extend outward toward the bone ends, called the *epiphyses.* As a bone reaches its ultimate length, the epiphyses close, and no further growth is possible. Scientists can use X-rays to determine how a

Catch-up growth
Accelerated growth that follows a period of delayed or stunting growth resulting from disease or malnutrition.

Skeletal maturity (bone age)
The degree of maturation of an individual as indicated by the extent of hardening of the bones.

The pace of growth during childhood and adolescence is influenced by both nature and nurture factors.

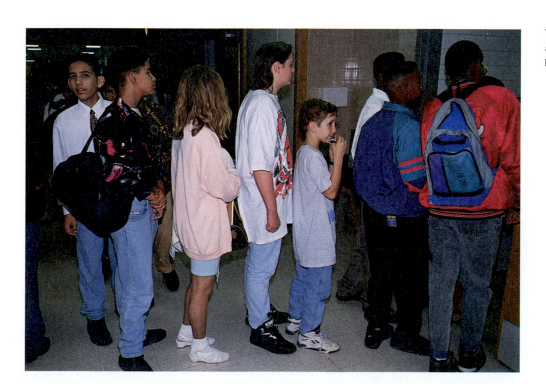

child's bone development compares with that of his or her peers and approximately how much more growth remains to occur (Tanner, 1990).

Changes in Body Proportion and Composition

Another aspect of growth rate concerns the rates at which different parts of the body develop. Figure 5.10 shows a graph of proportional growth of the body. Most noticeably, the relative size of the head changes from 50% of total body length at 2 months fetal age, to 25% at birth, and to only about 10% by adulthood. This shift reflects the cephalocaudal, or top-down, sequence of development described earlier.

We have seen that a spurt in height accompanies adolescence. More of this height comes from trunk growth than from leg growth. However, in one of the few violations of the cephalocaudal and proximodistal principles, leg growth occurs earlier than trunk growth by 6 to 9 months. Parents often wonder whether children at this stage will always be all hands and feet (Tanner, 1990).

Internal organs also follow individual paths of growth. Up to about 6 to 8 years of age, the brain grows much faster than the body in general and the reproductive organs grow much more slowly. Then the rate of brain growth slows to a gradual halt, whereas the reproductive system reaches a plateau between 5 and 12 years of age and surges at around 14 years of age.

The proportion of fat to muscle also changes with age and differs for boys and girls. The fetus begins to accumulate fat in the weeks before birth. This process continues until around 9 months after birth. After that, fat gradually declines until around 6 to 8 years of age. Girls have a bit more fat than boys at birth. This difference increases gradually through childhood until about 8 years of age and then increases more rapidly (Siervogel et al., 2000).

During the adolescent growth spurt, girls continue to gain fat faster than males. Muscle growth also occurs during adolescence, more strikingly for boys than for girls (Malina, 1990). However, because girls reach their growth spurt before males, there is a 2-year period in which girls, on average, have more muscle than boys. Changes in body

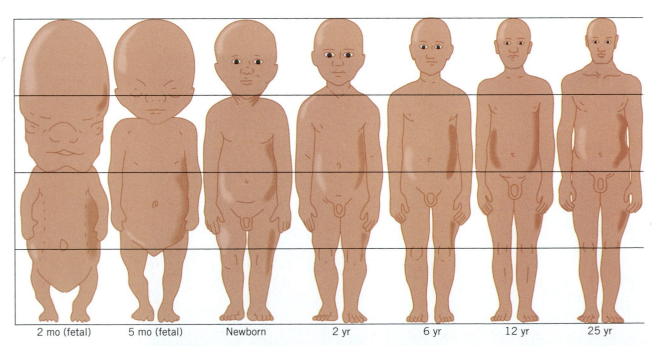

| 2 mo (fetal) | 5 mo (fetal) | Newborn | 2 yr | 6 yr | 12 yr | 25 yr |

Figure 5.10

Body proportions at several ages. From *Growth* by W. J. Robbins, S. Brady, A. G. Hogan, C. M. Jackson, and C. W. Greene, 1928, New Haven: Yale University Press, 118.

proportions that occur in adolescence result in greater shoulder width and muscular development in males and broader hips and more fat in females.

Puberty

We have seen that gender affects body size and composition. Now we look more closely at the physical aspects of gender in the growth years and especially in adolescence.

Changes during Puberty
After the fetal period, adolescence produces the greatest surge of differentiation between the two sexes. These changes occur when certain chemicals—hormones—provided by various endocrine glands are released into the bloodstream. Especially important glands for growth and sexual differentiation in adolescence are the gonads, the adrenals, and the thyroid. In addition, growth hormone, secreted by the pituitary gland, helps stimulate bone growth (Kulin, 1991; Paikoff & Brooks-Gunn, 1990).

The most significant aspect of development during adolescence is **puberty,** the series of changes that culminate in sexual maturity and the ability to reproduce. Puberty usually begins between the ages of 10 and 14, typically earlier for girls than for boys.

In males, the first sign of puberty, which occurs at around age 11 on average, is an enlargement of the testes and a change in the texture and color of the scrotum. Later, the penis enlarges, pubic hair appears, and sperm production begins, followed by the appearance of hair under the arms and on the face. Near the end of puberty, the larynx lengthens, causing the male voice to become deeper. This lengthening is sometimes evident in a breaking of the voice.

For females, the first sign of puberty is breast budding, which may occur as early as 8 years of age and as late as 13 years, followed by the appearance of pubic hair. Menarche occurs relatively late in puberty. In northern and central Europe and North America, 95% of girls begin menarche between 11 and 15 years of age. On average, African American girls begin slightly earlier than White girls (Biro et al., 2001). Usually, ovulation follows the onset of menarche by 1 or 2 years. The trend toward faster maturation has also been reflected in the age of menarche, which has decreased over the last century (Meredith, 1963; Tanner, 1987). Earlier maturation can be explained by better living conditions—better nourishment, better health care, and lowered incidence of disease.

Variations among adolescents in the timing of puberty can have a number of sources. Genes are clearly important, as is nutrition and general physical health. Even conditions in the home can affect the timing. In one study, girls whose home lives were characterized by high levels of stress (for example, discord between parents, absence of the father) were earlier to enter puberty than were girls who lived in less stressful home environments (Ellis & Garber, 2000).

How fast adolescents move through puberty varies as widely as when they start. For example, it may take a girl as few as 1.5 years or as many as 5 years to complete puberty. If we were to study a single class of boys and girls in elementary school, beginning when the first student began puberty and following the group until the last student finished puberty, chances are we would have to follow the group for a full 10 years (Petersen, 1987). We can imagine how much variation in maturation there would be in the middle years and how it might play out in social relations, self-image, and confidence.

Attitudes toward Puberty
Psychologists studying adolescence used to focus on physical changes. As investigators have learned more about the dynamics of adolescent change, however, they have increasingly emphasized social and cultural factors. More and more, investigators talk about biosocial or psychobiological factors in adolescence rather than only about biological factors (Graber, Brooks-Gunn, & Petersen, 1996).

Puberty
The period in which chemical and physical changes in the body occur that enable sexual reproduction.

Consider, for example, how girls react to the onset of menarche. This event usually heightens a girl's self-esteem and her prestige among peers. However, girls who are psychologically unprepared for menarche, perhaps because they lack information about it, have more negative feelings about its onset. Later in life, these girls are also more negative about menstruation, report more severe symptoms, and are more self-conscious about it than are other girls (Brooks-Gunn, 1987, 1991).

Social factors also influence how adolescents feel about the changes in their bodies and when they occur. At least in the United States, the ideal female is thin. But as we have seen, females add fat during puberty, and their hips broaden. In contrast, males add muscle and shoulder width, characteristics that better fit the preferred cultural image of males. Not surprisingly, then, early maturing females tend to be more dissatisfied with their bodies during puberty than late-maturing females, whereas the opposite is true for males (Crockett & Petersen, 1987; Graber et al., 1994; Ohring, Graber, & Brooks-Gunn, 2002).

A negative body image is not the only outcome linked to early or late maturity. Early maturity in girls is associated with a heightened probability of a number of problems, including depression, eating disorders, and substance abuse (Dick et al., 2000; Ge, Conger, & Elder, 2001a; Stice, Presnell, & Bearman, 2001). We should add, of course, that these are simply on-the-average relations; most early maturing girls escape such outcomes. For boys it is late maturity that tends to carry problems, including heightened anxiety and lower popularity among peers (Jones, 1965; Petersen, 1988). There is some evidence, however, that early maturity for boys may increase the probability of depression, just as is true for early maturing girls (Ge, Conger, & Elder, 2001b).

Only limited research exists on how early and late maturers succeed later in life. One longitudinal study indicates that the difficulties encountered by early maturing girls are not necessarily lasting ones; by early adulthood, the girls who had been early maturers were indistinguishable on most measures from their late maturing peers. They did, however, lag behind in educational attainment (Stattin & Magnusson, 1990). Another study reported that adolescent boys who had been early maturers had more stable careers than late maturers and that they scored higher on tests of sociability, dominance, self-control, and responsibility. On the positive side, late-maturing boys were more nurturant and seemed better able than earlier maturers to face their emotions and feelings (Brooks-Gunn & Reiter, 1990; Jones, 1965).

Factors that Affect Growth and Maturation

Our genes play a major part in our growth and physical maturation. Thus, children tend to resemble their parents—tall parents, for example, usually have taller children than do short parents. But like every other aspect of human development, growth and maturation are also influenced by the context of development.

Heredity Recall from Chapter 3 that investigators sometimes compare similarities in identical twins with similarities in fraternal twins to determine how much genetic factors influence particular behaviors. A similar strategy yields information about the role of heredity in the onset and pace of puberty and body structure.

One study of twins has been under way in Louisville, Kentucky, for over 40 years, and more than 500 twins have been studied. Identical twins have been found to become increasingly close in height up to around 4 years of age and to stabilize at a very high correlation of around .94. Fraternal twins of the same sex do the opposite. At birth, their correlation in height is about .77, but it drops to .59 at 2 years and to .49 at 9 years, at which point it stabilizes. A similar pattern exists for weight (Wilson, 1986). Identical twins are also more similar than fraternal twins in their spurts and lags in growth (Mueller, 1986).

Several other measures support the role of heredity in the rate of maturation. Identical twins display much higher similarity in the age of eruption of their teeth than do fraternal twins, and they are more similar in the pace of bone development, as well as in breast development in girls and testicular development in boys. The age of onset of menarche differs by less than 4 months in identical twins. One study revealed that even when identical twins were reared apart, the onset of menarche differed by an average of only 2.8 months. In contrast, fraternal twins reared together typically differ by 6 to 12 months in the age of onset of menarche. Such findings imply that genes play a substantial role in maturation, a conclusion also supported by similarities in the age of onset of menarche between mothers and daughters (Bailey & Garn, 1986).

If genetic factors influence maturation and eventual stature, we might expect to find maturational differences among genetic groups. In fact, we do. Asians reach puberty faster than do Europeans and move through it more quickly (but achieve a smaller stature). Africans proceed through adolescence at about the same pace as Europeans and Americans, but when they have equivalent quality of life, they reach a taller stature (see Figure 5.11) (Evelyth, 1986).

Nutrition   It should come as no surprise that relations have been found between the adequacy of a child's nutrition and various measures of that child's growth and development. Considering that about 40% of the world's children below age 5 are underweight, this is not a minor issue (Pollitt et al., 1996).

Poor nutrition is thought to be especially damaging during gestation and the early years of life, because brain growth is so rapid during this period (Georgieff & Rao, 2001). For example, children in Chile who died from malnutrition in their first or second year showed lower brain weight, less brain protein, fewer brain cells, and less myelin than expected (Balazs et al., 1986). Growth occurs in two ways: by increases in the number of cells and by increases in cell size. Increases in cell number usually characterize early growth, whereas increases in cell size are responsible for all growth after about 18 months. Thus, the impact of malnutrition may be different at different ages.

Even mild to moderate malnutrition can cause problems in children (Ricciuti, 1993). A major research project investigated the diets of children in Kenya, Egypt, and Mexico. The report concluded that even when children were consuming ample quantities of food, the quality of their diets affected their scores on various tests of cognitive and intellectual development. Deficiencies in certain vitamins (principally, vitamins A, B12, and D) and minerals (especially calcium, iron, and zinc) seemed to be most clearly involved (Sigman, 1995).

Recent studies indicate, however, that the effects of early malnutrition are not as irreversible as was once thought. Dietary correction and stimulating environments can

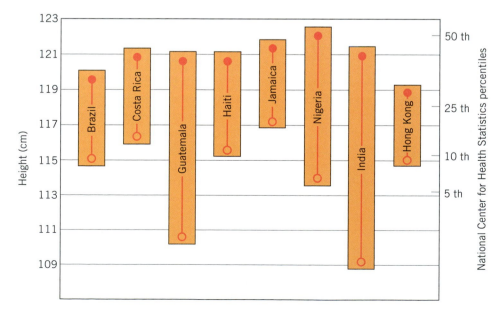

Figure 5.11

Average heights of 7-year-old boys in several countries. The solid circles at the top indicate the heights of boys from higher socioeconomic classes, and the open circles at the bottom indicate the heights of boys from lower socioeconomic classes. Adapted from "Genetics, Environment, and Growth: Issues in the Assessment of Nutritional Status" by R. Martorell, 1984. In A. Velasquez and H. Bourges (Eds.), *Genetic Factors in Nutrition* (p. 382), Orlando, FL: Academic Press. Copyright © 1984 by Academic Press. Adapted by permission.

Malnutrition, especially early in life, can have devastating effects.

have remarkable recuperative effects, although prevention is clearly better than treatment. One team of researchers, for example, provided nutritional supplements to pregnant women in rural Guatemalan villages where food resources were scarce and many villagers were underfed. Supplements were also given to the children during the first 2 years of life. Beneficial effects on various aspects of cognitive development were evident not only in childhood, and thus soon after the program was in effect, but also on follow-up tests in adolescence and early adulthood (Pollitt et al., 1993). Other studies with at-risk populations have verified the value of providing nutritional improvements during both pregnancy and the early childhood years (Grantham-McGregor, Ani, & Fernald, 2001).

Why does undernutrition affect intellectual development? Although direct biological effects on the brain seem to be involved, social and psychological factors may also play a role. For example, because poor nutrition reduces children's energy levels, it may limit their active exploration and learning. One theory also suggests that babies who are smaller in size and delayed in motor abilities—two common effects of early undernutrition—tend to be treated and cared for more like younger infants, thereby receiving less verbal and cognitive stimulation (Pollitt et al., 1993).

Eating disorders represent an area of nutrition that has received increasing attention in recent years (Bruch, 2001; Fairburn & Brownell, 2002; Polivy & Herman, 2002). With one such disorder, **anorexia nervosa,** the individual, most often a young female, voluntarily engages in severe dietary restriction to maintain a body physique that is extremely thin. Adolescent anorexics often have a distorted concept of nourishment and body image. The damaging effects of this self-starvation include muscle wasting, dry skin and hair, constipation, dehydration, and sleep disturbance. Sometimes growth and development are impaired, menstruation ceases, and breast development is permanently affected. Between 5 and 8% of individuals with anorexia die from starvation or suicide (Herzog et al., 2000; Schmidt, 2000).

Another eating disorder is **bulimia,** which involves binging on large quantities of food and then self-induced vomiting to purge the excess calories and maintain a normal weight level. This disorder often results in damage to teeth and gums, cracked and damaged lips, and serious imbalances in body fluids. Bulimics, like anorexics, also frequently have distorted concepts of food and body image, and they often have guilt, anxiety, and depression. Although they are typically more aware that they have a

Anorexia nervosa
A severe eating disorder, usually involving excessive weight loss through self-starvation, most often found in teenage girls.

Bulimia
A disorder of food binging and sometimes purging by self-induced vomiting, typically observed in teenage girls.

Eating disorders during adolescence often result from a preoccupation with weight and from distorted concepts of body image.

problem than are anorexics, this knowledge does not easily translate into behavior; indeed, impulsivity and lack of control are characteristics of the disorder (Leon, 1991; Polivy & Herman, 2002).

Obesity, or excess fat storage, is one of the most common disorders in the United States today. Obesity is usually defined as weight 20% or more over a standard weight for height. Obesity appears to be a particular problem among African Americans and Hispanic Americans (Pastor et al., 2002). It may result from genetic predisposition, overeating, or a combination of both, and it frequently has an early onset, by 4 or 5 years of age (Eichorn, 1970, 1979). In some instances parents may inadvertently contribute to the problem by their feeding practices — for example, by frequent admonitions to "clean your plate," or by making approval or rewards contingent on eating behavior (Fisher & Birch, 2001).

Obesity has several effects on development. Obese females tend to begin puberty earlier than do nonobese females, for example, and obese males hit their growth spurt earlier than do their counterparts. Obesity has psychological consequences as well. Obese children typically have poor bodily self-esteem, a finding that is evident as early as age 5 (Davison & Birch, 2002). Many obese children feel insecure and are overprotected by their parents. They frequently experience school difficulties, neuroses, and social problems. A vicious circle may become established in which social and psychological problems induce eating, and weight gain further contributes to the problems.

Obesity
A condition of excess fat storage; often defined as weight more than 20% over a standardized, ideal weight.

Abuse and Psychological Trauma

We have focused up to now on physical aspects of the context of growth and development, but psychological trauma can also impair growth. A failure-to-thrive syndrome has been described in infants who fail to gain weight for no obvious reasons other than psychological disturbances or maltreatment and abuse by parents. Frequently, these babies gain weight readily when their care is transferred to hospital personnel (Benoit, 1993; Drotar et al., 1990).

A report on 13 children between the ages of 3 and 11 years provides an example of how psychological trauma can affect growth. These children lived in homes that were unusually stressful as a result of marital problems or alcohol abuse, and there were several cases of child abuse. The children appeared to have abnormally low pituitary gland activity, and their growth rates were substantially impaired. Shortly after they were removed from their homes, the circulation of growth hormone from the pituitary increased, and the growth of most of the children accelerated (Powell, Brasel, & Blizzard, 1967). Thus, there is at least some environmental control over a characteristic that was once thought to be controlled almost exclusively by genetics.

To Recap . . .

Growth is continuous through childhood but does not proceed uniformly. The rate of growth gradually slows, then experiences a spurt at adolescence, and stops soon afterward. Growth rates vary widely among children, as do the heights ultimately reached. Different parts of the body develop at different rates, following a cephalocaudal progression. Body organs also vary in rates of maturation; the brain, for example, develops very early.

Boys and girls grow fairly similarly until adolescence. Girls typically experience the adolescent growth spurt and puberty earlier than do boys. Boys add more height once their growth spurt has begun, as well as more muscle mass and shoulder width. Girls add relatively more fat and hip width. The adolescent's attitude toward these changes may reflect social and cultural factors, such as the amount of information he or she has about the changes and the body image that society holds up as ideal. On average, relatively early pubertal onset is a risk factor for girls, whereas relatively late onset is a risk factor for boys.

Many factors influence growth and maturation. Genetic processes are clearly important, but such environmental factors as nutrition, disease, abuse, and psychological trauma also come into play. Some of these environmental variables, such as better nutrition, have accelerated growth rates in many developed countries during the 20th century.

CONCLUSION

This chapter concludes a set of three chapters that concern the more biological aspects of human development. In Chapters 3 and 4, we focused on genetics and prenatal development. In the present chapter, we discussed the behaviors and physical equipment the baby brings to the world and how this basic equipment develops through infancy, childhood, and adolescence.

Until recently, psychologists have not been very open to considering the physical and biological bases of behavior. Rather, a tension existed between the more physically based and the more psychologically based disciplines, with psychologists more focused on demonstrating that social and environmental factors influence behavior. However, the mood seems to be changing. As we have seen, biological influences that we might at first imagine would act on their own are found, on closer examination, to cooperate with environmental factors to produce their ultimate effect. We have seen many examples of this interdependence—for instance, in the effects of health care on birth mortality, of the family setting on the outcome of infants at risk, of prenatal exposure to cocaine on the newborn's state organization and rhythms, of practice on motor development, and of psychological trauma on growth. For this reason, many of the tensions that once existed between psychologists and biologists have largely disappeared, and the search is on to understand how biological factors and experience collaborate to influence human development. We will mention numerous instances of such collaboration as we move through the remaining topics in the book.

FOR THOUGHT AND DISCUSSION

1. Birthing practices in Western countries have changed in interesting ways. Until the mid-20th century, births generally took place at home with family members. Then there was a dramatic shift to delivering in hospitals, with impersonal medical procedures replacing traditional ones. Now the pendulum has swung back toward more natural methods in which the family once again is included. *What might be some advantages of this recent trend? What about disadvantages? Can you think of any other aspects of child-rearing that have displayed this same return to more traditional methods? Can you predict some that might do so?*

2. We pointed out in the text a possible evolutionary benefit of the palmar reflex: Newborns capable of supporting their own weight with their grip would have been able to cling tightly to the fur of their mothers as the mothers moved around. *What might the benefits of some of the other reflexes have been for our ancient ancestors? Can you think of any other explanations for these inborn reflexes?*

3. It is clear that the newborn is much more sophisticated and complex than was once believed. *Why do you think even trained professionals so grossly underestimated babies' abilities? Assume we continue to do so today. What other remarkable abilities might we someday discover that babies possess? Is there any danger of overestimating babies' abilities?*

4. We said that the development of the synapses in the brain goes on for a number of years after birth. *Why do you think humans have evolved this way, rather than with all of the connections already established? How would development be different if they were?*

VISUAL SUMMARY FOR CHAPTER 5
Physical Development: Birth, Motor Development, and Growth

Birth and the Perinatal Period
Indicators of Risk for Developmental Problems

Maternal and Family Characteristics
> A number of maternal and family factors, especially whether the mother receives prenatal care, are important in identifying babies at risk for developmental problems.

Physical Compromise of the Newborn
> Low birth weight is an important indicator of risk. Low-birth-weight babies may be preterm, or they may be small for gestational age (SGA).

Physical and Behavioral Assessment
> Newborn assessments, such as the Apgar exam and the Brazelton Neonatal Behavioral Assessment Scale, are also used to assess risk.

The Organized Newborn
Activity of Newborns

States
> The newborn's level of alertness can be categorized according to six states varying from quiet sleep to crying.

Rhythms
> The newborn's states occur in rhythmic cycles. A basic rest–activity cycle is coordinated with a longer sleep–wake cycle.

Reflexes
> Newborns possess a number of reflexes, some that last through life and others that disappear during the first year.

Congenitally Organized Behaviors
> Congenitally organized behaviors, including looking, sucking, and crying, are present in the newborn and differ from reflexes in that they are not easily attributable to a particular stimulus and are more adaptable.

Motor Development
Categories

Locomotion/Postural
> Control of trunk of the body and arms and legs for moving around.

Prehension
> Ability to use hands as tools.

Motor Development

Principles

Proximodistal ▸ Motor skills develop from center of the body to parts farther out.

Cephalocaudal ▸ Motor skills develop from head to feet.

Dynamic Systems Approach ▸ Individual motor skills develop when infants are motivated to accomplish a task and when they possess sufficient physical resources.

Stages ▸ During exploration, many different responses are tried somewhat randomly; during selection, responses are fine-tuned and coordinated.

Motor Development in Childhood

Fundamental Movement Skills ▸ Locomotor, manipulative, and stability.

Reaction Time ▸ Improves through preschool and elementary years.

The Human Brain

Three Stages in the Development of the Fetal Brain

Cell Production ▸ Most neurons are produced between 10 and 26 weeks after conception.

Cell Migration ▸ Following production, cells migrate to their proper locations, a process that is completed by 7 months gestational age.

Cell Elaboration ▸ Axons and dendrites form synapses with other cells, a process that continues for years.

Hemispheric Specialization

Left Hemisphere ▸ Prepared at birth to control language function in most people.

Right Hemisphere ▸ Prepared at birth to control spatial and mathematical functioning in most people.

Human Growth

Growth in Size, Proportion, and Composition ▸ Growth is continuous, but not uniform, throughout childhood. The rate of growth gradually slows, then spurts at adolescence and stops soon afterward. Different parts of the body, as well as body organs, develop at different rates.

Sex Differentiation and Puberty ▸ Boys and girls grow fairly similarly until puberty. Girls tend to experience the adolescence growth spurt and puberty earlier than boys. Once their growth spurt has begun, boys add more height, muscle mass, and shoulder width; girls add relatively more fat and hip width.

Factors Affecting Growth ▸ Human growth is influenced not only by heredity but also by environmental factors, such as nutrition, exercise, poverty, disease, and even abuse and psychological trauma.

6

Sensory and Perceptual Development

n 1991, noted neurologist Oliver Sachs received a phone call offering him a rare opportunity for scientific study. A 50-year-old man, blind since early childhood, had just undergone an operation that restored his sight. Sachs was invited to visit the man, Virgil, and his family and to help assess Virgil's progress in the weeks following the recovery of his vision.

As Sachs noted, Virgil's case history presented a real-life instance of a hypothetical situation posed more than 300 years earlier by a philosopher named Molyneux. Molyneux directed this question to the famous empiricist philosopher John Locke: A man is born blind, but is suddenly able to see as an adult. The man had learned to distinguish a sphere and a cube by touch when he was blind. Will he be able to recognize which is which by sight alone? Locke (1694/1824) answered no, arguing that experience is necessary to understand the relation between vision and touch (the empiricist, or nurture, position). Others predicted that the previously blind man would be able to identify the two objects by vision alone, because knowledge of the relations among properties of objects is inborn (the nativist, or nature, position). At issue was a central question in philosophy, which was later carried over to psychology: Are people born with innate, organized categories for perceiving the world, or must everything be experienced to be known?

Sachs's summary of his observations was published as an article in the New Yorker (Sachs, 1993). Virgil's experiences proved similar to those of other individuals who had gained or regained sight in adulthood (Gregory, 1978; Von Senden, 1960). Virgil could certainly see from the moment the bandages were removed, and he was sensitive to and interested in colors, shapes, and movements. He could make little sense, however, of what he saw—not only initially but for some time—and he was quite unable to recognize through sight objects with which he was familiar through touch. Furthermore, the attempt to cope with the world through a new perceptual mode brought conflicts and disappointments as well as gains, and over time Virgil used his vision less and less. For example, he reverted to eating as he had when blind, and he began to turn away from the mirror and close his eyes while shaving.

Cases such as Virgil's are fascinating; indeed, Virgil's story was the basis—with a fair amount of Hollywood reworking—of a movie titled *At First Sight*. Such clinical cases, however, offer only indirect and imperfect evidence with respect to the nature–nurture issues that inspired Molyneux's query. There are, after all, enormous differences between a 50-year-old man and a newborn baby, even if both are experiencing the world of vision for the first time. More direct evidence would come from studies of what the newborn perceives of his or her world. This type of evidence was unavailable in Molyneux and Locke's time, and indeed for many years after, but it is no longer unavailable today. In this chapter we discuss some exciting discoveries about perceptual development, especially about perception in infancy, that have emerged from contemporary child psychology. ■

ISSUES IN THE STUDY OF PERCEPTUAL DEVELOPMENT

Sensation
The experience resulting from the stimulation of a sense organ.

Perception
The interpretation of sensory stimulation based on experience.

Attention
The selection of particular sensory input for perceptual and cognitive processing and the exclusion of competing input.

To talk about perceptual development, we must first distinguish among three processes: sensation, perception, and attention. **Sensation** refers to the detection and discrimination of sensory information—for example, hearing and distinguishing high and low tones. **Perception** refers to the interpretation of sensations and involves recognition ("I've heard that song before") and identification ("That was thunder"). **Attention** refers to the selectivity of perception, as when a child fails to hear a parent calling because he is watching television.

Whether the focus is on sensation, perception, or attention, research on perceptual development addresses the same two general questions that underlie all research in child psychology: What are the most important changes that occur across the course of development, and how can we explain these changes? As we will see, an answer to the first question requires that we begin our examination very early in life. All of the sensory systems are operative from birth, and all achieve close to adult-level functioning by the end of infancy. It is for this reason that most of this chapter concentrates on the infant period. Infancy is, in the words of Bornstein and Arterberry (1999, p. 244), where "most of the 'action' . . . takes place."

The question of how to explain perceptual development is a particular form of one of the general issues introduced in Chapter 1: nature versus nurture. As the discussion of Molyneux and Locke illustrates, this question is an old one, for it was a central issue in philosophy centuries before psychology began to develop as a separate science. The empiricist or nurture position espoused by Locke was the forerunner of environmental/learning approaches to the study of infant perception. In such views, the child begins life with only minimal ability to take in and make sense of sensory information. The emphasis, rather, is on the role of experience in perceptual development. According to this view, a child builds perceptual impressions through associations. For example, a baby seeing a face for the first time sees no relation among the eyes, eyebrows, nose, mouth, ears, and hairline. It is only through experience that the baby comes to see all of these elements as belonging together and can eventually recognize a familiar face or distinguish one face from another.

Through experience babies also learn to connect sights with sounds, touch with vision, and so on. The sound of a human voice seems at first no more likely to accompany the sight of a face than does the sound of a horn. Only experience makes the combination of face and voice more natural than that of face and horn. So, along with Locke, learning theorists would answer Molyneux's question regarding the integration of the senses with a resounding no: The blind man must see and feel the sphere and the cube at the same time to understand the relations between the visual and tactile sensations.

As we will see, a strong version of the environmental/learning view of infant perception is not tenable. Nevertheless, modern research makes clear that experience does contribute to perceptual development, and does so from very early in life. Research on the central nervous system illustrates how experience can affect even single sensory cells—both their survival and the connections that form among them. Experience produces a kind of Darwinian survival-of-the-fittest battle among brain cells (Edelman, 1993). As we noted in Chapter 5, many of the neurons we are born with die early in life. Researchers believe that visual experience activates some cells, which survive, but that other cells are not activated, and these die or their synapses are trimmed back (Greenough & Black, 1999).

For example, each cell (neuron) in the visual area of the brain is stimulated by one type of visual element, such as vertical edges, but not by other elements, such as horizontal edges. Other brain cells respond to horizontal edges but are insensitive to vertical edges. Still other cells "like" angles, or diagonal lines, or other visual elements. Researchers believe that when a stimulus repeatedly activates combinations of such cells—as when a baby looks at a square—the connections among these cells grow stronger. Eventually, the cells fire in synchrony, and a person sees a whole square rather than a combination of lines and intersections (Hebb, 1949). The important point here is that these cells are sensitive to experience at a very early age (Antonini & Stryker, 1993).

In philosophy the empiricist position of Locke was countered by more nativist models, and the same has proved true for the learning approach within psychology. Many theorists believe (with, as we will see, a good deal of empirical support) that the biological contribution to perceptual development is considerably greater than the environmental/learning position allows (Spelke & Newport, 1998). Such theorists emphasize the natural equipment that animals and humans have evolved for gathering information from their world, equipment that is either present from the start of life or that emerges in the course of biological maturation.

A particularly influential position in this regard is the theory developed by James and Eleanor Gibson (Gibson, 1966; Gibson, 1969; Gibson & Pick, 2000). The Gibsons do not believe that perception involves combining pieces of input through experience, as in the traditional learning view. Instead, they argue that objects in the world give off physical energy that is already organized and can be perceived in its entirety. Perceptual development, they suggest, consists of a child's increasing sensitivity to the organization of this energy and to which properties of objects and people remain stable and which properties change.

In general, theorists such as the Gibsons would be likely to answer Molyneux's question with a yes, because they would assume that natural relations exist between vision and touch. For example, the Gibsonian analysis suggests that even infants should be sensitive to the synchrony of visual and auditory events, and this appears to be the case. When young babies watch people speak, they can detect when speakers' lip movements are not synchronized with the sounds that they hear (Kuhl & Meltzoff, 1988). (We discuss this research more fully later.) This ability is difficult to account for by traditional learning theories, which emphasize the need for certain sound–vision experiences. Such experiences are fairly limited for very young infants. Note that theorists generally assume that the earlier in development a perceptual skill emerges, the less likely it is that it has been acquired by experience.

Although the Gibsonian approach stresses the biological bases for perceptual development, the emphasis is not solely on nature. As the title of one of Eleanor Gibson's major works (*Principles of Perceptual Learning;* 1969) indicates, nurture plays an important role as well. With experience, infants and children become increasingly skilled at detecting the information available in sensory stimulation and thus at perceiving the world accurately. The approach is therefore definitely *interactionist*—as, indeed, are all contemporary approaches to the study of perceptual development.

The other two general issues introduced in Chapter 1 are also represented in research on perceptual development. Although departures from the norm (for example, visual or auditory impairments) can certainly be of great pragmatic importance, most work on perceptual development is toward the normative end of the normative-idiographic continuum. The developments of interest (for example, perception of depth, perception of size constancy) are not ones that typically show important individual differences; rather these are basic accomplishments demonstrated by virtually every

Babies' ability to perceive interesting objects, such as Mom's face, is a result of both nature and nurture.

member of the species. The focus, then, is on when and how they emerge in almost all children, not on individual differences among children.

The normative emphasis of most work on perceptual development sets the form taken by the third general issue: continuity-discontinuity. Because individual differences are seldom a focus, relatively few studies have examined the stability or predictability of individual differences over time (we will see some exceptions to this statement in Chapter 10). Instead, the challenge (still far from fully met, as we will see) has been to trace the gradual evolution of particular perceptual competencies as the child develops. How, for example—that is, through what phases and what processes—does a rudimentary form of size constancy present early in infancy evolve into the mature constancy of the older child or adult?

We will see these points illustrated frequently as we discuss major findings from the study of perceptual development. In what follows, we first examine the capacities that babies have for learning about the objects and people in their world and how these capacities develop. After we consider the perceptual modes (vision, touch, etc.) separately, we see how children coordinate information from these modes. We then discuss how the child integrates perception and attention with action in the smooth flow of behavior.

To Recap . . .

The study of perceptual development encompasses sensation (the detection of sensory information), perception (interpretation of that information), and attention (selection of what information is taken in). The question of how these processes develop is a form of the nature-nurture issue. Environmental/learning theories emphasize the role of experience. In this view, development occurs as babies learn through experience to construct increasingly complex perceptions from the separate input of the senses. Other theoretical positions, such as the model developed by the Gibsons, place considerably more emphasis on the biological bases for perceptual development. Learning through experience remains important in this approach, however—an interactionist stand that characterizes all contemporary theories of perceptual development.

Most research on perceptual development has a normative emphasis, in that the focus is on basic developments shown by virtually all children. How early forms of perceptual competence evolve into mature forms—a version of the continuity-discontinuity issue—is one of the challenging issues for the field.

TOUCH AND PAIN, SMELL AND TASTE, MOTION AND BALANCE

Now we turn to an examination of what young babies actually perceive. We have much less information about the sensory modes of touch, smell, taste, and body balance and motion than about hearing or vision. Nevertheless, these sensory capacities are vitally important to the survival of young organisms. In most animals, these capacities develop earlier than hearing and vision, so we consider them first.

Touch and Pain

Anyone who wonders whether the newborn baby senses touch or experiences pain should watch the baby's reaction to a heel prick for a blood sample or to circumcision (Hadjistavropoulos et al., 1994). The angry cry that follows the prick of the needle is a clear sign that the baby can feel pain, as are the physiological changes—for example, changes in blood cortisol level—that follow a medical procedure such as circumcision (Gunnar et al., 1985). Furthermore, the effects of early exposure to pain are not necessarily short-lived. Newborns who receive repeated needle pricks as part of a screening test for diabetes react more strongly to subsequent blood tests than do other newborns (Taddio et al., 2002). Male babies who are circumcised without anesthesia are more sensitve during vaccinations 4 to 6 months later (Taddio et al., 1997).

Touch plays an important role in early parent–child relations.

For years, standard medical practice was to perform neonatal surgical procedures without anesthesia, both because of doubts about whether newborns experience pain and because of concerns about the safety of anesthesia for the tiny neonate. Fortunately, advances in knowledge about the newborn period have spurred the search for effective forms of pain relief for this age group (Lander et al., 1997; Maxwell & Yaster, 1999).

Newborn babies also show touch reflexes such as those described in Chapter 5. In fact, the fetus displays the first sign of sensitivity to external stimulation through reactions to touch. As early as the 2nd month following conception, the fetus responds to stroking at the side of the mouth (tested in naturally aborted fetuses). Touch sensitivity increases over the first several days of life (Haith, 1986).

Touching is important for relations between children and adults. A hand placed on the newborn's chest can quiet a crying episode, and gentle stroking can soothe even premature babies (Oehler & Eckerman, 1988). For older infants, touching increases positive emotion and visual attention during interactions between infant and caregiver (Stack & Muir, 1992). It is interesting to note that parents can usually recognize their infant by touch alone within the first few days of life (Kaitz et al., 1993).

Haptic perception
The perceptual experience that results from active exploration of objects by touch.

Psychologists refer to the active, exploratory use of touch as **haptic perception.** Even neonates have some ability to acquire information about objects through touch, as shown by the fact that they habituate when the same object is placed repeatedly in their hand and dishabituate when the shape of the object is changed (Streri, Lhote, & Dutilleul, 2000). With age, infants assume an increasingly active role in acquiring information through touch, and they become increasingly skilled in doing so. By the end of the first year of life, infants can recognize a familiar object by exploration with the hand alone (Rose, Gottfried, & Bridger, 1981). Haptic perception continues to improve throughout the childhood years (Morrongiello et al., 1994b).

Smell and Taste

When can babies smell odors? How might we be able to tell? Researchers have examined this question by observing whether babies, when presented with a smell, will make a face, turn their heads, or do nothing at all. Even newborns turn their heads away from a cotton swab that smells bad (Rieser, Yonas, & Wikner, 1976). Babies produce positive facial expressions in response to banana, strawberry, and vanilla smells and negative expressions in response to smells of rotten eggs and fish (Crook, 1979; Steiner, 1979).

Thus, the newborn's sense of smell is keen, and it improves over the first few days of life (Lipsitt, Engen, & Kaye, 1963).

The infant uses this ability as early as the first week of life to distinguish the mother's smell. Three-day-old infants orient more toward a pad moistened with the mother's amniotic fluid than to a pad moistened with the fluid of another woman (Marlier, Schaal, & Soussingham, 1998). Six-day-olds turn more frequently toward the mother's breast pad than toward the pad of another woman (MacFarlane, 1975). Parents make use of olfactory cues as well. As with the sense of touch, parents can recognize their infant from smell alone within the first few days of life (Porter, Balogh, & Makin, 1988).

Babies are also sensitive to taste at birth. As the fluid that a baby sucks is sweetened, the baby sucks harder, consumes more, and tends to quiet faster from crying episodes (Blass & Smith, 1992; Smith et al., 1992). Even neonates who are born preterm prefer a sweetened solution, a finding that demonstrates that the relevant taste receptors are functioning before the normal term for birth (Smith & Blass, 1996).

As illustrated in Figure 6.1, newborn babies can distinguish among different tastes. At 2 hours of age, babies make different facial expressions when they taste sweet and nonsweet solutions, and they also differentiate sour, bitter, and salty tastes (Rosenstein & Oster, 1988). At around 4 months of age, they begin to prefer salty tastes, which they found aversive as newborns (Beauchamp et al., 1994).

The fact that newborns reject certain fluids and grimace in response to negative odors and tastes indicates that they come into the world with likes and dislikes. Within months, it can be a challenge to find the older infant's mouth with a spoon that contains something the infant has decided he dislikes just by looking at it.

Vestibular Sensitivity

Vestibular sensitivity refers to our ability to detect gravity and the motion of our bodies, which helps us maintain body posture. In adults, disturbance of the vestibular sense causes dizziness and an inability to remain standing in the dark.

Vestibular sensitivity
The perceptual experience that results from motion of the body and the pull of gravity.

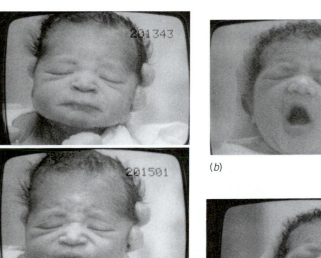

(a)

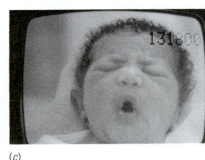

(b)

(c)

Figure 6.1

A newborn tasting (a) a sweet solution, (b) a bitter solution, and (c) a sour solution. From "Differential Facial Responses to Four Basic Tastes in Newborns" by D. Rosenstein and H. Oster, 1988, *Child Development, 59,* 1561–1563. Copyright © 1988 by the Society for Research in Child Development, Inc. Reprinted by permission.

Figure 6.2

Apparatus for testing infants' response to a conflict between visual and vestibular cues. When the wall moves toward the child, the visual cues suggest that the child is swaying forward, and the child compensates by leaning back. From "Infants' Sensitivity to Optical Flow for Controlling Posture" by B. I. Berten-thal and D. L. Bai, 1989, *Developmental Psychology, 25,* 939. Copyright © 1989 by the American Psychological Association. Reprinted by permission.

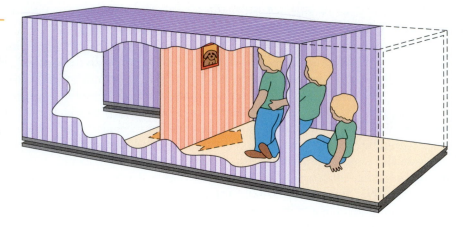

Newborns are sensitive to vestibular stimulation along all three axes of motion—front to back, up and down, and side to side (Reisman, 1987). The soothing properties of rocking and jiggling for crying babies clearly demonstrate this sensitivity. Postural adjustments can also affect a baby's alertness. For instance, babies are often more alert when in a vertical than when in a horizontal position (Korner & Thoman, 1970).

Several investigators have examined the relation between vestibular and visual perception in providing the infant with a sense of self-motion. Usually, visual cues and vestibular cues are consistent in telling us whether we are moving or stationary. However, sometimes conflict between these cues produces confusing effects. For example, if you are seated in a stopped train next to another stopped train, and then the other train begins to move forward, your train may seem to you to move backward. Your vision tells you one thing, while your vestibular sense tells you another. Vision wins out for a moment, but your stomach may take a turn when you realize what has happened. Pilots are taught to trust their instruments rather than their impressions, as both their sight and their vestibular sense may mislead them.

Figure 6.2 shows an apparatus used to test the relation between visual and vestibular cues in infancy. Infants who have begun to walk (typically about a year to a year and a half old) are placed in a room with walls that can move as the floor remains stationary. When the front and side walls move, visual cues tell the infant that she is moving forward, but vestibular cues indicate she is not moving at all. Apparently, the visual cues win out, as babies often fall backward in this situation (Lee & Aronson, 1974). A similar phenomenon occurs in babies who are old enough only to sit up (Bertenthal & Bai, 1989). Indeed, even newborns show some adjustment of their heads in response to visual cues that signal movement (Bertenthal & Clifton, 1998). Thus, some ability to use visual information to judge bodily position seems to be present very early in life.

 To Recap . . .

Touch and pain, smell and taste, and body balance and motion (vestibular sensitivity) are well developed at birth. Even the fetus is sensitive to touch, and touch sensitivity increases over the first days of life. Touch is a vital component of several adaptive reflexes and has important social effects as well. Babies use touch to explore the environment.

Newborns are sensitive to both smell and taste. They prefer pleasant odors to unpleasant ones and can distinguish their mother's body smells from those of other women. Similarly, babies suck harder to get sweeter fluid and consume more of it. As early as 2 hours after birth, babies can distinguish not only sweet but also sour, bitter, and salty tastes.

Newborns are also sensitive to vestibular stimulation, responding to both position and movement. Even older babies, however, tend to rely on vision when vestibular and vision cues contradict each other.

HEARING

Hearing is one of our most important senses, because a great deal of information about the world comes to us from sound alone. Cars approaching from behind, a ringing phone, music from a stereo, and, most important, human speech—all are perceived through the sense of hearing.

How do we know that a newborn baby can hear? As with smell and taste, we can exploit babies' naturally occurring responses to changes in stimulation. The baby may tighten his eyelids, for example, in response to a sound, or turn his head and eyes toward the source of the sound, or perhaps become quiet. Changes in the baby's heart rate and breathing also occur in response to sounds (Aslin, Pisoni, & Jusczyk, 1983).

Imagine that we are interested not just in whether babies can detect sounds but in their ability to discriminate among different sounds. Here the *habituation–dishabituation* procedure described in Chapter 1 can be especially informative. We might first present a particular sound (sound A) repeatedly until the baby habituates to it—that is, no longer shows much (if any) response. Then we present sound B. If the baby dishabituates in response to this change in stimulus, then we have good evidence that she can hear a difference between A and B.

The habituation technique is a general methodology that can be applied to any of the sensory modes. It provided the basis for several of the conclusions about touch and smell summarized in the preceding section. It also, as we will see, has been important in the study of vision.

Prenatal Hearing

Even the fetus can hear. Electrical recordings of brain responses demonstrate sound reception in fetuses as early as the 25th week after conception, about 3.5 months before full-term birth (Lecanuet, 1998; Parmelee & Sigman, 1983). These findings indicate that fetuses receive sound impulses. But how do they respond to sound?

Two investigators used ultrasound imaging to answer this question. (Ultrasound techniques, as mentioned in Chapter 4, create a picture of the fetus.) The images showed that although fetuses did not respond to auditory stimuli before 24 weeks after conception, after 28 weeks virtually all fetuses clamped their eyelids in response to sound. All the fetuses who did not respond (1 to 2%) were born with hearing deficits or serious impairments (Birnholz & Benacerraf, 1983).

But, we might ask, how good is the sound quality available to the fetus? One curious mother decided to answer this question by swallowing a microphone (she "drank the microphone," as she described it) and recording her own voice and other sounds. Although the stomach recording was muffled, various sounds could be discerned (Fukahara, Shimura, & Yamanouchi, 1988). As we might expect, the mother's speech was more audible than were sounds originating from outside, a finding that has emerged in other studies as well (Richards et al., 1992).

If some aspects of maternal speech are perceptible in the womb, might babies be affected by what they hear prenatally? A fascinating program of research by DeCasper, Fifer, and associates (DeCasper & Fifer, 1980; DeCasper & Spence, 1986; Fifer & Moon, 1995) suggests that the answer is yes. The initial study in the series (DeCasper & Fifer, 1980) reported a surprising finding: Babies less than 4 days old could discriminate their mothers' voices from strangers' voices (discrimination was shown by the fact that the babies altered their sucking rhythms more readily when their own mother's voice served as a reinforcer than they did when the reinforcer was the voice of a stranger).

One possible explanation for such early discrimination and preference for the mother is that the babies had become familiar with their mothers' voices in the womb. If this explanation is correct, we would expect no early preference for the father's voice, despite the fact that babies often hear the father in the days following birth. This, in fact, is the case: 4-day-old babies show no preference for their father's voice over that of a male stranger (DeCasper & Prescott, 1984).

The case for familiarity having come from fetal experience would be strengthened further if the infant could recognize a particular event that was only experienced before birth. DeCasper and Spence (1986) asked pregnant women to read aloud one of three stories each day in the last 6 weeks of pregnancy. When tested at 3 days of age, their babies showed a preference for the familiar story over a new story, whether it was the mother's voice reading the story or that of a stranger. This finding demonstrates a clear effect of prenatal experience, and it tells us as well that the fetus can become familiar not only with the mother's voice but also with some of the specific sound patterns that the mother produces.

Other research suggests that fetuses may also pick up more general aspects of their own native languages. Newborn French babies can discriminate a woman speaking French from the same woman speaking Russian; babies of non–French-speaking mothers, however, do not make the discrimination (Mehler et al., 1988). Finally, another study from the DeCasper group (DeCasper et al., 1994) reports heart-rate change to a familiar passage in third trimester *fetuses*—and thus effects of auditory experience that are evident even prior to birth.

Research on prenatal hearing and learning is an ongoing enterprise, and most investigators are cautious in drawing conclusions. Nevertheless, it seems clear that fetuses can hear more than once believed.

Sensitivity to Sound

Newborn babies appear to be less sensitive to sound than are adults (Aslin & Hunt, 2001). An adult, for example, can easily hear a whisper at a distance of about 4.5 feet; a newborn, however, requires a stimulus closer to normal conversational level to be able to hear at that distance. Fluid in the middle ear may be part of the problem.

How well a sound can be heard depends on its pitch. Adults can hear sounds of intermediate pitch better than sounds of high or low pitch. Newborn babies hear relatively better at low frequencies, but by 6 months of age their high-frequency sensitivity is as good as that of adults (Schneider & Trehub, 1985; Werner & Bargones, 1992). Sensitivity to sound increases until around 10 years of age. Sensitivity to higher frequencies, however, peaks earlier and does not improve beyond about 4 or 5 years of age (Trehub et al., 1988).

Sensitivity measurements determine how loud a sound must be for the infant to detect it. However, we are normally exposed to sounds that are much louder than this threshold level. For a full understanding of the infant's hearing capacity, we must also know how well the infant can discriminate sounds that differ in various characteristics, such as intensity, frequency, and duration.

Discriminating Sounds

Infants are able to distinguish differences in intensity, or loudness, at an early age. For example, after a 6-month-old becomes familiar with a sound approximately as loud as an ordinary conversation at a distance of about 3 feet, a small increase in intensity produces a noticeable change in heart rate (Moffitt, 1973). Twelve-month-olds can detect even very slight shifts in intensity (Trehub & Schneider, 1983).

How well do infants distinguish among sound frequencies? The fact that infants respond differently to sounds of different frequencies provides one kind of evidence of their ability to discriminate. Low-frequency tones are generally effective in quieting babies, whereas higher tones tend to distress them (Eisenberg, 1976). By 5 months of age, infants are almost as good as adults at distinguishing among high-frequency tones that vary only slightly (Werner & Bargones, 1992).

Babies are better at discriminating complex sounds than we might suspect. Infants as young as 4 months are sensitive to various properties of music, such as contour and rhythm, and they (like most adults) prefer consonant musical inputs to dissonant ones (Trainor & Heinmiller, 1998; Zentner & Kagan, 1998). By the middle of the first year babies can pick out melodies, even when the key changes (Trehub & Schellenberg, 1995). This means that they can perceive the relations among the frequencies, even when the frequencies themselves change because of the key change. Babies can also tell the difference between a lullaby and an adult-directed song, even when the song and lullaby are from a foreign culture (Trehub & Henderson, 1994). Indeed, from birth infants show a preference for lullaby-type input over adult songs (Masataka, 1999).

Babies are especially sensitive to the characteristics of sound that will be important for language perception. Young infants prefer to listen to sounds that fall within the frequency range of the human voice, and they can distinguish different speech sounds as early as 1 month of age (Aslin, Jusczyk, & Pisoni, 1998). We consider the issue of perception of speech more fully in Chapter 11.

Sound Localization

An important property of sounds is the direction from which they come. Even newborns distinguish very general sound location (Morrongiello et al., 1994a). They turn their eyes and heads toward a sound source to the left or right if the sound is relatively continuous. In one experiment, carried out in the delivery room by a scientist-parent, some evidence of ability to localize sounds was evident within 10 minutes of birth (Wertheimer, 1961)!

Research indicates that the localization response disappears around the 2nd month of life and reappears in the 3rd or 4th month in a more vigorous form. When the response reemerges, it is faster and more skilled, suggesting that a different brain center has taken control of this ability (Muir & Clifton, 1985). Localization is one of several behavioral systems that show such a U-shaped pattern of development in early infancy (Bever, 1982).

Over the first year and a half of life, babies make increasingly fine distinctions of auditory space (Ashmead et al., 1991; Morrongiello, 1988). To accomplish this feat, they must solve an interesting and very general problem of growing organisms, one of appropriate *recalibration,* or readjustment. The problem is that accurate sound localization depends in large part on the detection of the time difference between when sound arrives at the two ears. For example, a sound on the right produces energy that reaches the right ear before it reaches the left ear. With age, the head grows larger, so that the distance between the two ears increases. Therefore, a sound that comes from the same off-center location produces a greater time difference in an older child than in a younger child.

Because even the newborn displays some accuracy in locating sounds, the baby must perform a recalibration to accommodate growth at an older age, continually adjusting the relation between sound cues and what these cues mean for the location of the sound-producing object (Clifton et al., 1988; Morrongiello et al., 1994a). The need for readjustment presents a general problem for the baby in many action systems—eye movements, head movements, reaching, and walking, to name a few. And researchers still do not know how it happens.

To Recap . . .

The fetus can hear at least as early as several months prior to birth. Some prenatal auditory experiences, especially experience of the mother's voice, have effects that persist into infancy.

Although newborns appear to be less sensitive to sound than are adults, within the first year the infant's hearing at high frequencies is as good as the adult's. The infant can discriminate sounds on the basis of intensity, frequency, and duration. Especially important are sound discriminations that are central to the perception of speech. The baby's ability to localize sounds is present at birth and then fades somewhat, to reappear at 4 months in a more efficient form. This ability becomes more precise over the first 18 months of life.

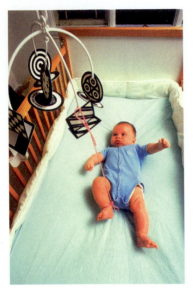

Infants find patterned stimuli interesting from early in life.

Visual acuity
The clarity with which visual images can be perceived.

Visual accommodation
The automatic adjustment of the lens of the eye to produce a focused image of an object on the light-sensitive tissue at the back of the eye.

VISION

Take a moment to look around and appreciate the richness and complexity of your visual environment. You can see variations in brightness and color and texture, and you can tell which surfaces are hard and which are soft. You can see dozens of objects and many items of function—light switches that can be flicked, containers that hold objects, shelves that support books, chairs that support people. Vision provides an immense amount of information about the world, and you know how to interpret this information easily.

Now, consider what this world must look like to a newborn baby. First, can the newborn see? If so, how well? When the baby can see well enough to make out objects, how does he or she know that one object is in front of another, that an object can serve as a container, or even that the container—say, a cup—is separate from the table on which it rests? How does the baby know that a tree seen through a window is outside the room rather than part of the glass? From this small sample of questions, you can see how much the baby must come to understand. In the past 3 decades, we have discovered a great deal about how this understanding develops. Here, we first consider two basic questions: How good is the newborn baby's vision, and how quickly does it improve?

Sensory Capabilities

We have known for some time that newborn babies can see something. New parents notice their baby often turns her head toward a source of light, such as a window. In the first days of life, awake babies also distinguish light intensity. They open their eyes widely in darkness and close them in bright light; typically, they choose to look at moderate light levels (Haith, 1980). Babies find visual movement especially attractive even at birth, and they become increasingly sensitive to movement over the first several months of life (Aslin & Shea, 1990; Nelson & Horowitz, 1987).

Visual Acuity   The newborn baby will look more at patterned than at unpatterned displays. For example, if we show a baby a picture of a black-and-white bull's-eye and a gray card that are equally bright, the baby will look more at the pattern than at the plain card (Fantz, 1961). We can use this pattern-looking tendency to measure the baby's **visual acuity,** or how sharply he can see things. (Box 6.1 describes how the technique for doing such research was developed.)

To measure visual acuity, we show the baby a gray picture next to a second picture that contains vertical, black-and-white stripes. Ordinarily, the baby looks longer at the striped picture. Over repeated presentations, we make the stripes more narrow and compressed, which makes them more difficult to distinguish from the gray picture. Eventually, the baby no longer looks more at the striped pattern, presumably because he can no longer tell the difference between the two pictures.

Using this approach, researchers have estimated that the newborn's acuity is about 20/400 to 20/800 (meaning that a normal-vision adult sees at 400 to 800 feet what the newborn sees at 20 feet), compared with normal adult acuity of 20/20 (Kellman & Banks, 1998; Maurer & Lewis, 2001). By 3 months of age, acuity improves to around 20/100; by 12 months, it approximates that of the adult (Hainline, 1998). Figure 6.4 shows how a picture of a face might look to infants at 1, 2, and 3 months of age from a distance of about 6 inches.

Why do younger infants have poorer vision? Early studies of infants younger than 1 month of age suggested that the lens of the eye did not vary its focus with distance, a process called **visual accommodation** (Haynes, White, & Held, 1965). Rather, the lens seemed to be fixed for optimal focus at a distance of about 7 to 8 inches. Because this is the typical distance of the mother's face from the baby's eyes during feeding, ethologists constructed a nice story about why evolution might use such a trick to ensure that the baby would be attracted to the mother's face.

What Do Babies See? The Work of Robert Fantz

A key problem in understanding perceptual development is that we cannot easily communicate with infants. People have wondered since the beginning of time what the newborn baby can see and when the baby can tell one color or face or shape from another.

Through much of the modern era of psychology, researchers have approached these questions somewhat indirectly. For example, an investigator might measure the heart rate or respiration of a baby looking at a picture of a face and then see whether changes occur when the baby looks at a picture of the facial features (mouth, eyes, nose) scrambled up in a different pattern; if so, the investigator might conclude that there is something special about faces for the infant. Other indirect approaches use learning procedures. If a baby can learn to turn her head right when a red stimulus appears and left for a blue stimulus, presumably the baby can discriminate between red and blue.

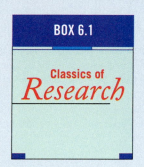

BOX 6.1

Classics of
Research

Robert Fantz made a discovery that profoundly affected research on infant vision (Fantz, 1961). Fantz observed that babies look at different things for different periods of time. He suggested simply measuring the amount of time babies looked at one display rather than another to determine what babies could see and discriminate in the displays. This direct approach would eliminate the need to use cumbersome electrodes to measure physiological changes or the tedium of training and learning procedures.

The procedure for measuring where babies look is straightforward. The researcher shows the baby two displays, side by side. With properly adjusted lighting, the researcher can see the reflection of these displays on the surface of the baby's eye, much as you can see the reflection of a window in daylight in the eyes of a person to whom you are talking. When the baby looks at one of the displays, that display is reflected from the surface of the eye over the black pupil opening. The researcher, using two stopwatches, can record how long the baby looks at each display. Figure 6.3 shows an early version of the Fantz apparatus.

This approach is labeled the **preference method,** because what we are interested in is whether the infant will show a preference—that is, look longer at one stimulus than

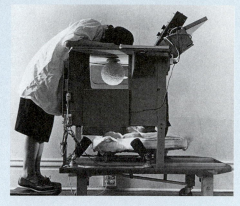

Figure 6.3

Apparatus used in the Fantz preference method to study infants' visual abilities. From "The Origin of Form Perception" by R. L. Fantz, 1961, *Scientific American, 204,* 66. Copyright © by Scientific American, Inc. Reprinted by permission. Photograph by David Linton.

at the other. If the infant does show a preference, we conclude that she can discriminate between the stimuli.

Researchers have used this powerful technique to study a host of issues concerning infant vision, including visual acuity, color perception, form perception, face recognition, and picture perception. Because an infant's interest in a particular visual display declines over time and recovers for novel stimuli, investigators have also been able to use this technique to study how an infant's memory develops and how various types of developmental problems (such as Down syndrome and prematurity) affect perceptual processing and memory (Bornstein & Sigman, 1986).

A remarkable fact about the Fantz discovery is how obvious it seems after the fact. Many great contributors to science have been able to see the obvious among the complex and to find significance in what others have overlooked.

Preference method

A research method for the study of visual ability in infancy. Two visual stimuli are presented simultaneously, and the amount of time the infant looks at each is measured.

Evolutionary explanations are often very seductive, but they can also be wrong, as this one was. In fact, the baby's lens is not fixed, but it does not vary with distance as the adult's does. At birth, the brain circuits that are responsible for accommodation are simply not sufficiently mature to pick up minor differences in the precision of focus. Thus, variations for focal distance in the early weeks of life are relatively useless. It appears to be only happenstance that the lens has a relatively fixed focus at around 7 to 8 inches. Accommodation improves between 1 and 3 months of age and is almost adultlike by 6 months of age (Hainline & Abramov, 1992).

Figure 6.4

Visual acuity improves dramatically during the first months of life, as illustrated in computer estimations of what a picture of a face looks like to 1-, 2-, and 3-month-olds at a distance of about 6 inches. All estimations were taken from the original, which illustrates adult acuity (seen on the far right). From "The Recognition of Facial Expressions in the First Two Years of Life: Mechanisms of Development" by Charles A. Nelson, *Child Development, 58,* Figure 1, 892. Copyright © 1987 by the Society for Research in Child Development, Inc. Reprinted by permission. These photos were made available by Martin Banks and Arthur Ginsburg.

Peripheral vision

The perception of visual input outside the area on which the individual is fixating.

Peripheral Vision   The part of the eye that provides acute vision covers a very small portion of the visual field—a circular area about the size of a quarter at arm's length. Yet our visual world seems continuous and complete; we do not see it as if we were looking through a long, quarter-size tube. This is because our **peripheral vision,** which is less detailed, covers much more of the visual field. The peripheral vision of the 1-month-old is much smaller than that of the adult, but significant improvement occurs by 3 months of age (Braddick & Atkinson, 1988).

Color Vision   When can babies see color? The answer is: In a limited way, from birth, but much better by 4 months.

Babies tend to look at colored objects, and that tendency has helped psychologists answer this question. Given optimal circumstances, newborns can make some color discriminations—red from green, for example, and both red and green from white (Adams, 1989; Adams & Courage, 1998). In most respects, however, early color perception is limited. Aspects of the visual system that mediate color perception are not mature at birth, and newborns are unable to see many of the contrasts that are available to adults (Adams, 1995). Like many forms of perception, however, color perception improves rapidly in the early months, and by 4 months infants' ability to perceive color appears equivalent to that of an adult (Teller & Bornstein, 1987).

Visual Pattern and Contrast

For years, many people believed that newborn babies were blind or at best capable merely of reflexively looking at a source of light. As suggested in the discussion of visual acuity, Robert Fantz proved them wrong. Even newborn babies looked longer at a patterned display than at a nonpatterned display, as shown in Figure 6.5.

Investigators later developed the techniques shown in Figure 6.6 to measure what parts of displays newborns look at. They discovered that newborns look primarily at high-contrast edges—for example, where black and white meet—and move their eyes back and forth over those contrast edges (Haith, 1980, 1991).

As babies get older, they prefer patterns that are more densely packed. Whereas 3-week-olds look longer at a 6-by-6 checkerboard than at a 12-by-12 or a 24-by-24 checkerboard, 6-week-olds are more likely to look longest at the intermediately complex display and 3-month-olds at the most complex display (Karmel & Maisel, 1975).

An early theory held that babies prefer increasing complexity (that is, more checks) as they get older and become more complex themselves. However, several investigators have pointed out that as the number of checks increases, so does the amount of

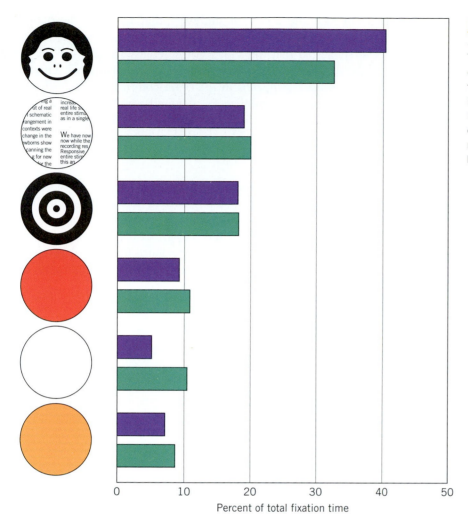

Figure 6.5

Stimuli that Robert Fantz showed to infants. The length of the purple bars indicates the average time that 2- to 3-month-olds looked at the stimulus, and the length of the green bars indicates looking time for 3- to 6-month-olds. From R. Fantz, 1961, "The origin of form perception," *Scientific American, 204,* 72. Copyright © 1961 by Scientific American. Reprinted by permission.

Percent of total fixation time

black–white edge in the display. Most investigators now believe that babies are attracted to the displays that offer the most edge contrasts that they can see at a particular age (Banks & Ginsburg, 1985). Why? Perhaps these findings suggest what babies are trying to accomplish with their visual behavior.

When babies move their eyes over edges, they activate cells of the visual areas of the brain. The strongest brain activity occurs when the baby adjusts the eye so that

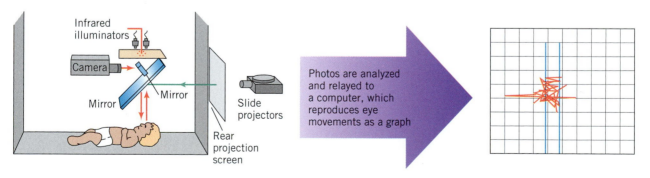

Figure 6.6

Studying how babies look at stimuli. A camera records the baby's eye movements as he looks at a reflected image. Pictures of the eye are then analyzed. Measurements of the positions of the center of the pupil and the reflected infrared light spots identify where the baby's eye fixated when the picture was taken. This information is relayed to a computer that reconstructs the baby's eye movements in graphic form. Shown is a reconstruction of a newborn's fixations on a vertical bar.

images of the edges fall near the center of the eye—that is, when the baby looks straight at the edges. Also, the more detail the baby can see, the stronger the activation. Haith (1980) has suggested that the baby's visual activity in early infancy reflects a biological "agenda" for the baby to keep brain-cell firing at a high level. This agenda makes sense because, as we have seen, cells in the brain compete to establish connections to other cells. Activity tends to stabilize the required connections, while inactive pathways deteriorate (Greenough & Black, 1999). Fortunately, this agenda brings the baby to areas of the visual display that are also psychologically meaningful. Edges provide information about the boundaries of objects, their relation in depth, and where they can be grasped.

Thus, the baby appears to be "programmed" to engage in visual activity that is very adaptive. This activity produces the sensory input needed to maintain and tune the neural apparatus and also focuses the baby's attention on the most informative parts of the visual world. Once again, we can see that the young infant is anything but passive. Even the newborn possesses tools to get necessary experience for normal development. And we can see again the interplay of nature and nurture as the potential routes for development provided by biology are shaped by experience.

Visual Relations

The agenda that biology sets for the newborn makes sense initially, but growing babies must move beyond simply exciting their own brains and begin to appreciate the organization among parts of the visual world. Mother's face, for example, needs to be seen as a whole, meaningful object rather than simply as eyebrows, eyes, ears, a nose, and so on.

Several lines of evidence suggest that although newborns are sensitive to very simple relations among stimuli, babies really begin to "put things together" between 1 and 3 months of age (Cohen, 1998; Haith, 1990). One example of the kind of research from which this conclusion is drawn is pictured in Figure 6.7. Infants were shown an arrangement of bars that formed a circular or square pattern. In some patterns, one bar was misaligned. To an adult, the one misaligned bar seems strange, because the adult sees all the other bars as going together. The misalignment had no effect on the visual fixations of 1-month-olds, but 3-month-olds looked longer around the displaced bar than around the properly aligned ones (Van Giffen & Haith, 1984). Thus, between 1 and 3 months of age, babies begin to see the organization in visual displays rather than only the details.

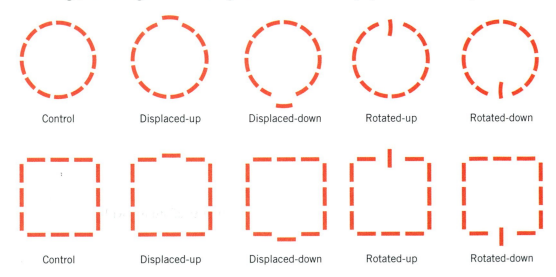

| Control | Displaced-up | Displaced-down | Rotated-up | Rotated-down |

| Control | Displaced-up | Displaced-down | Rotated-up | Rotated-down |

Figure 6.7

Stimuli used in the study by Van Giffen and Haith. Babies were shown the control stimulus three times, in alternation with one of the experimental figures. From "Infant Visual Response to Gestalt Geometric Forms" by K. Van Giffen and M. M. Haith, 1984, *Infant Behavior and Development, 7,* Figure 1, 338. Copyright © 1984 by Ablex Publishing Corp. Reprinted by permission.

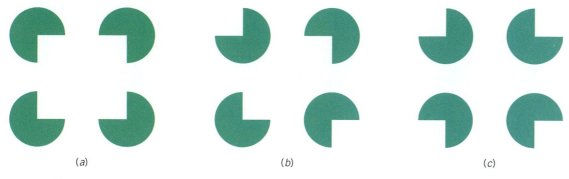

Figure 6.8

Stimuli used in studies by Bertenthal (all three stimuli) and Shapiro (*a* and *b* only). From "Development of Visual Organization: The Perception of Subjective Contours" by B. I. Bertenthal, J. J. Campos, and M. M. Haith, 1980, *Child Development, 51*, Figure 1, 1073. Copyright © 1980 by the Society for Research in Child Development, Inc. Reprinted by permission.

Of course, babies do not appreciate all possible visual relations by 3 months of age. As you can demonstrate to yourself by walking into a modern art gallery, the perception of organization takes time and effort and knowledge. Consider the display shown in Figure 6.8*a*. Adults report perceiving a square that overlays full circles at each of the corners in this display. They also report faint edges that connect the corners of the square, even though no such edges exist. Adults, of course, have considerable knowledge about such things as squares and how a square might block the view of circles behind it.

Babies looked at the arrangement in Figure 6.8*b* (the same elements, with some rotated to destroy the illusion) until their looking habituated. They then were tested for dishabituation with either the illusion stimulus in Figure 6.8*a* or the second nonillusion stimulus shown in Figure 6.8*c*. Both test stimuli involved a change in two corner elements, and hence we might expect them to be equally easy to discriminate. Five-month-old infants did not consistently detect either of these changes; however, 7-month-olds were able to detect the change when it involved the illusion in Figure 6.8*a*, indicating that they were able to group its elements perceptually in a way that the younger infants were not yet able to do (Bertenthal, Campos, & Haith, 1980).

This study and others like it demonstrate an important point: The perception of visual organization, like most developmental phenomena, is not something that happens all at once for all displays. The ability to appreciate visual organization begins between 1 and 3 months of age, but this ability continues to improve and is affected by both knowledge and the cues the environment provides (Condry, Smith, & Spelke, 2001; Kavsek, 2002; Needham, 2001).

Face Perception

Babies show an interest in faces or facelike stimuli from birth. As with perception of patterned stimuli in general, however, it has proved difficult to determine whether the newborn and young infant is responding to the face per se or simply to the interesting parts that make up the face. As Figure 6.9 shows, young infants' processing of faces is limited—they tend to look near the high-contrast borders of the face, and they pay relatively little attention to interior detail. In addition, a number of studies with infants in the first 2 or 3 months of life have failed to find a preference for faces over comparable nonface stimuli—that is, stimuli that are matched on dimensions such as contrast and brightness and curvature (Maurer, 1985).

Despite these cautions, recent evidence suggests that even newborns may be responsive to faces under some conditions. Figure 6.10 shows a set of stimuli used in this research. The stimuli were presented not statically but in motion across the infant's visual field, and the measure was of whether the babies moved their eyes or head to track the stimuli. The question was whether the facelike pattern would prove more interesting

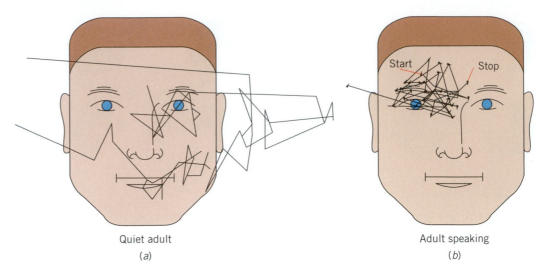

Quiet adult
(a)

Adult speaking
(b)

Figure 6.9

An apparatus similar to that shown in Figure 6.6 recorded a baby's fixations on a face. A computer reconstructed the baby's fixations on a face when (a) the adult was quiet and (b) the adult talked. A rotating arrow (b) shows the sequence of fixations and where the baby began and ended looking.

than the other targets. The answer was yes: Newborn babies, including some just a few minutes old, tracked the face more than they did the other stimuli (see Figure 6.10) (Johnson et al., 1991).

Since the Johnson et al. research, there have been several other demonstrations that newborn babies respond differentially to faces. These demonstrations include studies using the Fantz preference method, and thus measuring attention to static faces rather than tracking of moving faces (Cassia, Simion, & Umilta, 2001; Mondloch et al., 1999). There is also increasing evidence that it is really faceness and not other aspects of the stimulation that attract newborn attention (de Haan, 2001). On the other hand, it is important to note that response to faces in the early weeks of life, even if genuine, is fragile and limited in comparison to what it will eventually be. Indeed, the evidence suggests that different brain centers may underlie early and later response to faces (Johnson & de Haan, 2001).

By about 3 months of age, the preference for faces over comparable nonface stimuli is clearly established (Dannemiller & Stephens, 1988). By this age most babies also show a preference for a familiar face (typically mother's) over an unfamiliar one (Barrera

Figure 6.10

Stimuli and results from the Johnson et al. study of newborns' tendency to track moving objects. The babies moved their eyes and heads more in response to the face than in the response to the other two stimuli. From "Newborns' Preferential Tracking of Facelike Stimuli and Its Subsequent Decline" by M. H. Johnson, S. Ddziurawiec, H. Ellis, and J. Morton, 1991, *Cognition, 40,* 6. Copyright © 1991 by Elsevier Science Publishers. Reprinted by permission.

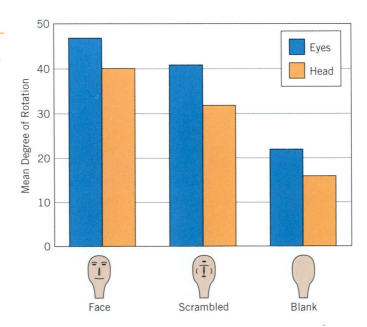

& Maurer, 1981). Interestingly, babies also show a preference for relatively attractive faces (as determined by adult ratings) over relatively unattractive ones (Langlois et al., 1987); this preference, in fact, is evident even in the newborn period (Slater et al., 1998). One possible explanation for this finding is that attractive faces are really a kind of average or composite of faces in general, a melding together and evening out of the range of human features. As such, they fit babies' developing image of the face better than do examples that deviate from the average, and for this reason they elicit more attention (Rubenstein, Kalakanis, & Langlois, 1999).

Several further developments in face perception are evident by the second half of the first year. Infants become capable of recognizing a face as the same despite changes in expression or orientation (Cohen & Strauss, 1979). They show an ability to classify faces on the basis of sex; for example, they habituate if shown a series of male faces but dishabituate if a female face appears (Fagan, 1976). They can even differentiate their own face from those of others and appear to recognize it as a familiar stimulus, as shown by the fact that they look more at the faces of other infants than at their own (although only when the faces are in motion; Legerstee, Anderson, & Schaffer, 1998). In addition, by 6 months of age infants, like older children and adults, show different forms of brain activity when processing faces than when responding to other sorts of stimuli (de Haan & Nelson, 1999).

Faces are not only interesting stimuli to view; they are also sources of social information. The sensitivity of babies to emotional expressions in faces grows slowly over the first 2 years of life (de Haan & Nelson, 1998; Walker-Andrews, 1997). Even 3-month-olds, however, may look longer at faces as the intensity of the smile increases. This tendency appears to depend on experience. Babies whose mothers call attention to themselves and smile when their babies look at them are the babies who show the strongest preferences for smiling faces (Kuchuk, Vibbert, & Bornstein, 1986). We will see in Chapter 12 that by the end of the first year, babies can differentiate a number of other expressions of emotion.

As with the study of infant vision in general, research on face perception reveals some surprising early competencies coupled with definite advances across the course of infancy. In Box 6.2 we consider some recent research that adds to the early competency part of the picture.

Objects and Their Properties

The ability of babies to appreciate the relations among visual elements—for example, lines, angles, and edges—is important for their perception of the objects that populate the world. But knowledge of objects involves more than the ability to perceive how the parts fit together to make a whole. In this section we discuss some further aspects of object perception that emerge during infancy.

The Constancies
As an object moves farther away from us, its image on the eye shrinks. Yet the object continues to appear the same size, at least up to a point. For example, a child standing in front of you seems shorter than an adult standing across the street, even though the child casts a larger image on your eyes than does the adult. This phenomenon is called **size constancy.**

Objects also change apparent shape as they rotate or as we move around them. **Shape constancy** refers to the stability of our perception in the face of changes in the shape of the image on the eye. Objects in the world continually change in brightness as well. Still, a dark dress continues to look dark whether it is dimly lit in a storeroom or brightly illuminated by direct sunlight. This is the phenomenon of **brightness constancy.** Finally, **color constancy** refers to the perception of a color as the same despite changes in the hue of light (for example, the fluorescent light of a department store versus sunlight).

Visual constancies are important because they address the fundamental question of how stable the world is for the infant. After all, without such constancies, each time a baby saw an object at a different distance, or in a different orientation, or in a different light, it would appear to be a different object. Instead of seeing only one mother, the

Size constancy
The experience that the physical size of an object remains the same even though the size of its projected image on the eye varies.

Shape constancy
The experience that the physical shape of an object remains the same even though the shape of its projected image on the eye varies.

Brightness constancy
The experience that the brightness of an object remains the same even though the amount of light it reflects back to the eye changes (because of shadows or changes in the illuminating light).

Color constancy
The experience that the color of an object remains the same even though the wavelengths it reflects back to the eye change (because of changes in the color of the illuminating light).

Can Newborns Recognize Their Mothers' Faces?

One of the important tasks of infancy is to learn to recognize and to prefer the primary caregiver, who in most instances is the baby's mother. We have seen that a preference for the mother's voice or the mother's odor emerges in the first few days of life. Might a preference for the mother's face also be present this early?

There are numerous reasons to think that the answer to this question will be no. In both the auditory and the olfactory realms, babies receive stimulation from the mother during the prenatal period, and thus they have a chance to acquire some familiarity with her characteristics prior to birth. In contrast, learning of the mother's face must clearly depend on experience following birth. As we have seen, newborns and young infants typically attend to only certain aspects of the face and ignore other aspects, especially the inner detail (recall Figure 6.9). Furthermore, they do not see what they do attend to at all clearly; on the most optimistic estimate, newborn visual acuity is only about one-10th that of the 20/20 optimal adult level (recall Figure 6.4).

Given this catalog of reasons to doubt early visual recognition of the mother, you have probably guessed by now that recent research suggests that newborns *do* recognize their mothers' faces. Babies as young as 2 days old have been shown to look more at their mothers' faces than at the face of a stranger (Bushnell, Sai, & Mullin, 1989; Pascalis et al., 1995). Newborn babies also alter their sucking patterns more readily to produce a view of their mother's face than to view the face of a stranger (Walton, Bower, & Bower, 1992).

BOX 6.2

On the
Cutting
EDGE

The investigators who conducted these studies have been careful to control for other possible bases for recognition of the mother, such as auditory or olfactory cues. Thus, the response really does seem to be to the mother's face.

How could a baby with such a limited visual system and such limited visual experience recognize the mother? The study by Pascalis et al. (1995) suggests an answer. After demonstrating the preference for the mother's face, the researchers redid the experiment, but with one difference: Now the women wore scarves that covered their hair and part of their foreheads. With the scarves in place, newborns could no longer distinguish their mother from a stranger. A subsequent study demonstrated that it is not until about 5 weeks of age that infants can recognize the mother when she is wearing a scarf (Bartrip, Morton, & de Schonen, 2001).

What this research suggests is that newborn recognition of the mother is not based on attention to the inner details of her face. Newborns seem to rely instead on more peripheral information, such as hairline and shape of head. Early recognition of the mother, like the early interest in facelike stimuli, is therefore crude and limited in comparison to the face perception of the older infant. Nevertheless, the recent research on response to the mother's face, like the research on face perception in general, suggests that newborn infants are more responsive to faces than psychologists once believed. And this early responsiveness seems clearly conducive to the important task of forming emotional ties with others.

---

infant would experience a different mother every time he saw her from a different angle. Fortunately for both baby and mother, the baby's visual world, as we will see, appears to be a good deal less chaotic than this.

Let us first consider size constancy. One approach to testing size constancy in very young infants is shown in Figure 6.11 (Slater, Mattock, & Brown, 1990). The stimuli are two cubes, one twice as large as the other. The baby first receives a series of familiarization trials in which one of the cubes is presented at different distances. For example, a baby might see the small cube at a distance of 23 cm, then at 53 cm, then at 38 cm, and so forth. Because both the distance and the size of the retinal image vary from trial to trial, the only constant element is the actual size of the cube. The test trials follow the familiarization phase. Now both cubes are presented simultaneously, but at different distances, with the larger cube twice as far away as the smaller one. The question of interest is whether the baby will show a preference by looking longer at one of the two cubes.

Before we describe the findings, it is worth taking a moment to think through the logic of the experiment. Why might the baby show a preference? The retinal image cannot be the basis for a preference, because the two cubes—as Figure 6.11*b* illustrates—project the same size image. The baby has not encountered the viewing distances before; thus, there is no reason to think that distance will be important. On the other hand, one of the cubes is familiar and the other is novel, and hence we might see a preference based on relative familiarity. Note, however, that the small cube will be familiar only if the baby has been able to perceive its constant size during the familiarization

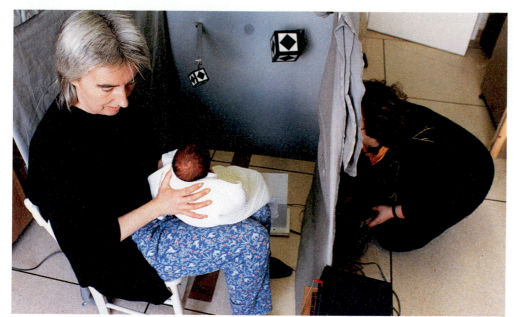

(a)

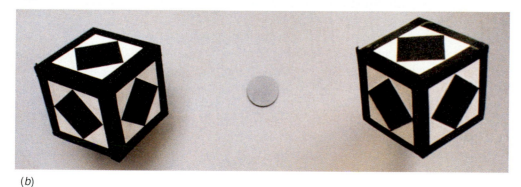

(b)

Figure 6.11

Procedure for testing size constancy in newborn babies. The top (*a*) shows the experimental arrangement, and the bottom (*b*) shows the stimuli for the critical test trial. From "Size Constancy at Birth: Newborn Infants' Responses to Retinal and Real Size" by A. Slater, A. Mattock, and E. Brown, 1990, *Journal of Experimental Child Psychology, 49,* 317, 318. Copyright © 1990 by Academic Press. Reprinted by permission.

trials. If, instead, size is perceived as changing every time distance changes, then both cubes will appear new on the test trials.

In fact, all of the newborn babies tested looked significantly longer at the larger cube. This finding tells us that they could see a difference between the two cubes, despite the equivalent retinal images. And the preference for the novel stimulus suggests that they did indeed find the small cube familiar and therefore less interesting. As noted, they could do so only if they perceived the constant size across presentations.

This study suggests, then, that some size constancy is present at birth. There is also evidence, based on a similar methodology, for some degree of shape constancy at birth (Slater & Morison, 1985). It is important to note, though, that "some constancy" is not complete constancy. Both size constancy and shape constancy are stronger and more easily demonstrated by 3 or 4 months of age than they are in the newborn. Indeed, the ability to judge the size of objects with changing distance improves up to at least 10 or 11 years of age (Day, 1987). Thus, constancy, like other perceptual accomplishments, is not an all-or-nothing affair.

To date, there have been no demonstrations that the other forms of constancy we identified—brightness constancy and color constancy—are present from birth. Brightness constancy, however, is evident as early as 7 weeks for objects that are not too small (Dannemiller, 1985), and some degree of color constancy is available by 4 months of age (Dannemiller & Hanko, 1987).

Object Continuity Our knowledge of objects extends beyond the various constancies. Because we understand principles of solidity and continuity, we see objects as continuous and whole even when our view is partially blocked. For example, when a person stands in front of a table, blocking the midsection of the table from our view, we naturally infer that the two ends of the table are connected. In a sense, we perceive a whole table. Do young infants also perceive objects as continuous and whole when they are partially blocked by other objects?

In one set of experiments, 4-month-old babies looked at a partially blocked object—for example, a long rod partly hidden by a block, as shown in the top of Figure 6.12*a*—until their interest declined. They then were shown the two stimuli at the bottom of Figure 6.12*a*: a continuous rod, paired with two rod pieces. Note that the latter stimulus is identical to what they were able to see with the block in place. Presumably, if the babies had perceived earlier that the rod was continuous, they should have looked longer at the two separated rods than at the more typical and familiar continuous rod. They did not, suggesting that they had not perceived a single whole rod behind the block (Spelke, 1985).

In a variation of this procedure, babies saw a bar move out from in front of a sphere that it had partially blocked, as illustrated in the top of Figure 6.12*b*. The movement of the bar revealed either a whole sphere or two separated sphere parts (bottom of Figure 6.12*b*). Again, the babies paid no special attention to the separated parts. The researchers tried several displays—including a face, as shown in Figure 6.12*c*—but had no success in demonstrating that infants could infer more about the objects than what they could see (Kellman & Spelke, 1983).

These findings seem amazing. Is it possible that babies see people as cut into pieces when they stand behind a table? Probably not. In all these studies, the partially hidden object was stationary, and so was the baby. In the real world, when we see one object partially blocked by another, our own movement produces more displacement of the closer object than of the "pieces" of the farther object. This is a clue that the blocked object is continuous. Furthermore, the blocked object itself may move, providing another clue. For example, infants who saw a sphere move behind a blocking rod (that is, the two parts of the sphere moved simultaneously) later looked at the separated sphere parts as though they had not seen them before. Under these conditions, infants apparently perceived the moving sphere as whole (Kellman, 1996; Spelke, 1988). Given

Figure 6.12

Some pictures used to study object perception in infants. From "Perception of Unity, Persistence, and Identity: Thoughts on Infants' Conceptions of Objects" by E. S. Spelke, 1985. In J. Mehler and R. Fox (Eds.), *Neonate Cognition: Beyond the Blooming Buzzing Confusion,* Figures 6.1, 6.2, and 6.3, pp. 91–93), Hillsdale, NJ: Erlbaum. Copyright © 1985 by Lawrence Erlbaum Associates. Reprinted by permission.

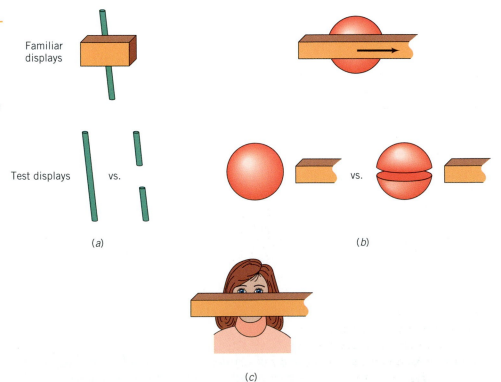

Familiar displays

Test displays

vs.

vs.

(*a*)   (*b*)

(*c*)

movement and other optimal cues (for example, use of a highly textured object), infants as young as 1 month can perceive the continuity of partially visible objects (Johnson, 1997; Johnson & Aslin, 1995; Kawabata et al., 1999). Newborns, however, cannot, which suggests that some experience may be necessary for this accomplishment (Slater et al., 1994, 1996).

Based on several experiments of the kind just described, Spelke has argued that infants in the early months of life understand object continuity, along with several other basic properties of objects. Some other properties, however (such as the effects of gravity), are not understood until the second year of life (Spelke, 1991; Spelke & Hermer, 1996; Spelke et al., 1992). We return to the question of what infants know about objects in Chapter 7.

The Spatial Layout

To this point, we have considered infants' fundamental perceptual capacities and their perception of patterns and objects. The visual world, however, consists of multiple objects—a landscape of objects and events that lie in particular spatial relations to one another (Gibson, 1988). To understand more about how babies perceive this richer world, we now consider the issues of depth and space perception.

Depth and Distance   As babies acquire the ability to move around, they also develop the capacity to get into trouble. One potential danger is falling over edges if they cannot perceive that a surface that supports them drops off. Eleanor Gibson and Richard Walk (1960) first tested infants' perception of depth by using a unique device called a **visual cliff,** shown in Figure 6.13.

The visual cliff consists of a sheet of Plexiglas on which the infant can crawl. A patterned cloth lies just beneath the clear surface on one side. Under the other side is the same cloth pattern, but it lies several feet below the clear surface. Infants able to crawl were placed on a small platform just at the edge of the boundary between "safe" and "deep." Although their mothers called to them from across the deep side, most infants were unwilling to cross, apparently because they perceived the depth and danger. Subsequent research has confirmed the pattern identified by Gibson and Walk. Most babies old enough to be tested avoid the deep side of the cliff, and by 9 or 10 months this avoidance response is quite strong (Bertenthal, Campos, & Kermoian, 1994).

Visual cliff
A research method for the study of depth perception in infancy. The infant is placed on a glass-covered table near an apparent dropoff, and perception of depth is inferred if the infant avoids the drop.

Figure 6.13

Around the time that babies develop skill in crawling, they become fearful of heights in the absence of support, as they display in their reluctance to cross a visual cliff.

When does the ability to perceive the depth of the deep side develop? An ingenious approach to this question, one that can be used with infants too young to crawl, involves measuring infants' heart rates as the experimenter lowers them to the clear surface of the visual cliff on both the deep and the safe sides. The heart rates of infants as young as 2 months of age slow when they are lowered to the deep side. This finding tells us that the babies notice the difference and are interested in it; there is no evidence, however, that they fear the depth. By 9 months the response is quite different. Now heart rate increases over the drop-off, suggesting that babies are afraid, and now most infants are also unwilling to cross over to the deep side (Campos, Bertenthal, & Kermoian, 1992; Campos et al., 1978).

The shift from interest to fear in response to drop-offs occurs after about 7 months of age. This is also the time when babies begin to take responsibility for their own movements—for instance, by crawling or by pushing themselves around in walkers. Might the two developments be related? Various kinds of evidence suggest that they are (Campos, Bertenthal, & Kermoian, 1992). For example, there is a correlation between crawling experience and fear of depth: Babies who have been crawling the longest are most likely to show the fear response on the visual cliff. There is also experimental evidence for a relationship: Babies who have been provided with walkers in which they can move themselves around show the fear response earlier. Apparently, moving about on one's own furnishes information about drop-offs and falls that is less readily available to the nonmobile infant. (We should add, however, that we are not advocating the use of walkers. Walkers have been linked to a heightened risk of injury in infancy, and the American Academy of Pediatrics has therefore called for a ban on their use.)

How are babies able to perceive depth? There are a number of perceptual cues for depth that babies might use. (Indeed, two researchers of the topic have written that "God must have loved depth cues, for He made so many of them"—Yonas & Granrud, 1985, p. 45.) Some cues are referred to as **pictorial cues** because they are the kind of information that can be conveyed in a picture. For example, railroad tracks appear to converge at a distant point, and this apparent nonparallelism creates an impression of depth. Objects that are nearer may hide objects that are farther along the same line of sight (a dime, held in the right position, can block an object as large as the moon). Finally, the relative size of objects provides a cue about their distance. If we see a picture in which a dog is larger than a car, we assume the car is farther away, and we can even judge their relative distance from one another because we know how big cars and dogs are (remember size constancy).

Another class of cues is **kinetic cues.** These are cues produced by movement, either of the observer or of the objects. Probably the most important kinetic cue is **motion parallax.** When we move, nearer objects appear to change position faster than do farther objects; similarly, when two objects move within our visual field, the nearer object appears to move faster. (You can verify this phenomenon by moving your head from side to side and noting the appearance of near and far objects.) Such differences in apparent movement furnish information about relative depth.

Moving objects provide additional cues when their movement puts them on a collision course with the observer. In this situation, as the size of the object in the eye increases, it blocks more and more of the background, and all the parts of the object get larger. You blink when an object approaches in this way, and so, it turns out, do babies as young as 1 month of age (Yonas, 1981).

Sensitivity to different depth cues develops at different ages (Yonas & Owsley, 1987). Babies can make some use of kinetic depth cues between 1 and 3 months of age; response to static pictorial cues, however, is not evident until 6 or 7 months. Similarly, by some behavioral measures (e.g., the blink response to an approaching object), perception of depth is present quite early; by others (e.g., fear on the visual cliff), it emerges considerably later. We can see again that there is no single answer to the "when" question for most developmental phenomena of interest. Perception of depth is a gradual, rather than instantaneous, achievement.

Keeping Track of Locations in Space

We will see in Chapter 13 that the young infant only gradually learns the distinction between the self and the external world of objects. Early in development, the baby understands the world egocentrically—that is,

---

Pictorial cues
Visual cues that indicate the relative distances of objects through static, picturelike information—for example, interposition of one object in front of another.

Kinetic cues
Visual cues that indicate the relative distances of objects through movement either of the objects or of the observer.

Motion parallax
An observer's experience that a closer object moves across the field of view faster than a more distant object when both objects are moving at the same speed or when the objects are stationary and the observer moves.

the understanding of space and objects is tied to the baby's own actions and body. Thus, the baby who finds an object to her right expects to find that object on her right again, even if she rotates her body. Gradually, babies learn to use stable landmarks in the environment to find objects, because these provide reliable cues that do not change as the baby moves around (Piaget, 1954).

A clever study by Linda Acredolo (1978) examined this issue for infants at 6, 11, and 16 months of age. In the wall to each side of the infant was a window. Infants learned to turn and look at one window—say, the one on the left—to make an interesting visual display appear. For half the infants, a colored star around the window where the display would appear served as a landmark. The remaining infants had no landmark.

After infants learned the left-turn response, their chair was rotated 180 degrees so that the correct response was now a right turn. If the babies were responding with reference only to their own body, they would continue to look to the left. If they could use the landmark or if they could compensate for the rotation of their body, they would look to the right. Whether or not the landmark was present, 6-month-olds turned to the left side—that is, they used their bodies as the frame of reference rather than the landmark. The 11-month-olds also tended to turn left when no landmark was present, but were able to use the landmark to respond when it was present. Finally, the oldest group responded correctly whether the landmark was present or not. Thus, there was a clear progression with age in the ability to use external referents to judge spatial location.

We have seen that one factor that affects how infants respond to depth is the opportunity to move themselves around. It seems plausible that moving on their own might also help infants keep track of spatial locations. In contrast, like passengers in a car, passively moved babies might not understand how they got from one place to another or the spatial consequences of the move.

It turns out that self-produced movement does facilitate understanding of locations. Performance on tasks such as that used by Acredolo (1978) is better when infants move on their own than when they are carried around the display (Benson & Uzgiris, 1985). And infants who have begun to crawl do better on such measures than do infants who are not yet crawling (Bertenthal, Campos, & Barrett, 1984).

The effects of self-produced movement extend to a number of other early developments in addition to the tasks considered here (Campos et al., 2000). Babies' control over their own movement through space apparently plays an important role in their mastery of the spatial world.

To Recap . . .

Newborns can see, although visual acuity does not approach adult levels until about 12 months of age. Peripheral vision and color vision are present in the early months of life. From birth, babies show interest in the visual contrasts presented by light–dark edges. At around 2 to 3 months of age, babies begin to prefer organized displays to simple visual detail and contrast.

An organized display of special interest is the human face. Although even newborns are responsive to faces, aspects of face perception continue to develop throughout the first year.

During the first 6 months of life, babies become quite sensitive to the properties of objects. They are able to appreciate that a single object offers many visual perspectives, as we can see in their ability to maintain size, shape, brightness, and color constancy. Babies in the first 6 months are also learning about further properties of objects, such as solidity and continuity. Initially, however, infants do not appear to infer that an object that is partially hidden from their view is continuous and whole unless they can see the object move.

Studies of how infants appreciate spatial layout illustrate several important principles. Infants become sensitive to several kinds of cues for determining the distance of objects, with kinetic cues becoming effective prior to static pictorial cues. Although babies can distinguish the deep and shallow sides of the visual cliff at around 2 to 3 months of age, their fear of depth develops only around the time they learn to crawl. During the first half year, babies organize space and the objects in it with reference to their own bodies. Later, they can use landmarks in the visual field. This accomplishment permits them to appreciate that objects occupy a stable location independent of their own activity.

INTERMODAL PERCEPTION

Up to this point, we have discussed the various perceptual modes separately. But, of course, we actually perceive most objects, people, and events in our world through more than one mode. A dog, for example, provides a great deal of visual information. It also supplies auditory information by barking, panting, and moving around. Touch may provide another cue as the dog sidles up against your leg. Unfortunately, the dog may stimulate yet another perceptual mode, smell, from a distance of several feet. Although these perceptual cues may sometimes be available simultaneously, you probably can tell that the dog is nearby with only a few of them, maybe even with one alone.

How the child comes to realize that cues from different senses "go together" has puzzled psychologists and philosophers for some time (Lewkowicz, 2000; Lickliter & Bahrick, 2000). As we will see in Chapter 7, Piaget (1952) argued that the sensory modes are largely separate at birth and that the baby integrates them only through experience. For example, the baby can relate touch and vision only when he learns to look at objects as his hand grasps them. In contrast, other theorists, such as the Gibsons (e.g., Gibson, 1988), have argued that some coordination of the senses is present from the start. There is, as we will see, some truth to both positions.

Researchers generally have approached infants' understanding of intermodal relations in one of two ways (Rose & Ruff, 1987). Many studies focus on how exploring in one mode triggers exploration in a different mode. Other studies focus on how input from different senses comes to indicate a single mental representation—how we know, for example, that a particular sight, touch, and smell all come from the same dog.

Exploratory Intermodal Relations

We appreciate the spatial location of objects through many sensory modes—vision, audition, touch, and sometimes even smell. Investigators have asked whether infants are born with a knowledge of space that is used by all the different sensory modes. If so, this shared knowledge could provide a basis for the intercoordination of the senses. For example, you know where to look when a person calls your name from behind or to the side. Will a newborn baby, who has had no opportunity to associate sound location and visual location, do the same?

As we mentioned earlier, the answer is yes. The newborn turns her eyes and head toward the sound of a voice or a rattle if the sound continues for several seconds (Ennouri & Bloch, 1996; Morrongiello et al., 1994a). And the interrelation among sensory modes is not limited to sound and vision. You will remember that one of the infant's earliest reflexes involves turning the head toward the cheek being stroked, an exploratory action that helps the newborn find the nipple. Similar relations exist between smell and vision—as noted, a 6-day-old baby will turn toward a breast pad that exudes the odor of the mother's milk (MacFarlane, 1975).

Babies explore novel objects with multiple modalities, including vision and touch (not necessarily a comforting tendency for household pets!).

An important form of exploratory relations among perceptual modes is the relation between vision and reaching. Infants' reaching for a rattle that they see illustrates how vision can trigger tactile exploration. Babies do not reach and grasp objects accurately before 4 or 5 months of age, but much earlier they move their arms in the right direction, perhaps as early as birth (Hofsten, 1982; White, Castle, & Held, 1964).

Such relations among the sensory modes are present at birth, presumably because they have evolutionary value. We call these *prepared relations*—relations for which the baby is predisposed by biology but that are also modifiable by experience. Some degree of modifiability is clearly necessary, so that the initially crude connections among perceptual modes can be sharpened by experience. Recall the notion of recalibration introduced earlier. If relations among the senses were fixed at birth, children would have no means by which they could adapt to such physical changes as the distance between their eyes and ears or the changing length of their arms and legs. In fact, all of the prepared relations that are evident in the newborn show substantial improvement across the course of infancy. Infants' localization of sounds, for example, is much more precise and flexible by 5 or 6 months of age than at birth (Morrongiello, 1994). Similarly, visually directed reaching becomes increasingly skilled and effective as infants gain more and more experience in acting on the world (Bertenthal & Clifton, 1998; Wentworth, Benson, & Haith, 2000).

The examples of exploratory activity described here support the idea that relations among the sensory modes exist quite early. Next, though, we must ask whether babies realize they are exploring the same object in the two modes. This question raises the issue of mental representation.

Intermodal Representation

How can we determine whether infants can use different perceptual modes to form a single mental representation of an object? Two kinds of evidence are informative. The first examines whether babies can transfer the benefit of experience from one mode to another. The second examines whether babies know that the same object is stimulating two modes. Psychologists have used these approaches to examine relations between haptic and visual perception and between vision and audition.

Haptic-Visual Relations
As noted earlier, haptic perception refers to active exploration by means of touch, as when a baby handles a rattle. Sucking can also be an important form of haptic exploration, especially for young infants.

Several researchers have investigated whether infants can transfer information gained from sucking to visual perception of the same object. Meltzoff and Borton (1979) provided 1-month-old infants an opportunity to suck on either a nubby (bumpy) nipple or a smooth nipple. They then presented the infants pictures of the nubby and smooth nipples, side by side. Infants looked longer at the nipple they had sucked. This finding suggests that cross-modal cues can specify the same object for infants at an amazingly early age, but we should be careful in reaching conclusions. Although some experimenters have reported similar findings (Gibson & Walker, 1984; Pecheux, Lepecq, & Salzarulo, 1988), others have been unable to replicate the results (Brown & Gottfried, 1986; Maurer, Stager, & Mondloch, 1999), and thus at present it is not clear how early such oral-visual matching is possible.

Infants have also been tested for the ability to recognize objects visually that they have previously explored only by hand. Whether this ability is present in the first half year of life is in doubt, but babies between 6 and 12 months of age clearly demonstrate that they can make the match (Rose & Orlian, 1991; Ruff & Kohler, 1978). Babies are also able to learn about an object visually and then recognize that object by touch, but the vision-to-touch connection is more difficult to make than is the touch-to-vision connection. Infants typically succeed only if they are allowed more time to explore the object or if they are already somewhat familiar with it (Bushnell, 1994; Rose, 1994).

An ingenious study examined whether babies can detect differences between what they feel and what they see. Babies were given the impression that they were reaching for an object reflected in a mirror, but they were actually reaching for an object hidden behind the mirror. On trick trials, babies felt a furry object while viewing a smooth object or vice versa. On nontrick trials, the objects matched. Whereas 8-month-olds did not show different facial expressions for trick and nontrick trials, 9.5- and 11-month-olds showed more surprise during the trick trials, indicating that they perceived the mismatch (Bushnell, 1982).

Auditory-Visual Relations
Can babies detect a correspondence between a sound and a visual event? Interestingly, babies naturally look at visual events that correspond to the sounds they hear. Researchers have capitalized on this tendency to explore the kinds of auditory-visual relations that babies appreciate.

For example, Spelke (1976) showed 4-month-old infants two films, side by side (Figure 6.14 shows the typical experimental arrangement in research of this sort). One film showed a person playing peekaboo, and the other showed a hand hitting a wooden block and a tambourine. A soundtrack was played that was appropriate to one of the films. Babies looked more at the film that matched the soundtrack, suggesting that they recognized the sight-sound correspondence.

Babies can also match auditory and visual events when the matching involves tempo and rhythm (Bahrick & Lickliter, 2000; Bahrick & Pickens, 1994). And by 4 months of age, babies have some idea about the types of sounds new objects will make when they bang together, a feat that requires knowledge of several properties of objects—for example, their hardness and whether one item or several items are involved in the collision (Bahrick, 1983, 1992).

Babies also appreciate auditory-visual relations that involve people. Babies look longer at their mother's face when they hear her voice than when they hear a stranger's voice (Cohen, 1974). As early as 3.5 months of age, babies look more at their mother when they hear her voice and more at their father when they hear his voice (Spelke & Owsley, 1979). By 4 months of age, babies look more at a male face when they hear a male voice and more at a female face when they hear a female voice, even when both faces and voices are unfamiliar (Walker-Andrews et al., 1991). By 4 months they also can match on the basis of age, directing attention to either an adult or a child speaker depending on whether the voice they hear is adultlike or childlike (Bahrick, Netto, & Hernandez-Reif, 1998).

Some sensitivities seem even more subtle. Spelke and Cortelyou (1981) showed 4-month-old infants two films with adult female strangers as speakers; in only one of the two films did the movement of the speaker's lips correspond to the sound track the babies heard. The infants looked more at the speaker whose lip movements were in synchrony with the sound. A series of studies by Kuhl and Meltzoff (1982, 1984, 1988) posed an even more challenging matching task. In this case the two speakers repeatedly pronounced two words that differed by just a single vowel—for example, one said *pop* and the other said *pep*. To match face and voice in this case the infant must engage in a kind of lip reading, mapping particular mouth movements onto particular sounds. Four-month-olds were able to do so: They looked longer at the speaker whose word was

Figure 6.14

Experimental arrangement used to study intermodal perception in infants. In the example shown, both faces are talking, but the soundtrack corresponds to the lip movements of only one of the speakers. From "The Bimodal Perception of Speech in Infancy" by P. K. Kuhl and A. N. Meltzoff, 1982, *Science, 218,* 1139. Copyright © 1982 by the AAAS. Reprinted by permission.

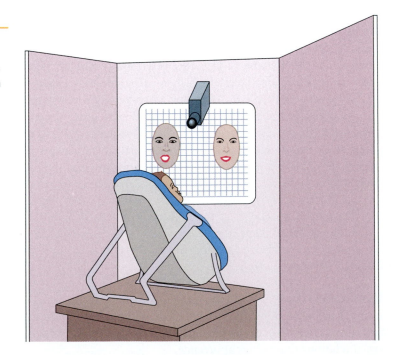

heard on the soundtrack. Indeed, a recent study suggests that *newborns* may be capable of such matching (Aldridge et al., 1999)!

Infants, then, are surprisingly good at picking up the commonality in cues from different senses. The baby's awareness that different cues from the same objects are coordinated greatly simplifies the task of organizing the overwhelming number of stimuli in the world into more manageable chunks. It is important to remember, though, that intermodal capabilities emerge at different times. At first, for example, infants simply appreciate that synchrony exists between visual and auditory events. More subtle forms of intermodal perception appear in steps as the baby matures (Lewkowicz & Lickliter, 1994).

We have discussed two basic approaches to the study of intermodal perception. Research on intermodal exploration has shown that babies come into the world with a number of inborn relations among sensory modes. Yet it also seems that forming mental representations of objects from the inputs of many perceptual modes requires some experience. As always, nature and nurture work together to guide development.

To Recap . . .

Most of our perceptual experience reflects the involvement of several sensory modes rather than a single one. Psychologists have wondered how children come to know that these perceptual cues "go together." In investigating this issue, they have focused on exploratory relations and mental representations.

Exploratory intermodal relations exist at birth, but they are tuned by experience. In the first half year of life, babies seem to have difficulty forming the same mental representation from different sensory modes. However, there is reasonable evidence that babies in the second half year do develop mental representations that bridge haptic and visual modes as well as auditory and visual modes. A general conclusion is that prepared relations between perceptual modes exist at birth, but that experience plays a significant role in tuning and elaborating these relations.

ATTENTION AND ACTION

Because sensory and perceptual processes are triggered by external stimuli, it may seem that these processes are passive and simply activated by events in the world. However, the perceptual modes are the mind's tools for gathering information about the environment, and the mind uses these tools actively. This is what we mean by *attention:* the active, selective taking in of some but not all of the potentially available information in a situation. Furthermore, perception is typically not an end in itself but a means toward the goal of operating on the world effectively: "We perceive in order to act and we act to perceive" (Pick, 1992, p. 791). In this final section of the chapter we examine the dynamic aspect of perception, considering both how action affects perception and how perception guides action. We begin with infancy and then move on to older children.

Infancy

Attention   Even newborn infants attend to mild sounds and sights. Their bodies become quieter, they stop what they are doing (such as sucking), they widen their eyes, and their heart rates slow (see Figure 6.15). These changes in behavior appear designed to optimize the baby's readiness to receive stimuli. First described by Sokolov (1960) as the **orienting reflex,** these changes can be observed, for example, when newborns attend to moving lights, to sounds that change gradually, or to sounds of low frequency (Haith, 1966). However, if the physical stimuli are too intense or the changes too

Orienting reflex
A natural reaction to novel stimuli that enhances stimulus processing and includes orientation of the eyes and ears to optimize stimulus reception, inhibition of ongoing activity, and a variety of physiological changes.

Defensive reflex
A natural reaction to novel stimuli that tends to protect the organism from further stimulation and that may include orientation of the stimulus receptors away from the stimulus source and a variety of physiological changes.

Selective attention
Concentration on a stimulus or event with attendant disregard for other stimuli or events.

abrupt, infants close their eyes and become agitated and their heart rates increase—a protective reaction called the **defensive reflex** (Graham & Clifton, 1966). The orienting and defensive reflexes appear to be the baby's earliest forms of positive and negative attention.

We have already discussed other indicators of newborns' attention, such as the tendency to look toward the location of a sound and to turn the head toward cheek stimulation or an attractive odor. Typically, however, investigators are more interested in the development of **selective attention,** the ability of the infant to focus on one stimulus rather than another. Even newborns have the capacity for at least a simple form of selective attention, choosing to look at displays of intermediate levels of brightness over extreme levels (Lewkowicz & Turkewitz, 1981) and at patterned over nonpatterned displays (Fantz, 1963). Newborns also adjust their sucking activity to hear their mother's voice rather than the voice of a woman unknown to them (DeCasper & Fifer, 1980). This capacity for selective attention provides a powerful tool for investigating infant perception, as we have already seen.

What controls the infant's attention? Two distinctions are useful in thinking about this question. One is a contrast that Leslie Cohen (1972) labels *attention getting* versus *attention holding*. Some aspects of stimulation are effective at capturing attention. Movement is an obvious example in the visual realm; a sudden noise is an obvious auditory example. Other aspects of stimulation are effective at maintaining attention beyond the initial taking in of the stimulus. A particular noise, for example, may quickly lose its fascination after the initial response to it. Suppose, however, that the noise is in some way puzzling or surprising (perhaps a sound coming for the first time from a previously silent toy). In this case attention may continue for some time in an attempt to make sense of the unexpected event.

The second distinction is related. Some properties of stimulation are *absolute*, in the sense that they can be specified independently of the perceiver. Movement is an example; so, in the visual realm, are contrast and curvature. In the early weeks of life it is primarily dimensions of this sort that seem to compel infant attention. Other properties of stimulation are *relative*, in the sense that they must be defined with respect to a

Figure 6.15

Examples of the orienting reflex in a young infant. Attention is high when a new stimulus first appears (pictures 1 and 2), then declines as the stimulus becomes familiar (pictures 4–6), then peaks again when the stimulus changes (picture 7). From *The World of the Newborn* by D. Maurer and C. Maurer, 1988, New York: Basic Books, pp. 128–129. Copyright © 1988 by Daphne Maurer and Charles Maurer.

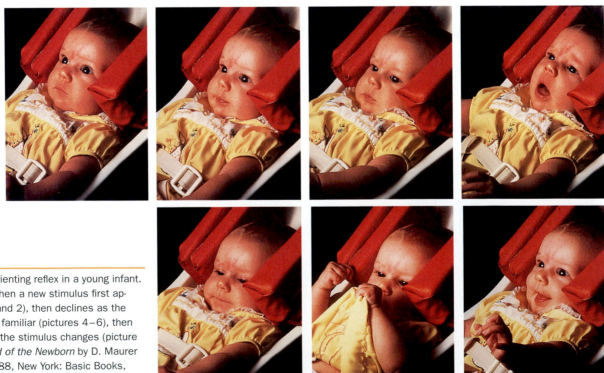

particular perceiver. Novelty is an example—a particular stimulus is not novel in an absolute sense; rather it is novel *to* someone who has never encountered it before. Surprise is another example—events are not surprising in themselves but rather *to* someone, given their fit with that person's expectations. From approximately 3 months on it is primarily events in this second category—in particular, events that are in some way new or discrepant or surprising—that are most interesting, indeed, not just during infancy but for children and adults as well (Kagan, 2002).

Action   We turn now to the relation between perception and action. The looking activity of young infants is a good example of the role that action plays in perception. When alert and active, young infants make new visual fixations two or three times each second. Newborn infants even search actively with their eyes in darkness, indicating that their perceptual system is active even when there is no stimulus to produce a reaction. They continue to search when a light is turned on until they find light–dark edges. When they do, they cross back and forth over those edges, adjusting their visual scanning as necessary. They seem to come into the world with a set of rules for acting:

1. If awake and the light is not too bright, open eyes.

2. If in darkness, search around.

3. If find light, search for contrasting edges.

4. If find edges, stay near them and cross back and forth over them.

5. As the clustering of edges increases, scan the edges more and more narrowly.

This inborn set of rules serves the biological function of activating visual cells in the brain and ensuring that cells form proper hookups with each other (Haith, 1980, 1991). Such rules also illustrate that from the earliest moments of a newborn's external life, action affects perception just as perception affects action.

Action can also anticipate perception. Recent research indicates that young infants can anticipate perceptual events before they occur, through the formation of expectations (Haith, 1994; Haith, Wentworth, & Canfield, 1993; Wentworth, Haith, & Hood, 2002). In these studies, infants see attractive pictures that flash in a preset pattern on a computer screen—for example, left-right-left-right. The question is whether they can learn the sequence and begin to look to the next location prior to the picture's appearance. The answer is yes, and quite quickly: After less than a minute of experience with such series, most infants move their eyes, during the delay period, to the place where the next picture will appear. By 2 months of age infants show such anticipatory behavior for a simple alternating pattern; by 3 months they can learn more complex sequences.

One interpretation of these findings is that infants form expectations to free themselves from simply reacting to each event as it occurs. The ability to anticipate future events is an important component of many kinds of cognitive activity throughout the lifespan (Haith et al., 1994). Apparently, such "future-oriented processing" begins very early.

Most of our discussion so far has concerned vision. Babies also use other action tools to investigate objects—for example, their mouths and tongues (Rochat, 1993) and, most obviously, their hands. We have seen that infants begin to use vision to direct their hands toward objects by about 4 months. From the onset of visually directed reaching babies show success at grasping not only stationary but also moving objects, an achievement that requires that they reach not to the present location but to an anticipated future site (Bertenthal, 1996; Hofsten, 1983). Thus reaching, like eye movements, is *prospective*—directed not just to current reality but to anticipated future reality.

When infants begin to move around by themselves, links between perception and action become even stronger. As we have seen, self-produced movement produces new experiences and sometimes new understandings—such as the onset of fear of heights (Campos et al., 1992). Moving around independently also requires new perceptual learning. This is so because babies in the first year of life have difficulty separating their perception of space from the actions they perform. For example, babies who are able to reach around a barrier for a hidden object have to relearn the task when they are required to crawl around the barrier to get it (Lockman, 1984; Lockman & Adams, 2001). Similarly, infants who can perceive and avoid a drop-off while in a sitting posture may respond differently when put in the posture for crawling (Adolph, 2000). Thus, what seem like very similar tasks to an adult do not at first seem similar to the baby. As infants gain more experience with the effects of their own movements, they gradually develop a more unified understanding of space.

Older Children

Attention   Although infants are capable of selective attention, there is a general shift with age from control of attention by external stimuli to stronger self-regulation based on the individual's own goals and intentions. Flavell (1985) identified four important aspects of attention that develop with age.

1. *Control* of attention improves with age as attention span increases and distractibility decreases. For example, children under 2.5 years of age are easily distracted from watching TV programs by toys in the room and other events in the house. Soon enough, however, it may become difficult to pull them away from the set (Anderson et al., 1986; Ruff, Capozzoli, & Weissberg, 1998).

2. *Adaptability* of attention to the task also changes. When an experimenter tells children to pay attention to a particular task, older children do so and disregard things that are not central to it. Younger children, however, focus on many more of the irrelevant aspects and so do not perform as well on the main task (Hagen & Hale, 1973; Miller, 1990).

3. Another feature of attentional change is *planfulness.* When an experimenter asks children to judge whether two complex pictures are the same, younger children often use a haphazard comparison strategy, not examining all the details before making a judgment. Older children are more systematic, comparing each detail across pictures, one by one (Vurpillot, 1968).

4. Finally, children become better at *adjusting* their attentional strategies as they gather information from a task. For example, experienced readers change their reading speed as the difficulty of the text changes, whereas younger readers tend to maintain a fairly regular reading speed regardless of difficulty (Day, 1975).

We saw that the study of children's eye movements demonstrates the interplay of action and perception very early in life. Eye movements are also informative in the study of older children. In one experiment, children were shown pairs of houses, such as those in Figure 6.16, and were asked to judge whether the houses in each pair were identical or different. The experimenter recorded the children's eye fixations and movements as they looked at the two houses. Each house had several windows of varying shapes with varying decorations. A thorough examination of the houses required comparing each window of the houses one by one.

Striking differences were found between children 4 and 9 years of age. The younger children appeared to have little or no plan for the task. Rather than comparing the corresponding windows in a pair of houses, the younger children often looked at windows in different locations, in a haphazard order, and did not check all windows before deciding the houses were the same. Older children, in contrast, scanned comparable windows, systematically checking each pair of windows before making a "same" decision. They were also more efficient, ending their inspection as soon as a difference between windows permitted them to say "different" (Vurpillot & Ball, 1979).

In general, studies of scanning and other forms of perceptual activity reveal increased carefulness in gathering information, more flexibility in search, and lowered distractibility as children move from the preschool to the middle-elementary school

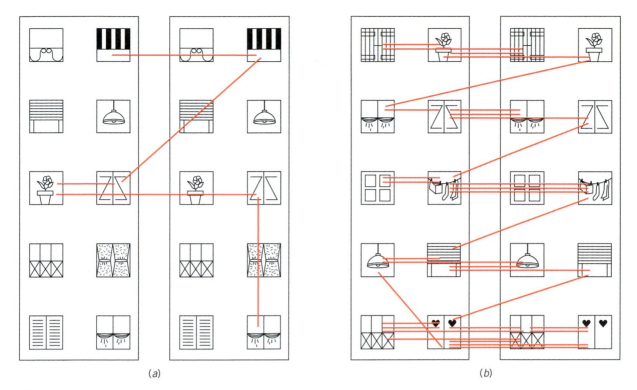

Figure 6.16

Reconstruction of a fixation sequence by (*a*) an inefficient child and (*b*) an efficient child. Their task was to judge whether the windows in two houses were identical or different. From "Extent of Visual Exploration and Number of Elements Present around the Stimulus in a Perceptual Differentiation Task" by E. Vurpillot, R. Castelo, and C. Renard, 1975, *Année Psychologique, 75,* Figure 2, 362–363. Reprinted by permission of Presses Universitaires de France.

years (Ruff & Rothbart, 1996). Such studies also reveal clear links between attention and learning and problem solving. Developmental improvements in attention are one source of differences between younger and older children in problem-solving prowess. Individual differences in attention at any age are one reason some children learn more effectively than others.

Developmental level is not the only contributor to how children deploy their attention. Barbara Rogoff and colleagues (Chavajay & Rogoff, 1999; Rogoff et al., 1993) observed toddlers (children 12 to 24 months old) in the United States and Mayan toddlers in Guatemala in situations in which there were potentially many stimuli and events to attend to. The Mayan toddlers were more likely than their American counterparts to attend simultaneously to two or three ongoing events, as opposed to focusing on a single thing at a time. One 12-month-old, for example, "skillfully closed things in a jar with his older sister, whistled on his toy whistle that his mother had mischievously slipped into his mouth, and at the same time watched a passing truck with interest" (Chavajay & Rogoff, 1999, p. 1080). The basis for the differences among the toddlers became evident from observations of the mothers' behavior: Mayan mothers, like their children, were more likely than the American sample to attend simultaneously to multiple events. The children's attentional patterns, then, reflected those of their mothers. We can see a theme from the sociocultural approach in this work: Children are socialized for forms of activity—in this case, patterns of attention—that are valued in the culture in which they are developing.

Action   We turn finally to some research that examines the relation between perception and various forms of skilled motor behavior. Action skills—behaviors that require physical coordination, such as reaching, walking, and catching—involve a complex interplay between perception and various parts of the motor system (Bertenthal & Clifton, 1998). The development of these skills is made more complicated by the fact that the growing body and limbs change in size, weight, and proportion. Perception plays a key role in the continuing adjustment required for skill development, providing feedback about the relative accuracy of performance. Feedback indicates the difference between reaching a goal (such as catching a ball) and not reaching it (missed it by 6 inches!).

One study examined how children of different ages adjust action to perception in the development of skill (Hay, 1984). Glass wedges placed in front of the eyes of 5- to 11-year-old children created a shift in the apparent location of visual objects (much like the apparent shift of underwater objects seen from above). If the child did not watch his arm as it moved toward the object, but simply reached directly for the object where it appeared to be, he would reach too far to one side and miss.

The 5-year-olds tended to make more direct reaches, correcting hand position only after the hand had reached the apparent position of the object. The 7-year-olds made slower or more hesitant reaches, with starts and stops followed by small corrections near the end. Children 9 and 11 years of age were more likely to begin with a direct movement, gradually slowing their reach as they approached the object, and making corrective movements near the end. Apparently, the 5-year-olds paid little attention to feedback, whereas the 7-year-olds overemphasized it, much as an unpracticed driver oversteers a sliding car. By 9 years of age, children used feedback more effectively.

This study revealed an expected improvement with age in the coordination between perception and action. In some contexts, however, the perceptual-action skills of the young child seem to outshine those of the adult. A visit to the local video-game arcade will convince any doubter that children are capable of highly sophisticated forms of perceptual-motor coordination. In fact, it is commonly assumed that children are more competent in such skills than are adults. However, we should not forget that children have more practice and are more motivated to engage in such activities.

One research team developed a technology for exploring this issue, as illustrated in Figure 6.17 (Roberts et al., 1991). Adults and 4-, 7-, and 12-year-olds played the video

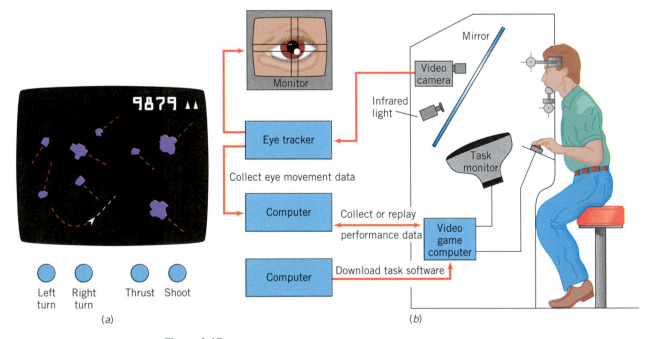

Figure 6.17

(*a*) In the Asteroids video game, a player controls a spaceship with buttons that can rotate the nose of the ship counterclockwise (left-turn button), rotate the nose clockwise (right-turn button), move the ship forward (thrust button), and fire missiles from the ship's nose. The object of the game is to destroy the moving asteroids with a missile and not to allow the asteroids to hit the ship. (*b*) As a person plays the game, a camera records the player's eye fixations. A computer records the screen presented to the player, the player's eye fixations, and the player's button presses 60 times each second. Researchers can analyze these data to find out precisely how looking and action are orchestrated.

ADHD: Helping Children with Attentional Problems

An important developmental achievement is the capacity to control and direct attention effectively. Not all children, however, master the challenges of attentional control as quickly or as fully as others. Anyone who has spent much time in elementary-school classrooms is familiar with children who constantly fidget and talk out inappropriately, who seem unable to stay in their seat or to concentrate for more than brief periods of time, and whose uncontrolled behavior detracts not only from their own but also from their classmates' learning.

Attention-deficit hyperactivity disorder (ADHD) is a relatively new label for what is almost certainly a very old problem. The term refers to a clinical syndrome characterized by the kinds of behavior patterns just described. Children with ADHD have great difficulty maintaining attention, they are often hyperactive, and their behavior has a generally uncontrolled and impulsive quality. These children perform poorly in school, and they often have difficulties in interpersonal relations as well. ADHD emerges early in childhood and can be a lifelong condition (American Psychiatric Association, 1994; Wender, 1995).

The diagnosis of ADHD has become increasingly common. Current estimates pf the proportion of school-age children in the United States with ADHD range from 4% to 12% (American Academy of Pediatrics, 2000). Boys are diagnosed with the disorder more often than are girls; it is unclear, however, whether this disparity reflects a genuine difference between the sexes or simply the fact that boys are more likely to show the disruptive behaviors that lead to clinical evaluation (Gaub & Carlson, 1997). The latter possibility is supported by the fact that gender differences are especially marked when teacher reports are the basis for identifying children for evaluation (Campbell, 2000).

The precise cause of ADHD remains a source of controversy (Faraone & Biedermann, 2000; Joseph, 2000). The evidence suggests that in most cases both nature and nurture contribute. The fact that ADHD tends to run in families suggests a biological component. Approximately 50% of children with ADHD have a relative with ADHD, usually a parent or sibling (Silver, 1999). In one study, 51% of identical twin pairs were concordant for ADHD—that is, if one twin had the disorder the other did as well (Goodman & Stevenson, 1989). Further evidence for the importance of biological factors

> **BOX 6.3**
>
> *Applications*

Attention-deficit hyperactivity disorder (ADHD)
A developmental disorder characterized by difficulty in sustaining attention, hyperactivity, and impulsive and uncontrolled behavior.

comes from studies of brain structure and functioning. Individuals with ADHD often show abnormalities in the frontal lobe of the cortex—the part of the brain responsible for attention and inhibition of behavior (Riccio et al., 1993; Zametkin et al., 1990).

Experience can also be important. The home lives of children with ADHD tend to be characterized by high levels of stress and parental punitiveness (Bernier & Siegel, 1994; Jacobvitz & Sroufe, 1987). The relationship between child and environment in most such cases is almost certainly transactional (Chapter 1): Aspects of parenting may contribute to the child's problems, but the presence of a difficult child also creates stress for the parents, whose attempts to cope may then make the child's problems even greater (Campbell, 2000). In some instances ADHD may have its origins even earlier in development—in the prenatal environment and the exposure of the fetus to teratogens such as alcohol and drugs (Silver, 1999).

Just as both nature and nurture may contribute to the emergence of ADHD, attempts to help children with ADHD may take both biological and environmental routes. One of the most common and effective treatments for these children is a biological one. Administration of stimulant drugs, such as Ritalin, has been used to treat ADHD since the 1930s. This treatment leads to improvement in approximately 80% of cases (Silver, 1999). Ritalin and similar drugs tend to decrease activity level and heighten attention—which, of course, is precisely the sort of change that children with ADHD need (Rapoport et al., 1978).

Although drug treatment can be an important part of a therapy program for ADHD, medication does not cure the condition, and medication alone is unlikely to give children with ADHD all the help they need. The most effective treatment programs combine medication with changes in the child's environment. Environmental interventions can take many forms. Among the approaches that have proved beneficial are operant conditioning of appropriate behaviors, modeling, and family-oriented forms of therapy (Barkley, 1998; Pelham & Hinshaw, 1992). As we would expect, interventions that involve both the school and the home tend to be most effective.

At present, there is no known cure for ADHD, and not even the best treatment programs can guarantee long-term success. Still, recent years have seen important advances in our ability to help children and families cope with one of the most common and debilitating childhood disorders.

game Asteroids over several sessions in the laboratory, so the researchers could observe them as the players evolved from novices to intermediates. The tasks in the game are to maneuver a spaceship so that it is not hit by flying rocks and to try to shoot down the rocks. The fast movement of the game makes it perceptually demanding, and the player uses several buttons to control turning and flying the spaceship and shooting its gun. A computer recorded all the game displays and all the players' actions, including eye movements, for later analysis.

People in all age groups initially simplified the task by using as few controls as possible—for example, pressing only the spaceship's right-turn and fire buttons. The younger groups maintained this strategy throughout and therefore never got much better. The older groups, however, tried new strategies with time, learning to move or fly the spaceship around the screen. The shift to new strategies had a short-term cost, because new flyers tended to run into things and destroy the spaceship. Ultimately, however, the ability to fly produced better performance.

We can see similarities to the earlier discussion of attention and eye-movement strategies. Here, too, development consists of increasing flexibility in the use of skills and increasing use of strategies. There is hope beyond elementary school, after all!

To Recap . . .

Perception, attention, and action are interwoven throughout life. From birth, some sensory stimuli arouse interest, or an orienting reflex, whereas others produce rejection, or a defensive reflex. Even newborns have some ability to be selective in what they attend to. In early infancy it is primarily absolute aspects of stimulation, such as movement and contour, that determine attention. Later, more relative aspects, such as novelty or surprise, assume greater importance.

Active use of perceptual skills is evident from birth. Newborns stimulate their developing brains through the inspection of high-contrast edges. Somewhat older babies develop expectations for regular events, which permit them to assume some control over their actions. Visually guided reach and self-produced locomotion dramatically change the opportunities that infants have to affect their own experience. Their control of their own movement through space contributes to their understanding of spatial stability.

Older children display better selective attention than do infants and young children. Four important aspects of attention that develop with age are control, adaptability, planfulness, and the ability to adjust with experience. Action tools also continue to develop through the school years. Increasingly, children make use of feedback to adapt to changing perception-action circumstances.

CONCLUSION

The issues that we have addressed in this chapter are long-standing—as the exchange between Molyneux and Locke with which we opened the chapter illustrates. What is new in the modern era are not the questions but the method of answering them. The last three decades have seen the development of powerful scientific methods for addressing what were once matters for purely philosophical speculation.

This research has taught us that many earlier ideas about infants were wrong. Many experts thought babies were blind and deaf at birth, an idea that lent support to the empiricist view that perceptual capacities were based solely on experience and learning. We now know that all the perceptual systems function even before the fetus has reached the age of normal-term birth. We live in the age of the "competent infant," in which many new capabilities have been discovered and infancy seems much less a period of perceptual disability than was once believed.

At the same time, we must be careful not to attribute too much skill to the infant. A recent "superbaby" craze (reinforced by articles in such widely read publications as *Time* and *Newsweek* magazines) has led many people to think that babies can do almost anything. However, even in terms of very basic sensory processes—in detecting and discriminating the physical energies that stimulate the receptors—it is clear that a newborn baby has a great deal left to accomplish. And as we have seen, perceptual skills must be increasingly refined.

It is useful to think of the baby as coming into the world with the essential tools for taking in and seeking out perceptual information. This is most obviously the case with eye movements. Other tools will soon mature, such as grasping, reaching, crawling, and walking. These tools are present at birth or mature during infancy in babies of every culture. However, the *content* of perception, the actual information gathered, is highly dependent on experience. Whether a baby becomes familiar with faces that are brown, yellow, or white or learns to understand French, Chinese, or English depends on the culture in which he or she is reared.

As in most cases, then, the diametrically opposed nature and nurture views are both correct. Evolution has provided a creature with all the tools necessary to collect information about the world. Experience determines exactly what that information will be.

FOR THOUGHT AND DISCUSSION

1. Molyneux's question concerned the relation between touch and vision. But it could have concerned other senses. *Think of some other combinations of senses for which we could ask the same question. Would the answers to these questions have the same implications for the nature–nurture issue as did Molyneux's original question?*

2. Investigators have demonstrated that some aspects of newborns' perceptual abilities appear to be innate, whereas others are acquired through experience. *Why is it important for research psychologists to be able to make these distinctions? What practical importance might the distinctions have?*

3. The development of the visual system appears to be influenced, in part, by experience. *If you were trying to optimize, or even accelerate, this development, how would you design a nursery for infants aged 1 month to 6 months?*

4. A prominent researcher of perception has written that "we perceive in order to act." *Think about the ways in which this statement applies to the ordinary activities of your day. How similar or different would the conclusions be for a 12-month-old baby? For a newborn baby?*

5. In discussing the interrelation of action and perception, we dealt mostly with laboratory findings. *Apply the concepts we described—intermodal perception, attentional strategies, and the relation between action and perception—to analyze an example of "real-life" athletic performance.*

VISUAL SUMMARY FOR CHAPTER 6
Sensory and Perceptual Development

Issues in the Study of Perceptual Development

The study of perceptual development encompasses sensation, perception, and attention. Research into all of these processes addresses two central question: What are the most important changes that occur across the course of development, and how can we explain these changes?

Nature vs. Nurture
> Although in explaining perceptual development, environmental/learning theories emphasize the role of experience and other models focus more on biological factors, an interactionist perspective characterizes all contemporary theories.

Normative vs. Idiographic
> Most research on perceptual development focuses on basic developments shown by virtually all children—a normative emphasis.

Touch and Pain, Smell and Taste, Motion and Balance

Touch and Pain
> The newborn is sensitive to touch, and this sensitivity increases over the first few days of life. Touch is important for several adaptive reflexes and for relations between children and adults. Infants and children use touch to explore the environment.

Smell and Taste
> Newborns are sensitive to both smell and taste. They prefer pleasant smells and can distinguish their mothers' smells from those of other women. They can distinguish among sweet, sour, bitter, and salty tastes.

Vestibular Sensitivity
> Newborns respond to both position and movement, as evident in the soothing properties of rocking and jiggling. When vestibular and visual cues contradict one another, babies tend to rely on vision.

Hearing

Sensitivity to Sound
> The fetus can hear several months prior to birth and may become familiar with sounds such as its mother's voice while in the womb. Newborns are not, however, as sensitive to sounds as adults. Sensitivity to sound, particularly high-pitched sounds, improves rapidly over the 1st year.

Discriminating Sounds
> Infants can discriminate sounds on the basis of intensity, frequency, and duration. Babies are especially sensitive to the characteristics of sound that will be important for speech perception.

Sound Localization
> The ability to localize sounds is present at birth, then fades somewhat, but reappears around 4 months in a more efficient form. This ability becomes more precise over the first 18 months of life.

Vision

Capabilities and Preferences

Visual acuity in the newborn is poor but improves with age, approaching adult levels at about 12 months of age. Peripheral vision and color vision are present in the newborn. Newborns are interested in high-contrast, light–dark edges; however, by 2 to 3 months organized displays and faces are of increasing interest.

Objects and Their Properties

During the first half year of life, babies become quite sensitive to the properties of objects. They are able to appreciate that a single object offers many visual perspectives, as evident in their ability to maintain size, shape, brightness, and color constancy. They are also learning about the solidity and continuity of objects, although initially they do not appear to infer that an object that is partly hidden from view is continuous and whole unless they can see the object move.

Spatial Perception

Babies use kinetic cues at an earlier age than static pictorial cues to judge depth and distance. Depth on the visual cliff can be detected by 2- to 3-month-old babies; however, fear of depth emerges only later in infancy, at about the time when babies learn to crawl. Babies younger than 6 months organize space and objects in it with reference to their own bodies, but older babies use landmarks in the visual field. The accomplishment allows them to appreciate that objects occupy a stable location independent of their own activity.

Intermodal Perception

Exploratory Intermodal Relations

Exploratory intermodal relations, such as turning toward a sound, are present in the newborn but are tuned by experience.

Intermodal Representation

In the first half year of life, babies have difficulty forming the same mental representation from different sensory modes. Older babies, however, develop mental representations that bridge haptic and visual modes, as well as the auditory and visual modes.

Attention and Action

Infancy

Even newborns have some ability to be selective in what they attend to. One model proposes that infants first attend to patterns and contours, then to discrepant stimuli, and then to events that require cognitive effort to be understood. Active use of perceptual skills is evident from birth. Newborns stimulate their developing brains through the inspection of high-contrast edges. Older babies develop expectations for regular events, allowing them to assume some control over their actions. Visually guided reach and self-produced locomotion dramatically change the opportunities that infants have to affect their own experience.

Older Children

Older children display better selective attention than do infants and young children. Four important aspects of attention that develop with age are control, adaptability, planfulness, and ability to adjust with experience. Action tools continue to develop through the school years. Increasingly, children make use of feedback to adpat to changing perception-action circumstances.

7

Cognitive Development: The Piagetian Approach

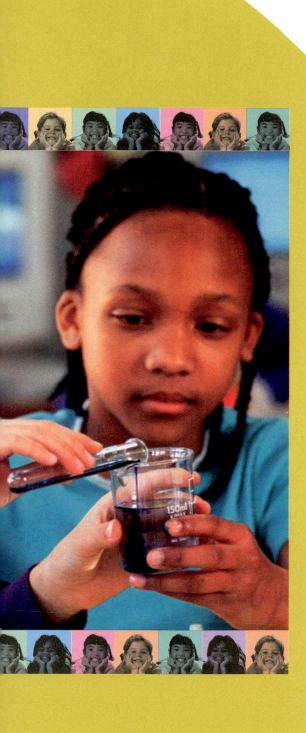

"*hy can I put my hand through water and not through soap?*"
"*Why doesn't butter stay on top of hot toast?*"
"*When I mix red and orange it makes brown, why?*"
"*Where was I before I was born?*"
"*When are all the days going to end?*"

As any parent knows, question asking is one of the most frequent activities of childhood. Child psychologists have long known this as well; in fact, some of the field's earliest scientific efforts were examinations of children's spontaneous questions. The examples above, which were collected by Paul Harris (2000), come from several of these pioneering studies, including some of the first work with children by the researcher on whom the present chapter concentrates, Jean Piaget.

As the examples make clear, children's questions come in many forms. Some concern mundane matters; others address issues of deep personal or scientific significance. Some questions are easily answerable; others pose issues that continue to challenge philosophers or scientists. The constant element is the search for understanding: the attempt to make sense of the many (really thousands!) of things that children do not at first know but must somehow come to understand. Across the next several chapters we consider how psychologists have attempted to make sense of children's sense-making efforts. ■

Cognition
Higher-order mental processes, such as reasoning and problem solving, through which humans attempt to understand the world.

We closed the last chapter with a message of both competence and limitations. We saw that the infant's perceptual abilities are considerably more impressive than psychologists once believed. But we saw as well that even the modern "superbaby" is not equivalent to an adult and that major improvements in perceptual ability occur within the short span of infancy. Determining the ways in which the perceptual world of the infant both resembles and differs from that of the adult is one of the most fascinating challenges in modern child psychology. So, too, is tracing the interplay of nature and nurture that transforms the "competent newborn" into the fully competent adult.

The same points apply, perhaps even more forcefully, to the subject of our next three chapters—children's cognitive development. By **cognition** we mean all the higher-order mental processes by which humans attempt to understand and adapt to their world—processes that go by such labels as *thinking, reasoning, learning,* and *problem solving.* Here, too, recent research has taught us that infants and young children are often far more competent than we used to believe. Yet the child's thinking may also differ from that of the adult in many ways, and these differences continue to intrigue and to baffle researchers and parents alike. Discovering the mixture of competence and limitations that characterizes thought at different points in childhood is one of the two great challenges that a researcher of cognitive development faces. The second is to discover how the limitations are overcome and how new forms of competence emerge. These challenges reflect the two general goals of developmental psychology identified in Chapter 1: to describe development and to explain it.

Across the next three chapters, we consider three general approaches to these questions. First, we focus on the cognitive-developmental approach, as represented by the work of Jean Piaget. We examine both Piaget's original theory and research and more recent studies that in some way test, modify, or extend the Piagetian position. In Chapter 8, we shift our attention to another major representative of the cognitive-developmental approach—the information-processing perspective. Finally, in Chapter 9 we consider the sociocultural approach. We will see that these perspectives are in many respects complementary rather than contradictory and that a full model of cognitive development requires insights gained from all three approaches.

PIAGET'S THEORY

As we saw in Chapter 1, Piaget's training included heavy doses of both biology and philosophy. From philosophy came much of the content of his work. Piaget's goal throughout his career was to use the study of children to answer basic philosophical questions about the nature and origins of knowledge. His research thus shows a consistent focus on what have long been central topics in philosophy: the child's understanding of space, time, and causality, of number and quantity, of classes and relations, of invariance and change. Undoubtedly one reason Piaget's studies have attracted so much attention is that they identify such basic and important forms of knowledge. Another reason is Piaget's surprising, and controversial, claim that these basic forms of knowledge often take a long time to develop.

From biology Piaget took ideas about both the structure and the function of intelligence. A basic principle in biology is that of *organization.* An organism is never simply a random collection of cells, tissues, and organs; rather, organisms are always highly organized systems. One job of the biologist is to discover what the underlying organization is. Piaget maintains that the same principle applies to human intelligence. For Piaget, the essence of intelligence does not lie in individually learned responses or isolated memories; the essence lies in the underlying organization. This organization takes the form of the various *cognitive structures* that the developing child constructs. The job of the psychologist is to discover what these structures are.

Biology also contributed to the functional side of Piaget's theory. Another basic biological principle is that of *adaptation.* All organisms adapt to the environment in which they must survive, often by means of very complex mechanisms. The biologist tries to discover what these mechanisms of adaptation are. Human intelligence, according to Piaget, is an adaptive phenomenon—indeed, it may be the primary means by which humans adapt to the environmental challenges they face.

Adaptation occurs through the complementary processes of *assimilation* and *accommodation.* Whenever we interact with the environment, we assimilate the environment to our current cognitive structures—that is, we fit it in or interpret it in terms of what we already understand. Yet at the same time we are continually accommodating our structures to fit with the environment—that is, altering our understanding to take account of new things. It is through innumerable instances of assimilation and accommodation that cognitive development occurs.

Piaget remains the field's most influential theorist of cognitive development. Many of his most important insights derived from his skill as an observer of children's behavior.

Table 7.1	Piaget's Four Periods of Development	
Period	**Ages (yrs)**	**Description**
Sensorimotor	0–2	Infants understand the world through the overt actions performed on it. These actions reflect the sensorimotor schemes. Across infancy, the schemes become progressively more complex and interrelated. Decentering occurs, and the infant comes to understand object permanence.
Preoperational	2–6	The child can now use representations rather than overt actions to solve problems. Thinking is consequently faster, more efficient, more mobile, and more socially sharable. The child's initial attempts at representational functioning also show limitations, including egocentrism and centration.
Concrete operational	6–12	The advent of operations allows the child to overcome the limitations of preoperational thought. Operations are a system of internal mental actions that underlie logical problem solving. The child comes to understand various forms of conservation, as well as classification and relational reasoning.
Formal operational	12–adult	The further development of operations leads to a capacity for hypothetical-deductive reasoning. Thought begins with possibility and works systematically and logically back to reality. The prototype for such logical reasoning is scientific problem solving.

The term *development* reflects one final influence from biology. Organisms are not static. Rather, they change, both across the lifetime of the individual and across the history of the species. One more task for the biologist, therefore, is to describe and explain the changes that occur. Intelligence, too, changes as the child develops, and the child psychologist must describe and explain these changes. For Piaget, there is no single organization or set of cognitive structures that defines childhood intelligence. As children develop, they construct qualitatively different structures, structures that allow a progressively better understanding of the world. These qualitatively different structures define the Piagetian *stages of development*. Thus Piaget, like many cognitive-developmentalists, was a stage theorist.

Piaget divided development into four general stages, or periods: sensorimotor, preoperational, concrete operational, and formal operational. These periods were introduced in Chapter 1 and are summarized in Table 7.1. Much of the rest of this chapter is devoted to a description of the Piagetian periods of development. Although we focus on Piaget, we also consider related research by others. We will be able to see, therefore, how contemporary research is building on and extending the important work begun by Piaget.

To Recap . . .

Piaget's approach to studying cognitive development was influenced by his training in both philosophy and biology. His training in philosophy led to an emphasis on basic forms of knowledge, such as concepts of space and causality. His training in biology led to the belief that intelligence reflects both organization—as knowledge is integrated into cognitive structures—and adaptation—as the child adjusts to challenges from the environment. Adaptation occurs through the complementary processes of assimilation and accommodation. As these processes lead to developmental change, children move through four qualitatively distinct stages, or periods, of cognitive functioning.

COGNITION DURING INFANCY: THE SENSORIMOTOR PERIOD

The first of Piaget's periods is the sensorimotor period. It is the period of infancy, extending from birth until about age 2.

You can gain some idea of the magnitude of cognitive advance during this period by imagining (or remembering, if you are a parent) the following two scenes: bringing a newborn home from the hospital and planning a 2-year-old's birthday party. Only 2 years separate the two events, yet how different are the sorts of things that one can do with, say to, and expect of the two children! It is Piaget's work that provides us with our most complete picture of exactly what the transformations are between birth and the end of infancy.

Studying Infant Intelligence

Piaget's conclusions about infant development are based on the study of his own three children from birth through the end of infancy (Piaget, 1951, 1952, 1954). His method of study combined naturalistic observation with experimental manipulation. Both Piaget and his wife, Valentine (herself a trained psychologist), spent many hours simply watching the everyday behavior of their babies. But these naturalistic observations were supplemented by frequent, small-scale experiments. If, for example, Piaget was interested in his daughter's ability to cope with obstacles, he would not necessarily wait until an obstacle happened along. Instead, he might interpose a barrier between daughter and favorite toy and then record her response to this challenge.

Piaget's methodology has both strengths and weaknesses. On the positive side, the method combines two attributes that are relatively rare in developmental research: the observation of behavior in the natural setting, and the longitudinal study of the same children as they develop. It seems clear that this approach (helped along, of course, by Piaget's genius) permitted insight into forms and sequences of development that could not have been gained solely from controlled laboratory study.

Perhaps the most obvious limitation of Piaget's method is his sample. A sample of three is a shaky basis for drawing conclusions about universals of human development—especially when all three are from the same family and are being observed by their own parents! It was clearly important for Piaget's observations to be replicated with larger and more representative samples and more objective techniques of data collection. A number of such replication studies now exist, and they are positive enough in general outline to tell us that Piaget's picture of infancy was reasonably accurate (Haith & Benson, 1998). The replications are by no means completely supportive, however. We note corrections and extensions as we go.

The Six Substages

Piaget divided the sensorimotor period into six substages. In the descriptions that follow, the ages should be taken simply as rough averages. What is important in a stage theory is not the age but the *sequence*—the order in which the stages come—which is assumed to be the same for all children.

Substage 1: Exercising Reflexes (Birth to 1 Month)
Piaget's label for the first substage reflects his predominantly negative conception of the newborn's abilities. In his view, the newborn's adaptive repertoire is limited to simple, biologically provided reflexes. Thus, the newborn sucks when a nipple rubs against the lips, grasps when an object grazes the palm, and orients when an appropriate visual stimulus appears. These behaviors are seen as automatic responses to particular environmental stimuli, and they show only slight change during the first month of life.

It should be clear from Chapter 5 that Piaget underestimated the newborn's behavioral competence. Indeed, most of what he labeled reflexes we would today refer to as congenitally organized behaviors, a term that reflects the complexity and the coordination that behaviors such as sucking and looking may show. Even in Piaget's view, however, these initial behaviors are important. They are important because they are the building blocks from which all future development proceeds. Development occurs as the behaviors are applied to more objects and events—in Piaget's terms, as babies assimilate more things—and as their behaviors begin to change in response to these new experiences—in Piaget's terms, as they begin to accommodate. As the initially inflexible behaviors begin to be modified by experience, the infant is entering the second of the sensorimotor substages.

Substage 2: Developing Schemes (1 to 4 Months)

As the infant changes, so does Piaget's terminology, from *reflexes* to *sensorimotor schemes*. We stressed earlier that Piaget sought to identify the cognitive structures that characterize a particular period of development. **Sensorimotor schemes** are the cognitive structures of infancy. The term refers to the skilled and generalizable action patterns with which the infant acts on and makes sense of the world. We can speak, for example, of a sucking scheme, in the sense that the infant has an organized pattern of sucking that can be applied to innumerable stimuli. Nipples, of course, are sucked, but so are rattles, stuffed toys, and fingers. Similarly, there is a grasping scheme, a skilled behavior of grasping that can be applied to virtually any object the infant encounters.

The notion of scheme captures an emphasis central to Piaget's theory—the role of action in intelligence. For Piaget, intelligence at every period of development involves some form of action on the world. During infancy, the actions are literal and overt. The infant knows the world through behaviors such as sucking, grasping, looking, and manipulating.

Schemes undergo two sorts of development during the second substage. First, individual schemes become progressively refined. The grasping of the 1-month-old is a rather primitive affair; the hard, thin rattle and the soft, fat stuffed toy may both be grasped in essentially the same way. The grasping of the 4-month-old is considerably more skilled and attuned to environmental variation. Such development does not stop at 4 months, of course. Particular schemes may continue to evolve throughout infancy.

The second change involves the coordination of initially independent schemes. Rather than being performed in isolation, the schemes are now combined into larger units. Of particular importance is the fact that schemes involving the different sensory modes—sight, hearing, touch, taste, smell—begin to be brought together. Thus, the infant hears a sound and turns toward the source of the sound, a coordination of hearing and vision. Or the infant looks at an object and then reaches out to grasp and manipulate it, a coordination of vision and touch.

Recent studies indicate that Piaget underestimated the degree of early coordination between the senses (Rochat, 2001). As we saw in Chapter 6, even newborns show a tendency to turn toward the source of a sound (Ennouri & Bloch, 1996). Other studies have suggested that the rudiments of visually directed reaching may be present quite early (Hofsten, 1982), as may the ability to achieve a primitive matching of tactile and visual input (Kaye & Bower, 1994). The competencies identified in these studies are limited, and they certainly do not negate Piaget's claim that intermodal coordination improves across the early months. But they do suggest that the beginnings of such coordination are present earlier than he believed.

Substage 3: Discovering Procedures (4 to 8 Months)

Although infants act on the environment from birth, their behavior in the first few months has an inner-directed quality. When a young baby manipulates a stuffed toy, for example, the baby's interest seems to lie more in the various finger movements being performed than in the toy itself. In Piaget's terms, the substage 2 infant uses schemes for the pure pleasure of using them—grasping for the sake of grasping, sucking for the sake of sucking, and so on. One characteristic of substage 3 is that the infant begins to show a clearer interest in the outer world. The schemes begin to be directed away from the baby's own body and toward exploration of the environment. Thus, the substage 3 infant who manipulates a toy does so because of a real interest in exploring that object.

One manifestation of this greater awareness of the environment is that the infant discovers procedures for reproducing interesting events. For example, the infant might accidentally kick a doll suspended above the crib, making the doll jump, and then spend

---

Sensorimotor schemes
Skilled and generalizable action patterns by which infants act on and understand the world. In Piaget's theory, the cognitive structures of infancy.

the next 10 minutes happily kicking and laughing. Or the infant might happen to create an interesting sound by rubbing a toy against the bassinet hood, thus initiating an activity that may continue indefinitely. The infant is beginning to develop a very important kind of knowledge—what he can do to produce desirable outcomes. That this knowledge is still far from perfectly developed is implied by the term *accidentally*. The substage 3 infant shows a kind of after-the-fact grasp of causality. Once the infant has accidentally hit on some interesting outcome, he may be able to reproduce it. What the infant cannot yet do is figure out in advance how to produce interesting effects.

Substage 4: Intentional Behavior (8 to 12 Months)

During substage 4 this after-the-fact restriction disappears. Now the infant first perceives some desirable goal and then figures out how to achieve it. In so doing, the infant demonstrates the first genuinely intentional behavior.

In Piaget's analysis, **intentional behavior** involves an ability to separate *means* and *end*. The infant must be able to use one scheme as a means to lead to some other scheme, which then becomes the goal, or end. The typical situation for studying intentional behavior involves response to obstacles. Suppose the baby is about to reach for a toy and we drop a pillow between hand and toy. How does the baby respond? Simple though this problem may seem, the infant before stage 4 cannot solve it. The younger infant may storm ineffectually at the pillow or may immediately activate the goal scheme—that is, do to the pillow what she would have done to the toy. What the substage 3 infant does not do—and the substage 4 infant does—is first push the pillow aside and then reach for the toy. This sort of adaptive problem solving requires a separation of means and end. The infant must use the push-aside scheme as a means to get to the reach-and-play scheme, the desired end.

Intentional behavior
In Piaget's theory, behavior in which the goal exists prior to the action selected to achieve it; made possible by the ability to separate means and end.

Substage 5: Novelty and Exploration (12 to 18 Months)

Piaget's name for substage 5 is "the discovery of new means through active exploration." The word *new* conveys a major difference between substage 4 and substage 5. The behavior of the substage 4 infant, although certainly intelligent, is essentially conservative. The infant at this stage tends to use mostly familiar schemes to produce a small range of mostly familiar effects. The substage 5 infant, in contrast, begins deliberately and systematically to vary her behaviors, thus creating both new schemes and new effects.

The advances of substage 5 are evident when the infant has some problem to solve. The infant now is not limited to reproducing previously successful solutions or slight variants of them. Instead, the infant can discover completely new solutions through a very active process of trial and error. Piaget documented, for example, how infants at this stage come to discover that a faraway goal can be retrieved by means of a string and that a stick can be used to push, pull, or otherwise act on some distant object. Note that these behaviors can be considered the first instances of a very important human achievement—the ability to use tools (Flavell, Miller, & Miller, 2002).

The substage 5 infant also experiments for the pure pleasure of experimentation. An example familiar to many parents is the "high-chair behavior" of the 1-year-old. The baby leans over the edge of her high chair and drops her spoon to the floor, carefully noting how it bounces. The parent retrieves and returns the spoon, whereupon the baby leans over the other side of the chair and drops the spoon again, perhaps with a bit more force this time. The parent again returns the spoon, and this time the baby flings it across the room—whereupon the exasperated parent gives up and removes either baby or spoon from the situation. For most of us, not being Piaget, it may be difficult to appreciate that cognitive development is occurring in this situation. Yet it is through such active experimentation that infants learn about the world.

Substage 6: Mental Representation (18 to 24 Months)

The first five sensorimotor substages are a time of remarkable cognitive progress. Yet there is still one more great advance to be made.

During the first five substages all of the infant's adaptation to the world occurs through overt behavior. Even the substage 5 infant's problem solving is based on trying out one behavior after another until a solution is reached. The advance that occurs at substage 6 is that the infant becomes capable for the first time of **representation**—of thinking about and acting on the world internally and not merely externally. It is this advance that will bring the sensorimotor period to an end.

Let us consider two examples. One involves Piaget's daughter Jacqueline, who is carrying some blades of grass through the house. The numbers at the start indicate her age—1 year, 8 months, 9 days.

> Jacqueline, at 1;8 (9) arrives at a closed door—with a blade of grass in each hand. She stretches out her right hand toward the knob but sees that she cannot turn it without letting go of the grass. She puts the grass on the floor, opens the door, picks up the grass again and enters. But when she wants to leave the room things become complicated. She puts the grass on the floor and grasps the doorknob. But then she perceives that in pulling the door toward her she will simultaneously chase away the grass which she placed between the door and the threshold. She therefore picks it up in order to put it outside the door's zone of movement. (Piaget, 1952, p. 339)

When Jacqueline pauses with her hand on the doorknob the second time, she is apparently doing two things. She is imagining the problem—the door sweeping over the grass. She is also imagining the solution—moving the grass beyond the sweep of the door. She is thus engaged in a kind of mental problem solving, based on an internal use of representations or symbols, that is not possible earlier in infancy.

The second example involves Piaget's other daughter, Lucienne. Lucienne (who is 16 months old) and her father are playing a game in which he hides a watch chain in a matchbox and she attempts to retrieve it. After several easy versions of the game, Piaget makes it harder. He reduces the opening of the matchbox to only 3 mm, too narrow for Lucienne to perform her usual solution of inserting a finger to hook part of the chain. How does the child respond?

> She looks at the slit with great attention; then, several times in succession, she opens and shuts her mouth, at first slightly, then wider and wider! Apparently Lucienne understands the existence of a cavity subjacent to the slit and wishes to enlarge that cavity. . . . Soon after this phase of plastic reflection, Lucienne unhesitatingly puts her finger in the slit and, instead of trying as before to reach the chain, she pulls so as to enlarge the opening. She succeeds and grasps the chain. (Piaget, 1952, pp. 337–338)

In Piaget's analysis, the opening of the mouth is a symbol for the opening of the matchbox, and it is this symbol that allows Lucienne to solve the problem. Note that Piaget apparently caught Lucienne during a transitional period. Had he tried the game a month or so earlier, the mouth opening would have been unlikely. Instead, Lucienne would probably have approached the problem in typical substage 5 fashion, experimenting through overt trial and error. Had he tried the game a month or so later, the mouth opening would again have been unlikely. An older Lucienne could generate and use a purely internal symbol. It is because Lucienne is transitional, on the brink of using representations but not yet very good at it, that she still has to externalize her symbol.

For Piaget, the onset of representation defines the movement from the sensorimotor period to the next period of development, the preoperational. We will have more to say about representational ability when we discuss the preoperational period.

Table 7.2 summarizes the six sensorimotor substages.

Object Permanence

Any brief summary of Piaget's sensorimotor studies necessarily omits many interesting aspects of infant development. But one aspect must receive some attention, both because of its importance in Piaget's theory and because it has been the target of dozens of follow-up studies. This is the phenomenon of object permanence.

Representation
The use of symbols to picture and act on the world internally.

As infants progress through the sensorimotor substages, they become increasingly skilled at acting on the environment to produce interesting outcomes.

A hallmark of sensorimotor stage 5 is the ability to experiment in new ways to produce novel outcomes.

The term **object permanence** refers to our knowledge that objects have a permanent existence that is independent of our perception of them. It is the knowledge that a toy does not cease to exist just because one can no longer feel it, or a rattle just because one can no longer hear it, or Mommy just because one can no longer see her. It is hard to imagine a more basic piece of knowledge than this. Yet Piaget's research suggests that infants do not at first understand object permanence and that this understanding develops only gradually across the entire span of infancy.

Object permanence
The knowledge that objects have a permanent existence that is independent of our perceptual contact with them. In Piaget's theory, a major achievement of the sensorimotor period.

Table 7.2	The Six Sensorimotor Substages	
Stage	**Ages (mos.)**	**Description**
1. Exercising reflexes	0–1	The infant is limited to exercising inborn reflexes—for example, sucking and grasping.
2. Developing schemes	1–4	The reflexes evolve into adaptive schemes. The schemes begin to be refined and coordinated.
3. Discovering procedures	4–8	Behavior becomes more outwardly oriented. The infant develops procedures for reproducing interesting events.
4. Intentional behavior	8–12	The first truly intentional behavior emerges. The infant can separate means and end in pursuit of a goal.
5. Novelty and exploration	12–18	The infant begins to vary the schemes systematically to produce new effects. Problems are solved through an active process of trial and error.
6. Mental representation	18–24	The capacity for representational or symbolic functioning emerges. Mental problem solving begins to replace overt trial and error.

Piaget described the development of object permanence in terms of the same six-stage progression that he used for the sensorimotor period as a whole. During the first two substages—that is, the first 3 or 4 months—babies show essentially no evidence that they realize objects exist apart from their own actions on them. Should a toy drop out of sight, for example, the 2-month-old acts for all the world as though it no longer exists. The young infant will not search for a vanished object and is likely instead to turn fairly quickly to some other activity. At most, the baby may follow an object with his eyes or stare for a while at the place where an object has just disappeared.

It is only during the third substage, at about 4 to 8 months, that babies begin to search for vanished objects. At first, however, the search shows a number of curious limitations. The infant may search, for example, if the object is partially hidden but not if it is totally hidden. The search may even depend on how much of the object is hidden. If only a corner of a sought-after toy is visible, the baby may sit perplexed. As soon as a bit more is revealed, however, the baby may happily reach out and retrieve the toy. Search may also depend on whether the infant's own action or something else makes the object disappear. The baby who pushes a toy over the edge of the high chair may look down at the floor to find it; should Papa Piaget do the pushing, however, search is less likely. For Piaget, this observation is evidence that the infant's knowledge of the object still depends on his or her action on it.

Substage 4 marks an important step forward with regard to object permanence. The infant now (at about 8 to 12 months) can search systematically and intelligently for hidden objects. The substage 4 infant searches even when the object is completely gone and even when it was not her own actions that made it disappear. Yet there are still limitations in the understanding of permanence, which are revealed when the infant must cope with more than one hiding place. Piaget might, for example, hide a toy under a pillow to his daughter's left two or three times, each time allowing her to retrieve it successfully. Then, with his daughter watching, he might hide the same toy under a blanket to her right. The baby would watch the toy disappear under the blanket and then turn and search under the pillow! What seemed to define the object was not its objective location, but the baby's previous success at finding it—it became "the thing that I found under the pillow." For Piaget, this behavior (which has come to be labeled the **A-not-B error**) is evidence that even at this substage, the baby's knowledge of objects is not freed from her own actions on them.

The infant does, of course, eventually overcome this limitation. The substage 5 infant (about 12 to 18 months) can handle the sort of multiple-hiding-place problems that baffle a younger baby. But there is still one more limitation. The infant can handle such problems only if the movements of the object are visible—that is, if he can see the object as it is moved from one hiding place to another. Suppose, however, that the movements are not visible—that the task involves what Piaget labeled *invisible displacements*. Piaget might hide a toy in his fist, for example, and then move the fist in succession through hiding places A, B, and C before bringing it out empty. To infer the movements of a hidden object, the infant must be able to represent the object when it is not visible. Solution of this problem is found only at substage 6, when the capacity for symbolic functioning emerges.

The work on object permanence illustrates two general themes in Piaget's approach to development. One is the notion of development as a process of **progressive decentering.** According to Piaget, the infant begins life in a state of profound **egocentrism;** that is, he literally cannot distinguish between himself and the outer world. The newborn and the young infant simply do not know what is specific to the self (one's own perceptions, actions, wishes, and so on) and what exists apart from the self. This egocentrism is reflected most obviously in the absence of object permanence. For the young baby, objects exist only to the extent that she is acting on them. Only gradually, across infancy, does the baby decenter and grow more aware of both self and world.

The second theme is the importance of **invariants** in development. We live in a world of constant flux, a world in which all sorts of things (what we can or cannot see,

A-not-B error
Infants' tendency to search in the original location in which an object was found rather than in its most recent hiding place. A characteristic of stage 4 of object permanence.

Progressive decentering
Piaget's term for the gradual decline in egocentrism that occurs across development.

Egocentrism
In infancy, an inability to distinguish the self (e.g., one's actions or perceptions) from the outer world. In later childhood, an inability to distinguish one's own perspective (e.g., visual experience, thoughts, feelings) from that of others.

Invariants
Aspects of the world that remain the same even though other aspects have changed. In Piaget's theory, different forms of invariants are understood at different stages of development.

Mastery of object permanence is a major achievement of infant cognitive development. The infant's search for vanished objects provides the clearest evidence that such knowledge is developing.

how things look, etc.) change from one moment to the next. Piaget maintained that one important kind of knowledge that the child must acquire is a knowledge of what it is that stays the same—remains invariant—in the face of constant change. The first and most basic cognitive invariant is object permanence—the realization that the existence of objects is invariant despite changes in our perceptual experience of them. We will encounter other, more advanced invariants when we discuss the later Piagetian stages.

Testing Piaget's Claims: More Recent Work on Infant Cognition

Piaget's studies continue to inspire a substantial proportion of the contemporary research on infant intelligence. Object permanence has been the most popular focus for such research, and we therefore begin with studies of infants' knowledge about objects, after which we broaden the discussion to other aspects of infant cognition.

Object Permanence
No researcher has questioned Piaget's assertion that the infant's understanding of objects is at first limited. Replication studies have amply confirmed Piaget's claims about the kinds of errors infants make when they must search for hidden objects (Harris, 1989). Nevertheless, many researchers have wondered whether the infant's understanding is really as limited as Piaget believed. A particular concern has been Piaget's emphasis on motor search behaviors in assessing object permanence—that is, behaviors such as lifting a cloth or pushing aside a screen. It seems logically possible that an infant may know perfectly well that an object still exists but simply fail to show the kinds of active search behaviors that Piaget required.

How else might we assess what infants know about objects? The most informative approach has made use of the habituation phenomenon described in Chapter 1. Habituation, you may recall, refers to a decline in response to a repeated stimulus; conversely, dishabituation refers to the recovery of response when the stimulus changes. Researchers have probed infants' understanding of objects by seeing what sorts of changes in objects they are likely to notice and dishabituate to. Of particular interest are infants' responses to impossible changes—that is, events that seem to violate the laws of object permanence.

A study by Baillargeon (1987a) provides an example. In this study, babies were first shown a screen that rotated, like a drawbridge, though a 180-degree arc (see Figure 7.1*a*). Although this event was initially quite interesting, after a number of repetitions the babies' attention dropped off, showing that they had habituated to the rotation. At this point a wooden box was placed directly in the path of the screen (see Figure 7.1*b*). Note that the baby could see the box at the start of a trial but that the box disappeared from view once the screen had reached its full height. In one experimental condition, labeled the "Possible event" in the figure, the screen rotated to the point at which it reached the box and then stopped—as indeed it should, given the fact that a solid object was in its path. In the other condition, labeled the "Impossible event," the screen rotated to the point of contact with the box and then kept right on going through its full 180-degree arc! (This outcome was made possible by a hidden platform that dropped the box out of the way.)

Any adult confronted with such an event would probably be quite surprised, because he or she would know that the box still existed behind the screen, even though it could no longer be seen. Infants as young as 4.5 months apparently possess the same knowledge. Their attention did not increase when they viewed the possible event; looking times shot up, however, when the screen appeared to pass magically through a solid object. The most obvious explanation for such recovery of interest is that the infants knew that the box must still exist and therefore expected the screen to stop.

Young infants know something about not only the existence but also the properties of hidden objects. In a further experiment, Baillargeon (1987b) replaced the hard and rigid box with a soft and compressible ball of gauze. Infants were not surprised by the continued rotation of the screen in the soft-object case, indicating that they

Figure 7.1

The Baillargeon test of object permanence. Infants were first habituated to the event shown in (*a*). Response was then measured to either the possible event in (*c*), in which the screen rotates to point of contact with the box and stops, or the impossible event in (*b*), in which the screen continues to move through the area occupied by the box. Adapted from "Object Permanence in 3 1/2- and 4 1/2-Month-Old Infants" by R. Baillargeon, 1987, *Developmental Psychology, 23,* 656. Copyright © 1987 by the American Psychological Association. Adapted by permission.

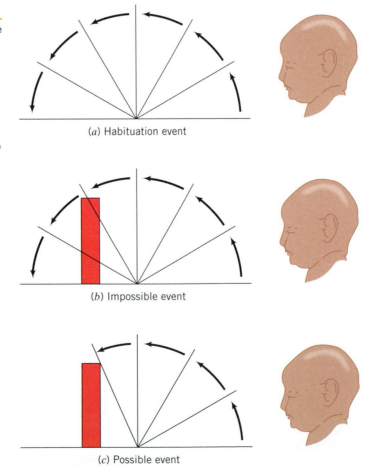

(*a*) Habituation event

(*b*) Impossible event

(*c*) Possible event

retained information about not only the presence but also the compressibility of the hidden object.

Infants can also retain and use information about the location of hidden objects. Baillargeon (1986) showed babies a toy car that moved along a track, disappeared behind a screen, and reemerged at the other end. Following habituation, the infants saw a box placed behind the screen, in one case next to the track (possible event) and in the other case directly on the track (impossible event). They then watched the car again make its journey from one side of the screen to the other. Infants looked longer at the impossible event, thus indicating that they remembered not only that the box still existed but where it was, and that they drew different implications from the two locations.

The experiments just described are but a few examples of the ingenious ways in which modern researchers have attempted to discover what young babies know about objects (Baillargeon, 1993, 1999, 2002; Spelke & Hermer, 1996). Having emphasized the positive picture that emerges from these studies, we should add two cautionary notes. The first is that the procedural innovations do not always result in successful performance. Baillargeon, for example, reports that young infants at first seem to possess a qualitative rather than quantitative appreciation of hidden objects—that is, they know that *some* object is still there, but have little ability to remember or reason about its quantitative properties once they can no longer see it. This means, for example, that they are not surprised if the drawbridge rotates somewhat farther than it should given the height of the concealed box, just so that it stops eventually; nor are they surprised if a large toy emerges from under a small cover, just so that *something* emerges (Baillargeon, 1994). Findings such as these confirm a general tenet of Piaget's approach to infant intelligence—that new knowledge does not emerge full-blown, but only gradually and through a series of progressively more mature forms.

The second caution is that not all researchers of infancy have been persuaded that studies such as Baillargeon's really demonstrate a basic knowledge of object permanence months earlier than Piaget believed (Bogartz, Shinskey, & Schilling, 2000; Haith, 1998; Haith & Benson, 1998). Criticisms of various sorts have been offered. Some researchers have argued that aspects of the procedure may result in artifactual success—that is, correct responses that do not really reflect knowledge of the hidden object. With respect to the drawbridge study, for example, it has been suggested that infants may find the movement of the screen inherently interesting, and thus look longer at the 180-degree rotation for this reason (Rivera, Wakeley, & Langer, 1999). Others have agreed that the success is genuine but have proposed that it can be explained through simpler processes than substage 4 object permanence. One possibility, for example, is that infants retain a mental image of the vanished object that persists for a few seconds after its disappearance; surprise then results from disconfirmation of this short-term perceptual expectancy, not from a violation of object permanence (Meltzoff & Moore, 1999a). Everyone, it seems fair to say, agrees that there is *some* underestimation in Piaget's account; at present, however, there is no agreement as to how much. Furthermore, no study to date has contradicted Piaget's claim that active search behaviors for hidden objects are absent prior to about 8 or 9 months. Why babies' ability to organize intelligent behaviors lags so far behind their initial knowledge is one of the most intriguing questions in modern infancy research (Bertenthal, 1996; Munakata et al., 1997).

Physical Knowledge   Object permanence is one important kind of physical knowledge. In this section we review several other kinds that also emerge, at least in their initial forms, during infancy.

Understanding of causality is a classic philosophical issue, to which Piaget devoted much attention. His conclusions about infants' knowledge of cause and effect were based largely on their ability to act effectively to produce desired outcomes—for example, to push aside an obstacle to attain a goal. As with object permanence, later studies have reduced the response demands on the infant, and as with object permanence, later studies have furnished a more positive picture of infant knowledge. The habituation methodology has again been informative. The most common strategy has been to habituate the infant to an event with a particular causal structure (for example, a red ball that strikes and propels a green ball) and then test for dishabituation to events that either preserve or violate that structure (for example, a green ball that propels a red ball). If the events are simple enough, infants as young as 6 or 7 months are sensitive to the causal relations (Cohen & Amsel, 1998; Leslie & Keeble, 1987).

Infants also have some appreciation of the laws of inertia and gravity. One method for probing such knowledge is shown in Figure 7.2*a*. Infants are first habituated to the first event shown in the figure—that is, a ball that is dropped behind a screen (depicted by the broken lines) and then revealed, once the screen is removed, to be resting on the floor. Following habituation, a table is placed in the ball's path, and one of two new events is presented. In the Consistent event (i.e., consistent with the laws of physics), removal of the screen reveals the ball resting on the table; in the Inconsistent event, the ball is again on the floor. The latter outcome is in a sense more familiar, because the ball appears in the same position in which it appears during habituation; to get there, however, it has had to pass magically through another solid object. Spelke and colleagues (1992) report that 4-month-old infants look longer at the Inconsistent event, suggesting that they understand the principles of object movement and are surprised by the magical outcome.

Figure 7.3 depicts another method for studying infants' understanding of gravity and support. The contrast is again between a Possible event (amount of contact between box and platform sufficient to support box) and an Impossible event (amount of contact insufficient, yet box remains perched on platform). By 6.5 months of age, infants look longer at the Impossible event, suggesting that they appreciate the relation between contact and support (Baillargeon, Kotovsky, & Needham, 1995).

We noted in discussing object permanence that the simplified procedures of modern research do not always lead to successful performance, especially if the focus is on very young infants. The same point applies to the topics considered in the present section. Infants of 3 or 4 months, for example, are not fazed by the Impossible event of Figure 7.3; for them, *any* degree of contact, at any orientation, is sufficient to provide support

Figure 7.2

Consistent and inconsistent events in Spelke et al.'s study of infants' understanding of object movement and gravity. From "Origins of Knowledge" by E. Spelke, K. Breinlinger, J. Macomber, and K. Jacobson, 1992, *Psychological Review, 99,* 611 and 621. Copyright © 1992 by the American Psychological Association. Reprinted by permission.

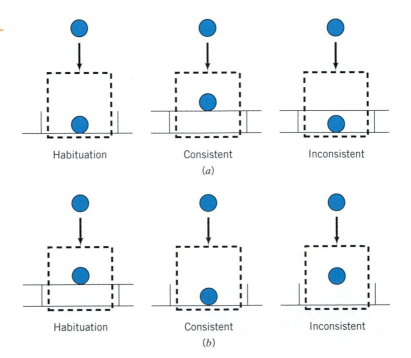

(Baillargeon et al., 1995). Or consider the events shown in Figure 7.2b. Here, in contrast to the procedure described earlier, a table is removed rather than added, and the Inconsistent event consists of the ball's magically floating at the height at which it once rested on the table. Spelke et al. (1992) report that 4-month-olds are apparently insensitive to this violation of gravity; they look more attentively at the Consistent outcome than at the Inconsistent one. Such findings are a valuable reminder: Infants may be more competent than we once believed, but there are still many gaps in their knowledge and many important developments still to occur.

Imitation   Among the many topics that Piaget explored in his sensorimotor studies was the development of imitation. He reported that imitation, like other sensorimotor accomplishments, had an extended developmental history, beginning with rudimentary and limited forms early in life and only slowly progressing toward the skilled behavioral system of the toddler or preschool child. Imitations in the first 6 or 8 months he considered to be especially limited. Infants of this age, according to Piaget, imitate only those behaviors that they already produce spontaneously and that they can see and hear themselves perform. Thus, the infant might imitate a movement such as finger wiggling, for which there is perceptible feedback. But we would not expect a young baby to be able to imitate a facial expression, such as opening the mouth or sticking out the tongue.

Some recent evidence has provided a strong challenge to this view. Across a series of studies, Meltzoff and Moore (1977, 1983, 1989, 1994, 1999b) have examined infants' ability to imitate facial expressions of a variety of sorts. Their procedure involves videotaping the infant's face as an adult model performs the target behaviors. The tapes are then scored by a rater who is unaware of the behavior being modeled (see Figure 7.4). Meltzoff and Moore report that even newborns can imitate both mouth opening and tongue protrusion, producing these behaviors reliably more often in response to the model than in the model's absence.

That modern research techniques often reveal greater competence than was evident to Piaget should be a familiar conclusion by now. The discrepancy in the Meltzoff and Moore studies, however, is especially striking—not just success far earlier than reported by Piaget, but the presence at birth of behavioral competencies that Piaget thought required many months of slow construction. In light of such a strong claim, it is not surprising that neonatal imitation has been the subject of dozens of recent studies. Some of this work provides support for Meltzoff and Moore's claims (e.g., Heimann, 1998; Reissland, 1988); other investigators, however, have reported difficulties in replication or cautions about the genuineness of the phenomenon (e.g., Anisfeld, 1996; Anisfeld et al., 2001; Jones, 1996). At present, therefore, the status of newborn imitation remains

Possible Event

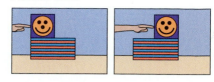

Impossible Event

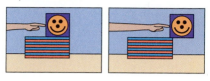

Figure 7.3

Possible and Impossible events in Baillargeon's study of infants' understanding of gravity and support. From *Current Directions in Psychological Science*, Vol. 3 (1994), p. 134, "How Do Infants Learn about the Physical World?" Fig. 1. Reprinted with permission of Cambridge University Press.

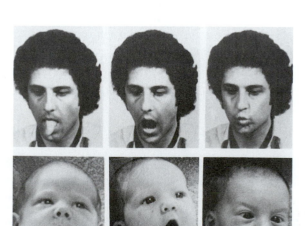

Figure 7.4

Adult model and infant response in Meltzoff and Moore's study of neonatal imitation. Even very young infants appear to imitate the adult's facial expressions. From "Imitation of Facial and Manual Gestures by Human Neonates" by A. N. Meltzoff and M. K. Moore, 1977, *Science, 298,* 75. Copyright © 1977 by the American Association for the Advancement of Science. Reprinted by permission.

controversial. If valid, however, Meltzoff and Moore's findings would constitute perhaps the most dramatic example of competence that exists earlier than Piaget claimed.

An Overall Evaluation

Piaget's work remains our most influential and informative account of infant cognitive development. Nevertheless, the more recent studies of infant cognition suggest several modifications to the initial Piagetian picture.

First, Piaget often underestimated the infant's ability. How great the underestimation is remains a matter of dispute. But when studies have suggested revisions in Piaget's age norms, the revisions have almost always been in a downward direction. This conclusion applies not just to the topics discussed here but to a wide range of infant developments (Courage & Howe, 2002; Lacerda, Hofsten, & Heimann, 2001).

Second, the primary reason for the discrepancy between Piaget's studies and modern work is methodological. Piaget's conclusions about infant knowledge were based largely on observations of overt motor behavior—that is, behaviors such as reaching, manipulating, bringing objects together, and in general acting on the world. With modern research techniques, such as the habituation procedure, the response demands on the infant are reduced considerably, and our picture of infant competence has correspondingly grown more positive.

A final conclusion is that this picture is not totally positive. Along with the demonstrations of unexpected competencies, modern studies have confirmed many of the limitations that were identified by Piaget. They also have at times revealed puzzling new gaps in infant competence—recall young infants' insensitivity to the quantitative features of objects, for example, or their apparent ignorance of the law of gravity. Our understanding of infant cognition has clearly progressed beyond the important beginning provided by Piaget; just as clearly, however, there is still much to learn.

To Recap . . .

The first of Piaget's stages is the sensorimotor period, which extends from birth until about age 2. Infant intelligence is characterized in terms of sensorimotor schemes, and development occurs through the processes of assimilation and accommodation—incorporating new elements into the schemes and modifying the schemes in response to new experiences. This conception of infant intelligence reflects Piaget's emphasis on the child's own actions as a source of knowledge.

The sensorimotor period is divided into six substages. The starting point consists of various inborn reflexes. The reflexes evolve into adaptive schemes, and the schemes become more refined, externally oriented, and intercoordinated as the infant develops. The culmination of the sensorimotor period is the onset of mental representation at substage 6.

An especially important sensorimotor achievement is object permanence: the knowledge that objects have a permanent existence. Piaget's research suggests that infants only gradually come to understand object permanence through a series of stages in which the existence of the object is freed from the infant's actions on it.

Later studies have largely confirmed the descriptive picture of infant cognition provided by Piaget. Such studies also indicate, however, that Piaget's methods often failed to capture early forms of infant competence, and they suggest that his explanation for developmental change is not totally correct.

THOUGHT IN THE PRESCHOOLER: THE PREOPERATIONAL PERIOD

The preoperational period extends from about age 2 to about age 6. The "about" is again important. Piagetian age norms are always rough guidelines, and particular children may develop more quickly or more slowly than the average.

We noted at the beginning of the chapter that childhood cognition is a mixture of competence and limitations. At no other time during development is this mixture—surprisingly adultlike abilities on the one hand and glaring, hard-to-believe errors on the other—quite so striking or so challenging to explain as it is during the preoperational period. Some of the most fascinating contemporary research in child psychology is directed at exploring the mysteries of the preoperational mind.

More about Representation

As we saw, the defining characteristic of the movement from the sensorimotor to the preoperational period is the onset of representational ability, or what Piaget called the **symbolic function.** Piaget defined the symbolic function as the ability to use one thing to represent something else—that is, to use one thing as a symbol to stand for some other thing, which then becomes the symbolized. Symbols can take a variety of forms. They can be motor movements, as when the opening of Lucienne's mouth symbolized the opening of the matchbox. They can be mental images, as may have been the case when Jacqueline thought through the blades-of-grass problem. They can be physical objects, as when a 3-year-old grabs a broom and rides it as if it were a horse. And, of course, they can be words.

What is the evidence that a general capacity for representational functioning emerges near the end of infancy? Piaget (1951) cited five kinds of behavior that become evident at this time, all of which seem to require representational ability, and none of which he had observed earlier in infancy. We have discussed two of these behaviors: the internal problem solving of substage 6, and the ability to handle the invisible displacements version of the object permanence problem. Another, discussed in Chapter 11, is the first appearance of words. Here Piaget stressed the ability not simply to label present objects but to talk about objects or events in their absence. The latter is clearly a symbolic achievement.

A fourth piece of evidence is the appearance of **deferred imitation.** Although babies imitate from early in life, they can at first imitate only models that are directly in front of them. Only near the end of infancy, according to Piaget, does the baby begin to imitate models from the past—for example, some behavior that an older sibling performed the week before. The ability to imitate behavior from the past clearly implies the capacity to store that behavior in some representational form.

The final index of the symbolic function is familiar to any parent. It is the emergence of **symbolic play.** Now is the time that the child's play begins to be enriched by the ability to use one thing in deliberate pretense to stand for something else. Now is the time that sticks turn into boats, sandpiles into cakes, and brooms into horses.

Was Piaget correct about the emergence of representational ability? We have seen that a consistent theme from modern research is that babies are often more capable than Piaget indicated. Such is probably the case as well with respect to the onset of representation (Mandler, 1998). Although the importance of the transition described by Piaget is not in dispute, more recent research indicates that some forms of representational functioning almost certainly emerge earlier in infancy than he believed. The recent studies of object permanence, for example, seem to demonstrate some capacity to represent and reason about unseen objects considerably earlier than Piaget predicted. Deferred imitation has been shown in babies as young as 6 months of age (Barr, Dowden, & Hayne, 1996) and there is suggestive evidence that simple forms may be present as early as 6 weeks (Meltzoff & Moore, 1994). Finally, there is intriguing evidence from studies of infants learning American Sign Language that the first genuinely symbolic signs may emerge as early as 6 or 7 months (Meier & Newport, 1990), and thus well before both the typical time for the first spoken words and the usual dating for Piaget's substage 6.

Symbolic function
The ability to use one thing (such as a mental image or word) as a symbol to represent something else.

Deferred imitation
Imitation of a model observed some time in the past.

Symbolic play
Form of play in which the child uses one thing in deliberate pretense to stand for something else.

One of the clearest signs of the preoperational child's representational skills is the emergence of symbolic play. With his newfound symbolic skills, the 3-year-old readily transforms a broom into a horse.

Strengths of Preoperational Thought

In Piaget's theory, the cognitive structures of later stages are always more powerful and more adaptive than those of earlier stages. Consequently, the onset of representational intelligence marks a major advance in the child's cognitive abilities.

Representational, in-the-head problem solving is superior to sensorimotor problem solving in a number of ways. Representational intelligence is considerably faster and more efficient. Rather than trying out all possible solutions overtly—a necessarily slow and error-prone process—the representational child can try them out internally, using representations rather than literal actions. When the representational child *does* act, the solution can be immediate and adaptive. Representational intelligence is also considerably more mobile. Sensorimotor intelligence is limited to the here and now—what is actually in front of the child to be acted on. With representational intelligence, however, the child can think about the past and imagine the future. The scope of cognitive activity is thus enormously expanded.

Representational intelligence is also socially sharable in a way that sensorimotor intelligence is not. With the acquisition of language, the child can communicate ideas to others and receive information from them in ways that are not possible without language. Piaget's theory does not place as much stress on either language or cultural transmission as do many other theories. Nevertheless, he did consistently cite social experience as one of the factors that account for development (Piaget, 1983). And both the extent and the nature of social experience change greatly once the child has entered the preoperational period.

The preoperational period is also a time of specific cognitive acquisitions. It is the time during which the child develops a form of knowledge that Piaget labeled **qualitative identity** (Piaget, 1968). Qualitative identity refers to the realization that the qualitative, or generic, nature of something is not changed by a change in its appearance. It is the realization, for example, that a wire remains the same wire even after it has been bent into a different shape or that water remains the same water even though it may look different after being poured from a glass to a pie pan. (Note, though, that the child does not yet realize that the length of the wire or the quantity of water remains the same—this is a more advanced form of knowledge.) It should be clear that qualitative identity, like object permanence, reflects a central Piagetian theme: the importance of mastering invariants in the environment.

A striking illustration of the phenomenon of qualitative identity can be found in a study by DeVries (1969). DeVries first exposed her preschool participants to a docile black cat. The cat was then transformed, by means of a very realistic mask, into a fierce-looking dog (see Figure 7.5). Following the transformation, DeVries questioned the children about what kind of animal they now saw. What kind of sound would it make, for example, and what kind of food would it like to eat? Most of the 3-year-olds seemed quite convinced that the cat had become a dog. In contrast, most of the 5- and 6-year-olds were able to overcome the perceptual cues and affirm qualitative identity. They realized that the cat was still a cat and would always remain a cat.

The achievements discussed here hardly exhaust the list of preoperational accomplishments. Indeed, one of Piaget's efforts during the last part of his career was to identify preoperational strengths that had been missed in his earlier studies (Beilin, 1992a, 1992b; Piaget, 1979, 1980). And when we turn to language development in Chapter 11, we will see that the years from 2 to 6 constitute a time of truly remarkable progress with respect to this critical and uniquely human ability.

Limitations of Preoperational Thought

Despite the positive features just noted, most of what Piaget had to say about preoperational thought concerns weaknesses rather than strengths. The weaknesses all stem from the fact that the child is attempting to operate on a new plane of cognitive functioning, that of representational intelligence. The 3-year-old who is quite skilled at the sensorimotor

Qualitative identity
The knowledge that the qualitative nature of something is not changed by a change in its appearance. In Piaget's theory, a preoperational achievement.

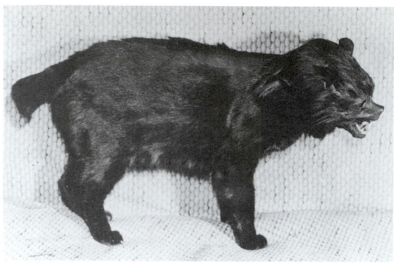

Figure 7.5

Cat transformed into dog, used by DeVries in the study of qualitative identity. Young preoperational children seem to believe that the cat has really become a dog; older preoperational children realize that the identity is unchanged. From "Constancy of Generic Identity in the Years Three to Six" by R. DeVries, 1969, *Monographs of the Society for Research in Child Development, 34* (3, Serial No. 127), 8. Copyright © 1969 by the Society for Research in Child Development. Reprinted by permission.

level turns out to be not at all skilled at purely mental reasoning and problem solving. Hence the term *preoperational*—to refer to the fact that the child lacks the "operations" that allow effective problem solving at the representational level.

Egocentrism   We saw that infancy begins in a state of profound egocentrism and that a major achievement of infancy is the gradual decentering through which the infant learns what is specific to the self and what exists apart from the self. The preoperational period also begins in a state of egocentrism but this time at a representational rather than a sensorimotor level. In Piaget's view, the young preoperational child has only a very limited ability to represent the psychological experiences of others—to break away from his own perspective to take the point of view of someone whose perspective is different from his own. Instead, the 3- or 4-year-old often acts as though everyone shares his particular point of view—sees what he sees, feels what he feels, knows what he knows, and so on. Note that egocentrism does not mean egotism or selfishness, but simply a difficulty in taking the point of view of another.

Preoperational egocentrism is evident in a variety of contexts. Perhaps the most apparent example is children's speech. Piaget's first book, *The Language and Thought of the Child* (1926), examined both naturally occurring conversations between children and experimentally elicited speech of various sorts. Piaget found that the children's speech was often hopelessly jumbled and hard to decipher, even when they clearly were trying their best to communicate.

Table 7.3 presents some examples from an experiment in which children attempted to retell a story (the phrases in brackets are Piaget's comments on their efforts). Piaget attributed such egocentric speech to the young child's basic cognitive egocentrism. Young children often fail to assume the perspective of their listener, acting instead as though the listener already knows everything that they know. Certainly anyone who has listened to a 3-year-old relate the events of her day has some appreciation for this claim.

Piaget also studied the child's ability to assume the visual perspective of another (Piaget & Inhelder, 1956). The best-known task for studying such visual perspective taking is the three-mountains problem pictured in Figure 7.6. After walking around the display, the child is seated on one side; the researchers then move a doll to various locations around the board. The child's task is to indicate what the doll would see from the

Table 7.3	Children Retell a Story: Some Piagetian Examples of Egocentric Speech

Story Presented to the Children

Once upon a time, there was a lady who was called Niobe, and who had 12 sons and daughters. She met a fairy who had only one son and no daughter. Then the lady laughed at the fairy because the fairy only had one boy. Then the fairy was very angry and fastened the lady to a rock. The lady cried for 10 years. In the end she turned to a rock, and her tears made a stream which still runs today.

Examples of Children's Reproductions

Met (6;4), talking of Niobe: "The lady laughed at this fairy because she [who?] only had one boy. The lady had 12 sons and 12 daughters. One day she [who?] laughed at her [at whom?]. She [who?] was angry and she [who?] fastened her beside a stream. She [?] cried for 50 months, and it made a great big stream." Impossible to tell who fastened, and who was fastened.

Gio (8 years old) "Once upon a time there was a lady who had 12 boys and 12 girls, and then a fairy a boy and a girl. And then Niobe wanted to have some more sons [than the fairy. Gio means by this that Niobe competed with the fairy, as was told in the text. But it will be seen how elliptical is his way in expressing it]. Then she [who?] was angry. She [who?] fastened her [whom?] to a stone. He [who?] turned into a rock, and then his tears [whose?] made a stream which is still running today."

SOURCE: Adapted from *The Language and Thought of the Child* by J. Piaget, 1926, New York: Harcourt Brace, pp. 99, 116, 121. Adapted by permission.

different locations. For many young children, the answer is clear: The doll would see exactly what they see. Again, the young child acts as though his or her own perspective is the only one possible.

Centration

Centration The concept of **centration** refers to the young child's tendency to focus on only one aspect of a problem at a time. As an example, let us consider what is perhaps the most famous Piagetian task—the **conservation** problem. Conservation is the realization that the quantitative properties of objects are not changed by a change in appearance.

The example that we examine is a conservation of number problem (Piaget & Szeminska, 1952). To construct such a problem, we might begin by laying out two rows of five chips, as shown in the first column of Figure 7.7. As long as the chips are arranged in one-to-one correspondence, even a 3- or 4-year-old can tell us that the two rows have the same number. But suppose that, while the child watches, we spread one of the rows so that it is longer than the other and then ask the child again about the number. Virtually every 3- and 4-year-old will say that the longer row now has more. If we ask the child why, the child finds the answer obvious—because it is longer. In Piaget's terms, the child *centrates* on the length of the row and hence fails to conserve the number.

Centration

Piaget's term for the young child's tendency to focus on only one aspect of a problem at a time, a perceptually biased form of responding that often results in incorrect judgments.

Conservation

The knowledge that the quantitative properties of an object or collection of objects are not changed by a change in appearance. In Piaget's theory, a concrete operational achievement.

Figure 7.6

Piaget's three-mountains problem for assessing visual perspective taking. The child's task is to judge how the display looks to someone viewing it from a different perspective. From *The Child's Conception of Space* by J. Piaget and B. Inhelder, 1956, London: Routledge and Kegan Paul, 211. Copyright © by Routledge and Kegan Paul. Reprinted by permission.

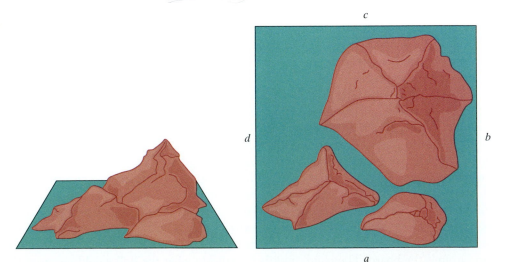

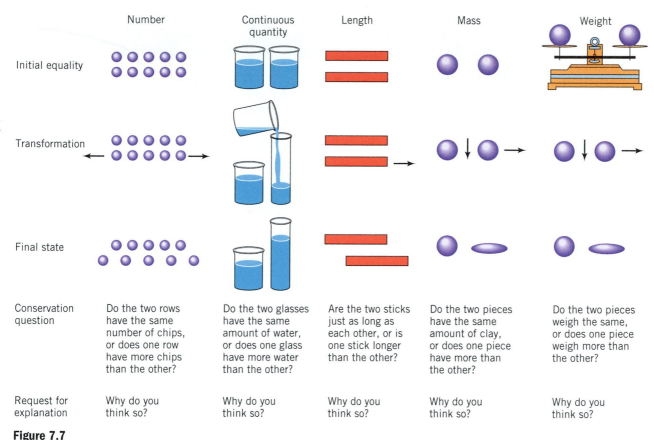

Figure 7.7

Examples of Piagetian conservation problems.

Centration, then, is a perceptually biased form of responding that is characteristic of young children. For the young child, what seems to be critical is how things look at the moment. The child's attention is captured by the most salient, or noticeable, element of the perceptual display, which in the number task is the length of the rows. Once her attention has been captured, the child finds it difficult to shift attention and take account of other information—for example, the fact that the rows differ not only in length but also in density. The result is that the child is easily fooled by appearance and often, as in the conservation task, arrives at the wrong answer.

Is the young child's thinking really as egocentric, as centrated, and as generally confused as Piaget claimed? A brief answer is "sometimes but by no means always." We provide a more complete answer after considering the next of the Piagetian periods.

 **To Recap . . .**

The second developmental period in Piaget's progression is the preoperational period. The onset of representational intelligence marks a major advance over sensorimotor functioning. The child's intellectual adaptations are now faster, more efficient, more mobile, and more socially sharable. The preoperational period is also a time of specific cognitive acquisitions, including mastery of qualitative identity.

The movement from sensorimotor to representational brings problems as well as advances, a fact that is signaled by the term *preoperational*. The young child's thinking is often egocentric, showing an inability to break away from his or her own perspective to adopt the perspective of others. The young child's thinking also shows centration, a tendency to be captured and misled by what is perceptually obvious. The child's failure to conserve is one manifestation of centration.

MIDDLE-CHILDHOOD INTELLIGENCE: THE CONCRETE OPERATIONAL PERIOD

The concrete operational period is the period of middle childhood. It extends from about age 6 to about age 11 or 12.

Discussions of the cognitive differences between preschoolers and grade-schoolers typically note a long list of contrasts (Flavell et al., 2002; Ginsburg & Opper, 1988). If forced to sum up the differences in a single phrase, however, most child psychologists would probably say something like "the older child is just more *logical*." This is not to say that preschoolers are totally illogical; that would be far from the truth. But the preschooler's attempts at logical reasoning are often scattered and incomplete, working impressively in some contexts but going badly astray in others. The young child seems to lack an overall logical system that can be applied with confidence to a wide range of problems, particularly the kinds of scientific and logical problems that Piaget stressed. The older child, in contrast, does possess such a system.

A Sampling of Tasks

For the most part, Piaget used the same tasks to study the preoperational and concrete operational periods. The difference between periods lies in the pattern of response. The preoperational child fails all the tasks, whereas the concrete operational child begins to succeed at them. The older child's success is not instantaneous, however. The concrete operational concepts differ in difficulty, and their mastery is spread across the entire period of middle childhood.

Conservation The conservation of number problem described earlier is just one example of a conservation task. Conservation can be examined in any quantitative domain. Indeed, Piaget and his co-workers studied just about every form of conservation that can be imagined. There are studies of conservation of mass, weight, and volume; of length, area, and distance; of time, speed, and movement (Piaget, 1969, 1970; Piaget & Inhelder, 1974; Piaget, Inhelder, & Szeminska, 1960). Some examples are shown in Figure 7.7. As can be seen, the typical starting point is a demonstration that two stimuli are equal on some quantitative dimension. While the child watches, one of the stimuli is transformed so that they no longer look equal. To conserve the quantity, the child must be able to overcome the misleading perceptual appearance. This is precisely what the preoperational child cannot do.

Different forms of conservation are mastered at different times. Conservation of number is typically one of the first to be acquired, appearing by about age 5 or 6. Conservation of mass and conservation of continuous quantity are also relatively early achievements. Conservation of length and conservation of weight are more difficult, typically coming 2 or 3 years after the first conservations. Other forms of conservation emerge still later.

Conservation represents another form of invariant. During the sensorimotor period, the infant masters the invariant of object permanence—the knowledge that the existence of objects is invariant. During the preoperational period, the child comes to understand qualitative identity—the knowledge that the qualitative nature of objects is invariant. During the concrete operational period, the child masters the various forms of conservation—the knowledge that quantitative properties of objects are invariant.

Classes Piaget's major work on classes is described in a book entitled *The Early Growth of Logic in the Child* (Inhelder & Piaget, 1964). The word *logic* is important. A number of investigators, both before and since Piaget, have studied how children form groups or classes when asked to sort an array of objects. Do they sort on the basis of color or shape, for example, and can they consistently follow whatever criteria they select? Piaget's focus, however, was not simply on the child's ability to group objects

One of the most basic forms of conservation is the conservation of quantity. To conserve quantity, the child must avoid centering on the misleading perceptual appearance.

sensibly. His interest was in the child's understanding of the structure or logic of any classification system formed.

The best-known task for probing the child's understanding of classes is the **class inclusion** problem. Suppose that we present the child with 20 wooden beads, 17 red and 3 white. The child agrees that some of the beads are red, some are white, and all are wooden. We then ask the child whether there are more red beads or more wooden beads. Or we might ask which would make a longer necklace, all the red beads or all the wooden beads.

However we word the question, the preoperational response is the same: "There are more red beads than wooden beads." The child is apparently unable to think about a bead as belonging simultaneously to both a subclass (all the red ones) and a superordinate class (all the wooden ones). Instead, once the child has focused on the perceptually salient subclass—the many red beads—the only comparison left is with the other subclass—the few white beads. Note again the role of centration in the preoperational child's thinking—the tendency to focus on what is perceptually obvious and to ignore other information. The result is that the child makes a fundamental logical error and judges that a subclass is larger than its superordinate class.

The concrete operational response is again quite different. The concrete operational child can solve this and other versions of the class inclusion problem. Furthermore, the concrete operational child, according to Piaget, appreciates the logical necessity of the class inclusion answer. The child knows not simply that there are not more roses than flowers or more dogs than animals. The child who truly understands the structure of classes knows that there can *never* be more roses or more dogs—that it is logically impossible for a subclass to be larger than the superordinate class (Miller, 1986).

Relations In addition to understanding classes, the child must come to understand the relations between classes. Thus, another large set of Piagetian tasks has to do with various aspects of relational reasoning.

A deceptively simple-looking problem in relational reasoning is the **seriation** task (Piaget & Szeminska, 1952). To study seriation of length, we might present 10 sticks of different lengths haphazardly arranged on a table. The child's task is to order the sticks in terms of length. We might expect that any child who is persistent enough will eventually arrive at the correct solution through trial and error. Yet most young children fail the task. They may end up with just two or three groups of "big" and "little" sticks rather than a completely ordered array. Or they may line up the tops of the sticks but completely ignore the bottoms. Even if the child succeeds through trial and error, he is unlikely to be able to solve further variants of the problem—for example, to insert new sticks into a completed array. What seriation requires, according to Piaget, is a systematic and logical approach in which the child is able to think of each stick as being simultaneously longer than the one that precedes it and shorter than the one that comes after it. It is this sort of two-dimensional, noncentrated approach to problem solving that the preoperational child lacks.

The preoperational child also fails to appreciate the **transitivity** of quantitative relations (Piaget et al., 1960). Suppose we work with three sticks—A, B, and C—that differ only slightly in length. We show the child that A is longer than B and that B is longer than C. We then ask about the relative lengths of A and C but do not allow the child to compare them perceptually. Solving this task requires the ability to add together the two premises (A > B and B > C) to deduce the correct answer (A > C). The concrete operational child has this ability (though not immediately—transitivity emerges at about age 7 or 8). The preoperational child does not, and so is likely to fall back on guessing or some other irrelevant strategy.

Note the similarity between transitivity and class inclusion. In both cases, the correct answer follows as a logically necessary implication from the information available. Thus, it is not simply a fact that A happens to be longer than C; if A is longer than B and B longer than C, then A *has* to be longer than C. We can see again Piaget's emphasis on very basic forms of logical reasoning.

Class inclusion
The knowledge that a subclass cannot be larger than the superordinate class that includes it. In Piaget's theory, a concrete operational achievement.

Understanding the nature of classes is an important achievement of the concrete operational period.

Seriation
The ability to order stimuli along some quantitative dimension, such as length. In Piaget's theory, a concrete operational achievement.

Transitivity
The ability to combine relations logically to deduce necessary conclusions—for example, if A > B and B > C, then A > C. In Piaget's theory, a concrete operational achievement.

The Concept of Operations

Interesting though the empirical studies may be, Piaget's primary purpose was never simply to document what children do or do not know. His goal was always to use children's overt performance as a guide to their underlying cognitive structures. During middle childhood, these structures are labeled *concrete operations*.

We will not attempt a complete presentation of Piaget's theory of concrete operations, both because the theory is very complicated and because the full model has not held up very well with time. Nevertheless, it is important to convey some idea of what Piaget meant by **operations**. Operations are in many respects similar to the sensorimotor schemes. One similarity is implied by the very name *operation*. An operation, like a sensorimotor scheme, always involves some form of action—*operating* on the world in order to understand it. Another similarity is that operations, like schemes, do not exist in isolation but are organized into a larger system of interrelated cognitive structures.

Operations
Piaget's term for the various forms of mental action through which older children solve problems and reason logically.

There are also differences between sensorimotor schemes and concrete operations. A major difference concerns how actions are expressed. Sensorimotor schemes are always expressed in overt action—reaching, grasping, manipulating, or the like. Operations, in contrast, are a system of *internal* actions. They are, in fact, the logical, in-the-head form of problem solving toward which the child has been slowly moving ever since the onset of representational intelligence.

Let us apply the notion of intelligence-as-internal-action to one of the concepts discussed earlier—working with classes, for example. Piaget argued that what a child knows about classes is a function of various mental actions that the child can perform. Simply to think about an object as belonging to a certain class is a form of action. Classes are not environmental givens; rather, they are cognitive constructions. To add together two subclasses (for example, red beads and white beads) to get the superordinate class (wooden beads) is a form of action. To compare the sizes of two subclasses, or of subclass and superordinate, is a form of action. In general, classification is a matter of mental activity—of creating and disbanding classes, comparing different classes, and logically adding, subtracting, or multiplying classes.

What about conservation? Piaget identified various mental actions through which the child might arrive at a correct conservation judgment. In the conservation of number task, the child might reason that the change in one dimension—say, the length of the row—is compensated by or canceled out by the change in the other dimension—the spacing between objects. Such reasoning by means of *compensation* involves a kind of logical multiplication of the two dimensions (increase in length times decrease in density implies no change in number). Or the child might reason that the spreading transformation can be undone and the starting point of equality reestablished, a form of reasoning that Piaget labeled *inversion* or *negation*.

Reversibility
Piaget's term for the power of operations to correct for potential disturbances and thus arrive at correct solutions to problems.

Both compensation and inversion are examples of a more general Piagetian notion, the concept of **reversibility.** Reversibility is a property of operational structures that allows the cognitive system to correct, or reverse, potential disturbances and thus to arrive at an adaptive, nondistorted understanding of the world. It is this power that concrete operational thought has and that preoperational thought lacks.

More on the Preoperational–Concrete Operational Contrast

Is young children's thinking really as riddled with deficiencies as Piaget claimed? Are the differences between early childhood and later childhood really so great? A number of recent research programs have suggested that the answer to both questions is no. Here we discuss research directed to three of the topics reviewed earlier—perspective taking, symbolic ability, and conservation.

Perspective Taking   We begin with the concept of visual perspective taking that Piaget's three-mountains task is meant to tap. As an examination of Figure 7.6 makes clear, the three-mountains task requires more than simply avoiding an egocentric response. To come up with the correct answer, the child must engage in a fairly complicated process of spatial calculation. Perhaps the young child's problems with this task tell us more about such spatial computation skills than about egocentrism.

When the task is simplified, young children often appear considerably less egocentric. Children as young as 3 can predict the other's viewpoint when familiar toys rather than Piagetian mountains serve as landmarks (Borke, 1975). Even 2-year-olds can demonstrate some awareness of the other's viewpoint in very simple situations. When asked to show another person a picture, for example, the 2-year-old holds the picture vertically so that its face is toward the viewer rather than toward the self (Lempers, Flavell, & Flavell, 1977). Similarly, 2-year-olds realize (popular myth notwithstanding) that the fact that *their* eyes are closed does not mean that other people also cannot see (Flavell, Shipstead, & Croft, 1980). Even 18-month-olds will point to objects that they want an adult to notice, a behavior that suggests some realization that the adult does not necessarily see what they see (Rheingold, Hay, & West, 1976). Eighteen-month-olds also show some awareness that others do not necessarily want what they want. Faced with an adult who (strangely!) has shown a preference for broccoli over Goldfish crackers, children this age offer the adult the broccoli, despite their own preference for crackers (Repacholi & Gopnik, 1997).

Children's ability to tailor their speech to the needs of others also turns out to be more advanced than one would expect from Piaget's accounts of egocentric speech. Four-year-olds use simpler speech when talking to 2-year-olds than when talking either to other 4-year-olds or to adults (Shatz & Gelman, 1973). Thus, they adjust the level of their communication to the cognitive resources of the listener. Indeed, even 2-year-olds talk somewhat differently to their infant siblings than to adults (Dunn & Kendrick, 1982). Children can also adjust to temporary variations in what the listener knows, as opposed to the general differences that exist between babies and adults. They describe an event differently, for example, depending on whether the adult to whom they are talking was present when the event occurred (Menig-Peterson, 1975), and they make different inferences about what listeners know and structure their communications differently in response to differences in listeners' past experiences (O'Neill, 1996).

Evidence for early perspective-taking skills is not limited to the studies reviewed here. The findings are quite general across a variety of different forms of perspective taking (Flavell, 1992b; Newcombe, 1989; Shantz, 1983). In no case is the 3- or 4-year-old's performance fully equivalent to that of the older child. But it is often more advanced than we once believed.

Symbolic Ability   Some impressive early accomplishments are also evident in the area of symbolic ability. The rudimentary forms of symbolic play that emerge by the end of infancy increase in both frequency and complexity across the preschool years (Corrigan, 1987; Howes, Unger, & Matheson, 1992). Whereas infants' first play efforts are limited to their own actions (e.g., pretending to go to sleep), eventually props of a variety of sorts can be incorporated. Initially the props must be physically close to their real-life counterparts; with development, more distant symbols can be utilized, including simply imagination in the absence of any prop. Initially most play episodes consist of isolated actions; eventually single acts of pretense evolve into sequences of related actions. And, of course, developments do not cease at age 5. Play is a ubiquitous childhood activity that is linked to numerous cognitive and social developments, and we therefore return to the topic at various points in later chapters.

Children also come to appreciate the representational nature of pictures. Although infants can recognize the correspondence between object and picture, they apparently do not yet realize that a picture is simply a symbolic depiction of the real thing. A 9-month-old presented with a realistic color photograph of an object pats and rubs the photo as though it were the object itself (DeLoache et al., 1998). By 19 months this confusion has disappeared, and pointing and vocalizing replace the manual exploration.

Other developments soon follow. Eighteen-month-olds do not care whether the picture they are viewing is right side up or upside down; by 30 months a preference for the standard upright orientation has emerged (DeLoache, Uttal, & Pierroutsakous, 2000). Two-year-olds realize that a picture can depict a real object, such as a dog; it is not until age 2.5, however, that children acquire the important insight that a picture can depict a *specific* real object, such as the family dog (DeLoache, Pierroutsakous, & Troseth, 1996). Finally, by age 3 or 4, children, like most adults, begin to take into account the artist's intent when identifying a picture (Bloom & Markson, 1998; Browne & Woolley, 2001). When presented, for example, with a drawing of a stick with an oval on top, they label it as either *lollipop* or *balloon*, depending on what they have been told the artist intended to draw, and they may vigorously object to the other (objectively equally valid) interpretation. The same emphasis on intent rather than product is evident when children themselves produce the picture, as anyone who has ever discussed a drawing with a 4-year-old knows.

The preschool child also makes some initial advances in the mastery of conventional symbol systems, such as maps and scale models (Huttenlocher, Newcombe, & Vasilyeva, 1999; Uttal, 2000). An especially interesting example in the latter category comes in a program of research by Judy DeLoache and associates (DeLoache, 2000, 2002; DeLoache, Miller, & Rosengren, 1997; DeLoache & Smith, 1999). The task is a hide-and-seek game: A Snoopy doll is hidden somewhere in the room, and the child's job is to find Snoopy. As Figure 7.8 shows, the room offers a number of possible hiding places, and thus the task is a challenging one. As the figure also shows, however, there is a helpful addition to the task: a model of the room that reproduces all of its features in miniature. There is also a miniature Snoopy, and he is to be hidden—as the experimenter carefully explains to the child—in the same place in his room as Big Snoopy is hiding in *his* room. The question is whether children can use this symbolic equivalence to solve the task. By 3 years of age they can: Once they see Little Snoopy disappear into his hiding place, they run immediately to the matching place in the real room to find Big Snoopy.

Although DeLoache's studies demonstrate some impressive symbolic competence by age 3, they also reveal a surprising early deficit. Children just a few months younger

Figure 7.8

Diagram of the experimental arrangement in the DeLoache research on early symbolic ability. The darkened areas in the scale model correspond to labeled items of furniture in the room. From "Young Children's Understanding of the Correspondence between a Scale Model and a Larger Space" by J. S. DeLoache, 1989, *Cognitive Development, 4,* 125. Copyright © 1989 by Ablex Publishing Company. Reprinted by permission.

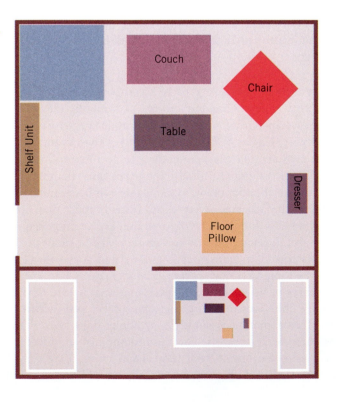

are unable to solve the Snoopy task. They fail despite apparently understanding the instructions and despite being highly motivated to find Snoopy—and despite the fact that they have been using symbols of various sorts for several months. Why the difficulty here? DeLoache argues that the challenge for the young child lies in the need for **dual representation,** which is the realization that an object can be represented in two ways simultaneously. In the find-Snoopy task the model and miniature dog are not only symbols for their life-size counterparts; they are also real objects in themselves. Two-year-olds are apparently unable to think about them as both objects and symbols simultaneously.

The dual representation hypothesis suggests an interesting prediction: that young children might show greater success if the symbol were less object-like—less a thing unto itself. This proves to be the case. When photographs of the room replace the scale model, children as young as 2.5 are able to use the symbols to find Snoopy. Conversely, when the real-object nature of the symbol is emphasized—for example, by allowing the children to play with the model before the search task—even older children may have difficulty appreciating the model's symbolic nature.

Dual representation
The realization that an object can be represented in two ways simultaneously.

Conservation   As we saw, the aspect of quantitative understanding that most interested Piaget was the child's ability to conserve quantities in the face of a perceptual change. Later studies have not disproved Piaget's contention that a full understanding of conservation is a concrete operational achievement. Recent work does suggest, however, that there may be earlier, partial forms of understanding that were missed in his studies.

As with perspective taking, investigators have simplified the conservation task in various ways. They have reduced the usual verbal demands, for example, by allowing the child to pick candies to eat or juice to drink rather than answer questions about "same" or "more." Or they have made the context for the question more natural and familiar by embedding the task within an ongoing game. Although such changes do not eliminate the nonconservation error completely, they often result in improved performance by supposedly preoperational 4- and 5-year-olds (Donaldson, 1982; Miller, 1976, 1982). Indeed, in simple situations even 3-year-olds can demonstrate some knowledge of the invariance of number. A study by Rochel Gelman (1972) provides a nice example.

Gelman's study makes use of the same violation-of-expectancy procedure that has proved informative in the study of infant cognition. In her study the 3-year-old participants first played a game in which they learned, over a series of trials, that a plate with three toy mice affixed to it was a "winner" and a plate with two toy mice was a "loser." Then, in a critical test trial, the three-mice plate was surreptitiously transformed while hidden. In some cases the length of the row was changed; in other cases one of the mice was removed. The children were unfazed by the change in length, continuing to treat the plate as a winner. An actual change in number, however, was responded to quite differently, eliciting surprise, search behaviors, and various attempts at an explanation (our favorite: "Jesus took it"). The children thus showed a recognition that number, at least in this situation, should remain invariant.

An Overall Evaluation   The consistent message that emerges from the studies just described is that the preschool child is more competent than Piaget's research and theory would lead us to believe. The studies and the content areas reviewed here represent just a small fraction of the evidence for this statement (Flavell, 1992a; Gelman & Baillargeon, 1983; Wellman & Gelman, 1998). Young children's relational reasoning, for example, has been shown to be more impressive than one might think from reading Piaget (e.g., Goswami, 1995), and the same is true for understanding of classes (e.g., Smith, 1979). In the concluding section of this chapter, we will see still further examples of impressive cognitive achievements during the preschool period.

This is not to say that Piaget's description of preoperational thinking is totally inaccurate. It is not. Young children *are* often egocentric, centrated, and illogical. They fail in a wide range of tasks on which older children succeed, and they often need simplified situations or special help to show whatever competence they possess. Piaget was correct in asserting that there are important limitations in early childhood thinking and important developmental changes between early childhood and middle childhood. But he may have somewhat misjudged the nature of both the limitations and the change.

To Recap . . .

The third developmental period in Piaget's theory is the period of concrete operations. During this period, the child gradually masters the different forms of conservation. The concrete operational child also comes to understand various aspects of classification (including class inclusion) and relational reasoning (including transitivity). Piaget attributed these and other achievements of middle childhood to the formation of concrete operations, an organized system of internal mental actions.

Recent research suggests that Piaget overstated the differences between early childhood and middle childhood. When tested in simplified situations, preschool children often show more competence than they show on standard Piagetian tasks. Young children are not as consistently egocentric as Piaget suggested, and they demonstrate rudiments of skills that will develop more fully during middle childhood.

ADOLESCENT AND ADULT: THE FORMAL OPERATIONAL PERIOD

Formal operations is the final period in Piaget's stage hierarchy. It can be given a beginning but not an end point, because once acquired, formal operations are assumed to last throughout the lifetime. The onset of the period is usually dated at about age 12 or 13, around the beginning of adolescence. But formal operations may emerge later than this or not at all. As we will see, the evidence suggests that not everyone reaches the formal operational period.

Characteristics of Formal Operational Thought

We have already discussed the meaning of the term *operations*. But what about the term *concrete?* The concrete part of the label refers to the basic limitation of concrete operational thought. As we have seen, the concrete operational child, in contrast to the sensorimotor child, does operate cognitively by means of representations rather than overt actions. Nevertheless, concrete operational children are still limited to dealing largely with what is directly in front of them—with what is concrete, tangible, real. What the child at this stage cannot yet do at all well is deal with the hypothetical—with the whole world of possibility rather than immediate reality.

Formal operational thinkers show no such limitation. The distinguishing characteristic of the formal operational period is the capacity for **hypothetical-deductive reasoning.** The formal operational thinker moves easily and surely through the world of what-ifs, might-bes, and if-thens. The adolescent, in fact, often seems more at home with the hypothetical—with imagined worlds, counterfactual propositions, life dreams and schemes—than in the world of mundane reality.

The *deductive* part of *hypothetical-deductive* is also important. To qualify as formal operational, thought must do more than simply imagine possibilities. The formal operational thinker possesses a rigorous logical system for evaluating hypotheses and deducing necessary outcomes. As the term *operations* implies, this system again involves various forms of mental action.

Piaget's favorite way of characterizing the difference between concrete operations and formal operations was to talk about a reversal in the relation between reality and possibility. For the concrete operational child, the starting point is always immediate reality. From this point, the child can make very limited extensions into the hypothetical. In a conservation of number task, for example, the child who imagines pushing the chips back together *is* going beyond what is immediately given but in a very limited way.

Hypothetical-deductive reasoning
A form of problem solving characterized by the ability to generate and test hypotheses and draw logical conclusions from the results of the tests. In Piaget's theory, a formal operational achievement.

For the formal operational thinker, in contrast, the starting point is the world of possibility—whatever it is that might be true. From this starting point in the possible, the thinker works back to what happens to be true in the situation under study.

A Research Example: Reasoning about Pendulums

Inhelder and Piaget's (1958) tasks for studying formal operations consist mostly of problems in scientific reasoning. In one task, for example, the participant must determine what factors (length, thickness, shape, and so on) influence the bending of a rod. In another, the task is to experiment with various chemical solutions to determine which combinations produce a specified outcome. Among the other content areas examined are projection of shadows, determinants of floating, conservation of motion, and laws of centrifugal force.

The example that we will describe is drawn from the domain of physics. In this task, the participant is shown a simple pendulum consisting of a weight hanging on a string. Various other weights and strings are also available for experimentation. The problem is to figure out what determines the frequency of oscillation of the pendulum—that is, how fast the pendulum swings back and forth. Is it the heaviness of the weight? The length of the string? The height from which the weight is dropped? The force with which it is pushed? Or perhaps some combination of two or more of these factors?

It turns out that the only factor that really has an effect is the length of the string. But the point is not that the formal operational thinker knows this in advance, because he or she probably does not. The point is that the formal operational thinker possesses a set of cognitive structures that will allow systematic solution of the problem. The solution requires first identifying each of the potentially important variables—weight, length, and so on—and then systematically testing them out, varying one factor at a time while holding other factors constant. The subject must be able to generate all the possible variables (and sometimes combinations of variables), keep track of what has been done and what remains to be done, and draw logical conclusions from the overall pattern of results. In the case of the pendulum, the performance of all relevant tests will lead to the conclusion that if the string is short the pendulum swings fast, and only if the string is short does the pendulum swing fast. Thus, the length is both a necessary and a sufficient determinant of oscillation.

As with all Piagetian stages, the achievements of formal operations are clearest when contrasted with the preceding period. The concrete operational child is unlikely to solve the pendulum problem. The 9- or 10-year-old faced with such a task will do some intelligent things, including accurately testing some of the possible variables. But the younger child is not able to generate and examine the full range of possibilities on which a logical conclusion depends. Instead, the child may find that a heavy weight on a short string swings fast and conclude that both the weight and length are important, a conclusion that is not valid in the absence of further tests.

Note that the formal operational approach to the problem embodies the kind of reversal between reality and possibility that Piaget stressed. The formal operational thinker begins by considering all the various possibilities—maybe the weight is important, maybe the length is important, and so on. At first, these are merely hypotheses; none of them is anything that has yet been observed, and most of them will turn out to be false. Yet it is only by systematically considering all the possibilities that the subject can determine what happens to be true. Thus, the movement of thought is from the possible to the real.

More Recent Work on Formal Operations

Research on formal operations has addressed the same general issues discussed with respect to earlier Piagetian stages. A basic question is whether Piaget accurately diagnosed what his participants knew. Later studies using the Inhelder and Piaget tasks have typically found lower levels of performance than Inhelder and Piaget reported (Shayer, Kucheman, & Wylam, 1976; Shayer & Wylam, 1978). Indeed some studies have found substantial proportions of adults who fail the usual formal operational tasks (Commons, Miller, & Kuhn, 1982).

The suggestion that Piaget may have *overestimated* ability runs counter to what we identified earlier as a common conclusion about Piagetian procedures—namely, that they typically lead to some underestimation of children's competence. Some researchers have suggested that underestimation may also occur at the formal operational level. The Inhelder and Piaget tasks are unfamiliar to most people, and the usual method of administering them may not elicit the individual's optimal performance. Studies have shown that the addition of a simple hint or prompt concerning the appropriate procedure can lead to a marked improvement on later trials (Danner & Day, 1977; Stone & Day, 1978). More extended training procedures, as well as other sorts of procedural simplifications, have elicited at least some elements of formal operational performance in children as young as 9 or 10 (Fabricius & Steffe, 1989; Kuhn, Ho, & Adams, 1979).

Another possible approach is to vary the content of the tasks. Perhaps people tend to be formal operational when reasoning about content that is interesting and familiar to them. For some people, the natural science problems used by Inhelder and Piaget may provide such content; others, however, may require tasks in literary analysis, or auto mechanics, or cooking. Piaget himself, in fact, suggested this possibility in one of his later articles about formal operations (Piaget, 1972). Although research to date is limited, there is some support for the idea. For example, De Lisi and Staudt (1980) demonstrated that college students' ability to reason at a formal operational level depended on the fit between academic training and specific task: Physics majors did best on the Inhelder and Piaget pendulum task; English majors excelled on a task involving analysis of literary style; and political science majors earned their highest scores on a problem in political reasoning.

Findings from cross-cultural research also illustrate the importance of specific experience. Although people from non-Western cultures seldom do well on the Inhelder and Piaget problems, they may show impressive levels of performance when operating in more familiar and culturally significant domains. For example, prior to the availability of magnetic compasses, Micronesian navigators sailed their canoes for hundreds of miles from one island to another without the aid of instruments, an achievement no Western sailor would attempt to duplicate. The navigators' ability to maintain course depended on a complex—and culturally transmitted—computational system in which star positions,

Formal operational reasoning is not limited to the science laboratory. The navigational achievements of Micronesian sailors depend on a complex system of computations and logical deductions.

rate of movement, and fixed reference points were systematically combined in ways that seem fully equivalent to the highest levels of performance shown by Inhelder and Piaget's participants (Hutchins, 1983).

Still one more indication that experience can be important comes from across-time comparisons of performance on formal-operational tasks. Flieller (1999) reports that adolescents tested in the 1990s earn higher scores on such measures than did comparable samples from the 1960s and early 1970s. The most plausible explanation for this rise in performance lies in changes in relevant experience across the 25-year span, perhaps especially improvements in education.

Level of performance has not been the only point of contention in follow-up work on formal operations. Piaget's theory of formal operational thought structures has also been subject to criticism, including many of the same criticisms made of his claims concerning concrete operations. The degree of within-stage consistency is an issue. Although some studies report fairly strong correlations among formal operational tasks (Eckstein & Shemesh, 1992), low to moderate relations are probably a more common finding (Martorano, 1977). Furthermore, the specific logical structures that Piaget believed underlie formal operational performance have been severely criticized by logicians (Braine & Rumaine, 1983; Ennis, 1976). As with earlier Piagetian stages, few dispute that Piaget identified interesting forms of thought or that his theory may partially explain what is happening. But the theory does not seem to be completely satisfactory, and debates about the best way to characterize this level of thinking therefore continue (Byrnes, 1988; Keating, 1988; Moshman, 1998).

To Recap . . .

The final period described by Piaget's theory is the period of formal operations, which typically begins around adolescence. The distinguishing characteristic of formal operations is the capacity for hypothetical-deductive reasoning. The formal operational thinker begins with possibility—all the hypotheses that might apply to the task under study—and ends with reality—the particular solution that a systematic and logical testing of hypotheses shows to be true. Such thinking is revealed most clearly in tasks that involve scientific reasoning, such as the pendulum problem.

Although later research has confirmed Piaget's general account of adolescent thought, questions have arisen concerning the adequacy of his assessment methods, with some researchers reporting poorer performance than that obtained by Piaget and some reporting better performance. Questions have also arisen concerning the accuracy of Piaget's specific model of formal operations.

GENERAL ISSUES

Despite the many corrections and qualifications that we have noted, Piaget's work remains the field's richest source for descriptions of children's thinking and how it changes with development. The descriptive picture of childhood cognition is not the only lasting influence of the approach, however. Piaget also identified some of the fundamental questions that a theory of development must address, and his theory sets forth some strong claims in his own answers to these questions. In the present section we consider the status of Piaget's claims with respect to three of the central issues in the study of cognitive development: whether development progresses through distinct stages, whether some aspects of development are universal across cultural settings, and how best to explain cognitive change.

Stages

Although we have described the Piagetian stages, we have not really discussed what it means to claim that there are stages of development. What must be true for a stage theory to be valid?

Most theorists agree that at least three criteria are important. One is that development include *qualitative* as well as quantitative changes—that is, changes in how the child thinks and not merely in how much the child knows or how quickly the child can do things.

Piagetian theorists maintain that development does in fact show qualitative change from one period to the next. They would argue, for example, that there is a qualitative, in-kind difference between a sensorimotor child, who must act out all her adaptation to the world, and a preoperational child, who can solve problems mentally through the use of symbols. Similarly, there is a qualitative difference between the preoperational response to a conservation task and the concrete operational response. Younger children treat conservation as a problem in perceptual estimation, always judging in terms of how things look. Older children do not even need to look at the stimuli; for them, conservation is a matter of logical reasoning, not of perceptual judgment.

A second criterion is that the stages follow an *invariant sequence*—each stage builds on the one before, and no stage can be attained until the preceding one has been mastered. It is impossible, for example, for the child to become preoperational without the sensorimotor developments that make representational thought possible. Similarly, concrete operations build on the achievements of the preoperational period. This claim of sequence applies not only to the four general periods but also to the substages within a period—for example, the six sensorimotor substages.

The final criterion has created the most problems. Piaget's theory maintains that each stage can be characterized by a set of interrelated cognitive structures—for example, the concrete operations of middle childhood. Once developed, these structures determine performance on a wide range of cognitive tasks. This position implies that there should be important *concurrences* in development. That is, if two or more abilities are determined by the same underlying structures, then they should emerge at the same time. Children's cognitive endeavors should show a good deal of consistency.

The problem for Piaget's theory is that children's performance is often far from consistent. They may, for example, succeed on some presumably concrete operational tasks yet fail totally on others. Piaget did not claim perfect consistency; he was the first, in fact, to demonstrate that various concrete operational concepts may be mastered at different times. Most commentators, however, believe that Piaget never satisfactorily explained the inconsistencies that his research uncovered. And research since his has revealed even more inconsistency in development, including instances in which abilities that Piaget explicitly claimed as concurrences are mastered at different times (de Ribaupierre, Rieben, & Lautrey, 1991; Jamison, 1977; Kreitler & Kreitler, 1989).

What, then, is the status of the concept of stage? The issue continues to be a source of debate (Fischer & Bidell, 1998; Lourenco & Machado, 1996; Miller, 2001). Some researchers believe that Piaget's stage model is basically accurate, even though specific details may need correcting. Others (including researchers whose work we discuss in the next chapter) believe that cognitive development does in fact occur in stages, but that the stages are different from those posited by Piaget. And still others believe that the concept of stage serves no useful purpose and should be abandoned.

Universality

We noted that Piaget's work is toward the normative end of the normative–idiographic continuum. For Piaget, however, the focus on similarities is not simply a methodological preference; rather, it is a claim about the nature of development. In Piaget's view, all children the world around pass through the same stages in the same order. And all children develop basic forms of knowledge, such as object permanence and conservation.

The study of development in other cultures provides a natural testing ground for the Piagetian claim of universality. We have long known that children growing up in the United States or Canada show the same basic patterns of development that Piaget first identified in children in Geneva some 50 or 60 years ago. But suppose we consider cultures in which children's experiences are markedly different from those that are typical in Western societies. Will development still follow the Piagetian mold?

The answer turns out to be yes and no. Research across a range of cultural settings indicates clearly that the specific experiences available to children can affect the development of Piagetian concepts in a variety of ways (Laboratory of Comparative Human Cognition, 1983; Rogoff & Chavajay, 1995). Culture can affect the rate of development: In some cultures development lags several years behind the norms reported in other settings. Culture can affect the final level of development: In some cultures, especially those without formal schooling, few if any individuals attain formal operations. Indeed, even the order in which certain abilities emerge may vary across cultures. For example, children from pottery-making families show precocious mastery of conservation of substance relative to other abilities (Price-Williams, Gordon, & Ramirez, 1969). Similarly, the extensive navigation through the spatial terrain that is part of life in nomadic societies is associated with accelerated development of spatial abilities in children from such groups (Dasen, 1975).

At the same time, cross-cultural research also provides some support for the Piagetian claim of universality. No one has found a culture in which children do not eventually acquire forms of knowledge such as object permanence and conservation, or in which children master conservation without going through an initial phase of nonconservation, or in which the order of the four general periods of development is reversed. Indeed, even some of the reported lags in rate of development disappear when the tests are made appropriate to the cultural setting—for example, when children are interviewed in their native language by a native speaker (Nyiti, 1982) or when the children themselves play an active role in the assessment situation (Greenfield, 1966).

Cross-cultural studies, then, reveal both variation and consistency, depending on which aspects of development we consider. The variations are informative, because they alert us to the importance of culturally variable experiences that were not addressed in Piaget's theory. A Piagetian could argue, however, that the variations operate on a bedrock of basic similarity.

Inuit children, and children of other nomadic cultures, have well-developed spatial abilities.

Cognitive Change

Most of Piaget's research was directed to the question that has been our focus throughout the chapter: What are the most important changes that occur in the course of cognitive development? In his theorizing, however, he also devoted considerable attention to the second general question that a theory of development must address: How can we explain the changes that our research has identified?

Piaget's position on the nature–nurture issue is definitely interactionist. In his theory, biology and experience act together to produce changes in the child's cognitive abilities.

More specifically, Piaget (1964, 1983) identified four general factors that contribute to cognitive change. Three of the factors are found to some extent in every theory of development. First, biological maturation plays a role. In any stage theory, biological factors contribute to both the nature and the timing of the stage changes. Learning and development occur within constraints set by the child's maturational level, and some kinds of development may be impossible until maturation has progressed sufficiently.

Experience is also important. Piaget divided experience into two categories: physical experience and social experience. The former includes the child's interactions with inanimate objects; the latter, the child's interactions with people. In both cases, Piaget stressed the importance of assimilation and action. Children must fit experiences, physical or social, into what they already understand. And they must actively construct new knowledge, as opposed to having knowledge imposed ready-made upon them.

Every theory talks in some way about maturation, physical experience, and social experience. The fourth factor is more uniquely Piagetian. **Equilibration** is another legacy of Piaget's biological training. Piaget used this term to refer to the general biological process of self-regulation. It was for him the most important of the four factors, the one that in a sense explained the other three.

Equilibration
Piaget's term for the biological process of self-regulation that propels the cognitive system to higher forms of equilibrium.

Equilibrium
A characteristic of a cognitive system in which assimilation and accommodation are in balance, thus permitting adaptive, nondistorted responses to the world.

What did Piaget mean by self-regulation? The notion is easiest to understand in conjunction with a closely related Piagetian construct, **equilibrium.** *Equilibrium* refers to balance within the cognitive system. It exists when the child's cognitive structures can respond to any environmental challenge without distortion or misunderstanding. In Piaget's theory, such an adaptive response implies a balance between assimilation and accommodation. The child neither distorts reality to make it fit existing structures (which would be an excess of assimilation) nor distorts current knowledge in an attempt to make sense of something new (which would be an excess of accommodation). It is the self-regulating process of equilibration that guards against such distortions and acts to maintain equilibrium.

Piaget cited equilibration as the ultimate explanation for several aspects of development. Equilibration accounts for the organization in development. As we saw, inputs from maturation and from various kinds of experience are not simply lumped together; rather, they are coordinated into cognitive structures. According to Piaget, there must be some more general factor that accounts for such coordination. This general factor is the self-regulating process of equilibration.

Piaget and Education

The Piagetian approach, with its grounding in basic issues in philosophy, has always been more theoretically than applicationally oriented. Yet Piaget wrote two books about education (Piaget, 1971, 1976), and others have written extensively about the educational implications of his work (Cowan, 1978; DeVries & Zan, 1994; Duckworth, 1987; Kamii & DeVries, 1993).

What do Piaget's theory and research have to say about education? Four principles are most often cited in discussions of Piagetian approaches to education. One is the importance of readiness. This principle follows from Piaget's emphasis on assimilation. Experience—educational or otherwise—does not simply happen to the child; rather, it must always be assimilated to current cognitive structures. A new experience will be beneficial only if the child can make some sense of it. Teaching that is too far beyond the child's level is unlikely to have any positive impact.

A second, related principle concerns the motivation for cognitive activity. Educational content that is too advanced is unlikely to be interesting, but the same applies to content that is too simple. What is needed is content that is slightly beyond the child's current level, so that it provides experiences familiar enough to be assimilated, yet challenging enough to provoke disequilibrium.

We can hardly work at the child's level unless we know what that level is. A third contribution from Piaget is a wealth of information about what a child does or does not know at different points in development. The message, to be sure, is in part negative—constraints on what can be taught before certain points, cautions about how much development can

BOX 7.1

Applications

be accelerated. More positively, Piaget's studies often identify steps and sequences through which particular content domains are mastered. We can thus determine not only where the child is but also the natural next steps for development.

A final principle is more functional. It concerns Piaget's emphasis on intelligence as action. Piaget distrusted educational methods that are too passive, too rote, or too verbal. In his view, education should build on the child's natural curiosity and natural tendency to act on the world to understand it. Knowledge is most meaningful when children construct it themselves rather than when it is imposed on them. This principle is expressed in the title of one of Piaget's books about education—*To Understand Is to Invent.*

The Piagetian approach to education stresses the child's own exploration and self-discovery.

Equilibration also explains motivation. In Piaget's view, the cognitive system seeks always to reach and maintain states of equilibrium, because equilibrium characterizes adaptive behavior. Suppose, however, that the child encounters some new event that cannot immediately be understood. This new event will evoke disequilibrium, or cognitive conflict—some sort of disturbing imbalance within the cognitive system. The child will feel a need to get rid of the conflict and will continue to think and act until the event is understood and equilibrium restored.

Equilibration accounts finally for the directionality in development—for the fact that development moves always in an upward, progressive direction. When disequilibrium exists, only certain kinds of resolution are satisfactory. Conceivably, the child could remove the disequilibrium by distorting the input or regressing to some lower level of understanding. But this does not happen. When equilibrium is restored, it exists at a higher, better level of understanding. It is in this way that misunderstanding evolves into understanding and lower stages into higher ones.

It should be clear that equilibration, at least as we have discussed it so far, is a *very* general notion. Even if the general construct makes sense, it does not tell us how specific cognitive changes come about. Piaget did attempt at various points to specify the equilibration process more exactly (Piaget, 1957, 1977). Most critics, however, have concluded that none of the versions is very satisfactory, and the theory remains vague and hard to test (Chapman, 1992; Zimmerman & Blom, 1983). A reasonable conclusion is that Piaget provided a general framework within which a theory of change could be constructed, but he himself never succeeded in filling in the framework.

To Recap . . .

A central claim of Piagetian theory is that development proceeds through a series of stages. This claim implies that there are qualitative changes with development, that the stages emerge in an invariant sequence, and that children's thinking will show important concurrences or consistencies. The last criterion poses the greatest challenge to the stage model, in that children's cognitive performance is often far from consistent.

Piaget's theory also posits important universals in development. Cross-cultural research provides mixed support for this claim. Such studies indicate that the speed and even the order with which abilities are mastered can vary across cultures. Such studies also suggest, however, that fundamental developments, such as object permanence and conservation, may be universal.

In addition to specifying important changes, a developmental theory must explain how the changes occur. Piaget identified four general factors that contribute to development: maturation, physical experience, social experience, and equilibration. Equilibration is the biological process of self-regulation—the tendency to move toward higher levels of equilibrium. The main criticism of this model has concerned lack of specificity.

NEW DIRECTIONS

As our discussions throughout this chapter should make clear, Piaget's tasks continue to be a fertile source for research in cognitive development. The influence of the Piagetian approach is not limited to the specific tasks and corresponding abilities examined in Piaget's own studies, however. The Piagetian legacy, rather, is a good deal more general, in that the basic cognitive-developmental approach initiated by Piaget has in recent years been extended to a number of interesting developments that received little if any attention in Piaget's own research. In this final section of the chapter we consider two such topics: children's understanding of concepts, and various developments that fall under the heading of "theory of mind."

Concepts

Take a moment to reflect on your experiences the next time you take a walk. Within a brief span of time you are likely to encounter dozens of distinct objects and events—grass, trees, dogs, and birds; running, flying, jumping; clouds, wind, and sun; perhaps happiness or excitement or fear. Some of these experiences will be identical to those you have encountered before (a familiar tree, for example), but most will be new—a bird you have never seen, a novel pattern of clouds. You will not be confused or overwhelmed by this newness, however; rather, you will automatically organize the ever-changing swirl around you into meaningful units that help you make sense of what is happening (a bird, a cloud, a smile, etc.).

Concept
A mental grouping of different items into a single category on the basis of some unifying similarity or set of similarities.

Your ability to cut the world up in this adaptive way is a reflection of the many concepts that you have developed and that you use every day. A **concept** is a mental grouping of different items into a single category on the basis of some underlying similarity—some common core that makes them all, in a sense, the same thing (all birds, all instances of happiness, etc.). Concepts are a fundamental way in which we organize the world, and thus their development in childhood is of clear interest. The question that we address now is how children organize their worlds. What bases do they use when judging things as similar, and how do these bases change with development?

Table 7.4 shows one approach to this question. The problems in the table are from an influential program of research by Gelman, Markman, and associates (Gelman, 2000;

Table 7.4	**Sample Items from Gelman and Markman's Studies of Children's Concepts**

This bird's legs get cold at night. (picture of flamingo)

This bat's legs stay warm at night. (picture of black bat)

See this bird. Do its legs get cold at night, like this bird, or do its legs stay warm at night, like this bat? (picture of blackbird, looks like the bat) (see pictures)

This fish stays under water to breathe. (picture of tropical fish)
This dolphin pops above the water to breathe. (picture of dolphin)
See this fish. Does it breathe under water, like this fish, or does it pop above the water to breathe, like this dolphin? (picture of shark, looks like the dolphin)

This puppy hides bones in the ground. (picture of brown dachshund)
This fox hides food in the ground. (picture of red fox)
See this puppy. Does it hide bones in the ground, like this puppy, or does it hide food in the ground, like this fox? (picture of red dog, looks like the fox)

SOURCE: From "Categories and Induction in Young Children" by S. A. Gelman and E. M. Markman, 1986, *Cognition, 23,* 183–209, with permission from Elsevier Science.

Gelman & Markman, 1986, 1987). The two possible bases for response should be clear. If perceptual similarity is taken to be critical, then the new item should be judged to be like the one that it most resembles. This means, for example, that the blackbird would be expected to have warm legs at night, just like the similar-looking bat. In contrast, if category membership is deemed more important, then the legs would be expected to be cold, just like those of the other bird. The contrast in these tasks is common in studies of children's concepts: between surface similarity and underlying essence as the basis for judging that things are the same.

Just as the contrast is common, so is the expectation that has guided much of the research on children's concepts. The expectation has been that young children will prove to be perceptually oriented, forming concepts on the basis of surface appearance rather than more basic commonalties. There is, certainly, support for this expectation. Piaget's studies furnish many instances of preschool children centrating on what is immediately obvious and ignoring what is beneath the surface. Some of the work we discuss in the next section will provide further examples of the young child's difficulties in moving beyond surface appearance.

What has been striking and informative in recent research on children's concepts are demonstrations that in many cases young children are *not* perceptually bound. Often, in fact, preschool children seem to cut the world up in essentially the same way as do adults. This, for example, was the major conclusion from the Gelman and Markman research summarized in Table 7.4. Despite the compelling perceptual cues, most 4-year-olds opted for category membership as the relevant basis for inference, judging that the bird's legs would get cold, that the shark would breathe under water, and so forth. A subsequent study using simplified procedures showed that even 2.5-year-olds had some ability to overlook perceptual appearance in favor of category membership (Gelman & Coley, 1990).

Why the more positive picture of preschoolers' competence in recent research? Two factors are probably important. One is the methods used. Many of the older studies based their conclusions about early concepts on children's response to explicit instructions to sort items into categories (e.g., "Show me which ones go together"). The Gelman and Markman procedure, in contrast, is tied to a natural, everyday use of concepts—drawing inferences about new instances from what is already known. Our concept of "dog," for example, allows us to form expectations with respect to a number of attributes (likely behaviors, preferred diet, internal organs, etc.) even for dogs we have never met—indeed, even for breeds of dogs we have never seen. The grounding of the response measure in this natural function of concepts may be one explanation for the impressive performance in recent research.

The type of concept at issue is probably important as well. Some studies have used arbitrary concepts created on the spot for the purposes of research—for example, the category of blue circles in a study of sorting behavior. There is nothing arbitrary, however, about the concepts that children naturally form—such concepts reflect important commonalties among real-life experiences that children extract as they attempt to make sense of the world. The focus on familiar and interesting material may also contribute to the good performance in recent research.

As the vignette that opened this section should make clear, concepts are far too plentiful and diverse to permit a case-by-case discussion of their development. We will, however, single out one general category that has been the target of much interesting recent research: children's concepts of biology. Questions of life—of living versus nonliving, of origins, of growth—have fascinated children for as long as they have fascinated scientists. They certainly fascinated Piaget—some of his earliest studies were directed to how children reason about biological phenomena (Piaget, 1929). As you might expect, the main message to emerge from these studies was one of confusions and misunderstandings. A basic confusion concerned a failure to distinguish between living and nonliving, a confusion reflected in a form of reasoning that Piaget

Animism
Piaget's term for the young child's tendency to attribute properties of life to nonliving things.

labeled **animism**: the tendency to attribute properties of life to nonliving things. The young child who indicates that the sun shines "because it wants to" is engaging in animistic thinking, as is the child who is concerned that a piece of paper will be hurt by being cut. Such reasoning, it should be clear, signals an important gap in biological understanding.

Studies since Piaget's have confirmed that young children do sometimes manifest animism in their thinking, along with a number of other confusions with regard to biological phenomena (Carey, 1985). Recent studies also indicate, however, that animism is less pervasive than Piaget believed and that the limitations in children's biological understanding are often accompanied by some unexpected strengths. Even 3-year-olds, for example, are fairly good at judging which things can move by themselves (i.e., animals) and which things cannot (e.g., statues, plants) (Massey & Gelman, 1988). Self-propelled movement is one distinguishing characteristic of animal life. Growth, in contrast, is a characteristic of both plants and animals, and preschool children also understand some of the basic facts about growth. They realize, for example, that only living things grow, that growth is inevitable (for example, you can't keep a baby pet small and cute just because you want to), and that growth is directional—that is, people, plants, and animals get bigger, not smaller, as they age (Inagaki & Hatano, 1987, 1996; Rosengren et al., 1991). They also have some appreciation of origins and kinship, realizing that dogs produce baby dogs, not cats, and that offspring generally resemble their parents (Springer, 1996; Springer & Keil, 1991). This understanding is, to be sure, far from complete, and there are disagreements about exactly what knowledge to attribute to preschoolers (Solomon et al., 1996). Still, there is clearly a stronger starting point than we once believed.

Children's understanding of biology is not only of theoretical interest. In Box 7.2 we consider the practical implications of one form of biological understanding.

Theory of Mind

Theory of mind
Thoughts and beliefs concerning the mental world.

We have seen that the preschool period is a time of impressive accomplishments in the domain of conceptual understanding. The preschool child also makes major strides with respect to a variety of forms of knowledge that fall under the heading of theory of mind. Psychologists use the term **theory of mind** to refer to children's understanding of the mental world—what they think about such phenomena as thoughts, beliefs, desires, and intentions. Do children realize, for example, that there is a distinction between the mental and the nonmental—that thoughts are in our minds and not part of the physical world? Do they realize, despite this distinction, that the mental and the nonmental are connected—that our experiences lead us to have certain thoughts and beliefs, and that these thoughts and beliefs in turn direct our behavior? Do they appreciate the distinctions among different mental states—the fact that to think something is not necessarily the same as to know something, or that the intention to achieve a goal is no guarantee that the goal will actually be reached?

Piaget (1929) was one of the first to explore questions of this sort. Contemporary researchers, however, have gone well beyond these Piagetian beginnings. In just the last decade, theory of mind has emerged as one of the most active arenas for research in cognitive development (Astington, 2000; Flavell, 1999; Flavell & Miller, 1998; Wellman, 2002).

False belief
The realization that people can hold beliefs that are not true. Such understanding, which is typically acquired during the preoperational period, provides evidence of the ability to distinguish the mental from the nonmental.

A topic of particular interest to theory-of-mind researchers has been the child's understanding of **false belief**: the realization that it is possible for people to hold beliefs that are not true. This topic is interesting because it provides evidence with respect to one of the issues identified in the preceding paragraph—the child's ability to separate the mental from the nonmental. Consider the scenario depicted in Figure 7.9. To any adult, the answer to the question of where Sally will search for her marble is obvious—in the basket, where she last saw it. She has no way, after all, of knowing that the marble

Beliefs about the Causes of Illness

Examinations of what children believe about growth or inheritance are relatively recent additions to the child psychology research literature. In contrast, one form of biological understanding has long been the subject of research attention, because it concerns knowledge that is of applied as well as theoretical importance. The topic is children's beliefs about the causes of illness.

Although Piaget himself never studied beliefs about illness, his stage model yields a number of predictions that guided early research on the topic. Probably the clearest prediction is that the understanding of young, preoperational children will be confused and incomplete. Preoperational children would be expected to focus on tangible and observable causes for illness, with little ability to conceptualize unseen contributors, such as germs. They would also be expected to reason inaccurately about cause and effect, perhaps generalizing particular causes too broadly or inferring causality from the mere proximity of some event to the onset of illness. And they would be expected to show a form of reasoning that Piaget labeled immanent justice. As we discuss more fully in Chapter 14, *immanent justice* refers to the belief that punishment automatically follows the occurrence of a misdeed. Young children who become ill may believe that they are being punished for being bad.

Research provides some support for all of these predictions (Bibace & Walsh, 1981; Kister & Patterson, 1980). Studies have shown, for example, that preschool children may offer vague or magical explanations for illness (e.g., colds come from the sun) and that they have only an incomplete grasp of more appropriate causal explanations. As Piaget's work would predict, young children often espouse a belief in immanent justice, claiming that getting sick is a punishment for being bad. As we would also expect from Piaget, there are clear changes in beliefs about illness with age, as children shed their initial confusions and gradually come to reason in more adultlike ways.

This is not to say, however, that understanding is totally absent in young children. As we have seen for many topics, the more sensitive assessment techniques of modern research often reveal previously unsuspected competencies in young children, and such has proved to be the case with regard to understanding of illness. Although young children's understanding is certainly not equivalent to that of older children or adults, it is more advanced than was once believed. Here are a few examples.

Perhaps the core knowledge with respect to illness concerns the role of germs and the conditions for contagion and contamination. Although they may be shaky on the specifics, even preschoolers possess some such knowledge. Most, for example, would refuse to drink a glass of milk with a cockroach in it; more impressively, most would also refuse to drink milk from which a cockroach has been recently removed, and thus for which there is no visible evidence of contamination (Siegal & Share, 1990). The mere proximity of a contaminant is not seen as sufficient, however, for children *will* drink from a glass that has a bug next to it, as long as they are certain that there has been no contact (Springer & Belk, 1994). Preschoolers realize that knowledge of the contaminant is not necessary for it to have an effect; thus, someone who unknowingly eats contaminated food will become just as sick as someone who is aware that the food is bad (Kalish, 1997). Preschoolers also realize—despite their budding appreciation of the importance of germs—that not all ailments are caused by germs. They judge, for example, that someone with a headache because of illness may be contagious, but that someone whose headache came from a blow to the head will not be (Kalish, 1996). Slightly older children come to another important form of understanding: that physical ailments can be transmitted by germs and contagion but that mental ailments cannot (Keil et al., 1999).

What are the implications of findings such as these for health practices with regard to children? Efforts to help children develop health-maintaining behaviors—and to cope with illness when it does occur—must build on knowledge of what children themselves think about the causes of illness. The earlier generation of studies identified confusions and gaps in knowledge that both parents and practicioners need to recognize. Young children should be helped, for example, to understand how particular causal agents work, and they should be reassured that they are not to blame if they become ill. Most generally, information about both specific illnesses and general health practices needs to be tailored to the child's level of understanding. What the recent research indicates, however, is that this starting-point understanding is greater than was once believed. Thus, even young children may be able to play a role in maintaining and restoring health (Siegal & Peterson, 1999).

One other point is important to note. Even when children's understanding is initially low, well-constructed health education programs may succeed in instilling relevant knowledge and related health-maintaining practices (Au, Romo, & DeWitt, 1999). The specific content area for which Au and colleagues demonstrate such educational effects is an important one indeed: children's understanding of the causes of AIDS.

BOX 7.2

Applications

Figure 7.9

Example of a false-belief task. To answer correctly, the child must realize that beliefs are mental representations that may differ from reality. From *Autism: Explaining the Enigma* by U. Frith, 1989, Oxford: Basil Blackwell, p. 160. Copyright © 1989 by Basil Blackwell. Reprinted with permission.

This is Sally.   This is Anne.

Sally has a basket.   Anne has a box.

Sally has a marble. She puts the marble into her basket.

Sally goes out for a walk.

Anne takes the marble out of the basket and puts it into the box.

Now Sally comes back.   She wants to play with her marble.

Where will Sally look for her marble?

has been moved during her absence. Note, however, that to arrive at this answer we must set aside our own knowledge of the true state of affairs to realize that Sally could believe something that differs from this true state—that she could hold a false belief. We can do this only if we realize that beliefs are mental representations that need not correspond to reality.

Three-year-old children typically have great difficulty understanding false beliefs. Most 3-year-olds fail tasks such as the one in Figure 7.9. Most 3-year-olds also have difficulty recapturing their own false beliefs. In another common false-belief task, children are shown a container that turns out to have unexpected contents—for example, a crayon box that actually holds candles. When asked what they initially believed was in the box, most 3-year-olds reply "candles," answering in terms of their current knowledge rather than their original, false belief. Four-year-olds are much more likely to understand that they can hold a belief that is false and that a representation can change even when the reality does not. They are also more likely to realize that others could hold false beliefs in tasks of either the crayon-box or hidden-marble sort.

Further evidence of the young child's difficulty in distinguishing representations from reality comes from another popular task in recent theory-of-mind research. As the name suggests, the **appearance–reality distinction** concerns the ability to distinguish between the way things appear and the way they really are. Suppose, for example, that we show a child a red car, cover the car with a filter that makes it look black, and then ask what color the car "really and truly is." A 3-year-old is likely to reply "black"; a 6-year-old will almost certainly (and perhaps scornfully) say "red." Suppose next that we present a stone disguised as an egg and ask what this strange object "looks like." The 3-year-old, knowing the "really and truly" in this case (the apparent egg really is a stone), answers "stone"; the 6-year-old, again showing a capacity to distinguish appearance from reality, replies "egg."

Problems in distinguishing appearance and reality are not limited to the visual realm. Children also come to realize that sounds or smells or touches may sometimes mislead, giving a false impression of their underlying source (Flavell, Flavell, & Green, 1983; Flavell, Green, & Flavell, 1989). And children must come to understand that people, as well as objects, can present misleading appearances—they may look nice, for example, when they are actually mean (Flavell et al., 1992). Of course the ability to make such distinctions is not complete by age 6; all of us remain susceptible to being fooled by misleading appearances. But the preschool child makes major strides in mastering this important kind of knowledge (Flavell, 1986).

As noted, tasks such as false belief and appearance-reality are of interest because they tap the basic realization that mental representations can be distinct from physical reality. But such tasks also speak to a further important realization: the understanding that mental and physical, although separate, are also linked—that is, that what we believe follows from what we experience. Consider again Figure 7.9. The only reason, after all, that Sally and Anne hold different beliefs is that they have had different experiences: Sally, having seen the first but not the second placement of her marble, believes it to be in the basket, whereas Anne, having seen the transfer, realizes that the box is the true location. As we saw, it is not until about age 4 that children are able to appreciate this connection between experience and belief.

Researchers have also probed more directly for children's understanding of where beliefs come from. Various questions have been of interest. Suppose, for example, that the child watches while one adult looks inside a box and a second adult merely stands by—can the child determine which adult now knows the contents of the box? Suppose that the child is one of the participants—can children make appropriate judgments of their own knowledge? Can children judge not only what they know but *how* they know? Can they recapture, for example, whether a particular belief was instilled through direct perception, or through inference, or through communication from someone else? Do they know what sorts of knowledge *can* come from different sources—for example, that vision is a good source for learning about color but not for learning about how objects feel—and that neither vision nor touch will work if the goal is to discover how something sounds?

Two general conclusions emerge from the studies of children's understanding of the origins of belief (Miller, 2000). First, the preschool period is again a time of important accomplishments. By age 5 most children have a basic understanding of how experience leads to belief and can handle at least most versions of the preceding problems. The second conclusion is perhaps more striking, given how obvious the experience–belief connection seems to any adult. The second conclusion is that this knowledge does in fact have to develop, for young preschoolers have only the shakiest grasp of how beliefs originate. Thus, 3-year-olds may be unable, seconds after learning the contents of a container, to indicate whether they learned through sight or touch or being told (O'Neill

Appearance – reality distinction Distinction between how objects appear and what they really are. Understanding the distinction implies an ability to judge both appearance and reality correctly when the two diverge.

& Chong, 2001). Asked how to determine the color of an unseen object, 3-year-olds may be quite content to explore via touch rather than sight (O'Neill, Astington, & Flavell, 1992). Even 4-year-olds may report that they have always known a fact that the experimenter in fact taught them just moments before (Taylor, Esbensen, & Bennett, 1994).

The tasks and findings discussed here are only a small sampling of the kinds of research being conducted under the theory-of-mind heading. Because most work to date has been with samples from industrialized Western cultures, one important effort is an attempt to determine whether similar phenomena and similar developmental changes

Theory of Mind in Infancy

BOX 7.3

On the
Cutting
EDGE

A 5-week-old infant imitates mouth openings produced by an adult but not similar-looking movements produced by an inanimate object (Legerstee, 1991). A 4-month-old reaches to retrieve an object that has just disappeared from view but vocalizes to bring back a person who has moved out of sight (Legerstee, 1994). A 7-month-old shows surprise when an inanimate object moves on its own—not, however, when a person moves (Spelke, Phillips, & Woodward, 1995).

Despite the concentration of research on the preschool period, no investigator of theory of mind believes that understanding of mental states begins to emerge only at age 3. As the examples just cited show, infants demonstrate an awareness that people are different from other objects from quite early in life. Indeed, in simpler form some ability to distinguish the social and nonsocial worlds is present from birth. Recall from Chapter 6 that infants only a day or two old find the human face and human voice especially interesting to look at or listen to.

Of course theory of mind encompasses more than simply a realization that people are somehow different from other things. The core understanding is *how* they are different—namely, that only people have mental states such as thoughts and desires and beliefs. Furthermore, these mental states, although distinct from the physical world, are also connected to it—that is, beliefs, desires, and so on are *about* something. How might infants show a dawning awareness of mental states and how they relate to the world? Consider the following two developments that are evident by about 1 year of age.

A mother and baby are playing together on the floor. At one point the mother turns her head and gazes toward the door of the room. The infant notices the mother's movement, stares for a moment at her face, and then turns and also gazes toward the door. This episode illustrates the phenomenon known as **joint attention:** the ability to follow into and share the attentional focus of someone else. It is an achievement of infancy, because it is not something that babies can do from the start. And it seems to imply some understanding, although probably only at an implicit level, of mother as a psychological being: Mommy is having an interesting visual experience, and if I look where she is looking, then I will, too.

Let us take our illustrative episode one step further. Suppose that what mother and baby see in the door is a stranger—some adult whom the baby has never encountered before. Uncertain how to respond, the baby turns back and looks at the mother's face. If the mother smiles and greets the stranger the baby will probably respond positively as well; on the other hand if the mother reacts with fear or distress there is a good chance that the baby's reaction will be also not be a happy one. The baby is engaging in **social referencing:** looking to another for cues about how to interpret and respond to an uncertain situation. Like joint attention, social referencing seems to imply some understanding that mother is experiencing a psychological state—in this case, an emotion that is relevant to the child's own emotional reaction. Like joint attention, social referencing is not present early in infancy but emerges around the end of the first year. And like joint attention, social referencing is specific to the human objects in the baby's environment. Infants do not follow the gaze of a favorite doll, and they do not turn to a teddy bear for guidance when trying to make sense of something new.

We should add that there are disagreements among researchers with respect to exactly when joint attention and social referencing emerge, and also with respect to how much knowledge about others' mental states such behaviors imply (Moore & Corkum, 1994; Repacholi, 1998; Tomasello, 1999). Even on the most positive reading, these achievements of infancy constitute a limited step into the mental world of others. Still, they may well be a starting point on which the accomplishments of the preschool period can build.

Joint attention
Using cues (such as direction of gaze) to identify and share the attentional focus of another.

Social referencing
Using information gained from other people to interpret uncertain situations and to regulate one's own behavior.

are evident in other cultural settings (Lillard, 1998; Vinden, 1999). Because most research to date has concentrated on the preschool period, another line of study involves extension to other age periods, exploring both developments beyond the preschool years (Bosacki & Astington, 1999; Chandler & Lalonde, 1996) and possible precursors and early forms in infancy and toddlerhood. We consider some of the work in the latter category in Box 7.3.

One of the most interesting of the ongoing research efforts concerns possible relations between theory-of-mind understanding and social behavior. It is certainly plausible that there could be a relation and in both directions—that children's understanding of the mental world can help them interact effectively with other people, but also that interactions with others can help teach children about belief and desire and other mental states. There is in fact evidence for both sorts of link. Several studies, for example, have reported a positive relation between number of siblings and false-belief understanding— that is, children from relatively large families are fastest, on the average, to master false belief (Jenkins & Astington, 1996; Perner, Ruffman, & Leekam, 1994; Peterson, 2000; Ruffman et al., 1998). Presumably, growing up in a household with several siblings heightens the probability of experiences (quarrels, appeals, tricks, etc.) through which children can learn about mental states in both other people and themselves.

Further evidence for links between theory-of-mind understanding and social behavior is provided by the phenomenon of childhood autism. Autism is a severe disorder, almost certainly biological in origin, that is characterized by a number of abnormalities in development, prominent among which are difficulties in social interaction. From early in life, children with autism show little interest in other people and little ability to form interpersonal relationships. They also, as recent research (e.g., Baron-Cohen, 1995; Frith, 1989) demonstrates, show marked deficiencies with regard to theory-of-mind understanding. Even when other aspects of mental functioning are relatively unimpaired, children with autism typically perform very poorly on theory-of-mind tasks. As Baron-Cohen (1995) observed, these children's insensitivity to the thoughts, wishes, and feelings of others is not surprising; they may literally not know that such psychological states exist. The consequences of such "mindblindness" (Baron-Cohen, 1995) are poignant testimony to the importance of theory of mind to normal social relations.

 **To Recap . . .**

The final section of the chapter considers ways in which modern researchers are building on and also extending the foundation laid down by Piaget. Studies of children's concepts examine the ways in which children organize their experiences into meaningful categories. Although such studies provide some support for Piaget's characterization of the perceptually oriented preschooler, they also have identified situations in which young children's concepts, like those of adults, reflect less obvious and more fundamental similarities among items.

Research under the theory-of-mind heading addresses children's knowledge about the mental world. Such research has revealed some striking limitations in young preschoolers' understanding of mental phenomena, including difficulties in appreciating false belief, in understanding the appearance–reality distinction, and in recognizing the sources of belief. Such research also reveals important advances in theory-of-mind understanding across the preschool years.

CONCLUSION

It is difficult in a single chapter to convey the impact of Piaget's work on the field of child psychology. American child psychologists began to discover Piaget in the late 1950s and the early 1960s, in part because translations of his books began to appear at this time and in part because of the publication of an excellent summary of Piaget's work by John Flavell (1963). Since that time, Piaget's writings have inspired literally thousands of studies of children's thinking. The tasks and findings described in this chapter are just a small sampling from this huge research yield (Chapman, 1988; Ginsburg & Opper, 1988; Modgil & Modgil, 1976).

Piaget's influence has also extended to the study of topics about which he himself had little to say. We considered two such topics—concepts and theory of mind—in the preceding section, and we will encounter many more in the chapters to come.

At the same time, the research effort of the past 30 years, perhaps inevitably, has revealed a number of problems in Piaget's research and theory. The major criticisms should be apparent by now. Piaget often underestimated children's ability, perhaps especially during the infant and preschool years. Development is not as orderly and consistent as Piaget's stage model seems to imply. Even if the concept of stages is valid, the logical models that Piaget used to characterize the stages are questionable. Finally, Piaget never offered a completely satisfactory explanation of cognitive change.

The information-processing perspective, to which we turn in the next chapter, is a major contemporary alternative to Piaget. Psychologists in this tradition do not necessarily deny the insights of Piaget's work; indeed, one subset of information-processing theorists label themselves neo-Piagetians to indicate that they are building on a foundation laid by Piaget. The information-processing approach does, however, offer a number of contrasts to Piaget that modern researchers have found attractive.

FOR THOUGHT AND DISCUSSION

1. Although Piaget's discussions of assimilation focus on infants and children, the process of assimilation is assumed to apply throughout the life span. *Can you think of recent examples from your own life in which your response to some new experience showed the operation of assimilation?*

2. Piaget suggested that children are often egocentric—that is, they are unable to break away from their own perspective to take the point of view of someone else. *Are adults also sometimes egocentric? Try to think of experiences you have had in which an adult (possibly yourself) demonstrated egnocentrism in his or her interactions with others.*

3. As we have seen, recent research, using simplified techniques, suggests that young children are more competent than Piget believed across a number of content areas (e.g., perspective taking, classification, conservation). *Consider the topic of false belief. Is it possible that young children are more competent here as well—that is—that they understand more about false belief than is indicated by the kind of experiments described in the text? How would you modify these experiments to probe for early knowledge?*

4. When tested with tasks of the sort described by Piaget, children younger than 5 or 6 typically fail to conserve quantities in the face of a misleading perceptual change. Such demonstrations, however, involve experimentally contrived situations in which children are explicitly asked about quantity. *Can you think of naturally occurring situations in which children might fail to conserve? More generally, can you think of real-life settings in which both the achievements and the limitations identified by Piaget might be demonstrated?*

5. Stage theories (such as Piaget's) imply that there should be a good deal of consistency in level of cognitive functioning, both within an individual and among individuals of the same age. *Think about the validity of this claim with respect to children you know. Are you more impressed by the similarities or differences among children of the same age? Are you more* *impressed by the consistency or inconsistency of any one child's level of thinking? Think about the claim with respect to yourself and your peers. Are you all in the same stage of cognitive development?*

6. Theory of mind includes the knowledge that other people have mental states (thoughts, beliefs, desires) and that these mental states may be different from one's own. *Imagine someone who lacked such knowledge. How would interactions with other people be affected?*

VISUAL SUMMARY FOR CHAPTER 7
Cognitive Development: The Piagetian Approach

Piaget's Theory

Grounding in Philosophy ▶ Emphasis on basic forms of knowledge, such as concepts of space and causality.

Grounding in Biology ▶ Belief that intelligence reflects both organization and adaptation. With development, children progress through four qualitatively distinct stages of cognitive functioning.

Cognition during Infancy: The Sensorimotor Period

Substage	Age	Description
1. Exercising Reflexes	Birth–1 month	The infant is limited to exercising inborn reflexes.
2. Developing Schemes	1–4 months	Reflexes evolve into adaptive schemes that begin to be refined and coordinated.
3. Discovering Procedures	4–8 months	Behavior becomes outwardly oriented and the infant develops procedures for reproducing interesting events.
4. Intentional Behavior	8–12 months	Intentional behavior emerges. The infant can separate means and end in pursuit of a goal.
5. Novelty and Exploration	12–18 months	The infant alters schemes to produce new effects. Trial and error is used to solve problems.
6. Mental Representation	18–24 months	The capacity for mental representation emerges. Mental problem solving begins to replace overt trial and error.

Development of Object Permanence

Object Permanence ▶ An especially important achievement of the sensorimotor period is the understanding that objects have a permanent existence independent of our perceptual contact with them. Piaget suggested that infants only gradually come to understand object permanence through a series of stages.

Criticism of Piaget's Account ▶ Although later studies have largely confirmed the descriptive picture provided by Piaget, they also indicate that Piaget's methods often failed to capture early forms of infant competence

Thought in the Preschooler: The Preoperational Period

Strengths and Limitations of Preoperational Thought ▶ The child's intellectual adaptations are faster, more efficient, more mobile, and more socially sharable than in the sensorimotor period. The preoperational period is also a time of specific cognitive acquisitions, including qualitative identity. However, the child lacks the operations that allow effective problem solving at the representational level. She has difficulty taking the perspective of others (egocentrism), tends to be captured and misled by what is perceptually obvious (centration), and shows a failure to conserve.

Recent research suggests that Piaget may have underestimated the abilities of the preoperational child. When tested in simplified situations, preschoolers often show more competence that on standard Piagetian tasks.

Middle-Childhood Intelligence: The Concrete Operational Period

Strengths and Limitations of Concrete Operational Thought

The child gradually masters the different forms of conservation, various aspects of classification, and relational reasoning. Concrete operational children are limited, however, to dealing with what is concrete, tangible, or real; they have difficulty thinking in terms of what is abstract or hypothetical.

Criticism of Piaget's Account

Many commentators feel that Piaget's account does not satisfactorily explain inconsistencies in the timing with which various concrete operational concepts emerge.

Adolescent and Adult: The Formal Operational Period

Strengths of Formal Operational Thought

The formal operational period is characterized by the capacity for hypothetical-deductive reasoning. Such thinking is revealed most clearly in tasks of scientific reasoning.

Criticism of Piaget's Account

Research has questioned the adequacy of some of Piaget's assessment methods. Some researchers report poorer performance than that obtained by Piaget, while others report better performance.

General Issues

Issue	Description	Criticisms
Stages of Development	Development proceeds through qualitatively distinct stages that emerge in an invariant sequence and that reflect important concurrences in children's thinking.	The last criterion poses the greatest challenge to the stage model, because children's cognitive performance is often inconsistent.
Universals of Development	All children pass through the same stages in the same order.	Some studies indicate that the speed and even the order in which abilities are mastered can vary across cultures.
Cognitive Change	Four general factors contribute to cognitive development: maturation, physical experience, social experience, and equilibration.	The main criticism of this model of cognitive change has concerned its lack of specificity.

New Directions

Children's Concepts

Studies of children's concepts provide some support for Piaget's characterization of the perceptually oriented preschooler. Such studies have also identified situations, however, in which young children's concepts, like those of adults, reflect less obvious and more fundamental similarities among items.

Theory of Mind

Research into children's knowledge about the mental world has revealed some striking limitations in young preschoolers' understanding of mental phenomena, including difficulties in appreciating false belief and in recognizing the sources of belief. Such research has also revealed important advances in theory-of-mind understanding across the preschool years.

8

Cognitive Development: The Information-Processing Approach

n three of the most prominent court cases of the last 20 years, the star witnesses were young children. In each case, the charge was child sexual abuse. The defendants in the Little Rascals case were the husband-and-wife owners of a preschool day care center. The initial allegation was limited: A mother of a

child at the center claimed that the husband had abused her son. Once parents and police began to question the children, however, the allegations quickly became more widespread. Eventually 90 children made claims of sexual or physical abuse, not only against the day care owners but also against several other adults in the community. Twelve children were among the witnesses when the case went to trial. Both the husband and wife were convicted of child sexual abuse.

The defendant in the Wee Care case was a female preschool teacher. Again, the initial charge was limited: A child made a comment during a pediatric exam that suggested that the teacher had sexually molested him. Once questioning began, however, a number of other children provided collaborative statements of abuse. Nineteen children testified at the trial, and the teacher was convicted of 115 counts of sexual abuse.

The defendants in the Country Walk case were the husband-and-wife proprietors of a babysitting service. Once again, an initial suspicion from one parent quickly escalated. Eventually dozens of children were questioned, and many provided stories of extreme ritualistic abuse. The husband was the main target of the claims, and he was eventually sentenced to six life terms in prison.

Although the children's testimony was sufficiently believable to contribute to the convictions in all three cases, there also were reasons for doubt. By the time of the testimony in court several years had elapsed since the alleged experiences. In many cases the children had been subjected to frequent and suggestive questioning. Their stories often changed over time, and some of their statements were clearly not true (for example, that they had been set on fire or forced to eat someone's head). Partly for this reason, the convictions in the Little Rascals and Wee Care cases were eventually reversed on appeal. That in the Country Walk case still stands. ■

Exactly how does memory work? How are memories stored and how are they retrieved? Questions like these are central to our understanding of human cognition. Such questions can also have important, real-life implications, as you can see in the examples just discussed and will see again when we return to the topic of children as witnesses later in the chapter.

The workings of memory and other basic psychological processes are the focus of scientists seeking to understand children's cognitive development from the information-processing perspective. As we noted in the preceding chapter, information processing has emerged as a major contemporary approach to the study of children's thinking.

In this chapter, we first summarize some of the most important characteristics of information-processing theory and research. We then move on to aspects of child development that have especially intrigued information-processing researchers. We consider several important areas of development, including memory, problem solving, and academic skills. The chapter concludes with the challenging issue of cognitive change.

THE NATURE OF THE APPROACH

As many commentators have noted, information processing is not a single theory but rather a general framework within which researchers have developed a number of specific theories (Klahr & MacWhinney, 1998; Miller, 2001; Siegler, 1998). The common core that unites the different theories is the shared assumption implied by the name of the approach: Thinking *is* information processing (Siegler, 1998). The information to be processed can take many forms across different contexts and developmental levels; it

Children's environments present information and cognitive challenges of many sorts. How children come to understand and to respond adaptively to these challenges are the concern of the information-processing approach.

might, for example, be a hard-to-work toy, a spatial landmark, a numerical symbol, or an instruction from the teacher. The processing can also take many forms depending on the demands of the task: attention to critical features, insertion into a conceptual category, comparison with past memory input. The goal of the information-processing approach is to specify such underlying psychological processes—and the developmental changes they undergo—as precisely as possible.

Two images are instructive in characterizing the information-processing approach. One is the flowchart. The other is the computer.

The Flowchart Metaphor

Figure 8.1 shows the symbolic representation of a typical information-processing theory. The particular theory, which deals with memory, contains a number of details that do not concern us here. But its general features are characteristic of the information-processing approach. The starting point is some environmental input, and the end point is some response output. Between stimulus and response a number of psychological processes intervene.

In the case of memory, the initial input is assumed to be acted on and transformed in various ways. Imagine, for example, that a 6-year-old in a first-grade classroom has just heard a word for the first time. This word enters the sensory register—in this case, the auditory register—where a literal image of a stimulus can be held for perhaps a second at most. The word then moves to short-term, or working, memory, which is the center for active and conscious processing. Although information typically stays for only a few seconds in short-term memory, various strategies (some of which we consider shortly) may prolong its lifetime considerably. Finally, the word may be transferred to long-term memory, where, as the name suggests, it can exist indefinitely. Getting the word to long-term memory is, of course, the teacher's goal when presenting a new term to be learned. And all of us in fact do have thousands of words stored in permanent memory.

As the figure indicates, more general psychological processes also play a role. Control processes of various sorts affect the maintenance of information and the movement from one store to another. Response-generating mechanisms are necessary to explain the eventual overt response—for example, the child's ability to say a recently learned word.

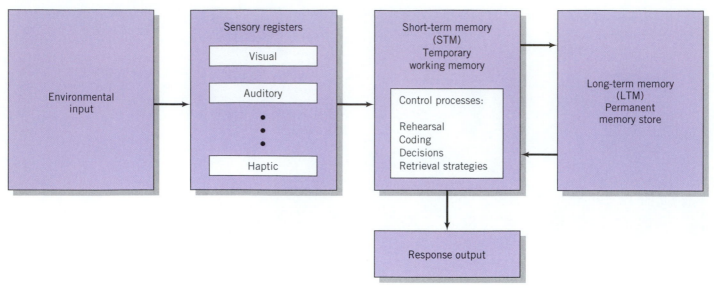

Figure 8.1

An example of an information-processing model of memory, which illustrates the kind of flowchart representation with which information-processing theorists attempt to describe the sequence of information processing. From "The Control of Short-Term Memory" by R. C. Atkinson and R. M. Shiffrin, 1971, *Scientific American, 225,* 82. Copyright credit Allen Beechel.

The origin of the term *flowchart* should be evident from this example. Information-processing theorists attempt to capture the orderly flow of information through the cognitive system. The origin of the term *information processing* should also be evident. Information is acted on, or processed, in various ways as it moves through the system. The external stimulus and external response—the concerns of traditional learning theory—are only the end points. The real goal of the psychologist—or so maintains the information-processing theorist—is to specify as completely and precisely as possible what comes between stimulus and response. And as our example suggests, even in a seemingly simple case, such as hearing a new word, quite a bit may be going on.

The Computer Metaphor

The preceding section described a cognitive system that can transform a variety of inputs into a variety of outputs in a systematic and intelligent way. In doing so, it uses stored information and stored rules of various sorts. What sort of intelligent system operates in this way? To anyone immersed in modern industrialized society, the answer should be obvious—a computer.

Information-processing theorists find the computer to be a useful tool on a variety of levels. At the most general level, the computer serves as a helpful metaphor for thinking about human cognition. Human and computer are alike in a number of ways. Both store representations or symbols and manipulate these symbols to solve problems. Both perform a variety of such manipulations in an incredibly rapid and powerful fashion. Despite this power, both are limited in the amount of information they can store and manipulate. Both, however, can learn from experience and modify their rule systems in a progressively adaptive direction. Understanding the operations of computer intelligence may thus lead to insights about human intelligence as well.

Information-processing theorists have drawn from computer technology in more specific ways as well. Any theorist of intelligence must decide on a language with which to formulate his or her theory. Information-processing theorists have often adopted preexisting computer languages for their theories. Such languages have the virtues of precision and (at least to the information-processing theorist) familiarity; they therefore are good vehicles for testing and communicating theories.

At the most specific level, the computer makes possible one of the prime methodologies of the information-processing approach—**computer simulation.** In a computer simulation, the researcher attempts to program a computer to produce some segment of intelligent behavior in the same way in which humans produce the behavior. The idea is to build into the computer program whatever knowledge and rules are thought to be important for the human problem solver. Suppose, for example, that we have a theory of how first-graders solve simple addition problems. We might program the computer to apply the rules that we think children use and then see how *it* responds to the same tasks. How successfully the program generates the target behavior—in this case, the pattern of first-grade responses—is a test of the investigator's theory of how children arrive at their answers.

Comparisons with Piaget

Because our most complete discussion of intelligence to this point has involved the Piagetian approach, comparing the information-processing approach with this view is instructive.

Information-processing approaches to child development share several similarities with Piaget's approach. The first similarity is in the content studied. Information-processing researchers recognize the importance of the concepts identified by Piaget, and much of their research involves attempts to apply information-processing techniques to Piagetian tasks and abilities. Second, similarity exists at a general theoretical level. Information-processing theories, like Piagetian theory, fall within the cognitive-developmental approach to child development. Information-processing theorists agree with Piaget that a complex system of mental rules underlies cognitive performance and that one job of the theorist is to discover what these rules are. Finally, some information-processing theorists follow Piaget in dividing development into distinct stages. Although the stages are not identical to Piaget's, they typically show some important similarities. Because of their grounding in Piaget, this group of information-processing theorists is often referred to as *neo-Piagetian* (Case & Okamoto, 1996; Demetriou, Shayer, & Efklides, 1993; Fischer & Bidell, 1998; Halford, 1993).

The issue of stages, however, also illustrates a difference between the information-processing and Piagetian approaches. Most information-processing theorists do not subscribe to a stage model of development. Furthermore, even those who may find stages useful differ in important ways from Piaget. The stages proposed by Piaget are the broadest, most general stages that the field of child psychology has seen. To say that a child is in the stage of concrete operations is to make a strong (and, as we saw, debatable) claim about how the child will perform on a wide range of cognitive tasks. Information-processing stage theories tend to be more limited in scope, focusing on specific skills and particular aspects of the child's development. A model might, for example, concentrate on the acquisition of spatial skills, without making any claims about the child's level of performance on other tasks. One way to summarize this difference is to say that the information-processing theorist's stages are more *domain-specific*—that is, more concerned with distinct aspects, or domains, of development.

Other differences between the information-processing and Piagetian approaches can be inferred from the flowchart and computer metaphors. Piaget's theoretical emphasis was always on the logical rules underlying problem solving, such as the concrete operations of middle childhood and the formal operations of adolescence. Piaget had little to say about many more process-oriented questions that are central to the information-processing researcher. How exactly does the child attend to new information? How is this information taken in and represented in memory? How is it retrieved in the service of problem solving? It would be difficult to construct a full flowchart model of problem solving, let alone a computer simulation, from Piaget's theoretical accounts. Information-processing theorists attempt to develop models that are more specific and more complete than those offered by Piaget.

Computer simulation
Programming a computer to perform a cognitive task in the same way in which humans are thought to perform it. An information-processing method for testing theories of underlying process.

These goals have both methodological and theoretical implications. Methodologically, the emphasis on precision and testability has led to a number of distinctive methods for studying children's thinking. We have already mentioned one such method—the computer simulation technique—and we describe others later. Theoretically, the emphasis on completeness has meant a concern with a variety of aspects of children's development in addition to the kinds of logical reasoning stressed by Piaget. Much of the work on attention discussed in Chapter 6 was carried out within an information-processing perspective. The same is true for much of the work on memory that we consider next.

To Recap . . .

The information-processing perspective is a major contemporary approach to the study of cognitive development. Information-processing researchers attempt to describe the underlying cognitive activities, or forms of information processing, that occur between stimulus input and response output. They draw from modern computer science, both for general ideas about human intelligence and for specific languages and methods with which to formulate and test their theories.

Like Piaget's theory, information-processing theories fall within the cognitive-developmental approach. In addition to sharing Piaget's emphasis on underlying rules or structures, information-processing researchers study many of the same concepts studied by Piaget, and some such researchers propose stage theories that have ties to Piaget's stages. Most information-processing theorists do not subscribe to the kinds of broad, general stages offered by Piaget, however. Their own models are more domain specific, and they attempt to construct models that are more precise, more complete, and more testable than those proposed by Piaget.

MEMORY IN INFANCY

Children can be affected by their experiences only if they can somehow retain information from these experiences over time. Questions of memory—of how information is taken in, stored, and retrieved—are therefore central to information-processing accounts of development. Because development starts in infancy, the examination of memory must also start with the infant.

We begin our discussion with a very basic question: Can babies remember? We have already encountered a number of findings that tell us the answer is yes. Many of the phenomena from Piaget's sensorimotor studies demonstrate the presence of memory—for example, the infant's ability to activate a familiar scheme when confronting a familiar object or to search for a plaything that has disappeared. Many of the findings from the study of infant perception discussed in Chapter 6 also imply the use of memory—for example, the infant's preference for the mother's voice. Much of the behavior that we as adults produce would be impossible if we did not remember and were not guided by past experience. The same is true of infants.

How well do babies remember? This question is harder to answer. Even a young infant's memory is in some respects surprisingly good. In other respects, however, infant memory is limited, and many important developmental advances have yet to come.

Psychologists distinguish between two basic forms of memory. **Recognition memory** refers to the realization that some perceptually present stimulus or event has been encountered before. You would be demonstrating recognition memory, for example, if you realized that you had already seen the flowchart memory model (Figure 8.1) when you encountered the same figure in some other book. **Recall memory** refers to the retrieval of some past stimulus or event when the stimulus or event is *not* perceptually present. You would be demonstrating recall memory if you were able to draw the flowchart model (or at least parts of it!) in the absence of any stimulus input. We begin with recognition, then move on to recall.

Recognition memory
The realization that some perceptually present stimulus or event has been encountered before.

Recall memory
The retrieval of some past stimulus or event that is not perceptually present.

Recognition Memory

Methods of Study How might we determine whether babies can recognize stimuli that they have encountered before? The most common method has been the habituation–dishabituation procedure. With this procedure, as you may recall, we examine the infant's response to a repeated stimulus; a decline in response as the stimulus becomes familiar is referred to as *habituation*. Such a decline in interest is possible only if the infant can recognize the repeated stimulus as something that has been experienced previously; if there were no such memory, every appearance of the stimulus would be experienced as a novel event. Similarly, *dishabituation*, or the recovery of response when the stimulus changes, can occur only if the infant is able to compare the new stimulus to some memory of the original.

Classical conditioning and operant conditioning have also been used to explore infant memory. As noted in Chapter 1, learning refers to the lasting effects of experience on behavior, and thus any demonstration of learning necessarily tells us something about memory as well.

One way in which operant conditioning has been employed to study infant memory is pictured in Figure 8.2. As the figure shows, the ribbon linking ankle and mobile confers a potential power on the infant—kicking the ankle will make the mobile jump. Infants as young as 2 months can learn this relation; the rate of kicking increases when the kicking pays off in the reinforcement of a dancing mobile (Rovee-Collier, 1987). Once this response has been established, various modifications can be introduced to probe the infant's memory. We can test for recognition of the training mobile, for example, by comparing response to a novel mobile with response to the familiar one. Or we can test the duration of the memory by seeing how the infant responds a day or a week or a month after the original conditioning.

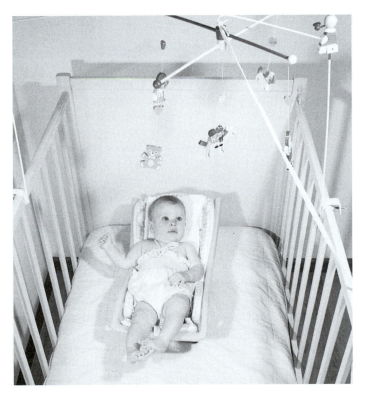 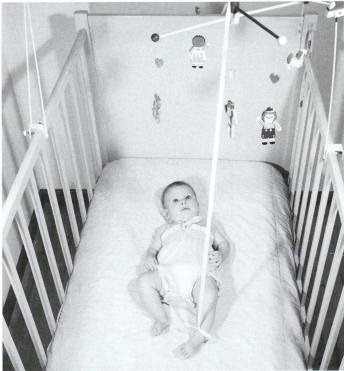

Figure 8.2

An experimental arrangement for studying infants' ability to learn and remember. When the ribbon is attached to the baby's ankle (as in the right-hand photo), kicking the leg makes the mobile above the crib move. Learning is shown by increased kicking whenever the ribbon is attached and the mobile is present. These photos were made available by Dr. C. K. Rovee-Collier.

Memory in Newborns   A number of questions about infant memory have been explored with these procedures. A natural first question is how early in life babies can remember. The answer seems clear—from birth (or possibly even earlier—recall the suggestion in Chapter 6 that babies may remember some events that they experienced prenatally). Habituation studies are one basis for this conclusion. Habituation is not easy to demonstrate in newborns, and for years infant researchers disagreed about whether such early habituation was possible (Slater, 1995). It now seems clear, however, that a newborn infant—given optimal circumstances—can show habituation across a range of modalities: visual (Slater et al., 1991), auditory (Zelazo, Weiss, & Tarquino, 1991), and tactile (Kisilevsky & Muir, 1984). Thus, newborns do possess some degree of recognition memory.

Conditioning studies are a further source of evidence for neonatal memory. As with habituation, conditioning can be difficult to produce in very young infants, and the question of whether newborns can be conditioned was a topic of debate for many years. Today, however, most researchers agree that both classical and operant conditioning are possible from birth (Lipsitt, 1990). We have already seen some examples of the latter. Recall the finding that newborns prefer a stimulus to which they have been exposed prenatally (DeCasper & Fifer, 1980). The newborns showed this preference by adjusting their sucking to produce the desired stimulus—for example, their own mothers' voices. Adjusting behavior to obtain reinforcement is a form of operant conditioning.

An example of classical conditioning in newborns is provided by a study in which 1- and 2-day-old infants received a sucrose solution delivered to the lips (Blass, Ganchrow, & Steiner, 1984). The solution functioned as an unconditioned stimulus that elicited the unconditioned response of sucking. The conditioned stimulus consisted of the experimenter's stroking the baby's forehead immediately before delivery of the sucrose. After a few pairings of the stroking with the solution, the babies began to suck in response to the stroking alone—a clear indication that conditioning had occurred.

Developmental Changes   Although memory may be present from birth, newborns' and young infants' memories are not as powerful as those of older infants. Developmental improvements of various sorts occur during the first year or so of life. One important change is in how long material can be retained. Most demonstrations of memory in newborns involve only a few seconds between presentation of a stimulus and the test for recognition of that stimulus. What such studies show, then, is very short-term memory. As infants develop, the length of time across which they can remember their experiences steadily increases, soon reaching impressive levels. By 5 months of age, babies can recognize a photo of a face, initially viewed for only 2 minutes, after a delay of 2 weeks (Fagan, 1973). With a more dynamic, moving stimulus, recognition has been demonstrated across a 3-month delay for babies who were only 3 months old at the time of initial exposure (Bahrick & Pickens, 1995). We should add, however, that even the newborn is not limited to very brief memories. Newborns can remember speech stimuli across a period of at least 24 hours (Swain, Zelazo, & Clifton, 1993). And the studies of memory for speech sounds experienced prenatally (DeCasper & Spence, 1991; see Chapter 6) have typically involved even longer intervals between the last prenatal exposure and the first postnatal test.

The mobile procedure shown in Figure 8.2 provides another approach to assessing the durability of infant memory. The question is how long babies can remember the association between kicking and the movement of the mobile. This procedure, too, reveals both impressive early capacity and developmental improvements in long-term memory with age (Rovee-Collier, 1999). Two-month-olds, for example, can remember the association for 3 days; by 3 months of age the span has stretched to 8 days; and by 6 months some retention is still evident 21 days after conditioning (Rovee-Collier & Shyi, 1992).

Memory is even better if the infant is given a brief reminder during the delay period. In a study by Sullivan (1982), the experimenter jiggled the mobile on the 13th day of the delay period while the infant simply watched. Infants given this reminder showed much more kicking on day 14 than did a control group that received no such help. Such

One of the most rewarding signs of infant memory is the baby's pleasure at recognizing his parents.

priming of memory through a brief reencounter with the original experience is referred to as **reactivation.** If the reminders are frequent enough, the original memory may be preserved indefinitely. In one study, for example, 2-month-olds who received periodic reactivation experiences still remembered the kicking response 5 months after initial exposure to the mobile (Rovee-Collier, Hartshorn, & DiRubbo, 1999). Naturally occurring instances of reactivation may be a major way in which forgetting is prevented and memories are kept alive (Rovee-Collier & Hayne, 1987).

In addition to duration, another basic question about memory concerns what information is retained. Babies' habituation to a stimulus tells us that they recognize *some* aspect of the stimulus, but it does not tell us exactly what they are remembering. This dimension of memory also shows developmental improvements across infancy. Older infants can remember both more information and more complex information than younger infants (Olson & Sherman, 1983). Older infants can also abstract and remember general categories of information and not just specific stimuli (Mandler, 2000). In one study, for example, 12- to 24-month-old infants were shown a series of pictures of various kinds of food (bread, hot dogs, salami, and so on). The infants were then given a choice of looking at either of two stimuli: a previously unseen item from the food category (an apple), or an item from a new category (a chair). Infants looked longer at the chair than at the apple, demonstrating that they recognized not just specific foods but the general category of food, and that they found a new category more interesting than a familiar one (Ross, 1980).

Even earlier success has been demonstrated for other, perceptually simpler kinds of categorical distinctions. By 4 months, for example, infants shown a series of dog pictures look more at a picture of a bird than they do at one of another dog (Quinn & Eimas, 1996; we should add, however, that telling dogs and cats apart is harder at this age). Infants as young as 3 months can distinguish animals from furniture, and they can even make some discriminations within each of these categories (Behl-Chadha, 1996; Quinn, 1999). Three-months-olds can also form simple categories based on color or shape (Hayne, 1996).

The ability to move beyond specific experiences to abstract more general categories is an essential component in our attempts to make sense of the world. The studies just reviewed suggest that this ability emerges very early.

Reactivation
The preservation of the memory for an event through reencounter with at least some portion of the event in the interval between initial experience and memory test.

Recall Memory

The research that we have described indicates clearly that recognition memory is present from birth. But what about recall? Can infants not only recognize familiar stimuli or events but also actively call such stimuli or events to mind?

Recall memory is considerably more difficult to study in infancy than is recognition memory, because infants cannot produce the responses that are used to study recall in older individuals (such as verbal reports or drawing). There is, in fact, no clear agreement on exactly what a young infant might do that would demonstrate recall and thus no agreement on exactly when recall emerges. It does seem clear that recall is present by the end of infancy, as many of the behaviors from Piaget's sensorimotor substage 6 imply. An infant could not show deferred imitation, for example, without the ability to recall a model from the past, nor could he or she produce words appropriately without some capacity for recall.

As we saw in our discussions of Piagetian research in Chapter 7, recent evidence suggests that simple forms of recall emerge earlier than Piaget proposed (Mandler, 1998). The infant's search for vanished objects is one kind of evidence. By the end of the first year most infants can find objects that are hidden in a single location (Piaget's substage 4 of object permanence). Most have also learned the permanent locations for familiar and valued objects, such as the cupboard in which a favorite cereal is kept (Ashmead & Perlmutter, 1980). The ability to find an object that one has not seen for days would certainly seem to imply some capacity for recall.

Studies of deferred imitation provide further evidence for recall memory in infancy. These studies indicate that the capacity to reproduce a model from the past emerges earlier than Piaget believed. By 6 months of age infants can imitate a novel action that they viewed a full 24 hours earlier (Barr, Dowden, & Hayne, 1996). By 14 months the retention span has stretched to one week (Meltzoff, 1988).

Infants can remember and imitate not only isolated behaviors but also simple sequences of action (Bauer, 2002; Bauer et al., 2000). Thirteen-month-olds, for example, can reproduce three-action sequences for such events as giving a teddy bear a bath (first place in tub, then wash with sponge, then dry with towel) or constructing a simple rattle (place ball in large cup, invert small cup into large, shake) (Bauer & Mandler, 1992). By 24 months children can remember sequences of five actions (Bauer & Travis, 1993), and by 30 months children can retain as many as eight separate steps (Bauer & Fivush, 1992). Memory for the order in which events occur is an important form of knowledge to which we will return. These studies indicate that such memory has its origins in infancy.

We saw that infants' ability to recognize familiar stimuli may eventually extend across a considerable period of time. The same appears to be true of early recall. Some memory for two-action sequences has been demonstrated after 6 months for infants who were only 10 months old at the time of initial learning (Carver & Bauer, 2001). Infants who are 16 months old at the time of learning show some recall of three-action sequences 8 months later (Bauer, Hertsgaard, & Dow, 1994). Even more impressive long-term memory is suggested in a study by McDonough and Mandler (1994). These researchers first taught their 11-month-old participants to imitate simple sequences of actions, as in the teddy bear and rattle tasks described earlier. When the infants were retested as 23-month-olds, they showed some ability to reproduce individual actions that they had seen modeled a full year earlier!

The studies just discussed are relevant to one of the classic puzzles in child psychology: the phenomenon of **infantile amnesia,** or the inability to remember experiences from the first 2 or 3 years of life. The absence of long-term memories from infancy would be easy to explain if infants did not form long-term memories; as we have just seen, however, this is not the case. Why, then, have all such memories disappeared by later in childhood? The earliest explanation to be put forth was Freud's proposal that the unavailability of early memories results from repression of

Memory for the order of events emerges early in life. Even 1-year-olds can remember simple sequences, such as the order to follow in giving a doll a bath.

Infantile amnesia

The inability to remember experiences from the first 2 or 3 years of life.

forbidden thoughts into the unconscious. Although few modern psychologists accept the Freudian position, there is little consensus on what the correct explanation may be, beyond a general agreement that several factors probably contribute (Howe, 2000; Newcombe et al., 2000). Among the contributors that have been proposed are immaturity of parts of the brain, qualitative differences between early and later memory systems (for example, nonverbal versus verbal), the lack of a sense of self in infancy, and the absence of a social system within which to share and rehearse memories. We return to the last of these possibilities when we discuss the social bases for early memories in Chapter 9.

To Recap . . .

Infants can remember from birth. Habituation, classical conditioning, and operant conditioning all imply memory, and all have been demonstrated in newborn babies. With development, the span of time across which the infant can retain material increases, as do the amount and the complexity of the material that can be retained.

Habituation and conditioning studies demonstrate recognition memory. Recall memory is more difficult to study in infancy, but recent research suggests that simple forms of recall probably emerge some time during the first year. Infants' ability to search for vanished objects provides one kind of evidence for this conclusion. Imitation of models from the past provides another.

MEMORY IN OLDER CHILDREN

Beyond infancy, most studies of how children remember have concentrated on various forms of recall. The most general change in this type of memory is an obvious one: Older children remember better than younger children. This fact was undoubtedly apparent to parents and teachers long before there was research to verify it. It has also long been apparent to test makers. All the IQ tests described in Chapter 10 include memory as one of their components. On the average, the older the child, the better the performance on such memory measures.

Developmental improvements in memory are of considerable practical importance, because they influence what parents and teachers expect of children and how they treat children. A 10-year-old can be entrusted with a string of verbal instructions that would overtax the memory of a 4-year-old. Such improvements are also of theoretical interest. How can we explain the fact that older children remember better than younger ones? Several kinds of explanation have been offered, and each seems to capture part of the basis for developmental change. Here we consider three possible contributors to the developmental improvement in memory: greater use of mnemonic strategies, greater knowledge about memory, and more powerful cognitive structures.

The Role of Strategies

Imagine that you are confronted with the following task. A list of words, such as that in Table 8.1, is presented to you at the rate of one every 5 seconds. There is a 30-second delay following the last word, and you must then recall as many of the words as possible. How might you proceed?

Adults faced with such a task are likely to do any of a variety of things to help themselves remember. They may say the words over and over again as the list is presented and during the delay period. They may seek to make the list more memorable by grouping the words into categories—noting, for example, that several of the items name foods and several others name animals. Or they may attempt to create associations among the words by imagining a scenario in which several of the words are linked—for example, a mental image of a cow eating a banana while riding a bicycle.

Table 8.1	Items to Be Recalled on a Short-Term Memory Test	
Cow		Truck
Tree		Hat
Banana		Bear
Bicycle		Apple
Dog		Flag
Orange		Horse

Mnemonic strategies
Techniques (such as rehearsal or organization) that people use in an attempt to remember something.

The approaches just sketched are examples of **mnemonic strategies.** A mnemonic strategy is any technique that people use in an attempt to help themselves remember something. The examples just given correspond, in fact, to three of the most often studied strategies in research on memory: *rehearsal* of the items to be recalled (the saying-over-and-over technique), *organization* of the items into conceptual categories (grouping into foods, animals, and so on), and *elaboration* of the items by linkage in some more general image or story (the picture of the cow on the bicycle).

Developmental Changes in Strategy Use   An increase in the tendency to use strategies is one important source of the improvements in memory that come with age. Dozens of studies have demonstrated that older children are more likely than younger children to generate and employ mnemonic strategies (Bjorklund, 1990; Schneider & Bjorklund, 1998). This finding holds for the three strategies just mentioned—rehearsal (Flavell, Beach, & Chinsky, 1966), organization (Hasselhorn, 1992), and elaboration (Kee & Guttentag, 1994). It also holds for other mnemonic strategies that develop across childhood—for example, the ability to direct one's attention and effort in optimal ways, such as by attending to central rather than irrelevant information (Miller, 1990) or by concentrating on difficult rather than easy items (Dufresne & Kobasigawa, 1989).

Do strategies work? The answer in general is yes. Children who use strategies show better recall than children who do not. Children do not always benefit from their initial attempts to employ a strategy, perhaps because executing a new strategy places too great a demand on their limited information-processing resources (Woody-Dorning & Miller, 2001). This failure of a recently developed strategy to facilitate recall is labeled a **utilization deficiency** (Bjorklund & Coyle, 1995; Miller & Seier, 1994). Usually, however, even young children derive some benefit from the use of strategies; their main problem is simply that they do not generate strategies in the first place. Before about age 5 or 6, it apparently simply does not occur to children that it makes sense to do something to help themselves remember. This failure to generate strategies spontaneously, even though the child is capable of executing and benefiting from a strategy, is referred to as a **production deficiency** (Flavell, 1970).

Utilization deficiency
The failure of a recently developed mnemonic strategy to facilitate recall.

Production deficiency
The failure to generate a mnemonic strategy spontaneously.

Strategies increase not only in frequency but also in complexity as children get older. Rehearsal is a relatively simple strategy and is, in fact, one of the first to emerge, typically appearing at about age 6 or 7. Organization appears somewhat later, and elaboration later still. There are also developmental changes in complexity within a particular strategy. Younger children's rehearsal efforts, for example, tend to be limited to naming each item as it appears. Older children are more likely to repeat larger chunks of the list each time ("cow," "cow-tree," "cow-tree-banana," and so on) (Ornstein, Naus, & Liberty, 1975). In general, older children can generate more complex strategies than younger children, they are better able to match particular strategy to particular task, and they are more skilled at executing their strategies—all of which contributes to their superior memory performance.

We noted that on many memory tasks children younger than 5 or 6 do not display strategies. Does this mean that the young child is totally incapable of generating a mnemonic strategy? Not at all. If the task is sufficiently simplified, even quite young children may show rudimentary strategies. In one study, 3-year-olds played a game in which they had to keep track of a toy dog that had been hidden under one of several cups. During the delay between hiding and retrieval, many of the children sat with their eyes glued to the critical cup and a finger planted firmly on it (Wellman, Ritter, & Flavell, 1975). These are simple strategies, to be sure, but they *are* strategies, and they are available to even young children. Furthermore, they work. Children who produced such strategies showed better recall than children who did not. Other studies using a similar hide-and-seek procedure have demonstrated that children as young as 18 to 24 months can produce and benefit from simple strategies (Wellman, 1988). The general conclusion to be drawn from such research should sound familiar from the discussion of preschoolers' strengths in Chapter 7. Young children are by no means as competent as older children—in memory or in logical reasoning. When tested in simple and familiar contexts, however, they can sometimes show surprising abilities.

Just as strategies may begin to develop earlier than experts once thought, so they may continue to develop beyond the grade-school years that have been the focus of most memory research. Complex mnemonic strategies continue to be refined well into adolescence and even adulthood (Pressley, Levin, & Bryant, 1983). Of particular interest to both researchers and teachers have been the various **study strategies** that students (or at least some students!) develop to cope with school material. Study strategies include specific techniques, such as note taking and outlining. They also include more general methods, such as allocation of study time to important or not-yet-mastered material and self-testing to determine what has been learned and what needs to be studied further.

As with strategies in general, study strategies improve with age. As children develop, the frequency with which they use such techniques increases, as does the complexity of the strategies they generate. And, again, as with strategies in general, study strategies are beneficial. Research reveals a clear relation between the use of appropriate study techniques and the quality of the child's learning (Paris & Oka, 1986; Pressley, Forrest-Pressley, & Elliot-Faust, 1988).

Clearly, the work on study strategies is not just of scientific interest; it also speaks to important applied questions concerning the bases for children's academic performance. If we can identify and help children whose study strategies are poor, then perhaps we can improve their chances of success in school. Such has proved to be the case. In recent years a number of intervention programs have verified the value of explicitly teaching study skills to children (Brown & Campione, 1990; Pressley et al., 1988).

Variability in Strategy Use   Although new and more complex strategies emerge with development, this does not mean that earlier strategies necessarily disappear. One interesting finding from recent memory research concerns the surprising variability in children's strategy use. Rather than employ a single preferred strategy, many children try out and combine several different approaches, sometimes generating as many as three or four strategies even within a single trial (Coyle, 2001; Coyle & Bjorklund, 1997). A particular child, for example, might not only rehearse the items to be remembered but also name the categories to which they belong and perhaps sort them into groups as well.

Why should children be so variable in their approach to memory tasks? It has been argued that such variability is adaptive, in that it provides experience from which children can eventually determine the optimal strategy for a particular task. According to this view, there is a kind of survival of the fittest with respect to mnemonic strategies, with experience operating to select the most effective techniques from the many possibilities that children initially explore. We return to this argument later in the chapter.

Research on strategies illustrates one important theme of the information-processing approach (Siegler, 1998). The child's—and, for that matter, the adult's—information-processing capacities are always limited. Only a limited amount of information can fit in short-term memory, for example, and this information typically can be held only briefly. If new information can be rehearsed, however, its lifetime can be extended considerably. If the child can think in terms of categories and not merely in terms of individual items, then much more can be retained. Much of development consists of the creation of techniques to overcome information-processing limitations and thereby increase the power of the cognitive system. Mnemonic strategies are a prime example of such techniques.

The Role of Metamemory

Although strategies are an important source of developmental improvements in memory, they are not the only contributor. What children know about memory also changes with age, and these changes in knowledge contribute to changes in memory.

Metamemory refers to knowledge about memory. It includes knowledge about memory in general—for example, the fact that recognition tasks are easier than recall

Study strategies
Mnemonic strategies (such as outlining and note taking) that students use in an attempt to remember school material.

Mnemonic strategies are not limited to laboratory settings. Study strategies can help to ensure that important material is remembered.

Metamemory
Knowledge about memory.

Watching Children Talk to Themselves: The Measurement of Mnemonic Strategies

The idea that strategies might be an important contributor to developmental improvements in memory is a long-standing one. For years, however, most of the evidence in support of this hypothesis was indirect. Rather than measure strategies directly, researchers inferred their contribution from different levels or different patterns of memory performance in younger and older children. A breakthrough in the study of mnemonic strategies came in the mid-1960s when John Flavell and colleagues devised a way to observe strategies directly (Flavell, Beach, & Chinsky, 1966).

The task that Flavell and associates used was similar to the one with which we opened the section on mnemonic strategies. The child was shown an array of seven pictures of common objects, the experimenter pointed to three of the seven pictures, there was a delay of 15 seconds, an array of the same pictures in a different spatial arrangement was presented, and the child's task was to point to the same three pictures in the same order. Rehearsal is a natural strategy for a task of this sort: saying the names of the target pictures over and over during the delay period. Furthermore, children, more than adults, tend to do the rehearsing overtly, saying the names out loud or at least moving their lips during the delay. Thus, the strategy was potentially observable.

Of course a child might be unlikely to rehearse if he realized that an experimenter was staring intently at his face. This problem was solved by having the child wear a toy space helmet with a visor that could be raised or lowered.

BOX 8.1

Classics of
Research

During the delay period the visor was lowered, thus preventing the child from seeing not only the pictures but also the staring experimenter. This experimenter had been trained in lip reading prior to the study, the goal, of course, being to ensure that even inaudible verbalizations could be correctly interpreted. Finally, the lip-reading task was simplified by the use of pictures whose labels required pronounced and distinct lip movements—for example, *pipe, moon, flag.*

Many of the children did indeed rehearse. Although some did so out loud, soundless mouth movements or soft whispering were more common; thus, the lip-reading skills were definitely needed. The probability of rehearsal increased markedly with age. Only 2 of 20 of the youngest children (5-year-olds) rehearsed, in comparison to about half of the 7-year-olds and almost all the 10-year-olds. Finally, rehearsal was in fact beneficial: Children who rehearsed performed better on the memory task than children who did not.

The Flavell et al. study was the first demonstration that the young child's problems on memory tasks are often a matter of production deficiency—that is, not a failure to benefit from a strategy but a failure to produce the strategy in the first place. Such a conclusion, of course, was dependent on a procedure that could measure whether strategies were or were not produced. More generally, the study was the forerunner of a number of attempts to measure strategies directly, both with respect to memory (e.g., Miller, 1990; Moely et al., 1969) and on other kinds of cognitive tasks (e.g., Siegler & Jenkins, 1989).

tasks or that a short list of items is easier to memorize than a long list. It also includes knowledge about one's own memory—for example, the ability to judge whether one has studied an assignment long enough to do well on an exam.

Developmental Changes in Metamemory Psychologists have been interested in metamemory for two general reasons. First, it is an important outcome of the child's cognitive development. Traditionally, research on cognitive development has concentrated on the child's understanding of external stimuli and events—in some cases physical stimuli (as in Piaget's conservation tasks) and in some cases social ones (as in studies of interpersonal understanding). Children's thinking is not limited to external stimuli, however; it also encompasses the internal, mental world. Flavell (1971) was among the first child psychologists to focus explicitly on "thinking about thinking," and he coined the term *metacognition* to refer to thoughts that have mental or psychological phenomena as their target. With metamemory, the focus is on thoughts about memory.

Children's thinking about memory changes in a variety of ways as they develop. Here we note just a few examples. A basic question is whether the child realizes that there is such a thing as memory. Even young children show some such knowledge. They may behave differently, for example, when told to remember something than when told simply to look, thus demonstrating some awareness that remembering may require special cognitive activities (Baker-Ward, Ornstein, & Holden, 1984). They also have some understanding of the relative difficulty of different memory tasks. By age 5 or 6, most children realize that familiar items are easier to remember than unfamiliar ones (Kreutzer, Leonard, & Flavell, 1975), that short lists are easier to learn than long ones (Wellman, 1977), that recognition is easier than recall (Speer & Flavell, 1979), and that forgetting becomes more likely over time (Lyon & Flavell, 1993).

In other respects, however, young children's metamemory is limited. They do not always behave differently when faced with an explicit request to remember (Appel et al., 1972). They do not yet understand many phenomena of memory, such as the fact that related items are easier to recall than unrelated ones (Kreutzer et al., 1975) or that remembering the gist of a story is easier than remembering the exact words (Kurtz & Borkowski, 1987). In addition, their assessment of their own mnemonic abilities is far too optimistic. In one study, for example, over half of the preschool and kindergarten participants predicted that they would be able to recall all 10 items from a list of 10, a performance that no child in fact came close to achieving (Flavell, Friedrichs, & Hoyt, 1970). Furthermore, young children do not adjust their expectations readily in response to feedback; even after recalling only 2 or 3 items on one trial, they may blithely assert that they will get all 10 on the next attempt (Yussen & Levy, 1975). Older children are both more modest and more realistic in assessing their own memories (Schneider & Pressley, 1997).

Effects of Metamemory on Memory Performance   The second general reason for interest in metamemory concerns its possible contribution to developmental changes in memory performance. We stated the argument at the beginning of this section. Older children know more about memory than do younger children; older children also remember better than do younger children. It is easy to see how these two facts might be related. Knowledge of the demands of different sorts of memory tasks should help the child select the best strategy for remembering. Knowledge of one's own memory should be important in deciding such things as how to allocate attention and what material to study further.

Obvious though the knowledge–behavior relationship seems, demonstrating it empirically has proved surprisingly difficult. Many early studies that assessed both metamemory and memory performance (usually focusing on the child's use of strategies) reported only modest correlations at best between the two (Cavanaugh & Perlmutter, 1982). Thus, the knowledge that children can demonstrate about memory does not always relate clearly to how they perform on memory tasks. The following quotation, taken from one of the first metamemory studies, suggests a possible reason for this discrepancy. Here, a little girl describes a wonderfully complex procedure for memorizing phone numbers (her metaknowledge), but then suggests at the end that her actual behavior might be quite different.

> Say the number is 633–8854. Then what I'd do is—say that my number is 633, so I won't have to remember that, really. And then I would think now I've got to remember 88. Now I'm 8 years old, so I can remember, say my age two times. Then I say how old my brother is, and how old he was last year. And that's how I'd usually remember that phone number. [Is that how you would most often remember a phone number?] Well, usually I write it down. (Kreutzer et al., 1975, p. 11)

Despite the difficulty in establishing knowledge–behavior links, most researchers remain convinced that the growth of metamemory is one source of developmental improvement in memory. It is simply hard to believe that what children know does not exert an important influence on how they behave. Indeed, more recent studies of the issue have been more successful than earlier work at identifying relations between knowledge and behavior (Schneider, 1999). One promising approach has been to train children in various forms of metamemory and then look for possible effects on subsequent memory performance (Ghatala et al., 1985; Pressley, Borkowski, & O'Sullivan, 1985). Such training does in fact improve memory.

Like the work on mnemonic strategies, research such as this has applied as well as theoretical implications. For example, it may prove possible to help children with memory problems by teaching them about memory itself. Indeed, some of the most successful of the strategy training programs discussed earlier included instruction in metamemory. Apparently, children are most likely to benefit from memory training if they learn not only what to do but why to do it.

The studies of metamemory illustrate a second general theme of the information-processing approach. We have stressed the information-processing theorist's emphasis on the many different processes that go into intelligent behavior. These processes do not occur in isolation, however, nor do they occur without direction. The child must somehow select and coordinate specific cognitive activities, and a full model of intelligence must explain how this selection and coordination occur. The case of mnemonic strategies provides a good illustration. A strategy such as rehearsal does not simply happen. Rather, other cognitive processes must decide that rehearsal is an appropriate strategy, monitor its execution, and evaluate its success. In short, some sort of "executive" must control the more specific forms of information processing. Work on metamemory is directed toward one sort of executive control—the child's knowledge of memory as a determinant of the ways in which he goes about remembering.

The Role of Knowledge

Our final explanation for developmental improvements in memory is perhaps the most straightforward. It concerns the effects of knowledge on memory. Memory and knowledge are in fact closely related. What we know about a topic is an important determinant of how well we learn and remember information about that topic. Older children generally know more about all sorts of things than do younger children; thus, older children generally remember better than younger children.

Studies that have attempted to specify the ways in which knowledge affects memory have taken a variety of directions. Here we discuss such research under two headings: constructive memory and expertise.

Constructive Memory   The notion of constructive memory is most easily introduced through example. Table 8.2 provides an example used in research with grade-school children. The children were first read the story and then asked the eight questions listed beneath it.

Any reader is likely to spot a difference between the first four questions and the last four. The first four tap verbatim memory for information that was given directly in the story. The last four, however, concern information that was never explicitly provided. We are never told, for example, that Linda likes to take care of animals. Yet any adult reader of the story knows that she does. So, it turns out, do most young children.

Constructive memory
Effects of the general knowledge system on how information is interpreted and thus remembered.

The ability to answer questions 5 through 8 is a function of **constructive memory.** Constructive memory refers to the ways in which people's general knowledge system interprets the information they take in and thus affects what they remember. The basic idea is that we do not simply record memories as a tape recorder would. Memory always involves acting on and integrating new experiences in light of what we already know— it always involves an attempt to *understand*, not just record. In our attempt to understand, we continually draw inferences and go beyond the information given. The eventual memory is therefore truly a construction, not merely a direct duplication of experience. This is why we, and the 6-year-old, can come away from the story in Table 8.2 knowing that Linda likes to take care of animals.

Let us consider another example. Eleven-year-olds were read sentences such as "His mother baked a cake" and "Her friend swept the kitchen floor" (Paris & Lindauer, 1976). Later they were asked to recall the sentences. Half the children were given

| Table 8.2 | **Story Used in Study of Constructive Memory with Children** |

Linda was playing with her new doll in front of her big red house. Suddenly she heard a strange sound coming from under the porch. It was the flapping of wings. Linda wanted to help so much, but she did not know what to do. She ran inside the house and grabbed a shoe box from the closet. Then Linda looked inside her desk until she found eight sheets of yellow paper. She cut the paper into little pieces and put them in the bottom of the box. Linda gently picked up the helpless creature and took it with her. Her teacher knew what to do.

1. Was Linda's doll new?
2. Did Linda grab a match box?
3. Was the strange sound coming from under the porch?
4. Was Linda playing behind her house?
5. Did Linda like to take care of animals?
6. Did Linda take what she found to the police station?
7. Did Linda find a frog?
8. Did Linda use a pair of scissors?

SOURCE: From "Integration and Inference in Children's Comprehension and Memory" by S. G. Paris, 1975. In F. Restle, R. Shiffrin, J. Castellan, H. Lindman, and D. Pisoni (Eds.), *Cognitive Theory*, Vol. 1, Mahwah, NJ: Erlbaum, p. 233. Copyright © 1975 by Lawrence Erlbaum Associates. Reprinted by permission.

retrieval cues—hints that might help them remember. The retrieval cues were the names of the instruments implied by the sentences—"oven" for the sentence about baking, "broom" for the sentence about sweeping, and so on. Children given the cues recalled more than children who received no such help. But why should such cues be helpful? The sentences, after all, did not contain the words *oven* and *broom*. The cues were helpful because the children had gone beyond the information given in the sentences to fill in the missing elements. Having already inferred what the instrument must be, they were easily able to use "oven" or "broom" as a cue to what they had actually heard. Indeed, these implicit cues were just as effective as explicit cues drawn directly from the sentences ("cake," "floor," and so on).

It seems clear that memory is constructive from early in life. At every age, children filter new experiences through their existing knowledge systems, and what they ultimately remember depends on how they interpret experiences. Constructive memory does change across childhood, however, and the changes are of two general sorts.

First, with increased age memory becomes even more constructive, as children become increasingly active in processing information and increasingly likely to draw inferences that allow them to go beyond the literal input. In the retrieval-cues study described, for example, 7- and 9-year-olds showed little benefit from the implicit cues that were so helpful for 11-year-olds. Although certainly capable of inferring "oven" from "baked a cake," the younger children apparently did not spontaneously make such inferences. Second, with increased age the complexity of the inferences that children can draw increases as their cognitive abilities increase. In the injured-bird story, for example, even most 5-year-olds could answer questions 7 and 8. Questions 5 and 6, however, require a somewhat higher-order inference and hence were solved at a slightly later age.

Another example of constructive memory will help make one final point. The example comes from Piaget's only research on memory. Piaget and Inhelder (1973) presented 3- to 8-year-old children with the stimulus shown in Figure 8.3*a*. The sticks in the figure constitute a *seriated array*—that is, an array in which the stimuli are perfectly ordered along some quantitative dimension, in this case length. As we saw in Chapter 7, Piaget's previous research had established that an understanding of seriation is a concrete operational achievement, typically coming at age 6 or 7.

One week after they had seen the sticks, the children were asked to draw what they had seen. Figure 8.3*b* shows the kinds of drawings that the youngest children produced.

Figure 8.3

Stimulus and typical responses in Piaget and Inhelder's study of constructive memory: (a) the seriated array presented to the children and (b) what 4- and 5-year-olds remembered a week later. The memory distortions result from the young child's preoperational assimilation of the stimulus.

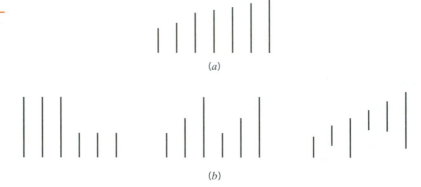

It can be seen that the children's memories were not only wrong but systematically wrong. Their drawings, in fact, corresponded exactly to the various errors that preoperational children make in attempting to solve the seriation task. Piaget's interpretation was that the children assimilated the input to their preoperational understanding of seriation. In so doing, they reworked and distorted the experience. The eventual memory thus reflected their understanding and not simply the literal stimulus.

The point that the Piagetian research makes is that constructive memory can operate in a negative as well as a positive direction. When some new experience is too advanced for the child, the child's memory of the experience is likely to be simplified and perhaps even distorted. Other factors besides cognitive level can sometimes result in such "constructive" distortions. It has been shown, for example, that children's beliefs about gender differences may influence how they process information about males and females. Children who viewed pictures in which gender-stereotypic activities were reversed (e.g., a girl sawing and a boy playing with dolls) showed a tendency on a later memory test to "correct" these images, reporting, for example, that it was the boy who did the sawing (Martin & Halverson, 1983). Similarly, children's beliefs about different ethnic groups can influence what they remember about members of those groups (Bigler & Liben, 1993), just as their stereotypes about old age can color their memories for particular elderly individuals (Davidson, Cameron, & Jergovic, 1995).

The constructive nature of memory, then, is, as Ornstein and Haden (2001, p. 204) put it, "a double-edged sword." In general, constructive memory is a positive force, helping us understand experience more adaptively. But in particular instances, constructive memory can distort and mislead. In Box 8.2 we discuss one situation in which it may be essential to know how accurate children's memories are.

Expertise   Like constructive memory, expertise is easiest to introduce through example. Imagine that you viewed each of the arrays pictured in Figure 8.4 for 10 seconds and then attempted to reproduce as much of each configuration as you could remember. If you do not play chess, the chances are that you would find the two arrays equally difficult to recall; both, after all, contain the same number and the same variety of stimuli. If you are a chess player, however, the top array would almost certainly be easier to remember. It would be easier because the pieces are in positions that might actually occur in a game, whereas those in the bottom array are randomly arranged. You could therefore draw on your knowledge of chess as you took in the information, stored it in memory, and retrieved it during reproduction.

Let us take our hypothetical study one step further. Imagine now that you are not only a chess player but an expert chess player. If so, several further predictions can be made. The odds are that your memory for the actual chess array will be even greater, that the discrepancy between actual and random will also be greater, and that you will easily surpass an average chess player, let alone a nonplayer, in your memory for the real positions.

Children's Eyewitness Testimony

It has been estimated that at least 100,000 children testify in court cases in the United States every year (Ceci & Bruck, 1998). This figure does not include the much larger number of instances in which children provide depositions or other kinds of evidence outside court. The cases in which children testify span a range of topics, but the most frequent category among criminal trials, accounting for about 13,000 cases each year, is child sexual abuse. In most instances of alleged abuse, the child witness is also the target of the abuse. In many, the child is the only witness.

Can the testimony of a young child be trusted? Should such testimony be admissible in court? As the figures just cited indicate—and the vignettes with which we opened the chapter confirm—questions like these can be critically important to answer.

BOX 8.2

Applications

They can also be very difficult to answer. Researchers who seek to study children's memory for abuse face some obvious challenges. Experiences of abuse are typically highly traumatic; they may continue for extended periods of time; and they often involve the child as a participant and not merely as a bystander. Furthermore, what children say about abuse may involve more than simply what they remember. Complex social and emotional factors may be important, such as the child's guilt about being a participant or reluctance to implicate a parent or friend. Questioning by a parent or authority figure may lead the child to particular responses, especially if questioners believe that they already know the truth or if, as advocates within the court system, they have an interest in a particular outcome. All these characteristics make memory for abuse different from the kinds of memory that psychologists usually study—or that they *can* easily study in an ethically acceptable way.

Researchers have tried in various ways to discover or devise memory tests that bear some similarity to the abuse situation. Some have created experimental settings that reproduce some elements of the real-life situations of interest—for example, a Simon Says game in which child and experimenter touch parts of each other's bodies (White, Leichtman, & Ceci, 1997). Others have focused on memory for naturally occurring traumatic experiences—for example, going to the dentist (Peters, 1991), receiving an injection (Goodman et al., 1991), or undergoing urinary catheterization (Quas et al., 1999). Although such experiences can hardly equal the trauma of abuse, they do capture some of its characteristics.

In many studies, researchers have also attempted to simulate the types of questioning that suspected victims of abuse must undergo. A child may be questioned several times across a period of weeks, for example, or the interviewer may include some deliberately leading questions in an attempt to determine how suggestible the child is. Children may be told to "keep a secret" about what happened to them during the experimental session (Bottoms et al., 1990), or a police officer rather than research assistant may do the questioning (Tobey & Goodman, 1992).

Such studies suggest several conclusions about children as witnesses (Bjorklund, 2000; Bottoms & Goodman, 1996; Ceci & Bruck, 1995, 1998; Eisen, Quas, & Goodman, 2002). First, research verifies that recall memory improves with age and that older children typically report more of their experiences than do younger children. The memories of 3-year-olds (the youngest age group tested in such research) are especially shaky. Second, as the delay between an event and questioning about it increases, the completeness and accuracy of recall decline; this is especially true for young children. In many real-life cases there are delays, often substantial ones, before children are first questioned, and so this finding is a cause for concern. Third, in at least some cases, young children are more suggestible than are older children or adults—that is, they are more likely to be influenced by leading questions from an adult authority figure. This finding indicates the need for caution in accepting the reports of young children who have undergone repeated and leading questioning, as is often true in investigations of suspected abuse.

On the other hand, in many studies memory differences between younger and older children or between children and adults are not very great. Age differences, as well as memory inaccuracies in general, are most likely when specific questions are used; conversely, they are minimized by the use of free recall measures that allow children to say what happened in their own words. Furthermore, the memory problems that children do show are mainly errors of omission rather than of commission—that is, they are more likely to fail to report certain details than they are to introduce false information. This finding suggests that any clearly spontaneous mentions of abuse by children should be taken very seriously.

Having offered these conclusions, we should add that there remains much controversy about exactly what the research shows and what the implications are for children's legal testimony. Fortunately, one point on which all researchers agree is that more study is necessary, and the topic of eyewitness memory is currently the focus of an extraordinarily active research effort. Among the topics being explored in this research is the issue of how best to question children in order to meet two goals: maximizing the accuracy of testimony and minimizing stress to the child (Goodman et al., 1992; Lamb & Poole, 1998; Poole & Lindsay, 2002) Having to provide testimony can add to the trauma of an already traumatic situation. It is therefore important to devise procedures that protect the child from further harm.

Thousands of children offer testimony in cases of alleged abuse every year. Ensuring the accuracy of their reports is a major challenge for those who interview children.

Figure 8.4

Meaningful and random configurations of chess pieces. Because they can make use of their knowledge of chess, chess players show better memory for the top array than for the bottom one. From "Chess Expertise and Memory for Chess Positions in Children and Adults" by W. Schneider, H. Gruber, A. Gold, and K. Opwis, 1993, *Journal of Experimental Child Psychology, 56,* p. 335. Copyright © 1993 by Academic Press. Reprinted by permission.

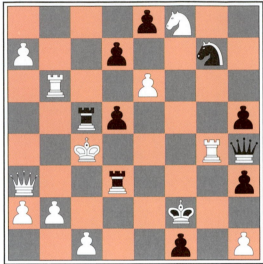

As you may have guessed, the kinds of results just sketched are not purely hypothetical; such outcomes have emerged in a number of research projects. The examples pictured in Figure 8.4 are from a study by Schneider and associates (1993). As have several similar studies, this study provided support for each of the expectations just discussed: Expert chess players showed better memory for real chess positions than for random ones; chess experts remembered chess configurations better than did chess novices; and the expert–novice differences were especially marked when real positions were the target.

The Schneider et al. study demonstrates the effects of expertise on memory. The term **expertise** (also sometimes called *content knowledge* or the *knowledge base*) refers to organized factual knowledge about some content domain—that is, what we know about some subject. In contrast to the knowledge embodied in Piagetian stages, expertise is content specific. Someone's expertise may be high with regard to chess or dinosaurs or birds but low when the topic turns to baseball or cooking or physics. When expertise is high, then memory also tends to be high. Variations in expertise contribute to variations in memory within individuals. Chess experts, for example, show better memory for chess positions and other chess-related information than they do for most other topics. Variations in expertise also contribute to differences in memory across individuals. Thus, chess experts remember more about chess than do chess novices, just as experts in baseball or cooking or physics remember more about their specialty than do most people. Finally, variations in expertise contribute to the aspect of memory that is our main concern here: developmental changes in memory across the span of childhood. Older

Expertise

Organized factual knowledge with respect to some content domain.

children possess more expertise for most topics than do younger children, and this greater expertise is one reason they remember more.

Expertise can affect memory in several ways. One way is through the form in which the knowledge is represented. In the case of chess, for example, experts store larger and more complex patterns of possible positions than do nonexperts, and this rich organizational structure helps them quickly make sense of positions that actually arise (Bedard & Chi, 1992). Another way is through effects on other contributors to memory, such as mnemonic strategies. Research has shown that children use strategies most effectively in content areas in which they are especially knowledgeable (Bjorklund, Muir-Broaddus, & Schneider 1990). Finally, perhaps the most general effect of expertise is on speed of processing. When knowledge about some domain is high, information relevant to that domain can be taken in and processed more rapidly, thus freeing cognitive resources for other activities, such as generating strategies (Bjorklund & Schneider, 1996).

An additional finding from the Schneider et al. study makes one more important point about expertise. In addition to the comparison of experts and novices, their study included an age dimension. Half the chess experts were adults and half were 10- to 13-year-old children; similarly, half the novices were adults and half were children. The design of the study (patterned after an earlier, classic study by Chi, 1978) therefore allowed the researchers to look separately at the effects of age and expertise, two factors that are usually closely linked and thus hard to pull apart. On memory tasks that did not involve chess, the adults, not surprisingly, demonstrated better memory than the children. On the memory-for-chess measure, however, expertise, not age, proved critical. Thus, the 10-year-old experts outshone the adult novices in reproducing chess positions—despite the fact that the adults in general had greater memory spans.

The point that this study makes is that in at least some instances it is expertise, and not other factors associated with age, that is critical to memory. Other researchers have also found that young participants can equal or even outperform older ones when the content is something they know well. Among the content areas for which child superiority has been demonstrated are dinosaurs (Chi & Koeske, 1983), cartoon figures (Lindberg, 1980), baseball (Recht & Leslie, 1988), and soccer (Schneider, Korkel, & Weinert, 1987).

The work on expertise brings us to another general theme of the information-processing approach. The role of factual knowledge is heavily stressed in contemporary

Knowledge about a particular content domain affects the ease with which information is processed and remembered. In some cases, children may possess greater expertise than adults.

information-processing accounts of not only memory but also reasoning and problem solving (Bjorklund, 1987; Chi, Glaser, & Farr, 1988). The argument is straightforward. The more children already know, the more they will understand of any new experience. The more they understand, the more they will remember. And the more they understand and remember, the more likely they are to reason and to solve problems in effective and adaptive ways.

To Recap . . .

Most examinations of memory beyond infancy have focused on recall memory, which improves with age across the childhood years. Three general explanations have been offered for this improvement. One source of improvement is the development of mnemonic strategies, such as rehearsal and organization. The tendency to use strategies, the complexity of the strategies, and the skill with which the strategies are executed all increase with age. The emphasis on strategies reflects one important theme of the information-processing approach—the existence of limits on information-processing resources and the need to develop techniques (such as mnemonic strategies) to overcome those limits.

A second approach to explaining developmental improvements stresses the child's metamemory, which includes knowledge about memory in general and about one's own memory in particular. Both sorts of knowledge increase with age. Although attempts to link metamemory to memory performance have sometimes been unsuccessful, recent evidence suggests that increases in knowledge do lead to improvements in performance. The work on metamemory reflects another theme of the information-processing approach—the need for executive control to select and coordinate cognitive activities.

A third approach stresses the effects of the general knowledge system on memory. Studies of constructive memory demonstrate that memory often involves inferences and constructions that go beyond the literal input. Older children are more likely to engage in such constructive processing than are younger children. Older children also possess greater content-specific expertise than do younger children, and this factor is another contributor to developmental improvements in memory.

NUMBER

We noted that information-processing studies of memory often have applied as well as theoretical value—the work on study strategies in school is a clear example. The same point applies to research directed to children's understanding of number. Making sense of numbers is a task to which children (and teachers) devote hundred of hours across many years in school. Research that informs us about the processes of children's mathematical thinking can help make these experiences happier ones for both teacher and child.

One point that relevant research makes is that children's understanding of number starts well before age 5 or 6. We therefore begin with developments that precede the first exposure to formal arithmetic in school, focusing first on infancy and then on the preschool period.

Infants' Response to Number

Until fairly recently, the idea that infants are at all sensitive to number is one that most child psychologists would have dismissed. This is no longer the case. Although there are, as we will see, disputes with regard to the extent of infant numerical competence, it now seems clear that some ability to respond to number is present from early in life.

What sorts of sensitivity to number might infants show? One basic question concerns the ability to discriminate between sets of different numerical size. A number of investigators have used the habituation-dishabituation methodology to probe for early ability to discriminate set sizes (Starkey & Cooper, 1980; Trehub, Thorpe, & Cohen, 1991; van Loosbroek & Smitsman, 1990; Xu & Spelke, 2000). In these studies, the infant is first repeatedly shown collections of a particular size (say, three objects) until attention drops off. A new set size (say, four objects) is then presented. Do infants notice the change? As long as the set sizes are small, as in the example, babies as young as 3 months apparently do. One study (Antell & Keating, 1983), in fact, reports successful discrimination of 2 versus 3 by newborns!

That infants can discriminate differences in set size is certainly impressive. Even more impressive is the suggestion that babies may be capable of very simple forms of arithmetic. Evidence derives from an extension of the Baillargeon possible event—impossible event procedure. In this case, however, the impossible event involves a violation of the laws of arithmetic. Figure 8.5 shows some examples—in the top part, a violation of the principles of addition; in the bottom part, a violation of subtraction.

Wynn (1992, 1995, 1998) reports that 5-month-old infants who witness such events react as we would expect them to react if they understood the arithmetical operations involved—that is, they show little dishabituation to the possible events but a marked recovery of interest when the rules of addition or subtraction are apparently violated. This outcome is certainly compatible with the hypothesis of early arithmetical competence; unfortunately, it does not definitively establish it. As some thought about Figure 8.5 should reveal, the impossible events in these studies encompass not only arithmetical impossibilities but also physical impossibilities—an object either magically disappears (in the Addition condition) or magically appears (in the Subtraction

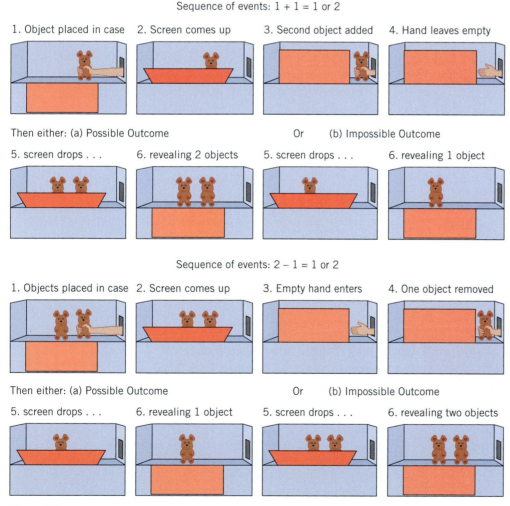

Figure 8.5

Possible and impossible outcomes in Wynn's study of infants' arithemetical competence. From "Addition and Subtraction by Human Infants" in *Nature* (1992) figure 1, p. 749. Reprinted by permission from *Nature*. Copyright © 1992 MacMillan Magazines Ltd.

condition). It is possible, therefore, that the infants' apparent surprise reflects their knowledge about objects rather than anything specific about number (Haith & Benson, 1998). Pulling apart these possibilities is a challenging task, and efforts therefore continue to specify exactly what, if anything, babies know about arithmetic (Cohen & Marks, 2002; Mix, Huttenlocher, & Levine, 2002; Wakeley, Rivera, & Langer, 2000).

Preschool Developments

Preschoolers, as we saw in Chapter 7, have only a very limited appreciation for the aspect of number on which Piaget concentrated: namely, the conservation of number in the face of a perceptual change. Preschoolers do, however, possess other sorts of numerical knowledge. In particular, research has demonstrated that their understanding of counting is more sophisticated than we might have expected.

Although counting is an automatic activity for most adults, accurate counting in fact depends on an appreciation of a number of underlying rules or principles. Rochel Gelman and associates (Gelman, 1982, 1991; Gelman & Gallistel, 1978) have identified five principles that a counting system must honor (see Table 8.3). As you can see, the first three principles deal with how to count, the fourth deals with what can be counted, and the fifth is a combination of features of the first four.

Research by Gelman and colleagues indicates that children as young as 3 or 4 have some understanding of these principles. Of course, preschoolers are unlikely to be able to verbalize the principles explicitly. But when asked to carry out counting tasks, they generally act in ways that accord with the principles (for example, applying just one number name to each item), and they also are able to spot violations of the principles when they watch others count. Young children, it is true, do not always follow the principles perfectly, and their specific ways of applying them may differ from those of adults (e.g., the 3-year-old who demonstrates the stable-order principle by always counting, "1, 2, 6"). Nevertheless, both Gelman's work and that of other researchers (e.g., Fuson, 1988; Sophian, 1995, 1998) indicate that counting is a systematic, rule-governed behavior from early in life. It is also a frequent activity—something that children the world around seem to do naturally, often for the pure pleasure of counting.

Arithmetic

We turn now to older children and the sorts of arithmetical problems that are the subject of instruction in school.

Suppose you were asked how you come up with answers to simple addition problems, such as 4 + 2 and 3 + 5. Your response would probably be that you simply know—that you have memorized the answer to such often-encountered problems. You

Table 8.3	What Young Children Know about Number: The Gelman and Gallistel Counting Principles
Principle	Description
One–one	Assign one and only one distinctive number name to each item to be counted.
Stable-order	Always recite the number names in the same order.
Cardinal	The final number name at the end of a counting sequence represents the number of items in the set.
Abstraction	The preceding counting principles can be applied to any set of entities, no matter how heterogeneous.
Order-irrelevance	The items in a set can be counted in any order.

SOURCE: Based on information from *The Child's Understanding of Number* by R. Gelman and C. R. Gallistel, 1978, Cambridge, MA: Harvard University Press.

would probably be right—all of us *have* memorized a number of basic arithmetical facts. But what about young children who are just beginning to learn about mathematics? How do they come up with their answers?

Many research programs have examined the strategies that children use to solve arithmetical problems (Ashcraft, 1990; Bisanz & LeFevre, 1990; Bjorklund & Rosenblum, 2001, 2002; Ginsburg, Klein, & Starkey, 1998). Here we concentrate on some research by Robert Siegler and associates (Siegler & Jenkins, 1989; Siegler & Shipley, 1995; Siegler & Shrager, 1984). Table 8.4 shows strategies that young children might use to solve the 3 + 5 problem. The retrieval strategy corresponds to the expected strategy for adults—retrieving from memory a previously memorized answer. Other possible strategies vary in both sophistication and likelihood of success.

How can we determine which strategy a child is using? Siegler and colleagues use a variety of techniques. One approach is simply to watch children as they work on the problems. Some strategies (putting up fingers, counting out loud) are overt and thus directly observable. Another approach is to ask children how they arrive at their answers. Although verbal reports are not infallible guides to mental processes (in children or anyone), they can provide useful information. Table 8.5 presents some examples of children's self-reports on their use of the min strategy, or the strategy of counting up from the larger of two addends (i.e., the two numbers to be added).

A third approach makes use of a central information-processing methodology: the measurement of response time as a guide to processes of solution. A child using the count-from-first-addend strategy, for example, should take longer to solve 3 + 7 than to solve 3 + 5; a child using the min strategy, however, should be equally quick on the two problems. Examination of response times across a range of problems can help specify the strategies being used.

One of the most interesting findings from the Siegler program of research concerns the diversity of strategies that children use. We might have expected that a child at any point in development would have a single method of solving addition problems. In fact, children typically employ a number of different strategies, sometimes going with one approach, sometimes trying something different.

Children's selection among strategies is not random but often adaptively geared to the problem at hand. They may, for example, use the retrieval strategy for simple and familiar problems but fall back on one of the more certain counting strategies when faced with a more complex task. In general, children seem to strive for a balance of speed and accuracy, selecting the fastest strategy that is likely to yield a correct response. With development, there is a predictable progression from less efficient to more efficient strate-

Counting on the fingers is one of the first arithmetical strategies that children develop.

Table 8.4	Children's Strategies for Solving Simple Addition Problems
Strategy	Typical Use of Strategy to Solve 3 + 5
Sum	Put up 3 fingers, put up 5 fingers, count fingers by saying "1, 2, 3, 4, 5, 6, 7, 8."
Finger recognition	Put up 3 fingers, put up 5 fingers, say "8" without counting.
Short-cut sum	Say "1, 2, 3, 4, 5, 6, 7, 8," perhaps simultaneously putting up one finger on each count.
Count-from-first-addend	Say "3, 4, 5, 6, 7, 8" or "4, 5, 6, 7, 8," perhaps simultaneously putting up one finger on each count.
Min (count-from-larger-addend)	Say "5, 6, 7, 8," or "6, 7, 8," perhaps simultaneously putting up one finger on each count beyond 5.
Retrieval	Say an answer and explain it by saying "I just knew it."
Guessing	Say an answer and explain it by saying "I guessed."
Decomposition	Say "3 + 5 is like 4 + 4, so it's 8."

SOURCE: Adapted from *How Children Discover New Strategies* by R. S. Siegler and E. Jenkins, 1989, Mahwah, NJ: Erlbaum, p. 59. Copyright © 1989 by Lawrence Erlbaum Associates. Adapted by permission.

Table 8.5	Protocols Illustrating Children's Use of the Min Strategy to Solve Addition Problems

Experimenter (E): How much is 6 + 3?

Lauren (L): (Long pause) Nine.

E: OK, how did you know that?

L: I think I said . . . I think I said . . . oops, um . . . I think he said . . . 8 was 1 and . . . um . . . I mean 7 was 1, 8 was 2, 9 was 3.

E: OK.

L: Six and three are nine.

E: How did you know to do that? Why didn't you count "1, 2, 3, 4, 5, 6, 7, 8, 9"? How come you did "6, 7, 8, 9"?

L: 'Cause then you have to count all those numbers.

E: OK, well how did you know you didn't have to count all of those numbers?

L: Why didn't . . . well I don't have to if I don't want to.

Experimenter (E): OK, Brittany, how much is 2 + 5?

Brittany (B): 2 + 5 — (whispers) — 6, 7 — it's 7.

E: How did you know that?

B: (excitedly) Never counted.

E: You didn't count?

B: Just said it — I just said after six something — seven — six, seven.

E: You did? Why did you say 6, 7?

B: 'Cause I wanted to see what it really was.

E: OK, well — so, did you — what — you didn't have to count at one, you didn't count, 1, 2, 3, you just said 6, 7?

B: Yeah — smart answer.

Experimenter (E): OK, Christian, How much is 1 + 24?

Christian (C): 1 + 24!?

E: Yep.

C: Umm . . . 25.

E: How did you know that?

C: I . . . counted in my head.

E: How did you count it in your head?

C: What was it again?

E: 1 + 24.

C: I went . . . 1, 2, 3, 4, 5, si . . . I went, 24 + 1, I, well. . . . I'll try to get you to understand, ok?

E: OK.

C: I went 24 + 1 . . . (whispers) 24 . . . (whispers) 25 . . . that's what I did.

E: OK, that's good, well why didn't you count 1, 2, 3, 4, 5, 6, 7, 8, 9, 10, all the way to 24?

C: Aww, that would take too long . . . silly.

SOURCE: From *How Children Discover New Strategies* by R. S. Siegler and E. Jenkins, 1989, Mahwah, NJ: Erlbaum, pp. 66, 80, 91. Copyright © 1989 by Lawrence Erlbaum Associates. Reprinted by permission.

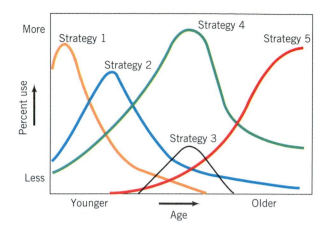

Figure 8.6

Siegler's overlapping waves model. From *Emerging Minds: The Process of Change in Children's Thinking* by R. S. Siegler, 1996, New York: Oxford University Press, p. 89. Copyright © 1996 by Oxford University Press. Reprinted by permission.

gies, culminating in the ability to retrieve answers from memory rather than continually having to calculate them anew. With development, speed and accuracy increase as well. These increases come in part from the emergence of more efficient strategies and in part from increased skill in executing any particular strategy.

These conclusions about strategies are not limited to the domain of addition. Both subtraction and division, for example, are also characterized by the use of multiple strategies rather than a single, consistent approach (Siegler, 1996). So too is reading (Siegler, 1988). So, as we saw earlier in this chapter, are many memory tasks.

Siegler (1996, 2000) captures these points about strategies in his "overlapping waves" model, depicted in Figure 8.6. The contrast drawn is with a strong version of a stage theory (what Siegler refers to as a staircase model), in which at any point children have a single way of solving a problem and in which lower-level approaches are abruptly replaced by higher ones. In fact, children often have multiple ways of solving problems, and the transitions across development are often gradual rather than abrupt.

The research discussed in this section has implications for teaching arithmetic. Perhaps the most general implication is that teachers should be sensitive to the beliefs and strategies that children bring to the classroom setting. We have seen that learning about numbers begins very early in life; thus, it is not surprising that even first-graders have their own strategies for solving arithmetic problems.

Teachers should realize, furthermore, that not all first-graders will have the same strategies and that instruction, as far as possible, should be adjusted to the individual child's level of development. Lower-level strategies, such as counting on one's fingers, should not necessarily be discouraged; children may need experience with the simpler strategies to arrive at answers that they can eventually retrieve from memory. The general principle is one that emerges also in discussions of the implications of Piaget's work for education: Be sensitive to the natural sequence of development and to the need for advanced knowledge to build on lower-level understanding.

To Recap . . .

Understanding of number begins to emerge well before the first formal instruction in school. Infants are sensitive to differences in set size and may (although this point is controversial) be capable of appreciating simple arithmetical operations. Preschool children demonstrate knowledge of the basic principles that underlie counting, even though their own counting efforts may often go astray.

Studies of arithmetic in school-aged children indicate that children develop a variety of strategies to solve arithmetical problems and that they typically use several strategies rather than just one, a notion that is captured in Siegler's overlapping waves model. With increased age, there is a gradual ascendance of more efficient strategies (such as retrieval) over less effective ones.

PROBLEM SOLVING

No one has to read a textbook to learn that children's problem-solving abilities improve dramatically across childhood. The tasks that the school system sets for its students, the ways in which parents attempt to reason with and control their children, the opportunities and the expectations that society in general holds—all are quite different for 15-year-olds than for 5-year-olds. As with the study of memory, the challenge for the researcher is to describe exactly how children's abilities change—and then to explain why these changes come about.

Children's problem-solving abilities in fact change in many ways as they develop (DeLoache, Miller, & Pierroutsaksos, 1998; Ellis & Siegler, 1994). Here we consider developments under three headings. We begin with the idea that some kinds of problem solving may be explained by the formation of rules for combining information and making judgments. We then discuss situations in which reasoning by analogy is an effective problem-solving strategy. We conclude with a central theme in information-processing theorizing—the contribution of memory to children's problem solving.

The Development of Rules

Rules
Procedures for acting on the environment and solving problems.

Robert Siegler (1978, 1981) has proposed that some important aspects of children's cognitive development can be characterized in terms of the construction of **rules.** Rules are procedures for acting on the environment and solving problems. They take the form of "if . . . then" statements. If A is the case, do X; if B is the case, do Y; and so forth. A simple and familiar example concerns the rules for behavior at traffic lights: If the light is green, proceed; if the light is red, stop (unfortunately, rules for yellow lights seem to be more variable!).

The rules for traffic lights are relatively simple ones, and in early childhood it is primarily simple rules with which children must deal. We begin with some recent research on preschoolers' ability to follow simple rules of the if-then sort. We then move on to some of the more complex forms of rule-based reasoning that emerge later in development.

Preschoolers' Rule-Based Reasoning
Although young children—as we hope is by now clear—have many cognitive strengths, there are times when they surprise us with what they cannot yet do or do not yet understand. Piaget's work furnishes numerous examples; so does research under the heading of theory of mind. Some recent studies by Zelazo and Frye (1998; Frye, 1999; Zelazo, 1999) provide another striking example.

The basic task in this research—*labeled the dimensional-change card sort*—is illustrated in Figure 8.7. The child is given a series of cards that vary in both shape and color and is instructed to sort them by one of the two dimensions. If the task is the "color game," for example, then the instructions will be to put the red ones in the box with the red picture and the blue ones in the box with the blue picture. Most 3-year-olds readily learn this task. After several such trials the rule changes: Now the task becomes the "shape game," and the instructions are to put the cars in one box and the flowers in the other. Most 4-year-olds easily make the switch. Most 3-year-olds do not. Even when they receive the new instructions at the start of every trial, and even when they themselves succeed in verbalizing the new rule, 3-year-olds continue to sort according to the original rule.

What the dimensional-change task shows is that 3-year-olds *are* capable of rule-based problem solving but with some definite limitations. Three-year-olds can handle two simple rules at a time—for example, if red, do this; if blue, do this. Even this, it is worth noting, is an accomplishment; 2-year-olds are able to learn and follow only one rule at a time. What the 3-year-old cannot yet do is to embed these simple rules within a more complex rule system, in which selection of one of the simple rules is contingent

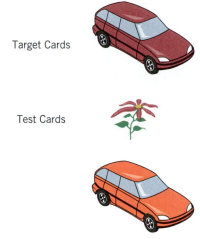

Target Cards

Test Cards

Figure 8.7

Dimensional card sort task used in Zelazo and Frye's study of early rule following. From "Cognitive Complexity and Control: II. The Development of Executive Function in Childhood," by P. D. Zelazo and D. Frye, 1998, *Current Directions in Psychological Science, 7,* 122. Copyright © 1998 by Cambridge University Press. Reprinted by permission.

on a prior, higher-order rule. Successful performance on the change trials requires this sort of embedded rule structure. The child must be able to reason in the following way: If this is the color game (higher-order rule), then if red do this and if blue do this; if this is the shape game, then if car do this and if flower do this.

In addition to illustrating the sorts of rules that young children can follow, the dimensional-change task suggests some general conclusions about contributors to children's problem solving. Success on the task requires a number of component processes. The child must have sufficient short-term memory capacity to keep in mind several rules at the same time. The child must be capable of inhibiting the original response once a new response is called for. Finally—and in Zelazo and Frye's (1998) analysis most critically—the child must have sufficient metacognitive ability to reflect on the rules that he or she has learned and to note the relations among them. The term **executive function** refers to general problem solving components of this sort—to components such as memory and inhibition and self-awareness that play a role in virtually every form of reasoning and problem solving. Recent research has shown that developmental improvements in executive function contribute to developmental advances on a wide range of cognitive tasks (Hughes, 2002; Keenan, 2000).

Executive function
General components of problem solving, such as short-term memory, metacognitive awareness, and inhibition.

Reasoning about Balance   Many situations, of course, require more thought than does sorting by shape or color, and it is these more complex situations to which research with older children has been directed. Figure 8.8 presents one example—a balance-scale problem originally devised by Inhelder and Piaget (1958) to study formal operational reasoning. The child is shown a simple balance scale on which varying numbers of weights can be placed at varying distances from the fulcrum. The task is to predict whether the scale will balance or whether one side or the other will go down. Successfully performing the task requires that the child realize that both weight and distance are important and that he or she know how to combine the two factors in cases of conflict. The original Piagetian research revealed that children of different ages gave quite different responses to the task, which Piaget analyzed in terms of the logical structures of concrete and formal operations.

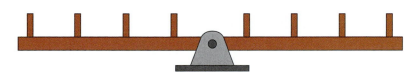

Figure 8.8

Balance scale used in Siegler's research. Metal disks can be placed on any of the eight pegs.

Siegler (1976, 1978) used the same task but a different methodology and form of analysis. He began by carefully considering all the various ways in which children might go about attempting to solve the balance-scale problem. Such *task analysis* is a characteristic information-processing methodology (Kail & Bisanz, 1982). Based on this task analysis, Siegler identified four rules that children might use in solving balance problems.

At the simplest level, rule 1, the child judges that the side with more weights will go down or that, if the number of weights on each side is equal, the scale will balance. The child using rule 2 also judges solely in terms of number of weights when the weights on each side are different; if the weights are equal, however, the rule 2 child can also take distance into account. The rule 3 child always considers both weight and distance and is correct whenever one or both are equal. If the two factors are in conflict, however (i.e., more weight on one side, greater distance on the other), the child becomes confused, does not know how to resolve the conflict, and (in Siegler's words) "muddles through." Finally, the rule 4 child has mastered the weight-times-distance rule: Downward force equals amount of weight multiplied by distance from the fulcrum. The rule 4 child can therefore solve any version of the task.

A task analysis identifies possible ways of responding, but it does not tell us whether children actually use these approaches. Siegler's next step, therefore, was to test the psychological reality of the proposed rules. He devised six types of balance-scale problems, carefully constructed to yield different patterns of response across the different rules. Both the problem types and the predicted responses are shown in Table 8.6.

Siegler presented five versions of each problem type to children ranging in age from 5 to 17. Fully 90% of the children followed one of the four rules consistently. (We should note, though, that subsequent studies have some times found evidence for more than four rules—Boom, Hoijink, & Kunnen, 2001; Tudge, 1992). As expected, the complexity of the preferred rule increased with age; most 5-year-olds used rule 1, whereas by age 17, rules 3 and 4 were most common. Finally, a particularly interesting

Table 8.6	**Types of Problems and Predicted Responses on the Siegler Balance-Scale Task**

	RULE			
Problem Type	**I**	**II**	**III**	**IV**
Balance	100	100	100	100
Weight	100	100	100	100
Distance	0 (Should say "Balance")	100	100	100
Conflict–weight	100	100	33 (Chance responding)	100
Conflict–distance	0 (Should say "Right down")	0 (Should say "Right down")	33 (Chance responding)	100
Conflict–balance	0 (Should say "Right down")	0 (Should say "Right down")	33 (Chance responding)	100

SOURCE: From "The Origins of Scientific Reasoning" by R. S. Siegler, 1978. In R. S. Siegler (Ed.), *Children's Thinking: What Develops?*, Mahwah, NJ: Erlbaum, p. 115. Copyright © 1978 by Lawrence Erlbaum Associates. Reprinted by permission.

finding was that accurate performance on the problems involving conflict actually declined with age. Although declines with age are normally unexpected, this finding fit nicely with the predictions of the rule analysis. As you can see in Table 8.6, the developmentally primitive rules 1 and 2 yield perfect performance on these problems, whereas the more advanced rule 3 results only in chance performance.

Siegler and others have applied his *rule-assessment methodology* to a number of tasks in addition to the balance-scale task (Klahr & Robinson, 1981; Ravn & Gelman, 1984). Siegler's (1981) own research has demonstrated the value of rules in explaining performance on a variety of Piagetian problems—for example, conservation of number and conservation of continuous quantity. The explanation is, to be sure, in some respects similar to Piaget's. In the case of conservation, for example, Siegler and Piaget agree that children solve the problem through mental action that logically combines information from both relevant dimensions (e.g., height and width in the case of quantity). There are, however, two differences between Siegler's and Piaget's accounts, differences that in general divide the information-processing and Piagetian approaches. One concerns specificity and testability. Rules are more precisely defined than are Piagetian operations, and the rule-assessment methodology provides a more rigorous test of a proposed explanation than is typically the case in Piagetian research. The second difference is theoretical. Operations are general structures that are assumed to determine performance on a wide range of tasks, and the expectation therefore is that children will be consistent in their level of performance. Rules, however, may be more domain specific, and there is no assumption that performance will necessarily be consistent from one task to another. Siegler in fact finds that the same child may use rules of different levels on different tasks.

Reasoning by Analogy

To many students, the term *analogical reasoning* doubtless conjures up images of the SAT or similar tests and complex verbal problems of the A is to B as C is to ? sort. In fact, the scope of the concept is a good deal broader than this. **Analogical reasoning** refers to a form of problem solving in which the solution is achieved through recognition of a similarity between the new problem (such as figuring out the relation between C and D) and an already understood problem (such as the relation between A and B). Some forms of such reasoning, including many verbal analogies, are indeed complex and late to develop, which is why analogies are a common item on standardized tests. Some forms, however, are evident very early in development. Here we consider two examples, one with infants and one with preschoolers.

Chen, Sanchez, and Campbell (1997) used the following task with 10- to 13-month-olds (see Figure 8.9). Infants were presented with an attractive toy, such as the toy car pictured on the right side of the figure. Two factors, however, prevented them from immediately grasping and playing with the toy: A barrier intervened between infant and toy, and the toy was in any case too far away to reach. To solve the problem, therefore, the infant needed to push aside the barrier, grasp the string connected to the toy (while ignoring the other, nonhelpful string), and pull the toy within range. The infants were first given a chance to solve the problem on their own, and few could do so. When a parent then modeled the solution, however, many more infants succeeded.

The test for analogical problem solving followed. The infants received a series of further problems that retained the same general solution structure as the original problem but varied a number of specific perceptual features—for example (as the figure shows), a different goal object, a different-colored barrier, a different string arrangement. The question was whether they could recognize the relation between the original problem and the new one and transfer the original solution appropriately. Not all could, especially at the younger end of the 10- to 13-month span. By the third problem, however, the average success rate had risen to better than 60%, a figure much higher than

Analogical reasoning
A form of problem solving in which the solution is achieved through recognition of the similarity between the new problem and some already understood problem.

Figure 8.9

Configuration of problems in Chen et al.'s study of analogical problem solving in infants. From "From Beyond to Within Their Grasp: The Rudiments of Analogical Problem Solving in 10- and 13-Month-Olds" by Z. Chen, R. P. Sanchez, & T. Campbell, 1997, *Developmental Psychology, 33,* 792. Copyright © 1997 by the American Psychogical Association. Reprinted by permission.

performance on the initial trial. Although they obviously could not put the process in words, the infants seemed to be engaging in reasoning of the following sort: "This barrier is like the one I pushed aside before, and this string is like the one I pulled before, and so if I want to get this new toy . . ."

As children develop, the sorts of relations they can recognize across problems become progressively less dependent on perceptual similarity; they also are more likely to be embedded in language. Consider an example of analogical problem solving in preschoolers (Brown, Kane, & Echols, 1986). Children first heard a story in which a genie needed to transport some jewels over a wall and into a bottle. The genie solved her problem by rolling up a piece of posterboard so that it formed a tube, placing one end of the tube in the mouth of the bottle, and rolling the jewels through the tube and into the bottle. The children were then asked to demonstrate a solution to the following problem: The Easter Bunny needs to transport his eggs across a river and into a basket on the other side. Despite the presence of a piece of posterboard, few 3-year-olds spontaneously recognized the analogy to the genie task, although with help (for example, questioning about the central elements in each story) some eventually succeeded. Five-year-olds were much more likely to recognize the relevance of the original story and to hit immediately on an analogical solution to the new task.

These examples of early analogical reasoning are obviously very simple, and they do not negate the fact that important developmental advances occur in this form of problem solving. To a good extent, however, what seems to develop is not the basic capacity to reason by analogy, which appears to be present from early in life, but rather knowledge about the particular items and particular relations that enter into particular analogies (Goswami, 1992, 1996). The point here is a simple one: If the child does not yet know what A or B is, then he or she cannot use the relation between A and B to reason analogically about C and D. We saw that what is known about a topic can be important for memory. The same point applies to problem solving.

The Contribution of Memory to Problem Solving

We have noted that some information-processing theorists are labeled neo-Piagetian because their ideas are especially closely tied to those of Piaget. In this section we examine one such theory, that of Robbie Case (1985, 1992; Case & Okamoto, 1996).

Like Piaget, Case divides development into distinct stages—stages in many respects similar to Piaget's. A major difference between the two approaches is the emphasis that Case places on memory. In his theory, the total problem-solving resources available to the child are divided into two components—operating space and short-term storage space.

The term **operating space** refers to the resources necessary to carry out whatever cognitive operations are being employed for the problem at hand. In the case of the Siegler balance-scale task, for example, a child who used rule 2 would first count the number of weights on each side of the fulcrum. Assuming that the weights were equal, the child would then count the number of pegs from the fulcrum. Finally, the child would use the information about weight or distance to predict which side would go down. Each of these operations would require a certain amount of operating space. Note that the term *space* is used somewhat metaphorically, for there is no reference to some actual physical area in the brain. The reference, rather, is to how much of the available mental energy must be used for the activity in question.

Performing operations is one part of problem solving; remembering the results of those operations is another part. The phrase **short-term storage space** refers to the resources the child needs to store results from previous operations while carrying out new ones. The rule 2 child, for example, would need to remember both the overall goal of the task and the results of each preceding operation to execute the sequence just described. Without such memory, there could be little hope of a successful solution.

The balance scale is just one of many problems whose solution depends on combining results from several cognitive operations. Such combining is possible only if short-term storage space is sufficient to hold all the relevant results. In Case's theory, limitations in short-term storage space are a major determinant of young children's difficulties in problem solving. Because they can keep track of only a few things at a time, young children can do only a few things at a time. Correspondingly, advances in problem solving occur as short-term storage space expands, and the child can begin to combine operations that previously could only be performed separately. More generally, the stage progressions in Case's theory are defined largely in terms of the new combinations made possible by increases in short-term storage capacity.

Why does short-term storage capacity increase? There are two possible explanations. One possibility, shown in Figure 8.10*a*, is that total problem-solving resources expand with age. As total resources grow, so does the space available for short-term storage. In this view, older children simply have more resources available to them. Thus, it is not surprising that they can remember more and do more.

Plausible though this model may seem, Case's research leads him to prefer a second possibility. This possibility, shown in Figure 8.10*b*, is that the growth in storage capacity

Operating space

In Case's theory, the resources necessary to carry out cognitive operations.

Short-term storage space

In Case's theory, the resources necessary to store results from previous cognitive operations while carrying out new ones.

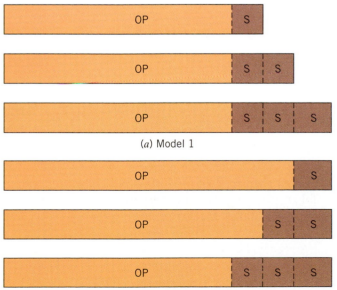

(*a*) Model 1

(*b*) Model 2

Figure 8.10

Two models for explaining developmental increases in short-term storage space. (*a*) In model 1, the total processing resources increase with age. (*b*) In model 2, processing resources remain constant, but operating space decreases.

results from a decrease in the space used to perform operations. Cognitive resources must always be divided between the two components of operations and storage; if fewer resources are needed for one component, then more are available for the other. In this second view, developmental changes in storage result from increases in the efficiency with which operations are performed. As children develop, they become more skilled at executing cognitive operations. Hence, they have more space left over for storage, and they can do more and more.

Accepting this second explanation leads naturally to another question: Why does operational efficiency increase? Case proposes two contributors. One is practice. With practice, cognitive activities of many sorts become more skilled and efficient. Thus, what once took effort and attention may eventually become automatic and routine. (We return to this notion, called *automatization,* in our discussion of cognitive change.) The second factor is biological maturation. Children develop at about the same pace, and this similarity suggests a biological contribution to development. Furthermore, Case notes that major changes in brain development occur at about the same time as the stage-to-stage transitions identified in his theory. Finally, research indicates that speed of information processing increases at a regular rate from early childhood to adulthood (Kail, 1991, 2000; Miller & Vernon, 1997). This increase in speed is so consistent across tasks and across samples that it appears to be maturational in origin.

Case's theory is one of the most ambitious information-processing efforts to date, and not all aspects of it have won acceptance. Its most general claim, however, is widely held: Memory improves as children develop, and improvements in memory contribute to improvements in reasoning and problem solving.

To Recap . . .

Like memory, children's problem solving improves dramatically over the childhood years. The development of rules is one contributor to developmental change. Even preschoolers are capable of using simple if-then rules, although they initially have difficulty with more complex, embedded rule systems. In older children response to a variety of tasks can be formulated in terms of the mental rules that guide responding. Solution of balance-scale problems is an example.

Reasoning by analogy is a basic form of problem solving that appears to be available to children from early in life. Much of the improvement in this form of reasoning with development reflects increased knowledge about the items and relations that enter into analogies.

Memory is a third important contributor to problem solving. Solutions to many problems require the ability to combine results from a number of cognitive operations. This is possible only if the child has sufficient short-term storage space to remember past results while performing new operations. Older children have greater storage capacity than do younger children, and so they are capable of more complex forms of reasoning and problem solving.

COGNITIVE CHANGE

In Chapter 7 we concluded that Piaget never succeeded in providing a satisfactory theory of cognitive change. Much the same criticism has been leveled against information-processing theorists (Miller, 2001). Most information-processing accounts have been more successful at specifying the various levels or states of understanding through which the cognitive system moves than at explaining the transition from one state to another.

In this section we consider some of the explanations for cognitive change that *have* been offered in information-processing theories to date (Klahr & MacWhinney, 1998; McClelland & Siegler, 2001; Siegler, 1996, 1998). We begin by discussing the methods that researchers in this tradition use to study change. We then consider several specific mechanisms of change that have been proposed by information-processing theorists.

Methods of Study

Information-processing researchers have utilized a variety of techniques to study the process of change. Here we concentrate on two methods that have been emphasized in recent information-processing research: microgenetic techniques and the creation of self-modifying computer simulations.

Microgenetic Techniques

As we saw when we introduced the microgenetic method in Chapter 2, a microgenetic study begins with the selection of a sample of children who are thought to be in a transitional phase for the knowledge being studied—that is, close to moving to a higher level of understanding. The children are observed as they attempt to solve a variety of problems that assess the abilities of interest. Typically, there are many such problems in each experimental session and several such sessions across a period of weeks or months. The goal is to observe processes of change as the change occurs—something that is usually not possible when we assess children only once or twice.

An analogy that Siegler (1996) uses in contrasting microgenetic techniques with the standard longitudinal approach is the difference between a snapshot and a movie. With longitudinal research we get snapshots—pictures of the cognitive system at different points in time. With microgenetic research we get a movie—a continuous record of change over time.

An example of a microgenetic study is provided by some of the work on arithmetical strategies discussed earlier in the chapter. Siegler and Jenkins (1989) selected 10 children who did not yet use the min strategy (that is, counting up from the larger addend) when solving simple arithmetic problems. These children then participated in three experimental sessions per week across a period of 11 weeks. During each session they attempted to solve seven addition problems; across sessions there was a gradual increase in the complexity of the problems presented. Both videotapes of the children's performance and direct questioning were used to infer the strategies underlying their answers. Through this approach, Siegler and Jenkins were able to document the gradual discovery of the min strategy by 7 of the 8 children who made it through all 11 weeks. Because of their extensive observational records, they knew when and how the strategy first appeared, as well as what preceded it and to what it subsequently led. The examples in Table 8.5 include the first appearance of the strategy for one of the children, Brittany.

In discussing the strengths of the microgenetic approach, Siegler (1996) identifies five issues related to cognitive change for which microgenetic techniques can provide valuable data. Such techniques can inform us about the *path* of cognitive change: the sequences and levels through which children move in acquiring new knowledge. They can provide information about the *rate* of change: how quickly or slowly different forms of knowledge are mastered. Microgenetic findings speak to the issue of *breadth* of change: when a new competency (such as a particular arithmetical strategy) is acquired, how narrowly or broadly it is applied. They are relevant to the question of possible *variability* in the pattern of change: Do all children follow the same route in mastering a new concept? As we have seen, a major conclusion from microgenetic research is that often children do not; there can be substantial variability en route to the same end point. Finally, microgenetic methods can provide information about the *sources* of change: the experiences and processes through which new knowledge is constructed.

Self-Modifying Computer Simulations

Earlier in the chapter we described the computer simulation methodology—the creation of computer programs that attempt to reproduce certain aspects of human cognition. As we saw, such simulations offer a powerful method for testing theories of underlying process. Nevertheless, many simulations are limited in that they are static; at best they tell us what the cognitive system is like at one point in development. A relatively recent development is the creation of programs that can actually change from one level of understanding to another.

Many of the first such efforts are collected in a book edited by Simon and Halford (1995). Although the research programs summarized vary in many ways, they do have several elements in common. Each includes a set of rules intended to model the starting-point level of understanding of a child who has not yet mastered the knowledge—for example, a rule system that uses only the length of the row when judging number and hence fails conservation-of-number tasks. Each also includes mechanisms for changing the initial rules in response to experience—for example, the capacity to benefit from experiences of counting and measurement in the case of conservation and thereby to construct more complex rules. Each includes tests in which the program is exposed to the relevant experiences and both its immediate and more long-term responses are recorded. Finally, each reports some success at modeling the acquisition of new knowledge—that is, in creating programs that modify their own rule systems with experience and hence change from lower to higher levels of understanding. Among the forms of knowledge for which change has been successfully modeled are conservation, transitivity, physical reasoning, and arithmetic.

Many of the ongoing efforts to create self-modifying systems take an approach labeled **connectionism**. Connectionism is a relatively recent development within the information-processing perspective, adopted by some but not all researchers in this tradition. Recall our discussion of the flowchart and computer as metaphors for human cognition. The starting point for advocates of connectionism is a basic limitation with regard to these metaphors: namely, that they *are* simply metaphors. That is, the human brain is not in fact a flowchart with different boxes, nor is it a digital computer. Chapter 5 discussed what it in fact is: an extraordinarily complex system of neural connections.

Connectionism attempts to mirror this aspect of the human brain. Rather than strings of symbols, therefore, connectionist computer programs take the form of *artificial neural networks*. Such networks consist of multiple interconnected processing units, just as the brain consists of multiple interconnected neurons. The units are arranged in layers, including an input layer that takes in information about the task facing the system and an output layer that generates an eventual response. Connections among units vary in strength, just as is true for connections among neurons in the brain. When the amount of activation received from its connecting units is sufficient, a unit fires, just as is

Connectionism

Creation of artificial neural networks, embodied in computer programs, that solve cognitive tasks and modify their solutions in response to experience. A methodological and theoretical approach adopted by a subset of information-processing researchers.

Figure 8.11

Artificial neural network for connectionist modeling of response to the balance-scale task. The input units code the information about weight and distance, the hidden units represent the system's current weighting of these factors, and the activation of the output units determines the response. From "A Connectionist Perspective on Knowledge and Development" by J. L. McClelland, 1995. In T. J. Simon & G. S. Halford (Eds.), *Developing Cognitive Competence: New Approaches to Process Modeling*, Hillsdale, NJ: Erlbaum. Copyright © 1995 by Lawrence Erlbaum Associates. Reprinted by permission.

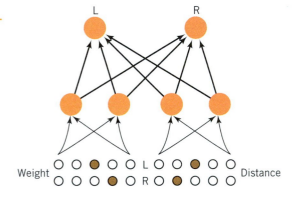

Using the Hands to Read the Mind

Cognitive change is a continuous process that begins the moment the baby enters the world. Children—and indeed any of us—are continually adapting to new challenges and forging new forms of understanding. For any particular kind of cognitive advance, however, there often are especially sensitive periods for change—transitional phases during which children are ready to overcome past limits and benefit from new experiences. Identifying such transitional phases is important both theoretically, in terms of our understanding of how change comes about, and pragmatically, in terms of our ability to help children who are ready to learn.

A recent program of research by Goldin-Meadow and associates (Goldin-Meadow, 2000, 2001; Goldin-Meadow, Alibali, & Church, 1993) offers some intriguing evidence with respect to one possible index of readiness for change. Most assessments of children's knowledge focus on a single response measure—typically verbal judgments in response to some task. The Goldin-Meadow group also elicits verbal judgments, but they add to such measures an observational recording of children's spontaneous gestures as they attempt to solve the problem. They are especially interested in what they label **gesture-speech mismatches**—that is, instances in which the information conveyed by the gesture does not match that expressed in the verbal judgment. These are cases in which the mouth is saying one thing and the hand something else.

One set of tasks used to explore such mismatches was drawn from Piaget's work (Church & Goldin-Meadow, 1986). The children in the study responded to a battery of conservation problems, and their gestures were recorded in addition to the standard judgments and explanations. Many of the children did in fact gesture when explaining their answers—for example, cupping their hands to indicate the width of the container on a continuous-quantity task. In many cases, the gesture was in accord with the verbal judgment; for some children, however, it was not. Some nonconservers, for example, referred only to the heights of the containers in their explanations, yet simultaneously signaled the difference in width with their accompanying gestures. Furthermore, a subsequent training study revealed that it was these "dis-

BOX 8.3

On the
Cutting
EDGE

Gesture–speech mismatches

Instances in which the meaning conveyed by speech and the meaning conveyed by an accompanying gesture are in conflict. Thought to be an indicator of readiness for change.

cordant" children who were most likely to benefit from conservation training. Thus, gesture–speech mismatch proved to be an index of readiness for change.

Why might gesture–speech mismatch be predictive of change? Goldin-Meadow et al. (1993) argue that such mismatches are a direct reflection of a knowledge state in transition. Children who are not yet close to mastering a concept are typically content with a simple and consistent basis for response—tall things have more, for example, in the case of conservation. The more advanced, transitional child, however, has reached the point of holding two conflicting beliefs about the phenomenon, and both beliefs come through in the response to the task. In the case of conservation, the discordant child, in contrast to his or her more solidly preoperational peer, has begun to sense that width as well as height is important and is struggling to reconcile these competing bases for response. Because both dimensions are in fact important, this child is closer to arriving at the correct answer than is the more confident and consistent nonconserver.

It is important to note that demonstrations of gesture–speech mismatch are not limited to conservation tasks. Indeed, one attractive feature of the measure as an index of readiness for change is that it is not tied to any particular task, or, for that matter to any particular age period. Among the other domains in which gesture–speech mismatches have been shown to be predictive of change are word learning in toddlers (Gershkoff-Stowe & Smith, 1997), arithmetical reasoning in grade-schoolers (Perry, Church, & Goldin-Meadow, 1988), formal operational reasoning in adolescents (Stone, Webb, & Mahootian, 1991), and understanding of physics in adults (Perry & Elder, 1997).

We noted that researchers have been able to use mismatches to predict which children will benefit from experimentally provided training. But we must also ask whether the measure has any more general utility—that is, are these cues that teachers and parents can naturally detect and use in their interactions with children? The answer is yes: Even untrained adults have been shown to be sensitive to mismatches in their assessments of children's knowledge, and to be above chance, after watching both speech and gestures, in their predictions of which children are ready to master a new concept (Alibali, Flevares, & Goldin-Meadow, 1997; Goldin-Meadow & Sandhofer, 1999). The first step in helping children learn is knowing which children are ready to learn.

true of neurons in the brain. It is the sum of the activated units that determines response to the task. With experience, connection strengths and patterns of activation are modified, which is how learning occurs and new responses eventually replace old.

As a brief (and simplified) example of how such a program works, let us use a task with which we are already familiar: the balance scale problem. Figure 8.11 shows a segment of a connectionist approach to this task (McClelland, 1995). As you know, the relevant inputs for the balance task are the number of weights on each side of the balance, along with their distance from the fulcrum. The program includes 20 input units to represent this information; their settings signal the particular weights-distances configuration that must be judged on a particular trial. The program also includes output units for the eventual judgment: either right side down or left side down or balance. Finally, the hidden units encode the system's current weightings for weight and distance information. The hidden units thus mediate between input and output: Depending on their setting, a particular input sets up a particular pattern of activation in the output units, and it is this activation that determines the response. With experience—in particular, with feedback about the correctness of different judgments—the weightings are adjusted and responses gradually change. In the simulation, the program began, as do children, by responding in terms of weight only (rule 1) and progressed, as do children, through rules 2 and 3 to a partial version of rule 4.

The balance task is just one of a number of content areas to which the connectionist approach has been applied. Other topics include infant perception (Mareschal & Johnson, 2002), object permanence (Munakata, 1998), Piagetian concrete operational concepts (Buckingham & Shultz, 2000), and language (MacWhinney & Chang, 1995). We will see an application to language in Chapter 11.

Mechanisms of Change

As noted, information-processing theorists have proposed a number of different change mechanisms. Here we discuss four: encoding, automatization, strategy construction, and strategy selection. We then consider a general characteristic that these and other specific mechanisms may have in common.

Encoding
Attending to and forming internal representations of certain features of the environment. A mechanism of change in information-processing theories.

Siegler (1991) defines **encoding** as "identifying the most important features of objects and events and using the features to form internal representations" (p. 10). Encoding is thus related to what we normally mean by *attention*, but it carries some further implications as well. One is the idea that information processing is always active rather than passive, because the child attends to only some features of the environment and uses only some features to arrive at judgments. The other is the emphasis on how the child interprets or represents the encoded information. Encoding involves not simply attending to but also forming some sort of representation of what has been attended to, and it is this representation that guides subsequent problem solving.

Let us consider how the concept of encoding can be applied to the balance-scale task. Recall that children who use rule 1 base their judgments solely on the number of weights. Siegler (1976) tested such children's encoding of the relevant information. First, he allowed the children to observe an arrangement of the scale for 10 seconds. Then he covered the scale, brought another scale forward, and asked the children to reproduce the arrangement that they had just seen. Both 5-year-old and 8-year-old rule 1 users were tested.

Siegler found that the 5-year-olds could reproduce only the weights and not the distances, evidence that they had encoded only weight. The 5-year-olds also failed to benefit from training trials that showed them the results of various configurations of weight and distance. As Siegler notes, the children's failure to learn from training is not surprising given that they never encoded the critical information. The 8-year-olds, in contrast, were able to encode both weight and distance, even though they did not yet use distance information in making their judgments. Because of their sensitivity to both variables, the 8-year-olds were able to benefit from the same training that had been ineffective with the 5-year-olds.

Automatization
An increase in the efficiency with which cognitive operations are executed as a result of practice. A mechanism of change in information-processing theories.

A second mechanism is **automatization.** As noted in the context of Case's (1985) theory of the role of memory in problem solving, there is a characteristic progression in the development of any cognitive skill. At first, the skill—precisely because it is new—requires considerable attention and effort, and few resources may be left for any other sort of cognitive processing. With practice, however, execution of the skill becomes more automatic, cognitive resources are freed, and more advanced forms of problem solving become possible. Automatization is a primary mechanism by which the cognitive system overcomes inherent limitations on the amount of information that can be processed.

The same can be said for a third mechanism, **strategy construction.** Like automatization, strategies serve to overcome processing limitations by increasing the efficiency with which information is handled. The child who realizes the organization inherent in a set of items, for example, may need to remember only the general categories and not every individual item. Similarly, a child who has developed the min strategy for adding numbers will need to count just twice rather than eight times when adding 2 plus 8.

A final, closely related mechanism is **strategy selection.** As we have seen, children often try out a variety of strategies when they are in the process of developing a new form of competence. We discussed examples with respect to both memory and arithmetic, and the same finding has emerged for other kinds of problem-solving as well (Ellis, 1997; Rosengren & Braswell, 2001). Given this multiplicity of approaches, a main task for development is selecting the strategy or combination of strategies that provides the optimal approach to problem solution. Over time, these relatively effective approaches come to be used more and more, whereas less effective strategies are gradually discarded. There is, in short, a survival of the fittest: Strategies that work are the ones that are maintained.

If the preceding passage reminded you of a theory from another discipline of science, the similarity was deliberate. Siegler (1996) argues that cognitive development across the course of childhood is in many respects parallel to biological evolution in the history of a species. In both evolution and development, change builds on initial diversity and variation. In the case of evolution, the diversity is in the distribution of genes within a species; in development, it lies in the variation in problem-solving approaches (multiple strategies, different encodings, etc.) that characterize the initial response to a task. In both evolution and development, the initial variation is followed by selection based on differential success: reproductive success in the case of evolution, problem-solving success in the case of development. And in both evolution and development, successful variants are preserved and passed on—to the next generation in the evolution of species, to future problem-solving efforts in the development of the child. In Siegler's analysis, the parallels between biology and psychology are not surprising, because they follow from the similar tasks of evolution and development: to produce adaptive change over time.

Strategy construction
The creation of strategies for processing and remembering information. A mechanism of change in information-processing theories.

Strategy selection
Progressively greater use of relatively effective strategies in comparison to relatively ineffective ones. A mechanism of change in information-processing theories.

To Recap . . .

Information-processing researchers use a variety of methods to study cognitive change, two of which have been especially important in recent research. Microgenetic studies involve repeated observations, typically in multiple sessions across weeks or months, of children's problem-solving efforts. This approach offers the possibility of observing change as it occurs. Self-modifying computer simulations are computer programs whose purpose is to model the change from one level of understanding to another. In the connectionist approach, such programs are written in the form of artificial neural networks.

Mechanisms that seem to be important for cognitive change include encoding, automatization, strategy construction, and strategy selection. Developmental advances in encoding make developmental advances in reasoning possible. Automatization frees resources for other cognitive activities. Strategy construction helps overcome the limitations of the information-processing system, and strategy selection ensures that the most effective strategies are used. A set of general principles that may unite these and other change mechanisms can be drawn from the theory of biological evolution. Cognitive development, like evolution, involves the progressive selection and preservation of adaptive variations from an initial pool of possibilities.

CONCLUSION

The information-processing approach has been a major position in the study of cognitive development for several decades now. During that time, it has achieved some noteworthy successes, as our discussions throughout this chapter should make clear. Nevertheless, even its strongest advocates clearly regard their efforts as work in progress—already fruitful, to be sure, but with much still to be done. In that spirit, we focus here on some of the challenges that remain for workers in this tradition. We discuss three.

One challenge concerns scope. Information-processing research has addressed many different aspects of child development. Information-processing theories have been more limited. To date, information-processing theorists have been most successful at constructing precise models of specific, but also somewhat limited, aspects of child development—what Klahr and MacWhinney (1998) refer to as "toy versions" of the larger domains of interest. There is as yet no information-processing theory that rivals Piaget's theory in the scope of phenomena it encompasses.

A second challenge relates to the computer metaphor that has guided so much work in this tradition. One obvious difference between humans and computers concerns the social context for intelligent behavior. Humans, unlike computers, interact constantly with other humans, and these interactions are both an important context for exercising cognitive skills and one of the sources of those skills. Information-processing conceptions, it is true, have begun to influence the study of social behavior; we will see a number of examples in the later chapters of the book. Information-processing researchers have also begun to explore the social contributors to information-processing skills. Nevertheless, the social world has been a relatively neglected topic for most information-processing researchers.

A final challenge relates to the issue with which we concluded our discussion: cognitive change. Despite much recent attention to the question, information-processing theorists are still far from producing a completely satisfactory explanation of how cognitive change comes about. On the other hand, they have generated both specific models of the change process and the methods for testing the models. Thus, they seem clearly to be moving in the right direction.

FOR THOUGHT AND DISCUSSION

1. The term *infantile amnesia* refers to our inability to remember events from the first 2 or 3 years of life. *Think about your own earliest memories. What sorts of events do they include? Why do you think that you remember these events and not numerous others from early childhood? How confident are you that these early memories are accurate?*

2. Mnemonic strategies are techniques that both children and adults use to help themselves remember something. *How often do you employ mnemonic strategies? In what situations are you most likely to use strategies, and what forms do the strategies take? How much of what you remember comes from the deliberate use of strategies?*

3. The accuracy of children's eyewitness testimony is an important and controversial topic. *Imagine that you had the task of designing the program of questioning for a young (say, 4- or 5-year-old) suspected victim of abuse. How would you proceed?*

4. We noted the centrality of the computer metaphor to the ways in which information-processing researchers think about and study cognition. *Do you perceive possible limitations to the computer metaphor—that is, aspects of human cognition that cannot be captured in a computer program? If so, what are the differences that you see between human intelligence and computer intelligence?*

5. We discussed implications of information-processing ideas for the teaching of arithmetic in childhood. *Think about the possible application of the approach to another academic subject, such as reading, writing, or science. How would an information-processing researcher study the topic, and what sorts of conclusions might he or she offer?*

6. In Chapter 7 we discussed the Piagetian approach to cognitive change and the constructs of assimilation, accommodation, and equilibration. In the present chapter we considered the information-processing approach and the notions of encoding, automatization, and strategy construction. *How similar or different do you perceive these two approaches as being? Do you prefer one or the other set of change mechanisms? If so, why?*

VISUAL SUMMARY FOR CHAPTER 8
Cognitive Development:
The Information-Processing Approach

The Nature of the Approach

The Flowchart Metaphor ▶ Information-processing theorists often employ a flowchart metaphor to describe the flow of information through the cognitive system, specifying the processes that occur between environmental input and response output.

The Computer Metaphor ▶ The computer can serve as a useful metaphor for thinking about human cognition and can also provide a method for simulating the processes underlying cognition and cognitive change.

Comparisons with Piaget ▶ Information-processing theories share Piaget's concern with cognitive development, his emphasis on underlying rules and structures, and, in some cases, his use of stages to describe development. Most information-processing theorists, however, do not subscribe to Piaget's broad, general stages, developing instead domain-specific models that are more precise, more complete, and more testable.

Memory in Infancy

Recognition Memory ▶ Habituation and conditioning studies demonstrate recognition memory—the realization that a perceptually present stimulus or event has been encountered before—in newborns. With development, the span of time across which the infant can retain material increases, as does the amount and complexity of the material that can be retained.

Recall Memory ▶ Recall memory—the retrieval of some past stimulus or event even when it is not perceptually present—is more difficult to study in infancy. Recent research suggests that simple forms of recall (e.g., the ability to search for vanished objects or the imitation of models from the past) may emerge by the end of the first year.

Memory in Older Children
Three Sources of Improvement in Memory across the Childhood Years

The Role of Strategies ▶ One source of improvement is the development of mnemonic strategies, such as rehearsal and organization. The tendency to use strategies, the complexity of strategies, and the skill with which strategies are executed all increase with age. The emphasis on strategies reflects one important theme in information-processing research—the existence of limits in information-processing resources and the need to develop techniques to overcome the limits.

The Role of Metamemory ▶ Metamemory includes knowledge about memory in general and one's own memory in particular. Such knowledge increases with age and can lead to improvements in memory performance. Research into metamemory reflects another theme of the information-processing approach—the need for executive control to select and coordinate cognitive activities.

The Role of Knowledge ▶ Memory in older children is more likely to involve inferences and constructions that go beyond the literal input (constructive memory) than in younger children. Older children also possess greater content-specific expertise, which contributes to memory performance.

Number

Infants' Response to Number ▶ Infants are sensitive to differences in set size and may be capable of appreciating certain simple arithmetic operations.

Preschool Developments ▶ Preschool children demonstrate knowledge of the basic principles that underlie counting, even though they may not be able to count accurately.

Arithmetic ▶ School-age children develop a variety of strategies to solve arithmetic problems and typically use several strategies. With increasing age comes a gradual ascendance of more efficient strategies over less effective ones.

Problem Solving
Factors that Contribute to Age-Related Improvements in Problem Solving

Development of Rules ▶ The development of mental rules that guide responding is one contributor to cognitive change. Solution of balance-scale problems, for example, consistently follows one of four general rules, and the complexity and appropriateness of the rules increase with age.

Reasoning by Analogy ▶ Reasoning by analogy, which involves recognition of similarities between a new problem and a problem already solved, is a basic form of problem solving that appears to be available to children early in life. Developmental improvements reflect increased knowledge about the items and relations that enter into analogies.

Contribution of Memory ▶ Older children have greater storage capacity needed to remember past results while performing new operations. They are thus capable of more complex forms of reasoning and problem solving than younger children. This growth in storage capacity results from an increase in operational efficiency, which in turn results from both biological maturation and practice at executing operations.

Cognitive Change

Methods of Study ▶ Microgenetic studies and self-modifying computer simulations are two methods of study that have been especially important in recent research studying cognitive change. Microgenetic studies offer the possibility of observing change as it occurs, through repeated observations across weeks or months of children's problem-solving efforts. Self-modifying computer simulations are computer programs whose purpose is to model the change from one level of understanding to another.

Mechanisms of Change ▶ Encoding, automatization, strategy construction, and strategy selection are mechanisms that seem important for cognitive change. Developmental advances in encoding make developmental advances in reasoning possible. Automatization frees resources for other cognitive activities. Strategy construction helps overcome the limitations of the information-processing system, and strategy selection ensures that the most effective strategies are used.

9

Cognitive Development: The Sociocultural Approach

When 8-year-old Tommisheon Davidson awoke on Wednesday, March 7, 2001, he most likely assumed it would be just another unremarkable day in third grade. But before the day ended, this Detroit, Michigan, student had helped his mother, Kimberly Jones, deliver a baby.

Kimberly's due date was more than a week away, but because her contractions had increased throughout the day, she decided it would be best if she headed to the hospital. Kimberly sent her husband to pick up a relative to stay with Tommy and his 2-year-old brother, Malik. While her husband was out, Kimberly realized the baby was coming more quickly than expected and that she would be giving birth at home with only Tommy at her side.

Tommy called 911 on the cordless phone, and the operator told him what to do. The operator said to collect some towels to keep the baby warm and to find a string to tie the umbilical cord 6 to 8 inches from the baby's belly. Finding the towels and even a suitable string weren't too hard—Tommy used a shoelace from one of his sneakers. Tying the knot didn't prove to be too much of a problem either, since Tommy had "this camping thing that tells you how to tie knots." The challenge was figuring out 6 to 8 inches. Like many children his age, Tommy had not yet mastered the intricacies of measurement, so Tommy and his mother did the measuring together. Happily, Micah Makayla (4 pounds, 14 ounces) arrived in good health, and Tommy's heroics will forever be part of the Davidson-Jones family lore.

Although few of the problems children encounter are as dramatic as delivering a baby, many other features of the situation in which Tommy found himself on March 7 are typical of children's problem solving. The problems children face arise during purposeful activity with valued goals, and whether those goals are achieved is a matter of real consequence. Children also typically solve problems with the assistance of other people—a parent, teacher, older sibling, or classmate. These people may actually be present in the physical setting, or they may render aid from a distance like the emergency operator or the author of the camping manual Tommy used. And, to solve problems successfully, children often have to master cultural tools and artifacts, including symbol systems, cultural conventions, and material tools.

How children become competent at using cultural tools and artifacts in purposeful activity—and, in turn, how these tools and artifacts contribute to cognitive development—is the focus of cognitive researchers working from the sociocultural perspective. In this chapter, we first summarize the most important characteristics of the sociocultural approach to development. We then consider several areas of development that have been studied extensively by sociocultural researchers. We conclude with a discussion of challenges faced by scholars working within the framework of sociocultural theory. ■

NATURE OF THE APPROACH

Culture
The accumulated knowledge of a people encoded in their language and embodied in the physical artifacts, beliefs, values, customs, institutions, and activities passed down from one generation to the next.

Like the information-processing approach described in the last chapter, the sociocultural approach is not a single theory but a family of theoretical frameworks. The common core that unites these theories is a focus on the social and cultural foundations of developmental processes. According to the sociocultural approach, individuals inherit their environments as much as they inherit their genes. These environments are organized by **culture**—the accumulated body of knowledge of a people encoded in language and embodied in the beliefs, values, norms, rituals, physical artifacts, institutions, and activities that are passed down from one generation to the next (Cole, 1996). Throughout the life course, biological and cultural aspects of development act in concert. Individual growth and development are the products of the coordination of these two organized, dynamic systems. Thus, socioculturalists believe that individual development must be understood in—and cannot be separated from—its social and cultural/historical context (Cole, 1996; Gauvain, 1998; Rogoff, 2003; Schweder et al., 1998; Valsiner, 1997).

Many researchers working within the framework of the sociocultural approach have been heavily influenced by the work of Soviet scholars, most notably Lev Vygotsky. Three themes in Vygotsky's writings have proved especially influential in guiding contemporary sociocultural theory and research (Wertsch, 1981). The first theme is that individual mental development has its origins in social sources. The second is that human thought and action are mediated by cultural tools. The third is that the study of mental functioning requires the study of change across multiple levels ranging from momentary learning to species history. We discuss each of these themes in more detail next.

The Social Origins of Thought

According to Vygotsky, children acquire knowledge and cognitive skills by participating in cultural activities with more experienced partners. During these interactions, children are introduced to new ways of thinking. Initially, children experience these modes of thinking in collaboration with others. Over time, children internalize the skills and use them independently.

Vygotsky believed the most productive interactions occur in what he termed "the zone of proximal (potential) development." The **zone of proximal development** is the distance between what a child can accomplish on his or her own and what the child can achieve under the guidance of an adult or in collaboration with a more capable peer. The zone of proximal development involves activities that are slightly beyond the child's current capabilities but can be accomplished with help. Interactions within the zone of proximal development promote growth because the social support allows children to extend current skills to a higher level of competence.

As we will see throughout this chapter, sociocultural researchers have devoted considerable attention to the ways in which other people support and encourage children's development. One way experienced partners assist children's learning is through a process known as scaffolding (Wood, Bruner, & Ross, 1976). During **scaffolding,** more capable partners adjust the level of help in response to the child's level of performance, moving to more direct, explicit forms of teaching if the child falters and to less direct, more demanding forms of teaching as the child moves closer to independent mastery. Scaffolding appears to be effective not only in producing immediate success but also in instilling the skills necessary for independent problem solving in the future.

Scaffolding best captures the processes involved in deliberate instruction. Much of what children come to know is not the result of explicit teaching, however, but rather a by-product of participating in routine cultural activities. These cultural activities—be they household chores, economic pursuits, or religious practices—may well serve as learning opportunities, but that is not their primary function.

Barbara Rogoff (1990) coined the term **guided participation** to describe the process by which young children become competent by participating in everyday, purposeful activities under the guidance of more experienced partners. As in scaffolding, the more expert partner is sensitive to the capabilities of the learners and structures tasks accordingly by assigning simple chores and adapting tools to their abilities. As children grow more competent, their roles and responsibilities change. In the process, so does their understanding of the task.

In Box 9.1, we describe new research on the ways parents support the development of children's scientific reasoning in informal settings.

Tools and Artifacts

A second theme in Vygotsky's writings is that human thought and action are mediated by material and symbolic tools (Vygotsky, 1981). *Tools,* in this context, refers to all the means individuals have at their disposal to achieve desired goals, from simple objects (such as sticks and rope) to complex technological devices (such as telephones and calculators). Tools also include representations such as maps, sign and symbol systems such

Zone of proximal development
The distance between what a child can accomplish independently and what the child can accomplish with the help of an adult or more capable peer.

Scaffolding
A method of teaching in which the adult adjusts the level of help provided in relation to the child's level of performance, the goal being to encourage independent performance.

Guided participation
The process by which young children become competent by participating in everyday, purposeful activities under the guidance of more experienced partners.

Guided participation in activities with a parent is an important source of cultural skills and values.

Family Learning in Museums

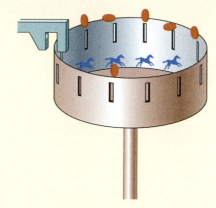

An increasingly popular family activity is a trip to the museum. There are currently more than 16,000 museums in the United States. These museums attract 2.3 million visitors *per day,* and more than half of the visits involve families (AAM, 2002; Dierking & Falk, 1994). Indeed, one recent survey showed that museums rank in the top three family vacation destinations. Given the popularity of museums among families and educational experts alike (Gardner, 1991), it is no wonder that research in museums has exploded (Falk & Dierking, 2000; Leinhardt, Crowley, & Knutson, 2002; Paris, 2002).

Among the issues that researchers have begun to explore are the ways in which children's social interactions in the museum setting shape their experience. In one recent study, Kevin Crowley, Maureen Callanan, and their associates observed 4- to 8-year-old children at an interactive exhibit at the San Jose Children's Museum (Crowley et al., 2001). The exhibit in question is known as a zoetrope (see Figure 9.1). The zoetrope, a common attraction in science museums, is a simple animation device that was developed in 19th century Europe. The device produces an illusion of motion when one looks through the slots of the spinning drum, and provides an opportunity for children to explore how cartoons, movies, and videos work.

Of particular interest to Crowley, Callanan, and their colleagues was whether and how parents would support their children's interactions with the zoetrope. According to the sociocultural approach, children learn most effectively when their efforts are guided by more expert partners. Parents support children's learning by managing their attention, simplifying the task, regulating frustration, modeling appropriate action, offering useful hints, and helping the child interpret outcomes.

The results of this study support the idea that children's performance is enhanced when working with an adult partner. Children who explored the zoetrope with parents spent more time at the exhibit than those who engaged with the device alone or with one or more peers. They were also more likely to manipulate the device properly, and were therefore more likely to produce the intended effect–the illusion of motion. They were more likely to experiment with changing the direction of spin and animation as well.

Parent–child pairs were also more likely to talk about the device together (the "conversations" among peers typically involved one child talking and the other[s] not listening). Furthermore the kinds of comments the parents offered were of

the sort that we would expect to promote children's understanding. In about one-third of the exchanges, the parents explained how the device worked. They also helped the children draw connections to familiar experiences (e.g., cartoons) and, in some cases, even introduced scientific principles responsible for the illusion: "Because your mind . . . your eye . . . sees each little picture and each one's different from the other one, but your mind puts it all in a big row" (Crowley et al., 2001, p. 728).

Clearly, museums and other informal science settings and activities such as planetariums, zoos, and television shows like *Bill Nye the Science Guy* are valuable opportunities for parents to help children learn factual scientific information and to practice scientific reasoning skills. Perhaps just as important, however, may be the messages parents convey about the value and excitement of science when they join their children in science activities (Crowley & Galco, 2001; Goodnow, 1990; Gottfried, Fleming, & Gottfried, 1998). After all, the renowned evolutionary theorist Stephen Jay Gould took his first steps toward a career in paleontology when he visited the American Museum of Natural History in New York with his father at age 5. Gould once wrote, "I dreamed of becoming a scientist, in general, and a paleontologist, in particular, ever since the Tyrannosaurus skeleton awed and scared me" (Yoon, 2002, p. 1).

Figure 9.1

Zoetrope in the interactive science exhibit at the San Jose Children's Discovery Museum. From "Shared Scientific Thinking in Everyday Parent-Child Activity," *Science Education,* by K. Crowley et al., 2001. Copyright © 2001. Reprinted by permission.

---

as language, and social practices such as routines and rituals that organize and structure human activity.

Children learn how to use these cultural tools through interactions with parents, teachers, and more experienced peers. As a result of using these tools—first in cooperation with others and later independently—the child develops **higher mental functions**—complex mental processes that are intentional, self-regulated, and mediated by language and other sign systems. Examples include focused attention, deliberate memory, and verbal thinking. Vygotsky believed that the particular structure and content

Higher mental functions
Complex mental processes that are intentional, self-regulated, and mediated by language and other sign systems.

of higher mental functions vary with social experience. Importantly, cultural tools for thinking both enhance and transform mental capabilities. Formal tools and systems for measuring time or distance, for example, enhance human thinking by improving accuracy. As children learn how to use these tools, their thinking is transformed, and they come to think about time and distance differently—that is, in units such as minutes, seconds, inches, or meters.

According to Vygotsky, the most powerful tool is language. Language is the primary means by which mature members of a cultural community pass knowledge and values surrounding cultural practices on to succeeding generations. Language also functions as a tool in its own right.

The Cultural-Historical Context of Development

The third theme in Vygotsky's writing is that to understand human cognition, we need to understand its origins and the transitions it has undergone over time (Wertsch & Kanner, 1995). Vygotsky proposed the study of development over four interrelated time frames—microgenetic, ontogenetic, phylogenetic, and cultural/historical. **Ontogenetic development** is development across years of an individual's life, such as childhood, whereas **microgenetic development** is moment-to-moment learning of individuals as they work on specific problems. As we have seen in the preceding chapters, developmental psychologists most often concern themselves with ontogenetic and microgenetic development.

Phylogenetic development is the development of the species. Existing human capabilities, including the ability to create human culture, are products of biological evolution. Of particular interest to sociocultural theorists are the capabilities that distinguish humans from other animals. These include the use of tools such as language and social-cognitive abilities that support learning in social contexts.

Cultural/historical development occurs over decades and centuries and leaves a legacy of tools and artifacts, value systems, institutions, and practices. Individual development unfolds in a particular cultural and historical niche that itself is dynamic and changing. As noted earlier, socioculturalists believe that individual development must be studied in its cultural context. Moreover, the sociocultural approach is unique among developmental theories in studying how changes in cultural practices and institutions (e.g., the introduction of formal schooling, move to a market economy, invention of new technologies) shape the human mind.

Comparisons with Cognitive-Developmental Theories

The sociocultural approach is similar in several ways to the cognitive-developmental theories of Piaget and information processing. Socioculturalists and researchers working within the framework of cognitive-developmental theories study many of the same aspects of mental functioning, including attention, memory, conceptual understanding, and academic skills such as mathematics, scientific reasoning, and literacy. Both approaches view the child as an active participant in his or her own development (as opposed to a passive recipient of environmental input), and both hold that the individual undergoes qualitative as well as quantitative change over the course of development (Miller, 2001).

The approaches differ, however, in several key respects. Perhaps most significant are views regarding the mechanisms of change. The Piagetian and information processing approaches focus on processes internal to the individual child, such as the reorganization of cognitive structures and increased speed of processing information. Sociocultural theorists, in contrast, believe developmental change is socially mediated. According to this perspective, development is the result of interactions with other people and the tools and artifacts that are the products of human culture. In this view, both children and their caregivers are active participants in the process of development.

Ontogenetic development
Development across years of an individual's life, such as childhood.

Microgenetic development
Moment-to-moment learning of individuals as they work on specific problems.

Phylogenetic development
Development of the species.

Cultural/historical development
Development that occurs over decades and centuries and leaves a legacy of tools and artifacts, value systems, institutions, and practices.

Another difference between the approaches is in what develops. Cognitive-developmental theories view cognitive development as changes in internal mental capabilities. Sociocultural theories situate thinking in practice. In this perspective, the development of a given skill cannot be isolated from the purposes to which it is put. Children learn not only the skill but values surrounding its use. As Goodnow (1990) notes: "We do not simply learn to solve problems. We learn also what problems are worth solving, and what counts as an elegant rather than simply an acceptable solution" (p. 260). What develops, then, is a culturally constructed system of knowledge that includes goals, values, and motivation (Miller, 2001).

Another issue that distinguishes the sociocultural approach involves the specificity of cognitive development. As we have seen, Piaget believed that development proceeds through a series of stages, which are consistent among children of every culture.

Most information-processing theorists do not subscribe to these kinds of broad, general stages and instead recognize a great deal of variability in performance. Sociocultural theories also anticipate a great deal of variability in performance. Socioculturalists accept the possibility that cognitive development could occur in stage-like fashion if cultures organized children's experiences in that way. They do not believe that there are universal stages in children's cognitive development, however, and even question whether there is some ideal endpoint in development (Rogoff, 1998, 2003).

✔ To Recap . . .

According to the sociocultural approach, cognitive development is fundamentally a social and cultural process. Contemporary adherents to this perspective have been strongly influenced by the writings of the Soviet scholar Lev Vygotsky, who argued that children's cognitive capabilities develop during supportive interactions with other people in the "zone of proximal development." It is in these interactions that children learn to use the products of cultural history, including tools and artifacts devised to aid in human problem solving. Children initially use these tools in collaborative interactions with experienced community members. These tools are gradually internalized and in the process transform children's thought.

Like cognitive-developmental theories, the sociocultural approach focuses on the development of intellectual skills. The approaches are also similar in that both believe the child to be an active participant in development and that development involves both quantitative and qualitative change. The approaches differ, however, in their views on how change occurs, what changes with development, and the universality of cognitive processes.

OBJECT EXPLORATION, TOOL USE, AND PLAY

In our earlier discussion of Piaget's theory (Chapter 7), we described how interactions with objects change over the course of infancy. According to the cognitive-developmental approach, developmental differences in the ways infants use objects in play and problem solving reflect fundamental changes in underlying cognitive abilities. Whereas adherents of the cognitive-developmental approach look inside the child to account for changes in infants' interactions with objects, sociocultural researchers focus on cultural practices that shape those encounters. These practices dictate how much contact infants have with objects, which objects young children have access to, and whether they use the objects in work or play, in solitary activity or jointly with others.

In the discussion that follows, we describe the social and cultural contexts of two broad categories of object use: (1) object exploration and nonsymbolic play and (2) symbolic play. Exploration and nonsymbolic play include object manipulation, exploration, and the functional uses of objects (e.g., building structures out of blocks, using a shovel to dig a hole in the ground). Symbolic play includes pretending with and without objects. Our discussion here focuses primarily on the first 4 years of life and emphasizes cognitive aspects of play. Additional discussions of play can be found in Chapters 15 and 16.

Exploratory and Nonsymbolic Play

Access to Objects   The number and types of objects infants and toddlers are allowed to explore vary widely among cultures. Some communities, such as one Mayan village in rural Guatemala, provide infants with few toys and actively restrict exploration of other objects (Gaskins, 1999). Others, such as the !Kung (now Ju'/hoansi), a hunter-gatherer society of Africa, allow infants access to a variety of objects, including twigs, grass, stones, and household implements (Bakeman et al., 1990). In still other cultures, caregivers encourage infants to manipulate tools used by older children and adults in productive work or miniature versions of tools fashioned by adults for small hands (Lancy, 1996). The Aka, a hunter-gatherer group in the tropical rain forests of the Central African Republic, for example, begin to teach their infants how to use sharp objects, such as knives, digging sticks, and axes, before the children reach their first birthday (Hewlett, 1992).

In wealthy, industrialized societies, caregivers provide infants with an abundant supply of specially manufactured toys and structure their joint play episodes around these toys (Whiting & Edwards, 1988). For example, one study of native-born Canadian infants reported the babies to have an average of 27 toys by the time they were 3 months of age. By 9 months, they averaged nearly 60 toys (Pomerleau, Malcuit, & Sabatier, 1991)!

In other cultural communities, object play takes a back seat to social interaction, as illustrated by this depiction of the environment of infants and toddlers in a working-class African American community in the Southern United States:

> During their first year, children are lap sitters, and spend their waking hours in the laps of adults or on the hips of older children; they have no occasions to sit alone and play with baby toys. As children become mobile and move about on their own, they are in demand by older children and adults of the community as toys themselves. They are looked on as entertainers, and all of their waking hours are spent in the company of others. (Heath, 1983, pp. 76–77)

According to the sociocultural approach, these variations in children's early experiences with objects can only be understood within a broad cultural context that includes the physical environment (e.g., whether infants spend their time indoors or outdoors), social environment (e.g., whether the infants are usually in the company of other children or adults or are alone), and customs of child care (e.g., whether infants are free to move about or physically restrained) (Super & Harkness, 1986). It may seem unwise, for example, to put potentially dangerous objects such as knives and axes in the hands of infants—especially to those of us who endured blunt-nosed safety scissors through much of elementary school. But the practice is common in cultures where infants are rarely beyond arm's reach of a caregiver and have many opportunities to observe the tools being used by older children and adults (Rogoff, 2003).

Parental Beliefs   Cultural beliefs about the nature of children and development also shape infants' experiences with objects. The !Kung believe that small children teach themselves by exploring the world and so rarely restrict their interactions with objects (Bakeman et al., 1990). The Maya believe that development is preprogrammed—it just "comes out by itself" as a natural consequence of participation in daily life. Consequently, caregivers make little effort to structure experiences in a way that will improve or hasten children's development (Gaskins, 1999). Middle-income North American parents, in contrast, see stimulation of their infants' intellectual and social development as an important part of the parental role. Robert LeVine and associates have labeled this view the "American pedagogical" model: "The American white middle-income mother sees herself as a teacher, among other things, and the infant as a pupil whose readiness for early education should be in the forefront of maternal attention" (LeVine et al., 1994, p. 250).

North American parents view object play as one means by which to promote infant development (Young, 1991). Or, as one West African mother commented to a Western researcher: "We give them toys to play with. You give them toys to learn something for the future" (Rabain-Jamin, 1994). Observations of parent–infant object play support this portrait of the American parent (Bornstein et al., 1999; Rogoff et al., 1993).

Implications of Object Play for Development
The differing cultural ideas about the role of object play in development lead to an obvious question: Do different cultural practices have different developmental results? Specifically, does toy play during the early years foster cognitive development? Evidence is mixed. Studies have shown a positive relationship between infants' access to toys and their performance on assessments of cognitive development during infancy and early childhood (Bradley et al. 1994; Yarrow, Rubenstein, & Pedersen, 1975). And the amount and quality of infants' object play alone and with caregivers predicts children's current and subsequent performance on various measures of cognitive competence (Belsky, Goode, & Most, 1980; Tamis-LeMonda & Bornstein, 1991; van den Boom, 1994; Yarrow et al., 1983).

Evidence from other studies, however, suggests that early experience exploring objects may not be essential for normal cognitive development. Despite wide cultural differences in access to objects, infants the world over follow the same sequence of sensorimotor development and use the same procedures to manipulate and explore objects (e.g., mouthing, squeezing, dropping).

Delays in object manipulation and exploration have been reported among infants in cultures that restrict access to objects during the first year, but these delays can be hard to interpret. For instance, the lags in development may be due to poor health. Infants whose physical well-being is compromised show diminished interest in objects and receive less encouragement to explore objects from caregivers (LeVine et al., 1994; Wachs, 2000). Reports of developmental delays are also typically based on formal assessments; such measurements may not accurately assess infant competencies because of various factors associated with the unusualness of the testing situation (Power, 2000).

There is also evidence that the link between the availability of toys and performance on measures of cognitive ability varies across cultural groups. Though the provision of toys during infancy is highly predictive of the intellectual capabilities of white North American children, for example, access to toys does not predict the intelligence test performance of Hispanic children (Bradley et al., 1994).

These findings highlight again the importance of examining object play in its broader cultural context. European American parents believe object play is important for their children's cognitive development. They also use objects as a "stage" for interacting with their infants. In this context, toys may provide an accurate measure of the amount and quality of stimulation infants receive from caregivers. But object play is only one means of stimulating infant development. A caregiving environment that is responsive and rich in social stimulation can also promote children's cognitive development.

The Social Context of Object Play
We have seen that the effects of infants' early interactions with objects on the development of general cognitive abilities remain a matter of debate. Nevertheless, these early encounters with objects are important opportunities for infants to learn about cultural tools and artifacts, particularly when those encounters involve other people. As would be predicted by sociocultural theory, infants spend more time exploring objects and engage in more focused and complex exploration when interacting with caregivers than when playing alone (Lockman & McHale, 1989; Tamis-LeMonda & Bornstein, 1991; Hofsten & Siddiqui, 1993). Infants and toddlers are also far more likely to use objects as tools to solve problems (e.g., using a stick to retrieve an out-of-reach toy) by seeing others use them than by discovering how to do so on their own (Chen & Siegler, 2000; Tomasello, Savage-Rumbaugh, & Kruger, 1993). Joint play with caregivers or older children appears to be particularly important for the development of pretend play, a topic we discuss in more detail later.

So far, our discussion of object play has emphasized the opportunities it offers for learning and cognitive growth. Joint object play can also enhance the development of social skills. The extent to which caregivers emphasize the social versus the cognitive benefits of object play varies across cultures. In some cultures, caregivers use object play as an opportunity to promote social interaction and affiliation, rather than to enhance children's cognitive and language development. A cuddly teddy bear, for example, can be used to tickle or tease, not just serve as the focus of instruction (e.g., "Where are the teddy bear's eyes?" "What does a bear say?"). And a parent presented with a toy phone can respond by showing the child how to push the buttons and make it ring or by pretending to call grandma (or, of course, both).

Japanese mothers are more likely to emphasize the social aspects of play, whereas U.S. mothers tend to use object play as a means to teach infants about the world and how to explore it on their own (Tamis-LeMonda et al., 1992). These differences in mother-infant play are consistent with a substantial research literature that contrasts socialization practices in Japan with those in Western nations, particularly the United States.

Some scholars believe that the different socialization practices are rooted in cultural conceptions of the self (Markus & Kitayama, 1991, 1998). Middle-income American culture is described as having an **independent orientation.** Cultures with this orientation emphasize individuality, self-expression, and personal achievement. Cultures with an **interdependent orientation** (such as Japan) focus on the self's role within a broader social network and emphasize interpersonal connectedness, social obligation, and conformity. As we will see throughout this text, these different social orientations are believed to have widespread implications for children's development.

Symbolic Play

Symbolic or pretend play is the "voluntary transformation of the here and now" (Garvey, 1990). Pretend play can take several forms, including actions with real objects or **replica toys** that resemble real objects (e.g., pretending to eat from a real or a toy spoon) and object transformations in which an object is used to represent something else (e.g., using a block as a boat). Pretense can also involve imagined objects or characters, such as feeding a baby with an unseen bottle or hiding from an invisible monster. Pretend play also includes **imaginary companions,** fantasy friends with names and stable personalities that remain a part of children's lives for months or even years.

In **solitary pretense,** children pretend by themselves. Solitary pretense can be quite simple or very complex, as when a preschooler acts out a complicated drama with a collection of dolls and stuffed animals. Most often, however, children's pretense involves other (real) people. The most complex type of joint pretense, **sociodramatic play,** occurs when two or more people enact a variety of related roles (e.g., mother and baby, driver and passenger, pet and owner).

The Frequency of Symbolic Play
Symbolic play can be found in every society, but there are wide cultural variations in when, where, and how often it occurs (Power, 2000; Roopnarine et al., 1998; Schwartzman, 1978). The capacity for pretense coincides with the growth of other cognitive skills (e.g., language, memory, imitative abilities) that together make it possible for children to begin to participate in a variety of cultural activities besides play.

The extent to which children engage in pretend play depends, in part, on the significance caregivers place on play relative to these other, competing activities. In many societies, such as the Mayan community described earlier (Gaskins, 1999), caregivers depend on small children to perform important chores, such as tending livestock or the garden and running errands. In these cultures, children's work responsibilities allow them little time for pretend play.

In other cultures, caregivers dismiss pretend play as mere amusement and do little to encourage it. For example, Jo Ann Farver and her associates found that Korean American children whose parents had recently emigrated to Los Angeles engaged in pretend play less often than European American children both at home and at school (Farver, 1999). They traced the differences to adult beliefs about the value of play. Whereas the European American parents and teachers valued the

Independent orientation
A focus on the self's individuality, self-expression, and personal achievement.

Interdependent orientation
A focus on the self's role within a broader social network, marked by an emphasis on interpersonal connectedness, social obligation, and conformity.

Replica toys
Toys that resemble real objects, such as dishes, dolls, and vehicles.

Imaginary companions
Fantasy friends with names and stable personalities that remain a part of children's lives for months or even years.

Solitary pretense
Pretend play engaged in by a child playing alone.

Sociodramatic play
Play in which two or more people enact a variety of related roles.

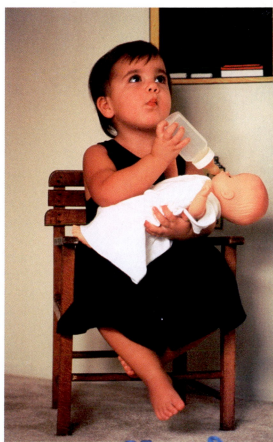

Replica toys can be a source of support for pretend play.

educational and cognitive benefits of play, the Korean American adults viewed memorization, hard work, and task persistence as a means to academic success. These beliefs were reflected in the ways adults structured children's activities. Korean American teachers provided few toys or materials likely to encourage social pretense and limited play opportunities to periods of outdoor activity. Children spent much of their indoor time seated at tables working quietly and independently on academic tasks. At the end of the day, children were given homework assignments to complete in the evening with their parents' help. European American teachers, in contrast, believed that play was "children's work" and provided children many opportunities for play and social interaction.

Interestingly, the differences between the play of the Korean American and European American children were most pronounced in unstructured, free-play settings. When children were provided a set of attractive toys to play with (a castle with its accessories), the differences disappeared.

The Social Context of Symbolic Play

Until recently, most theory and research on children's pretense was based on Piaget's theory and, consequently, focused on solitary play. Observational studies in everyday settings, however, reveal that most pretend play takes place in a social context with other people acting as either spectators or partners. Who those other people are varies across cultures. In many cultures, parents are not viewed as appropriate play partners. Guatemalan mothers laugh with embarrassment at the idea of playing with their children, as this is the role of other children or perhaps grandparents (Göncü, Mistry, & Mosier, 2000; Rogoff et al., 1993). Italian mothers also view play as the province of children or extended family members (New, 1994). Mexican mothers attach no particular value to play and rarely engage in pretense with their children (Farver & Howes, 1993).

In cultures where adults believe pretend play facilitates development, caregivers tend to view their own participation in play as both appropriate and desirable and participate actively in children's pretending (Haight, Parke, & Black, 1997). Parent–child pretend play is common among middle-income Turkish families, in Argentina, in China, and, of course, in European American communities (Bornstein et al., 1999; Göncü et al., 2000; Haight et al., 1999).

Observations in European American homes suggest that children's earliest play partner is most often the mother (Bornstein et al., 1996; Haight & Miller, 1993; Tudge, Lee, & Putnam, 1995). As with nonsymbolic play, symbolic play is more advanced when adult partners are involved. Toddlers' play episodes last longer when they are playing with an adult partner than when they are playing alone and include a greater diversity of themes and more complex sequences (Fiese, 1990; O'Connell & Bretherton; 1984; O'Reilly & Bornstein, 1993; Slade, 1987).

One study of a common type of pretense, "mother–baby" play, illustrates the various ways in which mothers scaffold toddlers' pretense (Miller & Garvey, 1984). Mothers in this study offered a good deal of explicit instruction and direction as to how the toddlers should behave (e.g, "Pat the baby") and what they should say (e.g., "Go 'aw' ") when playing the role of "mother." The real mothers also asked questions (e.g., "What's the baby doing?") that helped extend the play. As the toddlers grew older, mothers encouraged more complex pretense. For example, a mother might direct a 2-year-old to simply feed the baby but would tell an older child to heat the milk before feeding and to burp the baby periodically (and why).

The mothers also helped the toddlers incorporate objects into pretense (e.g., "Here. Use this as a baby bottle"). Indeed, nearly all symbolic play between mothers and their 1- and 2-year-old children revolves around objects, most often replica toys such as dolls, dishes, and vehicles (Dunn & Dale, 1984; Haight and Miller, 1993).

The central role of objects in early symbolic play between mothers and their young children is interesting because children under the age of 3 rarely spontaneously engage in symbolic object play, at least when observed under experimental conditions (e.g., Fenson & Ramsay 1981; Slade, 1987; Watson & Fischer, 1987). These

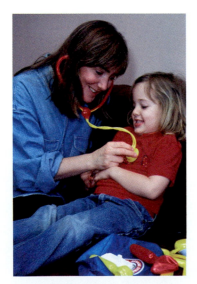

In some cultures, parents are frequent participants in their children's early pretend play.

findings suggest that children learn to use objects symbolically when playing with others and only later use objects symbolically on their own (Striano, Tomasello, & Rochat, 2001).

As noted earlier, in many cultures, children's most frequent playmates are siblings and peers, not adult caregivers. Researchers have documented important differences between sibling and mother–child play (Farver & Wimbarti, 1995; Youngblade & Dunn; 1995). First, objects play a less central role in the pretend play of siblings than in parent–toddler play. Second, the play themes differ. Mother–toddler play tends to involve domestic routines. Sibling play includes more diverse themes and is more likely to incorporate themes involving danger. Third, siblings and mothers tend to adopt different roles in play. Mothers are most often spectators, offering comments and suggestions "from the outside." Siblings, in contrast, are more active participants in the pretense, performing pretend actions and adopting complementary roles, such as the baby, father, train driver, or pilot. Fourth, parent–toddler play is often more subdued than sibling play.

Perhaps because siblings are generally more willing to entertain fantasy than mothers, pretend play with siblings is often more advanced than mother–child play. In addition, siblings are sometimes more skilled at scaffolding play than mothers. This may be particularly true in situations where older children are the primary caretakers of younger siblings, siblings have a cooperative and caring relationship, and mothers are not children's regular play partners (Farver, 1993; Farver & Wimbarti, 1995).

Themes in Pretense   Worldwide, the most common themes enacted in toddlers' pretense are those centered around domestic life (e.g., cooking, eating, child care), adult work activities (e.g., hunting, planting, fishing), and adult rituals (e.g., marriage, dancing) (Power, 2000). The details of these themes, however, are culturally specific. In India, for example, children enact traditional celebrations and folk tales (Roopnarine et al., 1994), whereas children in the Marquesas Islands pretend to paddle canoes and to hunt and fish (Martini, 1994). Korean American children focus on family themes, whereas American children enact fantastic and dangerous play themes (Farver, 1999). As the play episode shown in Table 9.1 suggests, this may be because American children's opportunities to observe their parents and other adult models engaged in everyday activities are limited relative to children's access to TV and movies.

Implications of Symbolic Play for Development

Many developmental psychologists believe that symbolic play makes important contributions to children's cognitive and social development. Vygotksy (1978), for example, argued that play functions as a zone of proximal development in which children can think and behave in ways more advanced than is possible outside of the context of play. "In play, a child is always above his average age, above his daily behavior; in play it is as though he were a head taller than himself" (p. 102).

There is some evidence to support Vygotsky's claim. Children can show higher levels of performance when cognitive tasks are embedded in a play context. For example, in one study, 4- and 5-year-old children were either shown a set of toys and asked to remember them or permitted to play with the toys (Newman, 1990). During the "remember" condition, the children used rehearsal to help them remember the items, repeatedly touching and naming each item. During the "play" condition, children spontaneously organized many of the items. Much of this organization arose from pretense—for example, putting the toy shoes on the toy doll and pretending to feed her the toy banana. Not surprisingly, the use of the more advanced organizational strategy produced better recall than the less mature rehearsal strategy.

In other research, experimenters presented 4- to 6-year-old children a series of logical problems in which they had to reason from two premises to reach a conclusion (Dias

Table 9.1	A Play Episode

Andrew:	This gonna be a spaceship. Y'wanna play?
Jeremy:	(drags the oven to the middle of the floor) This is the computer terminal.
Paul:	Put it over here.
Andrew:	(speaking into a silver slipper) Pilot to crew. Pilot to crew, ready for landing. Snow Planet down below.
	Watch out! It exploded!
	Darth Vader is coming!
	Millennium Falcon, where are you?
	E-e-k! V-e-e-p! Erk! Erk!!
	Get the light sabers!
	(Andrew runs to the woodbench. He grabs two long sticks and slams them on the painting table.) Quick! Emergency! Where's the red paint? (Mary Ann looks doubtful but hands him her paintbrush.)
Andrew:	Thanks, miss, I won't forget this. (He paints a red tip on each stick and rushes back to the doll corner.) Am I too late?
Paul:	Just in time. Darth Vader found us, but we got away. Wait, he might be invisible (kicking a pile of clothes).
Franklin:	(turning an unseen steering wheel, making a siren sound, and staring through squinty eyes) M-m-m . . . M-m-m . . . Darth Vader, he escapin'! Follow me men. Ah knows his plan. M-m-m . . . K-k-k . . . P-p-ah-ah. Ah blowed his ship to pieces! He back on Death Star.
Ned:	(gazing with admiration at Franklin, repeats quietly) He back on Death Star.

SOURCE: Adapted from *Boys and Girls: Superheroes in the Doll Corner* by V. G. Paley, 1984, Chicago: University of Chicago Press, pp. 8–9. Copyright © 1984 by the University of Chicago Press. Reprinted by permission.

& Harris, 1988, 1990). Sometimes, such as in the following problem, one of the premises ran counter to reality:

> All milk is black.
>
> Jane is drinking milk.
>
> Is her milk white?

The experimenter read the problems to half of the children in a matter-of-fact tone of voice. For the other children, the experimenter introduced the problem by saying, "Let's pretend that I am from another planet" and read the problem using the kind of intonation ordinarily used when telling a story. Children in the first condition had great difficulty reasoning according to the premises of the problem. They said, for example, that Jane's milk was white and justified their answer by asserting their knowledge about milk. Children in the "let's pretend" condition were much more successful. Further, the kinds of justifications they offered showed that they had entered into the hypothetical nature of the task (e.g., "because I'm pretending that milk is black").

These studies show that children can perform at more advanced levels during pretend play than in other contexts. But many psychologists, teachers, and parents believe that the benefits of pretense are much more far-reaching than this. Over the years, researchers have linked pretend play to the development of a number of intellectual abilities, including perception, attention, memory, problem solving, logical reasoning, language, literacy, and creative thinking (Berk, 2001; Frost, Worthman, & Reifel, 2001).

Given the importance psychologists and educators have ascribed to pretend play, the evidence that pretense makes unique contributions to children' cognitive development is weaker than we might expect. Most research on the benefits of symbolic play is correlational. So, for example, it is difficult to know whether, say, pretend play promotes the development of representational skills helpful to children as they learn to read or whether children with more advanced representational skills, including language, are more inclined to participate in pretense (Power, 2000).

According to sociocultural theory, children develop skills in the context of particular activities. From this perspective, we would not anticipate that participation in pretend play would have general effects on children's cognitive development; rather, it would have specific effects. Just as nonsymbolic object play may yield few benefits for general cognitive growth but nonetheless teach children a great deal about objects, symbolic play may do little to promote intellectual growth broadly defined yet teach children a great deal about pretense and related processes.

What kinds of cognitive skills would most likely be implicated in pretend play? One possible candidate is children's "theory of mind" (Chapter 7). Joint pretense offers children many opportunities to learn about the minds of others. Children may learn about other minds when setting the stage for the pretense, negotiating with other children about who will play whom, discussing what the props will stand for, and deciding what events will take place (Lillard, 2001).

Evidence for a link between social pretend play and children's theory of mind is suggestive. For example, children with siblings (playmates) are twice as likely to demonstrate knowledge of false beliefs as peers without siblings (Perner, Ruffman, & Leekam, 1994). Youngblade and Dunn (1995) found that toddlers who engaged in more social pretense with siblings at 30 months of age performed better on false-belief tasks administered 6 months later than children who engaged in joint pretense less often. And recently, Schwebel and associates (Schwebel, Rosen, & Singer, 1999) found that children who engaged in joint pretense more frequently performed better on appearance-reality tasks, even when verbal intelligence was controlled, whereas involvement in solitary pretense was not predictive of children's performance on theory of mind tasks. As with the bulk of research on children's play, these studies are correlational, and the results must be interpreted with caution. Nonetheless, the findings support the sociocultural perspective that children co-construct an understanding of the mind through joint activity with others (Göncü, 1993).

To Recap . . .

Although play is universal to children all over the world, cultures vary widely in the amount of time children devote to play, who participates in play, and the nature of children's play. These variations are shaped by the physical and social settings in which children spend their time, customs of child rearing, and parental beliefs about children, development, and the value of play.

Children learn to play and explore objects by interacting with more experienced partners. Infants and toddlers spend more time exploring objects and manipulate them in more complex ways when interacting with caregivers than when playing alone. Children's pretense is also more sustained, elaborate, and sophisticated when a caregiver is party to the play.

Siblings are also frequent play partners, especially as children grow older. Sibling play differs from adult–child play in the importance of objects, the themes enacted, and the roles adopted by participants. The themes enacted in children's play reflect the world they live in and include both universal and culturally specific aspects.

Many studies find links between play and children's current and subsequent cognitive competence. Because most of the research is correlational, it does not support firm cause–effect conclusions. Children's participation in cultural activities that involve objects either as problem-solving tools or toys does promote specific knowledge about how to use objects in work and in play, however.

MEMORY

In Chapter 8, we described several ways in which children's memory changes with age. Information-processing theorists conceptualize these improvements as the accomplishments of individuals and localize the causes of changes within the child. In contrast, sociocultural theorists view memory as a fundamentally social and cultural phenomenon. According to this perspective, both *what* children remember and *how* they remember are rooted in cultural practices (Nelson & Fivush, 2000).

Researchers working within the framework of the sociocultural approach are most interested in what Vygotsky (1978) termed **mediated memory.** Mediated memory involves remembering that relies on cultural tools and artifacts that support memory development and use. Mediational tools relevant to memory include verbal rehearsal, categorization schemes, list making, diagrams, chants, scripts, and narratives (stories). Children grow competent at using these tools by participating in cultural activities with more experienced members of the community. In the section that follows, we discuss the development of one such mediational tool—memory strategies.

Mediated memory
Remembering that relies on cultural tools and artifacts.

Strategies

As noted in Chapter 8, older children are more likely than younger children to use strategies such as rehearsal, organization, and elaboration. Why these particular strategies, and why does their use increase with age? To answer these questions, sociocultural researchers look to the kinds of activities common to children that might induce the use of memory strategies. One nearly universal activity, in Western cultures at least, is formal schooling.

One of the most common activities in school is committing information to memory—often information that (at least from the student's perspective) may seem disconnected and arbitrary. Perhaps this experience instills skills that serve schooled children well when they respond to typical laboratory measures of memory, which often involve somewhat arbitrary and context-free material.

To test whether experience in Western-style schools promotes the development of mnemonic strategies, researchers traveled to developing societies where levels of education vary widely. The researchers consistently found that children and adults with little or no schooling were far less likely than their schooled peers to spontaneously generate mnemonic strategies on list learning and other standard memory tasks. As a consequence, they were less successful in their recall efforts (Cole & Scribner, 1977; Mistry, 1997).

Although these findings are suggestive, factors other than schooling may have been responsible for the differences in performance. Individuals who attend school and those who do not are likely to differ in a number of ways. Those who attend school, for example, may come from wealthier, more modernized families (Rogoff, 1981) or may differ in general intelligence.

A more conclusive test of schooling and memory development would be to study participants equivalent on all measures except years of schooling. How can this be accomplished, especially in cultures where nearly every child receives some form of schooling? One way is to use a clever technique known as the **school cut-off design** (Morrison, Smith, & Dow-Ehrensberger, 1995).

In nearly all public school systems, children need to reach a certain age (e.g., 5 years) by a certain date (e.g., October 1) before they are permitted entry into school. A child whose birthday falls before the cut-off date, say on September 15, would enter kindergarten, whereas his neighbor with a birthday on October 15 would wait 1 year before beginning school. The cut-off design involves comparing children whose birthdays fall just slightly before and just slightly after the cut-off date for admittance to school. These children are within 1 month of each other in average age but differ in amount of schooling by 1 full year.

School cut-off design
Research technique that compares children who are close in age but differ in school experience by one year.

Morrison and colleagues presented the two groups of children a series of recall tasks in which they were shown a set of nine pictures, one at a time, for about 5 seconds. The tester named each object depicted as she showed it. After all the pictures were shown, the children were asked to recall as many as they could.

The children were tested three times. They were first tested at the beginning of the school year. This was the beginning of first grade for the children who had made the cut-off date a year earlier and the beginning of kindergarten for those who had not. Next, they were tested at the end of the school year. Finally, they were tested 1 year later, following grade one for those who had entered kindergarten and second grade for those who had begun the study in first grade.

As can be seen in Figure 9.2, there were no group differences in performance at the beginning of the school year. When tested at the end of the school year, those who had completed first grade recalled more pictures than those who had spent the year in kindergarten. The kindergartners showed no improvement over the year. One year later, the recall performance of the children who had just completed first grade had improved significantly, whereas the performance of those who completed second grade remained unchanged.

These findings suggest that something about the first-grade curriculum promotes the development of memory strategies, such as verbal rehearsal. The findings do not, however, reveal whether children discovered memory strategies on their own while working on first-grade assignments or whether other people taught them to use the strategies, as would be predicted by sociocultural theories.

Other research offers support for the idea that parents and teachers explicitly teach children memory strategies. For instance, in one study, mothers and their 6- to 8-year-old children worked together on two versions of a memory task (Rogoff, Ellis, & Gardner, 1984; Rogoff & Gauvain, 1986). Each task involved sorting 18 items into categories. One version involved putting grocery items away on shelves in a mock kitchen. The other involved sorting photographs of common household objects into specified compartments in a box. The experimenters provided the mothers a cue sheet that indicated the proper location of each group of items, but the mothers were not given any rationale for the groupings. After all the items were placed, the children were asked to sort and replace another set of groceries or photographs that included some of the original items and some new ones.

Most mothers in this study provided a great deal of mnemonic instruction. They generated labels for the categories (e.g., "snack foods," "cleaning things"), elaborated on the relationship between different items within each category, and encouraged active rehearsal (e.g., "Now what goes in the blue box? . . . *Good,* now say that again so you can remember it." (Rogoff et al., 1984, p. 198). Instruction on mnemonic techniques helped the children when they later performed the task on their own. Those whose mothers provided the most mnemonic guidance placed the greatest number of items in their correct locations, whereas those whose mothers provided less help did not spontaneously generate the category structures on their own (see also Göncü & Rogoff, 1998).

Further evidence that the use of memory strategies is socialized comes from cross-cultural comparisons of American and German students. German elementary school students tend to use more organizational strategies at a younger age than American children (Schneider et al., 1986). German parents and teachers are more likely than their American counterparts to report actively encouraging strategy development (Carr et al., 1989; Kurtz et al., 1990).

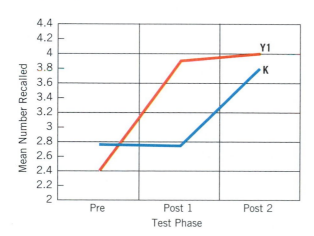

Figure 9.2

Mean number of Pictures recalled by the kindergarten (K) and young grade-one (Y1) groups across the three testing intervals. Adapted from "Education and Cognitive Development: A Natural Experiment," *Developmental Psychology, 31,* p. 794, by F. J. Morrison, L. Smith, & M. Dow-Ehrensberger, 1995, Washington, DC: American Psychological Association. Copyright © by American Psychological Association. Reprinted by permission.

Interestingly, memory techniques that serve us well on academic tasks may do little to promote recall on other kinds of memory problems. In one study, for example, 9-year-old Guatemalan Mayan children were asked to reproduce the placement of 20 familiar objects that they had viewed within a scale model of a Guatemalan terrain (see Figure 9.3). Memory for spatial locations is a natural development in any culture, and the children showed impressive levels of recall; indeed, their performance was slightly better than that of a sample of American 9-year-olds who responded to a similar task using stimuli drawn from their culture (Rogoff & Waddell, 1982).

Many of the American children were apparently hampered by an attempt to rehearse the information prior to the recall test. Although rehearsal is often a helpful strategy, it is not an optimal approach to problems of spatial memory. The Guatemalan children did not bring this bias to the task—and hence may have been quicker to hit on a more appropriate strategy.

Event memory

Recall of things that have happened.

Event Memory

As we have seen, much of the research on children's memory has focused on developmental changes in the ability to remember facts (e.g., phone numbers, word lists, details of stories). In everyday life, however, much of what people remember involves things that happen, or events. From the first days of life, our experience of events is socially constructed. The first events infants experience involve other people. Furthermore, these events are entirely produced and directed by adults. As Katherine Nelson observes, "children are first of all participants in other people's activities and secondarily actors on their own" (Nelson, 1996, p. 96).

During the first months of life, many of the events that infants experience recur over and over again. These include caregiving routines (e.g., feeding, bathing, dressing) and, in some cultures, ritual games such as peek-a-boo. Initially, these routines are entirely under the control of the caregiver. Gradually, however, the infant plays a larger and larger participatory role under the guidance of others who provide signs and cues as to what the infant should expect next. By the end of the first year, infants behave in ways that indicate they have internalized these social routines (Nelson, 1996).

Figure 9.3

Mayan child and tester in the Rogoff and Waddell study of spatial memory. The child's task was to place the objects in their original positions in the panorama. From *Apprenticeship in Thinking* by B. Rogoff, 1990, New York: Oxford University Press, p. 49. Copyright © 1990 by Oxford University Press. Reprinted by permission.

Mental representations of routine events such as bath time, trips to the grocery store, going to bed at night, and birthday parties are called scripts. We can define a **script** as a representation of the typical sequence of actions and events in some familiar context. Each of us, for example, possesses a restaurant script, which represents the typical sequence of events in dining at a restaurant: entering the restaurant, sitting down, ordering the meal, eating, paying, and leaving. Our restaurant script, like scripts in general, is not tied to any specific example. Rather, it is a general representation that can apply to any number of restaurants.

Scripts are valuable because they help us predict what will happen during routine events. This knowledge allows children to actively participate in events and offers stability to children's daily lives (Flavell, Miller, & Miller, 2002). Young children are especially sensitive to the order in which events occur. As many caregivers can attest, young children often grow upset when daily routines are disrupted, such as when they arrive later than usual to daycare or a new babysitter leaves out an element in the nightly bedtime ritual. Children also find it easiest to learn new scripts when the events in the script follow a natural logical or causal sequence (Bauer, 1992; Fivush, Kuebli, & Clubb, 1992).

Although young children's script reports are similar in many ways to those of older children and adults, there are also developmental differences. Table 9.2 presents some examples of children's birthday-party scripts, elicited in response to the question, "What happens when you have a birthday party?" The numbers in parentheses indicate the age of the child. As you can see, scripts increase in both completeness and complexity as children develop.

Much of the interest in children's scripts concerns their effects on memory. Scripts are both product and process of the constructive nature of the memory system described in Chapter 8. They are product in the sense that they reflect the child's abstraction, from numerous specific experiences, of the essential general features of some familiar event. Once formed, however, scripts influence how future experiences are processed and remembered (Davidson, 1996). As with constructive memory in general, the effects of scripts on memory are mixed. For the most part, scripts—like knowledge in general—aid the memory process. A script can, however, lead to memory distortions, as when some unexpected event is reworked to fit an established script. Furthermore, by focusing on what usually happens, children may lose information about specific episodes of a

Script
A representation of the typical sequence of actions and events in some familiar context.

Table 9.2	**Examples of Children's Birthday Party Scripts**

You cook a cake and eat it. (3 yr, 1 mo)

Well, you get a cake and some ice cream and then some birthday (?) and then you get some clowns and then you get some paper hats, the animal hats and then and then you sing, "Happy Birthday to you," and then they give you some presents and then you play with them and then that's the end and they they go home and they do what they wanta. (4 yr, 9 mo)

First, uhm . . . you're getting ready for the kids to come, like puttin' balloons up and and putting out party plates and making cake. And then all the people come you've asked. Give you presents and then you have lunch or whatever you have. Then . . . uhm . . . then you open your presents. Or you can open your presents anytime. Uhm . . . you could . . . after you open the presents, then it's probably time to go home. If you're like at Foote Park or something, then it's time to go home and you have to drive all the people home. Then you go home too. (6 yr, 7 mo)

Well, first you open your mail box, and you get some mail. And then you see that there's an invitation for you. Read the invitation. Then you ask your parents if you can go. Then you . . . uhm . . . go to the birthday party and you get a ride there, and after you get there you usually wait for everyone else to come. Then usually they always want to open one of the presents. Sometimes then they have three games, then they have the birthday cake, then sometimes they open up the other presents or they could open them up all at once. After that they like to play some more games and then maybe your parents come to pick you up. And then you go home. (8 yr, 10 mo)

SOURCE: From "Generalized Event Representations: Basic Building Blocks of Cognitive Development" by K. Nelson and J. Gruendel, 1981. In M. E. Lamb and A. L. Brown (Eds.), *Advances in Developmental Psychology, Vol. 1,* Hillsdale, NJ: Erlbaum, p. 135. Copyright © 1981 by Lawrence Erlbaum Associates. Reprinted by permission.

Scripts are representations of the typical structure of familiar events. Even preschoolers may have learned a simple making-cookies script.

routine event such as a day at school, dinner at home, or an afternoon at the park (Farrar & Goodman, 1992). Young children are better able to answer the general question "what happens?" (e.g., at school, during dinner) than the specific question "what happened yesterday?" (Hudson & Nelson, 1986). Children can recall details about specific episodes, however, if prompted with cues that help differentiate the event from all previous instances (Hudson & Fivush, 1984; Nelson, 1986; Pillemer, Picariello, & Pruett, 1994).

That prompts and cues help children recall past events highlights another way in which event knowledge is social. Children often discuss events they have experienced with other people. Talking about one's day is a frequent topic of dinner table conversation in working- and middle-income families (Bluma-Kulka & Snow, 1992). These conversations about past events, especially with a capable partner who can skillfully guide the discussion, promote more complete and accurate recall. In one study, for example, researchers interviewed 4- and 5-year-old children 3 weeks after the children had experienced a surprise event—the classroom visit of their former teacher and her new baby. Children who had talked about the event in greater detail with their mothers the day of the visit later provided a more complete and accurate account of the event to the researcher than children whose conversations with their mothers were more spare (Leichtman et al., 2000).

Talking about events *while* they are occurring can also promote better memory for the events. For example, Tessler and Nelson (1994) compared what mothers and their preschoolers talked about during a trip to a museum with what the children remembered about the event when interviewed 1 week later. The children recalled none of the exhibits they had seen but had not talked about with their mothers, nor did they remember what the mothers talked about on their own. The children only recalled exhibits that mothers and children talked about together.

Memory talk serves several additional functions. Talking about past events, both shared and unshared, can promote social solidarity and emotional closeness. In the process of talking about events, caregivers and others convey to children cultural values about what is worth remembering. Children also learn the form for how to talk about memories through participating in discussions of past events with adults. A number of scholars now believe that the ability to construct a coherent and organized report of past events underlies another very important achievement—the development of autobiographical memory (Fivush, 2001; Hudson, 1990; Nelson, 1993a; Welch-Ross, 1995).

Autobiographical Memory

Autobiographical memory
Specific, personal, and long-lasting memory regarding the self.

The term **autobiographical memory** refers to memories that are specific, personal, and long-lasting—memories that are part of one's life history, that have to do with the self. A child who can recount a typical day at school is demonstrating script memory. A child who can remember the time he broke his arm on the playground, won the geography bee, or helped his mother delivery a baby is demonstrating autobiographical memory.

Researchers have identified two broad styles that parents use to elicit talk about specific memories with young children. We should note that these styles, shown in Table 9.3, are really points along a continuum. As the examples suggest, parents in the *elaborative* category provide a richer narrative structure than do parents in the *repetitive* category. Not only do they furnish more information in their own speech, but they also make more extended and supportive efforts to elicit information from their children. They also talk more often about the past than do repetitive parents. The child of an elaborative parent is therefore given more chance to be an active participant in conversations about the past, as well as more chance to be successful in recall efforts. Such a child is also provided with more general and more frequent models of how to remember and talk about past experience.

As we might expect, then, children of elaborative parents are generally more successful at recalling past events than are children of repetitive parents, not only in conversations with their own parents but also when tested by an independent adult (Fivush, 1991; Nelson, 1993b). Children of elaborative parents are also more likely to approximate an adult-like narrative style, marked by clear temporal and causal relations and

Table 9.3	Examples of Elaborative and Repetitive Styles in Conversations between Parent (P) and Child (C)

Elaborative

P: Did we see any big fishes? What kind of fishes?

C: Big, big, big.

P: And what's their names?

C: I don't know.

P: You remember the names of the fishes. What we called them. Michael's favorite kind of fish. Big mean ugly fish.

C: Yeah.

P: What kind is it?

C: Um, ba.,

P: A ssshark?

C: Yeah.

P: Remember the sharks?

C: Yeah.

P: Do you? What else did we see in the big tank at the aquarium?

C: I don't know.

P: Remember when we first came in, remember when we first came in the aquarium? And we looked down and there were a whole bunch of birdies in the water? Remember the names of the birdies?

C: Ducks!

P: Nooo! They weren't ducks. They had on little suits. Penguins. Remember, what did the penguins do?

C: I don't know.

P: You don't remember?

C: No.

P: Remember them jumping off the rocks and swimming in the water?

C: Yeah.

P: Real fast. You were watching them jump in the water, hm.

C: Yeah.

Repetitive

P: How did we get to Florida, do you remember?

C: Yes.

P: How did we get there? What did we do? You remember?

C: Yeah.

P: You want to sit up here in my lap?

C: No.

P: Oh, okay. Remember when we went to Florida, how did we get there? We went in the—?

C: The ocean.

P: Well, be, when we got to Florida we went to the ocean, that's right, but how did we get down to Florida? Did we drive our car?

C: Yes.

P: No, think again, I don't think we drove to Florida. How did we get down there, remember, we took a great big—? Do you remember?

SOURCE: From "Parental Styles of Talking about the Past" by E. Reese and R. Fivush, 1993, *Developmental Psychology, 29*, p. 606. Copyright © 1993 by the American Psychological Association. Reprinted by permission.

helpful orienting and contextual information (e.g., "Remember when we . . . ?"). In general, children who engage in such conversations with their parents seem to be learning not only what to remember but *how* to remember—that is, how to organize and communicate their memories of the past.

How parents talk with children about the past clearly influences both how much children recall and how they report their memories. Is it possible that the way parents reminisce with their children also affects other aspects of autobiographical memory, such as what children remember or even the age of first memory? (See Figure 9.4.)

To address these questions, researchers have compared parent-child memory talk across cultures. As with the cross-cultural studies of play discussed earlier in this chapter, researchers have been particularly interested in the contrast between cultures characterized as independently versus interdependently oriented (Markus & Kitayama, 1991, 1998). Recall that independently oriented cultures (such as the United States) place more emphasis on the individual self, whereas interdependently oriented cultures emphasize the self's role within a broader social network. Therefore, we would expect parents in the United States to use conversations about the past to reinforce children's individuality and personal uniqueness, whereas parents in Asian cultures would use the opportunity to promote social values such as obligations to others and moral behavior.

Studies undertaken by a number of different researchers, using a variety of methods and working in different East Asian communities, provide support for this distinction. For example, Peggy Miller and her associates (Miller, Fung, & Mintz, 1996; P. J. Miller et al., 1997) used participant observation to study spontaneous memory talk among middle-income mothers and young children in Chicago and Taipei, Taiwan. Although there were many important similarities between the two groups, the Chinese families were more likely to tell stories about the child's past transgressions and use these stories to impart moral and behavioral standards, such as obedience to authority and responsibility toward others.

In another study, researchers solicited memory talk from European American mother–child pairs in Boston and Chinese dyads in Beijing (Wang, Leichtman, & Davies, 2000). Table 9.4 includes excerpts from two of the mother–child pairs. As you can see, American mothers were more likely to adopt the elaborative style described earlier and to make frequent references to children's personal preferences, judgments, and opinions, whereas Chinese mothers used the repetitive style of memory talk and referred more frequently to moral rules and behavioral standards. A study of Korean families reported similar results (Mullen & Yi, 1995).

Evidence linking these cultural differences in memory talk to autobiographical memory is indirect but suggestive. For example, American children include more

Figure 9.4

Parent–child conversations lay the foundation for autobiographical memory. (©Baby Blues Partnership. Reprinted with Special Permission of King Features Syndicate.)

Table 9.4	Examples of Reminiscing among American and Chinese Mothers and Children

American Dyad

M: What did we do when you went camping?

C: At the beach.

M: Uh-huh.

C: And a big rock of I couldn't get up and so Dad had to carry me.

M: Daddy carried you up that big rock.

C: Yeah, um and Daddy was fine.

M: Oh yeah, he was just fine. And what about um was it a beautifully sunny day we had our picnic?

C: Yeah, um, and it started to rain.

M: And then what happened?

C: The sun came up again.

M: But we had to go back through the woods, right?

C: Yeah.

M: Where did we sleep when we went camping?

C: In the tent!

M: In a tent. And what did we climb inside?

C: Sleeping bags.

M: And you have your very own, don't you? Yeah. Is there anything else about camping that you really liked?

C: Swimming.

M: Swimming. And how about the camp fire. Did you like the fire? What did we cook over the fire? Marshmallows, right?

C: Marshmallows! Yummy!

Chinese Dyad

M: Do you remember that Mom took you to the Fandole park last time?

C: I remember.

M: Tell Mom what were there in the Fandole?

C: There were toys.

M: What else?

C: There was food.

M: Right. When we went to Fandole park, did you ask Mom to carry you on the way?

C: I didn't. If I got tired, I would still keep on going ahead bravely.

M: Oh, right. When we rode on the bus, what did you see? We saw big wide roads. What else?

C: We also saw a big round circle.

M: Right. What else did we see on the way there?

C: Um.

M: Tell Mom, when a Mom takes her child to cross the street, where should they look?

C: Look to their left and right. Look at the zebra lines.

M: Right. We must walk on the zebra lines. Did you behave well that day?

C: Yes.

SOURCE: From "Sharing Memories and Telling Stories: American and Chinese Mothers and Their 3-Year-Olds" by Q. Wang, M. D. Leichtman, & K. I. Davies, 2000, *Memory, 8,* pp. 169–170. Copyright © 2000 by Psychology Press Ltd. Reprinted by permission.

references to preferences, thoughts, emotions, and evaluations and fewer references to other people in their recollections of past events than do Korean and Chinese children. Asian children also tend to give more "bare-bones" accounts than their American counterparts, who generally offer rich, elaborate narratives (Han, Leichtman, & Wang, 1998). Interestingly, Asian adults also report later childhood memories than do Caucasian adults (Mullen, 1994; Wang, 2001). These findings lend support to the idea that the ability to construct a coherent, organized account of personally significant events underlies the development of autobiographical memory.

To Recap . . .

Research on memory from the sociocultural perspective focuses primarily on mediated memory—that is, remembering that involves cultural tools and artifacts designed to aid memory, such as mnemonic techniques, scripts, and narratives.

Evidence suggests that children learn to use these mediational tools while participating in cultural activities with more experienced partners. The use of memory strategies is associated with experience in school. Parents and teachers explicitly teach children techniques to help them recall word lists, facts, and the other kinds of decontextualized information that is often the focus of school instruction.

Besides learning to remember facts, children learn to remember events. Memory for events is mediated by mental representations known as scripts. Children's scripts evolve from their participation in routine, everyday events. Scripts generally aid memory but can sometimes impair recall, as when an unusual event is distorted to fit an existing script or the details of a recurring event merge with other instances of the same event.

Talking with other people about events enhances recall and determines, in part, which details of the event will be incorporated into long-term memory. Conversations about past events also promote the development of autobiographical memory—that is, memory about the self. Children who talk frequently and in an elaborative style with their parents tend to report earlier first memories and to recall greater amounts of information.

SELF-REGULATION

As we have seen, much of children's memory is socialized. Another capability that has its roots in social interaction is self-regulation. In this section, we discuss two kinds of self-regulation that are particularly valuable in children's problem solving—planning and private speech.

Planning

According to the sociocultural approach, children learn to plan by participating in activities with other people who model planning behavior and support children's own planning efforts. There is significant evidence that interactions with parents contribute to the development of children's planning skills. From the first year onward, parents regularly talk to their children about future events. Even though parents recognize that very young children are unlikely to understand much about what they are saying (time concepts like yesterday and tomorrow are difficult for young children), parents believe that talking about the future is instructive. Though much of this "future talk" focuses on the events of that day or the next, parents sometimes talk about activities weeks or months away. It is noteworthy that parents devote far more time to talking about future events than events that happened in the past (Benson, 1984; Benson, Talmi, & Haith, in press; Lucariello & Nelson, 1987).

Children also learn about planning by participating in recurring events, such as bath time and birthday parties. Preschoolers construct more complete plans when they have a script for the event (Hudson & Fivush, 1991). Indeed, when asked "What kinds of things are planned?" 5-year-olds most often report daily routines such as going to bed and getting dressed in the morning. Nine- and 11-year-olds, in contrast, most often report planning chores, interpersonal relationships, and achievement-related activities (Kreitler & Kreitler, 1987).

Planning how to solve a problem and monitoring and modifying plans as circumstances and goals change can themselves be difficult problems (Deloache, Miller, & Pierroutsakos, 1998). Not surprisingly, children formulate much better plans when collaborating with an adult than when planning alone. For instance, Mary Gauvain and Barbara Rogoff (1989) observed planning on a problem-solving task that required children to retrieve a set of items from the shelves of a model grocery store. When working on the task alone, 5-year-olds tended to jump right in and retrieve items one by one with little regard for the efficiency of their routes. Those working with an adult partner, in contrast, were encouraged to scan the shelves before they began to retrieve the items. These children were more likely than children working alone to organize their routes in advance and to follow efficient routes through the model store.

Talking about their plans (e.g., comparing the lengths of alternative routes) with their adult partners helped children's planning, both during the collaboration and later when planning shopping routes on their own. These findings suggest that solving problems collaboratively with more experienced partners promotes the development of planning skills, especially when the partners talk about what they are doing.

In laboratory studies, skilled planning is usually characterized as planning in advance of action. But in everyday life, goals often emerge or must be modified in the course of an activity. In these cases, skilled planning requires flexibility. Consider, for example, a trip to a real supermarket. You might enter the store with one plan in mind only to discover some unforeseen problems. There may be a long line at the deli counter, a shattered jar of spaghetti sauce on the floor in aisle 2, and an ice cream section in desperate need of restocking. If you stick to your original plan, you will end up wasting time while you wait in the deli line, for the sauce to be mopped up, and for the ice cream case to be refilled. In these kinds of situations, the best plan is a flexible plan.

A study of Girl Scout cookie sales involving two troops of 10- and 11-year-old Scouts illustrates how much planning in everyday settings can differ from planning in the laboratory (Rogoff, Baker-Sennett, & Matusov, 1994; Rogoff et al., 1995, 2002). This study also serves as a good example of the wide range of methods used to study thinking in cultural context.

The researchers in this study functioned as "participant observers" and underwent training to serve as "cookie chairs" so they could be intimately involved in the cookie-selling enterprise. They also tape-recorded Scout meetings and interviewed the girls throughout the 2-month sales period. In addition, the Scouts were outfitted with tape recorders to carry around and record their sales and deliveries.

This study revealed much about the contextual supports that assist children in everyday problem solving (e.g., color-coded order forms), a topic we return to later. As the following example suggests, it also showed how strategies judged as superior in laboratory settings do not necessarily work as well in everyday settings:

> One girl began her delivery by separating out each customer's order and marking it with a Post-It note showing address and amount due, then lining up all the customers' orders according to their addresses, creating an efficient route around her neighborhood. She lined up dozens of groups of orders on the sidewalk in front of her house, asked her mother which addresses would be closest to which others, then stacked the linear array in *reverse order* in a wagon (to have the beginning of the route on top) (Rogoff et al., 1994, p. 366).

At first glance, this appears to be a brilliant plan (and quite impressive for a 10-year-old). But when the Scout began to deliver the cookies, she discovered that many of her customers were not at home. The orders became disorganized, and she found it difficult to keep track of the many boxes of cookies. In subsequent deliveries, the Scout used a more flexible strategy that involved smaller orders and much backtracking. Nonetheless, in the end, it proved to be a better plan.

To fully understand the processes of planning involved in this particular cultural practice, it is also important to place it in its in broader cultural-historical context (Bronfenbrenner & Morris, 1998; Modell & Elder, 2002). It is unlikely that the Scout would have faced the same sorts of difficulties had she been delivering cookies 30 years ago, when many children had mothers waiting for them at home after school. Today's Scouts have to face not only the challenge of delivering to customers who are not home but also their own hectic schedules, which keep them away from home until dark. To compound problems, neighborhoods are less safe and often less "neighborly" than they were in decades past. Fortunately, some of the Scouts' problems may be mitigated by advances in technology (e.g., e-mail, answering machines, desktop publishing) and changing cultural practices (e.g., parents taking order forms to their places of employment).

As these findings suggest, cultures vary in the need for planning and the kinds of activities to be planned. Cultures also vary in the value placed on planful action and in the ways in which they define "intelligence" (Sternberg, 2000). In European American cultures, intelligence is usually associated with speed (Berry, 1984; Goodnow, 1976, 1984; Kagan & Kogan, 1970). Other cultures, such as the Navajo, value slow, considered action over speed (Cazden & John, 1971). Children reared in cultures that encourage thoughtful over fast performance may plan more than those from cultures that place a priority on speed. For instance, Ellis and Schneiders (1989) observed planning among groups of Navajo and European American children as they solved a three-dimensional maze designed to resemble a rural scene with buildings, livestock, and vehicles. The Navajo children planned nearly 10 times as long as the European-American children and made fewer errors as a result.

In general, younger children are less likely to plan than older children, and there are a host of reasons why this is the case. One important factor is that younger children are less able to inhibit action and so find it difficult to disengage from a problem in order to plan. One way that young children control impulsive action is by talking to themselves out loud—a behavior now generally referred to as **private speech** (Berk, 2001).

Private speech
Speech children produce and direct toward themselves during a problem-solving activity.

Private Speech

Vygotsky (1934/1962) proposed that young children's private speech grows out of their interactions with parents and other adults as they work together on various tasks. Much of a parent's speech in such situations involves guiding and regulating the child. Over the course of many such interactions, children begin to use their parents' instructional comments (although not always in versions as complete or well formed) to direct their own behavior. Gradually, the controlling speech becomes internalized as thought, and children eventually produce silent statements similar to the verbal ones. Vygotsky thus viewed self-regulation as developing out of the child's social interactions—a process he called **sociogenesis** (Van der Veer & Valsiner, 1988).

Sociogenesis
The process of acquiring knowledge or skills through social interactions.

Vygotsky further posited that early on, when the border between social and private speech is fuzzy, the same factors that encourage speech to other people would promote greater amounts of private speech. To test this hypothesis, Vygotsky created a series of situations that discouraged or prevented social interaction and then measured preschoolers' private speech. In one experiment, he placed children in a very noisy classroom. In others, he surrounded children with peers who spoke a foreign language or who were deaf and had no oral language. In each situation, and in settings where children were isolated at a table by themselves or placed with unfamiliar peers, self-talk declined significantly. Conversely, private speech increases when children are in the presence of responsive social partners (Goudena, 1987).

A number of other factors have shown to affect the frequency with which children talk to themselves while solving problems. Private speech occurs most often on tasks that are challenging but not impossibly difficult (Behrend, Rosengren, & Perlmutter, 1989; Berk & Garvin, 1984; Kohlberg, Yaeger, & Hjertholm, 1968). It is most evident at the beginning of a new task and at other times when children have the greatest difficulty, but it decreases (becomes internalized) as they master the task (Berk, 1994; Meichenbaum & Goodman, 1979).

Children with learning and behavior problems tend to rely on private speech for a longer period of time than their peers (Berk & Landau, 1993; Winsler et al., 1999). Researchers have also found that in middle and later childhood a greater proportion of private speech takes the form of whispering, presumably reflecting its gradual internalization (Duncan & Pratt, 1997; Frauenglass & Diaz, 1985).

To Recap . . .

Both children's planning and their private speech have roots in social interaction. Parents begin to talk about plans with their children from the time the children are very young and long before they can fully appreciate the significance of the plans. Parents also scaffold the development of children's planning skills as they participate jointly in everyday routines and problem-solving activities.

Children also learn how to regulate their own behavior using private speech by working on tasks under the guidance of an adult. Over time, children adopt the instructional comments originally offered by the adult as their own. Although private speech is used by individuals of all ages and in all kinds of situations, it is observed most frequently among preschoolers and on problems or parts of problems that are challenging but not overwhelming.

PEER INTERACTION AND COGNITIVE CHANGE

Clearly, adults, especially parents, contribute much to children's cognitive development. But peers and siblings play an important role in the development of children's thinking as well. Much of what children know about the world is learned during interactions with other children. This includes factual knowledge (e.g., details about dinosaurs, celebrity gossip), strategies (e.g., mnemonic techniques, ways to beat video games), and subtle social information (e.g., how to dress "cool"). Through their interactions with peers and siblings, children can also develop a deeper understanding of not just factual information but concepts—for example, principles of justice. In this section, we discuss the processes involved in peer learning.

Peer learning has been an active area of study in developmental psychology for nearly three decades (see Azmitia, 1996; De Lisi & Goldbeck, 1999; Garton, 1992; Hogan & Tudge, 1999; Rogoff, 1998, for reviews). As one recent review noted, it is also hard to exaggerate the interest in peer learning in today's schools (Webb & Palincsar, 1996). This interest is fueled by a belief that group work often promotes greater understanding and higher levels of achievement than solitary efforts and by a growing appreciation of the importance of collaborative skills in settings outside of school, such as research laboratories, medical practices, manufacturing firms, and the corporate world (Hinds & Kiesler, 2002).

Research on peer interaction and cognitive change spans a wide variety of learning arrangements. In this section, we sample four broad categories of peer learning: teaching (tutoring), collaboration, small group interaction, and whole-class discussion. Although the term *peer* technically refers to individuals who are comparable in age or task expertise, researchers working in this area often use the word to describe any problem-solving interactions among children, including those involving children who differ in age, ability, or task knowledge. For ease of discussion, we adopt that convention here as well.

Peer Teaching

One way children learn from other children is through direct instruction, or teaching. Peer teaching can be formal, such as when older students are assigned to tutor younger children in school, or informal, as when siblings teach younger brothers and sisters how to play games or perform household chores. In peer teaching, one child is presumed to have some competence or knowledge that the second child lacks. For this reason, tutoring usually involves pairings of children who differ in age by 2 to 3 years. Sometimes, however, more capable children are assigned to teach same-age peers.

Processes of Peer Teaching   Though peer teaching was popular long before Vygotsky's theory became influential, many of its current supporters use Vygotsky's theory to promote its use. Specifically, they point to Vygotsky's idea that children learn new ways of thinking through their interactions with adults *or more capable peers* who skillfully guide their problem solving in the zone of proximal development. Some advocates of peer tutoring suggest that peers are better able than adults to offer assistance within the zone of proximal development (Juel, 1996). However, research shows that child teachers are often quite unskilled at scaffolding others' learning. The problem appears to lie in children's inability to provide instruction that is sensitive to learners' needs.

Sometimes the problem is that child teachers provide too little assistance. For example, when one 8-year-old was asked to teach a younger child the classification/memory task described earlier (in which photographs were sorted in specified boxes), the teaching closely resembled a guessing game, "Now where does this go? . . . Nope, try again . . . umh-unh . . . [shakes head no] . . . No. Think a little bit, think a little, don't just guess. Which one do you think this will go with?" (Ellis & Rogoff, 1986, p. 321). More often, as depicted in Table 9.5, children provide too *much* assistance and

Table 9.5	A Peer Teaching Episode
Novice:	You gotta let me help. You said you would.
Expert:	I will, after I finish this.
Novice:	[Sighs, sits back, crosses arms around chest and frowns. Some 20 seconds later, takes some Legos and begins building a section of the model. When completed, he hands it to the expert] I built this for our house.
Expert:	I'm the builder. You find Legos when I tell you, okay? Give me a yellow two-dot.
Novice:	I want to be a builder too. She [the experimenter] said work together. My window is good.
Expert:	Well, it's not going on my house [moves his building out of reach of the novice.]
Novice:	[Starts shaking the table, making it impossible for the expert to continue building.]
Expert:	Stop it! If you don't quit it we won't get finished. I'm almost done with the door.
Novice:	[Stops shaking the table, observes the expert until he finishes the door.] My turn! My turn!
Expert:	It's not time for your window yet.
Novice:	But it's the only thing [left] . . . and the roofs but the window goes first. How about I do the window and you the roof? Here [offers roof pieces].
Expert:	You'll mess it up. I gotta do it.
Novice:	No, I know how. See? It's the same [points to window and to model].
Expert:	Well, you don't know how to put it on.
Novice:	Yeah I do!
Expert:	If you want me to use your window you gotta let me put it on.
Novice:	[Sighs, puts head down on arms, and disengages from the interaction. Eighteen seconds later, he starts pelting the expert with Legos. When the expert lifts his hands to protect himself, the novice quickly reaches over and smashes the Lego building to pieces.]

SOURCE: Adapted from "Peer Interactive Minds: Developmental, Theoretical, and Methodological Issues" by M. Azmitia, 1996. *Interactive Minds: Life-Span Perspectives on the Social Foundation of Cognition*, p. 142. Copyright © 1996 by Cambridge University Press. Reprinted by permission.

frequently take over the problem entirely (McLane, 1987; Perez-Granados & Callanan, 1997; Perlmutter et al., 1989; Wood et al., 1995).

Why are child teachers relatively insensitive to learners' needs? One possibility is that children lack the self-regulatory skills to step back and let their partner solve the problem, particularly when the task is highly engaging (Azmitia, 1996). A related possibility is that the multiple demands of both solving the problem and teaching the solution to someone else overwhelm child teachers (Azmitia & Perlmutter, 1989). Even when children have been trained and can expertly solve the problem they are to teach, though, they typically do not actively engage the learner in the problem solution. And without active involvement in the problem-solving process, learners tend to show little cognitive growth (Radziszewska & Rogoff, 1991).

Another possibility is that children lack the social cognitive skills required for effective teaching. For children (or adults) to provide helpful instruction, they must be able to think about the learner's thinking (Tomasello et al., 1993; Wood et al., 1995). However, thinking analytically about their own and others' reasoning continues to be a challenge for children throughout elementary school. They find it especially difficult to reason about thinking they know to be incorrect, particularly when their own understanding is new and fragile (Chandler & Lalonde, 1996; Ellis & Johns, 1999; S. A. Miller et al., 1997; Piaget, 1932).

Yet another explanation for the relatively poor instruction provided by child teachers lies in socialization practices. Investigations that have shown children to be relatively ineffective teachers have typically involved European American children. As discussed earlier, European American communities tend to promote an independent orientation that encourages children to pursue individual achievement and to assert their independence and individuality. These values may make it especially difficult for young teachers and learners to coordinate their efforts. In contrast, children in cultures that embrace an interdependent orientation—especially those in which children are frequent caregivers of younger siblings—may show fewer of the limitations observed among European American children (Ellis & Gauvain, 1992; Farver, 1999; Rogoff, 1998; Zukow-Goldring, 1995).

So far, our discussion has focused solely on the child teacher and his or her ability to effectively scaffold instruction. This view of children as teachers is consistent with Vygotsky's theory, but it does overlook the contributions the learner makes to the instructional interaction. As discussed earlier in our treatment of guided participation, in many cultures, children are expected to learn by watching (Rogoff et al., 2003).

Studies show that children begin to learn by watching peers at least by the second year of life. In one study, for example, experimenters taught 14-month-old peer "experts" how to manipulate some unfamiliar objects in novel ways (Hanna & Meltzoff, 1993). The experts were then placed at a table with a group of their peers and encouraged to model the newly learned actions. When tested 2 days later in a new setting (their homes), the peers were able to duplicate the actions the expert had performed earlier.

Benefits of Peer Teaching Evaluations of school-based tutoring programs demonstrate that peer teaching can yield both cognitive and social benefits (Allen, 1976; Gartner, Kohler, & Riessman, 1971; Topping, 1988). Perhaps most interesting is that teachers (or tutors) often show gains as great as or even greater than those shown by the children they teach. This can be explained in part by the cognitive processes involved in teaching. In the process of generating explanations, teachers elaborate on their own reasoning. This produces richer representations and may reveal inconsistencies in the way they think about problems. If you ever *really* want to understand something, try to teach it to someone else.

Serving in the teacher role is also associated with positive social and emotional outcomes, such as increased confidence and improved attitudes toward learning. Consequently, many experts believe peer tutoring is most effective when children have opportunities to act as both teacher and learner. In addition, many experts believe that peer teaching is better suited for practicing existing skills and consolidating old knowledge than for generating new conceptual understanding (Damon, 1984; Sharan, 1984).

Collaboration

Another type of peer learning is collaboration. Collaboration differs in important, if sometimes subtle, ways from peer teaching (Foot & Howe, 1998). In peer teaching, the teacher is the authority and the source of correct knowledge that is to be conveyed to the less capable partner. In collaborative interactions, in contrast, partners begin with roughly the same levels of competence and, in the process of interacting, create new knowledge.

Many theorists believe that collaboration is more likely to promote long-lasting conceptual change than tutoring. In tutoring, the learner may simply go along with what the expert says without giving it much thought or even understanding the expert's point of view. Children may feel more comfortable questioning the ideas proposed by another person as well as more motivated to understand them in collaborative interactions marked by an equal distribution of power and knowledge (Bearison & Dorval, 2002; Damon, 1984; Hatano & Iagnaki, 1991).

Piaget's View   Much of the initial interest in collaboration was based on Piaget's theory (Piaget, 1932). Piaget proposed that during peer interaction, children are exposed to ways of thinking about problems or issues that conflict with their own. Piagetians call cognitive conflict induced by social interaction **sociocognitive conflict** (Bearison, 1982; Doise & Mugny, 1984; Piaget, 1932).

According to this perspective, cognitive change occurs when children work to reconcile the discrepancy between their views and those held by peers. Piaget (1977) laid out three conditions necessary for cognitive change. One, the partners need a common language and system of ideas. Two, they need to be able to "conserve" their own point of view so that they can defend it without contradicting themselves. Three, there must be reciprocity between partners so that each feels free to express his or her point of view.

An assumption that underlies Piagetian studies of peer collaboration is that individuals will be persuaded by the most logical and cogent arguments. Because these arguments are more likely to be associated with correct understanding than flawed reasoning, it follows that partners will be convinced of the correct answer and will move forward in their thinking.

To illustrate, consider a study by Miller and Brownell (1975). In this study, second-graders worked in pairs on Piagetian conservation tasks. Miller and Brownell found that conservers and nonconservers asserted their views equally often but that conservers were able to offer a greater variety of arguments to support their answers. Consequently, nonconservers were more likely to be convinced by their conserving partners than the other way around. This pattern of change—nonconservers advancing and conservers staying the same—has been replicated many times (Murray, 1982). As we shall see, however, discussions among collaborating peers are often much less involved than those reported by Miller and Brownell. Furthermore, children sometimes regress in their reasoning following collaboration.

Sociocultural Approach   In the Piagetian account of collaboration, the mechanism of cognitive change is conflict and resolution. According to the sociocultural approach, cognitive change is the result of cooperation and coordination. Partners negotiate—or coconstruct—new understanding as they clarify, refine, extend, and build on each other's reasoning (Forman & Cazden, 1985; Forman & McPhail, 1993). From this perspective, it matters less that partners hold divergent views on a problem (although that can be helpful) than that they establish **intersubjectivity**—a commitment to find common ground on which to build shared understanding (Rommetveit, 1979).

The sociocultural approach to collaboration differs from the Piagetian view in several other ways as well (Tudge & Rogoff, 1989). One important difference is the age at which children are believed to be able to participate in collaborative exchanges. Piaget (1977)

Sociocognitive conflict
Cognitive conflict that arises during social interaction.

Intersubjectivity
A commitment to find common ground on which to build shared understanding.

In simple situations, even young children can collaborate successfully.

believed that children could not engage in productive collaborations until the period of concrete operations, when they overcame the egocentrism of the preschool years.

Many socioculturalists, in contrast, believe young children can collaborative effectively. As we have already seen, young children are quite able to collaborate in play (Corsaro, 1985; Garvey, 1990; Verba, 1994). They can also coordinate their actions to solve simple problems (e.g., operating toys that require multiple hands) that do not depend heavily on discussion (e.g., Ashley & Tomasello, 1998; Brownell & Carriger, 1990; Charlesworth & Dzur, 1987).

There is also some evidence that older preschoolers can collaborate on problems that require verbal negotiation (Cooper, 1980). For instance, Heather Holmes-Lonergan (2003) observed 4- to 5.5-year-olds as they worked together on several problem-solving tasks (e.g., model building, making a bead necklace). The children in this study talked about how to complete the tasks with their partners, helped each other deal with problems and mistakes, coordinated the division of materials and labor, and gave explanations. The children also solved the problems correctly 70% of the time.

These early collaborative exchanges are not likely to induce the kind of fundamental cognitive restructuring envisioned by Piaget. Nonetheless, collaboration during the preschool years can provide valuable opportunities to acquire behavioral strategies and to begin to develop the social and communicative abilities required for more complex collaborations in the future.

Factors Associated with Productive Collaboration Studies of collaboration on Piagetian tasks, mathematical problem solving, scientific reasoning, and even writing show that students who work on problems with partners of relatively equal ability often produce solutions superior to those of individuals working alone. In addition, collaboration can promote a deeper understanding of the problem or concept that lasts over time. Collaboration does not always lead to such positive results, however. Sometimes, collaboration even leads to regressions in thinking (Forman & McPhail, 1993; Levin & Druyan, 1993; Tudge, 1989, 1992).

What are the characteristics of successful collaborations? According to both Piagetians and advocates of the sociocultural approach, successful collaboration depends, first and foremost, on a commitment to deepening understanding. Therefore, many of the factors that undermine effective peer teaching (e.g., pursuit of individual goals) also derail collaboration.

Research also shows that the most productive collaborations tend to be those characterized by lively discussion and debate (Dimant & Bearison, 1991; Kruger 1993). Unfortunately, in the absence of adult intervention, the quality of discussions among partners often leaves much to be desired (Mercer, 1996; Teasley, 1995). For example, Russell (1982) reports that the average interaction between the 5- to 8-year-old conservers and nonconservers in his study lasted only about 40 seconds and consisted of little more than "Same size, okay? Ready!"

Another condition that can influence the outcome of collaboration is the relationship between partners. Collaborations among friends tend to be more successful than those involving strangers or acquaintances (Nelson & Aboud, 1985; Newcomb & Brady, 1982). For instance, Azmitia and Montgomery (1993) found that pairs of adolescent friends assigned to solve a scientific reasoning problem were more likely to justify their propositions, discuss task concepts and solutions, and evaluate their outcomes than were pairs of acquaintances. Collaborations among acquaintances tended to disintegrate when the problems grew difficult. In contrast, pairs of friends were able to support each other's involvement by asking questions, offering encouragement, and making statements to the effect that "We're in this together."

Friendship does not *always* lay the foundation for productive interactions, however. Sometimes, partners are afraid to disagree with friends because it might disrupt the relationship (Forman, 1992; Palincsar & Herrenkohl, 1999). For example, Azmitia (1996) reports that one young study participant admitted he feared that if he did not let his partner "run" things, his partner would tell others not to play with him when they returned to the classroom.

Whether collaboration facilitates or hinders cognitive change also depends on the understanding partners bring to the task. Collaborations tend to be more successful when one partner has a more advanced understanding of the problem than when neither partner understands it very well at all (Perret-Clermont, 1980). Collaborations in which partners hold incorrect but different views also tend to be more productive than those in which partners both embrace the same incorrect reasoning. In the latter case, partners often end up reinforcing their shared erroneous thinking, in part because they are unable to generate alternative ways of thinking about the problem (Ellis, Siegler, & Klahr, 1993; Howe, Rodgers, & Tolmie, 1990; Howe, Tolmie, & Rodgers, 1992).

Collaboration—just like instruction—is most likely to induce cognitive change when children's understanding is in a state of transition (Murphy & Messer, 2000; Pine & Messer, 1998). Conversely, hearing another point of view will likely induce little change when an individual is deeply wedded to his or her current way of thinking. Some studies also suggest that change is most likely when a partner expresses ideas just beyond the other's current level of understanding—that is, in the zone of proximal development (Bell, Grossen, & Perret-Clermont, 1985; Kuhn, 1972; Mackie, 1983; Mugny & Doise, 1978).

Finally, collaboration is most likely to yield positive benefits on reasoning tasks that require discovery and reflection. Tasks that involve rote memorization or skill acquisition may be better mastered via peer teaching or individual practice (Kobayashi, 1994; Phelps & Damon, 1989).

Peer Learning in Classrooms

Another context in which children learn with peers is the classroom. Research on peer interaction in classroom settings has taken on a new look in recent years as educators have come to view academic disciplines as cultural communities (Brown, 1997; Brown, Collins, & Duguid, 1989; Lave & Wenger, 1991). According to this perspective, to be competent in a discipline requires that students be socialized to think, talk, and act like a member of that cultural community. Because "real" mathematicians and scientists do their work in social settings, it follows that students should learn to do so as well.

To do math and science with other people, children need to master the discourse styles used in those communities. As we have already noted, however, children often struggle to engage in meaningful discussions with peers, particularly when the content is

Table 9.6	Discussion of Photosynthesis among Fourth- and Fifth-Grade Students
Brandon:	How about leaf cells and oxygen — Leaf cells
Steve:	Release
Brandon:	Leaf cells give off
Steve:	Release
Sam:	Give off
Steve:	Release, release, release!
Sam:	Release? — Give off is easier
Brandon:	Give off
Steve:	Okay give off
Sam:	Majority wins!

SOURCE: Adapted from "Using Explanatory Knowledge During Collaborative Problem Solving in Science" by E. B. Coleman, 1998. *Journal of the Learning Sciences, 7*, p. 406, Copyright © 1998 by Lawrence Erlbaum Associates, Inc. Reprinted by permission.

challenging. Consider, for example, the discussion of photosynthesis among a group of fourth- and fifth-grade students shown in Table 9.6.

Although conversations among actual scientists *sometimes* deteriorate to the level depicted in this excerpt, the situation is far from ideal. Consequently, teachers and researchers have devised a variety of techniques that structure or scaffold students' group problem-solving interactions (Brown & Palincsar, 1989; O'Donnell & King, 1999). For instance, even the poorly coordinated discussion of photosynthesis excerpted in Table 9.6 was salvaged by the use of prescribed prompts printed on cards that the students were instructed to ask either themselves or their partners as they worked on each task. Following Sam's announcement, "Majority wins!" Brandon selected the prompt that read "Explain why your answer is correct or wrong." In response, Sam offered the following explanation, which is quite an improvement over the earlier discussion:

> Okay, my answer is correct because leaf cells are the only parts of the plant that can give off oxygen — The roots cannot because the oxygen would get stuck in the soil — And then we would not be able to breathe it and um the entire population would be dead. (Coleman, 1998, pp. 406–407)

Students who participated in groups supported by the scaffolded explanation–based intervention developed more accurate understanding of photosynthesis than students in a control group whose interactions were not scaffolded. Similar findings have been reported in other studies designed to improve the quality of children's discussions of scientific phenomena (Palincsar & Herrenkohl, 1999).

Whole-class discussions offer another opportunity for teachers to model appropriate discourse and scaffold student discussion. The teacher can, for example, rephrase student responses, perhaps introducing new, more formal terminology or elaborating on the answer in a way that redirects the discussion. She can ask students to clarify or expand on their own reasoning, and she can request students to evaluate other students' answers (Forman & Ansell, 2002; O'Connor, 1996).

Unfortunately, teachers in the United States often fail to take advantage of the opportunities afforded by whole-class discussion, preferring instead to rely on the conventional format in which the teacher is the authority who does most of the explaining and most of the evaluation of student responses. Students have few opportunities to learn from peers in classrooms organized in this fashion.

Japanese classrooms provide an interesting contrast and suggest ways in which discussions can be organized to promote peer learning. For instance, in Japanese classrooms, students do most of the explaining (Stigler, Fernandez, & Yoshida, 1996). In addition, Japanese teachers are reluctant to provide explicit feedback regarding the correctness of student answers, preferring that students decide on the basis of the persuasiveness of the

Scaffolding Group Discussion:
The Hypothesis-Experiment-Instruction Method

A common concern voiced by teachers wary of using whole-class discussion to promote student learning in mathematics and science classrooms is that students may not be able to generate plausible solutions (most notably the correct one) worthy of discussion. One way to remedy this problem is through the use of a Japanese educational intervention known as *hypothesis-experiment-instruction.*

In this intervention, the teacher provides three or four plausible alternatives along with a problem. For example:

Taro drinks 1/2 liter of milk at breakfast and 1/5 liter at supper. How many liters of milk does he drink a day?

1/2 + 1/5 = 2/7, answer is 1/7 liter
0.5 + 0.2 = 0.7, answer is 0.7 liter
1/2 + 1/5 = 7/10, answer is 7/10 liter

BOX 9.2

Applications

Students are then asked to choose one of the solutions and to write down the reasons for their choices. Students' choices, counted by a show of hands, are tabulated on the blackboard. Next, one or two students who supported each alternative are invited to state the reasons for their choices, after which all students are invited to discuss them. During the discussion, the teacher acts as a neutral moderator, taking care not to endorse some ideas over others. Following the discussion, students are asked to choose an alternative once again.

Implementation of this intervention in Japanese mathematics and science classrooms has yielded positive results (Hatano & Inagaki, 1991; Inagaki, 1981; Inagaki, Hatano, & Morita, 1998). Children as young as fourth and fifth grade have proven able to generate in class discussion arguments for and against each alternative, including the correct answer. Despite the fact that only a small minority of students have an opportunity to speak, most students tend to shift toward the appropriate solution without feedback from the teacher. And, following the discussion, students accurately recall the reasonable explanations offered by their classmates.

These findings show that children can develop correct understanding through peer interaction without it being "authorized" by the teacher. This process is aided by the fact that students are more likely to be persuaded by classmates known to be high achievers than by less able students, and by those arguments that are received favorably by the greatest number of students.

The hypothesis-experiment-instruction method has been used effectively in groups as large as 40 to 45 students. Of particular interest is that, even in large groups, "silent" students are as likely to adopt the correct solution as students who are vocal. Inagaki and colleagues suggest that these students may actively try to find among the speakers an "agent" who "speaks" for them in the discussion and, if they can, participate vicariously in the discussion as a result. Even if they cannot find such an agent, students engage with others' arguments in their own minds. In the words of the researchers, "active participation is the prerequisite for the construction of knowledge, but it may take forms other than speaking out" (Inagaki et al., 1998, p. 523).

Might this method work equally well in American classrooms? Perhaps, but Kayoko Inagaki and colleagues caution that the success of this approach and of whole-class discussion more generally depends on two key variables highly associated with Japanese school culture (Hatano & Inagaki, 1998). First, students need to feel comfortable making mistakes and revealing confusions in public. This is possible in Japanese classrooms where all children, regardless of their academic achievements, are genuinely valued by their peers (Lewis, 1995). In this environment, children can expect moral support for their efforts to learn. Additionally, children recognize that they have a responsibility to contribute their ideas—even the wrong ones—to aid the group's success. Inagaki and colleagues argue that unless the teacher can create a climate in which mistakes are viewed positively, discussions that highlight student errors might prove devastating.

A second factor is what the authors call "socialization for listenership" (Inagaki et al., 1998). Japanese children come to school predisposed to learn from their peers. They listen to classmates eagerly and carefully, and do not grow frustrated or inattentive when not given an opportunity to express their own ideas, as long as they have some sense of participation. As the following comment by one frustrated child illustrates, American students often begrudge the amount of time devoted to discussion:

There's so much work and you're always doing conversations and I'm not learning anything. In kindergarten I got all information like a computer would. I can't do that now. I knew all I had to know for first and second grade in kindergarten. It's conversation, conversation, and we hardly get anything accomplished (Peter, Grade 2, quoted in Nicholls & Hazzard, 1993, p. 172).

Nurturing an appreciation for what others have to say—and the skill to learn from their peers—may prove an even more formidable challenge for teachers hoping to encourage class discussion than creating a climate in which students feel free to make mistakes.

arguments. Therefore, rather than providing the feedback herself, the Japanese teacher is likely to ask the speaker's classmates whether they agree with the response and to explain why. Although American students may shudder at the prospect of having their ideas the focus of public debate, this occurs as a matter of course in Japanese classrooms. We discuss this issue further in Box 9.2.

To Recap . . .

Peer interaction is an important vehicle for children's cognitive growth. Researchers have documented the ways in which various types of peer learning arrangements can promote children's cognitive development.

Peer teaching involves pairing children who are relatively expert in the task at hand with less capable peers. For a variety of reasons, children often find it a challenge to provide instruction that is sensitive to the learners' needs. Hence, peer teaching often leads to greater advances for the teacher than the learner and may be best suited for reinforcing existing knowledge.

In peer collaboration, pairs or groups of children with roughly equal—if different—knowledge work together to solve problems. Collaboration can promote conceptual change as children coordinate and build on the different ideas that they bring to the joint effort.

Children can also learn from peers in classroom activities in which the teacher models, guides, and structures children's discussions.

CULTURAL ARTIFACTS AND MATERIAL TOOLS

As we have seen throughout this chapter, an important part of cognitive development is becoming competent at using tools for thinking. For example, *mnemonic techniques* promote recall for facts, *scripts* help children plan for the future, and *language* helps children regulate their problem solving. So far, our discussions of cultural tools have focused primarily on how children come to use tools in the context of cultural activities. We have paid somewhat less attention to an equally important issue—how the tools themselves shape children's thinking and problem solving. This is the issue we turn to next.

To understand the relationship between tools and children's intellectual development, it is helpful to be able to identify specific features of the tools that might be associated with different types of thinking. Mathematics—with its rule-based structure—has been shown to be a particularly good domain for this kind of analysis. Cross-cultural research that allows the comparison of mathematical tools that are alike in some ways but different in others has also shed light on the issue. For these two reasons, our discussion of the effects of tools on children's cognitive development will rely heavily on cross-cultural studies of mathematical development.

Numeration Systems

It is well established that students in East Asian nations outperform U.S. and European students on standardized tests of mathematical achievement. Explanations for these cross-national differences focus most often on cultural values and beliefs reflected in family and classroom practices (e.g., Stevenson & Stigler, 1992; Stigler & Hiebert, 1999). As we discuss elsewhere in this chapter and in Chapter 10, these factors surely do contribute to the differences in mathematical competence observed among East Asian students and those in other industrialized nations. However, some scholars believe that another factor may contribute to the superior mathematical achievement of East Asian students—the language used in mathematics.

There are at least two ways that language might influence mathematical development. One is the structure of the number-naming system (Fuson & Kwon, 1992a; Miller & Paredes, 1996; Nunes, 1999). The other is the speed with which the number words can be pronounced. We discuss the structure of the number naming system first.

Structure of the System   Table 9.7 shows the number-naming system in six languages. All the systems depicted in the table are base-10 systems. In a base-10 system, each place in a number represents 10 times the value of the place to its right. So, for example, in the number 555, the 50 is 10 times the value 5, and 500 is 10 times the value of 50. This may seem obvious and even inevitable—after all, humans have 10 fingers and 10 toes—but people have developed counting systems based on 2, 4, 8, 12, 20, and even 60 (Miller & Paredes, 1996)!

In East Asian languages, the structure of the base-10 number system is clearly represented by the structure of the number names themselves. In Chinese, for instance, the number words for 11, 12, and 13 (*shi-yi, shi-er, she-san*) are translated as ten-one, ten-two, and ten-three, respectively. In English, in contrast, the "teen" number names are irregular. There is no clue to mark the boundary between 10 and 11 and, although the number names become systematic after 12, the order of the place value is reversed (e.g., when we say thirteen, the three comes first, but when we write 13, the three comes second).

One indication that young English speakers struggle to understand the structure of our number-naming system is apparent in their early counting. American preschoolers often produce idiosyncratic number names when counting above 20 (e.g., "twenty-eight, twenty-nine, twenty-ten, twenty-eleven, twenty-twelve"). Interestingly, Chinese preschoolers never make these kinds of mistakes (Miller & Stigler, 1987).

Table 9.7	Number Names in Six Languages					
Number	**English**	**French**	**Swedish**	**Chinese**	**Japanese**	**Korean**
1	one	un, une	en, ett	yi	ichi	il
2	two	deux	tvá	er	ni	ee
3	three	trois	tre	san	san	sam
4	four	quatre	fyra	si	shi	sah
5	five	cinq	fern	wu	go	oh
6	six	six	sex	liu	roku	yook
7	seven	sept	sju	qi	shichi	chil
8	eight	huit	átta	ba	hachi	pal
9	nine	neuf	nio	jui	kyu	goo
10	ten	dix	tio	shi	juu	shib
11	eleven	onze	elva	shi-yi	juu-ichi	shib-il
12	twelve	douze	tolv	shi-er	juu-ni	shib-ee
13	thirteen	treize	tretton	shi-san	juu-san	shib-sam
14	fourteen	quatorze	fjorton	shi-si	juu-shi	shib-sah
15	fifteen	quinze	femton	shi-wu	juu-go	shib-oh
16	sixteen	seize	sexton	shi-liu	juu-roku	shib-yook
17	seventeen	dix-sept	sjutton	shi-qi	juu-shichi	shib-chil
18	eighteen	dix-huit	arton	shi-ba	juu-hachi	shib-pal
19	nineteen	dix-neuf	nitton	shi-jui	juu-kyu	shib-goo
20	twenty	vingt	tjugo	er-shi	ni-juu	ee-shib
21	twenty-one	vingt et un	tjugoett	er-shi-yi	ni-juu-ichi	ee-shib-il
22	twenty-two	vingt-deux	tjugotva	er-shi-er	ni-juu-ni	ee-shib-ee
30	thirty	trente	trettio	san-shi	san-juu	sam-shib
40	forty	quarante	fyrtio	si-shi	shi-juu	sah-shib
50	fifty	cinquante	femtio	wu-shi	go-juu	oh-shib
60	sixty	soixante	sextio	liu-shi	roku-juu	yook-shib
70	seventy	soixante-dix	sjuttio	qi-shi.	shichi-juu	chil-shib
80	eighty	quatre-vingts	áttio	ba-shl	hachi-juu	pal-shib
90	ninety	quatre-vingt-dix	nittio	jui-shi	kyu-juu g	goo-shib

SOURCE: From "First Graders' Cognitive Representation of Number and Understanding of Place Value: Cross-National Comparisons—France, Japan, Korea, Sweden, and the United States" by I. Miura, Y. Okamoto, C. C. Kim, M. Steere, & M. Fayol, 1993, *Journal of Educational Psychology, 85*, p. 25. Copyright © 1993 by American Psychological Association. Reprinted by permission.

Kevin Miller and associates (Miller et al., 1995) reasoned that if the structure of number names underlies the differences in early counting between Chinese and American children, then the difference should emerge only when the structures of the systems differ—that is, after the number 10. Indeed, comparisons of counting skill among 3- to 5-year-old Chinese and American children revealed no differences at age 3, when only a minority of children in either culture count above 10. A large difference favoring the Chinese children emerged between the ages of 3 and 4 years and widened over the next year (see Figure 9.5).

Speed of Pronunciation   The second way in which language might influence mathematical development is the speed with which the number names can be pronounced. For instance, the basic Chinese number names are quite short and can be pronounced more quickly than English number names. The speed of number pronunciations, in turn, influences memory span for numbers. Number names that are short and simple place fewer demands on working memory than number names that are long and difficult to say. And indeed, Chinese children can retain two to three more digits in working memory than their American counterparts (Chen & Stevenson, 1988; Geary et al., 1993). It is important to note that this superiority is limited to memory span measures involving digits. Chinese children are not blessed with superior memories in general. When American and Chinese children are tested with words equivalent in length, the difference in their memory spans disappears (Stevenson et al., 1985).

David Geary and associates (Geary et al., 1993, 1996) speculated that the different working memory demands might lead Chinese and American children to choose different strategies when solving addition problems. You may recall from Chapter 8 that most children use a variety of strategies to solve arithmetic problems. These strategies vary in the demands they make on working memory. Strategies that are entirely verbal (i.e., "in the head") place greater demands on memory than those that rely on fingers. Geary and colleagues hypothesized that because the number names are shorter, verbal counting should be easier in Chinese than in English. Conversely, the longer English number names might necessitate greater reliance on finger counting.

To test this hypothesis, the researchers compared the strategy choices of Chinese and American children in kindergarten through third grade on single-digit addition problems. The children in the two cultures used the same types of strategies to solve the problems (counting fingers, verbal counting, retrieval, decomposition, etc.), but the frequency with which they used the various strategies differed. As expected, when they

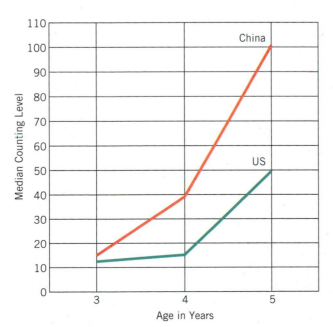

Figure 9.5

Median level of abstract counting by Chinese and American preschoolers. From "Preschool Origins of Cross-National Differences in Mathematical Competence: The Role of Number Naming Systems," *Psychological Science, 6,* by K. F. Miller, C. M. Smith, J. Zhu, & H. Zhang, 1995. Copyright © 1995 by American Psychological Society. Reprinted by permission.

counted, the Chinese children were most likely to use verbal counting, whereas the American children were most likely to count using their fingers.

As a whole, the results of these investigations suggest that features of the number-naming systems in Asian and non-Asian languages contribute to the ease with which young children learn to count and perform simple arithmetic. It is crucial, however, to place these findings in a broader cultural context. Asian and non-Asian cultures differ in numerous ways, including the importance ascribed to mathematical achievement and beliefs and practices regarding the teaching of math. The number-naming system is just one of many interrelated aspects of culture that shape children's mathematical development. Indeed, it may well be that *because* the number-naming system is so accessible, parents and teachers in Asian communities assume that all children can master it easily at a young age, thereby jump-starting an educational process that leads to superior mathematical achievement over time (Geary et al., 1996; Yang & Cobb, 1995).

These studies also illustrate a potential benefit of cross-cultural studies beyond learning more about how children come to understand mathematics in different cultures. Many English-speaking parents and teachers fail to appreciate the challenges children face when learning the number-naming system. As adults, we have been making the cognitive shift for so long that we automatically interpret the teens as 10 plus so many ones. By studying how children come to understand a symbol system with a different structure, researchers have been able to target what makes learning our own system so difficult. Teachers can use this knowledge to develop more effective instruction (Fuson & Kwon, 1992a, b).

Measurement

In addition to mastering some type of counting system, children in many cultures must become adept at using material tools that embody numerical information. Among these tools are those invented to help solve problems involving measurement (e.g., calendars, clocks, speedometers, thermometers, and rulers).

Measurement systems of various sorts have evolved over time to meet the changing needs of a particular people. The structure of the systems thus varies widely from culture to culture. As a result, children in different communities at different points in history face different conceptual challenges as they attempt to master the tools of their culture. At the same time, the structure of the tools can support or constrain the way children use them and ultimately shape the way children think about problems. To illustrate some of the processes involved in learning to use measuring tools, we will focus on one particular kind of measurement—the measurement of length.

Standard Unit of Measure
One of the key principles of measurement in modern, technological societies is the importance of a stable or constant unit of measurement, but this has not been true throughout history. Indeed, the original units of measure in the English system (e.g., inch, foot) were based on body parts. A *cubit*, for example, is the length between the tip of the middle finger and the point of the elbow, whereas a *fathom* is the length between fingertips when both arms are outstretched. The lengths of these measures were based on adult body parts, so naturally the measurements produced by children would not coincide with those of adults.

Body-part measuring systems are still in use today. For example, the Oksapmin of Papua New Guinea use what is called a *body-part enumeration system* (see Figure 9.6). In the Oksapmin system, number words are the names of parts of the body taken in a particular order. The word for 1 is also the word for the right thumb, the word for 14 is the nose, and so on until they reach the last finger of the left hand. The Oksapmin people use this system both to count items and to measure. Because people come in different sizes, the measurements produced by different individuals vary.

The absence of a standardized unit would appear to be a significant limitation, particularly when measurement takes place in a social context. Saxe and Moylan (1982) were curious whether the Oksapmin people recognized that the body-part system would

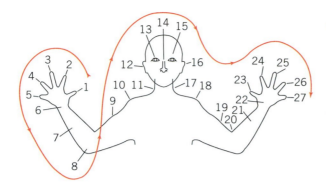

Figure 9.6

The Oksapmin of Papua New Guinea use a body-part numeration system. From "Body Parts as Numerals: A Developmental Analysis of Numeration Among the Oksapmin in Papua New Guinea," *Child Development, 52,* p. 307, by G. B. Saxe, 1981, Chicago: University of Chicago Press. Copyright © 1981 by University of Chicago Press. Reprinted by permission.

yield different measurements from one person to the next and whether people could make appropriate measurement conversions based on this recognition.

The researchers presented schooled and unschooled children and unschooled adults a set of stories describing a measurement activity common to their culture—determining the size of string bags. For some of the problems, the task was to determine whether a bag that measured to a specific point on the arm of one person (e.g., elbow) would be the same size as a bag that measured to the same point on someone else. The other set of problems required the participant to convert the measurement (e.g., would a bag that measured to the elbow of a tall father measure to the same spot or above or below that spot when placed on the arm of his young daughter?).

The findings revealed that understanding of equivalency was a fairly late development and was related to both schooling and experience in using the body-part measuring system. The unschooled children performed poorly on both kinds of stories. The schooled children (second- and sixth-graders) recognized that the size of bags would vary depending on the arm used to measure it, but they could not predict exactly how. Most of the adults, in contrast, could accurately predict both the size of a bag and how it would measure on arms of different lengths.

Researchers have also examined how an understanding of the importance of standard units develops in children in industrialized societies. Initially, children pay little attention to the size of measuring units, focusing instead on the number of units counted. For example, kindergartners who use counting as a means for measuring the passage of time conclude that the higher they have counted, the more time has passed, regardless of how fast they counted or from which number they started counting (Levin, 1989).

Similarly, when preschoolers were asked to divide a length of spaghetti equally among toy turtles, the children carefully distributed the spaghetti piece by piece among the turtles until it was gone without regard for the size of each piece (Miller, 1984). Although this strategy often resulted in each turtle's having the same *number* of spaghetti pieces, it did not ensure that the turtles had equivalent *amounts* of food. When children realized that one turtle had been short-changed, they simply took a piece of spaghetti from that turtle, cut it in two, and returned both pieces to the same turtle! (Devious caregivers sometimes take advantage of this conceptual limitation when resolving children's disputes over "who has more.")

Using Rulers Children's focus on number leads to similar errors when children use rulers. For instance, when young children are asked to compare quantities that have been measured with tools subdivided into different-sized units, they typically conclude that quantities associated with the greater number of units are larger, irrespective of unit size (Carpenter & Lewis, 1976; Hatano & Ito, 1965; Hiebert, 1981; Nunes & Bryant, 1996). And when given a choice between a properly designed ruler and a ruler that is incorrectly labeled or divided into units of varying size but ends in a higher number, kindergarten and first-grade children prefer the ruler with the higher number (Ellis & Siegler, 1995).

By second grade, most children recognize the importance of measuring with units of a constant size. Note that this recognition develops much earlier among schoolchildren in industrialized societies than among the Oksapmin people. The earlier development is likely due to both schooling and experience using rulers. Many teachers in early childhood classrooms explicitly teach the importance of equivalent units by having children measure with nonstandard units such as books, strips of paper, or hands and feet. The children then discuss, say, why a desk measured in "Michael" units differs in size from the same desk measured in "Sarah" units. Children may also abstract the importance of equal-sized units by using standard rulers. By second grade, they are likely to report that rulers divided into units that vary in size "look funny" (Ellis & Siegler, 1995).

Understanding the significance of a standard unit size is particularly important when measurement takes place in a social context. For people to coordinate their efforts in solving problems involving measurement, they must be using the *same* units. Lest you think this is a trivial problem, recall the fate of the $125 million Mars Climate Orbiter. It vanished on September 13, 1999, because the spacecraft was "speaking" to NASA engineers in metrics while the engineers on the ground were responding in nonmetric English!

The fact that young elementary school children recognize the importance of a stable unit of measurement does not necessarily mean that they fully understand the role of units in standard measuring tools (Piaget, Inhelder, & Szeminska, 1960). Sometimes it is obvious that children do not interpret the spaces on rulers as units, such as when children use a ruler as a pointer to mark off inch-sized units on the object to be measured. Conceptual confusions are harder to detect when a child produces an accurate measure. How can we know whether a child who reports that some item measures "6" or even "6 inches" in length is thinking about it in terms of units or simply reading off the number that corresponds to the end of the item?

Among the tools that cultures provide are those intended to help solve problems of measurement. Mastering such tools can be a challenge.

One approach is to ask children to measure with nonstandard measuring tools, such as rulers that begin at 3 or 4 instead of 0. Studies using this procedure show that most children in kindergarten through second grade simply read off the numeral that corresponds to the end of the object being measured. Only a few of the oldest children compensate in some way for the units missing at the beginning of the ruler (Ellis & Siegler, 1995; Nunes & Bryant, 1996).

Another way is to ask children to draw their own rulers (Nunes & Bryant, 1996). For instance, in one such study involving 5- and 6-year-old British students, nearly 90% of children placed the number 1 in correspondence with the first line on the ruler (see Figure 9.7). Similarly, when asked to measure using a ruler subdivided into units but lacking numeric labels, most children began counting from 1 and consequently produced measurements that were one unit off. Uncertainty about where to begin counting when using a ruler plagues children through much of elementary school (Ellis & Siegler, 1995). This confusion may reflect conventional counting procedures. After all, we rarely start counting from zero. But it does also raise questions about what children think they are counting when they use a ruler.

Research on children's measurement demonstrates the more general point that children can often use tools skillfully before they really understand them. This is due, in part, to the fact that tools are often designed in ways that scaffold or constrain the way they are used. For example, because it is more difficult to read numbers upside down than right-side up, children are encouraged to position rulers correctly. If children can count and recognize numbers, they are also likely to read rulers from left to right and to report measurements in terms of the number that aligns with the end of the item being measured, rather than the beginning.

Currency

Another cultural tool that has been studied extensively by socioculturalists is currency. Much of the interest in children's use of currency in problem solving arose from observations of street vendors in Brazil (Nunes, Carraher, & Schliemann, 1993; Saxe, 1988, 1991). In Brazil, candy selling is one of the occupations available to poor children (usually boys) who need to earn money to help their families survive. Children may enter the selling practice as early as age 5, and they may eventually work as many as 14

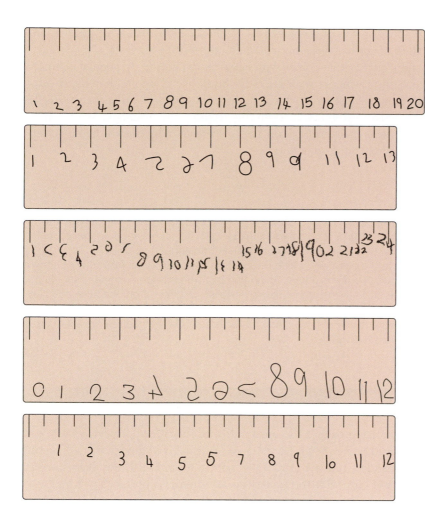

Figure 9.7

Examples of rulers labeled by 5- to 6-year-old children. From *Children Doing Mathematics,* by T. Nunes & P. Bryant, Oxford, UK: Blackwell, p. 88. Copyright © 1996 by Blackwell Press. Reprinted by permission.

hours per day and 60 or 70 hours per week. Many vendors either never go to school or leave school after a few years.

On the streets, child candy vendors perform a number of mathematical operations both quickly and accurately: representing the numerical values of different forms of currency, adding and subtracting units of various sizes, comparing ratios to determine optimal buying or selling prices (e.g., 3 for 500 versus 7 for 1,000), and adjusting over time for the ever-present inflation. In experimental tests, child candy vendors perform well on problems similar to those they encounter during selling but perform poorly on traditional school-type problems (Carraher, Carraher, & Schliemann, 1985; Saxe, 1991).

One reason that youthful street vendors calculate so well in the marketplace is that they order currency in a way that simplifies computation (Saxe, 1988). They also solve pricing problems by selling multiple units for specific bill denominations that are easy to manipulate mentally (Nunes, Schleimann, & Carraher, 1993; Saxe, 1991). This use of currency as an external problem-solving aid changes with development (Guberman, 1996). Although, when given a choice, vendors of all ages prefer to use currency as a problem-solving aid, it is most helpful to vendors with an intermediate level of skill who understand the currency system but have yet to make the shift from external aids to manipulating internal representations of quantity.

In addition to demonstrating the importance of cultural tools, the candy-selling studies illustrate another Vygotskian theme. This theme concerns the nurturing of children's intellectual development through the teaching and guidance provided by more competent members of the society. Candy vendors, especially the youngest ones, are not expected to master all the necessary mathematical tasks on their own. Help of various sorts is often provided. Parents may set the day's selling price before the child leaves the house. Storekeepers may help with various calculations. Peers and older siblings may provide both on-the-spot assistance and general models of how to proceed. As the child

Child candy vendors in Brazil must develop a number of mathematical skills in order to perform their task successfully.

grows older, these forms of assistance are gradually cut back. Older children are expected to do on their own what they once could do only with help.

One more change that comes with age is worth noting. In general, younger children are less competent vendors than are older ones. For example, they often offer just one price ratio rather than several, which might be expected to make their wares less attractive to prospective customers. Despite this seeming disadvantage, 6- to 7-year-old vendors make twice as many sales as do 12- to 15-year-olds. Clearly, being young and cute is one way to elicit help from adults.

To Recap . . .

Children's thinking grows more sophisticated as they master the tools provided by their culture. As they learn how to use these tools—which include symbol systems, material tools, and cultural practices—the way children think is transformed.

Tools vary in the ease with which they can be mastered. In some instances there are variations across cultures; for example, Asian number systems are in some respects easier to master than the English-language system. However, children often use even complex tools effectively long before they fully understand them because of the guidance of more capable members of their cultural communities and because tools themselves are often designed in ways that scaffold their use.

CONCLUSION

The sociocultural approach is the most recent of the three perspectives on cognitive development considered in detail in this book. Although Vygotsky was a contemporary of Jean Piaget, his ideas did not attract widespread attention in the West until the 1980s. Interest grew not only with the translation of some of Vygotsky's writings into English (a process that continues today) but with the publication of a number of interpretations of Vygotsy's ideas by a number of scholars.

In this chapter, we have glossed over the differences among the various approaches and the ways in which each diverges from Vygotksy's own views. Instead, we have focused on the commonalities among the various proponents of the sociocultural approach. These include an emphasis on the social origins of thought, the transformational powers of cultural tools and artifacts, and the importance of studying development in its cultural and historical context.

Over the past two decades, research from the sociocultural tradition has revealed much about the various ways in which culture and development are linked. However, as is true of advocates of the information-processing approach, researchers working within the sociocultural framework very much regard their efforts as work in progress. They, too, face significant challenges. We raise four of these challenges next.

Fans and critics alike have complained about the idealized portrayal of learning presented by those working within the sociocultural framework (Anderson, Reder, & Simon, 1996). As Goodnow (1996) observed, "one rarely finds, within Vygotskian-style analyses of learning, accounts of expert-novice interactions that depart from a picture of 'willing teachers/eager learners' " (p. 356). She points out that experts are not always so willing to give away all that they know. And novices are sometimes reluctant to take over responsibilities as soon as they have the competence to do so. To better understand the social origins of thought (and to have broader application to real-world learning), researchers need to examine learning in these less-than-optimal situations.

A second challenge has to do with the generality of learning. The issue is this: If intellectual skills are tied to specific cultural activities, how does one ever generalize knowledge learned in one context to another? To be sure, this issue of transfer has plagued Piagetians and information-processing theorists as well. But the problem takes on a somewhat different cast when competence itself is defined in terms of the individual-in-context (Anderson et al., 2000).

A third challenge faced by sociocultural researchers is how to effectively integrate across different levels or planes of analyses. In the vast majority of cultural research undertaken by psychologists, culture—or some aspect of culture, such as a particular tool or social arrangement—is treated not as a context but as an independent variable that affects or influences development. Few researchers collect data across multiple spheres of development as recommended by sociocultural theories (e.g., the micro-, meso-, exo-, and macrosystems in Bronfenbrenner's theory). In the absence of data from multiple levels of development, we may accumulate a great deal of fascinating information about lives in cultures around the world. This information may prove helpful in testing the universality of existing psychological theories. Nonetheless, this approach will offer only limited insights into the dynamic processes of development in cultural context.

Finally, to date, sociocultural researchers have paid little attention to developmental issues. In the words of Urie Bronfenbrenner, "In place of too much research on development 'out of context,' we now have a surfeit of studies on 'context without development'" (1986, p. 288). Developmental level, while in part a cultural construction, nonetheless influences the contexts that children inhabit, the nature of social interactions, and the effects of cultural-historical events on the child (Miller, 2001). And only recently have cultural psychologists begun to seriously address issues involving phylogenetic development (Tomasello, 1999).

FOR THOUGHT AND DISCUSSION

1. Sociocultural theories emphasize that learning is an inherently social process. *To illustrate this point, explain how a seemingly solitary activity—such as studying for a geography test—could be considered in fact a social activity.*

2. In many Western communities, child development experts place a great deal of importance on early exposure to a variety of objects, including toys. In other communities, object play is accorded less importance. *Might early experience with a variety of objects be more important is some cultures than others? Explain.*

3. We noted that the presence or absence of schooling is one important way in which cultures may differ in the opportunities they offer for the development of intellectual skills. *What are some other opportunities that may be present in some cultures and not others? Are there some aspects of cognitive development that you would expect not to vary across cultures? If so, what are they, and why would you expect them not to vary?*

4. In Western industrialized communities, children who solve problems quickly are generally viewed as more intelligent than children who are slower in coming to an answer. The value placed on speed is not universal, however. *What are some other cognitive values that might differ from culture to culture?*

5. Many teachers use peer learning in their classrooms. This practice is supported by a large body of evidence. *However, gifted students and their parents sometimes resent this practice, arguing that it holds the more capable students back. What do you think? Should peer learning be encouraged in schools? What are some of the problems you have experienced with peer learning? Under what conditions do you think it works best?*

6. When families reminisce about the past, they often retell the same events over and over again. These "family stories" reflect family values and beliefs and can shape how children come to view themselves. For example, we might imagine that recollections of the circumstances of Micah Makayla's birth will include references to Tommisheon's resourcefulness, courage, and intelligence. *What are some of your family stories? What "lessons" do your family stories convey?*

7. In this chapter, we described how a variety of tools and artifacts shape thinking. These include measurement tools, currency, classification schemes, and the like. *Describe how another tool or artifact not discussed in this chapter has changed the way you reason or solve problems.*

VISUAL SUMMARY FOR CHAPTER 9:
Cognitive Development: The Sociocultural Approach

The Nature of the Approach

Adherents to the sociocultural approach have been strongly influenced by the writings of the Soviet scholar Lev Vygotsky.

The Social Origins of Thought
> Cognitive development is fundamentally a social and cultural process. Children's cognitive capabilities develop during interactions with others in the zone of proximal development.

Tools and Artifacts
> Human thought and action are mediated by material and symbolic tools, especially language. Children learn to use these tools in collaborative interactions with more experienced others. The tools are gradually internalized and in the process transform children's thought.

Comparisons with Cognitive-Developmental Theories
> The sociocultural approach is similar to cognitive-developmental theories in focusing on the development of intellectual skills, viewing the child as an active participant in development, and considering development to involve both quantitative and qualitative change. The approaches differ in their views on how change occurs, what changes occur, and the universality of cognitive processes.

Object Exploration, Tool Use, and Play

Cultural Variation in Play
> Although play is universal across cultures, cultures vary in the amount of time children devote to play, who participates in play, and the nature of play. These variations are shaped by the physical and social settings in which children spend their time, customs of childrearing, and parental beliefs.

Interaction and Play
> Children learn to play and explore objects by interacting with more experienced partners. Infants and toddlers spend more time exploring objects and manipulate them in more complex ways when interacting with caregivers than when playing alone. Children's pretend play is also more sustained, elaborate, and sophisticated when a caregiver is involved. Siblings differ from adults as play partners in several respects: the importance of objects, the themes enacted, and the roles adopted.

Implications for Development
> Many studies find links between play and children's cognitive development. Because most of the research is correlational, however, it does not support firm cause–effect conclusions.

Memory

Sociocultural research on memory focuses primarily on mediated memory, which involves cultural tools and artifacts designed to aid memory. Children learn to use these tools while participating in cultural activities with more experienced partners.

Memory Strategies
> The use of memory strategies, such as rehearsal, organization, and elaboration, is associated with experience in school, where children are explicitly taught techniques to help them recall word lists, facts, and other such decontextualized information that is often the focus of school instruction.

Event Memory	Memory for events is mediated by scripts, which evolve from children's participation in routine, everyday events. Scripts generally aid memory but can impair memory when an unusual event is distorted to fit an existing script or when details of a recurring event merge with other instances of the same event. Talking with other people about events enhances recall and helps determine which details of the event will be remembered.
Autobiographical Memory	Conversations about past events also promote the development of autobiographical memory—memory about the self. Children who talk frequently and in an elaborative style with their parents tend to report earlier first memories and to recall more information.

Self-Regulation

Two kinds of self-regulation that are particularly valuable in problem solving are planning and private speech, both of which have their roots in social interaction.

Planning	Caregivers begin to talk about plans with their children when the children are very young, long before they can fully appreciate the significance of the plans. Caregivers also scaffold the development of children's planning skills as they participate jointly in everyday routines and problem-solving activities.
Private Speech	Children learn to use private speech by working on tasks under the guidance of an adult. Over time, the children adopt the instructional comments originally offered by the adult as their own. Private speech is observed most frequently among preschoolers and on problems that are challenging but not overwhelming.

Peer Interaction and Cognitive Change

Peer Teaching	Peer teaching involves pairing children who are relatively expert in the task at hand with less capable peers. Children often find it a challenge to provide instruction that is sensitive to learners' needs. Hence, peer teaching often leads to greater advances for the teacher than for the learner and may be best suited for reinforcing existing knowledge.
Collaboration	In peer collaboration, pairs or groups of children with roughly equal knowledge work together to solve problems. Collaboration can promote conceptual change as children coordinate and build on the different ideas that they bring to the joint effort.
Peer Learning in Classrooms	Children can also learn from peers in classroom activities in which the teacher models, guides, and structures children's discussions.

Cultural Artifacts and Material Tools

Children's thinking grows more sophisticated as they master the tools provided by their culture, such as number systems, measuring systems, and currency. Tools vary in the ease with which they can be mastered. However, children often use even complex tools effectively long before they fully understand them because of the guidance of more capable members of their communities and because tools themselves are often designed in ways that scaffold their use.

10

Intelligence and Schooling

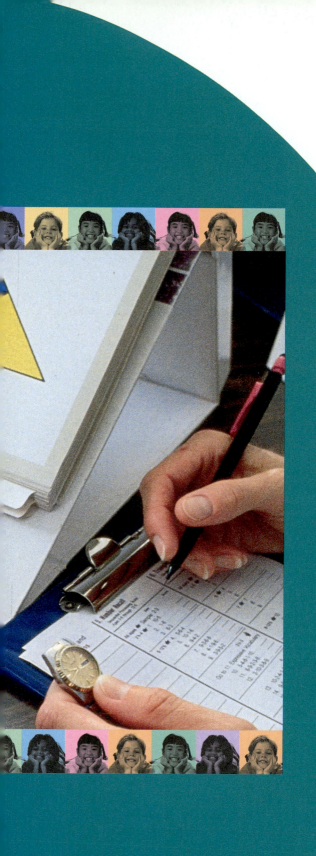

"**W**e pick out the brightest children, those with the most potential, and then send them off with the goats," explains Johnson Kinyago, a Masai herder in Kenya. "It takes brains to identify each animal, find water, and ward off cattle rustlers. School is for those who are less quick."

It is not difficult to understand why schools based on the model so prevalent in industrialized societies might seem irrelevant to the Masai, one of the few migratory groups remaining in East Africa. Traditionally, these herders have followed their cattle from place to place, setting up temporary camps, and the schooling they have valued has been the kind needed to pursue their nomadic lifestyle. For example, adult Masai would begin teaching 4- to 5-year-olds to look after animals by having them care for young lambs and calves. At age 5 to 7, children could look after older cows and accompany adults as they herded cattle. Eventually, boys could migrate long distances with the cattle, while girls helped their mothers with chores like drawing water and cutting wood.

Today, though, changes have begun to appear in this traditional way of life. The Masai do not have enough land to support their population, and years of drought have depleted the cattle herds, leaving many people dependent on food aid. In the view of some Masai, formal schooling has become necessary. "Land issues have caused a crisis . . . and this is threatening our whole people," says Peter Lowara, who works with a group called Osiligi.

"Unless we find alternatives we will die, which means we must become educated."

Osiligi ("hope" in Masai) is conducting informal classes for young Masai herders. In the classes, which meet for a few hours under the trees along the herders' migration routes, the subjects are Swahili, English, and math, along with animal husbandry, hygiene, and Masai culture. A few of the students will move on into the formal education system and eventually get jobs. The others will have edged a little closer to the modern world. "The thing is to control the pace of change," says James Legei of Osiligi.

For the Masai, changes in environment are making it necessary to change the content of schooling. It is likely that along with this change will come some change in the idea of what constitutes intelligence. The best reader, for example, will not necessarily be the best herder. In industrialized cultures, the definition of intelligence is strongly linked to formal schooling. As you will see, the well-known IQ test was formulated to predict success in school. But as you will also see, intelligence even in industrialized cultures can be defined in various ways. ■

Psychometric

An approach to the study of intelligence that emphasizes the use of standardized tests to identify individual differences among people.

In this chapter we consider the issues of intelligence and schooling. Our focus is on a particular approach to defining and measuring intelligence: the **psychometric,** or intelligence-test, approach. Consideration of this approach will both broaden our picture of children's intellectual development and immerse us in some of the most controversial issues in the field.

Why has the intelligence-test approach been so controversial? At least part of the answer lies in some important differences between this approach and the Piagetian, information-processing, and sociocultural perspectives. Some of the differences relate to the distinction between normative and idiographic approaches to development, one of the general issues identified in Chapter 1. Piaget's approach falls clearly under the normative heading, in that his emphasis was always on similarities in children's development—that is, forms of knowledge that all children develop and stages all children move through. Although information-processing researchers have paid more attention to individual differences than did Piaget, they also have tended to concentrate on basic processes that are common to all children.

In contrast, the main point of the intelligence-test approach is to identify differences in children's cognitive abilities. Furthermore, an IQ test identifies not merely differences but *ordered* differences—it says that one child is more or less intelligent than another or that a particular child is above or below average in intelligence. IQ tests thus involve an evaluative component that is impossible to escape, which is one reason that they have always been controversial. The evaluative nature of IQ provides a point of contrast not only with Piaget and information processing but also with the sociocultural perspective. As we have seen, sociocultural researchers often do identify differences in what children know or how they think; their emphasis, however, is on the cognitive strengths that children develop within a particular cultural setting, not on the deficiencies of one group relative to another.

Another difference between the intelligence-test approach and the other perspectives concerns purpose and uses. The research discussed in the three preceding chapters was very much theoretically oriented, its goal being to identify basic cognitive processes. We saw that such research has begun to have practical applications (e.g., effects on school curriculum); to date, however, such applications have been limited and secondary to the basic theoretical aims. In contrast, the psychometric approach has been pragmatically oriented from the start. As we will see, IQ tests were designed for practical purposes, and they have always had practical uses—most notably, to determine what kind of schooling a child is to receive. This factor, too, contributes to the controversy. Unlike many of psychologists' measures, IQ tests really can make a difference in a child's life.

In this chapter, we begin by reviewing what IQ tests for children look like, along with some of their strengths and weaknesses. We then move on to some of the theoretical issues that have been the focus of research in the psychometric tradition. Because of the importance of the question, we pay special attention to the role of experience in the development of intelligence, with a focus on schooling as it both contributes to and is affected by individual differences in intelligence. Although our emphasis is on IQ, we occasionally broaden the scope to include other ways to assess differences in intellectual ability. And in the final part of the chapter, we break away from the traditional IQ approach to consider some recent and exciting alternative approaches to studying intelligence.

THE NATURE OF IQ TESTS

Before we discuss results from the use of IQ tests, it is important to have some idea of how such tests are put together and what kinds of abilities they measure. We begin, therefore, with an overview of the history and construction of IQ tests. We take a brief look at several specific tests and then turn to the important question of how to evaluate such measures.

The Binet Approach to Measuring Intelligence

The first successful intelligence test was developed in Paris in 1905 by Alfred Binet and Theodore Simon. From the start, the IQ approach was tied in to success in school. Binet and Simon had been hired by the Paris school authorities to develop a test that could be given to children who were having difficulty in school. The goal was to distinguish between children who were capable, perhaps with extra help, of succeeding in school and children who were simply not intelligent enough to cope with the regular curriculum. Once the latter group had been identified, they could be placed in special classes from which they might benefit. This sort of tracking based on test performance has become controversial in recent years (Dornbusch, Glasgow, & Lin, 1996), but originally it had a quite humanitarian purpose.

Binet and Simon took a pragmatic approach to their task. They tried out a large number of possible items for their test, looking at performance across both a range of ages and a range of ability levels (i.e., children who were known to do well in school and children who were known to do poorly in school). All the items kept for the test were items on which older children, on the average, did better than younger children. Such improvement with age was one of Binet and Simon's criteria for a measure of childhood intelligence. These items also tended to differentiate between academically successful children and those who were less successful, which, of course, was the immediate purpose for which the test was designed. The test items, some of which appear in modified form on contemporary tests, included identification of parts of the body, naming of familiar objects, and distinguishing between abstract words—for example, indicating the difference between liking and respecting.

IQ tests were originally devised for purposes of school placement in Paris school systems in the early 1900s. Such educational applications remain important for contemporary IQ tests.

The Stanford-Binet Intelligence Scale (Roid, 2003) is the direct descendant of the original Binet-Simon test. It was developed in 1916 by Lewis Terman at Stanford University and has been revised several times since. The Stanford-Binet shares several features with Binet's original instrument. Although it can be used with adults, it is primarily a test of childhood intelligence, applicable to every age group within the span of childhood except infancy. It is a global measure of intelligence, designed to yield a single intelligence quotient, or IQ, score that summarizes the child's ability. And it stresses the kinds of verbal and academic skills that are important in school. Specifically, the current version of the Stanford-Binet assesses five general kinds of ability: quantitative reasoning, fluid reasoning, visual-spatial processing, knowledge, and working memory.

The Stanford-Binet—and indeed every other standardized test of intelligence—shares one other important feature with Binet's original test. We saw that Binet's approach to measuring intelligence was based on comparing the performances of different groups of children. All contemporary tests of intelligence are comparative, or relative, measures. There is no absolute metric for measuring intelligence, as there is for measuring height or weight. Instead, a child's IQ is a function of how that child's performance compares with the performance of other children the same age. Children who perform at the average for their age group have average IQs, which by convention are set at 100. Children who outperform their peers have above-average IQs; children who lag behind their age group have below-average IQs. The greater the discrepancy from average, the higher or lower the IQ will be.

Other Tests of Childhood Intelligence

The leading alternative to the Stanford-Binet is a series of tests developed by David Wechsler. There are two Wechsler tests designed for childhood: the Wechsler Intelligence Scale for Children (WISC-III), which is intended for ages 6 to 16, and the Wechsler Preschool and Primary Scale of Intelligence (WPPSI), which is intended for ages 4 to 6.5 (Wechsler, 1989, 1991). The Wechsler test bears many similarities to the Stanford-Binet, including a focus on academically relevant skills. One difference between the two tests is that the Wechsler is divided into a verbal scale (which includes items such as vocabulary and general information) and a performance scale (which includes items such as assembling a

Table 10.1	Types of Items Included on the Wechsler Intelligence Scale for Children—Third Edition

Subtest	**Verbal Scale**
Information	How many wings does a bird have? How many nickels make a dime? What is pepper?
Arithmetic	Sam had three pieces of candy and Joe gave him four more. How many pieces of candy did Sam have altogether? If two apples cost $.15, what will be the cost of a dozen apples?
Vocabulary	What is a _____? or What does .... mean? Hammer Protect Epidemic
Subtest	**Performance Scale**
Object assembly	Put the pieces together to make a familiar object.

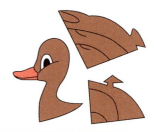

SOURCE: Adapted from *Wechsler Intelligence Scale for Children—Third Edition.* Copyright © 1991 by The Psychological Corporation. Reproduced by permission. All rights reserved.

puzzle and reproducing a design). The test therefore yields both an overall IQ and separate verbal and performance IQs. Some examples of the kinds of items included on the Wechsler test are shown in Table 10.1.

A relatively recent entry to the field of childhood assessment is a test developed by Kaufman and Kaufman (1983). The Kaufman Assessment Battery for Children, or K-ABC, marks an explicit effort to include cultural diversity and cultural fairness in the construction and administration of a test. The K-ABC thus attempts to answer one long-standing criticism of traditional IQ tests—namely, that such measures may discriminate against children from poor or minority families. The K-ABC also has a grounding in information-processing conceptions of intelligence, a grounding motivated by another criticism leveled at traditional measures, that they are empirically derived instruments that lack a clear theoretical rationale.

Other tests of childhood IQ focus on infancy, the one age period not encompassed by the Stanford-Binet and Wechsler tests. The best-known measure of infant development is the Bayley Scales of Infant Development (Bayley, 1993). Not surprisingly, measures of infant intelligence tend to stress sensorimotor skills, as opposed to the academic and verbal emphasis found in tests for older children. The Bayley test, for example, is divided into a motor scale (with items assessing control of the body, muscular coordination, manipulatory skill, and so on) and a mental scale (including items assessing sensory-perceptual acuity, vocalization, and memory). Table 10.2 presents some items from the mental scale.

Evaluating the Tests

How can we decide whether a test that claims to measure intelligence really does? A standardized test of intelligence—or indeed of any attribute—must meet two criteria: reliability and validity.

Reliability   The consistency or repeatability of measurement is referred to as **reliability.** Does the test give us a consistent picture of what the child can do? Or do scores on the test

Reliability
The consistency or repeatability of a measuring instrument. A necessary property of a standardized test.

| Table 10.2 | Examples of Items from the Bayley Scales of Infant Development |

Age Placement (in months)	Ability Measured	Procedure	Credit
1	Habituates to rattle	Shake rattle at regular intervals behind child's head	If child shows an initial alerting response that decreases over trials
6	Smiles at mirror image	Place mirror in front of child	If child smiles at image in mirror
12	Pushes car	Push toy car while child watches, then tell child, "Push the car, push the car like I did"	If child intentionally pushes car so that all four wheels stay on table
17–19	Uses two different words appropriately	Record the child's spontaneous word usage throughout the exam	If child uses two (nonimitative) words appropriately
23–25	Points to five pictures	Show pictures of 10 common objects (e.g., dog book, car), say "Show me the _____"	If child either correctly points to or names at least five pictures

SOURCE: From *Bayley Scales of Infant Development,* second edition. Copyright © 1993 by The Psychological Corporation. Reprinted by permission. All rights reserved.

fluctuate from one testing occasion to the next, perhaps sometimes coming out very high and sometimes very low? Clearly, a test that lacks reliability can hardly provide an accurate measure of the child's ability.

The notion of reliability does not mean that children's IQ scores can never change. Scores often do go up or down as children develop. Reliability refers to short-term consistency—that is, to the constancy of the measuring instrument, not of the child. The major tests of childhood IQ, such as the Stanford-Binet and Wechsler, do possess good reliability.

Validity
The accuracy with which a measuring instrument assesses the attribute it is designed to measure. A necessary property of a standardized test.

Validity   The second criterion that a test must meet is validity. The issue of **validity** is easy to summarize: Does the test measure what it claims to measure? Do scores on the Stanford-Binet, for example, really reflect individual differences in children's intelligence? Or do the scores have some other basis—perhaps differences in motivation, or in general test-taking ability, or in familiarity with the specific test content?

The validity of a test can be determined in various ways. The approach most commonly used for IQ tests is labeled *criterion validity*. To determine criterion validity, we first specify some external measure, or criterion, of the attribute that we are attempting to assess. We then see whether scores on the test relate to performance on this external criterion. For tests of childhood IQ, the most common external criterion has been performance in school or on standardized tests of academic ability. Tests such as the Stanford-Binet do in fact relate to academic performance, with typical correlations of about .5 to .6 (Brody, 1997; Sternberg, Grigorenko, & Bundy, 2001). Thus, on the average, the higher the child's IQ, the better the child does in school.

Academic performance is not the only correlate of IQ. IQ also correlates with most standard laboratory measures of learning and cognitive performance—not perfectly, to be sure, but with typical values of around .5 (Jensen, 1981). IQ in adulthood correlates, again at a midrange level, with indices of occupational status and with measures of job performance (Hunter & Hunter, 1984). Indeed, as we saw in the discussion of the Terman study of genius (Chapter 2), high IQ is associated with a wide range of favorable life outcomes. It is this ability to predict important aspects of everyday intelligent behavior that constitutes the argument for IQ tests as valid measures of intelligence.

It is important to note some qualifications to the points just made. Consider the relation between IQ and performance in school. A correlation of .5 indicates a moderate relation between IQ and academic performance. But if the correlation is only .5, there must also be a number of exceptions to this on-the-average relation—children with high IQs who do poorly in school, children with average or below-average IQs who do well in school. Knowing a child's IQ does not allow us to predict that child's school performance (or, indeed, anything else) with certainty. Furthermore, as we saw in Chapter 2, a correlation in itself does not allow us to determine the cause and effect. Thus, simply knowing that IQ correlates with school performance does not allow us to conclude that children do well or poorly in school *because* of their IQs. This is one possible explanation for the correlation, but it is not the only one. All we know for certain is that there is some relation between the two variables.

We can note finally that there is a kind of inbred relation between IQ tests and school performance. IQ tests for children were devised to predict school performance, and this is what they do (although not perfectly). Performance in school is important in our culture; so, too, is performance in the occupational contexts to which school success often leads. It is reasonable to argue, therefore, that IQ tests do measure something of what we mean by intelligence in our culture. But the qualifications implied by this wording are important. IQ tests may not tap cognitive skills that are important in other cultures, for example (as discussed in Chapter 7), the ability to navigate in a society in which sailing is important or (as discussed in Chapter 9) the ability to succeed as an urban candy vendor at an age when most Western children have barely started school. These tests may not even tap skills that are important for some subgroups within our culture, such as the ability to do chores on the family farm or to cope with the challenges of life in an inner-city ghetto. And for any individual, they at best measure *something* of intelligence, not everything that we would want this term to mean. The three preceding chapters considered numerous aspects of intelligence that are not well captured by IQ tests. Later in this chapter, we will see that even within the psychometric tradition there are a number of interesting alternatives to IQ.

IQ tests are most successful at measuring skills necessary for success in school. Such tests may not capture forms of intelligence that are important in other contexts.

To Recap . . .

The purpose of IQ tests is to measure individual differences in intellectual ability. Such tests were originally devised for practical purposes, and they have always had practical applications—school placement, for example. Such real-world applications contribute to the controversy that has always surrounded IQ tests.

Tests of intelligence must be both reliable and valid. The major IQ tests do possess satisfactory reliability. Whether the tests are valid measures of intelligence has been more difficult to determine. Tests of childhood IQ do relate to measures of academic performance, an important external criterion of childhood intelligence. The relation is not perfect, however. Furthermore, the academic focus of most IQ tests means that they may not be good measures of other kinds of intelligence.

ISSUES IN THE STUDY OF INTELLIGENCE

We have emphasized the pragmatic origins and uses of IQ tests. But the early pioneers of intelligence testing, including Binet, were also interested in theoretical questions about the nature of intelligence, and IQ tests have long served as another context, in addition to cognitive-developmental and sociocultural approaches, for addressing basic questions about cognitive development. In this section we consider some of the theoretical issues that have most intrigued researchers in the intelligence-test tradition.

Organization of Intelligence

The question of the organization or structure of intelligence is a basic issue that any approach to intelligence must confront. We have seen how Piagetian and information-processing researchers have examined this question. Psychometric researchers also study the organization of intelligence, but the methods they use are different from those we have encountered thus far.

In the psychometric approach, conclusions about the organization of intelligence are based on the individual differences that IQ tests elicit. The issue is whether these differences show consistent and interpretable patterns, patterns that can tell us something about how intelligence is organized.

Let us consider two opposed possibilities. Suppose that intelligence is a unitary trait—that is, that there is a single "general intelligence" that people possess in varying degrees. If so, then the particular task that we use to measure intelligence should not really matter. Some people—those who are high in general intelligence—will do well whatever the task, and some will do poorly whatever the task. This outcome would be reflected in uniformly high correlations among different measures of intelligence.

Consider now a very different hypothesis. Perhaps there is no such thing as general intelligence. Perhaps, instead, there are various specific intelligences—verbal intelligence, mathematical intelligence, spatial intelligence, and so on. People may be high in one form of intelligence but low in some other form. What happens, then, if we administer a test battery that assesses these different forms of intelligence? We no longer expect uniformly high correlations among our measures. Instead, a particular task should correlate most strongly with other tasks that are measuring the same kind of intelligence. Verbal tasks, for example, should correlate strongly with other verbal tasks, but weakly or not at all with measures of spatial ability.

The preceding example summarizes the psychometric approach to the organization of intelligence: determine how intelligence is organized by examining the pattern of correlations across different measures of intelligence. In practice, the approach is more complicated than this brief description suggests. Psychometric researchers use a complex statistical procedure called *factor analysis* to make sense of the large number of correlations that their research yields. There are disagreements about exactly how to carry out and interpret factor analyses, and results may vary depending on the method used. Results may also vary across different batteries of tasks or different samples of participants (Kail & Pellegrino, 1985). Thus, psychometric researchers provide no single, agreed-on answer to the structure question. But they have offered some interesting theories and related findings.

General versus Specific   We have already previewed the question that has generated the most interest and debate among researchers of the organization of intelligence: Is intelligence a single general ability, or does intelligence consist instead of a number of specific abilities?

The earliest proponent of the general-intelligence view was the inventor of factor analysis, Charles Spearman. Spearman proposed what has come to be called a *two-factor theory of intelligence* (Spearman, 1927). One factor is general intelligence, or **g**. In Spearman's view, g permeates every form of intellectual functioning and is the most important determinant of individual differences on any test of intelligence. The second factor is *s*, Spearman's label for specific abilities that contribute to performance on particular tasks. Spearman used his newly invented technique of factor analysis to analyze correlations among different measures of intelligence. His conclusion was that the consistently positive correlations across measures were evidence for the existence and importance of g.

g
General intelligence; g is assumed to determine performance on a wide range of intellectual measures.

Other theorists have argued for a more differentiated model. Louis Thurstone, for example, developed an intelligence test designed to assess seven primary mental abilities: verbal comprehension, verbal fluency, number, spatial visualization, memory, reasoning, and perceptual speed (Thurstone, 1938; Thurstone & Thurstone, 1962). Thurstone regarded these seven abilities as largely independent and equally important.

Seven is by no means the maximum number of abilities that have been proposed. In J. P. Guilford's structure of the intellect model, there are at least 180 somewhat distinct mental abilities (Guilford, 1988)!

Conclusions   What is the solution to the general-versus-specific dispute? As is often the case, the answer probably lies somewhere between extreme positions (Sternberg & Grigorenko, 2002b). The consistent finding of positive correlations among different measures of intelligence is evidence that something like general intelligence does exist. The fact that the correlations are far from perfect is evidence that more specific subskills also exist. This sort of solution is sometimes referred to as a **hierarchical model of intelligence**—intelligence is seen as organized in a hierarchical fashion, with broad, general abilities at the top of the hierarchy and more limited, specific skills nested underneath (Sternberg, 1985). This model probably corresponds to the intuitions that most of us hold about intelligence. We have some ability to order people, including ourselves, along some general dimension of intelligence. But we also realize that different people have different strengths and weaknesses and that we may outshine a particular peer in some respects yet lag behind in others.

Hierarchical model of intelligence
A model of the structure of intelligence in which intellectual abilities are seen as being organized hierarchically, with broad, general abilities at the top of the hierarchy and more specific skills nested underneath.

Stability of IQ

Do children's IQs remain stable as they develop, so that we can assume that a child who scores a 100 at age 4 will also score 100 at ages 8 or 12 or 20? Or can a child's IQ change? This is a question of both theoretical and practical importance.

Answering the question requires a longitudinal approach, in which the same children are tested repeatedly across some span of time. Researchers have conducted many longitudinal studies of IQ, including some essentially life-span efforts that began in the 1920s (Bayley, 1970). We therefore have quite a bit of data on this issue. Several conclusions emerge.

Prediction from Infancy   A first conclusion is that traditional tests of infant intelligence do not predict well to tests of later intelligence. The correlation between performance on the Bayley Scales, for example, and performance on later tests is typically close to 0 (Lipsitt, 1992; McCall, 1981). There are some exceptions to this statement: Very low scores on infant tests sometimes indicate some problem in development (Siegel, 1989), and scores on particular subparts of an infant test (such as items dealing with fine motor skills) may relate to measures of similar skills on childhood tests (Siegel, 1992). For the most part, however, individual differences in infant scores do not tell us much about how children will differ later in development.

Why should there be this gap between infant intelligence and later intelligence? The usual explanation stresses the differences in the content of infant tests and childhood tests (Brownell & Strauss, 1984). Tests such as the Stanford-Binet and WISC emphasize symbolic abilities (such as language) and abstract, higher-order reasoning and problem solving. Infant tests necessarily stress quite different things—manual dexterity, visual and auditory alertness, and so on. This explanation is related to the continuity-discontinuity issue introduced in Chapter 1. The argument is that there is a discontinuity in the nature of intelligence between infancy and later childhood. Intelligence in infancy requires different skills than those required by later intelligence, and thus it is not surprising that variations in infant development do not relate to variations in later development.

There is almost certainly some truth to the discontinuity argument. But to many psychologists, there is something unsatisfactory about any extreme version of the hypothesis. Surely there must be *some* continuity from infancy to childhood, *some* aspect of intelligence that is common across all age periods. But what might this common thread be?

Recent research suggests that the common thread may be response to novelty. This conclusion comes from longitudinal studies in which children who were first tested as infants are later assessed for childhood IQ. Investigators have reported positive relations between various measures of interest in and response to novelty in infancy and later measures of intelligence (Bornstein, 1998; Colombo, 1993; McCall & Carriger, 1993). For example, babies who show an especially strong preference for new compared with familiar stimuli tend to do well on later IQ tests (Fagan, 1992; Rose & Feldman, 1995). Similarly, babies who are especially quick to habituate to familiar stimuli tend to perform well on later tests (Slater et al., 1989). The relations that have been demonstrated are modest in size, with typical correlations in the range of .35 to .40. Nevertheless, these findings provide a first piece of evidence for some continuity in intelligence from infancy to later childhood.

As might be expected, the studies of response to novelty have led to the creation of a new approach to assessing infant intelligence. In the Fagan Test of Infant Intelligence (Fagan & Detterman, 1992; Fagan & Shepherd, 1986), babies are shown a picture to look at for a brief period, after which the original picture is paired with a slightly different, novel picture (see Figure 10.1). The measure of interest is how long the baby looks at the novel compared with the familiar. The greater the interest in novelty, the higher the score on the test. And the higher the Fagan score, the higher, on the average, the later IQ.

Prediction across Childhood   After infancy, scores from traditional IQ tests begin to correlate significantly from one age period to another. The correlation is not perfect, however. A typical set of findings is shown in Table 10.3.

Two rules for predicting stability in IQ can be abstracted from the data in the table. A first rule is that the degree of stability decreases as the time period between tests increases. Thus, we typically find more similarity in IQ between ages 3 and 6 than between ages 3 and 12. This pattern fits what we would expect from common sense: The longer we wait between tests, the more chance there is for some change to occur. Indeed, this pattern is not limited to IQ but applies generally whenever we measure stability or change across varying time periods (Nunnally, 1982).

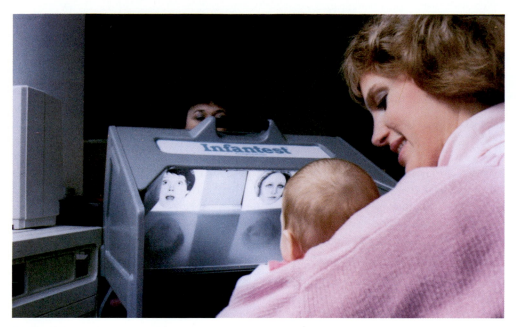

Figure 10.1

The Fagan Test of Infant Intelligence. Infants are first exposed to one of the two members of each stimulus pair, then given a chance to look at either the familiar stimulus or the novel alternative. A relatively strong preference for novelty correlates positively with later IQ. From "Predictive Validity of the Fagan Test of Infant Intelligence" by J. F. Fagan III, P. Shepherd, and C. Knevel, 1991, Meeting of the Society for Research in Child Development, Seattle. Copyright © 1993 by J. F. Fagan III. Reprinted by permission.

As an illustration of the second rule, consider a comparison between the 3-to-6 correlation and the 9-to-12 correlation. Both reflect a 3-year interval; hence by our first rule we would expect them to be equivalent. But the correlation is greater between 9 and 12 than it is between 3 and 6. In general, the older the child, the higher the correlation in IQ for any given span of time. This pattern, too, fits common sense. As children get older, major changes in their abilities relative to those of other children become less and less likely.

Another way to examine the stability question is to ask about the magnitude of changes in IQ. If children's IQs do change (and the less-than-perfect correlations tell us that they do), how large can the changes be? One study found that 79% of a sample of children shifted at least 21 points in IQ between the ages of 2.5 and 17. For 14% of the children, the change was 40 points or more (McCall, Applebaum, & Hogarty, 1973).

In summary, probably the most reasonable position on the stability issue is one that avoids extreme statements in either direction. It is not correct to suggest that IQ varies wildly as children develop and that childhood IQ therefore has no predictive value. IQ shows moderately good stability, and the stability increases as the child gets older. On

Table 10.3	Correlations in IQ across Different Ages				
Age	3	6	9	12	18
3		.57	.53	.36	.35
6			.80	.74	.61
9				.90	.76
12					.78

SOURCE: Based on information from "The Stability of Mental Test Performance between Two and Eighteen Years" by M. P. Honzik, J. W. MacFarlan, and L. Allen, *Journal of Experimental Education, 17,* p. 323, 1948. Reprinted with permission of the Helen Reid Educational Foundation. Published by Heldref Publications, 1319 Eighteenth St., N.W., Washington, D.C. 20036–1802. Copyright © 1948.

the other hand, it is also not correct to suggest that a child's IQ is fixed and unchangeable. IQs do change, and in some cases they change dramatically. We consider some of the reasons for change shortly.

Origins of Individual Differences

Our discussion of IQ has already touched on two of the issues introduced in Chapter 1—normative versus idiographic emphasis and continuity versus discontinuity. We turn next to the third and most general issue—nature versus nurture. The question of the origin of differences in intelligence has been perhaps the most common—and certainly the most heated—context for debates about the relative contributions of biology and experience to human development.

We first considered this question in Chapter 3 in the discussion of hereditary transmission. As we noted, researchers use three main approaches to study this question: family studies, adoption studies, and twin studies.

Family Studies   Family studies (also labeled kinship studies) capitalize on our knowledge of the degree of genetic relation among different sorts of relatives. Parent and child, for example, have 50% of their genes in common. Two siblings also share an average of 50% of their genes. For grandparent and grandchild, the average genetic overlap is 25%. For first cousins, the overlap is 12.5%. In general, if we know the type of relation between two people, we know their degree of genetic similarity. We can then see whether similarity in IQ relates to similarity in genes.

Similarity in IQ *does* relate to similarity in genes. Typical correlations in IQ across different degrees of relation are shown in Table 10.4. These findings fit nicely with what would be expected from a genetic model of intelligence.

Adoption Studies   The problem in interpreting the family studies, of course, is that genetic similarity is not the only possible explanation for similarity in IQ. The pattern shown in Table 10.4 might also be accounted for by environmental factors. Siblings, after all, usually share similar experiences. Parents are typically an important part of their children's environments. We would expect some relation between the parent's IQ and the child's IQ solely for environmental reasons.

You may recall that studies of adopted children offer a way to disentangle the genetic and environmental explanations for parent–child similarity. Two sets of correlations are relevant. One is the correlation between the adopted child's IQ and the biological parents' IQs. In this case, the usual genetic basis for a correlation remains, but the environmental basis is ruled out. The other correlation of interest is that between the adopted child's IQ and the adoptive parents' IQs. In this case, the environmental basis remains, but the genetic contribution is ruled out.

Table 10.4	Correlations in IQ as a Function of Degree of Genetic Relation
Relation	**Median Correlation**
Siblings	.55
Parent–child	.50
Grandparents–grandchild	.27
First cousins	.26
Second cousins	.16

SOURCE: Adapted from "Genetics and the Development of Intelligence" by S. Scarr-Salapatek, 1975. In F. D. Horowitz (Ed.), *Review of Child Development Research* (Vol. 4, p. 33), Chicago: University of Chicago Press. Copyright © 1975 by the University of Chicago Press. Adapted by permission.

Before discussing findings, we should note that adoption studies are not really as easy to interpret as this description suggests. In some cases, for example, when the separation of mother and infant does not occur at birth, the biological mother provides part of the postbirth environment. In all cases, the biological mother provides the prenatal environment, which — as we saw in Chapter 4 — can be important. There is also the possibility of selective placement, through which adoption agencies attempt to match characteristics of the adoptive parents with characteristics of the biological parents. To the extent that selective placement occurs, parent–child correlations cannot be clearly interpreted as either genetic or environmental (Horn, 1983).

Two main findings emerge from adoption studies (Plomin et al., 1997; Turkheimer, 1991). One concerns the pattern of correlations. Typically, the adopted child's IQ correlates more strongly with the IQs of the biological parents than with the IQs of the adoptive parents. This finding provides evidence for the importance of genetic factors. The biological parents make relatively little contribution to an adopted child's environment, but they do provide the child's genes. Recall from our discussion in Chapter 3 that studies of siblings paint a similar picture: stronger correlations for biological siblings than for children adopted into the same home.

The second finding concerns average level of IQ. In most studies the mean IQ for samples of adopted children falls in the range of 105 to 110 (Capron & Duyme, 1989; Scarr & Weinberg, 1983). Adopted children thus tend to have above-average IQs. Why should this be? The most plausible explanation is an environmental one. Parents who adopt children are not a random subset of the population of parents, nor are adoptive homes a random subset of the population of homes. Adoptive parents tend to be highly motivated parents, and adoptive homes tend to be privileged in various ways (such as having a large number of books available and access to good-quality schools for the children). These factors apparently boost the IQs of children who grow up in such

Adoptive homes often offer intellectually stimulating environments, and children who grow up in such homes tend to have above-average IQs.

settings. Thus, the adoption studies provide evidence for both genetic and environmental effects.

Twin Studies   The logic of the twin-study approach was explained in Chapter 3. There are two types of twins: monozygotic, or identical, twins, who are genetically identical, and dizygotic, or fraternal, twins, who have only a 50% genetic overlap and thus are no more related than are ordinary siblings. Researchers have compared correlations in IQ for members of identical twin pairs with correlations in IQ for members of fraternal twin pairs. If genes are important, the first set of correlations should be higher than the second.

The results from many such studies were summarized in Table 3.2 (see page 80). The consistent finding is that identical twins *are* more similar (McGue et al., 1993; Nichols, 1978). The same pattern emerges for tests of more specific abilities — for example, verbal and mathematical skills or spatial reasoning ability (Plomin, 1990).

Like family studies, twin studies are compatible with a genetic model, but they do not prove it correct. Environmental factors again provide an alternative explanation. Perhaps identical twins are treated more similarly than are fraternal twins. If so, the greater similarity in IQ may have an environmental rather than a genetic basis.

Researchers have tried in various ways to control for this environmental alternative. Some have attempted to measure aspects of the twins' environments to see whether identical twins are in fact treated more similarly than are fraternal twins. Investigators have concluded that such differential treatment is less marked than is often claimed; furthermore, to the extent that it does occur, it appears to be elicited by preexisting characteristics of the twins, such as the greater physical similarity or more similar temperaments of identical twins. In this view, then, the similarity between identical twins leads to their being treated similarly, not the reverse (Lytton, 1977, 1980).

The most widely cited attempt to control for environmental factors comes in the study of twins reared apart. If identical twins are separated early in life and reared in unrelated environments, then there is no environmental basis (other than prenatal experiences) for their developing similarly. The twins still share 100% of their genes, however. Should they still correlate in IQ, powerful evidence for the importance of genes would be gained.

Table 10.5 summarizes results from studies of twins reared apart. The values in the table indicate that separated twins correlate quite substantially in IQ. Indeed, the reported correlations are higher for identical twins reared apart than they are for fraternal twins reared in the same home (Bouchard, 1997; Segal, 1999)!

The Concept of Heritability   The three kinds of evidence that we have considered all point to the same conclusion: Both differences in genes and differences in environments can lead to differences in IQ. This conclusion is important, but very general. Can we go beyond a general statement that both factors are important to say something about their relative importance?

It is important to emphasize that the question of relative importance makes sense only when we are talking about differences among people. Any individual's intelligence clearly depends on both genes and environment, and there is no way, when talking about individual development, to disentangle the two factors or label one as more important than the other. We simply would not exist without both genes and environment, let alone have a height or weight or an IQ to explain.

Suppose, however, that we are studying a sample of people who differ in IQ and we wish to determine the origin of these differences. In this case, the question of relative importance *does* make sense. The differences among the members of our sample may be totally or predominantly genetic in origin, totally or predominantly environmental in origin, or a reflection of some more even mixture of genetic and environmental factors.

Researchers who attempt to determine relative importance make use of exactly the sorts of data that we have been discussing—kinship correlations, adoption studies, and twin studies. What they add to these data is a set of statistical procedures for calculating the heritability of IQ. The term **heritability** refers to the proportion of variance in a trait that can be attributed to genetic variance in the sample being studied. It is, in other words, an estimate of the extent to which differences among people come from differences in

Heritability
The proportion of variance in a trait (such as IQ) that can be attributed to genetic variance in the sample being studied.

Table 10.5	Correlations in IQ of Related and Unrelated Children Reared Together or Apart	
Relationship and Rearing Condition	**Average Correlation**	**Number of Pairs**
Identical twins reared together	.86	4,672
Fraternal twins reared together	.60	5,533
Siblings reared together	.47	26,473
Unrelated children reared together	.32	714
Identical twins reared apart	.72	65

SOURCE: Adapted from "Familial Studies of Intelligence: A Review" by T. J. Bouchard, Jr. and M. McGue, 1981, *Science*, p. 1056. Copyright © 1981 by the American Association for the Advancement of Science. Adapted by permission.

their genes as opposed to differences in their environments. The heritability statistic ranges from 0 (all of the differences are environmental in origin) to 1 (all of the differences are genetic in origin).

The most widely accepted contemporary estimates of the heritability of IQ place the value at about .4 to .7, with figures toward the lower end of the range more typical in childhood and somewhat higher values for adult samples (Grigorenko, 2000; Hay, 1999; Plomin et al., 1997). By these estimates, then, approximately half the variation in people's IQs results from differences in their genes. The conclusion that genes are important should come as no surprise in light of the evidence that we have reviewed. The heritability estimates follow directly from the findings just discussed—the similarity in IQ between identical twins, the correlations in IQ between adopted children and their biological parents, and so on.

It is important to note some limitations of the heritability statistic. First, heritability can be calculated in different ways, and the value obtained may vary depending on the method used and on the particular data that the researcher decides to emphasize. Second, whatever the heritability may be, the value is specific to the sample studied and cannot be generalized to other samples. The value is specific to the sample studied because it depends on two factors: the range of environmental differences in the sample, and the range of genetic differences in the sample. If we increase either range we give that factor more chance to have an effect; conversely, if we decrease either range we give that factor less chance to have an effect. In either case, we change the heritability.

Let us consider an example of this point, using not intelligence but height as the outcome we wish to explain. Imagine an island on which every person receives exactly 100% of his or her nutritional needs (Bjorklund, 2000). In this case, the heritability for height has to be close to 1, because there is no variability in the main environmental contributor to differences in height. If a factor does not vary in some sample of people, it cannot produce differences among those people. Suppose, however, that famine strikes the island. Some people still receive 100% of their nutritional needs; others, however, fall well short of this ideal. Over time, people in the first group grow taller than people in the second group. In this case, the heritability for height becomes less than 1, because environmental as well as genetic differences are now contributing to variations in height. Because the range of environmental differences has grown, the relative importance of genes and environment has changed.

The sample-specific nature of heritability has two further important implications. First, a particular heritability value—based as it is on the current range of genes and environments—tells us nothing for certain about what might happen in the future. In particular, heritability does not tell us about the possible effects of improvements in the environment. Height, for example, typically shows high heritability, yet average height has increased over the last 100 years, presumably because of improvements in nutrition (Angoff, 1988). Indeed, performance on IQ tests has improved steadily ever since the tests were first introduced, with an average gain of about 3 points per decade, which is one reason that the tests must be periodically revised and renormed. This phenomenon is known as the **Flynn Effect,** after the researcher who has most fully documented the changes in performance (Flynn, 1998, 1999). Thus, however high heritability may be, improvements in the environment could still lead to gains in children's intelligence.

Flynn Effect
Increase over time in the average level of performance on IQ tests.

Second, heritability tells us nothing for certain about comparisons between samples that were not included in the heritability estimate. Knowing what the heritability for height is on Island A, for example, does not tell us why its residents are taller or shorter than residents of Island B. Whatever the heritability may be within one group, differences between groups could result solely from differences in their genes, solely from differences in their environments, or from some combination of genes and environment. We will return to this point about comparisons between groups in our discussion of racial differences in IQ.

To Recap . . .

Organization is one major issue in the study of intelligence. Psychometric researchers draw inferences about how intelligence is organized from patterns of correlations across different measures of intelligence. Factor analyses of such correlations provide evidence both for general intelligence, which affects performance on many tasks, and for more specific abilities, which contribute to performance on specific tasks.

The question of the stability of IQ is another central issue in the psychometric approach to intelligence. Longitudinal studies indicate that traditional measures of infant IQ have little relation to later IQ. Recent evidence suggests, however, that response to novelty may provide a link between infancy and later childhood. After infancy, IQ begins to correlate from one age to another, and the stability increases as the child gets older. The correlations are not perfect, however, and substantial changes in IQ do sometimes occur.

The third classic issue in the psychometric approach concerns the origins of individual differences. Three methods of study have been prominent: family studies, adoption studies, and twin studies. All three methods suggest a substantial genetic contribution to individual differences in intelligence, yet all three also indicate the importance of the environment. Estimates of the heritability of IQ suggest that 40% to 70% of the variation among people is genetic in origin.

CONTRIBUTIONS OF THE FAMILY

In the preceding section we discussed some of the limitations of the heritability statistic. However, we have yet to note what is perhaps the most important limitation. At best, heritability estimates answer the question of how much: How much of the variation among people can be attributed to genetic or environmental factors? Such estimates tell us nothing about the processes by which genes or environments exert their effects. *How* is a genotype translated into a particular level of intelligence? And *how* do different environments shape different kinds of cognitive development?

We saw in Chapter 3 that researchers are just beginning to unravel the mysteries of genetic transmission. Some of the basic principles and mechanisms have been discovered, and more seem likely to yield their secrets in the near future. Our focus now is on the ways in which the environment affects intelligence. We begin with the contribution of home life to intellectual development.

Longitudinal Studies

Several kinds of research provide evidence about the contribution of family experience to children's intelligence. The longitudinal studies mentioned earlier are one source of evidence. Such studies have shown that IQ is not perfectly stable as children develop and that a particular child's IQ may go up or down by 30 or 40 points across childhood. Researchers have sought to discover whether these changes in IQ can be linked to characteristics of the children's environments.

Sameroff and associates, for example (Sameroff et al., 1993), followed a sample of children and their parents from the time the children were 4 until they reached the age of 14. Included at both time periods was an assessment of the extent to which the child's family life was characterized by each of the 10 risk factors listed in Table 10.6. At both age periods, the children's IQs were negatively related to the number of risk factors; that is, the more risk factors present, the lower, on average, the IQs. No single category of risk emerged as critical; rather, what seemed important was the accumulation of different forms of risk. Furthermore, risk at age 4 proved predictive of IQ at age 13. Children with difficult early environments were most likely to experience continued problems in intellectual adaptation. The negative impact of early risk, it is important to note, is not limited to IQ scores but extends as well to measures of language development and performance in school (Burchinal et al., 2000; Caughy, 1996).

Table 10.6	Risk Factors in the Sameroff et al. Study of Family Environment and IQ

Risk Factor	Description
Minority status	Family is African American or Puerto Rican.
Occupation	Head of household is unemployed or holds low-skilled occupation.
Mother's education	Mother did not complete high school.
Family size	Family has four or more children.
Father absence	Father is not present in the home.
Stressful life events	Family experienced at least 20 stressful events during the child's first 4 years.
Parenting perspectives	Parents hold relatively rigid and absolutist conceptions of children and child rearing.
Maternal anxiety	Mother is unusually high in anxiety.
Maternal mental health	Mother has relatively poor mental health.
Mother–child interaction	Mother shows little positive affect toward child.

SOURCE: Adapted from "Stability of Intelligence from Preschool to Adolescence: The Influence of Social and Family Risk Factors" by A. J. Sameroff, R. Seifer, A. Baldwin, and C. Baldwin, 1993, *Child Development, 64*, p. 85. Copyright © 1993 by the Society for Research in Child Development. Adapted by permission.

McCall and colleagues (1973) focused more directly on parents' contribution to stability or change in IQ. They analyzed patterns of IQ change for 80 children participating in a long-term longitudinal study. They found that two aspects of parental behavior showed the strongest relation to IQ change. Children who declined in IQ tended to have parents who made relatively little effort to stimulate them or to accelerate their development and who also fell at the extremes in their use of punishment (either very high or very low). In contrast, children who increased in IQ tended to have parents who emphasized intellectual acceleration and who were intermediate in the severity of their discipline. Thus, the most adaptive parental pattern appeared to be one that stressed stimulation and intellectual encouragement within a general context of structure and control. Similar conclusions have emerged from other studies of the child-rearing antecedents of intellectual competence (Wachs, 1992; White et al., 1978; Williams, 1998).

Research with the HOME

To identify the environmental contributors to intellectual development, we must have a way to assess the quality of the child's environment. Undoubtedly the most popular contemporary approach to measuring the home environment is an instrument called the **HOME (Home Observation for Measurement of the Environment)**. In this section we review findings from research with the HOME.

The infant version of the HOME, developed by Caldwell and Bradley (1979), consists of 45 items intended to tap the quality of the child's environment during the first 3 years. Each item is scored either yes (this feature is characteristic of the child's environment) or no (this feature is not characteristic). The 45 items are in turn grouped into six general subscales. The items and corresponding subscales are shown in Table 10.7. Scoring on the HOME is accomplished during a 1-hour home visit and is based on a combination of interviews with the mother and observation of mother–child interaction.

Of course, the infant environment, important though it may be, is not our only concern. There has long been a preschool version of the HOME as well. The preschool HOME is similar in structure to the infant scale but includes 55 items and eight subscales. More recent developments are HOME scales for the periods of middle childhood and adolescence (Bradley, 1994).

Do scores on the HOME relate to children's IQs? Many studies indicate that they do (Bradley, 1994, 1999; Gottfried, 1984a). In general, the higher the score on the HOME (that is, the greater the number of "yes" answers), the better the child's development.

HOME (Home Observation for Measurement of the Environment) An instrument for assessing the quality of the early home environment. Included are dimensions such as maternal involvement and variety of play materials.

Table 10.7	Items and Subscales on the HOME (Infant Version)

I. Emotional and Verbal Responsivity of Mother

1. Mother spontaneously vocalizes to child at least twice during visit (excluding scolding).
2. Mother responds to child's vocalizations with a verbal response.
3. Mother tells child the name of some object during visit or says name of person or object in a "teaching" style.
4. Mother's speech is distinct, clear, and audible.
5. Mother initiates verbal interchanges with observer— asks questions, makes spontaneous comments.
6. Mother expresses ideas freely and easily and uses statements of appropriate length for conversation (e.g., gives more than brief answers).
7. Mother permits child occasionally to engage in "messy" types of play.
8. Mother spontaneously praises child's qualities or behavior twice during visit.
9. When speaking of or to child, mother's voice conveys positive feelings.
10. Mother caresses or kisses child at least once during visit.
11. Mother shows some positive emotional responses to praise of child offered by visitor.

II. Avoidance of Restriction and Punishment

12. Mother does not shout at child during visit.
13. Mother does not express overt annoyance with or hostility toward child.
14. Mother neither slaps nor spanks child during visit.
15. Mother reports that no more than one instance of physical punishment occurred during the past week.
16. Mother does not scold or derogate child during visit.
17. Mother does not interfere with child's actions or restrict child's movements more than three times during visit.
18. At least 10 books are present and visible.
19. Family has a pet.

III. Organization of Physical and Temporal Environment

20. When mother is away, care is provided by one of three regular substitutes.
21. Someone takes child into grocery store at least once a week.

22. Child gets out of house at least four times a week.
23. Child is taken regularly to doctor's office or clinic.
24. Child has a special place in which to keep his toys and "treasures."
25. Child's play environment appears safe and free of hazards.

IV. Provision of Appropriate Play Materials

26. Child has some muscle-activity toys or equipment.
27. Child has push or pull toy.
28. Child has stroller or walker, kiddie car, scooter, or tricycle.
29. Mother provides toys or interesting activities for child during interview.
30. Provides learning equipment appropriate to age—cuddly toy or role–playing toys.
31. Provides learning equipment appropriate to age—mobile, table and chairs, high chair, play pen.
32. Provides eye–hand coordination toys—items to go in and out of receptacle, fit together toys, beads.
33. Provides eye–hand coordination toys that permit combinations—stacking or nesting toys, blocks or building toys.
34. Provides toys for literature or music.

V. Maternal Involvement with Child

35. Mother tends to keep child within visual range and to look at him often.
36. Mother "talks" to child while doing her work.
37. Mother consciously encourages developmental advances.
38. Mother invests "maturing" toys with value via her attention.
39. Mother structures child's play periods.
40. Mother provides toys that challenge child to develop new skills.

VI. Opportunities for Variety in Daily Stimulation

41. Father provides some caretaking every day.
42. Mother reads stories at least three times weekly.
43. Child eats at least one meal per day with mother and father.
44. Family visits or receives visits from relatives.
45. Child has three or more books of his or her own.

SOURCE: From "174 Children: A Study of the Relationship between Home Environment and Cognitive Development during the First 5 Years" by R. H. Bradley and B. M. Caldwell, 1982. In A. W. Gottfried (Ed.), *Home Environment and Early Cognitive Development,* New York: Academic Press, pp. 7–8. Copyright © 1984 by Academic Press. Reprinted by permission.

There is some evidence that each of the subscales correlates with IQ, although which scales predict most strongly varies some across studies and across age periods. Perhaps the most consistently important dimensions are parental involvement, play materials, and variety of stimulation (Gottfried, 1984b).

Measures on the HOME relate to contemporaneous measures of the child's intelligence. That is, scores on the infant version of the HOME correlate with infant intelligence (Barnard, Bee, & Hammond, 1984), scores on the preschool version correlate with preschool intelligence (Espy, Molfese, & DiLalla, 2001; Siegel, 1984), and scores on the middle childhood version correlate with childhood intelligence (Luster & Denbow, 1992).

Measures on the HOME also relate to future intelligence. In one study, for example, the correlation between HOME score at 6 months and IQ at 4.5 years was .50; the correlation between HOME at 24 months and IQ at 4.5 years was .63 (Bradley & Caldwell, 1984a). Other studies have demonstrated relations between HOME scores in infancy and both IQ and school performance during the grade-school years (Bradley & Caldwell, 1984b; Olson, Bates, & Kaskie, 1992). Thus, the quality of the child's early environment is predictive of various aspects of the child's later intelligence.

Although the HOME is a valuable source of evidence with respect to experience and intelligence, one caution should be noted. Research suggests that genetic factors may also contribute to findings with the HOME (Braungart, Fulker, & Plomin, 1992; Cherny, 1994; Cleveland et al., 2000). Genetically based characteristics of children may influence the HOME score itself, because such characteristics will affect the treatment that children receive from their parents (recall Bronfenbrenner's notion of developmentally generative characteristics, discussed in Chapter 1). And genetic characteristics of the parents may affect both the home environment and the child's intelligence, thus contributing to the correlation between HOME measures and children's IQs. The conclusion that both genes and environment are important for intelligence—and that the two factors are often very difficult to separate—should be familiar by now.

Cross-Cultural Research

As we discussed in Chapter 2, comparison of different cultures allows us to explore variations in experience and development that might not be evident within a single cultural setting. Some of the most interesting results from such comparisons concern performance on the kinds of academic measures that are often linked to IQ. Differences in mathematical achievement between Western and non-Western samples are especially striking.

American children, on average, do not perform well in mathematics. This conclusion has emerged from several surveys of cross-national differences in mathematics ability in recent years. The contrast with children from Asian countries is especially marked. For example, in one study of mathematics achievement in 20 countries, American 8th- and 12th-graders scored below the international average on virtually every measure taken (Garden, 1987; McKnight et al., 1987). Children from China and Japan, in contrast, were consistently near the top of the range. Other studies across the past two decades have provided a similar picture—disappointingly poor performance by American children, coupled with exceptional achievement for children from Asian countries (Geary, 1996; U.S. Department of Education, 2001).

Why do American children do so poorly in mathematics? It is tempting to indict the school system, and schools, as we discuss more fully in the next section, can be quite important. Some differences between Asians and Americans, however, are evident by age 5, before most children have even started school (Stevenson, Lee, & Stigler, 1986). Furthermore, Asian American students in the United States often outperform Caucasian students, even though both groups are moving through the same school systems (Sue & Ozaki, 1990). These findings suggest that schools are not the sole explanation; the family environment also contributes.

The most ambitious attempt to identify family bases for academic achievement is a program of research by Stevenson and associates (Chen & Stevenson, 1995; Stevenson, Chen, & Lee, 1993; Stevenson et al., 1990). The child participants for the initial phase of the project were first- and fifth-graders from the United States, China, and Japan. The children took a variety of achievement tests, and the results fit those of previous research—poorer performance in mathematics by American children than by children from China or

"Big deal, an A in math. That would be a D in any other country."

©The New Yorker Collection 1998 Mike Twohy from cartoonbank.com. All Rights Reserved.

Japan. Many of the 1st-graders were retested in 5th and 11th grade, and the original results were confirmed; if anything, the cross-national gap in achievement had widened.

The children's mothers also participated in the study, and it was their beliefs and practices that constituted the main focus of the research. The maternal interviews included a variety of questions designed to reveal differences among families and among cultures that might lead to differences in academic performance. Mothers were asked, for example, to judge how well their children were doing in school and to indicate how satisfied they were with this progress. They were asked to give their beliefs about the bases for school success—in particular, to judge the relative contributions of ability and effort to doing well in school. And they were asked about various experiences at home that might contribute to school success, such as parental help with homework or the provision of a quiet place to study.

The Stevenson group's assessments made clear that mothers in all three cultures are interested in and supportive of their children's academic development. At the same time, the maternal interviews revealed cross-cultural differences in beliefs and practices that might well contribute to the superior performance of Asian children. Asian mothers, for example, were more likely than American mothers to regard effort as more important than ability for success in school. The emphasis on effort in the Chinese and Japanese families appears to fit with general and long-standing cultural beliefs about the malleability of human nature and the possibility of improving oneself through hard work (Hong, 2001; Munro, 1977). In line with these beliefs, Asian mothers were more likely than American mothers to provide help for their children's academic endeavors. In China, for example, 96% of the children received help with homework (the figure in the United States was 67%), and fully 95% of Chinese fifth-graders and 98% of Japanese fifth-graders had their own desk at home at which to work (the figure for American children was 63%). Similar results emerged from a measure of time spent on academically related activities (e.g., reading, completing workbooks) outside school; Asian children spent more time in such endeavors than did American children.

Given the relatively poor performance of their children, American mothers might have been expected to be least satisfied with their children's academic achievement. In fact, just the reverse was true. American mothers were more satisfied with both their children's performance and their children's schools than were Chinese or Japanese mothers. American mothers also gave higher (and therefore less realistic) evaluations of their children's cognitive and academic abilities than did mothers in the other two cultures. This pattern suggests a basis for the failure of many American mothers to nurture optimal academic performance in their children. These mothers may believe that their children are doing better than they are doing and thus may be satisfied with levels of performance that are not that high. Furthermore, these mothers may believe that academic success is primarily a function of immutable ability rather than changeable effort and thus may see little point in encouraging their children to try harder.

Having presented the main conclusions of Stevenson et al.'s study, we should also note two qualifications (see also Hatano, 1990). First, the research does not claim that the child-rearing practices of the Asian cultures are producing generally superior children. American children do just as well as Chinese and Japanese children on measures of general intelligence, and differences in other domains of academic achievement are less marked and less consistent than those found for mathematics. In addition, the American children were more likely than their Asian counterparts to be involved in outside-of-school activities, such as music, art, and sports. Second, the research does not claim that the differences in mathematics result solely from differences among families. Schools are also important, and schools contribute to the superior performance of Asian children in mathematics. We discuss some of the important dimensions of schooling in the next section of the chapter.

To Recap . . .

The home environment is one context within which intellectual abilities develop. Longitudinal studies indicate that risk factors in the child's environment, such as family stresses, are predictive of declines in IQ over time. Studies that measure variations in the home environment (often using the HOME instrument) suggest that the quality of the experience within the home influences both current and future intellectual competence. Examinations of the bases for cross-national differences in mathematical achievement provide further evidence for the importance of parental values and practices.

SCHOOLING: VARIATIONS AND EFFECTS

The average American child spends approximately 15,000 hours in school between the ages of 5 and 18. Clearly, school is a major setting within which children in our society exercise—and develop—their intellectual abilities. What do we know about the impact of schooling on cognitive development? In addressing this question, we draw from the same two general kinds of evidence that were the focus of our discussions of the family. In this case we begin with comparisons of different cultures, after which we turn to variations within our own culture.

Cross-Cultural Studies

A difficulty in determining the effects of schooling in Western culture is its pervasiveness: Virtually every child goes to school. When we broaden our scope to encompass other cultures, this uniformity no longer holds. Of course, if we simply compare cultures with and without schooling, it will be difficult to interpret our results, because the cultures may differ in a number of ways apart from the presence or absence of school. Most informative, therefore, are cases in which only some children within a culture go to school or in which schooling has been recently introduced, allowing us to make a before-and-after comparison. Psychologists have been able to find and to study a number of such cases (Ceci, 1996; Cole, 1999). Several conclusions emerge.

A first conclusion is that some aspects of children's cognitive development seem to be more strongly and consistently affected by schooling than others. Many of the kinds of knowledge studied by Piaget fall in the relatively unaffected category. Schooling does sometimes influence the development of Piagetian concepts—most obviously, effects on the rate at which knowledge is acquired. Most studies, however, report no clear qualitative differences between schooled children and unschooled children in their mastery of such concepts as conservation, nor any lasting advantage for children who have been to school.

Other aspects of cognitive development appear to be affected more by schooling. Skill at various kinds of perceptual analysis can be facilitated by schooling—for example, the ability to match stimuli or to construct models of familiar patterns. Schooling can affect memory. Schooled children not only perform better on a variety of memory tasks but are also more likely to use mnemonic strategies to help themselves remember. Schooling affects how children classify objects. Children who have been to school are more likely to group objects in terms of general categories (e.g., all of the foods together) rather than functional or thematic relations (e.g., ice cream and spoon together). Similarly, schooling affects how children think about words and use language, with schooled children more likely to think in terms of general categories and abstract relations. Finally and perhaps most generally, schooling improves children's ability to reflect on their own cognitive processes—to think about thinking. As we saw in Chapter 8, such metacognition has emerged as an active area of current research interest.

Why does schooling produce these effects? Rogoff (1981) discusses four factors that may play roles. Perhaps the most obvious explanation is that schooling directly teaches many of the specific skills on which schooled children excel. Classification, for example,

An Early Study of the Effects of Schooling on Thinking

A central issue in the study of intelligence is whether people the world over all possess the same basic intellectual capacities or whether these capacities are profoundly shaped by cultural practices and institutions. The first systematic examination of this issue was an ambitious research project undertaken by A. R. Luria in Central Asia in the early 1930s (Luria, 1976, 1979).

At the time, many of the rural regions in Russia were undergoing a rapid social transformation. Although some of these regions could boast of an ancient high culture, most of the citizenry had long been dependent on wealthy landowners and powerful feudal lords. Few were able to read. Much changed following the Russian Revolution. Women were emancipated, schools were established, and a collectivist agricultural economy was introduced. Luria and a team of assistants took advantage of the changes taking place to compare the thinking and reasoning of nonliterate groups living in villages and groups who had begun to participate in the new social structure through schooling and participation in the collectivist economy.

Luria assessed a wide variety of cognitive skills, including perception, classification, and reasoning. In many respects, Luria followed procedures that cross-cultural researchers would advocate today. He conducted the experimental sessions in the local language in comfortable and familiar circumstances (e.g., around the evening campfire). And he avoided standard psychometric tests and tried to place the tasks in a familiar context using common materials.

Luria found striking differences between answers provided by the illiterate peasants and those offered by men and women with some schooling and experience in the new economy. As the following exchange shows, those without schooling tended to respond (or not) on the basis of personal experience:

In the Far North, where there is snow, all bears are white. Novaya Zemlya is in the Far North and there is always snow there. What colors are the bears there?
There are different sorts of bears.
[the syllogism is repeated]
I don't know. I've seen a black bear, I've never seen any others . . .
Each locality has its own animals: If it's white, they will be white. If it's yellow they will be yellow.
But what kinds of bears are there in Navaya Zemlya?
We always speak only of what we see; we don't talk about what we haven't seen.

BOX 10.1

Classics of Research

But what do my words imply?
Well, it's like this: our tsar isn't like yours, and yours isn't like ours. Your words can only be answered by someone who was there, and if a person wasn't there he can't say anything on the basis of your words.
But on the basis of my words—in the North, where there is always snow, the bears are white, can you gather what kind of bears there are in Navaya Zemlya?
If a man was sixty or eighty and had seen a white bear and had told about it, he could be believed, but I've never seen one and hence I can't say. That's my last word. Those who can tell, and those who didn't see can't say anything! (Luria, 1976, pp. 108–109)

Though the illiterate peasants performed somewhat better when the syllogisms related more directly to their everyday experiences, all of the villagers with some schooling and experience in the evolving economy were able to solve both familiar and unfamiliar logic problems by reasoning from the premises. On the basis of these and other data, Luria concluded that schooling and modernization led to qualitative shifts in reasoning.

After two expeditions, Luria returned to Moscow and made some of his findings public. The political climate at the time was not at all friendly toward Luria's conclusions. Although he clearly emphasized the benefits of collectivization, many people believed his results could be viewed as an insult to the Uzbeki people. Consequently, Luria's landmark study was not published until the 1970s (Cole, 1976).

Today, a growing number of researchers are traveling to distant cultures to test the universality of Western psychological theories. Like Luria, many of these researchers have found children and adults, especially those without schooling, to be quite perplexed by traditional psychological tasks. However, these researchers have also documented how well the same people could reason and solve problems in their daily lives. Recognizing the discrepancy in performance across contexts, many contemporary theorists have been unwilling to accept Luria's claim that schooling and modernization produce fundamental changes in modes of thinking (Cole, 1996; Rogoff, 2003). Exactly what does underlie cultural differences in performance on cognitive assessments continues to be debated. Nonetheless, the Central Asian study is highly regarded both for its unique historical value and for Luria's brilliant use of the clinical interview method (Cole, 1976).

is a common activity in school, and committing material to memory is even more common. A more general proposal is that schooling exerts its effects through its emphasis on the search for general rules—for universal systems of knowledge (such as mathematics) within which specific instances can be understood. A third possibility stresses the differences between teaching in school and teaching outside school. Teaching in school often involves the verbal transmission of information that is far removed from its everyday context, a style of instruction that may promote verbally based, abstract modes of thought. Finally, perhaps the most general explanation concerns a primary goal of most forms of schooling: the development of literacy. It has been argued that literacy, like verbally based teaching, promotes abstract, reflective styles of thinking. And reading, of course, can also be the door to a vast world of experiences and knowledge that could never be acquired firsthand (Stanovich, 1993).

Cross-cultural examinations of schooling are not limited to comparisons of present versus absent. Even when all children go to school, the type of schooling that children receive may vary across cultures, and these variations can be a source of cognitive differences. This point is relevant to the discrepancy in mathematics achievement between Chinese and Japanese children and American children. Studies of education in the three cultures make clear that the differences in family life discussed earlier are built on and magnified by the kinds of schooling that children in the three countries receive (Geary, 1995a; Stevenson & Stigler, 1992; Stigler & Hiebert, 1999). Children in China and Japan spend more time in school than do children in the U.S., with both longer school days and longer school years. In addition, classrooms in China and Japan typically devote more instructional time to mathematics than do classrooms in the United States; teachers and children in China and Japan spend a higher proportion of the allotted time actually teaching and doing mathematics as opposed to peripheral activities (e.g., handing out papers); children from China and Japan do more math homework than do American children; and mathematics textbooks and curricula are more challenging in Asia than they are in the United States. In light of these and other differences, it is perhaps not surprising that the achievement gap persists.

Amount of Schooling

We touched on some evidence about schooling in the United States in the points just made about cross-national differences. Here we take up the topic more fully. We begin with research on the amount of schooling, after which we turn to the more difficult question of the nature or quality of schooling.

It has long been known that there is a positive relation between number of years of education completed and IQ—that is, the more years of schooling people complete, the higher (on the average) are their IQs (Jencks, 1972). The usual explanation has been that more intelligent people stay in school longer. This factor is almost certainly part of the basis for the correlation. Recently, however, Stephen Ceci (1991, 1992; Ceci & Williams, 1997) has argued that the cause and effect may also flow in the opposite direction—that is, that schooling may actually increase IQ.

Ceci cites a variety of evidence in support of his conclusion. Here are three examples. First, children who drop out of school decline in IQ relative to children who stay in school, even when the two groups are initially equal in IQ. Second, children's IQs have been shown to decline slightly across the months of summer vacation and then to rise again during the school year. Third, children whose birthdays make them just barely old enough to qualify for school entry obtain higher IQ scores by age 8 than children whose birthdays make them fall just short. The point is that the two groups are virtually the same age, but one group has had a year more of schooling. This is the school cut-off approach discussed in Chapter 9. Using this approach, Morrison and colleagues (Christian, Bachnan, & Morrison 2001; Morrison, Griffith, & Alberts, 1997; Morrison, Smith, & Dow-Ehrensberger, 1995) have demonstrated that starting school relatively early can nurture a number of specific cognitive abilities.

In speculating about why schooling boosts IQ, Ceci draws on the cross-cultural evidence just discussed. We saw that schooling affects perceptual analysis, memory, language use, and classification. These skills, Ceci notes, are precisely the kinds of abilities that are stressed on IQ tests. This overlap is, of course, no accident: IQ tests were designed, in part, to predict school performance. It is not surprising, therefore, that being

Not only do IQ tests predict success in school; recent evidence suggests that schooling can increase IQ.

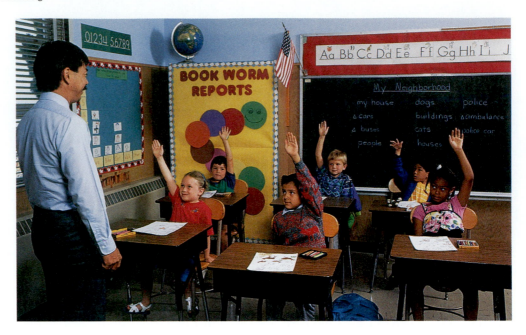

good at IQ-type skills is helpful in school. But it is also not surprising that experiences in school can nurture IQ.

Quality of Schooling

As might be expected, quality of schooling is more difficult than quantity to define and study (Eccles & Roeser, 1999; Good & Brophy, 2000). Despite the difficulties, however, few doubt that there can be important differences in the quality of the education that different children receive. Some schools consistently produce more successful outcomes than others—doing so even when the children being served are initially equivalent. And some teachers within a school consistently have happier and more productive classrooms than others.

Michael Rutter (1983) has provided one of the most helpful surveys of the research directed to quality of schooling. One of the interesting messages from his review concerns factors that do *not* make much of a difference. Rutter found little evidence, for example, that variations in school success (such as performance on standardized tests, attendance rates, and graduation rates) are associated with the financial or physical resources available to the school, with the overall size of the school, or with the size of the class within the school. This conclusion does not mean that such factors are never important—no one would advocate a class size of 50 for kindergartners. Indeed, more recent research indicates that small class size can sometimes be beneficial, especially in the early grades and perhaps especially for low-income students (Finn et al., 2001; Nye, Hedges, & Konstantopoulos, 2001). Nevertheless, the variations that are normally found along dimensions such as school and class size do not seem to be major contributors to school success.

What factors *do* influence school success? The dimensions that emerge as important in Rutter's review have to do mainly with emphasis and organization. Successful schools have a clear emphasis on academic goals, accompanied by clearly defined procedures for achieving those goals. Teachers plan the curriculum together, actively teach important content, assign and grade homework regularly, and in general hold high but realistic expectations for their students. Discipline within successful schools tends to be firm but fair—sufficient to maintain a focus on the task at hand but not so punitive as to arouse anxiety or resentment. Students in successful schools are helped to feel part of the school through opportunities to participate in school-related activities, as well as by the chance to have a voice in decisions concerning the school. Finally, teachers in successful schools manage their classrooms in an organized and efficient manner, maximizing the time spent on the lesson of the moment rather than on peripheral concerns (e.g., distributing papers, setting up equipment). As we saw, this same variable of classroom management proved important in the comparison of Asian and U.S. schools.

That organization and efficiency are desirable qualities in the school environment is not really in dispute; the challenge is how to achieve these characteristics. Other dimensions along which classrooms and schools vary are the subject of considerably more debate. One is the practice of **ability grouping**—that is, the separation of students who differ in ability (often as determined by standardized tests) into distinct groups for instruction. In the early school years, grouping is most likely to be at the within-class level—for example, the "red robins" and the "bluebirds" reading groups. By middle school and high school, grouping is more often at the between-class level—for example, separate curricula for college-bound and vocational-track students.

Is ability grouping a desirable educational practice? There is no simple answer to this question. The basic rationale behind the procedure—that instruction should be fit to the developmental level and interests of the student—is one with which no educator would disagree, and achieving such a fit is generally easier in a small and similar-ability group than in a diverse class of 30. Furthermore, some forms of ability grouping have been shown to work well for some students. In particular, placement in challenging educational tracks with peers of similar ability is generally beneficial for students of relatively high academic ability (Fuligni, Eccles, & Barber, 1995; Pallas et al., 1994).

Ability grouping is also sometimes beneficial for children whose academic performance or test scores consign them to lower-level tracks. In balance, however, the practice may carry more drawbacks than advantages for such children (Hallinan & Kubitschek, 1999; Oakes, Gamoran, & Page, 1992). One problem is that the assignment to a particular group may not always be an accurate reflection of the child's true ability or potential; even when objective measures are equated, low-income and minority children tend to be disproportionately represented in lower-level tracks (Dornbusch, 1994). Even when the placement is appropriate, children in lower-level tracks may not receive content that is sufficiently challenging to elicit their full potential, and the instruction they receive may not be of the same quality as that given their higher-track peers (Dornbusch et al., 1996; Dreeban & Barr, 1988). In addition, the negative labels that can accompany placement in the "slower" groups may adversely affect the child's self-image, which in turn may affect subsequent academic expectations and performance (Stipek, 2002). As we will see in Chapter 13, beliefs about one's competence can be a powerful contributor to how one actually performs.

Whether or not ability grouping is used, every school system necessarily makes decisions with regard to one basis for grouping students: namely, age of child. These decisions include the age at which formal schooling should begin (typically 5 years of age in American school systems) and the points at which movement will occur from one level or grade to the next (typically 1-year increments in American schools). In most communities, children do not remain in the same school throughout their educational careers, and thus decisions must also be made about how many transitions from one school to another there will be and when the transitions will occur. Most American students experience two transitions: from elementary school to either middle school (grades 6, 7, and 8) or junior high (grades 7 and 8 or 7, 8, and 9), and from middle school or junior high to high school.

The first of these transitions, in particular, can pose some special challenges. In part, these challenges stem from changes in the nature of schooling between elementary school and middle school or junior high. Most children now attend a school that is considerably larger than what they have been accustomed to. Rather than stay with a single teacher throughout the day, they now move from teacher to teacher for different subjects; as a result, there is less opportunity to form a close relationship with a supportive adult. Grading standards are typically more stringent than was formerly the case, and there is more emphasis on competition and comparison with peers. Teachers are more likely to provide instruction to entire classes rather than individual groups, and there is more emphasis on teacher control and discipline.

Ability grouping
Separation of students into groups of similar ability for purposes of instruction.

Jacquelynne Eccles and colleagues have argued that the inherent challenges posed by such changes in schooling are magnified by the developmental changes that occur during early adolescence (Eccles et al., 1993; Eccles, Lord, & Roeser, 1996; Eccles & Roeser, 1999). Early adolescence is a time of heightened self-consciousness, of a heightened desire and a heightened capacity for decision making and autonomy, of an increased concern with close peer relations, and of an increased need for supportive adults outside the home. It is, in short, a time when young people need exactly the sorts of things that the new structure of schooling tends to discourage. The relevant theoretical notion is labeled **stage–environment fit:** Development proceeds most smoothly when the environmental opportunities and challenges during a particular time period match the capacities and needs of the developing child. Eccles maintains that the typical middle school or junior high provides a poor fit for young adolescents.

Two general kinds of evidence provide support for this argument. First, early adolescence—and thus the middle school or junior high years—is a period of heightened risk for a number of psychological problems, including declines in self-esteem, lowered academic motivation, poorer academic performance, and increases in truancy and delinquency (Anderman & Midgley, 1997; Eccles & Roeser, 1999; Wigfield et al., 1991). Furthermore, these effects are not necessarily short-lived; declines in self-esteem during junior high are predictive of continued problems throughout high school (Eccles et al., 1997). Second, such negative outcomes are considerably less likely when students do not experience the typical post–grade school transition, either because they remain in the same school or because their new school incorporates positive features (e.g., the opportunity to form supportive relationships with teachers) that were typical of the earlier school experience (Roeser, Eccles, & Sameroff, 2000; Rudolph et al., 2001).

Contextual Contributors to Schooling

In Chapter 1 we introduced Bronfenbrenner's ecological systems theory (Bronfenbrenner, 1979). As we saw, schools fall within the environmental layer labeled the *microsystem,* as do families and peers. The *mesosystem* refers to interrelations among the child's microsystems. A consideration of schooling provides a clear illustration of the importance of the mesosystem, because the success of schooling depends very much on other important social contexts in the child's life.

Peers are important at the time of the first school transition: the entry into school at age 5 or 6. Children who have several good friends when they start kindergarten are happier in school than are children who lack such friendships; they develop more positive attitudes toward school; and they show greater gains in performance across the school year. Conversely, being rejected by peers is associated with unfavorable attitudes and poorer school performance (Ladd, 1990; Ladd, Birch, & Buhs, 1999; Ladd, Kochenderfer, & Coleman, 1996).

Peer relations remains important as children progress through school. Association with academically oriented peers promotes academic motivation and achievement; conversely, association with antisocial peers is linked to poor grades and dropping out of school (Fuligni et al., 2001; Ryan, 2001). Throughout grade school and high school, children who lack friends are less well adjusted in the classroom, show higher rates of absenteeism, and are more at risk for being retained at a grade (Coie et al., 1992; DeRosier, Kupersmidt, & Patterson, 1994). They are also less likely to complete school; across studies, socially unsuccessful children have been found to be two to eight times more likely to drop out of school than are children in general (Parker & Asher, 1987). (Recall from Chapter 9 that peers can also play a direct role in the educational process through instructional procedures such as collaborative learning and peer tutoring.)

The family is also important to success in school. We saw earlier the quality of the home environment is one contributor to the child's intellectual abilities, which of course are one contributor to performance in school. The importance of the family, however, extends

---

Stage–environment fit
Degree to which environmental circumstances match the capabilities and the needs of the child at particular points during development.

beyond simply stimulation of intellectual development. From the start of school, children's adjustment to school and their academic performance are linked to the quality of family relations and family support (Bradley et al., 2001; Cowan & Cowan, 2002; Entwisle & Alexander, 2000; Grolnick et al., 2000). A variety of aspects of family life are important, including the number of parents or other adults in the home, the stability of the family structure, the quality of relations with the parents, and the degree of parental support for academic achievement. These factors, in turn, affect a variety of outcomes in the school setting, ranging from adjustment to kindergarten to coping with the transition to middle school or junior high to the probability of dropping out of high school. It is worth noting that among the ways in which parents affect their children's school success is by influencing the peers with whom they associate, which, as we have seen, can be one contributor to academic attitudes and performance (Dishion & Bullock, 2002).

Parents' direct involvement with school is also important. Parents can take an active role in their children's schooling in a number of ways, including parent–teacher conferences, monitoring of and help with homework, and selection of curricular and eventual career-track options (Christenson & Sheridan, 2001; Epstein, 2002). The dimension of parental involvement, however, is itself an example of a contextual effect. On average, low-income and minority parents are less likely to be involved in their children's schooling than are middle-income parents. In many instances this lack of involvement is less a matter of interest and concern than of possibility—for parents who are coping with the challenges of poverty, dangerous neighborhoods, and uncertain employment, finding time and energy for their child's schooling may be an insurmountable task (Brooks-Gunn, Duncan, & Aber, 1997).

In addition to peers and parents, a final important context is the child's general cultural background. Because of the diversity of American society, different children often bring different experiences and beliefs and values to the school setting. The potential importance of this dimension is expressed in the **cultural compatibility hypothesis:** Classroom instruction will be most effective when it matches patterns of learning that are familiar in the child's culture (Slaughter-DeFoe et al., 1990; Tharp, 1989).

A nice example of this principle is found in a study of *wait-time*—the length of time one participant in a dialogue waits before responding to the other (White & Tharp, 1988). Navajo children tend to pause when giving answers, creating the impression (at least for Anglo teachers) that they have finished responding. The result is that Navajo children are often interrupted before they have completed their answers. In this case, the teacher's wait-time is too short. In contrast, native Hawaiian children prefer a short wait-time because in their culture prompt response and overlapping speech patterns are signs of interest and involvement. Teachers, however, often interpret the Hawaiian child's quick responses as rude interruptions, and their attempts to curtail such behavior may lead to general uncertainty and inhibition. Thus, in both cases, although in different ways, the teacher's unfamiliarity with the child's cultural background can create problems for the child in school.

Cultural compatibility hypothesis
The hypothesis that schooling will be most effective when methods of instruction are compatible with the child's cultural background.

✔ To Recap . . .

Schools as well as homes can affect children's intellectual development. Cross-cultural studies indicate that schooling promotes a number of cognitive skills, including memory, classification, and metacognition. Studies within our culture verify that both the quantity and the quality of schooling can be important. Successful schools or classrooms are characterized by efficiency, organization, and a strong academic emphasis. Less clear are the effects of ability grouping and the timing and nature of school transitions.

The success of schooling depends not only on the nature of the school but also on the contribution of other important social systems in the child's life. Peers and parents can both be important; in both instances, positive relations and support for academic achievement are related to school success. The fit between the school experience and the child's cultural background can also play a role.

SCHOOLING: EXPERIMENTAL INTERVENTIONS

Most of the research that we have considered to this point in the chapter—with regard to both families and schools—has concerned naturally occurring variations in children's experience. That is, different children grow up under different home circumstances, just as different children encounter different experiences in school, and researchers have attempted to determine the effects of these variations. Such research is valuable but also incomplete. Such studies lack experimental control, and therefore it is difficult to be certain of cause-and-effect relations. If we could experimentally manipulate the child's experiences, we could be much more certain about exactly what the critical factors and causal relations are.

For obvious ethical reasons, experimental manipulations of children's environments take one direction only. No researcher deliberately makes a child's environment worse. A number of investigators, however, have sought to improve children's environments and thereby enhance their intellectual development. The largest category of such intervention efforts—and the form on which we focus—have been directed to a specific population: young children (usually low-income and minority status) who are perceived as being at risk for school failure. The interventions involve provision of enriched environmental opportunities, and the goal is to enhance the children's prospects for success in school and in life beyond.

Of course, studies like this are not motivated only or even primarily by scientific considerations about cause and effect. Such studies are also of enormous applied value, because they address an issue that is of concern both to society in general and to millions of families and children. Indeed, the studies we are about to consider are among the most important forms of applied research in child psychology.

An Illustrative Intervention Project

The Abecedarian Project (Ramey et al., 2000; Ramey, Ramey, & Lanzi, 2001) is one of the most successful of the many intervention efforts that were launched in the 1960s and 1970s. Like many such projects, its focus was on low-income African American children and their families. Unlike many projects, however, it did not limit its intervention to the preschool years; rather, children were enrolled as infants, with an average age of 4 months at the start of the project. Half the infants were randomly assigned to the treatment group, and half were assigned to an untreated control group. The infants in the treatment group attended a specially constructed child-care center for 8 hours a day, 50 weeks a year. The center was of very high quality, with a low teacher-to-child ratio and a curriculum designed to promote cognitive development. Children remained in the center until age 5, with appropriate changes in the curriculum (e.g., an increased focus on language and academic skills) as they grew older. The children were also given nutritional supplements and health benefits, and their mothers received instruction in principles of child development. Finally, for half the sample aspects of the intervention remained in effect through the first 3 years of elementary school.

The Abecedarian Project had an immediate effect on IQ, with some differences between the treatment and control participants emerging as early as 6 months. The differences increased throughout the duration of the program; by preschool, the average IQ difference between treatment and control was 17 points. Although the superiority of the treatment participants decreased across the school years, it did not disappear; furthermore, the treatment participants consistently outperformed their counterparts on various measures of academic achievement. In the most recent follow-up, some effects of the intervention were still evident on cognitive and academic measures at age 21 (Campbell et al., 2001).

In addition to demonstrating the possibility for long-term success of intervention, the Abecedarian Project provides evidence with regard to the effects of variations in the timing and intensity of intervention. Some children in the project received intervention only during the preschool years, and some only during the early school years. Although there were some benefits in both cases, the greatest gains by far were shown by the children for whom intervention began early and extended late.

Project Head Start

The sample size for the Abecedarian Project was 111 children. Similarly modest sample sizes are true of most early intervention projects. Investigators seldom have the resources to include more than a fraction of the families that might benefit from their efforts. The hope has been that such programs can at least help some of the children in need, while perhaps also identifying general principles of intervention that can eventually be applied more broadly.

Project Head Start is enormously larger in scope. Head Start is a nationwide, federally funded intervention program directed primarily toward low-income preschool children and their families. It was launched in 1965 as part of President Lyndon Johnson's War on Poverty and, unlike many components of the War on Poverty, it continues today. There are approximately 2,500 Head Start centers spread across all 50 states.

Because Head Start is many centers rather than one, it can be difficult to say what Head Start "is." Nevertheless, several elements have characterized Head Start classrooms since the beginning of the program (Zigler & Muenchow, 1992). Head Start emphasizes family and community involvement. Parents are encouraged to volunteer in their children's classrooms and are also given a voice in decisions about the direction of the program. As part of this emphasis on family and community, Head Start attempts to avoid the "deficit" orientation that has characterized some interventions: Rather than seeking only to correct deficiencies in the child's background, Head Start is designed to build on existing interests and strengths. Although academic readiness is always part of a Head Start curriculum, other aspects of the child's development are stressed as well. Social skills are important, as is the development of self-confidence and motivation. So, too, is the child's physical development—an emphasis on nutrition and dental and medical care has been part of Head Start since its inception.

Does Head Start work? This question can be difficult to answer for any intervention. It is especially difficult in the case of Head Start, given the many different aspects of development that are stressed in the program, as well as the variations in how the general philosophy is implemented across centers. Initial evaluations of Head Start focused on IQ gain, and many commentators were dismayed when Head Start failed to produce lasting improvements in children's IQs (Westinghouse Learning Center, 1969). In the years since the initial assessment, however, it has become clear that Head Start, like intervention programs in general, can have a number of beneficial effects that are not captured by IQ scores (Lee et al., 1990; Zigler & Finn-Stevenson, 1999; Zigler & Styfco, 1993). These effects include greater success in school, better health status, gains in social competence, and increased involvement of the family in the child's education.

One other benefit of Head Start is worth noting. In addition to directly serving some 20 million children across the last 40 years, Head Start has functioned as a kind of national laboratory for designing and testing intervention programs for children and families (Zigler & Finn-Stevenson, 1999). A number of current social-policy initiatives had their origins in programs introduced as part of Head Start, including support programs for needy families and techniques for mainstreaming children with disabilities in regular classrooms. Head Start thus qualifies as not only the nation's largest social-policy effort but also its largest scientific experiment.

Overview

Head Start and other intervention projects of the sort just described have been in existence for nearly 40 years. What have they told us about the possibility of modifying intelligence by changing the environment? Reviews of the intervention literature support several general conclusions (Barnett, 1995; Brooks-Gunn, 2003; Consortium for Longitudinal Studies, 1983; Ramey et al., 2001).

Although preschool intervention projects typically have limited effects on IQ, they can increase children's chances for later success in school.

First, participation in intervention projects has an immediate positive effect on children's IQs. Children who have received intervention typically have higher IQs than children who have not, and the differences typically persist for at least a year or two after the program has ended. The effects, however, do show a definite tendency to diminish with time. Furthermore, no project has produced a generally superior level of intellectual functioning in its participants. The main effect of intervention seems to be to minimize the declines in IQ that the children would otherwise experience.

Second, positive effects of intervention are often more marked on measures other than IQ. Even in the absence of IQ gain, participation in early intervention is associated with higher scores on standardized achievement tests, lower probability of being assigned to special education classes, and lower probability of being retained in a grade. In some projects there is also evidence for positive effects on self-concept, achievement motivation, and maternal attitudes toward school. Such findings have reinforced long-standing criticisms of the practice of using IQ scores as the main index of the success of intervention (Schweinhart & Weikart, 1991; Travers & Light, 1982). Not only is IQ an incomplete measure of intellectual ability, but other kinds of effects (such as the effect on school performance) may be more important for the child's development. Furthermore, IQ tests cannot measure the nonintellectual benefits that some programs may have (improved nutritional status, better social competence, and so on).

A third set of conclusions concerns the specific features of intervention that produce positive effects. Ramey and Ramey (1998) identify six principles that capture much of what is known about the contributors to successful intervention. Table 10.8 summarizes

Table 10.8	Principles of Successful Intervention (Ramey & Ramey)
Principle	**Description**
Principle of developmental timing	Programs that begin early and extend later in development are more successful than those of briefer duration.
Principle of program intensity	Programs that are more intensive (with regard, for example, to number of hours and range of activities) are more effective than less intense programs.
Principle of direct provision of learning experiences	Programs that provide direct learning experiences to children are more effective than those that rely on indirect methods (e.g., parent training).
Principle of program breadth and flexibility	Programs that provide more comprehensive services and use multiple routes are more effective than progams that are narrower in focus.
Principle of individual differences	Some children show greater benefits from participation than do others.
Principle of environmental maintenance of development	Maintenance of positive effects over time depends on adequate environmental supports.

SOURCE: Adapted from "Early Intervention and Early Experience" by C. T. Ramey and S. L. Ramey, 1998, *American Psychologist, 53, pp. 109–120.* Copyright © 1998 by the American Psychological Association. Adapted by permission.

these principles. Note that the Abecedarian Project illustrates many of the principles, including the principle of developmental timing (the inception of the program in infancy rather than waiting for the preschool years) and the principle of program intensity (the year-long, 5-day-a week immersion in the program, as well as the incorporation of a number of aspects of the child's life). Note also the mixed message that emerges from this summary. On the positive side, it is clear that intervention programs *can* produce genuine and lasting benefits for children and their families, and that psychologists and educators have learned much about the factors that determine success. On the negative side, it is clear that success does not come easily; rather, a continued societal commitment will be required to ensure that the necessary resources are devoted to the task.

Race and Intelligence

The intervention programs we have just discussed have been directed overwhelmingly toward poor African American children. This emphasis reflects the fact that African American children are more likely than are Caucasian children to have problems in school. African American children also tend to perform more poorly than Caucasian children on IQ tests; the average difference is about 10 to 15 points (Loehlin, 2000). There is some evidence that the gap may have narrowed slightly in recent years (Vincent, 1991). Although current trends are less clear, there is also evidence that the differences in academic achievement declined during the 1970s and 1980s (Hauser, 1998).

Before we discuss possible bases for the IQ differences, we should note an important point about what such average differences do and do not tell us. The ranges of performance for different ethnic groups on IQ tests are completely overlapping, and there is much more variation within groups (that is, among Caucasian children or among African American children) than there is between groups (Suzuki & Valencia, 1997). There is no way, therefore, to predict anything about a child's abilities simply from knowing that child's race.

The issue of why average racial differences in IQ exist is perhaps the most controversial topic in developmental psychology. For years the commonly accepted explanation was an environmentalist one: The environments that African American children encounter are less likely than those of Caucasian children to promote the skills needed to do well on IQ tests. In 1969, however, Arthur Jensen published an article in which he suggested that genetic differences between races might also play a role (Jensen, 1969)—a position that he has since elaborated in a number of publications (Jensen, 1972, 1973, 1980, 1981). The appearance of the book *The Bell Curve* (Herrnstein & Murray, 1994) further fueled the debate. Although the authors of *The Bell Curve* are careful to state that the issue of racial differences remains unresolved, they do offer a variety of seemingly progenetic kinds of evidence—in the context of a generally strong statement about the importance both of IQ for success in society and of the genes as determinants of individual differences in IQ.

Why might anyone believe that genes contribute to racial differences in IQ? We can only briefly summarize this complex argument here. The starting point is the consistency of the racial differences in IQ. Such differences have appeared in dozens of studies and on a wide variety of tests. The differences do not seem to relate to the cultural loading of the test; they are found, for example, on nonverbal as well as verbal tests and on test items that do not seem to require any culture-specific knowledge. Nor are the differences explained by differences in social class, because controlling for social class results in only a small decrease in the discrepancy.

A further component of the argument comes from the data concerning heritability. Heritability for Caucasian samples, as we saw earlier, is high. Comparable studies with African American samples have also yielded substantial heritabilities (Scarr, 1981). It appears, therefore, that genes are an important source of individual differences within a race. Both Jensen and the authors of *The Bell Curve* acknowledge the points we made earlier—that heritability is always sample-specific and that heritability within one group cannot be applied directly to a comparison between two groups. What they offer, however, is a kind of plausibility argument. If genes are so important to differences within races, is it plausible that they make absolutely no contribution to differences between races? In

Stereotype Threat

One of the most perplexing and disturbing issues in the study of intelligence is the gap in test scores between African American and Caucasian students. Recent research has revealed one plausible contributor—a psychological process known as **stereotype threat** (Steele, 1997; Steele & Aronson, 1995).

Stereotype threat is the extra pressure people feel in situations in which their performance may confirm a negative stereotype about their group. In academic settings, individuals most vulnerable to stereotype threat are those who belong to groups perceived to be of lesser ability. In North America, a sizable portion of White Americans endorse the stereotype that African Americans are, on average, less intelligent than Whites (Aronson, Fried, & Good, 2002). Importantly, students can suffer stereotype threat even if they do not believe the stereotype.

Researchers have repeatedly docmented stereotype threat under controlled laboratory conditions. For example, in one early study, Steele and Aronson (1995) found that African American students performed significantly worse than Whites on a standardized test when the test was presented as diagnostic of their intellectual abilities. When the task was presented as a problem-solving task, the performance of the two groups was about equal. Simply asking students to indicate their race on a test form is sufficient to induce stereotype threat and impair the performance of African American students (Steele & Aronson, 1998).

Stereotype threat is not limited to African American students, however. It can affect the performance of any stereotyped social group. For instance, females tend to perform worse on assessments of mathematical ability when researchers evoke the stereotype that females are less capable in math (Spencer, Steele, & Quinn, 1999). Even White males, who normally do not suffer from stereotype threat, show impaired performance on difficult mathematics assessments when reminded of the stereotype that Whites are inferior to Asians at mathematics (Aronson et al., 1999).

Theorists believe stereotype threat undermines academic performance primarily in two ways. First, in the short run, it raises anxiety and impairs test performance. Under conditions of stereotype threat, African American college students report feeling more anxious; higher levels of anxiety have been confirmed by blood pressure measures (Blascovich et al., 2001; Steele & Aronson, 1995).

The second way stereotype threat hurts academic performance is via the means students use to cope with the threat it poses to their self-esteem. To protect themselves, students "disidentify," or disengage, from the threatened domain. Studies show that students tend to base their self-

Stereotype threat

Extra pressure people feel in situations in which their performance may confirm a negative stereotype held about their group.

BOX 10.2

On the
Cutting
E D G E

esteem on domains in which they can excel and devalue domains in which success is less likely (Eccles & Wigfield, 1995; Harter, 1999). Disengagement can be short-lived, as when a student discounts the importance of a poor exam score. It can also contribute to a general disidentification with academics over time (Major et al., 1998).

Researchers have explored several means of alleviating stereotype threat. One approach is to redefine the testing situation to make it less threatening (Steele & Aronson, 1995). Directly countering the stereotype also helps. For instance, when women are told that females perform just as well as males on specific kinds of math problems, their performance rises (Spencer et al., 1999). Drawing students' attention to the accomplishments of members of their group also appears to inoculate vulnerable students against the threat (McIntyre, Paulson, & Lord, 2003).

Although these manipulations have proved effective in laboratory settings, not all of them can be readily applied to real-world situations. For instance, it is not realistic to tell students that a test is not important. Researchers are now beginning to explore ways to reduce stereotype threat in real-world settings.

The aim of one large-scale intervention was to directly tackle Black students' fears that others hold negative views about their intellectual abilities by increasing interactions among Black and White students. The program, developed by Claude Steele and colleagues (Steele et al., in press), created a racially integrated "living and learning" community in a 250-student wing of a large dormitory. The program included weekly study groups, rap sessions that focused on the personal side of college life, and frequent mastery workshops.

Participation in the weekly discussions of the personal side of college life proved especially effective in reducing students' stereotype threat and improving grades. Why? Many of the students had only limited contact with members of groups other than their own prior to college. By providing students the opportunity to get to know members of other groups on a more personal level, the program helped students realize that they shared many of the same concerns about college life (e.g., the fear of not measuring up). The discussions also created a climate of trust that allowed students to reevaluate their thinking about the ways others treated or reacted to them. They came to appreciate that behavior that seems driven by stereotypes often is not. They also learned that although many people do hold stereotypes, the stereotypes often reflect inexperience or ignorance and not the worst kind of prejudice.

We know from decades of research that cultural stereotypes are very difficult to change, even among young children. However, the results of this intervention suggest that it is possible to create contexts—in classrooms and even entire schools—in which negative stereotypes are not felt to apply.

support of this position, they argue that the environmental factors known to be important for intelligence have not been shown to vary appreciably between Caucasians and African Americans. They maintain also that intervention programs designed to increase the intelligence of African American children have failed to do so. Thus, the environmentalist position, they maintain, has been tested and has failed.

Most developmental psychologists have not been persuaded by these arguments. Various replies are possible (Ceci, 1996; Dickens & Flynn, 2001; Fraser, 1995; Scarr, 1981). Many would contend that the plausibility argument drawn from the heritability data is simply not plausible. A high heritability value means simply that environmental differences are relatively unimportant *in the sample studied.* Even if differences among Caucasian children's environments have little impact, it is still possible that environmental differences between African Americans and Caucasians could produce a 10- to 15-point difference in IQ. Recall our example of Island A and Island B. Marked nutritional differences between the two islands might well lead to marked differences in height, no matter how high the heritabilities for each island alone. The same point applies to environmental effects on IQ. To many, this position is more plausible than is the claim that African American children's experiences do not differ in important ways from those of Caucasian children.

More direct evidence can also be cited.

1. Race is more a social classification than a biologically determined category (Fish, 2002). Many African Americans in the United States in fact have Caucasian ancestry in varying degrees. If genes contribute to group differences in IQ, then IQ scores among African Americans should be positively correlated with degree of Caucasian ancestry. So-called admixture studies, however, provide no support for this prediction (Scarr et al., 1977).

2. We noted that adopted children tend to have superior IQs. Similar effects have been reported in studies of transracial adoption—that is, African American children adopted into Caucasian homes. Although the interpretation of this research is somewhat controversial (Levin, 1994; Scarr & Weinberg, 1983; Waldman, Weinberg, & Scarr, 1994), it appears that rearing in what Scarr and Weinberg call the "culture of the test" (that is, homes and schools that promote the kinds of knowledge emphasized on IQ tests) diminishes the racial differences in IQ. Clearly, this finding is compatible with an environmentalist position.

3. Although intervention programs have not been as successful as hoped, at least some programs have produced genuine and long-term gains in African American children's intellectual competence. Furthermore, intervention programs to date do not exhaust what might be done. It is quite possible that future programs, building on the knowledge that has been gained, may yield more impressive effects.

To Recap . . .

Experimental interventions have been directed mainly toward children who are perceived as being at risk for school failure. A variety of intervention programs have had positive effects on children's development. Immediate effects are generally greater than are long-term ones, and effects on school performance are generally greater than are effects on IQ. Programs that introduce the greatest changes in the child's environment have generally had the greatest impact.

On average, African American children score lower than Caucasian children on IQ tests. Drawing on the generally high heritability of IQ, some authors have suggested that genetic factors may contribute to this difference. Most developmental psychologists disagree. Counterarguments include the inappropriateness of applying within-race heritabilities to between-race differences and the positive effect of transracial adoption on African American children's IQs.

ALTERNATIVE CONCEPTIONS OF INTELLIGENCE

In the discussion of intervention programs, we touched on some ways other than IQ to assess children's competence. In this section, we broaden the scope to consider some recent theories and programs of research that represent significant departures from the traditional IQ perspective.

Evolutionary Approaches

As we have seen, traditional approaches to intelligence primarily focus on abilities associated with success in school. School—and the disciplines taught in school—are, however, very recent developments. The human capacity to read and to write can be traced back fewer than 10,000 years. To this day, there are societies in which the majority of citizens cannot read and where formal education is unknown. Consequently, many theorists are dissatisfied with current formulations that define intelligence primarily in terms of school-related skills.

In recent years, there has been growing interest in understanding human intelligence in light of evolution. According to this perspective, intelligence is the ability to adapt to the environment. The issue is, *which* environment? Natural selection occurs over thousands of years. The changes that have occurred in modern times have occurred far too rapidly for humans to have had the opportunity to evolve cognitive capabilities specifically in response to them.

According to evolutionary theory, modern cognitive abilities reflect adaptations to the recurring pressures faced by our human ancestors during primeval times. Evolutionary psychologists label the environment that produced a species' evolved tendencies its **environment of evolutionary adaptiveness,** or **EEA** (Bowlby, 1969; Cosmides, Tooby, & Barkow, 1992). For humans, the EEA occurred two to three million years ago during the Pleistocene era, at which time humans and their protohuman ancestors lived as hunter-gatherers.

Based on studies of modern hunter-gatherer groups and observations of our closest genetic relatives, chimpanzees, evolutionary psychologists have painted a portrait of the lives of these early humans. They contend that early humans probably lived in small bands of 30 to 60 people and survived by gathering fruits, nuts, vegetables, and tubers; scavenging food left over from animal kills; and hunting. The social organization of the hunter-gatherer groups included a sexual division of labor, with females primarily responsible for food gathering and the care and nurturing of children and males primarily responsible for hunting. It is likely that some males had more than one mate, whereas others had no access to females. To survive, early humans had to cooperate and compete, both within groups and with people from the outside (Bjorklund & Pellegrini, 2002).

Of course, life has changed much over the past 100,000 years. But, as already noted, natural selection works too slowly for civilization and the associated changes in social roles, tools, and technology to have substantially affected the structure and organization of the human mind. What this means is that many of the problems our minds are designed to solve are not the ones common to modern life such as learning to read, solve algebra equations, and operate complex machines, but rather the problems our hunter-gatherer ancestors faced generation over generation.

What might those problems have been? Surely finding food would be one (along with knowing which foods to eat and which to avoid). And, our ancestors likely faced numerous problems centered around the complexities of social life, such as attracting and choosing mates, recognizing kin, and "mind-reading" (inferring other's motives, intentions, and knowledge) (Tooby & Cosmides, 1995).

Evolutionary psychologists believe that over many generations, humans evolved a neuropsychological system specially adapted to solving these "ancient" problems. Moreover, this system is organized into specialized modules or cognitive systems dedicated to solving certain kinds of problems—specifically, problems related to human survival and reproduction. These modules are not "preformed"; rather, they emerge with species-typical experience over the course of development.

One example of this approach is a model developed by David Geary (1998). As can be seen in Figure 10.2, Geary's model includes two overarching domains—social and ecological. These domains reflect the types of information that must be processed for humans to survive and reproduce in the natural habitat. Each of the domains consists of two more

Environment of evolutionary adaptiveness (EEA)
The environment that produced a species' evolved tendencies.

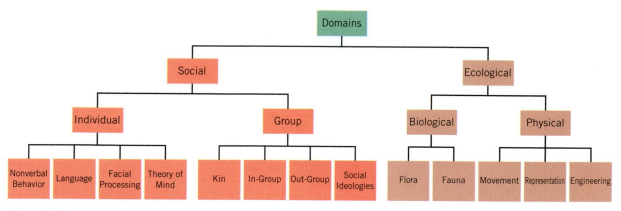

Figure 10.2

Proposed domains of the human mind. From *Male, Female: The Evolution of Human Sex Differences* by D. C. Geary, 1998, Washington, DC: American Psychological Association, p. 180. Copyright © 1998 by the American Psychological Association.

specific domains, each of which comprises even more specific domains. Thus, there are modules for language and for processing faces, a module for processing information about kin and a separate one for strangers, modules for plants and for moving through the physical world. Geary acknowledges that the list of domains is not complete. For instance, there is no domain for numerical information even though Geary himself believes such a domain exists. Indeed, some evolutionary psychologists believe the number of modules dedicated to solving specific types of adaptive problems to be quite large (Cosmides & Tooby, 2001).

Geary refers to the abilities shown in Figure 10.2 as biologically primary abilities. **Biologically primary abilities** have been shaped by natural selection and evolved to deal with problems faced by our ancestors (Geary, 1995b). These abilities (e.g., language, face recognition) are universal. They are found in all cultures and are acquired easily by all normally developing children in all but the most deprived environments. Indeed, children are highly motivated to master these abilities and actively pursue opportunities to do so through play, through social interaction, and through the exploration of objects and the environment (Geary, 2002).

Skills such as reading and higher mathematics are called biologically secondary abilities. **Biologically secondary abilities** are highly specialized neurocognitive systems that build on the primary secondary abilities. Reading, for example, builds on the cognitive and brain systems involved in language acquisition and production. Biologically secondary abilities are the product of culture, not biological evolution. Acquisition of these abilities depends on growing up in a culture that deliberately teaches the skills. For instance, children in illiterate cultures do not spontaneously learn to read. In contrast to biologically primary abilities, which most children readily (and happily) acquire without formal instruction, acquisition of biologically secondary abilities is much more variable. It also often depends on tedious practice and external inducements (Geary, 2002).

From the perspective of evolutionary theory, reading and the other skills taught in school are "unnatural." Consequently, it is understandable that some children have a good deal of difficulty mastering such skills as reading and higher mathematics. As we have seen, different cultures approach teaching mathematics somewhat differently. There are also a variety of ways to foster literacy. We describe various theoretical approaches to teaching reading in Box 10.3.

The idea that many human cognitive abilities are domain-specific or modularized is widely accepted by evolutionary psychologists. Most evolutionary psychologists do not endorse the idea of domain-general cognitive abilities or the notion of general intelligence. Moreover, because evolutionary psychology is primarily concerned with species-wide cognitive adaptations, they have devoted little attention to the topic that is at the heart of the psychometric approach: the study of individual differences in intelligence. Evolutionary psychologists have, however, devoted considerable attention to the study of gender differences in cognitive abilities, a topic that we will discuss in Chapter 15.

Biologically primary abilities
Evolved abilities shaped by natural selection to solve recurring problems faced by ancestral humans.

Biologically secondary abilities
Nonevolved abilities that coopt primary abilities for purposes other than the original evolution-based function and appear only in specific cultural contexts.

Approaches to Reading

One of the most important competencies children learn in school is the ability to read, which we define here as getting meaning from print (Rayner et al., 2001). How children learn to read is of considerable interest to psychologists, as well as parents, teachers, and policy makers. Psychologists have been studying reading and its development for over 100 years, producing tens of thousands of research articles on the topic (Hiebert & Raphael, 1996). Intense debates about the best methods for teaching reading recur regularly, involving not only professional educators but parents as well (Goodman, 1998; Loveless, 2001; Meyer, 2002). And concern with the high number of citizens who cannot read—and the economic consequences of illiteracy—is the centerpiece of current education reform (NICHD, 2000).

BOX 10.3

Applications

In this box, we describe how the four general theoretical frameworks we highlight throughout this text have been applied to the task of understanding and teaching reading.

Evolutionary and Biological Approaches

As we saw earlier, evolutionary psychologists view reading as an "unnatural skill" that depends on growing up in a community that deliberately teaches children how to read (Geary, 1995b). Evolutionary psychologists contrast reading with evolved abilities such as language, which most children are highly motivated to acquire and learn quite easily. Children are not, evolutionary psychologists argue, inherently (meaning biologically) motivated to learn to read. Consequently, we cannot assume that children's "natural curiosity" will lead them to spontaneously engage in the activities that will foster reading skills. Rather, parents and teachers must arrange opportunities for children to acquire the requisite skills and often will need to resort to inducements in order to motivate children to learn to read (Geary, 2002).

Evolutionary psychologists are generally concerned with species-wide abilities. There are, however, considerable individual differences in the ease with which children learn to read. Although much of this variation can be traced to environmental influences, there is growing evidence that biological factors contribute as well. For example, twin and family studies reliably show genetic influences on a variety of reading skills including phonemic awareness, word–reading, and phonological decoding (Byrne et al., 2002; Gayan & Olson, 2003; Wadsworth et al. 2002). And recent DNA studies have found evidence for a link between some types of reading disability and genes on several chromosomes (Plomin & Walker, 2003).

Genes are assumed to influence reading through their impact on brain functioning. Indeed, research using brain imaging has shown that when adults with developmental reading disabilities engage in tasks that involve phonological processing, their brain-wave patterns are different from those produced by normal readers engaging in phonological processing (Shaywitz et al., 1998).

One promising line of research suggests it may be possible to "re-wire" the brains of children with reading disabilities through extensive practice of specific reading skills. In one recent study (Temple et al., 2003), 8- to 12-year-old children with reading disabilities participated in an intensive 8-week computer-based training program that targeted the ability to distinguish between sounds that rhyme (e.g., "B" and "D"). Prior to training, the brains of these children and a control group of normal readers were scanned while the children performed a phonological processing task. As with the adult research, the scans revealed differences in the brain waves of the two groups of children. Following training, the children with reading problems showed improved performance on a number of language and reading tests. Moreover, the pattern of the activation in the children's brains fundamentally changed, becoming much more like that of good readers. This study is just one of a growing number of efforts to apply the cutting-edge tools of neuroscience to instruction.

Environmental/Learning Approaches

According to the environmental/learning view, reading development is subject to the same laws of learning as the acquisition of any other skilled behavior—meaning practice, reinforcement, and the like. This approach tends to emphasize specific reading skills in isolation, often neglecting comprehension (Hiebert & Raphael, 1996). The legacy of this approach is evident in workbook exercises and computer games that reinforce isolated skills. A recent review of computer-assisted instruction of beginning reading showed it to generally be effective (Blok et al., 2002). However, some critics contend that overuse of drill and practice can lead children to believe that reading is tedious and boring (Baker, Scher, & Mackler, 1997).

Reading incentive programs (e.g., *Million Minutes of Reading*; Pizza Hut's *BOOK IT!*) also have their roots in this tradition. There is considerable evidence that the amount children read influences future reading skill (Stanovich, 2000; Stanovich, Cunningham, & West, 1998). Thus, efforts to increase the amount children read are laudable. Nevertheless, there is also evidence that extrinsic rewards can undermine motivation and actually lead to decreases in rates of desirable behaviors (Fawson & Moore, 1999).

Cognitive-Developmental Approaches

Cognitive-developmental approaches to reading explain developmental changes in children's reading in terms of the development of the various mental processes involved in reading, such as memory, knowledge, and metacognitive strategies. In recent years, researchers working within the framework of information processing have focused much of their attention on one very important component of reading—phonological awareness. **Phonological awareness** refers to the child's knowledge of the internal sound structure of spoken words (Rayner et al., 2001). Examples of phonological awareness include the ability to hear the syllables within words (e.g., hearing "par" and "tee" as separate elements of *party*) and to identify words that rhyme (e.g., "light" and "kite").

An impressive body of correlational and experimental evidence links phonological awareness to reading ability. Children who begin school with strong phonological awareness read better in subsequent grades than peers with weaker phonological awareness (Rayner et al., 2001; Snow, Burns, & Griffin, 1998). Reading instruction that explicitly teaches phonological awareness through activities such as rhyming, segmenting sounds, and isolating the first sounds in words has been proved to foster children's phonological awareness and related reading skills (Rayner et al., 2001).

Phonological awareness
Knowledge of the internal sound structure of spoken words.

Piagetian research on the development of reading has focused on how children come to understand the representational functions of words and letters—in other words, that words and letters stand for something else (Hiebert & Raphael, 1998). Much of this work has focused on children's early writing. Children as young as 3 or 4 are aware that writing and drawing look different, although they are not exactly sure why. Initially, young children tend to believe that the forms of written words reflect their meanings. Thus, when asked to write the label for a small object, say caterpillar, they tend to make fewer or small marks. Conversely, they make more marks or larger marks when asked to write the word for a large object (e.g., elephant) (Tolchinsky-Landsmann & Levin, 1985).

Gradually, children's writing begins to reflect their growing understanding of the abstract relationship between letters and sounds. Their spellings now represent the sounds, or "phonemes," they hear, though they often omit vowels, as when *her* is spelled "hr" and *brother* is spelled "brutr." Reading experts believe that this early practice with writing can facilitate children's ability to segment words into sounds (Snow et al., 1998; Vernon & Ferreiro, 1999).

Sociocultural Approaches

Based on Vygosky's writings, sociocultural theorists view reading and literacy more generally as embedded in cultural practices. In contrast to the rather pessimistic view of children's motivation to read expressed by at least some evolutionary psychologists, those working within this framework believe that children are usually quite motivated to participate in the cultural practices of the adult world, including reading. Sociocultural approaches to reading emphasize the social and personal functions of literacy. Thus, sociocultural theorists contend that children should engage in "authentic practice" (e.g., reading the newspaper, writing e-mail, reading books for pleasure) and not contrived activities that enforce practice of specific reading skills in isolation (Au, 1997; O'Flahavan & Seidl, 1997; Lee & Smagorinsky, 2000).

Another important contribution of Vygotsky's theory to educational practice is the idea that learning is mediated by interactions with others. Thus, interventions modeled on sociocultural theory focus on the teacher's role as a mediator, use of instructional scaffolding, and the social systems in which children learn.

One example of the application of sociocultural theory to educational practice is an intervention called **dialogic reading** (Arnold et al., 1994; Lonigan et al., 1999). In typical book reading, the adult takes the lead role—the adult reads and the child listens. Dialogic reading involves a shift in roles, so that the child becomes the storyteller. In dialogic reading, the adult assumes the role of an active listener, posing questions, adding information, and prompting the child to increase the sophistication of his or her descriptions. Open-ended rather than yes/no questions are emphasized, as are questions that move the child beyond specific details to more general issues of motivation and meaning. And as the child's competence as a storyteller increases, so does the level of the adult's prompts and expectations. Studies of the effectiveness of dialogic reading consistently show significant improvements in preschoolers' language and early literacy skills (Whitehurst & Lonigan, 2001).

Dialogic reading
Form of joint picture-book reading in which the adult uses open-ended questions and other prompts to encourage the child to tell the story, with the goal of promoting linguistic skills.

A second application of sociocultural theory to reading instruction is **reciprocal teaching.** Reciprocal teaching is an instructional procedure that targets reading comprehension among older students. In reciprocal teaching, small groups of students learn to improve their reading comprehension through "scaffolded instruction" of strategies that promote comprehension and comprehension monitoring (Brown & Palincsar, 1989; Palincsar & Brown, 1984). The specific strategies are predicting, clarifying, questioning, and summarizing. The strategies are "scaffolded" by a dialogue leader, who may be a teacher or a student. Over time, the dialogue leader reduces his or her level of involvement, and other students in the group take over the role. The goal of reciprocal teaching is for students to internalize the four strategies so they are able to monitor and self-regulate their reading comprehension without assistance. Studies of reciprocal teaching among students of a wide range of ages and reading abilities have demonstrated its effectiveness (Rosenshine & Meister, 1994).

Reciprocal teaching
An instructional procedure in which students learn to monitor their understanding of text by observing and imitating strategies of predicting, clarifying, questioning, and summarizing.

Conclusion

For those who are good readers, reading feels almost effortless. It is almost impossible to look at a word and not read it (Rayner et al., 2001). Reading feels so natural to skilled readers that it seems as if it would be one of the simplest skills for a child to acquire. In fact, though, for many children, learning to read is extremely challenging and can take years of effort. Each of the approaches described here offers insights into ways in which parents and teachers can help children become successful readers.

Dynamic Testing

As we have seen, a central theme in the sociocultural approach to children's development is the cultural determination of individual development. In this view, much of what children learn is acquired from the culture around them, and much of the child's problem solving is mediated through adult help. This emphasis is captured in Vygotskian notion of the zone of proximal development, or what children can do with appropriate help from others.

From the sociocultural perspective, assessments of ability that focus on the child in isolation, as do IQ tests, are misleading. Such a focus at best captures the products of learning; it does not reveal the processes by which children acquire new skills. Furthermore, such a focus may miss important differences among children. Vygotsky used the following example to make this point. Imagine two children who each achieve a mental age of 7 on a standard intelligence test, and who therefore are equally intelligent from this perspective. With hints and prompts from an adult, however, one might be able to solve problems that are 2 years beyond his mental age, whereas the other can go only 6 months beyond. The two children have different zones of proximal development.

In recent years, a number of researchers have attempted to develop **dynamic assessments**—methods of assessing intelligence that build on the concept of the zone of proximal development and the child's ability to profit from instruction (Feuerstein et al., 1995; Lidz & Elliott, 2000; Sternberg & Grigorenko, 2002a; Tzuriel, 2001). Different investigators have taken somewhat different approaches. One common strategy, however, has been a *test-train-test procedure*. With this approach, the child first attempts to solve a set of problems on his or her own, much as on a standard IQ test. Following this determination of independent performance, the experimenter provides a standardized set of prompts designed to help the child arrive at an answer. The prompts are arranged in a graduated series, starting out fairly subtle and indirect and becoming progressively more explicit until the solution is reached. The child's zone for that kind of problem solving can be determined from the number of hints needed—the fewer the hints, the wider the zone. In the final phase, the child is presented with problems that vary in their similarity to those on which help was given. This final phase provides a measure of the child's ability to transfer the skills learned with adult help.

Studies using the approach have confirmed Vygotsky's claim that IQ tests provide an incomplete picture of children's intelligence. IQ scores do relate to both speed of initial learning and breadth of transfer. The relation is not perfect, however, and many children's ability to profit from help is not predicted by their IQs. Children, in short, are a good deal more variable than IQ tests indicate. In a sense, of course, this fact has always been known; we saw that IQ scores are a far from perfect predictor of school performance or any other important outcome. What dynamic assessments do is to specify one of the important dimensions not captured by IQ—the ability to profit from help provided by other people.

Assessing children's ability with standard IQ tests is relatively easy; there are many such instruments to choose among, and most can be administered in approximately 1 hour. Dynamic testing is more challenging on a number of dimensions: in the degree of training necessary to carry out such assessments, in the amount of time required to complete an assessment (up to 10 hours per child in some approaches), and in the interpretation of the results. Although several individual research programs have demonstrated the potential value of dynamic assessment, the approach has yet to result in a generally accepted, widely applied method of testing intelligence. Nevertheless, the approach remains, in the words of one recent evaluation, "a wonderful idea . . . with enormous promise" (Sternberg & Grigorenko, 2002a, p. viii).

Gardner's Multiple Intelligences

Howard Gardner (1983, 1993, 1999) has proposed a theory of intelligence that is in some respects similar to those of factor-analytic theorists, such as Thurstone and

Dynamic assessment
Method of assessing children's abilities derived from Vygotsky's concept of the zone of proximal development. Measures the child's ability to benefit from adult-provided assistance, typically in a test-train-retest design.

Guilford. Like these theorists, Gardner believes that intelligence is considerably more diversified and multifaceted than the notion of general intelligence admits. Unlike most psychometric researchers, however, Gardner does not rely solely on factor analyses of standardized tests to draw conclusions about different forms of intelligence. And the kinds of intelligence that he proposes go well beyond the ones that psychometric theorists usually consider.

Gardner's general thesis is that humans possess at least eight relatively distinct *intelligences,* defined as the "ability to solve problems or fashion products that are of consequence in a particular cultural setting or community" (Gardner, 1993, p. 15). We consider what some of these intelligences are shortly. First, however, we must ask about evidence. How can the existence of a distinct intelligence be demonstrated? Gardner suggests a number of kinds of evidence, or *signs,* that can help point the way. First, there must be experimental evidence in support of the intelligence. The factor-analytic studies discussed earlier are one possible experimental approach to distinguishing different sorts of intelligence; information-processing demonstrations of the distinctiveness of different cognitive domains (see Chapter 8) are another. Next, the intelligence should be specifiable in terms of a set of distinct core operations—that is, it should be possible to say what it "is." Third, the intelligence should show a distinct developmental history, progressing predictably from rudimentary to advanced. In addition, it should show a distinct evolutionary history, growing in complexity as the species grows more complex in the course of its evolution.

Two final signs discussed by Gardner concern deviations from the normal developmental path. Gardner argues that isolation by brain damage can be informative. For example, the fact that linguistic abilities can be either selectively impaired or selectively spared in cases of brain injury is evidence for a separate linguistic intelligence. Similarly, the existence of individuals with exceptional talents in one particular domain is a possible sign. In so-called savants, for example, remarkable mathematical ability may be coupled with subnormal general intelligence, suggesting that a distinct mathematical intelligence exists. And children who compose symphonies at age 10, as did Mozart and Mendelssohn, are evidence for a musical intelligence.

As noted, Gardner uses such evidence to propose the existence of at least eight distinct human intelligences. Table 10.9 summarizes the intelligences. Some are familiar. Gardner marshals evidence in support of a linguistic intelligence, a spatial intelligence,

Table 10.9	**Gardner's Multiple Intelligences**	
Type of Intelligence	**Description**	**Possible Vocations**
Linguistic	Sensitivity to spoken and written language, ability to use language to achieve goals	Writer, lawyer, poet
Logical-mathematical	Ability to analyze problems logically, carry out mathematical operations, investigate issues scientifically	Mathematician, scientist
Musical	Appreciation of musical patterns, skill in the composition and performance of music	Musician, composer
Bodily kinesthetic	Ability to use one's body or parts of the body (e.g., hands, feet) to solve problems or fashion products	Dancer, athlete, craftsperson
Spatial	Ability to perceive spatial relationships and manipulate patterns of space	Navigator, pilot, architect
Naturalist	Ability to recognize and classify flora and fauna	Biologist, naturalist
Interpersonal	Ability to understand the desires and intentions of other people and to work effectively with others	Clinician, salesperson, politician
Intrapersonal	Capacity to understand oneself and to use this understanding to direct one's life effectively	Relevant to almost any profession

SOURCE: Adapted from *Intelligence Reframed* by H. Gardner, 1999, New York: Basic Books.

and a logical-mathematical intelligence. Although the evidence that he uses is sometimes unusual (for example, an analysis of the drawings of a child with autism in the discussion of spatial intelligence; see Figure 10.3), these are forms of intelligence that are talked about in some way by every theorist.

Other intelligences are less familiar. We have already mentioned, for instance, the idea of a musical intelligence. In Gardner's view, musical ability meets all the signs for consideration as a distinct form of intelligence. Musical ability has both an evolutionary and a developmental history, it can appear in isolated form in cases of brain injury or musical prodigy, and it can be analyzed in terms of a set of core elements (pitch, rhythm, timbre, and so on). Similar arguments are offered in support of a bodily kinesthetic intelligence, a naturalist's intelligence, and two forms of personal intelligence—one (intrapersonal intelligence) concerned with understanding of the self, and one (interpersonal intelligence) concerned with understanding others.

We noted that the Vygotskian approach is beginning to have an impact on both psychological assessment and educational practice. The same is true of the theory of multiple intelligences. Recent years have seen the formation of a number of schools inspired by Gardner's framework, as well as the creation of methods of assessing children's abilities that encompass a wider range of skills and contexts than do IQ tests (Chen & Gardner, 1997; Kornhaber, 1994). As with the dynamic assessments inspired by Vygotsky, such efforts face formidable practical obstacles, and applications to date have been limited. Both approaches, however, have the potential to enrich our understanding of how children differ in intelligence, as well as to reveal and to nurture intellectual strengths that might not otherwise be apparent.

Figure 10.3

Drawing made by a 5-year-old girl with autism—one kind of evidence offered by Gardner in support of his theory of a distinct form of spatial intelligence. From *Frames of Mind: The Theory of Multiple Intelligence* by H. Gardner, 1983, New York: Basic Books, p. 189. Copyright © 1983 by Basic Books. Reprinted by permission.

Giftedness and Creativity

By one definition of *giftedness*, gifted children are simply those who score at the top of the IQ range—perhaps IQs of 130 or 140 or above. This is the most common definition in American school systems. It was also the definition in the Terman longitudinal study of genius (Box 2.1). As we saw, exceptional performance on childhood IQ tests was associated with a number of positive outcomes in the Terman research.

Not all psychologists agree that the standard IQ approach captures everything that the concept of giftedness should embody. Ellen Winner (1996, 2000) has been one of the most forceful advocates of an alternative approach to the study of gifted children. In Winner's view, high-IQ children represent only one form of giftedness—they are gifted with respect to the kinds of abilities (verbal skills, mathematical understanding, logical reasoning) that are stressed on IQ tests and in school. Even within the domain of IQ-type skills, however, such children are not necessarily exceptional across the board; a child, for example, might be gifted in math but only average on other dimensions. More generally, Winner argues that "global giftedness" is the exception rather than the rule; more typical is exceptional performance in just one domain of development. Furthermore, these domains, she maintains, include more than just the verbal and mathematical abilities valued in school. Primarily through analyses of dozens of case studies, Winner provides examples of giftedness not only in mathematics and language but also in art and in music. Figure 10.4 shows some of the drawings produced by one of the children identified as gifted in art.

Clearly, exceptional performance in some domain is the starting point for any conception of giftedness. Winner argues that gifted children display three further characteristics. One is *precocity*—gifted children not only possess exceptional abilities but demonstrate their abilities very early in development. The drawing of the cat in Figure 10.4 may not

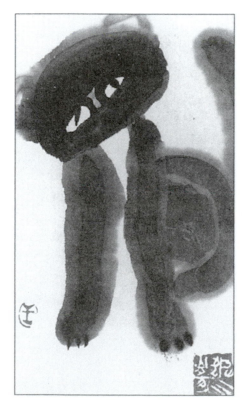

Figure 10.4

Drawings made by a young girl identified as gifted in art. The cat was drawn at age 3 and the monkeys at age 5. From *Gifted Children* by E. Winner, 1996, New York: Basic Books, pp. 84–85. Copyright © 1996 by Basic Books. Reprinted by permission.

seem remarkable in itself (even though it is probably better than most of us could do!); what is remarkable is that it was produced by a 3-year-old. A second characteristic is what Winner labels *marching to their own drummer*. Gifted children learn not only faster but in qualitatively different ways from children in general, and much of what they learn they discover for themselves, rather than acquiring from others. Finally, gifted children possess *a rage to master*—they are strongly motivated, perhaps even driven, to conquer their domain of interest. For example, the little girl who was the source for the drawings in Figure 10.4 produced 4,000 paintings in a span of 3 years!

Where does giftedness come from? Winner's answer is definitely of the nature *and* nurture sort—as is that of most psychologists and educators who have considered the question (e.g., Feldman, 1986; Gottfried et al., 1994). She dismisses as a "myth" the idea that parents or other environmental forces can turn any child into a gifted child. There must be a biological starting point, and only some children are born with the capacity to achieve exceptional levels in math or music or art. Biology is not sufficient, however; there must also be a supportive environment. It is true, as we have seen, that gifted children in part create their own environment. For their full potential to emerge, however, they cannot do it alone; they must receive help from parents, teachers, or other supportive adults.

If the definition of giftedness has been problematic for psychologists, that for *creativity* has proved to be even more so. At the adult level the meaning—if not the production—of creativity is fairly straightforward: Creativity involves the ability to generate novel outcomes that are valued in some context. But what can children do that merits the label *creative*, or that might be predictive of eventual adult creativity?

One approach emphasizes the distinction between convergent thinking and divergent thinking (Guilford, 1985; Wallach & Kogan, 1966). **Convergent thinking** is right-answer–oriented thinking—the form of thinking we engage in when faced with a task (e.g., a mathematical problem, a logical deduction) for which there is a single, definite solution. Convergent thinking is what IQ tests measure. In contrast, **divergent thinking** involves the ability to generate multiple and original possible solutions for tasks that do not have a single right answer. For example, thinking of unusual uses for a newspaper or coat hanger would be forms of divergent thinking, as would be coming up with different possible interpretations for a squiggle drawing.

The unusual uses and squiggles tasks are in fact among the tasks used to measure divergent thinking in childhood (Wallach & Kogan, 1966). Tasks like these do succeed in identifying individual differences in the capacity for divergent thinking, differences that are evident from early in childhood. Furthermore, these differences are only weakly if at all related to IQ. Thus, tests of divergent thinking meet one of the criteria for a measure of creativity: They appear to be tapping something other than simply intelligence in the IQ sense.

A capacity for divergent thinking is almost certainly necessary for creativity, but most investigators believe that it is not sufficient. There is, after all, a gap between generating lots of ideas for some topic and actually producing a genuinely creative product. Furthermore, measures of divergent thinking are at best weak predictors of real-world creative performance.

Most contemporary accounts of creativity are what Sternberg and Lubart (1996) label *confluence theories*, in that they stress the coming together or confluence of multiple contributors that must work together to make creativity possible. One example is the *investment theory* of creativity proposed by Sternberg and Lubart (1991, 1995). The basic idea of investment theory is implied by the name: Creativity requires a willingness to invest or commit a number of resources to the task at hand—to buy low, in the sense of pursuing novel or out-of-favor topics, and sell high, in the sense of persisting until a valued outcome is produced. The necessary cognitive resources include but are not limited to an aptitude for divergent thinking; also important are knowledge with regard to the specific problem domain and an ability to evaluate the adequacy of the ideas that one has generated. Cognitive factors, in turn, must be joined by the right sort of personality

Convergent thinking
Form of thinking whose goal is to discover the correct answer to problems with a definite solution—the form of thought emphasized on IQ tests.

Divergent thinking
Form of thinking whose goal is to generate multiple possible solutions for problems that do not have a single correct answer—the form of thought hypothesized to be important for creativity.

attributes—in particular, an ability to tolerate ambiguity and a willingness to take risks. There must be strong motivation to persist in the face of obstacles. And there must be a supportive environmental context.

The importance of this last contributor is worth reiterating. However strong the cognitive and personality resources may be, creative potential can flourish only if the environment provides the opportunity. We saw the same point with respect to giftedness, and of course it applies as well to other cognitive achievements, including intelligence in the IQ sense and performance in school. Cognitive abilities always develop and are expressed within an environmental context, and some children experience more supportive contexts than do others.

To Recap . . .

Dissatisfaction with the traditional IQ approach is reflected in several recent alternative approaches to intelligence. Evolutionary accounts contrast cognitive abilities that likely proved adaptive in the ancestral past with those necessary to survive in the modern world. Cognitive abilities that have been shaped by natural selection are called biologically primary abilities. These abilities are supported by dedicated neurocognitive systems and are readily acquired by children the world over. Biologically secondary abilities are culture-specific. Acquisition of these skills, which include reading and higher mathematics, requires deliberate instruction.

Sociocultural theorists emphasize what children can do with appropriate help from others. Theoretically, this emphasis is reflected in the concept of the zone of proximal development, and pragmatically it forms the basis for dynamic assessments, that is, assessments that add a social dimension to the evaluation of intellectual ability. Such assessments reveal individual differences among children that are not identified by standard IQ measures.

Gardner's theory of multiple intelligences suggests that certain forms of intelligence fall outside the scope of standard psychometric assessments. Based on a variety of evidence, Gardner posits the existence of eight relatively distinct human intelligences: linguistic, spatial, logical-mathematical, musical, bodily kinesthetic, naturalist, intrapersonal, and interpersonal.

Studies of giftedness and creativity attempt to identify forms of exceptional intellectual accomplishment that are not captured by IQ. Many psychologists believe that giftedness involves more than simply high IQ; children may be gifted in specific domains of development rather than in general, and these domains include abilities (e.g., in art or music) that are not part of standard conceptions of intelligence. Creativity also has been argued to require more than intelligence in the psychometric sense. Confluence models of creativity stress the convergence of multiple contributors to creativity, including divergent thinking, personality attributes, and motivation.

CONCLUSION

In 1994 the Board of Scientific Affairs of the American Psychological Association, impelled in part by the controversy surrounding *The Bell Curve,* formed a task force whose goal was to clarify the issues raised by the book. The committee set out to summarize and to evaluate the evidence with respect to the questions that have concerned us throughout this chapter: What is intelligence, where does it come from, why are there differences among individuals and among groups, and what effects does intelligence have? The task force was chaired by Ulric Neisser, and its members included many of the theorists and researchers whose work we have discussed.

The committee's report was published in the January 1996 issue of the *American Psychologist* (Neisser et al., 1996), and we recommend it highly for those with a continuing interest in the issues addressed in this chapter. We will not attempt to summarize all of the points made in the report, but we will note three of the general conclusions that the task force emphasizes, because they mirror conclusions that we have attempted to convey in our own discussion of the issues.

A first conclusion is that we have learned much about intelligence in the close to 100 years since intelligence tests first appeared. Much of the Neisser et al. article, like much of the current chapter, is devoted to documenting these gains in knowledge. As we noted at the outset of the chapter, the impact of the approach has been applied as well as theoretical—effects on school curricula, for example, or on the design and evaluation of intervention programs. Whether intelligence tests really rank, as one of their proponents has claimed, as "psychology's most telling accomplishment to date" (Herrnstein, 1971, p. 45) is debatable. But they certainly are among the most influential.

A second conclusion is that these undeniable achievements are accompanied by large areas of uncertainty and debate. The greatest uncertainty, not surprisingly, is associated with the hardest-to-study topics. Thus, we know, for example, that both genes and environment contribute to differences in IQ, as well as something about their typical relative contribution. But we still have much to learn about how genes or environments produce their effects. Nor do we know why there are on-average group differences on some measures of intellectual performance.

A final conclusion concerns limitations of another sort. IQ tests provide a sampling of intellectual abilities, but they do not exhaust the domain of human intelligence. As Neisser et al. (1996, p. 95) note, "We know much less about the forms of intelligence that tests do not easily assess: wisdom, creativity, practical knowledge, social skill, and the like." Furthermore, the psychometric focus on individual differences may cause us to lose track of the important ways in which all children are similar in their intellectual development. Similarly, the frequent focus on problems in development may cause us to miss the strengths that particular children possess. It is in this respect that the approaches to cognitive development we considered in the preceding three chapters provide a valuable complement to the intelligence-test perspective. These approaches concentrate on basic developments common to all children, and they remind us that all children show impressive intellectual achievements.

These points emerge even more clearly in the next chapter, when we turn to the topic of language development. We will see that the focus of most research on language has been on similarities rather than on differences among children. We will also see that mastery of language is a remarkable cognitive achievement—perhaps the most impressive achievement that the human species shows.

FOR THOUGHT AND DISCUSSION

1. We have tried in this chapter to present both the positive and the negative aspects of IQ tests. Some people, however, believe that the negative points so outweigh the positive that the tests should no longer be used. *Do you think that the use of IQ tests should be banned in schools and other applied settings? Why or why not? What would be gained and what would be lost if such tests were no longer used?*

2. One of the criticisms of the IQ approach to assessing intelligence is that a single score cannot capture the many different aspects of human intelligence. *What are your opinions with respect to the one intelligence versus many intelligences debate? How well does Gardner's theory of multiple intelligences apply to you or to people you know?*

3. Throughout the book, we consider a number of positions that suggest that people in part create their own environments—Bronfenbrenner's notion of developmentally generative or disruptive characteristics (Chapter 1), Bandura's model of reciprocal determinism (Chapter 1), and Scarr and McCartney's genotype–environment relationships (Chapter 3). *Consider the application of such models to the interpretation of studies of identical twins reared apart. Is similarity between separated identical twins necessarily a direct result of the genes? Does it make sense to try to identify separate contributions of genes and environment if the two factors are often correlated?*

4. The research discussed in this chapter addresses not only theoretical questions about the nature of intelligence but also practical questions about how best to nurture the intellectual development of all children. Intervention programs for children perceived to be at risk for later problems are a prime example of efforts in this second, applied category. *Imagine that you were to design an intervention program for an at-risk population, What would your program emphasize, and how would you evaluate its effects?*

5. We discuss what research has shown about the contribution of parents to their children's intellectual development. *Do any of the findings affect your ideas of how to interact with your children or of what you will do if you become a parent?*

6. The topic of creativity has long been a challenge for child psychologists. *Do you believe that creativity can be measured in childhood? If so, how? What are ways in which either parents or teachers might nurture the development of creativity?*

VISUAL SUMMARY FOR CHAPTER 10
Intelligence and Schooling

The Nature of IQ Tests

The Binet Approach

The first successful intelligence test was developed in 1905 by Binet and Simon. Its purpose was to measure individual differences in intellectual ability, to assist in school placement. The Stanford-Binet test is a direct descendant. Like other tests of intelligence, it compares a child's performance with that of other children.

Other Tests of Childhood Intelligence

The leading alternative to the Stanford-Binet is a series of tests developed by David Wechsler, which include the Wechsler Intelligence Scale for Children (WISC) and the Wechsler Preschool and Primary Scales of Intelligence (WPPSI). The Kaufman Assessment Battery for Children (K-ABC) includes an explicit attempt at cultural diversity and cultural fairness. Other tests include the Bayley Scales of Infant Development, which stresses sensorimotor skills in infancy.

Evaluating the Tests

The major IQ tests possess satisfactory reliability. Whether they are valid measures of intelligence has been more difficult to determine. Tests of childhood IQ do relate to measures of academic performance; however, the relation is not perfect. Moreover, the academic focus of most IQ tests means that they may not be good measures of other kinds of intelligence.

Issues in the Study of Intelligence

The Organization of Intelligence

Factor analysis provides evidence for both general intelligence, which affects performance on many tasks, and more specific abilities, which contribute to performance on specific tasks.

Stability of IQ

Infant IQ appears to have little relation to later IQ, a discontinuity in development usually attributed to differences in content between infant and childhood intelligence. Recent evidence suggests, however, that response to novelty may provide a link between infancy and later childhood. Beyond infancy, IQ does correlate from one age to another, although the correlations are not perfect.

Origins of Individual Differences

Family studies, adoption studies, and twin studies all suggest a substantial genetic contribution to individual differences in intelligence. All three methods also indicate the importance of the environment. It is estimated that 40% to 70% of the variation in IQ among people is genetic in origin.

Contributions of the Family

Longitudinal Studies

Longitudinal studies indicate that risk factors in the child's environment, such as family stresses, are predictive of declines in IQ over time.

Research with the HOME

Studies using the HOME, the most popular instrument for measuring the home environment, suggest that the quality of the child's experience within the home influences both current and future intellectual competence.

Cross-Cultural Research

Examinations of the bases for cross-national differences in mathematical achievement provide further evidence for the importance of parental values and practices.

Schooling: Variations and Effects

Cross-Cultural Studies
Cross-cultural research indicates that schooling promotes a number of cognitive skills, including memory, classification, and metacognition.

Amount of Schooling
There is a positive relation between number of years of education completed and IQ. The usual explanation has been that more intelligent people stay in school longer. In addition, however, schooling may actually increase IQ.

Quality of Schooling
The quality as well as the quantity of schooling can be important. Successful schools are characterized by efficiency, organization, and a strong academic emphasis. Less clear are the effects of ability grouping and the timing and nature of school transitions.

Contextual Contributors to Schooling
The success of schooling depends in part on the contribution of other important social systems, such as peers and parents. The fit between the school experience and the child's cultural background can also play a role.

Schooling: Experimental Interventions

Intervention Projects
Experimental interventions have been directed mainly toward children perceived to be at risk. A variety of intervention programs, such as the Abecedarian Project and Head Start, have had positive effects. Immediate effects are generally greater than long-term effects, and effects on school performance are generally greater than effects on IQ.

Race and Intelligence
On average, African American children score lower than White children on IQ tests. Some authors have suggested that genetic factors may play a role. Most developmental psychologists disagree. Counterarguments include the inappropriateness of applying within-race heritabilities to between-race differences and the positive effect of transracial adoption on African American children's IQs.

Alternative Conceptions of Intelligence
Dissatisfaction with the traditional IQ approach is reflected in several alternative approaches to intelligence.

Evolutionary Approaches
Evolutionary accounts contrast cognitive abilities that likely proved adaptive in the distant past with those necessary to survive in the modern world. Cognitive abilities shaped by natural selection, called biologically primary abilities, are readily acquired by all children. Biologically secondary abilities, such as reading, are culture-specific and require deliberate instruction.

Dynamic Testing
Sociocultural theorists emphasize what children can do with appropriate help from others. This emphasis forms the basis for dynamic assessments—assessments that add a social dimension to the evaluation of intellectual ability. Such assessments reveal individual differences that are not identified by standard IQ measures.

Gardner's Multiple Intelligences
Gardner's theory of multiple intelligences suggests that certain forms of intelligence fall outside the scope of standard psychometric assessments. Gardner posits the existence of eight relatively distinct human intelligences: linguistic, spatial, logical-mathematical, musical, bodily kinesthetic, naturalist, intrapersonal, and interpersonal.

Giftedness and Creativity
Both giftedness and creativity may involve more than simply high IQ. Children may be gifted in specific domains rather than in general, and these domains include abilities (e.g., art or music) that are not part of standard conceptions of intelligence. Confluence models of creativity stress the convergence of multiple contributors to creativity, including divergent thinking, personality attributes, and motivation.

11

Language Development

n the fifth century B.C.E., Greek historian Herodotus reported what may have been the first scientific experiment. According to Herodotus, Egyptian pharaoh Psammentichus had sought to determine which was the earliest (and therefore the most natural) human language. To answer this question,

the pharaoh ordered that two infants be reared in an isolated mountain hut without any exposure to language. If the infants nevertheless learned to speak, as the pharaoh believed they would, then the language that emerged must be the original human tongue. The infants did in fact eventually speak, and the first word uttered was *bekos,* which, it turned out, was the word for bread in the ancient language of Phrygia (now part of Turkey). The honor of the original language was therefore ceded to the Phrygians (Fromkin & Rodman, 1988).

The report by Herodotus is just one of many accounts of attempts, spread across many centuries, to identify the first human language. The reported results have varied. One experiment, carried out by King James IV of Scotland, led to the conclusion that the original language was Hebrew (Fromkin & Rodman, 1988). Another study was inconclusive because the isolated babies, deprived of social contact, died before they could produce any words (Ross & McLaughlin, 1949).

We will not attempt to solve the mystery of the first human language in this chapter. Our focus will be on how children today master the particular language to which they are exposed. We will see, however, that this problem is perhaps no less difficult than the one that confronted Psammentichus. The question of how children learn language is one of the most challenging and fascinating topics in the modern science of child psychology.

Any student who has spent 4 years in high school or college attempting to learn a second language can appreciate the struggle of trying to memorize how each verb is conjugated or what endings signify past, future, and subjunctive forms. Yet that very same student, during the first 4 years of life, very likely acquired the rudiments of his or her native language rather easily, with no textbooks, classroom instruction, or studying. How is such an impressive feat accomplished?

We can immediately rule out simple explanations of either the nature or nurture sort. The remarkable feat of language development would be easy to understand if language were simply an inherited ability that is passed along in the genes, emerging according to a biological timetable. As we saw in Chapter 1, even animals with very limited cognitive capabilities can display extremely complex behavior if it is the product of millions of years of evolution. Various properties of language rule out such an explanation, however. One is its **productivity.** Whereas communication in other species involves a small set of inborn messages that the animal can send and also recognize, humans can produce—and comprehend—an infinite number of sentences. Many of the statements we speak and hear every day are ones we have never used or encountered in exactly the same form, yet they give us little trouble. Such statements are obviously not the sorts of messages that are passed along genetically from generation to generation.

A second property of language that argues against a purely genetic explanation is its variety. Language consists not of one tongue used by all members of the species but of thousands of languages. Furthermore, different languages do not simply substitute one word for another; they use different grammatical structures. The word order used to ask a question in Japanese, for example, is different from the corresponding order in French. Yet children readily learn the particular language to which they are exposed. And a child of Japanese parents growing up in a French-speaking home will learn French, not Japanese. We are reminded of the story of the little American girl whose parents had just adopted a baby from Korea. "I can't wait until he gets older," she remarked, "so that he can teach me to speak Korean."* Whatever language abilities children inherit from their parents, the ability to speak and comprehend their native tongue is not one of them.

Productivity
The property of language that permits humans to produce and comprehend an infinite number of statements.

---

*We thank Harriet Rheingold for this story.

We can begin, then, by ruling out a simple nature solution to the fascinating puzzle of human language. Clearly, language must be at least in part learned. But some of the same properties of language that argue against a direct genetic explanation also pose problems for any simple learning account. Language, as we said, is infinitely productive, and children continually produce and understand sentences that they have not encountered before. The rules that underlie such sentences are quite complex, yet children master them very quickly. And they do so even though their parents do not explicitly teach them most of the rules, nor (as we will see) do they necessarily provide clear models or reinforcements from which children might learn the rules. These arguments suggest that there may indeed be a strong biological basis on which experience operates.

Our coverage of the active field of language development focuses on the two traditional developmental issues. One is a description of the typical course of language development, beginning with the infant's earliest recognition abilities and continuing through children's first words, sentences, and more complex utterances. The second involves proposed explanations of language acquisition and the research findings that support them.

The chapter is divided into five parts. We begin by considering modern theories of language development. Next we examine what is known about the period before the child begins to speak—a period that many researchers feel is important in laying the groundwork for language development. In the remaining sections, we discuss the development of the three principal areas of language: its meaning (semantics), its structure (grammar), and its functions (pragmatics).

THEORIES OF LANGUAGE DEVELOPMENT

As we saw in our discussion of pharaoh Psammentichus and other early researchers, the theoretical debate over language development is not new. Today, the theoretical approaches to language follow roughly the four traditions we described in Chapter 1, including a biologically oriented model, cognitive approaches, sociocultural approaches, and environmental/learning analyses. Here we outline the fundamental ideas of these theories, and in later sections we examine what the data from research with children have to say about them.

Nativistic Theory

The modern debate over language development began around 1960. Before then, most American psychologists viewed language learning in terms of conditioning and learning principles. In his book *Verbal Behavior* (1957), B. F. Skinner argued that the same operant principles used to explain other forms of human behavior could be used to explain the acquisition of language.

The first important challenge to Skinner's views came from Noam Chomsky, a linguist at the Massachusetts Institute of Technology (MIT). The **nativistic theory** of language development proposed by Chomsky puts heavy emphasis on inborn processes and biological mechanisms, in contrast to the environmentalist emphasis of Skinner's theory. Chomsky and other nativistic theorists contend that language acquisition must have a strong biological basis, because young children acquire language so rapidly and so easily, and during a period of development when their cognitive abilities are still rather unsophisticated (Chomsky, 1959, 1965; Lenneberg, 1967; Pinker, 1994). These theorists rule out the possibility that language is acquired by means of rewards, punishments, and imitation for several reasons.

First, adults do not appear to reinforce or punish children for the accuracy of their speech (a point we will discuss again shortly), as an environmental analysis would seem to suggest. In addition, learning by imitation would require that children be exposed to consistently good models of speech and language. However, much of the everyday adult speech that children hear is not well formed and accurate but includes short pieces of sentences,

Nativistic theory
A theory of language development, originated by Chomsky, that stresses innate mechanisms separate from cognitive processes.

hesitating stops and starts, slang words, and errors of many types. The productivity property of language also argues against learning by imitation because children produce many statements they have never heard spoken precisely in that way. Similarly, they cannot be imitating adult speech when they produce forms such as "Mommy goed here" or "me up."

A final argument comes from linguistic analyses of human language. Such analyses reveal that the rules we use in speaking or comprehending language are extremely complex. But adults do not specifically teach children these rules. None of us, in fact, could accurately describe the intricate system of language regulations we use so effortlessly to produce and understand good speech and to recognize when speech is not good. These problems and others have led theorists in this tradition to conclude that environmental/learning accounts of language development are inadequate. The only alternative, they suggest, is that children are born with special brain mechanisms—separate from other cognitive processes—that allow them to acquire language quickly and easily.

According to Chomsky's original model, language can be described in terms of two types of structures. A language's **surface structure** consists of the rules governing the way that words and phrases can be arranged, which may vary considerably from one language to another. The **deep structure** of language, in contrast, refers to the inborn rules humans possess that underlie *any* language system. Language acquisition, therefore, requires a speech-analyzing mechanism, which Chomsky called the **language acquisition device (LAD).** Whenever a child hears speech—good, bad, or whatever—this hypothetical brain mechanism begins to develop a **transformational grammar** that translates the surface structure of the language into the deep structure that the child can comprehend. The development of these transformational rules is assumed to take place over several years, explaining why the child's initial language skills are rather limited, but also why they progress so rapidly.

We should note that more recent models in this tradition have diverged in various ways from Chomsky's original formulation. Chomsky's own theory has undergone many specific changes over the years, but the general claims that are relevant for language acquisition have remained the same (Chomsky, 1995, 2000). Thus, the current version of the theory still maintains that language is an extraordinarily complex system with a number of nonobvious or "deep" features, that many of these features are universal across the languages of the world, and that children start the task of language learning with innate knowledge of these universal features. Experience, then, does not teach children language; rather, it simply tells them how the universal features are expressed in the language that they are learning. This emphasis on the natural, biologically prepared nature of language development is well captured in the title of a book devoted to this position: *The Language Instinct* (Pinker, 1994).

The nativistic model solves several of the problems of an environmental approach. The rewards and punishments that would be necessary to operantly condition children's speech are not important to this model. Rather, children need only a few critical bits of speech input to develop a grammar and thus to trigger a great deal of language development. Once children grasp the structural rules, or grammar, of the language, they can understand and produce an infinite number of sentences. In addition, according to this model, the analyzing and processing mechanisms needed have evolved specifically for language acquisition and are concerned only with the abstract structure of speech (e.g., subject-verb-object), not with its meaning or content. These two points mean that language acquisition should put few demands on children's cognitive abilities, making highly sophisticated language learning possible in a cognitively immature organism.

Chomsky's approach dominated language research and theory throughout the 1960s, and it remains a major position today. Beginning around 1970, however, alternative views of language development began to emerge. These views have a number of points in common. In particular, each places more emphasis on the environmental contributors to language acquisition than does the nativistic approach; in addition, the various models overlap in the assumptions they make and the kinds of evidence they cite. Nevertheless, there are also differences among them in emphases and specific claims, differences that correspond to general themes of the remaining three theoretical approaches.

Surface structure
Chomsky's term for the way words and phrases are arranged in spoken languages.

Deep structure
Chomsky's term for the inborn knowledge humans possess about the properties of language.

Language acquisition device (LAD)
Chomsky's proposed brain mechanism for analyzing speech input; the mechanism that allows young children to acquire quickly the language to which they are exposed.

Transformational grammar
A set of rules developed by the LAD to translate a language's surface structure to a deep structure that the child can innately understand.

Noam Chomsky's nativistic theory dominated research on language acquisition throughout the 1960s.

Environmental/Learning Approaches

We saw that Skinner's analysis of language behavior fell out of favor when Chomsky convincingly argued that the environment alone cannot explain the facts of normal language development. Nevertheless, learning-based approaches to this topic did not stop. Contemporary work in this tradition differs in two main ways from its predecessors.

First, most work is now directed by more cognitively oriented theories of learning than the operant conditioning model of Skinner. In particular, more recent work has been grounded in Bandura's social-cognitive model (see Chapter 1), with its emphasis on observational learning and related cognitive processes (Zimmerman, 1983). Chomsky argued that children cannot learn language simply by imitating what they hear because they can produce and understand an unlimited number of new sentences. But as we saw in Chapter 1, social-learning theorists have shown that learning by imitation need not involve exact copying. They argue, therefore, that modeling and observational learning may account for the kind of rule-based system that children come to use (Bandura, 1986; Whitehurst & DeBaryshe, 1989).

The second difference concerns evidence for the role of environmental factors. As we saw, one of Chomsky's most important criticisms of Skinner's approach was that the environment does not present the child with a good model of language from which to learn. But research has shown that people do not talk to infants or young children the same way they talk to proficient speakers. Instead, mothers (and fathers, and even older children) use a distinct style of speech termed **motherese.** Motherese (also referred to as *infant-directed speech*) is characterized by slow, careful pronunciation and exaggerated intonation. It consists primarily of familiar words, there is much repetition, and sentences tend to be short, simple, and grammatically accurate (Hampson & Nelson, 1993; Snow & Ferguson, 1977). These findings indicate that the input children receive may well be clearer and more helpful than Chomsky claimed.

Motherese
Simplified speech directed at very young children by adults and older children.

Finally, nativistic theorists have argued that parents do not specifically train children in the rules of language. Yet recent analyses of parent–child interactions indicate that parents do sometimes respond to the grammatical accuracy of their children's speech, providing them a variety of forms of feedback and instruction (Moerk, 2000). Taken together, these findings suggest that social and environmental factors may play a significant role in children's language acquisition.

Cognitive-Developmental Models

The major emphasis of the cognitive-developmental approach to language is, not surprisingly, on cognitive contributors to language acquisition. Whereas nativistic theorists believe that language does not depend on children's general cognitive abilities and is more or less separate from them, cognitive theorists assume that even very young children have a good deal of knowledge about the world and that they use this knowledge to help them learn language. These researchers contend that children do not simply acquire a set of abstract linguistic rules. Rather, they acquire language forms that they can "map onto" cognitive concepts they already possess.

Some cognitive language research has been based on Piaget's theory (Bates & Snyder, 1985). Most interest has centered on the transition from the later sensorimotor abilities of the toddler to the early preoperational abilities of the preschooler—a time when children are just beginning to combine words into two- and three-word phrases. This research has examined the relations between certain mental operations and corresponding language forms (Gopnik & Meltzoff, 1996; Tamis-Lemonda & Bornstein, 1994). For example, it appears that infants need a concept of object permanence before they begin using disappearance words, such as *all-gone* (Gopnik & Meltzoff, 1987). Similarly, the kinds of meanings that children convey in their earliest sentences (e.g., agents acting on objects) correspond closely to the kinds of understanding that they have developed during the sensorimotor period.

A second cognitive approach is based on a belief that children use their early cognitive concepts as a means of extracting the rules of language from the speech they hear.

Recall that the nativistic view is that children analyze speech into its abstract, grammatical structure. This cognitive model, in contrast, holds that children first analyze speech into meaning-based, or *semantic*, concepts that involve relations among objects, actions, and events. According to this view, children have a very early understanding of concepts such as *agent* (the person who performs an action), *action* (something that is done to a person or object), and *patient* (the person who is acted on). When young children hear speech, they presumably analyze it into these cognitive concepts, focusing, for example, on who did what to whom. They then develop simple rules regarding these concepts—such as "agents are usually named at the beginning of a statement"—that they use to guide their own speech (Bowerman, 1976).

A third cognitive approach stems from recent connectionist work within the information-processing perspective. As we saw in Chapter 8, connectionism involves the creation of self-modifying computer simulations in the form of artificial neural networks, the goal being to model forms of learning that humans show. The child's mastery of grammatical rules has been one of the most important targets for connectionist efforts. We consider a specific example later in the chapter.

Sociocultural Approaches

The sociocultural approach to language stresses the cognitive abilities children bring to the task of language acquisition in conjunction with a supportive and helpful social environment. It thus shares emphases with the two approaches just discussed. Nevertheless, it also adds some distinctive themes of its own.

One emphasis is on the functional basis for language acquisition and language use (MacWhinney & Bates, 1993; Ninio & Snow, 1999). Sociocultural theorists maintain that the child's primary motivation for acquiring language is social interaction—to communicate ideas and to be understood. The emphasis is thus on *pragmatics*, or the uses to which language is put. Children are seen as inherently social beings, and language is a primary way by which they enter into and affect their social world.

A further, related emphasis is on the preverbal origins of language acquisition. Social interaction begins at birth, and children therefore have many opportunities to learn about the nature of language well before the first words appear. Jerome Bruner (1983, 1999) has proposed that the typical social environment of infants (in most cases their parents) in fact provides many structured opportunities for language learning to take place. These opportunities make up what Bruner (in deliberate contrast to Chomsky's LAD) refers to as **LASS,** or the **language acquisition support system.**

The central component of the LASS is the *format.* Formats are similar to the scripts we discussed in Chapter 9. They consist of structured social interactions, or routines, that commonly take place between infants and their mothers. Familiar formats include looking at books together, playing naming games ("Where's your nose?" "Where's your mouth?") and action games (peekaboo and hide-and-seek), and singing songs with gestures ("The Itsy Bitsy Spider"). Such activities appear to be common across a range of cultures. Variations of the peekaboo game, for example, were found in all 17 cultural settings examined by Fernald and O'Neill (1993).

The format allows a child to learn specific language elements within a very restricted context—usually simply by memorizing words and their corresponding actions. Gradually, the parent may change the formats so that they include more elements or require a greater contribution from the child. In this way, additional language can be learned and previously acquired responses can be applied in new ways. Within these formatted interactions, the parent also provides other sorts of scaffolding for language acquisition, such as simplifying speech, using repetition, and correcting the child's inaccurate or incomplete statements (Snow, Perlmann, & Nathan, 1987).

A final emphasis of the sociocultural approach is on the rich set of social-cognitive abilities that both children and adults bring to the interactions that underlie language

Language acquisition support system (LASS)
Bruner's proposed process by which parents provide children assistance in learning language.

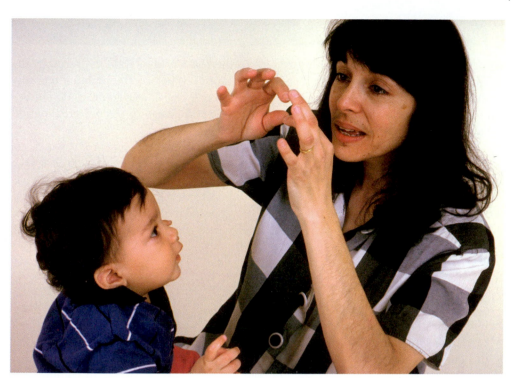

Jerome Bruner believes that young children learn language through structured play experiences called formats.

learning (Snow, 1999; Tomasello, 2001). Children's ability to learn from others is a central theme of the approach, not just with respect to language but in general; it is no surprise, therefore, that children are seen as possessing special sensitivity to the messages they receive from other people. In particular, as we will see, work under the theory of mind heading (see Chapter 7) documents a number of social-cognitive skills that can help explain the accomplishments of language acquisition.

To Recap . . .

Until about 1960, the leading theory of language development was Skinner's conditioning and learning account. Since then, the four major traditions have offered additional models.

The evolutionary tradition is represented by Chomsky's nativistic theory. This model holds that learning explanations are inadequate to account for language development. Instead, nativistic theorists propose that language is acquired by way of an inborn language acquisition device (LAD), which transforms the surface structure of the language into an internal deep structure that the child innately understands. In this view, language learning is essentially independent of the child's general cognitive abilities.

Contemporary environmental/learning accounts of language emphasize more complex forms of learning than did Skinner. Bandura's model of observational learning is seen as especially relevant. Such accounts also contend that the environment can provide children with the experiences necessary to acquire language.

Cognitive-developmental theorists believe that children's early knowledge and concepts play an important role in language development. Piagetians have attempted to link advances in sensorimotor and early preoperational abilities to corresponding language skills. Others contend that when children hear speech, they analyze it according to its content before extracting its grammatical structure.

Socioculturalist theorists argue that children's primary motivation to acquire language is to gain a tool for communication. Parents facilitate this process by providing a language acquisition support system (LASS), through which children acquire specific language elements as parts of games or songs. The approach also emphasizes the social-cognitive skills that both child and parent bring to the task of language learning.

THE PREVERBAL PERIOD

From the abstract world of theories, we turn to the real world of children learning language. Development in many areas begins at birth or even before. But children typically do not produce their first identifiable word until about 1 year of age, and they do not begin to combine words until about 18 months. Just how important is the preverbal period in language development?

Some theorists have argued that the process of language development is discontinuous, with the events of the preverbal period having little connection to later language learning (Bickerton, 1984; Shatz, 1983). Most, however, believe that language acquisition represents a continuous process and that abilities developed during infancy form the building blocks of the language skills that appear later on (Bloom, 1998; Hirsh-Pasek & Golinkoff, 1996). As we will see, much recent evidence supports the continuity point of view.

Speech Perception

Before babies can learn language, they must be able to perceive the sounds through which language works. How early is perception of speech sounds apparent? The answer to this question takes us into the area of **phonology,** the study of speech sounds.

Human speech actually consists of a continuous stream of sound. To comprehend language, the listener therefore must divide this stream into segments of various sorts, including syllables, words, and statements. The listener must also attend to other characteristics of speech, such as rising and falling intonations, pauses between words and phrases, and stress placed at different points.

Phonologists characterize speech in several ways. Speech therapists, for example, are most concerned with *phonetic* properties, which refer to the different kinds of sounds that can be articulated by our vocal apparatus—the lips, tongue, larynx, and so on. Articulation skills develop in a predictable order, with some sounds, such as *r*, appearing later than others (which explains why a young child might be heard to say, "The wabbit is wunning").

A more important characteristic of speech for infants learning language, however, is its *phonemic* properties. These are the contrasts in speech sounds that change the meaning of what is heard. Not all sound differences produce different meanings. The *a* in the word *car*, for example, sounds very different when spoken by someone from Mississippi and someone from Brooklyn. But they represent a single **phoneme** because they fall within a class of sounds that all convey the same meaning. As a result, an English-speaking listener would recognize both words as meaning "automobile."

If a sound variation crosses the boundary from one phoneme category to another, however, a different meaning is produced, as when *car* becomes *core*. The sound difference between these two words may actually be smaller than that between the two regional pronunciations of *car* we just described. But *car* and *core* are perceived as different words—that is, words with different meanings—because in English they represent different phoneme categories. The English language, in fact, uses about 45 phonemes. Other languages use more or fewer. According to Pinker (1994), the range extends from as few as 11 (in Polynesian) to as many as 141 (in the Khoisan or "Bushman" language).

This topic is important for our understanding of language development because research has shown that babies are surprisingly skilled in this area. From an early age, they show evidence of **categorical perception**—the ability to discriminate when two sounds represent two different phonemes and when, instead, they lie within the same phonemic category. This ability has been investigated extensively in infants and has been demonstrated across a wide range of speech sounds in babies as young as 1 month (Aslin, Jusczyk, & Pisoni, 1998; Jusczyk, 1997). Indeed, infants have been shown to display categorical perception of some speech contrasts found only in languages they have never

Phonology
The study of speech sounds.

Phoneme
A sound contrast that changes meaning.

Categorical perception
The ability to detect differences in speech sounds that correspond to differences in meaning; the ability to discriminate phonemic boundaries.

heard (Trehub, 1976). These findings suggest that categorical perception is an innate ability and thus universal among children. But biology is only part of the story.

Experience also plays a role in early speech perception. Two-day-old infants already show a preference for hearing their own language (Moon, Cooper, & Fifer, 1993). Studies indicate that the more babies are exposed to a language, the sharper their phonemic discriminations become (Kuhl, 2001). Conversely, lack of exposure may dull these abilities. For example, the distinction between the sounds *r* and *l*, which is not a phonemic contrast in the Japanese language, is a well-known problem for Japanese speakers. Studies show that adult Japanese not only have difficulty pronouncing these sounds but also struggle to discriminate them (Miyawaki et al., 1975). Young infants, however, have no difficulty discriminating this contrast, suggesting that children learning Japanese gradually lose the ability as a result of having little need to use it (Eimas, 1975). In fact, more recent research specifies exactly when the loss occurs: 7-month-old Japanese infants can make the *r* versus *l* discrimination; 11-month-olds cannot (Kuhl, 2001). This pattern turns out to be a general one, now demonstrated across a variety of speech contrasts and a variety of languages. By the end of the first year, babies lose a good deal of their ability to discriminate sound contrasts that are not present in the language to which they have been exposed (Best, 1995; Werker & Tees, 1999).

Experience with language also helps babies conquer the formidable task, mentioned earlier, of segmenting the continuous stream of speech they hear into individual words. Recent research indicates that babies bring some impressive skills to this task. One cue to word boundaries is frequency of co-occurrence: The syllables that make up a word (for example, *ba* and *by* in *baby*) occur together more often in speech than do syllables that span adjacent words (for example, *ty* and *ba* in *pretty baby*). By 8 months of age, infants can abstract and use such frequency information to distinguish common from less common patterns of speech sounds (Aslin, Saffran, & Newport, 1999). Recognizing which sounds occur together is a critical step in isolating individual words from the ongoing speech stream.

Any language provides additional cues about word boundaries beyond simple frequencies of occurrence. A further cue that babies learning English use is the location of a word's stress. In English, most words are stressed on the first syllable. By 9 months of age, American babies prefer listening to words stressed on the first syllable, presumably because this is the pattern they are used to hearing (Jusczyk, Cutler, & Redanz, 1993). In addition, they are more successful at segmenting words from the speech stream when the emphasis is on the first syllable (e.g., *kingdom, hamlet*) than when it comes later (e.g., *device, guitar*) (Jusczyk, Houston, & Newsome, 1999).

Research on infant speech perception, then, suggests the influence of both nature and nurture. Perhaps from birth, babies possess an ability to discriminate a wide range of speech contrasts. They are, in the words of one leading researcher, "universal linguists" (Kuhl, 1991). But the environment very quickly begins to fine-tune these discriminations, eliminating those that are not needed and improving the child's ability to use those that remain.

Listening Preferences

Babies not only discriminate various types and properties of speech but also prefer some speech sounds to others. As might be expected, infants prefer normal speech to either jumbled words or music (Colombo & Bundy, 1981; Glenn, Cunningham, & Joyce, 1981). They also prefer listening to their mothers' voices over virtually any other type of sound (DeCasper & Fifer, 1980; Mehler et al., 1978).

Perhaps even more theoretically important is the *type* of speech that infants prefer. We noted earlier that adults talk to babies differently than they talk to other adults, utilizing the style of speech that has been labeled *motherese*. Several research teams have presented babies with recordings of mothers speaking to their infants and mothers speaking to other adults. These investigators report that infants consistently prefer the

Babies have identifiable listening preferences, such as preferring the mother's voice to that of other adults.

mother-to-baby talk (Cooper & Aslin, 1990; Fernald, 1993; Pegg, Werker, & McLeod, 1992). This preference is evident in the first days of life, although young infants are not yet sensitive to all the tone-of-voice cues to which older babies respond (Cooper & Aslin, 1994). Interestingly, the phenomenon is not limited to the auditory medium. Deaf mothers of deaf infants use a form of motherese in the sign language they direct to their babies, slowing down and exaggerating their gestures, and their babies are more attentive to such input than they are to adult-directed signs (Masataka, 1996). Indeed, even hearing infants who have never been exposed to signs find the motherese form of sign language especially interesting (Masataka, 1998).

The findings from studies of motherese are important because they suggest that the adjustments speakers make when talking to an infant may actually increase the likelihood that the baby will be listening. But the benefits of motherese extend beyond simply heightening interest in the speech signal. Infants make a variety of discriminations more readily when the input takes the form of motherese than when the speech is of the adult-to-adult sort. For example, the early preference we noted for the mother's voice is most evident when the speech is in motherese (Mehler et al., 1978). Similarly, infants discriminate phonemic categories more easily when listening to motherese than when listening to adult-directed speech (Karzon, 1985), and they are better at detecting boundaries between clauses (Kemler Nelson et al., 1989). Thus, adults' natural way of talking to babies may help babies take the initial steps toward making sense of speech.

Early Sounds

Before babies speak words, they produce other sounds. This process is not random; rather, children's preverbal sounds follow a reasonably predictable course (Blake, 2000; Oller, 2000). The very earliest sounds consist of nonspeech utterances that include whimpers and cries, burps, grunts, and other physiological noises. At about 2 months of age, babies begin to produce one-syllable vowel sounds known as **cooing**—*ah*, *oo*, and occasionally a consonant-vowel combination such as *goo*. Whereas the earlier sounds usually signaled some form of discomfort, these new sounds frequently are accompanied by smiling or laughing and seem to convey more positive emotions (Blount, 1982).

Cooing
A stage in the preverbal period, beginning at about 2 months, when babies primarily produce one-syllable vowel sounds.

At about 6 months of age, **reduplicated babbling** appears (Ferguson, 1983). Here, the infant strings together several identical sounds, as in *bababababa*. In the months that follow, the baby adds more and more sounds, including some that occur only in other languages. Research indicates, in fact, that the babbling of children from different language backgrounds is very similar (Locke, 1989).

As infants approach the end of the first year, their babbling loses its duplicated quality, and they begin to combine different sounds, as in *da-doo* or *boo-nee*. This later phase of babbling is characterized by "speechiness"—that is, it begins to include certain fundamental qualities of speech. For example, babies add changing intonation to their sounds, so that their babbling includes the same patterns of rising and falling pitch that we might hear in adult speech (Clumeck, 1980). In addition, many of the sounds that infants produce late in the babbling period are sounds that they will display when they first begin to produce words (Vihman & Miller, 1988).

Babbling is so similar among infants of different language groups that biological mechanisms undoubtedly play a major role. But when infants finally begin to speak, they say only words from the language they have been hearing. Does this mean that speech emerges separately from babbling? Or, instead, does the form of babbling steadily gravitate toward the language the child hears—a theoretical notion called **babbling drift** (Brown, 1958b)? Evidence has been reported on both sides of this issue, but it seems to be accumulating in favor of the drift hypothesis (Blake, 2000; Boysson-Bardies, 1999; Locke, 1993). In either case, this issue nicely illustrates the difference between the continuity and discontinuity views of children's preverbal abilities.

The possible role of environmental factors in babbling has also led researchers to examine the vocalizations of deaf infants. If babies do not hear speech, will they still display babbling? The answer is yes, but the nature and course of babbling are not identical to the typical pattern for hearing children. Differences are most marked near the end of the babbling stage and include a delay in the onset of reduplicated babbling and a reduced number of well-formed syllables (Oller & Eilers, 1988). Such findings suggest that although early babbling is probably guided by innate mechanisms, hearing speech may be a necessary experience for the emergence of the more complex aspects of later babbling.

What about infants who are prevented from babbling? This unusual situation can occur, for example, in children who have severe respiratory problems and must breathe through a surgically implanted tube in the trachea. Clinical studies of such cases show that when the tube is eventually removed and normal breathing is resumed, the child's ability to articulate words lags behind that of age-mates for some time. This finding suggests that the opportunity to babble may provide important practice in the development of articulation. Also, the sounds produced by these children resemble those of deaf children, suggesting further that hearing one's own speech (that is, babbling), along with the speech of others, may be necessary for articulatory skills to develop properly (Locke & Pearson, 1990).

At least one type of babbling, however, does not require vocal skills. Deaf children learning sign language have been shown to display a sort of gestural babbling, producing partial forms of appropriate hand and finger gestures (Petitto & Marentette, 1991). This finding, too, supports the belief that early babbling has a strong biological basis.

Gestures and Nonverbal Responses

Gestures are an important component of human communication (McNeill, 1992). As early as the preverbal period, hearing infants use gestures, combined with other nonverbal responses, to perform many of the functions of vocal language (Acredolo & Goodwyn, 1990; Adamson, 1995).

One basic function of language is to make *requests*. Infants first use gestural responses for communicating requests at about 8 to 10 months, usually with their mothers (Bruner, Roy, & Ratner, 1982). Babies who want their mother to bring a toy, join in a

Reduplicated babbling
A stage in the preverbal period, beginning at about 6 months, when infants produce strings of identical sounds, such as *dadada*.

Babbling drift
A hypothesis that infants' babbling gradually gravitates toward the language they are hearing and soon will speak.

Gestures serve many purposes as children acquire language.

game, or open a box learn to signal these desires with various nonverbal behaviors. For example, a baby who wants a toy may reach toward it while looking back and forth between the toy and his mother. Sometimes the reaching includes fussing or crying, which stops when the mother complies with the request (Bates, Camaioni, & Volterra, 1975).

A second function of early gestures is *referential communication*—that is, talking about something in the environment (Bates, O'Connell, & Shore, 1987). This form of behavior usually appears at about 11 or 12 months and may initially involve only *showing,* in which the baby holds up objects for adults' acknowledgment. From showing, it may evolve into *giving,* in which the baby offers objects to the adult, again apparently for approval or comment. Eventually, infants develop *pointing* and *labeling*—the baby uses a gesture to draw attention to an object, such as a cat that has just walked into the room, while producing a vocalization and alternating glances between the adult and the object (Leung & Rheingold, 1981).

Not all infant gestures are used for communicating; some are used for *symbolizing* objects or events (Acredelo et al., 1999). For example, a child may put her fist to her ear and speak into it as if it were a telephone or hold her arms out to signify an airplane. Children also use gestures to label events (clapping hands to mean "game show") or to label attributes of objects (raising arms to mean "big"). These gestures frequently are not directed at anyone else—in fact, they often occur when the child is alone—and serve primarily to name things, not to communicate the names to others.

Is this early system of gestures related to the emergence of language? The answer seems to be yes. When words first appear, gesture labeling and word labeling are positively correlated—that is, children who do more gesturing also tend to use more words (Blake, 2000). In addition, teaching infants and toddlers a simple system of symbolic gestures has been shown to facilitate the mastery of spoken language (Goodwyn, Acredolo, & Brown, 2000). Apparently, infants seek to communicate through whatever means they have available, and initially they have more control over the movements of their hands than over the products of their vocal apparatus. Gestures are thus a natural early step on the road of communication. When spoken language does emerge, it can build on this gestural starting point.

Studies of deaf children provide an interesting addendum to work on the development of gestures. Deaf children who learn sign language do, of course, eventually master a gestural system that far surpasses that of hearing children. The striking finding concerns deaf children who, at least for a while, are not exposed to a conventional sign system. Despite the absence of the usual supports for language, many such children spontaneously develop a complex gestural system with many of the properties of spoken language (Goldin-Meadow & Mylander, 1984). We can see again a conclusion that emerged from studies of babbling in deaf children: Humans seem to be born with a strong tendency to develop language if at all possible.

Transition to Words

At about 12 months of age, most children utter what their parents consider to be their first word. Students unfamiliar with infants might assume that one morning a baby looks up from his cereal and says "granola." But in fact, the production of words appears to involve a more gradual and continuous process (Bates et al., 1987; Vihman & Miller, 1988).

Late in their first year, infants begin to utter specific sounds (or sound combinations) with increasing frequency—for example, *dee-dee.* Parents often notice that these sounds have become favorites for the child. Soon the baby begins to attach these utterances to particular objects, situations, or people, such as calling the television dee-dee (Kent & Bauer, 1985). At this point, such sounds would seem to be functioning as words for the child. But parents may not attribute much significance to this phase because none of the infant's words correspond to any of their own. Finally, though, the child begins to produce an utterance, even if it is a bit distorted, that the parents recognize, calling the television *dee-vee*. The parents jubilantly record this event as a milestone in the baby's development (Dore, 1985).

The continuity view of language development finds support during this period as well. For example, children more quickly learn words that involve sounds and syllables they are already using, suggesting that early speech builds on babbling skills (Schwartz et al., 1987). Additional evidence is that other preverbal communication forms do not immediately stop when words appear. For some time after the baby's first words, babbling continues, along with communicative and symbolic gesturing (Vihman & Miller, 1988). Together, these findings suggest that the transition between the preverbal period and the emergence of speech is relatively smooth and continuous rather than abrupt and discontinuous. And they add to the growing belief that the preverbal period serves as an important jumping-off point for later language development.

To Recap . . .

The importance of the preverbal period in language development is emphasized by continuity theorists, who view language development as growing out of earlier nonverbal communication. Several kinds of evidence support this view.

Research in early speech perception has shown that babies are born with categorical perception of many speech contrasts, including some that do not occur in their own language. Exposure to specific contrasts of their own language sharpens their ability to discriminate these contrasts, while the ability to discriminate other contrasts declines. Babies prefer speech to other sounds and particularly like the rising and falling intonations many adults use when speaking to young children. This motherese also enhances their ability to make various speech discriminations.

The first sounds of newborns are cries and physiological noises. Cooing sounds appear at about 2 months. Reduplicated babbling begins at 6 months and includes a wide variety of sounds. Near the end of the first year, babbling becomes more speechlike in its sounds and intonations and begins to converge on the sounds used in the speech environment around the baby.

Gestures serve many pragmatic functions for infants. Preverbal gestures initially take the form of requests and referential communication and later function as symbols to label objects, events, and attributes.

Early words only gradually replace babbling, gestures, and other nonverbal forms of communication. The combined evidence appears to support a growing consensus that the preverbal period is important for the development of later language.

SEMANTICS

Once children have begun speaking, their use of language expands at a breathtaking rate. We begin our look at this period of language development with the concept of **semantics,** the study of the meanings conveyed in language. Semantics encompasses both the meanings of individual words and the meanings expressed by words in combination.

Semantics
The study of meaning in language.

A well-known investigator of children's language recounts how her 18-month-old daughter began to use the word *hi* to mean that some sort of cloth was covering her hands or feet (for example, her hands were inside a shirt or a blanket was laid across her feet). The child apparently had come to make this unlikely association as a result of her mother's showing her a finger puppet that nodded its head and said "hi." Rather than interpreting the word as a greeting, the child had instead assumed that it meant the mother's fingers were covered by a cloth (Bowerman, 1976).

This anecdote illustrates two points about semantic development. The first is that learning the meaning of words is not as simple a task as it might appear, especially around the age of 2. Not only do children hear adults speaking thousands of different words (one estimate is that 2-year-olds hear 20,000 to 40,000 words per day! [Chapman et al., 1992]), but they also must learn that words are of different types, such as those that stand for objects ("hat" and "Mommy"), actions ("eat" and "talk"), and states ("happy" and "red").

Second, the more psychologists study word learning, the more they come to realize how closely this process is tied to children's concept development. Names of things (such as "cat") usually label an entire class of things (the family's pet kitten, a stuffed toy, Garfield), as do names of actions, states, and so on. Furthermore, the same thing can be called by many different names (for example, animal, horse, stallion, and Champ). How the young child knows what class of things to attach a new word to and how this learning develops are issues of considerable importance to understanding language acquisition (Bloom, 1993).

Early Lexical Development

The acquisition of words and their meanings typically begins in the baby's second year. Infants' first words usually name things that are familiar or important to them, such as food, toys, and family members. These words, we will see, also serve a variety of pragmatic functions, including requesting things, asking questions, and complaining. In this section, we examine the emergence of children's first words and the importance of the errors children make when attempting to relate words to objects and events in their world.

First Words and the Naming Explosion

By the age of 18 months, children possess an average **lexicon,** or vocabulary, of about 50 spoken words and about 100 words that they understand (Benedict, 1979). There are, however, substantial individual differences, a point to which we return shortly.

At around this time, many children display what has been termed the **naming explosion,** in which they begin to label everything in sight. Some psychologists believe that this burst of vocabulary is related to the child's emerging ability to categorize objects (Goldfield & Reznick, 1990; Poulin-Dubois, Graham, & Sippola, 1995). Word learning continues rapidly for the next few years, and by the age of 6, children have a lexicon of about 10,000 words (Anglin, 1993)—which means that they have learned, on average, six new words a day between the ages of 18 months and 6 years.

Semantic development proceeds faster for comprehension than for production. Children typically comprehend words before they begin to produce them, and they comprehend more words than they normally speak (Rescorla, 1981). This pattern is evident from the very beginning and continues into adulthood.

What sorts of words are present in children's early lexicons? Table 11.1 provides some typical examples. For most children, nouns (especially object words) predominate, and nouns remain more common than verbs and action words throughout language development. In most languages, in fact, nouns are understood earlier, spoken earlier and more frequently, and even pronounced better (Camarata & Leonard, 1986; Gentner, 1982; Nelson, Hampson, & Shaw, 1993).

Lexicon
A vocabulary, or repertoire of words.

Naming explosion
A period of language development, beginning at about 18 months, when children suddenly begin to acquire words (especially labels) at a high rate.

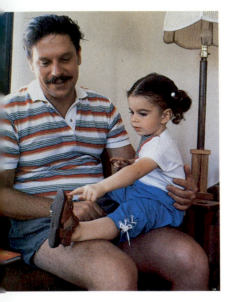

Children's first words usually label common objects.

Table 11.1	Typical Early Words: The First Words in Five Children's Lexicons
Child	**Words**
Jane	Daddy, Mommy, Daniel, girl, ball, cracker, cookie, that, school, bye
Leslie	Daddy, ball, duck, doggie, kitty, donkey, bottle, apple, thank you, bowwow
Lisa	Daddy, Mommy, Daisy, puppy, ball, see, hi, yes, where
Paul	Daddy, Mommy, Papa, boat, truck, map, this, sit, umm
Mark	Ma, dog, milk, water, car, here, bye-bye, no

SOURCE: Adapted from "Structure and Strategy in Learning to Talk" by K. Nelson, 1973, *Monographs of the Society for Research in Child Development, 38* (Serial No. 149). Copyright © 1973 by the Society for Research in Child Development, Inc., University of Michigan, Center for Human Growth & Development.

Individual and Cultural Differences   Despite the commonalities just noted, children do not all follow the same pattern of lexical development. Indeed, one of the major changes in the study of language development in recent years has been the realization that there are important individual differences in how children go about the task of learning language (Goldfield & Snow, 2001; Pine, Lieven, & Rowland, 1997; Shore, 1995).

One obvious difference is in the size of children's early vocabularies. We would expect, of course, that young children will vary in how quickly they learn words; the extent of the variation, however, may be surprising. In the most thorough examination of the issue (Fenson et al., 1994), the number of words produced at 16 months ranged from 0 to 347. At 25 months the range was from 7 to 668. Comparable differences were found for children's comprehension of words.

There are differences not only in the number but in the types of words that are found in children's early lexicons. The nouns-first pattern described earlier is not universal. Two kinds of early development have been identified (McCabe, 1989; Nelson, 1973). Some children, who display what is called a **referential style,** do follow the nouns-first mode. These children produce a large proportion of nouns, especially object names, and use language primarily to label things. Other children display an **expressive style.** This style includes a larger mix of word types, more "frozen phrases" (e.g., "What's that?" "Lemmee see"), and a greater emphasis on language as a pragmatic tool for expressing needs and for social interaction. The two groups seem to have somewhat different ideas about the purpose of language, with referential children focusing on its informational function and expressive children more concerned with interpersonal uses. On average (and, of course, with many exceptions), referential children are more likely to be girls, firstborns, and from middle- or upper-income homes.

What could produce these two different patterns of early language acquisition? One influential model stresses the contexts within which language learning takes place and the interplay of biological and environmental factors (Nelson, 1985; Shore, 1995). This contextual explanation stresses the *transactional* nature of development discussed in Chapter 1. Certain characteristics that differentiate children with the two styles—such as gender and birth order—affect the type of language environment to which the children are exposed. For example, in some samples parents have been found to speak to their infant daughters more than to their infant sons, using more complex language and more supportive forms of speech (Gleason & Ely, 2002; Leaper, Anderson, & Sanders, 1998). Similarly, parents tend to spend more time with firstborns than with later-born children, and speech to firstborns includes more learning devices and greater attention to the development of language abilities (Jones & Adamson, 1987). These different environments in turn lead children to develop either a referential or an expressive pattern of vocabulary acquisition.

Just as there are differences among children within a culture, so are there differences across cultures and languages. The nouns-first pattern, for example, is more marked in children learning English than is the case in several other languages whose early acquisition has been studied. Children learning Korean, for instance, are slower on average to acquire object names than are children learning English, and the same is true of children learning Mandarin Chinese (Choi, 1997, 2000; Kim, McGregor, & Thompson, 2000; Tardif, Gelman, & Xu, 1999). On the other hand, children in both cultures are faster to acquire verbs than are children in English-speaking homes. These differences, in turn, relate to differences in the kinds of speech input that parents in the different cultures provide. American parents tend to include a high proportion of object labels in speech to their children; they are also more likely to elicit nouns than verbs when prompting the child to produce words (Goldfield, 2000). In contrast, parents in Korea and China include a higher proportion of verbs in their speech than do English-speaking parents, and they also provide more cues to the meanings of verbs. The general conclusion is the same as that for individual differences within a culture: Children learn best the words for which their parents provide helpful input.

Referential style
Vocabulary acquired during the naming explosion that involves a large proportion of nouns and object labels.

Expressive style
Vocabulary acquired during the naming explosion that emphasizes the pragmatic functions of language.

Overextension
An early language error in which children use labels they already know for things whose names they do not yet know.

Underextension
An early language error in which children fail to apply labels they know to things for which the labels are appropriate.

Coining
Children's creation of new words to label objects or events for which the correct label is not known.

Holophrase
A single word used to express a larger idea; common during the second year of life.

The Nature of Children's Early Words   Psychologists have learned a great deal about children's semantic development by examining the kinds of errors they make. Word learning typically begins with a child's attaching a specific label to a specific object, such as learning that the pet poodle is a "doggie." Next, the child begins to extend that label to other examples of the same object, using "doggie" to label the dogs he or she sees in books or on TV. These extensions demonstrate that the child is forming an object category called *doggie* that is defined by certain features.

Most children, however, make errors when attempting to extend these early labels and may also use "doggie" to describe a cat, a fox, a rabbit, and so on. Such **overextensions** are very common in the early stages of semantic development in many languages (Rescorla, 1980). Why they occur is not certain. One obvious possibility is that children's initial categories are simply too broad; they do not yet understand the specific features that define the concept. However, this explanation does not fit very well with the fact that overextensions are more common in production than in comprehension. For example, a child who calls an apple a ball might, if shown an apple, a ball, and a pear, be able to *point* to the apple (Naigles & Gelman, 1995; Thomson & Chapman, 1977).

If overextensions do not always reflect a lack of understanding, then maybe they reflect a lack of vocabulary. If she does not know the word *apple,* a child may use the name of a similar object, such as "ball," simply to achieve the communication function of talking about the object. Such errors may also result from momentary memory problems: a failure to retrieve the correct label under the time pressure of generating a word. In fact, the evidence suggests that all of these factors contribute to overextension errors (Behrend, 1988; Gershkoff-Stowe, 2001; Hoek, Ingram, & Gibson, 1986).

Another type of semantic error involves applying labels too narrowly, rather than too broadly. A child who has learned to apply the label "bird" to robins and wrens, for example, may not apply it to ostriches. Such **underextensions** are less common in production than are overextensions. Underextensions are frequent, however, in comprehension. For example, when shown a group of different animals, young children often do not point to the ostrich in response to the instruction "show me a bird," but instead select a nonmember of the category, such as a butterfly (Kay & Anglin, 1982).

Both overextensions and underextensions are indications that children, for a while, use words differently than do adults. **Coining** occurs when children create new words that are not part of the adult language. We saw earlier that children sometimes name an unfamiliar object by overextending the label of a similar object. Thus, a child who sees a lawn rake for the first time may call it a fork, even though the child understands that the label is not correct. But another device that children use to deal with gaps in their vocabulary is simply to coin a new name for the object. Our first-time viewer of a rake might instead call it a grass-comb. Here are some more examples, taken from reports by Clark (1995) and Becker (1994): "fix-man" for mechanic, "many talls" for height, "nose-beard" for mustache. Word coining is common in young children, gradually decreasing as their lexicon grows (Windsor, 1993). Such inventiveness provides a nice example of a point that we will reencounter frequently: the creativity that children bring to the task of language learning.

A final characteristic of children's utterances during the one-word phase concerns their communicative function. We might expect that when children produce one-word utterances they are simply labeling objects in their environment—thus "ball" means "that's a ball," "Daddy" means "that's Daddy," and so forth. Although this is sometimes true, it is not always the case, especially near the end of the one-word phase. Instead, sometimes young children use one word to express an entire sentence or idea—thus "ball" might mean "I want the ball," or "the ball hit me," or perhaps any of several other meanings. We call such words **holophrases,** meaning single-word sentences (Dore, 1985). Making sense of them—for either parent or psychologist—must clearly depend on context and the use of whatever extralinguistic cues there may be to the child's intended meaning.

First Word Combinations   Children begin to combine words as they approach age 2. As with holophrases, they may sometimes use the same phrase to express different meanings, depending on its function. For example, "Daddy hat" may represent a name for an article of clothing, a demand for the father to take off his hat, or perhaps a simple description of the father's putting on his hat (Bloom, 1973). Again, contextual cues are important in interpreting what the child is trying to communicate.

Some functions of early word combinations are given in Table 11.2. Studies in various cultures reveal that the same dozen or so functions appear first in a variety of languages (Bowerman, 1975; Brown, 1973). This cross-language commonality suggests that the kinds of things children attempt to communicate during this period are influenced by their level of cognitive development. Because cognitive development is similar across different cultures, so too are aspects of early language.

Mechanisms of Semantic Development

Since the early 1970s, a variety of explanations for semantic development have been proposed. We discuss several potential contributors to early word learning. We begin with the proposal that children use grammatical cues to help determine the meanings of certain words. We then consider the claim that children are predisposed, perhaps by biology, to interpret words in certain ways. Finally, we consider the environmental contributors to word learning, focusing both on what parents do to help their children learn words and on the social-cognitive skills that children bring to the task of word learning.

Grammatical Cues   In our discussion of theories, we saw that cognitive-developmental theorists have argued that children use their knowledge of the meaning or semantics of utterances to help figure out the grammatical structure. In such cases, learning of grammar builds on a prior knowledge of semantics. But the reverse direction is also possible. Perhaps once children have mastered some aspects of grammar, they can use this knowledge to make sense of new words.

How might this process work? Imagine that a child who does not yet know the word *spatula* hears the sentence, "Give me the spatula." From its placement following "the," the child can use her knowledge of grammar to infer that *spatula* is a noun and probably the name of an object. If the spatula is the only nearby object whose name she

Table 11.2	Some Functions of First Word Combinations	
Function	**Purpose**	**Examples**
Nomination	Naming, labeling, or identifying	Bunny. Ernie.
Negation	Rejecting or denying	No nap. No wet.
Nonexistence	Describing something that is gone or finished	No milk. All-gone story.
Recurrence	Describing or demanding the repetition of something	More pat-a-cake. More milk.
Entity–attribute	Describing a characteristic of an object	Ball big.
Possessor–possession	Naming two nouns, the first possessing the second	Mommy sock.
Agent–action	Describing a person performing an action	Daddy jump.
Action–object	Describing an action being performed on an object	Hit ball.
Agent–patient	Describing a person doing something to another person	Oscar Bert.
Action–patient	Describing an action being performed on a person	Feed baby.
Entity–location	Naming a noun and its place	Ball up. Baby chair.

Table 11.3	Syntactic Cues to Word Meaning	
Syntactic Cues	**Usual Type of Meaning**	**Examples**
"This is a *fep*/the *fep*."	Individual members of a category	cat, forest
"These are *feps*."	Multiple members of a category	cats, forests
"This is *fep*."	Specific individual	Fido, John
"This is some *fep*."	Nonindivuated stuff	water, sand
"John *feps*."	Action with one participant	sleeps, stands
"John *feps* Bill."	Action with two participants	hits, kisses
"This thing is *feppy*."	Property	big, good
"The dog is *fep* the table."	Spatial relationship	on, near

SOURCE: From *How Children Learn the Meanings of Words* (p. 205) by P. Bloom, 2000, Cambridge, MA: MIT Press. Copyright © 2000 by the MIT Press. Reprinted by permission.

does not know, then the child is in position to make a correct name-object pairing and thus learn a new word. Suppose instead that the child already knows the word *spatula* and hears the sentence "Give me the gray spatula." From the fact that it follows an article and precedes a noun, the child can determine that *gray* must be an adjective. If further cues indicate what type of adjective is at issue (e.g., "Give me the gray spatula, not the white one"), then the child may learn a new color term.

There are, in fact, numerous grammatical cues to word meaning, in English and in other languages (Bloom, 1996, 2000). Table 11.3 summarizes some of the most important examples in English.

Can children use such information? The usual approach to this question has been to do experimental studies in which children have a chance to learn a new word based on the grammatical cues available in a sentence. Studies of this sort demonstrate that children can exploit a variety of grammatical cues—including all those listed in the table—to narrow down the possible meanings of new words (Bloom, 1996; Gleitman & Gillette, 1999; Hall, Lee, & Belanger, 2001). This process is called **syntactic bootstrapping** because the child's prior knowledge of grammar underlies, or "bootstraps," learning of semantics. Young children, with their more limited grasp of grammar, utilize such cues less successfully than do older children, and grammar alone is seldom a sufficient basis for determining meaning. But it can be helpful.

Syntactic bootstrapping
A proposed mechanism of semantic development in which children use syntactic cues to infer the meanings of words.

Fast-mapping
A process in which children acquire the meaning of a word after a brief exposure.

Constraints We saw that most children have learned thousands of words by the time they start school. Most of these are words that no one has explicitly taught them. And in some cases the learning is quite rapid. Children as young as 3 can sometimes acquire at least a partial meaning of a word after only one exposure to it, a process called **fast-mapping** (Carey, 1977; Heibeck & Markman, 1987). Preschoolers can even use this process when watching TV programs, demonstrating in some studies a very rapid acquisition of new words used by the story characters (Rice & Woodsmall, 1988).

But note how difficult this task really is. When a child sees a cat and hears Mommy say, "There's kitty," how does the child know that *kitty* refers to the cat rather than, say, its ears, its color, or its behavior? How does the child know that the reference is to the cat alone, not to the cat on the sofa, or the cat with its toy? In any situation in which a child hears a new word, there are many logically possible meanings for that word. How does the child avoid the many false directions and zero in on the one correct meaning?

Some psychologists contend that children can accomplish this task only if they are predisposed to relate labels to objects in particular ways. That is, when children hear a new word, they automatically make certain assumptions (usually accurate) regarding

Children can sometimes acquire the meaning of a new word from only a brief exposure, a process called fast-mapping.

what it probably means. The assumptions, or **constraints,** rule out the many false possibilities and thus permit children to acquire the meanings of new words quickly (Markman, 1991; Waxman, 1990). Several such constraints have been proposed to govern early word learning (Hollich, Hirsh-Pasek, & Golinkoff, 2000; Woodward & Markman, 1998). Here we consider two.

According to **lexical contrast theory** (Clark, 1987, 1993), when children hear an unfamiliar word, they automatically assume the new word has a meaning different from that of any word they already know. This assumption motivates them to learn exactly what the new word means. A second part of this theory holds that when a choice must be made, children always replace their current meanings or categories with those they decide are more conventional or accepted. For example, a child who has been assuming that foxes are called "dogs" should, on learning that "fox" has its own separate meaning, replace the incorrect label, "dog," with the correct label, "fox." This mechanism helps bring the child's categories in line with those of adults. There is evidence from both naturalistic and experimental studies that children often do honor the principle of contrast.

The **principle of mutual exclusivity** (Markman, 1989, 1991) states simply that children believe that objects can have only one name. So when a youngster hears a new word, she is more likely to attach it to an unknown object than to an object for which she already has a label. This strategy has the advantage of limiting the possible choices when a child is trying to attach meaning to a new word. Suppose, for example, that a toddler knows "kitty" but not "doggie." If her mother points in the direction of a cat and dog and says, "See the doggie," the child should assume, based on mutual exclusivity, that "doggie" cannot refer to the cat because she already knows a name for cats. She is therefore more likely to attach the label to the correct referent.

As with lexical contrast, research indicates that young children often do adhere to the principle of mutual exclusivity and that doing so can be helpful in learning new words (Merriman, 1997; Woodward & Markman, 1998). Interestingly, some of the support for the principle comes not from the successes but from the difficulties that young children sometimes have in learning words. For example, the strategy causes temporary problems as children encounter the hierarchical nature of word categories. A dog, for instance, can also be called an animal, a mammal, a beagle, and so forth. Two-year-olds sometimes balk at referring to their pet pooches by more than one name, which is what we would expect if they believe that objects can have only a single label (Gelman, Wilcox, & Clark, 1989; Mervis, 1987).

Although mutual exclusivity and other proposed constraints seem to account well for some aspects of early word learning, we should note that not all psychologists are convinced that the notion of constraints is really helpful (Bloom, 1998; Deak, 2000; Nelson, 1988). Disagreements revolve around several points: whether children's word learning biases really are as consistent and strong as the label "constraint" implies; whether, assuming that constraints exist, they are present from the start of word learning or emerge only later; and whether, again assuming their existence, constraints are innate or derived from experience. There are also concerns about the scope of such explanations—that is, how much of early word learning they can account for. Constraints positions have focused on how children learn nouns, yet children clearly must learn other types of words as well (Tomasello & Merriman, 1995). Finally, even if constraints provide a helpful start toward word learning, we still need to know how children use the speech around them to figure out exactly what words mean. We turn to this question next.

The Contribution of Parents
Whatever innate predispositions children may bring to the task of semantic development, experience is clearly necessary to complete the process. Children are not born knowing the meanings of any specific words; rather, they can learn words only if their social environment provides them with sufficient

Constraints
Implicit assumptions about word meanings that are hypothesized to narrow down the possibilities that children must consider and hence to facilitate the task of word learning.

Lexical contrast theory
A theory of semantic development holding that (1) children automatically assume that a new word has a meaning different from that of any other word they know and (2) children always choose word meanings that are generally accepted over more individualized meanings.

Principle of mutual exclusivity
A proposed principle of semantic development stating that children assume that an object can have only one name.

information about what different words mean. What do parents do that might help their children in this task?

Undoubtedly one important process is *modeling*. Although children sometimes make up their own words, much of what they say reflects what they have heard. We have already seen that children's early words tend to be those that are used most frequently by their parents. Furthermore, the more speech parents address to young children, the faster their early vocabularies grow (Hoff & Naigles, 2002; Snow, 1999).

The specific labels that children attach to objects can also be affected by parental modeling. Not surprisingly, children tend to learn such words as *dog* before they learn either *animal* (the superordinate category under which dogs fall) or *poodle* (a subordinate category within the category of dogs). At least part of the basis for this ordering lies in parents' labeling practices—parents are more likely to say "Look at the dog" than either "Look at the animal" or "Look at the poodle" (Callanan, 1985). Furthermore, when parents do use subordinate labels for objects, they usually do so for nontypical examples—such as identifying a robin as a bird but an ostrich as an ostrich (White, 1982). This suggests one explanation for children's underextensions: They may fail to extend a label to nontypical examples of a category because they seldom hear anyone use the label for such examples. If a child has never heard ostriches called birds, it is not surprising if his own use of *bird* does not include ostriches.

Parents' modeling of words can occur either incidentally, in the normal course of conversation, or explicitly, in an attempt to teach the child a new word. In what has been called the Original Word Game (Brown, 1958a), parents sometimes do, in fact, specifically show a child an object, tell the child its name, encourage the child to say the name, and then provide feedback as to the accuracy of the child's responses. This kind of modeling is given most often to infants and occurs less as children grow older (Goddard, Durkin, & Rutter, 1985). With older children, most labels occur in a less structured fashion, simply in everyday conversations between parent and child (Howe, 1981). Whether intended as teaching or not, however, such conversations can be a rich source of information about word meaning. Indeed, as we saw earlier, even labels encountered on TV can help children learn new words.

Social-Cognitive Contributors   Whatever the source or intent of a label, children can learn its meaning only if they can figure out what the speaker is referring to. This is the problem we considered earlier in our discussion of constraints: How does the child know that *kitty* refers to the cat rather than to any number of other logically possible alternatives? It is here that the social-cognitive abilities stressed by the sociocultural approach enter in.

Part of the answer to this puzzle seems to lie in parents' sensitivity to their child's interest and attention. Studies of parent–child interaction indicate that parents talk most about objects or events to which their children are already attending (Harris, Jones, & Grant, 1983) and that children are most successful at learning new words when parents have accurately judged their focus of attention (Tomasello & Farrar, 1986). In the "kitty" example, the argument is that the mother would not have said "kitty" if the child's attention had been focused on the cat's ears, the nearby dog, or any of the other features of the situation. Because the parent labels what the child is attending to, the child is in a good position to link label and referent.

Furthermore, children themselves play an active role in this process. The child's role is important, because even the most sensitive parent is not always going to be successful in judging his or her child's attentional focus. Recall, however, the early theory-of-mind developments discussed in Box 7.3. This work reveals that the process goes in both directions: From late in the first year infants are surprisingly good at discerning the *parent's* focus and thereby linking what the parent says with the correct object or event (Baldwin, 1995; Baldwin & Moses, 2001). And from early in life it is children, not parents, who initiate and direct many of the conversations from which words and other aspects of language are learned (Bloom et al., 1996).

To Recap . . .

Semantic development is the study of how children learn words and their meanings. At first, children acquire words slowly. But when their lexicons reach about 50 spoken words, their vocabularies typically increase rapidly, a phenomenon known as the naming explosion. Comprehension of words generally precedes production, and both children and adults understand more words than they speak. Nouns make up the majority of children's early lexicons, but even very early there are differences among children in the proportion of nouns used, which relate to factors such as culture, social class, and gender.

Children's language errors help explain their learning processes. Overextension, a common error, appears to occur for several reasons: Children may not yet understand a concept, they may lack the vocabulary to express the concept, or they may fail to retrieve the correct word from memory. Underextensions are less common in word production than are overextensions, although they occur frequently in comprehension. Children sometimes fill gaps in their vocabularies by coining new words. They also may use their one-word utterances as holophrases that convey a meaning similar to a full sentence.

Several models of word learning have been proposed. Some researchers have examined children's ability to use grammatical information to infer the meanings of new words. Experimental studies indicate that grammatical cues of a variety of sorts can be helpful. Other researchers have argued that various predispositions or constraints are necessary to explain how children rule out the many logically possible meanings for any word. Lexical contrast theory is based on two ideas: Children assume that new words have different meanings from familiar words, and they adopt generally accepted meanings over more individualized meanings. The mutual exclusivity hypothesis holds that children believe that objects can have only one name.

Children's learning of category labels is aided by parents' modeling, whether direct or in the course of day-to-day interaction. Children play an active part in this process, initiating conversations and following the parent's attentional focus.

GRAMMAR

All human languages are structured and follow certain rules called **grammar.** Many of these rules seem arbitrary, such as the English rule that adding *-ed* to a verb puts it in the past tense. But as nativistic theorists suggest, some rules may have a biological basis—that is, languages appear to be structured in such a way that humans learn them very easily.

Understanding the acquisition of grammar has posed one of the major challenges to language researchers. As noted at the beginning of the chapter, children are not explicitly taught the structure of their language (at least not before school age), yet they learn it very quickly. Making this feat all the more impressive is the fact that most adults, even those who are well educated, cannot describe our complex linguistic rules in any detail.

The grammar of most languages involves three principal devices: word order, inflections, and intonation. Word order, called **syntax,** is most important for the English language and thus the aspect of grammar on which we focus here. The sentences "John hit the car" versus "The car hit John" or "I did pay" versus "Did I pay?" illustrate how necessary it is to take into account the order of words. **Inflections** are certain endings added to words to modify their meanings. Common examples include plural endings (cat*s*), possessive endings (Mary*'s*), and past-tense endings (work*ed*). Some languages rely much more heavily than does English on inflections to communicate meaning. (In Turkish, a verb can have up to 3,000 different inflections!) Finally, *intonation* can alter grammar. A rising tone at the end of a sentence, for example, can transform a statement into a question. Again, some languages make greater use of this device than does English. In Chinese, for example, rising or falling tones serve to distinguish certain vowels from others.

Grammar
The study of the structural properties of language, including syntax, inflection, and intonation.

Syntax
The aspect of grammar that involves word order.

Inflections
The aspect of grammar that involves adding endings to words to modify their meaning.

Sharing Language Data: The CHILDES System

BOX 11.1

On the Cutting EDGE

There is probably no topic in child psychology for which naturalistic observation has been as important as in the study of child language. Most of what we know about children's early linguistic competence has come from detailed analyses of how young children naturally talk.

Although the studies of spontaneous speech have been enormously valuable, such studies also pose formidable challenges. It is a time-consuming enterprise to record, transcribe, and analyze even an hour or two of speech, let alone the dozens of hours that may be necessary to obtain a sufficient sample of utterances. If the study is longitudinal, as most such studies have been, then the challenges of data collection are multiplied. Given these challenges, it not surprising that the typical sample size in studies of this sort is 2 or 3 children.

A major advance in the study of child language came with the creation of **CHILDES,** which stands for **Child Language Data Exchange System** (MacWhinney, 1999, 2000). As the name suggests, the purpose of CHILDES is to share data. CHILDES brings together in a computerized format, and makes available to interested researchers, the original data from dozens of studies of child language spanning the past 40 years. In addition to studies of children learning English, CHILDES now includes samples of early child speech from 25 other languages. The database also includes samples from children learning two languages simultaneously, as well as samples from children with various forms of language impairment. The existence of such a resource means that a researcher interested in a particular topic may be able to examine it though analysis of already collected data, rather than by gathering new data. It also means that conclusions can be based on dozens of children rather than just one or two.

In addition to the data store, CHILDES includes two other components whose purpose is to facilitate both use of the data set and eventual scientific communication. One is CHAT, which stands for Codes for the Human Analysis of Transcripts. One of the challenges in studying spontaneous speech is to devise a transcription system that can capture everything of interest in an accurate fashion; in addition, one of the challenges in comparing or combining different studies has always been to cope with the different transcription systems that different investigators use. CHAT solves these problems by providing a common method of transcription for every study in the data base. Table 11.4 reproduces an example of a small segment of a transcript in CHAT format. Note that the example—like most of the records in CHILDES—includes not only the child's speech but also the speech of the adults in the setting and information about the context for the interaction.

The second component is CLAN, which stands for Computerized Language Analysis. CLAN consists of a set of programs that execute commonly used forms of data analysis. The Frequency program, for example, can be used to tally the number of instances of linguistic forms of interest—for example, the number of occurrences of personal pronouns or inflections, or how often particular syntactic structures are used. Other programs can analyze sequences and contingencies across utterances—for example, how often a mother's question elicits an answer from the child, as opposed to an irrelevant remark or no response at all.

The CHILDES database is available for use by any interested researchers. Presently, close to 1,000 published studies cite CHILDES as their main source of data. One requirement for using CHILDES, however, is that any new transcripts be contributed to the data set. The system is therefore a self-generating one: As it nurtures research, CHILDES grows itself.

CHILDES (Child Language Data Support System)
A computerized data-sharing system that makes available the transcribed records from dozens of studies of children's spontaneous speech.

Development of Grammar

Children's acquisition of knowledge about the structure of their language involves several distinct phases. And as with semantic development, children's errors often reveal a great deal about the rule-learning processes they are using.

Most children do not begin to combine words into the first simple sentences until about 18 months. Various precursors to sentence formation may be evident prior to this point, however. As we saw, the meanings and pragmatic functions that children convey with their one-word utterances expand across the one-word phase, moving from simple labels to more sentence-like communications. Also, near the end of this period many children begin to produce many single-word utterances in a row. Now the child may use one word to call the mother's attention to an object, and then a second word to comment on the object (e.g., "milk hot"). These multiple one-word utterances can be distinguished from the two-word sentences that will soon appear by the longer pause that

Table 11.4	Sample Transcript from CHILDES

Age of APR: 2;1.0
Birth of APR: 22-APR-1981
Date: 25-May-1983
Participants: APR April Child, MOT Mother, ROY Roy Investigator, TOM Tom Camera Operator
Situation: April and her mother are in the living room of the apartment sitting on the couch by the coffee table. On the coffee table there are books and toys.
*APR: who's that?
%com: looking at Tom
*MOT: what?
*APR: who's that?
*MOT: what's what honey?
*APR: who's that?
*MOT: point to it.
*MOT: who's that?
%gpx: points to Tom
*APR: who's that?
*MOT: who is that?
*APR: Pam.
*MOT: no # Tom.
*APR: Tom.
*MOT: right # not Pam.
*MOT: say Tom again.
*APR: Tom.
*MOT: right # Tom.
*APR: what's that?
%gpx: pointing to Tom again
*MOT: who is that?
*APR: rainbow # rainbow
*MOT: rainbow?
*MOT: oh yes # rainbow # he's got a rainbow on his shirt.
%gpx: April points to Roy.
*APR: who's that?
*MOT: who is that?
*APR: Roy
*APR: Roy's name is the best.

NOTE: com refers to a comment about the preceding utterance. gpx refers to a gesture. A hash mark (#) indicates a pause.

occurs between the words (Branigan, 1979). The child seems to be on the brink of producing sentences—just not quite ready to put the parts together.

Early Word Combinations   By age 2, most children have overcome this limitation and are producing two- and three-word sentences, such as "Mommy chair" and "all-gone cookie." Investigators have discovered that children's first word combinations are not random but follow certain patterns or orders. As a result, much research has been devoted to trying to understand these earliest indications of grammatical knowledge.

The principal method of investigation used has been to collect samples of a child's speech—usually in the natural environment—and to analyze its structure. Many such studies are longitudinal, with samples gathered over a period of months or years to examine how grammar evolves (Bates & Carnevale, 1993). An important recent development has been the creation of a computerized data-sharing system, which makes available the data from dozens of such investigations. Box 11.1 describes this development more fully.

Researchers have also devised a number of ingenious experimental techniques to probe for knowledge that may not be evident in children's spontaneous speech (McDaniel, McKee, & Cairns, 1997; Menn & Ratner, 2000). Such techniques can be used to assess children's comprehension of different linguistic forms, as well as their ability to produce forms that may not occur in a spontaneous speech sample.

The first syntactic rules that many children develop seem to be built around individual words. For example, a child may say "all-gone doggie," "all-gone milk," and "all-gone Mommy," using "all-gone + _____" as a basic rule (Maratsos, 1983). Children display a degree of individuality in these rules, however. Another child might develop rules around other words, for example "_____ + on" or "I + _____" (Bloom, Lightbrown, & Hood, 1975; Braine, 1976). Furthermore, not all children begin with the "familiar word + _____" formula; some show a greater variety of items and combinations in their initial sentences. We can see again that there are individual differences in how children go about learning language.

The next phase of grammatical development is the emergence of **telegraphic speech.** As the child's sentences grow from two to three or four words and beyond, they begin to resemble telegram messages. That is, they leave out unnecessary function words, such as *a, the,* and *of,* and also certain parts of words, such as endings and unstressed syllables. Thus, a child who hears "Billy, we're going to the parade" may repeat "Billy go 'rade." Over time, however, the telegraphic nature of children's speech greatly diminishes, as children expand their utterances and add more and more elements of the adult language (Bowerman, 1982).

We noted that children take somewhat different approaches to early sentence construction. One consistent characteristic, however, is an emphasis on word order. No child ever generates sentences by randomly combining all the words in her lexicon in all possible ways; rather, only certain orders and certain combinations appear in children's early utterances. Indeed, even children who are not yet producing sentences are responsive to word order in the sentences they hear (Hirsh-Pasek & Golinkoff, 1996; Mandel, Kemler Nelson, & Jusczyk, 1996). From the start, therefore, children seem to be sensitive to one of the basic properties of grammar.

Overregularization

As mentioned, the rule learning at the core of children's acquisition of grammar also is evident in certain types of mistakes they make. A good example involves inflections. The English language uses inflectional rules to change a verb to the past tense (-*ed* is added, as in talk*ed* and play*ed*) and a noun from singular to plural (-*s* or -*es* is added, as in cup*s* and dish*es*). But unfortunately for English-speaking children, our language also contains a large number of irregular forms that are exceptions to these rules—the verb forms *go-went, eat-ate,* and *see-saw,* for example, and the noun forms *mouse-mice, foot-feet,* and *sheep-sheep.*

At first, children may produce a correct irregular form if it is part of a chunk of adult speech that they are copying. Thus, even 2-year-olds may be heard to say "ate" or "feet." But as they begin to learn the inflectional rules of the language, children tend to **overregularization,** sometimes applying the rules to nouns and verbs that have irregular forms. Now the child will be heard to say "I knowed her" or "Look at the mans."

Telegraphic speech
Speech from which unnecessary function words (e.g., *in, the, with*) are omitted; common during early language learning.

Overregularization
An early structural language error in which children apply inflectional rules to irregular forms (e.g., adding -*ed* to *say*).

Interestingly, the correct forms do not altogether disappear, so that a child may at one time say "I ate" and at another time say "I eated." Eventually, the correct and incorrect forms may merge, and the child may begin to produce words such as "wented" and "mices." The final disappearance of the overregularized forms seems to take place word by word, with some errors persisting longer than others (Marcus, 1996).

Although such forms as "mans" or "eated" may be quite noticeable to the adults around the child, overregularizations in fact occur in only a minority of the cases in which children cope with irregular words. One extensive survey, based on more than 11,000 past tense utterances, reported overregularizations in only about 4% of the possible instances (Marcus et al., 1992). Nevertheless, overregularizations are informative because they tell us something about the creativity of child language. A word such as *eated* could not be an imitation of anything the child has heard. Instead, the errors children make suggest that they are not merely imitating but developing a system of rules.

Overregularizations are not limited to grammar. Similar phenomena are evident in phonological and semantic development. An example from the latter domain is the child who creates "yesternight" in analogy with "yesterday" (Maratsos, 1976). Nor are overregularizations limited to children who are learning English; indeed, such errors may be more striking in more highly inflected languages that offer more opportunity for children to go astray (Slobin, 1985b). (An early study of children's understanding of inflections is described in Box 11.2.)

Characterizing Children's Language   All researchers of child language agree that some sort of structured rule system underlies even the earliest sentences that children produce. What they do not agree on is how best to characterize the system. Two opposing positions exist.

One possibility, favored by cognitively oriented researchers, is that children's early sentences are organized in terms of meaning-based, or semantic, categories (Schlesinger, 1988). These categories, in turn, reflect the kinds of cognitive concepts that the 2- or 3 year-old child has come to understand. The small set of basic meanings that appear consistently in children's first sentences are compatible with this cognitive model (see Table 11.2).

The other possibility, favored by nativistic researchers, is that even the earliest sentences reflect knowledge of abstract grammatical categories, such as subject, verb, and object (Valian, 1986). In this view, syntax, not semantics, underlies sentence formation.

As an example of how these models differ, consider the sentences in Table 11.5. The sentences in the left column all lend themselves to a similar semantic description. Each includes at least two components of a basic three-part structure: an *agent* (e.g., Jamie) who *acts* (e.g., hits) on a *patient,* or recipient of the action (e.g., ball). Each sentence can also be analyzed as consisting of certain syntactic categories (nouns and verbs) and syntactic relations (subject-verb, verb-object). But—or at least so many researchers argue—there is no reason to credit the child with such abstract grammatical knowledge as long as a simpler, semantically based system can account for all the sentences that we hear.

Table 11.5	Sample Sentences
Jamie hits ball.	Jamie is hit.
Baby drinks juice.	Jamie has freckles.
Mommy play.	Baby liked juice.
Throw ball.	Thunder scary.

But consider now the sentences in the right column. Now there is no longer a one-to-one relation between a semantic description and a syntactic one. In the first sentence, for example, "Jamie" is the semantic patient (because she is the one receiving the action) but the grammatical subject. In the second sentence, "Jamie" is again the subject but now is the possessor of an attribute rather than an agent who performs an action. In both the second and third sentences, the verb is no longer an action word, and in the fourth, the subject is no longer an object name.

The debate about how to characterize early language centers on whether children's initial knowledge about language is limited to consistent meanings or extends to the abstract categories represented in the second group of sentences. As you might expect, semantic analyses find their strongest support with regard to children's *initial* sentences, which are much more likely to consist of combinations of the "Mommy play" sort than

Adding Endings to "Wugs" and Things

Even before the appearance of Chomsky's critique of learning theories of language acquisition, other researchers had questioned the early view that language is learned piecemeal through reinforcement of early babbling or imitation of adult speech. One alternative possibility was that children develop general rules that regulate their early speech productions.

To explore this possibility, Jean Berko, a doctoral student at MIT, conducted a simple but ingenious experiment (Berko, 1958). Children ages 4 through 7 were shown a series of pictures of nonsense objects and activities that had been given nonsense names—the most famous perhaps was a small, birdlike creature that Berko called a "wug," shown in Figure 11.1.

The aspect of grammar that Berko examined was inflectional endings—such as adding the *s* or *z* sound to create the plural (cat*s*, dog*s*) and the *d* or *t* sound to create the past tense (play*ed*, walk*ed*). To investigate a child's use of inflectional endings, Berko might have presented the child with a sequence similar to the following:

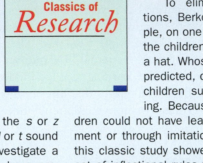

BOX 11.2

Classics of *Research*

"This is a cup. Now there is another one. There are two of them. There are two _____."

But what if the child added the correct ending sound to the word? Would that demonstrate that the child knew the rule for plurals? Perhaps. But it could simply mean that the child had previously been reinforced for saying "cups" when more than one was present or that the child was imitating her parents' use of this plural form.

To eliminate these alternative explanations, Berko used nonsense terms. For example, on one trial examining possessive endings, the children were told: "This is a bik who owns a hat. Whose hat is it? It is the _____." As predicted, on this and many of the other trials, children supplied the correct inflectional ending. Because these terms were new, the children could not have learned them either through reinforcement or through imitation of what they had heard. Rather, this classic study showed that the children had acquired a set of inflectional rules that they could systematically apply even to unfamiliar words.

they are to include such constructions as "is hit" or "baby liked" (de Villiers, 1980; Maratsos, 1988). In addition, children's earliest sentences, although occasionally creative constructions, keep fairly close to the adult models around them; they do not yet show the full productivity that will eventually characterize the child's language (Tomasello, 2000). It is possible, therefore—or at least some researchers maintain—to account for them with a fairly limited set of rules.

Even in the case of the earliest sentences, however, there are disputes about whether a semantic analysis is sufficient to capture all of the child's knowledge (Radford, 1990). And most researchers agree that soon thereafter some grammatical competence must be assumed, not only to account for utterances such as those in the right column of Table 11.5 but also to explain the emergence of more complex sentence forms, such as passives and negations. Exactly when, and how, knowledge of grammar emerges remains one of the most actively debated topics in the study of child language (de Villiers & de Villiers, 1999; Maratsos, 1998).

Mechanisms of Grammar Acquisition

As we have just suggested, no area of language development is more complex than that of grammar. As with semantics, many explanations for the mastery of grammar have been proposed. Rather than attempting to examine them all, we focus on those that are currently of greatest interest to language researchers.

Semantic Bootstrapping   One proposed model of the acquisition of grammar grows out of the semantics versus syntax debate discussed in the preceding section. Even most cognitively oriented researchers agree that children eventually master a system of grammatical rules. What they maintain, however, is that this acquisition builds on prior semantic understanding. According to this view, children first learn semantic categories, such as agent and action, which follow naturally from early achievements in cognitive

Figure 11.1

An example of a stimulus used to demonstrate that children's early use of inflectional endings involves rules. From "The Child's Learning of English Morphology" by J. Berko, 1958, *Word, 14,* 155. Reprinted by permission of Jean Berko Gleason.

This is a wug.

Now there is another one.

There are two of them.

There are two _____.

development. Once these categories are established, young language learners can begin to note that other words can perform the same roles in sentences as the words that make up their own utterances. For example, nouns in general, not just object labels, can serve as the subject of a sentence or can follow the word *the*. Similarly, verbs in general, not just action words, can be the predicate of a sentence or can precede the object or patient. In this way, abstract grammatical categories slowly grow out of what was at first a purely semantic system.

Earlier we discussed the notion of syntactic bootstrapping: the idea that children use their knowledge of grammar to help learn about semantics. The form of learning just discussed is known as **semantic bootstrapping:** use of knowledge of semantics to help learn about grammar (Bowerman, 1988; Pinker, 1987). The two kinds of learning are not, of course, incompatible; as language develops, the various components might well build on each other in a back-and-forth, reciprocal fashion. Given the complexity of language acquisition, it certainly makes sense that children would make use of any source of information available to them.

Semantic bootstrapping has a role even in many nativistic accounts of language acquisition (Pinker, 1987). Theorists in this tradition, however, do not believe that children's initial categories are purely semantic or that meaning alone is sufficient to teach children about syntax. Their view, rather, is that much of the basic structure of language—in particular, those aspects that are universal across languages—is innate. The reasons for this claim are the arguments given earlier: the apparent unlearnability of many language rules, given the complex, nonobvious nature of the rules and the very limited evidence available to children. Experience remains necessary in this view—not to teach the child the rules, however, but simply to indicate how the rules are expressed in his or her language.

Semantic bootstrapping
A proposed mechanism of grammatical development in which children use semantic cues to infer aspects of grammar.

Strategies The position just discussed assumes that children possess innate knowledge about the rules of language. An alternative possibility is that children's innate endowment consists not of rules but of cognitive strategies that allow them to acquire the rules rapidly.

One proposal of this type is based on the notion of **operating principles** (Slobin, 1982, 1985a). After studying more than 40 languages, Slobin extracted a number of strategies, which he called operating principles, that describe how to learn the rules of any language. Among the most important strategies are (1) "Pay attention to the order of words," (2) "Avoid exceptions," and (3) "Pay attention to the ends of words."

We have already seen that children increasingly focus on word order, or syntax, in speech. And children's overregularizations may result in part from their avoiding exceptions and applying inflectional rules across the board. Evidence supporting children's use of the third operating principle was reported in an interesting study.

The method used to address this issue involved teaching English-speaking children several artificial language rules and examining which were acquired most easily. First, the children were taught the names of two new animals—"wugs" and "fips" (Figure 11.2). Next, they learned two new verbs—"pum" (meaning to toss an animal vertically into the air) and "bem" (meaning to toss an animal horizontally across the table surface). Finally, the children were taught two variations of these verbs. If the animal's actions were observed by one other animal, the verbs describing them were "pumabo" or "bemabo"; if the animal's actions were observed by several other animals, the verbs became "akipum" or "akibem." The researchers hypothesized that if children use a strategy of paying attention to the ends of words, the verbs with a suffix (-*abo*) should be acquired more quickly than the verbs with a prefix (*aki-*). In support of Slobin's model, children learned the suffixed verbs more easily (Daneman & Case, 1981).

Slobin's full model includes more than 40 operating principles. These principles comprise what Slobin (1985a) refers to as the child's **language-making capacity,** or **LMC.** In contrast to Chomsky's LAD, the LMC does not consist of innate knowledge about the rules of language. What it consists of, rather, are learning strategies for rapidly acquiring such knowledge.

A more recent proposal that involves strategies for acquiring grammar is the **competition model** (Bates & MacWhinney, 1987; MacWhinney, 1987; MacWhinney & Chang, 1995). The competition model is a blend of sociocultural and information-processing approaches. According to this account, young children hearing speech examine the various grammatical cues of their language, such as word order, endings, and intonation, and then focus on the one they believe is most useful for learning the structure of the language. The cue they select can vary from one language to another and, significantly, is thought to change as the child matures.

Initially, children focus on the cue that is most *available*. In English and French, for example, children's first attempts to learn grammar involve word order. Because

---

Operating principle

A hypothetical innate strategy for analyzing language input and discovering grammatical structure.

Language-making capacity (LMC)

Slobin's proposed set of strategies or learning principles that underlie the acquisition of language.

Competition model

A proposed strategy children use for learning grammar in which they weight possible cues in terms of availability and relilability.

Figure 11.2

Artificial language concepts, along with these two imaginary animals, were used to compare children's acquisition of suffixed and prefixed verbs. From "Syntactic Form, Semantic Complexity, and Short-Term Memory: Influences on Children's Acquisition of New Linguistic Structures" by M. Daneman and R. Case, 1981, *Developmental Psychology, 17,* 369. Copyright © 1981 by the American Psychological Association. Reprinted by permission.

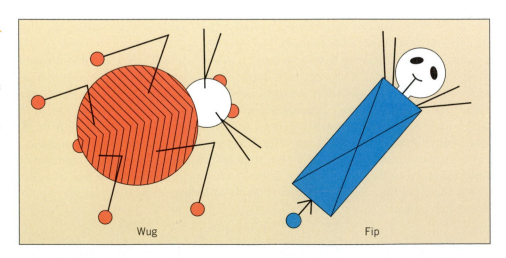

word order is important in these languages, it is a cue that is frequently available to provide information useful for learning language rules. In Turkish, in contrast, word order is less important, and language-learning children typically focus first on the inflections in the speech they hear. In the second stage, children select the cues that are most *reliable,* meaning those that most consistently provide clues to grammatical structure. In the final stage, children note cues that are in *conflict* with one another and then focus on the one that most often "wins out" and best reveals the language's structure.

The sociocultural origins of the competition model are evident in two emphases. One emphasis is on the helpful input provided by the adults in the speech environment around the child, input that helps the child make adaptive choices among the cues. The other emphasis is on the pragmatic bases for language acquisition and use. Children's mastery of language is motivated by the various uses to which language can be put, and pragmatic cues are among the cues that they use in learning language.

The information-processing aspect of the competition model is seen in the use of computer simulations to embody and to test the model's propositions. These simulations are in the form of artificial neural networks; they thus provide another example of the connectionist approach introduced in Chapter 8. As we saw, in connectionist simulations learning involves the adjustment of activation strengths with experience, as shifting patterns of connections among the underlying units gradually make some responses more likely and some less so. An example in the domain of language is mastery of the English past tense. Proponents of the competition model have demonstrated that a computer programmed with the strategies identified in the model and given appropriate linguistic input shows patterns of acquisition of the past tense that are similar to those shown by children, including a phase of overregularization errors prior to full mastery (MacWhinney & Leinbach, 1991).

Note that in this approach neither the computer program nor children are seen as acquiring discrete rules for language (such as add *-ed* to make a verb past tense); what they acquire, rather, are patterns of response that fit the cues available to them. This approach therefore stands in marked contrast to more traditional rule-based accounts of language acquisition. Whether connectionist models can account for all of the phenomena for which rule-based accounts were developed is currently a subject of dispute (Klahr & MacWhinney, 1998; Marcus 2001; Pinker, 1999). But they clearly provide an ongoing challenge to the traditional view.

Environmental Bases   Any theory of grammatical development, even the most strongly nativistic one, must include some contribution from learning and experience. We conclude our discussion of mechanisms, therefore, by considering the role of the environment, especially of the child's parents, in the mastery of grammar.

We can begin by asking what kind of language input parents provide to children. Recall that Chomsky claimed children should have difficulty extracting structural rules from everyday speech because such speech typically provides poor models of good language. But research has now demonstrated that both adults and children change aspects of their speech when talking to babies and toddlers (Newport, 1977; Snow & Ferguson, 1977). This is the *motherese* speaking style, already discussed at various points. Motherese, you may recall, includes helpful-looking adjustments of a variety of sorts. Mothers tend to speak slowly and use short utterances, often three words or fewer. Usually the words are pronounced very clearly, and the speech rarely contains grammatical errors. When talking about an object or situation, mothers label it frequently and use a good deal of repetition in their descriptions and comments. And the focus of their speech usually is on the here and now, rather than on more distant or abstract events.

Fathers display many of the same speech adjustments, although they generally are less sensitive to the infant's level of linguistic development (McLaughlin et al., 1983; Ratner, 1988). In fact, some researchers have suggested that the father's speech serves as a bridge between the fine-tuned adjustments of the mother and the complex and erratic

The form of speech known as motherese is one of many ways in which parents help their children master language.

speech of the outside world (Gleason & Weintraub, 1978; Mannle & Tomasello, 1987; Tomasello, Conti-Ramsden, & Ewert, 1990).

But do all these speech adjustments have any effect on the child's language development? We noted earlier that some aspects of phonological development, such as the ability to discriminate phonemes, can be facilitated by motherese. The evidence with respect to grammatical development is less clear. Attempts to find a convincing connection between the overall degree of maternal speech adjustment and the child's level of language development have failed to discover a strong relation (Murray, Johnson, & Peters, 1990; Valian, 1999). And attempts to uncover positive effects of more specific speech changes (length of utterance, amount of repetition, and so on) have offered only scattered support (Furrow, Nelson, & Benedict, 1979; Hoff-Ginsberg, 1990; Hoff-Ginsberg & Shatz, 1982).

Do these results mean that simplifications in the speech directed toward language-learning children are of little value? Not necessarily. One possibility is that some *minimum* amount of simplification is important, but the additional degree of motherese provided to some children is of no extra benefit (Scarborough & Wyckoff, 1986). Another possibility is that the methods and measures used by researchers have simply not been appropriate or sensitive enough to detect all the relations that exist between the adults' input and the children's output (Schwartz & Camarata, 1985; Snow et al., 1987). At present, therefore, the role of motherese in grammatical development remains to be established.

We turn now to one of the contributors discussed with respect to semantic development: parental modeling. We know, of course, that imitation of parental models cannot be the whole story. As Chomsky pointed out, our ability to produce entirely novel statements means that language must be based on more than merely copying what we hear. In addition, young children produce word combinations that they have probably not heard ("all-gone Daddy"), along with overregularizations not found in adult speech ("I hurted my foots"). These forms clearly do not arise from imitation in any simple sense.

But perhaps those imitations that occur are *progressive*. That is, perhaps when youngsters do repeat their parents' comments, they tend to imitate language structures more complex than those they use themselves. These structures may then begin to find their way into the children's own spontaneous speech. Whether this is the case seems to depend on how *imitation* is defined.

When imitation is defined as immediate and exact copying of an utterance, several findings emerge. The first is that most children display very little imitation, although a few imitate a great deal (Bloom, Hood, & Lightbrown, 1974). Furthermore, such imitations are rarely progressive. In fact, they often are even shorter and less complex than the syntax the child usually uses (Ervin, 1964; Tager-Flusberg & Calkins, 1990). Finally, the proportion of immediate and exact imitations declines over the first few years of language learning (Kuczaj, 1982).

A different picture emerges when imitation is defined more broadly. For example, we might look for *expanded imitations,* in which the child adds something to the utterance that was just heard; or *deferred imitations,* in which the copying occurs at some later time; or *selective imitations,* in which the child imitates the general form of a language structure, such as a prepositional phrase, but uses different words (Snow, 1983; Whitehurst & Novak, 1973). The research evidence suggests that these forms of imitation sometimes *are* progressive. Thus, at least in some cases, a more advanced language structure does first appear in a child's imitation of adult speech and then gradually finds its way into the child's spontaneous, nonimitative speech (Bloom 1974; Snow & Goldfield, 1983).

The final mechanism we consider that might help children master grammar is feedback, or correction in response to utterances that are grammatically incorrect. Such feedback is called *negative evidence* because it provides information about what is *not* correct in language (in contrast, parental modeling of correct language provides what is called *positive evidence*). The question of negative evidence is important, because it relates to a central claim in the Chomskian approach to language acquisition. Nativistic theorists maintain that some grammatical rules could be learned only if negative evidence is available; otherwise children could never avoid all the false starts and wrong directions that are compatible with the speech input they hear. They also claim that children do not receive such feedback—and thus that knowledge of the rules must be innate.

Do children receive negative evidence? The answer to this question is not a simple yes or no. Indeed, the issue of negative evidence is one of the most controversial topics in the study of language development (Bohannon et al., 1996; Morgan, Bonamo, & Travis, 1995; Valian, 1996).

Parents rarely respond to their children's ungrammatical statements with simple disapproval, such as "No, you didn't say that right." Instead, feedback regarding the accuracy of a child's remark usually involves its content, or truth value, such as "No, the block isn't red, it's blue" (Brown & Hanlon, 1970; Demetras, Post, & Snow, 1986). Thus, most children apparently do not receive the kind of negative evidence that nativistic theorists have stressed. But parents do provide helpful feedback in more subtle ways (Bohannon & Stanowicz, 1988; Moerk, 2000; Strapp, 1999).

Research has shown, for example, that mothers frequently respond to their children's ill-formed statements (such as "Mouses runned in hole, Mommy!") in one of three ways. **Expansions** involve repeating the child's incorrect statement in a corrected or more complete form ("Yes, the mice ran into the hole!"). **Recasts** involve restating the child's remark using a different structure ("Didn't those mice run into that hole!"). **Clarification questions** signal that the listener did not understand the comment and that the child should attempt the communication again ("What happened? What did those mice do?") (Demetras et al., 1986; Hirsh-Pasek, Treiman, & Schneiderman, 1984; Penner, 1987).

Are these forms of feedback helpful? Research suggests that they are. Children appear to be sensitive to such parental responses; it has been shown, for example, that they are much more likely to imitate a correct grammatical form following a parental recast than following ordinary speech (Farrar, 1992). And there is evidence, from both experimental and correlational studies, that providing children with such feedback can accelerate the development of correct grammar (Farrar, 1990, 1992; Moerk, 1996).

Expansion
A repetition of speech in which errors are corrected and statements are elaborated.

Recast
A response to speech that restates it using a different structure.

Clarification question
A response that indicates that a listener did not understand a statement.

Is Language Separate from General Cognitive Ability? The Message from Williams Syndrome

Carl is an extremely friendly 8-year-old who approaches strangers as though they were longtime friends. He likes to talk, his vocabulary is varied, and he speaks in complete sentences. He also demonstrates impressive sensitivity to the feelings of others. Despite these accomplishments, however, Carl's abilities in most respects fall well below those of a typical 8-year-old. He cannot yet tie his shoelaces or fasten small buttons, he cannot reproduce simple spatial patterns, and he struggles to produce a recognizable drawing. His IQ is 54, which places him in the moderately to severely retarded range (Mervis et al., 1999).

Carl has *Williams syndrome,* a genetically based disorder that occurs once per 20,000 births. As the description of Carl suggests, individuals with Williams syndrome show a very uneven profile of cognitive abilities. Their IQs are well below average, they have difficulty maintaining attention, and they experience special difficulty with spatial and numerical problem solving. Yet they demonstrate both interest and skill when social stimuli are the target; they are especially good, for example, at face processing. And their proficiency with language far surpasses what would be expected given their level of general intelligence. It also surpasses that found in other syndromes that produce similar levels of intelligence. Individuals with Down syndrome, for example, seldom achieve the level of language mastery that is typical in Williams syndrome (Harris et al., 1997).

Williams syndrome has been of interest to students of language because of its relevance to one of the central claims in Chomsky's nativistic theory. Recall that Chomsky argued that language is made possible by specially selected mental faculties that are largely independent of other cognitive abilities. This position implies that is should be possible to find instances in which language and general intelligence are dissociated—either impairments in language despite generally good intelligence or intact language in the face of serious intellectual deficits. A disorder labeled *specific language impairment* provides an example in the first category. Children with specific language impairment have normal intelligence by most measures but are seriously delayed in mastery of language (Fletcher, 1999). Williams syndrome

BOX 11.3

On the
Cutting
EDGE

has been cited by nativistic theorists as evidence for the second sort of dissociation (Pinker, 1999).

That Williams syndrome results in a strikingly uneven pattern of abilities is not in dispute. Indeed, the general conclusion that emerges from study of the syndrome is compatible with arguments that we have seen at various points throughout the book. We saw in Chapter 7 that Piaget's general stage model has been challenged by demonstrations that children's cognitive performance is often uneven across different tasks. We saw in Chapter 8 that an emphasis on the domain-specific nature of cognitive development is a characteristic of many information-processing theories of development. Recall also the discussion of Gardner's theory of separate intelligences in Chapter 10.

Whether Williams syndrome really provides evidence for the kind of separate language faculty proposed by nativistic theorists is more controversial. Although their eventual linguistic achievements are impressive, individuals with Williams syndrome are slower than most children to move through the initial phases of language mastery (Paterson et al., 1999). In addition, there is evidence that the path they take to mastery may be in some ways different from the typical path. For example, toddlers with Williams syndrome produce far fewer gestures than do normally developing toddlers, and they are less likely to engage in joint attention with their caregivers (Laing et al., 2002). They are also less likely to abide by the constraints (e.g., lexical contrast) that seem to govern much early word learning in normal development (Karmiloff & Karmiloff-Smith, 2001). Many researchers believe that mastery of language in this population is dependent—more than is true in normal development—on the attributes that people with Williams syndrome *do* possess: namely, good auditory memory coupled with intense social interest.

Whatever their ultimate implication for theories of language development, the achievements of individuals with Williams syndrome do mirror a central theme of this chapter. Children strive to master language, and they are flexible and resourceful learners who use whatever means may be available to them in this effort.

✓ *To Recap . . .*

Grammar is the study of the rules of language structure. These rules include such devices as word order (syntax), inflections, and intonation. The growth of grammar can be seen as children's speech steadily increases in length and complexity. Children's two-word utterances, which appear around the end of the second year, often display rules built around individual words—for example, combining "all-gone" with various nouns. As sentences grow longer, telegraphic speech emerges. When children first learn inflectional rules, they overregularize them, applying the regular forms even to irregular words. Children's early sentences are systematic and rule-governed, but researchers disagree as to whether semantic or grammatical knowledge accounts for their systematic nature.

Many explanations of how grammar develops have been proposed. The semantic bootstrapping hypothesis maintains that children use their knowledge of semantics (e.g., that agents act on objects) to figure out rules of syntax (e.g., the categories of nouns and verbs). In contrast, nativistic theorists maintain that children's language reflects syntactic and not merely semantic knowledge from the start and that innate knowledge about the principles of grammar makes language acquisition possible.

An alternative to inborn knowledge is inborn linguistic strategies. Operating principles for acquiring language have been derived from the study of many languages and are supported by observations and experimental investigations of children's language learning. The competition model, which focuses on how cues to grammatical structure are selected, finds support in connectionist simulations of grammatical change.

Environmental influences on grammatical development have also been investigated. Both mothers and fathers use motherese in talking to babies and young children. Attempts to link the use of this simplified speech style to progress in language development have met with mixed success.

Imitation can take several forms. Most important for language learning are the expanded, deferred, and selective forms, which introduce new grammatical constructions to some children. Another environmental factor is feedback. Although parents rarely respond to children's ungrammatical statements with disapproval, they commonly expand, recast, or ask for clarification of ill-formed statements. Such responses have been shown to be of some value for children's language development.

PRAGMATICS

We have seen that language has both structure (grammar) and meaning (semantics). But it also performs functions, in that it gets people to do things we would like them to do. When a toddler points to the refrigerator and says "cup," for example, she is not as likely to be labeling the refrigerator as she is to be asking her mother to fetch her cup of juice. The study of the social uses of language is called **pragmatics** (Ninio & Snow, 1996).

As we saw, it is the sociocultural approach that has placed the greatest stress on the pragmatic aspect of language development. From this perspective, children do not learn language simply because of an innate quest to understand linguistic structure. Instead, they are motivated to acquire language because it provides them with a very powerful tool—the ability to communicate with others easily and to achieve their goals effectively (Ninio & Snow, 1999).

To be effective communicators, children first must learn to express their needs or desires in ways that can be understood by others. In the beginning, babies cannot always accomplish this, and sometimes their attempts to convey their wants are frustrated by their parents' failure to understand exactly what is being requested. This frustration is an important motivator for the child to acquire skills that will make communication easier. But the process operates in the other direction as well. Effective communication also involves understanding what parents and others are saying in order to follow their directions, answer their questions, or comply with their requests. Communication, of course, is a two-way street.

We begin our discussion of pragmatics with a look at how children use speech to control others and to get their own way. Then we examine the development of conversation skills and the ability to communicate effectively with others.

Speech Acts

Before acquiring speech, infants use other tools for communication, such as crying, facial expressions, and gestures (Reddy, 1999; Sachs, 2001). In one study, mothers engaged in a turn-taking game (for example, taking turns squeezing a squeak toy) with their 1-year-old babies. Once the game was going smoothly, they were instructed not to take

Pragmatics
The study of the social uses of language.

a turn and simply to sit silently and motionlessly. The babies reacted by performing a variety of behaviors clearly designed to communicate to the mother that it was her turn. These included vocalizing at her, pointing to the toy, and picking up the toy and giving it to her (Ross & Lollis, 1987).

With the acquisition of language, children add verbal responses to this repertoire of communication devices. Now children achieve various goals by directing words and phrases at other people. Such pragmatic uses of language are referred to as **speech acts** (Astington, 1988; Dore, 1976). Researchers have found that even the earliest words that infants utter usually serve several pragmatic functions (Bretherton, 1988). "Mama," for example, is generally first used both to call the mother and to request things from her (as when the baby says "mama" while pointing to a toy on a shelf). In time, this word also begins to serve the more common purpose of naming the parent (Ninio & Snow, 1988). Later in the one-word period, babies begin to use relational words—those connecting several objects or events—in a number of pragmatic ways. For example, "more" may be used to request that an activity be continued as well as to describe a block being added to a pile (McCune-Nicolich, 1981).

As children's cognitive and linguistic abilities grow, so, too, do the range and effectiveness of their speech acts. In one longitudinal study, the number of communicative attempts per minute more than doubled between 14 and 32 months, and the number of different types of speech acts more than tripled. In addition, the proportion of attempts that were judged as interpretable—and therefore more likely to be successful—rose from 47% to 94% (Snow et al., 1996).

Adults also produce speech acts, which must be comprehended by the language-learning infant if adult and child are to communicate effectively. The comprehension side of communication also improves greatly with development. The child's task is complicated, however, by the fact that the function of some speech he or she hears may not be obvious. When a mother says, "May I open it for you?" she is not really asking the child a question as much as she is offering help. And when she says, "I didn't mean to break it," she is doing more than describing her intentions; she is actually apologizing to the baby. We will return to this aspect of pragmatics shortly.

Discourse

Regardless of what theory of language acquisition they favor, all researchers agree that language is most often used in social contexts. Speech during social interaction is called **discourse** or, more commonly, conversation (Hicks, 1996).

When people have conversations, they must, of course, adhere to the grammatical rules of the language if they are to understand one another. But they also must follow certain social rules of discourse. The most obvious of these is turn taking, with each participant alternating between the roles of speaker and of listener. This basic rule of conversation is one of the first acquired by children. As we have seen, it may actually be learned during the preverbal period (Collis, 1985).

Some other rules of discourse are more difficult, however, and are learned later. One of these is the "answer obviousness" rule. Some statements that are phrased as questions may actually be intended as directives, such as, "Could you hand me that pencil?" How do listeners know in these situations which function the speaker intends? Most often, we solve the problem by considering the context in which the remark is made (Shatz & McCloskey, 1984). For example, we would very likely treat the remark as a directive if the speaker were about to write a note, if a pencil were visible but out of the speaker's reach, and if the pencil were within our reach. Another kind of cue we often use in such situations, however, is the obviousness of the answer. Because we realize that the speaker in our example knows that we could pass the pencil, we do not treat the remark as a request for information. Instead, we view it as a directive. Discourse rules of this sort are clearly more difficult to learn than is turn taking, and the answer-obviousness rule is not apparent in children until about age 5 (Abbeduto, Davies, & Furman, 1988).

Speech act
An instance of speech used to perform pragmatic functions, such as requesting or complaining.

Discourse
Language used in social interactions; conversation.

Other discourse rules appear even later. For example, understanding that in a conversation one should (1) say something that relates to what the speaker has just said, (2) say something that is relevant to the topic under discussion, and (3) say something that has not already been said involves discourse rules that most children do not use consistently until 6 or 7 years of age (Conti & Camras, 1984).

Social Referential Communication

An even more advanced conversational skill involves the ability to effectively communicate information about something that is not known to the other participant in the conversation, as when one child describes his or her new computer game to a classmate in such a way that the other child understands how it is played. This form of communication is called **social referential communication.** In formal terms, such communication occurs when a speaker sends a message that is comprehended by a listener. The communication is social because it occurs between two people; it is referential because the message is in a symbolic form (the child is using language to convey the information and not simply showing the classmate what to do); and it is communication because it is understood by the listener (Whitehurst & Sonnenschein, 1985).

Research on social referential communication has been conducted primarily in laboratory settings. To study this process, researchers have generally used a task of the following sort (see Figure 11.3). Two children sit across from one another at a table, separated by a screen or partition. One child is designated the speaker, the other the listener. Both children are given identical sets of stimuli, such as blocks of different sizes, patterns, or colors. The speaker's task is to send messages that describe a block. The listener's task is to use the messages to select the correct block from the available array. In some experiments, the listener can ask questions or comment on the usefulness of the speaker's descriptions. The success of the communication is measured by how often the listener selects the correct item. Using this procedure, psychologists have been able to identify many of the factors that influence children's communication abilities.

For children to engage in social referential communication effectively—as speakers or as listeners—they must learn a number of important skills. In the role of speaker, children must become aware of listener cues, meaning simply that they must adjust messages to meet the needs of the listener. For example, if the listener is far away, the message should be loud; if the listener is running out the door, the message should be brief; and if the listener is someone of high status (for example, a teacher or a preacher), the message should be polite.

Social referential communication
A form of communication in which a speaker sends a message that is comprehended by a listener.

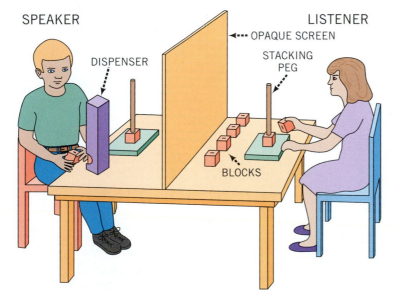

SPEAKER   LISTENER

DISPENSER   OPAQUE SCREEN

STACKING PEG

BLOCKS

Figure 11.3

Example of an arrangement used to study social referential communication in children. The speaker's task is to describe the target object in his set clearly enough so that the listener can pick the same object in her set. From "The Development of Communication: Competence as a Function of Age" by R. M. Krauss and S. Glucksberg, 1969, *Child Development, 40,* 259. Copyright © 1969 by the Society for Research in Child Development. Reprinted by permission.

A good example of a young child's failure to take listener cues into account is the little boy who talks with his grandmother on the phone and answers her questions by nodding his head. The same phenomenon is evident in experimental tasks of the sort pictured in Figure 11.3 when young children in the speaker role say, "It's this one," or perhaps simply point to the intended target.

Although children are often insensitive to the characteristics of the listener, they do sometimes adjust their speech in response to one important listener characteristic— namely, age. We have seen that adults tend to use the simplified motherese style of speech when talking to young children. So, it turns out, do children; children as young as 4 simplify their speech when addressing toddlers or infants (Sachs & Devin, 1976; Shatz & Gelman, 1973). As we would expect, this ability improves as children grow older. Fifth-graders, for example, make more effective speech modifications when talking to younger children than do first-graders (Sonnenschein, 1988). Even grade-schoolers, however, still show a tendency to overestimate the comprehension abilities of young listeners (Miller, Hardin, & Montgomery, in press; Montgomery, 1993).

Another useful listener cue involves *common ground*, the information shared by the speaker and listener. If the listener, for example, knows the speaker's birthday, then the message "Come over on my birthday" will be sufficient; if the listener does not possess the information, the message will be inadequate. Kindergartners have some understanding of the common-ground principle, but this ability, too, improves with age (Ackerman & Silver, 1990; Ackerman, Szymanski, & Silver, 1990).

Perhaps the most important listener cues involve feedback. If the listener does not appear to be comprehending, the speaker should change the message and try again. In simple situations with very clear cues, even 2-year-olds show some ability to adjust their messages when a listener has misunderstood (Ferrier, Dunham, & Dunham, 2000; Shwe & Markman, 1997). In general, however, sensitivity to listener feedback is limited in young children, who often persist with the same types of messages even when the listener is clearly not understanding (Robinson, 1981).

As listeners, children need to learn certain rules as well. Like speakers, listeners must be aware of context cues, including the information that has previously been sent and the nature of the array from which the referent is to be chosen. In addition, when a message is not informative, the child must learn to recognize this fact and communicate

To become effective communicators, young children must acquire both speaker skills and listener skills.

Language Differences in School:
Teaching (and Learning) One Language or Two?

Approximately 6 million children in the United States live in households in which a language other than English is spoken. When these children enter the school system they present an obvious challenge for educators. What is the best way to educate so-called Limited English-Proficient (LEP) children?

Approaches to this problem take a variety of forms, but they divide into two general categories (Brisk, 1998; Hakuta, 1999). Programs that follow a *bilingual model* utilize both the minority and the majority language for instruction. There are many variants of such programs depending on the specific emphases and time course (structured immersion, transitional bilingual education, two-way bilingual education, etc.); the common element, however, is the use of two languages. The second category, in contrast, consists of *majority-only* programs. Here, as the name suggests, instruction occurs in English only, and use of the minority language is minimized and may even be explicitly discouraged. As Bialystok (2001) notes, in United States schools even programs in the first category are not truly bilingual, in the sense of granting equal weight over time to two languages (as is the practice in many other countries). The goal, rather, is to prepare students as quickly as possible for instruction in English only.

Although the types of programs employed often reflect political rather than educational factors, policy makers typically attempt to support their decisions with scientific data regarding bilingual learning. One of the most important questions has been whether children learning two languages have more difficulty learning the majority language. For many scientists, answering this question requires a basic understanding of how the bilingual process works.

One theory has been that bilingual children initially approach the task of learning two languages as if they were learning only one. That is, they do not separate the two forms of speech input but develop a single language system that includes elements of each. Only with increasing age do these children presumably learn to differentiate the two tongues, gradually treating them as independent languages (Volterra & Taeschner, 1978).

This theory has principally grown out of the observation that younger bilingual children display a good deal of *code-mixing,* or combining forms from the two languages within the same utterance (Redlinger & Park, 1980). Mixing occurs at all levels of speech, including articulation, vocabulary, inflections, and syntax. The assumption has been that mixing reflects confusion on the part of the bilingual child, who cannot separate the two languages. A related finding is that children in bilingual homes acquire both languages more slowly than do peers who are learning only one language, although this lag gradually disappears and the children's proficiency in both languages eventually reaches that of monolingual children (Oller & Pearson, 2002).

More recent research strongly challenges the single-system hypothesis (Bialystok, 2001; Genesee, Nicoladis, & Paradis, 1995). Studies of infant speech perception, for example, indicate clearly that babies can differentiate sounds and phonemes found in different languages (Eilers & Oller, 1988; Moon et al., 1993). By 4 months of age, infants growing up in bilingual homes can differentiate sounds from the two languages, even when the languages are rhythmically similar (Bosch & Sebastian-Galles, 2001). Hence, perceptual confusion does not appear to be a problem.

It has also been suggested that children's substitution of a word in one language for the same word in the second language may simply reflect the overextension principle. Thus, the child may substitute in this way if he or she does not know the appropriate word in the second language or if it is simply easier to do so (Vihman, 1985). Furthermore, modeling by parents has been implicated in children's language mixing. Studies of bilingual children's home environments indicate that their parents often speak to them using parts of both languages simultaneously and that parents generally respond positively to the child's code-mixing (Goodz, 1989; Lanza, 1997). It is not surprising, then, that bilingual children often mix parts of their two languages.

Another claim of the older research literature was that bilingualism results in cognitive deficits. Theoretically, the bases for this claim were the slower growth of language skills in bilingual children and the suggestion that hearing and learning two languages confuses children. Empirically, the claim found support in studies that reported on-the-average cognitive deficits in samples of bilingual children. It has now become clear, however, that various methodological weaknesses (concentration on low-income samples, use of inappropriate measures) render the results of the earlier research suspect. Bilingual children, in fact, have been shown to be more advanced in some areas of cognition than monolingual children (Bialystok, 2001).

It appears, then, that exposure to two languages does not present an unusually difficult challenge to young children, who can apparently separate and acquire both systems. This would suggest that majority-only educational policies, in which nonnative children are required from the start of school to use and learn only the majority language, may be misguided. Indeed, research that compares different approaches to educating bilingual children generally favors some form of transitional approach, in which both languages are utilized at the early grades and children can gradually develop competence in the majority language (Genesee, 1994; Greene, 1998). Note that in addition to its purely academic benefits, this approach has the virtue of acknowledging the value of the child's family and cultural background.

BOX 11.4

Applications

Research indicates that teaching nonnative children in their own language does not interfere with their learning of the majority language.

the problem. Children as young as 5 can sometimes detect when a message is poorly constructed or when critical information is missing. At this age, however, they will often proceed with the inadequate information, whereas by age 7 they are more likely to seek clarification or additional information from the speaker (Ackerman, 1993).

Most of the conclusions just discussed were derived from the sorts of experimental measures pictured in Figure 11.3. We should add, therefore, that children's communicative performance, as either speaker or listener, is often more impressive in the natural environment (e.g., talking with a parent, playing with friends) than it is on unfamiliar laboratory tasks (Warren & McCloskey, 1997). As is often the case, what we conclude about children's abilities depends on the context in which we assess those abilities. On the other hand, difficulties in communicating clearly do not disappear in the natural setting—as anyone who has tried to carry on a conversation with a 4-year-old can attest.

How referential communication skills develop is an important question. Environmental factors certainly play a role. One study, for example, found that children whose mothers provided them specific feedback regarding how their messages were inadequate developed their communication skills most rapidly (Robinson, 1981). But such skills must also depend on the emergence of certain cognitive abilities. For example, as children's egocentric view of the world decreases, they develop a better appreciation for how another person might view a situation. And as their theory of mind understanding improves (see Chapter 7), they come to realize that listeners with different cognitive capabilities (such as children versus adults) may interpret the same information differently (Chandler & Lalonde, 1996; Taylor, Cartwright, & Bowden, 1991).

✓ To Recap . . .

Pragmatics is the study of the social uses of language. It is based on the sociocultural view that children are motivated to acquire language in order to communicate their wants and needs more effectively. Effective communication abilities involve both speaker skills and listener skills.

Infants at first communicate with crying, gestures, and so on. As they acquire language, they add speech acts to their nonverbal communication skills. They also learn to comprehend speech acts of others.

The ability to communicate effectively involves learning rules of discourse. Turn taking is one of the earliest discourse rules acquired by infants. Others, such as the answer-obviousness rule, are more difficult to learn and are not apparent in children until several years later.

Social referential communication occurs when a speaker sends a message that is understood by a listener. Effective communication of this sort involves speaker skills, such as adjusting the messages to the demands of the listener and the context, and listener skills, such as recognizing and communicating when messages are ambiguous. Both sets of skills improve with development.

CONCLUSION

Developmental psychologists, like researchers in the other natural sciences, attempt to identify processes that are general and fundamental. Rather than considering each event or behavior unique, scientists search for principles and laws that can explain and interrelate them across the many domains of human development.

During the 1960s, the study of language became an exception to this approach. Language was believed to be different, requiring special mechanisms and processes independent of other behaviors. The basic cognitive and learning processes that psychologists used to explain other aspects of development were thought to be inadequate, and even irrelevant, in explaining language acquisition. Perhaps this separation occurred because the nativistic model was developed outside traditional psychology, by theorists who were trained primarily in linguistic structure rather than human behavior. As we have seen throughout this chapter, however, the situation has changed considerably.

With the development of new theoretical models and better research techniques, language study has come back into the mainstream of child psychology. The view that language is either independent of cognitive abilities or insensitive to social and environmental factors no longer finds much support among developmental researchers. This is not to say that language does not possess its own unique characteristics, as nativist theorists continue to emphasize. But there can be little doubt that language development is very much interrelated with other developmental processes that both affect and are affected by it.

FOR THOUGHT AND DISCUSSION

1. One of the puzzles of human language is this: If language has such a strong biological basis, why are there so many different languages spoken around the world? *How do you think so many languages developed? Do you think the number of languages will change as time goes by? If so, in which direction? Why do you think people in, say, Brooklyn have accents so different from people only several hundred miles away in, say, Boston?*

2. The study of language acquisition has attracted more research than any other single area of developmental psychology. *Why do you think this is true? If you were studying children, what might attract you to investigate their language development?*

3. The growing number of immigrants in many countries is resulting in large numbers of children growing up in households that do not speak the majority language. *Do you think schools should teach in more than one language so that these children will not be at an immediate disadvantage? Or should schools teach the majority language alone?*

4. Most adults simplify their speech (using motherese) when speaking to children although it is not entirely clear why this occurs. *The next time you speak to a child note whether you make such adjustments. If you do, try to identify exactly what is motivating this behavior. In addition, try speaking to a child without making such adjustments. Does this cause any problems or offer any insights into why motherese occurs?*

5. Whether language is unique to humans is a question that persists in developmental psychology. *Why do you think this issue continues to be pursued? If we can train apes (or other species) to use complex language, what value might this have? What kinds of questions might we want to ask them?*

VISUAL SUMMARY FOR CHAPTER 11
Language Development

Theories of Language Development

Theory	Explanation
Nativistic	The nativistic approach holds that language is acquired by way of an inborn language acquisition device (LAD) that transforms the surface structure of the language into an internal deep structure that the child innately understands.
Environmental/ Learning	Skinner proposed an operant conditioning model of language development. Current environmental/learning accounts, such as Bandura's model of observational learning, emphasize more complex forms of learning. Such accounts also contend that the environment can provide children with the experiences necessary to acquire language.
Cognitive-Developmental	Piagetians link advances in cognitive abilities to language development. Others hold that when children hear speech, they analyze it according to its content before extracting its grammatical structure.
Sociocultural	Sociocultural theorists argue that children's primary motivation for acquiring language is to gain a tool for communication. Caregivers facilitate this process by providing a language acquisition support system (LASS), through which children acquire specific language elements. The sociocultural approach also emphasizes the social-cognitive skills that both child and caregiver bring to language learning.

The Preverbal Period

Speech Perception and Listening Preferences	Babies are born with categorical perception of many speech contrasts, including some that do not occur in their own language. Exposure to specific contrasts of their own language sharpens their ability to discriminate these contrasts, while the ability to discriminate other contrasts declines. Babies prefer speech to other sounds and particularly like the rising and falling intonations many adults use when speaking to young children. Such motherese enhances their ability to make various speech discriminations.
Early Sounds and Gestures	The first sounds of newborns are cries and physiological noises. Cooing appears at about 2 months; reduplicated babbling begins at 6 months. Near the end of the first year, babbling becomes more speechlike in sound and intonation. Gestures serve many pragmatic functions for infants, initially taking the form of requests and referential communication, and later functioning as symbols to label objects, events, and attributes.

Semantics

Early Lexical Development

> At around 18 months, children's vocabularies increase dramatically, with nouns comprising the majority of children's early lexicons. There are individual differences in the proportion of nouns children use, however, related to such factors as social class, gender, and birth order. Common errors in early word use include overextensions, underextensions, and coining. Young children often use holophrases—single words that express an entire sentence or idea.

Mechanisms of Semantic Development

> Some researchers have proposed that children use grammatical information to infer the possible meanings of new words, a process labeled syntactic bootstrapping. Other have argued that various constraints are necessary to explain how children rule out the many possible meanings for any word. Lexical contrast theory holds that children assume that new words have different meanings from familiar words and that they adopt generally accepted meanings over more individualized meanings. The mutual exclusivily hypothesis holds that children believe that objects have only one name. Children's learning of category labels is aided by parents' modeling, whether direct or in the course of day-to-day interactions.

Grammar

Development of Grammar

> Two-word utterances appear around the end of the second year. As sentences grow longer, telegraphic speech emerges. When children first learn inflectional rules, they overregularize them, applying regular forms even to irregular words.

Mechanisms of Grammar Acquisition

> The semantic bootstrapping hypothesis holds that children use their knowledge of semantics to figure out rules of syntax. Nativistic theorists maintain that innate knowledge about the principles of grammar makes language acquisition possible. Some researchers have argued for the importance of innate strategies, such as operating principles for acquiring language and the competition model. Grammar acquisition may also be facilitated by environmental factors, such as motherese, imitation, and feedback.

Pragmatics

Speech Acts

> Infants at first communicate with crying, gestures, etc. As they acquire language, they add speech acts—pragmatic uses of language—to their nonverbal communication skills, and they learn to comprehend speech acts of others.

Discourse

> To communicate effectively, children must learn rules of discourse. Some rules are simple and are acquired early, but others are complex and are learned later.

Social Referential Communication

> Social referential communication involves sending a message that is understood by a listener. Effective social referential communication requires speaker skills, such as adjusting the message to the demands of the listener, as well as listener skills, such as recognizing and communicating when messages are ambiguous.

12

Early Social and Emotional Development

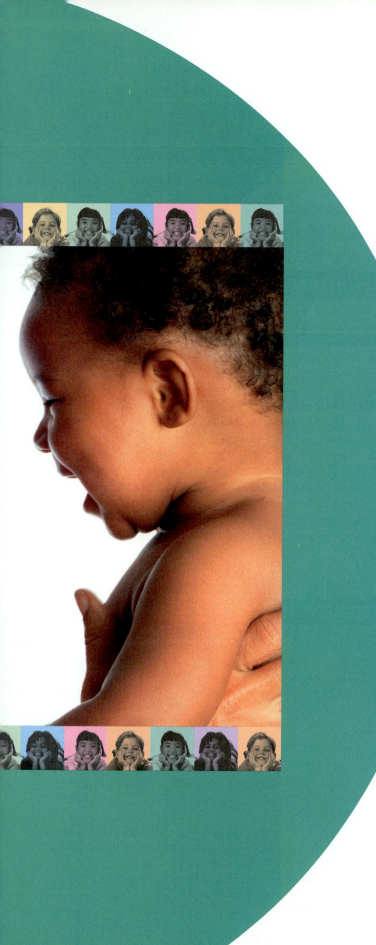

t's a fact of life in the United States—every day, millions of infants and preschool children spend time in day care centers. But how does day care affect a young child's social and emotional development, and how does it compare with being raised at home? Jennifer Ireland was a 19-year-old college student

in 1994 when her baby daughter, Maranda, became the focus of a custody battle centering on precisely these issues.

Shortly after Maranda was born to Jennifer and her boyfriend, the couple split up. Jennifer went on to start her freshman year at the University of Michigan, taking Maranda with her. The two lived in campus housing, and Maranda was cared for in the university's child care center. Maranda's father—who was still living at home with his parents—responded by suing for custody of the toddler. He claimed that Maranda would be better off living with him and being cared for by his mother, a full-time homemaker. The judge agreed and placed Maranda in her father's custody, ruling that a child is better off being raised in a home with a single caregiver than in a group setting.

Does the research evidence support the judge's claim? And what effect would such a decision have on life in the United States today? In the view of a lawyer for the American Civil Liberties Union, which helped Jennifer appeal the court's decision, the judge's "ruling had to be overturned, or else it would have sent shock waves to every single parent who works and uses day care." In 1995, the state court of appeals reversed the judge's order, holding that there is no convincing evidence that day care is harmful to young children or is necessarily less beneficial than being raised at home. The couple eventually agreed to share custody of the little girl.

In this chapter, we explore the issues at the center of this case, along with related issues, as we examine children's early social and emotional development. Family life in recent years has certainly been changing in some fundamental ways, and understanding the role played by the mother and other caregivers during the child's first months and years of life is thus more important than ever to psychologists, policy makers, and parents. As we will see, this area is very complex, and many questions—including those surrounding day care—have not been entirely resolved. Nevertheless, research is yielding some interesting and important answers. ■

Humans are a very social species. We organize into groups ranging in size from families to communities to nations, and we spend a good deal of time interacting with one another. From early on, children form many social relationships. Some of these relationships, such as those with occasional baby-sitters, are very brief and of little consequence. But others, such as those with family members and certain friends, will last for many years and may affect children's later development and personality in important ways (Caspi, 1998; Thompson, 1998).

Understanding social development has not been easy, however, because the complexity of social interaction poses certain obstacles to its scientific study. Consider the following mother–infant interaction, which represents the relatively simple dyadic, or two-person, situation. A mother talks to her baby and he begins to smile; when she moves a toy in front of him, the baby follows it with his eyes; and when she makes a strange face at him, he becomes still and stares attentively.

What causes these changes in the baby's behavior? Clearly the changes are being determined, or caused, by what the mother is doing. But there is more to the interaction than that because the influence here is undoubtedly bidirectional. That is, the baby's responses also influence the mother's behavior. For example, if the baby gazes at her with apparent interest, the mother is likely to continue what she is doing. If the baby begins to act bored, she may step up her actions, perhaps tickling him or adding attention-getting vocalizations. If the baby begins to fret, the mother may tone down her responses or even end the interaction altogether.

This relatively simple example illustrates the challenge that faces psychologists in their attempts to identify the determinants of social interactions. In the case of the baby's behavior, certainly one determinant is the mother's behavior. But the baby's behavior and personal characteristics affect the kinds of things the mother does. In that sense, then, the baby is a *producer* of his own environment (Lerner, 1982).

We have already encountered this general idea in earlier chapters—first, in Chapter 1, when we discussed Bandura's model of reciprocal determinism and Bronfenbrenner's notion of developmentally generative and disruptive behaviors, and then in Chapter 3, in the behavior-genetic models of Scarr and Plomin. The essential point here is that psychologists have come to understand that human social behavior is *transactional*—each person's actions both affect and are affected by the actions of others. We will see many examples of this in the remainder of the book.

This chapter is the first of five that deal with children's social and personality development. We focus here on social interactions during the child's first 2 years of life. To begin, we survey the approaches of the four major theoretical traditions to infant social development. Next, we consider how the infant and caregiver develop an early communication system as they learn to regulate one another's behavior. Then we look at the baby's temperament, or individual style of responding. Finally, we examine the topic that traditionally has been of greatest interest to researchers—the nature of the attachment process that produces the unique emotional bond between caregiver and child.

Children's social interactions are transactional. They not only respond to their environment, they also influence it.

THEORIES OF EARLY SOCIAL DEVELOPMENT

Social development during the first 2 years of life is distinctive in several important ways. First, although children eventually come to have many social contacts—family, friends, teachers, and so on—the social world of infants in most Western cultures has traditionally consisted of relatively few individuals, such as the mother, father, and siblings. Second, these initial relationships appear to be more influential and to have longer-term effects on the child's social, personality, and even cognitive development than do many of the relationships that develop later on. Finally, children appear to develop strong emotional relationships—especially with the mother but also with the father and others—more easily and intensely during the infant years, suggesting that early social development may involve psychological processes that are different from those that operate later in life.

Researchers from each of the four major theoretical approaches have taken an interest in early social development. And, as you might expect, their different views have led them to pursue different questions and aspects of this area. Much of the focus has been on the attachment process, which we discuss in detail later in the chapter.

Evolutionary and Biological Approaches

According to the evolutionary family of approaches, the social behaviors we observe in today's infants and caregivers represent millions of years of gradual adaptation to the environment. Much of this work has involved other species, with theorizing regarding human development based largely on the views of John Bowlby, discussed in Chapter 1 (Bretherton, 1995).

In contrast to the young of many other species, human infants are relatively helpless at birth and for years remain unable to survive on their own. If babies are not fed, sheltered, and protected, they will certainly die. And because humans produce comparatively few offspring (whereas fish, for example, lay thousands of eggs), our species would quickly become extinct if a high percentage of babies did not survive long enough to reproduce.

Evolutionary theorists believe that the process of natural selection has provided infants and mothers with an innate system of behaviors designed to ensure the infant's survival (Ainsworth & Bowlby, 1991). Perhaps the most important of these built-in behaviors is for the infant to develop a relationship with the **primary caregiver**—

Primary caregiver
The person, usually the mother, with whom the infant develops the major attachment relationship.

usually the mother—that accomplishes two goals: keeps her nearby and motivates her to provide adequate caregiving. For the first 6 or 7 months, the baby can remain close to the mother only by drawing her near. Crying is by far the most effective behavior for doing this. Later, as locomotor abilities develop, the child can stay near the mother by crawling or running after her.

The infant promotes caregiving behaviors in several ways. One is by making interactions very pleasant for the mother, such as by smiling, vocalizing, and making eye contact with her. Proper caregiving is also encouraged when babies reduce signs of distress in response to the mother's attention, such as when they stop fussing when picked up. Finally, some ethologists believe that the physical appearance of babies—large heads, round faces, and chubby legs—may also serve to maintain the mother's interactions because she innately finds these features "cute" (Alley, 1983). Interestingly, researchers have found that the preference for babylike features is found in both adult men and women but is most prominent in women. Moreover, development is characterized by a shift from a preference for adult features in middle childhood to favoring infant features beginning in early adolescence, corresponding with the onset of the ability to reproduce (Fullard & Reiling, 1976).

The caregiver, too, presumably has built-in mechanisms for doing what is necessary for the infant's survival. This individual's job is to "read" the infant's signals and decide what is wrong, what to do in response, and when it has been effective. Innate caregiving patterns are obvious with other mammals, where mothers of even first litters appear to know exactly how to care for their young. As we saw in Chapter 1, ethologists characterize these more complex sequences of innate behaviors as modal action patterns and assume that they are triggered by certain stimuli (such as the sound or smell of the newborn pups). It is not easy to determine what portion of the caregiving provided by human mothers is innate, however, because new mothers in most cultures typically acquire much of this information through social sources (e.g., by observing or conversing with other mothers).

The behaviors that serve to keep mother and baby together during the early weeks and months of life emerge as part of an *attachment process* that also includes a strong emotional bond. The baby, at first, emits care-seeking behaviors to virtually anyone. But if the mother responds to these bids in a sensitive and consistent way, the baby gradually comes to use the mother as a source of comfort and reassurance when upset and a secure base from which to explore the world. As we will discuss in more detail, this behavior characterizes what is known as a "secure" attachment. Bowlby and others of this tradition believe further that the attachment process in humans occurs during a sensitive

According to ethologists, aspects of babies' physical appearance may be innately "cute" and so elicit caregiving.

period in the baby's development, as is the case for the imprinting process that produces attachment in some other species (Scott, 1987).

According to Bowlby and most adherents of attachment theory, sensitive, responsive mothers and securely attached infants are nature's prototype, shaped by forces in our evolutionary past (Chisolm, 1996). Less responsive mothers—or infants who do not seek out their mothers for comfort and reassurance—are viewed as abnormal and maladaptive. More recently, however, a number of evolutionary theorists have questioned the premise that there is a single, species-appropriate type of mother–infant relationship (Chisolm, 1996; Hrdy, 1999; Lamb et al., 1985). To understand their objections, it is helpful to recall some of the work that shaped Bowlby's thinking.

Bowlby's model of the mother–infant relationship was heavily influenced by observations of modern hunter-gatherer groups, such as the !Kung (now known as the Ju'/hoansi). Many evolutionary theorists believe these groups live much as our ancestors did. Therefore, the way these groups deal with environmental constraints should reflect the pressures faced by our ancestors in the evolutionary past. !Kung infants, it should be noted, were in physical contact with their mothers 70–80% of the time during their first year of life (Konner, 1972).

Of course, it is impossible to know very much about the features of the environments in which humans evolved. However, contemporary evolutionary psychologists increasingly suspect that the environment was not quite as ideal as Bowlby imagined. It was probably highly unstable, with unpredictable changes in climate and habitat (Bjorklund & Pellegrini, 2002). Consequently, many evolutionary psychologists contend that humans are equipped with a flexible behavioral repertoire that allows persons to form social bonds that are adaptive given local ecological and social conditions. Indeed, studies of modern hunter-gatherer groups other than the !Kung show considerable variability in the nature of early social relationships (Hewlett et al., 2000; Tronick, Morelli, & Ivey, 1992).

Studies of attachment in high-risk samples in modern industrialized societies provide further support for the idea that whether a particular form of attachment relationship is adaptive or maladaptive depends on the situation. For instance, children who form a secure attachment with a severely depressed caregiver place themselves at risk for psychological problems, whereas children who do not form a close attachment are less at risk (Radke-Yarrow et al., 1995).

Environmental/Learning Approaches

Environmentally oriented theorists do not deny that infants and mothers possess many built-in responses that may contribute to early caregiving and the attachment process. But the main concern of these theorists is with the infant's **socialization**—the process by which a child's behavior is molded to fit with the society's roles, beliefs, and expectations (Bugental & Goodnow, 1998; Maccoby, 1992). Socialization is assumed to continue throughout childhood, and is thought to affect many of the child's more complex social behaviors, such as moral development and interactions with peers. The process, however, begins in infancy and can be observed in the way the baby's first social interactions are influenced by others.

Socialization
The process through which society molds the child's beliefs, expectations, and behavior.

According to the environmental/learning view, caregiver–infant social behaviors result from interaction between the two individuals, with each influencing the behavior of the other. Rather than appealing to special evolutionary mechanisms unique to this area, however, psychologists of this tradition assume that these interactions can be explained by social-learning processes, including reinforcement, punishment, and observational learning (Gewirtz & Pelaez-Nogueras, 1992a; Hay et al., 1985).

For example, this approach contends that infants produce behaviors that encourage the mother to approach and remain close (crying, smiling, vocalizing, and so on) because these behaviors result in either positive reinforcement (milk, a rattle, or being rocked) or negative reinforcement (the removal of a wet diaper). Similarly, the mother learns to respond to these behaviors because they also result in either negative reinforcement (the baby stops crying) or positive reinforcement (the baby smiles, coos, and clings).

Much of the evidence supporting the social-learning model derives from studies showing that infant social behaviors can be influenced by reinforcement processes. Infant vocalizations, for example, will increase if reinforced and decrease if subjected to an extinction procedure (Poulson & Nunes, 1988). The same is true for infant smiling (Etzel & Gewirtz, 1967; Zelazo, 1971). Likewise, certain behaviors common in infants, such as separation protest and social referencing (both of which we will discuss later in the chapter), can be produced through conditioning processes (Gewirtz & Pelaez-Nogueras, 1991, 1992b). And similar experiments have demonstrated that infant behaviors can serve to increase (reinforce) or decrease (punish) the social behavior of the caregiver (Gewirtz & Boyd, 1976, 1977). Together, these studies show that it is theoretically possible to explain changes in caregiver–infant interaction by applying social-learning principles. But exactly how important such principles are in the development of the typical infant–caregiver relationship remains unresolved (Hay, 1986; Schaffer, 1986).

Cognitive-Developmental Approaches

Social cognition
Knowledge of the social world and interpersonal relationships.

The cognitive-developmental tradition contends that to understand children's early social development we should search for the cognitive processes that underlie social behaviors. This approach is based on the concept of **social cognition** (Flavell & Miller, 1998), which refers to children's and adults' understanding of human behavior and social interactions. For example, it explores how children learn to predict another person's behavior by appreciating what the other person is thinking, what he or she believes to be true, or what he or she wants to achieve. Social cognition is thought to begin in infancy, such as with a baby's ability to follow and make use of another person's eye gaze or to reference his or her facial expression or vocal intonation for clues about how to react to novel stimuli. Ways in which these behaviors may demonstrate a budding theory of mind are discussed in Chapter 7.

Internal working model
An infant's and a caregiver's cognitive conception of each other, which they use to form expectations and predictions.

As applied to attachment, the cognitive tradition overlaps somewhat with the evolutionary approach in that both are concerned with how infants and mothers cognitively represent their relationships with each other (Main, Kaplan, & Cassidy, 1985). Some theorists believe that infants and caregivers develop **internal working models** of each other and use these models to interpret events and predict what will happen (Bowlby, 1973; Bretherton, 1987, 1993). For example, an infant may develop expectations regarding the mother's behavior as a result of the type of treatment she provides. If she responds quickly and reliably to the infant's signals of distress or care seeking, the baby may develop the expectation that the mother will be available if needed and so will be less likely to cry when left alone (Lamb, Ketterlinus, & Fracasso, 1992; Pipp, 1990). Likewise, the caregiver may develop an internal working model of the infant that leads her to expect the baby will be eager to interact with her. As a result, she may become more likely to play with the infant (Crowell & Feldman, 1991; George & Solomon, 1989). Internal working models are also important for the infant's development of a sense of self, a topic we consider in the next chapter.

Sociocultural Approaches

Sociocultural approaches to early social and emotional development focus on the solutions cultures devise to deal with one basic universal reality—that the survival of infants depends on bonds with caregivers who will protect and nurture them (Rogoff, 2003).

Like adherents to the theoretical approaches described earlier, sociocultural theorists acknowledge that infants and mothers possess many built-in responses that shape early caregiving and the attachment process. At the same time, however, variations in caregiving arrangements observed across cultures and history show that early development is due not to biology alone but to the interaction of biology with culture.

As is true of environmental/learning approaches, sociocultural perspectives on early social and emotional development focus on socialization practices. However, sociocultural approaches diverge from the traditional environmental/learning view in their scope. Environmental/learning theorists primarily focus on the interactions between infants and their caregivers. Sociocultural theorists contend that to understand these interactions, it is essential to place them in a cultural context. Consequently, sociocultural studies of early development focus on levels or contexts of development beyond the infant or the infant–caregiver dyad.

Theorists have proposed several frameworks to help organize research on early development in its cultural context. One of these frameworks, described in Chapter 1, is Bronfenbrenner's bioecological model (Bronfenbrenner & Ceci, 1994; Bronfenbrenner & Morris, 1998). This model stresses the interactions of a changing organism in a changing environment composed of immediate settings and the larger social and cultural contexts in which the settings are embedded. Of particular interest are the ways in which various spheres—the home, the school, the parents' workplace, the local community, national policies—interact and shape development.

Indeed, studies show that conditions outside of the caregiver–infant dyad can influence the quality of the relationship. For example, family stress, family support, employment, and changes in supplemental childcare have all been shown to affect the mother–infant relationship either directly or indirectly through the marital relationship (Corwyn & Bradley, 1999; Fish, 2001; Thompson, Lamb, & Estes, 1982; van Bakel & Riksen-Walraven, 2002; Vondra, Hommerding, & Shaw; 1999).

Another framework for considering early development in its cultural context was proposed by Beatrice Whiting and John Whiting (1975). Whiting and Whiting's psychocultural model focuses on the relations between the development of individuals and features of their immediate environments, their social partners, and institutional and cultural systems and values. In contrast to Bronfenbrenner's model, in which contexts are nested in one another, this model portrays development as the product of a chain of social and cultural circumstances. The chain begins with the local ecology (climate, flora, fauna, terrain), which leads, over time, to the development of maintenance systems, such as subsistence activities, social organization, and division of labor. These activities determine children's immediate environments—the settings they inhabit, who they encounter in those settings, and how they spend their time. According to this model, it is the features of these settings, rather than social interaction itself, that mold children's social development.

Working from this model, Whiting and Whiting observed child-rearing in six communities in India, Kenya, Mexico, and the United States that differed in social complexity, domestic living arrangements, economic activities, and cultural belief systems (Whiting & Whiting, 1975). This investigation, known as the Six Cultures study, as well as a later extension of the study (Whiting & Edwards, 1988), revealed both similarities and differences in caregiving practices around the world. In all cultures, mothers functioned as the primary caregivers. However, there was wide variation in the amount of time infants and toddlers spent in the care of others, including fathers and older siblings. This, in turn, was determined by living arrangements, the mother's workload, and the division of labor between husbands and wives.

A third model, known as the "developmental niche," was devised by Charles Super and Sara Harkness to provide a framework for thinking about parenting as a culturally constructed interface between the larger environment and the development of children. The developmental niche is composed of three subsystems: the physical and social settings in which the child lives, cultural customs of child care and child-rearing, and the psychology of the caregivers. The psychology of the caregivers includes their beliefs regarding the nature and needs of children, their child-rearing goals, and their understanding concerning effective rearing techniques (Super & Harkness, 1986, 1997, 2002).

As we see throughout this and subsequent chapters, socialization practices are largely compatible with parental child-rearing goals and beliefs. For instance, in cultures with high infant mortality rates, the parental goal is to maximize survival. Parents tend to have more children than in communities with low child mortality rates and to provide very attentive physical care during the first 2 or 3 years, when the children are at greatest risk (LeVine, 1988; LeVine et al., 1994). For example, among the Gussi, an agricultural group in tropical Africa, infants are fed on demand, sleep with the mother, and are almost always in someone's arms. Gussi mothers respond to infant cries and frets very quickly.

To Recap . . .

Early social development differs from later social interactions in that infants have fewer social relationships (at least, in traditional Western cultures); these relationships often have long-term significance and infants form them very easily. The transactional nature of social interactions has made social development a challenge to researchers.

Ethologists contend that evolution has provided many of the responses necessary for the infant's survival. Babies are programmed by nature to produce behaviors that keep the mother close at hand and encourage her to provide appropriate caregiving. The mother, in turn, is biologically predisposed to read and respond to the infant's signals. Infant–mother attachment results from these innate behaviors. Whereas most adherents of attachment theory consider sensitive, responsive mothers and securely attached infants to be nature's prototype, more recent evolutionary theory holds that attachment need not follow one pattern and may develop differently depending on environmental variables.

Social-learning theorists assume that mother–infant attachment responses result from social-learning processes, with the infant and caregiver each providing consequences for the other's behavior.

Cognitive explanations of early social development consider cognitive development an important influence on social development. Some psychologists contend that children's social behavior reflects their social cognition and that babies and mothers develop expectations, or internal working models, regarding each other's behavior.

Sociocultural approaches are similar to environmental/learning models but broader in scope. Among these approaches are Bronfenbrenner's bioecological model, the psychocultural model of Whiting and Whiting, and Super and Harkness's developmental niche. Although these models vary, all share a focus on the sociocultural contexts of social and emotional development, ranging from the immediate environment to the overall culture.

MUTUAL REGULATION BETWEEN INFANTS AND CAREGIVERS

The attachment process that becomes so evident by the end of the baby's first year has roots in early infancy (Malatesta et al., 1989). Right from birth, mothers and newborns begin to interact in ways that will draw them into a close emotional relationship. A most important feature of these early interactions is that each individual both influences the other's behavior and adjusts to it, producing a smooth-running system of mutual regulation (Bornstein & Tamis-LaMonda, 1990; Tronick, 1989).

The key to the development of this two-way system is effective communication between the infant and the caregiver. Chapter 11 described how babies use gestures and babbling to send messages even before they can speak. But the baby's ability to convey wants and needs and to mobilize the caregiver into action begins even earlier.

Crying

By far the most important form of communication for the newborn is crying. Not only is crying one of the baby's strongest and clearest responses, but it is one to which caregivers appear to be especially responsive (Demos, 1986). Crying is part of the infant's larger affective communication system, which we discuss next. But because it has generated so much research on its own, we consider crying here separately.

Darwin believed that crying in newborns evolved as a means of providing the mother with information about the baby's state or condition (Darwin, 1872). Ethologists today continue to assume that crying serves as a stimulus to trigger innate caregiving behaviors by the mother (Eibl-Eibesfeldt, 1989; Zeifman, 2001). Learning theorists point out that crying (like sucking and some other early, reflexlike behaviors) also soon comes under the baby's voluntary control. When this occurs, crying becomes modifiable by its consequences—that is, it can be conditioned. If a baby's crying results in his caregiver's presence (as it often does), he or she may learn to use this response purposefully as a way of summoning care (Gewirtz, 1991).

For crying to serve as a form of communication, two conditions are necessary. First, different types of cries should communicate different messages. And they do; babies have separate cries for pain, hunger, and fear (Wasz-Hockert, Michelsson, & Lind, 1985). In addition, variations in cries can convey other information. For example, as the pitch of crying increases, adult listeners tend to perceive the baby's problem as becoming more serious and urgent (Leger et al., 1996; Zeskind & Marshall, 1988).

The other condition necessary for crying to be communicative is that listeners must be able to discriminate one type from another. Caregivers must understand whether the baby is saying, for example, "I'm hungry," "I'm wet," or "I'm frightened." As we saw in Chapter 5, there is some debate about exactly which dimensions adults are sensitive to. Nevertheless, a number of studies have reported that adult listeners can be quite good at interpreting babies' cries. This ability is based in part on experience. In general, parents and other adults who have spent time around newborns are better at decoding infant crying than are adults with little experience (Green, Jones, & Gustafson, 1987; Gustafson & Harris, 1990). Similarly, mothers of 4-month-olds are better skilled in this area than are mothers of 1-month-olds (Freeburg & Lippman, 1986).

The communication role of crying thus has elements of both nature and nurture. At first, crying is innately elicited by various internal stimuli (such as hunger) and external stimuli (such as a diaper pin). Such crying serves primarily to draw the mother near. With experience, however, the caregiver becomes more accurate at reading the information in these signals, and babies learn to use the crying response as a means of controlling the mother's attention and care.

Emotions and the Affective System

Research on crying indicates that many of the early messages sent by babies involve "dislikes." Newborns also can communicate "likes," using behaviors such as smiling, vocalizing, and gazing at an object they find interesting (Brazelton, 1982). These aversions and preferences are the internal reactions, or feelings, we call **emotions.** On seeing his mother, for example, an infant might experience joy, which might be followed by anger as she prepares to leave, sadness when she is gone, and fear when he hears an unfamiliar sound. Some researchers believe that emotions also carry with them a readiness for action—the child experiences a particular feeling in preparation for doing something (Campos et al., 1994; Saarni, Mumme, & Campos, 1998).

The outward expression of emotions is called **affect.** Many theorists believe that initially a close correspondence exists between what babies feel and what they express. That is, early on, affect accurately reveals emotion (Malatesta et al., 1989). It is widely believed that the infant's ability to display different affective states is an important component in the mutual regulation between babies and their mothers (Adamson & Bakeman, 1991; Fogel & Thelen, 1987).

Emotion
An internal reaction or feeling, which may be either positive (such as joy) or negative (such as anger), and may reflect a readiness for action.

Affect
The outward expression of emotions through facial expressions, gestures, intonation, and the like.

Development and Expression of Emotions Although affective responses can take a number of forms, such as gestures and vocalizations, much of our understanding of babies' early emotional development has come about through the study of facial expressions (Malatesta, Izard, & Camras, 1991). Even newborns possess all the facial muscle movements necessary to produce virtually any adult emotional expression. Researchers have developed detailed coding procedures for assessing babies' facial expressions, involving separate ratings for the brow, eye, and mouth regions (Izard, 1989).

Babies' facial expressions of the basic emotions appear at different points in development (Camras, Malatesta, & Izard, 1991; Ekman, 1993). There is some disagreement about exactly what these basic emotions are (Izard, 1993; Sroufe, 1996), but we will consider several that have been mentioned frequently.

From birth, babies can indicate *distress* by crying and *interest* by staring attentively. As we saw in Chapter 6, one stimulus that reliably elicits interest is the human face, illustrating how evolution encourages infant–mother interaction right from the beginning. Another inborn facial expression is *disgust*, which is elicited by unpleasant tastes or odors, usually signaling to the caregiver that feeding is not going the way it should (Rosenstein & Oster, 1988; Steiner, 1979).

By 10 to 12 weeks of age, smiling (reflecting *pleasure*) appears in response to the human voice or a moving face (Haviland & Lelwica, 1987). Researchers have identified different types of smiles in babies, varying according to the components of lip retraction, cheek raising, and jaw dropping. Recent research suggests that 6- and 12-month-old infants display different smiles in response to different types of pleasure, such as the enjoyment of different components of a face-to-face mother–child interaction, including anticipation of the mother's behavior and satisfaction after its completion (Fogel et al., 2000). This further suggests that the positive emotional experience of children is rather complex even midway through the first year of life.

Sadness and *anger*—demonstrated experimentally by removing a teething toy or by restraining the baby's arm—are first evident in facial expressions at 3 or 4 months (Lewis, Alessandri, & Sullivan, 1990; Stenberg, Campos, & Emde, 1983). Facial expressions indicating fear do not appear until about 7 months, and more complex affective responses, such as those for guilt, shame, and embarrassment, are not apparent until the second year of life (Tangney & Fischer, 1995).

Because they are assumed to reflect the infant's emotions, an infant's expressions can be used to infer how the baby is feeling about a situation. For example, researchers taught babies to pull a string tied to one arm to produce a pleasant visual and auditory stimulus. The babies displayed expressions of joy during the learning process but displayed expressions of anger when the pulling no longer produced a reward (Lewis et al., 1990; Sullivan, Lewis, & Alessandri, 1992). Thus, the infants appeared to experience the two situations in much the same way adults would. Nevertheless, researchers cannot be certain that babies' affective responses are identical to those of adults, and we clearly have more to learn in this area (Izard et al., 1995; Oster, Hegley, & Nagel, 1992).

Socialization of Emotions The emergence of emotions in infancy is guided primarily by biological processes and is universal across cultures (Izard, 1995). However, even in early infancy, this development is shaped by cultural practices. In cultures where infants are in nearly constant physical contact with caregivers, they have little need to express their emotions. For example, among the Inuit of Arctic Quebec, infants are almost always found in a pouch inside their mother's parka. Under these circumstances, small postural changes or movements are sufficient to elicit a response from caregivers. Indeed, observers often remark how little infants cry in communities where they are constantly held. Martha Crago, who studies language acquisition among the Inuit noted:

> Infants wiggle and their mothers know they have awakened. They squirm and their mothers sense their hunger or discomfort. In some homes, I found the babies hardly

needed to cry to have their needs known and responded to. I remember being with one family and finding that a whole day had gone by and I had never heard the one-month-old peep. Her mother would be carrying her in [her parka] and for no reason that was perceptible to me the infant would be taken out and fed. (Crago, 1988, p. 204)

Modeling is another way in which emotions are socialized. Most mothers, for example, display only a few facial expressions to their babies, most of which are positive (Malatesta, 1985). The babies, in turn, tend to match these expressions (Haviland & Lelwica, 1987). This is particularly true in Japan, where the expression of negative emotion is discouraged. Japanese parents model restraint of emotion and actively avoid confrontations and contests of will in which negative emotions are likely to be expressed. When Japanese parents do oppose their children, they tend to express it indirectly via silence, indifference, or shunning (Azuma, 1996; Lebra, 1994; Miyake et al., 1986).

Socialization of emotions also occurs through reinforcement processes. Mothers more often respond positively to infants' expressions of pleasure than to their displays of distress (Keller & Scholmerich, 1987; Malatesta, 1985). This process, perhaps in combination with the modeling just described, may be one reason that over the course of the first year infants' positive emotional signals typically increase while their negative responses decrease (Malatesta et al., 1989).

Older infants and preschoolers generally learn to identify and label their emotions through everyday experiences. For example, parents frequently point out how a child is feeling ("You seem to be angry with Mommy" or "That baby must be feeling upset about dropping her ice cream cone") (Denham, Zoller, & Couchoud, 1994; Smiley & Huttenlocher, 1989).

At first, as mentioned, babies' affective expressions closely mirror their emotions, but over time children learn to control their affective displays, so that what they express may not necessarily reflect what they are feeling (Saarni, 1989, 1990, 1999). Such attempts to conceal emotions often result from children's increased understanding of their culture's emotional **display rules**—the expectations or attitudes regarding the expression of affect (Davis, 1995; Malatesta & Haviland, 1982; Underwood, Coie, & Herbsman, 1992), which children begin to show an understanding of as early as age 2 (Lewis & Michaelson, 1985). For example, boys may learn that displaying fear or pain is not seen as appropriate for them, and so they often try to inhibit such expressions of emotion.

Display rules
The expectations and attitudes a society holds toward the expression of affect.

Recognizing Emotions
Just as the baby influences the mother through the display of affective responses, the mother can influence the baby. But before this form of regulation can occur, the baby must be able to recognize and interpret the mother's responses, a task that is more difficult than simply producing one's own expressions of emotion (Denham, 1998).

An infant's ability to recognize facial expressions of emotion seems to develop in stages (Baldwin & Moses, 1996; Nelson, 1987; Walker-Andrews, 1997). Babies younger than 6 weeks are not very good at scanning faces for detail. As a result, they do not recognize different emotional expressions (Field & Walden, 1982). Soon after, however, infants begin to show evidence of discriminating facial expressions of emotions. For example, babies who have been habituated to a photo of a smiling face show renewed attention when the photo is changed to one depicting a frowning face (Barrera & Maurer, 1981). Babies of this age discriminate even better when they view talking faces displaying various emotions—although under these circumstances the voice may also provide important cues (Caron, Caron, & MacLean, 1988).

But do babies in this second stage have any real understanding of the emotions that are being expressed? Probably not. It is more likely that they simply can tell that the faces look different, without appreciating that a sad look represents unhappiness or a smiling face joy. Once infants reach 5 to 6 months of age, however, they appear to develop a clearer understanding of the meanings of emotional expressions. This is shown, for example, by the fact that at this age babies begin to display the same emotion as displayed on the face they are viewing (smiling at a happy face) and prefer some emotional expressions to others (Balaban, 1995; Haviland & Lelwica, 1987; Izard et al., 1995; Ludemann, 1991).

Near the end of the first year, infants begin to use information about other people's emotional expressions to regulate their own behavior—the social referencing process described in Chapter 7 (Feinman et al., 1992; Klinnert et al., 1983). Babies are especially likely to look to their mothers or fathers for this type of guidance when they are uncertain what to do next, such as when they encounter an unfamiliar object or person. They then use the parent's expression as a guide to how to react in the situation.

In a study that illustrates this process very clearly, 1-year-old infants and their mothers were studied as they interacted on the visual-cliff apparatus described in Chapter 6. The baby was placed on the shallow side, and the mother and an attractive toy were positioned at the deep end. This situation appeared to produce uncertainty in the infants, who generally responded cautiously and frequently looked up at their mothers as if attempting to gain information as to how to respond. The mothers were trained to produce a number of affective facial expressions, including fear, happiness, anger, interest, and sadness.

The question of interest to the researchers was whether the mother's expression would regulate the infant's behavior on the visual cliff. The results indicate that it did. When the mother expressed joy or interest, most babies crossed over to the deeper side to reach her. If she expressed fear or anger, however, very few of them ventured onto the deep portion of the apparatus (Sorce et al., 1985). Similar results have been found when mothers were instructed to express different emotions toward an unfamiliar person or a new toy—babies' willingness to approach and interact with the person or toy depended on the nature of the mother's reaction—both her facial expression and her vocal intonation (Baldwin & Moses, 1994; Boccia & Campos, 1989; Mumme, Fernald, & Herrera, 1996). Thus, babies as young as 1 year old appear to be able to use another person's emotional reactions as a gauge for understanding the environment and adjusting to it.

Research has found that infants may bring some awareness of the social context into play in social-referencing situations and that this ability develops across the first year of life. For example, when presented with the ambiguous novel stimulus of a barking toy dog, 10-month-olds were likely to look at their mothers' faces only if the mother was attending to them, whereas 7-month-olds did not make this distinction (Striano & Rochat, 2000).

Finally, mothers have been shown to use the infant's tendency for social referencing to their advantage. In a study examining the emergence of emotions, mothers were asked how they usually responded when an event—such as abruptly encountering an unfamiliar animal or hearing a loud sound—caused their baby to display surprise. Many mothers reported that immediately after exhibiting surprise, the baby appeared for a moment uncertain as to how to respond and then entered a state of either joy or distress. If during that brief moment the mother communicated a positive reaction to the infant, perhaps by smiling or speaking in a pleasant voice, the baby's response was more likely to be a pleasant one and distress avoided (Klinnert et al., 1984). This study and others suggest that mothers intuitively understand (or perhaps have learned through experience) that their babies look to them when feeling uncertain and that they have some ability to influence the infants' responses to the situation (Hornik & Gunnar, 1988).

Face-to-Face Interactions

During the first 3 or 4 months of life, much of the infant's contact with the caregiver involves face-to-face interactions, such as those that occur during feeding, diapering, and, in some cultures, play. Western psychologists have come to attach considerable significance to these early interactions, believing that they are fundamental to the development of an effective communication system between mother and baby and ultimately to the development of a strong attachment relationship (Brazelton & Yogman, 1986; Isabella, 1993, 1994).

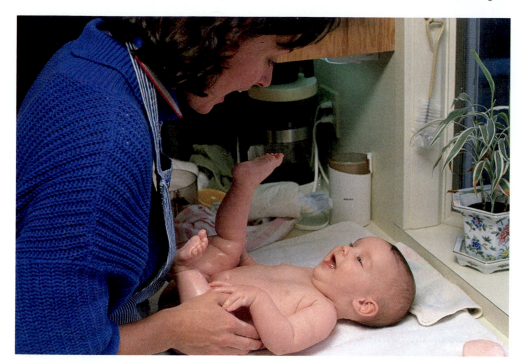

Face-to-face interactions during the early months appear to play an important role in the development of infant-caregiver attachment.

Researchers can closely investigate these early dyadic interactions in laboratory settings. The baby and mother sit facing each other, with the mother typically instructed to play with the infant in her normal fashion. As they interact, one camera videotapes the mother's face, and another videotapes the baby's. By replaying the two tapes side by side—often comparing only one frame at a time—investigators can examine the interactions in great detail. This technique, known as **microanalysis,** has helped reveal the subtle ways in which infant and mother influence one another (Kaye, 1982; Lamb, Thompson, & Frodi, 1982). Study of these early interactions has revealed two principal features that are characteristic of both newborn behavior in general and mother–infant dyadic exchanges in particular: cycles and patterns.

Microanalysis
A research technique for studying dyadic interactions, in which two individuals are simultaneously videotaped with different cameras and then the tapes are examined side by side.

Mother–Infant Interaction Cycles

Newborns appear to cycle from states of attention and interest to states of inattention and avoidance. During the attention phase, they make eye contact with the caregiver and often display positive affect, such as by smiling and vocalizing, whereas during the inattention phase they avoid eye contact and are more likely to show distress. Some psychologists believe that periods of attention can become too arousing and stressful for infants and that infants keep this stimulation under control by turning away and perhaps by self-comforting, for instance, by putting the thumb in the mouth (Field, 1987; Gianino & Tronick, 1988). Early face-to-face interactions are important because they reveal the baby's capability for emotion regulation, whereby the infant increases positive feelings and decreases negative feelings by adjusting his or her behavior (Fox, 1994; Thompson, Flood, & Lundquist, 1995).

Mother–Infant Interaction Patterns

Early interactions produce patterns of behavior between the caregiver and the infant. As the mother comes to recognize the baby's cycles of attention and inattention, she adjusts her behavior to them. Microanalytic studies of mother–infant interaction during the first 4 months have shown that mothers gradually learn to concentrate their affective displays (talking, tickling, and smiling) during those times when the baby is attending to them. When the baby looks away, the mother's responses decline. Soon the infant and mother develop an **interactional synchrony** in behavior, so that they are both "on" or both "off" at about the same time (Kaye, 1982). In this way, the mother maximizes her opportunities to "teach" the baby, and the baby can regulate the amount of interaction that takes place.

Interactional synchrony
The smooth intermeshing of behaviors between mother and baby.

Once a synchronous pattern has developed between mother and baby, a second pattern begins to emerge. The mother waits for the baby to respond, and then she responds back. Sometimes these responses are imitative (the mother produces the same sound that the baby has just made), sometimes they are repetitive (she wiggles the baby's toes after each response), and sometimes they take other forms. But all of them serve to "answer" the infant's responses. This *turn-taking* pattern between caregivers and babies may represent the first conversational "dialogues," which later become more obvious as speech and language develop (Beebe et al., 1988; Masataka, 1993; Mayer & Tronick, 1985). Babies appear to enjoy turn-taking episodes, often displaying a good deal of smiling and positive vocalizations.

Cultural Variations   Although the patterns of social interaction just discussed are observed in many cultures, they are not universal. Face-to-face encounters like those described are characteristic of cultures that view infants as social beings and as proper conversational partners—albeit partners with little to say—from shortly after birth. Not all cultures attribute the same capabilities to young infants. The existence of cultural variations in early mother–infant interaction suggests there is not just one pathway to the formation of emotional bonds between infants and others as Western theories often suppose.

For example, the Kaluli people who live in the tropical rainforest of Papua New Guinea see their babies as helpless creatures who have "no understanding." Consequently, Kaluli do not engage in conversational dialogues with them. The mothers are, however, highly attentive to their infants' cries and physical needs. Infants nurse on demand, although mothers often combine nursing with other activities and largely direct their attention elsewhere. Kaluli mothers do greet their infants by name and use expressive vocalizations, but they avoid looking into the babies' eyes while doing so. The Kaluli believe it impolite to look into a person's eyes when speaking to him or her and associate the act with witchcraft. And, although Kaluli mothers are almost always holding or carrying their infants, they tend to face them outward so the infants can see and be seen by others (Ochs & Schieffelin, 1984). The practice of facing infants outward is common to many cultures, including some African American communities (Heath, 1983; Martini & Kirkpatrick, 1981; Sostek et al., 1981). The practice serves to encourage triadic (three-person) or multiparty interactions and reflects a more general cultural orientation toward embeddedness in a complex social world.

There are also variations in the developmental course of face-to-face interactions in cultures where they do occur. In middle-income European American households, simple face-to-face interaction between the mother and baby peaks at about 3 to 4 months. After that, mothers increasingly direct their infant's attention outward toward objects and events in the world (Adamson & Bakeman, 1991; Lamb, Morrison, & Malkin, 1987). Japanese mothers, in contrast, continue to solicit their infants' attention and use objects to direct the babies' attention inward toward themselves for many months to come (Bornstein, Tal, & Tamis-LaMonda, 1991; Bornstein et al., 1990).

When Interaction Is Disrupted   Another issue with face-to-face interactions is what happens when they are disrupted. A revealing experimental technique involves having the mother present the baby with no expression at all. The results of this *still-face* procedure have been fairly consistent across a number of studies (Cohn & Tronick, 1983; Ellsworth, Muir, & Hains, 1993; Segal et al., 1995; Toda & Fogel, 1993). Generally, babies at first attempt to engage the mother's attention, sometimes by pointing, vocalizing, or looking at her inquisitively. When the mother fails to respond, the infants usually begin to show signs of distress and protest, and they reduce their overall level of positive affect and often gaze in a different direction. These findings are consistent with the belief that the infant and mother develop an interaction pattern within the first few months that becomes comfortable for both of them. When one member of the pair (in this case, the mother) violates that pattern, however, the system is disrupted, and the other member (here, the baby) has difficulty coping with the new interactional style.

The importance of a smooth-running pattern of infant–caregiver interactions can also be seen in studies with mothers who are clinically depressed. These mothers have been found to be much less positive or responsive to their babies, and they do not synchronize well with the infants' behaviors. The babies, in turn, are less active and attentive and spend much of their time crying or displaying other forms of distress (Cohn et al., 1990; Field et al., 1990; Murray et al., 1996). Importantly, however, such infants do not display this sort of behavior with their nursery teachers (Pelaez-Nogueras et al., 1994), suggesting that it is indeed the absence of a synchronous relationship with the caregiver that causes the infants to respond in this way.

An interesting sidelight involves the issue of child abuse. Although it is not clear why, preterm infants have been shown to be at greater risk for abuse than full-term babies. It is possible that this problem results in part from a failure of the infant and caregiver to develop a good communication system. In support of this view, studies have shown that preterm babies spend more time asleep, are less alert when awake, are more quickly overaroused by social stimulation, and spend more time averting their gaze from the caregiver. In turn, their mothers spend less time in face-to-face interaction with them, smile at and touch them less, and are less skilled at reading their emotional signals (Kropp & Haynes, 1987; Lester, Hoffman, & Brazelton, 1985; Malatesta et al., 1986). It is important to point out that prematurity does not necessarily prevent the development of a secure attachment relationship (van IJzendoorn et al., 1992). Nevertheless, the apparent disruption of normal face-to-face affective interaction that results from prematurity may interfere with the establishment of a strong mutual regulation system between mother and baby, possibly increasing the likelihood of abuse.

Investigators have also explored how individual differences among full-term infants produce variation in mother–infant interactive behaviors. In one study, mothers of 2- and 3-month-old infants were observed interacting with their babies, and researchers noted their levels of **affect mirroring,** or the degree to which they gauged their communicative behaviors to respond to input from their infants (Legerstee & Varghese, 2001). Infant behavior patterns corresponded to the level of maternal affect mirroring, with the infants of mothers high in this measure displaying more positive affect, attention toward their mothers, and social expectancy (preference for responsive input, smiles, and the like) than infants of mothers low in affect mirroring.

Affect mirroring
The degree to which caregivers gauge their communicative behaviors to respond to input from their infants.

To Recap . . .

The attachment between mother and infant begins at birth and depends in part on communication. At first, babies use crying to communicate. But soon, other elements of the affective system come into play. The mother and infant regulate each other's behavior through their affective expressions and their recognition of the affective expressions of the other.

Babies begin to express relatively simple emotions facially within the first 3 months; expression of emotions that require more cognitive sophistication occurs later. Infants also begin to discriminate facial expressions within the first half year of life. Their understanding of these expressions is not obvious until the second half year, however, and they do not use this understanding to guide their own behavior until the end of the first year.

Microanalytic studies of mother–infant face-to-face interaction reveal that mothers can be quite adept at synchronizing their behaviors to babies' cycles of attention and inattention. There are cultural variations in the occurrence and developmental course of face-to-face interactions. In cultures where face-to-face interactions are common, these exchanges gradually develop into a turn-taking pattern, which may represent the earliest form of conversation. They also reflect infants' ability to regulate their emotions. Experimentally altering the mothers' natural behavior toward the child produces negative reactions in the child, who has come to expect a particular form of interaction.

TEMPERAMENT

The child's role in infant–caregiver interactions is greatly influenced by his or her personality. For example, mothers often respond differently to happy, friendly babies who like to cuddle than to fussy, irritable babies who squirm when held. For infants, personality does not yet include many components that are evident later on, such as beliefs, attitudes, and values. For this reason, the study of infant personality is generally restricted to emotional expressiveness and responsiveness to environmental stimulation. These components of personality are called **temperament** (Rothbart & Bates, 1998).

Temperament is meant to describe the baby's behavioral style, reflecting not so much *what* babies do as *how* they do it. For example, two babies may both enjoy riding in a mechanical swing, but one may react exuberantly, shrieking with delight, whereas the other may remain calm and even fall asleep. Most researchers view temperament as simply one of the many individual differences, or traits, that make each child unique (Bates & Wachs, 1994).

Temperament
The aspect of personality studied in infants, which includes their emotional expressiveness and responsiveness to stimulation.

Defining Temperament

Psychologists' definitions of temperament vary considerably (Goldsmith et al., 1987). We begin, therefore, simply by considering three questions that have guided their attempts to define this concept.

Is Temperament Inherited?
A fundamental question is whether babies inherit their response styles, just as they inherit the shapes of their noses or the color of their hair. There is considerable support for this idea.

We saw in Chapter 3 that studies comparing identical twins with fraternal twins provide strong evidence that at least some portion of temperament is transferred through the genes. Identical twins have been found to be more similar to each other than fraternal twins on a variety of behavioral measures, ranging from descriptions by parents of the baby's irritability to ratings by trained observers of the child's reactions to strangers to laboratory tests of the infant's fear responses on the visual-cliff apparatus. Twin studies also have found genetic effects in temperament traits among toddlers and preschoolers (Emde et al., 1992; Goldsmith, Buss, & Lemery, 1997; Plomin et al., 1993; Robinson et al., 1992).

We will see, though, that there is some disagreement over which behaviors best represent an infant's temperament, and not all these behaviors have been shown to have a genetic basis (Goldsmith et al., 1997). In addition, even if aspects of temperament are inherited, they may also be influenced by the child's environment.

Is Temperament Stable?
Regardless of the origins of temperament, another theoretical question is whether it remains constant over the years. Does the fearful baby who cries at an unfamiliar face at 6 months also shy away from new people at 20 months and avoid playmates at 42 months? This kind of stability over time and across situations has traditionally been viewed as an important defining component of responses that reflect temperament.

Research suggests that certain aspects of infants' behavioral style do indeed remain reasonably stable over time. A longitudinal study over 7 years found that observational assessment of infant temperament was related to parent reports of the children's temperaments at age 7 on several dimensions: fear, frustration-anger, and approach tendencies (Rothbart, Derryberry, & Hershey, 2000). Other research has suggested a link between early and later negative emotionality (such as fear or fussiness), reactions to new situations or people, and attention span (Guerin & Gottfried, 1994; Pedlow et al., 1993; Ruddy, 1993). Not all measures of temperament, however, display this sort of stability.

The question of stability—or lack thereof—has been of interest to both nature and nurture theorists (Hooker et al., 1987). Those who favor a genetic model of temperament argue that when some aspect of a child's response style is found to be stable across years, this stability is most easily explained by assuming that the trait is simply part of the child's genetic structure. Environmentalists, however, contend that such stability could just as easily result from the child's remaining in a fairly constant environment (Bates, 1987; Wachs, 1988).

Lack of stability in temperament likewise can be handled by both nature and nurture models. Changes in behavioral style obviously could result from changes in the child's environment. But studies have also shown that genetically related children tend to show similar *patterns of change* in some temperamental behaviors, which could mean that temperament develops according to some genetic plan (Eaton, 1994; Matheny, 1989). More research on this issue is needed.

Is Temperament Evident Early in Life?

Is Temperament Evident Early in Life? A third question that has been important in defining temperament is whether the child's response style is apparent from very early on. Again, the evidence is mixed. Recent research has found that certain characteristics of the fetus—such as heart rate and activity level—are reasonably stable during the last months of pregnancy and also fairly good predictors of how the mother later rates her infant's temperament (DiPietro et al., 1996; Eaton & Saudino, 1992). These data would seem to suggest that temperament begins in the womb. However, only some of the temperamental differences among newborns—usually those involving irritability and other forms of negative responding—are still observable after several years (Plomin et al., 1993; Riese, 1987; Stifter & Fox, 1990; Worobey & Blajda, 1989); most early differences disappear. In addition, not all behaviors that are assumed to reflect temperament are evident this early (Bates, 1987).

In sum, although many psychologists believe that temperamental behaviors are genetic, stable, and apparent early, not all agree. And the research evidence at this point does not settle the issue. We will see in the sections that follow, however, that the absence of a formal, agreed-on definition has not prevented researchers from pursuing many investigations of children's temperament.

Conceptualizing Temperament

Since systematic studies of infant temperament began in the middle of the 20th century, researchers have focused on different answers to the question of how best to conceptualize temperament. In this section, we examine three models of temperament and then describe some research concerning the physiological processes involved.

An Early Approach: Goodness of Fit

An Early Approach: Goodness of Fit The oldest and perhaps most widely used classification of temperament was developed in the 1950s by two pediatricians, Alexander Thomas and Stella Chess. An important overarching dimension identified by this pair concerns the **goodness of fit** between the baby's response style and his or her physical and social surroundings (Thomas & Chess, 1977). The degree of goodness of fit determines the degree of influence of infant temperament on later development. This notion meshes well with the transactional view of early social development and has become an important concept in temperament research (Sanson, Hemphill, & Smart, 2002; Seifer, 2000; Wachs, 1994; Windle & Lerner, 1986).

Thomas and Chess's research project, named the **New York Longitudinal Study (NYLS),** has continued for more than 30 years and represents one of the most important longitudinal efforts in modern child psychology (Thomas & Chess, 1986; Thomas, Chess, & Birch, 1968). The research began as an effort to predict children's psychological adjustment by identifying potential problems early. The strategy was to develop categories of infant temperament and then to examine whether these categories related to the child's social and emotional development at later ages. After extensive interviews with parents of infants, Thomas and Chess identified three clusters of characteristics

Goodness of fit
A concept describing the relation between a baby's temperament and his or her social and environmental surroundings.

New York Longitudinal Study (NYLS)
A well-known longitudinal project conducted by Thomas and Chess to study infant temperament and its implications for later psychological adjustment.

that occurred frequently, leading them to conclude that they had identified three early behavioral styles. They labeled these styles "easy," "difficult," and "slow to warm up."

The *easy baby* is rhythmic and usually has regular patterns of eating, sleeping, and toileting. He or she adapts well to changing situations and generally has a positive, happy mood. Easy babies are willing to approach new objects or people, and their reactions (of all types) are typically of low to moderate intensity. About 40% of the babies studied were classified by Thomas and Chess as this type.

The *difficult baby* is just the opposite. His schedules are less predictable, he is uncomfortable when situations change, and he often cries or displays a negative mood. He also withdraws from new experiences and reacts intensely to most environmental stimulation. This pattern was evident in about 10% of the infants.

The *slow-to-warm-up baby*, too, adapts poorly to changing situations and tends to withdraw from unfamiliar people or objects. She is typically less active, however, and responds at a relatively low intensity. About 15% of the babies were classified as this type. (The remaining 35% of the infants in the project did not fit into any of these three categories.)

Although the NYLS approach remains a widely used method of categorizing infant temperament, it does have its critics. One problem is its heavy reliance on parental report as a means of obtaining information. Parents' descriptions of their babies' behavior have the advantage of reflecting a wide range of situations, but this method is also open to biases of several sorts. Some parents are undoubtedly more objective than others, and some are better than others at observing and describing what their children do. Parents also may tend to report what they assume the researchers would like to hear, presenting, for example, a consistent description of the infant from one interview to the next or portraying the child in a more positive than realistic light. And parents' descriptions sometimes reflect their own reactions to the infant's behavior. Some parents, for example, might describe a response style as stubborn that other parents would describe as self-assured (Bates & Bayles, 1984; Kagan, 1994).

An alternative to the interview is the questionnaire, which asks parents to respond to a series of objective questions about the child's typical behavior and reactions to situations. The best-known questionnaires have been designed according to the NYLS classification scheme (Carey & McDevitt, 1978; Fullard, McDevitt, & Carey, 1984; Medoff-Cooper, Carey, & McDevitt, 1993). Questionnaires offer the advantage of producing quantitative information that can be easily summarized and compared. But they suffer from some of the same potential biases as parent interviews, and they involve additional issues, including how well the parents understand the questions, how well they can compare their child with others (as some of the items require), and how they are feeling about the child when they fill out the instrument (Mebert, 1991; Rothbart & Goldsmith, 1985).

EAS Model Another popular method of classifying infant temperament has been developed by a research team headed by Robert Plomin (Buss & Plomin, 1984, 1986). This model is strongly biological in its approach, viewing temperament as inherited personality traits that show an early onset. According to these researchers, a baby's temperament can be measured along a few main dimensions. Because these theorists originally identified emotionality, activity, and sociability as the key components, this classification scheme has been commonly referred to as the **EAS model.** A fourth component, shyness, has often been included as well.

Emotionality in this model refers to how quickly a baby becomes aroused and responds negatively to stimulation from the environment. A baby rating high on this dimension, for example, would be awakened easily by a sudden noise and would cry intensely in reaction. Plomin believes that differences on this dimension represent inherited differences in infants' nervous systems, with some infants having a quicker "trigger" and automatically experiencing greater arousal than others. During the first few months of life, emotionality is revealed through general distress reactions (such as

EAS model
Plomin and Buss's theory of temperament, which holds that temperament can be measured along the dimensions of emotionality, activity, and sociability.

crying) in unpleasant situations. Later in the first year, emotionality begins to evolve toward either fear or anger responses. Which behavioral style develops, Plomin contends, depends on the infant's experiences.

Activity describes the baby's tempo and energy use. Babies rating high on this dimension are moving all the time, exploring new places, and frequently seeking out vigorous activities. Like most definitions of temperamental traits, this one describes only how the baby behaves and not precisely what the baby likes to do. The researchers use the analogy of the controls of an automobile: The activity level presumably determines how fast the infant can go, but the environment determines the direction that the infant will take.

Sociability refers to an infant's preference for being with other people. Babies rating high on this dimension do not like to spend time alone and often initiate contact and interaction with others. This trait is not meant to describe the closeness of a baby's relationship with the caregiver or other significant people, which is assumed to be greatly influenced by the child's experiences. It is simply a measure of how much a given child innately prefers the stimulation derived from people rather than from things, and it is perhaps most clearly assessed in the baby's reactions to unfamiliar people, when the strength of a prior relationship does not come into play.

Finally, *shyness* refers to the child's response to unfamiliar persons, both at home and elsewhere. It is more a measure of wariness than of social activity, which is what the sociability scale measures. Researchers have supported the inclusion of separate subscales for shyness and sociability (Boer & Westenberg, 1994) and found evidence for the stability of the EAS-based temperament measures from ages 18 months through 50 months (Mathiesen & Tambs, 1999).

Although the EAS model views temperament as a biological concept, the researchers are interactionist in their conception of social development. In their view, although the baby's levels of key temperamental characteristics may be determined by genes, the baby's overall social development will depend on how these characteristics interact with characteristics of the social and physical environment.

To measure temperament according to this model, the EAS Temperament Survey is used. This is typically a written questionnaire completed by a child's parents that asks about the child's behavioral patterns.

Rothbart's Model   A third model of temperament has been proposed by Mary Rothbart. This model also has a strong biological flavor, viewing temperament as reflecting inborn differences in infants' physiological functioning. It, too, employs a parent questionnaire to assess an infant's temperament, although this information is supplemented by laboratory measures and by data collected in the home by professional observers (Goldsmith & Rothbart, 1991). Rothbart views temperament as consisting of individual differences in two areas—reactivity and self-regulation (Rothbart & Bates, 1998).

Reactivity is similar to Plomin's dimension of emotionality in that it refers to how easily and intensely a baby responds to stimulation. The major difference is that Rothbart also includes positive arousal, as illustrated by a baby's smiling and laughing at a new toy.

The other component of temperament according to this model is the baby's ability to increase or reduce this reactivity. This ability, termed *self-regulation,* is assumed to be inborn and to vary from child to child. Control of arousal by infants can take a number of forms, such as how long a baby looks at a stimulating object before turning away or how he or she approaches and explores it. The specific behaviors used for self-regulation change as the baby gets older, but the underlying temperamental trait presumably determines the infant's success in achieving it (Rothbart & Posner, 1985).

In a study that illustrates reactivity and self-regulation (LaGasse, Gruber, & Lipsitt, 1989), 2-day-old babies were tested to determine how intensely they sucked on an artificial nipple to obtain sweetened water. Individual babies' reactions to this positive stimulation differed considerably. At 18 months, the intensity of the same babies' reactions to unfamiliar people and situations was examined and found to be positively correlated with their earlier behavior—that is, those who had reacted intensely to the positive stimulation also responded intensely to the aversive stimulation. The researchers interpreted these results as reflecting a stable temperamental trait involving both reactivity and self-regulation. Babies who rated high on this trait were better able both to maximize their exposure to the positive stimulation (by sucking harder) and to minimize their exposure to the aversive stimulation (by withdrawing and hiding).

Like the schemes previously described, Rothbart's model is interactionist. Even though the reactivity and self-regulation abilities of babies differ from birth, the child's caregivers and physical surroundings are assumed to play major roles in determining the path that development will take.

An Emphasis on Physiological Processes   Some investigators have focused on physiological contributions to temperament and have deemphasized the role of environmental factors. Of particular interest have been individual differences in *stress reactivity*, which is often evidenced by increased levels of the hormone cortisol. For example, high cortisol response has been found to be associated with being prone to distress at various points during the first 13 months of life (Gunnar et al., 1989, 1992, 1996). Similarly, high cortisol response to stressors may be associated with high emotionality at 4 and 8 months of age (Ramsay & Lewis, 1996). Furthermore, how mothers respond to the infants' distress does not appear to make a substantial difference. There may still be an important maternal contribution, however—in keeping infants away from likely stressful situations, for example (Lewis & Ramsay, 2001).

Overall, researchers interested in the physiological aspects of temperament have focused on negative emotionality. Researchers today tend to agree that extremely shy and inhibited children tend to have greater stress reactivity and that indications of this tendency are present early in infancy (Rosenbaum et al., 1993; Schmidt & Fox, 1998; Schmidt et al., 1997, 1999). We return to the topic of inhibition later in this section. Evidence is also gathering that stress reactivity may be related to aggression; to extroverted, sensation-seeking behaviors; and to low self-control (Dettling, Gunnar, & Donzella, 1999; Gunnar et al., 1997; Tout et al., 1998).

Of course, an important issue relevant to any research on physiology and temperament concerns the direction of causation. Are rises in cortisol, for example, a cause of the behaviors that constitute temperament, or are they simply markers of a child's temperamental tendencies?

Temperament and Social Interactions

Although, as noted, physiological responses have been the focus of some researchers, most researchers who study temperament have at least some appreciation for the interactional role of temperament and early social development. An infant's social interactions are influenced not only by personality but also by the degree to which these characteristics match the demands or expectations of the environment (Putnam, Sanson, & Rothbart, 2002; Sanson & Rothbart, 1995). For example, if a mother's personality is very methodical, she may have considerable difficulty with a baby whose behavioral style is irregular and unpatterned. As a result, she may frequently attempt to do certain things, such as feed or put the baby down for a nap, when the child is not interested, perhaps producing repeated conflict and tension for both of them. That same baby, however, may develop a smoother relationship with a mother whose own behavior is not very structured. A mismatch can similarly occur with the physical environment. A baby who has a high activity level, for example, may have trouble living in a small apartment, and a baby who has a low threshold for distraction may not do well in a noisy neighborhood.

The match between the baby's temperament and the mother's personality can influence how successfully attachment develops.

The quality of children's social interactions, as we have seen, can also affect their cognitive development. Thus, temperamental characteristics of the child come into play in this area of development as well. One research team found that when mothers viewed their infants as having a more difficult temperament, they tended to provide them with fewer learning and discovery opportunities during their daily interactions (Gauvain & Fagot, 1995). Importantly, follow-up observations at age 5 revealed that these children did not perform as well on tasks involving cognitive problem solving (Fagot & Gauvain, 1997).

The interactional model of temperament and social relationships has implications for the role that infant personality may play in the attachment process too. We consider this issue later in the chapter.

Temperament and Behavior Problems

We mentioned earlier that the NYLS project was motivated by the search for early predictors of children's psychological adjustment. Other investigators have taken a similar clinical approach to investigations of temperament. Most of this work has focused on two categories of infant personality: the level of difficulty and the level of inhibition (Bates, Wachs, & Emde, 1994; Newman et al., 1997).

Difficult Infants   Thomas and Chess reported early in their longitudinal study that babies classified as difficult displayed more behavior problems during early childhood than did infants in the other categories (Thomas, Chess, & Birch, 1968). This finding has spurred a number of investigations aimed at determining whether this classification scheme might serve as an early screening device for identifying children at risk for later problems (Rothbart, Posner, & Hershey, 1995).

Interestingly, in a follow-up of their original longitudinal subjects, Thomas and Chess (1984) indicated that the majority of those who displayed temperamental difficulties during early childhood showed no evidence of these difficulties by early adulthood. Others have reported similar findings (Korn, 1984; Lee & Bates, 1985). Nevertheless, it remains useful to ask whether assessments of a difficult temperament during infancy and early childhood correlate positively with reports of behavior and adjustment problems in later childhood, adolescence, or even adulthood. Some studies have indeed reported such correlations (e.g., Bates et al., 1991; Caspi et al., 1995, 1996; Goldsmith et al., 2001; Halverson & Deal, 2001; Rothbart, Ahadi, & Hershey, 1994; Tubman et al., 1992). But exactly why difficult infants tend to develop these sorts of problems later on remains unresolved.

One possibility is that those aspects of the baby's temperament that produce the classification of difficult, such as frequent crying and irritability, increase the chances that parents will respond to the infant in a less than optimal manner, leading to problems in the child–caregiver relationship and ultimately to behavior problems in the child. This explanation is related to the goodness-of-fit concept described earlier (Bates, 1990; Chess & Thomas, 1987).

A very different explanation is that the positive correlation lies primarily in the eyes of the beholders (that is, the parents). According to this analysis, the fact that some parents rate their babies as difficult and later report them as having behavior problems results from the parents' attitudes, expectations, or approaches to child-rearing, not from the child's characteristics (Garrison & Earls, 1987; Sanson, Prior, & Kyrios, 1990). Several studies, for example, have found that a baby's temperament during the first year—as measured by parent questionnaires—could be accurately predicted by assessment of the mother's personality characteristics and expectations when the child was still in the uterus (e.g., Diener, Goldstein, & Mangelsdorf, 1995; Mebert, 1989, 1991; Vaughn et al., 1987)!

Finally, having a "difficult" temperament—although perhaps posing certain long-term risks—nevertheless may afford children some ethological advantages. For example, a cross-cultural study of babies during a drought in East Africa found that those classified as difficult were most likely to survive, presumably because they were most demanding of attention and care from their mothers (DeVries & Sameroff, 1984).

Inhibited Infants   Inhibition has for several years been a focus of investigation by researchers (Asendorpf, 1990, 1994; Kagan, Snidman, & Arcus, 1993). **Inhibition** can be defined as a tendency to quickly respond in a negative manner to an unfamiliar situation. For example, an inhibited baby would be cautious when presented with a toy very different from any he or she had previously encountered. As inhibited children approach 1 year of age, they become more timid, shy, and fearful, especially when encountering new situations or people (Schmidt & Fox, 1997). Like difficult babies, inhibited infants also are at risk for a variety of behavior problems in later childhood and beyond (Kagan, 1997; Rubin & Asendorpf, 1993).

The best-known research on inhibited children has been conducted by Jerome Kagan and his colleagues (Kagan, 1994, 1998). Kagan's research has involved an impressive longitudinal study designed to determine whether certain behaviors and physiological responses of inhibited children display an early onset and are stable over childhood (Kagan, Snidman, & Arcus, 1992).

Kagan's approach was to first identify groups of 2-year-olds who were either very inhibited or very uninhibited. He did this by observing how a large group of children reacted in a laboratory setting with unfamiliar people or objects. About 15% of the children responded to the new situations in a very timid manner and were thus selected for study. The 15% who responded in the most outgoing and fearless manner were used for comparison. The children were studied again at 5.5 years and at 7.5 years to see whether their early response styles were still apparent, as we would expect if inhibition is a stable trait (Reznick et al., 1986).

Two sorts of measurement were used. The first was a set of behavioral measures, including children's performance on a series of problem-solving tasks with an unfamiliar adult, their interactions with unfamiliar peers, and their social behavior in school. On these measures, about 75% of the children who had been identified as inhibited or uninhibited displayed behaviors consistent with their classification even 6 years later. In addition, most of the inhibited children were found to have developed other fears or anxieties, such as fear of the dark or fear of going away to camp (Kagan, Reznick, Snidman, Gibbons, & Johnson, 1988).

Suspecting that inhibition might have a biological basis, the researchers also looked at a number of physiological responses (such as heart rate and pupil dilation) that are commonly associated with human stress reactions (Kagan, Reznick, & Snidman, 1987; Schmidt & Fox, 1997; Schwartz et al., 2003). The physiological data were reasonably consistent with the behavioral findings. Children identified at age 2 as being inhibited continued to show evidence of greater physiological arousal in new situations as second graders (Kagan, Reznick, & Snidman, 1988). These studies suggest that some timid children may be displaying a temperamental trait that has been apparent from infancy, has remained reasonably stable over the years, and has a biological basis. Findings in Sweden by other researchers support these conclusions (Broberg, Lamb, & Hwang, 1990; Kerr, Lambert, & Bem, 1996; Kerr et al., 1994).

Even if true, however, these results tell only part of the story. For example, only those children at the extremes of inhibition displayed the sort of stability that is presumed characteristic of a temperamental trait; the rest of the children's levels of inhibition varied considerably over time (Kagan, Reznick, & Gibbons, 1989; Reznick et al., 1989). And even within the extreme groups, some children's inhibition did not remain constant.

Shyness and timidity, like a difficult temperament, also can be influenced by factors related to experience and socialization. Several studies have found, for example, that babies who display the negative emotionality characteristic of this trait during the early months are more likely to reduce their crying and fussing if their mothers are sensitive,

Inhibition
The tendency to quickly respond in a negative manner to an unfamiliar situation.

Inhibition is a personality style that appears to have a biological basis, but it is likely also affected by socialization influences.

responsive, and highly involved with them (Belsky, Fish, & Isabella, 1991; Matheny, 1986; Washington, Minde, & Goldberg, 1986).

 **To Recap . . .**

Temperament refers to an infant's overall style of responding. No single definition of temperament exists, but many researchers assume it is genetically based, stable, and evident early in life.

Investigators have taken different approaches to temperament research. The NYLS project involved a longitudinal study designed to identify the early correlates of later social and emotional problems. Based on parent interviews, this approach has identified three temperament types: the easy baby, the difficult baby, and the slow-to-warm-up baby. It has been criticized, however, for its overreliance on parental reports. Plomin's EAS model has a strong biological orientation. It defines temperament as the baby's emotionality, activity, sociability, and shyness. Rothbart contends that temperament reflects the infant's reactivity (emotionality) and self-regulation (ability to control the emotionality). A growing body of research focuses on physiological components of temperament, with particular emphasis on stress reactivity.

Temperament is assumed to affect mother–child interactions through goodness-of-fit— the degree to which there is a match between the infant's temperamental characteristics and the physical and social environment. The quality of these interactions, in turn, can influence the child's cognitive development. Temperament is also assumed to be involved in children's later behavioral problems. Infants classified as difficult have been shown to be at risk for behavior disorders. Timid children may be displaying an early temperamental trait, inhibition, which is apparent in both their behavioral interactions and their physiological responses to stressful situations.

ATTACHMENT

We come at last to the topic that is most central to this chapter. How do mothers and babies develop the intense emotional relationship that characterizes infancy and early childhood? We have seen that this process appears to be continuous, beginning with the earliest mother–infant interactions. In particular, the development of the affective system—which is at the heart of infant–caregiver mutual regulation—is important in setting the stage for the social relationship that is about to form. The baby's temperament undoubtedly plays a role in this process as well.

Developmental Course of Attachment

The infant's attachment to the caregiver can first be clearly observed at 6 to 8 months of age. However, the actual process begins shortly after birth and continues well beyond this time. Here we describe three general phases of attachment development that roughly correspond to those proposed in several theoretical models of this process (Bowlby, 1982; Schaffer & Emerson, 1964).

Phase 1 (Birth–2 Months): Indiscriminate Social Responsiveness

At first, babies do not focus their attention exclusively on their mothers and will at times respond positively to anyone. Nevertheless, they do behave in ways that are important for the development of an attachment relationship with the caregiver. Infants come into the world with a number of built-in responses designed to draw the mother near (such as crying) and keep her close at hand (quieting and smiling, for example). And although babies in this stage may not reserve their sociability solely for the caregiver, they clearly can recognize her. As we saw in Chapter 6, the newborn prefers to look at the mother (or at a photograph of her) rather than at a stranger within only a few days after birth (Bushnell, Sai, & Mullin, 1989; Pascalis et al., 1995).

Caregivers, too, very quickly learn to recognize their babies. Within hours after giving birth, for example, mothers can identify their own children solely on the basis of smell (Kaitz et al., 1987) or by touching a hand or cheek (Kaitz et al., 1992, 1993).

An important difference, however, is that although the baby displays attachment only after some months have passed, the mother's emotional bond to the baby develops very quickly. Some believe that **maternal bonding** occurs during a sensitive period immediately following birth and requires skin-to-skin contact with the baby (Klaus & Kennell, 1976; Klaus, Kennell, & Klaus, 1995). Based on this view, many hospitals and neonatal intensive care units have made it easier for mothers to spend more time with their newborns during the presumably crucial first hours and days of life.

Research indicates, however, that although such early contact may be important for some mothers under some circumstances, it certainly does not appear necessary for a strong maternal bond (Eyer, 1992; Goldberg, 1983; Lamb & Hwang, 1982; Myers, 1987; Svejda, Pannabecker, & Emde, 1982). Mothers and babies separated during the first days after birth by illness are just as likely as pairs not separated to develop strong attachment relationships (Rode et al., 1981). This also holds true for mothers and their adopted babies (Brodzinsky, Lang, & Smith, 1995).

Phase 2 (2–7 Months): Discriminate Social Responsiveness

During the second stage, infants become more interested in the caregiver and other familiar people and direct their social responses to them. Although strangers continue to be accepted, they now assume a second-class status.

Across this period, the infant and caregiver develop interactional patterns that permit them to communicate and that establish a unique relationship between them. The child develops a cognitive representation, or internal working model, of the caregiver based on how reliable and trustworthy she is seen to be (Bretherton, 1993). The baby also looks to the mother when anxious or uncertain for information regarding how he or she should feel—the social-referencing process described earlier—and the mother uses this communication system to exert some control over the child (Ainsworth, 1992).

Also important to the attachment process, babies now begin to develop a sense of self and to understand that they are separate from the rest of the world and that they can do things to affect it. We discuss these processes in detail in the chapter that follows.

Phase 3 (8–24 Months): Focused Attachment

The attachment bond becomes clearest in the third quarter of the first year and remains very strong until about age 2. The appearance of attachment behaviors is very much tied to development in two other

Maternal bonding
The mother's emotional attachment to the child, which appears shortly after birth and which some theorists believe develops through early contact during a sensitive period.

areas. One of these is emotional. At about this time, fear begins to emerge as a dominant emotion. With improvements in memory and other cognitive functions, babies begin to recognize what is strange or unfamiliar, and they generally react to such experiences negatively (Thompson & Limber, 1990). **Wariness of strangers** becomes common, often causing the baby to cry and retreat to the mother. Being apart from the caregiver produces **separation protest,** which also involves crying and sometimes searching after the mother. Both forms of distress are typically reduced once the baby is back in contact with the caregiver.

The other related development is physical. At about 6 to 8 months, most babies begin to crawl. This ability gives infants their first opportunity to have considerable control over where they are, and it is crucial in the attachment process—the baby no longer needs to rely on crying or related behaviors to gain proximity to his or her mother but can crawl to her and follow her around.

The full-blown attachment process becomes evident when the infant puts these two developments together and begins to treat the mother as a secure base. Now the infant's increased mobility allows her to regulate feelings of fear and insecurity by controlling the distance between her and the caregiver. When she is feeling secure, she ventures boldly from the mother to explore her environment, but when an unfamiliar person or situation appears, she returns to the mother for comfort and security (Bowlby, 1988).

The development of this sort of attachment bond between infant and caregiver is now well established. But psychologists are still learning exactly how it develops and what effects it has on the child's later development (Stevenson-Hinde & Verschueren, 2002; Thompson, 1998; Waters et al., 1995).

Assessing Attachment

To study the attachment process, researchers must have reliable and valid methods for assessing the nature and quality of the infant–caregiver relationship. Two major methods have been developed for this purpose: the Strange Situation procedure and the Attachment Q-Set.

Strange Situation Procedure

The older and more popular way of assessing the strength and quality of the attachment relationship is the **Strange Situation procedure.** This method was developed in the 1960s by Mary Ainsworth as part of a longitudinal study of the attachment process (Ainsworth & Wittig, 1969).

The Strange Situation is a laboratory procedure that involves studying the child interacting with the mother and with an adult stranger in an unfamiliar setting. This approach ensures that the situation will be at least mildly stressful for the child and so will elicit secure-base attachment behaviors toward the caregiver. The procedure is typically conducted when the infant is about 12 months of age, a point at which the attachment relationship should be clearly established. Of particular interest are the baby's reactions when separated from the mother and when reunited with her.

The method consists of eight episodes, summarized in Table 12.1. Episode 1 simply involves introducing the caregiver and baby to the laboratory room, which contains several chairs and an array of toys and is designed to encourage exploration by the infant. Observers are positioned behind one-way windows, where they can observe and videotape the behaviors of the infant for later scoring. The next two episodes provide preseparation experiences for the baby. In episode 2, the caregiver and infant are alone, and the observers note the baby's willingness to explore the new toys and situation. In episode 3, a stranger joins them; after 1 minute of silence the stranger begins a conversation with the caregiver and also attempts to engage the baby in play.

Episode 4 represents the first separation, in which the caregiver leaves the child alone with the stranger. This episode may last for 3 minutes but is cut short if the baby shows too much distress. Episode 5 involves the return of the caregiver and the departure of the stranger. How the infant reacts to the reunion with the caregiver is carefully

Wariness of strangers
A general fear of unfamiliar people that appears in many infants at around 8 months of age and indicates the formation of the attachment bond.

Separation protest
Crying and searching by infants separated from their mothers; an indication of the formation of the attachment bond.

One clear sign that attachment has developed is the infant's reluctance to separate from her caregiver.

Strange Situation procedure
Ainsworth's laboratory procedure for assessing the strength of the attachment relationship by observing the infant's reactions to a series of structured episodes involving the mother and a stranger.

Table 12.1	Strange Situation Procedure		
Episode Number	**Persons Present**	**Duration**	**Brief Description of Action**
1	Mother, baby, and observer	30 sec.	Observer introduces mother and baby to experimental room, then leaves.
2	Mother and baby	3 min.	Mother is nonparticipant while baby explores. If necessary, play is stimulated after 2 min.
3	Stranger, mother, and baby	3 min.	Stranger enters. Min. 1: stranger silent. Min. 2: stranger converses with mother. Min. 3: stranger approaches baby. After 3 min., mother leaves unobtrusively.
4	Stranger and baby	3 min. or less[a]	First separation episode. Stranger's behavior is geared to that of baby.
5	Mother and baby	3 min. or more[b]	First reunion episode. Mother greets and comforts baby, then tries to settle baby again in play. Mother then leaves, saying bye-bye.
6	Baby alone	3 min. or less[a]	Second separation episode.
7	Stranger and baby	3 min. or less[a]	Continuation of second separation. Stranger enters and gears behavior to that of baby.
8	Mother and baby	3 min.	Second reunion episode. Mother enters, greets baby, then picks baby up. Meanwhile, stranger leaves unobtrusively.

[a]Episode is curtailed if the baby is unduly distressed.
[b]Episode is prolonged if more time is required for the baby to become reinvolved in play.

noted. The caregiver remains with the infant for at least 3 minutes, offering comfort and reassurance, and attempts to get the baby reinvolved with the toys.

In episode 6, the second separation takes place. Now the caregiver leaves the baby alone in the room, again for a maximum of 3 minutes, depending on the child's level of distress. The stranger returns in episode 7 and attempts to interact with the baby. Episode 8 is the second reunion, during which the caregiver greets and picks up the baby, while the stranger leaves.

Three patterns of responses were originally found to describe most infants who have undergone this procedure (Ainsworth, 1983; Thompson, 1998). Infants exhibiting pattern B are considered to be securely attached to the caregiver. They feel secure enough to explore freely during the preseparation episodes, but they display distress when the caregiver leaves and respond enthusiastically when she returns. In Ainsworth's original sample, about 65% of babies tested react in this manner. Pattern A babies are described as insecure–avoidant. They generally show little distress at separation, and when the caregiver returns, they tend to avoid her. This pattern represents about 20% of infants. Pattern C babies are termed insecure–resistant. They give evidence of distress throughout the procedure, particularly during separation. Reunions with the caregiver produce a mixture of relief at seeing her and anger directed toward her. Only about 15% of infants respond in this way.

Most infants have been found to fit into Ainsworth's three original categories of attachment. However, these three categories proved insufficient to account for all types of mother–infant interaction patterns (Main & Hesse, 1990; Main & Solomon, 1990). More recently, researchers have described a fourth type of attachment, dubbed *insecure–disorganized/disoriented* (pattern D) (Main & Hesse, 1990). The infant with this attachment pattern displays an unpredictable, distressed response to separation from the mother. The pattern is thought to emerge as a by-product of unusual, disrupted maternal behaviors. For example, mothers of children classified as disorganized are more likely to show both withdrawing behaviors (Lyons-Ruth et al., 1999) and frightening behaviors (Schuengel et al., 1999) in the Strange Situation. Maltreatment in infancy is associated with a higher incidence of disorganized attachment patterns (Barnett et al., 1999). Furthermore, the fear and disorganization evident in infants showing this pattern endure over time: Children who had received a disorganized classification as infants were found to display continued maladjusted behaviors as 6-year-olds (Hesse & Main, 2000).

It is important to understand that although the Strange Situation focuses on the infant's behavior, it is designed to assess the quality of the relationship between caregiver and baby. Pattern B infants are assumed to have developed a secure, healthy attachment to the caregiver, whereas the relationships developed by pattern A, C, and D infants are assumed to be less than optimal.

An important advantage of this procedure is that it is very structured and so can be applied in the same way at different times and by different researchers. Because it is videotaped, it also can be reobserved by other researchers or for other reasons. The major disadvantages are that it involves only a very brief sampling of the child's interactions, it occurs in an unfamiliar setting and environment, and the mother's behavior is strictly directed.

Attachment Q-Set   An alternative approach to assessing attachment that avoids the problems just mentioned is the **Attachment Q-Set (AQS)** (Solomon & George, 1999; Waters, 1995; Waters & Deane, 1985). Rather than studying attachment in the laboratory, this evaluation is conducted in the home and over a much longer period of time.

The procedure usually involves trained observers who visit the infant and mother in their own home, sometimes more than once, and observe their interactions in a variety of typical activities. After completing several hours of observation, each observer evaluates the nature and quality of the mother–baby relationship using the Q-sort method—a rating technique used in social science research in which prepared statements are sorted into categories. Sometimes the mothers themselves serve as the observers and evaluators.

The AQS consists of 90 items, each describing the behavior of an infant or young child (ages 1–5) interacting with the mother (e.g., "Child enjoys climbing all over the mother when they play" or "When child returns to mother after playing, he is sometimes fussy for no clear reason"). Each item is printed on a card, and the observer is instructed to sort the 90 cards into 9 piles ranging from "least like the child" (piles 1–3) to "most like the child" (piles 7–9).

When the cards have all been sorted, the researcher compares the observer's profile of the child with a profile of a "securely attached child" prepared by experts in the field. The higher the correlation with the expert description, the more securely attached the child is assumed to be.

The AQS would seem to offer an important advantage over the Strange Situation procedure in that it involves a much wider array of behaviors on the part of both the mother and the baby (Pederson & Moran, 1995). Nevertheless, studies that have included both methods have generally found that they classify children in about the same way (Pederson & Moran, 1996; Seifer et al., 1996; Vaughn & Waters, 1990).

Cultural Differences in Attachment   Most of the early work on attachment was done in the United States. But as this research spread to other countries and cultures, it became obvious that attachment to some degree varies with the cultural context in which it develops (Harwood, Miller, & Irizarry, 1995; Main, 1990). This conclusion was

Attachment Q-Set (AQS)
A method of assessing attachment in which cards bearing descriptions of the child's interactions with the caregiver are sorted into categories to create a profile of the child.

initially based on studies using the Strange Situation procedure and has since been confirmed by research involving the Q-Set approach, demonstrating that the differences may not be merely methodological (Sagi et al., 1995).

What cross-cultural contrasts have researchers found? A notable example is work undertaken in Germany. Because Germany's Western industrialized culture is not widely different from American culture, we might expect patterns of attachment in these two cultures to be very similar. Researchers have found, however, that in the German samples fewer infant–caregiver pairs display the secure (pattern B) attachment and more are classified as pattern A, or insecure–avoidant. This difference does not appear to result from less maternal sensitivity among German mothers. Rather, the investigators speculated that German mothers' emphasis on building independence in their children resulted in the infants' appearing less interested in their mothers during reunions (Grossmann & Grossmann, 1990; Grossmann et al., 1985).

Very different results have been reported in studies of Japanese children, which have found a higher percentage of pattern C, or insecure-resistant, attachments. In the Japanese culture, mothers rarely leave their babies with others, so the Strange Situation procedure may prove more stressful for the infants (Miyake, Chen, & Campos, 1985; Takahashi, 1986, 1990).

Whatever the pattern of attachment displayed in a particular culture, it is clear that cultural differences exist. Furthermore, differences exist among the subcultures within a single country. Researchers have reported, for example, that African American children often do not seem to find the Strange Situation procedure particularly stressful, likely because child care is often shared by multiple family members and is not the sole province of the mother (Jackson, 1993). These differences appear compatible with the view of evolutionary psychologists, mentioned earlier, that the social bonds infants form with caregivers are flexible, depending partly on the particular environment in which they live.

Determinants of Attachment

The measures of attachment we have been discussing raise two important questions: What factors produce different patterns of attachment between infant and caregiver, and what significance do they have for the child's development? The first issue involves the origin of patterns of attachment. Several factors have been suggested as determining what kind of attachment relationship develops (Belsky, Rosenberger, & Crnic, 1995; Cummings & Cummings, 2002).

Parental Responsiveness Many theorists believe that the major influence on the quality of attachment is the parents' responsiveness to the baby (Belsky, 1999; Braungart-Rieker et al., 2001). Mothers who are more sensitive to their infants' needs and who adjust their behavior to that of their babies are believed more likely to develop a secure attachment relationship (Ainsworth, 1983; Isabella, 1994; Pederson & Moran, 1995).

Examples of such interactions can be seen in certain everyday situations, such as feeding. Pattern B infants have mothers who are more responsive to their signals—feeding them at a comfortable pace, recognizing when they are done or ready for more, and recognizing their taste or texture preferences (Ainsworth et al., 1978; Egeland & Farber, 1984). Another revealing situation involves responsiveness to crying. Mothers of pattern B babies are less likely to ignore their crying, are quicker to respond, and are more effective in comforting the child (Belsky, Rovine, & Taylor, 1984; Del Carmen et al., 1993). A third situation involves the mother's bodily contact with the infant. When mothers of pattern B babies are holding them, they tend to be more affectionate, playful, and tender toward the children (Anisfeld et al., 1990; Tracy & Ainsworth, 1981).

In face-to-face interactions, pattern B infants have caregivers who more easily synchronize their actions to mesh with those of the baby (interactional synchrony and turn taking), which also serves to lengthen their time together (Isabella & Belsky, 1991; Isabella, Belsky, & von Eye, 1989; Kiser et al., 1986). Finally, overall levels of accep-

Mother Love: Harlow's Studies of Attachment

Much of the early work on attachment involved other species, in part because this research often was conducted by ethologists—scientists who traditionally study behavior in a wide range of animal species. But the focus on other species also reflects the fact that some questions cannot easily be addressed by research with humans. A classic study conducted in the 1950s by Harry Harlow at the University of Wisconsin illustrates this point.

BOX 12.1

Classics of *Research*

Harlow was interested in determining the role of feeding in the attachment process. Many psychologists at that time accepted the learning-theory view that a baby's emotional attachment to the mother is based on her role as a powerful reinforcer. Not only does she provide the infant with social stimulation, remove wet diapers, and comfort him when he is upset, she is, perhaps most important, the source of the baby's nourishment. Because food is so fundamental to sustaining life, many researchers assumed that the baby becomes emotionally drawn to the mother as a result of her being associated with food.

To test this hypothesis, a psychologist would need to manipulate when, how, and by whom a baby is fed. For ethical reasons, we cannot conduct such research with human babies. Harlow approached the issue using what he felt was the best available alternative—baby rhesus monkeys. In addition to feeding, Harlow suspected that the opportunity to cuddle with the mother would also influence the attachment process. So he conducted the following study.

A group of rhesus monkeys were removed from their mothers immediately after birth and raised in a laboratory with two surrogate "mothers" constructed of wood and wire. One of the surrogates was covered with terry cloth to which the baby monkey could cling; the other surrogate was made only of a wire mesh. For half the infants, food was made available in a bottle on the cloth mother; for the other monkeys, food was attached to the wire mother. To assess the infant's "love" for the mothers, Harlow used two measures: the amount of time spent with each surrogate, and the degree to which the mother provided the baby monkey with security in fear-producing situations.

The results were dramatic and surprising. The baby monkeys spent an average of 17 to 18 hours a day on the cloth mother and less than 1 hour a day on the wire mother, regardless of which mother provided the food. Likewise, when frightened, the monkeys consistently sought out the cloth mother for security; when only the wire mother was available to them, the infants seemed to find little comfort in its presence (Harlow & Harlow, 1966). Harlow's research thus demonstrated that the most important factor in the development of attachment in rhesus monkeys is not feeding but the opportunity to cling and snuggle, which he called contact comfort.

The relevance of these findings to our species remains unclear, partly because we cannot replicate Harlow's procedures by depriving human babies of contact with their caregivers. But this classic research did prompt investigators to begin examining factors other than conditioning and learning principles in their search for the determinants of human attachment. It also served as a reminder that even widely held ideas regarding the causes of behavior should not be accepted without scientific verification.

Harry Harlow found that contact comfort, rather than feeding, was the most important determinant of a rhesus monkey's attachment to its caregiver.

tance, rejection, and sensitivity by mothers across a variety of everyday activities have been shown to predict which of the three attachment classifications their babies will exhibit in the Strange Situation (De Wolff & van IJzendoorn, 1997; Pederson & Moran, 1996; Rosen & Rothbaum, 1993; Seifer et al., 1996).

Still other kinds of evidence link the caregiver's behavior to the quality of the attachment relationship. For example, babies can develop different attachment relationships with different caregivers (e.g., the mother, the father, professional caregivers),

Secure attachments are most likely to develop when the caregiver is sensitive and responsive to the infant's needs.

which should not be surprising if caregivers respond differently to the child (Howes & Hamilton, 1992; Sagi et al., 1995; van IJzendoorn & De Wolff, 1997).

Also, as mentioned, the proportion of infants in different attachment classifications varies from culture to culture, again presumably as a result of different caregiving practices (Sagi et al., 1995; van IJzendoorn & Kroonenberg, 1988). Finally, interventions designed to increase mothers' sensitivity to their infants have also produced more secure attachment relationships between them (van den Boom, 1994, 1995; van IJzendoorn, Juffer, & Duyvesteyn, 1995).

It seems clear, then, that the security of the relationship between the infant and the caregiver depends heavily on the kinds of care the child receives. Yet it should also be clear by this point that the infant has more than a little to do with how her mother treats her.

Attachment across Generations   It is reasonable to ask why some mothers respond more sensitively to their babies than do others. One answer seems to involve the mother's recollections of her own childhood experiences. The idea is that individuals form a working model of close relationships as young children, a prototype that endures with time and affects various close relationships in the future, both with romantic partners and with their own children (Roisman et al., 2001). One approach to studying this phenomenon has been to have mothers describe their childhood attachment relationships using an instrument called the **Adult Attachment Interview,** data that are then used to classify mothers as displaying one of four attachment styles (George, Kaplan, & Main, 1985; Main & Goldwyn, 1998).

Autonomous mothers present an objective and balanced picture of their childhood, noting both the positive and negative experiences; *dismissing* mothers claim to have difficulty recalling their childhoods and appear to assign little significance to them; *preoccupied* mothers tend to dwell on their early experiences, often describing them in a confused and highly emotional manner; and *unresolved* mothers have experienced attachment-related trauma that they have not yet resolved, such as the loss of or abuse from a mother or father.

The assumption underlying this research is that mothers' memories and feelings regarding their own attachment security will be expressed in their caregiving toward their child and so affect the infant–caregiver relationship. Several studies have shown that these classifications are indeed reasonably good predictors of the patterns of attachment

Adult Attachment Interview
An instrument used to assess an adult's childhood recollections of the attachment relationship with the primary caregiver.

these mothers form with their own babies (Posada et al., 1995; van IJzendoorn, 1992, 1995). Even more impressive, they can predict both forward and backward—that is, mothers' interviews during pregnancy predict their later attachment to their infants (Steele, Steele, & Fonagy, 1996; Ward & Carlson, 1995) and mothers' interviews when their children are age 6 correlate positively with their attachments when the children were only 12 months old (Main et al., 1985).

Other research has suggested that the impact of adults' memories of their childhood attachment patterns is importantly mediated by the nature of the current family environment (Cowan et al., 1996). A dysfunctional working model of close relationships may make one more likely to become involved in a marriage characterized by conflict, a reality that may in turn make adults poor communicators and less effective parents.

Temperament and Attachment   We have seen that an infant's temperament can affect how the child interacts with the caregiver, as well as in other social situations. Some researchers believe that temperament may therefore play a role in the attachment process. This could happen in two different ways (Seifer & Schiller, 1995).

First, the infant's temperament may interfere with a valid assessment of his or her attachment classification. For example, some researchers suspect that infants who are fearful and inhibited tend frequently to be classified as pattern C in the Strange Situation procedure—not because they actually have this sort of relationship with the caregiver but because their overreaction to the unfamiliar situation gives the appearance of insecure attachment (Calkins & Fox, 1992; Kagan, 1994; Thompson, Connell, & Bridges, 1988). Temperamental characteristics involving activity level, distractibility, or soothability likewise are suspected to affect ratings in the Strange Situation (Goldsmith & Harman, 1994). This problem does not appear to be serious, however, and use of the Q-Set methodology has helped address it (Rothbart & Bates, 1998).

The more important role for temperament is that it may directly affect the type of attachment relationship the child develops with the caregiver. This idea relates to the goodness-of-fit concept discussed earlier in the chapter. For example, babies who are irritable or have other characteristics of a difficult temperamental style might be a challenge to respond to in a prompt and sensitive manner. Another possibility is that a baby's temperament may influence how sensitive the child is to the mother's caregiving—such that the same type of caregiving could be received differently by different infants. Either of these situations could result in a child being less likely to develop a secure attachment with the mother.

There is some evidence that temperament may affect the attachment relationship in the second, more direct way (Seifer et al., 1996; van den Boom, 1994). For example, babies who tend to be more irritable or who less readily orient themselves to people or objects may be more likely to develop insecure attachments (Spangler & Grossmann, 1993; Susman-Stillman et al., 1996). However, other researchers continue to find no clear temperament-attachment link (Vaughn & Bost, 1999). Thus, the precise relationship at work here remains uncertain.

Consequences of Attachment

Another major issue in attachment research concerns a simple question: Why does it matter? One answer to this important question is that securely attached infants display a variety of other positive characteristics not found in infants whose caregiver relationships are of lower quality. These include features of both cognitive and social development, as will be discussed. Precisely why a secure attachment with the caregiver has these effects is not entirely understood. But it is likely that, as a result of being secure in the caregiver's presence, the infant feels comfortable in exploring the surrounding social and physical environment and thus develops important cognitive and social skills.

Ross Thompson (2000) cautions, however, that when we consider the mechanisms by which early attachment may produce long-term consequences, we must remember that early influence develops in context. In other words, attachment relationships do not exist in isolation. They are importantly shaped by the child's changing levels of cognitive understanding, as well as by other features of the parent–child relationship, such as how conflict is handled. The influence of attachment over time, therefore, may depend on several influential variables.

Cognitive Competence   Several experiments have shown that securely attached infants later become better problem solvers and show less negative affect in response to challenges (Frankel & Bates, 1990; Jacobsen, Edelstein, & Hofmann, 1994; Matas, Arend, & Sroufe, 1978). Securely attached infants also have been reported to be more curious, do more exploring, and engage in more symbolic play as toddlers. The quality and duration of play remained virtually unchanged by the mother's involvement for insecurely attached children, whereas securely attached children's play was enhanced by having Mom at their side (Hazen & Durrett, 1982; Slade, 1987). In addition, one study reported that the cognitive competence of children at 4 years of age can be predicted by their mothers' responsiveness toward them (and presumably the quality of their attachment relationship) at 3 months of age (Lewis, 1993).

Other research has found cognitive benefits associated with secure attachment in older children. Seven-year-olds in Iceland who were classified as securely attached based on their responses to a story about separation were more likely than their peers to display multiple positive characteristics at ages 9, 12, and 15 years (Jacobsen & Hofmann, 1997). These included possession of a strong sense of self, attentiveness in school, and higher grades.

Social Competence   Securely attached infants also seem to be more socially competent. For example, they tend to be more cooperative and obedient, and they have better relations with their peers (Cassidy et al., 1996; Fagot, 1997; Kerns, 1994). In addition, securely attached babies are less likely to develop emotional or behavior problems than are insecurely attached infants (Erickson, Sroufe, & Egeland, 1985; Lewis et al., 1984). Securely attached children tend to be better at regulating their emotions (Conteras et al., 2000) and are more skilled as preschoolers in understanding emotions (Laible & Thompson, 1998).

Secure attachment has been found to confer benefits on children's self-knowledge as well. Differences in self-knowledge (self-recognition, knowledge of one's gender and name) between securely and insecurely attached children have been shown to emerge by 2 years of age. Securely attached children also showed more knowledge of their mothers (Pipp, Easterbrooks, & Harmon, 1992).

In contrast, insecurely attached children are more likely than their securely attached counterparts to be biased in interpreting the behavior of other people (Cassidy et al., 1996). At age 5, insecurely attached children are likely to interpret another's behavior as indicating hostility. Being bumped by another child, for example, might connote ill will to an insecurely attached child but might be interpreted merely as an accident by a securely attached child.

There is evidence that the social benefit conferred on securely attached children may be associated with the relatively more sensitive and responsive caregiving provided by their mothers. Mothers of securely attached children have been found to be relatively adept in modulating the style and degree of the feedback they provide to their children during a cognitive task, favoring positive over negative comments and intervening only when asked. Mothers of insecurely attached children tended to be less skilled at recognizing their children's level of competence and responding appropriately (Meins, 1997).

It is important to note that this body of evidence does not mean that insecurely attached babies are doomed to problems. It has been shown, for example, that these babies seem to benefit from day care experiences, suggesting that environmental influences play an important role in the development of their later social competence (Egeland & Heister, 1995).

To Recap . . .

Infant–caregiver attachment develops in three stages. Between birth and 2 months of age, babies respond socially to almost anyone. From ages 2 to 7 months, infants direct social responses principally to familiar people, and they develop a unique affective communication system with the caregiver. Clear-cut attachment becomes evident at 6 to 8 months. At this point, the infant is wary of strangers, protests separation, and uses the mother as a source of comfort and a secure base. The appearance of attachment is related to the emergence of two other developmental milestones: the emergence of fear as a major emotion, and the ability to crawl.

Two principal methods are used to assess the quality of the infant–caregiver attachment relationship. Ainsworth's Strange Situation procedure is conducted in the laboratory and produces three common patterns of infant response: pattern A, or insecure–avoidant; pattern B, or securely attached; and pattern C, or insecure–resistant. Most babies display pattern B, but the proportion of infants in each classification varies across cultures, apparently reflecting different attitudes toward child-rearing. Because Ainsworth's three original categories proved insufficient to account for all types of mother–infant interaction, researchers have described a fourth type of attachment, insecure–disorganized/disoriented (pattern D). The Attachment Q-Set method assesses the infant–caregiver relationship over a wider range of behaviors and situations.

The quality of the infant–caregiver attachment relationship appears to result primarily from the caregiver's responsiveness. Mothers who are more sensitive to their babies' signals and who adjust their behavior to mesh with that of their children are more likely to develop secure attachment relationships. The mother's recollections of her childhood and the infant's temperament also play a role.

Secure attachment to the caregiver has several positive effects on the child's development. Pattern B babies generally display greater cognitive and social competence than do babies who are less securely attached.

EFFECTS OF EARLY EXPERIENCE

An important issue in the discussion of early social development concerns the magnitude of its impact over time. In earlier sections of this chapter, we discussed how social elements like early temperament and relationships may influence various aspects of a child's future. Next, we focus on special circumstances to further explain how early experience helps lay the groundwork for later social, emotional, and cognitive development.

Effects of Early Day Care

One of the most obvious societal changes in the United States in the latter part of the 20th century involved the increased number of women working outside the home and leaving some of the job of child rearing to others, such as those who provide care in day-care centers (Scarr, 1998). In the United States in 1997, for example, 79% of children under the age of 3 years regularly spent time in nonparental care, with 39% in care for 35 or more hours per week (Capizzano & Adams, 2000). Two topics that have generated a great deal of interest and debate concern what happens to the mother–infant attachment process under these circumstances (Clarke-Stewart, Gruber, & Fitzgerald, 1994; Lamb, 1998; McCartney, 1990) and whether particular features of child care are associated with negative outcomes (Brooks-Gunn, Han, & Waldfogel, 2002).

Early studies reported that infants whose mothers were employed were less likely than those whose mothers stayed at home to be classified as securely attached in the Ainsworth Strange Situation procedure (e.g., Barglow, Vaughn, & Molitor, 1987; Belsky, 1988; Belsky & Rovine, 1988; Lamb, Sternberg, & Prodromidis, 1992). And infants whose mothers worked full-time were less likely to be securely attached than those whose mothers worked part-time (Clarke-Stewart, 1989). Such evidence suggested that leaving infants with day-care providers might be inadvisable, although child development experts were hardly in agreement on the issue.

One objection had to do with the use of the Strange Situation to assess the effects of day care. As indicated earlier, the Strange Situation has been used frequently to

Time in day care is becoming a more common experience for U.S. children. For many, such experience begins early in life.

assess the attachment relationship, and there is some disagreement about exactly what it measures. We have also seen that an important requirement of Ainsworth's method is that the infant must experience it as somewhat stressful. This experience of stress is what causes the baby to show anxiety when the mother leaves and to greet her enthusiastically when she returns—reactions that lead to the baby's being classified as securely attached.

The problem with using this method to assess the impact of maternal employment is that infants left frequently in day care may not find the Strange Situation particularly stress-inducing. After all, their mothers routinely leave them with others and then later return to pick them up. Perhaps after babies have gained enough experience with this routine, the Strange Situation does not evoke the level of anxiety necessary for them to display the secure-base behaviors normally indicating secure attachment.

The debate over day care was further fueled by newer findings that failed to replicate the results of earlier investigations (Burchinal et al., 1992; Roggman, et al., 1994; Stifter, Coulehan, & Fish, 1993). Why the negative effects of day care seemed to disappear was unclear. One possible reason was that the number of mothers of infants in the workforce had increased over time; therefore, the working-mother group may have become more similar to the mothers who stayed at home than in previous years. Other possibilities were that publicizing the potential negative effects of early day care had led parents to be more selective in choosing day-care arrangements or to consider more carefully their own role in their children's development, leading to improvement in the quality of the home environment. The later studies of infant day care were also stronger methodologically than the early studies, which had often involved small numbers of children and lacked adequate controls.

To help resolve the debate, the U.S. federal government funded a large-scale longitudinal study to explore a variety of outcomes associated with the onset, duration, and quality of day care. The study enrolled over 1,000 children shortly after birth in 10 localities across the nation (Little Rock, Arkansas; Irvine, California; Lawrence, Kansas; Boston, Massachusetts; Philadelphia and Pittsburgh, Pennsylvania; Charlottesville, Virginia; Morganton, North Carolina; Seattle, Washington; and Madison, Wisconsin). The NICHD Early Child Care Research Network has issued regular reports of its findings since the study began in 1994. Regarding the impact of day care on attachment status, no evidence was found that placing a child in day care *in itself* affects the security of the child's attachment to the caregiver one way or the other at 15 months of age (NICHD Early Child Care Research Network, 1997a).

Evidence does indicate, however, that a child whose mother is low in sensitivity is more likely to be classified as insecurely attached when (1) the day-care center also does not provide a high level of care, (2) the child spends a great deal of time in day care, or (3) the child has had many different child-care arrangements. A related finding is that boys are more likely to be classified as insecurely attached when they spend a great deal of time in day care, whereas girls are more likely to receive such a classification when they spend little time in day care.

The NICHD research team also made direct observations of mother–child interaction when the children were 6, 15, 24, and 36 months of age (NICHD Early Child Care Research Network, 1999). This study found that infants and toddlers in more hours of care experienced somewhat less sensitive mothering and were less positively engaged with their mothers than children not in child care. However, the lesser amount of maternal sensitivity was not of sufficient magnitude to disrupt the formation of a secure infant attachment. Moreover, children in higher-quality programs experienced greater maternal sensitivity, regardless of the number of hours in care. It may be that using higher-quality day care provides mothers with role models for involved caregiving or emotional support. This, in turn, allows her to be more emotionally available to her child.

Investigators involved with the NICHD study have also focused on the cognitive characteristics of children in early day care. One recent study examined school readiness skills (e.g., children's knowledge of color, letters, numbers) among European American children at 3 years (Brooks-Gunn, Han, & Waldfogel, 2002). Children placed in day care before 9 months of age were found to have lower school readiness scores on average around the time of their third birthdays, and the effect was greater for infants who spent more than 30 hours per week in day care. As with the effects of day care on attachment, the negative effects of early and full-time child care were larger for children with mothers who were less sensitive and for boys (compared with girls).

Recent analyses, however, have found that the quality of care is again important (NICHD Early Child Care Research Network, 2002). Compared with children in lower-quality care, those in higher-quality care, in care that improved in quality over time, and in center-based arrangements had better language, cognitive, and pre-academic skills at age 4.5. However, children who spent more hours in out-of-home care were reported to have more behavior problems at age 4, 5, and during the kindergarten year regardless of program quality (NICHD 2003).

Results from the NICHD study and other investigations indicate that early child care is associated with both risks and benefits even when such factors as ethnicity, family income and education, and parenting quality are controlled for. Yet unless major governmental or business policy changes permit mothers (or perhaps fathers) to be supported while they stay at home with their newborns, most infants and children will spend part of their early years in nonparental care (Carnegie Task Force, 1994; Clark et al., 1997). Consequently, many researchers and policy makers have shifted their attention to ways to improve the quality of the care children receive (National Research Council & Institute of Medicine, 2000; National Research Council, 2001). We describe one such effort in Box 12.2.

Effects of Trauma

Posttraumatic stress disorder (PTSD) is a disorder in which a particularly stressful event results in later emotional symptoms, including reexperiencing of the event, decreased responsiveness to the outside world, a tendency to be easily startled, and nightmares. Like adults, children are susceptible to developing PTSD following such traumatic events as earthquakes (Pynoos et al., 1993), school shootings (Pynoos, Frederick, & Nader, 1987), and floods (Green et al., 1994).

Fostering Positive Teacher-Child Relationships during Early Childhood

Most research on attachment has concentrated on children's relationships with their parents. And, as we have seen, secure attachments with parents have been linked to later social and cognitive competence. Young children, however, spend a good deal of time with day-care providers or preschool teachers. Does the quality of their relationships with these caregivers have similar long-term effects?

Recent research suggests that it does. Compared with peers who have negative relationships with teachers, children who are emotionally close to their teachers during early childhood begin school with better school readiness skills, achieve more academically, and have better relations with peers (Burchinal et al., 2002; Howes, Hamilton, & Philipsen, 1998; Peisner-Feinberg et al., 2001). One longitudinal study even documented effects lasting through the end of elementary school (Hamre & Pianta, 2000).

Attachment theory offers some insight into why the effects of these early relationships are so long lasting. According to attachment theory, young children are better able to attend to and learn from adults with whom they have close relationships than from adults with whom they have detached or conflicted relationships (Pianta, 1999). Thus, children who have positive relations with caregivers are more likely to engage in the kinds of interactions that foster the language skills and other competencies required to succeed during the first years of school.

Moreover, the relationships children form with nonparental caregivers and teachers during early childhood support the development of an *internal working model* of teacher-child relationships that will help organize children's interactions with teachers and other adults during later school years. Children whose early experience suggests that adults cannot be trusted to care for them or to help them are prone to distrust the teachers they encounter later.

Unfortunately, estimates suggest that fewer than half of children in typical community child care have emotionally secure relationships with caregivers, and the numbers are even lower for children who come from difficult life circumstances—maltreatment, parental psychopathology, substance

BOX 12.2

Applications

abuse, and poverty (Howes, Galinsky, & Kontos, 1998; Howes & Ritchie, 1999). Research also suggests that day-care providers and teachers vary widely in their ability to foster positive relationships with the children under their care (Howes & Hamilton, 1992).

As with parent-child attachment, children are more likely to form secure bonds with caregivers who are sensitive and responsive to their needs. Teachers, like parents, naturally vary in their sensitivity (Kontos, Howes, & Galinsky, 1996). We have seen that short-term attachment intervention programs with mothers can be quite effective in changing maternal sensitivity and children's attachment (Van IJzendoorn, Juffer, & Duyvesteyn, 1995). Might similar, targeted interventions increase the sensitivity of child-care providers as well?

To examine this question, researchers (Howes, Galinsky, & Kontos, 1998) implemented an intervention in a day-care center located on-site at a large corporation. All of the caregivers at the center participated in an intensive 20-hour training program designed to encourage positive interactions with the children. Thirty-six children participated in the study. The 36 were randomly selected from a larger number of children whose families were willing to have them participate.

Observers rated caregiver sensitivity and children's attachment security before and 6 months following the intervention. At the first observation, 25 of the 36 children were deemed to have insecure attachments with the classroom teacher. Following the intervention, 21 of these children had secure relations with the caregiver. Analysis of the ratings of teacher sensitivity showed that the caregivers of children who became secure or stayed secure increased in sensitivity and decreased in detachment during their interactions with the children.

These findings suggest that modest interventions can increase caregivers' sensitivity to children and thereby foster the kinds of close relationships that are linked to positive developmental outcomes years later. These relationships may be especially valuable for children who lack opportunities to form secure emotional bonds with other adults in their lives (Howes & Ritchie, 2002; Pianta, 1999).

Rates of PTSD are significant, often initially affecting at least a third of exposed children. One recent study found that these events are not strongly associated with the onset of psychiatric disorders in children (Sandberg et al., 2001). Nevertheless, evidence suggests that the effects may linger into adulthood; clinicians have noted an association between recalled childhood trauma and adult depression (Hill, 2003).

A major area of research interest has been the effect of war on children. Here again, significant stress reactions are not rare. For example, one study found that 70% of Kuwaiti children reported moderate to severe posttraumatic stress following the first Gulf War (Nader et al., 1993), and PTSD was noted in a quarter of Bosnian adolescents and Kurdish children, all displaced from their homelands during times of conflict

Traumatic experiences—such as exposure to war—can have lasting effects on children's development.

(Ahmad, 1992; Weine et al., 1995). The effect of witnessing violence in war may be additive: that is, the more children witness, the more likely they are to suffer ill effects (Allwood, Bell-Dolan, & Husain, 2002).

Researchers have attempted to identify which specific factors associated with traumatic experiences make stress reactions more likely. In the case of war, evidence suggests that relocation and the disruption of school life or peer relationships that accompanies relocation may be especially important—more so than other potential factors, such as parenting and overall family functioning (Thabet & Vostanis, 1999).

Effects of Abuse

Although the family is typically a source of security and protection for the young child, sometimes it can be just the opposite. Child abuse is a tragic reality of some households, and it is a problem that may be growing (Emery & Laumann-Billings, 1998).

Abuse and neglect have major developmental consequences for growing children. By 1 year of age, maltreated infants tend to lag in both social and cognitive development, and these problems typically continue into childhood and adolescence (Trickett & McBride-Chang, 1995). Many developmental researchers believe that these deficits result from the lack of a secure attachment relationship with the mother. A great deal of recent research has focused on the attachment process in infants who have been abused or are at risk for abuse (Cicchetti & Carlson, 1989; Rogosch et al., 1995).

Sensitive and responsive caregiving growing out of mutual infant–caregiver regulation is thought to provide the basis for secure attachment. But, as noted, many abusive mothers fail to develop a smooth and effective communication system with their infants. Although babies will become attached even to mothers whose caregiving is of poor quality, the attachment relationship suffers. Perhaps for this reason, the insecure attachment patterns occur more frequently among maltreated infants (Carlson et al., 1989; Rogosch et al., 1995).

Some mothers maltreat their infants in ways that involve physical punishment, active hostility, and intrusiveness into the baby's world. Rather than synchronizing their behavior with that of the child, they often insensitively forge ahead with whatever they are doing (such as feeding a baby before he or she is hungry), focusing more on their own needs than on those of the infant. This caregiving style has been referred to as *overstimulating* and has been linked to physical abuse, such as beating and battering, and to the insecure–avoidant pattern of attachment (pattern A). In contrast, the insensitive care of some mothers takes the form of withdrawal and underinvolvement. This style, termed *understimulating*, has been associated with physical and emotional neglect and appears to be a cause of the insecure–resistant pattern of attachment (pattern C) (Belsky, Rovine, & Taylor, 1984; Lyons-Ruth, Connell, & Zoll, 1989).

Maltreated infants cannot always be classified according to Ainsworth's three original patterns because they often fail to display any coherent pattern of reactions to the Strange Situation. These infants frequently exhibit elements of each category, sometimes accompanied by bizarre responses, such as freezing, assuming unusual postures or expressions, and making interrupted or mistimed movements. Such behaviors, which are sometimes also seen in nonabused children, led to the development of the fourth classification, disorganized, or pattern D, described earlier (Main & Solomon, 1986, 1990). These children are especially at risk for developing aggression and antisocial behavior problems (Lyons-Ruth, Alpern, & Repacholi, 1993).

The conclusions that can be drawn from research on abused children support a transactional model of attachment (Crittenden & Ainsworth, 1989). Evolution has provided that babies will become attached even to caregivers who provide minimal or deviant care, but the interactions between these mothers and babies clearly affect the quality of the relationship that develops. This in turn affects the child's later social, emotional, and cognitive development (van IJzendoorn et al., 1992).

Effects of Childhood Hospitalization

Hospitalization is another experience that we might expect to be stressful for children. Hospital stays of more than 7 days have become less frequent overall in the past 20 years. Still, this trend is not universal. Though extended hospitalizations for injuries have decreased, those for mental disorders have increased (Chabra & Chavez, 2000). Early research (Rutter, 1976) found that a hospital stay per se does not necessarily cause problems over time. Ten-year-olds who had been hospitalized for 7 or fewer days before age 5 were no more likely than other children to suffer from maladjustment or other behavioral difficulties. However, repeated hospitalization was associated with varied behavior problems years down the road. In addition, recent research has found evidence for adverse effects of repeated hospitalizations on the families of children suffering from asthma, including greater financial strain and relatively high levels of conflict (Chen et al., 2003).

Parents' attitudes about a child's hospitalization can be an important determinant of the quality of the child's experience (Whelan & Kirkby, 2000). Parent stress can match and even exceed that of children, making it an important concern when considering issues relevant to hospitalization.

Another issue that influences the effect of hospitalization on children is, not surprisingly, the condition for which the child is receiving treatment. Specific characteristics of a child's illness are likely to influence the emotional impact of the illness and the hospitalizations associated with it. Mrazek (1991) identified several such illness-specific risk factors, such as time of onset, the degree of deformity or disability it produces, and the prognosis for the future.

To Recap . . .

Researchers have investigated several sorts of special circumstances in childhood to determine their impact on later social, emotional, and cognitive development.

One such circumstance concerns children whose mothers work outside the home and leave some of the job of child-rearing to others. Early studies on the results of this practice reported that infants whose mothers were employed were less likely than those whose mothers stayed at home to be classified as securely attached. Later studies failed to replicate these findings, however; and a large-scale governmental study found no evidence that placing a child in day care *in itself* affects the security of the child's attachment to the caregiver.

Childhood trauma from such events as natural disasters and war has been associated with adult psychiatric disorders, particularly depression. In addition, abuse and neglect have major negative effects on both social and cognitive development. Many researchers believe that these effects result from the lack of a secure attachment relationship with the mother. Childhood hospitalization, although not a problem in and of itself, can be associated with adverse outcomes, especially when hospitalizations occur repeatedly over time.

CONCLUSION

We said at the beginning of this chapter that social development is a complex topic. By now, that should be very clear. But it is important to understand that this complexity is of two different types.

The first concerns social interactions themselves. Because these behaviors are transactional—with people continually affecting one another—it becomes difficult to separate the causes of social behaviors from their effects. Even in the infant–mother relationship, as we have seen, social influences can be subtle and highly interrelated. Identifying the determinants of the baby's and the mother's behavior thus can be a very challenging task.

The second reason this topic is so complex is that social development is affected by more than social influences. How the child interacts with other people is the result of biological processes, cognitive abilities, and nonsocial environmental factors—in addition to the influences of others in the child's world. Only recently have psychologists begun to appreciate the extent to which these nonsocial factors are involved in the development of social relationships, as we shall continue to see in later chapters.

In this chapter, we have focused on the attachment process and the developmental events that lead up to it. Other social relationships and processes also occur during infancy, and we consider those in the chapters that follow. In addition, we examine social development beyond the early years as the child grows away from the caregiver and the home to become a member of the larger society.

FOR THOUGHT AND DISCUSSION

1. The modern study of social development assumes that parent-child interactions are bidirectional and transactional. *Think of some examples of children's behavior (such as exploration) that might previously have been explained one way but now could be interpreted differently.*

2. Temperamental differences are assumed by many researchers to be stable over time. *How would you characterize your own personality style? Do you think it has been stable since you were a child? Which aspects, if any, have changed?*

3. A growing number of children spend time in day care. Research has shown that the quality of day care affects children's development. *Should our society ensure that all day-care centers provide high-quality services? If so, who should pay for this? Employers? Federal or state governments?*

4. Interventions to increase maternal sensitivity can have positive effects on both mothers' behavior and infant-mother attachment. *Do you believe that parent training programs should be more broadly implemented? What are arguments for and against interventions designed to improve parenting?*

5. The trend to postpone childbearing has resulted in many children having older parents. *What do you see as some advantages and disadvantages for these children? What benefits and problems might result for the parents in being older?*

VISUAL SUMMARY FOR CHAPTER 12
Early Social and Emotional Development

Theories of Early Social Development

Theory	Explanation
Evolutionary and Biological Approaches	Ethologists contend that evolution has produced behaviors in mothers and infants that result in secure attachment. More recent evolutionary theory holds that attachment need not follow one pattern.
Environmental/ Learning Approaches	Mother–infant attachment responses result from socal-learning processes, with the infant and caregiver each providing consequences for the other's behavior.
Cognitive-Developmental Approaches	Cognitive-developmental approaches emphasize the role of social cognition, or the understanding of human behavior and social interactions. Some theorists contend that babies and mothers develop internal working models regarding each other's behavior.
Sociocultural Approaches	Sociocultural approaches focus on the sociocultural contexts of social and emotional development and include Bronfenbrenner's bioecological model, the psychocultural model of Whiting and Whiting, and Super and Harkness's developmental niche theory.

Mutual Regulation between Infants and Caregivers

Crying	Babies use different cries to communicate different messages. Caregivers, with experience, become more accurate at reading these messages.
Emotions and the Affective System	Babies begin to express relatively simple emotions within the first 3 months. Infants also begin to discriminate facial expressions within the first half year of life, although their understanding of these expressions is not obvious until the second half year.
Face-to-Face Interactions	Microanalytic studies of face-to-face interactions between mothers and babies show that mothers can be adept at synchronizing their behaviors to babies' cycles of attention and inattention. There are cultural variations in the occurrence and developmental course of face-to-face interactions. In cultures where they are common, they develop into a turn-taking pattern, perhaps the earliest form of conversation.

Temperament

Types of Temperament	The NYLS identified three temperament types: the easy baby, the difficult baby, and the slow-to-warm-up baby. Plomin's EAS model defines temperament in terms of emotionality, activity, sociability, and shyness. Rothbart contends that temperament reflects the infant's reactivity and self-regulation.

Consequences of Temperament

Temperament may influence mother–child interactions through goodness-of-fit, the match between the infant's temperament and the physical and social environment. The quality of these interactions, in turn, can influence the child's cognitive development. Temperament may also be involved in children's later behavior problems and in how they react to stressful situations.

Attachment

Developmental Course of Attachment

Infant–caregiver attachment develops in three stages. In the first stage, indiscriminate social responsiveness (birth–2 months), infants respond socially to almost anyone. In the second stage, discriminate social responsiveness (2–7 months), infants direct social responses principally to familiar people and develop a unique affective communication system with their caregiver. In the third stage, focused attachment (8–24 months), infants are wary of strangers, protest separation, and use the mother as a source of comfort and a secure base.

Assessing Attachment

Ainsworth's Strange Situation procedure is conducted in the laboratory. Ainsworth originally identified three patterns of infant response: pattern A, or insecure–avoidant; pattern B, or securely attached; and pattern C, or insecure–resistant. Because these three categories proved insufficient to account for all types of responses, researchers described a fourth type: insecure–disorganized/disoriented (pattern D). The AQS procedure involves observing infants and their mothers in their homes and evaluating the nature and quality of their relationships using the Q-sort method.

Determinants and Consequences of Attachment

The quality of the infant–caregiver attachment relationship appears to result primarily from the caregiver's responsiveness. The infant's temperament also plays a role, as do the mother's recollections of her own childhood. Secure attachment has positive effects on the child's cognitive and social development.

Effects of Early Experience

Effects of Early Day Care

Early studies reported that infants whose mothers were employed outside the home were less likely to be securely attached than infants whose mothers stayed at home. Later studies failed to replicate these findings, however; and a large-scale government study found no evidence that placing a child in day care in itself affects the security of the child's attachment.

Effects of Trauma, Abuse, and Hospitalization

Childhood trauma from such events as natural disasters and war has been associated with adult psychiatric disorders, particularly depression. Abuse and neglect have major negative effects on both social and cognitive development. Hospitalization, although it can sometimes be associated with adverse outcomes, does not present a problem in and of itself.

13

Development of the Self

Theories of the Self
- Cognitive-Developmental Approaches
- Environmental/Learning Approaches
- Evolutionary and Biological Approaches

- Sociocultural Approaches

Self-Knowledge
- Discovery of the Self in Infancy
- Self-Recognition
- Developmental Changes in Self-Descriptions

Self-Evaluation
- Measuring Self-Esteem
- The Developmental Progression of Self-Esteem
- Gender Differences in Self-Esteem
- Academic Self-Concept

Self-Regulation
- The Emergence of Self-Control
- Compliance
- Resistance to Temptation
- Delay of Gratification

Conclusion

"**A**nyone can cook aloo gobi," wails Jess. "But who can bend a ball like Beckham?" Jess (Jesminder Bjamra), a passionate soccer player, comes from a traditional Indian family. Her parents are Sikhs who fled from Uganda to England. Beckham is David Beckham, one of England's premier professional soccer players, Jess's idol.

The passage is from the 2002 film *Bend It Like Beckham.* The main characters in the movie are two athletically gifted 18-year-old girls, Jess and Jules, who dream about playing professional soccer in America. At the moment, though, their best option is playing on a community women's team where the girls have a chance to be noticed by American scouts.

There is a catch, though. Jess's family is impatient with her obsession with the sport. Her father disapproves of her running "half-naked" in front of men. Her mother, in the meantime, insists that Jess learn the wifely art of cooking perfect chapatis, while harboring hopes that her daughter will study law and marry a nice boy. To play, Jess must erect a wall of lies between her and her family. But not to play would be to deny the very core of her being.

Bend It Like Beckham is a story of the clash of aspirations between immigrant parents and assimilated children. At its heart, however, is another theme common to moviegoers—the story of a young person who follows a dream despite seemingly insurmountable odds. Every generation has several such films—*Saturday Night Fever, Flashdance, Rocky, Rudy, Working Girl, Billy Elliot, Legally Blonde*—in which the protagonist struggles against barriers of social class or culture, gender, family expectations, or all in combination for self-fulfillment. These films may hold special appeal to Western audiences, who by and large endorse the maxim "To thine own self be true." What, though, is the self? We address that question in this chapter. ■

Existential self
The "I" component of the self, which is concerned with the subjective experience of existing.

Categorical self
The "Me" component of the self, which involves one's objective personal characteristics.

Self-system
The set of interrelated processes—self-knowledge, self-evaluation, and self-regulation—that make up the self.

Self-knowledge (self-awareness)
The part of the self-system concerned with children's knowledge about themselves.

Self-evaluation
The part of the self-system concerned with children's opinions of themselves and their abilities.

Self-regulation
The part of the self-system concerned with self-control.

Over the years, psychologists have conceptualized the self using several schemes. One early and influential view, first proposed by Williams James (1890, 1892), divides the self into two major components: subjective "I" and objective "me." The "I," or **existential self,** is the subjective experiencer of the world, whereas the "Me," or **categorical self,** is an objective entity seen and evaluated in the world. The *I* includes a sense of personal identity, a sense of being able to do things (personal agency), and an awareness of one's continuing existence across time (Blasi & Glodis, 1995; Moore & Lemmon, 2001). The *Me* includes traits such as physical appearance, personality traits, and cognitive abilities (Lewis, 1994).

A more recent conceptualization posits that the "self" is a broad concept that can be divided into three distinct but interrelated elements: self-knowledge, self-evaluation, and self-regulation (Harter, 1983). Together, these compose the **self-system.**

- **Self-knowledge,** also referred to as **self-awareness,** is concerned with the questions: What do children know about themselves as distinct, enduring individuals? When do they acquire this knowledge? How is this knowledge related to their understanding of other aspects of their social and physical environments?

- **Self-evaluation** concerns the questions: Does the child have high or low self-esteem? What factors influence children's opinions of themselves? How do these opinions affect their behavior?

- Finally, **self-regulation** is concerned with the questions: How and when do children acquire self-control? What variables influence this process?

Our coverage of the self in this chapter focuses on these three major elements. Throughout the chapter, we also maintain our interest in the themes that have guided our discussions in other areas: what the four principal theoretical traditions have to say about this topic, how it looks from the nature and the nurture perspectives, and how researchers have investigated it.

THEORIES OF THE SELF

The three components of the self-system cover a very broad range of topics and issues. Perhaps for that reason, no theoretical perspective has explained all aspects of this complex area. In this section, we begin by considering what each of the major theories has to say about the self—approaches that will be revisited in later sections of the chapter as well.

Cognitive-Developmental Approaches

The concept of the self and its relation to other aspects of development have been of considerable interest to cognitive-developmental psychologists. Those working from the framework of information-processing theory focus on how children's cognitive abilities to process information limit and shape the development of the self. Other theorists have proposed normative models of self-development based largely on Piaget's theory (Case, 1985, 1992; Fischer, 1980; Harter, 1990; Selman, 1980).

Information-Processing Model   Children's information-processing abilities—how they encode, interpret, and remember information—contribute to the creation of self-relevant cognitive structures that in turn influence how further information is processed. Specifically, researchers believe that over time each child develops a **self-schema,** an internal notion of "who I am," composed of the various features and characteristics. As a child encounters new information, the self-schema works to filter, interpret, and organize that information. Whenever we encounter new events or information, we attempt to understand them in terms of these cognitive structures. Support for the existence of such structures is found in studies showing that people are better able to recall words and events that they can apply to themselves than to recall descriptors that do not seem to relate to them (Pullybank et al., 1985; Skowronski et al., 1995).

Self-schema
An internal cognitive portrait of the self used to organize information about the self.

For example, developmental psychologists have wondered whether being asked to process information in a self-relevant way would influence children's memory for that information. Specifically, researchers presented children with lists of words spoken one at a time. Half the words were followed by the question, "Is this word like you?" and the other half were followed by, "Is this a long word?" As predicted, answering the first question, regarding the word's relatedness to oneself, made children more likely to recall the word later than did the second question, which was neutral in regard to the self.

A second variable focused on how children's levels of self-esteem and depression influence their memories. Half the words presented to the children described positive personal traits (brave, helpful, and so on); the other half described negative personal traits (such as lonely and ugly). Again as predicted, children who were high in self-esteem and were not depressed showed better recall of the positive traits, whereas depressed children with low self-esteem showed better recall of the negative traits (Hammen & Zupan, 1984; Zupan, Hammen, & Jaenicke, 1987). Similar recent research has found that children of depressed mothers also are more likely to remember negative self-information than positive (Taylor & Ingram, 1999).

This type of research illustrates how powerfully children's self-schemas can influence how they relate to the world around them. For example, children whose self-esteem is high are apparently more attuned to information that is consistent with a positive view of themselves. They may be likely to notice compliments, which, in turn, should further enhance their self-image. Children low in self-esteem, in contrast, are more aware of information that confirms their negative feelings and thus likely serves to decrease self-esteem even more.

A Developmental Model: Selman's Work on Self-Awareness   A detailed account of children's self-awareness has been presented by Robert Selman (1980). In the tradition of other cognitive-developmental theories, the model was developed from extensive clinical interviews with children and emphasizes development through stages.

Selman presented children of various ages with brief stories in which the main character faces a conflict or dilemma. The children were then asked a series of questions regarding what the character was thinking and feeling and how the dilemma would be resolved. The focus was not so much on the children's solutions as on the type of reasoning they used to arrive at the solutions.

Using these responses, Selman identified a five-stage progression in self-awareness. The model includes some assumptions that are common to most stage theories. That is, the stages (1) follow a fixed sequence through which all children pass with no regression to earlier stages, (2) are consistent across different problems and situations, (3) are universal across cultures, and (4) develop as a result of changes in the child's cognitive abilities (Gurucharri & Selman, 1982).

The five stages are summarized briefly below. Note that Selman's stages begin with the infant's awareness of only the physical self and progress gradually to greater appreciation for other features of the self, such as an understanding of the potential for a private or "hidden" self, which appears in middle childhood, and the recognition in adolescence that the self may include unconscious components.

Level 0 (Infancy): Children understand their physical existence but do not display an awareness of a separate psychological existence. The child does not, for example, distinguish between physical behavior (such as crying) and simultaneous emotional feelings (such as being sad).

Level 1 (Early Childhood): The child now separates psychological states from behavior and believes that thoughts can control actions. But the child also believes that inner thoughts and feelings are directly represented in outward appearance and behavior, so that someone's self can be known simply by observing the person's actions and statements (for example, that a person who is whistling and smiling must be happy).

Level 2 (Middle Childhood): The child appreciates that feelings and motives can be different from behavior and thus that the self can to some degree be hidden from others; it cannot, however, be hidden from oneself.

Level 3 (Preadolescence): Children in later childhood show a growing belief that the self represents a stable component of personality. They believe that people can observe and evaluate their inner selves, suggesting that the mind (which does the observing) is somehow separate from the self (which is observed).

Level 4 (Adolescence): Ultimately, the adolescent comes to believe that the self cannot ever be completely known because some aspects of personality remain at an unconscious level.

Environmental/Learning Approaches

Social-learning theorists have proposed a number of psychological processes that are relevant to the self. Two theoretical models have been developed by Albert Bandura, one involving self-evaluation, the other, self-regulation.

Bandura's self-evaluation model is built around the concept of **self-efficacy,** a person's ability, as judged by that person, to carry out various behaviors and acts (Bandura, 1997, 2001). Bandura observes that just as infants and young children do not understand the operations of the physical and social world very well, they do not know much about their own skills and abilities. Studies have shown, for example, that parents (and teachers) can predict how well children will perform on academic tasks much better than can children themselves (Miller & Davis, 1992; Stipek & MacIver, 1989). Similarly, in everyday situations parents must frequently warn children, for example, that they are swimming out too far, or that a particular library book will be too difficult for them to understand, or that they can never finish the largest ice cream sundae on the menu. Such verbal instructions from parents, along with many trial-and-error experiences, help young children

Self-efficacy
Bandura's term for people's ability to succeed at various tasks, as judged by the people themselves.

gradually learn the limits of their talents and capabilities—that is, accurately judge their self-efficacy (Plumert, 1995).

As children grow, two other mechanisms promote the development of self-efficacy judgments. One is modeling, which children come to use as a way of estimating the likelihood of success at a task. For example, a child might reason, "If that little girl [who is my size and age] can jump over that fence, I can probably do it, too." Using vicarious experiences in this way obviously involves somewhat sophisticated cognitive abilities, in that the child must determine the appropriate models and situations for making comparisons.

Another way in which children learn to estimate their potential for success is through awareness of internal bodily reactions. For example, feelings of emotional arousal (e.g., tension, a nervous stomach, or a fast heart rate) frequently become associated with failures. Bandura believes that as a result, children begin to interpret these feelings as indications of fear, anxiety, or lack of confidence, and they learn to use them to decide that failure is close at hand. Again, using this type of information requires a fairly high level of cognitive processing, and so is more common in older children (Bandura & Schunk, 1981; Schunk, 1983).

Self-efficacy judgments are important because they are believed to affect children's behavior significantly. Bandura contends, for example, that greater feelings of self-efficacy produce increased effort and persistence on a task and thus, ultimately, a higher level of performance. This concept is especially relevant in the area of children's academic achievement and how it relates to their self-evaluations—a topic we discuss later in the chapter.

Bandura also has proposed a theoretical mechanism to explain the development of self-regulation (Bandura, 1991). Early on, children's behavior is only externally controlled through such processes as modeling, consequences (reinforcement and punishment), and direct instruction. With experience, however, children learn to anticipate the reactions of others, and they use this knowledge to self-regulate their behavior. For example, as a child learns (through external processes) how the teacher expects her to behave in the classroom, she begins to monitor her behavior to conform to these expectations. Gradually, the child internalizes the rules, and they become her own personal standards. Now the child's behavior comes under the control of her **evaluative self-reactions**—that is, the child notes whether her behavior has met her personal standards and then applies self-sanctions in the form of self-approval ("I did well today") or self-disapproval ("I shouldn't have done that"). According to Bandura, self-regulation occurs as children become motivated to behave in ways that match their internal standards and that lead to feelings of self-satisfaction.

Evaluative self-reactions
Bandura's term for consequences people apply to themselves as a result of meeting or failing to meet their personal standards.

Evolutionary and Biological Approaches

Two approaches to the self fall under the framework of evolutionary and biological approaches—Bowlby's attachment theory and evolutionary psychology. Historically, Bowlby's theory has proved the more influential.

Bowlby's Attachment Theory   In his landmark writings on attachment, John Bowlby discussed his belief that the sense of self begins to develop within the context of infant–caregiver interactions and is promoted by responsive caregiving. These ideas have been elaborated by more recent developmental theorists (Bretherton, 1993; Cicchetti, 1991; Lewis, 1987). For example, responsive caregiving leads to a more secure attachment between baby and mother, which in turn should affect the infant's development of an internal working model of the self (as well as of the mother) (Bretherton, 1993; Pipp, 1990, 1993). Babies whose caregivers are sensitive and responsive should construct an internal model of the self as lovable and worthy of attention; babies whose caregivers are neglectful and insensitive should form models of the self as unworthy (Sroufe, 1990). We will see shortly that evidence from both normal and clinical populations of children provides support for these ideas.

Evolutionary Psychology In recent years, evolutionary psychologists have taken up the issue of the self. Researchers working within this framework are interested in three questions: (1) At what point in human evolution did the modern self emerge? (2) What is the adaptive function of having a self? (3) What is the neuropsychological basis of the self?

To address the first question, evolutionary psychologists explore the existence of self-consciousness among nonhuman species. Although evolutionary theorists have long suspected that species others than humans may possess a self-concept (Darwin, 1871/1896), documenting self-consciousness among species who cannot talk about the self challenged researchers for decades (Dewsbury, 1984).

Great strides in the study of animal self-awareness occurred in 1970 with the publication of a paper on primate mirror self-recognition by Gordon Gallup, Jr. As described in Box 13.1, Gallup described an experimental procedure that provided compelling evidence that chimpanzees are able to recognize their images in mirrors. Since Gallup's pioneering study, scientists have tested many other species for mirror self-recognition. These include a wide variety of primates, fish, birds, dolphins, and even elephants (presumably using a *very* large mirror!). Among primates, only hominids (orangutan, bonobo, chimpanzee) show clear evidence of self-recognition (the evidence regarding gorillas is mixed) (Inoue-Nakamura, 2001). Studies using variations on the mark test suggest bottle-nosed dolphins may also have the capacity for self-recognition (Herman, 2002; Marten & Psarakos, 1994).

Although some skeptics remain (e.g., Heyes, 1994), most scientists agree that chimpanzees and several other great apes and perhaps dolphins have some kind of rudimentary self-concept. The exact nature of this self-concept is, however, hotly debated (Gallup, Anderson, & Shillito, 2002; Povinelli & Bering, 2002; Tomasello, 1999).

The Monkey in the Mirror: Primate Self-Recognition

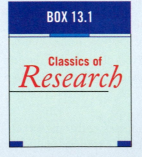

BOX 13.1

Classics of
Research

The concept of the self was at one time held to be a uniquely human capacity. In the late 1960s, Gordon Gallup, Jr., decided to test this claim by assessing whether chimpanzees have the capacity for self-recognition—a very basic aspect of the self. One way to measure self-recognition is to observe reactions to one's image in a mirror.

There had been reports of home-reared apes using mirrors to explore their teeth (Mitchell, 2003). However, these observations and those of babies playing with mirrors were open to interpretation. Both apes and babies might enjoy interacting with mirror images without recognizing the image as themselves. Researchers needed a technique that would allow them to make the distinction.

Gallup (1970) first gave several preadolescent chimpanzees 10 days of individualized exposure to mirrors. In each case, the chimp initially reacted to its reflection as if the reflection were another chimp (e.g., bobbing, vocalizing, threatening). After about 3 days, however, the chimpanzees began to behave in ways similar to the reports of home-reared apes and suggestive of self-recognition. For instance, they would pick food from between their teeth, make bubbles, and manipulate wads of food with their lips while watching their images in the mirror.

To test whether the chimpanzees had truly learned to recognize their own images, Gallup devised what has come to be known as the *mark test*. Gallup anesthetized each animal and applied red dye to an eyebrow ridge and to the opposite ear. On waking, the chimpanzees at first almost never touched the marks. Then, however, the mirror was reintroduced, and the chimps began to touch the marks frequently. Clearly, they related the marks they saw in the mirror to their own bodies.

Gallup's study has had an enduring effect on developmental psychology. Though researchers had long been interested in babies' reactions to their mirror images (e.g., Gesell, 1925; Shirley, 1933), they were reluctant to conclude that an infant recognized the image until he or she could label it (e.g., "It's me!"). As we have seen, reliance on verbal measures of understanding often underestimates what infants really know. The mark test pioneered by Gallup provided researchers a tool to assess self-recognition among preverbal infants. (Interestingly, unbeknownst to Gallup, Beulah Amsterdam [1972] was using a similar technique with human infants at about the same time.) Although researchers now employ a variety of techniques to assess children's self-recognition, the mark test is still in use today.

The second question of interest to evolutionary psychologists concerns how (or why) the self evolved. Many evolutionary psychologists believe that human intellectual capabilities were shaped by selection pressures associated with living in a group with a complex social organization (Bjorklund & Pellegrini, 2002; Cosmides & Tooby, 1992). According to this perspective, self-awareness is important because it lays the foundation for other capabilities required for group living, most notably the ability to understand the mental states of others. Indeed, the species that show self-recognition do live in complex social groups. However, other species (e.g., spotted hyenas) live in social groups and do not exhibit self-awareness (Holekamp & Engh, 2002).

The third question of interest to evolutionary psychologists is the neurological basis of the self. As described in earlier chapters, evolutionary psychologists generally believe that evolved human capabilities are encapsulated in modules in the brain. Studies of children with autism—who exhibit impairment in both self-recognition and the ability to draw inferences about others' mental states—provide some support for the modularized view of self-knowledge (Baron-Cohen, 2000).

Further evidence can be found in studies of clinical patients with damage to specific regions in the frontal cortex. These individuals show impairments in the ability to recognize their own faces and to engage in self-evaluation, as well as in autobiographical memory (Breen, 1999, cited in Gallup et al., 2002; Keenan & Wheeler, in press). There is also some evidence that gorillas, who may not show self-recognition, have a smaller, less well-developed frontal cortex than the other great apes, which do have the capacity for self-recognition (Semendeferi, 1999). However, recent studies of normal adults using brain-imaging techniques suggest that a neural network involving both right and left hemisphere brain structures is involved in self-recognition (Kircher et al., 2001). These findings caution against taking an overly simplistic view of the way the brain is involved in various kinds of self-understanding.

Sociocultural Approaches

The sociocultural approach focuses on the socialization of the self and self-understanding through participation in cultural practices, customs, and institutions. Socialization practices reflect each culture's model of the self. These models, in turn, derive from societal ideals and values and vary from culture to culture.

Cultural Models of the Self
Cultural models of the self vary across a number of dimensions (Cross & Gore, 2003; Hallowell, 1955; Neisser, 1988). Of these, the most extensively documented is the relation of the self to others. As we saw in Chapter 9, cultural communities with roots in Western European traditions tend to draw a clear distinction between the self and others. In this view, the self is independent, self-contained, and autonomous. In many other cultures, the boundary between the self and others is less clearly drawn. In this model, which is common in many East Asian, Central and South American, and Native American groups, the self and others are seen as interdependent or interconnected.

Although the self–other dimension has been most widely studied cross-culturally, conceptions of the self vary in other ways as well. Cultures differ in the age at which they assign "selfhood" or person-status to an individual. For instance, in some cultures, children are not considered "persons" until they are several months or even years old (Riesman, 1992).

Even more dramatic variations are found in how cultures perceive the self through space and time. Some American Indian societies believe that the self may leave the body and metamorphose into other forms, such as an eagle or bear (Hallowell, 1955). Cultures that endorse the idea of reincarnation believe that a self may have previously inhabited other bodies (Barth, 1997). And, of course, there is considerable cultural variation in beliefs about the existence of the self after biological death.

Cultures also vary in terms of the ideal self. In European American communities, for example, the ideal person is independent. In these communities, individuals strive to

In contrast to the autonomous view of the self stressed in Western thought, many cultures view self and others as interdependent.

distinguish themselves from the crowd. Personal economic and psychological needs take precedence over those of the group. In contrast, in many East Asian societies, the ideal person is closely connected with others. In these communities, individuals strive to conform, maintain harmonious interpersonal relations, and bring favor to the family (Ho, 1995; Markus & Kitayama, 1991; Tu, 1994).

Although every culture provides a broad outline of the ideal self, cultures also provide some options. The range of possible selves varies widely across cultures. In diverse, heterogeneous cultures, there is a veritable supermarket of identities from which to choose (Mathews, 1996). In others, there are relatively few options (e.g., for a woman—wife and mother, nun, prostitute) (Cross & Gore, 2003).

Cultural Shaping of the Self   From the first days of an infant's life, caregivers adopt practices that are largely compatible with their own cultural views of the self. Consider, for example, sleeping arrangements. From the first weeks of life, most European American infants sleep in their own beds, often in their own rooms (Morelli et al., 1992; Shweder, Jensen, & Goldstein, 1995). Although parents offer a variety of reasons for this practice (including safety concerns), a significant number believe that sleeping apart trains children to be independent (Morelli et al., 1992).

Autonomy training pervades other aspects of child-rearing as well. For instance, European American parents begin to teach children they have the right to an opinion by offering choices (e.g., "Do you want the red cup or the blue cup?") long before children can properly reply (Markus & Kitayama, 1994). Once a child is old enough to engage in conversation, middle-income mothers try not to infringe on the child's right to articulate his or her point of view, even if the child is mistaken or fabricating events (Wiley et al., 1998).

Adult reactions to disputes among children provide further evidence for the socialization of an autonomous self in European American communities. When siblings tussle over video game controls or the favored seat in the car, middle-income mothers often respond by establishing rules for equal, separate turn-taking. In the process, children learn to defend their individual rights and to respect the rights of others (Rogoff, 2003).

In contrast, in cultures that hold a model of the self that emphasizes the interconnectedness of the self with others, caregivers adopt socialization practices compatible with this view. In Japan, for example, infants and toddlers sleep next to their mothers and later with siblings or other family members. In contrast to European American parents, who believe children are born too dependent and need to be socialized for independence, Japanese parents believe children are born too independent. Co-sleeping is viewed as one means by which to foster healthy dependence and close bonds with others (Caudill & Weinstein, 1969).

Whereas European American children are encouraged to speak up and defend their individual rights, children in Japan are taught to rely on others to sense and meet their needs and, in turn, to empathize and be sensitive to the needs of others (Markus & Kitayama, 1994; Roland, 1988). These values are also reflected in adult reactions to children's disputes. Japanese children are taught to sacrifice their personal interest for the sake of interpersonal harmony and that "to lose is to win" (Lebra, 1976; Zahn-Waxler et al., 1996).

To Recap . . .

The self-system can be divided into three components: self-knowledge, self-evaluation, and self-regulation. Cognitive-developmental theorists have offered several models concerning the development of the self. Information-processing theorists view the self as part of the larger memory system. Children are believed to construct self-schemas, which they use to organize information related to the self and which influence how they perceive and interact with the world. Based on interviews with children, Selman proposed a five-stage model that begins with the infant's being unable to differentiate the physical and psychological selves and ends with the adolescent's believing that aspects of the self remain unconscious and unknowable.

Social-learning theory has contributed two models of the self, both proposed by Bandura. Self-efficacy judgments—judgments concerning one's own ability to succeed at various tasks—are assumed to be inaccurate in early childhood but to improve gradually with the help of four processes: verbal instruction from parents and other adults, success and failure experiences, observation of relevant models, and monitoring of internal bodily reactions. Self-efficacy judgments appear to have important effects on children's behavior. Self-regulation is assumed to occur when children internalize standards they have acquired through external processes and then use evaluative self-reactions to keep their behavior consistent with these standards.

Evolutionary and biological perspectives on the self include Bowlby's attachment theory and evolutionary psychology. According to Bowlby, infants construct an internal working model of the self through their interactions with caregivers. Children whose caregivers are responsive to their needs develop a working model of the self as worthy and lovable. Evolutionary psychologists are interested in the evolutionary roots of the self. Research from this perspective focuses on the nature of self-understanding and self-related behaviors among nonhuman species.

According to the sociocultural approach, the self is shaped through participation in cultural practices that reflect cultural models of the self. Cross-cultural studies show striking variability in cultural models of the self. The dimension of the self that has been most widely studied is the relation of the self to others.

SELF-KNOWLEDGE

Our look at the research evidence on the self-system begins with perhaps the most basic questions: What do children know about the self, and when do they know it? It is not uncommon to hear a toddler proudly announce that he is a big boy or that his name is Jeremy. But he may, as yet, have very little understanding of his physical characteristics (heavy or slight), his personality (shy or bold), or his living conditions (middle-income or poor). As we will see, children's self-knowledge develops steadily across the childhood years and is interwoven with the development of other cognitive and socialization processes.

Discovery of the Self in Infancy

When does a baby first understand that he exists separately from the surrounding world? This question has long been of interest in developmental psychology. Some researchers believe that babies have an inborn awareness of their existence or at least that awareness develops within the first weeks of life (Butterworth, 1995; Gibson, 1993; Samuels, 1986). Others argue that none of what babies do requires us to assume they have self-awareness prior to their first birthday (Kagan, 1991). Unfortunately, like many issues involving non-verbal infants, this one is not easily settled.

The Role of Perception Perceptual processes are thought to play an important role in infants' first coming to recognize their separateness (Butterworth, 1990, 1995; Neisser, 1993, 1995; Rochat, 2001). For example, we have seen that within only weeks after birth, infants can imitate certain adult facial expressions. This finding has been interpreted to mean that newborns can connect sensory (visual) input with the corresponding motor responses—a capability that lays the groundwork for their realizing that they can interact with and affect the world around them (Meltzoff & Moore, 1995).

By 3 months of age, infants seem to perceive that they control their own body movements. One study had babies seated in an apparatus in which they could see live images of their legs transmitted on two TV monitors in front of them. Different images—sometimes reversed or upside down—were presented on each TV, and it was clear from the babies' looking responses that they could easily detect when the timing or direction of the leg movements they viewed did not correspond to what they were doing (Rochat & Morgan, 1995). Similar research has reported the same findings with infants' arm movements (Schmuckler, 1995).

Studies of perception also have shown that in the months that follow, the self becomes much more clearly defined. As we saw in Chapter 6, when 6-month-olds are taught to look for an object located in one position relative to themselves—say, to the left—and then are rotated to the opposite orientation—so that the object is to their right—they continue to search for the object by looking left. The addition of visual cues or landmarks to encourage more appropriate searching has little effect on babies of this age (Acredolo, 1985). This approach, of course, results in unsuccessful searching and gradually gives way to more effective, environmentally guided perceptual strategies as the baby approaches 1 year. But in using themselves as anchor points when searching, young infants demonstrate at least a crude awareness of their own separate existence.

Personal agency
The understanding that one can be the cause of events.

Personal Agency Along with infants' knowledge that they exist apart from the things around them comes an understanding of **personal agency**—that is, an understanding that they can be the agents or causes of events that occur in their worlds. Now babies move toys and put things in their mouths and bang blocks, all suggesting an awareness both that they are separate from these things and that they can do something with them (Case, 1991; Connell & Wellborn, 1991). Personal agency also appears to develop through babies' early interactions with caregivers (Emde et al., 1991; Sroufe, 1990). Theorists concur that when parents are more sensitive and responsive to their infants' signals, babies more quickly develop an understanding of the impact they can have on their environments (e.g., "I can make Mommy come by crying").

A related question has been whether babies first acquire an understanding of the self or of the mother. In one study, babies aged 6 months and older watched an adult model eat a Cheerio. They were then given one and instructed either to feed it to themselves or to feed it to their mothers. Significantly more babies at each age level were able to follow the first instruction than were able to follow the second (Pipp, Fischer, & Jennings, 1987).

These findings are consistent with others in showing that infants learn to direct actions or speech toward themselves before they direct those same responses toward their mothers or others (Bretherton & Beeghly, 1982; Huttenlocher, Smiley, & Charney, 1983), suggesting that with respect to agency, self-knowledge ("I can do it to me") precedes mother-knowledge ("I can do it to her"). This difference reverses by age 2, when toddlers are better able to direct actions toward their mothers and other objects than toward themselves. This change may result from older infants' becoming more self-conscious (Lewis, 1995) and therefore less comfortable with directing actions toward themselves. Or it may reflect the child's increasing focus on interpersonal relations and newly emerging capacity for play (Pipp-Siegel & Foltz, 1997).

Self-Recognition

As babies approach age 2, they display an increasing awareness of the self. Perhaps the form of self-knowledge that has attracted the most research is infants' ability to recognize what they look like.

Visual Self-Recognition in Infancy

A number of researchers have investigated the development of **visual self-recognition** by examining babies' reactions to mirror reflections. The major issue in this research concerns whether babies actually recognize the reflected images as themselves.

During their first year, babies will smile and vocalize at their mirror reflections (Fischer, 1980; Schulman & Kaplowitz, 1977). There is some evidence that babies distinguish between their own images and that of another child. When infants as young as 3 months of age are shown still images of themselves and another baby, they exhibit a clear preference for looking at the other child, indicating not only that they can discriminate between the two images but that their own is familiar to them (Bahrick, 1995).

By about 5 months of age, this procedure reveals another interesting finding. When the image a baby normally sees in a mirror is altered (such as by placing colored marks on the cheeks of both babies), the looking preference changes, and infants spend more time looking at their own images (Legerstee, Anderson, & Schaffer, 1998). Whether babies this young realize that what they are seeing is themselves, however, is not known.

One sure way to know if a toddler recognizes herself in a mirror is if she labels the image ("It's me!" or "Amy!"). Pronouns such as *me* and *mine*, as well as the child's name, enter the child's vocabulary during the second year of life (Bates, 1990; Stipek, Gralinski, & Kopp, 1990). By the second birthday, most children can apply these labels to their reflections in mirrors. But researchers have long been curious as to whether children recognize mirror images as themselves even before they can apply the appropriate labels.

To investigate whether an infant understands that the image in the mirror is him- or herself, psychologists use the mark test described earlier (Box 13.1). A colored mark is surreptitiously placed on the infant's face in a location where she could not normally see it, such as on her forehead. The baby is then placed before a mirror, and the investigators note whether she attempts to touch the mark. If she does, they conclude that she understands that the marked face in the mirror is her own. Using this measure, researchers have not found self-recognition in infants under 15 months of age; self-recognition does not occur reliably until about 24 months (Brooks-Gunn & Lewis, 1984; Bullock & Lutkenhaus, 1990).

Visual self-recognition has also been investigated with a variety of other techniques, including comparing infants' reactions to videotapes or photographs of themselves with their reactions to tapes or photos of similar peers (Bigelow, 1981; Johnson, 1983) and having infants point to pictures of themselves in a group after hearing their names (Bertenthal & Fischer, 1978; Damon & Hart, 1982). Evidence from these measures places self-recognition several months later than do the mirror-technique findings (Fischer, 1980).

Self-Recognition over Time

Daniel Povinelli and colleagues (see Povinelli, 2001) have undertaken several studies aimed at exploring how self-recognition endures over time, with some surprising results. In one study (Povinelli, 1995), 2- to 4-year-old children were asked to play a game in which the experimenter repeatedly praised each child and patted him or her on the head. This provided an opportunity to place a large colorful sticker on the child's head. Just minutes later, the child was invited to watch a videotape of the game, which clearly showed the experimenter placing the sticker on the child's head, and the child then playing for a few minutes adorned with the sticker.

Visual self-recognition
The ability to recognize oneself; often studied in babies by having them look into mirrors.

Visual self-recognition has been the most commonly used method of assessing infants' and toddlers' self-awareness.

None of the 2-year-olds searched for the stickers on their own bodies, and only 25% of the 3-year-olds did so—even though they typically could label their video image with a confident "That's me!" An important distinction characterized the 4-year-olds, who not only searched for the stickers most of the time but did so immediately on seeing the videotape showing the sticker placement.

Povinelli concluded that a young child does not connect his or her current physical self with the selves that existed at various points in the past. This idea was supported by the results of another study, in which the children were shown live video feedback instead of the delayed feedback described earlier. In this case, the 2- and 3-year-olds began to reach for the stickers when they saw the stickers being placed on their heads. Evidently, the children did not respond in the same way to the delayed feedback because, although they recognized the delayed images as sharing physical characteristics with their present selves, the images did not move as the children were moving (Povinelli, 1995).

These findings and others have been discussed as evidence that experimental procedures that require children to use mirror or video information and reach for a spot of rouge or other mark on themselves may underestimate the dawning of self-recognition, because these actions require several accompanying cognitive achievements. Indeed, mark-directed behavior is thought to reflect more than self-recognition; it may signify a broad shift in cognitive development as the child approaches 2 years of age (Courage & Howe, 2002).

Individual Differences in Self-Recognition Regardless of the method used, self-recognition appears at different ages for different infants. What could be the source of these differences? One hypothesis is that self-recognition relates to temperament. Specifically, babies who react strongly in stress situations (and so are usually classified as difficult) are thought to develop a sense of self earlier than do other babies in order to deal better with the intensity of the stimulation they experience. Consistent with this idea, infants who react most strongly to vaccinations at 6 months of age also are most likely to show mirror self-recognition at 18 months of age (Lewis & Ramsay, 1997).

Another source of individual differences in self-recognition is attachment. Researchers have confirmed that children who are securely attached have a better understanding of both personal agency and physical characteristics than do children in other attachment classifications (Pipp, Easterbrooks, & Harmon, 1992; Verschueren, Marcoen, & Schoefs, 1996). Thus, a secure attachment relationship appears to promote the development of the self.

Why might this be? As we indicated earlier, some psychologists believe that mother–child interaction provides an infant the opportunity to first develop a concept of a separate self. And as mentioned in Chapter 12, a secure attachment to the caregiver promotes exploration and cognitive development in the baby—all factors that may contribute to the development of self-recognition.

One research team has sought to investigate the relationship between attachment and self-recognition in cases where children have been abused and neglected. The maltreated infants were found to be less securely attached and displayed less evidence of self-recognition (Schneider-Rosen & Cicchetti, 1984, 1991). Moreover, the maltreated infants responded more negatively to their mirror reflections, which the researchers speculate may indicate the beginnings of a low sense of self-worth (Cicchetti et al., 1990). Other research with abused children has found that their language is less likely to involve descriptions of themselves or of their internal states and feelings (Cicchetti, 1991; Coster et al., 1989).

Self-Awareness and Awareness of Others One consequence of infants' increasing awareness of their own identities may be a greater awareness of the separateness and distinctiveness of others. That is, as we become more self-aware, we should simultaneously become more other-aware. There is some evidence that infants draw distinctions between themselves and others at a very young age. In one study, for example, infants 4 months of age responded differently to a live video of an adult mimicking their behavior than to their own live video image. In this study, infants' behaviors toward the mimicker were more social than were their reactions to their own image, with more smiling and longer gazes. In addition, when the video images of both the infants and their adult mimickers were frozen for 1 minute, infants made more attempts to re-engage the adult image, suggesting recognition that another person—but not one's own image—is a potential social partner. This difference was present in both 4- and 9-month-old children, with a large increase in re-engagement behaviors across the two ages (Rochat & Striano, 2002).

Further evidence for children's developing appreciation of the existence and individuality of others can be found in an early type of play termed *synchronic imitation*. In synchronic imitation, preverbal children play with similar toys in a similar fashion (Eckerman & Stein, 1990; Nadel & Fontaine, 1989). For example, one toddler might bang a spoon. This is followed by another toddler banging her spoon, which is followed by the first toddler banging his spoon, and on and on to the great glee of all (except perhaps the daycare provider). To synchronize his play with that of a peer, a child must have some understanding of the other child's intentions and behavior. This type of play would thus seem to require some degree of self- and other-awareness. Consistent with this view, 18-month-olds who give evidence of mirror self-recognition display more synchronic imitation with same-age peers (and also with adults) than do infants who do not recognize themselves in the mirror (Asendorpf & Baudonniere, 1993; Asendorpf, Warkentin, & Baudonniere, 1996).

Self-recognition has also been linked to the emergence of the self-conscious emotions of embarrassment, pride, shame, empathy, and guilt (Kagan, 1981; Lewis, 1993, 2000). To experience this class of emotions, children need to be able to evaluate the self relative to some social standard. A number of studies have linked these affective experiences with the development of prosocial behavior and a moral sense (Kochanska et al., 2002; Zahn-Waxler et al., 1992). We return to this topic in Chapter 14.

Developmental Changes in Self-Descriptions

Psychologists have typically assessed older children's self-knowledge by examining their descriptions of themselves. This method has taken various forms, ranging from very unstructured interviews, which might include such general questions as "Who are you?" to very structured questionnaires, which might require answers to such written items as "How old are you?" and "What is your favorite outdoor game?" Regardless of the method used, researchers have found a relatively predictable pattern of development (Damon & Hart, 1992; Harter, 1998).

By the age of 2, many children display knowledge of some of their most basic characteristics. For example, they know whether they are girls or boys and that they are children rather than adults (Harter, 1988a; Lewis, 1981). These category labels are undoubtedly learned through modeling and other learning processes, as children repeatedly hear themselves referred to with phrases such as "my little boy" or as they receive approval when they correctly state their age or other personal characteristic. But as we will see, cognitive development also plays a role in the self-discovery process.

In the preschool years, as shown in Table 13.1, self-descriptions usually involve physical features, possessions, and preferences (Case, 1992; Hart & Damon, 1985). Thus a 4-year-old might say that she lives in a big house, has a dog, and likes ice cream. This information, however, is not always completely accurate, and children's descriptions are often unrealistically positive. During this period there is a focus on objective, here-and-now attributes—a finding that corresponds well with Piaget's description of preoperational children's view of the world.

But it is incorrect to assume, as some psychologists have, that children of this age can comprehend only specific characteristics of themselves and do not understand more general traits, such as being messy or having a big appetite. The self-description a young child offers seems to depend heavily on how the information is sought. Children give

Table 13.1	Children's Self-Descriptions during Three Age Periods		
Age Period	**Piagetian Stage**	**Focus of Self-Descriptions**	**Examples**
Early childhood	Preoperational	Physical characteristics, possessions, preferences	"I have freckles." "My cat is white." "I like pizza."
Middle and later childhood	Concrete operations	Behavioral traits and abilities, emotions, category membership	"I'm a good singer." "I'm a happy kid." "I'm a cheerleader."
Adolescence	Formal operations	Attitudes, personality attributes (sometimes opposing or associated with different roles), beliefs	"I'm patriotic." "I can be persuasive." "I support gun control."

more general responses when questions are structured to encourage generality ("Tell me how you are at school with your friends") than when questions seek more specific information ("Tell me what you did at school with friends today") (Eder, 1989, 1990).

In middle childhood, self-descriptions change in several ways, reflecting the shift to concrete operational abilities (Harter, 1994; Markus & Nurius, 1984). Rather than limiting their statements to the here and now and the physical, 6- to 10-year-olds begin to talk about less tangible characteristics, such as emotions ("Sometimes I feel sad"), and to combine separate attributes (good at climbing, jumping, and running) into an overall category ("I'm a good athlete"). The accuracy of children's information also improves during this period, although they generally continue to stress their positive, rather than negative, characteristics (Phillips & Zimmerman, 1990; Ruble & Dweck, 1995).

In later childhood, descriptions may be based on social comparisons with others, as children evaluate their skills or talents relative to those of friends or classmates ("I'm the best skater on the street") (Moretti & Higgins, 1990; Ruble & Frey, 1991). Children also can include opposing attributes, such as "I'm good at spelling, but bad at math," in their descriptions. But the earlier tendency to stress positive attributes now sometimes gives way to more intense negative self-evaluations and more general feelings of low self-worth (Harter, 1998).

As children enter adolescence, their self-descriptions continue to change (Harter, Whitesell, & Junkin, 1998). The formal operational child thinks and self-describes in more abstract and hypothetical terms. Rather than focusing on physical characteristics and possessions (as in early childhood) or on behavioral traits and abilities (as in middle and later childhood), the adolescent is concerned with attitudes ("I hate chemistry"), personality attributes ("I'm a curious person"), and beliefs involving hypothetical situations ("If I meet someone who has a different idea about something, I try to be tolerant of it") (Hart & Fegley, 1995; Rosenberg, 1986b).

By middle adolescence, the self typically differentiates into more roles. For example, adolescents give different responses when asked to describe themselves in the classroom, at home, and with friends. Sometimes these differences involve opposing or conflicting attributes, such as being shy in the classroom but outgoing with friends. For the first time, such conflicts produce feelings of confusion and distress (Harter & Monsour, 1992).

Later in adolescence, these opposing characteristics are often combined into single personality styles ("cheerful" and "sad" are combined into "moody"), and this more complex view of the self comes to be viewed as legitimate and normal (Harter, 1997). Adolescents now can display **false self behavior,** meaning that, when necessary, they can purposely behave ("act") in ways that do not reflect their true selves (Harter et al., 1996). The limits of self-development are not yet known, but the self apparently continues to differentiate throughout adolescence and adulthood (Block & Robins, 1993; Hart & Yates, 1996; Harter, 1999).

Adolescence is also the time when many youth begin to explore their cultural heritage and its relevance for their identity. Most of what is known about the development

False self behavior
Behaving in a way that is knowingly different from how one's true self would behave.

of cultural identity is based on studies of ethnic-minority youth. According to one model (Phinney & Kohatsu, 1997), there are three phases in ethnic identity development. During the initial phase, young people give little consideration to their cultural or ethnic identities. One reason may be that race and ethnicity are simply not sufficiently salient to warrant their attention. Alternatively, they may refuse to consider what it means to belong to an ethnic minority and may simply adopt the views of others without question. In the words of one Mexican American male, "I don't go looking for my culture. I just go by what my parents say and do, and what they tell me to do, the way they are" (Phinney, 1993, p. 68).

During the second phase, however, adolescents grow increasingly interested in learning about their ethnic and cultural heritage and the role it may play in their lives. Transition to this phase may be triggered by personal experiences with prejudice, stereotypes, or racism. Growing awareness of the discrepancies between the values of the

Globalization and the "Cultural Self": Are We All Bicultural Now?

There is no doubt the world is growing smaller. Advances in telecommunications and the increased presence of global media—recorded music, movies, television, and the Internet—have connected cultures and world regions in ways unknown in the past. The West largely defines this emerging global culture and its values: Western values of individualism, competition, freedom of choice, openness to change, and tolerance of difference. These values often collide with the values of traditional cultures (Friedman, 2000; Giddens, 2000). People the world over now face the challenge of somehow adapting both to this global culture and to their local culture, even as the local culture is in a state of flux. This is especially true of adolescents, who are less wedded to tradition than adults and more interested in global media (Dasen, 2000; Schlegel, 2001).

In recent years, a growing number of theorists have begun to explore the implications of globalization for psychological development. Among them is Jeffrey Arnett (2002). According to Arnett, the primary psychological impact of globalization is on identity, or how people think

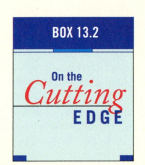

BOX 13.2

On the
Cutting
EDGE

about themselves in relation to the social world. Arnett contends that globalization affects identity development in a variety of ways. His most intriguing claim is that most adolescents in the world now develop a bicultural identity.

This bicultural identity includes a local identity that is based on the traditions of the community where adolescents grow up and a global identity that offers a sense of belonging to a worldwide culture and includes awareness of the values, beliefs, and practices of the global culture. In India, for example, highly educated young adults simultaneously participate in the high-tech business world and adhere to long-standing Indian traditions such as arranged marriages and caring for parents in old age (Verma & Saraswathi, 2002). These adults develop one identity to succeed in the fast-paced worldwide economy and maintain a second identity with respect to their families and personal lives.

The idea of a bicultural identity is not new. There is considerable evidence, for example, that individuals exposed to two cultures as immigrants or members of ethnic minority groups can develop two distinct self-representations (LaFromboise, Coleman, & Gerton, 1993; Sussman, 2000). Moreover, some research suggests that immigrants who adopt a bicultural identity fare better psychologically than those who assimilate the new culture, separate themselves from the new culture, or identify with neither culture (Berry, 1997).

Whether the concept of biculturalism can be fruitfully applied to globalization awaits further study. Arnett believes that several issues are worthy of consideration. Does the tendency to develop a bicultural identity vary with age? Under what circumstances do people develop a bicultural identity versus a *hybrid identity* (Hermans & Kempen, 1998), in which elements of two or more cultures are merged into a single identity? And does the addition of a global identity yield the same psychological benefits as does the development of a bicultural identity for immigrants and ethnic minorities?

The spread of globalization means that many children are exposed to a global as well as a local culture as they develop.

dominant culture and the minority culture or exposure to role models or to the history or culture of one's group may also inspire exploration of cultural identity. This process of exploration may lead to the third phase, in which the adolescent commits to his or her ethnic identity (Spencer & Markstrom-Adams, 1990).

Not all ethnic-minority adolescents develop a strong ethnic identity. For some, the process of exploration leads to a lessening of ethnic ties. Others develop a bicultural identity that includes identification with both the majority culture and their ethnic culture (Berry, 1997).

To date, as suggested earlier, researchers have paid little attention to the development of cultural identity among children and adolescents of the majority culture. However, a number of theorists have recently proposed that nearly everyone—not just members of racial or ethnic minority groups—participates in more than one cultural community (Arnett, 2002; Rogoff, 2003). For example, many people regard themselves as members of a national—or even global—community and of more local or specific communities defined by regional values and traditions (e.g., southern, rural) and religion, as well as ethnic heritage (such as Scottish descent). We discuss the implications of globalization and the self in further detail in Box 13.2.

To Recap . . .

Children's knowledge about the self increases steadily through childhood. It is not yet known whether babies are born with any understanding of the self. Perceptual processes, such as those involved in neonatal imitation, likely play an important role in early self-development. During the second half of the first year, babies begin to display a sense of personal agency by acting on toys and other objects in their environments.

As infants approach the end of their second year, they begin to show recognition of themselves. Research with mirrors and videotapes indicates reliable self-recognition by about 2 years of age. Not until about 4 years of age do children display recognition of self-images videotaped earlier, however. It may be that experimental procedures that require children to use mirror or video information underestimate the dawning of self-recognition because these actions require several accompanying cognitive achievements.

Individual differences are found in the development of self-recognition. Self-recognition may occur earlier in babies with difficult temperaments. Research with maltreated infants suggests that self-recognition is influenced by the security of the infant–caregiver attachment.

Increases in self-awareness are accompanied by increases in other-awareness. Infants who display self-recognition are also more likely to engage in synchronic imitation and to help someone in distress.

Self-knowledge in children beyond the infant years has been assessed principally through examination of their self-descriptions. Self-descriptions by preschoolers reflect preoperational thinking and typically include references only to objective, here-and-now characteristics. In middle childhood, the concrete operational child focuses to a greater degree on nontangible characteristics, such as emotions, and on membership in various categories. Adolescents' formal operational abilities lead to more abstract and hypothetical self-descriptions, concerned often with attitudes, personality characteristics, and personal beliefs, sometimes involving conflicting attributes. During adolescence, many youth grow increasingly interested in and committed to their ethnic and cultural identities.

SELF-EVALUATION

As children grow, they not only come to understand more about themselves but also begin to evaluate this information. Participation in school or on athletic teams encourages children to compare themselves with other children and also with their images of who they would like to be. Such self-evaluations usually bring both good news and bad, as children come to recognize their strengths and weaknesses and their positive and negative attributes. Self-evaluation, like self-knowledge, develops as children grow and is influenced by both cognitive and socialization variables (Ruble et al., 1990).

Measuring Self-Esteem

The opinions children develop about themselves have been referred to as their **self-esteem,** or **self-worth** (Harter, 1985a, 1987). Self-esteem is assumed to include not only children's cognitive judgments of their abilities but also their affective reactions (pride, shame, etc.) to these self-evaluations.

This concept is not new. Two traditional views of self-esteem have long been part of the developmental literature. According to the idea of the **looking-glass self** (Cooley, 1902), the psychological portraits we paint of ourselves are based on how we think others see us. That is, we view other people's reactions to us as "reflections" of who we are. The **competence** view of the self (James, 1892) holds that our level of self-esteem results from a combination of what we would like to achieve and how confident we feel about achieving it—an idea very similar to the more recent concept of self-efficacy (Harter, 1988a; Novick, Cauce, & Grove, 1996).

Methods of Measurement
The most common method of assessing children's self-esteem has been through questionnaires. Typically, such instruments present children with a list of questions designed to tap their opinions of themselves in a variety of situations or contexts (such as "Are you usually willing to help when a friend needs a favor?" and "Do you think you are artistic?"). The responses to these questions can be combined and analyzed to produce an overall score that represents the child's level of self-esteem (Keith & Bracken, 1996).

Attempts to capture self-esteem in a single score, however, have met with the same problems as attempts to describe children's intelligence with a single IQ score. Intuitively, it seems unlikely that children would evaluate themselves similarly in all areas—academics, appearance, athletics, and so on. And research has demonstrated that evaluations across different areas are usually not consistent (Harter, 1985a; Rosenberg, 1986a).

An alternative to the single-score method is to divide children's lives conceptually into a number of domains (social skills, physical skills, and so on) and then assess children's self-evaluations separately in each. The results are then reported as a profile across the various domains. We consider an example of this approach next.

Harter's *Self-Perception Profile for Children*
Susan Harter has developed a set of popular instruments for measuring self-esteem at various stages of development. Each instrument assesses self-evaluations in specific domains as well as overall self-worth. For instance, the *Self-Perception Profile for Children* (Harter, 1985b), designed for children ages 8 and older, assesses children's opinions of their overall worth as well as their self-evaluations in five separate domains: scholastic competence, athletic competence, social acceptance, behavioral conduct, and physical appearance. Three additional domains—close friendship, romantic appeal, and job competence—are included on the adolescent version of the scale (Harter, 1988b). There are also versions for use with college students and adults, which include an even greater number of domains (Harter, 1999).

Each item on the questionnaire presents two related statements, one describing a competent child and the other a less competent child. A child completing the instrument selects the statement that best describes him or her and then marks the box indicating whether the statement is "really true for me" or "sort of true for me." Figure 13.1 shows sample items from the scholastic competence area and the domain of behavioral conduct.

Children respond to six items in each of the six areas, and their scores are used to construct a profile of their self-esteem. Results allow the researcher to note both global self-worth and differences from one domain to the next. It should be noted that the tester cannot simply sum an individual's scores across the separate domains to obtain a score of global self-worth. The "global" score reflects responses to its own separate scale. In addition, the global score is imperfectly predicted by responses to the other scales.

Self-esteem (self-worth)
A person's evaluation of the self and the affective reactions to that evaluation.

Looking-glass self
The conception of the self based on how one thinks others see him or her.

Competence
Self-evaluation that includes both what one would like to achieve and one's confidence in being able to achieve it.

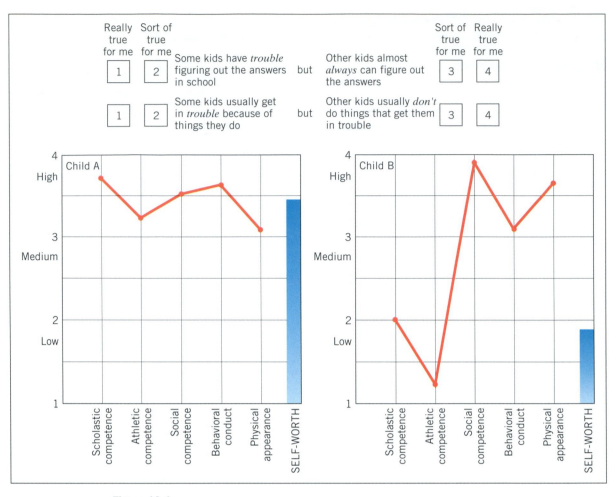

Figure 13.1

Two sample items from the *Self-Perception Profile* and examples of the scoring profiles from two children. Used by permission.

To assess the looking-glass self, Harter constructed additional items that asked children to rate how they believed other people felt about them. Consistent with that model, youngsters who felt others had high regard for them also rated themselves high on the self-worth items. To examine the competence view of the self, she asked children to rate how important each of the five areas was to them. In support of this model, children who rated themselves as very competent in areas they felt were important also had high self-worth scores (Harter, 1986). Harter concluded from her research that older children's feelings of self-esteem are based on both how they believe others evaluate them and how they evaluate themselves (Harter, 1988a, 1990).

Preschoolers differ from older children in their levels of self-understanding, their self-descriptions, and their general cognitive development. Measuring their self-concepts thus presents a unique challenge. For younger children between the ages of 4 and 7, Harter modified the *Self-Perception Profile* to create the *Pictorial Scale of Perceived Competence and Social Acceptance* (Harter & Pike, 1984). As shown in Figure 13.2, its items consist of pictures—for example, a girl who is good at puzzles (left) and a girl who is not good at puzzles (right). The child points to the circle indicating whether a picture is a little like her (small circle) or a lot like her (large circle). Because children below age 8 may not be able to form an overall judgment of their self-worth, only four individual content areas are assessed.

Harter's pictorial scale has been used widely to assess children's self-evaluations in early childhood education and intervention programs. Recent research has raised questions about the validity and applicability of the assessment tool, however. Some researchers have argued that there is no evidence of its being developmentally appropriate for preschool-age

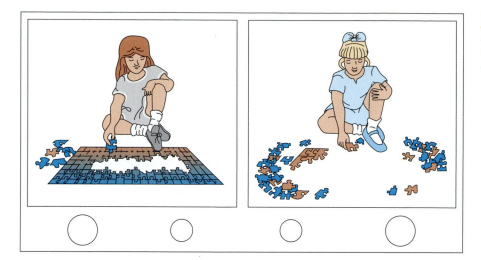

Figure 13.2

A sample item from the version of the *Self-Perception* Profile used with younger children. Used by permission.

children and have further concluded that it is poorly suited for use with some minority populations, such as children in urban Head Start programs (Fantuzzo et al., 1996).

Marsh's *Self-Description Questionnaire*   Another principal measure of the self is the *Self-Description Questionnaire* (SDQ), developed by Herbert Marsh and colleagues (Marsh et al., 1984; see also Marsh, 1990, 1993). This measure is based on the belief that individuals develop a multidimensional and hierarchical self-concept. Different versions have been devised for preadolescents, adolescents, young adults (see Byrne, 1996), and, more recently, preschool-age children (Marsh, Ellis, & Craven, 2002).

The new version for 4- to 5-year-olds uses an interview procedure in which the child is first asked a "yes" or "no" question, such as the following:

Can you run fast?

Do you like the way you look?

Do you have lots of friends?

Do your parents smile at you a lot?

Are you good at counting?

After answering "yes" or "no," the child is asked to clarify whether he or she means "yes/no always" or "yes/no sometimes." Using this procedure, preschoolers are able to distinguish among different aspects of self-concept (specifically, physical ability, appearance, relationships with peers, relationships with parents, verbal skills, and math skills).

The Developmental Progression of Self-Esteem

The developmental course of self-esteem is relatively clear. Although very young children may not have a well-developed sense of overall self-worth, the self-esteem scores of preschool and kindergarten children are generally high. Self-esteem drops slightly during the first years of elementary school. During middle and later childhood, self-esteem scores are generally stable, with perhaps a small trend toward improvement (Cairns & Cairns, 1988; Dunn, 1994). But the transition to adolescence often poses problems. Many investigators have found that at about age 11 or 12, self-esteem scores dip, only to increase again over the subsequent years (Harter, 1990; Twenge & Campbell, 2001; Wigfield et al., 1991). Several explanations have been offered for the drop in self-esteem in early adolescence.

Increased Self-Consciousness   One factor that may play a role in the temporary deterioration of self-esteem is the child's level of **self-consciousness,** or concern about the opinions of others (Tangney & Fischer, 1995). Cognitive-developmental theorists suggest that this tendency increases with the emergence of formal operational abilities.

Self-consciousness
A concern about the opinions others hold about one.

Early adolescence is a time of increased self-consciousness—and often lower self-esteem.

At this stage, children become so much better at taking the perspective of others that they develop a preoccupation with how other people regard their appearance, behavior, and so forth (Elkind, 1980; Hart, 1988). The increased self-consciousness leads to more critical self-evaluations, which in turn lower self-esteem (Adams, Abraham, & Markstrom, 1987; Rosenberg, 1985).

Changes Associated with Puberty The dip in self-worth among early adolescents may also be caused in part by the biological changes associated with puberty. Some researchers have suggested that pubertal changes produce physical and psychological stress in children that leads to depression and other negative emotional states (Simmons & Blyth, 1987). Other evidence has shown that the relationship between puberty and depression is connected with the young person's body image, self-esteem, and experience of stressful life events (Marcotte et al., 2002). Thus, the physical changes associated with puberty likely represent one element of a complex array of factors that dampen self-esteem in early adolescence.

Changing Schools An environmental variable that contributes to a drop in self-esteem involves whether children remain in their own school or move to a new one following sixth grade. Several studies report that moving to a new school usually produces a noticeable decline in self-esteem scores, especially if the new school is large and ethnically diverse (Blyth, Simmons, & Carlton-Ford, 1983; Simmons, Carlton-Ford, & Blyth, 1987). Children who remain in the same school show no such change (Rosenberg, 1986b). This phenomenon appears to affect a wide range of young people: A study of youth in poor urban settings, for example, found that the drop in self-esteem associated with the transition to junior high school was present regardless of ethnicity or gender (Seidman et al., 1994). We consider the role that changing schools plays in academic problems in a later section.

Gender Differences in Self-Esteem

We have seen that psychologists have identified broad trends in self-esteem in children and in the way self-esteem typically changes with age. We should note, however, that girls and boys exhibit some differences in self-esteem measures.

In self-evaluative judgments across different domains, boys show much less variability than girls from one domain to the next (Harter, 1999). Although girls typically evaluate their conduct in a more positive light than do boys, they provide much more negative assessments of their physical appearance and athletic competence. These gender differences are consistent among cultures and across development, holding from elementary school through college. Females' perceptions of their athletic abilities are thought to arise from the traditionally greater emphasis on males' athletic prowess and participation, whereas their low ratings of their own physical appearance are believed to stem from the greater emphasis on female appearance and the more limited yet unrealistic expectations of what constitutes female beauty.

The developmental course of self-esteem also differs for boys and girls. Here again, self-ratings of perceived physical appearance are a source of male-female contrast. Beginning in the fourth grade, girls' perceptions of their physical attractiveness decline markedly, so that by the last half of high school, girls have dramatically lower self-ratings than do boys, whose scores decline only a little with age. This trend may be particularly troubling given that perceived physical appearance has been shown to be an effective predictor of global self-worth (Harter, 1999). It is important to note, however, that the dramatic decline in perceived physical appearance was found in several samples of predominantly Caucasian females. Research with adults has found that African American women typically rate their appearance more favorably than do Caucasian women.

Academic Self-Concept

Academic self-concept
The part of self-esteem involving children's perceptions of their academic abilities.

The factors affecting self-esteem have also been investigated in the classroom, especially with regard to children's perceptions of their academic competence, or **academic self-concept.** We review some of these findings next.

Age and Gender Differences   Prior to entering school, children have no basis for an academic self-concept. Some research has examined the reactions of infants and preschoolers to other sorts of achievement tasks, however, and has found that a developmental progression does exist (Stipek, Recchia, & McClintic, 1992). Infants, for example, have little understanding of success and failure and so do not behave in ways that give any evidence of self-evaluation. However, even before the age of 2, children begin to show that they anticipate how adults will react to their achievements, such as when they look up for approval after making a stack of blocks. They also express delight at their successes and display negative reactions to their failures. By age 3, most children prefer to engage in activities at which they win rather than lose.

Children's academic self-concept generally is highest in kindergarten and steadily declines through at least fourth grade. This trend has been noted in children's spontaneous classroom comments to other students (Ruble & Frey, 1987), in their statements during interviews (Benenson & Dweck, 1986), and in their responses to questionnaires (Butler, 1990; Eccles et al., 1993). One cause of this decline may be as simple as the fact that older children realize that bragging is not socially appropriate and so increasingly avoid giving glowing descriptions of their abilities (Ruble & Frey, 1987).

Dweck's Motivational Model of Achievement   Children's academic self-concept, of course, derives mainly from their academic performance. Those who do well in school are likely to develop high opinions of their competence, whereas poor performers are likely to develop low opinions. How well a child performs in school depends partly on his or her academic abilities and partly on the amount of effort and motivation the child puts forth.

Based on over 20 years of research, Carol Dweck and her colleagues have developed a theoretical model that attempts to explain the complex role that motivation plays in children's academic success (Dweck, 1999). The model focuses on two patterns of motivation that have been observed in both younger and older children and that are reflected in their affect, cognitions, and behavior.

Motivation Patterns   Children in achievement situations generally react to failure experiences in one of two ways (Diener & Dweck, 1978, 1980). Some children display a *mastery-oriented* pattern. Despite having just failed at a task or problem, these children retain a positive mood and express high expectations for success on future attempts. As a result, they tend to persist at the task and they seek out similar challenging problems. This motivational pattern usually leads to improved academic performance over time.

Other children, however, display a *helpless* pattern. When they encounter failure, their affect conveys sadness or disappointment, and they express doubt that they can ever succeed at the task. These children show little persistence in the activity and tend to avoid similar

Performance in school is one important contributor to academic self-concept. Academic self-concept can in turn affect how well children do in school.

challenges in the future. Academic performance in these children often remains considerably below what it could be. What could produce these very different responses to failure?

Dweck's model proposes that at the heart of the problem are children's feelings of self-worth. Children who develop the helpless pattern typically believe that their self-worth depends on the approval and positive judgments of others. As a way of validating their self-worth, they seek out situations in which success involves receiving such approval. If the situation instead produces failure, these children view the absence of approval as a blow to their "goodness" as a person (self-worth), which then leads to the helpless pattern of negative affect, low expectations for future success, low persistence, and avoidance of similar situations.

In contrast, children who develop the mastery-oriented pattern do not believe that their self-worth depends on the opinions of others. They tend to seek out situations in which, whether successful or not, they will learn from their experiences. When these children fail, therefore, they view it simply as an opportunity to improve their ability on the task and so display the opposite pattern of affect, expectations, and persistence.

The Development of Motivation: Work with Preschool Children   Dweck and colleagues have examined the achievement motivation of preschool-age children and have found that even at these young ages, children display patterns of persistence or helplessness. In these studies, 4- and 5-year-olds were asked to solve several puzzles, but only one could actually be solved. The others had been modified—for example, in a jigsaw puzzle, pieces might have been removed and pieces from a different puzzle added. After spending time with the puzzles, children were given the opportunity to indicate which one they would like to play with again. More than a third of the children said they would like to work on the single solved puzzle again, despite having just completed it.

Interestingly, when asked to explain their choice, these "nonpersisters" did not say that the solved puzzle was challenging or that repeating it would provide them with good practice. Instead, these young children said things like "Because it was the easiest" or "Because I already know how to do it." These children also displayed negative affect toward the task and expressed lower expectations for success on another task. Children who chose to persist on one of the unsolved puzzles showed the more positive pattern of reactions (Smiley & Dweck, 1994).

Children's Implicit Theories of Intelligence   In older children, the model becomes more complex. Beyond 10 years of age or so, children's cognitive abilities permit them to develop certain self-conceptions (Dweck & Leggett, 1988). One of these is a "theory of intelligence." Some children come to believe in an **entity model,** in which the amount of a person's intelligence is fixed and unchangeable. Others subscribe to an **incremental model,** in which a person's intelligence can grow with experience and learning. A second self-conception involves children's "attributions for success or failure." Some children believe that success or failure results primarily from the amount of ability a person has; other children believe it depends on the amount of effort a person applies to a task.

Children who develop the helpless pattern, as we might expect, generally believe that the amount of their intelligence is fixed (entity model) and that their lack of success derives from a lack of ability. These two beliefs combine to give the child little reason for optimism in the face of failure—after all, ability is unchangeable and the child simply has too little of it. Predictably, then, these children feel helpless and hopeless.

A very different outlook, however, results from the two opposite beliefs, which are generally held by mastery-oriented children. If intelligence can grow (incremental model) and success depends largely on one's effort, then failure experiences need not lead to feelings of despair or pessimism. These children believe they can do better next time simply by trying harder.

Research has likewise supported this portion of the model. For example, one study found that fifth-grade children who displayed elements of the helpless pattern (nonpersistence and low expectations for future success) following failure on a task were more

Entity model
The belief that a person's intelligence is fixed and unchangeable.

Incremental model
The belief that a person's intelligence can grow through experience and learning.

likely to hold the entity view of intelligence, whereas children displaying the mastery-oriented pattern tended to believe in the incremental view (Cain & Dweck, 1995).

Studies also revealed that girls—especially bright girls—are especially vulnerable to the helpless pattern. Girls are also more likely to hold an entity theory of intelligence. Compared with boys, girls more often pick tasks at which they can perform well and show impairment when tasks grow difficult. When the going gets tough, girls are also more likely to blame their abilities (Dweck, 1999). We speculate about a possible cause of this gender difference in the following section.

The Effects of Praise and Criticism   Another important component of Dweck's model of achievement motivation concerns caregivers' responses to children's performance. How are failures and successes handled? What aspects of the child's performance are the targets of praise or criticism? The answers to such questions have been found to be of substantial consequence. In fact, Dweck (1999) asserts that the feedback children receive from adults is the source of patterns of motivation, having more impact than the child's temperament.

As you might expect, Dweck's team hypothesized that criticism could have a negative impact on children. Specifically, the researchers targeted criticism that judged the children themselves—their stable traits rather than their situation-specific effort. In contrast, criticism that focused on the children's effort or strategies was thought to promote the desirable mastery-oriented motivational pattern. What about praise? Here, too, the researchers hypothesized that praise directed toward the child's efforts or problem-solving processes would be beneficial, just as with criticism. Praise could end up having a negative impact, they argued, when focused on children's enduring traits.

To test these hypotheses, kindergartners participated in a role-playing exercise in which they imagined they had done some well-intentioned act for their teacher that ended up being a disappointment. For example, in one scenario, the children imagined creating a picture of a family and then realizing that a child in the painting had no feet:

> You spend a lot of time painting a picture of a family to give to your teacher. You pick out colors you think are nice and carefully draw each person. As you are about to give it to your teacher you say to yourself, "Uh oh, one of the kids has no feet." But you worked really hard on the picture and want to give it to her. You say, "Teacher, here's a picture for you." (Heyman, Cain, & Dweck, 1992, p. 404)

Interestingly, noting a flaw like this did not produce particular concern for kindergartners on their own. Reactions changed, however, when the scenario included criticism from the teacher, who the children were told had said, "What, no feet? I don't call this drawing the right way. I'm disappointed."

About a third of the young children responded to this input by lowering their own evaluation of the painting: What they thought was fine before was now judged to be inadequate. Children with this downward reaction also reported more negative emotion than the other children and were less willing to persist on the task, evidence of a helpless reaction (Dweck, 1999). These helpless children also imagined that their painting's shortcoming would elicit negative reactions from their parents and teachers, suggesting that their parents would respond with statements such as "You are very bad" or "That's bad work." Finally, this negativity extended to these children's self-evaluations: Nearly two-thirds of the helpless children said that their performance indicated they were not being good kids—a sentiment shared by fewer than 10% of the mastery-oriented children. Thus, it appears that a strong relationship exists between the child's motivation pattern and his or her reactions to criticism.

Dweck and colleagues have also demonstrated effects of differing kinds of criticism and praise using hypothetical scenarios as described above (Kamins & Dweck, 1999). Feedback was provided in response to children's errors. Some children received criticism that offered information about their strategy use—for example, "Maybe you should think of another way to do it." Other criticism focused on the child's behavior ("That's not what I call doing it the right way") or on the child as a whole ("I'm disappointed in you"). Children who received strategy-specific feedback fared the best, giving their work the highest self-rating, reporting the most positive overall feelings, and providing the best solutions for future improvement.

Analogous results were found for children's responses to praise. Receiving person-oriented praise was actually associated with increased vulnerability to failure, whereas praise directed at effort or strategy use produced the most mastery-oriented responses. In explaining these findings, Dweck proposes that believing that one is good when one does something correctly leaves one open to the alternative conclusion that one is bad when failure results. Thus, despite the common intuition that praise is bound to be beneficial for children, research suggests that certain forms of praise can in fact have later negative consequences.

Dweck also contends that performance-based praise may underlie girls' greater vulnerability to helplessness. Girls are usually the stars of elementary school. According to Dweck, young girls—especially bright ones—are likely fed a steady diet of praise during the early years of school. They are, after all, generally better behaved than boys and comply more readily with adult requests. Moreover, very capable girls are unlikely to struggle very much with the academic demands of the first years of school. The lesson girls may learn is that they can measure their traits from the outcomes and praise they receive.

Because the requirements of the classroom are less compatible with the needs of the average boy, they are more likely to experience both failure and criticism. These early difficulties may, however, prove advantageous over time, because through them boys learn that persistence can lead to success.

The Role of Social Comparisons

We have seen that academic self-image is affected by children's academic performance and by the types of attributions they make regarding failure. But the general decline over the elementary grades in children's self-evaluations of competence may involve yet another factor.

Children, like adults, contrast their abilities with those of others and draw conclusions about themselves from those assessments—a process called **social comparison** (Suls & Wills, 1991). This process begins as early as kindergarten, but its function changes with age (Pomerantz et al., 1995; Stipek, 1992).

Kindergartners use what their classmates are doing or saying primarily as a way of making friends or learning how things are done. For example, a child may comment to a classmate that they are coloring on the same page of their books. Social comparisons, at this point, do not appear to have much impact on the child's self-image (Aboud, 1985; Stipek & Tannatt, 1984). As children proceed through the early grades, however, their social comparisons increasingly involve academic performance, and they begin to use the comparisons to evaluate their own competence relative to others (Butler, 1992; Pomerantz et al., 1995).

By second grade, children's spontaneous self-evaluative remarks become positively correlated with the number of social comparisons they make; that is, children with lower opinions of their competence make fewer social comparisons (Ruble & Frey, 1991). Why? One interpretation of this finding is that in continually comparing their performance with that of peers, many children unhappily discover that their work is not as good as they had believed. A child who once found great pleasure in drawing may discover that his artwork is not as attractive as that of his classmates. As a result, he may lower his opinion of his drawings but also begin to avoid comparing his work with that of other children. If this interpretation is correct, we would expect academically successful children to seek out more information about their performance than children who are lower achievers. And research has found just that: High-achieving students show more interest in comparing their performance with that of classmates and also in discovering the correct answers to problems (Ruble & Flett, 1988).

This developmental change in the use of social comparisons is not inevitable, however, and can be influenced by the atmosphere of the educational environment. For example, in Israel the communal kibbutz environment places more emphasis on cooperative than on competitive learning and fosters concern with mastering skills rather than with surpassing others. As a result, even older children in the kibbutz environment have been found to use social comparison primarily as a means of acquiring new abilities and much less for self-evaluation (Butler & Ruzany, 1993).

Social comparison
Comparing one's abilities to those of others.

Calvin and Hobbes   by Bill Watterson

Children's willingness to make social comparisons is related to their academic competence. (CALVIN AND HOBBES copyright 1993 Watterson. Reprinted with permission of UNIVERSAL PRESS SYNDICATE. All rights reserved.)

The relation between social comparison and academic self-concept, then, is bidirectional. Social comparisons can affect children's self-image by giving them information about how they are performing relative to other children. But children's self-image may affect their willingness to engage in social comparisons, depending on how pleasant or unpleasant they expect the resulting information to be (Pomerantz et al., 1995).

Parenting Styles   Children's academic self-concept is also affected by the attitudes, expectations, and behaviors of their parents. Studies have shown that parents' perceptions of their children's academic abilities are one of the best predictors of the children's self-perceptions of ability (Eccles et al., 2000; Lamborn et al., 1991; Midgett et al., 2002; Oosterwegel & Oppenheimer, 1993; Phillips & Zimmerman, 1990).

How do such expectations produce their effects on children's self-perceptions? One likely possibility lies in the way in which parents interact with children on academic tasks. One general style of discipline (which we discuss more fully in Chapter 16) is labeled *authoritative*. We know that parents who display an authoritative style tend to use more scaffolding techniques when working with their children (Pratt et al., 1988) and that these children, in turn, tend to be more cognitively competent (Baumrind, 1989, 1991).

To determine whether differences in parents' interaction styles also influence academic self-concept, researchers in one study observed academically successful students working on several tasks with either their mothers or their fathers (Wagner & Phillips, 1992). The children were divided into those whose academic self-concepts were high and those whose academic self-concepts were low. No differences in interaction style were found among the mothers of these two groups; however, marked differences were found among the fathers. The fathers of children with high academic self-concept were warmer and more supportive in their interactions than were the fathers of the other children. This finding is consistent with other research in which college students recalled that continuing support from their fathers was instrumental in their success in school (Schaffer & Blatt, 1990).

Effects of Academic Self-Concept   Children's perception of their academic competence has perhaps been of such interest to psychologists because of its applied value—academic self-concept strongly influences academic achievement (Byrne, 1996; Nolen-Hoeksema, Girgus, & Seligman, 1986). Studies examining feelings of competence and perceived self-efficacy report that children who view themselves as academically skilled are more motivated to succeed, more persistent in their work, and more willing to seek out challenging tasks or problems (Boggiano, Main, & Katz, 1988; Harter, 1988a; Harter & Connell, 1984; Schunk, 1984). A high academic self-concept, even when it is an overestimate of the child's abilities, also correlates positively with (and probably contributes to) a high level of self-esteem (Connell & Ilardi, 1987; Harter, 1985a).

Children with low opinions of their academic abilities are less motivated to work. One study found that even among children whose academic skills were high, those who held an incorrectly low opinion of their competence approached new tasks with less effort and optimism than did their classmates (Phillips, 1984, 1987). Thus, for some children, academic success may hinge as much on academic self-concept as it does on academic ability. We describe one approach to shaping students' conceptions of their academic selves in Box 13.3.

Research suggests that fathers may be especially important contributors to children's academic self-concept.

Possible Selves and Academic Achievement

I want to be smart and hope to get a scholarship to college and to graduate from college and own a business. . . . I want to be out on my own too. I want to have an apartment. [Eventually] I want to build me a house and have children. (Kerpelman, Shoffner, & Ross-Griffin, 2002, p. 294)

This comment was offered by one adolescent in response to the question "Who do you expect to become during the next 5 years?" Among the ways in which the self-concept grows more differentiated during adolescence is its relation to time. In contrast to younger children, adolescents are able to think flexibly about the self in terms of the past, present, and future. Future-oriented components of the self are referred to as **possible selves.** Possible selves represent a person's goals and embody dreams, hopes, and fears (Markus & Nurius, 1986). Possible selves include hoped-for selves and feared selves. Hoped-for selves represent "what we would like to become." These selves are domain-specific (e.g., career, family) and include abstract goals as well as the scripts, plans, and strategies for achieving the goals. Feared selves are the possible selves that an individual does *not* want to become. Together, hoped-for and feared selves motivate behavior as people are energized to pursue images they hope for and strive to avoid images they fear (Oyserman & Markus, 1990).

A growing number of researchers are beginning to examine adolescent educational aspirations and achievement in light of the theory of possible selves (e.g., Kerpelman et al., 2002; Packard & Nguyen, 2003; Yowell, 2000, 2002). The reasoning behind this approach is quite straightforward. Adolescents who view their future selves as academically successful should be motivated to engage in behaviors that lead to success in school and avoid behaviors (e.g., truancy, substance use) that interfere with academic achievement. Conversely, adolescents who do not include an academically

BOX 13.3

successful self among their possible selves should be less motivated to engage in behavior associated with school success. Indeed, studies have documented a link between possible selves and academic behaviors and achievement (Oyserman, Gant, & Ager, 1995; Oyserman & Markus, 1990; Oyserman & Saltz, 1993).

Given the established link between school-focused possible selves and academic performance, might it be possible to improve a student's engagement in school and, ultimately, academic performance by targeting his or her academic self-concept? Daphna Oyserman and colleagues (Oyserman, Terry, & Bybee, 2002) developed an after-school intervention to do just that. The 9-week intervention, *Schools-to-Jobs,* involved a sequence of activities focused on helping adolescents (1) create and detail academically successful possible selves; (2) connect possible selves for the coming year to specific strategies to attain these selves; (3) connect their short-term possible selves and strategies to adult possible selves; and (4) develop skills to effectively work with others to attain these possible selves.

The researchers implemented the intervention with three cohorts of low-income urban African American middle-school students. Evaluation of the intervention showed that, compared with a control group that received no intervention, students in the *Schools-to-Jobs* program reported better school attendance and more bonding to school (e.g., "I feel I really belong at school"). They also expressed more concern about doing well in school, more "balanced" possible selves, and more realistic strategies for achieving these possible selves.

The findings to date suggest that the *Schools-to-Jobs* program can positively impact student attitudes toward school. Additional research is needed to document more specific behavioral changes and to see whether the effects of the intervention last over time. Meanwhile, this study offers a promising means to foster educational achievement—especially among youth lacking role models and mentors who embody and reinforce the long-term importance of school success.

Possible selves

Concepts of the self in the future that represent one's goals and embody dreams, hopes, and fears.

The value of academic success to the child may seem obvious, but its effects can reach beyond the classroom. For example, research indicates that when children have academic (and social) failure experiences at school, their relations with their parents often suffer—the children tend to become more demanding and unreasonable, while the parents become more disapproving and punitive (Repetti, 1996). These home experiences, in turn, may further erode the child's attitude toward school, in effect producing a vicious circle.

✔️ To Recap . . .

The opinions children form about themselves constitute their self-esteem. Researchers have often measured self-esteem through questionnaires. The most popular of these is Susan Harter's *Self-Perception Profile for Children,* appropriate for school-age children, which creates a profile of children's self-esteem across a number of different domains. Measures have also been created to measure self-esteem in preschool-age children using picture-based and/or interview methods.

Kindergartners tend to have a relatively high level of self-esteem, which remains stable until early adolescence. At about age 11 or 12, children report a dip in self-esteem, which has been attributed to several changes that typify adolescence, including an increase in self-consciousness. Boys and girls show differences in self-esteem.

An important component of self-esteem is a feeling of competence. Academic self-concept, representing the child's perceived competence in the classroom, has been of particular interest to researchers. The academic self-image of the kindergartner is high, but it steadily decreases through at least the fourth grade.

Dweck has developed a theoretical model describing the complex role that motivation plays in academic achievement. According to the model, mastery-oriented children remain positive and persistent because they view failure experiences as opportunities to learn, whereas helpless children become pessimistic and avoid future challenges because they view failures as signs of low self-worth. In older children, conceptions of intelligence and attributions for failure (effort or ability) affect academic motivation. The types of feedback children receive in response to their performances can also have a significant impact, with feedback directed at the process or strategies the child used having the most positive overall effect.

As children move through the early grades, they increasingly use social comparisons in developing academic self-concepts. This process may explain the general decline in academic self-image, because many children must lower their assessments of their abilities as they compare themselves with other children. Parents' interaction styles also influence children's academic self-concepts.

Academic self-concept influences children's academic achievement. High self-image improves motivation and success, and low self-image reduces them, even among children whose low self-image inaccurately reflects their high academic ability.

SELF-REGULATION

We have examined how growing children gain knowledge of the self and how their continual evaluation of this knowledge produces a positive or negative view of the self. In this section, we consider a third process—how the self comes to regulate, or control, children's behavior.

Self-regulation is a crucial aspect of human development. If children did not learn to control their own behavior—to avoid the things they must avoid, to wait for the things they cannot have right away, to alter strategies that are not working—they would be constantly at the mercy of the moment-to-moment pushes and pulls of their environments. They would simply be "weathervanes," as Bandura puts it (1986, p. 335). The development of self-control is one of the child's most impressive accomplishments. Self-control indicates at the very least that the child knows what demands are made by the surrounding world, realizes what behaviors relate to those demands, and understands how to adjust behaviors to meet the demands (Vaughn, Kopp, & Krakow, 1984). How does such self-control develop, and what are its effects?

The Emergence of Self-Control

During early infancy, self-regulation mostly involves involuntary biological processes (Rothbart & Posner, 1985; Stifter & Braungart, 1995). For instance, babies reflexively squint in response to a bright light. And even young infants control sensory input by turning away or even falling asleep when stimulation from caregivers or surroundings becomes overwhelming. Such responses serve important regulatory functions, but there is no evidence that the infants who engage in them are cognitively aware of what is happening.

By the beginning of the second year, babies have developed many voluntary behaviors and can act on their environments in purposeful ways. Children act to accomplish things or to produce outcomes, such as when a baby grabs for a toy he or she would like to play with or pushes over a tower of blocks to watch it crash to the floor. But at this point, the child's ability to monitor behaviors and to adjust them as necessary is still limited (Bullock & Lutkenhaus, 1988).

During the third year, most children begin to consistently regulate their activities with respect to producing outcomes. They pay attention to simple standards set by others or by themselves and monitor their activities with respect to those standards. For instance, a child making a birthday cake out of sand may try several combinations of mud, water, sticks, and grass to get it just right. As children come to recognize standards, they also begin to react affectively when they meet or fail to meet them. Thus, we begin to see the expression of the self-conscious emotions of pride, shame, guilt, and embarrassment (Lewis, 1993, 2000).

The changes in self-regulation observed during the early years reflect two important developments. First, regulation shifts from external to internal control. Initially, caregivers largely regulate children's behavior either directly or indirectly by supporting or scaffolding children's own efforts at self-regulation. Gradually, however, regulation shifts to the child. Second, self-control grows more elaborate and sophisticated. These issues are discussed in more detail below.

Compliance

Compliance
The child's ability to go along with requests or adopt the standards of behavior espoused by caregivers.

One of the earliest indices of self-control is compliance. **Compliance** refers to children's ability to go along with requests or adopt the standards of behavior espoused by caregivers (Kopp, 1982). Children begin to understand caregiver wishes and expectations around the end of the first year (Kaler & Kopp, 1980). However, during the months that follow, children are more likely to refuse, ignore, or subvert parents' behavioral requests than comply with them.

The kinds of situations in which parents expect compliance vary widely. For instance, sometimes caregivers direct children to stop or refrain from doing something—for example, playing with the electric socket, interrupting when mom is on the phone, going in the street. To comply with these requests, children must be able to inhibit a behavior. In other situations, parents want their children to perform desired behavior such as brushing teeth, saying "thank you," and helping with chores (Gralinski & Kopp, 1993; Kochanska & Aksan, 1995).

To study the development of compliance, researchers look at children's behavior in both kinds of situations (termed "Don't" and "Do" situations). For example, in one recent study, Grazyna Kochanska and colleagues (Kochanska, Coy, & Murray, 2001) followed a group of children longitudinally from shortly after their first birthdays until age 4. As can be seen in Figure 13.3, compliance in the "Don't" situations increased dramatically during the second year of life. By the time they were 4, children complied with parental prohibitions nearly 80% of the time. In contrast, compliance in the "Do" situation was far more difficult to achieve.

Moreover, the quality of children's compliance differed between the two contexts. In the "Don't" situation, children usually complied wholeheartedly. Kochanska terms this **committed compliance**. Committed compliance describes children's behavior when they embrace the caregiver's agenda, adopt it as their own, and follow caregiver directives in a self-regulated ways (e.g., saying "No, no, don't touch").

Committed compliance
Compliant behavior that results from a child's internalizing the instruction of an adult; results in positive emotion.

Situational compliance
Obedience that results from a child's awareness of an adult's will in a particular situation and does not reflect enduring behavioral change.

Compliance in the "Do" situation was less likely and usually achieved grudgingly. In this type of compliance, termed **situational compliance,** children essentially cooperate with parental directives but with little enthusiasm. Situational compliance also requires a good deal of sustained caregiver support, such as reminding the child to continue or framing the activity (e.g., toy cleanup) as some kind of game. Situational compliance is often fleeting and disappears if caregivers grow distracted, leave the room, or otherwise withdraw control.

It is clear that "Do" requests are more challenging for young children than "Don't" demands. Why this is so is open to interpretation. One possibility is that the neuropsychological correlates that underlie the ability to inhibit a behavior mature before those required to sustain a prolonged flow of behavior (Rothbart, 1989). Another possibility is that parents impose "Don't" commands earlier and expect children to comply with them at a younger age than "Do" commands. It is noteworthy that many "Don't" commands involve safety issues (e.g., "*Don't* jump on the bed;" "*Don't* poke the dog;" "*Don't* touch the stove").

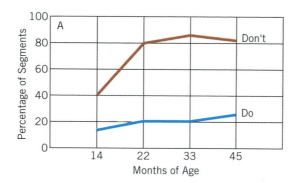

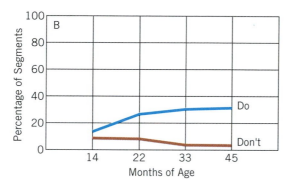

Figure 13.3

Mean percentage of (A) committed and (B) situational compliance at 14, 22, 33, and 45 months in the Do and Don't contexts. From "The Development of Self-Regulation in the First Four Years of Life," by G. Kochanska, K. C. Coy, and K. T. Murray, 2001, *Child Development, 72,* 1101. Copyright © by the Society for Research in Child Development. Reprinted by permission.

There are also striking individual differences in the ease with which parents and children achieve compliance. Some children are eager to comply with caregivers, whereas others readily comply with one parent but not the other. For other children, achieving compliance is a struggle regardless of who else is involved in the interaction. What might underlie these differences?

One contributing factor may be children's temperament. As discussed in Chapter 12, children vary along a number of temperament dimensions, including fearfulness and the ability to regulate their behavior (inhibitory control). We might expect that children who are more cautious or who are able to inhibit a dominant response would be more compliant. And, indeed, researchers have found links between various temperament measures and compliance (Kochanska, Murray, & Coy, 1997; Rothbart, Ahadi, & Evans, 2000). It is simply more difficult to get some children to comply than others.

Another factor that matters a great deal is the quality of the relationship between the parent and the child. Children are most likely to comply in dyads marked by a happy mood and in which partners are mutually responsive to one another's needs and desires (Kochanska, 2002). Longitudinal studies show that mothers in dyads with a mutually responsive orientation have a history of being responsive to their children's signals of need, signs of distress, bids for attention, and social overtures (Kochanska, 1997). During the second year, children whose mothers were responsive to their needs tend to adopt a similar attitude — or what Kochanska terms a *responsive stance* — toward maternal wishes. Children with a responsive stance happily embrace the mother's agenda and eagerly comply with her requests. Kochanska believes that a responsive stance is an intermediate step between simple cooperation and genuine internalization of parental values and standards.

Studies of Japanese mother–child relations provide additional support for Kochanska's model of compliance. As we have seen, the mother–child relationship in Japan is unusually close. Mothers are highly responsive (even indulgent in the view of many Westerners) to infants' needs. Japanese parents try to avoid direct confrontations and contests of will with their children, rarely scold them directly, and often back down when children resist their requests (Lebra, 1994; Vogel, 1963/1991). Although giving children such a free reign might seem destined to create demanding tyrants, Japanese children, in fact, make fewer demands on parents, give fewer commands, and are less likely to assert that they will not obey (Caudill & Schooler, 1973). Indeed, the "terrible twos," a phenomenon American parents are led to believe is unavoidable and normative, is virtually unheard of in Japan.

To understand why Japanese children tend to be more compliant than their American counterparts and at a younger age, we can return to Kochanska's model. The goal of Japanese parenting techniques is to encourage children to *want* to adhere to parental and societal values and standards (Fogel, Stevenson, & Messinger, 1992; Rothbaum et al., 2000). In other words, by virtue of creating a warm, close, and responsive parent–child relationship, Japanese parents are in effect fostering a receptive stance.

American parents, in contrast, try to *convince* children to go along with parental requests (Fogel et al., 1992). To convince them, American parents are often forced to resort to power assertion or appeals to the parents' authority. Power assertion encompasses a range of behaviors, including taking toys from children, spanking, and verbal threats. As we discuss in greater depth in Chapter 14, although power assertion is often effective in the short run (e.g., a child who is slapped upon touching an attractive toy will likely stop immediately), it is less likely to promote the internalization of values and standards than other techniques.

There are undoubtedly many reasons why Japanese and American parents adopt such different approaches to the socialization of self-control. Nonetheless, a number of theorists contend that the American approach is a natural outgrowth of the joint emphasis on autonomy and independence (Fogel et al., 1992; Rogoff, 2003; Rothbaum et al., 2000). As we have seen, parents begin to encourage children to assert their own wishes and desires from a very early age. It should not be surprising, then, to discover that toddlers and preschoolers have their own opinions about a variety of issues, including the reasonableness of parental requests and directives!

Resistance to Temptation

As children grow older and spend more time outside of the immediate supervision of adults, they learn to inhibit forbidden behaviors, even when no one is watching them. How does this kind of self-control come about?

Forbidden-toy technique

An experimental procedure for studying children's resistance to temptation in which the child is left alone with an attractive toy and instructed not to play with it.

A common method for studying resistance to temptation uses the **forbidden-toy technique.** Note that this is similar to the "Don't" situation already described. Typically, an experimenter puts a child in a room where there is an attractive toy and tells the child not to touch or play with the toy. Outside the room, observers monitor the child's behavior through a two-way mirror. The investigators usually are interested in how long the child waits before breaking the rule or how much time the child spends playing with the forbidden toy.

Researchers have explored whether having children produce self-instructional statements during their waiting time affects their ability to resist temptation. In one study, 3- to 7-year-old children were placed in a room with several attractive toys on a table behind them and were instructed not to turn around and look at the toys while the experimenter was out of the room. Some of the children were also told that, to help them keep from looking, they should repeat out loud a relevant statement, such as "I must not turn around." Children in a second group were told to use an irrelevant self-instruction, such as "hickory, dickory, dock." Those in a third group were given no self-instructional advice and waited silently. For younger children, producing a verbal self-instruction led to greater resistance than remaining silent. But the semantic content of the instruction did not matter—the relevant and irrelevant instructions worked equally well. For older children, the content of the self-instruction did make a difference, with the relevant statement proving most effective (Hartig & Kanfer, 1973).

Several other factors have also been shown to influence children's behavior in forbidden-toy settings. For example, seeing an adult model break the rule and play with the toy makes children more likely to do so (Grusec et al., 1979). On the other hand, providing children with a good rationale for following the prohibition ("Don't touch the toy; it's fragile and might break") increases the likelihood that they will resist (Parke, 1977), as does teaching children to develop their own plans or strategies for dealing with the temptation (Patterson, 1982).

Delay of Gratification

Another popular approach to studying children's self-control has been the **delay-of-gratification technique.** Typically, the child is presented with two choices: a small reward that is available immediately or a larger reward that can only be obtained later. This situation is analogous to many choices children (and adults) encounter every day. Should I use this week's allowance to buy a small toy or combine it with next week's and buy a larger toy? Should I eat this snack now or save my appetite for a better meal later? Perhaps because this experimental task is a bit more complex than that involving resistance to temptation, more factors have been shown to influence children's ability to delay gratification (Mischel, Shoda, & Rodriguez, 1989).

In one study, while waiting for the better reward, children were directed to produce either a relevant statement ("I am waiting for the marshmallow"), an irrelevant statement ("one, two, three"), or nothing. Once again, either of the self-statements increased waiting time for younger children, but only the relevant verbalizations were of assistance to the older children (Karniol & Miller, 1981).

Another method for helping children delay gratification is to reduce or alter the attention they pay to the tempting object (the smaller but immediately available reward) (Mischel et al., 1989). When the object is out of sight, for example, children will wait much longer. The same is true when they spend the waiting time playing with a toy or engaging in some other distracting activity. Even when they are thinking about the tempting object, children will wait longer if they are instructed to think only about certain of its objective properties (say, the shape or color of a candy bar) rather than about its appealing properties (the candy bar's smell or taste).

As children grow older, their understanding of these delay strategies increases. For example, when presented with various waiting techniques and asked to select the ones that would work best, preschoolers display little knowledge of what strategies would be more effective. Third-graders, however, show an impressive understanding. And by sixth grade, the large majority of children clearly seem to know that redirecting one's attention from the reward and various other forms of distraction are the methods most useful in delaying gratification (Mischel et al., 1989; Yates, Yates, & Beasley, 1987).

Children's use of distraction strategies in other contexts may be related to their ability to delay gratification. Toddlers who were able to use self-distraction to cope with a period of separation from their mother were found to be able to delay gratification at age 5 for longer periods than were children who did not show that early coping ability (Sethi et al., 2000). These researchers also explored how delay of gratification is related to children's reactions to their mother's behavior in a play setting. The key predictor of preschool delay of gratification was toddlers' response to their mothers: The greatest success in delay of gratification at age 5 was observed in the children who as toddlers had distanced themselves from controlling mothers or those who had engaged themselves with noncontrolling mothers. Thus, the ability to delay gratification may be an indication of a child who is generally well equipped to navigate social experiences and adjust his or her responses to best fit a situation.

Not surprisingly, then, the ability to delay gratification has been linked to children's social competence as well. Children who respond impulsively often experience problems in their social interactions with other children, in part because they fail to acquire all the necessary information about a situation before making a decision (Eisenberg, Pidada, & Liew, 2001; Frankel & Feinberg, 2002; Hughes et al., 2000). One study investigated the relation between a child's ability to delay gratification (in the standard tasks described here) and how many witness statements the child chose to hear before deciding whether another child was guilty of having caused a problem. As predicted, those children who were good at delaying gratification also waited to hear more testimony before making their decisions (Gronau & Waas, 1997).

Finally, children's ability to cope with temptation in this type of experimental situation appears to reflect a surprisingly stable personality characteristic. In one study, adolescents

Delay-of-gratification technique
An experimental procedure for studying children's ability to postpone a smaller, immediate reward in order to obtain a larger, delayed one.

The ability to delay gratification appears to be a personality trait that remains quite stable over the years.

who had participated as preschoolers in delay-of-gratification research of the type described earlier were studied again 10 years later. Parents were asked to complete several questionnaires concerned with aspects of their children's present cognitive skills, social competence, and ability to cope with stress.

The results indicated that children who had been better at delaying gratification in their early years were much more likely to be rated by parents as stronger in each of these three areas. For example, the children who had waited the longest during the experimental procedures (especially those who had spontaneously developed good coping strategies) were now reported to be the most academically successful, the best at getting along with peers, the best at coping with problems, and the most confident and self-reliant (Mischel, Shoda, & Peake, 1988; Shoda, Mischel, & Peake, 1990). These rather remarkable findings indicate that a child's early ability to delay gratification may be one long-term predictor of that child's eventual success and happiness.

 To Recap . . .

The development of self-regulation is a major achievement. Little meaningful self-regulation is evident during the first year of life, but children during the third year consistently regulate their activities with respect to producing outcomes. The changes in self-regulation observed during the early years reflect two important developments: a shift from external to internal control and an increase in the sophistication of self-control.

Compliance is an early index of self-control. Research has indicated that children display two contrasting types of compliance to authority: committed compliance and situational compliance. Only committed compliance, wherein the child adopts the caregiver's viewpoint as his or her own, can be considered a demonstration of self-regulation. Investigators are still exploring what factors lead to this deeper form of compliance.

Resistance-to-temptation studies examine the common situation in which children must withhold a prohibited behavior. Using the forbidden-toy technique, investigators have found that the ability to resist temptation is influenced by a number of factors, including appropriate self-statements, modeling, and a good rationale or plan for resisting the prohibited act.

Delay-of-gratification studies examine children's ability to forgo smaller, immediate rewards in order to receive larger, delayed ones. Factors that affect waiting time include self-statements and various methods of reducing attention to the tempting, immediately available reward. Children's understanding of effective delay strategies increases as they get older. The ability to delay gratification during the preschool years has been linked with parents' ratings of their adolescents' cognitive, social, and coping abilities.

CONCLUSION

This chapter has covered a variety of topics that may seem only loosely connected to one another. Why a baby watches herself in a mirror may seem unrelated to why she does or does not give up a smaller reward to wait for a larger one in kindergarten or why she lowers her opinion of herself in junior high school. The lack of an immediately obvious connection between these aspects of child development reflects the fact that the self has only recently become a topic of major research interest.

Our examination of the self has, however, nicely illustrated an important theme of this book and of modern child psychology: Social and cognitive development are so interdependent that it is difficult to study either one alone. Although for clarity we have often discussed these two domains separately, it should be apparent that one cannot be completely understood without the other. We have seen, for example, that children's growing knowledge about themselves and their increasingly accurate evaluations of their abilities have major influences on their interactions with other people. On the other hand, social interactions play an important role in the development of children's thinking and problem-solving skills. This theme emerged in earlier chapters and will continue to find its way into our discussions as we look further at children's social development.

FOR THOUGHT AND DISCUSSION

1. Our awareness of who we are involves both the subjective I-self and the objective Me-self. *Think about who you are. Which of these two selves do you tend to focus on? Why do you think this is the case? Would you guess this is true for everyone?*

2. Our self-efficacy judgments are believed to influence our behavior. *Can you think of several things you recently decided to not do as a direct result of your own self-efficacy judgments? Do you think that following these judgments is always wise?*

3. In recent studies, Carol Dweck and colleagues have shown that praise in the form of statements such as "I'm proud of you" and "You are really smart" places children at a significant disadvantage when faced with later setbacks. Instead, Dweck recommends that parents and teachers offer praise that focuses on children's effort (e.g., "You worked very hard"), strategies (e.g., "You found a good way to do this"), skills, and knowledge. *Do you think it is always ill-advised to praise children's intelligence? Do you think the effects of this type of praise might vary with children's age and circumstances? Given that it is almost automatic for American adults to praise children in this fashion, might there be other ways to foster a mastery-orientation without abandoning person-oriented praise?*

4. Presumably, the self continues to differentiate beyond the adolescent years. *Have you begun to think about yourself in any new ways since entering college? What additional "selves" might you expect to emerge as you grow older (such as the "parent-self")?*

5. Bandura noted that in the absence of self-control we would all be "weathervanes." *What exactly did he mean by this? Give some everyday examples. Do other species demonstrate self-control? Give examples of some behavior that supports your answer.*

6. Children who are better at delaying gratification grow up to be more competent in a variety of ways. *Why do you think this ability is so important?*

VISUAL SUMMARY FOR CHAPTER 13
Development of the Self

Theories of the Self

The self-system can be divided into three components: self-knowledge, self-evaluation, and self-regulation.

Cognitive-Developmental Approaches ▶ Cognitive-developmental theorists have offered several models concerning self-development. Information-processing theorists view the self as part of the larger memory system. Selman proposed a 5-stage model of self-awareness.

Environmental/Learning Approaches ▶ Bandura proposed a model of self-evaluation built around children's developing sense of self-efficacy. Bandura also proposed an explanation for the development of self-regulation that involves a shift from external control of behavior to internal control.

Evolutionary and Biological Approaches ▶ Bowlby's attachment theory holds that infants construct an internal working model of the self through their interactions with caregivers. Evolutionary psychologists are interested in the evolutionary roots of the self and focus their research on self-understanding and self-related behaviors among nonhuman species.

Sociocultural Approaches ▶ According to sociocultural theorists, the self is shaped through participation in cultural practices that reflect cultural models of the self.

Self-Knowledge

Discovery of the Self in Infancy ▶ It is not yet known whether newborns have an understanding of the self. During the second half of the first year, babies begin to display a sense of personal agency by acting on toys and other objects. Toward the end of the second year, they begin to show recognition of themselves in mirrors and videotapes.

Developmental Changes in Self-Descriptions ▶ Self-descriptions by preschoolers reflect preoperational thinking and typically include references only to objective, here-and-now characteristics. In middle childhood, the concrete operational child focuses to a greater degree on nontangible characteristics, such as emotions, and on membership in various categories. Adolescents' formal operational abilities lead to more abstract and hypothetical self-descriptions, concerned with attitudes, personality characteristics, and personal beliefs, sometimes involving conflicting attributes.

Self-Evaluation

Measuring Self-Worth

> The opinions children form about themselves make up their self-esteem. The most popular measure of self-esteem in Susan Harter's *Self-Perception Profile for Children*, which creates a profile of children's self-esteem across a number of different domains.

The Stability of Self-Worth

> Kindergartners tend to have a relatively high level of self-esteem, which remains stable until early adolescence. At about age 11 or 12, children report a dip in self-esteem, which has been attributed to several changes that typify adolescence, including an increase in self-consciousness.

Academic Self-Concept

Dweck's Motivational Model of Achievement

> Dweck's model distinguishes between mastery-oriented and helpless patterns. Mastery-oriented children remain positive and persistent because they view failure experiences as opportunities to learn, whereas helpless children become pessimistic and avoid future challenges because they view failures as signs of low self-worth.

Influences on Academic Self-Concept

> As children move through the early grades, they increasingly use social comparisons in developing academic self-concepts. Many children must lower their assessments of their abilities as they compare them with those of other children. Parents' interaction styles also influence children's academic self-concept.

Effects of Academic Self-Concept

> Academic self-concept influences children's academic achievement. High self-image improves motivation and success and low self-image reduces them, even among children whose low self-image inaccurately reflects their high academic ability.

Self-Regulation

The Emergence of Self-Control

> Little meaningful self-regulation is evident during the first year of life. Changes through the third year reflect two important developments: a shift from external to internal control and an increase in the sophistication of self-control.

Compliance

> Children display two contrasting types of compliance to authority: committed compliance and situational compliance. Only committed compliance, wherein the child adopts the caregiver's viewpoint as his or her own, can be considered a demonstration of self-regulation.

Resistance to Temptation

> Resistance-to-temptation studies examine situations in which children must withold a prohibited behavior. The ability to resist temptation is influenced by a number of factors, including appropriate self-statements, modeling, and a good rationale for resisting the prohibited act.

Delay of Gratification

> Delay-of-gratification studies examine children's ability to forgo smaller immediate rewards to receive larger delayed ones. Factors that affect waiting time include self-statements and various methods of reducing attention to the tempting, immediately available reward. Children's understanding of effective delay strategies increases as they get older. The ability to delay gratification during the preschool years has been linked with cognitive, social, and coping abilities in adolescence.

14

Moral Development

ut our fish said, "No! No!
Make that cat go away!
Tell that Cat in the Hat
You do NOT want to play.

He should not be here.
He should not be about.
He should not be here
When your mother is out!"[1]

Many readers will recognize this excerpt from the well-loved children's book, *The Cat in the Hat.* It is a cold and rainy day; mother is out, and Sally and her brother are bored. A mischievous cat appears on the doorstep with promises of "good games" and amusing "tricks" that will undoubtedly annoy mother. Despite the warnings of the fish (the parental voice), the children let the cat into the house and all kinds of chaos ensues. The children grow concerned, but the cat shows up with an amazing machine that restores order and all is well, except, perhaps, the children's state of mind. They wonder—should we tell mother, or not? (And, the author asks, would you?)

Generations of children have felt the rush of adrenaline as the cat breaks rule after rule in this story and its sequel, *The Cat in the Hat Comes Back.* The stories appeal strongly to children who are old enough to know about family and societal rules and to spend increasing amounts of time unsupervised and outside of direct adult control. They delight in imagining what they might do—if they could be certain they would not be caught. Would they eat cake in the bathtub? Fly kites in the house? Juggle mother's china? Try on father's shoes?

The violations depicted by Dr. Seuss are relatively minor—and that is part of their appeal to young listeners. As we discuss shortly, by the time children are old enough to appreciate Dr. Seuss, they can already distinguish between the fanciful infractions of the Cat in the Hat and more serious transgressions, and most children would not find these latter sorts of violations so amusing. Why this is so, and how children come to understand various kinds of rules and to follow them even when parents or other authority figures are not around, is the focus of this chapter. ■

Morality involves issues of right and wrong, good and evil. If any society is going to survive, it must have rules that make clear to its citizens what is permitted and what is prohibited. Children's moral development involves the ways in which they come to understand and follow (or not follow) the rules of their social world. Until fairly recently, the study of moral development was left primarily to philosophers and religious scholars. Today, developmental psychologists also have a great deal of interest in this topic.

Contemporary research focuses on three facets of morality—affect, cognition, and behavior. Research on affect focuses on the emotions associated with moral behavior, such as empathy and guilt. Research into the cognitive underpinnings of moral development investigates how children think about what they and others do. Studies of this type focus on children's ability to examine a situation and to decide such questions as whether a person's behavior was appropriate and whether the person should be punished. Ultimately, of course, researchers aim to explain children's behavior—for example, why children steal, which children are more likely to start fights, and what factors promote sharing and cooperation among youngsters.

Increasingly, models of moral development incorporate all three facets. Historically, however, each of these facets has been studied in isolation. This is due in part to the ways the four major approaches to development have conceptualized moral development.

---

[1]From THE CAT IN THE HAT by Dr. Seuss, copyright TM and copyright © by Dr. Seuss Enterprises, L. P. 1957, renewed 1985. Used by permission of Random House Children's Books, a division of Random House, Inc.

THEORIES OF MORAL DEVELOPMENT

Two theoretical issues have dominated the study of moral development. One is whether children's moral beliefs and behaviors reside in the child and simply emerge over time or whether they reside in the culture and are transmitted to the child. The second issue involves the generality of moral rules. If they emerge from the child, they must have a large biological component, making them universal for all members of our species. On the other hand, if they develop within the social group, they are more arbitrary and thus can vary from one culture to the next. These two questions lie at the heart of much of the research on this topic.

Cognitive-Developmental Approaches

The cognitive tradition has been most concerned with the development of children's *moral reasoning* as they struggle with issues involving moral rules and social conventions. Some of these issues, such as physician-assisted suicide or the death penalty, are complex, with compelling arguments on both sides. Older children and adults will often examine the various arguments and weigh the evidence on all sides. As we have seen, however, young children often have difficulty taking multiple perspectives into account. They tend to consider only some of the information at hand and arrive at fairly simplistic solutions. Based on these observations, cognitive developmentalists have concluded that advances in moral reasoning abilities depend heavily on children's improving cognitive abilities. Their advancing moral understanding, in turn, is thought to produce more mature moral behaviors.

Three models have guided most of the cognitive research on moral development. Like so much else in developmental psychology, this line of inquiry began with the pioneering work of Jean Piaget.

Piaget's Theory   Piaget had just a brief foray into the realm of children's reasoning about moral issues, but his groundbreaking studies have proved very influential. Piaget's model of moral development grew out of his early work with children in Geneva, Switzerland, during the 1920s and 1930s. To investigate how children's conceptions of morality develop, Piaget used two very different methods.

One was a naturalistic approach in which he observed children playing common street games, such as marbles. Piaget closely examined how youngsters created and

Piaget studied common children's games as a way of examining children's conceptions of rules.

Moral dilemmas
Stories used by Piaget and others to assess children's levels of moral reasoning.

enforced the rules of their games, and he questioned them about circumstances under which the rules could be modified or even ignored. The second approach was more experimental and involved presenting individual children with **moral dilemmas** to solve. These took the form of short stories in which the child had to determine which of two characters was "naughtier." For example, in one story a little boy named Augustine accidentally makes a large ink stain on the tablecloth while trying to be helpful and fill his father's ink pot, whereas a little boy named Julian makes a small ink spot on the tablecloth while engaging in the forbidden act of playing with his father's pen.

From this research, Piaget developed a four-stage model of moral development that focused on the way children follow rules (Piaget, 1932). In the first stage (2 to 4 years), children have no real conception of morality. Much of their behavior involves play and imaginative games that have no formal rules, although at times they may invent certain restrictions as part of the play (e.g., all green blocks must be put in the same pail). The idea of following someone else's rules does not appear consistently until the second stage (5 to 7 years). When rule following emerges, children approach the concept in an absolute manner. Social rules are viewed as heteronomous (or externally dictated) commands presented by people in authority (usually parents), and they cannot be changed. Children in this second stage, called the stage of **moral realism,** do not think to question the purpose or correctness of a rule, even though they may not like to follow it. Thus, Piaget observed that younger children playing marble games were usually very inflexible about changing any rules, even if it would have made the game more convenient or more fun.

Moral realism
Piaget's second stage of moral development, in which children's reasoning is based on objective and physical aspects of a situation and is often inflexible.

Piaget noted two interesting characteristics that grow out of this absolutist orientation. Most children in the second stage evaluate moral situations only in terms of their physical and objective consequences. These children saw acts causing more damage as more morally wrong than acts causing less damage, regardless of the character's motives or intentions. Hence, the helpful Augustine was usually seen as naughtier than the disobedient Julian because he made the larger ink stain.

Another characteristic of this stage is **immanent justice.** Because these children believe so firmly in the authority of a rule, they feel that punishment must always occur when the rule is broken. Thus, if a child steals a cookie when no one is looking and then loses his baseball the following day, he may assume that he has been punished for the theft.

Immanent justice
Literally, inherent justice; refers to the expectation of children in Piaget's stage of moral realism that punishment must follow any rule violation, including those that appear to go undetected.

In Piaget's third stage (8 to 11 years), the child gradually realizes that rules are agreements created by people to help or protect one another. Obeying these rules is

A belief in immanent justice characterizes children's reasoning in Piaget's stage of moral realism.

PEANUTS reprinted by permission of United Features Syndicate, Inc.

no longer viewed as simply following someone else's orders but as an autonomous or personal decision to cooperate with others. Piaget observed, for example, that third-stage children could adapt marble-game rules if necessary to fit the circumstances of the moment (too many players, too few marbles, and so on).

Furthermore, at this stage children's more advanced cognitive abilities allow new factors to enter into their moral evaluations. What a person was trying or meaning to do—that is, the person's motives or intentions—may become as important as the outcome of the behavior. Accordingly, with increasing age, children were more likely to judge Julian's forbidden behavior naughtier, even though it caused less damage. Because the morality of following a rule is now evaluated in relation to other factors in the situation, Piaget referred to this third level as the stage of **moral relativism.**

In the final stage, which Piaget discussed only briefly, children become capable of developing new rules when the circumstances require it. They also begin to extend their moral reasoning beyond the personal level to larger societal and political concerns.

Piaget believed that both cognitive factors and social experience underlie the development of moral reasoning. As children move away from the egocentrism of early childhood, they become better able to evaluate the morality of a situation from multiple perspectives. Thus, the narrow focusing on unchangeable rules and objective consequences gives way to a broader, more flexible view of the world as the child gets older.

Piaget also emphasized the importance of social experiences in children's moral development. Of particular importance are children's interactions with peers. During their early years, children learn that parents usually dictate and enforce the rules of behavior. In their desire to please their parents, children adopt the belief that they live in a world where rules must be followed. But the one-way nature of this rule system keeps children from expressing their own points of view or appreciating that there can be different opinions on moral questions. Piaget believed that through their interactions with peers, children learn that there can be several perspectives on an issue and that rules are the result of negotiating, compromising, and respecting the points of view of other people.

Kohlberg's Model   A second influential cognitive theory of moral development was proposed by Lawrence Kohlberg, who drew much of his inspiration and methodology from Piaget's earlier work (Colby & Kohlberg, 1987; Kohlberg, 1969, 1981). Like Piaget, Kohlberg rejected the idea that moral development is a simple transmission of moral rules from parents and other adults to children.

Kohlberg's method, like Piaget's, involved presenting research participants with moral dilemmas to assess their level of moral reasoning. But Kohlberg's stories did not require a simple choice as to who was naughtier. Instead, they presented the child with a dilemma in which a story character must choose, for example, between obeying a law (or rule) and breaking the law for the benefit of an individual person. For example, in one story a poor man named Heinz must choose between stealing medicine from a drugstore to save the life of his sick wife and letting her die. For each dilemma, the child is asked to indicate what the character should do and why. In Kohlberg's model, the second question is more important because it presumably reveals the subject's level of reasoning.

From his research, Kohlberg concluded that moral reasoning develops in three predictable levels, termed **preconventional, conventional,** and **postconventional.** Within each level are two stages, each of which can be divided into a social perspective component and a moral content component. The model is described in Table 14.1. In his later writings, Kohlberg suggested that the sixth stage is actually more theoretical than real. Few individuals attain this level, and none of the individuals that Kohlberg studied ever displayed it. Nevertheless, Kohlberg speculated that a seventh stage of moral development might also exist that goes beyond conventional moral reasoning and enters the realm of religious faith (Kohlberg, Levine, & Hewer, 1983).

An important aspect of Kohlberg's model is how the two components of each stage interact. The social perspective component indicates the point of view from which the

Moral relativism
Piaget's third stage of moral development, in which children view rules as agreements that can be altered and consider people's motives or intentions when evaluating their moral conduct.

Preconventional level
Kohlberg's first two stages of moral development. Moral reasoning is based on the assumption that individuals must serve their own needs.

Conventional level
Kohlberg's third and fourth stages of moral development. Moral reasoning is based on the view that a social system must be based on laws and regulations.

Postconventional level
Kohlberg's final stages of moral development. Moral reasoning is based on the assumption that the value, dignity, and rights of each individual person must be maintained.

Table 14.1	Kohlberg's Stage Model of Moral Reasoning

	Social Perspective	Moral Content
Level I Preconventional		
Stage 1: Heteronomous morality ("Morality derives from power and authority.")	Children cannot consider more than one person's perspective. They tend to be egocentric, assuming that their feelings are shared by everyone.	This stage is equivalent to Piaget's moral realism. Evaluations of morality are absolute and focus on physical and objective characteristics of a situation. Morality is defined only by authority figures, whose rules must be obeyed.
Stage 2: Individualism and instrumental purpose ("Morality means looking out for yourself.")	Children understand that people have different needs and points of view, although they cannot yet put themselves in the other's place. Other people are assumed to serve their own self-interests.	Moral behavior is seen as valuable if it serves one's own interests. Children obey rules or cooperate with peers with an eye toward what they will get in return. Social interactions are viewed as deals and arrangements that involve concrete gains.
Level II Conventional		
Stage 3: Interpersonal conformity ("Morality means doing what makes you liked.")	People can view situations from another's perspective. They understand that an agreement between two people can be more important than each individual's self-interest.	The focus is on conformity to what most people believe is right behavior. Rules should be obeyed so that people you care about will approve of you. Interpersonal relations are based on the Golden Rule ("Do unto others . . .").
Stage 4: Law and order ("What's right is what's legal.")	People view morality from the perspective of the social system and what is necessary to keep it working. Individual needs are not considered more important than maintaining the social order.	Morality is based on strict adherence to laws and on performing one's duty. Rules are seen as applying to everyone equally and as being the correct means of resolving interpersonal conflicts.
Level III Postconventional		
Stage 5: Social contract ("Human rights take precedence over laws.")	People take the perspective of all individuals living in a social system. They understand that not everyone shares their own values and ideas but that all have an equal right to exist.	Morality is based on protecting each individual's human rights. The emphasis is on maintaining a social system that will do so. Laws are created to protect (rather than restrict) individual freedoms, and they should be changed as necessary. Behavior that harms society is wrong, even if it is not illegal.
Stage 6: Universal ethical principles ("Morality is a matter of personal conscience.")	People view moral decisions from the perspective of personal principles of fairness and justice. They believe each person has personal worth and should be respected, regardless of ideas or characteristics. The progression from stage 5 to stage 6 can be thought of as a move from a social-directed to an inner-directed perspective.	It is assumed that there are universal principles of morality that are above the law, such as justice and respect for human dignity. Human life is valued above all else.

SOURCE: Based on information from L. Kohlberg, "Moral Stages and Moralization: The Cognitive-Development Approach," 1976, in T. Likona (Ed.), *Moral Development and Behavior: Theory, Research, and Social Issues* (New York: Holt, Rinehart and Winston).

moral decision is made. For example, the child in the first stage is egocentric and sees all situations from a personal point of view. With development, the child becomes better able to appreciate the dilemma from the perspective of others or in terms of what is best for society as a whole. Advances in this area are thought to be related to the individual's cognitive development. But advances in perspective taking are not sufficient for moral reasoning to advance. They must be accompanied by development of the moral content component, which is assumed to be more strongly influenced by the child's experiences with moral situations. Kohlberg's theory thus resembles Piaget's in assuming that moral development results from a combination of improving cognitive skills and repeated encounters with moral issues.

Movement from stage to stage in Kohlberg's model closely follows the Piagetian process of accommodation. Movement occurs when the child can no longer handle new information within her current view of the world—or, in Piagetian terms, when she can no longer assimilate new information within her existing structure of schemes. Kohlberg's model places particular importance on *role-taking* opportunities, which occur when children participate in decision-making situations with others and exchange differing points of view on moral questions. The contrasting viewpoints produce cognitive conflict, which the child eventually resolves by reorganizing his or her thinking into a more advanced stage of reasoning. This process occurs gradually, so although any individual's reasoning can be generally classified into one of the stages, he or she may approach certain moral issues at a higher or lower stage.

Several other characteristics of Kohlberg's stage model are similar to Piaget's theory. For instance, each stage forms a *structured whole*, with children in that stage generally responding consistently to different dilemmas and situations. Also, the stages follow an *invariant sequence*, so all children experience them in the same order and with no regression to earlier stages. Finally, the progression of stages is *universal* for all people and all cultures.

Turiel's Model   Turiel's model has much in common with those of Piaget and Kohlberg, including the methods used to assess children's reasoning. Like Piaget and Kohlberg, Turiel and colleagues interview children about hypothetical situations. Some of these stories involve themes highly reminiscent of those in the stories of Piaget and Kohlberg (e.g., stealing, breaking a promise). Others involve other rule violations, such as undressing on the playground, not saying grace before snack, a boy's wanting to become a nurse and care for infants when he grows up, and the like (Turiel, Killen, & Helwig, 1987). The stories are designed to depict rule violations in three distinct *domains*.

The *moral domain* is concerned with people's rights and welfare. Issues concerning fairness and justice, such as lying, stealing, and killing, fall into this category. The *social domain* involves **social conventions,** the rules that guide social relations among people. Being polite, wearing appropriate clothing, and addressing people using the proper titles (Mrs. Jones, Dr. Brown, etc.) are behaviors that characterize this domain. There are also *matters of personal choice*, in which individual preferences take priority. These issues do not violate the rights of others or harm others, and they are not socially regulated (or only weakly so). In many American families, these issues include one's hairstyle, choice of friends, and leisure activities.

A central premise of Turiel's model is that children can distinguish among these domains from a very early age. Of particular interest is the distinction between moral rules and social conventions. In the models of Piaget and Kohlberg, rules and conventions initially fall within a single domain for children and do not divide into separate cognitive categories until later on. In fact, by age 3, children in many societies understand that moral violations (e.g., hitting another child) are more wrong than violations of social conventions (e.g., eating ice cream with fingers). And by age 4, children assert that a moral transgression would be wrong even if an adult did not see it and there was no rule to prohibit it (Smetana & Braeges, 1990).

How do children come to make these distinctions? According to Turiel, children's understanding of issues within the moral domain is thought to result from their social interactions—especially with peers—through both being victims of immoral acts and witnessing the consequences of such acts for others. Children's understanding of social conventions is assumed to result from their having experiences in a variety of social settings, where the conventions often differ from one setting to another. One very important context involves culture. The domain model predicts that children in all cultures will distinguish between the moral and conventional domains at an early age but that particular social conventions may vary from one culture to the next (Turiel, 2002; Turiel & Wainryb, 1994; Wainryb, 1993).

Social conventions
Rules used by a society to govern everyday behavior and maintain order.

Evolutionary and Biological Approaches

As we have seen, cognitive-developmental theorists view reasoning as the primary determinant of moral behavior. Theorists working within the evolutionary approach have a markedly different perspective. Much of their work has involved relating human behavior to that observed in other species, whose intellectual capabilities are very different from those of humans. Scientists working within this tradition contend that there must be some biological basis for human morality, because every known human culture has developed some kind of moral system to structure interactions among members. Moreover, they argue, it is implausible that the capacity for moral behavior suddenly appeared among humans in the absence of any semblance of moral behavior in other species. Thus, evolutionary theorists believe the rudiments of human morality must exist in the behavior of nonhuman primates. The behaviors that have attracted most of their attention include altruism (or prosocial behavior) and aggression (de Waal, 1996; Hinde, 1986; MacDonald, 1988b).

Altruism   Altruistic behaviors are those that benefit someone else but offer no obvious benefit—and perhaps even some cost—to the individual performing them. Giving money to a charity, sharing a candy bar, and risking one's life to save someone else's are examples. As mentioned in Chapter 1, this prosocial behavior has been a particular challenge to classical evolutionary models because self-sacrifice would not seem to fit with Darwin's proposed mechanisms. How can a behavior that does not increase a person's own chances of survival and reproduction be passed on in the species? It would seem, instead, that people who act selfishly and think first about themselves would be more likely to survive to pass along their genes. This dilemma, called the **paradox of altruism,** was discussed by Darwin and has been studied and debated ever since (Campbell & Christopher, 1996; Krebs, 1987; MacDonald, 1988a; Post et al., 2002).

Sociobiologists have attempted to resolve this problem by adding two concepts to Darwin's notion of survival of the fittest (Dawkins, 1976; Maynard Smith, 1976). **Kin selection** proposes that humans (and some other animals) behave in ways that increase the chances for the survival and reproduction of their genes rather than of themselves. A person can pass on genes either by reproducing or by increasing the reproductive chances of someone who has the same or similar genes. The more genes the second individual shares with the first, the more reasonable it becomes to try to save that individual's life (and reproductive capability). Therefore, we would predict that a mother should be more likely to risk her life for her child than for her husband, because her child shares many of her genes. Similarly, any family member, or kin, should be favored over any unrelated individual.

But people perform acts of altruism directed toward nonfamily members every day. How does evolutionary theory explain such behavior? Here, a process called **reciprocal altruism** comes into play. According to this idea, people are genetically programmed to be helpful because (1) it increases the likelihood that they will someday in turn receive aid from the person they helped or from some other altruistic member of their group, or (2) by helping someone else in their social group, they help ensure that genes similar to their own will be passed on in the species (Trivers, 1971, 1983).

Aggression   Aggression and mechanisms for controlling aggression have been another favorite area of research. One function of aggression is, again, to increase the likelihood of survival of an individual's genes—believed by some to be the most important evolutionary function of any behavior. Aggression serves this purpose in many ways, such as by helping the individual obtain food, protect the young, or preserve valuable hunting territory. In such cases, evolutionary processes clearly favor the stronger, smarter, or more skillful members of the species.

Aggression in many species can lead to physical combat. Some conflicts, however, do not progress to this point but are resolved when one animal displays threatening

Paradox of altruism
The logical dilemma faced by ethological theorists who try to reconcile self-sacrificial behavior with the concepts of natural selection and survival of the fittest.

Kin selection
A proposed mechanism by which an individual's altruistic behavior toward kin increases the likelihood of the survival of genes similar to those of the individual.

Reciprocal altruism
A proposed mechanism by which an individual's altruistic behavior toward members of the social group may promote the survival of the individual's genes through reciprocation by others or may ensure the survival of similar genes.

gestures (such as certain facial expressions and body postures) and the other animal backs down, perhaps making submissive gestures. Such behaviors also have adaptive value for both individuals—the attacker gains possession of the desired property, and the retreating animal avoids injury or death. In some species that form social groups, such as monkeys, a **dominance hierarchy** develops, in which each member of the group fits somewhere on a dominance ladder. Each monkey controls those lower in the hierarchy (often simply by threats) but submits to those higher on the ladder. Even though initially created through aggression, such a structure ultimately reduces the overall physical conflict that might otherwise occur in the group (Pellegrini & Bartini, 2001; Strayer & Noel, 1986). The structure and function of dominance hierarchies in children's social interactions has been a favorite focus of ethologists, as we will see in Chapter 16.

Dominance hierarchies are one way of managing conflicts of interest among group members. In recent years, ethologists have expanded their focus to include nonaggressive methods of managing conflict (Aureli & de Waal, 2000). For example, high-ranking male chimpanzees intervene in fights among juveniles and come to the aid of low-ranking females under attack. Researchers have also observed chimpanzees massively bark in protest when an adult male punishes a juvenile too roughly. And many primates have a repertoire of "peacemaking" behaviors, including special calls, facial expressions, and rituals such as kissing and embracing that serve to restore damaged relationships following conflicts. These more advanced methods of conflict management require the ability to keep track of past social exchanges and, some ethologists believe, at least a rudimentary capacity for empathy and sympathy (Flack & de Waal, 2000). As we will see, these emotions play a key role in linking moral reasoning to moral action among humans.

Environmental/Learning Approaches

The environmental/learning approach also has much to say about moral development. The essence of the social-learning view is that the social behaviors we traditionally label in terms of moral development are acquired and maintained through the same principles that govern most other behaviors. Although social-learning theorists agree that these processes are affected by developmental advances in cognitive abilities (Perry & Perry, 1983), they emphasize environmental mechanisms such as reinforcement, punishment, and observational learning (modeling and imitation). This emphasis argues against a stage model of development in which moral behaviors emerge according to an internal timetable that is universal for all children. Instead, it predicts that behaviors should develop more individually, depending primarily on each child's social environment and personal experiences.

Most of the research within the social-learning tradition has involved *moral conduct*—both prosocial and antisocial behaviors—rather than moral reasoning. This difference has resulted principally because social-learning theorists, unlike cognitive developmentalists, believe that moral reasoning and moral conduct are somewhat independent processes that can be influenced by different factors. As a result, social-learning theorists are less inclined to expect a child's moral behavior to show consistency across situations or between knowledge and conduct (Gewirtz & Pelaez-Nogueras, 1991).

The principal spokesperson for the social-learning account of moral development has been Albert Bandura, and most of the research conducted within this tradition is based on his views (Bandura, 1986, 1989, 1991b). Bandura's theory, described in Chapter 1, holds that reinforcement and punishment are major processes by which children acquire moral behaviors. In simplest terms, children are more likely to produce behaviors (prosocial or antisocial) that are approved or rewarded and tend to inhibit behaviors that are ignored or punished. In addition, children come to discriminate the reinforcement possibilities that exist in different settings, such as the praise parents provide for good grades versus the pressure peers may exert for skipping school.

Dominance hierarchy
A structured social group in which members higher on the dominance ladder control those who are lower, initially through aggression and conflict, but eventually simply through threats.

Another process that Bandura considers crucial for understanding moral development is observational learning. Children learn many of the rules and practices of their social world by watching others, such as parents and peers (Brody & Shaffer, 1982; Mills & Grusec, 1988). Also of interest is the role of the media and how children's behavior is affected by what they observe on television or read in books and magazines (Berkowitz, 1993; Huesmann & Eron, 1986).

With development, reinforcement and observational processes become internalized, and children learn to use them to regulate their own behavior. As we saw in Chapter 13, Bandura proposes that, through the use of evaluative self-reactions and self-sanctions, children come to regulate their behavior to match the moral standards they set for themselves.

We will have much to say about the contributions of social-learning researchers when we discuss children's prosocial development and aggression later in the chapter.

Sociocultural Approaches

The sociocultural approach to moral development focuses on how children come to understand moral and social rules and abide by them in the context of everyday activities. Like those working within the framework of social-learning theory, sociocultural researchers view moral development as a process of socialization. Sociocultural theorists believe children develop moral understanding during their interactions with parents and other more mature members of their communities. During these interactions, adults and other partners scaffold children's moral development by making salient the features of moral situations that are important for children to understand. Sometimes caregivers and others make explicit reference to rules (e.g., "Never hit small children"). Other times, the message is tacit, and children must draw inferences based on others' reactions to their transgressions. And, in some situations, caregivers engage in lengthy discussions with children that highlight why some act is right or wrong. In these ways, the moral concepts of a culture are communicated to children (Buzzelli, 1995; Edwards, 1987; Shweder, Mahapatra, & Miller, 1987; Tappan, 1997).

The sociocultural approach views moral concepts as part of a child's cultural heritage—much like conceptions of the self, norms for emotional expression, and language—that have been passed on from generation to generation. This does not mean that socioculturalists endorse the idea that cultures "stamp" their moral codes onto the young. Rather, like cognitive developmentalists, those working within this framework acknowledge that children actively construct their understanding of morality. But whereas cognitive developmentalists see this as a largely individual process fueled by children's social experiences, socioculturalists regard the process itself as a social one in which other people assist children's moral development by structuring and interpreting situations through the lens of a particular—not necessarily universal—moral system.

Much sociocultural research on moral development focuses on children's involvement in moral situations that naturally arise during everyday life. For example, researchers have devoted considerable attention to the ways caregivers foster children's moral development in the context of sibling interactions (Dunn, 1987; Edwards, 1987; Whiting & Edwards, 1988). Of growing interest is how participation in cultural institutions (such as schools, churches, and community service organizations) contributes to children's moral development (Eccles & Barber, 1999; Lewis, 1995; Youniss, McLellan, & Mazer, 2001). And, in keeping with Bronfenbrenner's ecological model, researchers working within this tradition are also concerned with how aspects of parents' lives, such as the nature of their employment, directly and indirectly affect children's involvement in prosocial and antisocial activities (Elder & Conger, 2000; Fletcher, Elder, & Mekos, 2000). We consider these contexts of children's moral development in greater detail later.

To Recap . . .

Cognitive developmentalists are most concerned with moral reasoning. They argue that moral development depends on cognitive development. In addition, moral development is marked by consistency across situations and between moral thought and moral conduct, and it proceeds through stages.

Piaget proposed a four-stage model. Children in the first stage show very little understanding of rule following. In the stage of moral realism, children view rules as absolute and base their moral evaluations largely on physical and objective aspects of a situation. Increased interaction with peers combines with a movement away from egocentric thinking in the stage of moral relativism, during which children approach rules more flexibly and are able to take subjective factors into account. In the final stage, moral reasoning can extend to hypothetical situations and to issues in the larger society.

Kohlberg's model consists of three levels of moral reasoning—preconventional, conventional, and postconventional—each composed of two stages. The two components of each stage, social perspective and moral content, represent cognitive and environmental influences, respectively. According to Kohlberg, movement from stage to stage occurs when the child experiences cognitive conflict; each stage represents a structured whole; the stages follow an invariant sequence; and the model is universal across cultures and sexes.

Turiel believes that children's moral reasoning involves several domains of social cognition, that even very young children can distinguish issues in the moral and societal domains, and that understanding such issues is influenced by their context and situational factors.

The evolutionary approach explains moral development in terms of evolutionary principles. For the so-called paradox of altruism, sociobiologists have argued that self-sacrificial behavior can be explained by a focus on the survival of the genes, rather than of the individual, through the processes of kin selection and reciprocal altruism. In the area of aggression, ethologists have been especially interested in how primate social groups—including humans—regulate conflict through dominance hierarchies and nonaggressive means of resolving disputes.

Social-learning theory emphasizes environmental influences on moral development and is most concerned with moral conduct. Bandura has been the most influential proponent of this view. Reinforcement and punishment principles, along with observational learning processes and self-regulation, are assumed to be the major determinants of children's moral behavior according to the social-learning model.

The sociocultural approach focuses on both moral reasoning and moral behavior. This approach emphasizes children's moral development in the context of everyday activities, such as family interactions and participation in cultural institutions. Sociocultural theorists view moral development as a social process in which other people assist children's moral development by structuring and interpreting situations for them.

MORAL REASONING

How well has research evidence supported the theories we have just examined? We investigate this question, along with other issues, with reference to three important topic areas: moral reasoning, prosocial behavior, and aggression. We begin with a discussion of research on children's moral reasoning.

Evaluating Piaget's Model

Piaget's account of children's moral development has generally fared well empirically. Numerous studies show that with age, children increasingly consider motives and intentions when evaluating the morality of actions (Berg & Mussen, 1975; Lickona, 1976). In addition, various cognitive measures, including perspective-taking and mental state understanding, have been associated with children's level of moral judgment (Dunn & Herrera, 1997; Kurdek, 1980).

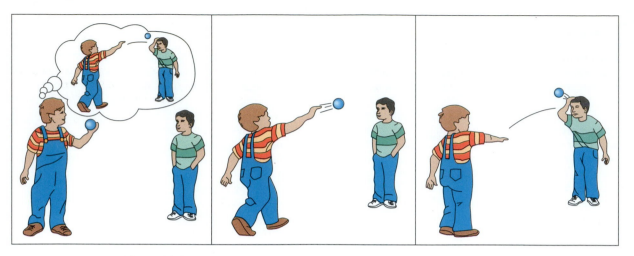

Figure 14.1

An example of drawings used to convey motive, action, and outcome in stories. When pictures such as these accompany stories involving moral dilemmas, even 4- to 6-year-olds sometimes use story characters' motives as a basis for evaluating their behavior. From "Factors Influencing Young Children's Use of Motives and Outcomes as Moral Criteria," by S. A. Nelson, 1980, *Child Development, 51,* 823–829. Copyright © 1980 by the Society for Research in Child Development. Reprinted by permission.

Piaget's idea that peer relations are an important context for moral development is also supported by research. As we discuss in detail later, children's peer relations provide many opportunities to tackle moral issues, such as kindness and unkindness, exclusion from play, failure to share, and so forth. Moreover, research supports Piaget's contention that children can achieve advances in moral reasoning via discussions with peers (Kruger, 1992; Walker, Hennig, & Krettenauer, 2000). And, consistent with his prediction, children with punitive parents who reinforce strict adherence to rules tend to display less mature moral reasoning and behavior (Hoffman, 1983, 2000; Walker & Taylor, 1991).

That said, some aspects of Piaget's theory have not held up well to scrutiny. As will become clear, parents play a far more important role—and a different one—in the development of children's morality than envisioned by Piaget. Piaget also appears to have underestimated the moral reasoning abilities of young children. For example, when Piaget's dilemmas are presented in ways that make intentions more *salient* by, say, stating the intention at the end of the story or adding pictures like that shown in Figure 14.1, even young children can take motives into account (Chandler, Greenspan, & Barenboim, 1973; Helwig, Zelazo, & Wilson, 2001; Jones & Thomson, 2001).

Other research shows that even young children consider a variety of factors in addition to motives and damage when assessing a character's morality. For example, young children believe that taking a toy from a friend is more wrong than taking a toy from a nonfriend (Slomkowski & Killen, 1992). Most important, children in many societies judge the breaking of moral rules more harshly that the violation of social conventions.

Evaluating Kohlberg's Model

Like Piaget's model of moral development, Kohlberg's theory is supported by a good deal of empirical research. Studies that use Kohlberg's methods and criteria for scoring responses generally show that individuals progress through the sequence proposed by Kohlberg in the predicted order (Armon & Dawson, 1997; Rest et al., 1999; Walker, 1989). One of the most convincing studies is an investigation that followed a group of boys from age 10 through adulthood (Colby et al., 1983). As shown in Figure 14.2, at age 10, the boys primarily used preconventional reasoning—emphasizing obeying authority or acting in one's own self-interest. From the ages of 14 to 24, Stage 3 reasoning predominated. During these years, they were concerned with conforming to expectations to win

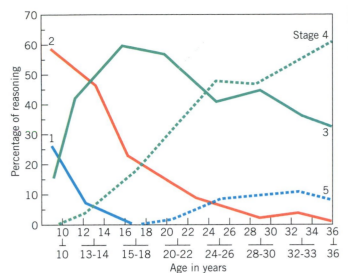

Figure 14.2

Mean percentage of moral reasoning by age group. From A. Colby, L. Kohlberg, J. C. Gibbs, and M. Lieberman, "A Longitudinal Study of Moral Judgment," 1983, *Monographs of the Society for Research in Child Development, 48,* 1–2. Reprinted by permission.

others' approval. Even by age 36, only a small number were reasoning at the postconventional (Stage 5) level.

There is also support for the idea that individuals will consistently apply the same level of moral reasoning across a range of problems (Walker & Taylor, 1991). A typical study, for example, found that 60% of the time, the reasoning of research participants across a series of moral dilemmas involved only one stage, and 90% of the time it involved two adjacent stages (Walker, DeVries, & Trevarthen, 1987). Nevertheless, an individual's level of reasoning is not always consistent. It can even be influenced by characteristics of the dilemma itself, such as whether the dilemma involves general moral issues or personally experienced problems (Carpendale & Krebs, 1995; Teo, Becker, & Edelstein, 1995).

A larger question raised by Kohlberg's theory is whether the model is universal, applying equally well to people of all cultures. Studies in nontechnological societies, for example, show that individuals rarely progress to the fifth stage, although many people in more technologically advanced cultures do make this progression (Snarey, 1985). This finding is not a major problem for Kohlberg's theory, which incorporates the idea that culture and experiences help determine what stage a person ultimately reaches (Kohlberg, 1984). A more serious concern is that Kohlberg's moral dilemmas do not adequately address certain moral issues and concepts found in other cultures (Snarey & Keljo, 1991).

In some Chinese cultures, for example, the conflict between what is right for the individual and what is right for society is not ideally resolved by choosing one over the other (as is required in Kohlberg's hypothetical dilemmas). Instead, the most appropriate solution is thought to be reconciling the two interests by arriving at a compromise solution (Dien, 1982). And according to Hindu beliefs in India, the very fact that Heinz finds himself in a dilemma is an indication of his prior sins or negligence, which he will not escape by committing further sinful actions, such as stealing (Shweder & Much, 1987). Kohlberg's model, then, is not applicable to everyone in these cultures.

Applicability should be universal not only across cultures but between sexes as well. Recall that Kohlberg's theory focuses on justice reasoning as the best indicator of moral development. In one early study, Kohlberg reported that the moral reasoning of females generally was not as advanced as that of males (Kohlberg & Kramer, 1969). Not surprisingly, the notion that females engage in less sophisticated moral reasoning than males was not well received, particularly by women. In response, Carol Gilligan asserted that women's moral reasoning is not lower than that of males, just different from it. Specifically, Gilligan claimed that females are socialized to an "ethic of care" that is devalued in Kohlberg's system. She argued that females evaluate Kohlberg's dilemmas in terms of issues of responsibility and care—whether someone has an *obligation* to do something based on the value of a personal relationship rather than on whether someone has the right to do something based on laws or rules (Gilligan, 1982).

Contrary to Kohlberg's early findings and Gilligan's premise, research has provided little evidence that males and females score differently on Kohlberg's tasks at any age (Dawson, 2002; Jadack et al., 1995; Walker, 1991, 1995). Moreover, themes of justice and care appear in the responses of both sexes. However, consistent with Gilligan's views, females do tend to focus more on issues of caring about other people in their moral judgments (Garrod, Beal, & Shin, 1990; Gilligan & Attanucci, 1988; Smetana, Killen, & Turiel, 1991). This is particularly true when individuals reflect on moral issues in their own lives (Jaffee & Hyde, 2000; Wark & Krebs, 1996).

Evaluating Turiel's Model

Turiel's model, too, is supported by a considerable body of evidence. The claims that moral reasoning involves several independent domains of social cognition and that children distinguish between them from an early age have found support in many studies. For example, preschool children in the United States generally believe that breaking a moral rule (such as stealing) is always wrong, whereas breaking a social convention (such as eating with your hands) depends on the setting and situation. Likewise, they believe that it is wrong to do something immoral whether or not an explicit rule about it exists; ignoring a social convention, however, is acceptable if there is no specific rule prohibiting it. Similarly, in situations involving harm and justice (moral rules), children judge that peers, parents, and other adults all have the authority to intervene to protect another person. And they believe it is illegitimate for a teacher or other authority figure to compel a child to violate moral rules. In contrast, children believe teachers and other authority figures have the right to make their own rules in their own arenas of influence. So teachers can make rules in the classroom but not in children's homes. Finally, when asked which is more wrong, a minor moral misdeed (stealing an eraser) or a major social-conventional transgression (wearing pajamas to school), most children choose the former (Catron & Masters, 1993; Laupta & Turiel, 1993; Smetana & Braeges, 1990; Smetana, Schlagman, & Adams, 1993; Tisak & Turiel, 1988).

Turiel's belief that children's moral reasoning will be influenced by the context in which it takes place similarly has much support (Turiel & Wainryb, 1994). For example, when the violation is presented as part of a story, children view the breaking of a moral rule as always wrong. However, when the same rule is broken within their real-life experience, children are more willing to consider other factors (such as motives or intentions) in determining the wrongness of the act (Smetana et al., 1993). Likewise, physical harm (pushing someone down) is viewed by children as always wrong, whereas psychological harm (calling someone stupid) is viewed as wrong when it occurs in real life but as much more acceptable when it occurs as part of a game (Helwig, Hildebrandt, & Turiel, 1995).

Children in Western societies appear to reason in ways consistent with Turiel's model. But do children in all cultures of the world draw similar distinctions among moral rules, social conventions, and matters of personal choice; and do they make these distinctions at similar ages? The evidence here is intriguing and the focus of considerable debate. On the one hand, researchers using culturally appropriate versions of Turiel's stories have replicated his findings in a diverse array of societies (Turiel, 1998). Still, research also shows considerable cultural variability in how children classify various kinds of rule violations. For example, compared with middle-income children, those in lower-income families are less likely to draw clear distinctions between moral rules and social conventions and view fewer issues as matters of personal choice (Nucci, 1997). These findings suggest that there are some acts involving harm and justice that are universally regarded as wrong (e.g., breaking promises, destroying property) but that the category of moral transgressions may be wider in some cultures than others.

A problem with this interpretation is that actions that are unjust or that harm other people are not always judged to be immoral, whereas other acts that seemingly harm no

Table 14.2	Transgressions Rated Most and Least Serious by Hindu Brahman 8- To 10-Year-Olds

Serious Transgressions

The day after his father's death, the eldest son had a haircut and ate chicken.

A family member eats beef regularly.

A widow in a community eats fish two or three times a week.

Less Serious Transgressions

A person meets a foreigner who is wearing a watch. He asks how much it costs and whether the foreigner will give it to him.

In school, a girl drew a picture. One of her classmates came, took it, and tore it up.

Not a Transgression

A boy played hooky from school. The teacher told the boy's father and the father warned the boy not to do it again. But the boy did it again, and the father beat him with a cane (the father's actions).

SOURCE: Based on information from R. A. Shweder, M. Mahapatra, and J. G. Miller, "Culture and Moral Development," 1987, in J. Kagan and S. Lamb (Eds.), *The Development of Morality in Young Children* (pp. 40–41), Chicago: University of Chicago Press.

one are. To illustrate, consider some of the transgressions rated as most and least serious by Hindu Brahman 8- to 10-year-olds (see Table 14.2). To understand how a child would come to judge a widow's eating fish as seriously wrong, it is necessary to place judgments of morality in a broader context of beliefs, including religious beliefs. Hindu beliefs specify that eating fish will stimulate the sexual appetite and lead the widow to behave immorally instead of fulfilling her obligation to seek salvation so she can be reunited with the soul of her husband (Shweder et al., 1987). Instances such as these have led some critics to question whether the tendency to draw clear distinctions among moral, social, and personal is culturally universal.

Researchers working within Turiel's social-cognitive domain approach have responded to this criticism by expanding their focus beyond straightforward rule transgressions to complex issues that involve the coordination of fairness and rights with judgments about social group, customs, norms, conventions, and personal choice. These issues include democracy and rights (Prencipe & Helwig, 2002), acts of subversion and oppression (Turiel, 2002), and religion (Nucci & Turiel, 1993).

In addition, there is a growing body of literature on how people of different ages evaluate decisions based on beliefs that differ from their own (Wainryb, 1993; Wainryb & Ford, 1998; Wainryb, Shaw, & Maianu, 1998). In these studies, people are asked to evaluate the actions of people who believe to be true such things as that misbehaving children are possessed by evil spirits, that mental retardation is contagious, and that only by enduring physical hardship do boys become men. These studies consistently show that from childhood onward, people are remarkably tolerant of seemingly immoral behavior based on factual beliefs that differ from their own. However, at no age do individuals view alternative moral beliefs as justification for immoral behavior.

Distributive Justice and Retributive Justice

We have been focusing on the ideas of Piaget, Kohlberg, and Turiel, but the moral concepts assessed by their methods are not the only areas of moral reasoning that have been of interest to psychologists. Here we briefly consider research on two other aspects of children's moral reasoning: distributive justice and retributive justice.

Distributive Justice   The question of how to distribute a limited amount of resources among a group of deserving people—called *distributive justice* (Damon, 1983)—is usually assessed using a reward-allocation task. In the typical study, a group of children perform a task together for which they are to receive some sort of payment.

One child is then asked to divide the pay among the participants. Usually the situation is designed so that the children have performed different amounts of work.

Children's reasoning regarding distributive justice appears to develop in several stages. Up to about 4 years of age, children's reward distribution is characterized by self-interest; they tend to take a large portion of the earnings for themselves, regardless of the amount of work they contributed. At 5 or 6 years of age, children begin to divide rewards according to an equality principle, with all children receiving the same share, whatever their input. By about 7 years of age, children start to use equity as the basis for reward allocation; children who did more work are given more of the reward, although not always in the correct proportions.

Children's allocation of rewards appears to be influenced not only by their cognitive development—for example, their understanding of proportions—but also by situational variables. For example, children distribute more reward to those whom they consider to be in greater need or whom they see as kind and helpful (Enright et al., 1984; McGillicuddy-De Lisi, Watkins, & Vinchur, 1994; Nisan, 1984). Also, if children believe they will interact again with someone who has done relatively little work, they tend to reward that person using the equality rule rather than the more advanced equity rule (Graziano, 1987).

Retributive Justice   Children's concepts of justice have also been examined with a view toward determining what factors children use in assigning blame or responsibility—that is, their concept of *retributive justice.* Even young children appear to approach such problems in essentially the same way as adults.

When presented with a story about a character who broke a rule, both children and adults first examine whether any harm or damage was done. If none occurred, they typically do not pursue the issue of responsibility and justice. When damage is perceived to have occurred, people in both age groups then attempt to determine whether the story character was responsible. If no blame can be assigned to the character, punishment typically is not considered necessary. If, however, the character is deemed responsible for the harm, both children and adults proceed to the questions of whether punishment is warranted and, if so, how much. At both ages, then, they appear to follow a three-step line of reasoning: harm? responsibility? punishment? (Shultz & Darley, 1991; Shultz & Wright, 1985; Shultz, Wright, & Schleifer, 1986).

Although their approach to punishment situations may be similar to that of adults, children predict that adults' approach will be different from their own. For example, when children were presented with several stories in which a character had bad intentions and produced a bad outcome, they rated the character's behavior negatively. When asked to predict how adults would evaluate the behavior, the children predicted that the adults would also view the behavior negatively but would focus more on the outcome of the bad behaviors than on the character's motives and would evaluate the character's behavior more harshly than they had. These predictions proved to be inaccurate when the children's parents were then also asked to rate the story characters (Saltzstein et al., 1987).

These findings indicate that children's moral reasoning in situations involving responsibility for damage does not represent a simple imitation of what they expect from adults. Furthermore, children's predictions about the harshness of adults' judgments may reflect their view of adults as the creators and enforcers of social rules.

Social and Family Influences on Moral Reasoning

Researchers working within each of the four theoretical traditions agree that social factors play a role in moral development, although they disagree as to the nature and importance of that role. In this section, we consider several of the most important functions of the social world in the development of morality.

Peers   Both Piaget and Kohlberg argued that children's interactions with peers are an important impetus for moral growth. Researchers have examined this issue using a

variety of approaches. One indirect test of the role of peers in children's moral development is whether children who have greater peer experience engage in more advanced moral reasoning. And, indeed, correlational studies generally have demonstrated a positive relation between aspects of a child's peer interactions (such as popularity) and the child's level of moral maturity (Dunn, Cutting, & Demetriou, 2000; Enright & Satterfield, 1980; Schonert-Reichl, 1999). It is likely, however, that the direction of influence between peer relations and moral development goes both ways: Children who reason competently about moral issues are likely to be attractive companions and friends.

Other researchers have followed in Piaget's footsteps and observed children's social interactions around moral events. There have been numerous studies of this type in homes, in schools, and on playgrounds involving children as young as age 2 through junior high (Much & Shweder, 1978; Nucci & Nucci, 1982a, 1982b; Nucci & Turiel, 1978; Turiel, 2002). These studies consistently show that situations involving issues of fairness and harm arise frequently in children's interactions with peers. Moreover, from a very early age, children respond to moral transgressions, usually by talking about the injury or loss experienced by the victim and asking the perpetrator to consider how it would feel to be the victim of the transgression. More work on children's moral reasoning about peer relations is described in Box 14.1.

Other researchers have examined the impact of peer interaction on moral reasoning using an experimental approach (Berkowitz, Gibbs, & Broughton, 1980; Kruger 1992; Kruger & Tomasello, 1986; Walker et al., 2000). In these studies—which typically involve older elementary school children or adolescents—researchers begin by interviewing children individually about some type of moral dilemma. Various materials have been used, including Kohlberg's dilemmas and situations personally experienced by the interviewees. The children are then paired with peer partners and asked to discuss and reach consensus about the dilemmas. Following the discussion, each partner is interviewed again, sometimes months or even years later.

Studies using this approach show that discussing moral issues with peers can foster advances in children's moral reasoning. Findings also suggest that interactions among peers with somewhat different perspective on the problems are most beneficial (Berkowitz, et al., 1980). And there is some evidence that peer interactions that promote moral growth differ in important ways from parent–child interactions associated with higher levels of moral reasoning (Walker et al., 2000).

Children's Reasoning about Peer Exclusion

Exclusion by peers is a normal experience for most children. As early as the preschool years, children prefer some playmates to others. During middle childhood and adolescence, children sort into social groups or cliques that—by definition—include some people and exclude others. Many groups organized for children by adults also practice exclusion. Girls are excluded from the Boy Scouts, for example, and less skilled soccer players are excluded from the traveling team.

Peer exclusion has some elements of a moral situation. After all, as anyone who has ever been excluded by others knows, exclusion can cause harm. Being excluded makes a child feel bad (psychological harm). It can also restrict opportunities to acquire valuable skills and knowledge and to form social relationships that can facilitate professional and social advancement later in life. Considered from this perspective, exclusion can also be unfair. Acts of exclusion that occur in the absence of harmful *intent,* however, may not appropriately be classified as moral events.

Are children and adolescents aware of the moral complexities of exclusion? In earlier work, researchers established that most people generally view the choice of friends as a personal—not a moral—issue (Nucci, 1996; Smetana & Bitz, 1996). But what if a child refuses to consider someone as a potential friend not on the basis of shared interests or likability but because of gender or race? Do children view this as a personal decision because it concerns friendship? Or do they view it as a moral transgression because it may hurt feelings or depend on unfair criteria?

To study this issue, Melanie Killen and colleagues interviewed nearly 300 4th-, 7th-, and 10th-grade public school students in a suburban area in Maryland. The students were from working-class and middle-income homes and from ethnically diverse schools (Killen et al., 2002). The researchers presented the students six scenarios depicting exclusion in three contexts—friendship, the peer group, and the school.

BOX 14.1

On the
Cutting
EDGE

In half of the scenarios, the exclusion was based on gender, and in half it was based on race.

The friendship scenario involved a White boy who did not want to be friends with a new neighbor because the neighbor was either a girl or Black. The peer group scenario involved a music club, either all boys or all Whites, whose members did not want to let a girl or a Black join. The school scenario involved a town that did not allow girls or Blacks to go to school. After hearing each scenario, students were asked whether it was "Okay" to exclude the child and were also asked to explain their answer.

At all ages, children and adolescents judged exclusion differently depending on whether it occurred in the context of a friendship, the peer group, or the school. The students almost universally regarded exclusion in school on the basis of either gender or race as unacceptable. In the friendship and peer group contexts, children judged exclusion on the basis of gender as less negative than exclusion on the basis of race (see Figure 14.3).

The justifications children offered for the judgments also varied somewhat across the three contexts, though it should be noted that most justified their judgments in terms of moral rules. Students were especially likely to refer to fairness in response to exclusion in school. As one fourth-grade boy responded, "It's not all right because it's not like girls have this certain disease. There is no difference between anybody and everybody should be able to go to school" (p. 52).

Justifications based on personal choice appeared only in the friendship context, and most often when exclusion was based on gender. "I think it's up to him even though I don't think it's very nice for him to not hang out with Sally just because she's a girl. But I do think it's his choice" (10th-grade male) (p. 52).

References to social convention, or group functioning, occurred most often in the context of the peer group, espe-

Parents As we have seen, discussions of moral issues with peers can foster moral growth. Research shows that dialogues with parents can as well (Holstein, 1972; Parikh, 1980). For example, in one impressive investigation, Lawrence Walker and John Taylor recruited children ranging in age from 6 to 16, along with their parents, to participate in two laboratory sessions 2 years apart. First, both parents and children responded individually to a set of Kohlberg's moral dilemmas and a second, real-life dilemma they had recently experienced in their own lives.

Following the individual interviews, the children and their parents were asked to discuss one of the Kohlberg dilemmas on which they had displayed some disagreement during the individual interviews, as well as a real-life dilemma that had been volunteered by the child. (The experimenters asked for the children's permission first.) The same procedure was repeated 2 years later.

The study resulted in a number of interesting findings. One was that parents lowered their level of reasoning during the family conversations, whereas children raised theirs. These findings are consistent with Vygotsky's notion of a zone of proximal development. By aiming their reasoning at—but not beyond—the upper bounds of the child's capabilities, parents provided a scaffold for the child's acquisition of a more advanced moral understanding.

cially with respect to exclusion on the basis of gender. "I think that Mike and his friends are right for not letting her in the club because it's their club. . . . If she wanted to make her own group, then she can do it and make it so no boys are allowed" (seventh-grade boy) (p. 56).

A particularly interesting finding was that although children of all ages viewed exclusion negatively, older children were less likely to express a negative view. Compared with the younger students, 10th-graders were less likely to evaluate exclusion in the context of friendships and the peer group negatively. This was especially true for exclusion based on gender.

This study raises a number of intriguing questions. One question has to do with a long-standing issue in the study of moral development—the relationship between moral reasoning and moral behavior. The children in this study were remarkably uniform in the opposition to exclusion, and they explained their opposition in terms of moral rules. In real life, however, most children do practice exclusion. More research is needed

to understand how children and adolescents reconcile their moral beliefs about exclusion with their social practices.

Another question is whether the same findings would emerge in a different sample or geographic region. The students in this study lived in a suburb among families of varied cultural backgrounds and attended ethnically diverse schools. As one African American adolescent put it, "I live with Cambodians, Ethiopians, and Asians, all kinds of people, and everyone has a heart" (p. 99). Perhaps these experiences fostered a greater appreciation for moral issues related to race (Pettigrew & Tropp, 2000).

Finally, what are we to make of the finding that negative ratings of exclusion in the context of friendship and peer relations decline with age? The answers to all these questions await further study. In the meantime, one thing is clear—friendships and peer groups are important contexts for the development of children's moral reasoning.

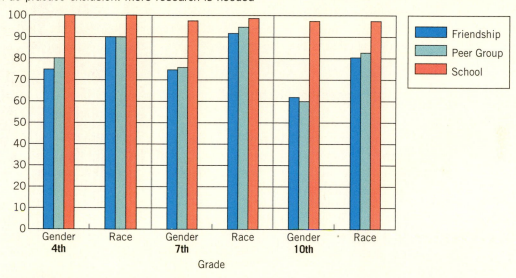

Figure 14.3

Proportion of negative judgments about exclusion by gender and race. Based on M. Killen, J. Lee-Kim, H. McGlothin, and C. Stangor, 2002, "How Children and Adolescents Evaluate Gender and Racial Exclusion," *Monographs of the Society for Research in Child Development, 67,* 4.

Walker and Taylor also found that the nature of the interactions differed across the two kinds of dilemmas. When discussing the hypothetical dilemma, parents tended to challenge children's reasoning and adopt a rather opinionated lecturing-type style. During discussions of the child's real-life dilemma, in contrast, parents tended to be more supportive, focusing on drawing out the child's opinion and coming to understand it. Interestingly, the quality of the interactions on the real-life dilemmas—but not the hypothetical ones—predicted children's moral reasoning 2 years later (Walker & Taylor, 1991).

Another way parents influence children's moral understanding is through discipline for misconduct. When parents punish children, they generally hope that children will not only avoid engaging in the inappropriate behaviors again but also gradually assume responsibility for enforcing the rules. As we saw in the previous chapter, the development of self-regulation often involves learning to control the desire to engage in forbidden behavior. And just as Vygotskians and others have argued, children seem to accomplish this by *internalizing* the rules and prohibitions presented by their parents (Buzzelli, 1995; Hoffman, 1994; Tappan, 1997).

The effectiveness of discipline in promoting internalization of the parents' values and morals depends on a number of factors (Grusec & Goodnow, 1994). One involves the style of punishment parents employ. Three general classes of parental discipline have been identified (Hoffman, 1970, 1984). *Power assertion* involves the use of commands, threats, and physical force. *Love withdrawal* refers to the use of verbal disapproval, ridicule, or the withholding of affection from the child. *Induction* involves reasoning with the child to explain why certain behaviors are prohibited and often encourages feelings of guilt in the child by pointing out how the misbehavior may have caused harm or distress to someone else.

Evidence from several studies indicates that American children who have been disciplined with an induction approach display the most advanced levels of moral reasoning; love-withdrawal techniques result in somewhat lower levels, and power assertion produces the least mature forms of reasoning (Boyes & Allen, 1993; Hart, 1988b; Weiss et al., 1992).

Another factor that affects how well discipline promotes internalization involves the child's temperament. Recent studies have identified *fearfulness* as an inborn trait that influences whether children will internalize their parents' rules (Kochanska, 1993, 1995, 1997). For fearful children, who are prone to being timid and anxious, gentle discipline and the avoidance of power tactics seem best to promote the development of conscience (internalization) in the child. For fearless children, the best disciplinary approach capitalizes on the child's positive motivation to accept the parents' values and so involves a cooperative and responsive approach by the adult. The goodness-of-fit concept discussed in Chapter 12 thus applies here as well. The type of discipline that is most effective with a particular child is the one that best "fits" with the child's personality and temperament (Kochanska & Thompson, 1997).

Moral Reasoning and Moral Conduct

A central issue in the study of moral development is the relationship between moral reasoning and moral behavior. When this issue is raised, the scenario that typically comes to mind is one in which an individual presumed to possess sophisticated powers of moral reasoning—a politician, a religious figure, or a business leader, for example—

A Study in Moral Character: Are There "Good Kids" and "Bad Kids"?

Are there "good kids" and "bad kids," or does children's morality depend on the situation and circumstances in which they find themselves? This question formed the basis for a classic early study of children's character, conducted by Hugh Hartshorne and Mark May (1928–1930). The question these researchers raised is really one of cross-situational consistency. We might state it this way: Does morality represent a consistent personality trait that each of us carries with us? Cognitive-developmental theorists, we have seen, expect cross-situational consistency to be high because they assume that children's moral behavior is guided by their current levels of moral reasoning. Environmental/learning theorists expect much less consistency, arguing that children's behavior is more likely to be influenced by the risks and rewards that exist in a given situation.

Hartshorne and May explored this problem by exposing over 10,000 children (ages 8 to 16) to situations that provided opportunities for dishonesty. The settings ranged from homes to schools to churches, and the behaviors of interest were various forms of lying, cheating, and stealing. Each situation was designed so that dishonest behavior would "pay

BOX 14.2

Classics of
Research

off" for the child, but the apparent risk of being detected varied; in reality, the researchers were always aware of whether the child was being honest. The children were also interviewed as to their attitudes regarding dishonesty.

The results seemed very straightforward at the time. The investigators reported almost no consistency across situations for the children they studied. The fact that a child stole in one context was not useful in predicting whether the child would cheat in another. And there was very little correspondence between children's verbal pronouncements of moral values and their actual behavior. Hartshorne and May thus concluded that children's moral behavior does not reflect a personality trait but is situation-specific, depending primarily on the circumstances at hand.

This conclusion has since been modified to some degree. A reanalysis of the project's data indicated that some degree of consistency did exist particularly for situations that were similar to one another (Burton, 1963, 1984). Nevertheless, it remained clear that the children observed in this classic study were, for the most part, willing to adjust their moral conduct to fit the demands of the moment.

engages in immoral activity. But when we study moral development among children, we often see that the opposite can also be true—children often behave in moral ways without being able to explain very clearly why.

The different theoretical perspectives address this issue somewhat differently. Piaget believed that thought follows from action, and so he anticipated that children's behavior should initially at least be more advanced than their reasoning. Kohlberg, in contrast, believed that moral thought and moral action should be consistent (although not perfectly so), and he claimed that the evidence shows that they are (Kohlberg, 1987; Kohlberg & Candee, 1984). Social-learning theorists make a different prediction. They argue that moral reasoning and conduct may show some correspondence but that the correspondence need not be very strong, because what children say and what they do involve somewhat independent processes (Bandura, 1991b; Liebert, 1984).

The evidence on this question has not supported Kohlberg's position. Studies based on Kohlberg's method have found only a modest relation between a child's level of moral reasoning and the child's moral behavior (Blasi, 1980, 1983; Rholes & Lane, 1985; Straughan, 1986). In most children, this relation simply does not hold.

Children's moral behavior is undoubtedly influenced by many factors. One of the most important is one we have largely neglected so far—moral affect or emotions. We consider the role of affect in the discussions of the development of prosocial and aggressive behavior that follow.

To Recap . . .

Research generally supports Piaget's model but suggests that he somewhat underestimated younger children's moral reasoning. When, in the classic moral dilemmas, the story characters' motives are made salient, even preschoolers can use this information as a basis for moral evaluations.

Experimental studies generally support Kohlberg's contention that moral reasoning displays consistency across situations and that children proceed through the stages in an invariant order. The universality of the model is less well documented, and in some cultures Kohlberg's theory clearly does not apply.

Turiel's domain theory likewise has found support in experimental studies. Research suggests that children do distinguish between moral and societal rules from an early age. Their moral reasoning also appears to be influenced by contextual factors, including culture.

Children's allocation of rewards seems to follow a predictable sequence, moving from self-interest to equality and then to equity, but it is also influenced by situational variables. Children's reasoning about application of punishment uses much the same pattern found in adults: Was harm done? If so, was the person in question responsible? If so, is punishment warranted?

Interactions with peers, especially in situations of moral conflict, stimulate the development of moral reasoning. Dialogue with parents, particularly about real-life dilemmas, also fosters moral growth. Parental disciplinary techniques affect moral reasoning and the degree to which children internalize parents' standards. Induction is most effective in stimulating moral development and internalization among children in the United States. The temperamental trait of fearfulness in the child helps determine the type of discipline that will promote the development of conscience.

The relation between moral reasoning and moral behavior is a fundamental issue in moral development research. Kohlberg asserted that the two should be closely related, but this assertion has been largely unsupported.

PROSOCIAL BEHAVIOR

We turn now to moral conduct—how children act as opposed to how they think. Specifically, we examine **prosocial behavior**—those acts that society considers desirable and attempts to encourage in children. Three forms of prosocial behavior that have been studied extensively are helping (which includes comforting and caregiving), sharing, and

Prosocial behavior
The aspect of moral conduct that includes socially desirable behaviors, such as sharing, helping, and cooperating; often used interchangeably with altruism by modern researchers.

conflict resolution (Eisenberg & Fabes, 1998). It is widely believe that the roots of prosocial behavior lie in the capacity to feel empathy and sympathy, and so we begin our discussion of prosocial development with these topics.

Empathy and Sympathy

Most theorists acknowledge that moral action requires more than moral thoughts; it also requires what have come to be known as moral emotions. Two of the moral emotions are empathy and sympathy. **Empathy** is the ability to vicariously experience another's emotional state or condition. **Sympathy,** in contrast, involves feeling concern for another in reaction to his or her situation or emotional state without necessarily sharing the same emotions (Eisenberg, 1986). As we saw earlier, evolutionary theorists believe that the capacity to feel these emotions is present in some nonhuman primate species (Flack & de Waal, 2000).

Martin Hoffman (2000) has proposed a five-stage model of the development of empathy. A precursor of empathy is apparent during the first months of life when infants reflexively cry on hearing the cries of other infants. Interestingly, infants do not cry when they hear their own tape-recorded crying, nor do they react as strongly to equally noxious nonsocial stimuli (Martin & Clark, 1982; Sagi & Hoffman, 1976).

In the second stage, infants respond to another's distress as though they themselves were in distress. During this developmental interval, infants feel empathic distress but lack clear boundaries between the self and others. Consequently, infants respond to others' distress by comforting themselves (e.g., sucking their thumbs) or seeking comfort from caregivers.

During the third stage, as children develop a sense of themselves as distinct individuals, their reactions to others' distress change. When confronted with someone who is distressed, they realize the distress is the other's, not their own. However, because young children have difficulty distinguishing between their own and others' thoughts and feelings, the help they offer tends to reflect what they would like and not necessarily what is most helpful to the other person. For example, one 14-month-old responded to a crying friend with a sad look, then gently took the friend's hand and brought him to his own mother, although the friend's mother was nearby (Hoffman, 1978, 2000). Hoffman contends that during this stage, children begin to feel sympathy for others.

During the fourth stage of empathy development, children come closer to feeling what others are actually feeling because they are now understand that other people have inner states that are different from their own. Children can now offer more appropriate

Empathy
The ability to vicariously experience another's emotional state or condition.

Sympathy
Feeling of concern for another in reaction to the other's situation or emotional state, not necessarily involving an experience of the other's emotional state.

Empathy involves the ability not only to understand someone else's feelings, but also to share them.

help and comfort, though we should note that the understanding that emerges during this stage is not *always* put to its best use. A child may, for example, understand very well why a sibling is distressed and how best to comfort her—and choose to do the exact opposite (Dunn, 1988)!

During the final stage, which emerges in middle childhood, children are able to consider the broader features of other people's lives. Thus, they are able to empathize with those they imagine to have generally sad or unpleasant lives because of illness, poverty, and the like. Children at this age are also able to classify people into groups and so come to comprehend the plight of entire classes of people, such as the homeless, social outcasts, and victims of war.

Development of Prosocial Behavior

We look next at the development of prosocial behavior in the three major areas mentioned earlier: helping, sharing, and conflict resolution.

Helping   The results of empirical studies on the development of early helping behavior are largely consistent with Hoffman's five-stage theory of the development of empathy. Of particular note are a series of longitudinal studies conducted by Carolyn Zahn-Waxler and colleagues that tracked changes in children's reactions to others' distress during the second and third years of life (Zahn-Waxler & Radke-Yarrow, 1982; Zahn-Waxler et al., 1992; Zahn-Waxler et al., 2001).

Each of the studies involved maternal reports of their children's reactions when confronted with the distress of another in the context of everyday activities. In some of the studies, these reports were supplemented by home and laboratory visits during which mothers and experimenters staged events designed to elicit concern. For example, the mother might pretend to cry, cough, or choke, or feign an injury to her knee. Coders recorded the children's reactions to the incidents. Typical behaviors included hugs or kisses, words of comfort (e.g., "You be okay"), putting on a bandage, asking if the mother was all right, facial expressions of concern, and expressions of personal distress.

As Hoffman's theory predicts, when confronted with someone distressed, the younger toddlers primarily became distressed themselves. But many of the older toddlers actually attempted to help the victim, although the help was not always appropriate, as when one youngster tried to feed his cereal to his ailing father (Zahn-Waxler, Radke-Yarrow, et al., 1992). As the children grew older, both the frequency and sophistication of the helping increased. With age, children were increasingly likely to express their concern verbally, fetch a bandage or a blanket, or ask an adult to intervene.

Similar age-related increases in helping have been reported in studies of siblings and peers. Young children show an increased tendency to comfort a sibling in distress between the ages of 15 and 36 months—but only if the child was not the cause of the sibling's distress (Dunn, 1988). Observations in preschools reveal that young children will also comfort peers in distress, especially if the pair have an ongoing friendly relationship (Farver & Branstetter, 1994).

Further evidence for the early development of prosocial behavior comes from observations of children as they follow parents and older siblings about during their daily activities (Rogoff, 1990, 2003). Toddlers are often eager to help others perform household chores (Rheingold, 1982). There are, however, cultural variations in how often young children have the opportunity to "pitch in" and how others respond to their offers of help. In communities where children are integrated into the lives of adults, toddlers' imitation of adult activities is expected and encouraged, and even small children are assigned simple chores (Rogoff, 2003). As we will see shortly, studies in a variety of cultures show that participation in chores is associated with prosocial behavior (Elder & Conger, 2000; Whiting & Whiting, 1975).

Together, these findings paint a very positive picture of the prosocial tendencies of young children. But are older children and adolescents equally enthusiastic helpers? Research suggest that generally they are: Helping actually increases with age. Moreover, compared with younger children, older children and adolescents are more likely to help even at some cost to themselves, perhaps because older children are better able to recognize possible physical, psychological, or moral gains from assisting others (Eisenberg & Fabes, 1998).

Of course, individuals—whatever their age—do not always offer to help even when they could. Obstacles to helping at all ages include not knowing how to help, lack of confidence in one's ability to help, and fear that helping will make the situation worse or otherwise be unappreciated. Additionally, children and adolescents sometimes fail to help because they feel that someone else is responsible or that it is not appropriate for them to help (Eisenberg & Fabes, 1998). Studies show that children are more likely to help when they have been shown how to assist and when they have been assigned responsibility to help (Peterson, 1983a, 1983b; Staub, 1971). We return to this topic later in our discussion of intervention programs aimed at peer bullying and victimization.

Sharing   Another prosocial behavior that is of considerable interest to researchers and caregivers alike is sharing. As we all know, young children do not always readily share. Still, like helping, sharing emerges remarkably early. Babies as young as 1 year will often hand a toy or some of their food to their mother or to another child. Sharing can serve a variety of interpersonal functions. For young children who have as yet only limited verbal capabilities, sharing is one way in which to initiate or maintain social interactions with adults or peers (Eckerman, Davis, & Didow, 1989; Hay et al., 1995). It also may be a means by which children resolve conflicts among themselves (Butovskaya et al., 2000; Caplan et al., 1991). Children are especially likely to share when they are involved in a give-and-take relationship with the other person and have experienced some "receiving" as well as "giving" (Hay & Murray, 1982; Levitt et al., 1985). Interestingly, similar "rules" appear to guide food sharing and grooming among chimpanzees (de Waal, 1997, 2000). Finally, as with helping, older children are more likely to share than are younger ones (e.g., Benenson et al., 2003; Eisenberg & Fabes, 1998).

Conflict Resolution   A third type of prosocial behavior is conflict resolution. Although estimates vary, conflict among peers and sibling appears to be a fairly regular occurrence during childhood and adolescence (Buhrmester & Furman, 1990; DeHart, 1999; Hartup et al., 1988; Hay, 1984; Laursen & Collins, 1994). Because many of these conflicts occur away from adult eyes, there must be some mechanism in place to keep children's conflicts from escalating out of control.

Conflict is in fact resolved in a variety of ways. The methods can be placed in three broad categories. *Negotiation* includes compromise and intervention by a third party, such as another peer or a teacher. *Disengagement* includes withdrawal (walking away from the dispute) and shifting the focus or topic. *Coercion* occurs when one party gives in to the demands of another, sometimes in response to threats or other aggressive ploys (Jensen-Campbell, Graziano, & Hair, 1996; Vuchinich, 1990).

A recent meta-analysis of studies of peer conflict among North American samples examined how use of these resolution strategies changes with age (Laursen, Finkelstein, & Betts, 2001). Children tend to resolve disputes with coercion and to refrain from disengagement. Adolescents, in contrast, tend to favor negotiation, and they employ disengagement and coercion equally often. Young adults strongly favor negotiation and use coercion infrequently. The study also showed that children tend to display higher conflict resolution skills when reasoning about hypothetical dilemmas than in actual disputes, where even adolescents tend to rely on coercive techniques. The particular methods used also vary depending on the relationship (e.g., friends, acquaintances). We discuss this issue further in Chapter 16.

The developmental trends revealed by the meta-analysis make sense. As children's verbal abilities, understanding of mental and emotional states, and self-regulatory capacities advance, we would expect greater use of negotiation. The meta-analysis is limited, however, in that the studies examined failed to consider the aftermath of peer conflict.

Of growing interest are the ways children "make peace" with one another following conflict (Verbeek, Hartup, & Collins, 2000).

Postconflict peacemaking behaviors vary considerably, both among nonhuman primates and human children. **Peacemaking** refers to a friendly postconflict reunion between former opponents. Peacemaking can follow the conflict immediately or can occur after a delay or cooling-off period. In some species, peacemaking involves conspicuous behaviors that are rarely observed in other social contexts, whereas in other species the behaviors are more implicit (de Waal, 1993). Studies show that children use both explicit and implicit behaviors to reconcile with peers. We have already mentioned one—sharing toys. Others include invitations to play, apologies, and hugs.

Recent studies of peacemaking reveal interesting cultural variations, as well as some peacemaking techniques not previously found among North American samples (Butovskaya et al., 2000). Research teams observed postconflict reunions among children in daycare centers and schools in four diverse cultural communities. The samples—all middle-income—included preschool-age children in large cities in the United States and Sweden and 6- and 7-year-old elementary school children in two Russian communities. One group was composed of ethnic Russians living in a large city. The other group was composed of Kalmyk children. Traditionally nomadic herdsman, Kalmyks now live in villages and towns near the Caspian Sea. Town and village residents often regard themselves as kin. Kalmyks practice Lamaism, a form of Buddhism.

The observations revealed significant peacemaking in each of the four communities. Opponents were more likely to seek each other out for peaceful interaction than children who had not engaged in conflict, and the interaction usually was initiated within 2 minutes of the conflict. Older children were more inclined to make peace than younger children. This was most readily observed among the Swedish sample, which included children ranging in age from 3 to 6 years. Postconflict peacemaking occurred 60% of the time among 5- and 6-year-olds and 42% of the time among 4-year-olds, compared with only 17% of the time among 3-year-olds.

When compared with their Russian counterparts, the Kalmyk children showed a greater peacemaking tendency. This tendency may reflect the stronger emphasis the Kalmyk place on peaceful coexistence, perhaps because of their religion or their social organization. Kalmyk and Russian children also used ritualized peacemaking rhymes, called *mirilka*. During the peacemaking rituals, children held hands and recited rhymes, such as "Make peace, make peace, don't fight, if you fight, I'll bite, and we can't bite since we're friends" (Butovskaya et al., 2000, p. 249). Sometimes, Kalmyk peers brought the opponents together and encouraged them to recite the rhymes.

Across the four cultural groups, girls and boys did not differ in their peacemaking tendency. However, girls and boys sometimes differed in the methods they used to make peace. One approach that was used often by boys but rarely by girls was acting silly to make others laugh. We briefly consider the general issue of sex differences in prosocial behavior next.

Peacemaking
A friendly postconflict reunion between former opponents often characterized by invitations to play, hugs, apologies, object sharing, and silliness.

Gender Differences in Prosocial Behavior
One of the most widely held gender stereotypes is that females are more kind, generous, and caring than males (Eagly, Wood, & Diekman, 2000; Shigetomi, Hartmann, & Gelfand, 1981). In fact, however, empirical evidence suggests only a modest sex difference favoring girls (Eagly & Crowley, 1987; Eisenberg & Fabes, 1998). As infants and toddlers, girls tend to display more personal distress, empathy, and other expressions of concern than boys, though the difference is not great (Zahn-Waxler et al., 2001). Sex differences in empathy grow larger with age and are greatest when measured by self-report. Girls are also more likely to be kind and considerate but are not more inclined to share, comfort, or help (Eisenberg & Fabes, 1998).

Biological Determinants of Prosocial Behavior

We earlier discussed evolutionary explanations of a species-wide capacity for prosocial behavior, but individual differences in prosocial behavior also exist. Some children seem

Although girls have the reputation of being more generous, research indicates that girls are only slightly more altruistic than boys.

inordinately caring and compassionate, whereas others appear to care little about the welfare of other beings. Are these differences solely due to socialization, or might biological factors also play a role?

There is some evidence that genetic factors do contribute to individual differences in prosocial behavior. Studies involving adult twins have found greater similarity in self-reported empathy and altruism among pairs of identical twins than among fraternal twin pairs (Davis, Luce, & Kraus, 1994; Rushton et al., 1986). Similar findings were reported in a recent study of toddler twins (Zahn-Waxler et al., 2001). Identical twins received more similar scores on measures of empathic concern and prosocial behavior than did fraternal twins.

Researchers doubt there is a gene for kindness, so how might genetic factors produce differences in prosocial behavior? Individual differences in prosocial responding are likely related to differences in temperament. Studies have linked children's tendencies to feel negative emotions such as anxiety, sadness, and guilt, as well as their responses to these emotions, with their tendency to feel empathy and sympathy. Children who experience negative emotions but are not overcome by them are especially likely to feel sympathy for the plight of others. In contrast, children who are overcome by high levels of negative emotions tend to focus on themselves (Eisenberg et al., 1998; Eisenberg et al., 2000). Of course, feeling bad is not always sufficient to prompt action. Inhibited or cautious children may not always be able to bring themselves to help someone even if they want to (Barrett & Yarrow, 1977; Denham & Couchoud, 1991).

Cognitive and Affective Determinants of Prosocial Behavior

Although the capacity for prosocial behavior is grounded to some extent in biology, there exists extensive evidence that other factors also play a role. In this section, we consider cognitive and emotional factors that may affect prosocial development.

Empathy   Early studies that relied on self-report found little relation between empathy and prosocial behavior (Eisenberg & Miller, 1987). In recent years, however, the assessment of empathy has focused on physiological responses. Researchers have, for example, measured children's emotional arousal and facial expressions as they viewed videotapes designed to induce feelings of sympathy for a story character. Children whose responses were strongest were shown to be most likely to share or to display other prosocial behaviors when given the opportunity (Eisenberg & Fabes, 1998; Fabes et al., 1994; Miller et al., 1996).

Prosocial Reasoning

We have seen that cognitive-developmental psychologists believe that moral reasoning processes lie at the heart of moral development. Their models would predict, then, a positive relation between a child's moral reasoning and his or her altruistic behavior (Krebs & Van Hesteren, 1994).

Investigations of this issue have typically evaluated the child's level of moral reasoning through the use of *prosocial dilemmas*. These stories differ from those of Piaget and Kohlberg in that they place less emphasis on breaking rules or laws. Instead, the story character usually must decide whether to help someone, often at some personal expense. For example, one story requires a little girl to choose between helping a hurt child and being on time for a birthday party (Eisenberg, 1982).

Investigations comparing children's prosocial reasoning with their prosocial behavior have generally found a small positive relation (Eisenberg, 1986, 1987; Eisenberg et al., 1995). This finding is similar to studies pertaining to Kohlberg's justice reasoning dilemmas, which reveal a modest relation between how children think about moral issues and how they act.

Mental State Understanding

The ability to understand a situation from someone else's point of view is also basic to cognitive-developmental explanations of prosocial behavior. For example, in several studies, children who were better at telling a story from another person's point of view were more prosocial with peers (Eisenberg, 1986, 1987; Eisenberg et al., 1995). Understanding (but not necessarily experiencing) the feelings and emotions of another person is also correlated with prosocial behavior (Garner, Jones, & Miner, 1994; Moore & Eisenberg, 1984). And children who do well as preschoolers on various types of "mind-reading" tasks (for example, the false belief tasks described in Chapter 7) are better able to resolve conflicts with friends during elementary school (Dunn, 1999).

Sociocultural and Family Determinants of Prosocial Behavior

Over the course of childhood and adolescence, prosocial behaviors increase in frequency. Clearly, developmental changes in children's affective and cognitive capabilities contribute to this increase. But increases in prosocial responding also coincide with changes in children's social experiences. Among these are changes in the settings children inhabit, the roles they play, the kinds of activities they engage in, and the expectations of others. In this section, we describe some ways that children's social experiences contribute to prosocial development. We begin the discussion with opportunities for prosocial behavior.

Opportunities for Prosocial Behavior

One context in which children can practice prosocial behavior is the home. Do children who routinely perform chores and contribute to the functioning of the household develop a stronger prosocial orientation than peers not assigned chores? The answer appears to be a qualified yes, if their work involves benefits to other family members (Grusec, Goodnow, & Cohen, 1996) One source of supporting evidence is the Six Cultures Study described in Chapter 12 (Whiting & Whiting, 1975). In this study, researchers observed children between the ages of 3 and 11 in six different countries. They found that children in Kenya, Mexico, and the Philippines displayed more nurturant behavior (e.g., offering help and support) than children in Okinawa, India, or the United States. The factor most strongly associated with nurturing behavior was the assignment of chores to children, especially the care of infants. Moreover, the degree to which children within each culture participated in the infant care and household work was predictive of their level of nurturance.

There are a number of plausible reasons why participation in child care and household work might foster a prosocial orientation. One possibility, suggested by the researchers themselves, is that infants naturally elicit nurturant behavior (whereas caring for older children may elicit controlling, aggressive behavior). A more recent study of Iowa farm youth suggests some other possibilities (Elder & Conger, 2000).

This study followed more than 400 seventh-graders over a period of 6 years during a time when many Iowa farmers were struggling economically. As is true in many farm families, the farm youth in this study made a significant economic contribution to the household through their labor on the farm and the money they earned by raising livestock or in part-time jobs. Even as seventh-graders, the adolescents took their responsibilities quite seriously. Most rated their chores as very important, a higher rating than that provided by agemates from nonfarm families. When interviewed as 12th-graders about what made their work important, many of the youth focused on the importance of being counted on and the experience of being interconnected with others. As one boy noted, "If I help the family, it saves the family money as whole. So we can take the money we save . . . and apply it to maybe . . . a new truck" (Elder & Conger, 2000, p. 90).

The opportunity to fulfill productive roles also fostered a sense of adult status among the farm youth. For many adolescents, voluntary community service may serve a similar function and provide an opportunity to practice helping others and perhaps increase feelings of prosocial commitment (Johnson et al., 1998; Yates & Youniss, 1996).

Communication of Values   Another way parents may foster a prosocial orientation is through the values they communicate to children (Grusec & Goodnow, 1994). As we have already seen, children whose parents employ inductive techniques and talk with them about the impact of their actions on others display more mature moral reasoning than parents who use other disciplinary techniques (Hoffman, 1975; Krevans & Gibbs, 1996). Compelling support for the power of parental communication of values comes from studies of people who show unusual levels of altruism. For example, during interviews after World War II, individuals who risked their own lives to rescue Jews from the Nazis in Europe often reported having learned values of caring, generosity, and respect for all human life from their parents and other influential adults. Neighbors who were not involved in rescue activities mentioned learning these values far less often (Oliner & Oliner, 1988).

Modeling   Of course, children learn not only from what parents say but also from what they do. Laboratory studies have shown that children share more or are more helpful after observing a model performing similar behaviors (e.g., Eron & Huesmann, 1986; Lipscomb, McAllister, & Bregman, 1985; Radke-Yarrow & Zahn-Waxler, 1986). Children are especially likely to imitate adults with whom they have a positive relationship.

Some psychologists have attempted to use modeling in applied settings to increase prosocial behavior. Children's educational television, for example, often includes moral themes and prosocial messages (Jordan, Schmitt, & Woodard, 2001) A recent meta-analysis of 34 studies (with a total sample of over 5,000 children) found that viewing prosocial TV programming has a modest effect on prosocial behavior. The effects were greater with the use of supplemental materials, such as guided lessons, games, and general discussion designed to enhance program content (Mares & Woodard, in press).

Reinforcement   Will children be more altruistic if their altruism is reinforced? This straightforward question has been answered positively many times in laboratory studies, demonstrating clear effects of reward and praise on children's prosocial behaviors (Eisenberg & Murphy, 1995; Gelfand & Hartmann, 1982). Praise is especially effective in promoting altruism if it emphasizes that the child is a generous or helpful person ("You were a very nice girl for sharing your candy") (Mills & Grusec, 1989). Applied psychologists have used reward programs as a way of increasing prosocial behaviors in the classroom and other naturalistic settings (CPPRG, 1999; Walker, Colvin, & Ramsey, 1995).

But do reinforcement processes play a role in maintaining altruism under everyday circumstances, when no psychologist is involved? One study investigating preschool children's naturally occurring altruistic behavior found that peers often responded positively to this type of behavior, such as by smiling, thanking the child, or doing something nice in return (Eisenberg et al., 1981). Similar research conducted in home settings has indicated that mothers, like peers, often respond to altruistic behavior with some form of praise or verbal approval (Eisenberg et al., 1992; Mills & Grusec, 1988). Recent research shows that parental reinforcement is key to adolescent involvement in community activities, particularly when the parents themselves do not participate (Fletcher, Elder, & Mekos, 2000). And older siblings who are cooperative and helpful also tend to promote prosocial interactions among younger family members (Dunn & Munn, 1986).

Finally, even in the absence of external rewards or approval, reinforcement processes can still be in operation. Witnessing the joy experienced by someone we have just helped, for example, or sharing that person's relief from distress can reinforce our helping behavior. Whether pure altruism ever occurs remains a matter of debate, but there can be no doubt that much of children's prosocial behavior occurs because it rewards the giver as well as the receiver.

To Recap . . .

Many theorists believe the roots of prosocial, or altruistic, behaviors lie in the capacity for empathy and sympathy. Hoffman has proposed a five-stage theory of empathy development. During the first stage, infants cry reflexively on hearing another infant cry. During the next stage, others' distress produces personal distress, and infants respond by seeking comfort themselves. In the third stage, toddlers interpret the distress of another correctly but often respond inappropriately because of limited ability to understand others' mental states. In the fourth stage, children recognize others' distress and now respond in appropriate ways. In the fifth stage, children empathize with the general conditions of people's lives and with classes of largely unknown people.

Major categories of prosocial behavior are helping, sharing, and conflict resolution. Clear evidence for helping behavior emerges during the second year of life, when toddlers try to comfort others who are distressed. Generally, helping increases over the course of childhood and adolescence. Sharing also emerges early—by the end of the first year of life. Sharing serves a number of interpersonal functions. Children are most likely to share with friends and those who have given them help in the past. Like helping, sharing increases with age. Another prosocial skill is conflict resolution. During childhood, children tend to use coercion to resolve conflicts. This gradually gives way to the more prosocial approach of negotiation. Studies of children's peacemaking show that children are able to resolve past conflicts and repair damaged relationships.

There is little empirical support for a gender difference in prosocial behavior, although girls tend to display more empathy and concern for others. This sex difference is largest on self-report measures.

Biology, affect, cognition, and socialization all contribute to the development of prosocial behavior. It is believed that genes influence prosocial development through temperament. Studies have shown modest relations between prosocial behavior and empathetic distress (measured physiologically), prosocial reasoning, and children's mental state understanding. Parents contribute to children's prosocial development by providing opportunities to practice prosocial behaviors and by modeling and reinforcing prosocial behavior.

AGGRESSION

Aggression
Behavior that is intended to cause harm to persons or property and that is not socially justifiable.

At the opposite end of the spectrum from prosocial behavior is the antisocial behavior of **aggression.** Whether it takes the form of destroying a preschool playmate's block tower, teasing and taunting by a fourth-grader, or fighting between teenage gangs, aggression is a common and important aspect of child development that has been studied extensively (Coie & Dodge, 1998; Loeber & Farrington, 1998).

Defining Aggression

Psychologists define *aggression* as behavior that is intended to cause harm to persons or property and that is not socially justifiable. Notice that by this definition aggression is always based on a social judgment that takes into account both the individual's motives and the context in which the behavior occurs (Coie & Dodge, 1998; Parke & Slaby, 1983).

Hostile (retaliatory) aggression
Aggression whose purpose is to cause pain or injury.

Instrumental aggression
Aggression whose purpose is to obtain something desired.

Relational aggression
Aggression designed to damage or disrupt social relationships.

Aggression can be divided into types based on its form and function. For example, verbal aggression, involving name calling, teasing, threats, and so forth, can be distinguished from physical aggression, such as hitting, kicking, and biting. In addition, aggression aimed specifically at inflicting pain or harm is termed **hostile aggression** (or **retaliatory aggression,** if it is carried out in response to the aggression of someone else), whereas aggressive behavior whose purpose is to obtain something (e.g., shoving another child away from a desired toy) is termed **instrumental aggression** (Berkowitz, 1993). A form of aggression that has been studied extensively in recent years is **relational aggression,** whose purpose is to damage or manipulate social relationships, such as through rumor spreading, threats to withdraw friendship, or social exclusion (Crick, 1995; Crick & Grotpeter, 1995).

Age and Gender Differences in Aggression

The various types of aggression are worth distinguishing because they occur in different proportions among children of different ages and sexes. Children begin to use physical aggression, such as hitting and pushing, to resolve conflicts by the end of their second year of life (Tremblay et al., 1999). Physical and instrumental aggression decline over the preschool years, whereas verbal and hostile aggression become more common.

The decline in physical aggression in the preschool years coincides with an improved ability to resolve conflicts verbally and to control emotions and actions. Most children continue to show a decline in overt physical aggression during elementary school, although some children manifest serious problems with aggression and other forms of antisocial behavior at this age (Cairns et al., 1989; Loeber & Hay, 1993). This decline continues for most children through adolescence, although there is a marked increase in serious acts of violence (Coie & Dodge, 1998; Haapasalo & Tremblay, 1994). Adolescent violent crime peaks at age 17, when 29% of males and 12% of females report engaging in at least one serious violent act. As can be seen in Figure 14.4, there is a large difference in the number of males and females who engage in violent behavior during adolescence and early adulthood. This sex difference in rates of aggression begins long before adolescence and is observed in all cultures of the world. Boys begin to display more physical and verbal aggression as preschoolers and continue to do so throughout the elementary-school years (Loeber & Hay, 1997).

Also, beginning with the preschool years and extending into adolescence, girls display more relational aggression than boys do (Crick et al., 1999; Crick, Bigbee, & Howes, 1996; Crick, Casas, & Mosher, 1997). In the later elementary grades, another gender difference begins to become apparent. Aggression by boys toward other boys becomes increasingly physical in nature, but aggression by boys toward girls drops markedly. Aggression by girls remains primarily relational and is directed

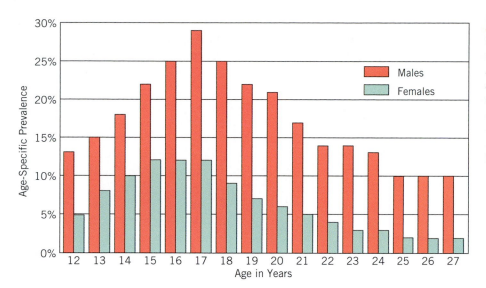

Figure 14.4

Prevalence of self-reported violence for males and females of different ages. From J. D. Coie and K. A. Dodge, "Aggression and Antisocial Behavior," 1998, in W. Damon (Series Ed.) & N. Eisenberg (Vol. Ed.), *Handbook of Child Psychology: Volume 3. Social, Emotional, and Personality Development* (5th ed.), New York: Wiley. Reprinted by permission.

predominantly toward other girls (Cairns et al., 1989; Galen & Underwood, 1997; Underwood, 2003).

Biological Determinants of Aggression

Much of the research on children's aggression has been concerned with identifying its causes. Here we consider the determinants that have primarily a biological basis and then move on to social and cognitive influences.

An individual's level of aggression has proved to be remarkably stable over many years (Farrington, 1994; Loeber & Stouthamer-Loeber, 1998). Longitudinal research indicates that peer nominations of aggression at age 8 are good predictors of aggression and various other antisocial behaviors at age 30 (Eron et al., 1987). This degree of stability lends itself well to a genetic or biological explanation of the behavior. Among the mechanisms that have been suggested are hormones, genes, and inborn temperament styles.

Hormones   The fact that males in all cultures of the world are more aggressive than females certainly suggests that hormones play some role in the development of aggression. And, indeed, numerous studies have shown a link between levels of testosterone and *adult* aggressiveness (Archer, 1991). Evidence for a link between hormone levels and aggression among adolescent samples, however, is mixed. Some studies have found that boys rated as more aggressive by their peers or parents have higher-than-average levels of testosterone (Olweus et al., 1988; Sussman et al., 1987), whereas other studies have found no evidence that increases in testosterone are related to increases in aggression (Halpern et al., 1994). To further complicate matters, there is some evidence that testosterone levels are more closely linked to social dominance than aggression per se and that

In boys aggression is often physical, whereas in girls it is often verbal.

hormone levels can change in response to particular kinds of competitive experiences (Coie & Dodge, 1998). If hormone levels do contribute to individual differences in aggression, the process is likely to be indirect and to vary with developmental status (Archer, 1994).

Genes   The strongest evidence that aggression is genetically mediated comes from work with animals in which scientists (or animal breeders) breed animals specifically to be high or low in aggressiveness (Cairns, MacCombie, & Hood, 1983). The situation appears to be far more complicated in humans, for whom environmental factors play a key role in the development of aggression and for whom the behaviors regarded as aggressive vary widely in form and function.

Nonetheless, there is evidence that genes do play a role in human aggression. Numerous studies of adult twins have reported more similar levels of aggression among identical (monozygotic) twins than among fraternal (dizygotic) twins or other siblings (DiLalla, 2002). Recent twin studies involving children have also demonstrated significant genetic effects on aggression (Deater-Deckard & Plomin, 1999; Taylor, Iacono, & McGue, 2001; Vierikko et al., 2003). Moreover, genes have a stronger influence on aggression than on other forms of antisocial behavior, such as delinquency. In addition, they play a stronger role during childhood and adulthood than during adolescence, when environmental factors matter a great deal (Miles & Carey, 1997).

Temperament   One manifestation of genetic effects is temperament. We saw in Chapter 12 that some babies are born with "difficult" response styles. They fuss, cry, and are more demanding than other infants of the same age. This personality dimension is quite stable across childhood, prompting researchers to investigate whether it bears some relation to the development of aggressive behavior.

One team of researchers tested this hypothesis by asking a group of mothers to rate their 6-month-old infants on a temperament questionnaire that allowed the researchers to identify difficult babies. Over the course of the next 5 years, the same mothers periodically evaluated their children's aggressive behavior. As predicted, the early temperament ratings were quite good predictors of which children would display greater amounts of aggression (Bates et al., 1991). More recent longitudinal studies have reported similar results extending into adolescence (Caspi et al., 1995; Olson et al., 2000).

As children move into the preschool years, other temperament dimensions, such as impulsivity and poor regulatory control, become predictive of later aggressiveness. Children who are highly impulsive during early childhood are more likely to engage in fighting and delinquency during early adolescence, aggression and criminal activity during late adolescence, and violence in adulthood (Caspi et al., 1995; Tremblay et al., 1994).

Why might these early temperament dimensions be predictive of later antisocial behavior? One possibility is that a difficult early temperament reflects an underlying problem that is stable and manifests itself in different ways at different ages. Another possibility is that difficult babies are not really difficult; they are just seen that way by parents. Parents may either directly or indirectly communicate to such children that they are difficult, which may motivate the children to behave in ways that match parental expectations. Still another possibility is that children with difficult temperaments elicit or evoke harsh and punitive parenting. Evidence for such a phenomenon has been reported (Ge et al., 1996; O'Connor et al., 1998; Rubin et al., 2003). We discuss the impact of parenting on the development of aggression next.

Sociocultural and Family Determinants of Aggression

Social and situational factors are very important determinants of aggressive behavior. One common argument against the ethologists' claim that aggression is innate in humans, for example, is that there are some cultures in which interpersonal conflict is very rare (Montague, 1968).

As might be expected, social-learning theorists believe that aggression is controlled largely by learning principles (Bandura, 1986, 1989, 1994). Their research indicates, for example, that gender differences in physical aggression may result because boys—by their own report—expect less disapproval for this sort of behavior and are less bothered by the disapproval when it occurs (Boldizar, Perry, & Perry, 1989; Perry, Perry, & Weiss, 1989). Environmental influences can also be illustrated by a consideration of two familiar contexts in which aggressive behavior develops: family interactions and the viewing of violence on television.

Family Processes   Children's aggression often stems from their interactions with parents and siblings. Parents of aggressive children have been found to deal with misbehavior more through power-assertion methods of discipline, using physical punishment, than through verbal explanation or reasoning (Chamberlain & Patterson, 1995; Rubin, Stewart, & Chen, 1995; Schwartz et al., 1997). For social-learning theorists, this finding suggests that two processes may be at work in these situations. First, the parents may be modeling aggressive behavior to their children, who go on to imitate what they see. Second, these parents may be interacting with their children in ways that actually promote aggression. There is evidence that these processes may continue from one generation to the next, with aggressive, socially withdrawn children more likely to have aggressive children themselves (Serbin et al., 2002).

An example of the first of these processes can be found in a study of two neighboring communities in Mexico. In one village, the level of adult conflict and violence was very high, whereas the other village was unusually peaceful and nonviolent. As predicted, the behavior of the children in these communities paralleled that of the adults. In the violent village, children engaged in more frequent play fighting and real aggression, suggesting that they were imitating the behaviors they observed in their parents and other adults (Fry, 1988).

The second process is illustrated by a series of observational studies conducted by Gerald Patterson and his colleagues (Patterson, 1982; Patterson, Reid, & Dishion, 1992; Snyder & Patterson, 1995). Patterson found that families of aggressive children commonly display a troublesome pattern of interactions, which he terms **coercive family process**. These households are characterized by very few friendly, cooperative comments or behaviors and by a high number of hostile and negative responses. Commonly, the parents spend a good deal of time scolding, berating, or threatening the children, and the children nag or disobey the parents and tease or frustrate one another.

In such environments, aggression is used as a means of stopping or escaping from these sorts of aversive experiences. For example, a little girl may tease and taunt her brother, who punches her to make her stop, which leads his mother to spank him for punching his sister. Thus, both the children and parents use aggression to control one another and to get what they want.

Patterson refers to this pattern as *coercion* because the family members achieve their goals through threats, commands, and other coercive behaviors rather than through cooperative, prosocial means. Young boys who learn this style of interaction at home—and who fail to learn more positive interpersonal skills—also display aggression in other settings and often go on to delinquency and other serious forms of antisocial behavior (Conger et al., 1994; DeBaryshe, Patterson, & Capaldi, 1993; Patterson, 1995; Vuchinich, Bank, & Patterson, 1992). The relation between this sort of parenting and later aggression in young girls is not as clear, for reasons that are not yet understood (Keenan & Shaw, 1997; McFayden-Ketchum et al., 1996).

Peer Relations   Aggression is considered a social problem primarily because it causes harm to others. But psychologists have also warned that aggressive children, by failing to acquire appropriate social skills, run the risk of being rejected by their peer group and becoming outcasts (Asher & Coie, 1990; Lochman & Wayland, 1994).

Coercive family process
Gerald Patterson's term for the method by which some families control one another through aggression and other coercive means.

We will see in Chapter 16 that these concerns have some foundation. Aggressive children often have poor interpersonal skills, and aggression runs high among unpopular, rejected children (although the cause-and-effect relation probably operates in both directions). But does this mean that highly aggressive children never have friends? Or that they are never members of stable social groups?

These questions were addressed in a large-scale study of the social patterns of aggressive children (Cairns et al., 1988). To begin, the researchers identified a group of boys and girls in the fourth and seventh grades as very aggressive, based on reports from their teachers, principals, and counselors. Next, for comparison, the researchers selected a group of nonaggressive children who were similar in age, gender, race, and other related characteristics. The social patterns of the two groups were measured by a number of means, including interviews with classmates, ratings by teachers, and self-ratings.

The data from these measures were analyzed to answer several questions. First, did the children group themselves into social clusters, in which certain children spent a great deal of time together? If so, which children were members of these groups? Were any of the clusters made up predominantly of aggressive children? Finally, how often were aggressive children nominated as "best friends" by their classmates?

The results proved somewhat surprising. In the social clusters that were identified, aggressive individuals were just as likely to be members as those who were nonaggressive. Children high in aggression often tended to hang around together, forming their own clusters. And aggressive children had just as many peer nominations as best friend as did nonaggressive children. The best-friend relationships, however, involved aggressive children nominating one another and nonaggressive children nominating one another.

These findings, once again, demonstrate how studies of children in their natural environments often turn up unexpected results. The widely held belief that aggressive behavior automatically sentences a child to a life of social isolation is clearly overstated. Many aggressive children have networks of friends who are similar to themselves. Although these clusters may encourage and thus perpetuate antisocial behavior, they also appear to provide friendships and social support. Thus, although many aggressive children may fail to develop good interpersonal skills and may be rejected by their peers, some are socially competent enough to make and maintain friends.

Violence on Television   The prevalence of violence on television is well documented. Surveys of TV programming from the early 1970s to the early 1990s revealed that over 70% of children's prime time programs and over 90% of Saturday morning dramatic programming depicted violent acts. The average number of violent acts per hour was 5.3 during prime time and 23 on Saturday mornings (Huston & Wright, 1998).

The amount of aggression and violence shown on TV is particularly striking in light of the amount of TV children watch—about 24 hours per week for the typical school-age child (Comstock & Scharrer, 2001). The number of violent acts viewed during these hours adds up—by age 21, the average child has witnessed about 8,000 television murders (Huston & Wright, 1998).

Beginning with Bandura in the 1960s, researchers have repeatedly demonstrated that children can learn new forms of aggression, and can be stimulated to perform them, by viewing a violent film model (Bandura, 1973, 1983, 1994). But does the average child really become more aggressive simply as a result of watching a typical diet of current network programming? The answer, based on dozens of studies and reports, appears to be yes (Bushman & Huesmann, 2001; Comstock & Scharrer, 1999). Moreover, the effects of violence can take several forms.

The most obvious effect is that children imitate the violent acts they see. They are especially likely to do so when the violence is performed by the "good guys" and also when the aggression successfully achieves its purpose. A somewhat less obvious effect is that TV violence increases the likelihood of all other forms of aggression in children, even those that do not resemble the behavior of the television models. And the effects

© Etta Hulme / Reprinted by permission of NEA, Inc.

Violence on television has been shown to be a common cause of children's aggression.

are long term—one study, for example, found that the amount of violence boys view at age 8 is a good predictor of their level of crime at age 30 (Huesmann & Miller, 1994). Similarly, researchers have reported that viewing TV violence from ages 6 to 10 was associated with elevated aggressive behavior 15 years later in young adulthood (Huesmann et al., 2003). Moreover, this relationship was true for both boys and girls and held regardless of factors such as socioeconomic status and intellectual ability. The relation between violence and aggression appears to be circular: Television violence stimulates aggression, and more aggressive children also tend to watch more violent television (Huesmann, Lagerspetz, & Eron, 1984). Finally, violence on TV can also make children more tolerant of aggression and less bothered by it (Parke & Slaby, 1983).

Exposure to Real-Life Violence Not all the violence children witness comes in the form of movies or TV programs. Many children experience repeated violence first-hand in their everyday lives. Sometimes it occurs in the home among family members, perhaps in the form of spouse or child abuse. And increasingly, children around the world are exposed to political, ethnic, or community violence (Cairns, 1987, 1996; Garbarino et al., 1992; Garbarino & Kostelny, 1996; Kostelny & Garbarino, 1994; Leavitt & Fox, 1993; Straker, 1992).

What happens to children whose development takes place in the context of such violence? It is well documented that stress is an important risk factor for children's health and normal development (Garmezy & Rutter, 1983; Haggerty et al., 1994). This would suggest that living in a violent environment should increase the chances of negative outcomes for children. But another possibility is that children who are exposed repeatedly to violent events might develop psychological mechanisms that protect or buffer them from the possible negative effects of these dangerous environments. Which model does the research evidence support? Most of the studies on this question have been conducted in only the last few decades, leaving much more work to do. We can, however, consider what researchers know so far.

Psychologists have typically approached this issue by identifying children who have been exposed to real-life violence and then comparing their development with that of children who have not had these direct experiences. Of greatest interest have been any subsequent psychological or behavioral problems, such as aggression, anxiety and phobias, depression, and the like. Typically, this information is gathered by interviewing parents or teachers or by having them complete a questionnaire regarding the child's behavior problems. The children themselves may be interviewed about their personal experiences and their feelings about the events taking place around them. Sometimes they are asked to draw pictures depicting where they live and what it is like to live there. These drawings, like the one shown in Figure 14.5, frequently reveal children's perceptions of, and ideas about, the world in which they live.

Figure 14.5

Drawing by a 9-year-old Palestinian child, revealing feelings of victimization. Note the soldiers with guns standing over the small children near their house. From "Coping with the Consequences of Living in Danger: The Case of Palestinian Children and Youth," by K. Kostelny & J. Garbarino, 1994, *International Journal of Behavioral Development, 17,* 595–611.

The overriding conclusion is that even when children are not physically injured by real-life violence, they are often invisible or silent victims of the traumatic events (Groves et al., 1993; Osofsky, 1995a, 1995b). Younger children in particular seem to be more strongly affected in these situations. Common problems reveal evidence of fear and anxiety—such as withdrawal, constant crying and clinging, sleep disturbances, and bed-wetting—with boys somewhat more vulnerable to these problems than girls. Such children also tend to display increased use of aggressive words, aggressive play, and a general preoccupation with aggressive themes.

Children who have a secure relationship with one or both parents generally fare the best in these environments, whereas any conflict or animosity within the family increases the likelihood that the children will be affected by the violence.

Cognitive and Affective Influences on Aggression

Any complete understanding of children's aggression must include the cognitive processes that control it. Much research in this area has involved the development of social cognition, or how children come to understand the social world in which they live.

Aggression is a subject with which most youngsters are familiar. From an early age, children can identify aggressive behavior and realize that it is considered undesirable. Even first graders show strong agreement on peer nominations of aggression (Younger & Piccinin, 1989; Younger, Schwartzman, & Ledingham, 1985). By the age of 5, children can comprehend more complex forms of aggressive behavior, such as **displaced aggression,** in which a child who has been the object of aggression reacts by striking out at something else (Miller & DeMarie-Dreblow, 1990; Weiss & Miller, 1983).

Aggressive children (especially boys) show certain cognitive differences from their classmates. For example, their levels of moral reasoning and empathy (Cohen & Strayer, 1996) tend to be lower, and they are less likely to take into account a character's motives when making a moral judgment (Sanvitale, Saltzstein, & Fish, 1989). In addition, aggressive children often display a "self-protective" interpretation of their social world; that is, they tend to minimize the negative feelings that other children have toward them (Zabriski & Coie, 1996). Consistent with this idea is the finding that children who have positively biased self-perceptions (believing themselves to be more socially accepted than their peers report them to be) are more likely to show high levels of both physical and relational aggression than are children without such a bias (David & Kistner, 2000).

Displaced aggression

Retaliatory aggression directed at a person or object other than the one against whom retaliation is desired.

Aggressive children also have been found to differ in two other aspects of social cognition (Dodge & Crick, 1990). One of these is attributions. Kenneth Dodge and his associates, using an information-processing model, found that aggressive children have difficulty reading social cues in the environment (Crick & Dodge, 1994; Dodge & Crick, 1990; Quiggle et al., 1992). Their studies typically involve videotaped episodes in which one child is harmed or provoked by a peer whose intentions are unclear. In these situations, aggressive children are much more likely to attribute hostile or malicious motives to the provoker. And when cues are provided to suggest that the provoker's intentions are not hostile, aggressive children have more difficulty understanding and using these cues (Dodge & Crick, 1990; Dodge & Somberg, 1987). Thus, these children may be aggressive because they do not view the world in the same way that most children do (Waas, 1988; Waldman, 1996). Children whose aggression stems from these sorts of attributional problems are most likely to display hostile aggression (Crick & Dodge, 1996) (defined earlier as aggression whose main purpose is to inflict harm).

Dodge believes that aggressive children also frequently have difficulty with another aspect of their social information processing—deciding how to respond to a provocation from another child (Dodge & Crick, 1990). In such situations, these children are most likely to select an aggressive response as the best way to respond, apparently because they believe that this approach will produce the most positive outcomes. Aggressive children with this type of processing difficulty are most likely to display instrumental aggression, whose purpose, we have seen, is to obtain something (Crick & Dodge, 1996).

The studies described in this section, together with the research already discussed, indicate that aggression is a complex social behavior with biological, social, and cognitive elements. This complexity has made the task of preventing or reducing the frequency of aggression a major challenge.

Controlling Aggression

Parents, teachers, and public officials often look to developmental psychology for help in solving real-life problems. This has been very much the case with regard to reducing juvenile violence and aggression, a task in which legal and judicial methods have generally failed. Despite enormous attention to the issue, however, the contributions of developmental psychology to violence prevention have been largely disappointing (Pettit & Dodge, 2003). This can be attributed to several factors, including naïveté about the complexity of the problem, insufficient attention to the broader contexts of troubled children's lives, and overoptimism regarding the power of intervention, particularly among older youth.

In recent years, however, considerable progress has been made in understanding the development of antisocial behavior. We have learned that antisocial youth may follow one of a number of routes, or "developmental trajectories" (Lacourse et al., 2002). Consequently, "one-size-fits-all" interventions are unlikely to work equally well with all children. We also have learned that preventing the development of antisocial behavior in the first place is generally more effective than treating youth after they have begun to engage in problem behavior (Fields & McNamara, 2003). And we have learned much about which kinds of interventions do work—and which do not. We discuss some approaches next.

Catharsis   It was once believed that aggression is a means of venting steam and that it can thus be prevented by having the aggressive child channel energy into other behaviors or experience aggression vicariously. Hitting a punching bag or watching a wrestling match, then, could take the place of engaging in aggressive behaviors. Psychoanalytic theory refers to these substitute behaviors as forms of **catharsis**. The cathartic process has been used to defend the existence of violent TV programs and aggression-related toys (Feshbach & Singer, 1971).

Research evidence, however, does not support this theory. As we have seen, viewing violence on TV increases rather than decreases the probability of aggression. And studies

Catharsis
The psychoanalytic belief that the likelihood of aggression can be reduced by viewing aggression or by engaging in high-energy behavior.

with both children and adults indicate that engaging in high-activity behaviors does not make aggression any less likely (Bushman, 2002; Geen, 1983). Not surprisingly, methods aimed at curbing aggression through catharsis have generally proved ineffective (Parke & Slaby, 1983).

Parent Training   It is well established that parents' child-rearing methods are related to their children's aggression (Coie & Dodge, 1998; Stormshak et al., 2000). One of the most straightforward and successful approaches to handling this source of aggression has been the use of parent training techniques (Forehand & Kotchick, 2002; Kazdin, 2002; Reid, 1993). Drawing on principles of behavior modification, psychologists have trained parents in more effective ways of interacting with their children. Parents learn to reduce the use of negative remarks, such as threats and commands, and replace them with positive statements and verbal approval of children's prosocial behaviors. They are also trained in applying nonphysical punishment in a consistent and reasonable manner when discipline is required. The results of this form of intervention have often been dramatic in changing both the parents' and the children's behavior.

Social-Cognitive Methods   Another way to reduce aggression is to focus on cognitive and affective processes, which tend to be different for aggressive children. This approach has been used with children ranging in age from preschoolers to adolescents.

One cognitive approach involves preventing aggression through training in problem-solving techniques. This method teaches children to deal with problem situations more effectively by first generating and examining various strategies for confronting the problem and then following a systematic plan for dealing with it. With younger children, problem-solving training often is begun in a laboratory setting. The children first hear stories in which a character faces potential conflict and then are trained to analyze the problem and develop constructive solutions. Gradually, the children are encouraged to apply these new skills in real-life situations (Lochman et al., 1984; Shure, 1989). Similar programs have been used with aggressive adolescents (Goldstein & Glick, 1994; Guerra & Slaby, 1990).

One limitation of this approach is that for many aggressive children, the difficulty lies not in their ability to generate multiple and appropriate solutions to interpersonal conflicts but in their ability to execute the behaviors. Often, heightened emotion interferes with children's ability to inhibit aggressive actions. Laboratory studies with adults have shown that if this emotional response can be replaced with an incompatible response, such as empathy, aggression can be prevented or decreased (Baron, 1983). Similarly, programs for increasing children's empathy—by teaching them to take the perspective of the other child and to experience that child's emotional reactions—have found some success in reducing conflict and aggression (Feshbach & Feshbach, 1982; Frey, Hirschstein, & Guzzo, 2000; Gibbs, 2003).

A third approach is to focus on the attributions children make about others' behavior (Graham & Hoehn, 1995; Graham, Hudley, & Williams, 1992; Graham & Juvonen, 1998b). The premise of this approach—like the attributional model of Dodge described earlier—is that aggressive children are likely to interpret ambiguous, provocative actions by their peers (such as bumping into them in the school hallway) as intentional and hostile. This attribution produces anger, which then gives rise to aggressive, retaliatory behavior.

Using this model as a basis, researchers developed a cognitive intervention program designed to interrupt the sequence leading up to the aggression (Hudley & Graham, 1993). The study involved urban African American children in grades 4 to 6 who had been selected on the basis of teacher and peer ratings of their aggression. Most of the children had been rated high on aggression, but some had been rated low (so that not all children selected to participate in the study were stigmatized as problem students). Each research participant was assigned to one of three groups: an experimental group that received attribution training, an attention control group that received training only in academic skills, and a second control group that received no training.

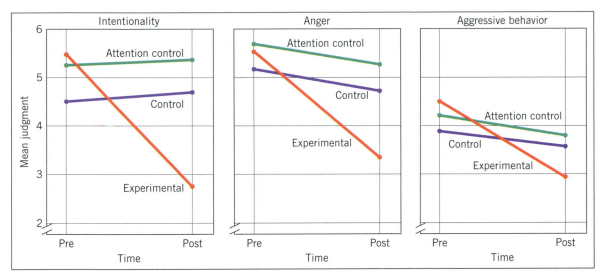

Figure 14.6

Results of an intervention study with African American children. The experimental group received attributional training and decreased the most on the three measures of interest. Adapted from "An Attributional Intervention to Reduce Peer-Directed Aggression among African-American Boys," by C. Hudley & S. Graham, 1993, *Child Development, 64,* 124–138. Copyright © 1993 by the Society for Research in Child Development. Reprinted by permission.

The attribution training involved teaching the children to recognize cues to another person's intentions (such as facial expressions), to encourage nonhostile attributions when the peer's actions were ambiguous (for example, "he probably did it by accident"), and to generate nonaggressive responses to the peer's behavior. The training continued for 6 weeks and included a variety of methods, such as storytelling, role playing, videos, and group brainstorming.

Before and after the training, all research participants were given a series of assessments designed to determine how likely they were to (a) attribute hostile intentions in an ambiguous situation, (b) become angry in response to such attributions, and (c) respond with aggressive behavior. The data for those children initially rated high on aggression are shown in Figure 14.6. Obviously, the attributional training worked very well. On each of the three measures, children in the experimental group scored the lowest on the posttest that followed the training and showed by far the greatest change. These data suggest not only that attributions play a role in producing aggression toward peers in everyday classroom situations but also that cognitive interventions designed to change these attributions can reduce such aggression.

The researchers caution, however, that other factors in the situation should not be overlooked. One is that not all aggression is directed toward peers and that this approach may not reduce problems involving vandalism, defiance of authority, theft, and so forth. Perhaps a more important point is that given the extremely difficult conditions under which many of these urban children live, attributing hostile intentions to peer provocations may often be accurate, and retaliating with aggression may be a useful survival response in this setting.

School-Based Universal Programs   An alternative approach to controlling aggression is to shift the focus away from the individual child and toward the school—one of the primary socialization contexts of children's lives. Several intervention programs share a common goal of reducing aggressive behavior and increasing prosocial behavior by altering the social environment of the school (Battistich et al., 2000; Flannery et al., 2003; Grossman et al., 1997; Nucci, 2001). Although the specifics of the programs differ, all aim to create caring school communities. In contrast to the other intervention efforts we have described so far, these so-called universal interventions involve all children

Bullying and Victimization in School

According to surveys, 40% to 80% of students experience unpleasantness at the hands of peers, including humiliation, taunting, threats, and social ostracism at school (Bosworth, Espelage, & Simon, 1999; Hoover, Oliver, & Hazler, 1992; Juvonen & Graham, 2001). For most students, these negative experiences are relatively infrequent and have no serious impact on long-term adjustment. For others, however, victimization is frequent and longstanding. One recent study estimates that approximately 10% of students are picked on and harassed by peers at least two to three times per month. A sizable number are bullied several times per week, and many of these victims are tormented by peers for years (Sohlberg & Olweus, 2003). Not surprisingly, these children are at heightened risk for a variety of problems, including loneliness, depression, anxiety, low self-esteem, peer rejection, and academic difficulties (Ladd & Ladd, 2001).

In recent years, investigators have devoted considerable effort to understanding the phenomena of peer bullying and victimization. One thing we have learned is that bullying is largely a group phenomenon. Studies show that peers are present during the vast majority of bullying episodes (Atlas & Pepler, 1998; Hawkins, Pepler, & Craig, 2001; Olweus, 2001). Despite their presence, students seldom intervene and put a halt to attacks on peers:

> The leaders . . . made it a point to give [Mick] a new derogatory nickname each day—"Brillo" and "Helmet" were two—making fun of his hair, of course. They all thought it was hilarious. Sometimes they'd start to chant—"Don't let Mick eat"—and it was like a rallying cry. They would blow snot on his sandwich or simply steal his food. One day they stole a bee from the biology lab and put it in his tuna sandwich. I didn't join in the teasing, but looking back on it, I can't believe I just sat there and let it happen around me. (Kindlon & Thompson, 1999, p. 7)

BOX 14.3

Applications

Why do students so often stand by and watch as others are teased, assaulted, and humiliated by peers? Research suggests that most children do not support the practice of bullying, find it uncomfortable to watch, and admire peers who try to stop it (Charach, Pepler, & Ziegler, 1995; Rigby & Slee, 1993). Nonetheless, while a significant minority of youth report that they know they should try to halt bullying, peers intervene only 10% to 20% of the time (Atlas & Pepler, 1998; Hawkins et al., 2001; Salmivalli, 2001).

One reason children choose not to intervene is that they believe that victims bring harassment on themselves. Children may elicit attacks by showing off, tattling, spreading rumors, or otherwise behaving obnoxiously (Graham & Juvonen, 1998a; Olweus, 2001). In such cases, children (and often adults) may feel that—to some degree—the victim "deserves" the rough treatment. Of course, even children who behave badly have the right to a safe school environment.

It is noteworthy, too, that provocative victims (or "bully/victims") constitute only a minority of children who are picked on by peers. Research consistently shows that most (80%) victims do not actively provoke others but rather are perceived as weak and vulnerable (Olweus, 2001). Even

in a classroom or school and not just children deemed to have problem behaviors. Key to the success of the programs is helping teachers foster a prosocial orientation among students toward classmates and their community. Universal interventions have been shown to have positive effects, although the impact on children with serious problems with aggression is modest (Greenberg, Domitrovich, & Bumbarger, 2001).

Comprehensive Interventions Although numerous interventions have proved promising in the short term, the challenge is to maintain the reduction in aggression and other antisocial behaviors over time. Increasingly, psychologists believe that effective treatment of antisocial and aggressive children requires a multifaceted approach that addresses parenting skills, teacher-parent communication, the social behaviors and reasoning skills of at-risk children, and the behaviors of peers.

One of the most intensive comprehensive programs is the Fast Track intervention. Fast Track targets children who display problem behaviors at the beginning of elementary school. The intervention is designed to address the multiple problems that characterize these "early-starting" aggressive children: They tend to come from poor families and neighborhoods, experience ineffective parenting, have poor relations with peers, do poorly in school, and attend schools that cannot control disruptive and violent behavior. The program seeks to improve these various areas of children's lives.

these victims may be seen as bringing on attacks by appearing weak and by failing to defend themselves (Graham & Juvonen, 1998a). Boys, in particular, are unlikely to come to the aid of peers who express fear (Terwogt, 2002).

Students also fail to stop bullying because they fear the group will turn on them if they do. As one fifth-grade boy observed,

> It's a real risk if you want to try to stick up for someone because you could get rejected from the group or whatever. Some people do, and nothing happens because they are so high up that other people listen to them. But most people would just find themselves in the same boat. And, we've all been there before, so we know what that's like. (Adler & Adler, 1998, pp. 67–68)

As understanding of bullying has grown, it has become increasingly clear that it is unreasonable to expect students to work out peer problems on their own. Researchers have developed a number of school-based programs designed to reduce school bullying. One of the most successful of these programs is a large-scale intervention implemented by Dan Olweus and colleagues in Norwegian schools.

The Olweus intervention program has four major goals (Olweus, 1997). The first is to increase awareness of the bullying problem. Second, the program aims to actively involve teachers and parents. Implicit in this goal is the recognition that adults have some responsibility to control what goes on among students at school. A third goal is to develop clear rules against bullying. These rules include explicit statements that bullying is not allowed, that students are to help those who are bullied, and that students should attempt to include in their activities peers who are easily left out. A final goal is to provide support and protection of victims.

These four goals are translated into specific actions. Teachers and parents are provided information on what is generally known about the causes and consequences of bullying and victimization, as well as information specific to their school setting gleaned from student responses to (anonymous) questionnaires about bullying at their school. The latter information helps school staff to increase supervision for those times and locations when and where bullying has occurred most often at school (for example, lunch and break times).

Steps are also implemented in the classroom. Each classroom establishes and enforces clear rules against bullying, and teachers regularly hold meetings with students to discuss bullying. When students violate class rules and bully others, teachers intervene swiftly and seriously. They sit down and discuss the incident with bullies and victims and their parents.

Finally, teachers work directly with victims and their parents. Teachers help victims learn how to assert themselves in the classroom and how to respond effectively to taunts and threats. They also help victims' parents find ways to improve their children's relations with peers by establishing new peer contacts or acquiring the social skills required to maintain existing friendships. Teachers also support victims by enlisting the help of neutral or well-adjusted peers to alleviate the victims' predicaments in various ways.

Olweus has reported between 50% and 70% declines in bullying in Norwegian schools that have implemented the intervention, while control schools generally show increases in bullying (Olweus, 1997, 2001). The Olweus program was recently selected as a model intervention program by a panel of U.S. experts, and it is currently being tested in a number of schools in the United States as part of a violence prevention initiative supported by the Department of Justice. Whether the intervention proves as successful in U.S. schools as in those in Norway remains to be seen. Regardless of the results of this particular investigation, reducing levels of bullying in American schools is sure to be a national priority for years to come.

Fast Track begins in first grade and continues through grade 10. It includes both a universal curriculum for all children and a specialized program that targets high-risk children and their families. The universal curriculum fosters emotion regulation and prosocial skills in the regular education classroom. The specialized program includes weekly enrichment sessions during school hours. High-risk children and their parents participate in these sessions, which are designed to further advance children's social skills and peer relations and to improve parenting skills, parent–child relations, and the parent–school partnership. The children also receive academic tutoring. In addition, the program includes home visits designed to develop trusting relationships with the parents and children and to promote general problem-solving skills for the entire family (CPPRG, 1992, 1999).

Does Fast Track work? A longitudinal study designed to assess the effectiveness of this comprehensive program was initiated in 1990. Nearly 900 first-graders with behavior problems were randomly assigned to intervention (Fast Track) or control classrooms. Results of ongoing evaluations are promising. By fourth grade, 48% of children in the control group had been placed in special education, compared with 36% of children in the intervention group. The intervention also lowered arrest rates. By eighth grade, 42% of the control group had been arrested, contrasting with 38% of Fast Track children. And among children in ninth grade, the intervention reduced serious conduct disorders by more than a third, from 21% to 13% (CPPRG, 2002; Crawford, 2002).

Fast Track is an expensive program. Is the reduction in rates of serious antisocial behavior obtained so far worth the cost? Kenneth Dodge, one of the program directors, thinks so. He observes, "If each career criminal costs society $1.3 million and the Fast Track program costs $40,000 per child, the program will prove to be a wise economic investment if just 3% of children are saved from careers of violent crime" (Crawford, 2002, p. 38).

To Recap . . .

Aggression is often defined as behavior that is intended to cause harm and that is not socially justifiable. This definition always involves a social judgment. Aggression can be classified as verbal versus physical, as instrumental versus hostile or retaliatory, or as relational. To measure aggression, researchers may use direct observation or the peer-nomination method.

In preschoolers, physical and instrumental aggression gradually give way to verbal and hostile aggression. In school-age children, the overall level of aggression tends to decrease with age. Boys are more aggressive than girls, especially toward one another; girls display more relational aggression.

The fact that aggression is a very stable characteristic over the life span lends itself to a biological explanation of aggressive behavior. One such explanation of aggression has linked it to blood levels of the hormone testosterone. There is some evidence for a genetic basis for aggression, which may in part be manifested through a "difficult" temperament.

Situational factors are assumed to influence aggression by way of the social-learning principles of reinforcement, punishment, and observational learning. The families of aggressive children engage in an ongoing pattern of coercive interactions in which members control one another through aggressive behavior. Violence on television also increases the likelihood of aggression in child viewers. The effects may include direct imitation of the violent behavior, an increase in overall aggression, and an increase in children's tolerance of aggression in others.

Aggressive children appear to be deficient in a number of cognitive areas, including moral reasoning and empathy. These children have difficulty interpreting social cues. They are more likely to attribute hostile motives to other children and to select responses involving aggression.

Various methods have been used in attempts to control children's aggression. Techniques based on the catharsis model have been of little value. Methods designed to teach parents more effective ways to discipline and interact with their children have proved successful, as have cognitive approaches aimed at directly changing children's beliefs and attitudes and interventions that foster a caring school climate. Multifaceted interventions that incorporate features of each of these other interventions are especially promising.

CONCLUSION

At the beginning of this chapter, we noted that two issues have dominated the study of moral development. One issue is whether morality lies within the child and simply emerges over time or is transmitted from adults and society to the child. The second is whether moral rules are universal, shared by all cultures.

Developmental psychology has made significant progress in understanding these two issues since Piaget initiated the study of children's moral reasoning in the 1930s. With respect to the first question, the most accurate answer is probably *neither*. Scientists now believe that humans are born with the capacity to experience emotions that underlie moral behavior. However, the development of a moral sense and ultimately moral behavior depends on a complex interplay between cognitive abilities and experience with other people who themselves adhere to a moral code and enforce compliance among others.

We have also learned much about the second question, although here, too, the issue is far more complex than envisioned by early researchers. Moral rules are universal in the sense that every known culture has a legacy of agreed-upon rules that structure the interactions among members. At the same time, there exists considerable cultural variation in these rules. Moreover, this variation is not as insignificant as was once believed (e.g., variations in levels of moral reasoning achieved in different cultures). Widely divergent beliefs permeate cultural ideologies around the world and are the basis on which people justify such acts as widow burning and infanticide.

Earlier in the chapter, we mentioned research by Wainryb and colleagues on how children and adults reason about moral beliefs that differ from their own. These studies show that, beginning in childhood, people wrestle with the issue of what makes beliefs with which they disagree more or less legitimate. One consistent finding is that beginning as young as age 3, people do not judge moral beliefs that differ from their own as legitimate grounds on which to base actions that they would consider immoral (Wainryb, 2000).

Whether or not cultural differences in moral reasoning can be interpreted in terms of a core set of principles such as harm and justice continues to be a matter of debate among theorists. But the issue of cultural differences in moral belief systems is not just of academic interest. The terrorist attacks of September 11, 2001—and the increased awareness of living conditions in other parts of the world that followed—force us to confront face to face the fact that people hold very different beliefs about the morality of particular actions. Coming to terms with this knowledge will likely prove a challenge for generations to come.

FOR THOUGHT AND DISCUSSION

1. Parents and teachers of preschoolers are often concerned with two goals: reducing aggressive behavior and promoting prosocial behavior. *What kind of advice would child development experts from each of the four major theoretical frameworks offer to help socializing agents achieve these goals?*

2. As we have seen, individuals differ in the way that they categorize various types of rule violations. What one person views as a moral issue, another person may see as a matter of personal choice. Moreover, differences in how people categorize issues can make it very difficult to reach consensus about appropriate behavior. *What are some issues that Americans of different ages often classify differently?*

3. Fortunately, few of us face moral dilemmas like that of poor Heinz, who had to choose between stealing a drug or letting his wife die. Nonetheless, moral decisions arise frequently in everyday life. *Think about a moral dilemma you faced in your life. How does your dilemma compare with those used in research studies? How would you rate your reasoning and action according to Kohlberg's stages?*

4. Some psychologists believe that pure altruism does not exist and that all of our acts of kindness are really based on getting something in return. *Do you believe that pure altruism ever occurs? If so, try to generate an example of an altruistic act in which no reward of any sort is possible.*

5. The world seems to be prepetually at war. Whenever one dispute is settled, another erupts. *Do you believe that humans are innately aggressive and therefore that wars are inevitable? If not, how do you explain the constant presence of international conflict?*

6. For children living in some inner-city neighborhoods, responding to aggression with retaliation may be a useful survival response. *Under such circumstances, would there be any justification for intervention programs to encourage such behavior (or at least not discourage it)? Can you think of other potential responses that might be encouraged in an intervention program for this type of situation?*

7. Some nations (for example, Sweden) have adopted laws against bullying in schools or are currently discussing the possibility. The United States is not one of these nations. *Do you believe that such laws are a good idea? Are there aspects of American culture that lead Americans to be less concerned about bullying than is true in other nations?*

VISUAL SUMMARY FOR CHAPTER 14
Moral Development

Theories of Moral Development

Cognitive-Developmental Approaches
Cognitive developmentalists are most concerned with moral reasoning. Piaget proposed a four-stage model which focused on the way children understand and follow rules. Kohlberg proposed a model that consists of three levels—preconventional, conventional, and postconventional—each composed of two stages. Turiel believes that children's moral reasoning involves several domains of social cognition and that even very young children can distinguish issues in the moral and societal domains.

Evolutionary and Biological Approaches
Sociobiologists have argued that altruism can be explained by a focus on the survival of the genes, rather than of the individual. In the area of aggression, ethologists have been interested in how primate social groups regulate conflict through dominance hierarchies and nonaggressive means of resolving disputes.

Environmental/ Learning Approaches
Social-learning theory is most concerned with moral conduct, explaining moral behavior with reference to reinforcement and punishment principles, along with observational learning processes and self-regulation.

Sociocultural Approaches
Sociocultural theorists view moral development as a social process in which other people, in the context of everyday activities such as family interactions and participation in cultural institutions, assist children's moral development by structuring and interpreting situations for them.

Moral Reasoning

Evaluating Piaget's Model
Research generally supports Piaget's model but suggests that he somewhat underestimated younger children's moral reasoning. When motives are made salient, even preschoolers can use this information as a basis for moral evaluations.

Evaluating Kohlberg's Model
Research generally supports Kohlberg's model but raises questions about the universality of the model. There are cultures where Kohlberg's theory clearly does not apply.

Evaluating Turiel's Model
Experimental studies support Turiel's domain theory. Research suggests that children from an early age distinguish between moral and societal rules. Their moral reasoning also appears to be influenced by contextual factors, including culture.

Distributive and Retributive Justice
Children's allocation of rewards follows a predictable sequence, moving from self-interest (up to age 4), to equality (ages 5 and 6), and then to equity (age 7 and older). Children's reasoning about punishment uses much the same pattern found in adults: Was harm done? If so, is punishment warranted?

Social and Family Influences on Moral Reasoning
Interactions with peers stimulate the development of moral reasoning. Parental discipline techniques also affect moral reasoning and internalization of parents' standards. The temperamental trait of fearfulness helps determine the type of discipline that promotes the development of conscience.

| **Moral Reasoning and Moral Conduct** | ▶ | The relation between moral reasoning and moral behavior is a fundamental issue in moral development research. Kohlberg asserted that the two should be closely related, but this assertion has been largely unsupported. |

Prosocial Behavior

| **Empathy and Sympathy** | ▶ | Many theorists believe the roots of prosocial behaviors lie in the capacity for empathy and sympathy. Hoffman has proposed a five-stage model of empathy development, culminating in the ability to empathize with the general conditions of people's lives and with classes of largely unknown people. |

| **Development of Prosocial Behavior** | ▶ | Major categories of prosocial behavior are helping, sharing, and conflict resolution. Both helping and sharing emerge early and increase with age. Conflict resolution during childhood is often accomplished through coercion, but this gradually gives way to the more prosocial approach of negotiation. Studies of children's peacemaking show that children are able to resolve past conflicts and repair damaged relationships. There is little empirical support for a gender difference in prosocial behavior. |

| **Determinants of Prosocial Behavior** | ▶ | Biology, affect, cognition, and socialization all contribute to the development of prosocial behavior. It is believed that genes influence prosocial development through temperament. Studies have shown modest relations between prosocial behavior and empathetic distress, prosocial reasoning, and mental state understanding. Parents contribute to prosocial development by providing opportunities to practice prosocial behaviors and by modeling and reinforcing prosocial behavior. |

Aggression

| **Age and Gender Differences in Aggression** | ▶ | In preschoolers, physical and instrumental aggression decrease relative to verbal and hostile aggression. In school-age children, the overall level of aggression tends to decrease with age. Males are more aggressive than females, especially toward one another; females display more relational aggression. |

| **Biological Determinants of Aggression** | ▶ | One biological explanation has linked aggression to blood levels of testosterone. There is some evidence for a genetic basis for aggression, which may in part be manifested through a "difficult" temperament. |

| **Sociocultural and Family Determinants of Aggression** | ▶ | Situational factors influence aggression by way of reinforcement, punishment, and observational learning. The families of aggressive children engage in an ongoing pattern of coercive interactions in which members control one another through forms of aggressive behavior. Violence on television also increases the likelihood of aggression. |

| **Cognitive and Affective Influences on Aggression** | ▶ | Aggressive children appear deficient in a number of cognitive areas, including moral reasoning and empathy. They have difficulty interpreting social cues and are more likely to attribute hostile motives to other children and to choose responses involving aggression. |

| **Controlling Aggression** | ▶ | Various methods have been used in attempts to control children's aggression. Teaching parents effective ways to discipline and interact with their children has been very successful, as have cognitive approaches aimed at directly changing children's beliefs and attitudes. Multifaceted approaches are especially promising. |

15

Gender-Role Development and Sex Differences

Sages and quacks throughout recorded history have offered couples advice on how to influence the sex of their offspring. Aristotle counseled ancient Greek males desirous of a son to tie off their left testicles. Since the 13th century, Chinese women have consulted an astrology chart to determine when they are most likely to conceive a boy or a girl.

German folklore recommends that couples hoping for a daughter place a wooden spoon under the mattress before intercourse. And, in recent decades, books and magazines describing low-tech sex selection methods (e.g., manipulating the timing of copulation) have become best-sellers. Now, with the discovery of new sperm-sorting technologies, we are about to embark on an era in which prospective parents will be able to determine with 100% certainty whether they have a baby boy or baby girl.

Would you take advantage of this emerging technology? The medical body that oversees physicians involved in reproductive health—the American Society of Reproductive Medicine—expects that many people will. Anticipating growing demand for this procedure, the ASRM has declared it ethical to offer sex selection to parents for reasons unrelated to the health of the baby or the mother (Ethics Committee of the ASRM, 2001).

Critics have raised numerous objections to the decision of the ASRM. Some fear sex selection will lead to a preponderance of one gender or a particular type of family configuration (e.g., older brother–younger sister sibling pairs). Others worry about the possibility of psychological harm to sex-selected offspring in cases where the child's behavior fails to meet parents' gender-specific expectations. And still other opponents argue that the opportunity to choose the sex of children focuses undue attention on a nonessential human characteristic and will ultimately promote and reinforce gender bias.

Currently, the ASRM proposes to offer non-medical sex selection only to parents who already have offspring of one gender and wish to have a child of the opposite sex. They note that most parents interested in sex selection do not favor one sex over another but are hoping for a "balanced" family that includes at least one child of each gender. According to the ASRM, this preference for children of each gender reflects a basic truth about human nature—that there are well-established physical and psychological differences between male and female children. These differences, the doctors assert, shape parents' child-rearing experiences. Raising boys is simply different from raising girls, they argue, and parents who wish to have both kinds of experience have the right to use available technologies to make that desire a reality. ■

Most psychologists would agree that in many ways, rearing boys *is* different from rearing girls. Psychologists disagree, often strenuously, about why this is the case, however. In this chapter, we consider various aspects of gender-role development and sex differences, including the origin of sex differences, how gender roles develop and what they mean, and why this area has attracted so much attention. First, however, we should clarify the terminology we will be using throughout the chapter.

When to use the label *gender* rather than *sex* has been a matter of some debate among psychologists (Deaux, 1993; Ruble & Martin, 1998). In this chapter, we use them interchangeably to refer to an individual's biological maleness or femaleness. The biological process through which these physical differences emerge is called **sex differentiation.** When we refer to a sex difference, however, we are saying simply that males and females differ on the particular personality trait or psychological characteristic under discussion; we are not assuming anything about the biological or environmental origins of that difference.

The term **gender role** (or *sex-role stereotype*) refers to a pattern or set of behaviors considered appropriate for males or females within a particular culture (Deaux, 1993; Gentile, 1993). In most cultures, for example, the male gender role is characterized by

Sex differentiation
The biological process through which physical differences between sexes emerge.

Gender role
A pattern or set of behaviors considered appropriate for males or females within a particular culture.

© 2002, Baby Blues Partnership. Distributed by King Features Syndicate

Raising boys is different from raising girls, but why?

such traits as leadership, independence, and aggressiveness, whereas females are expected to be nurturing, dependent, and sensitive (Best, 2001; Williams & Best, 1990). **Sex typing** is the process by which children develop the behaviors and attitudes considered appropriate for their gender. This process is assumed to involve a combination of biological, cognitive, and social mechanisms (Huston, 1985; Powlishta et al., 2001).

Sex typing

The process by which children develop the behaviors and attitudes considered appropriate for their gender.

THEORIES OF GENDER-ROLE DEVELOPMENT AND SEX DIFFERENCES

The study of gender roles has covered many different questions and issues. And as usual, theorists from the four major traditions have had different things to say about the nature and causes of this aspect of development.

Evolutionary and Biological Approaches

The evolutionary and biological family of theories focuses on the contributions of innate biological factors to the development of sex differences, gender roles, and sexual orientation. Evolutionary theory provides a broad framework for studying sex differences, whereas research on more immediate biological processes provides insight into the mechanisms by which sex differences are expressed in each succeeding generation.

Evolutionary Approaches   As we have seen, evolutionary approaches to development focus on the adaptive function of behaviors and traits. Most evolved adaptations are species-wide and occur in both males and females. For instance, both male and female infants evolved a capacity to form attachments with caregivers. To understand sex differences, however, evolutionary theorists must address why behaviors adaptive for one sex may not be adaptive for the other. To answer this question, evolutionary theorists point to the different roles males and females play in reproduction.

One way in which the reproductive roles of males and females differ is in the relative investment each makes to parenting and to mating (Trivers, 1972). For females, each copulation brings with it the possibility of conception and 9 months of pregnancy. In traditional societies and in our ancestral past, it also means several years of nursing. Thus, females have a large potential investment in each copulation. In theory, males need to invest little more than sperm and the energy required for copulation. As a result of these differences in parental investment, natural selection favored somewhat different reproductive strategies for females and males. Females evolved to be choosier about their mates and to invest more in parenting, whereas males, who invest much less in individual offspring, evolved to focus their reproductive efforts largely on mating (Buss & Kenrick, 1998; Kenrick & Luce, 2000).

Support for the evolutionary origins of human sex differences can be found in ethological studies that show similar behavior patterns among the females and males of many nonhuman species. Evolutionary theorists contend that sex differences that emerge during childhood reflect and help the young prepare for later reproductive roles

(Geary & Bjorklund, 2000). Thus, higher rates of aggression and dominance displays by boys are seen as preparation for adult male competition over mates. And girls' greater inhibitory control reflects the challenges they will face in choosing mates and caring for young, demanding infants (Bjorklund & Kipp, 1996; Geary, 1998).

Psychobiological Approach   Clearly, modern sex differences reflect the evolutionary past. But to understand how this past is expressed in each succeeding generation, we must look to more immediate causes, such as genes, hormones, and brain structure and organization.

Researchers interested in the biological underpinnings of sex differences have concentrated much of their attention on hormones. During the prenatal period, fetal hormones guide the development of male or female reproductive organs and external genitals. There is growing evidence that prenatal sex hormones also affect the organization of the central nervous system (e.g., the size of brain structures, connections between nerve cells). Sex hormones after puberty are believed to activate the neural systems and behavioral patterns laid down earlier.

Hormones contribute not only to behavioral differences between males and females but also to differences within each sex. Individual differences in masculinity and femininity are sometimes due to hormonal disorders. Other differences are due to naturally occurring variations in hormone levels. In addition, hormone levels can be influenced by innumerable environmental factors, such as outside temperature, immunological reactions, and maternal stress.

The idea that biology and experience interact in development is not unique to evolutionary accounts. It characterizes the sociocultural approach as well. We turn to this approach next.

Sociocultural Approaches

According to the sociocultural approach, gender roles develop as children participate in and prepare for the adult roles they are expected to play in their communities (Rogoff, 2003). Gender differences arise because, in most cultures, males and females occupy very different social roles (Eagly & Wood, 1999; Eagly, Wood, & Diekman, 2000; Wood & Eagly, 2002). Historically, these social roles have been closely tied to biological differences between males and females—in particular, differences in child-bearing and child-rearing and differences in size and strength.

Worldwide, women are more responsible for child care and household duties, whereas men are more responsible for the provision of resources acquired through hunting, warfare, or, in modern societies, paid employment (Barry, Bacon, & Child, 1957; D'Andrade, 1966; Murdock, 1967). The gender roles of girls and boys parallel those of the adults around them and exert a powerful influence on how children spend their time, with whom, and where. Like their mothers, girls around the world devote more time to child care and household chores than do boys. Boys, in contrast, spend more time in unsupervised activities and play (Larson & Verma, 1999). Compared with boys, girls are also more likely to be found at home or close to home (Weisner, 1996; Whiting & Edwards, 1988).

Sociocultural theorists contend that sex differences observed among children and adults *follow* from the roles commonly held by females versus males. This view contrasts with that of evolutionary psychologists, who believe that intrinsic, inborn differences between the sexes give rise to and maintain gender roles. To be sure, sociocultural theorists acknowledge that females and males have biological differences that may affect what activities they pursue. They point out, however, that male and female roles vary among cultures, which indicates that the roles cannot be fixed aspects of male and female inheritance.

Although sociocultural theorists reject the idea that sex differences reflect evolved psychological dispositions, they believe that humans have evolved capacities that make it especially easy to learn gender roles. These capacities include a tendency to organize the world into categories such as "male" and "female" and the ability to acquire culture (Tomasello, 1999).

Sociocultural theorists also recognize that gender roles affect behavior through cognitive and social processes. Exactly how these processes operate is the focus of the remaining two perspectives—the cognitive-developmental and environmental/learning approaches.

Cognitive-Developmental Approaches

The cognitive-developmental approach to gender-role development focuses on the child's understanding of the concepts of male and female and his or her ability to identify with one of them. These models emphasize the child's growing knowledge regarding gender and gender roles and how this knowledge translates into the sex-typed behaviors that we commonly observe (Liben & Bigler, 2002; Martin, Ruble, & Szkrybalo, 2002).

Kohlberg's Stage Model
The earliest cognitive developmental model of gender-role development was proposed by Lawrence Kohlberg (1966). Kohlberg believed that children construct their gender identity from what they see and hear around them. Once established, this gender identity serves to organize and regulate children's gender learning and behavior.

A key component of Kohlberg's model is the development of **gender constancy**—the belief that one's own gender is fixed and irreversible (Kohlberg & Ullian, 1974; Slaby & Frey, 1975). This understanding is similar to the Piagetian concept of conservation of physical properties discussed in Chapter 7. Children who have achieved gender constancy understand that their sex is a permanent attribute tied to biological properties and that changes in superficial characteristics such as hair length, clothing, or activities will not turn them into a member of the opposite sex.

Kohlberg proposed that gender constancy develops in three stages—**gender identity** ("I am a boy/girl"), **gender stability** ("I will grow up to be a man/woman"), and **gender consistency** ("I cannot change my sex"). Furthermore, according to Kohlberg's theory, children reliably behave in gender-typed ways only after they have developed gender constancy—not until about 6 years of age and, in some cultures, even later (Bhana, 1984; De Lisi & Gallagher, 1991; Munroe, Shimmin, & Munroe, 1984).

Gender constancy
The belief that one's own gender is fixed and irreversible.

Gender identity
The ability to categorize oneself as male or female.

Gender stability
The awareness that all boys grow up to be men and all girls become women.

Gender consistency
The recognition that an individual's gender remains the same despite changes in dress, hairstyle, activities, or personality.

Gender stability refers to the understanding that boys grow up to be men and girls grow up to be women.

Studies of the development of gender constancy in societies as diverse as Egypt, Kenya, and Nepal, as well as North America, have confirmed that children the world over do indeed progress through Kohlberg's stages in the proposed order (see Gibbons, 2000, for a review). The idea that gender constancy precedes children's adherence to gender norms is not, however, supported by empirical research. Children show gender-typed toy preferences, emulate same-sex models, and reward peers for gender-appropriate behavior years before they understand that gender is a permanent, unchanging attribute.

Moreover, although numerous studies have shown significant relationships between levels of gender constancy and gender-appropriate preferences and behaviors, other studies have failed to demonstrate a link or have found stronger relationships at lower — rather than higher — levels of gender constancy, quite the opposite of what Kohlberg originally proposed (Ruble & Martin, 1998).

Gender Schema Theory   Theorists working within the framework of information processing have proposed an alternative theory of gender-role development based on the concept of schemas. Proponents of this approach explain developmental changes in children's gender-role behavior in terms of mental models that organize children's experiences concerning gender. Specifically, children form **gender schemas** — cognitive representations of the characteristics associated with being either male or female (Bem, 1981; Liben & Signorella, 1987; Martin & Halverson, 1987).

According to this theory, children categorize gender-relevant stimuli (people, toys, activities) as "for girls" or "for boys." These schemas result principally from two factors: the child's inborn tendency to organize and classify information from the environment and the preponderance of gender-distinguishing cues (such as clothing, names, and occupations) that make these concepts easily identifiable.

The child then adopts one of the schemas — girl or boy. This self-schema, in turn, affects the child in two ways. First, it prompts the child to pay greater attention to information relevant to his or her own gender. A girl may notice television ads for a new Barbie doll, for example, whereas a boy may be more attuned to commercials announcing the release of a new action hero movie. Second, it influences the child's self-regulated behavior. For instance, a girl may decide to play with Barbie dolls and a boy to take karate lessons (Bem, 1993; Martin, 1993; Powlishta, 1995).

Gender schema theory has much in common with Kohlberg's theory. In both approaches, for example, children are motivated to behave in ways that are consistent with what they know or believe about gender. An important difference between the two theories, however, is the level of knowledge or understanding required for the child to begin to act in accordance with gender norms. Kohlberg believed that children do not behave in sex-typed ways until they achieve gender constancy, a milestone not typically attained until 6 years of age or later. According to gender schema theory, children begin to organize their experience and behave in ways compatible with gender norms once they can identify themselves as male or female — an achievement typically reached between the ages of 2 and 3.

What does research have to say about gender schema theory? As we discuss in more detail later, there is considerable evidence that young children do use gender as a means to categorize their world and that knowledge of gender categories influences children's processing of information. The link between gender-role knowledge and gender-typed behavior is less straightforward. For example, children often show gender-typed toy preferences even before they can label themselves as girls or boys or identify specific toys as being more appropriate or typical for one gender or the other. Gender schema theorists argue, however, that these children may know more about gender roles than they are given credit for; that is, standard means of assessing gender knowledge may underestimate what children understand about gender (Levy, 1999; Liben & Bigler, 2002; Martin et al., 2002).

Another potential problem with the theory is that greater amounts of gender role knowledge do not always translate into more gender-typed behavior. That is, some

Gender schemas
Cognitive representations of the characteristics associated with being either male or female.

children show impressive knowledge of gender-role stereotypes but nonetheless choose to behave in non-gender-typed ways. Gender schema theorists do not view this finding as a serious threat to the theory, noting that a variety of situational factors influence whether children will match their behavior to their gender knowledge structures (Martin, 1993; Martin et al., 2002).

It is also the case that some children develop *idiosyncratic gender schemas,* or gender schemas that include dimensions more typically associated with the opposite sex. For instance, a "tomboy" may have a schema that is different from the schemas of more typical girls. This schema would likely allow the child greater flexibility than a more traditional gender schema. Nonetheless, it would influence her to behave in certain ways rather than others (Liben & Bigler, 2002).

Environmental/Learning Approaches

Within the environmental/learning family of theories, social-learning theorists view gender roles as primarily learned patterns of behavior that are acquired through experience (Lott & Maluso, 2001). According to this approach, many sex-typed behaviors are products of the same learning principles that govern other social behaviors, including reinforcement processes, observational learning, and self-regulation (Bandura, 1989, 1991; Bussey & Bandura, 1999). Little boys, for example, are more likely to behave in traditionally masculine ways because they receive social approval for this type of behavior and disapproval when they exhibit traditionally feminine behavior or preferences. They also observe and imitate models in their environments—ranging from parents to classmates to TV characters—who display gender-related behaviors. And, by learning to anticipate how others will respond to their behavior, they gradually internalize standards regarding what are appropriate and inappropriate gender behaviors and then self-regulate their behavior to conform to these standards.

Social-learning theorists do not deny that biological distinctions separate males and females, but they argue that many of the sex differences in children's social behavior and cognitive abilities are not inevitable results of their genetic makeup. Nor do they deny that children develop a cognitive understanding of different gender roles. But this understanding, they believe, is not necessarily the cause of the sex differences we observe in behavior, especially during early childhood (Bandura, 1991; Bussey & Bandura, 1999).

Alexia Fotopoulos spent her early years traveling with her mother Danielle and the other members of the Carolina Courage, a professional women's soccer team. Will Alexia's gender schemas for females include sports?

To Recap . . .

The biological approach to gender development includes the general framework of evolutionary theory as well as a focus on specific biological mechanisms, such as genes, hormones, and brain functioning. According to the evolutionary approach, modern sex differences reflect the different reproductive challenges faced by males and females in the ancestral past.

The sociocultural approach contends that sex differences follow from the different social roles that males and females play in each society. Proponents of the sociocultural approach place somewhat less emphasis on biological factors than do proponents of the evolutionary approach. They emphasize, however, that gender-role behavior is readily acquired by children who have inherited evolved tendencies to categorize the world and acquire culture.

The cognitive-developmental tradition has generated two theoretical approaches to gender-role development. One is Kohlberg's stage model, in which children's understanding of gender-role issues proceeds through three stages: gender identity, gender stability, and gender consistency. The other is based on the information-processing concept of the gender schema. The gender schema is a cognitive representation of gender believed to help children organize gender-related information, regulate their gender-role behavior, and make inferences regarding gender-role issues.

Social learning theory views gender-role behaviors as simply another class of social responses acquired and maintained by learning principles, including reinforcement, modeling, and self-regulation. Sex differences in this view are not inevitable and may change with environmental conditions.

SOME PERCEIVED AND REAL SEX DIFFERENCES

In this section, we discuss sex differences that are commonly observed during childhood or adolescence. We begin with some guidance on how to interpret research on sex differences. As you may have noticed, studies sometimes yield conflicting results. This is certainly true of research on sex differences. To give just one example, some studies find that parents talk more to girls, others report that parents talk more to boys, and yet others find no differences in the amount of speech parents direct to sons and daughters. How do we know which results to believe?

To help make sense of discrepant results, researchers employ meta-analysis, a technique described in Chapter 2 (Box 2.2). In meta-analysis, researchers apply statistical rules to a group of studies that all examine the same thing. Because meta-analysis is based on large amounts of data collected by numerous researchers under widely varying conditions, researchers are better able to draw firm conclusions about the phenomena under study. Meta-analyses are not available for every behavior and attribute that has attracted the attention of researchers interested in sex differences, but as you read our discussion of sex differences, you should pay special attention to those differences supported by studies that have used meta-analysis.

Another thought to keep in mind is that sex differences represent only the average difference across all males and females. To illustrate the point, consider Figure 15.1, which shows two possible patterns of sex differences. In (a), males and females differ so markedly that there is no overlap in their scores. When the topic of sex differences is raised, the picture represented by graph (a) may come to mind. Be aware, though, that this pattern virtually *never* arises in real life, despite what we might be led to believe by books with such titles as *Men Are from Mars; Women Are from Venus!*

In (b), females, on average, outperform males, but there is considerable overlap between males and females. In this situation, many females are more different from other females than they are from the average male. Conversely, many males are more different from other males than they are from the average female. The general pattern depicted in (b) is the most common—although, of course, which gender outperforms the other varies with the task or domain. In general, then, the average differences between males and females are actually smaller than the variability within each sex.

In conclusion, we caution you not to assume that the differences discussed here primarily reflect innate biological differences. All sex differences are best conceived of as the product of biological and environmental processes acting in concert.

Physical Differences

Physical differences include differences in physical maturity and vulnerability, in activity level, and in motor development.

Physical Maturity and Vulnerability
At birth, the female newborn generally is healthier and more developmentally advanced than the male, despite being somewhat

Figure 15.1

The discussion of sex differences focuses on the differences between males and females on average. Generally, the difference within each sex is larger than the difference between males and females, as shown in (b).

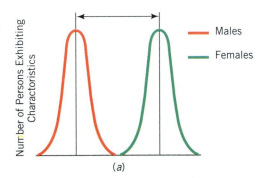

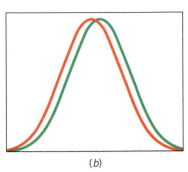

smaller and lighter. Although she is less muscular and somewhat more sensitive to pain, she is better coordinated neurologically and physically (Garai & Scheinfeld, 1968; Lundqvist & Sabel, 2000; Reinisch & Sanders, 1992; Tanner, 1990). On average, females also reach developmental milestones earlier than males. For instance, girls lose their first tooth at a younger age and begin (and end) puberty sooner.

Males are physically more vulnerable than females from conception on. They are more likely to be miscarried, to suffer from physical and mental illnesses and various kinds of hereditary abnormalities, and to die in infancy (Hartung & Widiger, 1998; Jacklin, 1989). Males are also more likely to suffer physical injuries. This probably reflects a constellation of factors, including boys' higher activity level and greater risk-taking tendencies (Byrnes, Miller, & Schafer, 1999; Laing & Logan, 1999).

Activity Level   On average, boys have higher activity levels than girls. This sex difference first emerges during the prenatal period; male fetuses are more active in the womb (Almli, Ball, & Wheeler, 2001; DiPietro et al., 1996). Meta-analytic studies show that this difference is maintained through infancy and childhood (Campbell & Eaton, 1999; Eaton & Enns, 1986). Interestingly, sex differences in activity level are small when children are playing alone. Boys' activity levels increase substantially when they are in the company of other boys—as any casual observer of a preschool classroom, birthday party, or school lunch line can attest (Maccoby, 1998).

Motor Development   During infancy, sex differences in motor development are minimal. Sex differences in large and fine motor development are evident in early childhood, however. Boys have the edge in skills that require strength. By age 5, boys can jump farther, run faster, and throw farther than girls. Beginning in the preschool years, boys are also able to throw more accurately than girls. This sex differences increases during adolescence, in part because of physical changes and in part because of practice.

Girls, in turn, have an advantage in gross motor skills, such as hopping and skipping, that require a combination of balance and precise movement. Girls also have better fine motor skills and so initially have an easier time tying shoes and performing tasks required in school, such as writing, cutting paper, and the like.

Cognitive Differences

According to popular stereotypes, girls are better at verbal tasks, whereas boys are better at mathematics. In fact, studies using meta-analysis reveal that the differences between males and females in these two cognitive domains are quite small (Hyde, Fennema, & Lamon, 1990; Hyde & Linn, 1988). Furthermore, the differences that do exist are often restricted to specific age groups, to specific kinds of tasks, or to very high-achieving groups. Nevertheless, some differences are observed.

Language and Verbal Abilities   There is little doubt that young females outperform young males in some kinds of verbal skills (Feingold, 1992, 1993). Female infants produce more sounds at an earlier age than do males (Harris, 1977); they use words sooner; and the size of their early vocabularies is larger (Bauer, Goldfield, & Reznick, 2002; Galsworthy et al., 2000; Huttenlocher et al., 1991). On a variety of measures of grammar and language complexity (sentence length, use of pronouns, use of conjunctions, and so on), girls begin to show marked superiority at about 2 years of age, and the differences continue through adolescence (Koenigsknecht & Friedman, 1976; Schacter et al., 1978).

Throughout the school years, females achieve higher scores in reading and writing (Campbell, Hombo, & Mazzeo, 2000; Halpern, 2000). Early differences in learning to read may originate in sex differences in the ability to detect the sounds of language (phonology), as females outperform males across a range of phonological tasks (Majeres, 1999). Recent reports of performance on standardized exams of reading and writing show that females continue to outperform males at the end of high school (National Center for Education Statistics, 1997; Willingham et al., 1997).

One source of the gender gap in reading and writing is that males are more likely than females to have serious problems with speech and written language. Compared with girls, boys are more likely to suffer from language difficulties, such as stuttering. They are also more likely to have dyslexia and other types of learning disorders that make learning to read and write difficult (Miles, Haslum, & Wheeler, 1998; Nass, 1993).

There is considerable evidence that sex differences in verbal and language abilities are biologically based. Of particular importance is brain **lateralization**—the specialization of functions in the right and left hemispheres. Scientists believe that prenatal exposure to high levels of testosterone—which occurs normally during the development of male fetuses—slows the development of the left hemisphere and enhances the development of the right hemisphere (Rosen, Galaburda, & Sherman, 1990). This process may produce two results significant for sex differences in cognitive abilities.

One is that the right hemisphere is relatively more established in males. You may recall from Chapter 5 that the right hemisphere is specialized for quantitative and spatial tasks. This may help account for the male advantage in spatial tasks. Second, the brains of females are less lateralized. Female superiority on verbal and language tasks may derive from the fact that they use both hemispheres to process language, whereas males' language processing tends to be localized in the left hemisphere. We return to the topic of lateralization in a later section.

Although language skills appear to have biological underpinnings, environment plays a significant role as well. Girls usually experience a richer language environment than boys. A recent meta-analysis of mother–child talk showed that mothers vocalize more to daughters, imitate their vocalizations more, and generally maintain a higher level of mother–infant vocal exchange (Leaper, Anderson, & Sanders, 1998). Parents also believe daughters to have greater reading ability than sons, even when actual ability differences do not support this belief (Eccles, Arbreton, et al., 1993; Wigfield et al., 2002).

Quantitative Abilities

During elementary school girls and boys are equally interested in mathematics (Andre et al., 1999; Eccles, Jacobs, et al., 1993; Folling-Albers & Hartinger, 1998; Wigfield et al., 1997). Even at this young age, however, females and males appear to excel at different kinds of mathematics. Throughout elementary and junior high school, girls are better at computational problems, whereas boys do better with mathematical reasoning (Hyde et al., 1990; Seong, Bauer, & Sullivan, 1998).

By adolescence, males express greater interest in mathematics than do females (Gardner, 1998; Wigfield et al., 2002). They also begin to perform significantly better than females, at least when measured on standardized exams. On average, males achieve higher scores on SAT mathematics exams than females, whereas females tend to receive higher grades in mathematics courses (Benbow, 1992; Snyder & Hoffman, 2000). The sex difference in performance on standardized exams is especially marked among students of very high ability (Benbow, 1992; Bielinksi & Davison, 1998; Willingham & Cole, 1997).

Recent studies in the United States shed some light on male–female differences. These studies looked at how girls and boys solve mathematical problems—not just whether they solve them correctly or not. Compared with boys, first-grade girls are more likely to use simple strategies (e.g., counting on one's fingers) that are almost certain to produce correct solutions. Boys, in contrast, tend to use more sophisticated strategies, such as retrieval, but as a result are at greater risk for making mistakes (Carr & Jessup, 1997; Carr, Jessup, & Fuller, 1999).

Some researchers believe that these early differences in the types of strategies preferred by girls and boys contribute to differences in mathematical achievement that persist over time. Despite their earlier "failures," by third grade, boys are better able to

Lateralization
The specialization of functions in the right and left hemispheres of the brain.

rapidly and automatically retrieve correct answers to arithmetic problems. This ability may lay the foundation for later-developing mathematical competencies. How quickly students retrieve mathematical facts is predictive of their performance on both computational and mathematical reasoning tasks (Geary et al., 2000; Royer et al., 1999). Speedy retrieval may especially advantage males on timed tests, such as college entrance exams.

There is also a sex difference in the kinds of strategies used to solve mathematical reasoning problems. Starting in first grade, girls are more likely to use concrete strategies, such as counting, whereas boys use more abstract approaches (Fennema et al., 1998). By third grade, girls prefer the conventional strategies taught in school, whereas boys are more likely to use logic, estimation, or some kind of unconventional strategy (Hopkins, McGillicuddy-De Lisi, & De Lisi, 1997).

Differences in strategy preferences can also help explain why females tend to perform better in mathematics courses yet obtain lower scores than males on standardized exams. Although the orthodox approaches used by girls tend to produce correct solutions on conventional problems, they are less likely to yield good results on unconventional ones (see Table 15.1 for an illustration). Consequently, females may perform well on school exams designed to test whether they can correctly apply a taught strategy, but they are less able to solve trickier problems that require a novel approach. Conversely, although mathematics teachers may not always appreciate the creative solutions offered by male students, those approaches may confer an advantage on males outside of the classroom (Gallagher & De Lisi, 1994; Gallagher et al., 2000).

Why boys and girls approach mathematical problems differently is not well understood. One possibility is that girls rely on safe strategies because they fear making mistakes. Indeed, some studies have suggested that girls have less confidence in their mathematical abilities than do boys (Pajares & Miller, 1994; Stipek & Gralinski, 1991;

Table 15.1	Two Types of SAT Math Problems

Whereas Problem 1 is easily solved using a formula, Problem 2 is more easily solved using nonconventional procedures. Females tend to have better success with the first type of problem.

Problem 1.

P   Q   R
———————————→
4/n   5/n   1/4

If PQ = QR on the number line above, what is the length of PR?

(A) 1/12
(B) 1/9
(C) 1/8
(D) 1/6
(E) 3/16

Answer: (A) 1/12

Problem 2.

A blend of coffee is made by mixing Colombian coffee at $8 a pound with espresso coffee at $3 a pound. If the blend is worth 45¢ a pound, how many pounds of the Colombian coffee are needed to make 50 pounds of the blend?

(A) 20
(B) 25
(C) 30
(D) 35
(E) 40

Answer: (A) 20

SOURCE: Adapted from A. M. Gallagher and R. De Lisi, "Gender Differences in Scholastic Aptitude Test Mathematics Problem Solving among High-Ability Students," *Journal of Educational Psychology, 86,* 1994, 204–211. Adapted by permission.

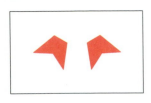

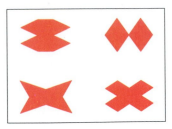

Figure 15.2

In this spatial transformation task, children select which of the four cards shows what the two pieces in the top card would look like if placed together. *Source:* S. C. Levine, J. Huttenlocher, A. Taylor, and A. Langrock, "Early Sex Differences in Spatial Skill," *Developmental Psychology, 35,* 1999, 940–949.

Wigfield et al., 1997). However, more recent work suggests that the gender gap in beliefs involving mathematical competence is decreasing (Jacobs et al., 2002; Marsh & Yeung, 1998). Another possibility is that females are more concerned with following rules and meeting teacher expectations (Dweck, 1999). Still another possibility is that sex differences in mathematics performance are related to underlying differences in spatial abilities (Casey, Nuttal, & Pezaris, 1997; Nuttal & Pezaris, 2001). We turn to this topic next.

Spatial Abilities As we have already noted, males repeatedly outperform females in tasks involving spatial abilities (Feingold, 1993; Halpern, 2000). Some sex differences in spatial abilities are observed as early as the preschool years. On average, boys outperform girls on the Maze Subtest of the Weschler Preschool and Primary Scale of Intelligence (Fairweather & Butterworth, 1977; Wechsler, 1967). Four-year-old boys also outperform girls on spatial transformation tasks like that shown in Figure 15.2 and show superior performance on three-dimensional spatial tasks such as copying Lego models (Levine et al., 1999; McGuiness & Morley, 1991).

There is some evidence that sex differences in spatial abilities increase in adolescence and adulthood, although the extent of the difference varies with the task (Voyer, Voyer, & Bryden, 1995). One type of task on which adolescent and adult males and females differ markedly involves mental rotation (Linn & Petersen, 1986; Masters & Sanders, 1993). An example of a mental-rotation task appears in Figure 15.3. Another task at which females generally have more difficulty is the water-level task, shown in Figure 15.4 (Vasta & Liben, 1996).

What might account for this pervasive sex difference? One explanation, as we have already noted, emphasizes the biological explanation of brain lateralization. The right hemisphere is specialized for quantitative and spatial tasks, and the development of the right hemisphere is promoted by male hormones. Another explanation, which emphasizes experiential factors, is that, from early childhood on, males are more likely to participate in activities that promote spatial skills. They spend more time building with blocks, constructing models, and playing computer and video games and sports (Baenninger & Newcombe, 1989, 1995; Serbin et al., 1990; Subrahmanyam & Greenfield, 1994; Subrahmanyam et al., 2001).

Nora Newcombe, an expert on the development of spatial cognition, has recently argued that the debate over the origins of sex differences in spatial abilities, though interesting—at least to scientists who study such things—has diverted attention from a more important point, which is that spatial skills are trainable (Newcombe, Mathason, & Terlecki, 2002). It is widely accepted that spatial skills are important in daily life (e.g., hooking up the computer, packing the trunk of the car), as well as in various professions, such as science, engineering, and medicine (Gardner, 1993; Shea, Lubinski, & Benbow,

Figure 15.3

A mental-rotation task in which one must decide whether the two objects are the same (as in *a*) or different (as in *b*).

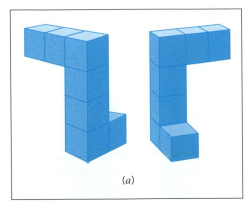

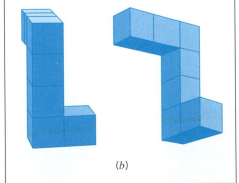

(a)

(b)

2001). Consequently, Newcombe believes society would benefit if more people developed better spatial skills. This raises an interesting question—should spatial reasoning be taught in school? That is the topic of Box 15.1.

Should Schools Teach Visual-Spatial Skills?

One of the most robust and reliable findings in research on sex differences is a male advantage on tasks that involve spatial reasoning, such as mental rotation and spatial visualization. At the same time, there is ample evidence that certain experiences promote the development of spatial skills (Baenninger & Newcombe, 1989, 1995).

Cross-cultural research shows superior spatial abilities among children and adults in cultures that depend heavily on hunting and other activities that require extensive travel (Dasen, 1975). Moreover, when females travel and hunt as frequently as males, they exhibit comparable spatial skills (Berry, 1966).

Everyday, practical experience performing tasks that entail spatial demands also enhances spatial competence in modern societies. For instance, Ross Vasta and colleagues (Vasta et al., 1997) found that individuals in occupations that provide extensive experience with liquids in containers—namely, bartenders and servers—perform better than adults of equal age, gender, and education on the water-level task depicted in Figure 15.4.

Experience playing computer and video games has also been linked to spatial competence. Under naturalistic conditions, it is difficult to know whether time spent playing these games promotes the development of spatial skills or whether children (and adults) with better spatial skills enjoy playing those games more and so devote more time to them. Although the latter is probably true, experimental research supports the idea that playing some kinds of games does enhance spatial competence (Okagaki & Frensch, 1994).

A recent study that tracked children's cognitive development over the course of the first 2 years of elementary school supports the idea that some kinds of activities promote the development of spatial abilities (Huttenlocher, Levine, & Vevea, 1998). Children in this study were tested

BOX 15.1

Applications

four times—October of kindergarten, April of kindergarten, October of first grade, and April of first grade. Children's spatial skills increased over the 2-year period, but most children showed greater growth during the months they were in school (October through April) than when they were mostly at home. These findings suggest that typical school activities, such as puzzle play and basic geometry instruction, facilitate children's development of spatial competence. Interestingly, children who entered kindergarten with very strong spatial abilities did not improve differentially during the school year. This suggests that the home environments of these spatially gifted children may have included more opportunities to practice spatial skills than the home environments of the other children.

Training studies provide further evidence for the effect of experience on spatial abilities. In one study, female college students were taught how to solve the water-level problem (Vasta, Knott, & Gaze, 1996). This task has proved notoriously difficult for college-age women; estimates suggest that up to 50% of them do not recognize that the water level will remain horizontal when the container is tilted (Halpern, 2000). Simply by receiving practice on a series of problems of increasing complexity (and no feedback), females were able to solve problems as accurately as males.

The fact that spatial skills can be taught has led some theorists to argue that spatial thinking should be included in the school curriculum. Schools offer remedial programs for reading—an area in which boys are at increased risk for educational failure. Significant numbers of girls—and more than a few boys—exhibit serious deficiencies in spatial competence. Yet schools generally make little effort to address these limitations (Halpern, 2000). Given the importance of spatial abilities for success in our increasingly technological world, should not schools direct efforts at promoting these skills as well?

Figure 15.4

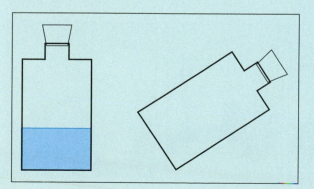

Predict how the water will look when the bottle is tilted.

Social and Personality Differences

We turn next to social and personality differences between boys and girls, including differences in temperament, emotional development, self-control, aggression, prosocial behavior, activities and interests, and friends and companions.

Temperament As we saw in Chapter 12, infants are born with a basic personality, or temperament. Some babies are easygoing, whereas others are often fussy and irritable. It is clear that temperament varies from infant to infant. But are some dimensions of infant temperament more typical of females while others more typical of males?

From the first days of life, female newborns seem better equipped for social interaction than their male counterparts. Female infants maintain greater eye contact with caregivers than males (Connellan et al., 2000; Hittleman & Dickes, 1979). By 3 months of age, they engage in more face-to-face communication (Lavelli & Fogel, 2002). Female babies also smile more during social interactions (Cossette et al., 1996). And these differences persist into adulthood. Adult women maintain eye contact and smile more during social exchanges than do adult males (Hall, 1984; LaFrance, Hecht, & Paluck, 2003).

Although these differences may seem compelling, there is no evidence to suggest that females are inherently more sociable than males (Maccoby, 1998; Mathiesen & Tambs, 1999; McCrae et al., 2002). What appears to be a female propensity for social interaction during the first months of infancy is most likely related to male infants' greater fussiness and irritability and their less-developed ability to regulate their emotional states (Calkins et al., 2002; Weinberg et al., 1999).

Emotional Development As they grow older, both boys and girls become better able to manage their emotions. This improvement is due to both biological maturation and the development of emotion regulation strategies (Compas et al., 2001). Sex differences in the strategies used to regulate emotional state have been observed among children as young as age 2. In one study, for example, toddlers were promised an attractive toy but made to wait before being allowed to play with it. The girls coped with the stress of the situation by seeking comfort from their mothers, whereas the boys were more likely to distract themselves by playing with the other objects in the room (Raver, 1996).

This gender difference in coping style grows larger over the course of childhood (Broderick, 1998; Copeland & Hess, 1995). By adolescence, these behavioral styles are incorporated into gender scripts. Adolescents expect females to turn to other people when upset and males to find something else to do (Broderick & Korteland, 2002). A recent meta-analysis of the adult coping literature confirms the same pattern in adulthood. Females are more likely to seek social support and talk about upsetting events. Males, in contrast, are more likely to employ distraction or to engage in some kind of physical activity (Tamres, Janicki, & Helgeson, 2002).

Males and females tend to use different coping strategies. Females prefer to talk about problems, whereas males tend to prefer to use distraction or physical activity.

© 2003, ZITS Partnership. Distributed by King Features Syndicate

One possible reason girls talk about their feelings with other people more than boys is that they are socialized to do so (Fivush & Buckner, 2000). Studies of parent–child reminiscing in Western cultures find that mothers and fathers talk more about the emotional aspects of events with daughters than with sons (Eisenberg, 1999; Fivush, 1998; Flannagan & Perese, 1998). Most intriguing is that parents seem to highlight sadness when talking with daughters (Chance & Fiese, 1999; Fivush & Buckner, 2000; Kuebli & Fivush, 1992). This focus on sadness does not appear to be elicited by the girls themselves, as young girls and boys mention sadness equally often. Later in childhood, however, females are more likely to report feeling sad than are males (Hughes & Dunn, 2002).

There are gender differences in the expression of other negative emotions as well. Parent–child conversations about anger are more common with sons than daughters (Brody, 1999; Fivush, 1991). Boys are also more likely to express anger, both in face-to-face interactions and when describing past events (Hubbard, 2001; Peterson & Biggs, 2001). In addition, boys are more likely to deny feeling afraid. For example, one male space camper, asked if he would like to go into space following the destruction of the *Columbia* shuttle in 2003, replied: "Nooooooo, I'm just not a space person. Not that I'm scared or anything" (Halbfinger, 2003, p. 23).

Boys are also less likely to follow cultural display rules regarding the expression of disappointment. For instance, upon receiving a disappointing gift, girls are better able to mask their disappointment and look pleased. Boys not only are more likely to show disappointment in this situation but also are less capable of hiding it, even when given incentives to do so (Cole, 1986; Davis, 1995; McDowell, O'Neil, & Parke, 2000).

Self-Control   As we saw in Chapter 13, the emergence of self-control is one of the hallmark achievements of the preschool period. Children with self-control are able to inhibit impulsive and aggressive behavior, delay immediate gratification, and comply with caregiver requests and prohibitions.

There is some evidence that girls develop self-regulatory capabilities more rapidly than boys. During early childhood, boys have considerably more difficulty than girls with tasks that demand impulse control—for example, whispering on command, walking slowly on a line, and playing games such as Simon says (Kochanska et al., 1996). Girls also have been found to comply more readily and at a younger age than boys with parental requests to perform unpleasant tasks, such as picking up toys, and prohibitions against touching attractive or dangerous objects (Kochanska & Askan, 1995; Kochanska, Coy, & Murray, 2001; Kuczynski & Kochanska, 1990).

Children with limited self-control are at risk for problem behaviors, such as angry outbursts and other kinds of disruptive actions. Prior to age 4 or 5, girls and boys engage in disruptive and impulsive behavior equally often (Achenbach, Edelbrock, & Howell, 1987). After this age, however, striking sex differences are found. Whereas most girls show a steady decline in problem behaviors, boys show a lesser decline and, in some cases, even an increase (Prior et al., 1993).

Aggression   Perhaps the clearest and largest sex difference in behavior is that males generally display more aggression than do females—especially the more violent varieties. For example, FBI statistics indicate that in the United States, males commit about 88% of the murders and 87% of the aggravated assaults. Most other countries and cultures report similar statistics (Kenrick & Trost, 1993). A recent study of over 4,500 preschoolers in eight countries found that males were universally reported to be markedly more aggressive than females (LaFreniere et al., 2002).

When less violent forms of aggression are considered, however, the situation becomes more complex (Eagly & Steffen, 1986; Hyde, 1984, 1986). Preschool and elementary-school males display more physical aggression, such as kicking, pinching, and hitting, than do females of the same age. They are also more likely to engage in oppositional behavior and to damage property. Females, in contrast, are more likely to use relational and social forms of aggression (Crick et al., 2001; Offord, Lipman, & Duku, 2001; Underwood, 2003).

Prosocial Behavior   We saw in the previous chapter that females are generally rated as more generous, helpful, and cooperative than boys by their teachers and peers (Shigetomi, Hartmann, & Gelfand, 1981; Zarbatany et al., 1985). Some evidence does suggest that females have better affective perspective-taking abilities and experience more empathy (Dodge & Feldman, 1990; Zahn-Waxler et al., 1992; Zahn-Waxler, Robinson, & Emde, 1992). But when researchers have examined children's actual behavior, they have found few sex differences (Eagly & Crowley, 1986; Eisenberg, Martin, & Fabes, 1996); so if a difference exists in this area, it is very small.

Activities and Interests   Gender differences in activity preferences emerge between the first and second birthdays. Boys show more interest in blocks, transportation toys (such as trucks and airplanes), and objects that can be manipulated. They also engage in more large-motor activities, including rough-and-tumble play (DiPietro, 1981; O'Brien & Huston, 1985; Roopnarine, 1984).

Girls prefer doll play, dress-up, artwork, and domestic activities, such as sewing and cooking. They also prefer more sedentary activities, such as reading and drawing, over more vigorous ones. This sex difference in participation in vigorous physical activity is maintained throughout childhood and adolescence (Bradley et al., 2000). However, whereas males tend to stick to a rather narrowly defined group of toys and games, females display a wider range of interests and are more likely than males to engage in activities preferred by the opposite sex (Bussey & Bandura, 1992; Eisenberg, Tryon, & Cameron, 1984; Fagot & Leinbach, 1993).

Because sex differences in play preferences emerge so early, it is tempting to believe that somehow boys are born to prefer mechanical toys and girls to prefer dolls. As we shall see, however, parents encourage sex-typed play from the first months of life. This is especially true for boys, who experience considerable pressure from both parents and peers to play with toys deemed appropriate for their sex.

In addition to differing in play preferences, boys and girls exhibit sex-stereotyped television preferences (Huston & Wright, 1998). Boys prefer noneducational cartoons, action programs, and sports. Girls lose interest in noneducational cartoons before boys and prefer shows with relationship themes (Wright et al., 2001).

Beginning during the preschool years, boys use computers more than girls do (Funk, Germann, & Buchman, 1997; Greenfield, 1994; Huston et al., 1999; Rideout et al., 1999). One national survey of children age 2 to 18 found the gender difference to lie in computer use in school. While more boys than girls reported using (or were reported by parents to have used) computers in school the day before, there were no differences in the percentage using computers outside of school (Roberts et al., 1999). These findings are consistent with the results of other studies indicating that boys tend to monopolize computers in the classroom, particularly in periods of uncontrolled access (Cassell & Jenkins, 1998; Kinnear, 1995; Schofield, 1995).

Boys spend far more time playing computer and video games than do girls (Harrell et al., 1997; Roberts et al., 1999; Wright et al., 2001). This gender gap reflects in part a disparity in the availability of games that appeal to boys and girls (Subrahmanyam & Greenfield, 1998). An analysis of popular Nintendo and Sega Genesis games revealed that nearly 80% had aggressive or violent themes (Dietz, 1998). These themes appeal primarily to boys, who often prefer violent games, including those that depict realistic human violence (Funk et al., 1997; Gailey, 1996).

With the exception of computer gaming, boys and girls use computers similarly. During adolescence, there are no sex differences in the use of the computer for chatting, visiting web sites, using e-mail, doing schoolwork, or using the computer in a job (Gallup Poll, 1997; Roberts et al., 1999). Recent evidence also suggests that adolescent males and females are equally confident about their computer abilities and equally skilled (Gallup Poll, 1997; North & Noyes, 2002).

Gender similarities—and differences—are also apparent in other leisure activities. Lynne Zarbatany and associates asked middle-income Canadian fifth- and sixth-graders to keep track of the activities they enjoyed with peers (but not siblings) over a period of one week (Zarbatany, Hartmann, & Rankin, 1990). Included among the many activities that boys and girls devoted equivalent amounts of time to were noncontact sports, watching TV and listening to music, talking with friends (face to face), and just hanging out. Girls reported spending more time on the phone, shopping, and talking about fashion, whereas boys spent more time playing contact sports.

There are also some gender differences in children's academic interests. Beginning in elementary school, girls are more interested in reading and music than boys, whereas boys express greater interest in sports. At this age, however, girls and boys are equally interested in mathematics and science (Andre et al., 1999; Eccles, Jacobs, et al., 1993; Folling-Albers & Hartinger, 1998; Wigfield et al., 1997).

By adolescence, males express greater interest in mathematics and science than do females (Gardner, 1998; Wigfield et al, 2002). A recent cross-national study (based on data collected in 1990–91) confirmed the same pattern of interests in the United States, Japan, and Taiwan. Interestingly, the sex difference was smaller in the United States than in the two Asian communities. The researchers attributed the cultural difference to the more egalitarian gender roles found in the United States (Evans, Schweingruber, & Stevenson, 2002). In addition, recent studies reveal that the gender difference in interest in mathematics and science is decreasing in the United States. One survey of a national sample found that although 59% of male adolescents reported preferring mathematics and science over English and social studies, 53% of females did as well (Gallup Poll, 1997).

Although many females are as interested in science as males, their specific interests *within* the domain of science differ. Male students tend to be more interested in the physical sciences. Female students, in contrast, tend to express more interest in the biological sciences (Adamson et al., 1998; Burkam, Lee, & Smerdon, 1997; Jones, Howe, & Rua, 2000).

By adolescence, boys typically express more interest in science—especially the physical sciences—than do girls.

Friends and Companions   Children's social relationships show striking sex differences. Beginning in early childhood, boys play in larger groups, whereas girls generally limit their group size to two or three. Boys report having a greater number of friends, whereas girls have fewer but more intimate friendships.

Boys' and girls' groups are also characterized by different interactional processes. Interactions among girls tend to involve more self-disclosure and intimacy (Brown, Way, & Duff, 1999; Lansford & Parker, 1999). Social interaction among boys often involves issues of dominance and leadership, whereas girls' interactions stress turn taking and equal participation by group members (Benenson, 1993; Benenson, Apostoleris, & Parnass, 1997; Maccoby, 1990, 1995).

When attempting to resolve a conflict or influence others to do something, boys take a more heavy-handed approach, often using threats or physical force. Girls are more likely to use verbal persuasion or to abandon the conflict altogether (Leaper, Tenenbaum, & Shaffer, 1999; Miller, Danaher, & Forbes, 1986; Pettit et al., 1990; Sheldon, 1990, 1992).

To Recap . . .

Sex differences are found in several physical, cognitive, and social areas. In the physical area, females generally are healthier and more developmentally advanced than males at birth and reach developmental milestones earlier. Males are more physically active—especially when in the company of other males—and more vulnerable to illness and injury.

In the cognitive area, females outperform males in rate of language acquisition. Generally, females also learn to read more easily. Recent studies show females outperform males on language and reading assessment through the high school years. Parental expectations and child-rearing practices combine with biological factors to produce this difference.

Boys and girls are initially equally interested in mathematics, but they excel in different aspects of mathematics from an early age. Girls tend to outperform males in mathematical computation, whereas males show superior performance on mathematical reasoning. On average, males also outperform females on spatial tasks from early childhood on. During adolescence, males begin to exhibit both greater interest and performance in mathematics, at least when assessed on standardized exams. Both socialization and biological factors have been implicated in sex differences in quantitative and spatial abilities.

In the area of social and personality differences, male infants are initially more fussy and less able to regulate their arousal than female infants. Perhaps in part as a result, female infants appear better equipped for social interaction. There is no evidence for sex differences in temperament over the long term, however.

Beginning in childhood, males and females use different strategies to regulate their emotions. Females tend to talk about their feelings with others, whereas males tend to use distraction or physical activity. Females are generally more emotionally expressive than males and talk more often about feeling sad. Males more readily express anger. These differences reflect differences in the kinds of conversations parents have with their children.

Females exhibit greater self-control than males. During early childhood, girls appear better able to control their impulses and comply more readily with parental requests. Girls also have a reputation for being more altruistic, helpful, and cooperative, but few sex differences in these behaviors have actually been observed. Males display more physical aggression during childhood, whereas females display more social and relational aggression.

To some extent, males and females prefer different activities. Boys tend to enjoy more active play, as well as television and computer games with violent or aggressive themes. Girls enjoy more sedentary play and tend to role-play more domestic themes. Males and females also have different academic interests. These differences appear to be influenced by cultural attitudes and opportunities to pursue different roles.

Girls have fewer, more intimate friends, whereas boys have more numerous friends. Girls also tend to prefer activities that involve smaller groups, whereas boys prefer those that require more participants. Interaction styles also differ: Girls tend to be somewhat more concerned with equal participation, and boys are concerned with issues of dominance.

BIOLOGICAL INFLUENCES ON GENDER-ROLE DEVELOPMENT

Research has clearly shown the existence of a number of sex differences. Understanding the origins of those differences has proved a greater challenge. In the following sections, we discuss how biological factors and socialization contribute to the development of sex differences and gender-role development. We turn first to biological factors. These include the genetic, structural, and physiological processes that distinguish males and females.

Like most other species, humans exhibit *sexual dimorphism*—that is, the male and female are biologically different for the purpose of reproduction. As noted earlier, the process through which these biological differences emerge is called *sex differentiation*. Many of the biological influences on gender-role development appear to result from nature's preparing the individual in this way to participate in the reproduction process.

Genetic Influences

As we explained in Chapter 3, the sex chromosomes—known as the X and the Y chromosomes—determine whether we develop as boys or girls. The X chromosome is of about average size as chromosomes go and carries a good deal of genetic material, whereas the Y chromosome is much smaller and has many fewer genes. When the pair of sex chromosomes inherited from the parents consists of two X chromosomes (XX), the person is female; when it is made up of one of each type (XY), the person is male.

The sex chromosomes have no influence at all on the fertilized zygote for about 6 weeks. At that point, if the embryo is genetically male (XY), the Y chromosome causes a portion of the embryo to become the male gonadal structure—the testes. Once this is accomplished, the Y chromosome does not appear to play any further role in the process of sex differentiation. If the embryo is genetically female (XX), the sex chromosomes produce no change at 6 weeks. At 10 to 12 weeks, however, one X chromosome causes a portion of the embryo to become female gonads—the ovaries. From this point on, sex differentiation is guided primarily by the hormones produced by the testes and the ovaries. This process does not always work as it should. When problems occur, the embryo may have an unusual arrangement of sex chromosomes. We described the physical and psychological characteristics of several such disorders in Chapter 3.

In addition to genes on the sex chromosomes, there are other genes that can affect males and females differently. Usually, this occurs when the expression of a trait requires the presence of certain levels of sex hormones. Such traits are called **sex-limited traits**. The gene for baldness, for example, may be carried by either men or women, but the characteristic appears primarily in men because high levels of male hormones are needed for it to be expressed.

Sex-Limited traits
Genes that affect males and females differently but that are not carried on the sex chromosomes.

Hormonal Influences

A major step in sex differentiation begins when the newly formed embryonic gonads begin to secrete hormones of different types. Up until about the third month of gestation, the internal sex organs of the fetus can become either male or female. When a Y chromosome causes testes to develop in the embryo, these glands secrete hormones called *androgens*, which cause the male internal reproductive organs to grow (they also secrete a chemical that causes the female organs to shrink). At 5 months, if androgens are present, the external sex organs also develop as male, producing a penis and scrotal sac. If androgens are not present at 3 months, the internal sex organs, and later the external sex organs, develop as female. The hormones produced mainly by the ovaries, estrogen and progesterone, do not play their principal role in sex differentiation until puberty.

Somewhere between 3 and 8 months after conception, sex hormones are believed to affect the development and organization of the fetal brain. The two major types of organizing effects involve hormonal regulation (how often the body releases various hormones) and brain lateralization.

Hormonal Regulation and Abnormalities   In adult humans, the pituitary gland controls the production of hormones by the gonads. One effect of these hormones is to activate certain social behaviors, including aggression, maternal behaviors, and sexual activity. Some theorists believe that sex differences in these and other social behaviors may be largely controlled by such hormones (Hines & Green, 1991).

In support of this idea, researchers have given pregnant hamsters or monkeys extra doses of testosterone (a type of androgen), for example, and found that the female offspring tended to be more aggressive, dominant, and exploratory—characteristics more common in males of the species (Hines, 1982).

Recent advances in means available to measure hormone levels in humans have made it possible to examine whether naturally occurring variations in testosterone during the prenatal period are related to the gender-role behavior of offspring (Hines et al.,

2002). Researchers measured testosterone levels in maternal blood samples obtained during routine prenatal care. When the children were 3 years of age, their parents completed a questionnaire concerning their children's involvement with sex-typed toys, games, and activities. Among girls, higher levels of testosterone during the prenatal period were linked with lower levels of sex typing. There was no relationship between prenatal testosterone levels and boys' gender-role behavior, however.

Another way to study the effects of hormones on development is to study cases where hormonal processes go awry. One such hormonal abnormality, **congenital adrenal hyperplasia (CAH),** occurs when too much androgen is produced during pregnancy. CAH usually results from an inherited enzyme deficiency that causes the adrenal glands to produce androgens, regardless of the presence or absence of testes (Breedlove & Hampson, 2002). This problem typically begins after the internal sex organs have been formed but before the external sex organs appear. The effects of the extra dose of androgens on males are fairly mild. These boys are somewhat more inclined toward intense physical activity than are normal boys, but they do not appear to be more aggressive or antisocial (Berenbaum & Hines, 1992; Berenbaum & Snyder, 1995; Hines & Kaufman, 1994).

If, however, the fetus is genetically female (XX), she will have ovaries and normal internal sex organs, but the excessive androgen will cause the external organs to develop in a masculine direction. Often the clitoris will be very large, resembling a penis, and sometimes a scrotal sac will develop (although it will be empty, because there are no testes).

In a number of reported cases, such females have been mistaken at birth for males and raised as boys (Money & Annecillo, 1987). In most cases, however, the problem is discovered at birth and corrected by surgically changing the external sex organs and by administering drugs to reduce the high levels of androgens. Although these procedures return the girls to biological normality, the early androgen exposure appears to have some long-term effects. CAH females often have better spatial abilities (but poorer verbal skills) than normal females (Kelso et al., 2000). Many of these girls also become "tomboys," preferring rough outdoor play and traditional male-stereotyped toys, while having little interest in dolls, jewelry, or activities typical of young females (Leveroni & Berenbaum, 1998).

Another type of hormonal disorder is known as androgen insensitivity. **Androgen insensitivity** is a genetic defect in males that prevents the body cells from responding to androgens, the masculinizing hormones. The testes will produce hormones, but neither internal nor external male sex organs will develop. The substance that usually shrinks the potential female internal sex organs will be effective, however, leaving the fetus with neither a uterus nor an internal male system. The external organs will develop as female. Studies have shown that androgen-insensitive individuals are generally feminine in appearance, preferences, and abilities (Breedlove & Hampson, 2002).

Taken together, evidence from animals and humans suggests that fetal sex hormones play an important part in producing differences between males and females. But hormonal processes are complex, and scientists still do not understand exactly how they interact with socialization processes.

Brain Lateralization

As we discussed earlier, the human brain is divided into left and right hemispheres that perform different functions. The left half both controls and receives information from the right side of the body, including the right ear, hand, and foot and the right visual field of each eye. The right hemisphere controls and receives information from the left side. The left hemisphere is primarily responsible for language and speech processes, whereas the right side appears to be more involved with quantitative and spatial abilities (Springer & Deutsch, 1998).

Because the division of these functions corresponds to the cognitive sex differences discussed earlier, some psychologists believe that differences in brain laterality may be important for understanding certain differences in male and female behavior. As noted earlier, some data suggest that males are more lateralized—that is, their left and right hemispheres function more independently—than are females (Bryden, 1982; McGlone, 1980).

Congenital adrenal hyperplasia (CAH)

A recessive genetic disorder in which the adrenal glands produce unusually high levels of male hormones known as androgens.

Androgen insensitivity

A genetic defect in males that prevents the body cells from responding to androgens, the masculinizing hormones.

Prenatal Influences on Gender Identity: The Case of David Reimer

BOX 15.2

Classics of
Research

In 1963, one of a pair of identical 7-month-old twin boys suffered severe injury to his penis following an accident during routine surgery. Learning that it would not be possible to reconstruct the penis, the anguished parents sought advice from Dr. John Money, a leading sex researcher at Johns Hopkins University. The parents asked if it would be better for their son to live as a physically deformed male or as a female.

Dr. Money recommended that the child be transformed into a female through surgical construction of female genitalia followed in later years by further surgery and hormone treatments. In the hope of giving their baby the best chance for a normal life, the parents agreed and proceeded to raise their son—renamed Brenda—as a girl, assured by the doctors that she would remain unaware of her original biology.

The details of this extraordinary case were first made public in 1972 (Money & Ehrhardt, 1972). In the report, the authors mentioned Brenda's tomboyishness but focused primarily on the ways in which her behavior and interests conformed to female stereotypes, especially in contrast to those of her identical twin brother. In this and subsequent updates on the twins' development, the intervention was portrayed as an unqualified success (Money, 1975).

The case received a great deal of attention in both the scientific literature and the popular press. *Time* magazine opined, "This dramatic case provides strong support for a major contention of women's liberationists: that conventional patterns of masculine and feminine behavior can be altered. It also casts doubt on the theory that major sexual differences, psychological as well as anatomical, are immutably set by the genes at conception" (*Time,* 1973, cited in Colapinto, 2000, p. 69).

In reality, the case turned out to offer strong support for the biological determinants of psychological gender. From early on, Brenda displayed more interest in toys and activities commonly preferred by boys despite the parents' best efforts to encourage stereotypically female interests and behavior. Everyone, including her twin brother, Brian, noticed Brenda's masculinity.

When I say there was nothing feminine about Brenda," Brian laughs, "I mean there was *nothing* feminine. She walked like a guy. Sat with her legs apart. She talked about guy things, didn't give a crap about cleaning house, getting married, wearing makeup. We both wanted to play with guys, build forts and have snowball fights and play army. She'd get a skipping rope for a gift, and the only thing we'd use *that* for was to tie people up, whip people with it. (Colapinto, 2000, pp. 57–58)

Brenda's tomboy looks and mannerisms elicited daily teasing and ridicule from peers as early as kindergarten. During early adolescence, Brenda made a brief but concerted effort to look and act more feminine, but the result was an appearance so unusual that even strangers would stop and stare. Moreover, Brenda did not *feel* like a girl—she felt like a freak.

Finally, Brenda rebelled. She abandoned her efforts to dress and behave like a girl, resisted the annual visits to Johns Hopkins, and refused to undergo the vaginal surgery needed to complete her transformation. When Brenda was 14, the physicians assigned to her case declared the sex reassignment a total failure and advised Brenda's father to tell her the truth. Brenda decided immediately to take steps to return to her original gender as a male and took the name David. By all accounts, David emerged as a fairly well-adjusted heterosexual male. He eventually married and became a devoted father to two adopted children.

It would be 20 years before the rest of the world learned the truth about the twins. Milton Diamond, a biologist who specialized in the effects of prenatal sex hormones on development and who had for years expressed skepticism about the case, and Keith Sigmundson, a psychiatrist who had been involved in the twins' treatment, convinced David to go public with his story (Diamond & Sigmundson, 1997).

In retrospect, one of the most remarkable aspects of this case is that so many people readily accepted the premise that it would be easy to change a normal, healthy baby boy into a girl. Why weren't there more skeptics like Diamond? One explanation is the prevailing zeitgeist in the United States in the 1960s and early 1970s. At the time, the idea that sexual orientation and sex-typed behavior were primarily the products of socialization resonated with Americans, whose gender-role expectations were changing dramatically. Today, the zeitgeist is far different. Indeed, now many scholars argue that experiential factors, rather than biological ones, are at risk of being overlooked (Lewontin, 2000; Oyama, 2000).

Studies of language and verbal abilities provide some support for the idea that brain lateralization plays a role in gender differences. For example, sex differences in hemisphere specialization have been found in both 3- and 6-month-old infants. When they responded to recordings of a voice speaking, female infants showed stronger brain-wave reactions to right-ear (left-hemisphere) presentations, whereas male infants showed stronger reactions to left-ear (right-hemisphere) presentations (Shucard & Shucard, 1990; Shucard et al., 1981). At 2 and 3 years of age, both sexes begin to process verbal stimuli (such as spoken words) through the right ear and nonverbal stimuli (such as music) through the left ear (Harper & Kraft, 1986; Kamptner, Kraft, & Harper, 1984). But at this point, males begin to show evidence of greater lateralization than females—for example, performing much better in response to verbal stimuli presented in the right ear than the left ear but showing the opposite tendency for nonverbal stimuli (Kraft, 1984).

Other research has reported that verbal abilities in males whose left hemispheres have been damaged (such as through strokes or tumors) are much more impaired than are those in females with a similar degree of damage in that area (McGlone, 1980; Sasanuma, 1980). More recently, studies using functional magnetic resonance imaging have shown that when males perform phonological tasks, activation is more localized to a specific region of the left hemisphere, whereas females show more bilateral activation (Shaywitz et al., 1995). These results suggest that language functioning in females is more equally spread between the two hemispheres.

The role of brain lateralization in spatial abilities has also been examined in a study of children's haptic (touch) performance. Children in the study first felt a pair of hidden shapes, one with each hand, for 10 seconds. They were then asked to pick out the two shapes from a visual display. For boys, left-hand (right-hemisphere) performance was better than right-hand performance. For girls, left- and right-hand performance were equal (Witelson, 1976).

The evidence that males seem to be more lateralized than females does not in itself provide a simple explanation of verbal and spatial sex differences. It does, however, suggest that some sex differences may literally exist in our brains.

To Recap . . .

In humans, the male and female are different for the purpose of reproduction, a characteristic called sexual dimorphism. The process through which these differences emerge is called sex differentiation.

The sex chromosomes—the X and Y chromosomes—determine whether an embryo develops as male or female. Abnormalities can produce individuals with unusual sex chromosome arrangements. In addition, other genes can affect males and females differently. Usually, this occurs when the expression of a trait requires the presence of certain levels of sex hormones. Such traits are called sex-limited traits.

The principal fetal hormones are androgens in males and progesterone and estrogens in females. The production of androgens by the testes is necessary for the embryo to develop as male. Androgens also affect the organization of the fetal brain.

Hormonal abnormalities in humans illustrate the role of hormones in gender-related behaviors. Congenital adrenal hyperplasia (CAH) results from the overproduction of androgens during gestation. Even with treatment, the personalities of CAH females remain masculinized. CAH males are much less affected. Androgen insensitivity involves a failure of the body cells to respond to androgens. The personalities of androgen-insensitive males are feminized.

Brain lateralization refers to specialization in function of the brain hemispheres. The right hemisphere is principally involved with quantitative and spatial abilities, and the left hemisphere is more involved with verbal abilities. Males appear to be more lateralized than females. This sex difference may be related to behavioral sex differences on verbal and spatial tasks.

SOCIALIZATION AND GENDER-ROLE DEVELOPMENT

Clearly, biological factors make important contributions to gender-role development. They do not, however, operate in isolation. Rather, biological processes interact with environmental forces in shaping gender development. We now turn to these environmental forces.

Environmental influences on the development of gender are usually viewed in terms of socialization. The socialization of gender occurs on multiple levels, ranging from the societal to the self. In the following sections, we highlight two means of socialization—modeling and differential treatment of boys and girls.

Socialization by Society

In all cultures, children are socialized to gender roles, although the specifics of the roles may differ across time and place. One way children learn about gender roles is through modeling, by observing those around them. In addition, girls and boys may experience differential treatment.

Modeling   As we have seen in earlier chapters, modeling is a powerful means of transmitting values, attitudes, beliefs, and behavioral practices from generation to generation (Bandura, 1986). Gender knowledge is no exception.

In many societies, the media have greatly expanded the variety of models available to children. Television, especially, communicates a great deal about social practices and behavior. Analyses of the contents of both network programs and commercials—in the United States and around the world—indicate that TV has generally portrayed characters in very traditional gender roles (Allan & Coltrane, 1996; Craig, 1992; Furnam, Abramsky, & Gunter, 1997; Gilly, 1988; Signorielli, 2001; Signorelli & Bacue, 1999). This is especially the case for children's noneducational cartoons (Leaper et al., 2002; Thompson & Zerbinos, 1995, 1997). Thus, it should not be surprising that children who are the heaviest TV viewers also hold the most stereotyped perceptions of male and female sex roles (Luecke-Aleksa et al., 1995; McGhee & Frueh, 1980; Signorella, Bigler, & Liben, 1993).

Differential Treatment   A second mechanism for the socialization of gender roles is differential treatment of males and females. Differential treatment can take various forms (Bussey & Bandura, 1999; Leaper, 2002). One is direct instruction, or the guided participation of the child in cultural practices (Rogoff, 1990). In some cultures, access to formal education and apprenticeships differs for males and females. Cultures also have a sexual division of labor, although the specific tasks assigned to each gender and the extent to which tasks are shared across genders vary widely across cultures.

A second type of differential treatment involves the opportunities and experiences available to males and females. For instance, worldwide, boys are generally granted greater autonomy than girls. They have greater freedom of movement and can be found farther from home without adult supervision (Whiting & Edwards, 1988). As a consequence, males have greater opportunities to explore the environment, pursue risky adventures, and work out interpersonal conflicts without adult intervention.

A third type of differential treatment concerns the expectations societies have for boys and for girls. Different expectations translate into different opportunities and

In many societies, the media are an important source of information about male and female roles.

Society makes distinctions between males and females right from infancy.

different socialization pressures. In Japan, for example, the expectations for self-control are greater for girls than for boys. Consequently, girls exhibit greater self-regulatory capabilities at a younger age than do boys (Olson & Kashiwagi, 2000).

In recent years, there has been considerable interest in whether males and females experience differential treatment in one of the primary socialization settings for children—the school. Some evidence indicates that teachers do indeed treat male and female students differently. Of particular interest has been teacher attention. Studies show rather consistently that teachers give more attention to boys than to girls. However, much of the contact is negative. For instance, teachers criticize boys more often than girls for engaging in cross-sex activities (Etaugh, Collins, & Gerson, 1975; Fagot, 1977). Boys also receive more disapproval and scolding for misbehavior than girls (Huston, 1983; Pollack, 1998).

There is less consensus regarding positive attention. Some studies have found that teachers are more attentive to boys, call on them more often, and allow them more time to speak (AAUW, 1992; Duffy, Warren, & Walsh, 2001; Sadker & Sadker, 1994). However, other studies do not find a difference in the amount of attention teachers direct to male and females students (Kleinfeld, 1996). Interestingly, girls see themselves as participating in class as much as boys. Moreover, when asked whom teachers call on most often and pay the most attention to, the majority of both middle and high school males and females report a gender bias—favoring girls (AAUW/Greenberg-Lake, 1990; Harris, 1997).

If boys do receive more attention from teachers than girls, it may be in part because they actively elicit it. A majority of over 1,000 6th- through 12th-grade teachers responding to a survey reported that boys demanded more attention in the classroom than girls (Harris, 1997). And a recent observational study of middle school science classrooms found that half of the teachers did call on boys more often than girls. However, in these classrooms, the boys also volunteered to answer questions more frequently than their female classmates (Altermatt, Jovanovic, & Perry, 1998).

Like the parents described in the following section, teachers sometimes hold gender-stereotyped beliefs about the abilities of males and females. Some studies suggest that teachers attribute greater ability in math and science to males (Li, 1999), although other studies do not find a gender difference in teacher beliefs about ability (Helwig, Anderson, & Tindal, 2001). When teachers believe that male and female students are different in terms of ability or interest, it is reflected in the number and kinds of questions they ask of each gender, as well as the amount of encouragement they provide (She, 2000).

Evidence that males and females have different experiences in school has fostered concern that schools shortchange students of both genders. Some advocates argue that schools undermine girls' self-confidence and career aspirations and discourage interest in traditionally male domains such as math and science (AAUW, 1992; Oakes, 1990). Partly in response to these assertions, schools and other organizations have done much to transform the educational experiences of many females. With the exception of physics, female high school students now enroll in as many mathematics and science courses as males (Sanders, Koch, & Urso, 1997). And they achieve scores within 5 to 10 points of males on standardized tests of mathematics and science (National Center for Education Statistics, 1997).

Concern is now growing that schools are failing to meet the needs of males (AAUW, 2001; Gally, 2002; Lesko, 2000; Noble & Bradford, 2000; Skelton, 2001). Indeed, boys do appear to be falling behind girls in educational achievement. The gender gap in reading and writing has actually widened, with males scoring on average about 15 points lower than girls on standardized tests (National Center for Education Statistics, 1997).

Socialization by Parents

Parents, too, can influence children's learning about gender roles through modeling and through differential treatment.

Modeling   Because parents are typically important figures in children's lives, they are especially salient models for what it means to be male or female (Bussey & Bandura,

1999). As we have seen, however, there is no shortage of gender role models in children's lives. Thus, it can be difficult to isolate the effects of modeling by parents from other models, such as television characters, classmates, and other adults.

One way to address this issue is to examine gender-role development in families in which parents' roles deviate from traditional cultural norms. In such situations, parents model behavior different from what children typically observe in other settings. Researchers have examined gender-role development of children in single-parent households and alternative living arrangements (e.g., communes), as well as among children with lesbian parents and in families where mothers are employed. These studies find few differences in gender-role development among children from different types of families (Anderson, Amlie, & Ytteroy, 2002; Golombok et al., 2003; Serbin, Powlishta, & Gulko, 1993; Stevens et al., 2002; Stevenson & Black, 1988; Weisner & Wilson-Mitchell, 1990). And when differences are found, they tend to be small and specific to children of a particular age, gender, or socioeconomic status.

The fact that researchers have had so little luck linking variations in gender-role development to differences in parents' roles does not mean that no link is there. Rather, simply knowing whether a parent is, for example, married or employed reveals little about what children actually observe in the home. Studies that have examined parents' attitudes and behavior show that in homes where parents perform nontraditional jobs and chores, children do indeed hold less stereotyped ideas about the proper roles of men and women (Deutsch, Servis, & Payne, 2001; Hoffman & Youngblade, 1999; Serbin et al., 1993; Weisner, Garnier, & Loucky, 1994). Interestingly, however, even in homes where parents enthusiastically endorse egalitarian ideals, girls, and especially boys, often maintain strong preferences for sex-typed peers, toys, and clothing (Weisner & Wilson-Mitchell, 1990).

There is also evidence that African American children are less sex typed than European American children, perhaps because of the more egalitarian gender roles in African American families. African American children are more likely to have friends of the other sex (Kovacs, Parker, & Hoffman, 1996). And whereas European American girls exhibit more interest in babies than do their male counterparts, African American boys and girls both show as much interest in babies as European American girls (Reid & Trotter, 1993).

Differential Treatment   Another way parents may socialize gender differences is by treating sons and daughters differently. As with influences at the societal level, differential treatment by parents includes instruction, opportunities, and attitudes. For instance, parents are sometimes quite explicit in teaching sons or daughters skills traditionally associated with one or the other gender—as when fathers recruit sons, but not daughters, to help with home repairs. Differential treatment can also be largely unconscious. We have seen, for example, that parents talk about emotions differently with sons and daughters. Most parents are probably unaware of this difference. Nonetheless, a consequence of this differential treatment is that boys and girls learn different ways of expressing and coping with emotions.

Studies show that parents also offer sons and daughters different opportunities. The most notable example is children's play (Lytton & Romney, 1991). Parents tend to play differently with sons and daughters. During infancy, parents are more likely to physically stimulate boys than girls (Frisch, 1977; MacDonald & Parke, 1986). This emphasis on physical play with boys is maintained during early childhood. Both mothers and fathers tend to engage in more physical play with sons and pretend play with daughters; however, rough physical play is especially likely among fathers and sons (Jacklin, DiPietro, & Maccoby, 1984; Lindsey & Mize, 2001; Lindsey, Mize, & Pettit, 1997).

In wealthy cultures that place a premium on play, differential treatment is also apparent in parents' selection of toys (Lytton & Romney, 1991). Parents tend to give boys more sports equipment, vehicles, and tools, and girls more dolls and toy kitchen sets (Fisher-Thompson, 1993; Rheingold & Cook, 1975; Robinson & Morris, 1986). In many families, infants are given sex-typed toys within the first few months of life—long before they can express any kind of toy preferences themselves (Pomerleau et al., 1990).

Children begin to demonstrate preferences for same-sex toys between their first and second birthdays. Parents encourage gender-appropriate play during this period by more often offering gender-appropriate or neutral toys than those traditionally viewed as appropriate for the other sex (Caldera, Huston, & O'Brien, 1989; Eisenberg et al., 1985; Wood, Desmarais, & Gugula, 2002). Parents are likely to express approval (smile, act excited, comment approvingly) for gender-appropriate play and activities and to respond negatively to behaviors considered characteristic of the other sex (Fagot & Hagan, 1991; Fagot & Leinbach, 1987; Leaper et al., 1995).

Parents' gender typing of play tends to be stronger with sons than daughters. This is especially true of fathers. Fathers appear to be more concerned both that their male child be masculine and that their female child be feminine, whereas mothers tend to treat their sons and daughters alike (Fisher-Thompson, 1993; Jacklin et al., 1984; Turner & Gervai, 1995). These more rigid attitudes are expressed in fathers' descriptions of what constitutes appropriate gender-role behaviors as well as in their actual interactions with their sons and daughters (Bronstein, 1994; Lindsey et al., 1997; Siegal, 1987).

Sex typing of play is important because different kinds of play provide opportunities to acquire and practice different skills. Female-stereotyped play, such as pretense involving domestic themes, encourages nurturance and certain types of social understanding. Pretense also depends more heavily on language than the kinds of activities parents more often enjoy with sons—such as physical play and construction activities. In turn, these male-stereotyped activities foster a different set of knowledge and abilities, including visual-spatial skills and physical strength, endurance, and coordination.

As children move into the elementary school years, parents begin to provide them with other kinds of experiences, such as dance classes, music lessons, and sports activities. One ongoing study of a group of approximately 600 children has found that parents provide different experiences for sons and daughters (Eccles et al., 2000). As shown in Table 15.2, these experiences tend to reflect gender stereotypes and to parallel gender differences in interests and achievement that emerge in later childhood and adolescence. For example, parents are far more likely to encourage sons to either view or participate in sports. Conversely, they more often encourage daughters to read and take music and dance lessons.

Parents also often hold different expectations for sons and daughters. Even before newborns leave the hospital, parents use very different terms to describe their little boys (e.g., "firmer," "better coordinated," "stronger") (Rubin, Provenzano, & Luria, 1974). As infants become mobile, mothers tend to perceive their infant sons to have better crawling abilities—and daughters to have worse crawling skills—than they really do (Mondschein, Adolph, & Tamis-LeMonda, 2000). During middle childhood, parents rate sons as more capable in sports than daughters (Eccles et al., 2000). And when boys and girls achieve success in sports, parents attribute the success to different factors. Boys' sports achievements are attributed to "natural talent," whereas girls' achievements are attributed to hard work (Eccles, Jacobs, et al., 1993).

Parents hold different expectations for males and females in the academic realm as well. As noted earlier, parents believe daughters' reading ability to be greater than sons' (Eccles, Arbreton, et al., 1993; Wigfield et al., 2002). They also believe that mathematics is more natural for boys than for girls and tend to underestimate girls' mathematics abilities and overestimate boys' (Eccles et al., 2000). Similar findings have emerged in science (Tenenbaum & Leaper, 2003). As in mathematics, there is no gender difference in science aptitude or achievement during elementary school. Nonetheless, parents generally endorse the cultural stereotype that boys are better in science than girls.

Parents' gender-stereotyped expectations regarding children's abilities and interests contribute to children's gender-role development in two ways. First, as we have seen, these expectations lead parents to provide boys and girls with different opportunities to develop specific skills and competencies. Second, parents' views of their children's abilities influence children's own developing sense of competence and interest in different

Table 15.2	Parents' Provision of Experiences for Daughters and Sons (Grades 2, 3, and 5)		

Activity	Girls	Boys
Have child read to you	3.10	2.90
Play sports with child	2.63	3.36
Do active, outdoor activities with child	3.20	3.56
Take child to paid sporting event	1.71	1.91
Encourage child to do math- or science-related activities at home	4.01	4.35
Encourage child to work on or play with a computer outside of school	3.70	4.04
Encourage child to read	6.04	5.69
Encourage child to play competitive sports	3.58	4.43
Encourage child to play noncompetitive sports	4.54	4.94
Encourage child to take dance lessons	3.56	2.15
Encourage child to take dancing for fun	3.85	2.53
Encourage child to watch sports on TV	2.61	3.07
Encourage child to take music lessons	4.26	3.52
Encourage child to play a musical instrument	4.32	3.67
Enourage child to build, make, or fix things	3.83	4.67
Encourage child to learn cooking and other homemaking	4.01	3.59

Ratings were made on 7-point scales: 1 = never/strongly discourage; 7 = almost every day/strongly encourage. All differences between girls' and boys' means are significant at $p < .05$

SOURCE: Adapted from J. S. Eccles, C. Freedman-Doan, P. Frome, J. Jacobs, & K. S. Yoon (2000). "Gender-Role Socialization in the Family: A Longitudinal Approach," in T. Eckes & H. M. Trautner (Eds.), *The Developmental Social Psychology of Gender,* Mahwah, NJ: Erlbaum. Adapted by permission.

domains (Eccles et al., 2000; Tiedemann, 2000; Wigfield et al., 2002). Children whose parents rate their ability as low in a domain tend to also rate their own ability lower than it really is. Furthermore, in American society, where effort is generally viewed less positively than in many other cultures, children whose parents believe they will have to work hard to be successful at something are likely to lose interest and channel their efforts to domains where they believe they can excel more easily.

Socialization by Peers

The peer group is another powerful socialization force in children's lives. Studies consistently show that peers reinforce one another for engaging in gender-typed play and punish those who deviate from established norms. Although boys and girls are both criticized by peers for cross-sex play, the consequences are especially severe for boys (Carter & McCloskey, 1984; Lamb & Roopnarine, 1979; Zucker et al., 1995).

In one early study, Beverly Fagot (1977) observed children's reactions to cross-gender play in a number of preschool classrooms. Girls who enjoyed boys' activities were allowed to join boys' groups and went back and forth between girl and boy groups with relative ease. The story for boys was quite different. Boys had especially strong reactions to male classmates who violated gender norms. They taunted and teased those who played with the girls, using derogatory terms such as "sissy boy." When the "offending" boys tried to rejoin the boy groups, they were rejected, criticized, and physically threatened. The negative reactions continued throughout nursery school, even though most of the boys learned quite quickly to avoid playing with girls or in girls' activities.

The Influence of Opposite-Sex Siblings on Interests, Activities, and Behavior

Historically, most studies of socialization of gender roles have focused on parents, peers, or nonfamily influences, such as schools and the media. Recently, researchers have begun to explore the impact that siblings have on gender-role development. Of particular interest is the potential impact of having an opposite-sex sibling on interests, activities, and behavior.

Rust and colleagues (Rust et al., 2000) recently examined this question in a massive study of British children. Participants included over 2,000 3-year-olds with older siblings under the age of 12 and a comparable number of singletons (children without siblings). Parents completed a questionnaire that included items about children's toys, activities, and interpersonal characteristics. According to parents, preschoolers with same-sex older siblings engaged in more sex-typed play and exhibited more sex-typed interpersonal behavior than children with an older sibling of the opposite sex. The ratings of singletons fell between the two sibling groups.

Interestingly, having an older brother had a bigger effect on the younger siblings than having an older sister. Compared with singletons and children with older sisters, younger boys *and* girls with older brothers exhibited more masculinized toy and activity preferences and interpersonal characteristics and less feminized ones. Although boys with older sisters did exhibit more feminine interests and behaviors, the presence of an older sister did not decrease their masculine traits.

Why might having an older brother matter more? One possibility is that the activities of older brothers are more highly regarded. As we have seen, it is more acceptable for girls to behave like boys than for boys to behave like girls. And girls are more likely to imitate male models than boys are to imitate females.

Another possibility is that older brothers exert greater pressure on younger siblings to engage in the kinds of activities they prefer. We know from studies of preschool peer groups that boys—at least among European American samples—use more forceful control tactics than girls, and consequently have more influence over girls than girls have over boys. Younger brothers may be less influenced by their older sisters both because sanctions against cross-sex play are stronger for boys and because the older sisters are less successful (or perhaps less interested) in inducing their little brothers to play with them or at least to play what the girls want to play.

Other studies have examined the impact of opposite-sex siblings among older children and adolescents, who might be expected to spend less time together—and consequently have less influence on one another—than siblings do when they are young. The results of these studies suggest that older siblings continue to influence the gender-role development and behavior of their younger brothers and sisters. One study (McHale et al., 2001) even found that the gender-role orientations of older siblings (ages 10–12 years) were stronger predictors of second-borns' gender-role attitudes, sex-typed personality characteristics, and masculine leisure activities than were those of the parents.

Other research suggests that sibling influence can extend to one's relations with peers, at least among females. Compared with girls with older sisters, girls with older brothers reported more controlling behavior with their friends. These findings suggest that girls learn male-typical control strategies in their interactions with their older brothers, which they then utilize in their friendships (Updegraff, McHale, & Crouter, 2000).

The extent to which siblings contribute to one another's gender-role development will surely vary depending on a host of factors, including the quality of the relationship between the siblings, the amount of time they spend together, exposure to other socialization influences, and so forth. Moreover, some children may be more open to the influence of an opposite-sex sibling. For example, one recent study found that having a brother and the associated opportunities to engage in male-stereotyped play enhanced girls' spatial abilities, but only for girls believed to have an inherited predisposition to acquire spatial skills fairly easily. Girls for whom spatial tasks were expected to be challenging did not benefit from having a brother and, in fact, developed better spatial skills when there were no boys in the house (Casey, Nuttall, & Pezaris, 1999)!

BOX 15.3

On the Cutting EDGE

Research suggests that older brothers may be especially important contributors to their younger siblings' gender-role development.

Children actively maintain strictures against cross-sex interaction throughout middle childhood. One particularly revealing study of preadolescents at a summer camp described a set of "rules" that dictate children's interactions with members of the opposite sex (see Table 15.3). These guidelines have come to be known as "the cootie rules" because children observing them often behave as though they have been contaminated by just being near a member of the opposite sex (Sroufe et al., 1993). Basically, the rules state that one cannot freely choose to interact with a peer of the opposite sex, but they acknowledge that contact is sometimes inevitable or unavoidable. Under those circumstances, it is acceptable. Interestingly, children who adhere most closely to the rules and maintain them most actively are liked the most by peers and judged to be most socially competent by adults.

Given their proclivity to avoid contact with the other sex, it is not surprising that children spend much of their time in the company of same-sex peers. In simpler societies, gender segregation is imposed by adults, who manage children's lives in ways that separate boys and girls. For instance, in some societies, boys are assigned chores (such as herding) that take them away from home, whereas girls take on domestic duties that keep them near adult women and other girls (Whiting & Edwards, 1988). In other societies, children attend single-sex schools or are kept largely separate in other ways. As we have seen, however, gender segregation also prevails in societies where children are free to associate—indeed, are *encouraged* to associate—with opposite-sex peers. Gender segregation emerges around age 3 and is routinely observed in mixed-sex settings, such as daycare and preschool. Although children regularly play with the opposite sex in homes and in neighborhoods, there is apparently a very powerful tendency for children to seek out companions of the same sex and to avoid children of the opposite sex (Hartup, 1983; Leaper, 1994; Maccoby & Jacklin, 1974).

The causes of gender segregation are not well understood (Fagot, Rodgers, & Leinbach, 2000; Maccoby, 2000; Powlishta et al., 2001). One explanation is that children are naturally attracted to children with play styles that are compatible with their own. And, as we have seen, boys and girls exhibit rather distinct play styles beginning at an early age. Although there is some evidence to support this theory of gender segregation (Moller & Serbin, 1996), it cannot be the whole story. Children often react more positively to others of their same gender before they have had time to learn much about their play styles (Martin, 1989; Serbin & Sprafkin, 1986). Children also exhibit a preference for same-sex adults, for whom play styles are not as important (Serbin & Sprafkin,

Table 15.3	The "Cootie" Rules: Under What Circumstances Is It Permissible to Have Contact with the Other Gender in Middle Childhood?

Rule: The contact is accidental.
Example: You're not looking where you are going and you bump into someone.

Rule: The contact is incidental.
Example: You go to get some lemonade and wait while two children of the other gender get some. (There should be no conversation.)

Rule: The contact is in the guise of some clear and necessary purpose.
Example: You may say, "Pass the lemonade," to persons of the other gender at the next table. No interest in them is expressed.

Rule: An adult compels you to have contact.
Example: "Go get that map from X and Y and bring it to me."

Rule: You are accompanied by some of your own gender.
Two girls may talk to two boys though physical closeness with your own partner must be maintained and physical intimacy with the others is disallowed.

Rule: The interaction or contact is accompanied by disavowal.
You say someone is ugly or hurl some other insult or (more commonly for boys) push or throw something at them as you pass by.

SOURCE: L. A. Sroufe, C. Bennett, M. Englund, J. Urban, & S. Shulman, "The Significance of Gender Boundaries in Preadolescence: Contemporary Correlates and Antecedents of Boundary Relations and Maintenance," *Child Development, 64,* 1993, 455–466. Reprinted by permission.

1986). In addition, children's preference for same-sex companions extends beyond a willingness to play with them. Children exhibit an own-sex favoritism that colors their perception of a wide variety of sex-typed traits (Powlishta, 1995).

Whatever the causes of gender segregation may be, the consequences of same-sex gender groupings are very important for children's gender-role development. As we saw earlier, boy and girl groups differ in size, the nature of activities, and norms for social interaction. According to Eleanor Maccoby (1998), a prominent gender theorist, the dynamics of interaction in boys and girls groups are so different that the groups constitute separate "cultures of childhood." These "peer cultures," in turn, foster the development of distinct sets of social-emotional skills and propensities.

Others believe the gender segregation during early and middle childhood contributes to the development of sexual orientation (Bem, 1996, 2000). We return to this topic later.

Socialization by Self

So far, our discussion of socialization portrays children as largely responding passively to pressures from outside. However, a central premise of socialization accounts of gender-role development is that children participate actively in the process of socialization. Here we discuss two ways that children can be said to "self-socialize" their gender roles.

One way is through their selection of models. Although children of both genders can learn male and female gender stereotypes by viewing models, children tend to focus on models of their own gender. Children are better able to recall and imitate the behavior of same-sex models (Bussey & Bandura, 1984, 1992; Perry & Bussey, 1979). In addition, children are sensitive to the gender appropriateness of the model's activity. If a male child, for example, believes that a behavior is "female," he is unlikely to imitate it even if it is modeled by a male (Masters, 1979; Raskin & Israel, 1981).

The tendency to attend more to same-sex models is especially strong for boys, who often resist imitating behaviors modeled by females. In contrast, although girls prefer to imitate adult women, they will also imitate adult men (Bussey & Perry, 1982; Slaby & Frey, 1975). Generally, both boys and girls are more likely to imitate models perceived to be powerful. The greater likelihood of cross-sex imitation by girls than boys may reflect their perception that our culture invests males with higher status and greater rewards (Williams, 1987).

Second, external sanctions (such as negative reactions from parents and peers) are gradually internalized as self-sanctions. As children acquire knowledge about the likely consequences of gender-linked conduct, they come to regulate their actions accordingly (Bussey & Bandura, 1999). Children's regulation of their own sex-typed play was graphically illustrated in a study that examined preschoolers' reactions to opportunities to play with a variety of gender-typed toys or toys linked to the other gender (Bussey & Bandura, 1992). When only other-sex toys were available, some boys attempted to have the stereotypically feminine toys removed. When that failed, the boys did all they could to avoid playing with the toys. One boy was reported to fling the baby doll across the room and turn his back on it. Others transformed the toys into more masculine props, such as using the egg beater in the kitchen set as a drill or gun. Children's self-ratings correspond to these behavioral observations. At age 4, both boys and girls rated themselves more positively when they played with own-sex toys and negatively when they played with toys usually associated with the other sex.

Other studies show that young children adapt their toy preferences to win approval from peers (Serbin et al., 1979). In one recent study (Banerjee & Lintern, 2000), boys and girls between the ages of 4 and 9 described their activity and toy preferences twice—once when alone and once when facing a group of same-sex peers. Whereas the older children did not change their self-descriptions when in front of peers, younger boys presented themselves as more sex-typed in front of peers than they did when alone.

As you can see, the process of "self-socialization" requires a good deal of knowledge about gender and related attributes. What children know about gender and when they know it is the focus of the next section.

Sex differences in toy preferences and play patterns emerge vary early.

To Recap . . .

Gender-role socialization occurs at many levels—society, family, peer, and the self. Two mechanisms of socialization are modeling and differential treatment. Children readily acquire gender-appropriate conduct by observing those around them. In simpler societies, there is little variation in the behaviors children observe. In modern societies, children have an abundance of models to choose from, ranging from family members to characters depicted on television and other media outlets.

In all societies, males and females are treated somewhat differently. Differential treatment includes direct instruction and guided participation, the provision of opportunities and experiences, and expectations. Although the specifics vary from culture to culture, differential treatment fosters the development of different skills, abilities, and attitudes.

Peers are also a powerful socialization force. Of particular importance is the same-sex peer group. From an early age, children in all cultures spend much of their time with same-sex peers. Although the causes of gender segregation are not well understood, theorists believe it has important consequences for the development of gender-role behavior.

Children themselves contribute importantly to the socialization process through their selection of appropriate models and the application of self-sanctions to gender-linked behavior.

UNDERSTANDING GENDER ROLES AND STEREOTYPES

We have reviewed considerable evidence that socialization processes are involved in sex typing. In this section, we turn to the cognitive processes that influence gender-role development. Of particular interest is the developing child's increasing understanding of gender roles and stereotypes.

The Development of Gender Identity

We have already mentioned Kohlberg's stage model of gender constancy, which includes gender identity ("I am a boy/girl"), gender stability ("I will grow up to be a man/woman"), and gender consistency ("I cannot change my sex") (Kohlberg & Ullian, 1974; Slaby & Frey, 1975). Data from a number of studies have confirmed this theoretical progression. By 3 years of age, almost all children display gender identity. Gender stability follows at about 4 years of age, and gender consistency at about 5. Males and females progress through these stages at approximately the same rate (Bem, 1989; Fagot, 1985; Martin & Little, 1990). This progression has been demonstrated in a variety of cultures, although children in many non-Western cultures appear to proceed through the stages more slowly (Munroe, Shimmin, & Munroe, 1984).

The Development of Gender Knowledge

Recent research shows that children develop some knowledge about gender categories during the first 2 years of life. By just 2 months of age, infants can discriminate male and female voices (Jusczyk, Pisoni, & Mullennix, 1992). By the end of the first year, children are able to categorize people by gender on the basis of features such as voice pitch and hair length (Leinbach & Fagot, 1993; Patterson & Werker, 2002; Poulin-Dubois et al., 1994; Walker-Andrews et al., 1991).

Once the categories of male and female are established, children begin to associate other attributes with gender. By about 2, children can reliably sort pictures of males and females and their accessories (clothes, tools, and appliances) into separate piles and accurately point to pictures of things for males and things for females (Fagot, Leinbach, & Hagan, 1986; O'Brien & Huston, 1985). There is some evidence that toddlers also have some awareness of the typical activities of men and women at around age 2 (Poulin-Dubois et al., 2002). Within about 1 year, they are able to verbally label toys as for boys or for girls (Weinraub et al., 1984).

Over the course of early childhood, children begin to incorporate more abstract or metaphorical concepts into their gender stereotypes. For example, perhaps as early as age 2 and certainly by age 4, children come to associate hardness and items such as bears and eagles with boys and softness, flowers, butterflies, and the color pink with girls (Eichstedt et al., 2002; Leinbach, Hort, & Fagot, 1997). During middle childhood, children gradually add information about occupations, behavioral traits, and personality differences to their stereotypes (Best & Williams, 1993; Liben & Bigler, 2002; Serbin et al., 1993; Signorella et al., 1993).

Children's gender stereotypes mirror those of the adults in their cultural communities (Williams & Best, 1990). Cross-cultural studies show that male stereotypes are generally learned earlier than female stereotypes, although there are exceptions. Female stereotypes are learned earlier in Germany and in Latin/Catholic cultures (Brazil, Chile, Portugal, Venezuela), where the adult-defined female stereotype is more positive than the male (Best, 2001).

Flexibility of Gender Stereotypes

The rigidity or flexibility of children's gender stereotypes changes over the course of childhood. During the preschool years, most children view gender roles in inflexible, absolutist terms (consistent with preoperational thinking) and consider cross-sex behaviors to be serious violations of social standards.

By middle childhood, children generally have begun to view gender roles as socially determined rules and conventions that can be approached somewhat flexibly and broken without major consequences (Serbin et al., 1993; Stoddart & Turiel, 1985; Trautner, 1992). This flexibility reflects several developmental achievements, including more advanced classification skills (Bigler & Liben, 1992; Trautner, 1992), a growing awareness of the cultural relativity of gender norms (Carter & Patterson, 1982; Damon, 1977; Levy, Taylor, & Gelman, 1995; Stoddart & Turiel, 1985), and an increasingly sophisticated understanding of biology. For instance, one study presented children with a story of a baby who had been raised on an island with only members of the opposite sex. When asked which gender characteristics the baby would eventually display, children younger than age 9 or 10 predicted that the baby's biological sex would determine its later characteristics. Children above that age, in contrast, believed that the baby would be more influenced by the social environment and so would adopt the characteristics of the opposite sex (Taylor, 1996).

The transition to junior high school appears to increase adolescents' flexibility toward the roles of males and females. This may occur because the fairly dramatic change in setting and routine forces young adolescents to rethink many of their previous ideas (Katz & Ksansnak, 1994). Nevertheless, across the junior high and high school years, gender stereotypes become increasingly rigid again (Alfieri, Ruble, & Higgins, 1996).

Gender Knowledge and Behavior

We have seen that some forms of gender knowledge are present very early in childhood. But does this knowledge affect children's behavior? Evidence suggests that it does.

Toy Preferences   As suggested earlier, sex differences in children's play emerge between the first and second birthdays, before children of both sexes can reliably identify toys as being more appropriate or typical for girls or boys (Campbell, Shirley, & Caygill, 2002; Serbin et al., 2001). Consequently, gender knowledge is probably not critical for the emergence of sex-typed play. It does, however, exert considerable influence on children's play preferences as they grow older.

One way to study the effects of gender knowledge on children's play is to present children with toys described as being for boys (e.g., "I think boys like the toys in this box better than girls do") or for girls or for both boys and girls. Studies using this procedure show that by the preschool years, children spend more time exploring own-sex toys and rate own-sex toys as more attractive even if the opposite sex or neutral toys are actually more appealing—that is, *if* children remember the labels, and not all children do (Bradbard et al., 1986; Frey & Ruble, 1992; Martin, Eisenbud, & Rose, 1995).

Motivation   Gender labeling also influences children's motivation, accuracy, and expectancies for success. In one study (Montemayor, 1974), 6- to 8-year-old children were shown a novel game (Mr. Munchie) that involved throwing marbles into a clown's body. Some children were told that the game was a toy for boys, "like basketball." Others were told it was a girls' game, "like jacks"; and yet others were given no information about the game. Children performed better, reported liking the game more, and gave the game higher ratings when told the game was for their own sex versus the other sex.

Researchers have examined the impact of gender labels on children's motivation and performance on a variety of other tasks, including academic ones (Gold & Berger, 1978; Stein, Pohly, & Mueller, 1971). The results from these studies confirm that children, especially boys, are vulnerable to stereotypes at a young age. This vulnerability may have both short- and long-term effects. In the short term, children may be less inclined to try activities they deem appropriate for the opposite sex. Once children decide that an activity is more appropriate for the other sex (for example, that "reading is for girls"), their performance on the activity may suffer. In this way, the gender label serves to maintain both the stereotype and the sex difference (Carter & Levy, 1988; Levy & Carter, 1989).

Memory   Gender stereotypes influence what children remember. Children remember more about same-sex peers and activities than other-sex peers and activities (Ruble & Stangor, 1986; Signorella et al., 1993; Stangor & McMillan, 1992). Gender information also influences children's memory for scripted sequences of behaviors (Chapter 9). Boys, but not girls, show better memory for own-gender than other-gender scripts (Bauer, 1993; Boston & Levy, 1991; Levy & Fivush, 1993).

Children's recall is better when information is consistent with the gender schemas they have formed. For example, in several studies, children were shown a series of pictures or photographs, each depicting either a male or female performing a gender-stereotyped activity. The children later were shown two pictures and asked which one they had seen earlier. Children had more accurate memory for gender-consistent pictures (such as a woman ironing clothes) than for gender-inconsistent pictures (such as a man ironing clothes) (Bigler & Liben, 1990; Boston & Levy, 1991; Liben & Signorella, 1993). Children sometimes even misremember information so as to make it consistent with their stereotypes (Martin & Halverson, 1983; Signorella & Liben, 1984). These kinds of memory distortions appear to peak at about 5 to 6 years and then decline with age (Stangor & Ruble, 1987; Welch-Ross & Schmidt, 1996).

Social Judgments   Children—like adults—use gender knowledge to make inferences and judgments about other people. As was true of gender-related recall, young children are better able to make stereotypic inferences when given own-sex cues than other-sex cues. For example, a girl told about a child who likes to play with kitchen sets would likely infer that the same child would also like to play with dolls. She would be less likely, however, to draw appropriate inferences if told about a boy who likes to play with trucks.

By around age 8, children are able to use other-gender cues to draw inferences about the opposite sex. Developmental differences also emerge when children are presented conflicting information about another person, such as a boy who enjoys playing with dolls. Young children tend to reason simply on the basis of the child's gender and infer that because the unfamiliar child is a boy, he will probably like to play with trucks. Older children rely more on individuating information (e.g., the target child's individual interests, traits, appearance) and infer that this particular boy may not behave in sex-stereotyped ways (Berndt & Heller, 1986; Biernat, 1991; Martin, 1989).

A recent study of Chinese and Israeli school-age children shows that the extent to which children draw inferences that run counter to gender stereotypes also depends on cultural acceptance of behavior that deviates from the norm (Lobel et al., 2001). Chinese society places a high value on conformity to cultural norms and discourages individual differences. Chinese children, especially boys, are less likely to rely on individuating information than their Western counterparts and, hence, are more likely to infer that a boy with stereotypically feminine interests would have masculine toy and occupation preferences.

The range of possible inferences increases as children gain additional stereotypic information about the sexes. For example, when told of a boy who admired another child's bicycle, school-age boys and girls were likely to suggest that the boy was the kind of person who likes to steal things. In contrast, when the character was a girl, children were more likely to claim that she was simply trying to be friendly (Heyman, 2001).

To Recap . . .

Almost all children display gender identity by about age 3, gender stability by about age 4, and gender consistency by about age 5. Males and females progress through these stages at about the same rate, and the progression has been demonstrated in a variety of cultures, although children in many non-Western cultures appear to proceed through the stages more slowly.

Gender-role knowledge involves awareness of the concepts of male and female and their culturally defined stereotypes. Even young infants can learn to discriminate the categories of male and female. Children generally understand the basic male–female concept by age 2. Gender labeling of toys appears at age 3, and an awareness of sex-typed personality traits at about age 5.

Sex-typed labels affect children's behavior. When activities or objects are seen as being for one gender or the other, children prefer the same-sex activities and avoid the cross-sex ones. Children also tend to perform better on same-sex-labeled activities.

Children also use gender information to draw inferences about other people. As children get older, they increasingly view gender roles as socially determined, and their attitudes toward violations become more tolerant and flexible—if they live in a culture that encourages tolerance.

DEVELOPMENT OF SEXUAL RELATIONSHIPS AND BEHAVIOR

Throughout childhood, the dominant theme in children's relations with the opposite sex is segregation. As children move into adolescence, hetereosexual attraction becomes increasingly powerful, opposing the forces of cross-sex avoidance. There is, of course, marked individual variation in sexuality and **sexual orientation.** Nonetheless, most adolescents develop a sexual attraction to those of the opposite sex, and the peer culture of adolescence is dominated by a heterosexual orientation. In this section, we describe how adolescents manage the transition to adult sexual relationships. We begin with a discussion of the emergence of romantic and sexual interest.

Sexual orientation
A person's sexual preference. Heterosexuals are attracted to members of the opposite sex, and homosexuals are attracted to members of the same sex.

Emergence of Romantic and Sexual Interest

Children are aware of each other as potential romantic and sexual partners from early on. Romantic themes involving dating, courtship, and marriage dominate much of girls' play. In the meantime, boys engage in sexy "locker room" talk about girls' bodies (Maccoby, 1998). "Kiss-and-chase" games that are the mainstay of elementary school playgrounds in industrialized societies are observed in cultures around the world as well (Sutton-Smith & Roberts, 1973). During middle childhood when children are at the peak of opposite gender avoidance, children tease each other for "liking" or "loving" a child of the opposite sex (Maccoby, 1998; Thorne, 1993).

How do children move from these kinds of immature relationships to the sexually mature relationships of adulthood? Until recently, sexual maturation was highly regulated by cultural practices and prescribed social expectations. In some cultures, this remains true even today. But in many communities, young people must negotiate their entry into dating and sexuality with little direct support from parents or other adults. In these communities, the peer group serves as an important context for the development of heterosexual relationships.

Numerous theorists have found it helpful to consider the transition as a series of stages or phases (Brown, 1999; Dunphy, 1963; O'Sullivan, Graber, & Brooks-Gunn, 2001). Boys and girls typically report experiencing their first romantic interests, or "crushes," between the ages of 7 and 10. Most often, these crushes are directed at unavailable targets, such as teachers and celebrities.

Between the ages of 10 and 14 years, young people spend increasing amounts of time in mixed sex groups just "hanging out" and going places together. There is initially little intimacy in these encounters. Gradually, activities such as dances and parties that require more intimacy increase in frequency. Games with some sexual content (e.g., Spin the Bottle, Man Hunt, and Seven Minutes of Heaven) and kissing and touching breasts or genitals over clothes become more common (O'Sullivan et al., 2001). Nonetheless, having numerous peers around remains important to ensure that behavior remains within culturally acceptable bounds.

By middle adolescence (15 to 16 years), approximately half of U.S. adolescents are involved in a romantic relationship (Feiring, 1996). Nonetheless, couples continue to spend much of their time in mixed-sex groups that include peers involved in romantic relationships and other adolescents who are just friends.

During later adolescence, romantic relationships involve greater levels of emotional and sexual intimacy. The relationships are also longer in duration and involve more solitary activities than those observed in younger adolescents (O'Sullivan et al., 2001). Research generally reports significant correspondence between stages of dating (e.g., casual, steady, engaged) and sexual activity (e.g., kissing, petting, intercourse) (Jessor & Jessor, 1977; McCabe & Collins, 1984; Miller et al., 1986). National surveys show that by 12th grade, approximately 60% of youth in the United States have had sexual intercourse (Centers For Disease Cantrol, 2002). Most females and approximately 50% of males first experience intercourse within a committed relationship (Jessor & Jessor, 1977).

Both supporters and critics of stage models of the development of sexual and romantic bonds acknowledge that large numbers of adolescents do not conform to the normative model just described. Studies suggest there may be cultural differences in the order in which sexual behaviors emerge (Smith & Udry, 1985). Individuals who are developmentally "off-time" may explore their sexuality outside of the peer group. Gay, lesbian, and bisexual young people typically do not have their first same-sex sexual experience within a romantic relationship, in part because of the difficulty of dating someone of the same sex given the heterosexual orientation that dominates adolescent peer culture (Diamond, Savin-Williams, & Dube, 1999; Herdt & Boxer, 1993). And some adolescents may skip stages altogether or recycle through the various stages several times (Brown, 1999).

Origins of Sexual Orientation

As mentioned, most adolescents develop a heterosexual orientation. That said, homosexuality has been found in most cultures that have been studied (Ford & Beach, 1951). Surveys in North America and Europe estimate the percentage of men who identify themselves as gay to be around 3% to 5% of the population and the percentage of women who identify themselves as lesbian to be around 2% or 3% (Diamond, 1993). In addition, an unknown but significant number identify themselves as bisexual.

How does an erotic attraction to one or the other sex or both sexes develop? Perhaps because a heterosexual orientation is the norm—and makes so much sense from an evolutionary perspective—most research on the development of sexual orientation has focused on how some individuals develop an attraction to members of their own sex. Admittedly, this research focus is not a very satisfying state of affairs. After all, most children in modern societies learn to read, but that has not led researchers to study only children who do not. Nonetheless, researchers have generally looked at the development of a nonheterosexual orientation as a puzzle to be understood. To explain it, researchers have looked to both biological and socialization influences.

Biological Influences   Research on twins and families suggests that sexual orientation may be in part hereditary. Although concordance rates vary widely from study to study, the chances that both members of a pair of twins will have a homosexual orientation are significantly greater for identical (monozygotic) twins than for fraternal (dizygotic) twins (Hershberger, 2001; Zucker, 2001). Studies also find gay men and lesbian women to have more gay and lesbian siblings than heterosexuals. Moreover, gay males are more likely to have gay male siblings than lesbian siblings, whereas lesbian siblings are—to a lesser degree—more likely to have lesbian siblings than gay male siblings (Bailey & Bell, 1993; Bailey & Benishay, 1993; Bailey, Pillard, et al., 1993; Pillard, 1990).

How might genes influence the development of sexual orientation? Some researchers believe certain genes influence the production or impact of prenatal hormones. As we saw earlier, hormones produced by the newly formed testes masculinize the fetus, which includes both the development of the reproductive organs and the organization of the fetal brain. Some researchers believe that sexual orientation is established during this process (Meyer-Bahlberg, 1993; Reinisch, Ziemba-Davis, & Sanders, 1991).

As we have seen, however, hormone levels are influenced by both genetic and environmental factors. Whether a person is chromosomally male (XY) or female (XX), hormonal imbalances—such as those caused by CAH and androgen insensitivity—can affect the individual's gender-related behavior, personality traits, and sexual preferences (Berenbaum & Snyder, 1995; Dittmann et al., 1990; Zucker et al., 1996). And girls exposed to unusually high levels of masculinizing androgens because of drugs their mothers were prescribed to prevent miscarriage are more likely to develop a lesbian or bisexual orientation than girls whose mothers did not take the drugs (Meyer-Bahlberg et al., 1995). It is not known, however, whether the processes occurring in these individuals relate in any way to the hormonal processes of gays and lesbians unaffected by these disorders or drugs.

Further evidence to support the role of hormones in sexual orientation is the existence of a birth order difference between gay and heterosexual men (Hershberger, 2001). Specifically, homosexual boys tend to be later in birth order than heterosexual boys. Moreover, the later birth order of gay men depends only on the number of older brothers and not on the number of older sisters (Blanchard & Bogaert, 1996; Blanchard & Zucker, 1994; Blanchard et al., 2002). The birth order effect is believed to be due to a maternal immune reaction that lessens the impact of male androgens during the prenatal period (Blanchard & Klassen, 1997).

Socialization

An alternative explanation of sexual orientation involves socialization processes. In general, traditional socialization accounts of sexual orientation have not fared well empirically. There is little evidence, for example, that having a nonheterosexual parent predisposes a child to become gay or lesbian (Bailey & Dawood, 1998; Golombok & Tasker 1996; Gottman, 1990; Patterson, 1992; Tasker & Golombok, 1997). In one study of the sons of gay fathers, researchers found that the sons' identification as either gay or heterosexual was unrelated to the amount of time they had lived with their fathers, how accepting they were of their fathers' homosexuality, and the quality of their relationships with their fathers (Bailey, Nothnagel, & Wolfe, 1995). In general, the proportion of children reared by gay, lesbian, or bisexual parents who adopt a nonhetereosexual identity is comparable to that among children raised by heterosexual parents.

The fact that child-rearing alone is not enough to determine sexual orientation does not mean that socialization is irrelevant, however. Indeed, most scholars believe that sexual orientation is the product of interaction between biology and environment.

An Interactionist Model

Daryl Bem (1996, 2001) has offered one model of how biological factors and experience might interact in the development of sexual orientation. In Bem's model—termed the *Exotic-Becomes-Erotic (EBE) Theory*—sexual orientation is the culmination of a complex chain of events that begins with children's temperament. According to Bem, children's inborn temperament shapes their preferences for activities and play partners. As we have seen, some behavioral styles tend to be more characteristic of boys than girls. Specifically, boys tend to have, on average, higher activity levels. They are also more aggressive. Consequently, children higher in activity level and aggression are drawn to male-typical activities, whereas children who prefer quieter play are attracted to female-typical activities.

According to EBE theory, children not only prefer others like themselves but perceive children in the other group as different, unfamiliar, even "exotic." These feelings—which gender-conforming children have toward members of the opposite sex but which gender-nonconforming children have toward members of the same sex—are associated with heightened physiological arousal in the presence of the other-group children.

Initially, of course, children do not interpret this arousal in sexual or erotic terms. Rather, a male-typical child may experience arousal in the presence of girls as antipathy ("girls are yucky"). A female-typical child may experience arousal in the presence of boys as apprehension. Eventually, through a complex process involving maturational, cognitive, and situational factors, this physiological state comes to be experienced as erotic desire.

The idea that individuals come to be attracted to a class of people from whom they felt different in childhood is supported by retrospective interviews of gay men and lesbians and heterosexual adults. When asked about their childhoods, a majority of gay men and lesbians report feeling different from same-sex peers on gender-related characteristics, such as activity preferences. Heterosexual adults rarely report feeling different from same-sex peers because of gender-related characteristics (Bell, Weinberg, & Hammersmith, 1981; Savin-Williams, 1998).

Of course, the reliability of retrospective reports is subject to scrutiny. Regardless of their sexual orientation, adults may consciously or unconsciously reconstruct the past in ways that make sense given their current lifestyle. However, the significance of gender nonconformity for later sexual preference is also supported by prospective studies that follow children to adolescence or adulthood. Boys who grow up to be gay men are more likely to display feminine behaviors as children. They avoid rough-and-tumble activities, physical aggression, and competitive sports; like playing with girls; and are often regarded as "sissies" by their peers. Girls who grow up to be lesbian are more likely to display masculine behaviors as children (Bailey, Dunne, & Martin, 2000; Bailey, Miller, & Willerman, 1993; Bailey & Zucker, 1995).

Bem's model seems particularly well suited for explaining the sexual orientation of gay men and lesbian women who fit cultural stereotypes—that is, effeminate males and masculine females. But not everyone who is gay or lesbian fits these stereotypes. Can EBE theory explain individual differences in sexual orientation?

Bem contends that it can. The central tenet of EBE theory is that individuals feel different from a class of peers during childhood. What makes a child feel that way may differ across peer subcultures. To illustrate, Bem points to males who are highly interested in computers. In some peer cultures, these males would be regarded as highly masculine, whereas in others they would be regarded as gender-deviant. Bem also points out that an individual child may be gender-nonconforming in some ways but not feel different from peers if he or she conforms to other gender expectations that are more gender-defining in the culture. In addition, widespread cultural changes can produce cohort effects, and behaviors that are gender-nonconforming in one cohort can become more or less so in a later cohort.

Bem acknowledges that there may be multiple routes to adult sexual orientation and that EBE theory describes just one of them. He also admits that EBE theory may be completely wrong and that biological factors such as genes, prenatal hormones, and brain structure may indeed play a more direct and powerful role in the development of sexual orientation than accounted for in his theory (Bem, 2001). It is important to remember, however, that existing evidence for the biological origins of human sexual orientation remains correlational. Bem has made a valuable contribution to the study of the development of both heterosexual and nonheterosexual orientations by cautioning against the overly deterministic view of sexual orientation that is gaining popularity.

To Recap . . .

Children begin to exhibit interest in others as future sexual partners during middle childhood. Children's sexual relationships gradually evolve from "kiss and chase" games to crushes on unattainable figures (such as celebrities), to increasingly intimate involvements with people they know well. In many communities, adolescents negotiate this transition to intimate relations in the context of the mixed-sex peer group.

Although most children eventually develop a heterosexual orientation, a minority of children adopt a gay, lesbian, or bisexual orientation. Biological accounts of sexual orientation link sexual behavior and interest to genes and prenatal hormones. Although there is good evidence that both play a role in the development of nonheterosexual orientations, it is less clear how each influences the development of a heterosexual orientation.

There is little evidence that socialization alone shapes the development of sexual orientation or identity. The proportion of children reared by gay, lesbian, or bisexual parents who adopt a nonheterosexual identity is comparable to that among children raised by heterosexual parents. Most contemporary researchers believe that sexual orientation is influenced by both biology and environment, although the processes by which each contributes are far from understood.

CONCLUSION

The past three decades have seen dramatic changes in the roles of men and women worldwide. In many nations, the roles open to both women and men have expanded considerably. In North America, we are no longer surprised to learn that the next space mission will include a female, that the young mother next door is an army reservist, or that the best doctor in town is a woman. In many communities, the roles of men have also changed. Although still relatively uncommon, some fathers opt to be stay-at-home dads, and increasing numbers share child-care and household responsibilities with mothers. Attitudes toward sexual roles have also changed. Acceptance of gay, lesbian, and bisexual individuals is growing.

Science has made significant contributions to these societal changes. Early research revealed numerous ways in which child-rearing and educational practices blunted the aspirations of young girls. Changes in policies followed, accompanied by a wide range of intervention programs designed to foster gender equity in schools, sports, and the workplace. Studies showed that fathers—not just mothers or mother figures—can serve as primary caregivers. These findings have helped shaped decision making about child care among families and in the courts. And research on the origins of sexual orientation, including longitudinal investigations of children reared in gay and lesbian households, has proved influential in shaping both attitudes and laws regarding the rights of sexual minorities.

We have learned much about gender development during recent years, but numerous questions continue to intrigue the public and scientists alike. Why, for example, do females seem to enjoy caring for children more than males? Why are most of the students who commit violence in schools male? And why, despite the fact that males and females are more alike than different, do we often find each other so hard to understand?

Although scientists have not yet found firm answers to these questions, one thing has become clear—the process of gender development is far from simple. As in other areas of development, biological, cognitive, and sociocultural factors all play important parts in guiding the child's progress toward a sexual identity.

FOR THOUGHT AND DISCUSSION

1. Studies have shown that one result of developing gender schemas and associating ourselves with either the male or female schema is that we then become selectively attuned to information relevant to our gender. *Can you think of several examples of things in your everyday life that you pay attention to probably because they are related to your gender schema? Are there things that you probably ignore because they are part of the other gender schema? Repeat this exercise with another schema, besides gender, to which you relate.*

2. Research indicates that by the preschool years, girls and boys tend to play with different kinds of toys and engage in different sorts of play activities. *Should preschool or day-care teachers actively attempt to engage children in activities more typical of the other gender, even if the children resist doing so? For example, should boys be encouraged (or required) to spend time in the cooking area, even if they find this activity unappealing? If not, do you think there is another way for teachers to break down children's strong gender stereotypes?*

3. One reason males are better than females on some spatial tasks may be that they have had more experience with activities that promote the development of spatial skills. *What are some specific activities that you believe might do this? Can you think of any activities more common in females that could promote spatial skills and that would offer evidence counter to this hypothesis?*

4. According to the sociocultural approach, children learn the behaviors and attributes appropriate for their gender by participating in and observing others perform social roles. Most of the empirical work to date has focused on the kinds of chores children perform, particularly childcare. But children and adolescents occupy other social roles as well in school, in other cultural institutions, and in their leisure activities. *Describe some of these other social roles and the skills, attitudes, and behaviors they foster. Are some of these roles more typical of one gender than another? How important is it that males and females have equal access to various social roles?*

5. In this chapter, we described the debate about whether schools adequately meet the needs of both male and female students. One response to the debate has been to establish single-sex schools and classrooms. *Describe the theoretical and empirical support for single-sex schools. What criteria would you use to determine whether single-sex education "works"? Is there reason to believe that single-sex schooling would be more effective at some ages than others?*

6. There is considerable interest in the impact of media on the development of children's gender-role behavior and attitudes. But the media offer a plethora of models and these models often convey very different ideas about what it means to be male and female. *How important do you think the media are in shaping children's gender-role development? How do children decide which messages to "soak up" and which to ignore? Do you think parents and other adults have a responsibility to monitor the kinds of gender-role models children see?*

VISUAL SUMMARY FOR CHAPTER 15
Gender-Role Development and Sex Differences

Theories of Gender-Role Development

Evolutionary and Biological Approaches

According to evolutionary theorists, modern sex differences reflect the different reproductive challenges faced by males and females in the ancestral past. Researchers have also investigated the more immediate biological mechanisms of sex differences, such as genes, hormones, and brain functioning.

Sociocultural Approaches

The sociocultural approach contends that sex differences follow from the different social roles that males and females play in each society.

Cognitive-Developmental Approaches

Cognitive-developmental models include Kohlberg's stage model of children's understanding of gender-role issues, as well as information-processing models based on the concepts of the gender schema and gender script.

Environmental/ Learning Approaches

Social-learning theory views gender-role behaviors as simply another class of responses acquired and maintained by learning principles. In this view, sex differences are not inevitable and may change with environmental conditions.

Some Perceived and Real Sex Differences

Physical Differences

Females generally are healthier and more developmentally advanced than males at birth and reach developmental milestones earlier. Males are more physically active and more vulnerable to illness and injury.

Cognitive Differences

Male−female diferences have been found in rate of language acquisition, overall verbal abilities, math reasoning and computation, and performance on spatial tasks. Both socialization and biological factors likely play a role in these differences.

Social and Personality Differences

Males and females tend to use different strategies to regulate their emotions; females talk about their feelings and males use distraction or physical activity. Females are generally more emotionally expressive than males, although males more readily express anger. Males display more physical aggression, whereas females display more social and relational aggression. To some extent, males and females prefer different activities and academic interests. In the area of relationships, girls have fewer, more intimate friends and prefer activities that involve smaller groups, whereas boys have more numerous friends and prefer large-group activities.

Biological Influences on Gender-Role Development

Genetic Influences

Abnormalities in sex chromosomes can produce individuals with unusual sex chromosome arrangements. In addition, other genes can affect males and females differently. Usually, this occurs when the expression of a trait (called a sex-limited trait) requires the presence of certain levels of sex hormones.

Hormonal Influences	▶	The principal fetal hormones are androgens in males and progesterone and estrogens in females. Androgens also affect the organization of the fetal brain. Congenital adrenal hyperplasia (CAH) results from overproduction of androgens during gestation. The personalities of CAH females are masculinized. Androgen insensitivity involves a failure to respond to androgens. The personalities of males with androgen insensitivity are feminized.
Brain Lateralization	▶	The right hemisphere is largely involved with quantitative and spatial abilities. The left hemisphere is more involved with verbal abilities. Males appear to be more lateralized than females, a sex difference that may be related to behavioral sex differences on verbal and spatial tasks.

Socialization and Gender-Role Development
Gender-role socialization occurs at many levels. Two mechanisms of socialization are modeling and differential treatment.

Socialization by Society and Parents	▶	Males and females are treated differently in all societies, although the specifics of the differential treatment vary across cultures. Parents also treat their sons and daughters differently. Differential treatment includes direct instruction and guided participation, the provision of opportunities and experiences, and expectations. Differential treatment fosters the development of different skills, abilities, and attitudes.
Socialization by Peers	▶	Peers are a powerful socialization force. The same-sex peer group is especially important.
Socialization by Self	▶	Children contribute importantly to the socialization process through their selection of appropriate models and the application of self-sanctions to gender-linked behavior.

Understanding Gender Roles and Stereotypes

The Development of Gender Identity	▶	Almost all children display gender identity by about age 3, gender stability by about age 4, and gender consistency by about age 5. This progression has been demonstrated in both males and females and in a variety of cultures, although children in many non-Western cultures proceed through the stages more slowly.
The Development of Gender Knowledge	▶	Gender-role knowledge involves awareness of the concepts of male and female and their culturally defined stereotypes. Children generally understand the basic male–female concept by age 2. Gender labeling of toys appears at age 3, and an awareness of sex-typed personality traits at about age 5. Children's gender stereotypes change over the course of childhood, becoming more flexible.
Gender Knowledge and Behavior	▶	Sex-typed labels affect children's behavior. When activities or objects are seen as being for one gender or the other, children prefer the same-sex activities and avoid the cross-sex ones. Children also tend to perform better on same-sex-labeled activities.

Development of Sexual Relationships and Behavior

Emergence of Romantic and Sexual Interest	▶	Children's sexual relationships gradually evolve from "kiss and chase" games to crushes on unattainable figures to increasingly intimate involvements with people they know well. Adolescents often negotiate the transition to intimate relations in the context of the mixed-sex peer group.
Origins of Sexual Orientation	▶	Biological accounts of sexual orientation link sexual behavior and interest to genes and prenatal hormones. There is little evidence that socialization alone shapes the development of sexual orientation or identity, but most contemporary researchers believe that socialization plays a role in combination with biological factors.

16

Families and Peers

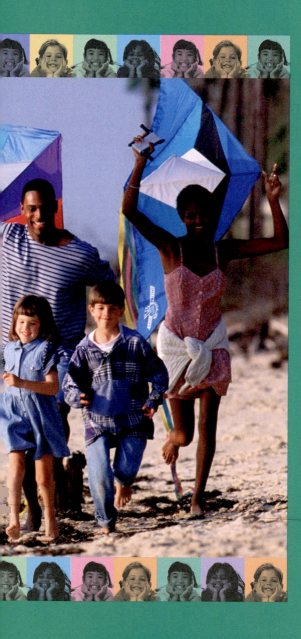

Stories of children abandoned or lost and left to raise themselves in the wild have long captured the Western imagination. We wonder: If a child were somehow able to find sustenance and protection from the elements, would she develop in much the same way as a child subject to the socializing influences of

parents, peers, and human culture? Or would she emerge a wild animal?

Remarkably, over the course of human history, several children have found themselves in circumstances much like these. Such cases provide unique insights into the importance of human socialization.

One of the best-documented cases occurred in the early 1900s in India. The Reverend A. J. L. Singh, a Christian missionary working in Calcutta, discovered two young girls living among wolves in the jungle outside a small village. Singh estimated the larger one to be about 8 years of age. He named her Kamala. The smaller one, whom Singh guessed to be about a year and a half, he named Amala.

Singh took the girls to an orphanage he operated with his wife. At the time of their rescue, the girls were half-savage, more like beasts than humans. They ate, drank, and walked like dogs. They seemed not to feel heat or cold and would shred the clothing the reverend and his wife compelled them to wear in the cold winter months. The girls showed no fear of the dark, preferring to explore the compound at night and stay indoors, sheltered from the sun, during the day. The girls also remained aloof and shy. Initially, they refused to interact with anyone. They were particularly uncomfortable around the other children, and the mere presence of another child in the room was enough to prevent them from even moving. When they were approached, they often made faces and bared their teeth.

Within about a year of their capture, both girls grew quite ill with dysentery, and the younger one, Amala, died. Kamala grieved for her young companion for a long time and was so detached from those around her that the missionary and his wife feared she would die of loneliness. Eventually, however, Kamala developed affection for Mrs. Singh and gradually acquired the rudiments of human behavior. She learned to walk upright, wear human clothing, use the toilet, and relate to the other children, and she even acquired a small vocabulary. But at the time of her death 8 years later, Kamala—although grown—functioned at the level of a child of a year and a half.

Kamala's fate resembled that of another famous "wild child," Victor, the Wild Boy of Aveyron, as well as the outcomes of more recent cases of children reared in isolation or abandoned to the streets. Although the outcomes vary somewhat depending on the extent of isolation, one thing is clear: Human children raised outside of human culture, without peers or family, never develop normal human capacities. Why this is so, and how family and peers influence development, is the focus of this chapter. ■

A central aspect of being human is being socialized by other humans—as the sad cases of Kamala and Victor make clear. Normal development requires a social world and social experiences of many forms and from very early in life. Children encounter many people who influence them as they develop. For most, however, the family and peer group are the principal agents of socialization. It is with family and peers that this final chapter is concerned.

THEORIES OF SOCIALIZATION

Socialization is one of the central issues in the field, and each of the major theoretical traditions has therefore had much to say about the topic. To a good extent, the pictures they provide complement rather than contradict one another.

Evolutionary Approaches

We have already seen some of the emphases that evolutionary approaches bring to the study of socialization. The overriding theme is that of a biological basis for adaptive behavior, a basis set by the evolutionary history of the species. This biological pretuning is evident very early. As we saw in Chapter 12, ethologists believe that evolution has provided infants with a number of characteristics, both physical and behavioral, that elicit appropriate caregiving responses from the adults around them and hence promote survival. Evolution has also provided adults with natural responses to these infant characteristics—for example, relieving the distress of a crying baby.

Although any adult is presumably set by evolution to respond to children in appropriate ways, theorists under the sociobiology and evolutionary psychology headings add two further ideas (Bjorklund, Younger, & Pellegrini, 2002). One is that parents are especially likely to engage in caregiving practices that promote the development of their children, because doing so serves to perpetuate their genes. (Of course there is no claim that this is a conscious motivation on parents' part.) The second, which we discussed in Chapter 15, is the idea that evolution has provided males and females with somewhat different priorities with regard to mating and subsequent child care. According to parental investment theory (Trivers, 1972), females have considerably more investment in the survival and well-being of particular offspring than do males. And indeed, in most cultures at most points in human history mothers have assumed a much greater role in child care than have fathers.

Ethologists also contend that there is an innate underpinning to many of the behaviors that children direct toward their peers. We have already seen this argument applied to two important classes of social behavior: altruism and aggression. Ethologists do not claim that such behaviors are totally under genetic control, because experience is clearly necessary for their emergence. But they do claim that there is an important biological basis, set by evolution, on which experience operates. Recall that in the case of aggression, evolution is also assumed to have built in various controls whose function is to prevent interspecies aggression from becoming too severe. We discussed one such control in Chapter 14: the formation of a dominance hierarchy, or a kind of social pecking order that determines who wins out over whom in social disputes. Once the hierarchy is established, disputes can be resolved simply through members' knowledge of their relative status and thus without use of force. A range of different species form dominance hierarchies, and so, as we saw, do human children (Bjorklund & Pellegrini, 2002). Such hierarchies are evident on the preschool playground (LaFreniere & Charlesworth, 1983), and they are also evident in the summer camp encounters of adolescents (Savin-Williams, 1987). We can see in the work on dominance hierarchies two emphases of the ethological approach: the value of comparative study and the importance of studying behavior in the natural setting.

Environmental/Learning Approaches

The goal of the environmental/learning approach has always been to identify basic learning principles that apply across a range of situations, age groups, and types of behavior. From this perspective, socialization does not require the discovery of new processes of learning; the task, rather, is to explain how the basic processes apply in the socialization context. Indeed, John Watson, whom we discussed as one of the pioneers of the approach in Chapter 1, wrote advice pamphlets in which he instructed parents in the application of the basic learning techniques that had been identified in laboratory study.

What has changed over the years in environmental/learning approaches to socialization is not the guiding philosophy but the particular forms of learning that are stressed. Early versions emphasized direct learning via reinforcement and punishment. Such processes remain important in contemporary accounts; clearly, one way in which parents influence their children is by reinforcing and thereby strengthening some behaviors and punishing and thereby weakening others. Often, of course, parents' delivery of reinforcing or punishing consequences is intentional, but this is not always the case—which means that parents may sometimes strengthen behavior that they do not wish to promote. Patterson's (1982) work on coercive processes in the home setting as antecedents of aggression (Chapter 14) provides one example.

In modern versions of social-learning theory—most notably, Bandura's work (Bandura, 1986, 1989)—reinforcement and punishment are joined by a third important socialization process: observational learning that results from exposure to a model. Another basic way that parents influence their children, therefore, is by providing models of behavior that may then affect the child's behavior. Again, parents may do this either intentionally or unintentionally, and the result may be either desirable or undesirable behavior on the child's part. The topic of aggression again provides an example of the latter; recall that physical punishment by parents is associated with heightened aggression in children, an outcome that may result from the aggressive model that a punitive parent provides.

Like parents, peers can affect a child's behavior and development in several ways. One way again is through reinforcement and punishment, and peers provide many reinforcing or punishing consequences as a child develops—attention, praise, acquiescence to the child's wishes, sharing or refusing to share, criticism, disapproval. Many of these consequences are, to be sure, unintended, but they may function as reinforcements or punishments nonetheless. Peers are also important as models of behavior; indeed, for some behaviors (e.g., forms of play) peers may be more important models than parents. Finally, peers contribute to the development of self-efficacy—children's conceptions of which behaviors they are capable of performing. One source of self-efficacy judgments is the child's observation of the behavior of others, and peers are clearly a natural comparison group.

Of course, none of the roles just cited is unique to peers. But peers may be especially important sources of such effects, especially as children grow older. The sheer amount of time spent with peers guarantees that any child will be exposed frequently to the behavior of other children and will experience frequent consequences from other children as the result of his or her behavior. Furthermore, the importance, for most children, of being accepted by other children guarantees that peers will be effective agents of reinforcement and punishment as well as potent models for a wide range of behaviors. And, of course, the behaviors that peers model and reinforce may differ from the behaviors that adults try to promote.

Cognitive-Developmental Approaches

Bandura's version of social-learning theory places considerably more emphasis on cognition than did its predecessors in the environmental/learning tradition. Nevertheless, it is within the cognitive-developmental approach, not surprisingly, that cognitive factors are accorded their most prominent role.

A cognitive emphasis in the study of parenting is a relatively recent emergence. The first wave of child-rearing studies were inspired primarily by either Freudian theory or learning theory, neither of which put much emphasis on how parents think about their children or the tasks of child-rearing. In Parke's (1978, p. 76) words, researchers proceeded as though "the cognitive capacities of the infant and parent could functionally be treated as similar."

Such is no longer the case. In recent years a substantial research literature has grown up devoted to the study of parents' beliefs about children (Bugental & Happeney, 2002; Goodnow, 2002; Miller, 1988, 1995). In retrospect, the general conclusions that emerge from this literature are perhaps not surprising. Parents do hold beliefs of various sorts, both about children in general and about their own children in particular. Some beliefs are conscious and explicit; others (such as the working models discussed in Chapter 12) may be largely implicit. There are marked individual differences among parents in the ways that they think about children, as well as on-the-average differences in belief systems across different cultures or subcultures (Harkness, Raeff, & Super, 2000; Sigel & McGillicuddy-De Lisi, 2002). Although the relation is far from perfect, beliefs do relate to parental behavior—for example, a belief (as in Piagetian theory) that children learn best through self-discovery is associated with nondirective, child-oriented methods of teaching (Sigel, 1986). Finally, parental beliefs also relate to children's development (Murphey, 1992). Again, the relation is far from perfect, but in general more accurate or sophisticated beliefs are associated with more positive developmental outcomes.

Contemporary approaches to child-rearing also emphasize the child's cognitive contribution. Rather than simply adhering (or failing to adhere) to parental directives, children are seen as striving to make sense of both their parents' positions and their own eventual behavior (Why should I clean my room? Why should I not hit other children?). The ways in which they do so change as their cognitive capacities change, which is one reason that a 12-year-old and a 3-year-old require somewhat different socialization practices. In general, from this perspective, socialization involves not only the teaching of specific behaviors but the transmission of general attitudes or belief systems—which is why the eventual effects may extend well beyond the specific contexts and issues that are the focus for socialization in childhood.

Cognitive-developmental theorists also address the role of peers in the socialization process. One example is Piaget's (1932) theory of how peers contribute to changes in moral reasoning, a theory discussed in Chapter 14. In Piaget's view, the child, lacking the power and authority of the adult, conforms to what he or she perceives to be the adult's views. The result is moral realism, characterized by a rigid conception of right and wrong. When the child interacts with peers, however, the relation is much more one of equals, and there is a continual need for cooperating, negotiating, and taking the point of view of the other. Interaction with peers, therefore, leads to the ability to consider different perspectives, an ability central to the more advanced form of reasoning known as moral relativism. More generally, interaction with peers is important in breaking down the child's egocentrism and encouraging more mature forms of thought.

Peers are also important in Kohlberg's (1987) theory of moral development. As in Piaget's theory, movement through Kohlberg's stages results partly from biological maturation. Achieving a new stage, however, requires not only a sufficient level of maturation but also experience with moral issues. Kohlberg especially stresses experiences in which the child encounters different points of view and thus is forced to consider and integrate different perspectives. Such experiences of cognitive conflict may be especially likely in the give-and-take of the peer group.

In addition to their role in promoting cognitive change, peers are important as objects of the child's thought. Thinking about other children falls under the heading of *social cognition*—the child's understanding of the social and interpersonal world. Social cognition is of interest both in itself and because of its possible effects on the child's social behavior. A basic principle of the cognitive-developmental approach is that the child's cognitive level is an important determinant of the child's behavior, including behavior toward other people. Thus, the cognitive theorist would expect older children to show more complex and mature forms of social behavior because of their greater cognitive maturity. And within an age group, the theorist would expect children who are advanced in their level of social reasoning to be advanced in their social behavior as well. Later in the chapter we will see how well these expectations are borne out by research.

Sociocultural Approaches

As we have seen in previous discussions of theories, sociocultural approaches share a number of assumptions with the other general theoretical traditions. Theorists under this heading certainly agree, for example, that parental models can be an important contributor to children's behavior, and that children's cognitive capacities affect both what they bring to and what they take away from socialization encounters. In the other approaches, however, development is seen as residing primarily in the child; it is affected by and often expressed within social contexts, but the child and the social world are separate entities. For sociocultural theorists, in contrast, development is always embedded within and inseparable from a social-cultural context. To a good extent, therefore, development *is* socialization.

Because of its inherently social emphasis, it is no accident that our earlier discussions of this approach have already said quite a bit about the roles of the family and the peer group in children's development. Recall that a key notion in both cases is the Vygotskian concept of the zone of proximal development. Parents can direct their child's development most successfully when they work within the child's zone for a particular domain, either through scaffolding in the case of explicit instructional encounters or through guided participation as they socialize the child in the ways of the home or the community more generally. Although our earlier discussion stressed effects on the child's cognitive development, the same principle applies to other developmental outcomes that parents attempt to instill—for example, assuming responsibilities around the household or behaving in prosocial ways toward a younger sibling.

As we saw in Chapter 9, peers are also important in sociocultural approaches to development. In contrast to cognitive-developmental theories, however, the emphasis is not on the clash of differing perspectives but on the transmission of knowledge or skills from a more expert to a less expert peer (Tudge & Rogoff, 1989). Thus, just as children benefit from interactions with a parent or teacher, they may also be helped to achieve new levels of understanding when they interact with a more competent peer.

Bronfenbrenner's (1979) ecological systems theory adds a further important point. Not only are children affected by the various microsystems (family, peers, school) within which they develop; also important are the ways in which these systems relate to one another—the layer referred to in Bronfenbrenner's model as the mesosystem. We will see several examples of this point later in the chapter. Bronfenbrenner's model also captures an emphasis that is central to theory and research in the sociocultural perspective: the importance of the macrosystem, or the general culture within which development occurs. Socialization practices often vary in important ways across cultures or subcultures; furthermore, the impact of a particular practice may differ across different cultural settings. We will see examples of these points as well.

To Recap . . .

The four major theoretical perspectives in child psychology offer their own distinct views on socialization. Evolutionary approaches reflect the assumption that evolution has provided an important innate basis for many social behaviors. Infants enter the world with characteristics that elicit appropriate caregiving, and adults in turn are equipped with natural responses to these characteristics. Many behaviors toward peers (such as altruism and aggression) are also assumed to have an innate underpinning that reflects the evolutionary history of the species.

The environmental/learning approach to socialization stresses the application of general learning principles. Both parents and peers can affect children's development in several ways. Both may reinforce or punish certain behaviors and thereby increase or decrease their likelihood. Both may serve as models who influence the child's subsequent behavior. Finally, peers in particular can be an important source for self-efficacy judgments.

The cognitive-developmental approach emphasizes the cognitive resources that both parents and children bring to the task of socialization. Parents hold beliefs of various sorts about children, beliefs that contribute to both their socialization practices and the child's development. Children, in turn, are active cognitive processors in socialization interchanges. Children also form beliefs about other children, and such beliefs are one determinant of how they behave toward peers. Interaction with peers can be an important impetus for cognitive change. Both Piaget and Kohlberg stress cognitive conflict with peers as one source of the ability to consider different points of view.

For theorists in the sociocultural perspective, development is always embedded within a social context, and thus questions of socialization are central to the approach. Both parents and peers can nurture development most effectively when they provide experiences that are within the child's zone of proximal development for the task in question. In addition to the various microsystems (such as family and peers) within which development occurs, the sociocultural approach stresses the relations among systems and the effects of the general culture on socialization and development.

SOCIALIZATION WITHIN THE FAMILY

For most children, the most important socialization context, especially in the early years, is the family. Our discussion of socialization begins, therefore, with life in the home. We focus first on the role of the parents. In the next section we will consider the contribution of other family members, as well as the effects of different kinds of family arrangements.

Parenting Styles

Research on child-rearing has always had a strong idiographic focus. Parents differ in how they socialize their children—indeed, the same parent may treat two children in the same family differently. The goal in most studies of child-rearing is twofold: to identify the important differences among parents and to determine what effects, if any, these variations have on children's development.

What are the significant dimensions along which parenting might vary? Although many distinctions have been proposed, two dimensions have consistently emerged as important (Maccoby & Martin, 1983). One is **parental warmth** (sometimes labeled *acceptance/responsiveness*)—the amount of support, affection, and encouragement the parent provides, as opposed to hostility, shame, or rejection. You will not be surprised to learn that a high standing on the dimension of parental warmth is generally associated with positive child outcomes. The second dimension is **parental control** (sometimes labeled *demandingness*)—the degree to which the child is monitored, disciplined, and regulated, as opposed to being left largely unsupervised. Control also appears in general to be beneficial, although the results are more variable and complex than those for warmth.

One reason that conclusions regarding control (and to some extent even those for warmth) vary is that the effects of any one aspect of parenting depend on other aspects of parenting—that is, the overall context within which it is expressed. This realization, in fact, reflects one of the major changes in the study of child-rearing over the years. Initially, studies of parenting tended to focus on specific parental behaviors in isolation— for example, method of feeding in infancy or amount of physical punishment in later childhood. Contemporary research is more likely to encompass multiple parental practices and dimensions in an attempt to capture the overall pattern of child-rearing— what is referred to as **parenting style.**

The most influential conceptualization of parenting style was developed by Diana Baumrind (1971, 1989, 1991). (Box 16.1 describes the original Baumrind research.) Baumrind's approach combines the dimensions of warmth and control to yield four parenting styles, which are summarized in Table 16.1. As can be seen, the **authoritative parenting** style is characterized by high standing on both warmth and control. Authoritative parents tend to be caring and sensitive toward their children, while at the same time setting clear limits and maintaining a predictable environment. They also provide rationales for why they expect certain behavior from the child. In contrast, the **authoritarian parenting** style couples high control with low warmth. Authoritarian parents are very demanding, they exercise strong control over their children's behavior, and they tend to enforce their demands with threats and punishments rather than reasons.

The **permissive parenting** style represents a third possible combination of the two dimensions. Permissive parents are high in warmth but low in control. These parents are loving and emotionally sensitive but set few limits on behavior and provide little in the way of structure or predictability. Finally, the **uninvolved parenting** style (also termed the **disengaged parenting** style) is the label for parents who are low on both dimensions. These parents set few limits on their children, but they also provide little in the way of attention, interest, or emotional support.

The Baumrind approach has proved successful at identifying individual differences among parents across a range of different populations and child ages. As noted, however, the measurement of parental characteristics is usually just the first step in stud-

Parental warmth
A dimension of parenting that reflects the amount of support, affection, and encouragement the parent provides to the child.

Parental control
A dimension of parenting that reflects the degree to which the child is monitored, disciplined, and regulated.

Parenting style
The overall pattern of child-rearing provided by a parent, typically defined by the combination of warmth and control that the parent demonstrates.

Authoritative parenting
A style of parenting characterized by firm control in the context of a warm and supportive relationship.

Authoritarian parenting
A style of parenting characterized by firm control in the context of a cold and demanding relationship.

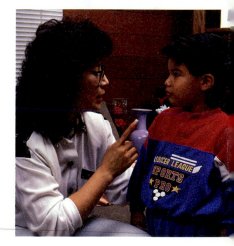

The authoritative style of child-rearing is characterized by firm control in the context of a warm and supportive relationship, as well as by frequent use of reasoning in disciplining the child.

Permissive parenting
A style of parenting characterized by low levels of control in the context of a warm and supportive relationship.

Uninvolved (disengaged) parenting
A style of parenting characterized by low levels of both control and warmth.

Parenting Styles: The Work of Diana Baumrind

The field of child psychology has seen literally thousands of studies of parental child-rearing practices, dating back more than 100 years. Probably no entry in this long list has been more influential than a series of studies carried out by Diana Baumrind almost 40 years ago (Baumrind, 1967, 1971; Baumrind & Black, 1967).

Any researcher of child-rearing must surmount at least two major challenges. One is getting accurate measures of parents' behavior. Child-rearing, after all, is something that occurs primarily in the privacy of the home, with parent and child as not only the only participants but the only witnesses. How can we learn what parents do with their children? Most researchers have solved this problem by asking parents what they do—that is, collecting self-reports of typical behavior, via either questionnaires or interviews.

Baumrind made use of parental reports in her research as well. The core of the measurement, however, came from direct observation of parent–child interactions. Trained observers visited the homes of the participants (4-year-old children and their parents) on two occasions for several hours at a time, during which they made extensive observations of the interactions between the parents and the child. The visits extended from about an hour before dinner until the child's bed time, a time deliberately selected because, in the researchers' words, it is a "period commonly known to produce instances of parent–child divergence." Certainly anyone who has been a parent of a preschooler can relate to this assertion.

Several hours of detailed observation of family interactions yield a wealth of information about both parent and child behavior. A second challenge in child-rearing research is to make sense of all this information—to abstract general principles and processes from the hundreds of specific inter-

BOX 16.1

Classics of
Research

changes between parent and child. Drawing partly from theory and partly from past research, Baumrind identified 15 "clusters" of parental behavior—that is, sets of interrelated behaviors that appeared to capture important dimensions of child-rearing and important differences among parents. Examples of the clusters include Directive versus Nondirective, Firm versus Lax Enforcement Policy, Encourages versus Discourages Independence, and Expresses Punitive versus Nurturant Behavior.

The next step was to determine whether the clusters—which themselves were composites of numerous specific behaviors—could be organized into larger, more general categories. Baumrind's answer was yes, and this aspect of the work yielded two conclusions that have affected the study of child-rearing ever since. One was the identification of the three general styles of child-rearing that we described in the text: authoritative, authoritarian, and permissive (the uninvolved category was a later addition). The second—made possible by the inclusion of a battery of child outcome measures—was a demonstration of the effects of the different styles. Baumrind reported that the authoritative style was consistently associated with the most positive child outcomes.

Since the original studies, the Baumrind approach to conceptualizing child-rearing has proved informative across a range of ages, specific measurement techniques, and cultural groups. As the text indicates, however, the extension of the approach to different groups has sometimes produced conclusions different from those that held for the White middle-income families that made up Baumrind's sample. It is worth noting that Baumrind herself anticipated such variation. Indeed, she was the first to demonstrate that a particular parental style could have different meaning in different cultural groups.

ies of parenting. A further step is to determine how the variations in parenting affect children's development. Here, too, the approach has proved very influential.

Baumrind reported, and later studies have largely confirmed, that the authoritative style was associated with the most positive child outcomes (Baumrind, 1971; Parke & Buriel, 1998; Steinberg, 2001). Children of authoritative parents tend to be curious, self-confident, and well behaved. They perform well in school, they are popular with peers, and they are responsive to parental messages. Their self-esteem is high, and their probability of engaging in deviant activities (e.g., drug use in adolescence) is low.

The other parenting styles are linked to more negative outcomes, although in somewhat different ways. Children of authoritarian parents tend to be anxious, easily upset, and low in self-confidence. They often react with anger and aggression when frustrated, a tendency that negatively affects their relations with peers. They are at risk for conduct problems, and their performance in school is typically not equal to that of children from authoritative families.

Just as the pattern for authoritarian rearing (anxious, aggressive, etc.) might be predicted from knowledge of the style, so the outcomes for children of permissive parents are what we might expect. These children tend to be impulsive, immature, and disobedient. They are overly dependent on adults, they do not persist well in the face of difficulty, and

Table 16.1	**Features of Parenting Styles**

Authoritative parenting

Accepting of child; frequent expressions of affection

High standards, but not overly restrictive, consistently enforced

Employs reason rather than force

Encourages child to express his or her point of view

Authoritarian parenting

Shows little warmth

High standards and a structured environment

Expects strict obedience

Uses harsh, punitive discipline

Rarely solicits the child's opinion

Permissive parenting

Highly accepting; frequent expressions of affection

Lax about rules, undemanding, inconsistent about discipline

Employs reason rather than force

Encourages child to express his or her point of view

Uninvolved parenting

Emotionally detached; withdrawn

Undemanding

---

they often do not do well in school. In adolescence they show a heightened probability of various forms of rebellious, antisocial behavior.

Finally, the uninvolved style seems to be associated with the most negative outcomes, which is not surprising, given that uninvolved parents are low in both warmth and control. Children of uninvolved parents often form insecure attachments in infancy, they show low social and academic competence as they develop, and they are at heightened risk for substance abuse and delinquency in adolescence. At the extreme, the uninvolved style becomes *neglect,* a form of child abuse associated with a range of negative outcomes.

We should qualify these conclusions in two ways. First, these are on-the-average findings, and as such they do not apply to every child. Not all instances of authoritative rearing lead to positive outcomes, and children whose parents exhibit one of the other styles are certainly not doomed to failure. Many such children turn out fine.

The second qualification is that effects of the different styles may vary across groups. We consider this issue next.

Ethnic and Cultural Differences

Most of the research just summarized was with White, predominantly middle-income families. Extension of the approach to other populations reveals both some similarities and some important differences.

Perhaps the clearest findings involve the authoritative and authoritarian styles. The authoritative style has been shown to be beneficial across a range of different populations. These include subgroups within the United States, such as African American, Hispanic American, and Asian American samples (Brody & Flor, 1998; Glasgow et al., 1997; Steinberg et al., 1991). They also include samples from other countries; China and India are among the societies studied (Chen, Liu, & Li, 2000; Pinto, Folkers, & Sines, 1991). On the other hand, the benefits of authoritative rearing—and the superiority of this style to other methods of child-rearing—are often smaller or less consistent in populations other than middle-income Western Whites. In some instances they vary for different members of the same ethnic group. For example, authoritative rearing appears to be generally beneficial for adolescents from second-generation Chinese American families. For first-generation families, however, few benefits are evident (Chao, 2001).

Conclusions regarding authoritarian rearing change in two ways when a wider range of settings and populations are taken into account. One concerns frequency: The authoritarian pattern is more common in many groups than is the case for the White samples that have been the focus of research. This is true for African American and Asian American samples in the United States, as well as for samples of Chinese parents and children (Greenberger & Chen, 1996; Parke & Buriel, 1998). Two factors—either alone or in combination—appear to account for this finding. One is cultural beliefs and values. In China, for example, family unity and respect for elders are central goals of socialization, and parental concern for children is expressed more through close supervision and frequent teaching than through displays of overt affection (Chao & Tseng, 2002). Many African American families within the United States share a similar emphasis on communal values, respect for parents and other adults, and close control of children's activities.

The other factor is economic and personal necessity. For families living in dangerous neighborhoods and under conditions of poverty, reasoning with the child and encouraging independence may be risky luxuries. Firm and immediate control may be a higher priority for parents in such circumstances—and may in fact make more sense for the overall well-being of the child (Furstenberg, 1993).

This last point suggests that in some contexts the authoritarian style might actually be beneficial for children's development. And this leads to the second way in which conclusions about authoritarian rearing have been found to vary across groups. Although an extreme standing on this dimension is probably not optimal in any context, authoritarian rearing does indeed have beneficial—or at least not clearly detrimental—effects in some contexts. This is the case, for example, for many African American samples within the United States (Lamborn, Dornbusch, & Steinberg, 1996), as well as for Chinese families in China and Chinese American families in the United States (Chao & Tseng, 2002). It is also at least sometimes the case for families living in poverty (Baldwin, Baldwin, & Cole, 1990).

What the variable results for authoritarian rearing suggest is that the meaning of a particular parental style cannot defined solely in terms of objective attributes, such as amount of physical discipline or expressions of overt affection. The meaning, rather, lies in how the parents' practices are interpreted by the child, which in turn depends on the overall cultural context within which they occur. One Asian American student makes this point well in talking about the firm and at times even punitive control that characterizes his culture's parenting: "That's how we know our parents love us" (Bronfenbrenner, 1993, p. 39).

The Role of Fathers

Our discussions to this point have been of "parents," but in fact most of the research has concentrated on mothers. There are theoretical reasons for this emphasis, in that the theories that have guided socialization research have stressed the mother. There are also pragmatic reasons—mothers in fact have typically been more involved in early child care than fathers.

But this is not to say, of course, that fathers are unimportant to children's lives. In recent years fathers have assumed an increased role in children's care, in part because of social changes that have allowed more mothers to enter the workforce (Pleck, 1997; Yeung et al., 2001). Recent years have also seen an increased research interest in the role of fathers in children's development (Lamb, 1997; Parke, 1996, 2002).

How do mothers and fathers typically compare in their caregiving activities? Any summary must be prefaced by the acknowledgment that there are wide variations across families and no single pattern is going to characterize all fathers. In general, however, fathers—despite the increased involvement in recent years—devote less time to child care than do mothers. Furthermore, the time that they do spend tends to be distributed differently. Although research suggests that most fathers are as skilled and sensitive in performing basic caregiving activities (e.g., feeding, diapering, putting to bed) as are mothers (Parke, 2002), most fathers do not in fact do such activities very often. Instead, fathers' interactions with their children tend to center around physical stimulation and play, especially with boys. This emphasis emerges early in infancy and continues through childhood (Russell & Russell, 1987). We should add, however, that the pattern is not universal. Although father as play partner is a common role across many cultures, there are exceptions. In Sweden, for example, there are no mother–father differences in the tendency to engage children in play (Lamb et al., 1982), and the same is true for Israeli kibbutz families (Sagi et al., 1985). In both instances, the society's egalitarian political views may account for the similarity in parental roles (although with definite limitations—mothers still perform most of the basic caregiving activities).

What fathers do with their children is one of the questions of interest in research on the father's role. The other question is what effects these paternal behaviors have. What do we know about fathers' contribution to children's development?

Some of the things we know were discussed in earlier chapters. In Chapter 15 we saw that fathers, on average, seem to hold stronger views about gender-appropriate behavior than do mothers and are more likely to treat boys and girls in ways that might promote sex differences in development. In Chapter 12 we saw that fathers as well as mothers can serve as attachment objects for infants. Almost all babies with a father in the home become attached to their fathers, and the probability of a secure attachment is as great with the father as with the mother (Van IJzendoorn & De Wolff, 1997). Furthermore, as we discuss more fully later in the chapter, secure attachment to the father is predictive of later positive outcomes in much the same way as is secure attachment to the mother.

More generally, how do children's relationship with the father compare to their relationship with the mother? Russell and Saebel (1997) review evidence from 116 studies that examined parent–child relationships as a function of both sex of parent and sex of child. In total, the studies span a range of ages and a variety of measures of parent–child relations. As we might expect, differences do occur on some measures for some samples—some children do have closer or more satisfactory or more intense relations with one parent than with the other. This conclusion has emerged in other reviews as well (Collins & Russell, 1991; Russell, Mize, & Bissaker, 2002). Nevertheless, the main message could be argued to be one of similarity: In the majority of cases, relations with the two parents—for both sons and daughters—are more alike than different.

Research on the effects of parenting style reveals one further mother–father similarity. In general, the attributes that characterize successful parenting for fathers turn out to be the same as those that are important for mothers—namely, a warm relation with the child, firm but not punitive control, frequent use of reasons. Thus, just as for mothers, it is the authoritative style of parenting that appears most adaptive for fathers' socialization of their children (Marsiglio et al., 2000).

The Child's Contribution

With rare exceptions, most child-rearing findings are correlational findings in that they reflect the relation between two constructs (parenting practices, child characteristics) that have been measured but not experimentally manipulated. Because the findings are correlational, they do not establish the cause-and-effect relation between the two constructs. The usual assumption—and the one we have adopted to this point—is that parenting style causes particular outcomes in children. But is the reverse also possible—that is, could characteristics of the child influence parenting style?

This causal direction is not only possible; it has been definitely established. Beginning with a classic paper by Richard Bell (1968), researchers have grown increasingly sensitive to the ways in which characteristics of the child can influence the parent's behavior. Perhaps the clearest example comes from the work on temperament discussed in Chapter 12. As we saw then, infants enter the world with somewhat different temperaments, including variations along dimensions (e.g., irritability, emotionality, sociability) that could clearly affect the ways parents interact with them. And such characterisitics do indeed affect parental behavior (Putnam, Sanson, & Rothbart, 2002). Infants with difficult temperaments, for example, receive more total caregiving time in the early months of life than do infants in general, presumably because their characteristics force attention in a way that those of easier-to-handle babies do not (Crockenberg, 1986). By the second half of the first year, however, mothers of difficult infants tend to soothe their infants less and to be generally less involved, presumably because they have too often found their efforts to be frustrating and unrewarding (van den Boom & Hoeksma, 1994). Other temperamental dimensions have also been shown to have predictable effects on parent behavior—activity level, for example, or inhibition/timidity.

Although any parent necessarily adapts to some extent to the child's characteristics, some parents do so more successfully than others. This is the notion of goodness of fit discussed in Chapter 12: the idea that development proceeds most successfully when parents are able to match their caregiving practices to the nature and needs of the child. The case of difficult temperament provides a good example. Early difficult temperament is moderately predictive both of continued difficult temperament and of various behavioral problems in later childhood (Gallagher, 2002). It is far from perfectly predictive, however, and parental response is one determining factor: Some parents are successful at gradually moderating their child's problematic attributes, whereas others respond to the child in ways that perpetuate or even aggravate the difficulties. Note the transactional nature of the developmental process: Characteristics of the child elicit particular behaviors from the parent, these parental behaviors in turn alter characteristics of the child, the child then brings a somewhat different set of characteristics to future socialization encounters with the parent, and so on throughout development.

As the point just made suggests, effects of children's characteristics on parental behavior are not limited to the early years or to inborn temperamental qualities. Child effects are a pervasive finding across a range of ages and socialization contexts. For example, children who display committed compliance (see Chapter 13) are likely to receive milder and more verbal forms of discipline than are children whose compliance is more of the forced, situational sort (Kochanska, 1997). Children who resist maternal requests elicit stronger demands and more restrictions from the mother than do children who are easier to control (Kuczynski & Kochanska, 1995). Adolescents who engage in antisocial behavior receive harsher forms of parental discipline than do adolescents who are better behaved (Neiderheiser et al., 1999).

Having stressed effects of the child on the parent, we should add that the fact that children can affect their parents does not mean that parent and child play equal roles or have equal impact in most socialization exchanges (Maccoby, 2002). Nor, of course, does it mean that parent–child correlations are due solely to effects of the child. But it does indicate the need for caution in interpreting any simple correlation between parental practices and children's development.

To Recap . . .

The goals of most child-rearing studies are to identify important differences among parents and to determine the effects of these variations on children's development. One influential approach identifies four general parenting styles that vary along the dimensions of warmth and control. The authoritative style is characterized by firm control in the context of a warm, supportive relationship. In contrast, the authoritarian style is high in control but low in warmth, the permissive style shows the opposite pattern of high warmth and low control, and the uninvolved style is low on both dimensions.

In general, the authoritative style is associated with the most positive developmental outcomes in both the social and cognitive domains. In somewhat different ways, each of the other styles places children at risk for a variety of negative outcomes. These effects are not inevitable, however, and they may vary across different populations. In particular, authoritarian parenting appears to have beneficial effects in some cultural contexts and under some environmental conditions.

Increasingly, studies of socialization are taking into account the father's contribution as well as that of the mother. Although paternal involvement has increased in recent years, fathers typically devote less time to child care than do mothers, and in many cultures their interactions with the child center around play rather than more general caregiving. Fathers can be effective caregivers, however, and the same attributes that characterize successful parenting for mothers (warmth, control) are important for fathers as well.

Most child-rearing studies are correlational, which means that the direction of cause and effect is uncertain. In some instances the causal direction is from child to parent, as characteristics of children influence the ways that parents treat them. Work on temperament provides the clearest example of this point.

THE FAMILY AS A SYSTEM

Determining what mothers or fathers do is important, but a sole focus on one or even both parents provides an incomplete picture of life in the family, for several reasons. Most obviously, most families contain more members than a child and two parents—siblings, most commonly, and perhaps grandparents and other family members as well. Furthermore, the impact of the characteristics and behaviors of any one family member can depend on the family system as a whole. For example, parenting practices take somewhat different form and have different effects when conflict between parents is high than when parental relations are more harmonious. Similarly, a parent's behavior toward a firstborn child typically changes in predictable (and, from the child's point of view, not desirable) ways when a second child arrives on the scene. Finally, not all families fit the two-parent, two-child "nuclear family" mold. Families come in many forms, and the different forms can have definite effects on how children develop.

In the present section of the chapter we consider aspects of family life that are not captured by a focus on parenting practices alone. We begin with a consideration of the role of siblings in children's development.

Siblings

In the United States and Europe, approximately 80% of children have siblings; most spend more time with their siblings than with their parents; and for many, relationships with siblings will be the longest lasting relationships they ever have (Dunn, 2002). What do we know about sibling relations and their possible effects on other aspects of development?

Relations among Siblings   One thing we know is that sibling relations come in many forms. Some of the variations are obvious and objective. Any child is either the older or the younger member of a sibling dyad. Siblings can be the same gender or different genders. They can be close in age or widely separated. And they can number only two or perhaps a dozen. The former, however, is a good deal more likely than the latter—the modal number of children for U.S. families is two, and only 6% of families have four or more children (Fields & Casper, 2001). Growing up with lots of siblings is a less common experience than was once the case.

More important than the differences just noted are variations in the *quality* of the sibling relationship—variations that are only weakly predicted by such characteristics as age spacing or gender composition. Some siblings have considerably closer and more positive relations than do others, and for many this remains true throughout development. Judy Dunn, a leading researcher of sibling relations, summarizes the differences as follows:

> Some siblings show affection, interest, cooperation, and support in the great majority of their interactions; when interviewed they describe their affection and positive feelings vividly. Other siblings show hostility, irritation, and aggressive behavior, and describe their dislike very clearly. Yet other children are ambivalent about their relations with their siblings, and show both hostility and positive interest in one another. (Dunn, 2002, p. 224)

Both conflict and cooperation are frequent components of silbling interaction.

What causes such striking variations? As is true for many aspects of development, temperament plays a role. Siblings typically get along best when they have similar temperaments—for example, both active and outgoing (Brody, 1996). Because temperament is only moderately heritable, many siblings will in fact not have similar temperaments. Furthermore, a difficult temperament for either member of a sibling pair is predictive of eventual difficulties in their relationship (Brody, Stoneman, & McCoy, 1994).

Parents can also be important. The same qualities that make up successful parenting in general—warmth, reasoning, firm but nonpunitive control—also enhance the probability of positive relations among siblings (Brody, 1998; Furman & Lanthier, 2002). The parents' own relationship can contribute as well. Positive relations among siblings are most likely when the husband–wife relationship is a positive one (MacKinnon, 1989).

General parenting practices are not the only way parents can affect sibling relations. Also important is the *equality* of parenting. Perhaps the strongest predictor of difficulty in the sibling relation is differential treatment by parents—that is, one sibling in general receiving more attention, more affection, weaker discipline, and so forth than the other sibling (Dunn, 2002; Furman & Lanthier, 2002). Not only is the existence of differential treatment important but also the child's *interpretation* of the treatment (Kowal & Kramer, 1997; Kowal et al., 2002). It is when children both perceive that they are being treated unequally and regard the differential treatment as unfair that difficulties in the sibling relation are most likely.

Changes with Development   For the first child in a family, sibling relations begin with the birth of a second child. It is not a happy time for most firstborns. The arrival of a second child is associated with a decline in both the amount and the positiveness of mother–child interaction for the firstborn (Baydar, Greek, & Brooks-Gunn, 1997). It is also associated with an increase in behavior problems for the older child. We can see here evidence for what has long been regarded as the most worrisome aspect of sibling relations: the existence of **sibling rivalry,** or negative, competitive feelings between two or more siblings.

Initially, a new sibling has little to offer to an older child in the family. By about a year of age, however, the younger sibling begins to present possibilities as a play partner, and by the time a baby brother or sister reaches age 2 or 3 most siblings are spending considerable amounts of time together. These interreactions tend to be marked by strong expressions of emotion on both sides of the sibling pair, with the balance of positive and negative emotions varying markedly across dyads. Dunn (1993) reports one case in which a sibling pair produced 56 conflicts in an hour!

Sibling rivalry
Feelings of competition, resentment, and jealousy that can arise between siblings.

As they develop, interactions between siblings change in various ways (Brody, 1996). Interactions become less physical and more verbal, and they also become more wide-ranging in their topics and concerns. In addition to serving as play partners, siblings begin to perform various other roles for each other. They can be sources of support in times of stress, as well as sources of advice or information when some problem arises. They provide help with school work, for example, and they consult each other on family issues and other personal matters (Tucker, McHale, & Crouter, 2001). Typically the provision of information or support flows from older to younger, but this is not always the case, especially as children grow older.

As children develop, there are changes in the balance or symmetry of their interactions and of their relationship more generally. Initially, older siblings take the lead in most dealings with their younger siblings, initiating both more positive and more negative actions and generally directing the course of the interaction; younger siblings, in turn, are more likely to give in to and to imitate their older partner (Teti, 1992). Such asymmetry lessens with age, and by adolescence the relations between siblings are typically more egalitarian. Now the younger sibling is sometimes the dominant member, and now the younger sibling can be the one who provides nurturance or help (Buhrmester & Furman, 1990).

Another change that is evident by adolescence is a decline in the relative importance of siblings as sources of intimacy or help. As we will see, by adolescence friends come to play these roles more often; children thus have less need to turn to their siblings when in need of emotional or instrumental support (Buhrmester & Furman, 1990).

Effects of Siblings   Siblings spend thousands of hours together as they grow up, they imitate each other frequently from early in life (Abramovitch, Corter, & Pepler, 1980), and they eventually exchange information and opinions (often conflicting ones!) on dozens of different issues. There are probably few aspects of development that are not potentially affected by growing up with siblings.

We have already touched on one of the cognitive benefits of siblings in both Chapters 8 and 9. Growing up with siblings—perhaps especially older siblings—is associated with accelerated development of various theory-of-mind skills (Ruffman et al., 1998). Sibling interactions are a frequent context for teasing, tricks, and sharing of emotions. It is no surprise, therefore, that such interactions can help children learn about other minds and how they can differ from their own.

In the theory-of-mind case the learning that occurs is largely incidental—a natural by-product of the kinds of interactions in which siblings engage. Siblings can also be effective teachers of one another. Indeed, research suggests that siblings may be both more likely to teach and more skillful in teaching a younger child in need than are peers, even older ones (Azmitia & Hesser, 1993). Many parents capitalize on this fact by entrusting an older child to convey a household chore or a social expectation (how to behave at church, what to say when Grandma gives you a gift) to a younger brother or sister.

Siblings can also affect aspects of each other's social development. The topic of gender-role development provides one obvious example. Siblings (especially older ones) are both models of gender-role behavior and potential agents of reinforcement or punishment for behaviors they see in their siblings. As we saw in Chapter 15, siblings do have an effect; in general (with some exceptions and complications), same-sex older siblings promote gender-typical behavior and opposite-sex siblings make counterstereotypical behavior more likely (McHale et al., 2001; Rust et al., 2000). The topic of peer relations provides another example. As we will see later in this chapter, the social skills and expectations that children first acquire in interactions with siblings affect—for better or for worse—how they behave and how successful they are when they enter the larger world of peers.

One more point is worth noting. We have drawn our (very partial) summary of sibling effects primarily from research in Western societies. In such societies, older siblings may occasionally take care of younger ones, but the caregiving role is not a generally expected, culturally mandated part of being an older sibling. When we broaden our scope to wider range of cultures the situation changes—older siblings serve as principal caregivers for younger children in a large number of the world's cultures (Zukow-Goldring, 2002). Millions of children the world around, therefore, receive much of their socialization in their early years not from adults but from older siblings. And of course the older siblings are themselves socialized by the adults of the community for the role of caregiver—a prime example of the guided participation model of cultural transmission stressed in the sociocultural approach to development.

Grandparents and Other Family Members

In the United States almost 6 million children live in a home with one or more grandparents—in some instances with one or more parents as well, and in some instances (about three quarters of the cases) with the grandparent as the primary caregiver (Bryson & Casper, 1999). Millions of other children, of course, make visits to and receive visits from grandparents, and surveys indicate that such contacts are moderately frequent in a majority of cases (Smith & Drew, 2002). Surveys also indicate that grandparents value their role: Being a grandparent is ranked as the third most important role in the grandparent's life, following spouse and parent (Kivett, 1985).

Grandparents can play many roles in their grandchildren's lives. They can be a source of emotional or financial support for the parents, and they can be mentors, playmates, baby-sitters, or substitute parents for grandchildren. In one survey, most grandchildren reported having done the following activities (among others) with their grandparents: having treats, playing games, going on trips, taking part in family events, joining in religious activities, talking about school, and learning about family history (Eisenberg, 1988).

How involved grandparents are in their grandchildren's lives depends on a number of factors. One such factor is family structure. In families with two parents, grandparents tend to stay more in the background and have less direct involvement with the grandchildren. When one parent is absent, however, the role of grandparents generally increases, and children similarly report an increased closeness to them. When there is no parent present (as is the case for more than 4 million U.S. children), the role of the grandparent is obviously maximal.

Another factor is gender. On average, grandmothers are more involved in and derive more satisfaction from the grandparent role than do grandfathers (Creasey & Koblewski, 1991; Somary & Stricker, 1998). Research on whether, and how, grandparenting varies as a function of gender of child or age of child has yet to yield consistent results (Smith & Drew, 2002). Such research, however, does reveal expectable changes with age in how children perceive their grandparents, from a view of the grandparent as a dispenser of gifts or treats in early childhood to an emphasis on companionship and support by late childhood and adolescence.

One situation in which the presence of a grandmother can be very important is that of teenage motherhood. Coresidence of daughter and mother becomes more likely when a new baby arrives, especially among African Americans, and a grandmother in the home can be a source of both expertise and welcome hands-on help (Stevens, 1984). Having a grandmother present is not always a benefit, however. In some cases the presence of her own mother can interfere with the new mother's becoming comfortable and effective in the parenting role, with detrimental effects on both her parenting skills and the child's development (Moore & Brooks-Gunn, 2002).

There are some cultures in which the presence of grandparents in the home is a good deal more typical than is the case for European American families. In China, for example, three-generation households are common (Shu, 1999), and the same is true for African American families in the United States. More generally, in many cultures—including again African Americans—the modal family pattern is not the nuclear family but the **extended family,** that is, a family unit that consists not only of children and parents but also of at least one and often several other adult relatives. For African Americans, the extended family is a legacy of family patterns in Africa, where newly married couples often join one of the parents' households rather than starting a household of their own.

Extended family
A family unit that consists not only of parents and children but also of at least one and sometimes several other adult relatives.

In many cultures, the extended family is a common—and often beneficial—arrangement.

As we would expect of any long-established cultural tradition, the extended family is associated with beneficial effects in cultures in which it is the norm. This is true for African Americans in the United States; the extended family structure has been shown to provide social and financial support to members of the younger generation, to facilitate the transmission of cultural history and values, and to reduce the probablility of negative developmental outcomes (Taylor, Casten, & Flickinger, 1993; Wilson, 1995). It is also true in a number of other parts of the world. In Sudan, for example, the nuclear family is a relatively recent development, and children who live in nuclear families have more problems in development than those growing up in the more culturally familiar extended family (El Hassan Al Awad & Sonuga-Barke, 1992). Similar findings have been reported for children in Korea (Hwang & St. James-Roberts, 1998).

Divorce

Divorce is an increasing reality in the lives of many children. Between 1960 and 1980 the divorce rate in the United States more than doubled, and at present almost half of new U.S. marriages end in divorce (Hetherington & Stanley-Hagan, 2002). Only about two-thirds of U.S. children now live in a two-parent home, and in some ethnic groups the percentage is considerably lower (U.S. Bureau of the Census, 2001).

Because much of what we will say about effects of divorce will be negative, we should begin with two qualifications. First, the findings to be discussed—and this is always the case in research on socialization—are on-the-average outcomes that do not apply to every child. Not all children are negatively affected by divorce, and the effects that do occur vary in severity across different children. Second, evaluations of the negative consequences of divorce must be placed in the context of the alternative, which in many cases is for parents to stay together in an unhappy marriage in which conflict in the home is a daily occurrence. Experts disagree with regard to the extent to which an unhappy marriage should be preserved for the sake of the children (Hetherington & Kelly, 2002; Wallerstein, Lewis, & Blakeslee, 2000); most, however, believe that in some instances divorce may be the better of two unfortunate alternatives.

Effects of Divorce   Children whose parents have divorced do not fare well when compared with children from intact families. Negative outcomes for children of divorce have been demonstrated across virtually every aspect of development that has been examined (Amato, 2001; Clarke-Stewart et al., 2000; Hetherington & Stanley-Hagan, 2002).

Effects are generally most evident in the time period immediately following the divorce (Hetherington, 1989). Typically, the first year or so following a divorce is a time of heightened anxiety, depression, and parent–child conflict. Often, both child and parent are struggling to adjust to new and stressful circumstances, and the negative reactions of each can affect the other in a cyclical, escalating fashion.

Although the obvious immediate effects of divorce generally dissipate with time, the consequences do not necessarily disappear. Children whose parents have divorced remain at risk for a variety of problems, including antisocial behavior, lower self-esteem, difficulties in school, and poor relations with both siblings and peers (Hetherington, Bridges, & Isabella, 1998). Effects may persist into adolesence, as shown by a heightened probability of precocious sexual activity, substance abuse, and school dropout (Hetherington & Clingempeel, 1992). They may also persist into adulthood: Children of divorce are more likely to have their own marriages end in divorce (Amato, 1996).

Effects of divorce vary to some extent as a function of both the age and the gender of the child. Preschool-age and early-school-age children are in some ways especially vulnerable, because they lack the cognitive resources necessary to understand the reasons for the divorce and may assume that they themselves were somehow to blame (Zill, Morrison, & Coiro, 1993). On the other hand, each segment of the developmental span presents its own vulnerabilities and possibilities for damage; adolescence, for example, can be an especially challenging time to cope with the dissolution of a marriage. Boys are typically more impacted by divorce than are girls, at least in terms of overt effects (for example, increased aggression, defiant behavior); girls, however, may be more vulnerable to effects of an internalizing sort, such as sadness and self-blame (Hetherington & Stanley-Hagan, 2002). Nevertheless, in most respects the negative consequences of divorce appear greater for boys than for girls.

Determinants of Effects Documenting effects is just one of the goals in research on divorce. A further important goal is to determine why the effects occur—and why outcomes are more positive for some children than for others.

Some of the effects associated with divorce result from conditions present prior to the divorce. It perhaps goes without saying that families in which the parents are on the verge of divorce do not present the most harmonious home atmosphere. Studies indicate that the problems shown by children of divorce were often at least somewhat evident prior to the parents' separation (Hetherington & Stanley-Hagan, 2002).

Changes in the child's experiences following the divorce are also important. Most obviously, one of the parents with whom the child has lived his or her entire life (typically the father) is no longer in the home, and thus a source of affection and support is no longer so readily available. In many cases the family's economic situation worsens appreciably, and the financial circumstances put additional stress on a mother who is now trying to cope with the role of single parent. Often the mother's parenting practices become harsher and less consistent, with predictable negative effects on the children's behavior (Hetherington & Kelly, 2002). More positively, when mothers are able to maintain an authoritative style of parenting, their children are more likely to adapt successfully following divorce (Wolchik et al., 2000).

The behavior of the noncustodial parent (in more than 80% of cases this is the father) is also important. Sheer amount of time with the father does not appear to be critical, but the quality of the time is. As we would expect, children generally adjust most successfully when the relationship with the father is warm and supportive (Amato & Gilbreth, 1999; Whiteside & Becker, 2000).

Although mother-only custody remains the usual outcome for divorces in the United States, joint custody—that is, equally shared rights and responsibilities for the two parents—is becoming increasingly common. As with any postdivorce arrangement, the success of joint custody depends on how committed and effective each parent is in the parenting role, as well as how successfully the parents are able to work together. In general, however, joint custody appears to increase the chances of successful adjustment following divorce (Bauserman, 2002).

Remarriage   Approximately 75% of divorced parents eventually remarry (although, sadly, an even higher proportion of these marriages than of first marriages will end in divorce) (Hetherington & Stanley-Hagan, 2002). The addition of a stepparent to the child's life brings both challenges and opportunities. When both parents bring children to the new marriage then there are stepsiblings as well, and still more new challenges. The conjuction of two families to form a new one is referred to as a **blended family.**

Initially, adjustment to the new family situation following remarriage is often shaky—for both child and stepparent. This is especially true during early adolescence (a shaky time in general for parenting!) and for girls' adjustment to a stepfather (Hetherington, 1993). Boys are more likely to adjust favorably to a stepfather, presumably because they perceive less threat to their relationship with the mother than do girls.

Because mothers usually obtain custody of the child following divorce, less is known about the effects of a new stepmother in the home. Studies indicate, however, that this situation can also be a difficult one—perhaps even more than the more typical new-stepfather case (Mekos, Hetherington, & Reiss, 1996). As with stepfathers, however, initial difficulties are often (though unfortunately not always) smoothed out with time. Important in both cases is the relationship between the newly married parents, as well as the support (or at least not active hostility) of the noncustodial biological parent.

Despite the difficulties just noted, stepparents can be a wonderful addition to the lives of children who have experienced a divorce. Especially when stepparents are involved with the children and skillful in their parenting efforts, positive effects on family life and children's development are evident (Hetherington & Stanley-Hagan, 2002). Unfortunately, stepparents, on average, are less involved and less skillful than parents in general; thus, not all children reap these potential benefits.

> **Blended family**
> A new family unit, resulting from re-marriage, that consists of parents and children from previously separate families.

Alternative Family Compositions

We have already touched on some of the many forms that families can take. Children can grow up with two parents, or one, or none. In the case of divorce and blended families they may eventually have more than two parents, with stepparents joining their lives in addition to the biological parents. The number of siblings in the home can vary from zero to many, and this too may change if the child becomes part of a blended family. Finally, the child may grow up as part of an extended family, with anywhere from one to perhaps half a dozen or so grandparents, aunts, and uncles as part of the family unit.

In the present section we consider two further variations in family composition: families created through adoption and families with gay or lesbian parents.

Adoption   In the United States approximately 2% to 4% of children are adopted (Brodzinsky & Pinderhughes, 2002). (The government does not maintain statistics on adoption, which is why the number is uncertain.) A slight majority are kinship adoptions; the rest go to families with whom they have no biological ties. Increasingly, adoptions from other countries have become common—up to 20,000 per year in recent years.

Adoptions occur for many reasons and under many circumstances and at many points in adopted children's lives—all of which complicate the task of determining what effects, if any, adoption has on children's development. It is clear that the majority of adopted children develop in ways that are indistinguishable from those of children being reared by their biological parents. Nevertheless, adoption is a risk factor for a number of negative outcomes—that is, adopted children are more likely, on average, to manifest problems than are children being reared by their biological parents. The problems that have been identified include learning disabilities and other academic difficulties, conduct problems, substance abuse, and various clinical syndromes (Ingersoll, 1997; Miller et al., 2000).

Almost certainly, a variety of causes contribute when problems do occur, including the difficult early environments that some children experience prior to adoption (Peters, Atkins, & McKay, 1999).

In the research just summarized, the comparison group is typically children who are being reared by their biological parents but who are otherwise similar to the adopted sample (same community, same ethnicity, etc.). Some researchers have questioned whether this is the most appropriate comparison to make. The other possibility is to ask how adopted children's development compares with what might be predicted had they stayed with their biological parents and grown up in their original environments. When this comparison is made, conclusions about adoption become more positive, for adopted children often do better than similar children who were not adopted (Brodzinsky & Pinderhughes, 2002; Hocksbergen, 1999). Thus, adoption can serve as a protective factor against the damaging effects of adverse environmental circumstances. Recall that we discussed one such effect in Chapter 10: higher IQs for adopted children than would be expected based on the background of their biological parents.

Gay and Lesbian Parenthood   Adoption, of course, is one of the methods through which individuals or couples who are lesbian or gay can add children to their family, although those who attempt to follow this route—especially gay men—face formidable challenges. More commonly, the children of gay or lesbian parents are the result of a previous heterosexual relationship of a parent who has now committed to a gay or lesbian sexual orientation.

Because of the fear of discrimination that prevents many lesbian or gay individuals from revealing their sexual orientation, the number of gay or lesbian parents is not known. Estimates of the number in the United States range from 1 to 5 million (Patterson, 2002). This means, of course that at least a million and possibly many more children are growing up in households with a gay or lesbian parent or parents. Some estimates place the number as high 10 to 14 million (Patterson, 1995).

Research on the possible effects of such a family structure is a fairly recent endeavor; such research faces a number of methodological challenges, and all who evaluate the research agree that more study is needed (Golombok, 2000, Patterson, 2002; Patterson & Chan, 1999). Thus far, however, the findings seem clear: There is no evidence that growing up with lesbian or gay parents has negative effects on children's development—or indeed any consistent effects of any sort that differentiate such children from those in other family arrangements. This conclusion holds across a range of outcomes, including self-esteem, intelligence, family relations, and peer relations. It holds as well for the most frequently examined outcomes: gender-role development and sexual identity. As we saw in Chapter 15, children of lesbian or gay parents are not in general either more or less strongly sex-typed than children of heterosexual parents, and as adolescents and young adults they appear no more likely to adopt a same-sex sexual orientation than are young adults in general.

To Recap . . .

Relations among siblings vary markedly in quality, from close and supportive to distant and at times hostile. The children's temperaments are one contributor to these variations; parental practices are another. With development, relations among siblings typically become broader in scope and more symmetrical. Growing up with siblings can affect a number of aspects of development, including theory-of-mind skills in the cognitive realm and gender-role development in the social realm.

Grandparents can play a variety of roles in their grandchildren's lives, from occasional play partner to principal caregiver. Grandmothers are typically more involved than are grandfathers, and in some cultures grandparents have greater involvement than in others. More generally, the extended family is the norm in a number of cultural settings, and in such settings the extended family is associated with positive developmental outcomes.

Divorce has become more prevalent in recent years and divorce is associated with a number of negative outcomes, both immediate and more long-term. Effects are not inevitable, however, and both their occurrence and their magnitude depend on a number of factors. Among these factors are the age and gender of the child, the parenting styles experienced by the child following divorce, and the postdivorce living circumstances, including whether one or both parents remarry.

Adopted children are at greater than average risk for a number of negative outcomes. Nevertheless, most adopted children turn out fine, and for many, outcomes are more posiitve than would have been the case had they stayed in their family of origin. Studies of children growing up with lesbian or gay parents have not demonstrated any consistent effects of such family arrangements, including effects on sexual orientation.

SOCIALIZATION BY PEERS

How do children interact with one another? What factors affect these interactions, and how do interactions with peers in turn affect other aspects of the child's development? To address these questions, we first consider how peer relations change as children grow older—that is, the developmental aspect of peer relations. We then discuss the various processes and contexts through which peers influence each other's development. In the next section we take up the important question of individual differences in the quality of peer relations.

Typical Peer Relations

Infancy Unlike older children, infants cannot spontaneously seek out their peers for companionship or pleasure. If infants find themselves together, it is because adults have placed them together. Adults often do place babies together, however, and the likelihood of such contact is increasing as more and more mothers enter the labor force (NICHD Early Child Care Research Network, 1997). Three or four infants may be cared for in the home of one mother, or half a dozen or so may occupy the infant room of a day-care center.

Interest in other children emerges quite early. Infants as young as 6 months look at, vocalize to, smile at, and touch other infants (Hay, 1985; Hay, Nash, & Pedersen, 1983). Such behaviors are, to be sure, limited in both frequency and complexity. They also have been characterized as *object-centered*, because infants' early interactions often center on some toy of mutual interest. Indeed, toys remain an important context for interaction

For many children, interaction with peers begins very early in life.

throughout infancy (at least in cultures that emphasize early object play—recall our discussion in Chapter 9).

Relations with peers change in various ways as babies develop (Brownell & Brown, 1992; Eckerman & Peterman, 2001). Initially simple and discrete behaviors, such as a touch, begin to be coordinated into more complex combinations, such as a touch in conjunction with a smile, perhaps followed by a vocalization. Reciprocity becomes more and more likely as one-way social acts evolve into more truly social interchanges. Bouts of mutual imitation develop, in which babies both imitate their partner and take pleasure in being imitated themselves (Howes, 1992). Positive emotional responses become more marked as infants begin to derive obvious enjoyment from the company and the behavior of their peers. Unfortunately, negative responses also become more evident, especially in disputes over toys. Nevertheless, most social interchanges among infants are positive. And the cognitive level of a child's play is generally higher when peers are present than when they are not (Rubenstein & Howes, 1976).

The Preschool Period We have already seen numerous differences between what infants can do and what preschoolers can do. It should be no surprise to learn that peer relations also differ between the two periods. The preschooler occupies a larger social world than the infant, with a greater number and variety of playmates (Howes, 1983, 1987). The preschooler's social world is also more differentiated—that is, the child can direct different behaviors to different social objects and form somewhat different relations with different peers (Ross & Lollis, 1989). The complexity of social interactions increases as symbolic forms of behavior begin to predominate over physical ones. The same goal that was once accomplished with a pull or a shove can now be achieved (at least sometimes) with a verbal request. Children also become more skilled at adjusting such communications to the different needs of different listeners (Garvey, 1986; Shatz & Gelman, 1973), and the first truly collaborative problem solving emerges (Brownell & Carriger, 1990; Holmes-Lonergan, 2003).

Much of the research concerned with peer relations during the preschool years has focused on children's play. One common approach to categorizing play is shown in Table 16.2. As you can see, the categories vary in the cognitive complexity of the play, ranging from the simple motor exercise of functional play to the give-and-take intricacies of games with rules. As would be expected, children of different ages are likely to engage in different types of play. Functional play emerges early and predominates during the infant and toddler years, whereas games with rules are infrequent among children younger than grade-school age (Rubin, Fein, & Vandenberg, 1983).

The category of **pretend play** has been of special interest to investigators of preschool development. Studies have demonstrated that both the frequency and the

Pretend play
A form of play in which children use an object or person as a symbol to stand for something else.

Table 16.2	Types of Play Classified According to Cognitive Level	
Type	**Description**	**Examples**
Functional	Simple, repetitive muscular movements performed with or without objects	Shaking a rattle; jumping up and down
Constructive	Manipulation of objects with intention of creating something	Building a tower of blocks; cutting and pasting pictures
Pretend	Use of an object or person to symbolize something that it is not	Pretending that a log is a boat; playing Batman and Robin with a friend
Games with rules	Playing games in accordance with prearranged rules and limits	Playing hopscotch; playing checkers

SOURCE: Based on information from *The Effects of Sociodramatic Play on Disadvantaged Preschool Children* by S. Smilansky, 1968, New York: Wiley.

Table 16.3	Types of Play Classified According to Social Level
Type	**Description**
Onlooker	Watching others play without participating oneself
Solitary	Playing alone and independently, with no attempt to get close to other children
Parallel	Playing alongside other children and with similar materials but with no real interaction or cooperation
Associative	Playing with other children in some common activity but without division of labor or subordination to some overall group goal
Cooperative	Playing in a group that is organized for the purpose of carrying out some activity or attaining some goal, with coordination of individual members' behavior in pursuit of the common goal

SOURCE: Based on information from "Social Participation among Preschool Children" by M. B. Parten, 1932, *Journal of Abnormal and Social Psychology, 27,* 243–269.

complexity of pretend play increase across the preschool years. Recall from our earlier discussions that both parents and siblings can be important contributors to the earliest forms of pretend play.

Another popular approach to categorizing play is shown in Table 16.3. Here, the focus is on the social organization rather than the cognitive level of the child's play. The usual assumption has been that the various types of play develop in the order shown in the table. Thus, 2-year-olds are most likely be found in solitary or onlooker behavior; in 5- and 6-year-olds, cooperative and associative play are common. A particularly interesting category is that of **parallel play,** in which two or more children play next to each other, using the same sorts of materials and perhaps even talking, yet without any genuine interaction. Anyone who has watched groups of 3- and 4-year-olds can verify that such "semisocial" play is common.

The categories listed in Table 16.3 were developed more than 70 years ago (Parten, 1932). Although recent research verifies that children today show the same general patterns of play, such research also suggests some qualifications and complexities in the developmental picture (Howes & Tonyan, 1999; Rubin, Bukowski, & Parker, 1998). Not all children progress in the order shown in the table; a child might move directly from

Parallel play
A form of play in which children play next to each other and with similar materials but with no real interaction or cooperation.

Parallel play is a familiar sight among preschoolers.

The most advanced form of social play is found in the cooperation and coordination of cooperative play.

Group
A collection of individuals who interact regularly in a consistent, structured fashion and who share values and a sense of belonging to the group.

Clique
A kind of group typical in adolescence, consisting usually of 5 to 10 members whose shared interests and behavior patterns set them apart from their peers.

solitary behavior to cooperative play, for example, without an intervening phase of parallel play (Smith, 1978). Nor do the early categories of play necessarily disappear as children grow older; solitary and parallel play are still common among 4- and 5-year-olds (Tieszen, 1979). What does change with age is the cognitive maturity of the play. The nonsocial play of 2- and 3-year-olds consists mainly of various kinds of functional play (see Table 16.2). Older children are more likely to embed even their nonsocial play in a constructive or dramatic context (Rubin, Watson, & Jambor, 1978). Because of this interplay of cognitive and social factors, modern scales to assess play typically include both cognitive and social dimensions (Howes, Unger, & Seidner, 1989; Rubin, 1989).

Later Childhood and Adolescence   As children develop, their play continues to evolve through the hierarchies shown in Tables 16.2 and 16.3. By age 8 or 9, children have become enthusiastic participants in games with rules, as any visit to a school playground or toy store will readily verify (Eifermann, 1971). By middle childhood, children's play is also more likely to fall within the most advanced of the categories in Table 16.3—cooperative play.

These changes in both the cognitive level and the social organization of play in turn relate to more general factors in the child's development. Increased experience with peers clearly plays a role as children spend more and more time with a wider variety of children. Indeed, effects of experience are evident well before this point; from infancy on, children with more extensive peer experience are more positive and skilled in peer play (Howes & James, 2002; NICHD Early Child Care Research Network, 2001). Advances in cognitive level also contribute. In particular, gains in perspective-taking skills during middle childhood may underlie both the newfound facility at games with rules and the general ability to interact cooperatively.

One of the most striking developmental changes in peer relations is the increased importance of groups as a context for peer interaction. For psychologists, the term **group** describes something more than just a collection of individuals. Hartup (1983) suggests the following criteria for determining that a group exists: "social interaction occurs regularly, values are shared over and above those maintained in society at large, individual members have a sense of belonging, and a structure exists to support the attitudes that members should have toward one another" (p. 144).

Preschool children occasionally interact in ways that seem to fit this definition. The same four boys, for example, may play together in similar ways every day, demonstrating clear leader-and-follower roles in their play as well as a clear sense of "we" versus "they" in their relations with those outside their group. Nevertheless, it is during the grade-school years that membership in groups assumes a clear significance in the lives of most children. Some such groups are formal ones with a substantial degree of adult input, such as Girl and Boy Scouts, 4-H, and Little League. Other groups are more informal, child-created, and child-directed, reflecting mutual interests of the group members. The culmination of this developmental progression can be seen in the **cliques** to which many adolescents belong—groups of perhaps 5 to 10 friends who interact frequently and whose shared interests and behavior patterns set them apart from both their peers and the adult world.

How does membership in a group affect peer relations? A classic study of this question is the Robbers Cave experiment (Sherif et al., 1961). For this study, 22 fifth-grade boys, initially unacquainted, were recruited to attend one of two summer camps. In each camp, the boys engaged in typical activities—hiking, sports, crafts, and the like. Thanks to the manipulation of the experimenters, they also coped with various unexpected challenges—for example, preparing a meal when the staff had failed to do so. In both camps, divisions of labor and cooperative problem solving ensued, both in response to immediate crises and with respect to longer-term group organization and group goals. Leaders and followers emerged. And both camps adopted names—Rattlers in one case, Eagles in the other.

Initially, neither group was aware of the other. After 5 days, however, the experimenters arranged for the two groups to meet "accidentally." A series of competitions (baseball, tug-of-war, and so on) followed, engineered so that neither group enjoyed

The Robbers Cave experiment is a classic study of group formation. M. Sherif, O.J. Harvey, B. Jack White, William R. Hood, Carolyn W. Sherif, photograph p. 103 from the Robbers Cave Experiment, © 1988 by Muzafer Sherif, Wesleyan University Press reprinted by permission of the University Press of New England.

more success than the other. The immediate effects of the competitions on group cohesiveness were detrimental; bickering followed any defeat, and the leader of one group was actually overthrown. Over time, however, the between-group competitions led to a heightened sense of within-group—"us" versus "them"—solidarity. At the same time, the rivalry between groups escalated, eventually reaching the point of physical violence. Only through cooperative efforts to solve further experimentally engineered crises (for example, a nonfunctioning water supply on a hot day) did the two groups begin to resolve their conflict and develop between-group friendships.

The Robbers Cave experiment suggests several conclusions about children's groups that are verified by more recent research (Bigler, Brown, & Markell, 2001; Fine, 1987; Nesdale & Flesser, 2001). Most generally, it is clear that children tend to form groups based on common interests and goals and that groups serve as a source of self-identity and gratification. Groups are organized, with rules and norms that must be adhered to and divisions of the members into leaders and followers. Work in support of common goals is one source of group cohesiveness; competition with other groups is another source. Between-group rivalry is clearly the most worrisome aspect of group functioning, since attitudes and behaviors toward outsiders may become quite negative. More positively, the same factors that promote within-group cohesion—in particular, working toward a common goal—can also serve to reduce between-group hostility.

Cognitive Contributions

We turn now to the role that cognitive development plays in peer relations. As the name suggests, cognitive factors are stressed most heavily in the cognitive-developmental approach. But any theoretical perspective must allow some role for cognitive factors. It seems obvious that how children think about peers must affect their behavior toward peers. The question is exactly how these factors contribute.

A reasonable first step is to ask which cognitive factors might be important. The most popular candidate has been perspective taking. The ability to adopt the perspective of another—to figure out what someone else feels, thinks, wishes, or the like—seems clearly relevant to the ability to interact with others. More broadly, researchers have stressed various aspects of social cognition—the child's thoughts and level of reasoning with respect to other people. How, for example, do children reason about the causes of other people's behavior, or about the morality of various behaviors, or about the nature

Social problem-solving skills
Skills needed to resolve social dilemmas.

of friendship (Shantz, 1983)? Finally, some investigators have moved closer to actual social interaction by focusing on **social problem-solving skills,** the skills needed to resolve social dilemmas (Rubin & Krasnor, 1986; Rubin & Rose-Krasnor, 1992). An example of an approach to assessing social problem-solving skills is shown in Table 16.4. Models of the skills needed to solve such problems have often been grounded in information-processing conceptions of the components—such as attention, representation, and memory—of problem solving in general (Dodge, 1986).

Skills such as those assessed by the tasks in Table 16.4 improve with age—as, of course, do perspective-taking and information-processing abilities more generally. The parallel changes with age in cognitive skills and peer relations are compatible with the idea that cognitive advances lead to social advances—as children can do more cognitively, they also can do more socially. This kind of evidence, however, is very indirect. Stronger support for the role of cognitive factors in peer relations would come from two further sorts of data. If the cognitive-developmental position is correct, we would expect to find cognitive-social links within an age group—children who are advanced in the relevant cognitive abilities should also be advanced in their peer relations. We would also expect that teaching children relevant cognitive skills would lead to advances in their social behavior as well.

Both kinds of evidence have in fact been obtained. Research has shown that there *is* a positive relation between level of cognitive development and level of peer relations. Perspective taking has been the most frequently examined cognitive variable, and a variety of forms of perspective taking have been shown to relate to how children interact (Kurdek, 1978). Measures of communication skill, both in speaking and listening, also relate positively to peer interaction (Gottman, Gonso, & Rasmussen, 1975). So do various measures of social cognition—for example, level of moral judgment (Blasi, 1980) and attributions concerning the intentions underlying behavior (Dodge, Murphy, & Buchsbaum, 1984). And so do measures of the kind of social problem-solving skills described in Table 16.4 (Yeates, Schultz, & Selman, 1991). Among the aspects of peer relations that have been found to relate to cognitive development are play (Rubin & Maioni, 1975), prosocial behavior (Wentzel & Erdley, 1993), and aggression (Rubin, Bream, & Rose-Krasnor, 1991).

Table 16.4	Examples of Items Used to Assess Children's Social Problem-Solving Skills	
Stimulus	**Narration**	**Questions**
Picture of one girl swinging and another girl standing nearby	This girl's name is Laurie, and this is Kathy. Laurie is five years old. Kathy is seven years old. Kathy is older than Laurie. Kathy has been on the swing for a long, long time. Laurie would really like to play on the swing.	What do you think Laurie could say or do so that she could play on the swing? If that didn't work, what else could Laurie do or say so that she could play on the swing? What do you think you would do or say if you wanted to play on the swing?
Picture of a boy riding a tricycle and a girl standing nearby	This boy's name is Bert and this girl's name is Erika. They are both five years old. Bert, the boy, has been on the tricycle for a long, long time. Erika, the girl, would like to ride the tricycle.	What do you think Erika could say or do so that she could ride the tricycle? If that didn't work, what else could Erika do or say so that she could have the tricycle? What do you think you would do or say if you wanted to ride on the tricycle?
Picture of a school setting with two girls sitting near each other	This girl's name is Kim and this is Jenny. Kim and Jenny are both five years old. They are both the same age. Kim and Jenny are in the same class at school, but this is Jenny's first day at the school. Jenny is a new girl in the class. Kim would like to get to know Jenny better.	What do you think Kim could say or do to get to know Jenny? If that didn't work, what else could Kim do or say to get to know Jenny? What do you think you would do or say to get to know Jenny?

SOURCE: Excerpted from *The Social Problem-Solving Test—Revised* (pp. 3, 4) by K. H. Rubin, 1988, Waterloo, Ontario: University of Waterloo Press. Copyright © 1988 by K. H. Rubin. Reprinted by permission.

In general, the results from studies that attempt to train relevant cognitive skills are compatible with those from correlational research. Not all training studies produce positive results, and the effects that do occur are generally modest in magnitude. Nevertheless, most of the evidence suggests that training in cognitive skills does have some effect on how children behave with peers. Training in perspective taking, for example, has been shown to lead to decreased aggression (Chandler, 1973) and increased helpfulness and cooperation (Iannotti, 1978). Teaching children social problem-solving skills has been shown to result in improvements in prosocial behavior and general social adjustment (Weissberg, 1985). Note that work of this sort has applied as well as scientific value, a point to which we return later.

Processes of Peer Influence

As they develop, children spend increasingly more time with peers, and they interact in increasingly varied and complex ways. How do experiences with peers affect children's development? We begin by considering some of the processes stressed in social-learning accounts of peer relations.

One important process is modeling. Children clearly imitate other children; one study in a preschool setting reports an average of 13 imitative acts per child per hour (Abramovitch & Grusec, 1978). A variety of behaviors have been shown to be susceptible to the effects of peer models, including compliance with adult instructions (Ross, 1971), sharing (Elliott & Vasta, 1970), social participation (O'Connor, 1972), and problem solving (Butler, 1996). Indeed, as we noted in our discussion of infancy, some capacity for imitative learning emerges even before the usual age for preschool attendance. Recent research has shown simple forms of peer imitation in children as young as 15 to 20 months (Asendorpf & Baudonniere, 1993; Eckerman, 1993).

Reinforcement, too, occurs frequently when children interact with each other (Charlesworth & Hartup, 1967; Furman & Gavin, 1989). Among the reinforcers children deliver are help giving, praise, smiling or laughing, affection, and compliance. Preschool children also deliver punishment to one another; examples include noncompliance, blaming, disapproval, physical attack, and ignoring. That such behaviors do function as reinforcements or punishments is suggested by children's reactions to them; reinforcers tend to elicit positive responses in their recipients, whereas punishments tend to elicit negative ones (Furman & Masters, 1980). The reinforcing or punishing nature of such events is also verified by their effects on subsequent behavior. Children are most likely to repeat a response that results in reinforcement and least likely to repeat one that results in punishment (Hartup, 1983); they are also most likely to continue to play with peers from whom they generally receive positive consequences (Snyder et al., 1996). Among the aspects of development that have been shown to be responsive to peer consequences are gender-typed behaviors (Lamb, Easterbrooks, & Holden, 1980), aggression (Patterson, Littman, & Bricker, 1967), modes of initiating interaction (Leiter, 1977), and on-task behavior in the classroom (Sage & Kindermann, 1999).

We noted earlier that children's reinforcement of their peers is often unintentional. The same is true, of course, for many instances of modeling. These processes are not necessarily inadvertent, however, even in children as young as preschool age. Research indicates that preschool children often use imitation of peers as a technique to win friends or to enter ongoing groups (Grusec & Abramovitch, 1982)—a successful technique, in that imitation is generally responded to positively. And anyone who has spent much time around young children is familiar with their deliberate manipulation of reinforcement through such promises as "I'll be your friend if . . ." and the corresponding threat "I won't be your friend unless . . ."

Conformity to Peers   We have seen that groups play an increasing role in most children's lives as they move through the late childhood and early adolescent years. To many adults, the importance of peer-group membership for the grade-schooler or adolescent raises the disturbing possibility that peers may come to outweigh parents as a source of behaviors and values. What do we know about the influence of peers in general and about the relative influence of peers and parents in particular?

The issue of peer influence turns out to be one of those "it depends" issues (Berndt, 1989a; Urberg, 1999). Peers can clearly be an important source of values. But how important they are depends on a number of factors. Peer influence varies with age, reaching a peak, at least by some measures, in early adolescence and declining thereafter (Berndt, 1979; Constanzo, 1970). Peer influence varies from child to child; some children are a good deal more susceptible to pressures from the peer group than are others (Berndt, 1996; Hartup, 1999). And peer influence, as well as the relative importance of peers and parents, varies from one area of life to another. In areas such as clothing, music, and choice of friends, peers are often more important than parents, especially by adolescence. In areas such as academic planning and occupational aspirations, however, parents usually have the dominant voice (Berndt, Miller, & Park, 1989; Sebald, 1989; Steinberg, 2001).

This discussion is not meant to imply that peers are never a negative influence. In particular cases, they clearly can be—in problem areas as serious as smoking (Urberg, Degirmencioglu, & Pilgrim, 1997), drinking (Cleveland & Wiebe, 2003), drug use (Dinges & Oetting, 1993; Mounts & Steinberg, 1995), bullying (Espelage, Holt, & Henkel, 2003), delinquency (Jessor & Jessor, 1977), and gang violence (Lahey et al., 1999). Despite these cautionary points, it is important to remember that membership in groups, in addition simply to being enjoyable for children, often nurtures positive behaviors and values, as well as promoting a number of social skills that will remain valuable throughout life. Furthermore, surveys reveal that the common perception of a clash in values between peers and parents is overstated; on most questions, peers and parents are more similar than different in their views (Brown, 1990; Newman, 1982). In part, this similarity results from the fact that parents help determine the peers with whom the child associates (Collins et al., 2000)—a point we return to shortly.

To Recap . . .

Children's peer relations undergo dramatic changes with development. Infants as young as 6 months show interest in and positive behaviors toward other babies, and as infants develop, their interactions with peers become more frequent, more complex, and more reciprocal.

During the preschool years, peer interactions continue to grow in frequency and complexity. Relations with peers become more differentiated, and symbolic forms of interaction begin to predominate over physical ones. Play increases in both cognitive level and social organization as cooperative play becomes increasingly likely. Development during the grade-school years is partly a continuation of trends present earlier. In addition, groups, both formal and informal, begin to assume a prominent role. Studies of children's groups reveal the importance of common interests and goals for group formation, as well as the importance of organization and agreed-on norms for effective group functioning.

A factor stressed especially in the cognitive-developmental approach to peer relations is the cognitive level of the child. Cognitive level is by no means a perfect predictor of peer interaction. Nevertheless, evidence from both correlational research and experimental training studies suggests that cognitive factors do contribute to peer relations.

As they interact more, children become important socializing agents for one another, especially by delivering reinforcements and punishments for particular behaviors and by serving as models.

Although the peer group can be an influential source of values and behavior, parents remain influential as well, and on most issues the views of peers and of parents are more similar than different.

VARIATIONS IN PEER RELATIONS

Our emphasis thus far has been on general processes in peer relations and general changes that accompany development. But peer relations do not follow a single general pattern. For some children, life in the peer group is a good deal more enjoyable and fulfilling than it is for others. In this section, our focus shifts to individual differences in the quality of peer relations. We begin with the most important peer relationship: friendship. We then consider status in the peer group more generally.

Friendship

According to the dictionary, the word *peer* means "equal." Clearly, however, some peers (to borrow from George Orwell's *Animal Farm*) are more equal than others. Relations among peers, like peers themselves, differ. In this section, we focus on the closest and most significant peer relationship—friendship. We begin by considering what children themselves mean by the word *friend*. We then examine how friendships are formed and how friendship influences children's behavior and development.

Conceptions of Friendship
Consider the following answers in response to the question "What is a friend?"

"A friend is a person you like. You play around with them."

"Friends don't snatch or act snobby, and they don't argue or disagree. If you're nice to them, they'll be nice to you."

"A person who helps you do things. When you need something, they get it. You do the same for them."

"Someone you can share things with and who shares things with you. Not material things; feelings. When you feel sad, she feels sad. They understand you."

"A stable, affective, dyadic relationship marked by preference, reciprocity, and shared positive affect."

It does not take much psychological insight to guess that these answers were given by respondents of different ages—or to figure out which is the definition offered by professional researchers. The first four answers (drawn from studies by Rubin, 1980, and Youniss and Volpe, 1978) came from children ranging in age from 6 to 13. The last (from Howes, 1987, p. 253) is typical of how psychologists define **friendship.**

Despite their diversity, the different definitions do share some common elements. All agree that there is something special about a friend that does not apply to peers in

Friendship
An enduring relationship between two individuals, characterized by loyalty, intimacy, and mutual affection.

The most important peer relationship is that of friendship.

general. All state or imply that friendship is not just any sort of relationship, but a relationship of affection—friends like each other. And all acknowledge that friendship is a two-way, reciprocal process. One child may like another child, but liking alone does not make one a friend. For friendship to exist, the affection must be returned.

As the examples indicate, the presence of these common elements does not rule out the possibility that children's reasoning about friendship might change with age. At a general level, a description of the changes that occur should sound familiar, because such changes parallel more general advances in the way children think about the world (Hartup & Abecassis, 2002; Rawlins, 1992). Young children's thinking about friendship tends to focus on concrete, external attributes—a friend is someone who is fun to play with and who shares things. Older children are more capable of penetrating beneath the surface to take into account more abstract aspects of friendship, such as caring for another person. For young children, friendship is often a momentary state dependent on specific acts just performed or about to be performed. Older children are more likely to see friendship as an enduring relationship that persists across time and even in the face of occasional conflicts. Finally, although even young children realize the importance of mutual liking between friends, qualities such as loyalty and intimacy do not become central in children's thinking about friendship until late childhood or adolescence.

Determinants of Friendship

Friends are not selected randomly. As children develop, they are exposed to many different people, but only a few of these potential friends ever become actual friends. On what basis are these selections made?

Studies of friendship formation show a rare unanimity in agreeing that one general factor is central to most friendship choices (Aboud & Mendelson, 1996; Hartup & Stevens, 1997). This factor is similarity. Children tend to pick friends who are similar to themselves. Similarity is not the only criterion used; children may sometimes seek out friends who are more popular than they are (Hirsch & Renders, 1986) or who have a higher socioeconomic status (Epstein, 1983). Nevertheless, similarity seems to be a major contributor to most friendship selections.

Various kinds of similarity are important. One is similarity in age. Friendships are most common among children who are close in age. Mixed-age friendships are found, of course, especially when children move outside the same-age groupings imposed by school (Epstein, 1989). Even when not constrained by adults, however, most children tend to pick friends who are about the same age (Berndt, 1988).

Similarity in gender is also important. As we saw in Chapter 15, a preference for same-sex friends emerges in the preschool years and becomes quite strong by middle childhood. Indeed, throughout much of childhood, gender is a better predictor of friendship choices than age (Epstein, 1986; Maccoby, 2000b). By adolescence, of course, cross-sex romantic relationships have begun to emerge (Shulman & Collins, 1997); even here, however, same-sex friendships continue to predominate (Hartup, 1993).

Finally, still another contributor to friendship choices is similarity in race. As with gender, a preference for same-race friends is evident as early as preschool and generally increases with age (Fishbein & Imai, 1993). It should be noted, however, that the strength of this tendency depends on a number of factors, including the degree of integration in both the school system and the neighborhood (Epstein, 1986).

Although the variables of age, gender, and race are important, they do not completely explain friendship selection. Most children encounter many peers who are similar to them in age, gender, and race, yet only some of these peers are selected as friends. What seems to be important in addition to general similarity to a peer is specific similarity in behaviors and interests—what psychologists call **behavioral homophyly**. In short, one reason that children become friends is that they like to do the same sorts of things.

This pattern is evident as early as the preschool period (Rubin et al., 1994), and it eventually extends to various settings in which children find themselves. Among older children, friends tend to be similar in their orientation toward school; they show correlations, for example, in educational aspirations and achievement test scores (Ide et al., 1981).

Behavioral homophyly
Similarity between peers in behaviors and interests. Such similarity is one determinant of friendship selection.

They also tend to be similar in what Berndt (1988) labels their "orientation toward children's culture," or what they like to do outside of school (music, sports, games, and so on). They tend to be similar in general behavior patterns and personality—for example, in the tendency to be shy or aggressive (Kupersmidt, DeRosier, & Patterson, 1995; Poulin et al., 1997). Finally, an important dimension of similarity for African American adolescents is ethnic identity, or the degree to which the adolescent identifies with the culture and values of his or her ethnic group (Hamm, 2000).

Although the relation between similarity and friendship is well established, the causal basis for the relation is less clear. There are two possibilities. Do children become friends because they have similar interests and preferences or do children develop similar interests and preferences because they are friends? Answering this question requires longitudinal study, in which patterns of similarity can be traced over time. Such studies suggest that the cause and effect flow in both directions (Epstein, 1989; Hartup, 1996). Children who later become friends are more similar initially than are children who do not become friends, indicating that similarity is indeed a determinant of friendship selection. But children who are friends become more similar over time, indicating that friendship also promotes further similarity.

What are the processes through which friendships are initially formed? A study by John Gottman (1983) provides an exceptionally detailed account.

The participants in Gottman's research were children between the ages of 3 and 9, none of whom knew one another at the start of the study. Pairs of same-aged children were randomly formed, and each pair then met in the home of one of the children for three play sessions across a period of 4 weeks. The questions were whether the children would become friends and, if so, what processes led to friendship formation.

Gottman found that some of the children did indeed become friends, whereas others did not. What aspects of the interaction differentiated the two groups? Several processes proved important. Children who became friends were more successful at establishing a *common-ground activity*—that is, agreeing on what to do—than were children who did not become friends. Eventual friends showed greater *communication clarity* and were more successful at *exchanging information* than were nonfriends. Eventual friends were more skillful at *resolving conflict*—an important skill, for conflict is frequent in young children's interactions. And eventual friends were more likely to engage in *self-disclosure*, or sharing of personal information about oneself.

Other studies of friendship formation support Gottman's conclusion that processes such as exchange of information and resolution of conflict play central roles (Grusec & Lytton, 1988). As we will see, processes of this sort do not disappear once a friendship has been formed. The same kinds of skills that help build a friendship are also central to the ways friends interact with each other.

Behavior with Friends   That behavior is different with friends than with nonfriends seems almost part of the definition of friendship. But exactly how does behavior differ as a function of friendship? Some differences are obvious. Children spend more time with friends than with nonfriends, and they typically derive more pleasure from interacting with friends (Newcomb & Bagwell, 1995). Friends, clearly, are fun to be with. In this section we focus on several further areas of possible differences between friends and nonfriends.

Prosocial Behavior   As we saw in Chapter 14, the term *prosocial behavior* refers to forms of conduct that society considers desirable and whose development is thus encouraged in children. Examples of prosocial behavior include helping someone in need, comforting someone in distress, and sharing with others. It seems reasonable to expect that such clearly positive behaviors will be more likely with friends than with peers in general.

For the most part, this commonsense prediction is borne out by research. Children share more with friends than with classmates who are merely acquaintances (Jones, 1985). Cooperation in carrying out some common task is generally greater among friends than nonfriends, as is equity in dividing any rewards that are obtained (Berndt,

1981). Even as early as the preschool years, children may cooperate and share more with friends than with nonfriends (Matsumoto et al., 1986), and they are more likely to offer help to a friend in distress than to a mere acquaintance (Costin & Jones, 1992). Preschoolers also deliver reinforcements more often to friends than to peers in general (Masters & Furman, 1981).

Despite this positive evidence, not all studies find that prosocial behaviors are more likely with friends. Berndt (1986) summarizes a series of studies in which elementary-school children actually shared less with friends than with acquaintances. According to Berndt, the critical element may be the presence of perceived competition with the friend. Research indicates that children believe friends should be equal (Tesser, 1984). Sharing too freely threatens this principle, because it may result in the friend "winning the contest" by ending up with the greater amount. Allowing a nonfriend to "win" is less threatening; hence, children are more willing to share with nonfriends. By adolescence, this "can't let him beat me" attitude has diminished, and sharing is more likely with friends even under competitive conditions.

Occasional conflicts are an inevitable part of friendship. But friends are skilled at defusing conflict and restoring positive relations.

Conflict   We turn next to a less positive side of peer interaction. The definition psychologists give to conflict is a broad one: Conflict occurs "when one person does something to which a second person objects" (Hay, 1984, p. 2). The core notion is thus one of opposition between individuals, a notion conveyed by words such as *refusing, denying, objecting,* and *disagreeing* (Hartup, 1992a).

Defined this broadly, conflict is clearly a frequent component of peer interaction (Shantz & Hartup, 1995). It is also a frequent component of interaction between friends; indeed, conflicts probably occur most often among friends (Shantz, 1987). This situation results, in part, simply because friends spend so much time together. But it also reflects the freedom and security that friends feel with one another, and thus their ability to criticize and to disagree without threatening the relationship (Hartup et al., 1993).

The important difference between friends and nonfriends, therefore, is not the probability of conflict but the ways conflict is handled (Laursen, Finkelstin, & Betts, 2001). Although exceptions certainly occur, conflicts are generally less heated among friends than among nonfriends. Friends use what Hartup (1992a) refers to as "softer" modes of managing conflict than do nonfriends: They are more likely to attempt to reason with the other person and less likely to get into extended chains of disagreement. They are also more likely to resolve the conflict in an equitable, mutually satisfactory way. And they are more likely to let bygones be bygones and to continue playing together following the conflict. We saw that the ability to resolve conflicts satisfactorily plays a role in forming a friendship. The findings just mentioned indicate that such skills are also important for maintaining a friendship. Indeed, the ability to overcome conflict and remain close can be seen as one definition of the term *friendship*.

Intimacy   The idea that intimacy is central to friendship is expressed clearly in the fourth of the quotations that opened the section on conceptions of friendship: A friend is someone with whom to share one's innermost thoughts and feelings. The quotation that expressed this view came from a 13-year-old, and it is usually not until late childhood or adolescence that the emphasis on intimacy in children's talk about friendship emerges.

Do friends in fact interact in more intimate ways than do nonfriends? Children's own statements about friendship provide one source of evidence. If a girl says she shares things with her best friend that she can share with no one else, there seems little reason to doubt the accuracy of her statement. In one series of studies, statements of this sort were absent among kindergartners, but were offered by approximately 40% of the sixth-grade participants (Berndt, 1986a).

Observations of children's interactions also provide evidence about the role of intimacy in friendship. Children who are friends or are in the process of becoming friends are more likely than nonfriends to talk about feelings and to engage in various forms of self-disclosure (Gottman, 1983). Because this difference emerges as early as the preschool years, these data suggest that intimacy may be a characteristic of friendship long before children begin to talk about intimacy as being important. On the other hand, the frequency of such intimate disclosures does increase as children grow older (Berndt & Perry, 1990; Buhrmester & Prager, 1995). And the importance of intimacy as a determinant of the quality of friendship is greater for adolescents than for younger children (Buhrmester, 1990; Hartup, 1993). It is worth noting that in addition to age differences there are gender differences in this aspect of friendship: Girls' friendships are characterized by a higher degree of intimacy than are those of boys (Buhrmester, 1996). This difference begins to emerge by middle childhood and increases into adolescence.

Effects of Friendship   Friendship, as we have seen, can have a number of positive effects on the ways in which children interact—effects, for example, on the likelihood of prosocial forms of behavior or on the probability of successful conflict resolution. The effects that we have discussed, however, have all been fairly immediate and short-term. In this section we turn to the more long-term impact of childhood friendship. Do children with many friends develop differently than children with few or no friends? Do children with high-quality friendships differ in their development from children whose friendships are less satisfactory?

Both common sense and the studies already discussed suggest that the answer to these questions should be positive. And research on the long-term consequences of friendship in fact confirms the commonsense expectation. We have already discussed one benefit of friendship: Children with satisfactory friendships adjust more successfully to school than do children who lack such support (see Chapter 10). Here we consider two others.

Self-Esteem   One effect of friendship is on the child's self-esteem. We saw in Chapter 13 that children vary in how positive they feel about different aspects of their lives (academic abilities, physical prowess, etc.). We saw also that the successes or failures a child experiences in a particular domain are one determinant of these feelings of self-worth. The specific example discussed was academic self-concept; as we would expect, children who do well in school tend to feel better about their academic competence than children who do less well.

Children's success in the peer group also affects self-esteem. The primary measure used in this research is the Self-Perception Profile for Children, which we described in Chapter 13. Not all examinations of the issue have found relations between friendship quality and self-esteem (Berndt, 2002). In most studies, however, children with relatively satisfactory friendships have been reported to have more positive scores on the Self-Perception Profile than do children who lack such friendships (Berndt & Keefe, 1995; Keefe & Berndt, 1996). As we might expect, the greatest differences tend to be on the social acceptance subscale, but the effects are not limited to perceptions of peer relations. Global self-worth—the most general index of self-evaluation—also tends to be higher in children who have satisfactory friendships.

Social Support   Perhaps the most general benefit of friendship is that it provides social support. The term **social support** refers to resources provided by other people in times of uncertainty or stress. We all need such support on occasion, even if the help is simply in the form of someone "being there" during a difficult time. Research with adults has shown that success in obtaining support is an important determinant of people's ability to cope with stress (Cohen & Wills, 1985).

Social support is also important in the lives of children (Bryant, 1985; Reid et al., 1989). The supports that children need can take a variety of forms, depending on the particular situation. One important category is *emotional support*—behaviors of others that offer needed comfort or reassurance and in general enhance the self-esteem of the recipient. Providing reassurance after a potentially embarrassing failure is a form of emotional support, as is lending a sympathetic ear when a friend has frustrations to vent. Other forms of support include *instrumental support* (provision of tangible resources to help solve

Social support
Resources (both tangible and intangible) provided by other people in times of uncertainty or stress.

practical tasks), *informational support* (provision of information or advice about how to cope with problems), and *companionship support* (sharing of activities and experiences).

Just as they can take many forms, supports can come from many sources. As we would expect, parents tend to be the most important sources of support for most children. A variety of other sources can also be important, however, including peers, siblings, grandparents, teachers, and even pets. Among peers, friends, not surprisingly, typically rank highest. In one study, friends were judged second only to parents as sources of emotional support, and friends headed the list when children were in need of companionship (Reid et al., 1989). Furthermore, the value of friends as sources of support increases as children grow older (Berndt, 1989b; Denton & Zarbatany, 1996). Older children, as we have seen, emphasize such qualities as intimacy and trust in their thinking about friendship and in their behavior with friends. It is not surprising, then, that development brings an increased tendency to turn to friends in times of need.

Popularity and Problems

Friendships do not exhaust the category of peer relations—for children or for any of us. In addition to the peers who become friends, children interact with a wide range of other children as they develop. They also form opinions—sometimes positive, sometimes negative—about many of these peers, and of course any child is him- or herself the subject of evaluation by other children in the peer group. In this section we consider a question that is of considerable importance in the lives of many children: What are the factors that determine whether a child is generally liked or disliked by other children?

Measuring Social Status

A first question concerns measurement. How can we determine which children are doing well in the peer group and which are not? The most common approach has been to ask children themselves, the assumption being that a child's peers should be the best judges of that child's standing among peers. Such peer-based evaluations of social standing are referred to as **sociometric techniques** (Asher & Hymel, 1981; Cillessen & Bukowski, 2000).

Researchers have used a variety of specific sociometric approaches. In the *nomination technique,* the child is asked to name some specific number of well-liked peers—for example, "Tell me the names of three kids in the class you especially like." The technique can also be directed to negative relations—"Tell me the names of three kids in the class you don't like very much." In the *rating-scale technique,* the child is asked to rate each of her classmates along the dimension of interest. The child might be asked, for example, to rate each classmate on a 5-point scale ranging from "really like to play with" to "really don't like to play with." Finally, in the paired-comparison technique, the child is presented with the names of two classmates at a time and asked to pick the one that he or she likes better. Because all pairs are eventually presented, the technique yields an overall measure of liking for each target child.

What is the evidence that sociometric measures yield a valid picture of a child's social standing? Sociometric scores correlate with teacher ratings of popularity or social competence—that is, the children who are identified by their peers as well liked also tend to be the ones whom teachers identify as popular (Green et al., 1980). Sociometric scores also correlate with direct observations of children's social interactions (Bukowski & Hoza, 1989). Even sociometric assessments by children as young as preschool age show correlations with such external measures and thus some evidence of validity (Denham & McKinley, 1993; Wu et al., 2001).

Popularity

However it is measured, *popularity* is easy to define. A popular child is one who is well liked by his or her peers. In terms of sociometric techniques, such children receive high ratings and are the objects of many positive and few, if any, negative choices. These children are sometimes referred to as the "stars" in sociometric classification systems (Gronlund, 1959). But what underlies such star status?

Sociometric techniques
Procedures for assessing children's social status based on evaluations by the peer group. Sociometric techniques may involve ratings of degree of liking, nominations of liked or disliked peers, or forced-choice judgments between pairs of peers.

Some examinations of this question have focused on relatively indirect predictors of popularity. Two factors, in particular, emerge as important. One is intellectual ability. Both IQ scores (Czeschlik & Rost, 1995) and measures of academic performance (Green et al., 1980) have been found to correlate with sociometric ratings. The second is physical attractiveness. On the average, relatively attractive children (as rated either by adults or by children themselves) are more popular than are relatively unattractive children (Langlois et al., 2000).

It is perhaps not surprising that intellectual ability correlates with popularity, given the importance of the school as a context for observation of peers. But why should physical attractiveness relate to popularity? Although no one knows for sure, an intriguing suggestion is that attractive and unattractive children may actually behave differently. In one study, 5-year-olds rated as unattractive showed more aggression and were more boisterous in their play than their more attractive counterparts (Langlois & Downs, 1979). Thus, part of the reason for the unattractive child's social problems may lie in the child's behavior. On the other hand, there is also ample evidence that both adults and children in U.S. society tend to hold a "beauty is good" stereotype, evaluating attractive individuals positively even in the absence of objective evidence (Ritts, Patterson, & Tubbs, 1992). Such stereotypes, moreover, may begin to operate very early. One study, for example, found that mothers of relatively attractive newborns responded more positively to their babies than did mothers whose infants were less attractive (Langlois et al., 1995). Thus, part of the basis for the unattractive child's difficulties may stem from stereotyped expectations about what attractive and unattractive people are like.

As noted, the research we have considered thus far has concerned relatively indirect predictors of popularity. We turn next to direct measures of behavior. Presumably, popular children become popular because they behave in ways that other children find attractive. What do we know about behavioral contributors to popularity?

In general, the behavioral correlates of popularity are not at all surprising. Popular children tend to be friendly, socially visible, outgoing in their behavior, and reinforcing in their interactions with others (Newcomb, Bukowski, & Pattee, 1993). At a more specific level, three sets of skills seem to be especially important (Asher, Renshaw, & Hymel, 1982). Popular children are skilled at *initiating interaction* with other children. They enter ongoing groups smoothly and set about making friends in a carefully paced but confident manner, not forcing themselves on other children but also not giving up at the slightest rebuff. Popular children are also skilled at *maintaining interaction*. They reinforce other children, show sensitivity to the needs and wishes of others, and communicate effectively in the role of both speaker and listener. Finally, popular children are skilled at *resolving conflict*. The popular child knows how to defuse touchy situations in ways agreeable to all parties, using reasoning rather than force and drawing on general principles of fairness and general rules for how people should interact.

This list of contributors to popularity should sound familiar. The kinds of social skills that help make a child popular are the same sorts of skills that we saw are important for forming and maintaining friendships. The concurrence is what we would expect—popular children are children who have the qualities desirable in a friend.

Problems in Peer Relations Popularity is the bright side of the sociometric picture. But not everyone is popular, and not everyone develops satisfactory friendships. Problems in peer relations are a topic not only of scientific interest but also of great practical importance in the lives of many children.

Popularity, as we saw, is easy to define. Problems, however, can take many forms, and different investigators have proposed different classification systems (Asher & Coie, 1990; Hymel et al., 2002; Newcomb et al., 1993).

One often-used system distinguishes rejected children, neglected children, and controversial children. The **rejected child** receives few positive but many negative nominations from his or her peers. The rejected child seems to be actively disliked. The **neglected child,** in contrast, receives few nominations of any sort, positive or negative, from peers. The neglected child seems to be less disliked than ignored. Finally, the

Rejected child
A child who receives few positive and many negative nominations in sociometric assessments by peers. Such children seem to be disliked by the peer group.

Neglected child
A child who receives few nominations of any sort, positive or negative, in sociometric assessments by peers. Such children seem to be ignored by the peer group.

Controversial child
A child who receives both many positive and many negative nominations in sociometric assessments by peers.

controversial child, as the name suggests, receives a mixed evaluation from the peer group, earning both positive and negative nominations. The rejected-neglected-controversial distinction has been the focus of much research, and so we begin by reviewing findings concerning these three groups. As we go, however, we also note some qualifications to the general conclusions, because not all children with problems fall clearly into one of these categories.

Studies of the behavior of rejected children suggest several ways in which the rejected child's behavior may contribute to his or her social difficulties (Cillessen et al., 1992; Coie, Dodge, & Kupersmidt, 1990; Rubin et al., 1998). Probably the most consistent correlate of peer rejection is aggression. Peers report, and behavioral observations confirm, that many rejected children are well above average in levels of aggression. Longitudinal studies indicate that the cause and effect flow in both directions: Aggression leads to being rejected by the peer group, but being rejected also increases later aggression (Dodge et al., 2003). More generally, rejected children often show behavior that is antisocial, inappropriate to the situation at hand, and disruptive of ongoing group activities. Their attempts to enter new groups or to make new friends tend to be especially maladroit, consisting of overly intrusive and even bizarre overtures whose outcome, predictably, is exactly the opposite of their intent (Putallaz & Wasserman, 1990).

The picture for neglected children is different (Coie & Kupersmidt, 1983). Neglected children are often perceived by their peers as being shy. This perception is not surprising, in that neglected children are less talkative and less socially active than are other children. Compared with most children, neglected children make fewer and more hesitant attempts to enter groups and make new friends. They also tend to give up quickly when their tentative and not very skilled efforts do not meet with success.

As befits their in-between sociometric status, controversial children typically show a mixture of positive and negative social behaviors (Newcomb et al., 1993). Like rejected children, controversial children tend to rank high on measures of aggression. But, like popular children, they also tend to score high on measures of sociability.

The patterns just described reflect typical, average differences among groups of children. As such, they do not apply to all rejected or neglected children. Only some neglected children, for example, show the shy behavioral style described; others are indistinguishable in their behaviors from sociometrically average children (Rubin, LeMare, & Lollis, 1990). Similarly, only some rejected children seem to earn their status through high aggression and lack of control; for others, social withdrawal appears to be a more important contributor (French, 1988, 1990). Some researchers have argued, in fact, that **social withdrawal**—that is, self-imposed isolation from the peer group—can be an important problem in itself, even in the absence of rejection or neglect (Rubin, 1993).

Social withdrawal
Self-imposed isolation from the peer group.

Finally, not all unpopular children are totally lacking in friends. As we saw in Chapter 14, aggressive, rejected children, in particular, may have a small set of close friends. These children are not generally liked by the peer group, however, and the friends they do have are often other aggressive children who are more likely to maintain than moderate their antisocial behavior (Cairns et al., 1988; Dishion, Andrews, & Crosby, 1995).

The message from this discussion is that problems in peer relations can take many forms and can have many sources. Is it possible, despite this diversity, that the various problems have a common underlying core? The common element that has been most often proposed is a cognitive one. Earlier we reviewed evidence indicating that social-cognitive skills are important for successful peer relations. Perhaps children with social problems acquire their status because they lack such skills. Simply put, such children do not know how to make or maintain friends.

Research to investigate the hypothesis that cognitive deficits underlie social problems is similar to the research discussed earlier in the chapter. Again, the findings are mixed. Not all studies find relations between cognitive and social skills, and when relations do emerge, they are seldom large (Crick & Dodge, 1994; Dodge & Feldman, 1990). Clearly, cognitive deficits are at best only one contributor to problems in peer relations. A variety of studies suggest, however, that cognitive problems do indeed contribute. Unpopular children are often lower in perspective-taking skills than are their more popular peers (Jennings, 1975). Rejected children have difficulty judging the intentions behind the behavior of others, a deficiency that may contribute to their high levels of aggression (Dodge, 1986). And both rejected and neglected children show deficits in the kind of social problem-solving skills illustrated in Table 16.4 (Rubin & Krasnor, 1986; Rubin & Rose-Krasnor, 1992). This finding makes sense, because the kinds of solutions such dilemmas call for are precisely the behaviors that rejected and neglected children fail to show.

Stability of Sociometric Status   An important question in the study of peer relations concerns the stability of sociometric status over time. Do popular children remain popular and unpopular children unpopular as they grow up? This question is of pragmatic as well as theoretical importance. Clearly, there is less reason for concern if children with problems are simply going to outgrow them as they develop.

Longitudinal studies indicate that children with problems do *not* automatically outgrow them (Cillessen, Bukowski, & Haselager, 2000; McDougall et al., 2001). Some, of course, do; early peer status is no more perfectly predictive of later development than is any other early childhood measure. For many children, however, early rejection or neglect or withdrawal does predict continuing rejection or neglect or withdrawal. The category of rejection is especially stable over time. And rejected children are the ones who are at greatest risk for a number of problems later in life, including juvenile delinquency, dropping out of school, and mental illness (Coie, in press; Laird et al., 2001; Parker et al., 1995). Although less is known about the long-term consequences of early social withdrawal, evidence suggests that withdrawn children are also at risk for later problems (Rubin, Burgess, & Coplan, 2002). (In Box 16.2 we consider intervention programs designed to help children who are having difficulty in the peer group.)

Interventions to Help Children with Problems

Problems in peer relations are not just a source of anxiety and unhappiness in childhood; such problems place children at greater than average risk for a variety of negative outcomes later in life. Can children who are having difficulty in the peer group be helped by intervention programs designed to improve their success?

A variety of intervention approaches have been tried (Ladd, Buhs, & Troop, 2002; Ramsey, 1991; Schneider, Rubin, & Ledingham, 1985). Some are grounded in social-learning theory. Modeling, for example, has been used in an attempt to increase social skills and social acceptance (Schunk, 1987). Shaping of desirable social behaviors through reinforcement has also been explored (O'Connor, 1972). Other approaches have their origins in cognitive-developmental theory. Included in this category are attempts to improve peer relations through teaching perspective-taking skills (Chandler, 1973) and through training in social problem-solving abilities (Pepler, King, & Byrd, 1991; Urbain & Kendell, 1980). Still other programs are more eclectic, encompassing a number of different training techniques in an effort to promote the needed social skills (Mize & Ladd, 1990).

A particularly interesting form of intervention is labeled **peer-mediated intervention** (Odom & Strain, 1984). This approach focuses not only on the target child but also on the group of peers with whom the child interacts. The attempt is to utilize responses from these other children (for example, offers to play, praise for desirable behavior) to promote more effective social behaviors in the target child.

Intervention efforts do have beneficial effects (Asher, Parker, & Walker, 1996; Erwin, 1993; Schneider & Byrne, 1985). All of the approaches we mentioned have yielded positive results in terms of both the social skills being taught and subsequent sociometric status. These effects are, to be sure, limited in various ways. Not all children benefit from intervention, and we have limited information about the long-term impact of such programs. Nevertheless, the picture is encouraging. Especially heartening is the fact that rejected children, who may be most at risk for later problems, can be helped through intervention to improve their social status (Asher, 1985).

It is interesting to note that one technique that has proved especially effective with rejected children is training in academic skills (Coie & Krehbiel, 1984). Apparently, the improvement in the rejected child's academic performance has a beneficial impact on the child's self-concept and general classroom behavior, changes that in turn affect how the peer group evaluates the child.

BOX 16.2

Applications

Peer-mediated intervention
Form of intervention for children with sociometric problems in which responses of the peer group are utilized to elicit more effective social behaviors from the target children.

Cultural Variations As with many topics in developmental psychology, most of what we know about the bases for children's sociometric standing comes from research in a narrow range of cultural settings. For example, in their 1993 review of the contributors to sociometric status, Newcomb and colleagues summarized results from 41 studies, 39 of which had been carried out in North America.

Fortunately, this situation is changing. Recent years have seen the extension of sociometric research to a number of new settings beyond the United States and Canada. The picture that emerges from these studies is in some respects similar to what is found with North American samples and in some respects different.

Let us first consider a major similarity. In North American samples, one of the strongest and most consistent predictors of peer rejection is aggression. This finding has proved to be general across a range of cultures. Similar aggression–rejection links have now been demonstrated in China (Chen, Rubin, & Li, 1995), Italy (Attili, Vermigli, & Schneider, 1997), the Netherlands (Cillessen et al., 1992), and Costa Rica (Kupersmidt & Trejos, 1987). These findings confirm what most of us would predict: Hitting other children is not an effective way to win friends or earn group approval, whatever the specific cultural setting in which the child is developing.

On the other hand, not all findings from North American samples have proved to be generalizable to other cultures. Recall that American children who are shy and reserved in their interactions with peers are at risk of being neglected by the peer group. In China, however, there is no association between a reserved pattern of behavior and neglect. To the contrary, Chinese children who are quiet and nonassertive tend to be above average in popularity. They also are rated by their teachers as especially competent, and they hold a disproportionate number of leadership positions within the school (Chen, 2002; Chen, Rubin, & Sun, 1992).

Why might a similar behavior pattern lead to such different outcomes in different cultures? The most likely answer concerns cultural values and expectations. In China, a cautious, self-restrained style of interpersonal interaction is regarded as a sign of competence and maturity (Ho, 1986). Adults therefore encourage such a behavior pattern in children, and children themselves come to value it and to reward it in their peers.

In a sense, then, the comparison of Chinese and American children reveals similarity as well as difference. In any culture there are expectations about appropriate forms of behavior—expectations held by children as well as adults. Children whose behavior is in accord with cultural values and expectations are the ones who are most likely to find acceptance in the peer group.

To Recap . . .

A particularly important peer relation is friendship. Children themselves agree with this assessment—from the preschool years on, children talk about friends as being different from peers in general. Children reason about friendship in increasingly sophisticated ways as they develop. Young children tend to think of friends in concrete terms as sources of immediate pleasure; older children are more likely to see friendship as an enduring relationship characterized by such attributes as intimacy and loyalty.

Children tend to pick friends who are similar to themselves. Similarities in age, gender, and race have all been shown to influence selection. Similarities of a more behavioral sort also play a role. Friends tend to be similar in academic orientation, and they often share the same outside-of-school interests. Studies of friendship formation suggest that a variety of processes contribute, including exchange of information, self-disclosure, and successful resolution of conflict.

Behavior with friends differs from that with nonfriends in a number of ways. Prosocial behaviors, such as sharing and helping, are generally more common with friends. Although conflict does not disappear once a friendship has been formed, resolution of conflict is usually more successful among friends than among nonfriends. Finally, sharing of intimate information is more likely among friends, and the importance of intimacy for friendship increases as children get older. Friendship can have long-term as well as immediate benefits. Among the aspects of development that are influenced by the quality of friendships are self-esteem and availability of social support in times of need.

Children show important individual differences in the quality of their peer relations. Typically, such differences have been assessed through sociometric techniques—judgments offered by the child's peers. Children are defined as popular if they are the objects of many positive and few negative judgments. Studies of the determinants of popularity have explored both relatively indirect predictors and more direct behavioral correlates. Variables in the first category that correlate with popularity include intellectual ability and physical attractiveness. The behavioral skills that seem to distinguish popular from less popular children are of three sorts: skill in initiating interaction, skill in maintaining interaction, and skill in resolving conflict.

Sociometric assessments also identify children with problems in peer relations. The rejected child receives few positive but many negative nominations from the peer group, whereas the controversial child receives many choices in both categories and the neglected child receives few nominations of any sort. Both rejected and neglected children show deficits in social skills, although their behavioral problems take different forms. Many (although not all) rejected children are characterized by aggressive, antisocial, and inappropriate behavior, whereas many (although again not all) neglected children are characterized by shy and withdrawn behavior.

FAMILY AND PEERS

For most children, the family and the peer group are the two most important microsystems within which development occurs. In this final section we consider how these two major social worlds relate. We begin by examining how children's relations with their siblings compare with their peer relations. We then explore the contribution of parents to children's peer relations.

Siblings and Peers

There are both obvious similarities and obvious differences in children's relations with their siblings and their relations with their peers, especially with their friends. On the one hand, both sibships and friendships are intimate, long-lasting relationships that are the context for frequent and varied interactions—usually positive in tone but including moments of conflict and rivalry as well. Both relationships involve partners who are close in age, and hence interactions are likely to be more egalitarian and symmetrical than are interactions with adults, such as parents or teachers.

On the other hand, siblings (unless they are twins) are not identical in age, and the younger–older contrast introduces a basic asymmetry not necessarily found with friends. Furthermore, siblings, unlike friends, are not together by choice and do not have the option of terminating the relationship if negative aspects begin to outweigh positive ones. As one researcher put it, "Siblings do not choose each other, very often do not trust or even like each other, and may be competing strongly for parental affection and interest; the sources of conflict and hostility in this relationship are likely to be very different from those leading to tension in a friendship" (Dunn, 1992, p. 7).

This analysis suggests that we should expect some similarity, but hardly perfect similarity, between sibling relations and peer relations. And this, in fact, is what research shows. Let us first consider some similarities. As we have seen, siblings clearly can perform the same roles and fulfill the same needs that are important among friends—as objects of pleasure or companionship, for instance, or as sources of affection, or as confidants for intimate interchanges (Buhrmester, 1992). Less positively, siblings, like friends, may also sometimes be targets for hostility and conflict; especially among younger children, conflicts among siblings are a depressingly familiar experience for many parents (Dunn, 1993). Some conflict is inevitable in any long-term, intimate relationship, and siblings, like friends, are no exception to this rule.

Along with these general similarities in sibling and peer relations come differences. Some differences follow from the differences in age between siblings and the contrasting roles played by the younger and older child. Sibling interchanges, especially early in development, tend to be less symmetrical and egalitarian than those among friends, both because of the younger–older contrast and because of the forced, not chosen nature of the sibling relationship. This factor also contributes to differences in the domain of conflict. Although conflicts occur in both relationships, they tend to be more frequent between siblings than between friends (Buhrmester, 1992), and they also take somewhat different forms in the two contexts. Children are less likely to reason with siblings than with friends, less likely to attempt to take the sibling's point of view, and more likely to judge perceived transgressions negatively when the perpetrator is a sibling (Slomkowski & Dunn, 1993). Again, the forced nature of the sibling relationship may account for the siblings–friends differences.

Our discussion so far has concerned general similarities or differences between sibling relations and peer relations. But it is also important to ask about within-child links between the two social worlds. Does a particular child tend to show the same sorts of behaviors with peers as with siblings? Does the overall quality of a child's peer relations mirror the quality of relations with siblings?

The answer turns out to be "sometimes but not always" (Dunn & McGuire, 1992). Research makes clear that there is no simple, direct carryover of relations forged with siblings to relations with peers. Indeed, some examinations of the issue report little if any association between how children behave with siblings and how they behave with peers (Abramovitch et al., 1986; Volling, Youngblade, & Belsky, 1997). Such findings demonstrate once again the importance of context for children's behavior—what we see in one social context does not necessarily hold true when we move to a different context.

In other studies, sibling–peer connections do emerge, but they are seldom strong. As we might expect, links tend to be greater with friendship (another intense, dyadic relationship) than with peer relations in general (Stocker & Dunn, 1990). In some cases the direction of the relation is positive. For example, studies have shown positive correlations between cooperation with siblings and cooperation with friends (Stocker & Mantz-Simmons, 1993), between aggression with siblings and aggression toward peers (Vandell et al., 1990), and between the overall quality of sibling relations and the quality of peer relations (Seginer, 1998). In other cases the direction is negative. For example, children with relatively hostile sibling relations sometimes form especially close friendships (Stocker & Dunn, 1990); similarly, children who are unpopular with peers may rank high on affection and companionship with their siblings (East & Rook, 1992). What seems to be happening in these cases is a kind of compensation: When one component of children's social world is unsatisfactory, they may try especially hard to obtain pleasure and support from other components.

Parents and Peers

In Chapter 10 we saw one example of Bronfenbrenner's (1979) concept of the mesosystem, or the interrelationships among the various microsystems in the child's life. There our focus was on the ways in which relations with parents and peers contribute to children's success in school. Here we take up another aspect of the mesosystem: relations between life with parents and life in the peer group. The specific question on which we focus is one of interest to any parent: What do parents do that helps or hinders their children's success with peers? The answer, we will see, is that parents do a variety of things that can be important (Kerns, Contreras, & Neal-Barnett, 2000; Parke & Ladd, 1992; Parke et al., 2002).

Early Contributors   Parents' contribution to peer relations can begin very early in life, before most children have even begun to interact with peers. As we saw in Chapter 12, infants differ in the security of the attachments they form with the caregiver, and these differences in turn relate to the sensitivity and responsiveness of caregiving practices. As we also saw, secure attachment in infancy is associated with a number of positive outcomes in later childhood, including various aspects of peer relations.

Children who were securely attached as infants tend to do well on measures of social competence and popularity later in childhood (Bohlin, Hagekull, & Rydell, 2000; Fagot, 1997; Kerns, Klepac, & Cole, 1996). Security of attachment is also related to quality of friendships; children with a history of secure attachment tend to form more harmonious and well-balanced friendships than do children with a history of less satisfactory attachments (Kerns, 1996; Youngblade & Belsky, 1992). Indeed, infant attachment is a stronger predictor of friendship quality than of general peer status (Schneider, Atkinson, & Tardif, 2001).

Most of the research on attachment security as a predictor of later developmental outcomes has concentrated on mothers. We know less, therefore, about the possible importance of early relations with fathers. The studies that do exist, however, suggest that a secure attachment with the father also relates positively to later success with peers (Schneider et al., 2001).

As we saw in Chapter 9, parents may also contribute to the development of the forms of play that occupy such a central position in children's early interactions with their peers. Before they embark on pretend or dramatic play with peers, many children have spent dozens of hours engaged in such play with their mothers and fathers at home. Observational studies verify that joint pretend play is a frequent activity in many households and that parents (mothers, in particular, in these studies) often assume a directive role in such play (Tamis-LeMonda, Uzgiris, & Bornstein, 2002). Research suggests, moreover, that children can acquire social skills in play with parents that carry over to later interactions with peers. It has been shown, for example, that parents' expression of positive emotions during play is linked to children's subsequent expression of positive emotions with peers, which in turn is related to acceptance by the peer group (Isley et al., 1999). Similarly, mothers' use of other-oriented reasoning in resolving conflicts with their children is related to the children's subsequent success in resolving conflicts with friends (Herrera & Dunn, 1997).

Parents as Managers   Parents' involvement in early play represents a relatively indirect contribution to eventual peer relations. Parents may also take a more direct role in promoting and managing their children's encounters with peers. Ladd (1992) identified four ways parents may influence the frequency and nature of peer interactions: (a) as *designers* of the child's environment, parents make choices that affect the availability of peers and the settings (such as a safe versus a hazardous neighborhood) within which peer interactions take place; (b) as *mediators*, parents arrange peer contacts for their children and regulate their choice of play partners; (c) as *supervisors*, parents monitor their children's peer interactions and offer guidance and support; and finally, (d) as *consultants*, parents provide more general advice and emotional support with respect to peer relations, especially in response to questions and concerns from the child.

Research indicates that parents vary in the frequency and the skill with which they perform these various roles and that these variations in parental behavior in turn relate to variations in children's peer relations (Ladd & Pettit, 2002). It has been found, for example, that peer acceptance in the preschool is related to the extent to which parents initiate play opportunities for their children (Ladd & Hart, 1992). Play among children, especially toddlers or preschoolers, proceeds more smoothly and happily when a parent is present to facilitate and direct (Bhavnagri & Parke, 1991). And play opportunities are more frequent and friendship networks larger when children grow up in safe neighborhoods with closely spaced houses than when conditions are less conducive to peer interaction (Medrich et al., 1982).

These conclusions are not limited to children growing up in the United States. Parents' initiation of peer contacts for their children has been shown to relate positively to peer acceptance in both Russia and China (Hart et al., 1998). Parental monitoring of interaction with peers has been found to be beneficial in a variety of cultural settings, including Denmark (Arnett & Balle-Jensen, 1993), Australia (Feldman et al., 1991), and China (Chen et al., 1998).

Parents' Child-Rearing Although these kinds of direct management can undoubtedly be important, most attempts to identify the parental contribution to peer relations have focused on general child-rearing strategies that either nurture or fail to nurture the social skills necessary for success with peers. Several dimensions emerge as important. One consistent correlate of sociometric status and social skills

Peer Relations as a Source of Resilience

It is well established that children exposed to aversive family environments during early childhood are at elevated risk for the development of behavior problems. Of course, exposure to difficult family experiences does not foreordain adjustment problems. Many children reared in difficult circumstances nonetheless show good adjustment later in life. Psychologists refer to children who adapt positively in the face of significant adversity as **resilient children** (Luthar, Cicchetti, & Becker, 2000; Masten et al., 1999).

Studies of resilient children have revealed that a variety of factors contribute to children's ability to overcome negative experiences. These include personal characteristics of the child (e.g., socially responsive temperament, high self-esteem), aspects of the family (e.g., the availability of alternative caregivers), and characteristics of the child's wider social network (e.g., supportive neighbors or social agencies) (Cochran & Niego, 2002; Werner & Smith, 1982). In one recent study, researchers explored whether peers might buffer children from the effects of exposure to a family environment characterized by high levels of marital conflict and physical aggression (Criss et al., 2002).

The investigation was part of a larger, longitudinal study of children's socialization known as the Child Development Project (Pettit et al., 2001). More than 550 children and their families in Tennessee and Indiana were recruited for the study when they registered for kindergarten. The families were primarily of middle-income and European American backgrounds. During the summer before children entered kindergarten, the parents were interviewed and completed questionnaires about a variety of issues. Based on the parents' responses, each family was rated on three dimensions of family adversity—ecological disadvantage, violent marital conflict, and harsh discipline.

Data on children's peer relations were collected during kindergarten and first grade. To assess children's peer relations, the researchers used two of the sociometric techniques described earlier. During individual interviews, children were shown a class roster and asked to nominate up to three peers they liked and three peers they disliked. They were also asked to rate how much they liked each peer. The measures provided an index of how much each child was generally liked by peers as well as his or her number of friends.

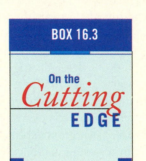

BOX 16.3

On the
Cutting
EDGE

Children's adjustment was based on teacher ratings. During the spring of grade 2, teachers completed the Child Behavior Checklist, a widely used checklist of behavior problems that includes such items as "gets in many fights" and "disobedient at school."

As expected, the researchers found that children exposed to higher levels of family adversity in early childhood exhibited greater numbers of problem behaviors in grade 2. However, children reared in adverse circumstances but who had positive peer relations displayed far fewer behavior problems than other children raised in comparable family situations. Moreover, the positive impact of peers was found for all three kinds of family adversity.

The results of this study suggest that positive peer relations can serve as a protective factor against family adversity. The findings also raise a number of intriguing questions. One question is how peer relations might moderate the effects of negative family environments. Theorists have proposed a number of explanations. One possibility is that positive peer relationships provide a "remedial" context in which children can practice certain skills not picked up at home (Price, 1996). For instance, a child whose parents are too overstressed to help the child learn how to manage his or her emotions may learn how to do so in the context of peer interaction.

Another possibility is that relationships with peers may foster the child's engagement in school and foster positive relations with teachers. A positive orientation toward school may in turn decrease the child's tendency toward social deviance.

A third possibility is that peers may serve as a form of "behavioral intervention." The negative reactions of peers, and possibly the peers' parents, to inappropriate behavior (e.g., aggression) may teach the at-risk child that behaviors that are normative in his or her own home are unacceptable outside of it.

Finally, children's relationships with peers may also indirectly modify parents' behaviors. By interacting with the parents of their children's friends, mothers may learn more effective means of discipline and of resolving marital conflicts (Fletcher et al., 1995). Establishing a network of relations with other parents may also reduce family stress by providing social support. Thus, peer relations may lead to improvements in the behavior of children at risk via their positive influence on parenting.

Resilient children
Children who adapt positively and develop well despite early environmental adversity.

is parental warmth (MacDonald, 1992). Children who come from homes that are characterized by high levels of warmth, nurturance, and emotional expressiveness tend to do well in the peer group; conversely, children whose home lives are less harmonious are at risk for peer problems as well. The extreme of the latter situation arises in cases of physical abuse or neglect. Children who have been abused show special difficulty in responding appropriately when peers exhibit signs of distress (Klimes-Dougan & Kistner, 1990). Children who have been maltreated also show heightened levels of aggressiveness and social withdrawal (Mueller & Silverman, 1989). Not surprisingly, abused children tend to fare poorly on sociometric measures, and their unskilled behavior with peers often perpetuates their difficulties (Bolger & Patterson, 2001; Cicchetti et al., 1992).

The parent's methods of controlling and disciplining the child can also be important (Dekovic & Janssens, 1992; Dishion, 1990; Hart et al., 1992). Parents of popular children tend to be intermediate in the degree of control they exert, neither rigidly directing the child's every action nor allowing too much leeway because of lack of time or interest. These parents are involved in the lives of their children, but the goal of their socialization seems to be to promote autonomy and not merely immediate compliance. When discipline becomes necessary, parents of popular children tend to prefer verbal rather than physical methods, reasoning with the child and negotiating rather than imposing solutions. In contrast, techniques of power assertion (threats and physical punishment) are likely to characterize the home lives of children with peer problems (Ladd & Pettit, 2002).

These conclusions about the contribution of parents to peer relations should not sound new or surprising. They fit with the general conclusions about the effects of parental practices discussed earlier in the chapter. They also fit with what we would expect from theory. Support for cognitive-developmental positions is evident in the value of rational, cognitively oriented techniques of control and discipline. Support for social-learning theory can be seen in the clear role of parental reinforcements and parental models in fostering social skills. Indeed, the importance of parents as models is perhaps the clearest conclusion to be drawn from studies of the family's contribution to peer relations. Parents who are warm and friendly and effective with others have children who are warm and friendly and effective with others.

In discussing links between family and peer experience, we have emphasized the contribution of parents to the child's success with peers. We should add, however, that effects can clearly flow in the other direction as well. In Box 16.3 we discuss some recent research that explores how satisfactory relations with peers can buttress children against the effects of family adversity.

To Recap . . .

Experiences within the family contribute to children's behavior with friends. Siblings are in many respects similar to peers as social objects, and sibling relations show many of the characteristics important in relations with peers, especially friends. Sibling relationships and friendships are different in some respects, however, and specific qualities of sibling relations are only sometimes reflected in relations with peers.

Parents can contribute to their children's behavior with peers in a number of ways. Secure attachment to the parent during infancy is associated with positive peer relations in later childhood. Parents' participation in early pretend play may facilitate the emergence of play with peers. Both the frequency and the nature of peer interactions may be affected by various parental actions, ranging from choice of neighborhood to direct initiation and management of peer encounters. Finally, parents' child-rearing practices can help instill the social skills necessary for success in the peer group. Among the parental practices that can be beneficial are creation of a warm and supportive family atmosphere, use of cognitively oriented techniques of discipline, and provision of models of socially appropriate actions in the parents' own behavior.

CONCLUSION

In 1998 Judith Harris published a book titled *The Nurture Assumption,* a book that quickly became one of the most talked about and controversial publications in the field. The book was an extension of an earlier article by Harris (1995), the opening lines of which set forth her basic thesis: "Do parents have any important long-term effects on the development of their child's personality? This article examines the relevant evidence and concludes that the answer is no" (p. 458). Rather than parents' practices being of any importance, Harris argued that children's development was shaped by two main forces: the genes with which they were born and experiences in the peer group as they grew up.

Most child psychologists have not been persuaded by Harris's arguments, and many in fact have offered explicit counterarguments to her position (e.g., Collins et al., 2000; Maccoby, 2000a, 2002; Vandell, 2000). As our discussions throughout this chapter suggest, we are not persuaded either. We believe that a substantial body of evidence indicates that parents can be important from birth, both in shaping eventual individual differences among children (the idiographic side of development) and in aiding the development of species-wide competencies and attributes (the normative side of development).

Whatever its ultimate fate, however, *The Nurture Assumption* does serve to provide a valuable reminder of several important points. One is that although parents may be important for their children's development they are very far from being *all-important.* Many factors contribute to making all of us what we ultimately become. These factors clearly include the two determinants emphasized by Harris: peers and genes. Psychology's growing appreciation of the importance of genetic factors was a theme of earlier chapters, and the potential contributions of peers should be clear from the discussions in this chapter. Nor do genes and peers exhaust the nonparental sources of children's development. If you need to be reminded of this point, simply look back at all the forces in the Bronfenbrenner ecological systems model (Figure 1.1).

A second point concerns the challenges in doing research on some of the most basic and important issues in the field, including socialization. If fundamental uncertainties still exist after a century of child-rearing research, it is not because of either lack of effort or lack of competence on psychologists' part. Rather, it is because child-rearing is considerably more difficult to study than are most topics that science addresses—indeed, more difficult than most topics within psychology.

A final point is that despite the challenges, the scientific method has brought genuine advances in our understanding of child-rearing specifically and of childhood more generally. There was a time when the expert scientific advice to parents about how to treat children was John Watson's (1928, p. 81) "Never hug or kiss them, never let them sit in your lap." We have come a long way since then. The same story could be told for dozens of other topics considered in this book. At the same time, there is still much to be learned about almost every topic we have considered. The power of the scientific approach is verified daily in the study of child psychology. But the mysteries of human development yield their secrets slowly.

FOR THOUGHT AND DISCUSSION

1. Most psychologists oppose the use of physical punishment. However, many parents believe that spanking is the most effective way to teach children right from wrong. Physical punishment is common among many cultural minorities including African Americans and some immigrant groups. Yet the use of physical punishment among these groups is not associated with the negative effects (e.g., high levels of aggression) found in European American communities. *How should psychologists and others in the helping professions respond to the use of spanking and others forms of physical punishment? Should they always try to prevent it and encourage caregivers to adopt parenting techniques endorsed by psychologists? Or should they offer different advice to different cultural groups?*

2. One of the best-established findings from child-rearing research is that frequent use of reasoning by parents is associated with positive development outcomes in children. Because the research is correlational, however, the direction of casuality is uncertain: Parents may be responding to, rather than shaping, characteristics of their children. *Suppose that you wished to determine whether reasoning is in fact an effective technique of socialization? What further kinds of evidence could you gather?*

3. Increasingly, couples are opting to have fathers stay home and take care of children full-time while mothers work—sometimes at highly demanding jobs that require long hours. *Do you think that children who spend their early years under the primary care of fathers rather than mothers will develop any differently from those who spend most of their time cared for by females? Do you think fathers and mothers are differentially important depending on children's ages?*

4. Each of the major theoretical positions emphasizes the role of peers in children's development. *But is experience with peers necessary for development? Imagine a scenario in which a child is reared solely in the company of loving and sensitive adults. Could such a child develop normally? Why or why not?*

5. Consider the topic of friendship selection. *Suppose you wished to determine how a group of kindergartners select playmates. How would you go about finding out? If you asked the children directly, what would you ask?*

6. Research indicates that initial similarity between children is one basis for friendship selection but that friends also become more similar over time. *Think about your own friendships, either past or present. To what extent have you sought out friends who were similar to yourself, and to what extent have you and your friends grown more similar across the course of the relationship?*

VISUAL SUMMARY FOR CHAPTER 16
Families and Peers

Theories of Socialization

Evolutionary Approaches
> Evolutionary approaches assume that many social behaviors—including caregiving by parents and certain behaviors toward peers, such as altruism and aggression—are based on innate characteristics reflecting the evolutionary history of the species.

Environmental/ Learning Approaches
> The environmental/learning approach stresses the application of general learning principles. Both parents and peers may reinforce or punish certain behaviors, thereby increasing or decreasing their likelihood. Both may also serve as models, and peers in particular can be an important source of self-efficacy judgments.

Cognitive- Developmental Approaches
> The cognitive-developmental approach emphasizes the cognitive resources of parents and children. Parental beliefs contribute to their socialization practices, and children are active cognitive processors in socialization interchanges. Children also form beliefs about other children, which help determine their behavior toward peers. Interaction with peers can also be an impetus for cognitive change.

Sociocultural Approaches
> Both parents and peers nurture development most effectively when they provide experiences within the child's zone of proximal development. In addition to the microsystems (such as family and peers) within which development occurs, the sociocultural approach stresses the relations among systems and the effect of the general culture.

Socialization within the Family

Parenting Styles
> One influential approach to parenting identifies four styles that vary along the dimensions of warmth and control: the authoritative, authoritarian, permissive, and uninvolved styles. In general, the authoritative style is associated with the most positive social and cognitive outcomes. However, the effects of the different styles may vary across different populations.

The Role of Fathers
> Fathers typically devote less time to child care than do mothers. Fathers can be effective caregivers, however, and the same attributes that characterize successful parenting for mothers (warmth, control) are important for fathers.

The Child's Contribution
> In some instances, the characteristics of children influence the ways that parents treat them. Work on temperament provides the clearest example of this point.

The Family as a System

Siblings
> Relations among siblings vary from close and supportive to distant and hostile. The children's temperaments are one contributor to variations; parental practices are another. With development, relations among siblings become broader in scope and more symmetrical. Growing up with siblings can affect such aspects of development as theory-of-mind skills and gender-role development.

Grandparents and Other Family Members
> Grandparents play a variety of roles, from occasional play partner to principal caregiver. Involvement of grandparents varies among cultures. More generally, the extended family is the norm in some cultural settings and in these settings is associated with positive developmental outcomes.

| **Divorce** | Divorce is associated with a number of negative outcomes, both immediate and long-term. These effects are not inevitable but depend on various factors, including the age and gender of the child, the parenting styles following the divorce, and the postdivorce living circumstances. |

| **Alternative Family Compositions** | Adopted children are at greater than average risk for a number of negative outcomes, although for many, outcomes are more positive than would have been the case had they stayed in their families of origin. Growing up with lesbian or gay parents has not been demonstrated to have any consistent effects, including effects on sexual orientation. |

Socialization by Peers

| **Typical Peer Relations** | Infants as young as 6 months show interest in and positive behaviors toward other babies. During the preschool years, relations with peers become more differentiated, and symbolic forms of interaction begin to predominate. Play increases in both cognitive level and social organization. During the grade-school years, these trends continue. In addition, groups begin to assume a prominent role. |

| **Cognitive Contributions** | Cognitive level is stressed especially in cognitive-developmental approaches to peer relations. Although cognitive level is by no means a perfect predictor of peer interaction, evidence suggests that cognitive factors do play a role. |

| **Processes of Peer Influence** | As they interact more, children become important socializing agents for one another, especially by delivering reinforcements and punishments for particular behaviors and by serving as models. Nevertheless, parents remain important; and on most issues, the views of peers and parents are more similar than different. |

Variations in Peer Relations

| **Friendship** | Children begin to differentiate friends from peers in the preschool years, and their reasoning about friendship becomes increasingly sophisticated as they develop. Children tend to pick friends who are similar to themselves. Processes that contribute to friendship formation include exchange of information, self-disclosure, and successful resolution of conflict. Behavior with friends differs from that with nonfriends in a number of ways. The quality of friendships affects self-esteem and availability of social support in times of need. |

| **Popularity** | Popularity is generally assessed through sociometric techniques—judgments offered by peers. Indirect predictors of popularity include intellectual ability and physical attractiveness. Direct behavioral correlates include skill in initiating interaction, maintaining interaction, and resolving conflict. |

| **Problems** | In sociometric measurements, rejected children receive few positive and many negative judgments; neglected children receive few positive or negative judgments; and controversial children receive many positive and many negative judgments. Many rejected children are characterized by aggressive, antisocial, and inappropriate behavior, whereas many neglected children are characterized by shy and withdrawn behavior. |

Family and Peers

| **Siblings and Peers** | Sibling relations show many of the characteristics important in relations with peers, especially friends. Sibling relations and friendships differ in some respects, however, and specific qualities of sibling relations are only sometimes reflected in relations with peers. |

| **Parents and Peers** | Parents contribute to their children's behavior with peers in a number of ways. Secure attachment in infancy is associated with positive peer relations later. Both the frequency and the nature of peer interactions may be affected by parental actions ranging from choice of neighborhood to management of peer encounters. Finally, parents' child-rearing practices can help instill social skills. |

Glossary

A

Ability grouping Separation of students into groups of similar ability for purposes of instruction.

Academic self-concept The part of self-esteem involving children's perceptions of their academic abilities.

Accommodation Changing existing cognitive structures to fit with new experiences. One of the two components of adaptation in Piaget's theory.

Active gene-environment correlation Situation in which genes and environment affect development similarly because children seek out experiences that are compatible with their genetic predispositions.

Adaptation The tendency to fit with the environment in ways that promote survival. One of the two biologically based functions stressed in Piaget's theory.

Adult Attachment Interview An instrument used to assess an adult's childhood recollections of the attachment relationship with the primary caregiver.

Affect The outward expression of emotions through facial expressions, gestures, intonation, and the like.

Affect mirroring The degree to which caregivers gauge their communicative behaviors to respond to input from their infants.

Age of viability The age (presently around 23 or 24 weeks) at which the infant has a chance to survive if born prematurely.

Aggression Behavior that is intended to cause harm to persons or property and that is not socially justifiable.

Alleles Genes for the same trait located in the same place on a pair of chromosomes.

Amniocentesis A procedure for collecting cells that lie in the amniotic fluid surrounding the fetus. A needle is passed through the mother's abdominal wall into the amniotic sac to gather discarded fetal cells. These cells can be examined for chromosomal and genetic defects.

Amniotic sac A fluid-containing watertight membrane that surrounds and protects the embryo and fetus.

Analogical reasoning A form of problem solving in which the solution is achieved through recognition of the similarity between the new problem and some already understood problem.

Animism Piaget's term for the young child's tendency to attribute properties of life to nonliving things.

Anorexia nervosa A severe eating disorder, usually involving excessive weight loss through self-starvation, most often found in teenage girls.

A-not-B error Infants' tendency to search in the original location in which an object was found rather than in its most recent hiding place. A characteristic of stage 4 of object permanence.

Anoxia A deficit of oxygen to the cells, which can produce brain or other tissue damage.

Apgar Exam An exam administered immediately after birth that assesses vital functions such as heart rate and respiration.

Appearance-reality distinction Distinction between how objects appear and what they really are. Understanding the distinction implies an ability to judge both appearance and reality correctly when the two diverge.

Assimilation Interpreting new experiences in terms of existing cognitive structures. One of the two components of adaptation in Piaget's theory.

At risk Describes babies who have a higher likelihood than other babies of experiencing developmental problems.

Attachment Q-Set (AQS) A method of assessing attachment in which cards bearing descriptions of the child's interactions with the caregiver are sorted into categories to create a profile of the child.

Attention The selection of particular sensory input for perceptual and cognitive processing and the exclusion of competing input.

Attention-deficit hyperactivity disorder (ADHD) A developmental disorder characterized by difficulty in sustaining attention, hyperactivity, and impulsive and uncontrolled behavior.

Authoritarian parenting A style of parenting characterized by firm control in the context of a cold and demanding relationship.

Authoritative parenting A style of parenting characterized by firm control in the context of a warm and supportive relationship.

Autobiographical memory Specific, personal, and long-lasting memory regarding the self.

Automatization An increase in the efficiency with which cognitive operations are executed as a result of practice. A mechanism of change in information-processing theories.

Autosomes The 22 pairs of human chromosomes, other than the sex chromosomes.

Axon A long fiber extending from the cell body in a neuron; conducts activity from the cell.

B

Babbling drift A hypothesis that infants' babbling gradually gravitates toward the language they are hearing and soon will speak.

Baby biography Method of study in which a parent studies the development of his or her own child.

Behavioral homophyly Similarity between peers in behaviors and interests. Such similarity is one determinant of friendship selection.

Behavior genetics The field of study that explores the role of genes in producing individual differences in behavior and development.

Behaviorism A theory of psychology, first advanced by John B. Watson, that human development results primarily from conditioning and learning processes.

Biologically primary abilities Evolved abilities shaped by natural selection to solve recurring problems faced by ancestral humans.

Biologically secondary abilities Non-evolved abilities that co-opt primary abilities for purposes other than the original evolution-based function and appear only in specific cultural contexts.

Blended family A new family unit, resulting from remarriage, that consists of parents and children from previously separate families.

Bone age The degree of maturation of an individual as indicated by the extent of hardening of the bones. Also called *skeletal maturity*.

Brain stem The lower part of the brain, closest to the spinal cord; includes the cerebellum, which is important for maintaining balance and coordination.

Brazelton Neonatal Behavioral Assessment The most comprehensive of newborn assessment instruments; assesses attention and social responsiveness, muscle tone and physical movement, control of alertness, and physiological response to stress.

Brightness constancy The experience that the brightness of an object remains the same even though the amount of light it reflects back to the eye changes (because of shadows or changes in the illuminating light).

Bulimia A disorder of food binging and sometimes purging by self-induced vomiting, typically observed in teenage girls.

C

Case study A research method that involves only a single individual, often with a focus on a clinical issue.

Catch-up growth Accelerated growth that follows a period of delayed or stunted growth resulting from disease or malnutrition.

Categorical perception The ability to detect differences in speech sounds that correspond to differences in meaning; the ability to discriminate phonemic boundaries.

Categorical self The "Me" component of the self, which involves one's objective personal characteristics.

Catharsis The psychoanalytic belief that the likelihood of aggression can be reduced by viewing aggression or by engaging in high-energy behavior.

Centration Piaget's term for the young child's tendency to focus on only one aspect of a problem at a time, a perceptually biased form of responding that often results in incorrect judgments.

Cephalocaudal Literally, head to tail. This principle of development refers to the tendency of body parts to mature in a head-to-foot progression.

Cerebral cortex The thin sheet of gray matter that covers the brain.

Cerebrum The highest brain center; includes both hemispheres of the brain and the interconnections between them.

Cesarean section Surgical delivery of the fetus directly from the uterus; performed when normal delivery is prohibited.

CHILDES (Child Language Data Support System) A computerized data-sharing system which makes available the transcribed records from dozens of studies of children's spontaneous speech.

Chorionic villus sampling (CVS) A procedure for gathering fetal cells earlier in pregnancy than is possible through amniocentesis. A tube is passed through the vagina and cervix so that fetal cells can be gathered at the site of the developing placenta.

Chromosomes Chemical strands in the cell nucleus that contain the genes. The nucleus of each human cell has 46 chromosomes, with the exception of the gametes, which have 23.

Chronosystem Bronfenbrenner's term for the passage of time as a context for studying human development.

Clarification question A response that indicates that a listener did not understand a statement.

Classical (respondent) conditioning A form of learning, involving reflexes, in which a neutral stimulus acquires the power to elicit a reflexive response (UCR) as a result of being associated (paired) with the naturally eliciting stimulus (UCS). The neutral stimulus then becomes a conditioned stimulus (CS).

Class inclusion The knowledge that a subclass cannot be larger than the superordinate class that includes it. In Piaget's theory, a concrete operational achievement.

Clique A kind of group typical in adolescence, consisting usually of 5 to 10 members whose shared interests and behavior patterns set them apart from their peers.

Codominance The case in which both alleles are dominant and each is completely expressed in the phenotype.

Coercive family process Gerald Patterson's term for the method by which some families control one another through aggression and other coercive means.

Cognition Higher-order mental processes, such as reasoning and problem solving, through which humans attempt to understand the world.

Cohort effect A problem sometimes found in cross-sectional research in which people of a given age are affected by factors unique to their generation.

Coining Children's creation of new words to label objects or events for which the correct label is not known.

Color constancy The experience that the color of an object remains the same even though the wavelengths it reflects back to the eye change (because of changes in the color of the illuminating light).

Committed compliance Compliant behavior which results from a child's internalizing the instruction of an adult; results in positive emotion.

Comparative research Research conducted with nonhuman species to provide information relevant to human development.

Competence Self-evaluation that includes both what one would like to achieve and one's confidence in being able to achieve it.

Competition model A proposed strategy children use for learning grammar in which they weight possible cues in terms of availability and reliability.

Compliance The child's ability to go along with requests or adopt the standards of behavior espoused by caregivers

Computer simulation Programming a computer to perform a cognitive task in the same way in which humans are thought to perform it. An information-processing method for testing theories of underlying process.

Concept A mental grouping of different items into a single category on the basis of some unifying similarity or set of similarities.

Conception The combining of the genetic material from a male gamete (sperm) and a female gamete (ovum); fertilization.

Concrete operations Form of intelligence in which mental operations make logical problem solving with concrete objects possible. The third of Piaget's periods, extending from about 6 to 11 years of age.

Conditioned stimulus (CS) A neutral stimulus that comes to elicit a response through a conditioning process in which it is consistently paired with another stimulus (UCS) that naturally evokes the response.

Congenital adrenal hyperplasia (CAH) A recessive genetic disorder in which the adrenal glands produce unusually high levels of male hormones known as androgens.

Congenitally organized behavior Early behaviors of newborns that do not require specific external stimulation and that show more adaptability than simple reflexes.

Connectionism Creation of artificial neural networks, embodied in computer programs, that solve cognitive tasks and that modify their solutions in response to experience. A methodological and theoretical approach adopted by a subset of information-processing researchers.

Conservation The knowledge that the quantitative properties of an object or collection of objects are not changed by a change in appearance. In Piaget's theory, a concrete operational achievement.

Constraints Implicit assumptions about word meanings that are hypothesized to narrow down the possibilities that children must consider and hence to facilitate the task of word learning.

Constructive memory Effects of the general knowledge system on how information is interpreted and thus remembered.

Constructivism Piaget's belief that children actively create knowledge rather than passively receive it from the environment.

Continuity versus discontinuity debate The scientific controversy regarding whether development is constant and connected (continuous) or uneven and disconnected (discontinuous).

Controversial child A child who receives both many positive and many negative nominations in sociometric assessments by peers.

Conventional level Kohlberg's third and fourth stages of moral development. Moral reasoning is based on the view that a social system must be based on laws and regulations.

Convergent thinking Form of thinking whose goal is to discover the correct answer to problems with a definite solution—the form of thought emphasized on IQ tests.

Cooing A stage in the preverbal period, beginning at about 2 months, when babies primarily produce one-syllable vowel sounds.

Correlation The relation between two variables, described in terms of direction and strength.

Correlation coefficient (r) A number between $+1.00$ and -1.00 that indicates the direction and strength of a correlation between two variables.

Cross-cultural studies Research designed to determine the influence of culture on some aspect of development and in which culture typically serves as an independent variable.

Crossing over The exchange of genetic material between pairs of chromosomes during meiosis.

Cross-sectional design A research method in which people of different ages are studied simultaneously to examine the effects of age on some aspect of behavior.

Cross-sequential design A research method combining longitudinal and cross-sectional designs.

Cultural compatibility hypothesis The hypothesis that schooling will be most effective when methods of instruction are compatible with the child's cultural background.

Cultural/historical development Development that occurs over decades and centuries and leaves a legacy of tools and artifacts, value systems, institutions, and practices.

Cultural psychology Study of a single culture from the perspective of members of that culture, the goal being to identify the values and practices important to the culture.

Cultural relativism The belief that each culture should be examined and evaluated on its own terms.

Culture The accumulated knowledge of a people encoded in their language and embodied in the physical artifacts, beliefs, values, customs, institutions, and activities passed down from one generation to the next.

D

Deep structure Chomsky's term for the inborn knowledge humans possess about the properties of language.

Defensive reflex A natural reaction to novel stimuli that tends to protect the organism from further stimulation and that may include orientation of the stimulus receptors away from the stimulus source and a variety of physiological changes.

Deferred imitation Imitation of a model observed some time in the past.

Delay-of-gratification technique An experimental procedure for studying children's ability to postpone a smaller, immediate reward in order to obtain a larger, delayed one.

Dendrite One of a net of short fibers extending out from the cell body in a neuron; receives activity from nearby cells and conducts that activity to the cell body.

Deoxyribonucleic acid (DNA) A stairlike, double-helix molecule that carries genetic information on chromosomes.

Dependent variable The variable that is predicted to be affected by an experimental manipulation. In psychology, usually some aspect of behavior.

Descriptive research Research based solely on observations, with no attempt to determine systematic relations among the variables.

Developmental pacing The rate at which spurts and plateaus occur in an individual's physical and mental development.

Developmental psychology The branch of psychology devoted to the study of changes in behavior and abilities over the course of development.

Dialectical process The process in Vygotsky's theory whereby children learn through problem-solving experiences shared with others.

Discourse Language used in social interactions; conversation.

Dishabituation The recovery of a habituated response that results from a change in the eliciting stimulus.

Displaced aggression Retaliatory aggression directed at a person or object other than the one against whom retaliation is desired.

Display rules The expectations and attitudes a society holds toward the expression of affect.

Divergent thinking Form of thinking whose goal is to generate multiple possible solutions for problems that do not have a single correct answer—the form of thought hypothesized to be important for creativity.

Dizygotic (DZ) twins Twins who develop from separately fertilized ova and who thus are no more genetically similar than are other siblings. Also called *fraternal twins*.

Dominance hierarchy A structured social group in which members higher on the dominance ladder control those who are lower, initially through aggression and conflict, but eventually simply through threats.

Dominant gene A relatively powerful allele whose characteristics are expressed in the phenotype regardless of the allele with which it is paired.

Dual representation The realization that an object can be represented in two ways simultaneously.

Dynamic assessment Method of assessing children's abilities derived from Vygotsky's concept of the zone of proximal development. Measures the child's ability to benefit from adult-provided assistance, typically in a test-train-retest design.

Dynamic systems Thelen's model of the development of motor skills, in which infants who are motivated to accomplish a task create a new motor behavior from their available physical abilities.

E

EAS model Plomin and Buss's theory of temperament, which holds that temperament can be measured along the dimensions of emotionality, activity, and sociability.

Ecological perspective An approach to studying development that focuses on individuals within their environmental contexts.

Egocentrism In infancy, an inability to distinguish the self (e.g., one's actions or perceptions) from the outer world. In later childhood, an inability to distinguish one's own perspective (e.g., visual experience, thoughts, feelings) from that of others.

Electroencephalograph (EEG) An instrument that measures brain activity by sensing minute electrical changes at the top of the skull.

Embryo The developing organism from the third week, when implantation is complete, through the eighth week after conception.

Emotion An internal reaction or feeling, which may be either positive (such as joy) or negative (such as anger), and may reflect a readiness for action.

Empathy The ability to vicariously experience another's emotional state or condition.

Encoding Attending to and forming internal representations of certain features of the environment. A mechanism of change in information-processing theories.

Entity model The belief that a person's intelligence is fixed and unchangeable.

Environment of evolutionary adaptiveness (EEA) The environment that produced a species' evolved tendencies.

Equilibration Piaget's term for the biological process of self-regulation that propels the cognitive system to higher and higher forms of equilibrium.

Equilibrium A characteristic of a cognitive system in which assimilation and accommodation are in balance, thus permitting adaptive, nondistorted responses to the world.

Ethnographic methods Methods of study employed in cultural psychology, in which the researcher lives as a member of a culture and gathers information about the culture through various techniques (e.g., observations, interviews) over an extended period of time.

Ethology The study of development from an evolutionary perspective.

Evaluative self-reactions Bandura's term for consequences people apply to themselves as a result of meeting or failing to meet their personal standards.

Event memory Recall of things that have happened.

Evocative gene-environment correlation Situation in which genes and environment affect development similarly because genetically set predispositions of the child elicit compatible experiences from the environment.

Evolutionary developmental psychology A branch of evolutionary psychology that encompasses the evolutionary origins of contemporary cognitive abilities as well as those that underlie social relations and social interactions.

Executive function General components of problem solving, such as short-term memory, metacognitive awareness, and inhibition.

Existential self The "I" component of the self, which is concerned with the subjective experience of existing.

Exosystem Social systems that can affect children but in which they do not participate directly. Bronfenbrenner's third layer of context.

Expansion A repetition of speech in which errors are corrected and statements are elaborated.

Expertise Organized factual knowledge with respect to some content domain.

Expressive style Vocabulary acquired during the naming explosion that emphasizes the pragmatic functions of language.

Extended family A family unit that consists not only of parents and children but also of at least one and sometimes several other adult relatives.

Extinction A process related to classical conditioning in which the conditioned stimulus (CS) gradually loses its power to elicit the response as a result of no longer being paired with the unconditioned stimulus (UCS).

F

False belief The realization that people can hold beliefs that are not true. Such understanding, which is typically acquired during the preoperational period, provides evidence of the ability to distinguish the mental from the nonmental.

False self behavior Behaving in a way that is knowingly different from how one's true self would behave.

Fast-mapping A process in which children acquire the meaning of a word after a brief exposure.

Fetal alcohol syndrome (FAS) A set of features in the infant and child caused by the mother's use of alcohol during pregnancy; typically includes facial malformations and other physical and mental disabilities.

Fetal distress A condition of abnormal stress in the fetus, reflected during the birth process in an abnormal fetal heart rate.

Fetus The developing organism from the ninth week to the 38th week after conception.

Flynn effect Increase over time in the average level of performance on IQ tests.

Forbidden-toy technique An experimental procedure for studying children's resistance to temptation in which the child is left alone with an attractive toy and instructed not to play with it.

Formal operations Form of intelligence in which higher-level mental operations make possible logical reasoning with respect to abstract and hypothetical events and not merely concrete objects. The fourth of Piaget's periods, beginning at about 11 years of age.

Fraternal twins Twins who develop from separately fertilized ova and who thus are no more genetically similar than are other siblings. Also called *dizygotic (DZ) twins*.

Friendship An enduring relationship between two individuals, characterized by loyalty, intimacy, and mutual affection.

G

g General intelligence; g is assumed to determine performance on a wide range of intellectual measures.

Gender consistency The recognition that an individual's gender remains the same despite changes in dress, hairstyle, activities, or personality.

Gender constancy The belief that one's own gender is fixed and irreversible.

Gender identity The ability to categorize oneself as male or female.

Gender role A pattern or set of behaviors considered appropriate for males or females within a particular culture.

Gender schemas Cognitive representations of the characteristics associated with being either male or female.

Gender stability The awareness that all boys grow up to be men and all girls become women.

Gene A segment of DNA on the chromosome that codes for the production of proteins. The basic unit of inheritance.

Genetic counseling The practice of advising prospective parents about genetic diseases and the likelihood that they might pass on defective genetic traits to their offspring.

Genomic imprinting The case in which the allele from one parent is biochemically silenced and only the allele from the other parent affects the phenotype.

Genotype The arrangement of genes underlying a trait.

Gesture-speech mismatch Instance in which the meaning conveyed by speech and the meaning conveyed by an accompanying gesture are in conflict. Thought to be an indicator of readiness for change.

Goodness of fit A concept describing the relation between a baby's temperament and her social and environmental surroundings.

Grammar The study of the structural properties of language, including syntax, inflection, and intonation.

Group A collection of individuals who interact regularly in a consistent, structured fashion and who share values and a sense of belonging to the group.

Guided participation The process by which young children become competent by participating in everyday, purposeful activities under the guidance of more experienced partners.

H

Habituation The decline or disappearance of a response as a result of repeated presentation of the eliciting stimulus. The simplest type of learning.

Haptic perception The perceptual experience that results from active exploration of objects by touch.

Heritability The proportion of variance in a trait (such as IQ) that can be attributed to genetic variance in the sample being studied.

Hierarchical model of intelligence A model of the structure of intelligence in which intellectual abilities are seen as being organized hierarchically, with broad, general abilities at the top of the hierarchy and more specific skills nested underneath.

Higher mental functions Complex mental processes that are intentional, self-regulated, and mediated by language and other sign systems.

Holophrase A single word used to express a larger idea; common during the second year of life.

HOME (Home Observation for Measurement of the Environment) An instrument for assessing the quality of the early home environment. Included are dimensions such as maternal involvement and variety of play materials.

Hostile (retaliatory) aggression Aggression whose purpose is to cause pain or injury.

Hypothesis A predicted relation between a phenomenon and a factor assumed to affect it that is not yet supported by a great deal of evidence. Hypotheses are tested in experimental investigations.

Hypothetical-deductive reasoning A form of problem solving characterized by the ability to generate and test hypotheses and draw logical conclusions from the results of the tests. In Piaget's theory, a formal operational achievement.

I

Identical twins Twins who develop from a single fertilized ovum and thus inherit identical genetic material. Also called *monozygotic (MZ) twins*.

Identification The Freudian process through which the child adopts the characteristics of the same-sex parent during the phallic stage.

Identity In Erikson's theory, the component of personality that develops across the eight stages of life and that motivates progress through the stages.

Imaginary companions Fantasy friends with names and stable personalities that remain a part of children's lives for months or even years.

Imitation Behavior of an observer that results from and is similar to the behavior of a model.

Immanent justice Literally, inherent justice; refers to the expectation of children in Piaget's stage of moral realism that punishment must follow any rule violation, including those that appear to go undetected.

Imprinting A biological process of some species in which the young acquire an emotional attachment to the mother through following.

Incomplete dominance The case in which a dominant gene does not completely suppress the effect of a recessive gene, which is then somewhat expressed in the phenotype.

Incremental model The belief that a person's intelligence can grow through experience and learning.

Independent orientation A focus on the self's individuality, self-expression, and personal achievement.

Independent variable The variable in an experiment that is systematically manipulated.

Infantile amnesia The inability to remember experiences from the first 2 or 3 years of life.

Inflections The aspect of grammar that involves adding endings to words to modify their meaning.

Inhibition The tendency to quickly respond in a negative manner to an unfamiliar situation.

Innate releasing mechanism A stimulus that triggers an innate sequence or pattern of behaviors.

Instrumental aggression Aggression whose purpose is to obtain something desired.

Intentional behavior In Piaget's theory, behavior in which the goal exists prior to the action selected to achieve it; made possible by the ability to separate means and end.

Interactional synchrony The smooth intermeshing of behaviors between mother and baby.

Interactionist perspective The theory that human development results from the combination of inborn processes and environmental factors.

Interdependent orientation A focus on the self's role within a broader social network, marked by an emphasis on interpersonal connectedness, social obligation, and conformity.

Internalization Vygotsky's term for the child's incorporation, primarily through language, of bodies of knowledge and tools of thought from the culture.

Internal working model An infant's and a caregiver's cognitive conception of each other, which they use to form expectations and predictions.

Intersubjectivity A commitment to find common ground on which to build shared understanding.

Invariants Aspects of the world that remain the same even though other aspects have changed. In Piaget's theory, different forms of invariants are understood at different stages of development.

J

Joint attention Using cues (such as direction of gaze) to identify and share the attentional focus of another.

K

Kinetic cues Visual cues that indicate the relative distances of objects through movement either of the objects or of the observer.

Kin selection A proposed mechanism by which an individual's altruistic behavior toward kin increases the likelihood of the survival of genes similar to those of the individual.

L

Language acquisition device (LAD) Chomsky's proposed brain mechanism for analyzing speech input; the mechanism that allows young children to acquire quickly the language to which they are exposed.

Language acquisition support system (LASS) Bruner's proposed process by which parents provide children assistance in learning language.

Language-Making Capacity (LMC) Slobin's proposed set of strategies or learning principles that underlie the acquisition of language.

Lateralization The specialization of functions in the right and left hemispheres of the brain.

Law (principle) A predicted relation between a phenomenon and a factor assumed to affect it that is supported by a good deal of scientific evidence.

Learning A relatively permanent change in behavior that results from practice or experience.

Lexical contrast theory A theory of semantic development holding that (1) children automatically assume that a new word has a meaning different from that of any other word they know and (2) children always choose word meanings that are generally accepted over more individualized meanings.

Lexicon A vocabulary, or repertoire of words.

Locomotion The movement of a person through space, such as walking and crawling.

Longitudinal design A research method in which the same individuals are studied repeatedly over time.

Looking-glass self The conception of the self based on how one thinks others see him or her.

M

Macrosystem The culture or subculture in which the child lives. Bronfenbrenner's fourth layer of context.

Maternal bonding The mother's emotional attachment to the child, which appears shortly after birth and which some theorists believe develops through early contact during a sensitive period.

Maturation The biological processes assumed by some theorists to be primarily responsible for human development.

Mediated memory Remembering that relies on cultural tools and artifacts.

Meiosis The process by which germ cells produce four gametes (sperm or ova), each with half the number of chromosomes of the parent cell.

Mesosystem The interrelationships among the child's microsystems. The second of Bronfenbrenner's layers of context.

Meta-analysis A method of reviewing the research literature on a given topic that to uses statistical procedures to establish the existence and the size of effects.

Metamemory Knowledge about memory.

Microanalysis A research technique for studying dyadic interactions, in which two individuals are simultaneously videotaped with different cameras, and then the tapes are examined side by side.

Microgenetic development Moment-to-moment learning of individuals as they work on specific problems.

Microgenetic method A research method in which a small number of individuals are observed repeatedly in order to study an expected change in a developmental process.

Microsystem The environmental system closest to the child, such as the family or school. The first of Bronfenbrenner's layers of context.

Midbrain A part of the brain that lies above the brain stem; serves as a relay station and as a control area for breathing and swallowing and houses part of the auditory and visual systems.

Mitosis The process by which body cells reproduce, resulting in two identical cells.

Mnemonic strategies Techniques (such as rehearsal or organization) that people use in an attempt to remember something.

Modal action pattern A sequence of behaviors elicited by a specific stimulus.

Monozygotic (MZ) twins Twins who develop from a single fertilized ovum and thus inherit identical genetic material. Also called *identical twins*.

Moral conduct The aspect of children's moral development concerned with behavior.

Moral dilemmas Stories used by Piaget and others to assess children's levels of moral reasoning.

Moral realism Piaget's second stage of moral development, in which children's reasoning is based on objective and physical aspects of a situation and is often inflexible.

Moral reasoning The aspect of children's moral development concerned with knowledge and understanding of moral issues and principles.

Moral relativism Piaget's third stage of moral development, in which children view rules as agreements that can be altered and consider people's motives or intentions when evaluating their moral conduct.

Moral rules Rules used by a society to protect individuals and to guarantee their rights.

Motherese Simplified speech directed at very young children by adults and older children.

Motion parallax An observer's experience that a closer object moves across the field of view faster than a more distant object when both objects are moving at the same speed or when the objects are stationary and the observer moves.

Myelin A sheath of fatty material that surrounds and insulates the axon, resulting in speedier transmission of neural activity.

N

Naming explosion A period of language development, beginning at about 18 months, when children suddenly begin to acquire words (especially labels) at a high rate.

Nativism The theory that human development results principally from inborn processes that guide the emergence of behaviors in a predictable manner.

Nativistic theory A theory of language development, originated by Chomsky, that stresses innate mechanisms separate from cognitive processes.

Natural selection An evolutionary process proposed by Charles Darwin in which characteristics of an individual that increase its chances of survival are more likely to be passed along to future generations.

Nature versus nurture debate The scientific controversy regarding whether the primary source of developmental change rests in biological (nature) factors or in environmental and experiential (nurture) factors.

Negative correlation A correlation in which two variables change in opposite directions.

Negative reinforcer A consequence that makes the behavior it follows more likely through the removal of something unpleasant.

Neglected child A child who receives few nominations of any sort, positive or negative, in sociometric assessments by peers. Such children seem to be ignored by the peer group.

Neuron A nerve cell, consisting of a cell body, axon, and dendrites. Neurons transmit activity from one part of the nervous system to another.

Neurotransmitter A chemical that transmits electrical activity from one neuron across the synapse to another neuron.

New York Longitudinal Study (NYLS) A well-known longitudinal project conducted by Thomas and Chess to study infant temperament and its implications for later psychological adjustment.

Nonshared environment A concept used in behavior genetics to refer to presumed aspects of the environment that children experience differently.

Normative versus idiographic development The question of whether research should focus on identifying commonalities in human development (normative development) or on the causes of individual differences (idiographic development).

Norms A timetable of age ranges indicating when normal growth and developmental milestones are typically reached.

O

Obesity A condition of excess fat storage; often defined as weight more than 20% over a standardized, ideal weight.

Object permanence The knowledge that objects have a permanent existence that is independent of our perceptual contact with them. In Piaget's theory, a major achievement of the sensorimotor period.

Objectivity A characteristic of scientific research; it requires that the procedures and subject matter of investigations should be formulated so that they could, in principle, be agreed on by everyone.

Observational learning A form of learning in which an observer's behavior changes as a result of observing a model.

Ontogenetic development Development across years of an individual's life, such as childhood.

O

Operant behaviors Voluntary behavior controlled by its consequences. The larger category of human behaviors.

Operant learning A form of learning in which the likelihood of an operant behavior changes as a result of its reinforcing or punishing consequences.

Operating principle A hypothetical innate strategy for analyzing language input and discovering grammatical structure.

Operating space In Case's theory, the resources necessary to carry out cognitive operations.

Operations Piaget's term for the various forms of mental action through which older children solve problems and reason logically.

Organization The tendency to integrate knowledge into interrelated cognitive structures. One of the two biologically based functions stressed in Piaget's theory.

Orienting reflex A natural reaction to novel stimuli that enhances stimulus processing and includes orientation of the eyes and ears to optimize stimulus reception, inhibition of ongoing activity, and a variety of physiological changes.

Overextension An early language error in which children use labels they already know for things whose names they do not yet know.

Overregularization An early structural language error in which children apply inflectional rules to irregular forms (e.g., adding -ed to say).

P

Paradox of altruism The logical dilemma faced by ethological theorists who try to reconcile self-sacrificial behavior with the concepts of natural selection and survival of the fittest.

Parallel play A form of play in which children play next to each other and with similar materials but with no real interaction or cooperation.

Parental control A dimension of parenting that reflects the degree to which the child is monitored, disciplined, and regulated.

Parental investment The time, energy, and resources required to produce and rear offspring that survive to reproductive age.

Parental warmth A dimension of parenting that reflects the amount of support, affection, and encouragement the parent provides to the child.

Parenting style The overall pattern of child rearing provided by a parent, typically defined by the combination of warmth and control that the parent demonstrates.

Passive gene-environment correlation Situation in which genes and environment affect development similarly because the genes the child receives from the parents are compatible with the environment the parents provide.

Peacemaking A friendly post-conflict reunion between former opponents, often characterized by invitations to play, hugs, apologies, object sharing, and silliness.

Peer-mediated intervention Form of intervention for children with sociometric problems in which responses of the peer group are utilized to elicit more effective social behaviors from the target children.

Perception The interpretation of sensory stimulation based on experience.

Perinatal period The events and environment surrounding the birth process.

Periods Piaget's term for the four general stages into which his theory divides development. Each period is a qualitatively distinct form of functioning that characterizes a wide range of cognitive activities.

Peripheral vision The perception of visual input outside the area on which the individual is fixating.

Permissive parenting A style of parenting characterized by low levels of control in the context of a warm and supportive relationship.

Personal agency The understanding that one can be the cause of events.

Phenotype The characteristic of a trait that is expressed or observable. The phenotype results from an interaction of genotype and environment.

Phoneme A sound contrast that changes meaning.

Phonology The study of speech sounds.

Phylogenetic development Development of the species.

Pictorial cues Visual cues that indicate the relative distances of objects through static, picturelike information—for example, interposition of one object in front of another.

Placenta An organ that forms where the embryo attaches to the uterus. This organ exchanges nutrients, oxygen, and wastes between the embryo or fetus and the mother through a very thin membrane that does not allow the passage of blood.

Polygenic inheritance The case in which a trait is determined by a number of genes.

Positive correlation A correlation in which two variables change in the same direction.

Positive reinforcer A consequence that makes the behavior it follows more likely through the presentation of something pleasant.

Postconventional level Kohlberg's final stages of moral development. Moral reasoning is based on the assumption that the value, dignity, and rights of each individual person must be maintained.

Postural development The increasing ability of the baby to control parts of his or her body, especially the head and the trunk.

Pragmatics The study of the social uses of language.

Preconventional level Kohlberg's first two stages of moral development. Moral reasoning is based on the assumption that individuals must serve their own needs.

Preference method A research method for the study of visual ability in infancy. Two visual stimuli are presented simultaneously, and the amount of time the infant looks at each is measured.

Prehension The ability to grasp and manipulate objects with the hands.

Preoperational Form of intelligence in which symbols and mental actions begin to replace objects and overt behaviors. The second of Piaget's periods, extending from about 2 to about 6 years old.

Pretend play A form of play in which children use an object or person as a symbol to stand for something else.

Preterm Describes babies born before the end of the normal gestation period.

Primary caregiver The person, usually the mother, with whom the infant develops the major attachment relationship.

Principle of mutual exclusivity A proposed principle of semantic development stating that children assume that an object can have only one name.

Private speech Speech children produce and direct toward themselves during a problem-solving activity.

Production deficiency The failure to generate a mnemonic strategy spontaneously.

Productivity The property of language that permits humans to produce and comprehend an infinite number of statements.

Progressive decentering Piaget's term for the gradual decline in egocentrism that occurs across development.

Prosocial behavior The aspect of moral conduct that includes socially desirable behaviors such as sharing, helping, and cooperating; often used interchangeably with altruism by modern researchers.

Proximal processes Bronfenbrenner and Ceci's term for interactions between the child and aspects of the microsystem that have positive effects on psychological functioning and that help maximize expression of the child's genetic potential.

Proximodistal Literally, near to far. This principle of development refers to the tendency of body parts to develop in a trunk-to-extremities direction.

Psychometric An approach to the study of intelligence that emphasizes the use of standardized tests to identify individual differences among people.

Puberty The period in which chemical and physical changes in the body occur that enable sexual reproduction.

Punisher A consequence that makes the behavior it follows less likely, either through the presentation of something unpleasant or the removal of something desirable.

Q

Qualitative identity The knowledge that the qualitative nature of something is not changed by a change in its appearance. In Piaget's theory, a preoperational achievement.

R

Rapid eye movement (REM) sleep A stage of light sleep in which the eyes move rapidly while the eyelids are closed.

Reaction range In Gottesman's model, the term for the range of ability or skill that is set by the genes. The value achieved within this range is determined by the environment.

Reactivation The preservation of the memory for an event through reencounter with at least some portion of the event in the interval between initial experience and memory test.

Recall memory The retrieval of some past stimulus or event that is not perceptually present.

Recapitulation theory An early biological notion, later adopted by psychologist G. Stanley Hall, that the development of the individual repeats the development of the species.

Recast A response to speech that restates it using a different structure.

Recessive gene A relatively weak allele whose characteristics are expressed in the phenotype only when it is paired with another recessive gene.

Reciprocal altruism A proposed mechanism by which an individual's altruistic behavior toward members of the social group may promote the survival of the individual's genes through reciprocation by others or may ensure the survival of similar genes.

Reciprocal determinism Albert Bandura's proposed process describing the interaction of a person's characteristics and abilities (P), behavior (B), and environment (E).

Recognition memory The realization that some perceptually present stimulus or event has been encountered before.

Reduplicated babbling A stage in the preverbal period, beginning at about 6 months, when infants produce strings of identical sounds, such as dadada.

Referential style Vocabulary acquired during the naming explosion that involves a large proportion of nouns and object labels.

Reflex A biological relation in which a specific stimulus reliably elicits a specific response; an automatic and stereotyped response to a specific stimulus.

Rejected child A child who receives few positive and many negative nominations in sociometric assessments by peers. Such children seem to be disliked by the peer group.

Relational aggression Aggression designed to damage or disrupt social relationships.

Reliability The consistency or repeatability of a measuring instrument. A necessary property of a standardized test.

Replica toys Toys that resemble real objects, such as dishes, dolls, and vehicles.

Representation The use of symbols to picture and act on the world internally.

Repression Freud's term for the process through which desires or motivations are driven into the unconscious, as typically occurs during the phallic stage.

Resilient children Children who adapt positively and develop well despite early environmental adversity.

Respondent behaviors Responses based on reflexes, which are controlled by specific eliciting stimuli. The smaller category of human behaviors.

Response inhibition The absence of a particular response that has just been modeled; often the result of vicarious punishment.

Reversal-replication (ABAB) design An experimental design in which the independent variable is systematically presented and removed several times. Can be used in studies involving very few research participants.

Reversibility Piaget's term for the power of operations to correct for potential disturbances and thus arrive at correct solutions to problems.

Rules Procedures for acting on the environment and solving problems.

S

Scaffolding A method of teaching in which the adult adjusts the level of help provided in relation to the child's level of performance, the goal being to encourage independent performance.

Scatter diagram A graphic illustration of a correlation between two variables.

Schemes Piaget's term for the cognitive structures of infancy. A scheme consists of a set of skilled, flexible action patterns through which the child understands the world.

School cut-off design Research technique that compares children who are close in age but differ in school experience by one year.

Scientific method The system of rules used by scientists to conduct and evaluate their research.

Script A representation of the typical sequence of actions and events in some familiar context.

Selective attention Concentration on a stimulus or event with attendant disregard for other stimuli or events.

Self-consciousness A concern about the opinions others hold about one.

Self-efficacy Bandura's term for people's ability to succeed at various tasks, as judged by the people themselves.

Self-esteem (self-worth) A person's evaluation of the self, and the affective reactions to that evaluation.

Self-evaluation The part of the self-system concerned with children's opinions of themselves and their abilities.

Self-knowledge (self-awareness) The part of the self-system concerned with children's knowledge about themselves.

Self-regulation The part of the self-system concerned with self-control.

Self-schema An internal cognitive portrait of the self used to organize information about the self.

Self-system The set of interrelated processes-self-knowledge, self-evaluation, and self-regulation—that make up the self.

Semantic bootstrapping A proposed mechanism of grammatical development in which children use semantic cues to infer aspects of grammar.

Semantics The study of meaning in language.

Sensation The experience resulting from the stimulation of a sense organ.

Sensitive period A period of development during which certain behaviors are more easily learned.

Sensorimotor Form of intelligence in which knowledge is based on physical interactions with people and objects. The first of Piaget's periods, extending from birth to about 2 years.

Sensorimotor schemes Skilled and generalizable action patterns by which infants act on and understand the world. In Piaget's theory, the cognitive structures of infancy.

Separation protest Crying and searching by infants separated from their mothers; an indication of the formation of the attachment bond.

Seriation The ability to order stimuli along some quantitative dimension, such as length. In Piaget's theory, a concrete operational achievement.

Sex chromosomes The pair of human chromosomes that determines one's sex. Females have two X chromosomes; males have an X and a Y.

Sex differentiation The biological process through which physical differences between sexes emerge.

Sex typing The process by which children develop the behaviors and attitudes considered appropriate for their gender.

Shape constancy The experience that the physical shape of an object remains the same even though the shape of its projected image on the eye varies.

Short-term storage space In Case's theory, the resources necessary to store results from previous cognitive operations while carrying out new ones.

Sibling rivalry Feelings of competition, resentment, and jealousy that can arise between siblings.

Situational compliance Obedience that results from a child's awareness of an adult's will in a particular situation and does not reflect enduring behavioral change.

Size constancy The experience that the physical size of an object remains the same even though the size of its projected image on the eye varies.

Skeletal maturity The degree of maturation of an individual as indicated by the extent of hardening of the bones. Also called *bone age*.

Small for gestational age (SGA) Describes babies born at a weight in the bottom 10% of babies of a particular gestational age.

Social cognition Knowledge of the social world and interpersonal relationships.

Social comparison Comparing one's abilities to those of others.

Social conventions Rules used by a society to govern everyday behavior and to maintain order.

Socialization The process through which society molds the child's beliefs, expectations, and behavior.

Social-learning theory A form of environmental/learning theory that adds observational learning to classical and operant learning as a process through which children's behavior changes.

Social problem-solving skills Skills needed to resolve social dilemmas.

Social referencing Using information gained from other people to interpret uncertain situations and to regulate one's own behavior.

Social referential communication A form of communication in which a speaker sends a message that is comprehended by a listener.

Social support Resources (both tangible and intangible) provided by other people in times of uncertainty or stress.

Social withdrawal Self-imposed isolation from the peer group.

Sociobiology A branch of biology that attempts to discover the evolutionary origins of social behavior.

Socio-cognitive conflict Cognitive conflict that arises during social interaction.

Sociodramatic play Play in which two or more people enact a variety of related roles.

Sociogenesis The process of acquiring knowledge or skills through social interactions.

Sociometric techniques Procedures for assessing children's social status based on evaluations by the peer group. Sociometric techniques may involve ratings of degree of liking, nominations of liked or disliked peers, or forced-choice judgments between pairs of peers.

Solitary pretense Pretend play engaged in by a child playing alone.

Speech act An instance of speech used to perform pragmatic functions, such as requesting or complaining.

Stage-environment fit Degree to which environmental circumstances match the capabilities and the needs of the child at particular points during development.

Stereotype threat Extra pressure people feel in situations in which their performance may confirm a negative stereotype held about their group.

Stimulus generalization A process related to classical conditioning in which stimuli that are similar to the conditioned stimulus (CS) also acquire the power to elicit the response.

Strange Situation procedure Ainsworth's laboratory procedure for assessing the strength of the attachment relationship by observing the infant's reactions to a series of structured episodes involving the mother and a stranger.

Strategy construction The creation of strategies for processing and remembering information. A mechanism of change in information-processing theories.

Strategy selection Progressively greater use of relatively effective strategies in comparison to relatively ineffective ones. A mechanism of change in information-processing theories.

Study strategies Mnemonic strategies (such as outlining and note taking) that students use in an attempt to remember school material.

Sudden Infant Death Syndrome (SIDS) The sudden and unexpected death of an otherwise healthy infant under the age of 1.

Surface structure Chomsky's term for the way words and phrases are arranged in spoken languages.

Symbolic function The ability to use one thing (such as a mental image or word) as a symbol to represent something else.

Symbolic play Form of play in which the child uses one thing in deliberate pretense to stand for something else.

Sympathy Feeling of concern for another in reaction to the other's situation or emotional state, not necessarily involving an experience of the other's emotional state.

Synapse The small space between neurons across which neural activity is communicated from one cell to another.

Syntactic bootstrapping A proposed mechanism of semantic development in which children use syntactic cues to infer the meanings of words.

Syntax The aspect of grammar that involves word order.

T

Tabula rasa Latin phrase, meaning "blank slate," used to describe the newborn's mind as entirely empty of inborn abilities, interests, or ideas.

Telegraphic speech Speech from which unnecessary function words (e.g., in, the, with) are omitted; common during early language learning.

Temperament The aspect of personality studied in infants, which includes their emotional expressiveness and responsiveness to stimulation.

Teratogen An agent that can cause abnormal development in the fetus.

Teratology The study of the effects of teratogens upon development.

Theory A broad set of statements describing the relation between a phenomenon and the factors assumed to affect it.

Theory of mind Thoughts and beliefs concerning the mental world.

Tools of intellectual adaptation Vygotsky's term for the techniques of thinking and problem solving that children internalize from their culture.

Transactional influence A bidirectional, or reciprocal, relationship in which individuals influence one another's behaviors.

Transformational grammar A set of rules developed by the LAD to translate a language's surface structure to a deep structure that the child innately understand.

Transitivity The ability to combine relations logically to deduce necessary conclusions—for example, if A > B and B > C, then A > C. In Piaget's theory, a concrete operational achievement.

U

Ultrasound imaging A noninvasive procedure for detecting physical defects in the fetus. A device that produces soundlike waves of energy is moved over the pregnant woman's abdomen, and reflections of these waves form an image of the fetus.

Umbilical cord A soft cable of tissue and blood vessels that connects the fetus to the placenta.

Unconditioned response (UCR) The response portion of a reflex, which is reliably elicited by a stimulus (UCS).

Unconditioned stimulus (UCS) The stimulus portion of a reflex, which reliably elicits a respondent behavior (UCR).

Underextension An early language error in which children fail to apply labels they know to things for which the labels are appropriate.

Uninvolved (disengaged) parenting A style of parenting characterized by low levels of both control and warmth.

Universals of development Aspects of development or behavior that are common to children everywhere.

Utilization deficiency The failure of a recently developed mnemonic strategy to facilitate recall.

V

Validity The accuracy with which a measuring instrument assesses the attribute that it is designed to measure. A necessary property of a standardized test.

Variable Any factor that can take on different values along a dimension.

Vestibular sensitivity The perceptual experience that results from motion of the body and the pull of gravity.

Vicarious punishment Punishing consequences experienced when viewing a model that affect an observer similarly.

Vicarious reinforcement Reinforcing consequences experienced when viewing a model that affect an observer similarly.

Visual accommodation The automatic adjustment of the lens of the eye to produce a focused image of an object on the light-sensitive tissue at the back of the eye.

Visual acuity The clarity with which visual images can be perceived.

Visual cliff A research method for the study of depth perception in infancy. The infant is placed on a glass-covered table near an apparent dropoff, and perception of depth is inferred if the infant avoids the drop.

Visual self-recognition The ability to recognize oneself; often studied in babies by having them look into mirrors.

W

Wariness of strangers A general fear of unfamiliar people that appears in many infants at around 8 months of age and indicates the formation of the attachment bond.

Z

Zeitgeist The spirit of the times, or the ideas shared by most scientists during a given period.

Zone of proximal development The distance between what a child can accomplish independently and what the child can accomplish with the help of an adult or more capable peer.

Zygote A fertilized ovum.

References

Abbeduto, L., Davies, B., & Furman, L. (1988). The development of speech act comprehension in mentally retarded individuals and nonretarded children. *Child Development, 59,* 1460–1472.

Abel, E. L. (1980). Fetal alcohol syndrome: Behavioral teratology. *Psychological Bulletin, 87,* 29–50.

Abel, E. L. (1981). Behavioral teratology of alcohol. *Psychological Bulletin, 90,* 564–581.

Aboud, F. E. (1985). Children's application of attribution principles to social comparisons. *Child Development, 56,* 682–688.

Aboud, F. E., & Mendelson, M. J. (1996). Determinants of friendship selection and quality: Links to child–mother attachment. In W. M. Bukowski, A. F. Newcomb, & W. W. Hartup (Eds.), *The company they keep: Friendship in childhood and adolescence.* New York: Cambridge University Press.

Abramovitch, R., Corter, C., & Pepler, D. J. (1980). Observation of mixed-sex sibling dyads. *Child Development, 51,* 217–229.

Abramovitch, R., Corter, C., Pepler, D. J., & Stanhope, L. (1986). Sibling and peer interaction: A final follow-up and a comparison. *Child Development, 57,* 217–229.

Abramovitch, R., Freedman, J. L., Thoden, K., & Nikolich, C. (1991). Children's capacity to consent to participation in psychological research: Empirical findings. *Child Development, 62,* 1100–1109.

Abramovitch, R., & Grusec, J. E. (1978). Peer imitation in a natural setting. *Child Development, 49,* 60–65.

Achenbach, T. M., Edelbrock, C., & Howell, C. T. (1987). Empirically based assessment of the behavioral/emotional problems of 2-and 3-year-old children. *Journal of Abnormal Child Psychology, 15,* 629–650.

Ackerman, B. P. (1993). Children's understanding of the speaker's meaning in referential communication. *Journal of Experimental Child Psychology, 55,* 56–86.

Ackerman, B. P., & Silver, S. (1990). Children's understanding of private keys in referential communication. *Journal of Experimental Child Psychology, 50,* 217–242.

Ackerman, B. P., Szymanski, J., & Silver, D. (1990). Children's use of common ground in interpreting ambiguous referential utterances. *Developmental Psychology, 26,* 234–245.

Acredolo, L. P. (1978). Development of spatial orientation in infancy. *Developmental Psychology, 14,* 224–234.

Acredolo, L. P. (1985). Coordinating perspectives on infant spatial orientation. In R. Cohen (Ed.), *The development of spatial cognition.* Hillsdale, NJ: Erlbaum.

Acredolo, L. P., & Goodwyn, S. W. (1990). Development of communicative gesturing. In R. Vasta (Ed.), *Annals of child development* (Vol. 7). Greenwich, CT: JAI Press.

Acredolo, L. P., Goodwyn, S. W., Horobin, K. D., & Emmons, Y. D. (1999). The signs and sounds of early language development. In L. Balter & C. S. Tamis-LeMonda (Eds.), *Child psychology: A handbook of contemporary issues.* Philadelphia: Psychology Press.

Adams, G. R., Abraham, K. G., & Markstrom, C. A. (1987). The relations among identity development, self-consciousness, and self-focusing during middle and late adolescence. *Developmental Psychology, 23,* 292–297.

Adams, R. J. (1989). Newborns' discrimination among mid- and long-wavelength stimuli. *Journal of Experimental Child Psychology, 47,* 130–141.

Adams, R. J. (1995). Further exploration of human neonatal chromatic-achromatic discrimination. *Journal of Experimental Child Psychology, 60,* 344–360.

Adams, R. J., & Courage, M. L. (1998). Human newborn color vision: Measurement with chromatic stimuli varying in excitation purity. *Journal of Experimental Child Psychology, 67,* 22–34.

Adamson, L. B. (1995). *Communication development during infancy.* Madison, WI: Brown & Benchmark.

Adamson, L. B., & Bakeman, R. (1991). The development of shared attention during infancy. In R. Vasta (Ed.), *Annals of child development* (Vol. 8). London: Kingsley.

Adamson, L. B., Foster, M. A., Roark, M. L., & Reed, D. B. (1998). Doing a science project: Gender differences during childhood. *Journal of Research in Science Teaching, 35,* 845–857.

Adler, P. A., & Adler, P. (1998). *Peer power: Preadolescent culture and identity.* New Brunswick, NJ: Rutgers University Press.

Adolph, K. E. (2000). Specificity of learning: Why infants fall over a veritable cliff. *Psychological Science, 11,* 290–295.

Ahmad, A. (1992). Symptoms of post-traumatic stress disorder among displaced Kurdish children in Iraq: Victims of man-made disaster after the Gulf war. *Nordic Journal of Psychiatry, 46,* 314–319.

Ainsworth, M. D. S. (1983). Patterns of infant–mother attachment as related to maternal care: Their early history and their contribution to continuity. In D. Magnusson & V. Allen (Eds.), *Human development: An interactional perspective.* New York: Academic Press.

Ainsworth, M. D. S. (1992). A consideration of social referencing in the context of attachment theory and research. In S. Feinman (Ed.), *Social referencing and the social construction of reality in infancy.* New York: Plenum.

Ainsworth, M. D. S., Blehar, M. C., Waters, E., & Wall, S. (1978). *Patterns of attachment: A psychological study of the Strange Situation.* Hillsdale, NJ: Erlbaum.

Ainsworth, M. D. S., & Bowlby, J. (1991). An ethological approach to personality development. *American Psychologist, 46,* 331–341.

Ainsworth, M. D. S., & Wittig, B. A. (1969). Attachment and exploratory behavior of one-year-olds in a strange situation. In B. M. Foss (Ed.), *Determinants of infant behavior* (Vol. 4). London: Methuen.

Alarcon, M., Plomin, R., Fulker, D. W., Corley, R., & DeFries, J. C. (1999). Molarity not modularity: Multivariate genetic analysis of specific cognitive abilities in parents and their 16-year-old children in the Colorado Adoption Project. *Cognitive Development, 14,* 175–193.

Aldridge, M. A., Braga, E. S., Walton, G. E., & Bower, T. G. R. (1999). The intermodal representation of speech in newborns. *Developmental Science, 2,* 42–46.

Alfieri, T., Ruble, D. N., & Higgins, E. T. (1996). Gender stereotypes during adolescence: Developmental changes and the transition to junior high school. *Developmental Psychology, 32,* 1129–1137.

Alibali, M. W., Flevares, L. M., & Goldin-Meadow, S. (1997). Assessing knowledge conveyed in gesture: Do teachers have the upper hand? *Journal of Educational Psychology, 89,* 183–193.

Allan, K., & Coltrane, S. (1996). Gender display in television commercials: A comparative study of television commercials in the 1950s and 1980s. *Sex Roles, 35,* 185–203.

Allen, V. L. (1976). *Children as teachers: Theory and research in tutoring.* New York: Academic Press.

Alley, T. R. (1983). Infantile head shape as an elicitor of adult protection. *Merrill-Palmer Quarterly, 29,* 411–427.

Allwood, M. A., Bell-Dolan, D., & Husain, S. A. (2002). Children's trauma and adjustment reactions to violent and nonviolent war experiences. *Journal of the American Academy of Child and Adolescent Psychiatry, 41,* 450–457.

Almli, C. R., Ball, R. H., & Wheeler, M. E. (2001). Human fetal and neonatal movement patterns: Gender differences and fetal-to-neonatal continuity. *Developmental Psychobiology, 38,* 252–273.

Als, H., Duffy, F. H., & McAnulty, G. B. (1988). Behavioral differences between preterm and full-term newborns as measured with the APIB System Scores: I. *Infant Behavior and Development, 11,* 305–318.

Altermatt, E. R., Jovanovic, J., & Perry, M. (1998). Bias or responsivity? Sex and achievement-level effects on teachers' classroom questioning practices. *Journal of Educational Psychology, 90,* 516–527.

Amato, P. R. (1996). Explaining the intergenerational transmission of divorce. *Journal of Marriage and the Family, 58,* 628–640.

Amato, P. R. (2001). Children of divorce in the 1990s: An update of the Amato and Keith (1991) meta-analysis. *Journal of Family Psychology, 15,* 355–370.

Amato, P. R., & Gilbreth, J. G. (1999). Nonresident fathers and children's well-being: A meta-analysis. *Journal of Marriage and the Family, 61,* 557–573.

American Academy of Pediatrics. (2000a). Changing concepts of sudden infant death syndrome: Implications for infant sleeping environment and sleep position. *Pediatrics, 105,* 650–656.

American Academy of Pediatrics. (2000b). Diagnosis and evaluation of the child with attention-deficit/hyperactivity disorder. *Pediatrics, 105,* 1158–1170.

American Association of Museums. (2002). About museums. www.aam-us.org.

American Association of University Women. (1992). *How schools shortchange girls: A study of major findings on girls and education.* Washington, DC: AAUW Educational Foundation, Wellesley College Center for Research on Women.

American Association of University Women. (2001). *Beyond the gender wars: A conversation about girls, boys, and education.* Washington, DC: AAUW.

American Association of University Women/Greenberg-Lake. (1990). *Expectations and aspirations: Gender roles and self-esteem.* (Data Report and Banners). Washington, DC: Greenberg-Lake.

American Psychiatric Association. (1994). *Diagnostic and statistical manual of mental disorders* (4th ed.). Washington, DC: APA.

American Psychological Association. (2002). Ethical principles of psychologists and code of conduct. *American Psychologist, 57,* 1060–1073.

Amsterdam, B. (1972). Mirror self-image reactions before the age of two. *Developmental Psychobiology, 5,* 297–305.

Anderman, E. M., & Midgley, C. (1997). Changes in achievement goal orientations, perceived academic competence, and grades across the transition to middle-level schools. *Contemporary Educational Psychology, 22,* 269–298.

Anderson, D. R., Lorch, E. P., Field, D. E., Collins, P. A., & Nathan, J. G. (1986). Television viewing at home: Age trends in visual attention and time with TV. *Child Development, 57,* 1024–1033.

Anderson, G. M., & Allison, D. J. (1990). Intrauterine growth retardation and the routine use of ultrasound. In R. B. Goldbloom & R. S. Lawrence (Eds.), *Preventing disease: Beyond the rhetoric.* New York: Springer-Verlag.

Anderson, J. R., Greeno, J. G., Reder, L. M., & Simon, H. A. (2000). Perspective on learning, thinking, and activity. *Educational Researcher, 29,* 11–13.

Anderson, J. R., Reder, L. M., & Simon, H. A. (1996). Situated learning and education. *Educational Researcher, 25,* 5–11.

Anderson, N., Amlie, C., & Ytteroy, E. A. (2002). Outcome for children with lesbian or gay parents: A review of studies from 1978 to 2000. *Scandinavian Journal of Psychology, 43,* 335–351.

Andre, T., Whigham, M., Hendrickson, A., & Chambers, S. (1999). Competency beliefs, positive affect, and gender stereotypes of elementary students and their parents about science versus other school subjects. *Journal of Research in Science Teaching, 36,* 719–747.

Anglin, J. M. (1993). Vocabulary development: A morphological analysis. *Monographs of the Society for Research in Child Development, 58*(10, Serial No. 238).

Angoff, W. H. (1988). The nature–nurture debate, aptitudes, and group differences. *American Psychologist, 43,* 713–720.

Anisfeld, E., Casper, V., Nozyce, M., & Cunningham, N. (1990). Does infant carrying promote attachment? An experimental study of the effects of increased physical contact on the development of attachment. *Child Development, 61,* 1617–1627.

Anisfeld, M. (1996). Only tongue protrusion modeling is matched by neonates. *Developmental Review, 16,* 149–161.

Anisfeld, M., Turkewitz, G., Rose, S. A., Rosenberg, F. R., Sheiber, F. J., Couturier-Fagan, D. A., et al. (2001). No compelling evidence that newborns imitate oral gestures. *Infancy, 2,* 111–122.

Antell, S. E., & Keating, D. P. (1983). Perception of numerical invariance in neonates. *Child Development, 54,* 695–701.

Antonini, A., & Stryker, M. P. (1993). Rapid remodeling of axonal arbors in the visual cortex. *Science, 260,* 1819–1821.

Apgar, V. (1953). A proposal for a new method of evaluation of the newborn infant. *Current Researches in Anesthesia and Analgesia, 32,* 260–267.

Appel, L. F., Cooper, R. G., McCarrell, N., Sims-Knight, J., Yussen, S. R., & Flavell, J. H. (1972). The development of the distinction between perceiving and memorizing. *Child Development, 43,* 1365–1381.

Appley, M. (1986). G. Stanley Hall: Vow on Mount Owen. In S. H. Hulse & B. F. Green (Eds.), *One hundred years of psychological research in America.* Baltimore: Johns Hopkins University Press.

Archer, J. (1991). The influence of testosterone on human aggression. *British Journal of Psychology, 82,* 1–28.

Archer, J. (1992). *Ethology and human development.* London: Harvester Wheatsheaf and Barnes & Noble.

Archer, J. (1994). Testosterone and aggression: A theoretical review. *Journal of Offender Rehabilitation, 21,* 3–39.

Armon, C., & Dawson, R. L. (1997). Developmental trajectories in moral reasoning across the lifespan. *Journal of Moral Education, 26,* 433–453.

Arnett, J. J. (2002). The psychology of globalization. *American Psychologist, 57,* 774–783.

Arnett, J., & Balle-Jensen, L. (1993). Cultural bases of risk behavior: Danish adolescents. *Child Development, 64,* 1842–1855.

Arnold, D. H., Lonigan, C. J., Whitehurst, G. J., & Epstein, J. N. (1994). Accelerating language development through picture book reading. Replication and extension to a videotape training format. *Journal of Educational Psychology, 86,* 235–243.

Aronson, J., Fried, C. B., & Good, C. (2002). Reducing the effects of stereotype threat on African American college students by shaping theories of intelligence. *Journal of Experimental Social Psychology, 38,* 113–125.

Aronson, J., Lustina, M., Good, C., Keough, K., Brown, J. L., & Steele, C. M. (1999). When White men can't do math: Necessary and sufficient factors in stereotype threat. *Journal of Experimental Social Psychology, 35,* 11–23.

Asendorpf, J. B. (1990). Development of inhibition during childhood: Evidence for situational specificity and a two-factor model. *Developmental Psychology, 26,* 721–730.

Asendorpf, J. B. (1994). The malleability of behavioral inhibition: A study of individual developmental functions. *Developmental Psychology, 30,* 912–919.

Asendorpf, J. B., & Baudonniere, P. (1993). Self-awareness and other-awareness: Mirror self-recognition and synchronic imitation among unfamiliar peers. *Developmental Psychology, 29,* 88–95.

Asendorpf, J. B., Warkentin, V., & Baudonniere, P. (1996). Self-awareness and other-awareness II: Mirror-self recognition, social contingency awareness, and synchronic imitation. *Developmental Psychology, 32,* 313–321.

Ashcraft, M. H. (1990). Strategic processing in children's mental arithmetic: A review and proposal. In D. F. Bjorklund (Ed.), *Children's strategies: Contemporary views of cognitive development.* Hillsdale, NJ: Erlbaum.

Asher, S. R. (1985). An evolving paradigm in social skill training research with children. In B. H. Schneider, K. H. Rubin, & J. E. Ledingham (Eds.), *Children's peer relations: Issues in assessment and intervention.* New York: Springer-Verlag.

Asher, S. R., & Coie, J. D. (Eds.). (1990). *Peer rejection in childhood.* New York: Cambridge University Press.

Asher, S. R., & Hymel, S. (1981). Children's social competence in peer relations: Sociometric and behavioral assessment. In J. D. Wine & M. D. Smye (Eds.), *Social competence.* New York: Guilford.

Asher, S. R., Parker, J. G., & Walker, D. L. (1996). Distinguishing friendship from acceptance: Implications for intervention and assessment. In W. M. Bukowski, A. F. Newcomb, & W. W. Hartup (Eds.), *The company they keep: Friendship in childhood and adolescence.* New York: Cambridge University Press.

Asher, S. R., Renshaw, P. D., & Hymel, S. (1982). Peer relations and the development of social skills. In S. G. Moore (Ed.), *The young child: Reviews of research* (Vol. 3). Washington, DC: National Association for the Education of Young Children.

Ashley, J. A., & Tomasello, M. (1998). Cooperative problem-solving and teaching in preschoolers. *Social Development, 7,* 143–163.

Ashmead, D. H., Davis, D. L., Whalen, T., & Odom, R. D. (1991). Sound localization and sensitivity to inter-aural time differences in human infants. *Child Development, 62,* 1211–1226.

Ashmead, D. H., & Perlmutter, M. (1980). Infant memory in everyday life. In M. Perlmutter (Ed.), *New directions for child development: No. 10. Children's memory.* San Francisco: Jossey-Bass.

Aslin, R. N., & Hunt, R. H. (2001). Development, plasticity, and learning in the auditory system. In C. A. Nelson & M. Luciana (Eds.), *Handbook of developmental cognitive neuroscience.* Cambridge, MA: MIT Press.

Aslin, R. N., Jusczyk, P. W., & Pisoni, D. B. (1998). Speech and auditory processing during infancy: Constraints on and precursors to language. In W. Damon (Series Ed.) & D. Kuhn & R. S. Siegler (Vol. Eds.), *Handbook of child psychology: Vol. 2. Cognition, perception, and language* (5th ed.). New York: Wiley.

Aslin, R. N., Pisoni, D. B., & Jusczyk, P. W. (1983). Auditory development and speech perception in infancy. In P. H. Mussen (Series Ed.) & M. M. Haith & J. J. Campos (Vol. Eds.), *Handbook of child psychology: Vol. 2. Infancy and developmental psychology* (4th ed.). New York: Wiley.

Aslin, R. N., Saffran, J. R., & Newport, E. L. (1999). Statistical learning in linguistic and nonlinguistic domains. In B. MacWhinney (Ed.), *The emergence of language.* Mahwah, NJ: Erlbaum.

Aslin, R. N., & Shea, S. L. (1990). Velocity thresholds in human infants: Implications for the perception of motion. *Developmental Psychology, 26,* 589–598.

Astington, J. W. (1988). Children's production of commissive speech acts. *Journal of Child Language, 15,* 411–423.

Astington, J. W. (Ed.). (2000). *Minds in the making.* Malden, MA: Blackwell.

Atkinson, R. C., & Shiffrin, R. M. (1971). The control of short-term memory. *Scientific American, 225,* 82.

Atlas, R. S., & Pepler, D. J. (1998). Observations of bullying in the classroom. *Journal of Educational Research, 92,* 86–99.

Attili, G., Vermigli, P., & Schneider, B. H. (1997). Peer acceptance and friendship patterns within a cross-cultural perspective. *International Journal of Behavioral Development, 21,* 277–288.

Au, K. H. (1997). A sociocultural model of reading instruction: The Kamehameha Elementary Education program. In S. A. Stahl & D. A. Hayes (Eds.), *Instructional models in reading.* Mahwah, NJ: Erlbaum.

Au, T. K., Romo, L. F., & DeWitt, J. E. (1999). Considering children's folkbiology in health education. In M. Siegal & C. C. Peterson (Eds.), *Children's understanding of biology and health.* New York: Cambridge University Press.

Aureli, F., & de Waal, F. B. M. (2000). *Natural conflict resolution.* Berkeley: University of California Press.

Azmitia, M. (1996). Peer interactive minds: Developmental, theoretical, and methodological issues. In P. B. Baltes & V. M. Staudinger (Eds.), *Interactive minds: Life-span perspectives on the social foundations of cognition.* New York: Cambridge University Press.

Azmitia, M., & Hesser, J. (1993). Why siblings are important agents of cognitive development: A comparison of siblings and peers. *Child Development, 64,* 430–444.

Azmitia, M., & Montgomery, R. (1993). Friendship, transactive dialogues, and the development of scientific reasoning. *Social Development, 2,* 202–221.

Azmitia, M., & Perlmutter, M. (1989). Social influences on children's cognition: State of the art and future directions. In H. W. Reese (Ed.), *Advances in child development and behavior,* (Vol. 22). San Diego, CA: Academic Press.

Azuma, H. (1996). Cross-national research on child development: The Hess-Azuma collaboration in retrospect. In D. Schwalb & B. Schwalb (Eds.). *Japanese childrearing: Two generations of scholarship.* New York: Guilford.

Baenninger, M., & Newcombe, N. (1989). The role of experience in spatial test performance: A meta-analysis. *Sex Roles, 20,* 327–344.

Baenninger, M., & Newcombe, N. (1995). Environmental input to the development of sex-related differences in spatial and mathematical ability. *Learning and Individual Differences, 7,* 363–382.

Bahrick, L. E. (1983). Infants' perception of substance and temporal synchrony in multimodal events. *Infant Behavior and Development, 6,* 429–451.

Bahrick, L. E. (1992). Infants' perceptual differentiation of amodal and modality-specific audio-visual relations. *Journal of Experimental Child Psychology, 53,* 180–199.

Bahrick, L. E. (1995). Intermodal origins of self-perception. In P. Rochat (Ed.), *The self in infancy: Theory and research.* Amsterdam: Elsevier.

Bahrick, L. E., & Lickliter, R. (2000). Intersensory redundancy guides attentional selectivity and perceptual learning in infancy. *Developmental Psychology, 36,* 190–201.

Bahrick, L. E., Netto, D., & Hernandez-Reif, M. (1998). Intermodal perception of adult and child faces and voices by infants. *Child Development, 69,* 1263–1275.

Bahrick, L. E., & Pickens, J. N. (1994). Amodal relations: The basis for intermodal perception and learning in infancy. In D. J. Lewkowicz & R. Lickliter (Eds.), *The development of intersensory perception: Comparative perspectives.* Hillsdale, NJ: Erlbaum.

Bahrick, L. E., & Pickens, J. N. (1995). Infant memory for object motion across a period of three months: Implications for a four-phase attention function. *Journal of Experimental Child Psychology, 59,* 343–371.

Bailey, J. M., & Bell, A. P. (1993). Familiality of female and male homosexuality. *Behavior Genetics, 23,* 313–322.

Bailey, J. M., & Benishay, D. (1993). Familial aggregation of female sexual orientation. *American Journal of Psychiatry, 150,* 272–277.

Bailey, J. M., & Dawood, K. (1998). Behavioral genetics, sexual orientation, and the family. In C. P. Patterson & A. R. D'Augelli (Eds.), *Lesbian, gay, and bisexual identities in families: Psychological perspectives.* New York: Oxford University Press.

Bailey, J. M., Dunne, M. P., & Martin, N. G. (2000). Genetic and environmental influences on sexual orientation and its correlates in an Australian twin sample. *Journal of Personality and Social Psychology, 78,* 524–536.

Bailey, J. M., Miller, J. S., & Willerman, L. (1993). Maternally rated childhood gender nonconformity in homosexuals and heterosexuals. *Archives of Sexual Behavior, 22,* 461–469.

Bailey, J. M., Nothnagel, J., & Wolfe, M. (1995). Retrospectively-measured individual differences in childhood sex-typed behavior among gay men: Correspondences between self and maternal reports. *Archives of Sexual Behavior, 24,* 613–622.

Bailey, J. M., Pillard, R. C., Neale, M. C., & Agyei, Y. (1993). Heritable factors influence sexual orientation in women. *Archives of General Psychiatry, 50,* 217–223.

Bailey, J. M., & Zucker, K. J. (1995). Childhood sex-typed behavior and sexual orientation: A conceptual analysis and quantitative review. *Developmental Psychology, 31,* 43–55.

Bailey, S. M., & Garn, S. M. (1986). The genetics of maturation. In F. Falkner & J. M. Tanner (Eds.), *Human growth: A comprehensive treatise.* New York: Plenum.

Baillargeon, R. (1986). Remembering the existence and the location of hidden objects: Object permanence in 6- and 8-month-old infants. *Cognition, 23,* 21–41.

Baillargeon, R. (1987a). Object permanence in 3 1/2- and 4 1/2-old-infants. *Developmental Psychology, 23,* 655–664.

Baillargeon, R. (1987b). Young infants' reasoning about the physical and spatial properties of a hidden object. *Cognitive Development, 2,* 179–200.

Baillargeon, R. (1993). The object concept revisited: New directions in the investigation of infants' physical knowledge. In H. W. Reese (Ed.), *Advances in child development and behavior* (Vol. 23). New York: Academic Press.

Baillargeon, R. (1994). How do infants learn about the physical world? *Current Directions in Psychological Science, 3,* 133–140.

Baillargeon, R. (1999). Young infants' expectations about hidden objects: A reply to three challenges. *Developmental Science, 2,* 115–132.

Baillargeon, R. (2002). The acquisition of physical knowledge in infancy: A summary in eight lessons. In U. Goswami (Ed.), *Blackwell handbook of childhood cognitive development.* Malden, MA: Blackwell.

Baillargeon, R., Kotovsky, L., & Needham, A. (1995). The acquisition of physical knowledge in infancy. In D. Sperber, D. Primack, & A. J. Primack (Eds.), *Causal cognition: A multidisciplinary debate.* New York: Clarendon Press.

Bakeman, R., Adamson, L. B., Konner, M., & Barr, R. G. (1990). !Kung infancy: The social context of object exploration. *Child Development, 61,* 794–809.

Baker, L., Scher, D., & Mackler, K. (1997). Home and family influences on motivations for reading. *Educational Psychologist, 32,* 69–82.

Baker-Ward, L., Ornstein, P. A., & Holden, D. J. (1984). The expression of memorization in early childhood. *Journal of Experimental Child Psychology, 37,* 555–575.

Balaban, M. T. (1995). Affective influences on startle in five-month-old infants: Reactions to facial expressions of emotion. *Child Development, 66,* 28–36.

Balazs, R., Jordan, T., Lewis, P. D., & Patel, A. J. (1986). Undernutrition and brain development. In F. Falkner & J. M. Tanner (Eds.), *Human growth: A comprehensive treatise.* New York: Plenum.

Baldwin, A., Baldwin, C., & Cole, R. E. (1990). Stress-resistant families and stress-resistant children. In J. E. Rolf, A. S. Masten, D. Cicchetti, K. N. Wechterlein, & S. Weintraub (Eds.), *Risk and protective factors in the development of psychopathology.* New York: Cambridge University Press.

Baldwin, D. A. (1995). Understanding the link between joint attention and language. In C. Moore & P. J. Dunham (Eds.), *Joint attention: Its origins and role in development.* Hillsdale, NJ: Erlbaum.

Baldwin, D. A., & Moses, L. J. (1994). Early understanding of referential intent and attentional focus: Evidence from language and emotion. In C. Lewis & P. Mitchell (Eds.), *Children's early understanding of mind.* Hillsdale, NJ: Erlbaum.

Baldwin, D. A., & Moses, L. J. (1996). The ontogeny of social information gathering. *Child Development, 67,* 1915–1939.

Baldwin, D. A., & Moses, L. J. (2001). Links between social understanding and early word learning: Challenges to current accounts. *Social Development, 10,* 309–329.

Bandura, A. (1965). Influence of models' reinforcement contingencies on the acquisition of imitative responses. *Journal of Personality and Social Psychology, 1,* 589–595.

Bandura, A. (1973). *Aggression: A social learning analysis.* Englewood Cliffs, NJ: Prentice Hall.

Bandura, A. (1977). *Social learning theory.* Englewood Cliffs, NJ: Prentice Hall.

Bandura, A. (1978). The self system in reciprocal determinism. *American Psychologist, 33,* 344–358.

Bandura, A. (1983). Psychological mechanisms of aggression. In R. G. Geen & E. I. Donnerstein (Eds.), *Aggression: Theoretical and empirical reviews* (Vol. 1). New York: Academic Press.

Bandura, A. (1986). *Social foundations of thought and action: A social cognitive theory.* Englewood Cliffs, NJ: Prentice Hall.

Bandura, A. (1989a). Regulation of cognitive processes through perceived self-efficacy. *Developmental Psychology, 25,* 729–735.

Bandura, A. (1989b). Social cognitive theory. In R. Vasta (Ed.), *Annals of child development* (Vol. 6). Greenwich, CT: JAI Press.

Bandura, A. (1991a). Self-regulation of motivation through anticipatory and self-regulatory mechanisms. In R. A. Dienstbier (Ed.), *Nebraska symposium on motivation: Vol. 38. Perspectives on motivation:* Lincoln: University of Nebraska Press.

Bandura, A. (1991b). Social cognitive theory of moral thought and action. In W. M. Kurtines & J. L. Gewirtz (Eds.), *Handbook of moral behavior and development: Vol. 1. Theory.* Hillsdale, NJ: Erlbaum.

Bandura, A. (1992). Social cognitive theory. In R. Vasta (Ed.), *Six theories of child development: Revised formulations and current issues.* London: Kingsley.

Bandura, A. (1994). Social cognitive theory of mass communication. In J. Bryant & D. Zillman (Eds.), *Media effects: Advances in theory and research.* Hillsdale, NJ: Erlbaum.

Bandura, A. (1997). *Self-efficacy: The exercise of control.* New York: W. H. Freeman.

Bandura, A. (2001). Social cognitive theory: An agentic perspective. *Annual Review of Psychology, 52,* 1–26.

Bandura, A., & Schunk, D. H. (1981). Cultivating competence, self-efficacy, and intrinsic interest through proximal self-motivation. *Journal of Personality and Social Psychology, 41,* 586–598.

Banerjee, R., & Lintern, V. (2000). Boys will be boys: The effect of social evaluation concerns on gender-typing. *Social Development, 9,* 397–408.

Banks, M. S., & Ginsburg, A. P. (1985). Infant visual preferences: A review and new theoretical treatment. In H. W. Reese (Ed.), *Advances in child development and behavior* (Vol. 19). Orlando, FL: Academic Press.

Bard, C., Hay, L., & Fleury, M. (1990). Timing and accuracy of visually directed movements in children: Control of direction and amplitude components. *Journal of Experimental Child Psychology, 50,* 102–118.

Barglow, P., Vaughn, B. E., & Molitor, N. (1987). Effects of maternal absence due to employment on the quality of infant–mother attachment. *Child Development, 58,* 945–954.

Barinaga, M. (1993). Death gives birth to the nervous system. But how? *Science, 259,* 762–763.

Barkley, R. A. (1998). *Attention-deficit hyperactivity disorder: A handbook for diagnosis and treatment* (2nd ed.). New York: Guilford.

Barkow, J. H., Cosmides, L., & Tooby, J. (Eds.). (1992). *The adapted mind: Evolutionary psychology and the generation of culture.* New York: Oxford University Press.

Barnard, K. E., Bee, H. L., & Hammond, M. A. (1984). Home environment and cognitive development in a healthy, low-risk sample: The Seattle study. In A. W. Gottfried (Ed.), *Home environment and early cognitive development.* New York: Academic Press.

Barnett, C. R., Leiderman, P. H., Grobstein, R., & Klaus, M. H. (1970). Neonatal separation: The maternal side of interactional deprivation. *Pediatrics, 45,* 197–205.

Barnett, D., Hunt, K. H., Butler, C. M., McCaskill, J. W. IV, Kaplan-Estrin, M., & Pipp-Siegel, S. (1999). Indices of attachment disorganization among toddlers with neurological and non-neurological problems. In J. Solomon & C. George (Eds.), *Attachment disorganization.* New York: Guilford.

Barnett, W. S. (1995). Long-term effects of early childhood programs on cognitive and school outcomes. In The Center for the Future of Children (Ed.), *The future of children.* Los Altos, CA: David and Lucile Packard Foundation.

Baron, R. A. (1983). The control of human aggression: A strategy based on incompatible responses. In R. G. Geen & E. I. Donnerstein (Eds.), *Aggression: Theoretical and empirical reviews* (Vol. 2). New York: Academic Press.

Baron-Cohen, S. (1995). *Mindblindness: An essay on autism and theory of mind.* Cambridge, MA: MIT Press.

Baron-Cohen, S. (2000). The cognitive neuroscience of autism: Evolutionary approaches. In M. Gassaniga (Ed.), *The new cognitive neurosciences* (2nd ed.). Cambridge, MA: MIT Press.

Barr, R., Dowden, A., & Hayne, H. (1996). Developmental changes in deferred imitation by 6- to 24-month-old infants. *Infant Behavior and Development, 19,* 159–170.

Barrera, M., & Maurer, D. (1981a). The perception of facial expressions by the three-month-old. *Child Development, 52,* 203–206.

Barrera, M., & Maurer, D. (1981b). Recognition of mother's photographed face by the three-month-old infant. *Child Development, 52,* 714–716.

Barrett, D. E., & Yarrow, M. R. (1977). Prosocial behavior, social inferential ability, and assertiveness in children. *Child Development, 48,* 475–481.

Barry, H. III, Bacon, M. K., & Child, I. L. (1957). A cross-cultural survey of some sex differences in socialization. *Journal of Abnormal and Social Psychology, 55,* 327–332.

Barth, F. (1997). How is the self conceptualized? Variations among cultures. In U. Neisser & D. A. Jopling (Eds.), *The conceptual self in context: Culture, experience, self-understanding.* Cambridge: Cambridge University Press.

Bartrip, J., Morton, J., & de Schonen, S. (2001). Response to mother's face in 3-week to 5-month-old infants. *British Journal of Developmental Psychology, 19,* 219–232.

Bates, E. (1990). Language about me and you: Pronominal reference and the emerging concept of self. In D. Cicchetti & M. Beeghly (Eds.), *The self in transition: Infancy to childhood.* Chicago: The University of Chicago Press.

Bates, E., Camaioni, L., & Volterra, V. (1975). The acquisition of performatives prior to speech. *Merrill-Palmer Quarterly, 21,* 205–226.

Bates, E., & Carnevale, G. F. (1993). New directions in research on language development. *Developmental Review, 13,* 436–470.

Bates, E., & MacWhinney, B. (1987). Competition, variation, language learning. In B. MacWhinney (Ed.), *Mechanisms of language acquisition.* Hillsdale, NJ: Erlbaum.

Bates, E., O'Connell, B., & Shore, C. (1987). Language and communication in infancy. In J. D. Osofsky (Ed.), *Handbook of infant development* (2nd ed.). New York: Wiley.

Bates, E., & Snyder, L. (1985). The cognitive hypothesis in language development. In I. Uzgiris & J. M. Hunt (Eds.), *Research with scales of psychological development in infancy.* Champaign-Urbana: University of Illinois Press.

Bates, J. E. (1987). Temperament in infancy. In J. D. Osofsky (Ed.), *Handbook of infant development* (2nd ed.). New York: Wiley.

Bates, J. E. (1990). Conceptual and empirical linkages between temperament and behavior problems: A commentary on the Sanson, Prior, and Kyrios study. *Merrill-Palmer Quarterly, 36,* 193–199.

Bates, J. E., & Bayles, K. (1984). Objective and subjective components in mothers' perceptions of their children from age 6 months to 3 years. *Merrill-Palmer Quarterly, 30,* 111–130.

Bates, J. E., Bayles, K., Bennett, D. S., Ridge, B., & Brown, M. M. (1991). Origins of externalizing behavior problems at eight years of age. In D. Pepler & K. H. Rubin (Eds.), *Development and treatment of childhood aggression.* Hillsdale, NJ: Erlbaum.

Bates, J. E., & Wachs, T. D. (Eds.) (1994). *Temperament: Individual differences at the interface of biology and behavior.* Washington, DC: American Psychological Association.

Bates, J. E., Wachs, T. D., & Emde R. N. (1994). Toward practical uses for biological concepts of temperament. In J. E. Bates & T. D. Wachs (Eds.), *Temperament: Individual differences at the interface of biology and behavior.* Washington, DC: American Psychological Association.

Battistich, V., Schaps, E., Watson, M., Solomon, D., & Lewis, C. (2000). Effects of the Child Development Project on students' drug use and other problem behaviors. *Journal of Primary Prevention, 21,* 75–99.

Bauer, D. J., Goldfield, B. A., & Reznick, J. S. (2002). Alternative approaches to analyzing individual differences in the rate of early vocabulary development. *Applied Psycholinguistics, 23,* 313–326.

Bauer, P. J. (1992). Holding it all together: How enabling relations facilitate young children's event recall. *Cognitive Development, 7,* 1–28.

Bauer, P. J. (1993). Memory for gender-consistent and gender-inconsistent event sequences by twenty-five-month-old children. *Child Development, 64,* 285–297.

Bauer, P. J. (2002). Early memory development. In U. Goswami (Ed.), *Blackwell handbook of childhood cognitive development.* Madden, MA: Blackwell Publishers.

Bauer, P. J., & Fivush, R. (1992). Constructing event representations: Building on a foundation of variation and enabling relations. *Cognitive Development, 2,* 381–401.

Bauer, P. J., Hertsgaard, L. A., & Dow, G. A. (1994). After 8 months have passed: Long-term recall of events by 1- to 2-year-old children. *Memory, 2,* 353–382.

Bauer, P. J., & Mandler, J. M. (1992). Putting the horse before the cart: The use of temporal order in recall of events by one-year-old children. *Developmental Psychology, 28,* 441–452.

Bauer, P. J., & Travis, L. L. (1993). The fabric of an event: Different sources of temporal invariance differentially affect 24-month-olds' recall. *Cognitive Development, 8,* 319–341.

Bauer, P. J., Wenner, J. A., Dropik, P. L., & Wewerka, S. S. (2000). Parameters of remembering and forgetting in the transition from infancy to early childhood. *Monographs of the Society for Research in Child Development, 65*(4, Serial No. 263).

Bauerfeld, S. L., & Lachenmeyer, J. R. (1992). Prenatal nutritional status and intellectual development: Critical review and evaluation. In B. B. Lahey & A. E. Kazdin (Eds.), *Advances in clinical child psychology* (Vol. 14). New York: Plenum.

Baumrind, D. (1967). Child care practices anteceding three patterns of preschool behavior. *Genetic Psychology Monographs, 75,* 43–88.

Baumrind, D. (1971). Current patterns of parental authority. *Developmental Psychology Monograph, 4,* 1–103.

Baumrind, D. (1989). Rearing competent children. In W. Damon (Ed.), *Child development today and tomorrow.* San Francisco: Jossey-Bass.

Baumrind, D. (1991). The influence of parenting style on adolescent competence and substance abuse. *Journal of Early Adolescence, 11,* 56–95.

Baumrind, D., & Black, A. E. (1967). Socialization practices associated with dimensions of competence in preschool boys and girls. *Child Development, 38,* 291–327.

Bauserman, M. (2002). Child adjustment in joint-custody versus sole-custody arrangements: A meta-analytic review. *Journal of Family Psychology, 16,* 91–102.

Baydar, N., Greek, A., & Brooks-Gunn, J. (1997). A longitudinal study of the effects of the birth of a sibling during the first 6 years of life. *Journal of Marriage and the Family, 59,* 939–956.

Bayley, N. (1956). Individual patterns of development. *Child Development, 27,* 45–74.

Bayley, N. (1969). *Manual for the Bayley Scales of Infant Development.* New York: Psychological Corporation.

Bayley, N. (1970). Development of mental abilities. In P. H. Mussen (Ed.), *Carmichael's manual of child psychology* (3rd ed., Vol. 1). New York: Wiley.

Bayley, N. (1993). *Bayley Scales of Infant Development: Birth to Two Years* (2nd ed.). New York: Psychological Corporation.

Bearison, D. (1982). New directions in studies of social interactions and cognitive growth. In F. C. Serafica (Ed.), *Social-cognitive development in context.* New York: Guilford.

Bearison, D., & Dorval, B. (2002). *Collaborative cognition: Children negotiating ways of knowing.* Westport, CT: Ablex.

Beauchamp, D. K., Cowart, B. J., Mennella, J. A., & Marsh, R. R. (1994). Infant salt taste: Developmental, methodological, and contextual factors. *Developmental Psychobiology, 27,* 353–365.

Becker, J. (1994). "Sneak-shoes," "sworders," and "nose-beards": A case study of lexical innovation. *First Language, 14,* 195–211.

Beckwith, L., & Parmelee, A. (1986). EEG patterns of preterm infants, home environment, and later IQ. *Child Development, 57,* 777–789.

Bedard, J., & Chi, M. T. H. (1992). Expertise. *Current Directions in Psychological Science, 1,* 135–139.

Beebe, B., Alson, D., Jaffe, J., Feldstein, S., & Crown, C. (1988). Vocal congruence in mother–infant play. *Journal of Psycholinguistic Research, 17,* 245–259.

Behl-Chadha, G. (1996). Basic-level and superordinate-like categorical representations in early infancy. *Cognition, 60,* 105–141.

Behrend, D. A. (1988). Overextensions in early language comprehension: Evidence from a signal detection approach. *Journal of Child Language, 15,* 63–75.

Behrend, D. A., Rosengren, K. A., & Perlmutter, M. (1989). A new look at children's private speech: The effects of age, task difficulty, and parental presence. *International Journal of Behavioral Development, 12,* 305–320.

Behrman, R. E., Kliegman, R. M., & Jenson, H. B. (Eds.). (2000). *Nelson textbook of pediatrics* (16th ed.). Philadelphia: W. B. Saunders.

Behrman, R. E., & Vaughan, V. C. III. (1987). *Nelson textbook of pediatrics* (3rd ed.). Philadelphia: Saunders.

Beier, E. G. (1991). Freud: Three contributions. In G. A. Kimble, M. Wertheimer, & C. L. White (Eds.), *Portraits of pioneers in psychology.* Hillsdale, NJ: Erlbaum.

Beilin, H. (1992a). Piaget's enduring contribution to developmental psychology. *Developmental Psychology, 28,* 191–204.

Beilin, H. (1992b). Piaget's new theory. In H. Beilin & P. B. Pufall (Eds.), *Piaget's theory: Prospects and possibilities.* Hillsdale, NJ: Erlbaum.

Bell, A. P., Weinberg, M. S., & Hammersmith, S. K. (1981). *Sexual preference: Its development in men and women.* Bloomington: Indiana University Press.

Bell, N., Grossen, M., & Perret-Clermont, A.-N. (1985) Sociocognitive conflict and intellectual growth. In M. Berkowitz (Ed.), *New directions for child development: No. 29. Peer conflict and psychological growth.* San Francisco: Jossey-Bass.

Bell, R. Q. (1968). A reinterpretation of the direction of effects of socialization. *Psychological Review, 75,* 81–95.

Bellinger, D. C., & Adams, H. F. (2001). Environmental pollutant exposures and children's cognitive abilities. In R. J. Sternberg & E. L. Grigorenko (Eds.), *Environmental effects on cognitive abilities.* Mahwah, NJ: Erlbaum.

Bellinger, D. C., Leviton, A., Needleman, H. L., Waternaux, C., & Rabinowitz, M. (1986). Low-level lead exposure and infant development in the first year. *Neurobehavioral Toxicology and Teratology, 8,* 151–161.

Belsky, J. (1988). The "effects" of infant day care reconsidered. *Early Childhood Research Quarterly, 3,* 235–272.

Belsky, J. (1999). Interactional and contextual determinants of attachment security. In J. Cassidy & P. R. Shaver (Eds.), *Handbook of attachment: Theory, research, and clinical applications.* New York: Guilford.

Belsky, J., Fish, M., & Isabella, R. (1991). Continuity and discontinuity in infant negative and positive emotionality: Family antecedents and attachment consequences. *Developmental Psychology, 27,* 421–431.

Belsky, J. Goode, M. K., & Most, R. K. (1980). Maternal stimulation and infant exploratory competence: Cross-sectional, correlational, and experimental analyses. *Child Development, 51,* 1168–1178.

Belsky, J., Rosenberger, K., & Crnic, K. (1995). The origins of attachment security: "Classical" and contextual determinants. In S. Goldberg, R. Muir, & J. Kerr (Eds.), *Attachment theory: Social, developmental, and clinical perspectives.* Hillsdale, NJ: Analytic Press.

Belsky, J., & Rovine, M. (1988). Nonmaternal care in the first year of life and infant–parent attachment security. *Child Development, 59,* 157–167.

Belsky, J., Rovine, M., & Taylor, D. G. (1984). The Pennsylvania Infant and Family Development Project; III. The origins of individual differences in infant–mother attachment: Maternal and infant contributions. *Child Development, 55,* 718–728.

Bem, D. J. (1996). Exotic becomes erotic: A developmental theory of sexual orientation. *Psychological Review, 103,* 320–335.

Bem, D. J. (2000). Exotic becomes erotic: Interpreting the biological correlates of sexual orientation. *Archives of Sexual Behavior, 29,* 531–548.

Bem, D. J. (2001). Exotic becomes erotic: Integrating biological and experiential antecedents of sexual orientation. In A. R. D'Augelli & C. J. Patterson (Eds.), *Lesbian, gay, and bisexual identities and youth: Psychological perspectives.* New York: Oxford University Press.

Bem, S. L. (1981). Gender schema theory: A cognitive account of sex typing. *Psychological Review, 88,* 354–364.

Bem, S. L. (1989). Genital knowledge and gender constancy in preschool children. *Child Development, 60,* 649–662.

Bem, S. L. (1993). *The lenses of gender: Transforming the debate on sexual inequality.* New Haven, CT: Yale University Press.

Benasich, A. A., & Brooks-Gunn, J. (1996). Maternal attitudes and knowledge of child-rearing: Associations with family and child outcomes. *Child Development, 67,* 1186–1205.

Benbow, C. P. (1992). Academic achievement in mathematics and science of students between ages 13 and 23: Are there differences among students in the top one percent of mathematical ability? *Journal of Educational Psychology, 84,* 51–61.

Benedict, H. (1979). Early lexical development: Comprehension and production. *Journal of Child Language, 6,* 183–200.

Benenson, J. F. (1993). Greater preference among females than males for dyadic interaction in early childhood. *Child Development, 64,* 544–555.

Benenson, J. F., Apostoleris, N. H., & Parnass, J. (1997). Age and sex differences in dyadic and group interaction in early childhood. *Developmental Psychology, 33,* 538–543.

Benenson, J. F., & Dweck, C. S. (1986). The development of trait explanations and self-evaluations in the academic and social domains. *Child Development, 57,* 1179–1187.

Benenson, J. F., Markovits, H., Roy, R., & Denko, P. (2003). Behavioural rules underlying learning to share: Effects of development and context. *International Journal of Behavioral Development, 27,* 116–121.

Benoit, D. (1993). Failure to thrive and feeding disorders. In C. H. Zeanah Jr. (Ed.), *Handbook of infant mental development.* New York: Guilford.

Benson, J. (1984). The origins of future orientation in the everyday lives of 9- to 36-month-old infants. In M. M. Haith, J. B., Benson, R. J. Roberts, & B. F. Pennington (Eds.), *The development of future-oriented processes.* Chicago: University of Chicago Press.

Benson, J. B. (1990). The significance and development of crawling in human infancy. In J. E. Clark & J. H. Humphrey (Eds.), *Advances in motor development research* (Vol. 3). New York: AMS Press.

Benson, J. B, Talmi, A., & Haith, M. M. (in press). The social and cultural context of the development of future orientation. In C. Raeff & J. B. Benson (Eds.), *Social and cognitive development in the context of individual, social, and cultural processes.* London: Routledge.

Benson, J. B., & Uzgiris, I. C. (1985). Effects of self-initiated locomotion on infant search activity. *Developmental Psychology, 21,* 923–931.

Berenbaum, S. A., & Hines, M. (1992). Early androgens are related to childhood sex-typed toy preferences. *Psychological Science, 3,* 203–206.

Berenbaum, S. A., & Snyder, E. (1995). Early hormonal influences on childhood sex-typed activity and playmate preferences: Implications for the development of sexual orientation. *Developmental Psychology, 31,* 31–42.

Berg, N. E., & Mussen, P. (1975). The origins and development of concepts of justice. *Journal of Social Issues, 31,* 183–201.

Berg, W. K., & Berg, K. M. (1987). Psychophysiological development in infancy. In J. Osofsky (Ed.), *Handbook of infant development* (2nd ed.). New York: Wiley.

Berk, L. (2001). *Awakening children's minds: How parents and teachers can make a difference.* New York: Oxford University Press.

Berk, L. E. (1994). Why children talk to themselves. *Scientific American, 271,* 78–83.

Berk, L. E., & Garvin, R. A. (1984). Development of private speech among low-income Appalachian children. *Developmental Psychology, 20,* 271–286.

Berk, L. E., & Landau, S. (1993). Private speech of learning disabled and normally achieving children in classroom academic and laboratory contexts. *Child Development, 64,* 556–571.

Berko, J. (1958). The child's learning of English morphology. *Word, 14,* 150–177.

Berkowitz, L. (1993). *Aggression: Its causes, consequences, and control.* New York: Academic Press.

Berkowitz, M. W., Gibbs, J. C., & Broughton, J. M. (1980). The relation of moral judgment stage disparity to developmental effects of peer dialogues. *Merrill–Palmer Quarterly, 26,* 341–357.

Berndt, T. J. (1979). Developmental changes in conformity to peers and parents. *Developmental Psychology, 15,* 608–616.

Berndt, T. J. (1981). Age changes and changes over time in prosocial intentions and behavior between friends. *Developmental Psychology, 17,* 408–416.

Berndt, T. J. (1986). Sharing between friends: Contexts and consequences. In E. C. Mueller & C. R. Cooper (Eds.), *Process and outcome in peer relationships.* New York: Academic Press.

Berndt, T. J. (1988). The nature and significance of children's friendships. In R. Vasta (Ed.), *Annals of child development* (Vol. 5). Greenwich, CT: JAI Press.

Berndt, T. J. (1989a). Friendships in childhood and adolescence. In W. Damon (Ed.), *Child development today and tomorrow.* San Francisco: Jossey-Bass.

Berndt, T. J. (1989b). Obtaining support from friends during childhood and adolescence. In D. Belle (Ed.), *Children's social networks and social supports.* New York: Wiley.

Berndt, T. J. (1996). Transitions in friendship and friends' influence. In J. A. Graber, J. Brooks-Gunn, & A. C. Petersen (Eds.), *Transitions through adolescence: Interpersonal domains and context.* Mahwah, NJ: Erlbaum

Berndt, T. J. (2002). Friendship quality and social development. *Current Directions in Psychological Science, 11,* 7–10.

Berndt, T. J., & Heller, K. A. (1986). Gender stereotypes and social inferences: A developmental study. *Journal of Personality and Social Psychology, 50,* 889–898.

Berndt, T. J., & Keefe, K. (1995). Friends' influence on adolescents' adjustment to school. *Child Development, 66,* 1312–1329.

Berndt, T. J., Miller, K. E., & Park, K. (1989). Adolescents' perceptions of friends' and parents' influence on aspects of their school adjustment. *Journal of Early Adolescence, 9,* 419–435.

Berndt, T. J., & Perry, T. B. (1990). Distinctive features and effects of adolescent friendships. In R. Montemayor, G. R. Adams, & T. P. Gullotta (Eds.), *From childhood to adolescence: A transitional period?* London: Sage.

Bernier, J. G., & Siegel, D. H. (1994). Attention-deficit hyperactivity disorder: A family ecological systems perspective. *Families in Society, 75,* 142–150.

Berry, J. B. (Ed.). (1997). *Handbook of cross-cultural psychology.* Boston: Allyn and Bacon.

Berry, J. W. (1966). Temne and Eskimo perceptual skills. *International Journal of Psychology, 1,* 207–229.

Berry, J. W. (1984). Towards a universal psychology of cognitive competence. *International Journal of Psychology, 19,* 335–361.

Berry, J. W. (1997). Immigration, acculturation, and adaptation. *International Journal of Applied Psychology, 46,* 5–34.

Bertenthal, B. I. (1996). Origins and early development of perception, action, and representation. *Annual Review of Psychology, 47,* 431–459.

Bertenthal, B. I., & Bai, D. L. (1989). Infants' sensitivity to optical flow for controlling posture. *Developmental Psychology, 25,* 936–945.

Bertenthal, B. I., Campos, J. J., & Barrett, K. (1984). Self-produced locomotion: An organizer of emotional, cognitive, and social development in infancy. In R. Emde & R. Harmon (Eds.), *Continuities and discontinuities in development.* New York: Plenum.

Bertenthal, B. I., Campos, J. J., & Haith, M. M. (1980). Development of visual organization: The perception of subjective contours. *Child Development, 51,* 1072–1080.

Bertenthal, B. I., Campos, J. J., & Kermoian, R. (1994). An epigenetic perspective on the development of self-produced locomotion and its consequences. *Current Directions in Psychological Science, 3,* 140–145.

Bertenthal, B. I., & Clifton, R. K. (1998). Perception and action. In W. Damon (Series Ed.) & D. Kuhn & R. S. Siegler (Vol. Eds.), *Handbook of child psychology: Vol. 2. Cognition, perception, and language* (5th ed.). New York: Wiley.

Bertenthal, B. I., & Fischer, K. W. (1978). Development of self-recognition in the infant. *Developmental Psychology, 11,* 44–50.

Best, C. T. (1995). Learning to perceive the sound pattern of English. In C. K. Rovee-Collier & L. P. Lipsitt (Eds.), *Advances in infancy research* (Vol. 9). Norwood, NJ: Ablex.

Best, D. L. (2001). Cross-cultural gender roles. In J. Worell (Ed.), *Encylopedia of women and gender* (Vol. 1). San Diego, CA: Academic Press.

Best, D. L., & Williams, J. E. (1993). A cross-cultural viewpoint. In A. E. Beall & R. J. Sternberg (Eds.), *The psychology of gender.* New York: Guilford.

Bever, T. G. (Ed.). (1982). *Regressions in mental development: Basic phenomena and theories.* Hillsdale, NJ: Erlbaum.

Bhana, K. (1984). The development of gender understanding in children. *South African Journal of Psychology, 14,* 10–13.

Bhavnagri, N., & Parke, R. D. (1991). Parents as direct facilitators of children's peer relationships: Effects of age of child and sex of parent. *Journal of Social and Personal Relationships, 8,* 423–440.

Bialystok, E. (2001). *Bilingualism in development: Language, literacy, and cognition.* New York: Cambridge University Press.

Bibace, R., & Walsh, M. E. (1983). Children's conceptions of illness. In R. Bibace & M. E. Walsh (Eds.), *New directions for child development: No. 14. Children's conceptions of health, illness, and bodily functions.* San Francisco: Jossey Bass.

Bickerton, D. (1984). The language bioprogram hypothesis. *Behavioral and Brain Sciences, 7,* 173–187.

Bielinski, J. C., & Davison, M. L. (1998). Gender differences by item difficulty interactions in multiple-choice mathematics items. *American Educational Research Journal, 35,* 455–476.

Biernat, M. (1991). A multicomponent, developmental analysis of sex typing. *Sex Roles, 24,* 567–586.

Bigelow, A. E. (1981). The correspondence between self- and image movement as a cue to self-recognition for young children. *Journal of Genetic Psychology, 139,* 11–26.

Bigler, R. S., Brown, C. S., & Markell, M. (2001). When groups are not created equal: Effects of group status on the formation of intergroup attitudes in children. *Child Development, 72,* 1151–1162.

Bigler, R. S., & Liben, L. S. (1990). The role of attitudes and interventions in gender-schematic processing. *Child Development, 61,* 1440–1452.

Bigler, R. S., & Liben, L. S. (1992). Cognitive mechanisms in children's gender stereotyping: Theoretical and educational implications of a cognitive-based intervention. *Child Development, 64,* 1351–1363.

Bigler, R. S., & Liben, L. S. (1993). A cognitive-developmental approach to social stereotyping and reconstructive memory in Euro-American children. *Child Development, 64,* 1507–1518.

Biological systems. (1988, June 10). *Science, 240,* p. 1383.

Birnholz, J. C., & Benacerraf, B. R. (1983). The development of human fetal hearing. *Science, 222,* 516–518.

Biro, F. M., McMahon, R. P., Striegel-Moore, R., Crawford, P. B., Obarzanek, E., Morrison, J. A., et al. (2001). Impact of timing of pubertal maturation on growth in black and white female adolescents: The National Heart, Lung, and Blood Institute Growth and Health Study. *Journal of Pediatrics, 138,* 636–643.

Bisanz, J., & Lefevre, J. (1990). Strategic and nonstrategic processing in the development of mathematical cognition. In D. F. Bjorklund (Ed.), *Children's strategies: Contemporary views of cognitive development.* Hillsdale, NJ: Erlbaum.

Bjorklund, D. F. (1987). How age changes in knowledge base contribute to the development of children's memory: An interpretive review. *Developmental Review, 7,* 93–130.

Bjorklund, D. F. (Ed.). (1990). *Children's strategies: Contemporary views of cognitive development.* Hillsdale, NJ: Erlbaum.

Bjorklund, D. F. (1997). The role of immaturity in human development. *Psychological Bulletin, 122,* 153–169.

Bjorklund, D. F. (2000a). *Children's thinking* (3rd ed.). Belmont, CA: Wadsworth.

Bjorklund, D. F. (Ed.). (2000b). *False-memory creation in children and adults: Theory, research, and implications.* Mahwah, NJ: Erlbaum.

Bjorklund, D. F., & Coyle, T. R. (1995). Utilization deficiencies in the development of memory strategies. In F. E. Weinert & W. Schneider (Eds.), *Memory performance and competencies: Issues in growth and development.* Mahwah, NJ: Erlbaum.

Bjorklund, D. F., & Kipp, K. (1996). Parental investment theory and gender differences in the evolution of inhibition mechanisms. *Psychological Bulletin, 120,* 163–188.

Bjorklund, D. F., Muir-Broaddus, J. E., & Schneider, W. (1990). The role of knowledge in the development of strategies. In D. F. Bjorklund (Ed.), *Children's strategies: Contemporary views of cognitive development.* Hillsdale, NJ: Erlbaum.

Bjorklund, D. F., & Pellegrini, A. D. (2000). Child development and evolutionary psychology. *Child Development, 71,* 1687–1708.

Bjorklund, D. F., & Pellegrini, A. D. (2002a). Evolutionary perspectives on social development. In P. K. Smith & C. H. Hart (Eds.), *Blackwell handbook of childhood social development.* Madden, MA: Blackwell Publishers.

Bjorklund, D. F., & Pellegrini, A. D. (2002b). *The origins of human nature: Evolutionary developmental psychology.* Washington, DC: American Psychological Association.

Bjorklund, D. F., & Rosenblum, K. E. (2001). Children's use of multiple and variable addition strategies in a game context. *Developmental Science, 4,* 184–194.

Bjorklund, D. F., & Rosenblum, K. E. (2002). Context effects in children's selection and use of simple arithmetic strategies. *Journal of Cognition and Development, 3,* 225–242.

Bjorklund, D. F., & Schneider, W. (1996) The interaction of knowledge, aptitude, and strategies in children's memory performance. In H. W. Reese (Ed.), *Advances in child development and behavior* (Vol. 26). San Diego, CA: Academic Press.

Bjorklund, D. F., Younger, J. L., & Pellegrini, A. D. (2002). The evolution of parenting and evolutionary approaches to childrearing. In M. H. Bornstein (Ed.), *Handbook of parenting* (2nd ed., Vol. 2). Mahwah, NJ: Erlbaum.

Blake, J. (2000). *Routes to child language.* New York: Cambridge University Press.

Blanchard, R., & Bogaert, A. F. (1996). Homosexuality in men and number of older brothers. *American Journal of Psychiatry, 153,* 27–31.

Blanchard, R., & Klassen, P. (1997). H-Y antigen and homosexuality in men. *Journal of Theoretical Biology, 185,* 373–378.

Blanchard, R., & Zucker, K. J. (1994). Reanalysis of Bell, Weinberg, and Hammersmith's data on birth order, sibling sex ratio, and parental age in homosexual men. *American Journal of Psychiatry, 151,* 1375–1376.

Blanchard, R., Zucker, K. J., Cavacas, A., Allin, S., Bradley, S. J., & Schachter, D. C. (2002). Fraternal birth order and birth weight in probably prehomosexual feminine boys. *Hormones and Behavior, 41,* 321–327.

Blascovich, J., Spencer, S. J., Quinn, D. M., & Steele, C. M. (2001). African Americans and high blood pressure: The role of stereotype threat. *Psychological Science, 12,* 225–229.

Blasi, A. (1980). Bridging moral cognition and moral action: A critical review of the literature. *Psychological Bulletin, 88,* 1–45.

Blasi, A. (1983). Moral cognition and moral action: A theoretical perspective. *Developmental Review, 3,* 178–210.

Blasi, A., & Glodis, K. (1995). The development of identity: A critical analysis from the perspective of the self as subject. *Developmental Review, 15,* 404–433.

Blass, E. M., Ganchrow, J. R., & Steiner, J. E. (1984). Classical conditioning in newborn humans 2–48 hours of age. *Infant Behavior and Development, 7,* 223–235.

Blass, E. M., & Smith, B. A. (1992). Differential effects of sucrose, fructose, glucose, and lactose. *Developmental Psychology, 28,* 804–810.

Block, J., & Robins, R. W. (1993). A longitudinal study of consistency and change in self-esteem from early adolescence to early adulthood. *Child Development, 64,* 909–923.

Blok, H., Oostdam, R., Otter, M. E., & Overmaat, M. (2002). Computer-assisted instruction in support of beginning reading instruction: A review. *Review of Educational Research, 72,* 101–130.

Bloom, L. (1973). *One word at a time.* The Hague, Netherlands: Mouton.

Bloom, L. (1993, Winter). Word learning. *SRCD Newsletter,* 1–13.

Bloom, L. (1998). Language acquisition in developmental contexts. In W. Damon (Series Ed.) & D. Kuhn & R. S. Siegler (Vol. Eds.), *Handbook of child psychology: Vol. 2. Cognition, perception, and language* (5th ed.). New York: Wiley.

Bloom, L., Hood, L., & Lightbrown, N. P. (1974). Imitation in language development: If, when, and why. *Cognitive Psychology, 6,* 380–420.

Bloom, L., Lightbrown, P., & Hood, L. (1975). Structure and variation in child language. *Monographs of the Society for Research in Child Development, 40*(2, Serial No. 160).

Bloom, L., Margulis, C., Tinker, E., & Fujita, N. (1996). Early conversations and word learning: Contributions from child and adult. *Child Development, 67,* 3154–3175.

Bloom, P. (1996). Controversies in language acquisition: Word learning and the part of speech. In R. Gelman & T. Au (Eds.), *Perceptual and cognitive development.* San Diego, CA: Academic Press.

Bloom, P. (2000). *How children learn the meanings of words.* Cambridge, MA: MIT Press.

Bloom, P., & Markson, L. (1998). Intention and analogy in children's naming of pictorial representations. *Psychological Science, 9,* 200–204.

Blount, B. G. (1982). The ontogeny of emotions and their vocal expression in infants. In S. A. Kuczaj (Ed.), *Language development* (Vol. 2). Hillsdale, NJ: Erlbaum.

Bluma-Kulka, S., & Snow, C. E. (1992). Developing autonomy for tellers, tales, and telling in family narrative events. *Journal of Narrative Life History, 2,* 187–217.

Blyth, D. A., Simmons, R. G., & Carlton-Ford, S. (1983). The adjustment of early adolescents to school transitions. *Journal of Early Adolescence, 3,* 105–120.

Boccia, M., & Campos, J. J. (1989). Maternal emotional signals, social referencing, and infants' reactions to strangers. In N. Eisenberg (Ed.), *New directions for child development: No. 44. Empathy and related emotional responses.* San Francisco: Jossey-Bass.

Boer, F., & Westenberg, P. M. (1994). The factor structure of the Buss and Plomin EAS Temperament Survey (Parental Ratings) in a Dutch sample of elementary school children. *Journal of Personality Assessment, 62,* 537–551.

Bogartz, R., Shinskey, J. L., & Schilling, T. H. (2000) Object permanence in five-and-a-half-month-old infants? *Infancy, 1,* 403–428.

Boggiano, A. K., Main, D. S., & Katz, P. A. (1988). Children's preference for challenge: The role of perceived competence and control. *Journal of Personality and Social Psychology, 54,* 134–141.

Bohannon, J. N. III, Padgett, R. J., Nelson, K. E., & Mark, M. (1996). Useful evidence on negative evidence. *Developmental Psychology, 32,* 551–555.

Bohannon, J. N. III, & Stanowicz, L. (1988). The issue of negative evidence: Adult responses to children's language errors. *Developmental Psychology, 24,* 684–689.

Bohlin, G., Hagekull, B., & Rydell, A. (2000). Attachment and social functioning: A longitudinal study from infancy to middle childhood. *Social Development, 9,* 24–39.

Boismer, J. D. (1977). Visual stimulation and wake–sleep behavior in human neonates. *Developmental Psychology, 10,* 219–227.

Boldizar, J. P., Perry, D. G., & Perry, L. C. (1989). Outcome values and aggression. *Child Development, 60,* 571–579.

Bolger, K. E., & Patterson, C. J. (2001). Developmental pathways from child maltreatment to peer rejection. *Child Development, 72,* 549–568.

Boom, I., Hoijink, H., & Kunnen, S. (2001). Rules in the balance: Classes, strategies, or rules for the balance scale task? *Cognitive Development, 16,* 717–735.

Borke, H. (1975). Piaget's mountains revisited: Changes in the egocentric landscape. *Developmental Psychology, 11,* 240–243.

Bornstein, M. H. (1998). Stability in mental development from early life: Methods, measures, models, meanings, and myths. In F. Simion & G. Butterworth (Eds.), *The development of sensory, motor and cognitive capacities in early infancy: From perception to cognition.* Hove, UK: Psychology Press.

Bornstein, M. H., & Arterberry, M. E. (1999). Perceptual development. In M. H. Bornstein & M. E. Lamb (Eds.), *Developmental psychology: An advanced textbook* (4th ed.) Mahwah, NJ: Erlbaum.

Bornstein, M. H., DiPietro, J. A., Hahn, C., Painter, K., Haynes, O. M., & Costigan, K. A. (2002). Prenatal cardiac function and postnatal cognitive development: An exploratory study. *Infancy, 3,* 475–494.

Bornstein, M. H., Haynes, O. M., O'Reilly, A. W., & Painter, K. M. (1996). Solitary and collaborative pretense play in early childhood: Sources of individual variation in the development of representational competence. *Child Development, 67,* 2910–2929.

Bornstein, M. H., Haynes, O. M., Pascual, L., Painter, K. M., & Galperin, C. (1999). Play in two societies: Pervasiveness of process, specificity of structure. *Child Development, 70,* 317–331.

Bornstein, M. H., & Sigman, M. D. (1986). Continuity in mental development from infancy. *Child Development, 57,* 251–274.

Bornstein, M. H., Tal, J., & Tamis-LaMonda, C. S. (1991). Parenting in cross-cultural perspective: The United States, France, and Japan. In M. H. Bornstein (Ed.), *Cultural approaches to parenting.* Hillsdale, NJ: Erlbaum.

Bornstein, M. H., & Tamis-LaMonda, C. S. (1990). Activities and interactions of mothers and their firstborn infants in the first six months of life: Covariation, stability, continuity, correspondence, and prediction. *Child Development, 61,* 1206–1217.

Bornstein, M. H., Toda, H., Azuma, C. S., Tamis-LeMonda, C. S., & Ogino, M. (1990). Mother and infant activity and interaction in Japan and in the United States: II. A comparative microanalysis of naturalistic exchanges focused on the organization of infant attention. *International Journal of Behavioral Development, 13,* 289–308.

Bosacki, S., & Astington, J. W. (1999). Theory of mind in preadolescence: Relations between social understanding and social competence. *Social Development, 8,* 237–255.

Bosch, L., & Sebastian-Galles, N. (2001). Evidence of early language discrimination abilities in infants from bilingual environments. *Infancy, 2,* 29–50.

Boston, M. B., & Levy, G. D. (1991). Changes and differences in preschoolers' understanding of gender scripts. *Cognitive Psychology, 6,* 417–432.

Bosworth, K., Espelage, D. L., & Simon, T. R. (1999). Factors associated with bullying behavior in middle school students. *Journal of Early Adolescence, 19,* 341–362.

Bottoms, B. L., & Goodman, G. S. (Eds.). (1996). *International perspectives on child abuse and children's testimony: Psychological research and law.* Thousand Oaks, CA: Sage.

Bottoms, B. L., Goodman, G. S., Schwartz-Kenney, B. M., Sachsenmaier, T., & Thomas, S. (1990, March). *Keeping secrets: Implications for children's testimony.* Paper presented at the American Psychology and Law Society Meeting, Williamsburg, VA.

Bouchard, T. J. Jr. (1997). IQ similarity in twins reared apart: Findings and responses to critics. In R. J. Sternberg & E. L. Grigorenko (Eds.), *Intelligence, heredity, and environment.* New York: Cambridge University Press.

Bouchard, T. J. Jr., Lykken, D. T., McGue, M., Segal, N. L., & Tellegen, A. (1990). Sources of human psychological differences: The Minnesota Study of Twins Reared Apart. *Science, 250,* 223–228.

Bouchard, T. J. Jr., & McGue, M. (1981). Familial studies of intelligence: A review. *Science, 212,* 1055–1059.

Bowerman, M. (1975). Cross-linguistic similarities at two stages of syntactic development. In E. H. Lenneberg & E. E. Lenneberg (Eds.), *Foundations of language: A multidisciplinary approach.* New York: Academic Press.

Bowerman, M. (1976). Semantic factors in the acquisition of rules for word use and sentence construction. In D. M. Morehead & A. E. Morehead (Eds.), *Normal and deficient child language.* Baltimore: University Park Press.

Bowerman, M. (1982). Reorganizational processes in lexical and syntactic development. In E. Wanner & L. R. Gleitman (Eds.), *Language acquisition: The state of the art.* New York: Cambridge University Press.

Bowerman M. (1988). Inducing the latent structure of language. In F. S. Kessel (Ed.), *The development of language and language researchers: Essays in honor of Roger Brown.* Hillsdale, NJ: Erlbaum.

Bowlby, J. (1969). *Attachment and loss: Vol. 1. Attachment.* New York: Basic Books.

Bowlby, J. (1973). *Attachment and loss: Vol. 2. Separation.* New York: Basic Books.

Bowlby, J. (1980). *Attachment and loss: Vol. 3. Loss.* New York: Basic Books.

Bowlby, J. (1982). *Attachment and loss: Vol. 1. Attachment* (2nd ed.). New York: Basic Books. (Original work published 1969)

Bowlby, J. (1988). *A secure base: Parent–child attachment and healthy human development.* New York: Basic Books.

Boyes, M. C., & Allen, S. G. (1993). Styles of parent–child interaction and moral reasoning in adolescence. *Merrill-Palmer Quarterly, 39,* 551–570.

Boysson-Bardies, B. (1999). *How language comes to children.* Cambridge, MA: MIT Press.

Brackbill, Y., Adams, G., Crowell, D. H., & Gray, M. L. (1966). Arousal level in neonates and preschool children under continuous auditory stimulation. *Journal of Experimental Child Psychology, 4,* 178–188.

Bradbard, M. R., Martin, C. L., Endsley, R. C., & Halverson, C. F. (1986). Influence of sex stereotypes on children's exploration and memory: A competence versus performance distinction. *Developmental Psychology, 22,* 481–486.

Braddick, O., & Atkinson, J. (1988). Sensory selectivity, attentional control, and cross-channel integration in early visual development. In A. Yonas (Ed.), *Minnesota symposia on child psychology: Vol. 20. Perceptual development in infancy.* Hillsdale, NJ: Erlbaum.

Bradley, C. B., McMurray, R. G., Harrell, J. S., & Deng, S. (2000). Changes in common activities of 3rd though 10th graders: The CHIC study. *Medicine and Science in Sports and Exercise, 32,* 2071–2078.

Bradley, R. H. (1994). The HOME inventory: Review and reflections. In H. W. Reese (Ed.), *Advances in child development and behavior* (Vol. 25). San Diego, CA: Academic Press.

Bradley, R. H. (1999). The home environment. In S. L. Friedman & T. D. Wachs (Eds.), *Measuring environment across the life span: Emerging methods and concepts.* Washington, DC: APA.

Bradley, R. H., & Caldwell, B. M. (1984a). 174 children: A study of the relationship between home environment and cognitive development during the first 5 years. In A. W. Gottfried (Ed.), *Home environment and early cognitive development.* New York: Academic Press.

Bradley, R. H., & Caldwell, B. M. (1984b). The relation of infants' home environments to achievement test performance in first grade: A follow-up study. *Child Development, 55,* 803–809.

Bradley, R. H., & Corwyn, R. F. (2002). Socioeconomic status and child development. *Annual Review of Psychology, 53,* 371–399.

Bradley, R. H., Corwyn, R. F., Burchinal, M., McAdoo, H. P., & Coll, C. G. (2001). The home environments of children in the United States Part II: Relations with behavioral development through age 13. *Child Development, 72,* 1868–1886.

Bradley, R. H., Mundfrom, D. J., Whiteside, L., Casey, P. H., & Barrett, K. (1994). A factor analytic study of the Infant-Toddler and Early Childhood versions of the HOME inventory administered to White, Black, and Hispanic American parents of children born preterm. *Child Development, 65,* 880–888.

Braine, M. D. S. (1976). Children's first word combinations. *Monographs of the Society for Research in Child Development, 41*(1, Serial No. 164).

Braine, M. D. S., & Rumain, B. (1983). Logical reasoning. In P. H. Mussen (Series Ed.) & J. H. Flavell & E. M. Markman (Vol. Eds.), *Handbook of child psychology: Vol. 3. Cognitive development* (4th ed.). New York: Wiley.

Branigan, G. (1979). Some reasons why successive single word utterances are not. *Journal of Child Language, 6,* 411–421.

Braungart, J. M., Fulker, D. W., & Plomin, R. (1992). Genetic mediation of the home environment during infancy: A sibling adoption study of the HOME. *Developmental Psychology, 28,* 1048–1055.

Braungart, J. M., Plomin, R., DeFries, J. C., & Fulker, D. W. (1992). Genetic influence on tester-rated infant temperament as assessed by Bayley's Infant Behavior Record: Non-adoptive and adoptive siblings and twins. *Developmental Psychology, 28,* 40–47.

Braungart-Rieker, J. M., Garwood, M. M., Powers, B. P., & Wang, X. (2001). Parental sensitivity, infant affect, and affect regulation: Predictors of later attachment. *Child Development, 72,* 252–270.

Brazelton, T. B. (1982). Joint regulation of neonate-parent behavior. In E. Z. Tronick (Ed.), *Social interchange in infancy: Affect, cognition, and communication.* Baltimore: University Park Press.

Brazelton, T. B., & Nugent, J. K. (1995). *Neonatal Behavioral Assessment Scale* (3rd ed.). London: Mac Keith Press.

Brazelton, T. B., & Yogman, M. W. (Eds.). (1986). *Affective development in infancy.* Norwood, NJ: Ablex.

Breedlove, S. M., & Hampson, E. (2002). Sexual differentiation of the brain and behavior. In J. B. Becker, S. M. Breedlove, D. Crews, & M. M. McCarthy (Eds.), *Behavioral endocrinology* (2nd ed). Cambridge, MA: MIT Press.

Bretherton, I. (1987). New perspectives on attachment relations: Security, communication, and internal working models. In J. D. Osofsky (Ed.), *Handbook of infant development* (2nd ed.). New York: Wiley.

Bretherton, I. (1988). How to do things with one word: The ontogenesis of intentional message making in infancy. In M. D. Smith & J. L. Locke (Eds.), *The emergent lexicon.* San Diego, CA: Academic Press.

Bretherton, I. (1993). From dialogue to internal working models: The co-construction of self in relationships. In C. A. Nelson (Ed.), *Minnesota symposia on child development: Vol. 26. Memory and affect in development.* Hillsdale, NJ: Erlbaum.

Bretherton, I. (1995). The origins of attachment theory: John Bowlby and Mary Ainsworth. In S. Goldberg, R. Muir, & J. Kerr (Eds.), *Attachment theory: Social, developmental, and clinical perspectives.* Hillsdale, NJ: Analytic Press.

Bretherton, I., & Beeghly, M. (1982). Talking about internal states: The acquisition of an explicit theory of mind. *Developmental Psychology, 18,* 906–921.

Brisk, M. (1998). *Bilingual education: From compensatory to quality schooling.* Mahwah, NJ: Erlbaum.

Broberg, A., Lamb, M. E., & Hwang, P. (1990). Inhibition: Its stability and correlates in sixteen- to forty-month-old children. *Child Development, 61,* 1153–1163.

Broderick, P. C. (1998). Early adolescent gender differences in the use of ruminative and distracting coping strategies. *Journal of Early Adolescence, 18,* 173–191.

Broderick, P. C., & Korteland, C. (2002). Coping style and depression in early adolescence: Relationships to gender, gender role, and implicit beliefs. *Sex Roles, 46,* 201–213.

Brody, G. H. (Ed.). (1996). *Sibling relationships: Their causes and consequences.* Norwood, NJ: Ablex.

Brody, G. H. (1998). Sibling relationship quality: Its causes and consequences. *Annual Review of Psychology, 49,* 1–24.

Brody, G.H., & Flor, D. L. (1998). Maternal resources, parenting practices, and child competence in rural single-parent African American families. *Child Development, 69,* 803–816.

Brody, G. H., & Shaffer, D. R. (1982). Contributions of parents and peers to children's moral socialization. *Developmental Review, 2,* 31–75.

Brody, G. H., Stoneman, Z., & McCoy, J. K. (1994). Forecasting sibling relationships in early adolescence from child temperament and family processes in middle childhood. *Child Development, 65,* 771–778.

Brody, L. R. (1999). *Gender, emotion, and the family.* Cambridge, MA: Harvard University Press.

Brody, N. (1997). Intelligence, schooling, and society. *American Psychologist, 52,* 1046–1050.

Brodzinsky, D. M., Lang, R., & Smith, D. W. (1995). Parenting adopted children. In M. H. Bornstein (Ed.), *Handbook of parenting: Vol. 3. Status and social conditions of parenting.* Mahwah, NJ: Erlbaum.

Brodzinsky, D. M., & Pinderhughes, E. (2002). Parenting and child development in adoptive families. In M. H. Bornstein (Ed.), *Handbook of parenting* (2nd ed., Vol. 1). Mahwah, NJ: Erlbaum.

Bronfenbrenner, U. (1979). *The ecology of human development: Experiments by nature and design.* Cambridge, MA: Harvard University Press.

Bronfenbrenner, U. (1986). Recent advances in research on human development. In R. K. Silbereisen, K. Eyferth, & G. Rudinger (Eds.), *Development as action in context: Problem behavior and normal youth development.* New York: Springer-Verlag.

Bronfenbrenner, U. (1992). Ecological systems theory. In R. Vasta (Ed.), *Six theories of child development: Revised formulations and current issues.* London: Kingsley.

Bronfenbrenner, U. (1993). The ecology of cognitive development: Research models and fugitive findings. In R. H. Wozniak & K. W. Fischer (Eds.), *Development in context.* Hillsdale, NJ: Erlbaum.

Bronfenbrenner, U. (1999). Environments in developmental perspective: Theoretical and operational models. In S. L. Friedman & T. D. Wachs (Eds.), *Measuring environment across the life span: Emerging methods and concepts.* Washington, DC: American Psychological Association.

Bronfenbrenner, U., & Ceci, S. J. (1994). Nature–nurture reconceptualized in developmental perspective: A bioecological model. *Psychological Review, 101,* 568–586.

Bronfenbrenner, U., & Morris, P. A. (1998). The ecology of developmental processes. In W. Damon (Series Ed.) & R. M. Lerner (Vol. Ed.), *Handbook of child psychology: Vol. 1. Theoretical models of human development* (5th ed.). New York: Wiley.

Bronstein, P. (1994). Differences in mothers' and fathers' behaviors toward children: Cross-cultural comparison. *Developmental Psychology, 20,* 995–1003.

Brooke, J. (1991, June 15). Signs of life in Brazil's industrial valley of death. *New York Times International,* p. 2.

Brooks-Gunn, J. (1987). Pubertal processes and girls' psychological adaptation. In R. M. Lerner & T. L. Foch

(Eds.), *Biological psychosocial interactions in early adolescence.* Hillsdale, NJ: Erlbaum.

Brooks-Gunn, J. (1991). Maturational timing variations in adolescent girls, consequences of. In R. M. Lerner, A. C. Petersen, & J. Brooks-Gunn (Eds.), *Encyclopedia of adolescence* (Vol. 2). New York: Garland.

Brooks-Gunn, J. (2003). Do you believe in magic? What we can expect from early childhood intervention programs. *Society for Research in Child Development Social Policy Report, 17* (1).

Brooks-Gunn, J., Duncan, G., & Aber, J. L. (Eds.). (1997). *Neighborhood poverty: Vol. 1. Context and consequences for children.* New York: Russell Sage Foundation.

Brooks-Gunn, J., Han, W., & Waldfogel, J. (2002). Maternal employment and child cognitive outcomes in the first three years of life: The NICHD Study of Early Child Care. *Child Development, 73,* 1052–1072.

Brooks-Gunn, J., & Lewis, M. (1984). The development of early visual self-recognition. *Developmental Review, 4,* 215–239.

Brooks-Gunn, J., & Reiter, E. O. (1990). The role of pubertal processes. In S. S. Feldman & G. R. Elliott (Eds.), *At the threshold: The developing adolescent.* Cambridge, MA: Harvard University Press.

Brown, A. L. (1997). Transforming schools into communities of thinking and learning about serious matters. *American Psychologist, 52,* 399–413.

Brown, A. L., & Campione, J. C. (1990). Communities of learning and thinking, or a context by any other name. In D. Kuhn (Ed.), *Developmental perspectives on teaching and learning thinking skills.* Basel, Switzerland: Karger.

Brown, A. L., Kane, M. J., & Echols, C. (1986). Young children's mental models determine analogical transfer across problems with a common goal structure. *Cognitive Development, 1,* 103–121.

Brown, A. L., & Palincsar, A. S. (1989). Guided cooperative learning and individual knowledge acquisition. In L. B. Resnick (Ed.), *Cognition and instruction: Issues and agendas.* Hillsdale, NJ: Erlbaum.

Brown, B. (1999). Optimizing expression of the common human genome for child development. *Current Directions in Psychological Science, 8,* 37–41.

Brown, B. B. (1990). Peer groups and peer cultures. In S. S. Feldman & G. R. Elliott (Eds.), *At the threshold: The developing adolescent.* Cambridge, MA: Harvard University Press.

Brown, B. B. (1999). "You're going out with *who?*": Peer group influences on adolescent romantic relationships. In W. Furman, B. B. Brown, & C. Feiring (Eds.), *The development of romantic relationships in adolescence.* Cambridge: Cambridge University Press.

Brown, J. S., Collins, A., & Duguid, P. (1989). Situated cognition and the culture of learning. *Educational Researcher, 18,* 32–42.

Brown, K. W., & Gottfried, A. W. (1986). Development of cross-modal transfer in early infancy. In L. P. Lipsitt & C. K. Rovee-Collier (Eds.), *Advances in infancy research* (Vol. 4). Norwood, NJ: Ablex.

Brown, L. M., Way, N., & Duff, J. L. (1999). The others in my I: Adolescent girls' friendships and peer relations. In N. G. Johnson, M. C. Roberts, & J. Worell (Eds.), *Beyond appearance: A new look at adolescent girls.* Washington, DC: American Psychological Association.

Brown, R. (1958a). How shall a thing be called? *Psychological Review, 65,* 14–21.

Brown, R. (1958b). *Words and things.* Glencoe, IL: Free Press.

Brown, R. (1973). *A first language: The early stages.* Cambridge, MA: Harvard University Press.

Brown, R., & Hanlon, C. (1970). Derivational complexity and order of acquisition in child speech. In J. R. Hayes

(Ed.), *Cognition and the development of language.* New York: Wiley.

Browne, C. A., & Woolley, J. D. (2001). Theory of mind in children's naming of drawings. *Journal of Cognition and Development, 2,* 389–411.

Brownell, C. A., & Brown, E. (1992). Peers and play in infants and toddlers. In V. B. Van Hasselt & M. Hersen (Eds.), *Handbook of social development.* New York: Plenum.

Brownell, C. A., & Carriger, M. S. (1990). Changes in cooperation and self-other differentiation during the second year. *Child Development, 61,* 1164–1174.

Brownell, C. A., & Strauss, M. A. (1984). Infant stimulation and development: Conceptual and empirical considerations. *Journal of Children in Contemporary Society, 6,* 109–130.

Bruch, H. (2001). *The golden cage: The enigma of anorexia nervosa.* Cambridge, MA: Harvard University Press.

Brum, G. D., & McKane, L. K. (1989). *Biology: Exploring life.* New York: Wiley.

Bruner, J. (1983). *Child's talk: Learning to use language.* New York: Norton.

Bruner, J. (1999). The intentionality of referring. In P. D. Zelazo, J. W. Astington, & D. R. Olson (Eds.), *Developing theories of intention.* Mahwah, NJ: Erlbaum.

Bruner, J., Roy, C., & Ratner, N. (1982). The beginnings of request. In K. E. Nelson (Ed.), *Children's language* (Vol. 3). Hillsdale, NJ: Erlbaum.

Bryant, B. K. (1985). The Neighborhood Walk: Sources of support in middle childhood. *Monographs of the Society for Research in Child Development, 50*(3, Serial No. 210).

Bryden, M. P. (1982). *Laterality: Functional asymmetry in the intact brain.* New York: Academic Press.

Bryson, K., & Casper, L. M. (1999). Coresident grandparents and grandchildren. *Current Population Reports.* Washington, DC: U.S. Department of Commerce.

Buckingham, D., & Shultz, T. R. (2000). The developmental course of distance, time, and velocity concepts: A generative connectionist model. *Journal of Cognition and Development, 1,* 305–345.

Bugental, D. B., & Goodnow, J. J. (1998). Socialization processes. In W. Damon (Series Ed.) & N. Eisenberg (Vol. Ed.), *Handbook of child psychology: Vol. 3. Social, emotional, and personality development* (5th ed.). New York: Wiley.

Bugental, D. B., & Happaney, K. (2002). Parental attributions. In M. H. Bornstein (Ed.), *Handbook of parenting* (2nd ed., Vol. 3). Mahwah, NJ: Erlbaum.

Buhrmester, D. (1990). Intimacy of friendship, interpersonal competence, and adjustment during preadolescence and adolescence. *Child Development, 61,* 1101–1111.

Buhrmester, D. (1992). The developmental courses of sibling and peer relationships. In F. Boer & J. Dunn (Eds.), *Children's sibling relationships: Developmental and clinical issues.* Hillsdale, NJ: Erlbaum.

Buhrmester, D. (1996). Need fulfillment, interpersonal competence, and the developmental contexts of early adolescent friendship. In W. M. Bukowski, A. F. Newcomb, & W. W. Hartup (Eds.), *The company they keep: Friendship in childhood and adolescence.* New York: Cambridge University Press.

Buhrmester, D., & Furman, W. (1990). Perceptions of sibling relationships during middle childhood and adolescence. *Child Development, 61,* 1387–1398.

Buhrmester, D., & Prager, K. (1995). Patterns and functions of self-disclosure during childhood and adolescence. In K. J. Rotenberg (Ed.), *Disclosure processes in children and adolescents.* New York: Cambridge University Press.

Bukowski, W. M., & Hoza, B. (1989). Popularity and friendship: Issues in theory, measurement, and outcome. In T. J. Berndt & G. W. Ladd (Eds.), *Peer relationships in child development.* New York: Wiley.

Bullock, M., & Lutkenhaus, P. (1988). The development of volitional behavior in the toddler years. *Child Development, 59,* 664–674.

Bullock, M., & Lutkenhaus, P. (1990). Who am I? Self-understanding in toddlers. *Merrill-Palmer Quarterly, 36,* 217–238.

Burchinal, M. R., Bryant, D. M., Lee, M. W., & Ramey, C. T. (1992). Early day care, infant-mother attachment, and maternal responsiveness in the infant's first year. *Early Childhood Research Quarterly, 7,* 383–396.

Burchinal, M. R., Peisner-Feinberg, E., Pianta, R., & Howes, C. (2002). Development of academic skills from preschool through second grade: Family and classroom predictors of developmental trajectories. *Journal of School Psychology, 40,* 415–436.

Burchinal, M. R., Roberts, J. E., Hooper, S., & Zeisel, S. A. (2000). Cumulative risk and early cognitive development: A comparison of statistical risk models. *Developmental Psychology, 36,* 793–807.

Burkam, D. T., Lee, V. E., & Smerdon, B. (1997). Gender and science learning early in high school: Subject matter and laboratory experiences. *American Educational Research Journal, 34,* 297–331.

Burton, R. V. (1963). The generality of honesty reconsidered. *Psychological Review, 70,* 481–499.

Burton, R. V. (1984). A paradox in theories and research in moral development. In W. M. Kurtines & J. L. Gewirtz (Eds.), *Morality, moral behavior, and moral development.* New York: Wiley.

Bushman, B. J. (2002). Does venting anger feed or extinguish the flame? Catharsis, rumination, distraction, anger and aggressive responding. *Personality and Social Psychology Bulletin, 28,* 724–731.

Bushman, B. J., & Huesmann, L. R. (2001). Effects of televised violence on aggression. In D. G. Singer & J. L. Singer (Eds.), *Handbook of children and the media.* Thousand Oaks, CA: Sage.

Bushnell, E. W. (1982). Visual-tactual knowledge in 8-, 9-, and 11-month-old infants. *Infant Behavior and Development, 5,* 63–75.

Bushnell, E. W. (1994). A dual-processing approach to cross-modal matching: Implications for development. In D. J. Lewkowicz & R. Lickliter (Eds.), *The development of intersensory perception: Comparative perspectives.* Hillsdale, NJ: Erlbaum.

Bushnell, I. W. R., Sai, F., & Mullin, J. T. (1989). Neonatal recognition of the mother's face. *British Journal of Developmental Psychology, 7,* 3–15.

Buss, A. H., & Plomin, R. (1984). *Temperament: Early developing personality traits.* Hillsdale, NJ: Erlbaum.

Buss, A. H., & Plomin, R. (1986). The EAS approach to temperament. In R. Plomin & J. Dunn (Eds.), *The study of temperament: Changes, continuities and challenges.* Hillsdale, NJ: Erlbaum.

Buss, D. M. (1999). *Evolutionary psychology: The new science of the mind.* Boston: Allyn and Bacon.

Buss, D. M., & Kenrick, D. T. (1998). Evolutionary social psychology. In D. T. Gilbert, S. T. Fiske, & G. Lindzey (Eds.), *The handbook of social psychology* (4th ed., Vol. 2). Boston: McGraw-Hill.

Bussey, K., & Bandura, A. (1984). Gender constancy, social power, and sex-linked modeling. *Journal of Personality and Social Psychology, 47,* 1292–1302.

Bussey, K., & Bandura, A. (1992). Self-regulatory mechanisms governing gender development. *Child Development, 63,* 1236–1250.

Bussey, K., & Bandura, A. (1999). Social-cognitive theory of gender development and differentiation. *Psychological Review, 106,* 676–713.

Bussey, K., & Perry, D. G. (1982). Same-sex imitation: The avoidance of cross-sex models or the acceptance of same-sex models? *Sex Roles, 8,* 773–784.

Butler, R. (1990). The effects of mastery and competitive conditions on self-assessment at different ages. *Child Development, 61,* 201–210.

Butler, R. (1992). What young people want to know when: The effects of mastery and ability on social information seeking. *Journal of Personality and Social Psychology, 62,* 934–943.

Butler, R. (1996). Effects of age and achievement goals on children's motives for attending to peer's work. *British Journal of Developmental Psychology, 14,* 1–18.

Butler, R., & Ruzany, N. (1993). Age and socialization effects on the development of social comparison motives and normative ability assessment in kibbutz and urban children. *Child Development, 64,* 532–543.

Butovskaya, M., Verbeek, P., Ljungberg, T., & Lunardini, A. (2000). A multicultural view of peacemaking among young children. In F. Aureli & F. B. M. de Waal (Eds.), *Natural conflict resolution.* Berkeley: University of California Press.

Butterworth, G. (1990). Self-perception in infancy. In D. Cicchetti & M. Beeghly (Eds.), *The self in transition: Infancy to childhood.* Chicago: University of Chicago Press.

Butterworth, G. (1995). The self as an object of consciousness in infancy. In P. Rochat (Ed.), *The self in infancy: Theory and research.* Amsterdam: Elsevier.

Buzzelli, C. A. (1995). Teacher-child discourse in the early childhood classroom: A dialogic model of self-regulation and moral development. In S. Reifel (Ed.), *Advances in early education and day care* (Vol. 7). Greenwich, CT: JAI Press.

Byrne, B. M. (1996). *Measuring self-concept across the life span: Issues and instrumentation.* Washington, DC: American Psychological Association.

Byrne, B., Delaland, C., Fielding-Barnsley, R., Quain, P., Samuelsson, S., Hoien, T., et al. (2002). Longitudinal twin study of early reading development in three countries: Preliminary results. *Annals of Dyslexia, 52,* 49–73.

Byrnes, J. P. (1988). Formal operations: A systematic reformulation. *Developmental Review, 8,* 66–87.

Byrnes, J. P., Miller, D. C., & Schafer, W. D. (1999). Gender differences in risk taking: A meta-analysis. *Psychological Bulletin, 125,* 367–383.

Cain, K. M., & Dweck, C. S. (1995). The relation between motivational patterns and achievement cognitions through the elementary years. *Merrill-Palmer Quarterly, 41,* 25–52.

Cairns, E. (1987). *Caught in crossfire: Children and the Northern Ireland conflict.* Belfast: Appletree Press.

Cairns, E. (1996). *Children and political violence.* Oxford: England: Blackwell.

Cairns, R. B., & Cairns, B. D. (1988). The sociogenesis of self concepts. In N. Bolger, A. Caspi, G. Downey, & M. Moorehouse (Eds.), *Persons in context: Developmental processes.* New York: Cambridge University Press.

Cairns, R. B., Cairns, B. D., Neckerman, H. J., Ferguson, L. L., & Gariepy, J. (1989). Growth and aggression: I. Childhood to early adolescence. *Developmental Psychology, 25,* 320–330.

Cairns, R. B., Cairns, B. D., Neckerman, H. J., Gest, S. D., & Gariepy, J. (1988). Social networks and aggressive behavior: Peer support or peer rejection? *Developmental Psychology, 24,* 815–823.

Cairns, R. B., MacCombie, D. J., & Hood, K. E. (1983). A developmental-genetic analysis of aggressive behavior in mice: I. Behavioral outcomes. *Journal of Comparative Psychology, 97,* 69–89.

Caldera, Y. M., Huston, A. C., & O'Brien, M. (1989). Social interactions and play patterns of parents and toddlers with feminine, masculine, and neutral toys. *Child Development, 60,* 70–76.

Caldwell, B. M., & Bradley, R. (1979). *Home observation for measurement of the environment.* Unpublished manuscript, University of Arkansas.

Calkins, S. D., Dedmon, S. E., Gill, K. L., Lomax, L. E., & Johnson, L. M. (2002). Frustration in infancy: Implications for emotion regulation, physiological processes, and temperament. *Infancy, 3,* 175–197.

Calkins, S. D., & Fox, N. A. (1992). The relations among infant temperament, security of attachment, and behavioral inhibition at twenty-four months. *Child Development, 63,* 1456–1472.

Callanan, M. A. (1985). How parents label objects for young children: The role of input in the acquisition of category hierarchies. *Child Development, 56,* 508–523.

Camarata, S., & Leonard, L. B. (1986). Young children pronounce object words more accurately than action words. *Journal of Child Language, 13,* 51–65.

Campbell, A., Shirley, L., & Caygill, L. (2002). Sex-typed preferences in three domains: Do two-year-olds need cognitive variables? *British Journal of Psychology, 93,* 203–217.

Campbell, D., & Eaton, W. O. (1999). Sex differences in the activity level of infants. *Infant and Child Development, 8,* 1–17.

Campbell, F. A., Pungello, E. P., Miller-Johnson, S., Burchinall, M., & Ramey, C. T. (2001). The development of cognitive and academic abilities: Growth curves from an early childhood educational experiment. *Developmental Psychology, 37,* 231–242.

Campbell, J. R., Hombo, C. M., & Mazzeo, J. (2000). *NAEP 1999 trends in academic progress: Three decades of student performance.* Washington, DC: U.S. Department of Education.

Campbell, R. L., & Christopher, J. C. (1996). Moral development theory: A critique of its Kantian presuppositions. *Developmental Review, 16,* 1–47.

Campbell, S. B. (2000). Attention-deficit/hyperactivity disorder: A developmental view. In A. Sameroff, M. Lewis, & S. M. Miller (Eds.), *Handbook of developmental psychopathology* (2nd ed.). New York: Plenum.

Campos, J. J., Anderson, D. I., Barbu-Roth, M. A., Hubbard, E. M., Hertenstein, M. J., & Witherington, D. (2000). Travel broadens the mind. *Infancy, 1,* 149–220.

Campos, J. J., Bertenthal, B. I., & Kermoian, R. (1992). Early experience and emotional development: The emergence of wariness of heights. *Psychological Science, 3,* 61–64.

Campos, J. J., Hiatt, S., Ramsay, D., Henderson, C., & Svejda, M. (1978). The emergence of fear on the visual cliff. In M. Lewis & L. Rosenblum (Eds.), *The origins of affect.* New York: Plenum.

Campos, J., Mumme, D., Kermoian, R., & Campos, R. (1994). A functionalist perspective on the nature of emotion. In N. Fox (Ed.), The development of emotion regulation: Biological and behavioral considerations. *Monographs of the Society for Research in Child Development, 59*(2–3, Serial No. 240).

Campos, R. G. (1989). Soothing pain-elicited distress in infants with swaddling and pacifiers. *Child Development, 60,* 781–792.

Camras, L. A., Malatesta, C. Z., & Izard, C. E. (1991). The development of facial expressions in infancy. In R. Felman & B. Rime (Eds.), *Fundamentals of nonverbal behavior.* Cambridge: Cambridge University Press.

Capizzano, J. & Adams, G. (2000, March). *The hours that children under five spend in child care: Variation across states. A report assessing the new federalism.* Washington, DC: Urban Institute.

Caplan, M., Vespo, J. E., Pedersen, J., & Hay, D. F. (1991). Conflict and its resolution in small groups of one- and two-year-olds. *Child Development, 62,* 1513–1524.

Capron, C., & Duyme, M. (1989). Assessment of effects of socio-economic status on IQ in a full cross-fostering study. *Nature, 340,* 552–554.

Cardon, L. R. (1994). Specific cognitive abilities. In J. C. DeFries, R. Plomin, & D. W. Fulker (Eds.), *Nature and* nurture during middle childhood. Oxford, England: Blackwell.

Carey, S. (1977). The child as word learner. In M. Halle, J. Bresnan, & G. A. Miller (Eds.), *Linguistic theory and psychological reality*. Cambridge, MA: MIT Press.

Carey, S. (1985). *Conceptual change in childhood*. Cambridge, MA: MIT Press.

Carey, W. B., & McDevitt, S. C. (1978). Revision of the Infant Temperament Questionnaire. *Pediatrics, 61*, 735–739.

Carlson, V., Cicchetti, D., Barnett, D., & Braunwald, K. G. (1989). Finding order in disorganization: Lessons from research on maltreated infants' attachments to their caregivers. In D. Cicchetti & V. Carlson (Eds.), *Child maltreatment: Theory and research on the causes and consequences of child abuse and neglect*. New York: Cambridge University Press.

Carmichael, S. L., & Shaw, G. M. (2000). Maternal life event stress and congenital anomalies. *Epidemiology, 11*, 30–35.

Carnegie Task Force. (1994). *Starting points: Meeting the needs of our youngest children*. New York: Carnegie Corporation of New York.

Caron, A. J., Caron, R. F., & MacLean, D. J. (1988). Infant discrimination of naturalistic emotional expressions: The role of face and voice. *Child Development, 59*, 604–616.

Carpendale, J. I. M., & Krebs, D. L. (1995). Variations in moral judgment as a function of type of dilemma and moral choice. *Journal of Personality, 63*, 289–313.

Carpenter, T. P., & Lewis, R. (1976). The development of the concept of a standard unit of measure in young children. *Journal for Research in Mathematics Education, 7*, 53–59.

Carr, M., & Jessup, D. L. (1997). Gender differences in first grade mathematics strategy use: Social and metacognitive influences. *Journal of Educational Psychology, 98*, 318–328.

Carr, M., Jessup, D. L., & Fuller, D. (1999). Gender differences in first-grade mathematics strategy use: Parent and teacher contributions. *Journal for Research in Mathematics Education, 30*, 20–46.

Carr, M., Kurtz, B. E., Schneider, W., Turner, L. A., & Borkowski, J. G. (1989). Strategy acquisition and transfer among American and German children: Environmental influences on meta-cognitive development. *Developmental Psychology, 25*, 765–771.

Carraher, T. N., Carraher, D. W., & Schliemann, A. D. (1985). Mathematics in the streets and schools. *British Journal of Developmental Psychology, 3*, 21–29.

Carter, D. B., & Levy, G. D. (1988). Cognitive aspects of early sex-role development: The influence of gender schemas on preschoolers' memories and preferences for sex-typed toys and activities. *Child Development, 59*, 782–792.

Carter, D. B., & McCloskey, L. A. (1984). Peers and maintenance of sex-typed behavior: The development of children's conceptions of cross-gender behavior in their peers. *Social Cognition, 2*, 294–314.

Carter, D. B., & Patterson, C. J. (1982). Sex roles as social conventions: The development of children's conceptions of sex-role stereotypes. *Developmental Psychology, 18*, 812–824.

Carver, L. J., & Bauer, P. J. (2001). The dawning of a past: The emergence of long-term explicit memory in infancy. *Journal of Experimental Psychology: General, 130*, 726–745.

Case, R. (1985). *Intellectual development*. New York. Academic Press.

Case, R. (1991). Stages in the development of the young child's first sense of self. *Developmental Review, 11*, 210–230.

Case, R. (1992). *The mind's staircase: Exploring the conceptual underpinnings of children's thought and knowledge*. Hillsdale, NJ: Erlbaum.

Case, R., & Okamoto, Y. (1996). The role of central conceptual structures in the development of children's thought. *Monographs of the Society for Research in Child Development, 61* (1–2, Serial No. 246).

Casey, B. J., & de Haan, M. (2002). Introduction: New methods in developmental science. *Developmental Science, 5*, 265–267.

Casey, M. B., Nuttall, R. L., & Pezaris, E. (1997). Mediators of gender differences in mathematics college entrance test scores: A comparison of spatial skills with internalized beliefs and anxieties. *Developmental Psychology, 33*, 669–680.

Casey, M. B., Nuttall, R. L., & Pezaris, E. (1999). Evidence in support of a model that predicts how biological and environmental factors interact to influence spatial skills. *Developmental Psychology, 35*, 1237–1247.

Caspi, A. (1998). Personality development across the life span. In W. Damon (Series Ed.) & N. Eisenberg (Vol. Ed.), *Handbook of child psychology: Vol. 3. Social, emotional, and personality development* (5th ed.). New York: Wiley.

Caspi, A., Henry, B., McGee, R. O., Moffitt, T. E., & Silva, P. A. (1995). Temperamental origins of child and adolescent behavior problems: From age 3 to age 15. *Child Development, 66*, 55–68.

Caspi, A., Moffitt, T. E., Newman, D. L., & Silva, P. A. (1996). Behavioral observations at age 3 predict adult psychiatric disorders: Longitudinal evidence from a birth cohort. *Archives of General Psychiatry, 53*, 1033–1039.

Cassell, J., & Jenkins, H. (1998). Chess for girls? Feminism and computer games. In J. Cassell & H. Jenkins (Eds.), *From Barbie to Mortal Kombat: Gender and computer games*. Cambridge, MA: MIT Press.

Cassia, V. M., Simion, F., & Umilta, C. (2001). Face preference at birth: The role of an orienting mechanism. *Developmental Science, 4*, 101–108.

Cassidy, J., Kirsh, S. J., Scolton, K. L., & Parke, R. D. (1996). Attachment and representations of peer relationships. *Developmental Psychology, 32*, 892–904.

Catron, T. F., & Masters, J. C. (1993). Mothers' and children's conceptualizations of corporal punishment. *Child Development, 64*, 1815–1828.

Caudill, W., & Schooler, C. (1973). Child behavior and child rearing in Japan and the United States: An interim report. *Journal of Nervous and Mental Disease, 157*, 323–338.

Caudill, W., & Weinstein, H. (1969). Maternal care and infant behavior in Japan and America. *Psychiatry: Journal for the Study of Interpersonal Processes, 32*, 12–43.

Caughy, M. O. (1996). Health and environmental effects on the academic readiness of school-age children. *Developmental Psychology, 32*, 515–522.

Cavanaugh, J. C., & Perlmutter, M. (1982). Metamemory: A critical examination. *Child Development, 53*, 11–28.

Cazden, C. B., & John, V. P. (1971). Learning in American Indian children. In M. Wax, S. Diamond, & F. Goering (Eds.), *Anthropological perspectives on education*. New York: Basic Books.

Ceci, S. J. (1991). How much does schooling influence general intelligence and its cognitive components? A reassessment of the evidence. *Developmental Psychology, 27*, 703–722.

Ceci, S. J. (1992, September/October). Schooling and intelligence. *Psychological Science Agenda*, pp. 7–9.

Ceci, S. J. (1996). *On intelligence: A bioecological treatise on intellectual development* (expanded ed.). Cambridge, MA: Harvard University Press.

Ceci, S. J., & Bruck, M. (1995). *Jeopardy in the courtroom: A scientific analysis of children's testimony*. Washington, DC: American Psychological Association.

Ceci, S. J., & Bruck, M. (1998). Children's testimony. In W. Damon (Series Ed.) & I. E. Sigel & K. A. Renninger (Vol. Eds.), *Handbook of child psychology: Vol. 4. Child psychology in practice* (5th ed.). New York: Wiley.

Ceci, S. J., & Williams, W. M. (1997). Schooling, intelligence, and income. *American Psychologist, 52*, 1051–1058.

Centers for Disease Control (2002). Trends in sexual risk behaviors among high school students-United States. *Morbidity and Mortality Report Weekly, 51*, 856–859.

Chabra, A., & Chavez, G. F. (2000). A comparison of long pediatric hospitalizations in 1985 and 1994. *Journal of Community Health: The Publication for Health Promotion & Disease Prevention, 25*(3), 199–210.

Chamberlain, P., & Patterson, G. R. (1995). Discipline and child compliance in parenting. In M. H. Bornstein (Ed.), *Handbook of parenting: Vol. 4. Applied and practical parenting*. Mahwah, NJ: Erlbaum.

Chance, C., & Fiese, B. H. (1999). Gender-stereotyped lessons about emotion in family narratives. *Narrative Inquiry, 9*, 243–255.

Chandler, M. J. (1973). Egocentrism and antisocial behavior: The assessment and training of social perspective-taking skills. *Developmental Psychology, 9*, 326–332.

Chandler, M. J., Greenspan, S., & Barenboim, C. (1973). Judgments of intentionality in response to videotaped and verbally presented moral dilemmas: The medium is the message. *Child Development, 44*, 315–320.

Chandler, M. J., & Lalonde, C. (1996). Shifting to an interpretive theory of mind: 5-to-7-year-olds' changing conceptions of mental life. In A. J. Sameroff & M. M. Haith (Eds.), *The five to seven year shift: The age of reason and responsibility*. Chicago: University of Chicago Press.

Chao, R. (2001). Extending the research on the consequences of parenting style for Chinese Americans and European Americans. *Child Development, 72*, 1832–1843.

Chao, R., & Tseng, V. (2002). Parenting of Asians. In M. H. Bornstein (Ed.), *Handbook of parenting* (2nd ed., Vol. 3). Mahwah, NJ: Erlbaum.

Chapman, M. (1988). *Constructive evolution: Origins and development of Piaget's thought*. Cambridge: Cambridge University Press.

Chapman, M. (1992). Equilibration and the dialectics of organization. In H. Beilin & P. B. Pufall (Eds.), *Piaget's theory: Prospects and possibilities*. Hillsdale, NJ: Erlbaum.

Chapman, R. S., Streim, N. W., Crais, E. R., Salmon, D., Strand, E. A., & Negri, N. A. (1992). Child talk: Assumptions of a developmental process model for early language learning. In R. A. Chapman (Ed.), *Processes in language acquisition and disorders*. St. Louis, MO: Mosby Year Book.

Charach, A., Pepler, D., & Ziegler, S. (1995). Bullying at school. *Education Canada, 37*, 12–18.

Charlesworth, R., & Hartup, W. W. (1967). Positive social reinforcement in the nursery school peer group. *Child Development, 38*, 993–1002.

Charlesworth, W. R. (1992). Darwin and developmental psychology: Past and present. *Developmental Psychology, 28*, 5–16.

Charlesworth, W. R., & Dzur, C. (1987). Gender comparisons of preschoolers' behavior and resource utilization in group problem solving. *Child Development, 58*, 191–200.

Chasnoff, I. J., Schnoll, S. H., Burns, W. J., & Burns, K. (1984). Maternal narcotic substance abuse during pregnancy: Effects on infant development. *Neurobehavioral Toxicology and Teratology, 6*, 277–280.

Chavajay, P., & Rogoff, B. (1999). Cultural variation in management of attention by children and their caregivers. *Developmental Psychology, 35*, 1079–1090.

Chen, C., Greenberger, E., Lester, J., Dong, Q., & Guo, M. (1998). A cross-cultural study of family and peer correlates of adolescent misconduct. *Developmental Psychology, 34,* 770–781.

Chen, C., & Stevenson, H. W. (1988). Cross-linguistic differences in digit span of preschool children. *Journal of Experimental Child Psychology, 46,* 150–158.

Chen, C., & Stevenson, H. W. (1995). Motivation and mathematics achievement: A comparative study of Asian-American, Caucasian-American, and East Asian high school students. *Child Development, 66,* 1215–1234.

Chen, E., Bloomberg, G. R., Fisher, E. B. Jr., & Strunk, R. C. (2003). Predictors of repeat hospitalizations in children with asthma: The role of psychosocial and socioenvironmental factors. *Health Psychology, 22,* 12–18.

Chen, J., & Gardner, H. (1997). Alternative assessment from a multiple intelligences theoretical perspective. In D. P. Flanagan, J. L. Genshaft, & P. L. Harrison (Eds.), *Contemporary intellectual assessment.* New York: Guilford.

Chen, X. (2002). Peer relationships and networks and socio-emotional adjustment: A Chinese perspective. In B. Cairns & T. Farmer (Eds.), *Social networks from a developmental perspective.* New York: Cambridge University Press.

Chen, X. Liu, M., & Li, D. (2000). Parental control, warmth, and indulgence and their relations to adjustment in Chinese children: A longitudinal study. *Journal of Family Psychology, 14,* 401–419.

Chen, X., Rubin, K. H., & Li, Z. (1995). Social functioning and adjustment in Chinese children: A longitudinal study. *Developmental Psychology, 31,* 531–539.

Chen, X., Rubin, K. H., & Sun, Y. (1992). Social reputation and peer relationships in Chinese and Canadian children: A cross-cultural study. *Child Development, 63,* 1336–1343.

Chen, Z., Sanchez, R. P., & Campbell, T. (1997). From beyond to within their grasp: The rudiments of analogical problem solving in 10- and 13-month-olds. *Developmental Psychology, 33,* 790–801.

Chen, Z., & Siegler, R. S. (2000). Across the great divide; Bridging the gap between understanding of toddlers' and older children's thinking. *Monographs of the Society for Research in Child Development, 65,* (2), Serial No. 261.

Cherny, S. S. (1994). Home environmental influences on general cognitive ability. In J. C. DeFries, R. Plomin, & D. W. Fulker (Eds.), *Nature and nurture during middle childhood.* Cambridge, MA: Blackwell.

Cherny, S. S., & Cardon, L. R. (1994). General cognitive ability. In J. C. DeFries, R. Plomin, & D. W. Fulker (Eds.), *Nature and nurture during middle childhood.* Oxford, England: Blackwell.

Cherny, S. S., Fulker, D. W., Corley, R. P., Plomin, R., & DeFries, J. C. (1994a). Continuity and change in infant shyness from 14 to 20 months. *Behavior Genetics, 24,* 365–379.

Cherny, S. S., Fulker, D. W., Emde, R. N., Robinson, J., Corley, R. P., Reznick, J. S., et al. (1994b). A developmental-genetic analysis of continuity and change in the Bayley mental development index from 14 to 24 months: The MacArthur Longitudinal Twin Study. *Psychological Science, 5,* 354–360.

Chess, S., & Thomas, A. (1987). *Origins and evolution of behavior disorders: From infancy to early adult life.* Cambridge, MA: Harvard University Press.

Chi, M. T. H. (1978). Knowledge structures and memory development. In R. S. Siegler (Ed.), *Children's thinking: What develops?* Hillsdale, NJ: Erlbaum.

Chi, M. T. H., Glaser, R., & Farr, M. J. (Eds.). (1988). *The nature of expertise.* Hillsdale, NJ: Erlbaum.

Chi, M. T. H., & Koeske, R. D. (1983). Network representation of a child's dinosaur knowledge. *Developmental Psychology, 19,* 29–39.

Children's Defense Fund. (2002). *The state of children in America's union: A 2002 action guide to leave no child behind.* Washington, DC: Children's Defense Fund.

Chisolm, J. S. (1996). The evolutionary ecology of attachment organization. *Human Nature, 7,* 1–38.

Choi, S. (1997). Language-specific input and early semantic development: Evidence from children learning Korean. In D. I. Slobin (Ed.), *The crosslinguisitic study of language acquisition: Vol. 5. Expanding the contexts.* Mahwah, NJ: Erlbaum.

Choi, S. (2000). Caregiver input in English and Korean: Use of nouns and verbs in book-reading and toy-play contexts. *Journal of Child Language, 27,* 69–96.

Chomsky, N. (1959). A review of B. F. Skinner's Verbal Behavior. *Language, 35,* 26–58.

Chomsky, N. (1965). *Aspects of the theory of syntax.* Cambridge, MA: MIT Press.

Chomsky, N. (1995). *The minimalist program.* Cambridge, MA: MIT Press.

Chomsky, N. (2000). *New horizons in the study of language and mind.* New York: Cambridge University Press.

Christenson, S. L., & Sheridan, S. M. (2001). *School and families.* New York: Guilford.

Christian, K., Bachnan, H. J., & Morrison, F. J. (2001). Schooling and cognitive development. In R. J. Sternberg & E. L. Grigorenko (Eds.), *Environmental effects on cognitive abilities.* Mahwah, NJ: Erlbaum.

Church, R. B., & Goldin-Meadow, S. (1986). The mismatch between gesture and speech as an index of transitional knowledge. *Cognition, 23,* 43–71.

Cicchetti, D. (1991). Fractures in the crystal: Developmental psychopathology and the emergence of self. *Developmental Review, 11,* 271–287.

Cicchetti, D., Beeghly, M., Carlson, V., & Toth, S. (1990). The emergence of self in atypical populations. In D. Cicchetti & M. Beeghly (Eds.), *The self in transition: Infancy to childhood.* Chicago: University of Chicago Press.

Cicchetti, D., & Carlson, V. (Eds.), (1989). *Child maltreatment: Theory and research on the causes and consequences of child abuse and neglect.* New York: Cambridge University Press.

Cicchetti, D., Lynch, M., Shonk, S., & Manly, J. T. (1992). An organizational perspective on peer relations in maltreated children. In R. D. Parke & G. W. Ladd (Eds.), *Family-peer relationships: Modes of linkage.* Hillsdale, NJ: Erlbaum.

Cillessen, A. H. N., & Bukowski, W. M. (Eds.). (2000). Recent advances in the measurement of acceptance and rejection in the peer system. *New directions for child and adolescent development: No. 88.*

Cillessen, A. H. N., Bukowski, W. M., & Haselager, G. J. T. (2000). Stability of sociometric categories. In A. H. N. Cillessen & W. M. Burkowski (Eds.), *New directions for child and adolescent development: No. 88. Recent advances in the measurement of acceptance and rejection in the peer system.* San Francisco: Jossey-Bass.

Cillessen, A. H. N., Van IJzendoorn, H. W., Van Lishout, C. F. M., & Hartup, W. W. (1992). Heterogeneity among peer-rejected boys: Subtypes and stabilities. *Child Development, 63,* 893–905.

Clarke, A. M., & Clarke, A. D. B. (1976). *Early experience: Myth and evidence.* London: Open Books Publishing.

Clark, E. V. (1987). The principle of contrast: A constraint on language acquisition. In B. MacWhinney (Ed.), *Mechanisms of language acquisition.* Hillsdale, NJ: Erlbaum.

Clark, E. V. (1993). *The lexicon in acquisition.* New York: Cambridge University Press.

Clark, E. V. (1995). Later lexical development and word learning. In P. Fletcher & B. MacWhinney (Eds.), *The handbook of child language.* Cambridge, MA: Blackwell.

Clark, R., Hyde, J. S., Essex, M. J., & Klein, M. H. (1997). Length of maternity leave and quality of mother–infant interactions. *Child Development, 68,* 364–383.

Clarke-Stewart, K. A. (1989). Infant day care: Maligned or malignant? *American Psychologist, 44,* 266–273.

Clarke-Stewart, K. A., Gruber, C. P., & Fitzgerald, L. M. (1994). *Children at home and in day care.* Hillsdale, NJ: Erlbaum.

Clarke-Stewart, K. A., Vandell, D. L., McCartney, K., Owen, M. T., & Booth, C. (2000). Effects of parental separation and divorce on very young children. *Journal of Family Psychology, 14,* 304–326.

Cleveland, H. H., Jacobson, K. C., Lipinski, J. J., & Rowe, D. C. (2000). Genetic and shared environmental contributions to the relationship between the HOME environment and adolescent achievement. *Intelligence, 28,* 69–86.

Cleveland, H. H., & Wiebe, R. P. (2003). The moderation of adolescent-to-peer similarity in tobacco and alcohol use by school levels of substance use. *Child Development, 74,* 279–291.

Clewell, W. H., Johnson, M. L., Meier, P. R., Newkirk, J. B., Zide, S. L., Hendee, R. W., et al. (1982). A surgical approach to the treatment of fetal hydrocephalus. *New England Journal of Medicine, 306,* 1320–1325.

Clifton, R. K., Gwiazda, J., Bauer, J. A., Clarkson, M. G., & Held, R. M. (1988). Growth in head size during infancy: Implications for sound localization. *Developmental Psychology, 24,* 477–483.

Clumeck, H. V. (1980). The acquisition of tone. In G. H. Yeni-Komshian, J. Kavanagh, & C. A. Ferguson (Eds.), *Child phonology: Vol. 1. Production.* New York: Academic Press.

Cochran, M., & Niego, S. (2002). Parenting and social networks. In M. H. Bornstein (Ed.), *Handbook of parenting* (2nd ed., Vol. 4). Mahwah, NJ: Erlbaum.

Cohen, D. (1979). *J. B. Watson: The founder of behaviorism.* London: Routledge & Kegan Paul.

Cohen, D., & Strayer, J. (1996). Empathy in conduct-disordered and comparison youth. *Developmental Psychology, 32,* 988–998.

Cohen, L. B. (1972). Attention-getting and attention-holding processes of infant visual preference. *Child Development, 43,* 869–879.

Cohen, L. B. (1998). An information-processing approach to infant perception and cognition. In F. Simion & G. Butterworth (Eds.), *The development of sensory, motor and cognitive capacities in early infancy: From perception to cognition.* Hove, UK: Psychology Press.

Cohen, L. B., & Amsel, G. (1998). Precursors to infants' perception of the causality of a simple event. *Infant Behavior and Development, 21,* 713–731.

Cohen, L. B., & Marks, K. S. (2002). How infants process addition and subtraction events. *Developmental Science, 5,* 186–212.

Cohen, L. B., & Strauss, M. S. (1979). Concept acquisition in the human infant. *Child Development, 50,* 419–424.

Cohen, S. E. (1974). Developmental differences in infants' attentional responses to face–voice incongruity of mother and stranger. *Child Development, 45,* 1155–1158.

Cohen, S., & Wills, T. A. (1985). Stress, social support, and the buffering hypothesis. *Psychological Bulletin, 98,* 310–357.

Cohn, J. F., Campbell, S. B., Matias, R., & Hopkins, J. (1990). Face-to-face interactions of postpartum depressed and nondepressed mother–infant pairs at 2 months. *Developmental Psychology, 26,* 15–23.

Cohn, J. F., & Tronick, E. Z. (1983). Three-month-old infants' reaction to simulated maternal depression. *Child Development, 54,* 185–193.

Coie, J. D. (in press). The impact of negative social experience on the development of antisocial behavior. In J. Kupersmidt & K. A. Dodge (Eds.), *Peer relations in childhood: From development to intervention to public policy.* Washington, DC: American Psychological Association.

Coie, J. D., & Dodge, K. A. (1998). Aggression and antisocial behavior. In W. Damon (Series Ed.) & N. Eisenberg (Vol. Ed.), *Handbook of child psychology: Vol. 3. Social, emotional, and personality development* (5th ed.). New York: Wiley.

Coie, J. D., Dodge, K. A., & Kupersmidt, J. B. (1990). Peer group behavior and social status. In S. R. Asher & J. D. Coie (Eds.), *Peer rejection in childhood.* New York: Cambridge University Press.

Coie, J. D., & Krehbiel, G. (1984). Effects of academic tutoring on the social status of low-achieving, socially rejected children. *Child Development, 55,* 1465–1478.

Coie, J. D., & Kupersmidt, J. (1983). A behavioral analysis of emerging social status in boys' groups. *Child Development, 54,* 1400–1416.

Coie, J. D., Lochman, J. E., Terry, R., & Hyman, C. (1992). Predicting early adolescent disorder from childhood aggression and peer rejection. *Journal of Consulting and Clinical Psychology, 60,* 783–792.

Colapinto, J. (2000). *As nature made him.* New York: HarperCollins.

Colby, A., & Kohlberg, L. (1987). *The measurement of moral judgment* (Vols. 1–2). New York: Cambridge University Press.

Colby A., Kohlberg, L., Gibbs, J. C., & Lieberman, M. (1983). A longitudinal study of moral judgment. *Monographs of the Society for Research in Child Development, 48*(1-2, Serial No. 200).

Cole, M. (1976). Foreword. In A. R. Luria. *Cognitive development: Its cultural and social foundations.* Cambridge, MA: Harvard University Press.

Cole, M. (1996). *Cultural psychology: A once and future discipline.* Cambridge, MA: Harvard University Press.

Cole, M. (1999). Culture in development. In M. H. Bornstein & M. E. Lamb (Eds.), *Developmental psychology: An advanced textbook* (4th ed.). Mahwah, NJ: Erlbaum.

Cole, M., & Scribner, S. (1977). Cross-cultural studies of memory and cognition. In R. V. Kail Jr., & J. W. Hagen (Eds.), *Perspectives on the development of memory and cognition.* Hillsdale, NJ: Erlbaum.

Cole, P. M. (1986). Children's spontaneous control of facial expression. *Child Development, 57,* 1309–1321.

Coleman, E. B. (1998). Using explanatory knowledge during collaborative problem solving in science. *Journal of the Learning Sciences, 7,* 387–427.

Collins, W. A., Maccoby, E. E., Steinberg, L., Hetherington, E. M., & Bornstein, M. H. (2000). Contemporary research on parenting: The case for nature *and* nurture. *American Psychologist, 55,* 218–232.

Collins, W. A., & Russell, G. (1991). Mother–child and father–child relationships in middle childhood and adolescence: A developmental analysis. *Developmental Review, 11,* 99–136.

Collis, G. M. (1985). On the origins of turn-taking: Alternation and meaning. In M. D. Barrett (Ed.), *Children's single-word speech.* New York: Wiley.

Colombo, J. (1993). *Infant cognition: Predicting later intellectual functioning.* Thousand Oaks, CA: Sage.

Colombo, J. (2001). The development of visual attention in infancy. *Annual Review of Psychology, 52,* 337–367.

Colombo, J., & Bundy, R. S. (1981). A method for the measurement of infant auditory selectivity. *Infant Behavior and Development, 4,* 219–223.

Colpin, H. (2002). Parenting and psychosocial development of IVF children: Review of the research literature. *Developmental Review, 22,* 644–673.

Committee for Ethical Conduct in Child Development Research. (1990, Winter). Report from the Committee for Ethical Conduct in Child Development Research. *SRCD Newsletter,* pp. 5–7.

Commons, M. L., Miller, P. M., & Kuhn, D. (1982). The relation between formal operational reasoning and academic course selection and performance among college freshmen and sophomores. *Journal of Applied Developmental Psychology, 3,* 1–10.

Compas, B. R., Conner-Smith, J. J., Saaltzman, H., Thomsen, A. H., & Wadsworth, M. E. (2001). Coping with stress during childhood and adolescence: Problems, progress, and potential in theory and development. *Psychological Bulletin, 127,* 87–127.

Comstock, G., & Scharrer, E. (1999*). Television: What's on, who's watching, and what it means.* San Diego, CA: Academic Press.

Comstock, G., & Scharrer, E. (2001). The use of television and other film-related media. In D. Singer & J. L. Singer (Eds.), *Handbook of children and the media.* Thousand Oaks, CA: Sage.

Condry, K. F., Smith, W. C., & Spelke, E. S. (2001). Development of perceptual organization. In F. Lacerda, C. von Hofsten, & M. Heimann (Eds.), *Emerging cognitive abilities in early infancy.* Mahwah, NJ: Erlbaum.

Conger, R. D., Ge, X., Elder, G. H., Lorenz, F. O., & Simons, R. L. (1994). Economic stress, coercive family process, and developmental problems of adolescents. *Child Development, 65,* 541–561.

Connell, J. P., & Ilardi, B. C. (1987.) Self-system concomitants of discrepancies between children's and teachers' evaluations of academic competence. *Child Development, 58,* 1297–1307.

Connell, J. P., & Wellborn, J. G. (1991). Competence, autonomy, and relatedness: A motivational analysis of self-system processes. In M. R. Gunnar & L. A. Sroufe (Eds.), *Minnesota symposia on child psychology: Vol. 23. Self processes and development.* Hillsdale, NJ: Erlbaum.

Connellan, J., Baron-Cohen, S., Wheelwright, S., Batki, A., & Ahluwalia, J. (2000). Sex differences in human neonatal social perception. *Infant Behavior and Development, 23,* 113–118.

Consortium for Longitudinal Studies. (1983). *As the twig is bent . . . lasting effects of preschool programs.* Hillsdale, NJ: Erlbaum.

Constanzo, P. R. (1970). Conformity development as a function of self-blame. *Journal of Personality and Social Psychology, 14,* 366–374.

Conteras, J. M., Kerns, K. A., Weimer, B. L., Gentzler, A. L., & Tomich, P. L. (2000). Emotion regulation as a mediator of associations between mother-child attachment and peer relationships in middle childhood. *Journal of Family Psychology, 14,* 111–124.

Conti, D. J., & Camras, L. A. (1984). Children's understanding of conversational principles. *Journal of Experimental Child Psychology, 38,* 456–463.

Cooley, C. H. (1902). *Human nature and the social order.* New York: Charles Scribner's Sons.

Cooper, C. R. (1980). Development of collaborative problem solving among preschool children. *Developmental Psychology, 16,* 433–440.

Cooper, N. G. (Ed.). (1994). *The human genome project: Deciphering the blueprint of heredity.* Mill Valley, CA: University Science Books.

Cooper, R. P., & Aslin, R. N. (1990). Preference for infant-directed speech in the first month after birth. *Child Development, 61,* 1584–1595.

Cooper, R. P., & Aslin, R. N. (1994). Developmental differences in infant attention to the spectral properties of infant-directed speech. *Child Development, 65,* 1663–1677.

Copeland, E. P., & Hess, R. S. (1995). Differences in young adolescents' coping strategies based on gender and ethnicity. *Journal of Early Adolescence, 15,* 203–219.

Corina, D. P., Vaid, J., & Bellugi, U. (1992). The linguistic basis of left hemisphere specialization. *Science, 255,* 1258–1260.

Cornelius, M. D., & Day, N. L. (2000). The effects of tobacco use during and after pregnancy on exposed children. *Alcohol Research and Health, 24,* 242–249.

Cornelius, M. D., Ryan, C. M., Day, N. L., Goldschmidt, L., & Willford, J. A. (2001). Prenatal tobacco effects on neuropsychological outcomes among preadolescents. *Journal of Developmental and Behavioral Pediatrics, 22,* 217–225.

Cornelius, M. D., Taylor, P., Geva, D., & Day, N. L. (1995). Prenatal tobacco exposure and marijuana use among adolescents: Effects on offspring gestational age, growth, and morphology. *Pediatrics, 95,* 738–743.

Corrigan, R. (1987). A developmental sequence of actor-object pretend play in young children. *Merrill-Palmer Quarterly, 33,* 87–106.

Corsaro, W. M. (1985). *Friendship and peer culture in the early years.* Norwood, NJ: Ablex.

Corwyn, R. F., & Bradley, R. H. (1999). Determinants of paternal and maternal investment in children. *Infant Mental Health, 20,* 238–256.

Cosmides, L., & Tooby, J. (1992). Cognitive adaptations for social exchange. In J. H. Barkow, L. Cosmides, & J. Tooby (Eds.), *The adapted mind: Evolutionary psychology and the generation of culture.* New York: Oxford University Press.

Cosmides, L., & Tooby, J. (2001). Unraveling the enigma of human intelligence: Evolutionary psychology and the multimodular mind. In R. J. Sternberg & J. C. Kaufman (Eds.), *The evolution of intelligence.* Mahwah, NJ: Erlbaum.

Cosmides, L., Tooby, J., & Barkow, J. (1992). Evolutionary psychology and conceptual integration. In J. Barkow, L. Cosmides, & L. Tooby (Eds.), *The adapted mind: Evolutionary psychology and the generation of culture.* New York: Oxford University Press.

Cossette, L., Pomerleau, A., Malcuit, F., & Kaczorowski, J. (1996). Emotional expressions of female and male infants in a social and nonsocial context. *Sex Roles, 35,* 693–710.

Coster, W. J., Gersten, M. S., Beeghly, M., & Cicchetti, D. (1989). Communicative functioning in maltreated toddlers. *Developmental Psychology, 25,* 1020–1029.

Costin, S. E., & Jones, D. C. (1992). Friendship as a facilitator of emotional responsiveness and prosocial interventions among young children. *Developmental Psychology, 28,* 941–947.

Courage, M. L., & Howe, M. L. (2002). From infant to child: The dynamics of cognitive change in the second year of life. *Psychological Bulletin, 128,* 250–277.

Cowan, P. A. (1978). *Piaget with feeling.* New York: Holt, Rinehart & Winston.

Cowan P. A., Cohn, D. A., Cowan, C. P., & Pearson, J. L. (1996). Parents' attachment histories and children's externalizing and internalizing behaviors: Exploring family systems models of linkage. *Journal of Consulting and Clinical Psychology, 64,* 53–63.

Cowan, P. A., & Cowan, C. P. (2002). What an intervention design reveals about how parents affect their children's academic achievement and behavior problems. In J. G. Borkowski, S. L. Ramey, & M. Bristol-Power (Eds.), *Parenting and the child's world: Influences on academic, intellectual, and social-emotional development.* Mahwah, NJ: Erlbaum.

Cox, B. D., & Lightfoot, C. (Eds.). (1997). *Sociogenetic perspectives on internalization.* Mahwah, NJ: Erlbaum.

Coyle, T. R. (2001). Factor analysis of variability measures in eight independent samples of children and adults. *Journal of Experimental Child Psychology, 78,* 330–358.

Coyle, T. R., & Bjorklund, D. F. (1997). Age differences in, and consequences of, multiple- and variable-strategy use on a multitrial sort-recall task. *Developmental Psychology, 33,* 372–380.

Cozby, P. C., Brown, K. W., Worden, P. E., & Kee, D. W. (1998). *Research methods in human development* (2nd ed.). Mountain View, CA: Mayfield.

CPPRG. (1992). A developmental and clinical model for the prevention of conduct disorder: The FAST Track Program. *Development and Psychopathology, 4,* 509–527.

CPPRG. (1999). Initial impact of the Fast Track prevention trial for conduct problems: I. The high-risk sample. *Journal of Consulting and Clinical Psychology, 67,* 631–647.

CPPRG. (2002). Evaluation of the first 3 years of the Fast Track prevention trial with children at high risk for adolescent conduct problems. *Journal of Abnormal Child Psychology, 30,* 19–35.

Crago, M. B. (1988). *Cultural context in the communicative interaction of young Inuit children.* Unpublished doctoral dissertation. McGill University.

Craig, R. S. (1992). The effect of television's daily part in gender portrayals in television commercials: A continuing analysis. *Sex Roles, 26,* 197–211.

Cravens, H. (1992). A scientific project locked in time: The Terman genetic studies of genius, 1920s–1950s. *American Psychologist, 47,* 183–189.

Crawford, N. (2002). Science-based program curbs violence in kids. *Monitor on Psychology, 33,* 38.

Creasey, G. L., & Koblewski, P. J. (1991). Adolescent grandchildren's relationships with maternal and paternal grandmothers and grandfathers. *Journal of Adolescence, 14,* 373–387.

Crick, N. R. (1995). Relational aggression: The role of intent attributions, feelings of distress, and provocation type. *Development and Psychopathology, 7,* 313–322.

Crick, N. R., Bigbee, M. A., & Howes, C. (1996). Gender differences in children's normative beliefs about aggression: How do I hurt thee? Let me count the ways. *Child Development, 67,* 1003–1014.

Crick, N. R., Casas, J. F., & Mosher, M. (1997). Relational and overt aggression in preschool. *Developmental Psychology, 33,* 579–588.

Crick, N. R., & Dodge, K. A. (1994). A review and reformulation of social information-processing mechanisms in children's social adjustment. *Psychological Bulletin, 115,* 74–101.

Crick, N. R., & Dodge, K. A. (1996). Social information-processing mechanisms in reactive and proactive aggression. *Child Development, 67,* 993–1002.

Crick, N. R., & Grotpeter, J. K. (1995). Relational aggression, gender, and social-psychological adjustment. *Child Development, 66,* 710–722.

Crick, N. R., Nelson, D. A., Morales, J. R., Cullerton-Sen, C., Cases, J. F., & Hickman, S. E. (2001). Relational victimization in childhood and adolescence: I hurt you through the grapevine. In J. Juvonen & S. Graham (Eds.), *Peer harassment in school: The plight of the vulnerable and the victimized.* New York: Guilford.

Crick, N. R., Werner, N. E., Casas, J. F., O'Brien, K. M., Nelson, D. A., Grotpeter, J. K., et al. (1999). Childhood aggression and gender: A new look at an old problem. In D. Bernstein (Ed.), *Nebraska symposium on motivation: Vol. 45. Gender and motivation.* Lincoln: University of Nebraska Press.

Criss, M. M., Pettit, G. S., Bates, J. E., Dodge, K. A., & Lapp, A. L. (2002). Family adversity, positive peer relationships, and children's externalizing behavior: A longitudinal perspective on risk and resilience. *Child Development, 73,* 1220–1237.

Crittenden, P. M., & Ainsworth, M. D. S. (1989). Child maltreatment and attachment theory. In D. Cicchetti & V. Carlson (Eds.), *Child maltreatment: Theory and research on the causes and consequences of child abuse and neglect.* New York: Cambridge University Press.

Crockenberg, S. B. (1986). Are temperamental differences in babies associated with predictable differences in care giving? In J. V. Lerner & R. M. Lerner (Eds.), *New directions for child development: No. 31. Temperament and social interaction during infancy and childhood.* San Francisco: Jossey-Bass.

Crockett, L. J., & Petersen, A. C. (1987). Pubertal status and psychosocial development: Findings from the early adolescence study. In R. M. Lerner & T. L. Foch (Eds.), *Biological psychosocial interactions in early adolescence.* Hillsdale, NJ: Erlbaum.

Crook, C. K. (1979). The organization and control of infant sucking. In H. W. Reese & L. P. Lipsitt (Eds.), *Advances in child development and behavior* (Vol. 14). New York: Academic Press.

Cross, S. E., & Gore, J. S. (2003). Cultural models of the self. In M. R. Leary & J. P. Tangney (Eds.), *Handbook of self and identity.* New York: Guilford.

Crouchman, M. (1985). What mothers know about their newborns' visual skills. *Developmental Medicine and Child Neurology, 27,* 455–460.

Crowell, J. A., & Feldman, S. S. (1991). Mothers' working models of attachment relationships and mother and child behavior during separation and reunion. *Developmental Psychology, 27,* 597–605.

Crowley, K., Callanan, M. A., Jipson, J., Galco, J., Topping, K., & Shrager, J. (2001). Shared scientific thinking in everyday parent-child activity. *Science Education, 85,* 712–732.

Crowley, K., & Galco, J. (2001). Everyday activity and the development of scientific thinking. In K. Crowley, C. D. Schunn, & T. Okada (Eds.), *Designing for science: Implications for everyday, classroom, and professional science.* Mahwah, NJ: Erlbaum.

Culhane, M., Fowler, M. G., Lee, S. S., McSherry, G., Brady, M., & O'Donnell, K. (1999). Lack of long-term effects of in utero exposure to zidovudine among uninfected children born to HIV-infected women. *Journal of the American Medical Association, 281,* 151–157.

Cummings, E. M., & Cummings, J. S. (2002). Parenting and attachment. In M. H. Bornstein (Ed.), *Handbook of parenting, Vol. 5* (2nd ed.). Mahwah, NJ: Erlbaum.

Cunningham, F. G., MacDonald, P. C., & Gant, N. F. (1989). *Williams obstetrics* (18th ed.). London: Appleton & Lange.

Curtin, S. C., & Park, M. M. (1999). Trends in the attendant, place, and timing of births and in the use of obstetric interventions: United States 1989–1997. *National Vital Statistics Report, 47* (27), 1–12.

Curtiss, S. (1977). *Genie: A psycholinguistic study of a modern day "wild child."* New York: Academic Press.

Czeschlik, T., & Rost, D. H. (1995). Sociometric types and children's intelligence. *British Journal of Developmental Psychology, 13,* 177–189.

D'Andrade, R. (1966). Sex differences and cultural institutions. In E. E. Maccoby (Ed.), *The development of sex differences.* Stanford, CA: Stanford University Press.

Damon, W. (1977). Measurement and social development. *Counseling Psychologist, 6,* 13–15.

Damon, W. (1983). *Social and personality development.* New York: Norton.

Damon, W. (1984). Peer education: The untapped potential. *Journal of Applied Developmental Psychology, 5,* 331–343.

Damon, W., & Hart, D. (1982). The development of self-understanding from infancy through adolescence. *Child Development, 53,* 841–864.

Damon, W., & Hart, D. (1992). Self-understanding and its role in social and moral development. In M. H. Bornstein, & M. E. Lamb (Eds.). *Developmental psychology: An advanced textbook* (3rd ed.). Hillsdale, NJ: Erlbaum.

Daneman, M., & Case, R. (1981). Syntactic form, semantic complexity, and short-term memory: Influences on children's acquisition of new linguistic structures. *Developmental Psychology, 17,* 367–378.

Dannemiller, J. L. (1985). The early phase of dark adaptation in human infants. *Vision Research, 25,* 207–212.

Dannemiller, J. L., & Hanko, S. A. (1987). A test of color constancy in 4-month-old infants. *Journal of Experimental Child Psychology, 44,* 255–267.

Dannemiller, J. L., & Stephens, B. R. (1988). A critical test of infant pattern preference models. *Child Development, 59,* 210–216.

Danner, F. W., & Day, M. C. (1977). Eliciting formal operations. *Child Development, 48,* 1600–1606.

Darwin, C. (1859). *The origin of species.* London: Murray.

Darwin, C. (1871/1896). *Descent of man.* New York: Appleton.

Darwin, C. (1872). *The expression of emotions in man and animals.* London: Murray.

Darwin, C. (1877). A biographical sketch of an infant. *Mind, 2,* 285–294.

Dasen, P. (2000). Rapid social change and the turmoil of adolescence: A cross-cultural perspective. *International Journal of Group Tensions, 29,* 17–49.

Dasen, P. R. (1975a). Concrete operational development in Canadian Eskimos. *International Journal of Psychology, 10,* 165–180.

Dasen, P. R. (1975b). Concrete operational development in three cultures. *Journal of Cross-Cultural Psychology, 6,* 156–172.

David, C. F., & Kistner, J. A. (2000). Do positive self-perceptions have a "dark side"? Examination of the link between perceptual bias and aggression. *Journal of Abnormal Child Psychology, 28,* 327–337.

Davidson, D. (1996). The role of schemata in children's memory. In H. W. Reese (Ed.), *Advances in child development and behavior* (Vol. 26). San Diego, CA: Academic Press.

Davidson, D., Cameron, P., & Jergovic, D. (1995). The effects of children's stereotypes on their memory for elderly individuals. *Merrill-Palmer Quarterly, 41,* 70–90.

Davies, W., Isles, A. R., & Wilkinson, L. S. (2001). Imprinted genes and mental dysfunction. *Annals of Medicine, 13,* 428–436.

Davis, M. H., Luce, C., & Kraus, S. J. (1994). The heritability of characteristics associated with dispositional empathy. *Journal of Personality, 62,* 369–391.

Davis, T. L. (1995). Gender differences in masking negative emotions: Ability or motivation? *Developmental Psychology, 31,* 660–667.

Davison, K. K., & Birch, L. L. (2002). Processes linking weight status and self-concept among girls from ages 5 to 7 years. *Developmental Psychology, 38,* 735–748.

Dawkins, R. (1976). *The selfish gene.* New York: Oxford University Press.

Dawson, T. L. (2002). New tools, new insights: Kohlberg's moral judgement stages revisited. *International Journal of Behavioral Development, 26,* 154–166.

Day, M. C. (1975). Developmental trends in visual scanning. In H. W. Reese (Ed.), *Advances in child development and behavior* (Vol. 10). New York: Academic Press.

Day, N. L., Richardson, G. A., Goldschmidt, L., & Cornelius, M. D. (2000). Effects of prenatal tobacco exposure on preschoolers' behavior. *Journal of Developmental and Behavioral Pediatrics, 21,* 180–188.

Day, R. H. (1987). Visual size constancy in infancy. In B. E. McKenzie & R. H. Day (Eds.), *Perceptual development in early infancy: Problems and issues.* Hillsdale, NJ: Erlbaum.

de Haan, M. (2001). The neuropsychology of face processing in infancy. In C. A. Nelson & M. Luciana (Eds.), *Handbook of developmental cognitive neuroscience.* Cambridge, MA: MIT Press.

de Haan, M., & Nelson, C. A. (1998). Discrimination and categorisation of facial expressions of emotions during infancy. In A. Slater (Ed.), *Perceptual development: Visual, auditory, and speech perception in infancy.* Hove, UK: Psychology Press.

de Haan, M., & Nelson, C. A. (1999). Brain activity differentiates face and object processing in 6-month-old infants. *Developmental Psychology, 35,* 1113–1121.

De Lisi, R., & Gallagher, A. M. (1991). Understanding of gender stability and constancy in Argentinean children. *Merrill-Palmer Quarterly, 37,* 483–502.

De Lisi, R., & Goldbeck, S. L. (1999). Implications of Piagetian theory for peer learning. In A. M. O'Donnell & A. King (Eds.), *Cognitive perspectives on peer learning.* Mahwah, NJ: Erlbaum.

De Lisi, R., & Staudt, J. (1980). Individual differences in college students' performance on formal operations tasks. *Journal of Applied Developmental Psychology, 1,* 201–208.

De Ribaupierre, A., Rieben, L., & Lautrey, J. (1991). Developmental change and individual differences: A longitudinal study using Piagetian tasks. *Genetic, Social, and General Psychology Monographs, 117,* 285–311.

de Villiers, J. G. (1980). The process of rule learning in child speech: A new look. In K. E. Nelson (Ed.), *Children's language* (Vol. 2). New York: Gardner.

de Villiers, J. G., & de Villiers, P. A. (1999). Language development. In M. H. Bornstein & M. E. Lamb (Eds.), *Developmental psychology: An advanced textbook* (4th ed.). Mahwah, NJ: Erlbaum.

de Waal, F. B. M. (1993). Reconciliation among primates: A review of empirical evidence and unresolved issues. In W. A. Mason & S. Mendoza (Eds.), *Primate social conflict.* Albany: State University of New York Press.

de Waal, F. B. M. (1996). *Good natured: The origins of right and wrong in humans and other animals.* Cambridge, MA: Harvard University Press.

de Waal, F. B. M. (1997). Food transfers through mesh in brown capuchins. *Journal of Comparative Psychology, 111,* 370–378.

de Waal, F. B. M. (2000). Primates-a natural heritage of conflict resolution. *Science, 289,* 586–590

De Wolff, M. S., & van IJzendoorn, M. H. (1997). Sensitivity and attachment: A meta-analysis on parental antecedents of infant attachment. *Child Development, 68,* 571–591.

Deak, G. O. (2000). Hunting the fox of word learning: Why "constraints" fail to capture it. *Developmental Review, 20,* 29–80.

Deater-Deckard, K., & Plomin, R. (1999). An adoption study of etiology of teacher and parent reports of externalizing behavior problems in middle childhood. *Child Development, 70,* 144–154.

Deaux, K. (1993). Sorry, wrong number-A reply to Gentile's call. Sex or gender? *Psychological Science, 4,* 125–126.

DeBaryshe, B. D., Patterson, G. R., & Capaldi, D. M. (1993). Performance model for academic achievement in early adolescent boys. *Developmental Psychology, 29,* 795–804.

DeCasper, A. J., & Fifer, W. P. (1980). Of human bonding: Newborns prefer their mothers' voices. *Science, 208,* 1174–1176.

DeCasper, A. J., & Prescott, P. A. (1984). Human newborns' perception of male voices: Preference, discrimination, and reinforcing value. *Developmental Psychobiology, 17,* 481–491.

DeCasper, A. J., & Spence, M. J. (1986). Newborns prefer a familiar story over an unfamiliar one. *Infant Behavior and Development, 9,* 133–150.

DeCasper, A. J., & Spence, M. J. (1991). Auditory mediated behavior during the perinatal period: A cognitive view. In M. J. S. Weiss & P. R. Zelazo (Eds.), *Newborn attention: Biological constraints and the influence of experience.* Norwood, NJ: Ablex.

DeCasper, A. J., Lecanuet, J.-P., Busnel, M.-C., Granier-Deferre, C., & Mau-Geais, R. (1994). Fetal reactions to recurrent maternal speech. *Infant Behavior and Development, 17,* 159–164.

DeFries, J. C., Plomin, R., & Fulker, D. W. (Eds.). (1994). *Nature and nurture during middle childhood.* Oxford, England: Blackwell.

DeHart, G. B. (1999). Conflict and averted conflict in preschoolers' interactions with siblings and friends. In W. A. Collins & B. Laursen (Eds.), *Minnesota symposia on child psychology: Vol. 30. Relationships as developmental contexts.* Mahwah, NJ: Erlbaum.

Dejin-Karlsson, E., Hanson, B. S., Estergen, P., Sjoeberg, N., & Marshal, K. (1998). Does passive smoking in early pregnancy increase the risk of small-for-gestational age infants? *American Journal of Public Health, 88,* 1523–1527.

Dekovic, M., & Janssens, J. M. A. M. (1992). Parents' child-drearing style and child's sociometric status. *Developmental Psychology, 28,* 925–932.

Del Carmen, R., Pedersen, F. A., Huffman, L. C., & Bryan, Y. E. (1993). Dyadic distress management predicts subsequent security of attachment. *Infant Behavior and Development, 16,* 131–147.

DeLoache, J. S. (1989). Young children's understanding of the correspondence between a scale model and a larger space. *Cognitive Development, 4,* 121–139.

DeLoache, J. S. (2000). Dual representation and young children's use of scale models. *Child Development, 71,* 329–338.

DeLoache, J. S. (2002). The symbol-mindedness of young children. In W. W. Hartup & R. A. Weinberg (Eds.), *Minnesota symposia on child psychology: Vol. 32. Child psychology in retrospect and prospect.* Mahwah, NJ: Erlbaum.

DeLoache, J. S., Miller, K. F., & Pierretsoukas, S. L. (1998). Reasoning and problem solving. In W. Damon (Series Ed.) & D. Kuhn & R. S. Siegler (Vol. Eds.), *Handbook of child psychology: Vol. 2. Cognition, perception, and language* (5th ed.). New York: Wiley.

DeLoache, J. S., Miller, K. F., & Rosengren, K. (1997). The credible shrinking room: Very young children's performance in symbolic and non-symbolic tasks. *Psychological Science, 8,* 308–313.

DeLoache, J. S., Pierroutsakos, S. L., & Troseth, G. L. (1996). The three "R's" of pictorial competence. In R. Vasta (Ed.), *Annals of child development* (Vol. 12). London: Jessica Kingsley Publishers.

DeLoache, J. S., Pierroutsakos, S. L., Uttal, D. H., Rosengren, K. S., & Gottlieb, A. (1998). Grasping the nature of pictures. *Psychological Science, 9,* 205–210.

DeLoache, J. S., & Smith, C. M. (1999). Early symbolic representation. In I. E. Sigel (Ed.), *Development of mental representation.* Mahwah, NJ: Erlbaum.

DeLoache, J. S., Uttal, D., & Pierroutsakos, S. L. (2000). What's up? The development of an orientation preference for picture books. *Journal of Cognition and Development, 1,* 81–95.

Demetras, M. J., Post, K. N., & Snow, C. E. (1986). Feedback to first language learners: The role of repetitions and clarification questions. *Journal of Child Language, 13,* 275–292.

Demetriou, A., Shayer, M., & Efklides, A. (Eds.). (1993). *Neo-Piagetian theories of cognitive development.* New York: Routledge.

Demos, V. (1986). Crying in early infancy: An illustration of the motivational function of affect. In T. B. Brazelton & M. Yogman (Eds.), *Affect and early infancy.* Norwood, NJ: Ablex.

Denenberg, V., & Thoman, E. (1981). Evidence for a functional role for active (REM) sleep in infancy. *Sleep, 4,* 185–191.

Denham, S. A. (1998). *Emotional development in young children.* New York: Guilford.

Denham, S. A., & Couchoud, E. A. (1991). Social-emotional predictors of preschoolers' responses to adult negative emotion. *Journal of Child Psychology and Psychiatry and Allied Disciplines, 32,* 595–608.

Denham, S. A., & McKinley, M. (1993). Sociometric nominations of preschoolers: A psychometric analysis. *Early Education and Development, 4,* 109–122.

Denham, S. A., Zoller, D., & Couchoud, E. A. (1994). Socialization of preschoolers' emotion understanding. *Developmental Psychology, 30,* 928–936.

Denkel-Schetter, C., Sagrestano, L. M., Feldman, P., & Killingsworth, C. (1996). Social support and pregnancy: A comprehensive review focusing on ethnicity and culture. In G. R. Pierce, B. R. Sarason, & I. G. Sarason (Eds.), *Handbook of social support and the family.* New York: Plenum.

Dennis, W. (1960). Causes of retardation among institutional children: Iran. *Journal of Genetic Psychology, 96,* 47–59.

Dennis, W., & Najarian, P. (1957). Infant development under environmental handicap. *Psychological Monographs, 71* (7, Whole No. 436).

Denton, K., & Zarbatany, L. (1996). Age differences in support processes in conversations between friends. *Child Development, 67,* 1360–1373.

DeRosier, M., Kupersmidt, J., & Patterson, C. (1994). Children's academic and behavioral adjustment as a function of the chronicity and proximity of peer rejection. *Child Development, 65,* 1799–1813.

Dettling, A. C., Gunnar, M. R., & Donzella, B. (1999). Cortisol levels of young children in full-day childcare centers: Relations with age and temperament. *Psychoneuroendocrinology, 24,* 519–536.

Deutsch, F. M., Servis, L. J., & Payne, J. D. (2001). Paternal participation in child care and its effects on children's self-esteem and attitudes toward gendered roles. *Journal of Family Issues, 22,* 1000–1024.

DeVries, M. W., & Sameroff, A. J. (1984). Culture and temperament: Influences on infant temperament in three East African societies. *American Journal of Orthopsychiatry, 54,* 83–96.

DeVries, R. (1969). Constancy of generic identity in the years three to six. *Monographs of the Society for Research in Child Development, 34* (3, Serial No. 127).

DeVries, R., & Zan, B. (1994). *Moral classrooms, moral children: Creating a constructivist atmosphere in early education.* New York: Teachers College Press.

Dewsbury, D. A. (1984). *Comparative psychology in the twentieth century.* Stroudsburg, PA: Hutchinson Ross.

Diamond, A., Prevor, M. B., Callender, G., & Druin, D. P. (1997). Prefrontal cortex cognitive deficits in children treated early and continuously for PKU. *Monographs of the Society for Research in Child Development, 62*(4, Serial No. 252).

Diamond, L. M., Savin-Williams, R. C., & Dubé, E. M. (1999). Sex, dating, passionate friendships, and romance: Intimate peer relations among lesbian, gay, and bisexual adolescents. In W. Furman, B. B. Brown, & C. Feiring (Eds.), *The development of romantic relationships in adolescence.* Cambridge: Cambridge University Press.

Diamond, M. (1993). Homosexuality and bisexuality in different populations. *Archives of Sexual Behavior, 22,* 291–310 .

Diamond, M., & Sigmundson, H. K. (1997). Sex reassignment at birth. Long-term review and clinical implications. *Archives of Pediatric Adolescent Medicine, 151,* 298–304.

Dias, M. G., & Harris, P. L (1988). The effect of make-believe play on deductive reasoning. *British Journal of Developmental Psychology, 6,* 207–221.

Dias, M. G., & Harris, P. L. (1990). The influence of the imagination on reasoning by young children. *British Journal of Developmental Psychology, 8,* 305–318.

Dick, D. M., Rose, R. J., Viken, R. J., & Kaprio, J. (2000). Pubertal timing and substance use: Associations between and within families across adolescence. *Developmental Psychology, 36,* 180–189.

Dickens, W. T., & Flynn, J. R. (2001). Heritability estimates versus large environmental effects: The IQ paradox resolved. *Psychological Review, 108,* 346–369.

Dick-Read, G. (1933). *Natural childbirth.* New York: Dell.

Dick-Read, G. (1944). *Childbirth without fear.* New York: Dell.

Dien, D. S. F. (1982). A Chinese perspective on Kohlberg's theory of moral development. *Developmental Review, 2,* 331–341.

Diener, C. I., & Dweck, C. S. (1978). An analysis of learned helplessness: Continuous changes in performance, strategy, and achievement cognitions following failure. *Journal of Personality and Social Psychology, 36,* 451–462.

Diener, C. I., & Dweck, C. S. (1980). An analysis of learned helplessness: II. The processing of success. *Journal of Personality and Social Psychology, 39,* 940–952.

Diener, M. L., Goldstein, L. H., & Mangelsdorf, S. C. (1995). The role of prenatal expectations in parents' reports of infant temperament. *Merrill-Palmer Quarterly, 41,* 172–190.

Dierking, L. D., & Falk, J. H. (1994). Family behavior and learning in informal science settings: A review of the research. *Science Education, 78,* 57–72.

Dietrich, K. N. (1999). Environmental toxicants and child development. In H. Tager-Flusberg (Ed.), *Neurodevelopmental disorders.* Boston: MIT Press.

Dietz, T. L. (1998). An examination of violence and gender role portrayals in video games: Implications for gender socialization and aggressive behavior. *Sex Roles, 38,* 425–442.

DiLalla, L. F. (2002). Behavior genetics of aggression in children: Review and future directions. *Developmental Review, 22,* 593–622.

Dimant, R. J., & Bearison, D. J. (1991). Development of formal reasoning during successive peer interactions. *Developmental Psychology, 27,* 277–284.

Dinges, M. M., & Oetting, E. R. (1993). Similarity in drug use patterns between adolescents and their friends. *Adolescence, 28,* 253–266.

DiPietro, J. (1981). Rough and tumble play: A function of gender. *Developmental Psychology, 17,* 50–58.

DiPietro, J. A., Bornstein, M. H., Costigan, K. A., Pressman, E. K., Hahn, C., Painter, K., et al. (2002). What does fetal movement predict about behavior during the first two years of life? *Developmental Psychobiology, 40,* 358–371.

DiPietro, J. A., Hodgson, D. M., Costigan, K. A., Hilton, S. C., & Johnson, T. R. B. (1996). Fetal neurobehavioral development. *Child Development, 67,* 2553–2567.

DiPietro, J. A., Hodgson, D. M., Costigan, K. A., & Johnson, T. R. B. (1996). Fetal antecedent of infant temperament. *Child Development, 67,* 2568–2583.

DiPietro, J. A., Suess, P. E., Wheeler, J. S., Smouse, P. H., & Newlin, D. B. (1995). Reactivity and regulation in cocaine-exposed neonates. *Infant Behavior and Development, 18,* 407–414.

Dishion, T. J. (1990). The family ecology of boys' peer relations in middle childhood. *Child Development, 61,* 874–892.

Dishion, T. J., Andrews, D. W., & Crosby, L. (1995). Antisocial boys and their friends in early adolescence: Relationship characteristics, quality, and interactional process. *Child Development, 66,* 139–151.

Dishion, T. J., & Bullock, B. M. (2002). Parenting and adolescent problem behavior: An ecological analysis of the nurturance hypothesis. In J. G. Borkowski, S. L. Ramey, & M. Bristol-Power (Eds.), *Parenting and the child's world: Influences on academic, intellectual, and social-emotional development.* Mahwah, NJ: Erlbaum.

Dittmann, R. W., Kappes, M. H., Kappes, M. E., Borger, D., Meyer-Bahlberg, H. F. L., Stegner, H., et al. (1990). Congenital adrenal hyperplasia: II. Gender-related behavior and attitudes in female patients and sisters. *Psychoneuroendocrinology, 15,* 410–420.

Dixon, R. A., & Lerner, R. M. (1999). History and systems in developmental psychology. In M. H. Bornstein & M. E. Lamb (Eds.), *Developmental psychology: An advanced textbook* (4th ed.). Mahwah, NJ: Erlbaum.

Dodge, K. A. (1986). A social information processing model of social competence in children. In M. Perlmutter (Ed.), *Minnesota symposia on child psychology: Vol. 18. Cognitive perspectives on children's social and behavioral development.* Hillsdale, NJ: Erlbaum.

Dodge, K. A., & Crick, N. R. (1990). Social-information processing bases of aggressive behavior in children. *Personality and Social Psychology Bulletin, 16,* 8–22.

Dodge, K. A., & Feldman, E. (1990). Issues in social cognition and sociometric status. In S. R. Asher & J. D. Coie, (Eds.), *Peer rejection in childhood.* New York: Cambridge University Press.

Dodge, K. A., Lansford, J. E., Burks, V. S., Bates, J. E., Pettit, G. S., Fontaine, R., et al. (2003). Peer rejection and social information-processing factors in the development of aggressive behavior problems in children. *Child Development, 74,* 374–393.

Dodge, K. A., Murphy, R. R., & Buchsbaum, K. (1984). The assessment of intention-cue detection skills in children: Implications for developmental psychopathology. *Child Development, 55,* 163–173.

Dodge, K. A., & Somberg, D. R. (1987). Hostile attributional biases among aggressive boys are exacerbated under conditions of threats to the self. *Child Development, 58,* 213–224.

Doise, W., & Mugny, G. (1984). *The social development of the intellect.* Oxford: Pergamon.

Donaldson, M. (1982). Conservation: What is the question? *British Journal of Psychology, 73,* 199–207.

Dore, J. (1976). Children's illocutionary acts. In R. Freedle (Ed.), *Comprehension and production.* Hillsdale, NJ: Erlbaum.

Dore, J. (1985). Holophrases revisited: Their "logical" development during dialog. In M. D. Barrett (Ed.), *Children's single-word speech.* New York: Wiley.

Dornbusch, S. M. (1994, February). *Off the track.* Presidential address presented at the meeting of the Meeting of the Society for Research in Adolescence, San Diego, CA.

Dornbusch, S. M., Glasgow, K. L., & Lin, I.-C. (1996). The social structure of schooling. *Annual Review of Psychology, 47,* 401–429.

Dougherty, T., & Haith, M. M. (1993, March). *Processing speed in infants and children: A component of IQ?* Paper presented at the meeting of the Society for Research in Child Development, New Orleans.

Dowling, M., & Bendell, D. (1988). Characteristics of small-for-gestational-age infants. *Infant Behavior and Development, 11,* 77.

Dreeban, R., & Barr, R. (1988). Classroom composition and the design of instruction. *Sociology of Education, 61,* 129–142.

Drotar, D. K., Eckerle, D., Satola, J., Pallotta, J., & Wyatt, B. (1990). Maternal interactional behavior with nonorganic failure-to-thrive infants: A case comparison study. *Child Abuse and Neglect, 14,* 41–51.

Duckworth, E. (1987). *The having of wonderful ideas and other essays on teaching and learning.* New York: Teachers College Press.

Duffy, F. H., Als, H., & McAnulty, G. B. (1990). Behavioral and electrophysiological evidence for gestational age effects in healthy preterm and full-term infants studied two weeks after expected due date. *Child Development, 61,* 1271–1286.

Duffy, J., Warren, K., & Walsh, M. (2001). Classroom interactions: Gender of teacher, gender of student, and classroom subject. *Sex Roles, 45,* 579–593.

Dufresne, A., & Kobasigawa, A. (1989). Children's spontaneous allocation of study time: Differential and sufficient aspects. *Journal of Experimental Child Psychology, 47,* 274–296.

Duncan, R. M., & Pratt, M. W. (1997). Microgenetic change in the quantity and quality of preschoolers' private speech. *International Journal of Behavioral Development, 20,* 367–383.

Dunn, J. (1987). The beginnings of moral understanding: Development in the second year. In J. Kagan & S. Lamb (Eds.), *The emergence of morality in young children.* Chicago: University of Chicago Press.

Dunn, J. (1988). *The beginnings of social understanding.* Cambridge, MA: Harvard University Press.

Dunn, J. (1992). Sisters and brothers: Current issues in developmental research. In F. Boer & J. Dunn (Eds.), *Children's sibling relationships: Developmental and clinical issues.* Hillsdale, NJ: Erlbaum.

Dunn, J. (1993). *Young children's close relationships.* Newbury Park, CA: Sage.

Dunn, J. (1994). Sibling relationships and perceived self-competence: Patterns of stability between childhood and early adolescence. In A. Sameroff & M. M. Haith (Eds.). *The five to seven year shift: The age of reason and responsibility.* Chicago: University of Chicago Press.

Dunn, J. (1999). Siblings, friends, and the development of social understanding. In W. A. Collins & B. Laursen (Eds.), *Minnesota symposia on child psychology: Vol. 30. Relationships as developmental contexts.* Mahwah, NJ: Erlbaum.

Dunn, J. (2002). Sibling relationships. In P. K. Smith & C. H. Hart (Eds.), *Blackwell handbook of childhood social development.* Madden, MA: Blackwell Publishers.

Dunn, J., Cutting, A. L., & Demetriou, H. (2000). Moral sensibility, understanding others, and children's friendship interactions in the preschool period. *British Journal of Developmental Psychology, 18,* 159–177.

Dunn, J., & Dale, N. (1984). I a Daddy: 2-year-olds' collaboration in joint pretend with sibling and with mother. In I. Bretherton (Ed.), *Symbolic play: The development of social understanding.* New York: Academic Press.

Dunn, J., & Herrera, C. (1997). Conflict resolution with friends, siblings, and mothers: A developmental perspective. *Aggressive Behavior, 23,* 343–357.

Dunn, J., & Kendrick, J. (1982). The speech of two-and three-year-olds to infant siblings: "Baby talk" and the context of communication. *Journal of Child Language, 9,* 579–595.

Dunn, J., & McGuire, S. (1992). Sibling and peer relationships in childhood. *Journal of Child Psychology and Psychiatry and Allied Disciplines, 33,* 67–105.

Dunn, J., & Munn, P. (1986). Siblings and the development of prosocial behaviors. *International Journal of Behavioral Development, 9,* 265–284.

Dunphy, D. C. (1963). The social structure of urban adolescent peer groups. *Sociometry, 26,* 230–246.

Dweck, C. S. (1999). *Self-theories: Their role in motivation, personality, and development.* Philadelphia: Psychology Press.

Dweck, C. S., & Leggett, E. L. (1988). A social-cognitive approach to motivation and personality. *Psychological Review, 95,* 256–273.

Eagly, A. H., & Crowley, M. (1986). Gender and helping behavior: A meta-analytic review of the social psychological literature. *Psychological Bulletin, 100,* 283–308.

Eagly, A. H., & Steffen, V. J. (1986). Gender and aggressive behavior: A meta-analytic review of the social psychological literature. *Psychological Bulletin, 100,* 309–330.

Eagly, A. H., & Wood, W. (1999). The origin of sex differences in human behavior: Evolved dispositions versus social roles. *American Psychologist, 54,* 408–423.

Eagly, A. H., Wood, W., & Diekman, A. B. (2000). Social role theory of sex differences and similarities: A current appraisal. In T. Eckes & H. M. Trautner (Eds.), *The developmental social psychology of gender.* Mahwah, NJ: Erlbaum.

East, P. L., & Rook, K. S. (1992). Compensatory patterns of support among children's peer relationships: A test using school friends, nonschool friends, and siblings. *Developmental Psychology, 28,* 163–172.

Eaton, W. O. (1994). Temperament, development, and the Five-Factor Model: Lessons from activity level. In C. F. Halverson Jr., G. A. Kohnstamm, & R. P. Martin (Eds.), *The developed structure of temperament and personality from infancy to adulthood.* Hillsdale, NJ: Erlbaum.

Eaton, W. O., & Enns, L. R. (1986). Sex differences in human motor activity level. *Psychological Bulletin, 100,* 19–28.

Eaton, W. O., & Saudino, K. J. (1992). Prenatal activity level as a temperament dimension? Individual differences and the developmental functions in fetal movement. *Infant Behavior and Development, 15,* 57–70.

Ebrahim, S. H., Floyd, R. L., Merritt, R. K., Decoufle, P., & Holtzman, D. (2000). Trends in pregnancy-related smoking rates in the United States, 1987–1996. *Journal of the American Medical Association, 283,* 361–366.

Eccles, J. S., Arbreton, A., Buchanan, C., Jacobs, J., Flanagan, C., Harold, R., et al. (1993). School and family effects on the ontogeny of children's interests, self-perceptions, and activity choice. In J. Jacobs (Ed.), *Nebraska symposium on motivation: Vol. 40. Developmental perspectives on motivation.* Lincoln: University of Nebraska Press.

Eccles, J. S., & Barber, B. L. (1999). Student council, volunteering, basketball, or marching band: What kind of extracurricular involvement matters? *Journal of Adolescent Research, 14,* 10–43.

Eccles, J. S., Freedman-Doan, C., Frome, P., Jacobs, J., & Yoon, K. S. (2000). Gender-role socialization in the family: A longitudinal approach. In T. Eckes & H. M. Trautner (Eds.), *The developmental social psychology of gender.* Mahwah, NJ: Erlbaum.

Eccles, J. S., Jacobs, J. E., Harold, R. D., Yoon, K. S., Arbreton, A., & Freedman-Doan, C. (1993). Parents and gender-role socialization during the middle childhood and adolescent years. In S. Oskamp & M. Costanzo (Eds.), *Gender issues in contemporary society.* Thousand Oaks, CA: Sage.

Eccles, J. S., Lord, S., & Roeser, R. W. (1996). Round holes, square pegs, rocky roads, and sore feet: The impact of stage/environment fit on young adolescents' experiences in schools and families. In D. Cicchetti & S. L. Toth (Eds.), *Rochester symposium on developmental psychopathology: Vol. 8. Adolescence: Opportunities and challenges.* Rochester, NY: University of Rochester Press.

Eccles, J. S., Lord, S., Roeser, R. W., Barber, B. L., & Jozefowicz, D. M. H. (1997). The association of school transitions in early adolescence with developmental trajectories through high school. In J. Schulenberg, J. Maggs, & K. Hurrelmann (Eds.), *Health risks and developmental transitions during adolescence.* New York: Cambridge University Press.

Eccles, J. S., Midgley, C., Wigfield, A., Buchanan, C. M., Reuman, D., Flanagan, C., et al. (1993). Development during adolescence: The impact of stage-environment fit on young adolescents' experiences in schools and in families. *American Psychologist, 48,* 90–101.

Eccles, J. S., & Roeser, R. W. (1999). School and community influences on human development. In M. H. Bornstein & M. E. Lamb (Eds.), *Developmental psychology: An advanced textbook* (4th ed.). Mahwah, NJ: Erlbaum.

Eccles, J. S., & Wigfield, A. (1995). In the mind of the actor: The structure of adolescents' achievement task values and expectancy related beliefs. *Personality and Social Psychology Bulletin, 21,* 215–225.

Eccles, J., Wigfield, A., Harold, R. D., & Blumenfeld, P. (1993). Age and gender differences in children's self- and task perceptions during elementary school. *Child Development, 64,* 830–847.

Eckerman, C. O. (1993). Imitation and toddlers' achievement of co-ordinated action with others. In J. Nadel & L. Camaioni (Eds.), *New perspectives in early communicative development.* New York: Routledge.

Eckerman, C. O., Davis, C. C., & Didow, S. (1989). Toddlers' emerging ways of achieving social coordinations with a peer. *Child Development, 60,* 440–453.

Eckerman, C. O., Hsu, H., Molitor, A., Leung, E. H. L., & Goldstein, R. F. (1999). Infant arousal in the enface exchange with a new partner: Effects of prematurity and perinatal biological risk. *Developmental Psychology, 35,* 282–293.

Eckerman, C. O., & Peterman, K. (2001). Peers and infant social/communicative development. In G. Bremner & A. Fogel (Eds.), *Blackwell handbook of infant development.* Malden, MA: Blackwell Publishers.

Eckerman, C. O., & Stein, M. R. (1990). How imitation begets imitation and toddlers' generation of games. *Developmental Psychology, 26,* 370–378.

Eckstein, S., & Shemesh, M. (1992). The rate of acquisition of formal operational schemata in adolescence: A secondary analysis. *Journal of Research in Science Teaching, 29,* 441–451.

Edelman, G. M. (1993). Neural Darwinism: Selection and reentrant signaling in higher brain function. *Neuron, 10,* 115–125.

Eder, R. A. (1989). The emergent personologist: The structure and content of 3 1/2-, 5 1/2-, and 7 1/2-year-olds' concepts of themselves and others. *Child Development, 60,* 1218–1228.

Eder, R. A. (1990). Uncovering young children's psychological selves: Individual and developmental differences. *Child Development, 61,* 849–863.

Edwards, C. (1987). Culture and the construction of moral values: A comparative ethnography of the moral encounters in two cultural settings. In J. Kagan & S. Lamb (Eds.), *The emergence of morality in young children.* Chicago: University of Chicago Press.

Egeland, B., & Farber, E. (1984). Infant–mother attachment: Factors related to its development and changes over time. *Child Development, 55,* 753–771.

Egeland, B., & Heister, M. (1995). The long-term consequences of infant day-care and mother–infant attachment. *Child Development, 66,* 474–485.

Eibl-Eibesfeldt, I. (1989). *Human ethology.* Hawthorne, NY: Aldine de Gruyter.

Eichorn, D. (1970). Physiological development. In P. H. Mussen (Ed.), *Carmichael's manual of child psychology* (3rd ed.). New York: Wiley.

Eichorn, D. (1979). Physical development: Current foci of research. In J. D. Osofsky (Ed.), *Handbook of infant development.* New York: Wiley.

Eichstedt, J. A., Serbin, L. A., Poulin-Dubois, D., & Sen, M. G. (2002). Of bears and men: Infants' knowledge of conventional and metaphorical gender stereotypes. *Infant Behavior and Development, 25,* 296–310.

Eifermann, R. R. (1971). Social play in childhood. In R. E. Herron & B. Sutton-Smith (Eds.), *Child's play.* New York: Wiley.

Eilers, R. E., & Oller, D. K. (1988). Precursors to speech: What is innate and what is acquired? In R. Vasta (Ed.), *Annals of child development* (Vol. 5). Greenwich, CT: JAI Press.

Eimas, P. D. (1975). Auditory and phonetic coding of the cues for speech: Discrimination of the [r-l] distinction by young infants. *Perception and Psychophysics, 18,* 341–347.

Eisen, M. L., Quas, J. A., & Goodman, G. S. (Eds.). (2002). *Memory and suggestibility in the forensic interview.* Mahwah, NJ: Erlbaum.

Eisenberg, A. (1999). Emotion talk among Mexican American and Anglo American mothers and children from two social classes. *Merrill-Palmer Quarterly, 45,* 267–284.

Eisenberg, A. R. (1988). Grandchildren's perspectives on relationships with grandparents: The influence of gender across generations. *Sex Roles, 19,* 205–217.

Eisenberg, N. (1982). The development of reasoning regarding prosocial behavior. In N. Eisenberg (Ed.), *The development of prosocial behavior.* New York: Academic Press.

Eisenberg, N. (1986). *Altruistic emotion, cognition, and behavior.* Hillsdale, NJ: Erlbaum.

Eisenberg, N. (1987). The relation of altruism and other moral behaviors to moral cognition: Methodological and conceptual issues. In N. Eisenberg & J. Strayer (Eds.), *Empathy and its development.* New York: Cambridge University Press.

Eisenberg, N., Cameron, E., Tryon, K., & Dodez, R. (1981). Socialization of prosocial behavior in the preschool classroom. *Developmental Psychology, 17,* 773–782.

Eisenberg, N., Carlo, G., Murphy, B., & Van Court, P. (1995). Prosocial development in late adolescence: A longitudinal study. *Child Development, 66,* 1179–1197.

Eisenberg, N., & Fabes, R. A. (1998). Prosocial development. In W. Damon (Series Ed.) & N. Eisenberg (Vol. Ed.), *Handbook of child psychology: Vol. 3. Social, emotional, and personality development* (5th ed.). New York: Wiley.

Eisenberg, N., Fabes, R. A., Carlo, G., & Troyer, D. (1992). The relations of maternal practices and characteristics to children's vicarious emotional responsiveness. *Child Development, 63,* 583–602.

Eisenberg, N., Fabes, R. A., Guthrie, I. K., & Reiser, M. (2000). Dispositional emotionality and regulation: Their role in predicting quality of social functioning. *Journal of Personality and Social Psychology, 78,* 136–157.

Eisenberg, N., Fabes, R. A., Shepard, S. A., Murphy, B. C., Jones, S., & Guthrie, I. K. (1998). Contemporaneous and longitudinal prediction of children's sympathy from dispositional regulation and emotionality *Developmental Psychology, 34,* 910–924.

Eisenberg, N., Martin, C. L., & Fabes, R. A. (1996). Gender development and gender effects. In D. C. Berliner & R. C. Calfee (Eds.), *Handbook of educational psychology.* New York: Macmillan Library Reference.

Eisenberg, N., & Miller, P. A. (1987). The relation of empathy to prosocial and related behaviors. *Psychological Bulletin, 101,* 91–119.

Eisenberg, N., & Murphy, B. (1995). Parenting and children's moral development. In M. H. Bornstein (Ed.), *Handbook of parenting: Vol. 4. Applied and practical parenting.* Mahwah, NJ: Erlbaum.

Eisenberg, N., Pidada, S., & Liew, J. (2001). The relations of regulation and negative emotionality to Indonesian children's social functioning. *Child Development, 72,* 1747–1763.

Eisenberg, N., Tryon, K., & Cameron, E. (1984). The relation of preschoolers' peer interaction to their sex-typed toy choices. *Child Development, 55,* 1044–1050.

Eisenberg, N., Wolchik, S. A., Hernandez, R., & Pasternack, J. F. (1985). Parental socialization of young children's play: A short-term longitudinal study. *Child Development, 56,* 1506–1513.

Eisenberg, R. B. (1976). *Auditory competence in early life.* Baltimore: University Park Press.

Ekman, P. (1993). Facial expression and emotion. *American Psychologist, 48*, 384–392.

El Abd, S., Turk, J., & Hill, P. (1995). Annotation: Psychological characteristics of Turner syndrome. *Journal of Child Psychology and Psychiatry, 36*, 1109–1125.

El Hassan Al Awad, A. M., & Sonuga-Barke, E. J. S. (1992). Childhood problems in a Sudanese City: A comparison of extended and nuclear families. *Child Development, 63*, 906–914.

Elder, G. H., & Caspi, A. (1988). Human development and social change: An emerging perspective on the life course. In N. Bolger, A. Caspi, G. Downey, & M. Moorehouse (Eds.), *Persons in context: Developmental processes*. New York: Cambridge University Press.

Elder, G. H., & Conger, R. D. (2000). *Children of the land*. Chicago: University of Chicago Press.

Elkind, D. (1980). Strategic interactions in early adolescence. In J. Adelson (Ed.), *Handbook of adolescent psychology*. New York: Wiley.

Elliott, R., & Vasta, R. (1970). The modeling of sharing: Effects associated with vicarious reinforcement, symbolization, age, and generalization. *Journal of Experimental Child Psychology, 10*, 8–15.

Ellis, B. J., & Garber, J. (2000). Psychosocial antecedents of variations in girls' pubertal timing: Maternal depression, stepfather presence, and marital and family stress. *Child Development, 71*, 485–501.

Ellis, S. (1997). Strategy choice in sociocultural context. *Developmental Review, 17*, 490–524.

Ellis, S., & Gauvain, M. (1992). Social and cultural influences on children's collaborative interactions. In L. T. Winegar, & J. Valsiner (Eds.), *Children's development within social context: Vol. 2. Research and methodology*. Hillsdale, NJ: Erlbaum.

Ellis, S., & Johns, M. (1999, April). *Children's understanding of others' wrong reasoning*. Paper presented at the meetings of the Society for Research in Child Development, Albuquerque.

Ellis, S., & Rogoff, B. (1986). Problem solving in children's management of instruction. In E. C. Mueller & C. R. Cooper (Eds.), *Processes and outcomes in peer relationships*. New York: Academic.

Ellis, S., & Schneiders, B. (1989, April). *Collaboration on children's instruction: A Navajo versus Anglo comparison*. Paper presented at the meetings of the Society for Research in Child Development, Kansas City, MO.

Ellis, S., & Siegler, R. S. (1994). Development of problem solving. In R. J. Siegler (Ed.), *Handbook of perception and cognition: Vol. 12. Thinking and problem solving*. New York: Academic Press.

Ellis, S., & Siegler, R. S. (1995, April). *Developmental changes in children's understanding of principles and procedures of measurement*. Paper presented at the meetings of the Society for Research in Child Development, Indianapolis, Indiana.

Ellis, S., Siegler, R. S., & Klahr, D. (1993, March). *Effects of feedback and collaboration on changes in children's use of mathematical rules*. Paper presented at the meetings of the Society for Research in Child Development, New Orleans.

Ellsworth, C. P., Muir, D. W., & Hains, S. M. J. (1993). Social competence and person-object differentiation: An analysis of the still-face effect. *Developmental Psychology, 29*, 63–73.

Elman, J., Bates, E., Johnson, M., Karmiloff-Smith, A., Parisi, D., & Plunkett, K. (1996). *Rethinking innateness*. Cambridge, MA: MIT Press.

Elmer-DeWitt, P. (1994, January 17). The genetic revolution. *Time*, pp. 46–53.

Emde, R. N. (1992). Individual meaning and increasing complexity: Contributions of Sigmund Freud and Renè Spitz to developmental psychology. *American Psychologist, 28*, 347–359

Emde, R. N., Biringen, Z., Clyman, R. B., & Oppenheim, D. (1991). The moral sense of infancy: Affective core and procedural knowledge. *Developmental Review, 11*, 251–270.

Emde, R. N., & Harmon, R. J. (Eds.). (1984). *Continuities and discontinuities in development*. New York: Plenum.

Emde, R. N., Plomin, R., Robinson, J., Corley, R., DeFries, J., Fulker, D. W., et al. (1992). Temperament, emotion, and cognition at fourteen months: The MacArthur Longitudinal Twin Study. *Child Development, 63*, 1437–1455.

Emde, R. N., Swedberg, J., & Suzuki, B. (1975). Human wakefulness and biological rhythms after birth. *Archives of General Psychiatry, 32*, 780–783.

Emery, R. E., & Laumann-Billings, L. (1998). An overview of the nature, causes, and consequences of abusive family relationships: Toward differentiating maltreatment and violence. *American Psychologist, 53*, 121–135.

Ennis, R. H. (1976). An alternative to Piaget's conceptualization of logical competence. *Child Development, 47*, 903–919.

Ennouri, K., & Bloch, H. (1996). Visual control of hand approach movements in newborns. *British Journal of Developmental Psychology, 14*, 327–338.

Enright, R. D., Bjerstedt, A., Enright, W. F., Levy, V. M., Lapsley, D. K., Buss, R. R., et al. (1984). Distributive justice development: Cross-cultural, contextual, and longitudinal evaluations. *Child Development, 55*, 1737–1751.

Enright, R. D., & Satterfield, S. J. (1980). An ecological validation of social cognitive development. *Child Development, 51*, 156–161.

Entwisle, D. R., & Alexander, K. L. (2000). Diversity in family structure: Effects on schooling. In D. H. Demo, K. R. Allen, & M. A. Fine (Eds.), *Handbook of family diversity*. New York: Oxford University Press.

Epstein, J. L. (1983). Selections of friends in differently organized schools and classrooms. In J. L. Epstein & M. Karweit (Eds.), *Friends in school*. New York: Academic Press.

Epstein, J. L. (1986). Friendship selection: Developmental and environmental influences. In E. C. Mueller & C. R. Cooper (Eds.), *Process and outcome in peer relationships*. New York: Academic Press.

Epstein, J. L. (1989). The selection of friends: Changes across the grades and in different school environments. In T. J. Berndt & G. W. Ladd (Eds.), *Peer relationships in child development*. New York: Wiley.

Epstein, J. L. (2002). *School, family, and community partnerships: Your handbook for action* (2nd ed.). Thousand Oaks, CA: Corwin Press.

Erickson, M. F., Sroufe, L. A., & Egeland, B. (1985). The relationship between quality of attachment and behavior problems in pre-school in a high-risk sample. In I. Bretherton & E. Waters (Eds.), Growing points of attachment theory and research. *Monographs of the Society for Research in Child Development, 50*(1–2, Serial No. 209).

Eron, L. D., & Huesmann, L. R. (1986). The role of television in the development of prosocial and antisocial behavior. In D. Olweus, J. Block, & M. Radke-Yarrow (Eds.), *Development of antisocial and prosocial behavior*. Orlando, FL: Academic Press.

Eron, L. D., Huesmann, L. R., Dubow, E., Romanoff, R., & Yarmel, R. W. (1987). Aggression and its correlates over 22 years. In D. H. Crowell, I. M. Evans, & C. R. O'Donnell (Eds.), *Childhood aggression and violence: Source of influence, prevention, and control*. New York: Plenum.

Ervin, S. M. (1964). Imitation and structural change in children's language. In E. H. Lenneberg (Ed.), *New directions in the study of language*. Cambridge, MA: MIT Press.

Erwin, P. (1993). *Friendship and peer relations in children*. Chichester, England: Wiley.

Eskanezi, B., Stapleton, A. L., Kharrazi, M., & Chee, W. (1999). Associations between maternal decaffeinated and caffeinated coffee consumption and fetal growth and gestational duration. *Epidemiology, 10*, 242–249.

Espelage, D. L., Holt, M. K., & Henkel, R. R. (2003). Examination of peer-group contextual effects on aggression during early adolescence. *Child Development, 74*, 205–220.

Espy, K. A., Molfese, V. J., & DiLalla, L. F. (2001). Effects of environmental measures on intelligence in young children: Growth curve modeling of longitudinal data. *Merrill-Palmer Quarterly, 47*, 42–73.

Etaugh, C., Collins, G., & Gerson, A. (1975). Reinforcement of sex-typed behaviors of two-year-old children in a nursery school setting. *Developmental Psychology, 11*, 255.

Ethics Committee of the American Society for Reproductive Medicine. (2001). Preconception gender selection for nonmedical reasons. *Fertility and Sterility, 75*, 861–864.

Etzel, B. C., & Gewirtz, J. L. (1967). Experimental modification of caretaker-maintained high rate operant crying in a 6- and a 20-week old infant (*Infans tyrannotearus*): Extinction of crying with reinforcement of eye contact and smiling. *Journal of Experimental Child Psychology, 5*, 303–317.

Evans, E. M., Schweingruber, H., & Stevenson, H. W. (2002). Gender differences in interest and knowledge acquisition: The United States, Taiwan, and Japan. *Sex Roles, 47*, 153–167.

Evelyth, P. B. (1986). Population differences in growth. In F. Falkner & J. M. Tanner (Eds.), *Human growth: A comprehensive treatise*. New York: Plenum.

Eyer, D. E. (1992). *Mother–infant bonding: A scientific fiction*. New Haven, CT: Yale University Press.

Fabes, R. A., Eisenberg, N., Karbon, M., Troyer, D., & Switzer, G. (1994). The relations of children's emotion regulation to their vicarious emotional responses and comforting behavior. *Child Development, 65*, 1678–1693.

Fabricius, W. V., & Steffe, L. (1989, April). *Considering all possible combinations: The early beginnings of a formal operational skill*. Paper presented at the meeting of the Society for Research in Child Development, Kansas City, MO.

Fagan J. F. III. (1973). Infants' delayed recognition memory and forgetting. *Journal of Experimental Child Psychology, 16*, 424–450.

Fagan, J. F. III (1976). Infants' recognition of invariant features of faces. *Child Development, 47*, 627–638.

Fagan, J. F. III. (1992). Intelligence: A theoretical viewpoint. *Current Directions in Psychological Science, 1*, 82–86.

Fagan, J. F. III, & Detterman, D. H. (1992). The Fagan Test of Infant Intelligence: A technical summary. *Journal of Applied Developmental Psychology, 13*, 173–193.

Fagan, J. F. III, & Shepherd, P. A. (1986). *The Fagan Test of Infant Intelligence: Training manual*. Cleveland, OH: Infantest Corporation.

Fagan, J. F. III, Shepherd, P., & Knevel, C. (1991, April). *Predictive validity of the Fagan Test of Infant Intelligence*. Meeting of the Society for Research in Child Development, Seattle.

Fagot, B. I. (1977). Consequences of moderate cross-gender behavior in preschool children. *Child Development, 48*, 902–907.

Fagot, B. I. (1985). Beyond the reinforcement principle: Another step toward understanding sex role development. *Developmental Psychology, 21*, 1097–1104.

Fagot, B. I. (1997), Attachment, parenting, and peer interactions of toddler children. *Developmental Psychology, 33*, 489–499.

Fagot, B. I., & Gauvain, M. (1997). Mother-child problem solving: Continuity through the early childhood years. *Developmental Psychology, 33,* 480–488.

Fagot, B. I., & Hagan, R. (1991). Observations of parent reactions to sex-stereotyped behaviors: Age and sex effects. *Child Development, 62,* 617–628.

Fagot, B. I., & Leinbach, M. D. (1987). Socialization of sex roles within the family. In D. B. Carter (Ed.), *Current conceptions of sex roles and sex typing: Theory and research.* New York: Praeger.

Fagot, B. I., & Leinbach, M. D. (1993). Gender-role development in young children: From discrimination to labeling. *Developmental Review, 13,* 205–224.

Fagot, B. I., Leinbach, M. D., & Hagan, R. (1986). Gender labeling and the adoption of sex-typed behaviors. *Developmental Psychology, 22,* 440–443.

Fagot, B. I., Rodgers, C. S., & Leinbach, M. D. (2000). Theories of gender socialization. In T. Eckes & H. M. Trautner (Eds.), *The developmental social psychology of gender.* Mahwah, NJ: Erlbaum.

Fairburn, C. G., & Brownell, K. D. (Eds.). (2002). *Eating disorders and obesity: A comprehensive handbook* (2nd ed.). New York: Guilford.

Fairweather, H., & Butterworth, G. (1977). The WPPSI at four years: A sex difference in verbal-performance discrepancies. *British Journal of Educational Psychology, 7,* 85–90.

Falk, J. H., & Dierking, L. D. (2000). *Learning from museums: Visitor experiences and the making of meaning.* Walnut Creek, CA: AltaMira Press.

Fantuzzo, J. W., McDermott, P. A., Manz, P. H., Hampton, V. R., & Burdick, N. A. (1996). The Pictorial Scale of Perceived Competence and Social Acceptance: Does it work with low-income urban children? *Child Development, 67,* 1071–1084.

Fantz, R. L. (1961). The origin of form perception. *Scientific American, 204,* 66–72.

Fantz, R. L. (1963). Pattern vision in newborn infants. *Science, 140,* 296–297.

Faraone, S. V., & Biederman, J. (2000). Nature, nurture, and attention deficit hyperactivity disorder. *Developmental Review, 20,* 568–581.

Farrar, M. J. (1990). Discourse and the acquisition of grammatical morphemes. *Journal of Child Language, 17,* 607–624.

Farrar, M. J. (1992). Negative evidence and grammatical morpheme acquisition. *Developmental Psychology, 28,* 90–98.

Farrar, M. J., & Goodman, G. S. (1990). Developmental differences in the relation between scripts and episodic memory: Do they exist? In R. Fivush & J. Hudson (Eds.), *Knowing and remembering in young children.* New York: Cambridge University Press.

Farrar, M. J., & Goodman, G. S. (1992). Developmental changes in event memory. *Child Development, 63,* 173–187.

Farrington, D. P. (1994). Childhood, adolescent, and adult features of violent males. In L. R. Huesmann (Ed.), *Aggressive behavior: Current perspectives.* New York: Plenum.

Farver, J. M. (1993). Cultural differences in scaffolding pretend play: A comparison of American and Mexican mother-child and sibling-child pairs. In K. MacDonald (Ed.), *Parent-child play: Descriptions and implications.* Albany, NY: State University of New York Press.

Farver, J. M. (1999). Activity setting analysis: A model for examining the role of culture in development. In A. Göncü (Ed.), *Children's engagement in the world: Sociocultural perspectives.* Cambridge: Cambridge University Press.

Farver, J. M., & Branstetter, W. H. (1994). Preschoolers' prosocial responses to their peers' distress. *Developmental Psychology, 30,* 334–341.

Farver, J. M., & Howes, C. (1993). Cultural differences in American and Mexican mother-child pretend play. *Merrill-Palmer Quarterly, 39,* 344–358.

Farver, J. M., & Wimbarti, S. (1995). Indonesian children's play with their mothers and older siblings. *Child Development, 66,* 1493–1503.

Fawson, P. C., & Moore, S. A. (1999). Reading incentive programs: Beliefs and practices. *Reading Psychology, 20,* 325–340.

Feingold, A. (1992). Sex differences in variability in intellectual abilities: A new look at an old controversy. *Review of Educational Research, 62,* 61–84.

Feingold, A. (1993). Cognitive gender differences: A developmental perspective. *Sex Roles, 29,* 91–112.

Feinman, S., Roberts, D., Hsieh, K., Sawyer, D., & Swanson, D. (1992). A critical review of social referencing in infancy. In S. Feinman (Ed.), *Social referencing and the social construction of reality in infancy.* New York: Plenum.

Feiring, C. (1996). Concepts of romance in 15-year-old adolescents. *Journal of Research on Adolescence, 6,* 181–200.

Feldman, D. H. (1986). *Nature's gambit: Child prodigies and the development of human potential.* New York: Basic Books.

Feldman, P. J., Dunkel-Schetter, C., Sandman, C. A., & Wadhwa, P. D. (2000). Maternal social support predicts birth weight and fetal growth in human pregnancy. *Psychosomatic Medicine, 62,* 715–725.

Feldman, S., Rosenthal, D. A., Mont-Reynauld, R., & Leung, K. (1991). Ain't misbehavin': Adolescent values and family environments as correlates of misconduct in Australia, Hong Kong, and the United States. *Journal of Research on Adolescence, 1,* 109–134.

Fennema, E., Carpenter, T. P., Jacobs, V. R., Franke, M. L., & Levi, L. W. (1998). A longitudinal study of gender differences in young children's mathematical thinking. *Educational Researcher, 27,* 6–11.

Fenson, L., Dale, P. S., Reznick, J. S., Bates E., Thal, D. J., & Pethick, S. J. (1994). Variability in early communicative development. *Monographs of the Society for Research in Child Development, 59*(5, Serial No. 242).

Fenson, L., & Ramsay, D. S. (1981). Effects of modeling action sequences on the play of twelve-, fifteen-, and nineteen-month-old children. *Child Development, 52,* 1028–1036.

Ferguson, C. A. (1983). Reduplication in child phonology. *Journal of Child Language, 10,* 239–243.

Fernald, A. (1993). Approval and disapproval: Infant responsiveness to vocal affect in familiar and unfamiliar languages. *Child Development, 64,* 657–674.

Fernald, A., & O'Neill, D. K. (1993). Peekaboo across cultures: How mothers and infants play with voices, faces, and expectations. In K. MacDonald (Ed.), *Parent-child play.* Albany: State University of New York Press.

Fernandes, O., Sabharwai, M., Smiley, T., Pastuszak, A., Koren, G., & Einarson, T. (1998). Moderate to heavy caffeine consumption during pregnancy and relationship to spontaneous abortion and abnormal fetal growth: A meta-analysis. *Reproductive Toxicology, 12,* 435–444.

Ferrier, S., Dunham, P., & Dunham, F. (2000). The confused robot: Two-year-olds' responses to breakdowns in conversation. *Social Development, 9,* 337–347.

Ferriera, A. J. (1969). *Prenatal environment.* Springfield, IL: Charles C. Thomas.

Feshbach, N. D., & Feshbach, S. (1982). Empathy training and the regulation of aggression: Potentialities and limitations. *Academic Psychology Bulletin, 4,* 399–413.

Feshbach, S., & Singer, R. D. (1971). *Television and aggression: An experimental field study.* San Francisco: Jossey-Bass.

Feuerstein, R., Rand, Y., Haywood, H. C., Kyram, L., & Hoffman, M. B. (1995). *Learning Propensity Assessment Device-manual.* Jerusalem: International Center for the Enhancement of Learning Potential.

Field, T. M. (1987). Affective and interactive disturbances in infants. In J. D. Osofsky (Ed.), *Handbook of infant development* (2nd ed.). New York: Wiley.

Field, T. M. (2001). *Touch.* Cambridge, MA: MIT Press.

Field, T. M., Healy, B., Goldstein, S., & Guthertz, M. (1990). Behavior-state matching and synchrony in mother–infant interactions of nondepressed versus depressed dyads. *Developmental Psychology, 26,* 7–14.

Field, T. M., & Walden, T. A. (1982). Production and perception of facial expressions in infancy and early childhood. In H. W. Reese & L. P. Lipsitt (Eds.), *Advances in child development and behavior* (Vol. 16). New York: Academic Press.

Fields, J., & Casper, L. M. (2001). *America's families and living arrangements: March 2000.* Washington, DC: U.S. Census Bureau.

Fields, S. A., & McNamara, J. R. (2003). The prevention of child and adolescent violence. A review. *Aggression and Violent Behavior, 8,* 61–91.

Fiese, B. H. (1990). Playful relationships: A contextual analysis of mother-toddler interaction and symbolic play. *Child Development, 61,* 1648–1656.

Fifer, W. P., & Moon, C. M. (1995). The effects of fetal experience with sound. In J.-P. Lecanuet, W. P. Fifer, N. A. Krasnegor, & W. P. Smotherman (Eds.), *Fetal development: A psychobiological perspective.* Hillsdale, NJ: Erlbaum.

Fine, G. A. (1987). *With the boys: Little League baseball and preadolescent culture.* Chicago: University of Chicago Press.

Finn, J. D., Gerber, S. B., Achilles, C. M., & Boyd-Zaharias, J. (2001). The enduring effects of small classes. *Teachers College Record, 103,* 145–183.

Finnegan, L. P., & Fehr, K. O. (1980). The effects of opiates, sedative-hypnotics, amphetamines, cannabis, and other psychoactive drugs on the fetus and newborn. In O. J. Kalant (Ed.), *Research advances in alcohol and drug problems: Vol. 5. Alcohol and drug problems in women.* New York: Plenum.

Fischer, K. W. (1980). A theory of cognitive development: The control and construction of hierarchies of skills. *Psychological Review, 87,* 477–531.

Fischer, K. W. & Bidell, T. R. (1998). Dynamic development of psychological structures in action and thought. In W. Damon (Series Ed.) & R. M. Lerner (Vol. Ed.), *Handbook of child psychology: Vol. 1. Theoretical models of human development* (5th ed.). New York: Wiley.

Fischer, K. W., & Bidell, T. R. (1998). Dynamic development of psychological structures in action and thought. In W. Damon (Series Ed.) & R. M. Lerner (Vol. Ed.), *Handbook of child psychology: Vol. 1. Theoretical models of human development* (5th ed.). New York: Wiley.

Fish, J. M. (2002). The myth of race. In J. M. Fish (Ed.), *Race and intelligence.* Mahwah, NJ: Erlbaum.

Fish, M. (2001). Attachment in low-SES rural Appalachian infants: Contextual, infant, and maternal interaction risk and protective factors. *Infant Mental Health Journal, 22,* 641–664.

Fishbein, H. D., & Imai, S. (1993). Preschoolers select playmates on the basis of gender and race. *Journal of Applied Developmental Psychology, 14,* 303–316.

Fisher, C. B., & Tryon, W. W. (Eds.). (1990). *Ethics in applied developmental psychology: Emerging issues in an emerging field.* Norwood, NJ: Ablex.

Fisher, J. O., & Birch, L. L. (2001). Early experience with food and eating: Implications for the development of eating disorders. In J. K. Thompson & L. Smolak (Eds.), *Body image, eating disorders, and obesity in youth: Assessment, prevention, and treatment.* Washington, DC: APA.

Fisher-Thompson, D. (1993). Adult toy purchases for children: Factors affecting sex-typed toy selection. *Journal of Applied Developmental Psychology, 14*, 385–406.

Fivush, R. (1991a). Gender and emotion in mother-child conversations about the past. *Journal of Narrative and Life History, 1*, 325–341.

Fivush, R. (1991b). The social construction of personal narratives. *Merrill-Palmer Quarterly, 37*, 59–81.

Fivush, R. (1998). Gendered narratives: Elaboration, structure, and emotion in parent-child reminiscing across the preschool years. In C. P. Thompson & D. J. Herrmann (Eds.), *Autobiographical memory: Theoretical and applied perspectives*. Mahwah, NJ: Erlbaum.

Fivush, R. (2001). Owning experience: Developing subjective perspective in autobiographical narratives. In C. Moore & K. Lemmon (Eds.), *The self in time: Developmental perspectives*. Mahwah, NJ: Erlbaum.

Fivush, R., & Buckner, J. P. (2000). Gender, sadness, and depression: The development of emotional focus through gendered discourse. In A. H. Fischer (Ed.), *Gender and emotion: Social psychological perspectives*. New York: Cambridge University Press.

Fivush, R., Kuebli, J., & Clubb, P. A. (1992). The structure of events and event representations: A developmental analysis. *Child Development, 63*, 188–201.

Flack, J. C., & de Waal, F. B. M. (2000). 'Any animal whatever': Darwinian building blocks of morality in monkeys and apes. In L. D. Katz (Ed.), *Evolutionary origins of morality: Cross disciplinary perspectives*. Thorveton, UK: Imprint Academic.

Flannagan, D., & Perese, S. (1998). Emotional references in mother-daughter and mother-son dyads' conversations about school. *Sex Roles, 39*, 353–367.

Flannery, D. J. Vazsonyi, A. T., Liau, A. K., Guo, S., Powell, K. E., Atha, H., et al. (2003). Initial behavior outcomes for the PeaceBuilders universal school-based violence prevention program. *Developmental Psychology, 39*, 292–308.

Flavell, J. H. (1963). *The developmental psychology of Jean Piaget*. Princeton, NJ: Van Nostrand.

Flavell, J. H. (1970). Developmental studies of mediated memory. In H. W. Reese & L. P. Lipsitt (Eds.), *Advances in child development and behavior* (Vol. 5). New York: Academic Press.

Flavell, J. H. (1971). First discussant's comments. What is memory development the development of? *Human Development, 14*, 272–278.

Flavell, J. H. (1985). *Cognitive development* (2nd ed.). Englewood Cliffs, NJ: Prentice Hall.

Flavell, J. H. (1986). Development of children's knowledge about the appearance-reality distinction. *American Psychologist, 41*, 418–425.

Flavell, J. H. (1992a). Cognitive development: Past, present, and future. *Developmental Psychology, 28*, 998–1005.

Flavell, J. H. (1992b). Perspectives on perspective taking. In H. Beilin & P. B. Pufall (Eds.), *Piaget's theory: Prospects and possibilities*. Hillsdale, NJ: Erlbaum.

Flavell, J. H. (1999). Cognitive development: Children's knowledge about the mind. *Annual Review of Psychology, 50*, 21–45.

Flavell, J. H., Beach, D. H., & Chinsky, J. M. (1966). Spontaneous verbal rehearsal in a memory task as a function of age. *Child Development, 37*, 283–299.

Flavell, J. H., Flavell, E. R., & Green, F. L. (1983). Development of the appearance-reality distinction. *Cognitive Psychology, 15*, 95–120.

Flavell, J. H., Friedrichs, A., & Hoyt, J. (1970). Developmental changes in memorization processes. *Cognitive Psychology, 1*, 324–340.

Flavell, J. H., Green, F. L., & Flavell, E. R. (1989). Young children's ability to differentiate appearance-reality and

level 2 perspective taking in the tactile modality. *Child Development, 60*, 201–213.

Flavell, J. H., Lindberg, N. A., Green, F. L., & Flavell. E. R. (1992). The development of children's understanding of the appearance-reality distinction between how people look and what they are really like. *Merrill-Palmer Quarterly, 38*, 513–524.

Flavell, J. H., & Miller, P. H. (1998). Social cognition. In W. Damon (Series Ed.) & D. Kuhn & R. S. Siegler (Vol. Eds.), *Handbook of child psychology: Vol. 2. Cognition, perception, and language* (5th ed.). New York: Wiley.

Flavell, J. H., Miller, P. H., & Miller, S. A. (2002). *Cognitive development* (4th ed.). Upper Saddle River, NJ: Prentice Hall.

Flavell, J. H., Shipstead, S. G., & Croft, K. (1980). What young children think you see when their eyes are closed. *Cognition, 8*, 369–387.

Fletcher, A. C., Darling, N.E., Steinberg, L., & Dornbusch, S. (1995). The company they keep: Relation of adolescents' adjustment and behavior to their friends' perceptions of authoritative parenting in the social network. *Developmental Psychology, 31*, 300–310.

Fletcher, A. C., Elder, G. H., & Mekos, D. (2000). Parental influences on adolescent involvement in community activities. *Journal of Research on Adolescence, 10*, 29–48.

Fletcher, P. (1999). Specific language impairment. In M. Barrett (Ed.), *The development of language*. Hove, UK: Psychology Press.

Flieller, A. (1999). Comparison of the development of formal thought in adolescent cohorts aged 10 to 15 years (1967–1999 and 1972–1993). *Developmental Psychology, 35*, 1048–1058.

Flynn, J. R. (1998). IQ gains over time: Toward finding the causes. In U. Neisser (Ed.), *The rising curve: Long-term gains in IQ and related measures*. Washington, DC: APA.

Flynn, J. R. (1999). Searching for justice: The discovery of IQ gains over time. *American Psychologist, 54*, 5–20.

Fogel, A., Nelson-Goens, G. C., Hsu, H., & Shapiro, A. F. (2000). Do different infant smiles reflect different positive emotions? *Social Development 9*, 497–520.

Fogel, A., Stevenson, M. B., & Messinger, D. (1992). A comparison of the parent-child relationship in Japan and the United States. In J. L. Roopnarine & D. B. Carter (Eds.), *Annual advances in applied developmental psychology: Vol. 5. Parent-child socialization in diverse cultures*. Norwood, NJ: Ablex.

Fogel, A., & Thelen, E. (1987). Development of early expressive and communicative action: Reinterpreting the evidence from a dynamic systems perspective. *Developmental Psychology, 23*, 747–761.

Folling-Albers, M., & Hartinger, A. (1998). Interest of boys and girls in elementary school. In L. Hoffman, A. Krap, K. A. Renninger, & J. Baumert (Eds.), *Interest and learning*. Kiel, Germany: Institute for Science Education.

Foot, H., & Howe, C. (1998). The psychoeducational basis of peer assisted learning. In K. Topping & S. Ehly (Eds.). *Peer-assisted learning*. Mahwah, NJ: Erlbaum.

Ford, C., & Beach, F. (1951). *Patterns of sexual behavior*. New York: Harper & Row.

Forehand, R., & Kotchick, B. A. (2002). Behavioral parent training: Current challenges and potential solutions. *Journal of Child and Family Studies, 11*, 377–384.

Forman, E. A. (1992). Discourse, intersubjectivity, and the development of peer collaboration: A Vygotskian approach. In L. T. Winegar & J. Valsiner (Eds.), *Children's development within social context: Vol. 1. Metatheory and theory*. Hillsdale, NJ: Erlbaum.

Forman, E. A., & Ansell, E. (2002). Orchestrating the multiple voices and inscriptions of a mathematics classroom. *Journal of the Learning Sciences, 11*, 251–274.

Forman, E. A., & Cazden, C. B. (1985). Exploring Vygotskian perspectives in education: The cognitive value of

peer interaction. In J. V. Wertsch (Ed.), *Culture, communication, and cognition: Vygotskian perspectives*. Cambridge: Cambridge University Press.

Forman, E. A., & McPhail, J. (1993). Vygotskian perspective in children's collaborative problem solving activity. In E. A. Forman, N. Minick, & C. A. Stone (Eds.), *Contexts for learning: Sociocultural dynamics in children's development*. Oxford: Oxford University Press.

Fox, N. A. (Ed.) (1994). The development of emotion regulation: Biological and behavioral considerations. *Monographs of the Society for Research in Child Development, 59*(2–3, Serial No. 240).

Francis, P. L., Self, P. A., & Horowitz, F. D. (1987). The behavioral assessment of the neonate: An overview. In J. D. Osofsky (Ed.), *Handbook of infant development* (2nd ed.). New York: Wiley.

Frankel, F., & Feinberg, D. (2002). Social problems associated with ADHD vs. ODD in children referred for friendship problems. *Child Psychiatry and Human Development, 33*, 125–146.

Frankel, K. A., & Bates, J. E. (1990). Mother–toddler problem solving: Antecedents of attachment, home behavior, and temperament. *Child Development, 61*, 810–819.

Frankenburg, W. K., & Dodds, J. (1967). The Denver Developmental Screening Test. *Journal of Pediatrics, 71*, 181–191.

Fraser, S. (Ed.). (1995). *The Bell Curve wars: Race, intelligence, and the future of America*. New York: Basic Books.

Frauenglass, M. H., & Diaz, R. M. (1985). Self-regulatory functions of children's speech: A critical analysis of recent challenges to Vygotsky's theory. *Developmental Psychology, 21*, 357–364.

Freeburg, T. J., & Lippman, M. Z. (1986). Factors influencing discrimination of infant cries. *Journal of Child Language, 13*, 3–13.

Freedland, R. L., & Bertenthal, B. I. (1994). Developmental stages in interlimb coordination: Transition to hands-and-knees crawling. *Psychological Science, 5*, 26–32.

French, D. C. (1988). Heterogeneity of peer-rejected boys: Aggressive and nonaggressive subtypes. *Child Development, 59*, 976–985.

French, D. C. (1990). Heterogeneity of peer-rejected girls. *Child Development, 61*, 2028–2031.

Frey, K. S., Hirschstein, M. K., & Guzzo, B. A. (2000). Second Step: Preventing aggression by promoting social competence. *Journal of Emotional and Behavioral Disorders, 8*, 102–112.

Frey, K. S., & Ruble, D. N. (1992). Gender constancy and the "cost" of sex-typed behavior: A test of the conflict hypothesis. *Developmental Psychology, 28*, 714–721.

Fried, P. A., O'Connell, C. M., & Watkinson, M. A. (1992). Sixty- and 72-month follow-up of children prenatally exposed to marijuana, cigarettes, and alcohol: Cognitive and language assessment. *Developmental and Behavioral Pediatrics, 13*, 383–391.

Friedman, H. S., Tucker, J. S., Schwartz, J. E., Tomlinson-Keasey, C., Martin, L. R., Wingard, D. L., et al. (1995). Psychosocial and behavioral predictors of longevity: The aging and death of the "Termites." *American Psychologist, 50*, 69–78.

Friedman, J. M. (1981). Genetic disease in the offspring of older fathers. *Obstetrics and Gynecology, 57*, 745–749.

Friedman, T. L. (2000). *The Lexus and the olive tree: Understanding globalization*. New York: Anchor.

Frisch, H. L. (1977). Sex stereotypes in adult–infant play. *Child Development, 48*, 1671–1675.

Frith, U. (1989). *Autism: Explaining the enigma*. Oxford, England: Basil Blackwell.

Frodi, A. M., Lamb, M. E., Leavitt, L. A., & Donovan, W. L. (1978). Fathers' and mothers' responses to infant smiles and cries. *Infant Behavior and Development, 1,* 187–198.

Fromkin, V., & Rodman, R. (1988). *An introduction to language* (4th ed.). New York: Holt, Rinehart, and Winston.

Frost, J. L., Worthman, S., & Reifel, S. (2001). *Play and child development.* Upper Saddle River, NJ: Prentice Hall.

Fry, D. P. (1988). Intercommunity differences in aggression among Zapotec children. *Child Development, 59,* 1008–1019.

Frye, D. (1999). Development of intention: The relation of executive function to theory of mind. In P. D. Zelazo, J. W. Astington, & D. R. Olson (Eds.), *Developing theories of intention.* Mahwah, NJ: Erlbaum.

Fukahara, H., Shimura, Y., & Yamanouchi, I. (1988, November). *The transmission of ambient noise and self-produced sound into the human body.* Poster presented at the second joint meeting of the Acoustical Society of America and the Acoustical Society of Japan, Honolulu.

Fuligni, A. J., Eccles, J. S., & Barber, B. L. (1995). The long-term effects of seventh-grade ability grouping in mathematics. *Journal of Early Adolescence, 15,* 58–89.

Fuligni, A. J., Eccles, J. S., Barber, B. L., & Clements, P. (2001). Early adolescent peer orientation and adjustment during high school. *Developmental Psychology, 27,* 28–36.

Fullard, W., & Reiling, A. M. (1976). An investigation of Lorenz's "babyness." *Child Development, 47,* 1191–1193.

Fullard, W., McDevitt, S. C., & Carey, W. B. (1984). Assessing temperament in one to three year old children. *Journal of Pediatric Psychology, 9,* 205–217.

Funk, J. B., Germann, J. N., & Buchman, D. D. (1997). Children and electronic games in the United States. *Trends in Communication 2,* 111–126.

Furman, W., & Gavin, L. A. (1989). Peers' influence on adjustment and development. In T. J. Berndt & G. W. Ladd (Eds.), *Peer relationships in child development.* New York: Wiley.

Furman, W., & Lanthier, R. (2002). Parenting siblings. In M. H. Bornstein (Ed.), *Handbook of parenting* (2nd ed., Vol. 1). Mahwah, NJ: Erlbaum.

Furman, W., & Masters, J. C. (1980). Affective consequences of social reinforcement, punishment, and neutral behavior. *Developmental Psychology, 16,* 100–104.

Furnam, A., Abramsky, S., & Gunter, B. (1997). A cross-cultural content analysis of children's television advertisements. *Sex Roles, 37,* 91–99.

Furrow, D., Nelson, K., & Benedict, H. (1979). Mothers' speech to children and syntactic development: Some simple relationships. *Journal of Child Language, 6,* 423–442.

Furstenberg, F. F. (1993). How families manage risk and opportunity in dangerous neighborhoods. In W. J. Wilson (Ed.), *Sociology and the public agenda.* Newbury Park, CA: Sage.

Fuson, K. (1988). *Children's counting and concepts of number.* New York: Springer-Verlag.

Fuson, K. C., & Kwon, Y. (1992a). Learning addition and subtraction: Effects of number words and other cultural tools. In J. Bideaud, C. Meljac, & J.-P. Fischer (Eds.), *Pathways to number: Children's developing numerical abilities.* Hillsdale, NJ: Erlbaum.

Fuson, K. C., & Kwon, Y. (1992b). Korean children's understanding of multidigit addition and subtraction. *Child Development, 63,* 491–506.

Gailey, C. W. (1996). Mediated messages: Gender, class, and cosmos in home video games. In P. M. Greenfield & R. R. Cocking (Eds.), *Interacting with video.* Norwood, NJ: Ablex.

Galen, B. R., & Underwood, M. K. (1997). A developmental investigation of social aggression among children. *Developmental Psychology, 33,* 589–600.

Gallagher, A. M., & De Lisi, R. (1994). Gender differences in Scholastic Aptitude Test-mathematics problem

solving among high-ability students. *Journal of Educational Psychology, 86,* 204–211.

Gallagher, A. M., De Lisi, R., Holst, P. C., McGillicuddy-De Lisi, A. V., Morely, M., & Cahalan, C. (2000). Gender differences in advanced mathematical problem solving. *Journal of Experimental Child Psychology, 75,* 165–190.

Gallagher, K. C. (2002). Does child temperament moderate the influence of parenting on adjustment? *Developmental Review, 22,* 623–643.

Gallahue, D. L., & Ozmun, J. C. (1995). *Understanding motor development: Infants, children, adolescents, adults* (3rd ed.). Madison, WI: Brown & Benchmark.

Gallup Poll. (1997). *U.S. teens and technology.* Retrieved February 9, 2003 from www.nsf.gov/od/lpa/nstw/teenov.htm.

Gallup, G. G. Jr. (1970). Chimpanzees: Self-recognition. *Science, 167,* 86–87.

Gallup, G. G. Jr., Anderson, J. R., & Shillito, D. J. (2002). The mirror test. In M. Bekoff, C. Allen, & G. M. Burghardt (Eds.), *The cognitive animal: Empirical and theoretical perspectives on animal cognition.* Cambridge, MA: MIT Press.

Gally, M. (2002, Jan. 23). Research: Boys to men. *Education Week.* Retrieved February 9, 2003 from www.edweek.org/ew/newstory.cfm?slug519boys.h21.

Galsworthy, M. J., Dionne, G., Dale, P. S., & Plomin, R. (2000). Sex differences in early verbal and non-verbal cognitive development. *Developmental Science, 3,* 206–215.

Garai, J. E., & Scheinfeld, A. (1968). Sex differences in mental and behavioral traits. *Genetic Psychology Monographs, 7,* 169–299.

Garbarino, J., & Kostelny, K. (1996). The effects of political violence on Palestinian children's behavior problems: A risk accumulation model. *Child Development, 67,* 33–45.

Garbarino, J., Dubrow, N., Kostelny, K., & Pardo, C. (1992). *Children in danger: Coping with the consequences of community violence.* San Francisco: Jossey-Bass.

Garden, R. A. (1987). The second IEA mathematics study. *Comparative Education Review, 31,* 47–68.

Gardner, H. (1983). *Frames of mind: The theory of multiple intelligences.* New York: Basic Books.

Gardner, H. (1991). *The unschooled mind: How children think and how schools should teach.* New York: Basic Books.

Gardner, H. (1993a). *Frames of mind: The theory of multiple intelligences* (10th anniversary ed.). New York: Basic Books.

Gardner, H. (1993b). *Multiple intelligences.* New York: Basic Books.

Gardner, H. (1999). *Intelligence reframed: Multiple intelligence in the 21st century.* New York: Basic Books.

Gardner, P. L. (1998). The development of males' and females' interest in science and technology. In L. Hoffman, A. Krap, K. A. Renninger, & J. Baumert (Eds.), *Interest and learning.* Kiel, Germany: Institute for Science Education.

Garmezy, N., & Rutter, M. (Eds.). (1983). *Stress, coping, and development in children.* New York: McGraw-Hill.

Garner, P. W., Jones, D. C., & Miner, J. L. (1994). Social competence among low-income preschoolers: Emotion socialization practices and social cognitive correlates. *Child Development, 65,* 622–637.

Garrison, W. T., & Earls, F. J. (1987). *Temperament and child psychopathology.* Newbury Park, CA: Sage.

Garrod, A., Beal, C., & Shin, P. (1990). The development of moral orientation in elementary school children. *Sex Roles, 22,* 13–26.

Gartner, A., Kohler, M. C., & Riessman, F. (1971). *Children teach children: Learning by teaching.* New York: Harper & Row.

Garton, A. (1992). *Social interaction and the development of language and cognition.* Hillsdale, NJ: Erlbaum.

Garvey, C. (1986). Peer relations and the growth of communication. In E. C. Mueller & C. R. Cooper (Eds.), *Process and outcome in peer relationships.* New York: Academic Press.

Garvey, C. (1990). *Play.* Cambridge, MA: Harvard University Press.

Gaskins, S. (1999). Children's daily lives in a Mayan village: A case study of culturally constructed roles and activities. In A. Göncü (Ed.), *Children's engagement in the world: Sociocultural perspectives.* New York: Cambridge.

Gaub, M., & Carlson, C. L. (1997). Gender differences in ADHD: A meta-analysis and critical review. *Journal of the American Academy of Child and Adolescent Psychiatry, 36,* 1036–1045.

Gauvain, M. (1998). Cognitive development in social and cultural context. *Current Directions in Psychological Science, 7,* 188–192.

Gauvain, M., & Fagot, B. I. (1995). Child temperament as a mediator of mother-toddler problem solving. *Social Development, 4,* 257–278.

Gauvain, M., & Rogoff, B. (1989). Collaborative planning solving and children's planning skills. *Developmental Psychology, 25,* 139–151.

Gayan, J., & Olson, R. K. (2003). Genetic and environmental influences on individual differences in printed word recognition. *Journal of Experimental Child Psychology, 84,* 97–123.

Ge, X., Conger, R. D., Cadoret, R. J., Neiderhiser, J. M., Yates, W., Troughton, E., & Stewart, M. A. (1996). The developmental interface between nature and nurture: A mutual influence model of child antisocial behavior and parents' behaviors. *Developmental Psychology, 32,* 574–589.

Ge, X., Conger, R. D., & Elder, G. H. Jr. (2001a). Pubertal transition, stressful life events, and the emergence of gender differences in adolescent depressive symptoms. *Developmental Psychology, 37,* 404–417.

Ge, X., Conger, R. D., & Elder, G. H. Jr. (2001b). The relation between puberty and psychological distress in adolescent boys. *Journal of Research on Adolescence, 11,* 49–70.

Geary, D. C. (1995a). *Children's mathematical development.* Washington, DC: American Psychological Association.

Geary, D. C. (1995b). Reflections of evolution and culture in children's cognition: Implications for mathematical development and instruction. *American Psychologist, 50,* 24–37.

Geary, D. C. (1996). International differences in mathematical achievement: Their nature, courses, and consequences. *Current Directions in Psychological Science, 5,* 133–137.

Geary, D. C. (1998). *Male, female: The evolution of human sex differences.* Washington, DC: American Psychological Association.

Geary, D. C. (2002). Principles of evolutionary educational psychology. *Learning and Individual Differences, 12,* 317–345.

Geary, D. C., & Bjorklund, D. F. (2000). Evolutionary developmental psychology. *Child Development, 71,* 57–65.

Geary, D. C., Bow-Thomas, C. C., Fan, L., & Siegler, R. S. (1993). Even before formal instruction, Chinese children outperform American children in mental addition. *Cognitive Development, 8,* 517–529.

Geary, D. C., Bow-Thomas, C. C., Fan, L., & Siegler, R. S. (1996). Development of arithmetical competencies in Chinese and American children: Influence of age, language, and schooling. *Child Development, 67,* 2022–2044.

Geary, D. C., & Huffman, K. J. (2002). Brain and cognitive evolution: Forms of modularity and functions of mind. *Psychological Bulletin, 128,* 667–698.

Geary, D. C., Saults, S. J., Liu, F., & Hoard, M. K. (2000). Sex differences in spatial cognition, computational fluency, and arithmetical reasoning. *Journal of Experimental Child Psychology, 77,* 337–353.

Geen, R. G. (1983). Aggression and television violence. In R. G. Geen & E. I. Donnerstein (Eds.), *Aggression: Theoretical and empirical reviews* (Vol. 2). New York: Academic Press.

Gelfand, D. M., & Hartmann, D. P. (1982). Response consequences and attributions: Two contributors to prosocial behavior. In N. Eisenberg (Ed.), *The development of prosocial behavior.* New York: Academic Press.

Gelman, R. (1972). Logical capacity of very young children: Number invariance rules. *Child Development, 43,* 75–90.

Gelman, R. (1982). Basic numerical abilities. In R. J. Sternberg (Ed.), *Advances in the psychology of human intelligence* (Vol. 1). Hillsdale, NJ: Erlbaum.

Gelman, R. (1991). Epigenetic foundations of knowledge structures: Initial and transcendent constructions. In S. Carey & R. Gelman (Eds.), *The epigenesis of mind.* Hillsdale, NJ: Erlbaum.

Gelman, R., & Baillargeon, R. (1983). A review of some Piagetian concepts. In P. H. Mussen (Series Ed.) & J. H. Flavell & E. M. Markman (Vol. Eds.), *Handbook of child psychology: Vol. 3. Cognitive development* (4th ed.). New York: Wiley.

Gelman, R., & Gallistel, C. R. (1978). *The child's understanding of number.* Cambridge, MA: Harvard University Press.

Gelman, S. A. (2000). The role of essentialism in children's concepts. In H. W. Reese (Ed.), *Advances in child development and behavior* (Vol. 27). San Diego, CA: Academic Press.

Gelman, S. A., & Coley, J. D. (1990). The importance of knowing a dodo is a bird: Categories and induction in 2-year-old children. *Developmental Psychology, 26,* 796–804.

Gelman, S. A., & Markman, E. M. (1986). Categories and induction in young children. *Cognition, 23,* 183–209.

Gelman, S. A., & Markman, E. M. (1987). Young children's inductions from natural kinds: The role of categories and experience. *Child Development, 58,* 1532–1541.

Gelman, S. A., Wilcox, S. A., & Clark, E. V. (1989). Conceptual and lexical hierarchies in young children. *Cognitive Development, 4,* 309–326.

Genesee, F. (Ed.). (1994). *Educating second language children.* New York: Cambridge University Press.

Genesee, F., Nicoladis, E., & Paradis, J. (1995). Language differentiation in early bilingual development. *Journal of Child Language, 22,* 611–631.

Genome International Sequencing Consortium. (2001). Initial sequencing and analyses of the human genome. *Nature, 409,* 860–921.

Gentile, D. A. (1993). Just what are sex and gender, anyway? A call for a new terminological standard. *Psychological Science, 4,* 120–122.

Gentner, D. (1982). Why nouns are learned before verbs: Linguistic relativity versus natural partitioning. In S. A. Kuczaj (Ed.), *Language development* (Vol. 2). Hillsdale, NJ: Erlbaum.

George, C., Kaplan, N., & Main, M. (1985). *The Adult Attachment Interview.* Unpublished manuscript, University of California, Department of Psychology, Berkeley.

George, C., & Solomon, J. (1989). Internal working models of parenting and security of attachment at age six. *Infant Mental Health Journal, 10,* 222–237.

Georgieff, M. K., & Rao, R. (2001). The role of nutrition in cognitive development. In C. A. Nelson & M. Luciana (Eds.), *Handbook of developmental cognitive neuroscience.* Cambridge, MA: MIT Press.

Gershkoff-Stowe, L. (2001). The course of children's naming errors in early word learning. *Journal of Cognition and Development, 2,* 131–155.

Gershkoff-Stowe, L., & Smith, L. B. (1997). A curvilinear trend in naming errors as a function of early vocabulary growth. *Cognitive Psychology, 34,* 37–71.

Gesell, A. (1925). *The mental growth of the pre-school child.* New York: Macmillan.

Gesell, A., & Thompson, H. (1929). Learning and growth in identical infant twins: An experimental study by the method of co-twin control. *Genetic Psychological Monographs, 6,* 1–24.

Gesell, A., & Thompson, H. (1938). *The psychology of early growth.* New York: Macmillan.

Gewirtz, J. L. (1991). Social influence on child and parent via stimulation and operant learning mechanisms. In M. Lewis & S. Feinman (Eds.), *Social influences and socialization in infancy.* New York: Plenum.

Gewirtz, J. L., & Boyd, E. F. (1976). Mother–infant interaction and its study. In H. W. Reese (Ed.), *Advances in child development and behavior* (Vol. 11). New York: Academic Press.

Gewirtz, J. L., & Boyd, E. F. (1977). Experiments on mother–infant interaction underlying mutual attachment acquisition: The infant conditions the mother. In T. Alloway, P. Pliner, & L. Kramer (Eds.), *Advances in the study of communication and affect: Vol. 3. Attachment behavior.* New York: Plenum.

Gewirtz, J. L., & Pelaez-Nogueras, M. (1991a). The attachment metaphor and the conditioning of infant separation protests. In J. L. Gewirtz & W. M. Kurtines (Eds.), *Intersections with attachment.* Hillsdale, NJ: Erlbaum.

Gewirtz, J. L., & Pelaez-Nogueras, M. (1991b). Proximal mechanisms underlying the acquisition of moral behavior patterns. In W. M. Kurtines & J. L. Gewirtz (Eds.), *Handbook of moral behavior and development: Vol. 1. Theory.* Hillsdale, NJ: Erlbaum.

Gewirtz, J. L., & Pelaez-Nogueras, M. (1992a). B. F. Skinner's legacy to human infant behavior and development. *American Psychologist, 47,* 1411–1422.

Gewirtz, J. L., & Pelaez-Nogueras, M. (1992b). Social referencing as a learned process. In S. Feinman (Ed.), *Social referencing and the social construction of reality in infancy.* New York: Plenum.

Ghatala, E. S., Levin, J. R., Pressley, M., & Lodice, M. G. (1985). Training cognitive strategy monitoring in children. *American Educational Research Journal, 22,* 199–216.

Gianino, A., & Tronick, E. Z. (1988). The mutual regulation model: The infant's self and interactive regulation coping and defense. In T. Field, P. McCabe, & N. Schneiderman (Eds.), *Stress and coping.* Hillsdale, NJ: Erlbaum.

Gibbons, J. L. (2000). Gender development in cross-cultural perspective. In T. Eckes & H. M. Trautner (Eds.), *The developmental social psychology of gender.* Mahwah, NJ: Erlbaum.

Gibbs, J. C. (2003). *Moral development and reality: Beyond the theories of Kohlberg and Hoffman.* Thousand Oaks, CA: Sage.

Gibson, E. J. (1969). *Principles of perceptual learning and development.* New York: Appleton-Century-Crofts.

Gibson, E. J. (1988). Exploratory behavior in the development of perceiving, acting, and the acquiring of knowledge. *Annual Review of Psychology, 39,* 1–41.

Gibson, E. J. (1993). Ontogenesis of the perceived self. In U. Neisser (Ed.), *The perceived self: Ecological and interpersonal sources of self-knowledge.* Cambridge, MA: Cambridge University Press.

Gibson, E. J., & Pick, A. (2000). *Perceptual learning and development: An ecological view.* New York: Oxford University Press.

Gibson, E. J., & Walk, R. D. (1960). The "visual cliff." *Scientific American, 202,* 64–71.

Gibson, E. J., & Walker, A. (1984). Development of knowledge of visual-tactual affordances of substance. *Child Development, 55,* 453–460.

Gibson, J. J. (1966). *The senses considered as perceptual systems.* Boston: Houghton Mifflin.

Giddens, A. (2000). *Runaway world: How globalization is reshaping our lives.* New York: Routledge.

Gilbert, W. M., Nesbitt, T. S., & Danielsen, B. (1999). Childbearing beyond age 40: Pregnancy outcomes in 24,032 cases. *Obstetrics and Gynecology, 93,* 9–14

Gilligan, C. (1982). *In a different voice: Psychological theory and women's development.* Cambridge, MA: Harvard University Press.

Gilligan, C., & Attanucci, J. (1988). Two moral orientations: Gender differences and similarities. *Merrill-Palmer Quarterly, 34,* 223–237.

Gilly, M. (1988). Gender roles in advertising: A comparison of television advertisements in Australia, Mexico, and the United States. *Journal of Marketing, 52,* 75–85.

Ginsburg, H. J., Klein, A., & Starkey, P. (1998). The development of children's mathematical thinking: Theory, research, and practice. In W. Damon (Series Ed.) & I. E. Sigel & K. A. Renninger (Vol. Eds.), *Handbook of child psychology: Vol. 4. Child psychology in practice* (5th ed.). New York: Wiley.

Ginsburg, H., & Opper, S. (1988). *Piaget's theory of intellectual development* (3rd ed.). Englewood Cliffs, NJ: Prentice Hall.

Giusti, R. M., Iwamoto, K., & Hatch, E. E. (1995). Diethylstilbestrol revisited: A review of the long-term health effects. *Annals of Internal Medicine, 122,* 778–788.

Glasgow, K. L., Dornbusch, S. M., Troyer, L., Steinberg, L., & Ritter, P. I. (1997). Parenting style, adolescents' attributions, and educational outcomes in nine heterogeneous high schools. *Child Development, 68,* 507–529.

Glassman, M. (1994). All things being equal: The two roads of Piaget and Vygotsky. *Developmental Review, 14,* 186–214.

Gleason, J. B., & Ely, R. (2002). Gender differences in language development. In A. McGillicuddy-De Lisi & R. De Lisi (Eds.), *Advances in applied developmental psychology: Vol. 21. Biology, society, and behavior: The development of sex differences in cognition.* Westport, CT: Ablex.

Gleason, J. B., & Weintraub, S. (1978). Input and the acquisition of communicative competence. In K. E. Nelson (Ed.), *Children's language* (Vol. 1). New York: Gardner.

Gleitman, L. R., & Gillette, J. (1999). The role of syntax in verb learning. In W. C. Ritchie & T. K. Bhatia (Eds.), *Handbook of child language acquisition.* San Diego, CA: Academic Press.

Glenn, S. M., Cunningham, C. C., & Joyce P. F. (1981). A study of auditory preferences in nonhandicapped infants and infants with Down's syndrome. *Child Development, 52,* 1303–1307.

Goddard, H. H. (1912). *The Kallikak family: A study in the heredity of feeble-mindedness.* New York: The Macmillan Company.

Goddard, M., Durkin, K., & Rutter, D. R. (1985). The semantic focus of maternal speech: A comment on Ninio and Bruner (1978). *Journal of Child Language, 12,* 209–213.

Gold, D., & Berger, C. (1978). Problem-solving performance of young boys and girls as a function of task appropriateness and sex identity. *Sex Roles, 4,* 183–193.

Goldberg, S. (1983). Parent–infant bonding: Another look. *Child Development, 54,* 1355–1382.

Goldenberg, R. L. (1995). Small for gestational age infants. In B. P. Sachs, R. Beard, E. Papiernik, & C. Russell (Eds.), *Reproductive health care for women and babies.* New York: Oxford University Press.

Goldfield, B. A. (2000). Nouns before verbs in comprehension vs. production: The view from pragmatics. *Journal of Child Language, 27,* 501–520.

Goldfield, B. A., & Reznick, J. S. (1990). Early lexical acquisition: Rate, content, and the vocabulary spurt. *Journal of Child Language, 17,* 171–183.

Goldfield, B. A., & Snow, C. E. (2001). Individual differences: Implications for the study of language acquisition. In J. B. Gleason (Ed.), *The development of language* (5th ed.). Boston: Allyn and Bacon.

Goldin-Meadow, S. (2000). Beyond words: The importance of gesture to researchers and learners. *Child Development, 71,* 231–239.

Goldin-Meadow, S. (2001). Giving the mind a hand: The role of gesture in cognitive change. In J. L. McClelland & R. S. Siegler (Eds.), *Mechanisms of cognitive development.* Mahwah, NJ: Erlbaum.

Goldin-Meadow, S., Alibali, M. W., & Church, R. B. (1993). Transitions in concept acquisition: Using the hand to read the mind. *Psychological Review, 100,* 279–297.

Goldin-Meadow, S., & Mylander, C. (1984). Gestural communication in deaf children: The effects and noneffects of parental input on early language development. *Monographs of the Society for Research in Child Development, 49*(3–4, Serial No. 207).

Goldin-Meadow, S., & Sandhofer, C. M. (1999). Gestures convey substantive information about a child's thoughts to ordinary listeners. *Developmental Science, 2,* 67–74.

Goldman, A. S. (1980). Critical periods of prenatal toxic insults. In R. H. Schwartz & S. J. Yaffe (Eds.), *Drug and chemical risks to the fetus and newborn.* New York: Alan R. Liss.

Goldsmith, H. H., Aksan, N., Essex, M., & Vandell, D. L. (2001).Temperament and socioemotional adjustment to kindergarten: A multi-informant perspective. In T. D. Wachs & G. A. Kohnstamm (Eds.), *Temperament in context.* Mahwah, NJ: Erlbaum.

Goldsmith, H. H., Buss, A. H., Plomin, R., Rothbart, M. K., Thomas, A., Chess, S., et al. Roundtable: What is temperament. Four approaches. *Child Development, 58,* 505–529.

Goldsmith, H. H., Buss, K. A., & Lemery, K. S. (1997). Toddler and childhood temperament: Expanded content, stronger genetic evidence, new evidence for the importance of environment. *Developmental Psychology, 33,* 891–905.

Goldsmith, H. H., & Harman, C. (1994). Temperament and attachment: Individuals and relationships. *Current Directions in Psychological Science, 3,* 53–57.

Goldsmith, H. H., & Rothbart, M. K. (1991) Contemporary instruments for assessing early temperament by questionnaire and in the laboratory. In J. Strelau & A. Angleitner (Eds.), *Explorations in temperament: International perspectives on theory and measurement.* New York: Plenum.

Goldstein, A. P., & Glick, B. (1994). Aggression replacement training: Curriculum and evaluation. *Simulation and Gaming, 25,* 9–26

Golombok, S. (2000). *Parenting: What really matters?* London: Routledge.

Golombok, S., Cook, R., Bish, A., & Murray, C. (1995). Families created by the new reproductive technologies: Quality of parenting and social and emotional development of the children. *Child Development, 66,* 285–298.

Golombok, S., MacCallum, F., & Goodman, E. (2001). The "test-tube" generation: Parent-child relationships and the psychological well-being of in vitro fertilization children at adolescence. *Child Development, 72,* 599–608.

Golombok, S., Perry, B., Burston, A., Murray, C., Mooney-Somers, J., Stevens, M., et al. (2003). Children with lesbian parents: A community study. *Developmental Psychology, 39,* 20–33.

Golombok, S., & Tasker, F. L. (1996). Do parents influence the sexual orientation of their children? Findings from a longitudinal study of lesbian families. *Developmental Psychology, 32,* 3–11.

Göncü, A. (1993). Development of intersubjectivity in social pretend play. *Human Development, 36,* 185–198.

Göncü, A., Mistry, J., & Mosier, C. (2000). Cultural variations in the play of toddlers. *International Journal of Behavioral Development, 24,* 321–329.

Göncü, A., & Rogoff, B. (1998). Children's categorization with varying adult support. *American Educational Research Journal, 35,* 333–349.

Good, T. L., & Brophy, J. E. (2000). *Looking in classrooms* (8th ed.). New York: Longman.

Goodman, G. S., Hirschmann, J. E., Hepps, D., & Rudy, L. (1991). Children's memory for stressful events. *Merrill-Palmer Quarterly, 37,* 109–158.

Goodman, G. S., Pyle Taub, S., Jones, D. P. H., England, P., Port, L. K., Rudy, L., et al. (1992). Testifying in criminal court. *Monographs of the Society for Research in Child Development, 57*(5, Serial No. 229).

Goodman, K. (1998). *In defense of good teaching: What teachers need to know about the "reading wars."* York, ME: Stenhouse Publishers.

Goodman, R., & Stevenson, J. (1989). A twin study of hyperactivity: II. The aetiological role of genes, family relationships, and perinatal adversity. *Journal of Child Psychology and Psychiatry, 30,* 691–709.

Goodnow, J. J. (1976). The nature of intelligent behavior: Questions raised by cross-cultural studies. In L. B. Resnick (Ed.), *The nature of intelligence.* Hillsdale, NJ: Erlbaum.

Goodnow, J. J. (1984). On being judged "intelligent." In P. S. Fry (Ed.), *Changing conceptions of intelligence and intellectual functioning: Current theory and research.* Amsterdam: Elsevier Press.

Goodnow, J. J. (1990). The socialization of cognition: What's involved? In J. W. Stigler, R. A. Shweder, & G. Herdt (Eds.), *Cultural psychology: Essays on comparative human development.* New York: Cambridge University Press.

Goodnow, J. J. (1996). Acceptable ignorance, negotiable disagreement: Alternative views of learning. In D. R. Olson & N. Torrance (Eds.), *The handbook of education and human development: New models of learning, teaching, and schooling.* Cambridge, MA: Blackwell.

Goodnow, J. J. (2002). Parents' knowledge and expectations: Using what we know. In M. H. Bornstein (Ed.), *Handbook of parenting* (2nd ed., Vol. 3). Mahwah, NJ: Erlbaum.

Goodwyn, S. L., Acredolo, L. P., & Brown, C. A. (2000). Impact of symbolic gesturing on early language development. *Journal of Nonverbal Behavior, 24,* 81–103.

Goodz, N. S. (1989). Parental language mixing in bilingual families. *Journal of Infant Mental Health, 10,* 25–34.

Gopnik, A., & Meltzoff, A. N. (1987). Early semantic developments and their relationship to object permanence, means–ends understanding and categorization. In K. Nelson & A. VanKleek (Eds.), *Children's language* (Vol. 6). Hillsdale, NJ: Erlbaum.

Gopnik, A., & Meltzoff, A. N. (1996). *Words, thoughts, and theories.* Cambridge, MA: MIT Press.

Gorman, K. S., & Pollitt, E. (1992). Relationship between weight and body proportionality at birth, growth during the first year of life, and cognitive development at 36, 48, and 60 months. *Infant Behavior and Development, 15,* 279–296.

Goswami, U. (1992). *Analogical reasoning in children.* Hove, UK: Erlbaum.

Goswami, U. (1995). Transitive relational mappings in three- and four-year-olds: The analogy of Goldilocks and the three bears. *Child Development, 66,* 877–892.

Goswami, U. (1996). Analogical reasoning and cognitive development. In H. W. Reese (Ed.), *Advances in child development and behavior* (Vol. 26). New York: Academic Press.

Gotlieb, S. J., Baisini, F. J., & Bray, N. W. (1988). Visual recognition memory in IVGR and normal birthweight infants. *Infant Behavior and Development, 11,* 223–228.

Gottesman, I. I. (1974). Developmental genetics and ontogenetic psychology: Overdue détente and propositions from a matchmaker. In A. Pick (Ed.), *Minnesota symposia on child psychology* (Vol. 8). Minneapolis: University of Minnesota Press.

Gottfried, A. E., Fleming, J. S., & Gottfried, A. W. (1998). Role of cognitively stimulating home environment in children's academic intrinsic motivation. *Child Development, 69,* 1448–1461.

Gottfried, A. W. (Ed.). (1984a). *Home environment and early cognitive development.* New York: Academic Press.

Gottfried, A. W. (1984b). Home environment and early cognitive development: Integration, meta-analyses, and conclusions. In A. W. Gottfried (Ed.), *Home environment and early cognitive development.* New York: Academic Press.

Gottfried, A. W., Gottfried, A. E., Bathurst, K., & Guerin, D. W. (1994). *Gifted IQ: Early developmental aspects.* New York: Plenum Press.

Gottlieb, G. (1998). Normally occurring environmental and behavioral influences on gene activity: From central dogma to probabilistic epigenesis. *Psychological Review, 105,* 792–802.

Gottman, J. M. (1983). How children become friends. *Monographs of the Society for Research in Child Development, 48*(3, Serial No. 201).

Gottman, J. M., Gonso, J., & Rasmussen, B. (1975). Social interaction, social competence, and friendship in children. *Child Development, 46,* 709–718.

Gottman, J. S. (1990). Children of gay and lesbian parents. In F. W. Bozett & M. B. Sussman (Eds.), *Homosexuality and family relations.* New York: Harrington Park Press.

Goudena, P. P. (1987). The social nature of private speech of preschoolers during problem solving. *International Journal of Behavioral Development, 10,* 187–206.

Graber, J. A., Brooks-Gunn, J., Paikoff, R. L., & Warren, M. P. (1994). Prediction of eating problems: An 8-year study of adolescent girls. *Developmental Psychology, 30,* 823–834.

Graber, J. A., Brooks-Gunn, J., & Petersen, A. C. (Eds.). (1996). *Transitions through adolescence: Interpersonal domains and context.* Mahwah, NJ: Erlbaum.

Graham, F. K., & Clifton, R. K. (1966). Heart-rate change as a component of the orienting response. *Psychological Bulletin, 65,* 305–320.

Graham, S., & Hoehn, S. (1995). Children's understanding of aggression and withdrawal as social stigmas: An attributional analysis. *Child Development, 66,* 1143–1161.

Graham, S., Hudley, C., & Williams, E. (1992). Attributional and emotional determinants of aggression among African-American and Latino young adolescents. *Developmental Psychology, 28,* 731–740.

Graham, S., & Juvonen, J. (1998a). Self-blame and peer victimization in middle school: An attributional analysis. *Developmental Psychology, 34,* 587–599.

Graham, S., & Juvonen, J. (1998b). A social cognitive perspective on peer aggression and victimization. In R. Vasta (Ed.), *Annals of child development* (Vol. 13). London: Kingsley.

Gralinski, J. H., & Kopp, C. B. (1993). Everyday rules for behavior: Mothers' requests to young children. *Developmental Psychology, 29,* 573–584.

Grantham-McGregor, S., Ani, C., & Fernald, L. (2001). The role of nutrition in intellectual development. In R. J. Sternberg & E. L. Grigorenko (Eds.), *Environmental effects on cognitive abilities.* Mahwah, NJ: Erlbaum.

Graziano, W. G. (1987). Lost in thought at the choice point: Cognition, context, and equity. In J. C. Masters & W. P. Smith (Eds.), *Social comparison, social justice, and relative deprivation.* Hillsdale, NJ: Erlbaum.

Green, B. L., Grace, M., Vary, J. G., Kramer, T., Gleser, G. C., & Leonard, A. (1994). Children of disaster in the second decade: A 17-year follow-up of Buffalo Creek survivors. *Journal of the American Academy of Child and Adolescent Psychiatry, 33,* 71–79.

Green, J. A., Jones, L. E., & Gustafson, G. E. (1987). Perception of cries by parents and nonparents: Relation to cry acoustics. *Developmental Psychology, 23,* 370–382.

Green, K. D., Forehand, R., Beck, S. J., & Vosk, B. (1980). An assessment of the relationship among measures of children's social competence and children's academic achievement. *Child Development, 51,* 1149–1156.

Greenberg, M. T., Domitrovich, C., & Bumbarger, B. (2001). The prevention of mental disorders in school-age children: Current state of the field. Prevention and Treatment, 4, Article 001a. Online article available at http://hournals.apa.org/prevention/volume4/pre004001a.html.

Greenberger, E., & Chen, C. (1996). Perceived family relationships and depressed mood in early and late adolescence: A comparison of European and Asian Americans. *Developmental Psychology, 32,* 707–716.

Greene, J. P. (1998). *A meta-analysis of the effectiveness of bilingual education.* Claremont, CA: Tomas Rivera Policy Institute.

Greenfield, P. M. (1966). On culture and conservation. In J. S. Bruner, R. R. Oliver, & P. M. Greenfield (Eds.), *Studies in cognitive growth.* New York: Wiley.

Greenfield, P.M. (1994). Video games as cultural artifacts. *Journal of Applied Developmental Psychology, 15,* 3–11.

Greenough, W. T., & Black, J. E. (1999). Experience, neural plasticity, and psychological development. In N. A. Fox, L. A. Leavitt, & J. G. Warhol (Eds.), *The role of early experience in infant development.* Pompton Plains, NJ: Johnson and Johnson Pediatric Institute.

Gregory, R. (1978). *Eye and brain: The psychology of seeing* (3rd ed.). New York: McGraw Hill.

Grigorenko, E. L. (2000). Heritability and intelligence. In R. J. Sternberg (Ed.), *Handbook of intelligence.* New York: Cambridge University Press.

Grolnick, W. S., Kurowski, C. O., Dunlap, K. G., & Hevey, C. (2000). Parental resources and the transition to junior high. *Journal of Research on Adolescence, 10,* 465–488.

Gronau, R. C., & Waas, G. A. (1997). Delay of gratification and cue utilization: An examination of children's social information processing. *Merrill-Palmer Quarterly, 43,* 305–322.

Gronlund, N. (1959). *Sociometry in the classroom.* New York: Harper.

Groome, L. J., Swiber, M. J., Atterbury, J. L., Bentz, L. S., & Holland, S. B. (1997). Similarities and differences in behavioral state organization during sleep periods in the perinatal infant before and after birth. *Child Development, 68,* 1–11.

Grossman, D., Neckerman, H., Koepsell, T., Liu, P. Y., Asher, K. N., Belands, K., et al. (1997). Effectiveness of a violence prevention curriculum among children in elementary school: A randomized controlled trial. *Journal of the American Medical Association, 277,* 1605–1611.

Grossmann, K. E., & Grossmann, K. (1990). The wider concept of attachment in cross-cultural research. *Human Development, 33,* 31–47.

Grossmann, K., Grossmann, K. E., Spangler, G., Suess, G., & Unzner, L. (1985). Maternal sensitivity and newborns' orientation responses as related to quality of attachment in northern Germany. In I. Bretherton & E. Waters (Eds.), Growing points of attachment theory and research. *Monographs of the Society for Research in Child Development, 50*(1–2, Serial No. 209).

Groves, B., Zuckerman, B., Marans, S., & Cohen, D. (1993). Silent victims: Children who witness violence. *Journal of the American Medical Association, 269,* 262–264.

Grusec, J. E., & Abramovitch, R. (1982). Imitation of peers and adults in a natural setting: A functional analysis. *Child Development, 53,* 636–642.

Grusec, J. E., & Goodnow, J. J. (1994). Impact of parental discipline methods on the child's internalization of values: A reconceptualization of current points of view. *Developmental Psychology, 30,* 4–19.

Grusec, J. E., Goodnow, J. J., & Cohen, L. (1996). Household work and the development of concern for others. *Developmental Psychology, 32,* 999–1007.

Grusec, J. E., Kuczynski, L., Rushton, J. P., & Simutis, Z. M. (1979). Learning resistance to temptation through observation. *Developmental Psychology, 15,* 233–240.

Grusec, J. E., & Lytton, H. (1988). *Social development: History, theory, and research.* New York: Springer-Verlag.

Guberman, S. R. (1996). The development of everyday mathematics in Brazilian children with limited formal education. *Child Development, 67,* 1609–1623.

Guerin, D. W., & Gottfried, A. W. (1994). Developmental stability and change in parent reports of temperament: A ten-year longitudinal investigation from infancy through preadolescence. *Merrill-Palmer Quarterly, 40,* 334–355.

Guerra, N. G., & Slaby, R. G. (1990). Cognitive mediators of aggression in adolescent offenders: 2. Intervention. *Developmental Psychology, 26,* 269–277.

Guilford, J. P. (1985). The structure-of-intellect model. In B. B. Wolman (Ed.), *Handbook of intelligence.* New York: Wiley.

Guilford, J. P. (1988). Some changes in the structure-of-the-intellect model. *Educational and Psychological Measurement, 48,* 1–4.

Guillemin, J. (1993). Cesarean birth: Social and political aspects. In B. K. Rothman (Ed.), *Encyclopedia of childbearing.* Phoenix, AZ: Oryx Press.

Gunnar, M. R., Brodersen, L., Krueger, K., & Rigatuso, J. (1996). Dampening of adrenocortical responses during infancy: Normative changes and individual differences. *Child Development, 67,* 877–889.

Gunnar, M. R., Fisch, R. O., & Malone, S. (1984). The effects of a pacifying stimulus on behavioral and adrenocortical responses to circumcision in the newborn. *Journal of the American Academy of Child Psychiatry, 23,* 34–38.

Gunnar, M. R., Larson, M. C., Hertsgaard, L., & Harris, M. L., (1992). The stressfulness of separation among nine-month-old infants: Effects of social context variables and infant temperament. *Child Development, 63,* 290–303.

Gunnar, M. R., Malone, S., Vance, G., & Fisch, R. O. (1985). Coping with aversive stimulation in the neonatal period: Quiet sleep and plasma cortisol levels during recovery from circumcision. *Child Development, 56,* 824–834.

Gunnar, M. R., Mangelsdorf, S., Larson, M., & Hertsgaard, L. (1989). Attachment, temperament, and adrenocortical activity in infancy: A study of psychoendocrine regulation. *Developmental Psychology, 25,* 355–363.

Gunnar, M. R., Tout, K., de Haan, M., & Pierce, S. (1997). Temperament, social competence, and adrenocortical activity in preschoolers. *Developmental Psychobiology, 31,* 65–85.

Gurucharri, C., & Selman, R. L. (1982). The development of interpersonal understanding during childhood, pread-

olescence, and adolescence: A longitudinal follow-up study. *Child Development, 53,* 924–927.

Gustafson, G. E., & Harris, K. L. (1990). Women's responses to young infants' cries. *Developmental Psychology, 26,* 144–152.

Gustafson, G. E., Wood, R. M., & Green, J. A. (2000). Can we hear the causes of infants' crying? In R. G. Barr, B. Hopkins, & J. A. Green (Eds.), *Crying as a sign, a symptom, and a signal: Clinical, emotional, and developmental aspects of infant and toddler crying.* New York: Cambridge University Press.

Haapasalo, J., & Tremblay, R. E. (1994). Physically aggressive boys from age 6 to 12: Family background, parenting behavior, and prediction of delinquency. *Journal of Consulting and Clinical Psychology, 62,* 1044–1052.

Hack, M., Klein, N. K., & Taylor, H. G. (1995). Long-term developmental outcomes of low birth weight infants. *The future of children* (Vol. 5, No. 1). Los Angeles: Packard Foundation.

Hadjistavropoulos, H. D., Craig, K. D., Grunau, R. V. E., & Johnston, C. C. (1994). Judging pain in newborns: Facial and cry determinants. *Journal of Pediatric Psychology, 19,* 485–491.

Haeckel, E. (1977). Last words on evolution. In D. N. Robinson (Ed.), *Significant contributions to the history of psychology: 1750–1920.* Washington, DC: University Publications of America. (Original work published 1906)

Hagen, J.W., & Hale, G. A. (1973). The development of attention in children. In A. D. Pick (Ed.), *Minnesota symposia on child psychology* (Vol. 7). Minneapolis: University of Minnesota Press.

Hagerman, R. J. (1996). Biomedical advances in developmental psychology: The case of Fragile X syndrome. *Developmental Psychology, 32,* 416–424.

Haggerty, R., Garmezy, N., Rutter, M., & Sherrod, L. R. (Eds.). (1994). *Stress, risk and resilience in children and adolescents: Processes, mechanisms, and interventions.* New York: Cambridge University Press.

Hahn, C. S., & DiPietro, J. A. (2001). In-vitro fertilization and the family: Quality of parenting, family functioning, and child psychosocial adjustment. *Developmental Psychology, 37,* 37–48.

Haight, W. L., & Miller, P. J. (1993). *Pretending at home: Early development in a sociocultural context.* Albany: State University of New York Press.

Haight, W. L., Parke, R. D., & Black, J. E. (1997). Mothers' and fathers' beliefs about and spontaneous participation in their toddlers' pretend play. *Merrill-Palmer Quarterly, 43,* 271–290.

Haight, W. L., Wang, X., Fung, H., Williams, K., & Mintz, J. (1999). Universal, developmental, and variable aspects of young children's play: A cross-cultural comparison of pretending at home. *Child Development, 70,* 1477–1488.

Hainline, L. (1998). The development of basic visual abilities. In A. Slater (Ed.), *Perceptual development: Visual, auditory, and speech perception in infancy.* Hove, UK: Psychology Press.

Hainline, L., & Abramov, I. (1992). Assessing visual development: Is infant vision good enough? In C. Rovee-Collier & L. P. Lipsitt (Eds.), *Advances in infancy research* (Vol. 7). Norwood, NJ: Ablex.

Haith, M. M. (1966). The response of the human newborn to visual movement. *Journal of Experimental Child Psychology, 3,* 235–243.

Haith, M. M. (1980). *Rules that babies look by.* Hillsdale, NJ: Erlbaum.

Haith, M. M. (1986). Sensory and perceptual processes in early infancy. *Journal of Pediatrics, 109,* 158–171.

Haith, M. M. (1990). Progress in the understanding of sensory and perceptual processes in early infancy. *Merrill-Palmer Quarterly, 36,* 1–26.

Haith, M. M. (1991). Gratuity, perception-action integration and future orientation in infant vision. In F. Kessel, A. Sameroff, & M. Bornstein (Eds.), *The past as prologue in developmental psychology: Essays in honor of William Kessen*. Hillsdale, NJ: Erlbaum.

Haith, M. M. (1994). Visual expectations as the first step toward the development of future-oriented processes. In M. M. Haith, J. B. Benson, R. J. Roberts Jr., & B. F. Pennington (Eds.), *The development of future-oriented processes*. Chicago: University of Chicago Press.

Haith, M. M. (1998). Who put the cog in infant cognition? *Infant Behavior and Development, 21*, 161–179.

Haith, M. M., & Benson, J. B. (1998). Infant cognition. In W. Damon (Series Ed.) & D. Kuhn & R. S. Siegler (Vol. Eds.), *Handbook of child psychology: Vol. 2. Cognition, perception, and language* (5th ed.). New York: Wiley.

Haith, M. M., Benson, J. B., Roberts, R. J. Jr., & Pennington, B. F. (Eds.). (1994). *The development of future-oriented processes*. Chicago: University of Chicago Press.

Haith, M. M., Wentworth, N., & Canfield, R. L. (1993). The formation of expectations in early infancy. In C. Rovee-Collier & L. P. Lipsitt (Eds.), *Advances in infancy research* (Vol. 8). Norwood, NJ: Ablex.

Hakuta, K. (1999). The debate on bilingual education. *Journal of Developmental and Behavioral Pediatrics, 20*, 36–37.

Halbfinger, D. M. (2003, Feb. 9). For students on a week at a fantasy space camp, the mission continues. *New York Times*, p. 23.

Halford, G. S. (1993). *Children's understanding: The development of mental models*. Hillsdale, NJ: Erlbaum.

Hall, D. G., Lee, S. C., & Belanger, J. (2001). Young children's use of syntactic cues to learn proper names and count nouns. *Developmental Psychology, 37*, 298–307.

Hall, J. A. (1984). *Nonverbal sex differences: Communication accuracy and expressive style*. Baltimore: Johns Hopkins Press.

Hallinan, M. T., & Kubitschek, W. N. (1999). Curriculum differentiation and high school achievement. *Social Psychology of Education, 3*, 41–62.

Hallowell, A. I. (1955). *Culture and experience*. Philadelphia: University of Pennsylvania Press.

Halpern, C. T., Udry, J. R., Campbell, B., & Suchindraw, C. (1994). Relationships between aggression and pubertal increases in testosterone: A panel analysis of adolescent males. *Social Biology, 40*, 8–24.

Halpern, D. F. (2000). *Sex differences in cognitive abilities* (3rd ed.) Mahwah, NJ: Erlbaum.

Halpern, L. F., MacLean, W. E. Jr., & Baumeister, A. A. (1995). Infant sleep–wake characteristics: Relation to neurological status and the prediction of developmental outcome. *Developmental Review, 15*, 255–291.

Halverson, C. F., & Deal, J. E. (2001). Temperamental change, parenting, and the family context. In T. D. Wachs & G. A. Kohnstamm (Eds.), *Temperament in context*. Mahwah, NJ: Erlbaum.

Hamm, J. V. (2000). Do birds of a feather flock together? The variable bases for African American, Asian American, and European American adolescents' selection of similar friends. *Developmental Psychology, 36*, 209–219.

Hammen, C., & Zupan, B. A. (1984). Self-schemas, depression, and the processing of personal information in children. *Journal of Experimental Child Psychology, 37*, 598–608.

Hampson, I., & Nelson, K. (1993). The relation of maternal language to variation in rate and style of language acquisition. *Journal of Child Language, 20*, 313–342.

Hamre, B., & Pianta, R. C. (2000). Early teacher–child relationships and children's social and academic outcomes through eighth grade. *Child Development, 72*, 625–638.

Han, J. J., Leichtman, M. D., & Wang, Q. (1998). Autobiographical memory in Korean, Chinese, and American children. *Developmental Psychology, 34*, 701–713.

Hanna, E., & Meltzoff, A. N. (1993). Peer imitation by toddlers in laboratory, home, and day-care contexts: Implications for social learning and memory. *Developmental Psychology, 29*, 701–710.

Hans, S. L. (1992). Maternal opioid use and child development. In I. S. Zagon & T. A. Slotkin (Eds.), *Maternal substance abuse and the developing nervous system*. San Diego, CA: Academic Press.

Harkness, S., Raeff, C., & Super, C. M. (Eds.). (2000). *New directions for child and adolescent development: No. 87. Variability in the social construction of the child*. San Francisco: Jossey-Bass.

Harlow, H. F., & Harlow, M. K. (1966). Learning to love. *American Scientist, 54*, 244–272.

Harper, L. V., & Kraft, R. H. (1986). Lateralization of receptive language in preschoolers: Test-retest reliability in a dichotic listening task. *Developmental Psychology, 22*, 553–556.

Harrell, J. S., Gansky, S. A., Bradley, C. B., & McMurray, R. G. (1997). Leisure time activities of elementary school children. *Nursing Research, 46*, 246–253.

Harris, J. R. (1995). Where is the child's environment? A group socialization theory of development. *Psychological Review, 102*, 458–489.

Harris, J. R. (1998). *The nurture assumption*. New York: Free Press.

Harris, L. (1997). *The Metropolitan Life survey of the American teacher 1997: Examining gender issues in public schools*. New York: Louis Harris and Associates.

Harris, L. J. (1977). Sex differences in the growth and use of language. In E. Donelson & J. E. Gullahorn (Eds.), *Women: A psychological perspective*. New York: Wiley.

Harris, M., Jones, D., & Grant, J. (1983). The nonverbal context of mothers' speech to infants. *First Language, 4*, 21–30.

Harris, N. G. S., Bellugi, U., Bates, E., Jones, W., & Rossen, M. (1997). Contrasting profiles of language development in children with Williams and Down syndromes. *Developmental Neuropsychology, 13*, 345–370.

Harris, P. L. (1989). Object permanence in infancy. In A. Slater & G. Bremner (Eds.), *Infant development*. Hillsdale, NJ: Erlbaum.

Harris, P. L. (2000). On not falling down to earth: Children's metaphysical questions. In K. S. Rosengren, C. N. Johnson, & P. L Harris (Eds.), *Imagining the impossible*. New York: Cambridge University Press.

Hart, C. H., DeWolf, D. M., Wozniak, P., & Burts, D. C. (1992). Maternal and paternal disciplinary styles: Relations with preschoolers' playground behavioral orientations and peer status. *Child Development, 63*, 879–892.

Hart, C. H., Yang, C., Nelson, D. A., Jin, S., Bazarskaya, N., Nelson, L., et al. (1998). Peer contact patterns, parenting practices, and preschoolers' social competence in China, Russia, and the United States. In P. T. Slee & K. Rigby (Eds.), *Children's peer relations*. London: Routledge.

Hart, D. (1988). The development of personal identity in adolescence: A philosophical dilemma approach. *Merrill-Palmer Quarterly, 34*, 105–114.

Hart, D. (1988b). A longitudinal study of adolescents' socialization and identification as predictors of adult moral judgment development. *Merrill-Palmer Quarterly, 34*, 245–260.

Hart, D., & Damon, W. (1985). Contrasts between understanding self and understanding others. In R. L. Leahy (Ed.), *The development of the self*. Orlando, FL: Academic Press.

Hart, D., & Fegley, S. (1995). Prosocial behavior and caring in adolescence: Relations to self-understanding and social judgment. *Child Development, 66*, 1346–1359.

Hart, D., & Yates, M. (1996). The interrelation of self and identity in adolescence: A developmental account. In R. Vasta (Ed.), *Annals of child development* (Vol. 12). London: Kingsley.

Harter, S. (1983). Developmental perspectives on the self-system. In P. H. Mussen (Series Ed.) & E. M. Hetherington (Vol. Ed.), *Handbook of child psychology. Vol. 4. Socialization, personality, and social development* (4th ed.). New York: Wiley.

Harter, S. (1985a). Competence as a dimension of self-evaluation: Toward a comprehensive model of self-worth. In R. L. Leahy (Ed.), *The development of the self* Orlando, FL: Academic Press.

Harter, S. (1985b) *The Self-Perception Profile for Children*. Denver, CO: University of Denver.

Harter, S. (1986). Processes underlying the construction, maintenance, and enhancement of the self-concept in children. In J. Suls & A. Greenwald (Eds.), *Psychological perspectives on the self* (Vol. 3). Hillsdale, NJ: Erlbaum.

Harter, S. (1987). The determinants and mediational role of global self-worth in children. In N. Eisenberg (Ed.), *Contemporary topics in developmental psychology*. New York: Wiley.

Harter, S. (1988a). Developmental processes in the construction of the self. In T. D. Yawkey & J. E. Johnson (Eds.), *Integrative processes and socialization: Early to middle childhood*. Hillsdale, NJ: Erlbaum.

Harter, S. (1988b) *The Self-Perception Profile for Adolescents*. Unpublished manual, University of Denver, Denver, CO.

Harter, S. (1990). Causes, correlates and the functional role of self-worth: A life-span perspective. In R. J. Sternberg & J. Kolligian (Eds.), *Competence considered*. New Haven, CT: Yale University Press.

Harter, S. (1994). Developmental changes in self-understanding across the 5 to 7 shift. In A. Sameroff & M. M. Haith (Eds.), *Reason and responsibility: The passage through childhood*. Chicago: University of Chicago Press.

Harter, S. (1997). The personal self in social context: Barriers to authenticity. In R. D. Ashmore & L. Jussim (Eds.), *Self and identity: Fundamental issues*. New York: Oxford University Press.

Harter, S. (1998). The development of self-representations. In W. Damon (Series Ed.) & N. Eisenberg (Vol. Ed.), *Handbook of child psychology: Vol. 3. Social, emotional, and personality development* (5th ed.). New York: Wiley.

Harter, S. (1999). *The construction of the self: A developmental perspective*. New York : Guilford.

Harter, S., & Connell, J. P. (1984). A model of the relationship among children's academic achievement and their self-perceptions of competence, control, and motivational orientation. In J. Nicholls (Ed.), *The development of achievement motivation*. Greenwich, CT: JAI Press.

Harter, S., Marold, D. B., Whitesell, N. R., & Cobbs, G. (1996). A model of the effects of perceived parent and peer support on adolescent false self behavior. *Child Development, 67*, 360–374.

Harter, S., & Monsour, A. (1992). Developmental analysis of conflict caused by opposing attributes in the adolescent self-portrait. *Developmental Psychology, 28*, 251–260.

Harter, S., & Pike, R. (1984). The Pictorial Scale of Perceived Competence and Social Acceptance for Young Children. *Child Development, 55*, 1969–1982.

Harter, S., Whitesell, N. R., & Junkin, L. J. (1998). Similarities and differences in domain-specific and global self-evaluation of learning-disabled, behaviorally disordered, and normally achieving adolescents. *American Educational Research Journal, 35*, 653–680.

Hartig, M., & Kanfer, F. H. (1973). The role of verbal self-instructions in children's resistance to temptation. *Journal of Personality and Social Psychology, 25*, 259–267.

Hartmann, D. P., & George, T. P. (1999). Design, measurement, and analysis in developmental research. In M. H. Bornstein & M. E. Lamb (Eds.), *Developmental psychology: An advanced textbook* (4th ed.). Mahwah, NJ: Erlbaum.

Hartshorne, H., & May, M. S. (1928–1930). *Studies in the nature of character* (3 vols.). New York: Macmillan.

Hartung, C. M., & Widiger, T. A. (1998). Gender differences in the diagnosis of mental disorders: Conclusions and controversies of the DSM-IV. *Psychological Bulletin, 123*, 260–278.

Hartup, W. W. (1983). Peer relations. In P. H. Mussen (Series Ed.) & E. M. Hetherington (Vol. Ed.), *Handbook of child psychology: Vol. 4. Socialization, personality, and social development* (4th ed.). New York: Wiley.

Hartup, W. W. (1992). Conflict and friendship relations. In C. U. Shantz & W. W. Hartup (Eds.), *Conflict in child and adolescent development*. Cambridge: Cambridge University Press.

Hartup, W. W. (1993). Adolescents and their friends. In B. Laursen (Ed.), *New directions for child development: No. 60. Close friendships in adolescence*. San Francisco: Jossey-Bass.

Hartup, W. W. (1996). The company they keep: Friendships and their developmental significance. *Child Development, 67*, 1–13.

Hartup, W. W. (1999). Constraints on peer socialization: Let me count the ways. *Merrill-Palmer Quarterly, 45*, 172–183.

Hartup, W. W., & Abecassis, M. (2002). Friends and enemies. In P. K. Smith & C. H. Hart (Eds.), *Blackwell handbook of childhood social development*. Madden, MA: Blackwell Publishers.

Hartup, W. W., French, D. C., Laursen, B., Johnson, M. K., & Ogawa, J. R. (1993). Conflict and friendship relations in middle childhood: Behavior in a closed-field situation. *Child Development, 64*, 445–454.

Hartup, W. W., Laursen, B., Stewart, M. I., & Eastenson, A. (1988). Conflict and the friendship relations of young children. *Child Development, 59*, 1590–1600.

Hartup, W. W., & Stevens, N. (1997). Friendships and adaptation in the life course. *Psychological Bulletin, 121*, 355–370.

Harwood, R. L., Miller, J. G., & Irizarry, N. L. (1995). *Culture and attachment*. New York: Guilford.

Hasselhorn, M. (1992). Task dependency and the role of category typicality and metamemory in the development of an organizational strategy. *Child Development, 63*, 202–214.

Hatano, G. (1990). Commentary: Toward the cultural psychology of mathematical cognition. *Monographs of the Society for Research in Child Development, 55*(1–2, Serial No. 221).

Hatano, G., & Inagaki, K. (1991). Sharing cognition through collective comprehension activity. In L. B. Resnick, J. M. Levine, & S. D. Teasley (Eds.), *Perspectives on socially shared cognition*. Washington, DC: American Psychological Association.

Hatano, G., & Inagaki, K. (1998). Cultural contexts of schooling revisited: A review of *The Learning Gap* from a cultural psychology perspective. In S. G. Paris & H. M. Wellman (Eds.), *Global prospects for education: Development, culture, and schooling*. Washington, DC: American Psychological Association.

Hatano, G., & Ito, Y. (1965). Development of length measuring behavior. *Japanese Journal of Psychology, 36*, 184–196.

Hauser, R. M. (1998). Trends in Black-White test score differentials: I. Uses and misuses of NAEP/SAT data. In U. Neisser (Ed.), *The rising curve*. Washington, DC: APA.

Haviland, J. M., & Lelwica, M. (1987). The induced affect response: 10-week-old infants' response to three emotion expressions. *Developmental Psychology, 23*, 97–104.

Hawkins, D. L., Pepler, D. J., & Craig, W. M. (2001). Naturalistic observations of peer interventions in bullying. *Social Development, 10*, 512–527.

Hay, D. (1999). The developmental genetics of intelligence. In M. Anderson (Ed.), *The development of intelligence*. Hove, UK: Psychology Press.

Hay, D. F. (1984). Social conflict in early childhood. In G. J. Whitehurst (Ed.), *Annals of child development* (Vol. 1). Greenwich, CT: JAI Press.

Hay, D. F. (1985). Learning to form relationships in infancy: Parallel attainments with parents and peers. *Developmental Review, 5*, 122–161.

Hay, D. F. (1986). Learning to be social: Some comments on Schaffer's "The child's entry into a social world." *Developmental Review, 6*, 107–114.

Hay, D. F. (1994). Prosocial development. *Journal of Child Psychology and Psychiatry, 35*, 29–71.

Hay, D. F., Castle, J., Stimsom, C., & Davies, L. (1995). The social construction of character in toddlerhood. In M. Killen & D. Hart (Eds.), *Morality in everyday life*. New York: Cambridge University Press.

Hay, D. F., & Murray, P. (1982). Giving and requesting: Social facilitation of infants' offers to adults. *Infant Behavior and Development, 5*, 301–310.

Hay, D. F., Murray, P., Cecire, S., & Nash, A. (1985). Social learning of social behavior in early life. *Child Development, 56*, 43–57.

Hay, D. F., Nash, A., & Pedersen, J. (1983). Interaction between six-month-old peers. *Child Development, 54*, 557–562.

Hay, L. (1984). Discontinuity in the development of motor control in children. In W. Prinz & A. F. Sanders (Eds.), *Cognition and motor processes*. Berlin: Springer-Verlag.

Hayne, H. (1996). Categorization in infancy. In C. Rovee-Collier & L. P. Lipsitt (Eds.), *Advances in infancy research* (Vol. 10). Norwood, NJ: Ablex.

Haynes, H., White, B. L., & Held, R. (1965). Visual accommodation in human infants. *Science, 148*, 528–530.

Hazen, N. L., & Durrett, M. E. (1982). Relationship of security of attachment to exploration and cognitive mapping abilities in 2-year-olds. *Developmental Psychology, 18*, 751–759.

Heath, S. B. (1983). *Ways with words: Language, life, and work in communities and classrooms*. New York: Cambridge University Press.

Hebb, D. O. (1949). *The organization of behavior*. New York: Wiley.

Heibeck, T., & Markman, E. M. (1987). Word learning in children: An examination of fast mapping. *Child Development, 58*, 1021–1034.

Heimann, M. (1998). Imitation in neonates, in older infants, and in children with autism: Feedback to theory. In S. Braten (Ed.), *Intersubjective communication and emotion in early ontogeny*. New York: Cambridge University Press.

Helwig, C. C., Hildebrandt, C., & Turiel, E. (1995). Children's judgments about psychological harm in social context. *Child Development, 66*, 1680–1693.

Helwig, C. C., Zelazo, P. D., & Wilson, M. (2001). Children's judgments of psychological harm in normal and noncanonical situations. *Child Development, 72*, 66–81.

Helwig, R., Anderson, L., & Tindal, G. (2001). Influence of elementary student gender on teachers' perceptions of mathematics achievement. *Journal of Educational Research, 95*, 93–102.

Henry, B., Caspi, A., Moffitt, T. E., & Silva, P. A. (1996). Temperamental and familial predictors of violent and nonviolent criminal convictions: Age 3 to age 18. *Developmental Psychology, 32*, 614–623.

Herdt, G., & Boxer, A. M. (1993). *Children of Horizons: How gay and lesbian teens are leading a new way out of the closet*. Boston: Beacon.

Herman, L. M. (2002). Exploring the cognitive world of the bottlenosed dolphin. In M. Bekoff, C. Allen, & G. M. Burghardt (Eds.), *The cognitive animal: Empirical and theoretical perspectives on animal cognition*. Cambridge, MA: MIT Press.

Hermans, H. J. M., & Kempen, H. J. G. (1998). Moving cultures: The perilous problems of cultural dichotomies in a globalizing society. *American Psychologist, 53*, 1111–1120.

Herrera, C., & Dunn, J. (1997). Early experiences with family conflict: Implications for arguments with a close friend. *Developmental Psychology, 33*, 869–881.

Herrnstein, R. J. (1971, September). I.Q. *Atlantic Monthly*, pp. 43–64.

Herrnstein, R. J., & Murray, C. (1994). *The bell curve: Intelligence and class structure in American life*. New York: Free Press.

Hershberger, S. L. (2001). Biological factors in the development of sexual orientation. In A. R. D'Augelli & C. J. Patterson (Eds.), *Lesbian, gay, and bisexual identities and youth: Psychological perspectives*. New York: Oxford University Press.

Herzog, D. B., Greenwood, D. N., Dorer, D. J., Flores, A. T., Ekeblad, E. R., Richards, A., et al. (2000). Mortality in eating disorders: A descriptive study. *International Journal of Eating Disorders, 28*, 20–26.

Hesse, E., & Main, M. (2000). Disorganized infant, child, and adult attachment: Collapse in behavioral and attentional strategies. *Journal of the American Psychoanalytic Association, 48*, 1097–1127.

Hetherington, E. M. (1989). Coping with family transitions: Winners, losers, and survivors. *Child Development, 60*, 1–14.

Hetherington, E. M. (1993). An overview of the Virginia longitudinal study of divorce and remarriage with a focus on early adolescence. *Journal of Family Psychology, 7*, 1–18.

Hetherington, E. M., Bridges, M., & Isabella, G. M. (1998). What matters? What does not? Five perspectives on the association between marital transitions and children's adjustment. *American Psychologist, 53*, 167–184.

Hetherington, E. M., & Clingempeel, W. G. (1992). Coping with marital transitions: A family systems perspective. *Monographs of the Society for Research in Child Development, 57*(Serial No. 227).

Hetherington, E. M., & Kelly, J. (2002). *For better or worse: Divorce reconsidered*. New York: Norton.

Hetherington, E. M., & Parke, R. D. (1979). *Child psychology: A contemporary viewpoint*. New York: McGraw-Hill.

Hetherington, E. M., Reiss, D., & Plomin, R. (Eds.). (1994). *Separate social worlds of siblings: The impact of nonshared environment on development*. Hillsdale, NJ: Erlbaum.

Hetherington, E. M., & Stanley-Hagan, M. S. (2002). Parenting in divorced and remarried families. In M. Bornstein (Ed.), *Handbook of parenting*. (2nd ed., Vol. 3). Mahwah, NJ: Erlbaum.

Hewlett, B. S. (1992). The parent-infant relationship and social-emotional development among the Aka pygmies. In J. L. Roopnarine & D. B. Carter (Eds.), *Annual advances in applied development psychology: Vol. 5. Parent-child socialization in diverse cultures*. Norwood, NJ: Ablex.

Hewlett, B. S., Lamb, M. E., Leyendecker, B., & Scholmerich, A. (2000). Internal working models, trust, and sharing among foragers. *Current Anthropology, 41*.

Heyes, C. M. (1994). Reflections on self-recognition in primates. *Animal Behaviour, 47*, 909–919.

Heyes, C., & Huber, L. (Eds.). (2000). *The evolution of cognition*. Cambridge, MA: MIT Press.

Heyman, G. (2001). Children's interpretation of ambiguous behavior: Evidence for a 'boys are bad' bias. *Social Development, 10,* 230–247.

Heyman, G. D., Dweck, C. S., & Cain, K. M. (1992). Young children's vulnerability to self-blame and helplessness: Relationship to beliefs about goodness. *Child Development, 63,* 401–415.

Hicks, D. (1996). *Discourse, learning, and schooling.* New York: Cambridge University Press.

Hiebert, E., & Raphael, T. E. (1996). Psychological perspectives on literacy and extensions to educational practice. In D. C. Berliner & R. C. Calfee (Eds.), *Handbook of educational psychology.* New York: Macmillan Library Reference.

Hiebert, E. H., & Raphael, T. E. (1998). *Early literacy instruction.* Fort Worth, TX: Harcourt Brace College Publishers.

Hiebert, J. (1981). Cognitive development and learning linear measurement. *Journal for Research in Mathematics Education, 12,* 197–211.

Hilgard, E. R. (1987). *Psychology in America: A historical survey.* San Diego, CA: Harcourt Brace Jovanovich.

Hill, J. (2003). Early identification of individuals at risk for antisocial personality disorder. *British Journal of Psychiatry 182*(Supp 144), s11–s14.

Hinde, R. A. (1986). Some implications of evolutionary theory and comparative data for the study of human prosocial and aggressive behavior. In D. Olweus, J. Block, & M. Radke-Yarrow (Eds.), *Development of antisocial and prosocial behavior.* New York: Academic Press.

Hinds, P., & Kiesler, S. (2002). *Distributed work.* Cambridge, MA: MIT Press.

Hines, M. (1982). Prenatal gonad hormones and sex differences in human behavior. *Psychological Bulletin, 92,* 56–80.

Hines, M., Golombok, S., Rust, J., Johnston, K. J., Golding, G., & the Avon Longitudinal Study of Parents and Children Study Team. (2002). Testosterone during pregnancy and gender role behavior in children: A longitudinal, population study. *Child Development, 73,* 1678–1687.

Hines, M., & Green, R. (1991). Human hormonal and neural correlates of sex-typed behaviors. *Review of Psychiatry, 10,* 536–555.

Hines, M., & Kaufman, F. R. (1994). Androgen and the development of human sex-typical behavior: Rough-and-tumble and sex of preferred playmates in children with congenital adrenal hyperplasia (CAH). *Child Development, 65,* 1042–1053.

Hirsch, B. J., & Renders, R. J. (1986). The challenge of adolescent friendships: A study of Lisa and her friends. In S. E. Hobfolk (Ed.), *Stress, social support, and women.* Washington, DC: Hemisphere.

Hirsh-Pasek, K., & Golinkoff, R. M. (1996). *The origins of grammar: Evidence from early language comprehension.* Cambridge, MA: MIT Press.

Hirsh-Pasek, K., Treiman, R., & Schneiderman, M. (1984). Brown and Hanlon revisited: Mothers' sensitivity to ungrammatical forms. *Journal of Child Language, 11,* 81–88.

Hittelman, J. H., & Dickes, R. (1979). Sex differences in neonatal eye contact time. *Merrill-Palmer Quarterly, 25,* 171–184.

Ho, D. Y. F. (1986). Chinese patterns of socialization: A critical review. In M. H. Bond (Ed.), *The psychology of Chinese people.* New York: Oxford University Press.

Ho, D. Y. F. (1995). Selfhood and identity in Confucianism, Taoism, Buddhism, and Hinduism: Contrasts with the West. *Journal for the Theory of Social Behavior, 25,* 115–139.

Hocksbergen, R. C. (1999). The importance of adoption for nurturing and enhancing the emotional and intellectual potential of children. *Adoption Quarterly, 1,* 29–42.

Hoek, D., Ingram, D., & Gibson, D. (1986). Some possible causes of children's early word overextensions. *Journal of Child Language, 13,* 477–494.

Hoff, E., & Naigles, L. (2002). How children use speech to acquire a lexicon. *Child Development, 73,* 418–433.

Hoff-Ginsberg, E. (1990). Maternal speech and the child's development of syntax: A further look. *Journal of Child Language, 17,* 85–99.

Hoff-Ginsberg, E., & Shatz, M. (1982). Linguistic input and the child's acquisition of language. *Psychological Bulletin, 92,* 3–26.

Hoffman, L. W., & Youngblade, L. M. (1999). *Mothers at work: Effects on children's well being.* New York: Cambridge University Press.

Hoffman, M. L. (1970). Moral development. In P. H. Mussen (Ed.), *Carmichael's manual of child psychology* (3rd ed., Vol. 2). New York: Wiley.

Hoffman, M. L. (1975). Altruistic behavior and the parent-child relationship. *Journal of Personality and Social Psychology, 31,* 937–943.

Hoffman, M. L. (1978). Empathy, its development and prosocial implications. In C. B. Keasey (Ed.), *Nebraska symposium on motivation* (Vol. 25). Lincoln: University of Nebraska Press.

Hoffman, M. L. (1983). Affective and cognitive processes in moral internalization: An information processing approach. In E. R. Higgins, D. Ruble, & W. Hartup (Eds.), *Social cognition and social development: A socio-cultural perspective.* New York: Cambridge University Press.

Hoffman, M. L. (1984). Empathy, its limitations, and its role in a comprehensive moral theory. In J. L. Gewirtz & W. Kurtines (Eds.), *Morality, moral development, and moral behavior.* New York: Wiley.

Hoffman, M. L. (1994). Discipline and internalization. *Developmental Psychology, 30,* 26-28.

Hoffman, M. L. (2000). *Empathy and moral development.* New York: Wiley.

Hofsten, C. Von (1982). Eye-hand coordination in the newborn. *Developmental Psychology, 18,* 450–461.

Hofsten, C. Von (1983). Catching skills in infancy. *Journal of Experimental Psychology: Human Perception and Performance, 9,* 75–85.

Hofsten, C. von, & Siddiqui, A. (1993). Using the mother's actions as a reference for object exploration in 6- and 12-month-old infants. *British Journal of Developmental Psychology, 11,* 61–74.

Hogan, D., & Tudge, J. R. H. (1999). Implications of Vygotsky's theory for peer learning. In A. M. O'Donnell & A. King (Eds.), *Cognitive perspectives on peer learning.* Mahwah, NJ: Erlbaum.

Hogge, W. A. (1990). Teratology. In I. R. Merkatz & J. E. Thompson (Eds.), *New perspectives on prenatal care.* New York: Elsevier.

Holden, C. (1986). High court says no to administration's Baby Doe rules. *Science, 232,* 1595–1596.

Holekamp, K. E., & Engh, A. L. (2002). Field studies of social cognition in spotted hyenas. In M. Bekoff, C. Allen, & G. M. Burghardt (Eds.), *The cognitive animal: Empirical and theoretical perspectives on animal cognition.* Cambridge, MA: MIT Press.

Hollich, G. J., Hirsh-Pasek, K., & Golinkoff, R. M. (2000). Breaking the language barrier: An emergentist coalition model of word learning. *Monographs of the Society for Research in Child Development, 65*(3, Serial No. 262).

Holmes, J. (1995). "Something there is that doesn't love a wall": John Bowlby, attachment theory, and psychoanalysis. In S. Goldberg, R. Muir, & J. Kerr (Eds.), *Attachment theory: Social, developmental, and clinical perspectives.* Hillsdale, NJ: Analytic Press.

Holmes-Lonergan, H. A. (2003). Preschool children's collaborative problem solving interactions: The role of gender, pair type, and task. *Sex Roles. 48,* 505–517.

Holstein, C. B. (1972). The relation of children's moral judgment level to that of their parents and to communication patterns in the family. In R. C. Smart & M. S. Smart (Eds.), *Readings in child development and relationships.* New York: Macmillan.

Hong, Y. (2001). Chinese students' teachers and students' inferences of effort and ability. In F. Salili, C. Chiu, & Y. Hong (Eds.), *Student motivation: The culture and context of learning.* New York: Plenum Publishers.

Honzik, M. P., MacFarlan, J. W., & Allen, L. (1948). The stability of mental test performance between two and eighteen years. *Journal of Experimental Education, 17,* 323.

Hooker, K., Nesselroade, D. W., Nesselroade, J. R., & Lerner, R. M. (1987). The structure of intraindividual temperament in the context of mother–child dyads: P-technique factor analyses of short-term change. *Developmental Psychology, 23,* 332–346.

Hoover, J. H., Oliver, R., & Hazler, R. J. (1992). Bullying: Perceptions of adolescent victims in the midwestern USA. *School Psychology International, 12,* 5–16.

Hopkins, B. (1991). Facilitating early motor development: An intracultural study of West Indian mothers and their infants living in Britain. In J. K. Nugent, B. M. Lester, & T. B. Brazelton (Eds.), *The cultural context of infancy: Vol. 2. Multicultural and interdisciplinary approaches to parent–infant relations.* Norwood, NJ: Ablex.

Hopkins, K. B., McGillicuddy-De Lisi, A. V., & De Lisi, R. (1997). Student gender and teaching methods as sources of variability in children's computational arithmetic performance. *Journal of Genetic Psychology, 158,* 333–345.

Horn, J. M. (1983). The Texas Adoption Project: Adopted children and their intellectual resemblance to biological and adoptive parents. *Child Development, 54,* 268–275.

Hornik, R., & Gunnar, M. R. (1988). A descriptive analysis of infant social referencing. *Child Development, 59,* 626–634.

Horowitz, F. D. (1992). John B. Watson's legacy: Learning and environment. *Developmental Psychology, 28,* 360–367.

Howe, C. (1981). *Acquiring language in a conversational context.* Orlando, FL: Academic Press.

Howe, C. J., Rodgers, C., & Tolmie, A. (1990). Physics in the primary school: Peer interaction and the understanding of floating and sinking. *European Journal of Psychology of Education, V,* 459–475.

Howe, C. J., Tolmie, A., & Rodgers, C. (1992). The acquisition of conceptual knowledge in science by primary school children: Group interaction and the understanding of motion down an inclined plane. *British Journal of Developmental Psychology, 10,* 113–130.

Howe, M. L. (2000). *The fate of early memories.* Washington, DC: American Psychological Association.

Howes, C. (1983). Patterns of friendship. *Child Development, 54,* 1041–1053.

Howes, C. (1987). Social competence with peers in young children: Developmental sequences. *Developmental Review, 7,* 252–272.

Howes, C. (1992). *The collaborative construction of pretend.* New York: SUNY Press.

Howes, C., Galinsky, E., & Kontos, S. (1998). Child care caregiver sensitivity and attachment. *Social Development, 7,* 25–36.

Howes, C., & Hamilton, C. E. (1992a). Children's relationships with caregivers: Mothers and child care teachers. *Child Development, 63,* 859–866.

Howes, C., & Hamilton, C. E. (1992b). Children's relationships with child care teachers: Stability and concordance with parental attachment. *Child Development 63,* 867–878.

Howes, C., Hamilton, C. E., & Philipsen, L. C. (1998). Stability and continuity of caregiver and child-peer relationships. *Child Development, 69,* 418–426.

Howes, C., & James, J. (2002). Children's social development within the socialization context of childcare and early childhood education. In P. K. Smith & C. H. Hart (Eds.), *Blackwell handbook of childhood social development*. Madden, MA: Blackwell Publishers.

Howes, C., & Ritchie, S. (1999). Attachment organizations in children with difficult life circumstances. *Development and Psychopathology, 11*, 251–268.

Howes, C., & Ritchie, S. (2002). *A matter of trust: Connecting teachers and learners in the early childhood classroom*. New York: Teachers College Press.

Howes, C., & Tonyan, H. (1999). Peer relations. In L. Balter & C. S. Tamis-Lemonda (Eds.), *Child psychology: A handbook of contemporary issues*. Philadelphia: Psychology Press.

Howes, C., Unger, O. A., & Matheson, C. C.. (1992). *The collaborative construction of pretend: Social pretend play functions*. Albany: State University of New York Press.

Howes, C., Unger, O., & Seidner, L. B. (1989). Social pretend play in toddlers. Parallels with social play and with solitary pretend. *Child Development, 60*, 77–84.

Hoy, E. A., Bill, J. M., & Sykes, D. H. (1988). Very low birthweight: A long-term developmental impairment? *International Journal of Behavioral Development, 11*, 37–67.

Hrdy, S. B. (1999). *Mother nature: A history of mothers, infants, and natural selection*. New York: Pantheon.

Hubbard, J. A. (2001). Emotion expression processes in children's peer interaction: The role of peer rejection, aggression, and gender. *Child Development, 72*, 1426–1438.

Hudley, C., & Graham, S. (1993). An attributional intervention to reduce peer-directed aggression among African-American boys. *Child Development, 64*, 124–138.

Hudson, J. (1990). The emergence of autobiographical memory in mother-child conversation. In R. Fivush & J. Hudson (Eds.), *Knowing and remembering in young children*. New York: Cambridge University Press.

Hudson, J., & Fivush, R. (1991). Planning in the preschool years: The emergence of plans from general event knowledge. *Cognitive Development, 6*, 393–415.

Hudson, J., & Nelson, K. (1986). Repeated encounters of a similar kind: Effects of familiarity on children's autobiographic memory. *Cognitive Development, 1*, 253–271.

Huesmann, L. R., & Eron, L. D. (1986). *Television and the aggressive child: A cross-national perspective*. Hillsdale, NJ: Erlbaum.

Huesmann, L. R., Lagerspetz, K., & Eron, L. D. (1984). Intervening variables in the television violence-aggression relation: Evidence from two countries. *Developmental Psychology, 20*, 746–775.

Huesmann, L. R., & Miller, L. S. (1994). Long-term effects of repeated exposure to media violence in childhood. In L. R. Huesmann (Ed.), *Aggressive behavior: Current perspectives*. New York: Plenum.

Huesmann, L. R., Moise-Titus, J., Podolski, C.-L., & Eron, L. D. (2003). Longitudinal relations between children's exposure to TV violence and their aggressive and violent behavior in young adulthood: 1977–1992. *Developmental Psychology, 39*, 201–221.

Hughes, C. (2002). Executive functions and development: Emerging themes. *Infant and Child Development, 11*, 201–209.

Hughes, C., & Dunn, J. (2002). 'When I say a naughty word'. A longitudinal study of young children's accounts of anger and sadness in themselves and close others. *British Journal of Developmental Psychology, 20*, 515–535.

Hughes, C., White, A., Sharpen, J., & Dunn, J. (2000). Antisocial, angry, and unsympathetic: "Hard-to-manage" preschoolers' peer problems and possible cognitive influences. *Journal of Child Psychology and Psychiatry and Allied Disciplines, 41*, 169–179.

Human Genome Project [special issue]. (2001, February 16). *Science, 291*.

Hunt, M. (1997). *How science takes stock: The study of meta-analysis*. New York: Russell Sage Foundation.

Hunter, J. E., & Hunter, R. F. (1984). Validity and utility of alternative predictors of job performance. *Psychological Bulletin, 96*, 72–98.

Hurley, J. C., & Underwood, M. K. (2002). Children's understanding of their research rights before and after debriefing: Informed assent, confidentiality, and stopping participation. *Child Development, 73*, 132–143.

Hurt, H., Malmud, E., Betancourt, L. M., & Brodsky, N. L. (2001). A prospective comparison of developmental outcome of children with in utero cocaine exposure and controls using the Battelle Developmental Inventory. *Journal of Developmental and Behavioral Pediatrics, 22*, 27–34.

Huston, A. C. (1983). Sex-typing. In P. H. Mussen (Series Ed.) & E. M. Hetherington (Vol. Ed.), *Handbook of child psychology: Vol. 4. Socialization, personality, and social development* (4th ed.). New York: Wiley.

Huston, A. C. (1985). The development of sex typing: Themes from recent research. *Developmental Review, 5*, 1–17.

Huston, A. C., & Wright, J. C. (1998). Mass media and children's development. In W. Damon (Series Ed.) & I. E. Sigel & K. A. Renninger (Vol. Eds.), *Handbook of child psychology: Vol. 4. Child psychology in practice* (5th ed.). New York: Wiley.

Huston, A. C., Wright, J. C., Marquis, J., & Green, S. B. (1999). How young children spend their time: Television and other activities. *Developmental Psychology, 35*, 912–925.

Hutchins, E. (1983). Understanding Micronesian navigation. In D. Gentner & A. Stevens (Eds.), *Mental models*. Hillsdale, NJ: Erlbaum.

Huttenlocher, J., Haight, W., Bryk, A., Seltzer, M., & Lyons, T. (1991). Early vocabulary growth: Relation to language input and gender. *Developmental Psychology, 27*, 236–248.

Huttenlocher, J., Levine, S., & Vevea, J. (1998). Environmental input and cognitive growth: A study using time-period comparisons. *Child Development, 69*, 1012–1029.

Huttenlocher, J., Newcombe, N., & Vasilyeva, M. (1999). Spatial scaling in young children. *Psychological Science, 10*, 393–398.

Huttenlocher, J., Smiley, P., & Charney, R. (1983). Emergence of action categories in the child: Evidence from verb meanings. *Psychological Review, 90*, 72–93.

Huttenlocher, P. R. (1990). Morphometric study of human cerebral cortex development. *Neuropsychologia, 28*, 517–527.

Hutton, N. (1996). Health prospects for children born to HIV-infected women. In R. R. Faden & N. E. Kass (Eds.), *HIV, AIDS, and childbearing*. New York: Oxford University Press.

Hwang, H. J., & St. James-Roberts, I. (1998). Emotional and behavioral problems in primary school children from nuclear and extended families in Korea. *Journal of Child Psychology and Psychiatry, 39*, 973–979.

Hyde, J. S. (1984). How large are gender differences in aggression? A developmental meta-analysis. *Developmental Psychology, 20*, 722–736.

Hyde, J. S. (1986). Gender differences in aggression. In J. S. Hyde & M. C. Linn (Eds.), *The psychology of gender: Advances through meta-analysis*. Baltimore: Johns Hopkins University Press.

Hyde, J. S., Fennema, E., & Lamon, S. J. (1990). Gender differences in mathematics performance: A meta-analysis. *Psychological Bulletin, 107*, 139–153.

Hyde, J. S., & Linn, M. C. (1988). Gender differences in verbal ability: A meta-analysis. *Psychological Bulletin, 104*, 53–69.

Hymel, S., Vaillancourt, T., McDougall, P., & Renshaw, P. D. (2002). Peer acceptance and rejection in childhood. In P. K. Smith & C. H. Hart (Eds.), *Blackwell handbook of childhood social development*. Madden, MA: Blackwell Publishers.

Iannotti, R. (1978). Effect of role-taking experiences on role taking, empathy, altruism, and aggression. *Developmental Psychology, 14*, 119–124.

Ide, J. K., Parkerson, J., Haertel, G. D., & Walberg, H. J. (1981). Peer group influence on educational outcomes: A quantitative synthesis. *Journal of Educational Psychology, 73*, 472–484.

Ike, N. (2000). Current thinking on XYY syndrome. *Psychiatric Annals, 30*, 91–95.

Inagaki, K. (1981). Facilitation of knowledge integration through classroom discussion. *Quarterly Newsletter of the Laboratory of Comparative Human Cognition, 3*, 26–28.

Inagaki, K., & Hatano, G. (1987). Young children's spontaneous personification as analogy. *Child Development, 58*, 1013–1020.

Inagaki, K., & Hatano, G. (1996). Young children's recognition of commonalities between animals and plants. *Child Development, 67*, 2823–2840.

Inagaki, K., Hatano, G., & Morita, F. (1998). Construction of mathematical knowledge through whole-class discussion. *Learning and Instruction, 8*, 503–526.

Infante-Rivard, C., Fernandez, A., Gauthier, R., & Rivard, C. (1993). Fetal loss associated with caffeine intake before and during pregnancy. *Journal of the American Medical Association, 270*, 2940–2943.

Ingersoll, B. D. (1997). Psychiatric disorders among adopted children: A review and commentary. *Adoption Quarterly, 1*, 57–73.

Inhelder, B., & Piaget, J. (1958). *The growth of logical thinking from childhood to adolescence*. New York: Basic Books.

Inhelder, B., & Piaget, J. (1964). *The early growth of logic in the child*. New York: Norton.

Inoue-Nakamura, N. (2001). Mirror self-recognition in primates: An ontogenetic and a phylogenetic approach. In T. Matsuzawa (Ed.), *Primate origins of human cognition and behavior*. New York: Springer-Verlag.

Isabella, R. A. (1993). Origins of attachment: Maternal interactive behavior across the first year. *Child Development, 64*, 605–621.

Isabella, R. A. (1994). The origins of infant–mother attachment: Maternal behavior and infant development. In R. Vasta (Ed.), *Annals of child development* (Vol. 10). London: Kingsley.

Isabella, R. A., & Belsky, J. (1991). Interactional synchrony and the origins of infant–mother attachment: A replication study. *Child Development, 62*, 373–384.

Isabella, R. A., Belsky, J., & Von Eye, A. (1989). Origins of infant–mother attachment: An examination of interactional synchrony during the infant's first year. *Developmental Psychology, 25*, 12–21.

Isley, S. L., O'Neil, R., Clatfelter, D., & Parke, R. (1999). Parent and child expressed affect and children's social competence: Modeling direct and indirect pathways. *Developmental Psychology, 35*, 547–560.

Izard, C. (1989). *The maximally discriminative facial movement coding system (MAX)* (rev. ed.). Newark: University of Delaware, Information Technologies and University Media Services.

Izard, C. (1993). Organizational and motivational functions of discrete emotions. In M. Lewis & J. Haviland (Eds.), *Handbook of emotions*. New York: Guilford.

Izard, C. (1995). Innate and universal facial expressions: Evidence from developmental and cross-cultural research. *Psychological Bulletin, 115*, 288–299.

Izard, C. E., Fantauzzo, C. A., Castle, J. M., Haynes, O. M., Rayias, M. F., & Putnam, P. H. (1995). The ontogeny and significance of infants' facial expressions in the first 9 months of life. *Developmental Psychology, 31,* 997–1013.

Jacklin, C. N. (1989). Female and male: Issues of gender. *American Psychologist, 44,* 127–133.

Jacklin, C. N., DiPietro, J. A., & Maccoby, E. E. (1984). Sex-typing behavior and sex-typing pressure in child/parent interactions. *Archives of Sexual Behavior, 13,* 413–425.

Jackson, J. F. (1993). Multiple caregiving among African Americans and infant attachment: The need for an emic approach. *Human Development, 36,* 87–102.

Jacobs, J. E., Lanza, S., Osgood, D. W., Eccles, J. S., & Wigfield, A. (2002). Changes in children's self-competence and values: Gender and domain differences across grades one though twelve. *Child Development, 73,* 509–527.

Jacobsen, T., Edelstein, W., & Hofmann, V. (1994). A longitudinal study of the relation between representations of attachment in childhood and cognitive functioning in childhood and adolescence. *Developmental Psychology, 30,* 112–124.

Jacobsen, T., & Hofmann, V. (1997). Children's attachment representations: Longitudinal relations to school behavior and academic competency in middle childhood and adolescence. *Developmental Psychology, 33,* 703–710.

Jacobson, J. L., & Jacobson, S. W. (1988). New methodologies for assessing the effects of prenatal toxic exposure on cognitive functioning in humans. In M. Evans (Ed.), *Toxic contaminants and ecosystem health: A Great Lakes focus.* New York: Wiley.

Jacobson, J. L., Jacobson, S. W., Padgett, R. J., Brimitt, G. A., & Billings, R. L. (1992). Effects of prenatal PCB exposure on cognitive processing efficiency and sustained attention. *Developmental Psychology, 28,* 297–306.

Jacobvitz, D., & Sroufe, L. A. (1987). The early caregiver-child relationship and attention-deficit disorder with hyperactivity in kindergarten: A prospective study. *Child Development, 58,* 1496–1504.

Jadack, R. A., Hyde, J. S., Moore, C. F., & Keller, M. L. (1995). Moral reasoning about sexually transmitted diseases. *Child Development, 66,* 167–177.

Jaffee, S., & Hyde, J. S. (2000). Gender differences in moral orientation: A meta-analysis. *Psychological Bulletin, 126,* 703–726.

Jahoda, G. (1993). *Crossroads between culture and mind: Continuities and changes in theories of human nature.* Cambridge, MA: Harvard University Press.

James, W. (1890). *Principles of psychology.* New York: Holt.

James, W. (1892). *Psychology: The briefer course.* New York: Holt.

Jamison, W. (1977). Developmental inter-relationships among concrete operational tasks: An investigation of Piaget's stage concept. *Journal of Experimental Child Psychology, 24,* 235–253.

Jaroff, L. (1989, March 20). The gene hunt. *Time,* pp. 62–67.

Jencks, C. (1972). *Inequality.* New York: Basic Books.

Jenkins, J. M., & Astington, J. W. (1996). Cognitive factors and family structure associated with theory of mind development in young children. *Developmental Psychology, 32,* 70–78.

Jennings, K. D. (1975). People versus object orientation, social behavior, and intellectual abilities in preschool children. *Developmental Psychology, 11,* 511–519.

Jensen, A. R. (1969). How much can we boost IQ and scholastic achievement? *Harvard Educational Review, 39,* 1–123.

Jensen, A. R. (1972). *Genetics and education.* New York: Harper & Row.

Jensen, A. R. (1973). *Educability and group differences.* New York: Harper & Row.

Jensen, A. R. (1980). *Bias in mental testing.* New York: Free Press.

Jensen, A. R. (1981). *Straight talk about mental tests.* New York: Free Press.

Jensen-Campbell, L. A., Graziano, W. G., & Hair, E. C. (1996). Personality and relationships as moderators of interpersonal conflict in adolescence. *Merrill-Palmer Quarterly, 42,* 148–164

Jessor, R., Colby, A., & Shweder, R. A. (Eds.). (1996). *Ethnography and human development: Context and meaning in social inquiry.* Chicago: University of Chicago Press.

Jessor, R., & Jessor, S. L. (1977). *Problem behavior and psychosocial development.* New York: Academic Press.

Johnson, D. B. (1983). Self-recognition in infants. *Infant Behavior and Development, 6,* 211–222.

Johnson, M. H. (2001). Functional brain development during infancy. In G. Bremner & A. Fogel (Eds.), *Blackwell handbook of infant development.* Malden, MA: Blackwell Publishers.

Johnson, M. H. (2002). Imaging techniques and their application in developmental psychology [Special issue]. *Developmental Science, 5*(3).

Johnson, M. H., & de Haan, M. (2001). Developing cortical specialisation for visual-cognitive function: The case of face recognition. In J. L. McClelland & R. S. Siegler (Eds.), *Mechanisms of cognitive development: Behavioural and neural perspectives.* Mahwah, NJ: Erlbaum.

Johnson, M. H., Dziurawiec, S., Ellis, H., & Morton, J. (1991). Newborns' preferential tracking of facelike stimuli and its subsequent decline. *Cognition, 40,* 1–19.

Johnson, M. K., Beebe, T., Mortimer, J. T., & Snyder, M. (1998). Volunteerism in adolescence: A process perspective. *Journal of Research on Adolescence, 8,* 309–332.

Johnson, S. P. (1997). Young infants' perception of object unity: Implications for development of attentional and cognitive skills. *Current Directions in Psychological Science, 6,* 5–11.

Johnson, S. P., & Aslin, R. N. (1995). Perception of object unity in 2-month-old infants. *Developmental Psychology, 31,* 739–745.

Jones, C., & Adamson, L. B. (1987). Language use in mother–child and mother–child–sibling interactions. *Child Development, 58,* 356–366.

Jones, C., & Lopez, R. (1990). Drug abuse and pregnancy. In I. R. Merkatz & J. E. Thompson (Eds.), *New perspectives on prenatal care.* New York: Elsevier.

Jones, D. C. (1985). Persuasive appeals and responses to appeals among friends and acquaintances. *Child Development, 56,* 757–763.

Jones, E. F., & Thomson, N. R. (2001). Action perception and outcome valence: Effects on children's inferences of intentionality and moral and liking judgments. *Journal of Genetic Psychology, 162,* 154–166.

Jones, K. L., Smith, D. W., Ulleland, C. N., & Streissguth, A. P. (1973). Pattern of malformation in offspring of chronic alcoholic mothers. *Lancet, 1,* 1267–1271.

Jones, M. C. (1924). A laboratory study of fear: The case of Peter. *Pedagogical Seminary, 31,* 308–315.

Jones, M. C. (1965). Psychological correlates of somatic development. *Child Development, 36,* 899–911.

Jones, M. G., Howe, A., & Rua, M. J. (2000). Gender differences in students' experiences, interests, and attitudes toward science and scientists. *Science Education, 84,* 180–192.

Jones, S. S. (1996). Imitation or exploration? Young infants' matching of adults' oral gestures. *Child Development, 67,* 1952–1969.

Joos, S. K., Pollitt, E., Mueller, W. H., & Albright, D. L. (1983). The Bacon Chow study: Maternal nutritional supplementation and infant behavioral development. *Child Development, 54,* 669–676.

Jordan, A. B., Schmitt, K. L., & Woodard, E. H. (2001). Developmental implications of commercial broadcasters' educational offerings. *Journal of Applied Developmental Psychology, 22,* 87–101.

Jordan, H. E., & Kindred, J. E. (1948). *Textbook of embryology* (5th ed.). New York: Apple-Century-Crofts.

Joseph, J. (2000). Not in their genes: A critical view of the genetics of attention-deficit hyperactivity disorder. *Developmental Review, 20,* 539–567.

Journal of Gene Medicine. (2002). Gene therapy clinical trials. *Journal of Gene Medicine Clinical Trial Website.* Retrieved November 6, 2002, from www.wiley.uk.co/genetherapy/clinical.

Juel, C. (1996). Learning to learn from effective tutors. In L. Schauble & R. Glaser (Eds.), *Innovations in learning: New environments for education.* Mahwah, NJ: Erlbaum.

Jusczyk, P. W. (1997). *The discovery of spoken language.* Cambridge, MA: MIT Press.

Jusczyk, P. W., Cutler, A., & Redanz, N. J. (1993). Infants' preference for the predominant stress patterns of English words. *Child Development, 64,* 675–687.

Jusczyk, P. W., Houston, D. M., & Newsome, M. (1999). The beginnings of word segmentation in English-learning infants. *Cognitive Psychology, 38,* 159–207.

Jusczyk, P. W., Pisoni, D. B., & Mullennix, J. (1992). Some consequences of stimulus variability on speech processing by 2-month-old infants. *Cognition, 43,* 253–291.

Juvonen, J., & Graham, S. (2001). Preface. In J. Juvonen & S. Graham (Eds.), *Peer harassment in school: The plight of the vulnerable and victimized.* New York: Guilford.

Kaback, M. M. (1982). Screening for reproductive counseling: Social, ethical, and medicolegal issues in the Tay-Sachs disease experience. In *Human genetics: Part B. Medical aspects.* New York: Alan R. Liss.

Kagan, J. (1981). *The second year: The emergence of self-awareness.* Cambridge, MA: Harvard University Press.

Kagan, J. (1991). The theoretical utility of constructs for self. *Developmental Review, 11,* 244–250.

Kagan, J. (1994). *Galen's prophecy.* New York: Basic Books.

Kagan, J. (1997). Temperament and the reactions to unfamiliarity. *Child Development, 68,* 139–143.

Kagan, J. (1998). Is there a self in infancy? In M. D. Ferrari & R. J. Sternberg (Eds.), *Self-awareness: Its nature and development.* New York: Guilford.

Kagan, J. (2002). *Surprise, uncertainty, and mental structures.* Cambridge, MA: Harvard University Press.

Kagan, J., & Kogan, N. (1970). Individual variation in cognitive processes. In P. H. Mussen (Ed.), *Carmichael's manual of child psychology,* (3rd ed., Vol. 1.) New York: Wiley.

Kagan, J., Reznick, J. S., & Gibbons, J. (1989). Inhibited and uninhibited types of children. *Child Development, 60,* 838–845.

Kagan, J., Reznick, J. S., & Snidman, N. (1987). The physiology and psychology of behavioral inhibition. *Child Development, 58,* 1459–1473.

Kagan, J., Reznick, J. S., & Snidman, N. (1988). Biological bases of childhood shyness. *Science, 240,* 167–171.

Kagan, J., Reznick, J. S., Snidman, N., Gibbons, J., & Johnson, M. O. (1988). Childhood derivatives of inhibition and lack of inhibition to the unfamiliar. *Child Development, 59,* 1580–1589.

Kagan, J., Snidman, N., & Arcus, D. M. (1992). Initial reactions to unfamiliarity. *Current Directions in Psychological Science, 1,* 171–174.

Kagan, J., Snidman, N., & Arcus, D. (1993). On the temperamental categories of inhibited and uninhibited children. In K. H. Rubin & J. B. Asendorpf (Eds.), *Social withdrawal, inhibition, and shyness.* Hillsdale, NJ: Erlbaum.

Kail, R. V. (1991). Developmental change in speed of processing during childhood and adolescence. *Psychological Bulletin, 109,* 490–501.

Kail, R. V. (2000). Speed of information processing: Developmental changes and links to intelligence. *Journal of School Psychology, 38,* 51–61.

Kail, R., & Bisanz, J. (1992). The information-processing perspective on cognitive development in childhood and adolescence. In R. J. Sternberg & C. A. Berg (Eds.), *Intellectual development.* New York: Cambridge University Press.

Kail, R., & Pellegrino, J. W. (1985). *Human intelligence: Perspectives and prospects.* New York: W. H. Freeman.

Kaitz, M., Good, A., Rokem, A. M., & Eidelman, A. I. (1987). Mothers' recognition of their newborns by olfactory cues. *Developmental Psychology, 20,* 587–591.

Kaitz, M., Lapidot, P., Bronner, R., & Eidelman, A. I. (1992). Parturient women can recognize their infants by touch. *Developmental Psychology, 28,* 35–39.

Kaitz, M., Meirov, H., Landman, I., & Eidelman, A. I. (1993). Infant recognition by tactile cues. *Infant Behavior and Development, 16,* 333–341.

Kaler, S. R., & Kopp, C. B. (1990). Compliance and comprehension in very young toddlers. *Child Development, 61,* 1997–2003.

Kalish, C. W. (1996). Causes and symptoms in preschoolers' conceptions of illness. *Child Development, 67,* 1647–1670.

Kalish, C. W. (1997). Preschoolers' understanding of mental and bodily reactions to contamination: What you don't know can hurt you but cannot sadden you. *Developmental Psychology, 33,* 79–91.

Kamii, C., & DeVries, R. (1993). *Physical knowledge in preschool education: Implications of Piaget's theory* (rev. ed.). New York: Teachers College Press.

Kamins, M. L., & Dweck, C. S. (1999). Person versus process praise and criticism: Implications for contingent self-worth and coping. *Developmental Psychology, 35,* 835–847.

Kamptner, L., Kraft, R. H., & Harper, L. V. (1984). Lateral specialization and social-verbal development in preschool children. *Brain and Cognition, 3,* 42–50.

Kandel, E. R., & O'Dell, T. J. (1992). Are adult mechanisms also used for development? *Science, 258,* 243–245.

Karmel, B. Z., & Maisel, E. B. (1975). A neuronal activity model for infant visual attention. In L. B. Cohen & P. Salapatek (Eds.), *Infant perception: From sensation to cognition: Vol. 1. Basic visual processes.* New York: Academic Press.

Karmiloff, K., & Karmiloff-Smith, A. (2001). *Pathways to language.* Cambridge, MA: Harvard University Press.

Karniol, R., & Miller, D. T. (1981). The development of self-control in children. In S. S. Brehm, S. M. Kassin, & F. X. Gibbons (Eds.), *Developmental social psychology: Theory and research.* New York: Oxford University Press.

Karzon, R. G. (1985). Discrimination of polysyllabic sequences by one- to four-month-old infants. *Journal of Experimental Child Psychology, 39,* 326–342.

Katz, P. A., & Ksansnak, K. R. (1994). Developmental aspects of gender role flexibility and traditionality in middle childhood and adolescence. *Developmental Psychology, 30,* 272–282.

Kaufman, A. S., & Kaufman, N. L. (1983). *Kaufman Assessment Battery for Children.* Circle Pines, MN: American Guidance Service.

Kavsek, M. J. (2002). The perception of static subjective contours in infancy. *Child Development, 73,* 331–344.

Kawabata, H., Gyoba, J., Inoue, H., & Ohtsubo, H. (1999). Visual completion of partly occluded grating in infants under one month of age. *Vision Research, 39,* 3586–3591.

Kawasaki, C., Nugent, J. K., Miyashita, H., Miyahara, H., & Brazelton, T. B. (1994). The cultural organization of infants' sleep. *Children's Environments, 11,* 135–141.

Kay, D. A., & Anglin, J. M. (1982). Overextension and underextension in the child's expressive and receptive speech. *Journal of Child Language, 9,* 83–98.

Kaye, K. (1982). *The mental and social life of babies.* Chicago: University of Chicago Press.

Kaye, K. L., & Bower, T. G. R. (1994). Learning and intermodal transfer of information in newborns. *Psychological Science, 5,* 286–288.

Kazdin, A. E. (2002). Psychosocial treatments for conduct disorder in children and adolescents. In P. E. Nathan & J. M. Gorman (Eds.), *A guide to treatments that work* (2nd ed.). London: Oxford University Press.

Keating, D. P. (1988). Byrnes' reformulation of Piaget's formal operations: Is what's left what's right? *Developmental Review, 8,* 376–384.

Kee, D. W., & Guttentag, R. (1994). Resource requirements of knowledge access and recall benefits of associative strategies. *Journal of Experimental Child Psychology, 57,* 211–223.

Keefe, K., & Berndt, T. J. (1996). Relations of friendship quality to self-esteem in early adolescence. *Journal of Early Adolescence, 16,* 110–129.

Keefe, M. R. (1987). Comparison of neonatal nighttime sleep–wake patterns in nursery versus rooming-in environments. *Nursing Research, 36,* 140–144.

Keenan, J. P., & Wheeler, M. (in press). The neuropsychology of self. In A. S. David & T. Kircher (Eds.), *The self and schizophrenia: A neuropsychological perspective.* Cambridge: Cambridge University Press.

Keenan, K., & Shaw, D. (1997). Developmental and social influences on young girls' early problem behavior. *Psychological Bulletin, 121,* 95–113.

Keenan, T. (2000). Mind, memory, and metacognition: The role of memory span in children's developing understanding of the mind. In J. W. Astington (Ed.), *Minds in the making: Essays in honor of David R. Olson.* Malden, MA: Blackwell Publishers.

Keil, F. C. (1998). Cognitive science and the origins of thought and knowledge. In W. Damon (Series Ed.) & R. M. Lerner (Vol. Ed.), *Handbook of child psychology: Vol. 1. Theoretical models of human development* (5th ed.). New York: Wiley.

Keil, F. C., Levin, D. T., Richman, B. A., & Gutheil, G. (1999). Mechanism and explanation in the development of biological thought: The case of disease. In D. Medin & S. Atran (Eds.), *Folkbiology* (pp. 285–319). Cambridge, MA: MIT Press.

Keith, L. K., & Bracken, B. A. (1996). Self-concept instrumentation: A historical and evaluative review. In B. A. Bracken (Ed.), *Handbook of self-concept: Developmental, social, and clinical considerations.* New York: Wiley.

Keller, H. & Scholmerich, A. (1987). Infant vocalizations and parental reactions during the first four months of life. *Developmental Psychology, 23,* 62–67.

Kellman, P. J. (1996). The origins of object perception. In R. Gelman & T. Au (Eds.), *Perceptual and cognitive development.* San Diego, CA: Academic Press.

Kellman, P. J., & Banks, M. (1998). Infant visual perception. In W. Damon (Series Ed.) & D. Kuhn & R. S. Siegler (Vol. Eds.), *Handbook of child psychology: Vol. 2. Cognition, perception, and language* (5th ed.). New York: Wiley.

Kellman, P. J., & Spelke, E. S. (1983). Perception of partly occluded objects in infancy. *Cognitive Psychology, 15,* 483–524.

Kelso, W. M., Nicholls, M. E. R., Warne, G. L., & Zacharin, M. (2000). Cerebral lateralization and cognitive functioning in patients with congenital adrenal hyperplasia. *Neuropsychology, 14,* 370–378.

Kemler Nelson, D. G., Hirsh-Pasek, K., Jusczyk, P., & Cassidy, K. W. (1989). How the prosodic cues in motherese might assist language learning. *Journal of Child Language, 16,* 55–68.

Kenrick, D. T., & Luce, C. L. (2000). An evolutionary life-history model of gender differences and similarities. In T. Eckes & H. M. Trautner (Eds.), *The developmental social psychology of gender.* Mahwah, NJ: Erlbaum.

Kenrick, D. T., & Trost, M. R. (1993). The evolutionary perspective. In A. E. Beall & R. J. Sternberg (Eds.), *The psychology of gender.* New York: Guilford.

Kent, R. D., & Bauer, H. R. (1985). Vocalizations of one-year-olds. *Journal of Child Language, 12,* 491–526.

Kerns, K. A. (1994). A longitudinal examination of links between mother-child attachment and children's friendships in early childhood. *Journal of Social and Personal Relationships, 11,* 379–381.

Kerns, K. A. (1996). Individual differences in friendship quality: Links to child–mother attachment. In W. M. Bukowski, A. F. Newcomb, & W. W. Hartup (Eds.), *The company they keep: Friendship in childhood and adolescence.* New York: Cambridge University Press.

Kerns, K. A., Contreras, J. M., & Neal-Barnett, A. M. (Eds.). (2000). *Family and peers: Linking two social worlds.* Westport, CT: Praeger.

Kerns, K. A., Klepac, L., & Cole, A. (1996). Peer relationships and preadolescents' perceptions of security in the child-mother relationship. *Developmental Psychology, 32,* 457–466.

Kerpelman, J. L., Shoffner, M. F., & Ross-Griffin, S. (2002). African American mothers' and daughters' beliefs about possible selves and their strategies for reaching the adolescents' future academic and career goals. *Journal of Youth and Adolescence, 31,* 289–302.

Kerr, M., Lambert, W. W., & Bem, D. J. (1996). Life course sequelae of childhood shyness in Sweden: Comparison with the United States. *Developmental Psychology, 32,* 1100–1105.

Kerr, M., Lambert, W. W., Stattin, H., & Klackenberg-Larsson, I. (1994). Stability of inhibition in a Swedish longitudinal sample. *Child Development, 65,* 138–146.

Killen, M., Lee-Kim, J., McGlothin, H., & Stangor, C. (2002). How children and adolescents evaluate gender and racial exclusion. *Monographs of the Society for Research in Child Development, 67,* 4 (Serial No. 271).

Kim, M., McGregor, K. K., & Thompson, C. K. (2000). Early lexical development in English- and Korean-speaking children: Language-general and language specific patterns. *Journal of Child Language, 27,* 225–254.

Kindlon, D., & Thompson, M. (1999). *Raising Cain: Protecting the emotional life of boys.* New York: Ballantine.

Kinnear, A. (1995). Introduction of microcomputers: A case study of patterns of use and children's perceptions. *Journal of Educational Computing Research, 13,* 27–40.

Kircher, T. J., Senior, C., Philips, M. L., Rabe-Hesketh, S., Benson, P. J., Bullmore, E. T., et al. (2001). Recognizing one's own face. *Cognition, 78,* B1–B15.

Kiser, L. J., Bates, J. E., Maslin, C. A., & Bayles, K. (1986). Mother–infant play at six months as a predictor of attachment security at thirteen months. *Journal of the American Academy of Child Psychiatry, 25,* 68–75.

Kisilevsky, B. S., & Muir, D. W. (1984). Neonatal habituation and dishabituation to tactile stimulation during sleep. *Developmental Psychology, 20,* 367–373.

Kister, M. C., & Patterson, C. J. (1980). Children's conceptions of the causes of illness: Understanding of contagion and use of immanent justice. *Child Development, 51,* 839–846.

Kivett, V. R. (1985). Grandfathers and grandchildren: Patterns of association, helping, and psychological closeness. *Family Relations, 34,* 565–571.

Klahr, D., & MacWhinney, B. (1998). Information processing. In W. Damon (Series Ed.) & D. Kuhn & R. S. Siegler (Vol. Eds.), *Handbook of child psychology: Vol. 2. Cognition, perception, and language* (5th ed.). New York: Wiley.

Klahr, D., & Robinson, M. (1981). Formal assessment of problem solving and planning processes in preschool children. *Cognitive Psychology, 13,* 113–148.

Klaus, M. H., & Kennell, J. H. (1976). *Maternal–infant bonding.* St. Louis, MO: Mosby.

Klaus, M. H., Kennell, J. H., & Klaus, P. H. (1995). *Bonding: Building the foundations of secure attachment and independence.* Reading, MA: Addison-Wesley.

Kleeman, W. J., Schlaud, M., Fieguth, A., Hiller, A. S., Rothamel, T., & Troger, H. D. (1999). Body and head position, covering of the head by bedding, and risk of sudden infant death syndrome (SIDS). *International Journal of Legal Medicine, 112,* 22–26.

Kleinfeld, J. S. (1996). The surprising ease of changing the belief that the schools shortchange girls. In R. J. Simon (Ed.), *From data to public policy: Affirmative action, sexual harassment, domestic violence and social welfare.* Lanham, MD: University Press of America.

Klimes-Dougan, B., & Kistner, J. (1990). Physically abused pre-schoolers' responses to peers' distress. *Developmental Psychology, 26,* 599–602.

Klinnert, M. D., Campos, J. J., Sorce, J. F., Emde, R. N., & Svejda, M. (1983). Emotions as behavior regulators: Social referencing in infancy. In R. Plutchik & H. Kellerman (Eds.), *Emotions in early development: Vol. 2. The emotions.* New York: Academic Press.

Klinnert, M. D., Sorce, J. F., Emde, R. N., Stenberg, C., & Gaensbauer, T. (1984). Continuities and change in early emotional life: Maternal perceptions of surprise, fear, and anger. In R. N. Emde & R. J. Harmon (Eds.), *Continuities and discontinuities in development.* New York: Plenum.

Kobayashi, Y. (1994). Concept acquisition and change through social interaction. *Human Development, 37,* 233–241.

Kochanska, G. (1993). Toward a synthesis of parental socialization and child temperament in early development of conscience. *Child Development, 64,* 325–347.

Kochanska, G. (1995). Children's temperament, mothers' discipline, and security of attachment: Multiple pathways to emerging internalization. *Child Development, 66,* 597–615.

Kochanska, G. (1997). Multiple pathways to conscience for children with different temperaments: From toddlerhood to age 5. *Developmental Psychology, 33,* 228–240.

Kochanska, G. (1997). Mutually responsive orientation between mothers and their young children: Implications for early socialization. *Child Development, 68,* 94–112.

Kochanska, G. (2002). Committed compliance, moral self, and internalization: A mediational model. *Developmental Psychology, 38,* 339–351.

Kochanska, G., & Aksan, N. (1995). Mother-child mutually positive affect, the quality of child compliance to requests and prohibitions, and maternal control as correlates of early internalization. *Child Development, 66,* 236–254.

Kochanska, G., Coy, K. C., & Murray, K. T. (2001). The development of self-regulation in the first four years of life. *Child Development, 72,* 1091–1111.

Kochanska, G., Gross, J. N., Li, M-H., & Nichols, K. E. (2002). Guilt in young children: Development, determinants, and relations with a broader system of standards. *Child Development, 73,* 461–482.

Kochanska, G., Murray, K., & Coy, K. C. (1997). Inhibitory control as a contributor to conscience in childhood: From toddler to early school age. *Child Development, 68,* 263–277.

Kochanska, G., Murray, K., Jacques, T. Y., Koenig, A. L., & Vandergeest, K.A. (1996). Inhibitory control in young children and its role in emerging internalization. *Child Development, 67,* 490–507.

Kochanska, G., & Thompson, R. A. (1997). The emergence and development of conscience in toddlerhood and early childhood. In J. E. Grusec & L. Kuczynski (Eds.), *Handbook of parenting and the transmission of values.* New York: Wiley.

Koenigsknecht, R. A., & Friedman, P. (1976). Syntax development in boys and girls. *Child Development, 47,* 1109–1115.

Kohlberg, L. (1966). A cognitive-developmental analysis of children's sex role concepts and attitudes. In E. E. Maccoby (Ed.), *The development of sex differences.* Stanford, CA: Stanford University Press.

Kohlberg, L. (1969). Stage and sequence: The cognitive-developmental approach to socialization. In D. A. Goslin (Ed.), *Handbook of socialization theory and research.* Chicago: Rand McNally.

Kohlberg, L. (1976). Moral stages and moralization: The cognitive-developmental approach. In T. Likona (Ed.), *Moral development and behavior: Theory, research, and social issues.* New York: Holt, Rinehart and Winston.

Kohlberg, L. (1981). *Essays on moral development: Vol. 1. The philosophy of moral development.* New York: Harper & Row.

Kohlberg, L. (1984). *The psychology of moral development: The nature and validity of moral stages.* San Francisco: Harper & Row.

Kohlberg, L. (1987). The development of moral judgment and moral action. In L. Kohlberg (Ed.), *Child psychology and childhood education: A cognitive-developmental view.* New York: Longman.

Kohlberg, L., & Candee, D. (1984). The relationship of moral judgment to moral action. In W. M. Kurtines & J. L. Gewirtz (Eds.), *Morality, moral behavior, and moral development.* New York: Wiley.

Kohlberg, L., & Kramer, R. (1969). Continuities and discontinuities in childhood and adult moral development. *Human Development, 12,* 93–120.

Kohlberg, L., Levine, C., & Hewer, A. (1983). *Moral stages: A current formulation and a response to critics.* Basel, Switzerland: Karger.

Kohlberg, L., & Ullian, D. Z. (1974). Stages in the development of psychosexual concepts and attitudes. In R. C. Friedman, R. M. Richart, & L. VandeWiele (Eds.), *Sex differences in behavior.* New York: Wiley.

Kohlberg, L., Yaeger, J., & Hjertholm, E. (1968). Private speech: Four studies and a review of theories. *Child Development, 39,* 817–826.

Kolb, B. (1989). Brain development, plasticity, and behavior. *American Psychologist, 44,* 1203–1212.

Konner, M. (1972). Aspects of the developmental ethology of a foraging people. In N. Blurton-Jones (Ed.), *Ethological studies of child behavior.* Cambridge: Cambridge University Press.

Konner, M. J. (1976). Maternal care, infant behavior and development among the Kung. In R. B. Lee & I. DeVore (Eds.), *Kalahari hunter-gatherers.* Cambridge, MA: Harvard University Press.

Konner, M. J. (2002). *The tangled wing* (2nd ed.). New York: W. H. Freeman.

Kontos, S., Howes, C., Galinsky, E. (1996). Does training make a difference to quality in family child care? *Early Childhood Research Quarterly, 11,* 427–445

Kopp, C. B. (1982). Antecedents of self-regulation: A developmental perspective. *Developmental Psychology, 18,* 199–214.

Kopp, C. B., & Krakow, J. B. (Eds.). (1982). *The child.* Reading, MA: Addison-Wesley.

Korn, S. J. (1984). Continuities and discontinuities in difficult/easy temperament: Infancy to young adulthood. *Merrill-Palmer Quarterly, 30,* 189–199.

Korner, A. F., & Thoman, E. (1970). Visual alertness in neonates as evoked by maternal care. *Journal of Experimental Child Psychology, 10,* 67–78.

Kornhaber, M. (1994). *The theory of multiple intelligences: Why and how schools use it.* Cambridge, MA: Harvard Graduate School of Education.

Kostelny, K., & Garbarino, J. (1994). Coping with the consequences of living in danger: The case of Palestinian children and youth. *International Journal of Behavioral Development, 17,* 595–611.

Kovacs, D. M., Parker, J. G., & Hoffman, L. W. (1996). Behavioral, affective, and social correlates of involvement in cross-sex friendship in elementary school. *Child Development, 67,* 2269–2286.

Kowal, A., & Kramer, L., (1997). Children's understanding of parental differential treatment. *Child Development, 68,* 113–126.

Kowal, A., Kramer, L., Krull, J. L., & Crick, N. R. (2002). Children's perceptions of the fairness of parental preferential treatment and their socioemotional well-being. *Journal of Family Psychology, 16,* 297–306.

Kozulin, A. (1990). *Vygotsky's psychology.* Cambridge, MA: Harvard University Press.

Kraft, R. H. (1984). Lateral specialization and verbal/spatial ability in preschool children: Age, sex and familial handedness differences. *Neuropsychologia, 22,* 319–335.

Krauss, R. M., & Glucksberg, S. (1964). The development of communication: Competence as a function of age. *Child Development, 40,* 255–266.

Krebs, D. (1987). The challenge of altruism in biology and psychology. In C. Crawford, M. Smith, & D. Krebs (Eds.), *Sociobiology and psychology: Ideas, issues, and applications.* Hillsdale, NJ: Erlbaum.

Krebs, D. L., & Van Hesteren, F. (1994). The development of altruism: Toward an integrative model. *Developmental Review, 14,* 103–158.

Kreitler, S., & Kreitler, H. (1987). Conceptions and processes of planning: The developmental perspective. In *Blueprints for thinking: The role of planning in cognitive development.* Cambridge: Cambridge University Press.

Kreitler, S., & Kreitler, H. (1989). Horizontal decalage: A problem and its solution. *Cognitive Development, 4,* 89–119.

Kreutzer, M. A., Leonard, C., & Flavell, J. H. (1975). An interview study of children's knowledge about memory. *Monographs of the Society for Research in Child Development, 40* (1, Serial No. 159).

Krevans, J., & Gibbs, J. C. (1996). Parents' use of inductive discipline: Relations to children's empathy and prosocial behavior. *Child Development, 67,* 3263–3277.

Kropp, J. P., & Haynes, O. M. (1987). Abusive and nonabusive mothers' ability to identify general and specific emotion signals of infants. *Child Development, 58,* 187–190.

Kruger, A. C. (1992). The effect of peer and adult-child transactive discussions on moral reasoning. *Merrill-Palmer Quarterly, 38,* 191–211.

Kruger, A. C. (1993). Peer collaboration: Conflict, cooperation, or both? *Social Development, 2,* 165–182.

Kruger, A. C., & Tomasello, M. (1986). Transactive discussions with peers and adults. *Developmental Psychology, 22,* 681–685.

Kuchuk, A., Vibbert, M., & Bornstein, M. H. (1986). The perception of smiling and its experiential correlates in three-month-old infants. *Child Development, 57,* 1054–1061.

Kuczaj, S. A. (1982). Language play and language acquisition. In H. W. Reese (Ed.), *Advances in child development and behavior* (Vol. 17). New York: Academic Press.

Kuczynski, L., & Kochanska, G. (1990). Development of children's noncompliance strategies from toddlerhood to age 5. *Developmental Psychology, 26,* 398–408.

Kuczynski, L., & Kochanska, G. (1995). Function and content of maternal demands: Developmental significance of early demands for competent action. *Child Development, 66,* 616–628.

Kuebli, J., & Fivush, R. (1992). Gender differences in parent-child conversations about past emotions. *Sex Roles, 27,* 683–698.

Kuhl, P. K. (1991). Perception, cognition, and the ontogenetic and phylogenetic emergence of human speech. In S. Brauth, W. Hall, & R. Dooling (Eds.), *Plasticity of development.* Cambridge, MA: MIT Press/Bradford Books.

Kuhl, P. K. (2001). Speech, language, and developmental change. In F. Lacerda, C. von Hofsten, & M. Heimann (Eds.), *Emerging cognitive abilities in early infancy.* Mahwah, NJ: Erlbaum.

Kuhl, P. K., & Meltzoff, A. N. (1982). The bimodal perception of speech in infancy. *Science, 218,* 1138–1141.

Kuhl, P. K., & Meltzoff, A. N. (1984). The intermodal representation of speech in infants. *Infant Behavior and Development, 7,* 361–381.

Kuhl, P. K., & Meltzoff, A. N. (1988). Speech as an intermodal object of perception. In A. Yonas (Ed.), *Minnesota symposia on child psychology: Vol. 20. Perceptual development in infancy.* Hillsdale, NJ: Erlbaum.

Kuhn, D. (1972). Mechanisms of change in the development of cognitive structures. *Child Development, 43,* 833–844.

Kuhn, D. (1995). Microgenetic study of change: What has it told us? *Psychological Science, 6,* 133–139.

Kuhn, D., Ho, V., & Adams, C. (1979). Formal reasoning among pre- and late-adolescents. *Child Development, 50,* 1128–1135.

Kulin, H. E. (1991). Puberty, hypothalamic-pituitary changes of. In R. M. Lerner, A. C. Peterson, & J. Brooks-Gunn (Eds.), *Encyclopedia of adolescence* (Vol. 2). New York: Garland.

Kuller, J. A. (1996). Chorionic villus sampling. In J. A. Kuller, N. C. Cheschier, & R. C. Cefalo (Eds.), *Prenatal diagnosis and reproductive genetics.* St. Louis, MO: Mosby.

Kupersmidt, J. B., & Trejos, S. L. (1987, April). *Behavioral correlates of sociometric status among Costa Rican children.* Paper presented at the meeting of the Society for Research in Child Development, Baltimore.

Kupersmidt, J. B., DeRosier, M. E., & Patterson, C. P. (1995). Similarity as the basis for children's friendships: The roles of sociometric status, aggressive and withdrawn behavior, academic achievement, and demographic characteristics. *Journal of Social and Personal Relationships, 12,* 439–452.

Kurdek, L. A. (1978). Perspective taking as the cognitive basis of children's moral development: A review of the literature. *Merrill-Palmer Quarterly, 34,* 3–28.

Kurdek, L. A. (1980). Developmental relations among children's perspective taking, moral judgment, and parent-rated behaviors. *Merrill-Palmer Quarterly, 26,* 103–121

Kurtz, B. E., & Borkowski, J. G. (1987). Development of strategic skills in impulsive and reflective children: A longitudinal study of metacognition. *Journal of Experimental Child Psychology, 43,* 129–148.

Kurtz, B. E., Schneider, W., Carr, M., & Rellinger, E. (1990). Strategy instruction and attributional beliefs in West Germany and the United States: Do teachers foster metacognitive development? *Contemporary Educational Psychology, 15,* 268–283.

Laboratory of Comparative Human Cognition. (1983). Culture and cognitive development. In P. H. Mussen (Series Ed.) & W. Kessen (Vol. Ed.), *Handbook of child psychology: Vol. 1. History, theory, and methods* (4th ed.). New York: Wiley.

Lacerda, F., Hofsten, C. V., & Heimann, M. (Eds.). (2001). *Emerging cognitive abilities in early infancy.* Mahwah, NJ: Erlbaum.

Lacourse, E., Cote, S., Nagin, D. S., Vitaro, F., Brendgen, M., & Tremblay, R. E. (2002). A longitudinal-experimental approach to testing theories of antisocial behavior development. *Development and Psychopathology, 14,* 909–924.

Ladd, B. K., & Ladd, G. W. (2001). Variations in peer victimization: Relations to children's maladjustment. In J. Juvonen & S. Graham (Eds.), *Peer harassment in school: The plight of the vulnerable and victimized.* New York: Guilford.

Ladd, G. W. (1990). Having friends, keeping friends, making friends, and being liked by peers in the classroom: Predictors of children's early school adjustment? *Child Development, 61,* 1081–1100.

Ladd, G. W. (1992). Themes and theories: Perspectives on processes in family-peer relationships. In R. D. Parke & G. W. Ladd (Eds.), *Family-peer relationships: Modes of linkage.* Hillsdale, NJ: Erlbaum.

Ladd, G. W., Birch, S. H., & Buhs, E. S. (1999). Children's social and scholastic lives in kindergarten: Related spheres of influence? *Child Development, 70,* 1373–1400.

Ladd, G. W., Buhs, E. S., & Troop, W. (2002). Children's interpersonal skills and relationships in school settings: Adaptive significance and implications for school-based prevention and intervention programs. In P. K. Smith & C. H. Hart (Eds.), *Blackwell handbook of childhood social development.* Madden, MA: Blackwell Publishers.

Ladd, G. W., & Hart, C. H. (1992). Creating informal play opportunities: Are parents' and preschoolers' initiations related to children's competence with peers? *Developmental Psychology, 28,* 1179–1187.

Ladd, G. W., Kochenderfer, B. J., & Coleman, C. C. (1996). Friendship quality as a predictor of young children's early school adjustment. *Child Development, 67,* 1103–1118.

Ladd, G. W., & Pettit, G. (2002). Parents' and children's peer relationships. In M. H. Bornstein (Ed.), *Handbook of parenting* (2nd ed., Vol. 5). Mahwah, NJ: Erlbaum.

LaFrance, M., Hecht, M. A., & Paluck, E. L. (2003). The contingent smile: A meta-analysis of sex differences in smiling. *Psychological Bulletin, 129,* 305–334.

LaFreniere, P., & Charlesworth, W. R. (1983). Dominance, attention, and affiliation in a preschool group: A nine-month longitudinal study. *Ethology and Sociobiology, 4,* 55–67.

LaFreniere, P., Masataka, N., Butovskaya, M., Chen, Q., Dessen, M. A., Atwanger, K., et al. (2002). Cross-cultural analysis of social competence and behavior problems in preschoolers. *Early Education and Development, 13,* 201–219.

LaFromboise, T., Coleman, H., & Gerton, J. (1993). Psychological impact of biculturalism: Evidence and theory. *Psychological Bulletin, 114,* 395–412.

LaGasse, L. L., Gruber, C. P., & Lipsitt, L. P. (1989). The infantile expression of avidity in relation to later assessments of inhibition and attachment. In J. S. Reznick (Ed.), *Perspectives on behavioral inhibition.* Chicago: University of Chicago Press.

Lahey, B. B., Gordon, R. A., Loeber, R., Stouthamer-Loeber, M., & Farrington, D. P. (1999). *Journal of Abnormal Child Psychology, 27,* 247–260.

Laible, D. J., & Thompson, R. A. (1998). Attachment and emotional understanding in preschool children. *Developmental Psychology, 34,* 1038–1045.

Laing, E., Butterworth, G., Ansari, D., Gsodl, M., Longhi, E., Panagiotaki, G., Peterson, S., et al. (2002). Atypical development of language and social communication in toddlers with Williams syndrome. *Developmental Science, 5,* 233–246.

Laing, G. J., & Logan, S. (1999). Patterns of unintentional injury in childhood and their relation to socio-economic factors. *Public Health, 113,* 291–294.

Laird, R. D., Jordan, K. Y., Dodge, K. A., Pettit, G. S., & Bates, J. E. (2001). Peer rejection in childhood, involve-ment with antisocial peers in early adolescence, and the development of externalizing behavior problems. *Development and Psychopathology, 13,* 337–354.

Lamaze, F. (1970). *Painless childbirth: Psychoprophylactic method.* Chicago: Henry Regnery.

Lamb, M. E. (Ed.). (1997). *The role of the father in child development* (3rd ed.). New York: Wiley.

Lamb, M. E. (1998). Nonparental child care: Context, quality, correlates, and consequences. In W. Damon (Series Ed.) & I. E. Sigel & K. A. Renninger (Vol. Eds.), *Handbook of child psychology: Vol. 4. Child psychology in practice* (5th ed.). New York: Wiley.

Lamb, M. E., Easterbrooks, M. A., & Holden, G. W. (1980). Reinforcement and punishment among preschoolers: Characteristics, effects, and correlates. *Child Development, 51,* 1230–1236.

Lamb, M. E., Frodi, A. M., Hwang, C. P., & Frodi, M. (1982). Varying degrees of paternal involvement in infant care: Attitudinal and behavioral correlates. In M. E. Lamb (Ed.), *Nontraditional families.* Hillsdale, NJ: Erlbaum.

Lamb, M. E., & Hwang, C. (1982). Maternal attachment and mother–neonate bonding: A critical review. In M. E. Lamb & A. L. Brown (Eds.), *Advances in developmental psychology* (Vol. 2). Hillsdale, NJ: Erlbaum.

Lamb, M. E., Ketterlinus, R. D., & Fracasso, M. P. (1992). Parent–child relationships. In M. H. Bornstein & M. E. Lamb (Eds.), *Developmental psychology: An advanced textbook* (3rd ed.). Hillsdale, NJ: Erlbaum.

Lamb, M. E., Morrison, D. C., & Malkin, C. M. (1987). The development of infant social expectations in face-to-face interaction: A longitudinal study. *Merrill-Palmer Quarterly, 33,* 241–254.

Lamb, M. E., & Poole, D. A. (1998). *Investigative interviews of children: A guide for helping professionals.* Washington, DC: American Psychological Association.

Lamb, M. E., & Roopnarine, J. L. (1979). Peer influences on sex-role development in preschoolers. *Child Development, 50,* 1219–1222.

Lamb, M. E., Sternberg, K., & Prodromidis, M. (1992). Nonmaternal care and the security of infant–mother attachment: A reanalysis of the data. *Infant Behavior and Development, 15,* 71–83.

Lamb, M. E., Thompson, R. A., & Frodi, A. M. (1982). Early social development. In R. Vasta (Ed.), *Strategies and techniques of child study.* New York: Academic Press.

Lamb, M. E., Thompson, R., Gardner, W., & Charnov, E. (1985). *Infant–mother attachment: The origin and developmental significance of individual differences in Strange Situation behavior.* Hillsdale, NJ: Erlbaum.

Lamborn, S. D., Dornbusch, S. M., & Steinberg, L. (1996). Ethnicity and community context as moderators of the relation between family decision making and adolescent adjustment. *Child Development, 67,* 283–301.

Lamborn, S. D., Mounts, N. S., Steinberg, L., & Dornbusch, S. M. (1991). Patterns of competence and adjustment among adolescents from authoritative, authoritarian, indulgent, and neglectful families. *Child Development, 62,* 1049–1065.

Lancy, D. F. (1996). *Playing on the mother ground: Cultural routines for children's development.* New York: Guilford.

Lander, J., Brady-Fryer, B., Metcalfe, J., Nazarali, S., & Muttitt, S. (1997). Comparison of ring block, dorsal penile nerve block, and topical anesthesia for neonatal circumcision: A randomized control trial. *Journal of the American Medical Association, 278,* 2157–2162.

Langer, O. (1990). Critical issues in diabetes and pregnancy. In I. R. Merkatz & J. E. Thompson (Eds.), *New perspectives on prenatal care.* New York: Elsevier.

Langlois, J. H., & Downs, A. C. (1979). Peer relations as a function of physical attractiveness: The eye of the beholder or behavioral reality? *Child Development, 50,* 409–418.

Langlois, J. H., Kalakanis, L., Rubenstein, A. J., Larson, A., Hallam, M., & Smoot, M. (2000). Maxims or myths of beauty: A meta-analytic and theoretical review. *Psychological Bulletin, 126,* 390–423.

Langlois, J. H., Ritter, J. M., Casey, R. J., & Sawin, D. B. (1995). Infant attractiveness predicts maternal behaviors and attitudes. *Developmental Psychology, 31,* 464–472.

Langlois, J. H., Roggman, L. A., Casey, R. J., Ritter, J. M., Reiser-Danner, L. A., & Jenkins, V. Y. (1987). Infant preference for attractive faces: Rudiments of a stereotype? *Developmental Psychology, 23,* 363–369.

Lansford, J. E., & Parker, J. G. (1999). Children's interactions in triads: Behavioral profiles and effects of gender and patterns of friendships among members. *Developmental Psychology, 35,* 80–93.

Lanza, E. (1997). *Language mixing in infant bilingualism: A sociolinguistic perspective.* Oxford: Oxford University Press.

Largo, R. H., Molinari, L., Weber, M., Pinto, L. C., & Duc, G. (1985). Early development of locomotion: Significance of prematurity, cerebral palsy and sex. *Developmental Medicine and Child Neurology, 27,* 183–191.

Larson, R. W., & Verma, S. (1999). How children and adolescents spend time across the world: Work, play and developmental opportunities. *Psychological Bulletin, 125,* 701–736.

Larsson, G., Bohlin, A. B., & Tunell, R. (1985). Prospective study of children exposed to variable amounts of alcohol in utero. *Archives of Disease in Childhood, 60,* 316–321.

Laupta, M., & Turiel, E. (1993). Children's concepts of authority and social contexts. *Journal of Educational Psychology, 85,* 191–197.

Laursen, B., & Collins, W. A. (1994). Interpersonal conflict during adolescence. *Psychological Bulletin, 115,* 197–209.

Laursen, B., Finkelstein, B. D., & Betts, N. T. (2001). A developmental meta-analysis of peer conflict resolution. *Developmental Review, 21,* 423–449.

Lave, J., & Wenger, E. (1991). *Situated learning: Legitimate peripheral participation.* New York: Cambridge University Press.

Lavelli, M., & Fogel, A. (2002). Developmental changes in mother-infant face-to-face communication: Birth to 3 months. *Developmental Psychology, 38,* 288–305.

Leaper, C. (Ed.). (1994). *New directions for child development: No. 65. Childhood gender segregation: Causes and consequences.* San Francisco: Jossey-Bass.

Leaper, C. (2002). Parenting girls and boys. In M. H. Bornstein (Ed.), *Handbook of parenting* (2nd ed., Vol. 1). Mahwah, NJ: Erlbaum.

Leaper, C., Anderson, K. J., & Sanders, P. (1998). Moderators of gender effects on parents' talk to their children: A meta-analysis. *Developmental Psychology, 34,* 3–27.

Leaper, C., Breed, L., Hoffman, L., & Perlman, C. A. (2002). Variations in the gender-stereotyped content of children's television cartoons across genres. *Journal of Applied Social Psychology, 32,* 1653–1662.

Leaper, C., Leve, L., Strasser, T., & Schwartz, R. (1995). Mother-child communication sequences: Play activity, child gender, and marital status effects. *Merrill-Palmer Quarterly, 41,* 307–327.

Leaper, C., Tenenbaum, H. R., & Shaffer, T. G. (1999). Communication patterns of African American girls and boys from low-income, urban background. *Child Development, 70,* 1489–1503.

Leavitt, L., & Fox, N. (Eds.). (1993). *Psychological effects of war and violence on children.* Hillsdale, NJ: Erlbaum.

Lebra, T. S. (1976). *Japanese patterns of behavior.* Honolulu: University Press of Hawaii.

Lebra, T. S. (1994). Mother and child in Japanese socialization: A Japan-U.S. comparison. In P. M. Greenfield & R. R. Cocking (Eds.), *Cross-cultural roots of minority child development.* Hillsdale, NJ: Erlbaum.

Lecanuet, J.-P. (1998). Fetal responses to auditory and speech stimuli. In A. Slater (Ed.), *Perceptual development: Visual, auditory, and speech perception in infancy.* Hove, UK: Psychology Press.

Lee, C., & Bates, J. E. (1985). Mother–child interaction at the age of two years and perceived difficult temperament. *Child Development, 56,* 1314–1325.

Lee, C. D., & Smagorinksy, P. (Eds.) (2000). *Vygotskian perspectives on literacy research: Constructing meaning through collaborative inquiry.* New York: Cambridge University Press.

Lee, D. N., & Aronson, E. (1974). Visual proprioceptive control of standing in human infants. *Perception and Psychophysics, 15,* 529–532.

Lee, V. E., Brooks-Gunn, J., Schnur, E., & Liaw, F.-R. (1990). Are Head Start effects sustained? A longitudinal follow-up comparison of disadvantaged children attending Head Start, no preschool, and other preschool programs. *Child Development, 61,* 495–507.

Leger, D. W., Thompson, R. A., Merritt, J. A., & Benz, J. J. (1996). Adult perception of emotion intensity in human infant cries: Effects of infant age and cry acoustics. *Child Development, 67,* 3238–3249.

Legerstee, M. (1991). The role of person and object in eliciting early imitation. *Journal of Experimental Child Psychology, 51,* 423–433.

Legerstee, M. (1994). Patterns of 4-month-old infant responses to hidden silent and sounding people and objects. *Early Development and Parenting, 3,* 71–80.

Legerstee, M., Anderson, D., & Schaffer, A. (1998). Five- and eight-month-old infants recognize their faces and voices as familiar and social stimuli. *Child Development, 69,* 37–50.

Legerstee, M., & Varghese, J. (2001). The role of maternal affect mirroring on social expectancies in three-month-old infants. *Child Development, 72,* 1301–1313.

Leichtman, M. D., Pillemer, D. B., Wang, Q., Koreishi, A., & Han, J. J. (2000). When baby Maisy came to school: Mothers' interview styles and preschoolers' event memories. *Cognitive Development, 15,* 99–114.

Leiderman, P. H., & Seashore, M. J. (1975). Mother-infant separation: Some delayed consequences. In *Parent-infant interaction* (CIBA Foundation Symposium No. 33). New York: Elsevier.

Leinbach, M. D., & Fagot, B. I. (1993). Categorical habituation to male and female faces: Gender schematic processing in infancy. *Infant Behavior and Development, 16,* 317–332.

Leinbach, M. D., Hort, B. E., & Fagot, B. I. (1997). Bears are for boys: Metaphorical associations in young children's gender stereotypes. *Cognitive Development, 12,* 107–130.

Leinhardt, G., Crowley, K., & Knutson, K. (2002). *Learning conversations in museums.* Mahwah, NJ: Erlbaum.

Leiter, M. P. (1977). A study of reciprocity in preschool play groups. *Child Development, 48,* 1288–1295.

Lemery, K., & Goldsmith, H. H. (1999). Genetically informative designs in the study of behavioral development. *International Journal of Behavioral Development, 23,* 293–317.

Lempers, J. D., Flavell, E. R., & Flavell, J. H. (1977). The development in very young children of tacit knowledge concerning visual perception. *Genetic Psychology Monographs, 95,* 3–53.

Lenneberg, E. H. (1967). *Biological foundations of language.* New York: Wiley.

Leon, G. R. (1991). Bulimia nervosa in adolescence. In R. M. Lerner, A. C. Petersen, & J. Brooks-Gunn (Eds.), *Encyclopedia of adolescence.* New York: Garland.

Lerner, R. M. (1982). Children and adolescents as producers of their own development. *Developmental Review, 2,* 342–370.

Lerner, R. M., & Von Eye, A. (1992). Sociobiology and human development: Arguments and evidence. *Human Development, 35,* 12–33.

Lesko, N. (Ed.). (2000). *Masculinities at school.* London: Sage.

Leslie, A. M., & Keeble, S. (1987). Do six-month-olds perceive causality? *Cognition, 25,* 265–288.

Lester, B. M. (1984). A biosocial model of infant crying. In L. P. Lipsitt (Ed.), *Advances in infancy research* (Vol. 3). Norwood, NJ: Ablex.

Lester, B. M. (2000). Prenatal cocaine exposure and child outcome: A model for the study of the infant at risk. *Israel Journal of Psychiatry and Related Sciences, 37,* 223–235.

Lester, B. M., Boukydis, C. F. Z., & Twomey, J. E. (2000). Maternal substance abuse and child outcome. In C. H. Zeanah Jr. (Ed.), *Handbook of infant mental health* (2nd ed.). New York: Guilford.

Lester, B. M., Hoffman, J., & Brazelton, T. B. (1985). The rhythmic structure of mother–infant interaction in term and preterm infants. *Child Development, 56,* 15–27.

Lester, B. M., & Tronick, E. Z. (2001). Behavioral assessment scales: The NICU Network Neurobehavioral Scale, the Neonatal Behavioral Assessment Scale, and the Assessment of the Preterm Infant's Behavior. In L. T. Singer & P. S. Zeskind (Eds.), *Biobehavioral assessment of the infant.* New York: Guilford Press.

Leung, E. H. L., & Rheingold, H. L. (1981). Development of pointing as a social gesture. *Developmental Psychology, 17,* 215–220.

Leveroni, C. L., & Berenbaum, S. A. (1998). Early androgen effects on interest in infants: Evidence from children with congenital adrenal hyperplasia. *Developmental Neuropsychology, 14,* 321–340.

Levin, I. (1989). Principles underlying time measurement: The development of children's constraints on counting time. In I. Levin & D. Zakay (Eds.), *Time and human cognition: A life-span perspective.* The Netherlands: Elsevier.

Levin, I., & Druyan, S. (1993). When sociocognitive transaction among peers fails: The case of misconceptions in science. *Child Development, 63,* 1571–1591.

Levin, M. (1994). Comment on the Minnesota Transracial Adoption Study. *Intelligence, 19,* 13–20.

LeVine, R. A. (1988). Human parental care: Universal goals, cultural strategies, individual behavior. In R. A. LeVine, P. M. Miller, & M. M. West (Eds.), *New directions for child development: No. 40. Parental behavior in diverse societies.* San Francisco: Jossey-Bass.

LeVine, R. A., Dixon, S., LeVine, S., Richman, A., Leiderman, P. H., Keefer, C. H., et al. (1994). *Child care and culture: Lessons from Africa.* Cambridge: Cambridge University Press.

Levine, S. C., Huttenlocher, J., Taylor, A., & Langrock, A. (1999). Early sex differences in spatial skill. *Developmental Psychology, 35,* 940–949.

Levitt, M. J., Weber, R. A., Clark, M. C., & McDonnell, P. (1985). Reciprocity of exchange in toddler sharing behavior. *Developmental Psychology, 21,* 122–123

Levy, G. (1999). Gender-typed and non-gender-typed category awareness in toddlers. *Sex Roles, 41,* 851–873.

Levy, G. D., & Carter, D. B. (1989). Gender schema, gender constancy, and gender-role knowledge: The roles of cognitive factors in preschoolers' gender-role stereotype attributions. *Developmental Psychology, 25,* 444–449.

Levy, G. D., & Fivush, R. (1993). Scripts and gender: A new approach for examining gender-role development. *Developmental Psychology, 13,* 126–146.

Levy, G. D., Taylor, M. G., & Gelman, S. A. (1995). Traditional and evaluative aspects of flexibility in gender roles, social conventions, moral rules, and physical laws. *Child Development, 66,* 515–531.

Levy, M., & Koren, G. (1992). Clinical toxicology of the neonate. *Seminars in Perinatology, 16,* 63–75.

Lewis, C. C. (1995). *Educating hearts and minds: Reflections on Japanese preschool and elementary education.* Cambridge: Cambridge University Press.

Lewis, L., & Ramsay, D. S. (1999). Effect of maternal soothing on infant stress response. *Child Development, 70,* 11–20.

Lewis, M. (1981). Self-knowledge: A social cognitive perspective on gender identity and sex-role development. In M. E. Lamb & L. R. Sherrod (Eds.), *Infant social cognition: Empirical and theoretical considerations.* Hillsdale, NJ: Erlbaum.

Lewis, M. (1987). Social development in infancy and early childhood. In J. D. Osofsky (Ed.), *Handbook of infant development* (2nd ed.). New York: Wiley.

Lewis, M. (1993a). Early socioemotional predictors of cognitive competence at 4 years. *Developmental Psychology, 29,* 1036–1045.

Lewis, M. (1993b). Self-conscious emotions: Embarrassment, pride, shame, and guilt. In M. Lewis & J. Haviland (Eds.), *The handbook of emotions.* New York: Guilford.

Lewis, M. (1994). Myself and me. In S. T. Parker, R. W. Mitchell, & M. L. Boccia (Eds.), *Self-awareness in animals and humans: Developmental perspectives.* New York: Cambridge University Press.

Lewis, M. (1995). Embarrassment: The emotion of self-exposure and evaluation. In J. Tangney & K. Fischer (Eds.), *Self-conscious emotions: The psychology of shame, guilt, embarrassment, and pride.* New York: Guilford.

Lewis, M. (2000). The emergence of human emotions. In M. Lewis & J. Haviland-Jones (Eds.), *Handbook of emotions* (2nd ed.). New York: Guilford.

Lewis, M., Alessandri, S. M., & Sullivan, M. W. (1990). Violation of expectancy, loss of control, and anger expression in young infants. *Developmental Psychology, 26,* 745–751.

Lewis, M., Feiring, C., McGuffog, C., & Jaskir, J. (1984). Predicting psychopathology in six-year-olds from early social relations. *Child Development, 55,* 123–136.

Lewis, M., & Michaelson, L. (1985). Faces as signs and symbols. In G. Zivin (Ed.), *Development of expressive behavior: Biological-environmental interaction.* New York: Academic Press.

Lewis, M., & Ramsey, D. S. (1997). Stress reactivity and self-recognition. *Child Development, 68,* 621–629.

Lewkowicz, D. J. (2000). The development of temporal intersensory perception: An epigenetic systems/limitations view. *Psychological Bulletin, 126,* 281–308.

Lewkowicz, D. J., & Lickliter, R. (Eds.). (1994). *The development of intersensory perception: Comparative perspectives.* Hillsdale, NJ: Erlbaum.

Lewkowicz, D. J., & Turkewitz, G. (1981). Intersensory interaction in newborns: Modification of visual preferences following exposure to sound. *Child Development, 52,* 827–832.

Lewontin, R. (2000). *It ain't necessarily so: The dream of the human genome and other illusions.* New York: New York Review of Books.

Li, Q. (1999). Teachers' beliefs and gender differences in mathematics: A review. *Educational Research, 41,* 63–76.

Liben, L. S., & Bigler, R. (2002). The developmental course of gender differentiation: Conceptualizing, measuring, and evaluating constructs and pathways. *Monographs of the Society for Research in Child Development, 67*(2, Serial No. 269).

Liben, L. S., & Signorella, M. L. (1980). Gender-related schemata and constructive memory in children. *Child Development, 51,* 11–18.

Liben, L. S., & Signorella, M. L. (Eds.). (1987). *New directions for child development: No. 38. Children's gender schemata.* San Francisco: Jossey-Bass.

Liben, L. S & Signorella, M. L. (1993). Gender-schematic processing in children: The role of initial interpretations of stimuli. *Developmental Psychology, 29,* 141–149.

Lickliter, R., & Bahrick, L. E. (2000). The development of infant intersensory perception: Advantages of a comparative convergent-operations approach. *Psychological Bulletin, 126,* 260–280.

Lickona, T. (Ed.). (1976). *Moral development and behavior: Theory, research, and social issues.* New York: Holt, Rinehart and Winston.

Lidz, C., & Elliott, J. G. (Eds.). (2000). *Dynamic assessment: Prevailing models and application.* New York: JAI Press.

Liebert, R. M. (1984). What develops in moral development? In W. M. Kurtines & J. L. Gewirtz (Eds.), *Morality, moral behavior, and moral development.* New York: Wiley.

Lillard, A. (1998). Ethnopsychologies: Cultural variations in theories of mind. *Psychological Bulletin, 123,* 3–32.

Lillard, A. (2001). Pretend play as twin earth: A social-cognitive analysis. *Developmental Review, 21,* 495–531.

Lindberg, M. A. (1980). Is knowledge base development a necessary and sufficient condition for memory development? *Journal of Experimental Child Psychology, 30,* 401–410.

Lindsey, E. W., & Mize, J. (2001). Contextual differences in parent-child play: Implications for children's gender role development. *Sex Roles, 44,* 155–176.

Lindsey, E. W., Mize, J., & Pettit, G. S. (1997). Differential play patterns of mothers and fathers of sons and daughters: Implications for children's gender role development. *Sex Roles, 37,* 643–661.

Linn, M. C., & Petersen, A. C. (1986). A meta-analysis of gender differences in spatial ability: Implications for mathematics and science achievement. In J. S. Hyde & M. C. Linn (Eds.), *The psychology of gender: Advances through meta-analysis.* Baltimore: Johns Hopkins University Press.

Lipscomb, T. J., McAllister, H. A., & Bregman, N. J. (1985). A developmental inquiry into the effects of multiple models on children's generosity. *Merrill-Palmer Quarterly, 31,* 335–344.

Lipsitt, L. P. (1990). Learning and memory in infants. *Merrill-Palmer Quarterly, 36,* 53–66.

Lipsitt, L. P. (1992). Discussion: The Bayley Scales of Infant Development: Issues of prediction and outcome revisited. In C. K. Rovee-Collier & L. P. Lipsitt (Eds.), *Advances in infancy research* (Vol. 7). Norwood, NJ: Ablex.

Lipsitt, L. P., Engen, T., & Kaye, H. (1963). Developmental changes in the olfactory threshold of the neonate. *Child Development, 34,* 371–376.

Lobel, M., Dunkel-Schetter, C., & Scrimshaw, S. C. M. (1992). Prenatal maternal stress and prematurity: A prospective study of socioeconomically disadvantaged women. *Health Psychology, 11*(1), 32–40.

Lobel, T. E., Gruber, R., Govrin, N., & Mashraki-Pedhatzur, S. (2001). Children's gender-related inferences and judgments: A cross-cultural study. *Developmental Psychology, 37,* 839–846.

Lochman, J. E., Burch, P. P., Curry, J. F., & Lampron, L. B. (1984). Treatment and generalization effects of cognitive-behavioral and goal-setting interventions with aggressive boys. *Journal of Consulting and Clinical Psychology, 52,* 915–916.

Lochman, J. E., & Wayland, K. (1994). Aggression, social acceptance and race as predictors of negative adolescent outcomes. *Journal of the American Academy of Child and Adolescent Psychiatry, 33,* 1026–1035.

Locke, J. (1824). *An essay concerning human understanding.* New York: Seaman. (Original work published 1694.)

Locke, J. L. (1989). Babbling and early speech: Continuity and individual differences. *First Language, 9,* 191–206.

Locke, J. L. (1993). *The child's path to spoken language.* Cambridge, MA: Harvard University Press.

Locke, J. L., & Pearson, D. M. (1990). Linguistic significance of babbling: Evidence from a tracheostomized infant. *Journal of Child Language, 17,* 1–16.

Lockman, J. J. (1984). The development of detour ability during infancy. *Child Development, 55,* 482–491.

Lockman, J. J., & Adams, C. D. (2001). Going around transparent and grid-like barriers: Detour ability as a perception-action skill. *Developmental Science, 4,* 463–471.

Lockman, J. J., & McHale, J. P. (1989). Object manipulation in infancy: Developmental and contextual determinants. In J. J. Lockman & N. L. Hazen (Eds.), *Action in social context: Perspectives on early development.* New York: Plenum.

Loeber, R., & Farrington, D. P. (Eds.). (1998). *Serious and violent juvenile offenders: Risk factors and successful interventions.* Thousand Oaks, CA: Sage.

Loeber, R., & Hay, D. F. (1993). Developmental approaches to aggression and conduct problems. In M. Rutter & D. F. Hay (Eds.), *Development through life: A handbook for clinicians.* Oxford: Blackwell Publishers.

Loeber, R., & Hay, D. F. (1997). Key issues in the development of aggression and violence from childhood to early adulthood. *Annual Review of Psychology, 48,* 371–410.

Loeber, R., & Stouthamer-Loeber, M. (1998). Development of juvenile aggression and violence: Some common misconceptions and controversies. *American Psychologist, 53,* 242–259.

Loehlin, J. C. (1992). *Genes and environment in personality development.* Newbury Park, CA: Sage.

Loehlin, J. C. (2000). Group differences in intelligence. In R. J. Sternberg (Ed.), *Handbook of intelligence.* New York: Cambridge University Press.

Lonigan, C. J., Anthony, J. L., Bloomfield, B. G., Dyer, S. M., & Samwel, C. S. (1999). Effects of two preschool shared reading interventions on the emergent literacy skills of children from low income families. *Journal of Early Intervention, 22,* 306–322.

Lorenz, K. Z. (1937). The companion in the bird's world. *Auk, 54,* 245–273.

Lorenz, K. Z. (1950). Innate behaviour patterns. *Symposia for the Study of Experimental Biology, 4,* 211–268.

Lott, B., & Maluso, D. (2001). Gender development: Social learning. In J. Worell (Ed.), *Encyclopedia of women and gender* (Vol. 1). San Diego, CA: Academic Press.

Lounsbury, M. L., & Bates, J. E. (1982). The cries of infants of differing levels of perceived temperamental difficultness: Acoustic properties and effects on listeners. *Child Development, 53,* 677–686.

Lourenco, O., & Machado, A. (1996). In defense of Piaget's theory: A reply to 10 common criticisms. *Psychological Review, 103,* 143–164.

Loveless, T. (Ed.) (2001). *The great curriculum debate: How should we teach reading and math?* Washington, DC: Brookings Institution Press.

Lowrey, G. H. (1978). *Growth and development of children* (7th ed.). Chicago: Yearbook Medical Publishers.

Lucariello, J., & Nelson, K. (1987). Remembering and planning talk between mothers and children. *Discourse Processes, 10,* 219–235.

Ludemann, P. M. (1991). Generalized discrimination of positive facial expressions by seven- and ten-month-old infants. *Child Development, 62,* 55–67.

Luecke-Aleksa, D., Anderson, D. R., Collins, P. A., & Schmitt, K. L. (1995). Gender constancy and television viewing. *Developmental Psychology, 31,* 773–780.

Lundqvist, C., & Sabel, K-G. (2000). Brief report: The Brazelton Neonatal Behavioral Assessment Scale detects differences among newborn infants of optimal health. *Journal of Pediatric Psychology, 25,* 577–582.

Luria, A. R. (1976). *Cognitive development: Its cultural and social foundations.* Cambridge, MA: Harvard University Press.

Luria, A. R. (1979). *The making of mind. A personal account of Soviet psychology.* Cambridge, MA: Harvard University Press.

Luster, T., & Denbow, E. (1992). Home environment and maternal intelligence as predictors of verbal intelligence: A comparison of preschool and school-age children. *Merrill-Palmer Quarterly, 38,* 151–175.

Luthar, S. S., Cicchetti, D., & Becker, B. (2000). The construct of resilience: A critical evaluation and guidelines for future work. *Child Development, 71,* 543–562.

Lyon, T. D., & Flavell, J. H. (1993). Young children's understanding of forgetting over time. *Child Development, 64,* 789–800.

Lyons-Ruth, K., Alpern, L., & Repacholi, B. (1993). Disorganized infant attachment classification and maternal psychosocial problems as predictors of hostile-aggressive behavior in the pre-school classroom. *Child Development, 64,* 572–585.

Lyons-Ruth, K., Bronfman, E., & Parsons, E. (1999). Maternal frightened, frightening, or atypical behavior and disorganized infant attachment patterns. In J. I. Vondra & D. Barnett (Eds.), *Atypical attachment in infancy and early childhood among children at developmental risk. Monographs of the Society for Research in Child Development, 64* (3, Serial No. 258).

Lyons-Ruth, K., Connell, D. B., & Zoll, D. (1989). Patterns of maternal behavior among infants at risk for abuse: Relations with infant attachment behavior and infant development at 12 months of age. In D. Cicchetti & V. Carlson (Eds.), *Child maltreatment: Theory and research on the causes and consequences of child abuse and neglect.* New York: Cambridge University Press.

Lytton, H. (1977). Do parents create, or respond to, differences in twins? *Developmental Psychology, 13,* 456–459.

Lytton, H. (1980). *Parent–child interaction: The socialization process observed in twin and singleton families.* New York: Plenum.

Lytton, H., & Romney, D. M. (1991). Parents' sex-related differential socialization of boys and girls: A meta-analysis. *Psychological Bulletin, 109,* 267–296.

Maccoby, E. E. (1990). Gender and relationships: A developmental account. *American Psychologist, 45,* 513–521.

Maccoby, E. E. (1992). The role of parents in the socialization of children: An historical overview. *Developmental Psychology, 28,* 1006–1017.

Maccoby, E. E. (1995). The two sexes and their social systems. In P. Moen, G. H. Elder, Jr., & K. Luscher (Eds.), *Examining lives in context: Perspectives on the ecology of human development.* Washington, DC: American Psychological Association.

Maccoby, E. E. (1998). *The two sexes: Growing up apart, coming together.* Cambridge, MA: Harvard University Press.

Maccoby, E. E. (2000a). Parenting and its effects on children: On reading and misreading behavior genetics. *Annual Review of Psychology, 51,* 1-27.

Maccoby, E. E. (2000b). Perspectives on gender development. *International Journal of Behavioral Development, 24,* 398–406.

Maccoby, E. E. (2002). Parenting effects: Issues and controversies. In J. G. Borkowski, S. L. Ramey, & M. Bristol-Power (Eds.), *Parenting and the child's world: Influences on academic, intellectual, and social-emotional development.* Mahwah, NJ: Erlbaum.

Maccoby, E. E., & Jacklin, C. N. (1974). *The psychology of sex differences.* Stanford, CA: Stanford University Press.

Maccoby, E. E., & Martin, J. A. (1983). Socialization in the context of the family: Parent–child interaction. In P. H. Mussen (Series Ed.) & E. M. Hetherington (Vol. Ed.), *Handbook of child psychology: Vol. 4. Socialization, personality, and social development* (4th ed.). New York: Wiley.

MacDonald, K. B. (1988a). The interfaces between sociobiology and developmental psychology. In K. B. MacDonald (Ed.), *Sociobiological perspectives on human development.* New York: Springer-Verlag.

MacDonald, K. B. (1988b). Sociobiology and the cognitive-developmental tradition in moral development research. In K. B. MacDonald (Ed.), *Sociobiological perspectives on human development.* New York: Springer-Verlag.

MacDonald, K. B. (1992). Warmth as a developmental construct: An evolutionary analysis. *Child Development, 63,* 753–773.

MacDonald, K., & Parke, R. D. (1986). Parent-child physical play: The effects of sex and age of children and parents. *Sex Roles, 15,* 367–378.

MacFarlane, A. (1975). Olfaction in the development of social preferences in the human neonate. In *Parent–infant interaction* (CIBA Foundation Symposium No. 33). Amsterdam: Elsevier.

Mackie, D. (1983). The effects of social interaction on conservation of spatial relations. *Journal of Cross-Cultural Psychology, 14,* 131–151.

MacKinnon, C. E. (1989). An observational investigation of sibling interactions in married and divorced families. *Developmental Psychology, 25,* 36–44.

MacWhinney, B. (1987). The competition model. In B. MacWhinney (Ed.), *Mechanisms of language acquisition.* Hillsdale, NJ: Erlbaum.

MacWhinney, B. (1999). The CHILDES system. In W. C. Ritchie & T. K. Bhatia (Eds.), *Handbook of child language acquisition.* San Diego, CA: Academic Press.

MacWhinney, B. (2000). *The CHILDES project: Tools for analyzing talk* (3rd ed.) Mahwah, NJ: Erlbaum.

MacWhinney, B., & Bates, E. (1993). *The crosslinguistic study of sentence processing.* Cambridge: Cambridge University Press.

MacWhinney, B., & Chang, F. (1995). Connectionism and language learning. In C. A. Nelson (Ed.), *Minnesota symposia on child psychology: Vol. 28. Basic and applied perspectives on learning, cognition, and development.* Mahwah, NJ: Erlbaum.

MacWhinney, B., & Leinbach, J. (1991). Implementations are not conceptualizations: Revising the verb learning model. *Cognition, 40,* 121–157.

Magnusson, D., Bergman, L. R., Rudiger, G., & Torestad, B. (Eds.). (1994). *Problems and methods in longitudinal research: Stability and change.* New York: Cambridge University Press.

Main, M. (1990). Cross-cultural studies of attachment organization: Recent studies, changing methodologies, and the concept of conditional strategies. *Human Development, 33,* 48–61.

Main, M., & Goldwyn, R. (1998). Adult attachment rating and classification systems. In M. Main (Ed.), *Assessing attachment through discourse, drawings, and reunion situations.* Cambridge: Cambridge University Press.

Main, M., & Hesse, E. (1990). Parents' unresolved traumatic experiences are related to infant disorganized attachment status: Is frightened and/or frightening behavior the linking mechanism? In M. T. Greenberg & D. Cicchetti (Eds.), *Attachment in the preschool years.* Chicago: University of Chicago Press.

Main M., Kaplan, N., & Cassidy, J. (1985). Security in infancy, childhood and adulthood: A move to the level of representation. In I. Bretherton & E. Waters (Eds.), *Growing points of attachment theory and research. Monographs of the Society for Research in Child Development, 50*(1–2, Serial No. 209).

Main, M., & Solomon, J. (1986). Discovery of a disorganized/disoriented attachment pattern. In T. B. Brazelton & M. W. Yogman (Eds.), *Affective development in infancy.* Norwood, NJ: Ablex.

Main M., & Solomon, J. (1990). Procedures for identifying infants as disorganized/disoriented during the Ainsworth Strange Situation. In M. Greenberg, D. Cicchetti, & M. Cummings (Eds.), *Attachment during the preschool years.* Chicago: University of Chicago Press.

Majeres, R. L. (1999). Sex differences in phonological processes: Speeded matching and word reading. *Memory and Cognition, 27,* 246–253.

Major, B., Spencer, S., Schmader, T., Wolfe, C., & Crocker, J. (1998). Coping with negative stereotypes about intellectual performance: The role of psychological disengagement. *Personality and Social Psychology Bulletin, 24,* 34–50.

Malatesta, C. Z. (1985). Developmental course of emotion expression in the human infant. In G. Zivin (Ed.), *Development of expressive behavior: Biological-environmental interaction.* New York: Academic Press.

Malatesta, C. Z., Culver, C., Tesman, J. R., & Shepard, B. (1989). The development of emotion expression during the first two years of life. *Monographs of the Society for Research in Child Development, 54*(1–2, Serial No. 219).

Malatesta, C. Z., Grigoryev, P., Lamb, C., Albin, M., & Culver, C. (1986). Emotion socialization and expressive development in preterm and full term infants. *Child Development, 57,* 316–330.

Malatesta, C. Z., & Haviland, J. M. (1982). Learning display rules: The socialization of emotion expression in infancy. *Child Development, 53,* 991–1003.

Malatesta, C. Z., Izard, C. E., & Camras, L. (1991). Conceptualizing early infant affect: Emotions as fact, fiction, or artifact? In K. Strongman (Ed.), *International review of studies on emotion.* New York: Wiley.

Malina, R. M. (1990). Physical growth and performance during the transitional years (9–16). In R. Montemayor, G. R. Adams, & T. Gullotta (Eds.), *From childhood to adolescence: Vol. 2. Advances in adolescent development.* London: Sage.

Mandel, D., Kemler Nelson, D. G., & Jusczyk, P. W. (1996). Infants remember the order of words in a spoken sentence. *Cognitive Development, 11,* 181–196.

Mandler, J. M. (1998). Representation. In W. Damon (Series Ed.) & D. Kuhn & R. S. Siegler (Vol. Eds.), *Handbook of child psychology: Vol. 2. Cognition, perception, and language* (5th ed.). New York: Wiley.

Mandler, J. M. (2000). Perceptual and conceptual processes in infancy. *Journal of Cognition and Development, 1,* 3–36.

Mandoki, M. W., Summer, G. S., Hoffman, R. P., & Riconda, D. L. (1991). A review of Klinefelter's syndrome in children and adolescents. *Journal of the American Academy of Child and Adolescent Psychiatry, 30,* 167–172.

Mangelsdorf, S. C., Plunkett, J. W., Dedrick, C. F., Berlin, M., Meisels, S. J., McHale, J. L., et al. (1996). Attachment security in very low birth weight infants. *Developmental Psychology, 32,* 914–920.

Manke, B., Saudino, K. J., & Grant, J. D. (2001). Extreme analyses of observed temperament dimensions. In R. N. Emde & J. K. Hewitt (Eds.), *Infancy to early childhood.* New York: Oxford University Press.

Mannino, D. M., Moorman, J. E., Kingsley, B., Rose, D., & Repace, J. (2001). Health effects related to environmental tobacco smoke exposure in the United States. *Archives of Pediatric and Adolescent Medicine, 155,* 36–41.

Mannle, S., & Tomasello, M. (1987). Fathers, siblings, and the Bridge Hypothesis. In K. E. Nelson & A. VanKleeck (Eds.), *Children's language* (Vol. 6). Hillsdale, NJ: Erlbaum.

Maratsos, M. (1976). *Language development: The acquisition of language structure.* Morristown, NJ: General Learning Press.

Maratsos, M. (1983). Some current issues in the study of the acquisition of grammar. In P. H. Mussen (Series Ed.) & J. H. Flavell & E. M. Markman (Vol. Eds.), *Handbook of child psychology: Vol. 3. Cognitive development* (4th ed.). New York: Wiley.

Maratsos, M. (1988). The acquisition of formal word classes. In Y. Levy, I. M. Schlesinger, & M. D. S. Braine (Eds.), *Categories and processes in language acquisition.* Hillsdale, NJ: Erlbaum.

Maratsos, M. (1998). The acquisition of grammar. In W. Damon (Series Ed.) & D. Kuhn & R. S. Siegler (Vol. Eds.), *Handbook of child psychology: Vol. 2. Cognition, perception, and language* (5th ed.). New York: Wiley.

March of Dimes (2001). *International comparison of infant mortality rates.* White Plains, NY: March of Dimes Birth Defects Foundation.

Marcotte, D., Fortin, L., Potvin, P., & Papillon, M. (2002). Gender differences in depressive symptoms during adolescence: Role of gender-typed characteristics, self-esteem, body image, stressful life events, and pubertal status. *Journal of Emotional and Behavioral Disorders, 10,* 29–42.

Marcus, G. F. (1996). Why do children say "breaked"? *Current Directions in Psychological Science, 5,* 81–85.

Marcus, G. F. (2001). *The algebraic mind: Integrating connectionism and cognitive science.* Cambridge, MA: MIT Press.

Marcus, G. F., Pinker, S., Ullman, M., Hollander, M., Rosen, T. J., & Xu, F. (1992). Overregularization in language acquisition. *Monographs of the Society for Research in Child Development, 57*(4, Serial No. 228).

Mares, L., & Woodard, E. (in press). The positive effects of television on children's social interactions. In R. Carveth & J. Bryant (Eds.), *Meta-analyses of media effects.* Mahwah, NJ: Erlbaum.

Mareschal, D., & Johnson, S. P. (2002). Learning to perceive object unity: A connectionist account. *Developmental Science, 5,* 151–185.

Markman, E. M. (1989). *Categorization and naming in children: Problems of induction.* Cambridge, MA: MIT Press.

Markman, E. M. (1991). The whole object, taxonomic, and mutual exclusivity assumptions as initial constraints on word meanings. In S. A. Gelman & J. P. Byrnes (Eds.), *Perspectives on language and thought: Interrelations in development.* Cambridge: Cambridge University Press.

Markus, H. R., & Kitayama, S. (1991). Culture and the self: Implications for cognition, emotion, and motivation. *Psychological Review, 98,* 224–253.

Markus, H. R., & Kitayama, S. (1994). A collective fear of the collective: Implications for selves and theories of selves. *Personality and Social Psychology Bulletin, 20,* 568–579.

Markus, H. R., & Kitayama, S. (1998). The cultural psychology of personality. *Journal of Cross-Cultural Psychology, 29,* 63–87.

Markus, H. R., & Nurius, P. S. (1984). Self-understanding and self-regulation in middle childhood. In W. A. Collins (Ed.), *Development during middle childhood: The years from six to twelve.* Washington, DC: National Academy Press.

Markus, H. R., & Nurius, P. S. (1986). Possible selves. *American Psychologist, 41,* 954–969.

Marlier, L., Schaal, B., & Soussignan, R. (1998). Neonatal responsiveness to the odor of amniotic and lacteal fluids: A test of perinatal chemosensory continuity. *Child Development, 69,* 611–623.

Marsh, H. W. (1990). A multidimensional, hierarchical model of self-concept: Theoretical and empirical justification. *Educational Psychology Review, 2,* 77–172.

Marsh, H. W. (1993). Academic self-concept: Theory, measurement, and research. In J. Suls (Ed.), *Psychological perspectives on the self* (Vol. 4). Hillsdale, NJ: Erlbaum.

Marsh, H. W, Barnes, J., Cairns, L., & Tidman, M. (1984). Self-Description Questionnaire: Age and sex effects in the structure and level of self-concept for preadolescent children. *Journal of Educational Psychology, 76,* 940–956.

Marsh, H. W, Ellis, L. A., & Craven, R. G. (2002). How do preschool children feel about themselves? Unraveling measurement and multidimensional self-concept structure. *Developmental Psychology, 38,* 376–393.

Marsh, H. W., & Yeung, A. S. (1998). Longitudinal structural equation models of academic self-concept and achievement: Gender differences in the development of math and English constructs. *American Educational Research Journal, 35,* 705–738.

Marsiglio, W., Amato, P., Day, R. D., & Lamb, M. E. (2000). Scholarship on fatherhood in the 1990s and beyond. *Journal of Marriage and the Family, 62,* 1173–1191.

Marten, K., & Psarakos, S. (1994). Evidence of self-awareness in the bottlenose dolphin (*Tursiops truncatus*). In S. T. Parker, R. W. Mitchell, & M. L. Boccia (Eds.), *Self-awareness in animals and humans: Developmental perspectives.* Cambridge: Cambridge University Press.

Martin, C. L. (1989). Children's use of gender-related information in making social judgments. *Developmental Psychology, 25,* 80–88.

Martin, C. L. (1993). New directions for investigating children's gender knowledge. *Developmental Review, 13,* 184–204.

Martin, C. L., Eisenbud, L., & Rose, H. (1995). Children's gender-based reasoning about toys. *Child Development, 66,* 1453–1471.

Martin, C. L., & Halverson, C. E. (1983a). The effects of sex-typing schemas on young children's memory. *Child Development, 54,* 563–574.

Martin, C. L., & Halverson, C. F. (1983b). Gender constancy: A methodological and theoretical analysis. *Sex Roles, 9,* 775–790.

Martin, C. L., & Halverson, C. F. (1987). The roles of cognition in sex role acquisition. In D. B. Carter (Ed.), *Current conceptions of sex roles and sex typing: Theory and research.* New York: Praeger.

Martin, C. L., & Little, J. K. (1990). The relation of gender understanding to children's sex-typed preferences and gender stereotypes. *Child Development, 61,* 1427–1439.

Martin, C. L., Ruble, D. N., & Szkrybalo, J. (2002). Cognitive theories of early gender development. *Psychological Bulletin, 128,* 903–933.

Martin, G. B., & Clark, R. D. (1982). Distress crying in neonates: Species and peer specificity. *Developmental Psychology, 18,* 3–9.

Martin, J. A., Hamilton, B. E., Ventura, S. J., Menacker, F., & Park, M. M. (2002). Births: Final data for 2000. *Centers for Disease Control: National Vital Statistics Reports, 50*(5).

Martin, J. A., Park, M. M., & Sutton, P. D. (2002). Births: Preliminary data for 2001. *Centers for Disease Control: National Vital Statistics Reports, 50*(10).

Martini, M. (1994). Peer interactions in Polynesia: A view from the Marquesas. In J. L. Roopnarine, J. E. Johnson, & F. H. Hooper (Eds.), *Children's play in diverse cultures.* Albany, NY: SUNY Press.

Martini, M., & Kirkpatrick, J. (1981). Early interactions in the Marquesas Isalnds. In T. M. Field, A. M. Sostek, P. Vietze, & P. H. Leiderman (Eds.), *Culture and early interactions.* Hillsdale, NJ: Erlbaum.

Martorano, S. C. (1977). A developmental analysis of performance on Piaget's formal operational tasks. *Developmental Psychology, 13,* 666–672.

Martorell, R. (1984). Genetics, environment, and growth: Issues in the assessment of nutritional status. In A. Velasquez & H. Bourges (Eds.), *Genetic factors in nutrition.* Orlando, FL: Academic Press.

Masataka, N. (1993). Effects of contingent and noncontingent maternal stimulation on the social behavior of three- to four-month-old Japanese infants. *Journal of Child Language, 20,* 303–312.

Masataka, N. (1996). Perception of motherese in a signed language by 6-month-old deaf infants. *Developmental Psychology, 32,* 874–879.

Masataka, N. (1998). Perception of motherese in Japanese sign language by 6-month-old hearing infants. *Developmental Psychology, 34,* 241–246.

Masataka, N. (1999). Preference for infant-directed singing in 2-day-old infants of deaf parents. *Developmental Psychology, 35,* 1001–1005.

Massey, C. M., & Gelman, R. (1988). Preschoolers' ability to decide whether a photographed unfamiliar object can move itself. *Developmental Psychology, 24,* 307–317.

Masten, A. S., Hubbard, J. J., Gest, S. D., Tellegen, A., Garmezy, N., & Ramiriez, M. (1999). Competence in the context of adversity: Pathways to resilience and maladaptation from childhood to late adolescence. *Development and Psychopathology, 11,* 143–169.

Masters, J. C. (1979). Modeling and labeling as integrated determinants of children's sex-typed imitative behavior. *Child Development, 50,* 364–371.

Masters, J. C., & Furman, W. (1981). Popularity, individual friendship selection, and specific peer interaction among children. *Developmental Psychology, 17,* 344–350.

Masters, M. S., & Sanders, B. (1993). Is the gender difference in mental rotation disappearing? *Behavior Genetics, 23,* 337–341.

Matas, L., Arend, R., & Sroufe, L. A. (1978). Continuity of adaptation in the second year: The relationship between quality of attachment and later competence. *Child Development, 49,* 547–556.

Matheny, A. P. Jr. (1986). Stability and change of infant temperament: Contributions from infant, mother, and family environment. In G. Kohnstamm (Ed.), *Temperament discussed.* Berwyn, PA: Swets North America.

Matheny, A. P. Jr. (1989). Children's behavioral inhibition over age and across situations: Genetic similarity for a trait during change. [Special issue]. *Journal of Personality, 57,* 215–235.

Mathews, G. (1996). The stuff of dreams, fading: Ikigai and "the Japanese self." *Ethos, 24,* 718–747.

Mathiesen, K. S., & Tambs, K. (1999). The EAS Temperament Questionnaire-factor structure, age trends, reliability, and stability in a Norwegian sample. *Journal of Child Psychology and Psychiatry and Allied Disciplines, 40,* 431–439.

Matsumoto, D., Haan, N., Yabrove, G., Theodorou, P., & Carney, C. C. (1986). Pre-schoolers' moral actions and emotions in Prisoner's Dilemma. *Developmental Psychology, 22,* 663–670.

Maurer, D. (1985). Infants' perception of facedness. In T. M. Field & N. A. Fox (Eds.), *Social perception in infants.* Norwood, NJ: Ablex.

Maurer, D., & Lewis, T. L. (2001). Visual acuity and spatial contrast sensitivity: Normal development and underlying mechanisms. In C. A. Nelson & M. Luciana (Eds.), *Handbook of developmental cognitive neuroscience.* Cambridge, MA: MIT Press.

Maurer, D., & Maurer, C. (1988). *The world of the newborn.* New York: Basic Books.

Maurer, D., Stager, C. L., & Mondloch, C. J. (1999). Cross-modal transfer of shape is difficult to demonstrate in one-month-olds. *Child Development, 70,* 1047–1057.

Maxwell, L. G., & Yaster, M. (1999). Anesthesia for neonatal circumcision: No more studies, just do it. *Journal of Adolescent and Pediatric Medicine, 153,* 444–445.

Mayer, N. K., & Tronick, E. Z. (1985). Mothers' turn-giving signals and infant turn-taking in mother–infant interaction. In T. M. Field & N. A. Fox (Eds.), *Social perception in infants.* Norwood, NJ: Ablex.

Mayes, L. C. (1992). Prenatal cocaine exposure and young children's development. *Annals, AAPSS, 521,* 11–27.

Mayes, L. C., & Fahy, T. (2001). Prenatal drug exposure and cognitive development. In R. J. Sternberg & E. L. Grigorenko (Eds.), *Environmental effects on cognitive abilities.* Mahwah, NJ: Erlbaum.

Maynard Smith, J. (1976). Group selection. *Quarterly Review of Biology, 51,* 277–283.

McCabe, A. E. (1989). Differential language learning styles in young children: The importance of context. *Developmental Review, 9,* 1–20.

McCabe, M. P., & Collins, J. K. (1984). Measurement of depth of desired and experienced sexual involvement at different stages of dating. *Journal of Sex Research, 20,* 377–390.

McCall, R. B. (1981). Early predictors of later IQ: The search continues. *Intelligence, 5,* 141–148.

McCall, R. B., Applebaum, M. I., & Hogarty, P. S. (1973). Developmental changes in mental performance. *Monographs of the Society for Research in Child Development, 38* (3, Serial No. 150).

McCall, R. B., & Carriger, M. S. (1993). A meta-analysis of infant habituation and recognition memory as predictors of later IQ. *Child Development, 64,* 57–79.

McCall, R. B., & Groark, C. J. (2000). The future of applied child development research and public policy. *Child Development, 71,* 197–204.

McCartney, K. (Ed.). (1990). *New directions for child development: No. 49. Child care and maternal employment: A social ecology approach.* San Francisco: Jossey-Bass.

McClelland, J. L. (1995). A connectionist perspective on knowledge and development. In T. J. Simon & G. S. Halford (Eds.), *Developing cognitive competence: New approaches to process modeling.* Hillsdale, NJ: Erlbaum.

McClelland, J. L., & Siegler, R. S. (Eds.). (2001). *Mechanisms of cognitive development.* Mahwah, NJ: Erlbaum.

McCrae, R. R., Costa, P. T. Jr., Terracciano, A., Parker, W. D., Mills, C. J., De Fruyt, F., et al. (2002). Personality trait development from age 12 to age 18: Longitudinal, cross-sectional and cross-cultural analyses. *Journal of Personality and Social Psychology, 83,* 1456–1468.

McCune-Nicolich, L. (1981). The cognitive bases of relational words in the single word period. *Journal of Child Language, 8,* 15–34.

McDaniel, D., McKee, C., & Cairns, H. S. (Eds.). (1997). *Methods for assessing children's syntax.* Cambridge, MA: MIT Press.

McDonough, L., & Mandler, J. M. (1994). Very long-term recall in infants: Infantile amnesia reconsidered. *Memory, 2,* 339–352.

McDougall, P., Hymel, S., Vaillancourt, T., & Mercer, L. (2001). The consequences of childhood peer rejection. In M. Leary (Ed.), *Interpersonal rejection.* London: Oxford University Press.

McDowell, D. J., O'Neil, R., & Parke, R. D. (2000). Display rule application in a disappointing situation and children's emotional reactivity. *Merrill-Palmer Quarterly, 46,* 306–324.

McFayden-Ketchum, S. A., Bates, J. E., Dodge, K. A., & Pettit, G. S. (1996). Patterns of change in early childhood aggressive-disruptive behavior: Gender differences in predictions from early coercive and affectionate mother-child interactions. *Child Development, 67,* 2417–2433.

McGhee, P. E., & Frueh, T. (1980). Television viewing and the learning of sex-role stereotypes. *Sex Roles, 6,* 179–188.

McGillicuddy-De Lisi, A. V., Watkins, C., & Vinchur, A. J. (1994). The effect of relationship on children's distributive justice reasoning. *Child Development, 65,* 1694–1700.

McGlone, J. (1980). Sex differences in human brain asymmetry: Critical survey. *Behavioral and Brain Sciences, 3,* 215–227.

McGraw, M. B. (1935). *Growth: A study of Johnny and Jimmy.* New York: Appleton-Century-Crofts.

McGraw, M. B. (1940). Suspension grasp behavior of the human infant. *American Journal of the Disabled Child, 60,* 799–811.

McGue, M., Bouchard, T. J. Jr., Iacono, W. G., & Lykken, D. T. (1993). Behavior genetics of cognitive ability: A life-span perspective. In R. Plomin & G. E. McClearn (Eds.), *Nature, nurture, and psychology.* Washington, DC: American Psychological Association.

McGue, M., & Lykken, D. T. (1992). Genetic influences on risk of divorce. *Psychological Science, 3,* 368–373.

McGuiness, D., & Morley, C. (1991). Sex differences in the development of visuo-spatial ability in pre-school children. *Journal of Mental Imagery, 15,* 143–150.

McHale, S. M., Updegraff, K. A., Helms-Erikson, H., & Crouter, A. C. (2001). Sibling influences on gender development in middle childhood and early adolescence: A longitudinal study. *Developmental Psychology, 37,* 115–125.

McIntyre, R. B., Paulson, R. M., & Lord, C. G. (2003). Alleviating women's mathematics stereotype threat through salience of group achievements. *Journal of Experimental Social Psychology, 39,* 83–90.

McKnight, C. C., Crosswhite, F. J., Dossey, J. A., Kifer, E., Swafford, J. O., Travers, K. J., & Cooney, T. J. (1987). *The underachieving curriculum: Assessing U.S. school mathematics from an international perspective.* Champaign, IL: Stipes.

McKusick, V. A. (1998). *Mendelian inheritance in man* (12th ed.). Baltimore: Johns Hopkins University Press.

McLane, J. (1987). Interaction, context, and the zone of proximal development. In M. Hickman (Ed.), *Social and functional approaches to language and thought.* San Diego, CA: Academic Press.

McLaughlin, B., White, D., McDevitt, T., & Raskin, R. (1983). Mothers' and fathers' speech to their young children: Similar or different? *Journal of Child Language, 10,* 245–252.

McNeill, D. (1992). *Hand and mind: What gestures reveal about thought.* Chicago: University of Chicago Press.

Mebert, C. J. (1989). Stability and change in parents' perceptions of infant temperament: Early pregnancy to 13.5 months postpartum. *Infant Behavior and Development, 2,* 237–244.

Mebert, C. J. (1991). Dimensions of subjectivity in parents' ratings of infant temperament. *Child Development, 62,* 352–361.

Medoff-Cooper, B., Carey, W. B., & McDevitt, S. C. (1993). The Early Infancy Temperament Questionnaire. *Journal of Developmental and Behavioral Pediatrics, 14,* 230–235.

Medrich, E. A., Roizen, J. A., Rubin, V., & Buckley, S. (1982). *The serious business of growing up: A study of children's lives outside school.* Berkeley: University of California Press.

Mehler, J., Bertoncine, J., Barriere, M., & Jassik-Gershenfeld, D. (1978). Infant recognition of mother's voice. *Perception, 7,* 491–497.

Mehler, J., Jusczyk, P. W., Lambertz, G., Halsted, N., Bertoncini, J., & Amiel-Tison, C. (1988). A precursor of language acquisition in young infants. *Cognition, 29,* 143–178.

Meichenbaum, D. H., & Goodman, J. (1971). Training impulsive children to talk to themselves: A means to develop self-control. *Journal of Personality and Social Psychology, 34,* 942–950.

Meier, R. P., & Newport, E. L. (1990). Out of the hands of babes: On a possible sign advantage in language acquisition. *Language, 66,* 1–23.

Meins, E. (1997). Security of attachment and maternal tutoring strategies: Interaction within the zone of proximal development. *British Journal of Developmental Psychology, 15,* 129–144.

Mekos, D., Hetherington, E. M., & Reiss, D. (1996). Sibling differences in problem behavior and parental treatment in nondivorced and remarried families. *Child Development, 67,* 2148–2165.

Meltzoff, A. N. (1988). Infant imitation after a 1-week delay: Long-term memory for novel and multiple stimuli. *Developmental Psychology, 24,* 470–476.

Meltzoff, A. N., & Borton, R. W. (1979). Intermodal matching by human neonates. *Nature, 282,* 403–404.

Meltzoff, A. N., & Moore, M. K. (1977). Imitation of facial and manual gestures by human neonates. *Science, 198,* 75–78.

Meltzoff, A. N., & Moore, M. K. (1983). Newborn infants imitate adult facial gestures. *Child Development, 54,* 702–709.

Meltzoff, A. N., & Moore, M. K. (1989). Imitation in newborn infants: Exploring the range of gestures imitated and the underlying mechanisms. *Developmental Psychology, 25,* 954–962.

Meltzoff, A. N., & Moore, M. K. (1994). Imitation, memory, and the representation of persons. *Infant Behavior and Development, 17,* 83–99.

Meltzoff, A. N., & Moore, M. K. (1995). A theory of the role of imitation in the emergence of self. In P. Rochat (Ed.), *The self in infancy: Theory and research.* Amsterdam: Elsevier.

Meltzoff, A. N., & Moore, M. K. (1999a). A new foundation for cognitive development in infancy: The birth of the representational infant. In E. K. Scholnick, K. Nelson, S. A. Gelman, & P. H. Miller (Eds.), *Conceptual development: Piaget's legacy.* Mahwah, NJ: Erlbaum.

Meltzoff, A. N., & Moore, M. K. (1999b). Persons and representation: Why infant imitation is important for theories of human development. In J. Nadel & G. Butterworth (Eds.), *Imitation in infancy.* Cambridge: Cambridge University Press.

Menacker, F., & Curtin, S. C. (2001). Trends in cesarean birth and vaginal birth after previous cesarean, 1991–99. *National Vital Statistics Reports, 49*(13).

Menard, S. (1991). *Longitudinal research.* Newbury Park, CA: Sage.

Menig-Peterson, C. L. (1975). The modification of communicative behaviors in preschool-aged children as a function of the listener's perspective. *Child Development, 46,* 1015–1018.

Menn, L., & Ratner, N. B. (Eds.). (2000). *Methods for studying language production.* Mahwah, NJ: Erlabaum.

Mercer, N. (1996). The quality of talk in children's collaborative activity in the classroom. *Learning and Instruction, 6,* 359–377.

Meredith, H. V. (1963). Change in the stature and body weight of North American boys during the last 80 years. In L. P. Lipsitt & C. C. Spiker (Eds.), *Advances in child development and behavior* (Vol. 1). New York: Academic Press.

Merriman, W. E. (1997). CALLED: A model of early word learning. In R. Vasta (Ed.), *Annals of child development* (Vol. 13). London: Kingsley.

Mervis, C. B. (1987). Child-basic object categories and early lexical development. In U. Neisser (Ed.), *Concepts and conceptual development: Ecological and intellectual factors in categorization.* New York: Cambridge University Press.

Mervis, C. B., Morris, C. A., Bertrand, J., & Robinson, B. F. (1999). Williams syndrome: Findings from an integrated program of research. In H. Tager-Flusberg (Ed.), *Neurodevelopmental disorders.* Cambridge, MA: MIT Press.

Meyer, R. J. (2002). *Phonics exposed: Understanding and resisting systematic direct intense phonics instruction*. Mahwah, NJ: Erlbaum.

Meyer-Bahlberg, H. F. L. (1993). Psychobiologic research on homosexuality. *Child and Adolescent Psychiatric Clinics of North America, 2*, 489–500.

Meyer-Bahlberg, H. F. L., Ehrhardt, A. A., Rosen, L. R., Gruen, R. S., Veridiano, N. P., Vann, F. H., et al. (1995). Prenatal estrogens and the development of homosexual orientation. *Developmental Psychology, 31*, 12–21.

Midgett, J., Ryan, B. A., Adams, G. R., & Corville-Smith (2002). Complicating achievement and self-esteem: Considering the joint effects of child characteristics and parent-child interactions. *Contemporary Educational Psychology, 27*, 132–143.

Miles, D. R., & Carey, G. (1997). Genetic and environmental architecture of human aggression. *Journal of Personality and Social Psychology, 72*, 207–217.

Miles, T. R., Haslum, M. N., & Wheeler, T. J. (1998). Gender ratio in dyslexia. *Annals of Dyslexia, 48*, 27–55.

Miller, B. C., Fan, X., Christensen, M., Grotevant, H. D., & van Dulmen, M. (2000). Comparison of adopted and nonadopted adolescents in a large, nationally representative sample. *Child Development, 71*, 1458–1473.

Miller, K. F. (1984). Child as the measurer of all things: Measurement procedures and the development of quantitative concepts. In C. Sophian (Ed.), *Origins of cognitive skills*. Hillsdale, NJ: Erlbaum.

Miller, K. F., & Paredes, D. R. (1996). On the shoulders of giants: Cultural tools and mathematical development. In R. Sternberg & T. Ben-Zeev (Eds.), *The nature of mathematical thinking*. Hillsdale, NJ: Erlbaum.

Miller, K. F., Smith, C. M., Zhu, J., & Zhang, H. (1995). Preschool origins of cross-national differences in mathematical competence: The role of number naming systems. *Psychological Science, 6*, 56–60.

Miller, K. F., & Stigler, J. W. (1987). Counting in Chinese: Cultural variation in a basic cognitive skill. *Cognitive Development, 2*, 279–305.

Miller, L. T., & Vernon, P. A. (1997). Developmental changes in speed of information processing in young children. *Developmental Psychology, 23*, 549–554.

Miller, P., & Garvey, C. (1984). Mother-baby role play: Its origins in social support. In I. Bretherton (Ed.), *Symbolic play: The development of social understanding*. New York: Academic Press.

Miller, P. A., Eisenberg, N., Fabes, R. A., & Shell, R. (1996). Relations of moral reasoning and vicarious emotion to young children's prosocial behavior toward peers and adults. *Developmental Psychology, 32*, 210–219.

Miller, P. H. (1990). The development of strategies of selective attention. In D. F. Bjorklund (Ed.), *Children's strategies: Contemporary views of cognitive development*. Hillsdale, NJ: Erlbaum.

Miller, P. H. (2001). *Theories of developmental psychology* (4th ed.). New York: Worth.

Miller, P. H., & Coyle, T. R. (1999). Developmental change: Lesson from microgenesis. In E. K. Scholnick, K. Nelson, S. A. Gelman, & P. H. Miller (Eds.), *Conceptual development: Piaget's legacy*. Mahwah, NJ: Erlbaum.

Miller, P. H., & DeMarie-Dreblow, D. (1990). Social-cognitive correlates of children's understanding of displaced aggression. *Journal of Experimental Child Psychology, 49*, 488–504.

Miller, P. H., & Seier, W. L. (1994). Strategy utilization deficiencies in children: When, where, and why? In H. W. Reese (Ed.), *Advances in child development and behavior* (Vol. 25). New York: Academic Press.

Miller, P. J., Fung, H., & Mintz, J. (1996). Self-construction through narrative practices: A Chinese and American comparison of early socialization. *Ethos, 24*, 237–280.

Miller, P. J., Wiley, A. R., Fung, H., & Liang, C. H. (1997). Personal storytelling as a medium of socialization in Chinese and American families. *Child Development, 68*, 557–568.

Miller, P. M., Danaher, D. L., & Forbes, D. (1986). Sex-related strategies for coping with interpersonal conflict in children aged five to seven. *Developmental Psychology, 22*, 543–548.

Miller, S. A. (1976). Nonverbal assessment of Piagetian concepts. *Psychological Bulletin, 83*, 405–430.

Miller, S. A. (1982). Cognitive development: A Piagetian perspective. In R. Vasta (Ed.), *Strategies and techniques of child study*. New York: Academic Press.

Miller, S. A. (1986). Certainty and necessity in the understanding of Piagetian concepts. *Developmental Psychology, 22*, 3–18.

Miller, S. A. (1988). Parents' beliefs about children's cognitive development. *Child Development, 59*, 259–285.

Miller, S. A. (1995). Parents' attributions for their children's behavior. *Child Development, 66*, 1557–1584.

Miller, S. A. (1998). *Developmental research methods* (2nd ed.). Upper Saddle River, NJ: Prentice Hall.

Miller, S. A. (2000). Children's understanding of preexisting differences in knowledge and belief. *Developmental Review, 20*, 227–282.

Miller, S. A., & Brownell, C. A. (1975). Peers, persuasion, and Piaget: Dyadic interaction between conservers and nonconservers. *Child Development, 46*, 992–997.

Miller, S. A., & Davis, T. L. (1992). Beliefs about children: A comparative study of mothers, teachers, peers, and self. *Child Development, 63*, 1251–1265.

Miller, S. A., Hardin, C. A., & Montgomery, D. E. (in press). Young children's understanding of the conditions for knowledge acquisition. *Journal of Cognition and Development*.

Miller, S. A., Holmes, H. A., Gitten, J., & Danbury, J. (1997). Children's understanding of false beliefs that result from developmental misconceptions. *Cognitive Development, 12*, 21–51.

Mills, R. S. L., & Grusec, J. E. (1988). Socialization from the perspective of the parent–child relationship. In S. Duck (Ed.), *Handbook of personal relationships*. Chichester, England: Wiley.

Mills, R. S. L., & Grusec, J. E. (1989). Cognitive, affective, and behavioral consequences of praising altruism. *Merrill-Palmer Quarterly, 35*, 299–326.

Minde, K. (1993). Prematurity and illness in infancy: Implications for development and intervention. In C. H. Zeanah Jr. (Ed.), *Handbook of infant mental development*. New York: Guilford.

Minde, K. (2000). Prematurity and serious medical conditions in infancy: Implications for development, behavior, and intervention. In C. H. Zeanah Jr. (Ed.), *Handbook of infant mental health* (2nd ed.). New York: Guilford.

Mischel, W., Shoda, Y., & Peake, P. K. (1988). The nature of adolescent competencies predicted by preschool delay of gratification. *Journal of Personality and Social Psychology, 54*, 687–696.

Mischel, W., Shoda, Y., & Rodriguez, M. L. (1989). Delay of gratification in children. *Science, 244*, 933–938.

Mistry, J. (1997). The development of remembering in cultural context. In N. Cowan (Ed.), *The development of memory in childhood*. Hove, East Sussex, UK: Psychology Press.

Mitchell, R. W. (2003). Subjectivity and self-recognition in animals. In M. R. Leary & J. P. Tangney (Eds.), *Handbook of self and identity*. New York: Guilford.

Mitzenheim, P. (1985). The importance of Rousseau's developmental thinking for child psychology. In G. Eckardt, W. G. Bringman, & L. Sprung (Eds.), *Contributions to a history of developmental psychology*. Berlin: Mouton.

Miura, I., Okamoto, Y., Kim, C. C., Steere, M., & Fayol, M. (1993). First graders' cognitive representation of number and understanding of place value: Cross-national comparisons-France, Japan, Korea, Sweden, and the United States. *Journal of Educational Psychology, 85*, 24–30.

Mix, K., Huttenlocher, J., & Levine, S. C. (2002). Multiple cues for quantification in infancy: Is number one of them? *Psychological Bulletin, 128*, 278–294.

Miyake, K., Campos, J., Bradshaw, D., & Kagan, J. (1986). Issues in sociocemotional development. In H. Stevenson, H. Azuma, & K. Hakuta (Eds.), *Child development and education in Japan*. New York: Freeman.

Miyake, K., Chen, S., & Campos, J. J. (1985). Infant temperament, mother's mode of interaction, and attachment in Japan: An interim report. In I. Bretherton & E. Waters (Eds.), Growing points of attachment theory and research. *Monographs of the Society for Research in Child Development, 50*(1–2), Serial No. 209.

Miyawaki, K., Strange, W., Verbrugge, R., Liberman, A. M., Jenkins, J. J., & Fujimura, O. (1975). An effect of linguistic experience: The discrimination of the [r] and [l] by native speakers of Japanese and English. *Perception and Psychophysics, 18*, 331–340.

Mize, J., & Ladd, G. W. (1990). A cognitive-social learning approach to social skill training with low-status preschool children. *Developmental Psychology, 26*, 388–397.

Modell, J., & Elder, G. H. (2002). Children develop in history: So what's new? In W. W. Hartup & R. A. Weinberg (Eds.), *Minnesota symposia on child psychology: Vol. 32. Child psychology in retrospect and prospect*. Mahwah, NJ: Erlbaum.

Modgil, S., & Modgil, C. (1976). *Piagetian research: Compilation and commentary* (Vols. 1–8). Windsor, England: NFER.

Moely, B. E., Olson, F. A., Halwes, T. G., & Flavell, J. H. (1969). Production deficiency in young children's clustered recall. *Developmental Psychology, 1*, 26–34.

Moen, P., Elder, G. H., & Luscher, K. (Eds.). (1995). *Examining lives in context: Perspectives on the ecology of human development*. Washington, DC: American Psychological Association.

Moerk, E. L. (1996). Input and learning processes in first language acquisition. In H. W. Reese (Ed.), *Advances in child development and behavior* (Vol. 26). San Diego, CA: Academic Press.

Moerk, E. L. (2000). *The guided acquisition of first language skills*. Stamford, CT: Ablex.

Moffitt, A. R. (1973). Intensity discrimination and cardiac reaction in young infants. *Developmental Psychology, 8*, 357–359.

Molfese, D. L., & Molfese, V. J. (1979). Hemispheric and stimulus differences as reflected in the cortical responses of newborn infants to speech stimuli. *Developmental Psychology, 15*, 505–511.

Moller, L., & Serbin, L. A. (1996). Antecedents of toddler gender segregation: Cognitive consonance, gender-typed toy preferences and behavioral compatibility. *Sex Roles, 35*, 445–460.

Mondloch, C. J., Lewis, T. L., Budreau, D. R., Maurer, D., Dannemiller, J. L., Stephens, B. R., & Kleiner-Gathercoal, K. A. (1999). Face perception during early infancy. *Psychological Science, 10*, 419–422.

Mondschein, E. R., Adolph, K. E., & Tamis-LeMonda, C. S. (2000). Gender bias in mothers' expectations about infant crawling. *Journal of Experimental Child Psychology, 77*, 304–316.

Money, J. C. (1975). Ablatio penis: Normal male infant sex-reassigned as a girl. *Archives of Sexual Behavior, 4*, 65–71.

Money, J. C., & Annecillo, C. (1987). Crucial period effect in psychoendocrinology: Two syndromes, abuse dwarfism and female (CVAH) hermaphroditism. In M. H. Bornstein (Ed.), *Sensitive periods in development: Interdisciplinary perspectives.* Hillsdale, NJ: Erlbaum.

Money, J. C., & Ehrhardt, A. A. (1972). *Man and woman, boy and girl.* Baltimore: Johns Hopkins University Press.

Montague, M. F. A. (1968). *Man and aggression.* New York: Oxford University Press.

Montemayor, R. (1974). Children's performance in a game and their attraction to it as a function of sex-typed labels. *Child Development, 45,* 152–156.

Montgomery, D. E. (1993). Young children's understanding of interpretive diversity between different-age listeners. *Developmental Psychology, 29,* 337–345.

Moon, C., Cooper, R. P., & Fifer, W. P. (1993). Two-day-olds prefer their native language. *Infant Behavior and Development, 16,* 495–500.

Moore, B. S., & Eisenberg, N. (1984). The development of altruism. In G. J. Whitehurst (Ed.), *Annals of child development* (Vol. 1). Greenwich, CT: JAI Press.

Moore, C., & Corkum, V. (1994). Social understanding at the end of the first year of life. *Developmental Review, 14,* 349–372.

Moore, C., & Lemmon, K. (Eds.). (2001). *The self in time: Developmental perspectives.* Mahwah, NJ: Erlbaum.

Moore, M. R., & Brooks-Gunn, J. (2002). Adolescent parenthood. In M. H. Bornstein (Ed.), *Handbook of parenting* (2nd ed., Vol. 3). Mahwah, NJ: Erlbaum.

Morell, V. (1993). The puzzle of the triple repeats. *Science, 260,* 1422–1423.

Morelli, G., Rogoff, B., Oppenheim, D., & Goldsmith, D. (1992). Cultural variations in infants' sleeping arrangements: Questions of independence. *Developmental Psychology, 28,* 604–613.

Moretti, M. M., & Higgins, E. T. (1990). The development of self-esteem vulnerabilities: Social and cognitive factors in developmental psychopathology. In R. J. Sternberg & J. Kolligian, Jr. (Eds.), *Competence considered.* New Haven, CT: Yale University Press.

Morgan, B., & Gibson, K. R. (1991). Nutritional and environmental interactions in brain development. In K. R. Gibson & A. C. Petersen (Eds.), *Brain maturation and cognitive development.* New York: Aldine de Gruyter.

Morgan, J. L., Bonamo, K. M., & Travis, L. L. (1995). Negative evidence on negative evidence. *Developmental Psychology, 31,* 180–197.

Morgane, P. J., Austin-LaFrance, R., Bronzino, J., Tonkiss, J., Diaz-Cintra, S., Cintra, L., et al. (1993). Prenatal malnutrition and development of the brain. *Neuroscience and Biobehavioral Reviews, 17,* 91–128.

Moro, E. (1918). Das erste Trimenon. *Munch. med. Wschr., 65,* 1147–1150.

Morrison, F. J., Griffith, E. M., & Alberts, D. M. (1997). Nature–nurture in the classroom: Entrance age, school readiness, and learning in children. *Developmental Psychology, 33,* 254–262.

Morrison, F. J., Smith, L., & Dow-Ehrensberger, M. (1995). Education and cognitive development. A natural experiment. *Developmental Psychology, 31,* 789–799.

Morrongiello, B. A. (1988). Infants' localization of sounds along two spatial dimensions: Horizontal and vertical axes. *Infant Behavior and Development, 11,* 127–143.

Morrongiello, B. A. (1994). Effects of colocation on auditory-visual interactions and cross-modal perception in infants. In D. J. Lewkowicz & R. Lickliter (Eds.), *The development of intersensory perception: Comparative perspectives.* Hillsdale, NJ: Erlbaum.

Morrongiello, B. A., Fenwick, K. D., Hiller, L., & Chance, G. (1994a). Sound localization in newborn human infants. *Developmental Psychobiology, 27,* 519–538.

Morrongiello, B. A., Humphrey, G. K., Timney, B., & Choi, J. (1994b). Tactual object exploration and recogni-

tion in blind and sighted children. *Perception, 23,* 833–848.

Moshman, D. (1998). Cognitive development beyond childhood. In D. Kuhn & R. S. Siegler (Vol. Eds.) & W. Damon (Series Ed.), *Handbook of child psychology: Vol. 2. Cognition, perception, and language* (5th ed.). New York: Wiley.

Mounts, N. S., & Steinberg, L. (1995). An ecological analysis of peer influence on adolescent grade point average and drug use. *Developmental Psychology, 31,* 915–922.

Mrazek, D. A. (1991). Chronic pediatric illness and multiple hospitalizations. In M. Lewis (Ed.), *Child and adolescent psychiatry: A comprehensive textbook.* Baltimore: Williams & Wilkins.

Much, N., & Shweder, R. A. (1978). Speaking of rules: The analysis of culture in breach. In W. Damon (Ed.), *New directions for child development: No. 2. Moral development.* San Francisco: Jossey-Bass.

Mueller, C. (1996). Multidisciplinary research of multimodal stimulation of premature infants: An integrative review of the literature. *Maternal-Child Nursing Journal, 24,* 18–31.

Mueller, E., & Silverman, N. (1989). Peer relations in maltreated children. In D. Cicchetti & V. Carlson (Eds.), *Child maltreatment: Theory and research on the causes and consequences of child abuse and neglect.* New York: Cambridge University Press.

Mueller, W. H. (1986). The genetics of size and shape in children and adults. In F. Falkner & J. M. Tanner (Eds.), *Human growth: A comprehensive treatise* (2nd ed., Vol. 3). New York: Plenum.

Mugny, G., & Doise, W. (1978). Socio-cognitive conflict and the structure of individual and collective performances. *European Journal of Social Psychology, 8,* 181–192.

Muir, D., & Clifton, R. K. (1985). Infants' orientation to the location of sound sources. In G. Gottlieb & N. A. Krasnegor (Eds.), *Measurement of audition and vision in the first year of postnatal life: A methodological overview.* Norwood, NJ: Ablex.

Mullen, M .K. (1994). Earliest recollections of childhood: A demographic analysis. *Cognition, 52,* 55–79.

Mullen, M. K., & Yi, S. (1995). The cultural context of talk about the past: Implications for the development of autobiographical memory. *Cognitive Development, 53,* 407–419.

Mumme, D. L., Fernald, A., & Herrera, C. (1996). Infants' responses to facial and vocal emotional signals in a social referencing paradigm. *Child Development, 67,* 3219–3237.

Munakata, Y. (1998). Infant perseveration and implications for object permanence theories: A PDP model of the AB task. *Developmental Science, 1,* 161–184.

Munakata, Y., McClelland, J. L., Johnson, M. H., & Siegler, R. S. (1997). Rethinking infant knowledge: Toward an adaptive process account of successes and failures in object permanence tasks. *Psychological Review, 104,* 686–713.

Munro, D. J. (1977). *The concept of man in contemporary China.* Ann Arbor: University of Michigan Press.

Munroe, R. H., Shimmin, H. S., & Munroe, R. L. (1984). Gender understanding and sex role preference in four cultures. *Developmental Psychology, 20,* 673–682.

Murata, P. J., McGlynn, E. A., Siu, A. L., & Brook, R. H. (1992). *Prenatal care.* Santa Monica, CA: Rand.

Murdock, G. P. (1967). *Ethnographic atlas.* Pittsburgh, PA: University of Pittsburgh Press.

Murphey, D. A. (1992). Constructing the child: Relations between parents' beliefs and child outcomes. *Developmental Review, 12,* 199–232.

Murphy, N., & Messer, D. (2000). Differential benefits from scaffolding and children working alone. *Educational Psychology, 20,* 17–31.

Murray, A. D., Johnson, J., & Peters, J. (1990). Fine-tuning of utterance length to preverbal infants: Effects on later language development. *Journal of Child Language, 17,* 511–525.

Murray, F. B. (1982). Learning and development through social interaction and conflict: A challenge to social learning theory. In L. Liben (Ed.), *Piaget and the foundation of knowledge.* Hillsdale, NJ: Erlbaum.

Murray, L., Fiori-Cowley, A., Hooper, R., & Cooper, P. (1996). The impact of postnatal depression and associated adversity on early mother–infant interactions and later outcome. *Child Development, 67,* 2512–2526.

Myers, B. J. (1987). Mother–infant bonding as a critical period. In M. H. Bornstein (Ed.), *Sensitive periods in development: Interdisciplinary perspectives.* Hillsdale, NJ: Erlbaum.

Nadel, J., & Fontaine, A. (1989). Communicating by imitation: A developmental and comparative approach to transitory social competence. In B. H. Schneider, G. Attili, J. Nadel, & R. P. Weissberg (Eds.), *Social competence in developmental perspective.* Dordrecht, Netherlands: Kluwer.

Nader, K., Pynoos, R., Fairbanks, L., Al-Ajeel, M., & Al-Asfour, A. (1993). A preliminary study of PTSD and grief among the children of Kuwait following the Gulf crisis. *British Journal of Clinical Psychology, 32,* 407–416.

Naeye, R. L., Diener, M. M., & Dellinger, W. S. (1969). Urban poverty: Effects on prenatal nutrition. *Science, 166,* 1026.

Naigles, L. G., & Gelman, S. A. (1995). Overextensions in comprehension and production revisited: Preferential-looking in a study of dog, cat, and cow. *Journal of Child Language, 22,* 19–46.

Nass, R. D. (1993). Sex differences in learning abilities and disabilities. *Annals of Dyslexia, 43,* 61–77.

Nathanielsz, P. W. (1995). The role of basic science in preventing low birth weight. *The future of children* (Vol. 5, No. 1). Los Angeles: Packard Foundation.

National Center for Education Statistics. (1997). *Digest of education statistics 1997* (NCES 98–015). Washington, DC: U.S. Department of Education.

National Research Council (2001). *Eager to learn: Educating our preschoolers.* Committee on Early Childhood Pedagogy, B. T. Bowman, M. S. Donovan, & M. S. Burns (Eds.). Commission on Behavioral and Social Sciences and Education. Washington, DC: National Academy Press.

National Research Council, and Institute of National Research Council and Institute of Medicine. (2000). *From neurons to neighborhoods: The science of early childhood development.* J. P. Shonkoff & D. A. Phillips (Eds.). Washington, DC: National Academy Press.

Needham, A. (2001). Object recognition and object segregation in 4.5-month-old infants. *Journal of Experimental Child Psychology, 78,* 3–24.

Needham, J. (1959). *A history of embryology.* Cambridge: Cambridge University Press.

Needleman, H. L., Schell, A. S., Bellinger, D., Leviton, A., & Alldred, E. N. (1990). The long-term effects of exposure to low doses of lead in childhood: An 11-year follow-up report. *New England Journal of Medicine, 322,* 83.

Neiderhiser, J. M., Reiss, D., Hetherington, E. M., & Plomin, R. (1999). Relationships between parenting and adolescent adjustment over time: Genetic and environmental contributions. *Developmental Psychology, 35,* 680–692.

Neisser, U. (1988). Five kinds of self-knowledge. *Philosophical Psychology, 1,* 35–39.

Neisser, U. (Ed.). (1993). *Ecological and interpersonal knowledge of self.* New York: Cambridge University Press.

Neisser, U. (1995). Criteria for an ecological self. In P. Rochat (Ed.), *The self in infancy: Theory and research.* Amsterdam: Elsevier.

Neisser, U., Boodoo, G., Bouchard, T. J. Jr., Boykin, A. W., Brody, N., Ceci, S. J., et al. (1996). Intelligence: Knowns and unknowns. *American Psychologist, 51,* 77–101.

Nelson, C. A. (1987). The recognition of facial expressions in the first two years of life: Mechanisms of development. *Child Development, 58,* 889–909.

Nelson, C. A., & Horowitz, F. D. (1987). Visual motion perception in infancy: A review and synthesis. In P. Salapatek & L. Cohen (Eds.), *Handbook of infant perception: Vol. 2. From perception to cognition.* New York: Academic Press.

Nelson, C. A., & Luciano, M. (Eds.). (2001). *Handbook of developmental cognitive neuroscience.* Cambridge, MA: MIT Press.

Nelson, E. A. S., Schiefenhoevel, W., & Haimerl, F. (2000). Child care practices in nonindustrialized societies. *Pediatrics, 105,* e75.

Nelson, J., & Aboud, F. (1985). The resolution of social conflict between friends. *Child Development, 56,* 1009–1017.

Nelson, K. (1973). Structure and strategy in learning to talk. *Monographs of the Society for Research in Child Development, 38*(1–2, Serial No. 149).

Nelson, K. (1985). *Making sense: The acquisition of shared meaning.* Orlando, FL: Academic Press.

Nelson, K. (1986). *Event knowledge: Structure and function in development.* Hillsdale, NJ: Erlbaum.

Nelson, K. (1988). Constraints on word learning? *Cognitive Development, 3,* 221–246.

Nelson, K. (1993a). The psychological and social origins of autobiographical memory. *Psychological Science, 4,* 7–14.

Nelson, K. (1993b). Events, narratives, memory: What develops? In C. A. Nelson (Ed.), *Minnesota symposia on child psychology: Vol. 26. Memory and affect in development.* Hillsdale, NJ: Erlbaum.

Nelson, K. (1996). *Language in cognitive development: The emergence of the mediated mind.* New York: Cambridge University Press.

Nelson, K., & Fivush, R. (2000). Socialization of memory. In E. Tulving, & F. I. M. Craik, (Eds.), *The Oxford handbook of memory.* New York: Oxford University Press.

Nelson, K., & Gruendel, J. (1981). Generalized event representations: Basic building blocks of cognitive development. In M. E. Lamb & A. L. Brown (Eds.), *Advances in developmental psychology* (Vol. 1). Hillsdale, NJ: Erlbaum.

Nelson, K., Hampson, J., & Shaw, L. K. (1993). Nouns in early lexicons: Evidence, explanations, and implications. *Journal of Child Language, 20,* 61–84.

Nelson, S. A. (1980). Factors influencing young children's use of motives and outcomes as moral criteria. *Child Development, 51,* 823–829.

Nesdale, D., & Flesser, D. (2001). Social identity and the development of children's group attitudes. *Child Development, 72,* 506–517.

New, R. S. (1994). Child's play–*una cosa naturale*: An Italian perspective. In J. L. Roopnarine, J. E. Johnson, & F. H. Hooper (Eds.), *Children's play in diverse cultures.* Albany: State University of New York Press.

Newcomb, A. F., & Bagwell, C. L. (1995). Children's friendship relations: A meta-analytic review. *Psychological Bulletin, 117,* 306–347.

Newcomb, A. F., & Brady, J. E. (1982). Mutuality in boys' friendship relations. *Child Development, 53,* 393–395.

Newcomb, A. F., Bukowski, W. M., & Pattee, L. (1993). Children's peer relations: A meta-analytic review of popular, rejected, neglected, controversial, and average sociometric status. *Psychological Bulletin, 113,* 99–128.

Newcombe, N. (1989). The development of spatial perspective taking. In H. W. Reese (Ed.), *Advances in child development and behavior* (Vol. 22). San Diego, CA: Academic Press.

Newcombe, N. S., Drummey, A. B., Fox, N. A., Lie, E., & Ottinger-Alberts, W. (2000). Remembering early childhood: How much, how, and why (or why not). *Current Directions in Psychological Science, 9,* 55–58.

Newcombe, N. S., Mathason, L., & Terlecki, M. (2002). Maximization of spatial competence: More important than finding the cause of sex differences. In A. V. McGillicuddy-De Lisi & R. De Lisi (Eds.), *Biology, society, and behavior: The development of sex differences in cognition.* Greenwich, CT: Ablex.

Newman, D. L., Caspi, A., Moffitt, T. E., & Silva, P. A. (1997). Antecedents of adult interpersonal functioning: Effects of individual differences in age 3 temperament. *Developmental Psychology, 33,* 206–217.

Newman, L. S. (1990). Intentional and unintentional memory in young children: Remembering vs. playing. *Journal of Experimental Child Psychology, 50,* 243–258.

Newman, P. R. (1982). The peer group. In B. B. Wolman (Ed.), *Handbook of developmental psychology.* Englewood Cliffs, NJ: Prentice Hall.

Newport, E. L. (1977). Motherese: The speech of mothers to young children. In N. J. Castellan, D. B. Pisoni, & G. Potts (Eds.), *Cognitive theory* (Vol. 2). Hillsdale, NJ: Erlbaum.

Newport, E. L. (1991). Contrasting concepts of the critical period for language. In S. Carey & R. Gelman (Eds.), *The epigenesis of mind: Essays on biology and cognition.* Hillsdale, NJ: Erlbaum.

NICHD (2000). *Report of the National Reading Panel. Teaching children to read: An evidence-based assessment of the scientific research on reading and its implications for reading instruction* (NIH Publication No. 00–4769). Washington, DC: U.S. Government Printing Office.

NICHD Early Child Care Research Network. (1997a). Child care in the first year of life. *Merrill-Palmer Quarterly, 43,* 340–360.

NICHD Early Child Care Research Network. (1997b). The effects of infant child care on infant-mother attachment security: Results of the NICHD Study of Early Child Care *Child Development, 68,* 860–879.

NICHD Early Child Care Research Network. (1999). Child care and mother-child interaction in the first three years of life. *Developmental Psychology, 35,* 1399–1413.

NICHD Early Child Care Research Network. (2001). Child care and children's peer interaction at 24 and 36 months: The NICHD Study of Early Child Care. *Child Development, 72,* 1478–1500.

NICHD Early Child Care Research Network. (2002). Early child care and children's development prior to school entry: Results from the NICHD Study of Early Child Care. *American Educational Research Journal, 39,* 133–164.

NICHD Early Child Care Research Network (2003). Does amount of time spent in child care predict socioemotional adjustment during the transition to kindergarten? *Child Development, 74,* 976–1005.

Nicholls, J. G., & Hazzard, S. P. (1993). *Education as adventure: Lessons from second grade.* New York: Teachers College Press.

Nichols, R. C. (1978). Heredity and environment: Major findings from twin studies of ability, personality and interest. *Homo, 29,* 158–173.

NIH (2000). *NIH Consensus Statement: Phenylketonuria: Screening and management.* Washington, DC: National Institutes of Health.

Ninio, A., & Snow, C. E. (1988). Language acquisition through language use: The functional sources of children's early utterances. In Y. Levy, I. M. Schlesinger, & M. D. S. Braine (Eds.), *Categories and processes in language acquisition.* Hillsdale, NJ: Erlbaum.

Ninio, A., & Snow, C. E. (1996). *Pragmatic development.* Boulder, CO: Westview Press.

Ninio, A., & Snow, C. E. (1999). The development of pragmatics: Learning to use language appropriately. In W. C. Ritchie & T. K. Bhatia (Eds.), *Handbook of child language acquisition.* San Diego, CA: Academic Press.

Nisan, M. (1984). Distributive justice and social norms. *Child Development, 55,* 1020–1029.

Noble, C., & Bradford, W. (2000). *Getting it right for boys . . . and girls.* London: Routledge.

Nolen-Hoeksema, S., Girgus, J. S., & Seligman, M. E. P. (1986). Learned helplessness in children: A longitudinal study of depression, achievement, and explanatory style. *Journal of Personality and Social Psychology, 51,* 435–442.

North, A. S., & Noyes, J. M. (2002). Gender influences on children's computer attitudes and cognition. *Computers in Human Behavior, 18,* 135–150.

Novick, N., Cauce, A. M., & Grove, K. (1996). Competence self-concept. In B. A. Bracken (Ed.), *Handbook of self-concept: Developmental, social, and clinical considerations.* New York: Wiley.

Nucci, L. P. (1996). Morality and the personal sphere of action. In E. S. Reed, E. Turiel, & T. Brown (Eds.), *Values and knowledge.* Hillsdale, NJ: Erlbaum.

Nucci, L. P. (1997). Culture, universals, and the personal. In H. D. Saltzstein (Ed.), *New directions for child development: No. 76. Culture as a context for moral development: New perspectives on the particular and the universal.* San Francisco: Jossey-Bass.

Nucci, L. P. (2001). *Education in the moral domain.* New York: Cambridge University Press.

Nucci, L. P., & Nucci, M. S. (1982a). Children's responses to moral and social conventional transgressions in free-play settings. *Child Development, 53,* 1337–1342.

Nucci, L. P., & Nucci, M. S. (1982b). Children's social interactions in the context of moral and conventional transgressions. *Child Development, 53,* 403–412.

Nucci, L. P., & Turiel, E. (1978). Social interactions and the development of social concepts in preschool children. *Child Development, 49,* 400–407.

Nucci, L., & Turiel, E. (1993). God's word, religious rules, and their relation to Christian and Jewish children's concepts of morality. *Child Development , 64,* 1475–1491.

Nunes, T. (1999). Mathematics learning as the socialization of the mind. *Mind, Culture, and Activity, 6,* 33–52.

Nunes, T., & Bryant, P. (1996). *Children doing mathematics.* Cambridge, MA: Blackwell.

Nunes, T., Schliemann, A. D., & Carraher, D. W., (1993). *Street mathematics and school mathematics.* New York: Cambridge University Press.

Nunnally, J. C. (1982). The study of human change: Measurement, research strategies, and methods of analysis. In B. B. Wolman (Ed.), *Handbook of developmental psychology.* Englewood Cliffs, NJ: Prentice Hall.

Nuttall, R. L., & Pezaris, E. (2001). Spatial-mechanical reasoning skills versus mathematical self-confidence as mediators of gender differences on mathematics subtests using cross-national gender-based items. *Journal for Research in Mathematics Education, 32,* 28–57.

Nye, B., Hedges, L. V., & Konstantopoulos, S. (2001). Are effects of small classes cumulative? Evidence from a Tennessee experiment. *Journal of Educational Research, 94,* 336–345.

Nyiti, R. M. (1982). The validity of "cultural differences explanations" for cross-cultural variation in the rate of Piagetian cognitive development. In D. A. Wagner & H. W. Stevenson (Eds.), *Cultural perspectives on child development.* San Francisco: W. H. Freeman.

O'Brien, M., & Huston, A. C. (1985). Development of sex-typed play behavior in toddlers. *Developmental Psychology, 21,* 866–871.

O'Connell, B., & Bretherton, I. (1984). Toddler's play, alone and with mother. The role of maternal guidance. In I. Bretherton (Ed.), *Symbolic play: The development of social understanding.* New York: Academic Press.

O'Connor, M. C. (1996). Managing the intermental: Classroom group discussion and the social context of learning. In D. I. Slobin, J. Gerhardt, A. Kyratzis, & J. Guo (Eds.), *Social interaction, social context, and language: Essays in honor of Susan Ervin-Tripp.* Mahwah, NJ: Erlbaum.

O'Connor, R. D. (1972). Relative efficacy of modeling, shaping, and the combined procedures for modification of social withdrawal. *Journal of Abnormal Psychology, 79,* 327–334.

O'Connor, T. G., Deater-Deckard, K., Fulker, D., Rutter, M., & Plomin, R. (1998). Genotype-environment correlations in late childhood and early adolescence: Antisocial behavioral problems and coercive parenting. *Developmental Psychology 34,* 970–981.

O'Connor, T. G., Heron, J., Golding, J., Beveridge, M., & Glover, V. (2002). Maternal antenatal anxiety and children's behavioural/emotional problems at 4 years. *British Journal of Psychiatry, 180,* 502–508.

O'Donnell, A. M., & King, A. (Eds.) (1999). *Cognitive perspectives on peer learning.* Mahwah, NJ: Erlbaum.

O'Flahavan, J. F., & Seidl, B. L. (1997). Fostering literate communities in school: A case for sociocultural approaches to reading instruction. In S. A. Stahl & D. A. Hayes (Eds.), *Instructional models in reading.* Mahwah, NJ: Erlbaum.

O'Neill, D. K. (1996). Two-year-olds' sensitivity to a parent's knowledge state when making requests. *Child Development, 67,* 659–677.

O'Neill, D. K., Astington, J. W., & Flavell, J. H. (1992). Young children's understanding of the role that sensory experiences play in knowledge acquisition. *Child Development, 63,* 474–490.

O'Neill, D. K., & Chong, S. C. F. (2001). Preschool children's difficulty understanding the types of information obtained through the five senses. *Child Development, 72,* 803–815.

O'Reilly, A. W., & Bornstein, M. H. (1993). Caregiver-child interaction in play. In M. H. Bornstein & A. W. O'Reilly (Eds.), *New directions in child development: No. 59. The role of play in the development of thought.* San Francisco: Jossey-Bass.

O'Sullivan, L. F., Graber, J. A., & Brooks-Gunn, J. (2001). Adolescent gender development. In J. Worell (Ed.), *Encyclopedia of women and gender* (Vol. 1). San Diego, CA: Academic Press.

Oakes, J. (1990). Opportunities, achievement, and choice: Women and minority students in science and mathematics. In C. B. Cazden (Ed.), *Review of research in education* (Vol. 16). Washington, DC: American Educational Research Association.

Oakes, J., Gamoran, A., & Page, R. N. (1992). Curriculum differentiation: Opportunities, outcomes, and meanings. In P. Jackson (Ed.), *Handbook of research on curriculum.* New York: Macmillan.

Ochs, E., & Schieffelin, B. B. (1984). Language acquisition and socialization: Three developmental stories and their implications. In R. Schweder & R. LeVine (Eds.), *Culture theory: Essays on mind, self, and emotion.* Cambridge: Cambridge University Press.

Odom, S. L., & Strain, P. S. (1984). Peer-mediated approaches to promoting children's social interaction: A review. *American Journal of Orthopsychiatry, 54,* 544–557.

Oehler, J. M., & Eckerman, C. D. (1988). Regulatory effects of human speech and touch in premature infants prior to term age. *Infant Behavior and Development, 11,* 249.

Offord, D. R., Lipman, E. L., & Duku, E. K. (2001). Epidemiology of problem behavior up to age 12 years. In R. Loeber & D. P. Farrington (Eds.), *Child delinquents: Development, intervention, and service needs.* Thousand Oaks, CA: Sage.

Ogle, A., & Mazzullo, L. (2002). *Before your pregnancy.* New York: Ballantine Books.

Ohring, R., Graber, J. A., & Brooks-Gunn, J. (2002). Girls' recurrent and concurrent body dissatisfaction: Correlates and consequences over 8 years. *International Journal of Eating Disorders, 31,* 404–415.

Okagaki, L., & Frensch, P. (1994). Effects of video game playing on measures of spatial performance: Gender effects in late adolescence. *Journal of Applied Developmental Psychology, 15,* 33–58.

Oliner, S. P., & Oliner, P. M. (1988). *The altruistic personality: Rescuers of Jews in Nazi Europe.* New York: Free Press.

Oller, D. K. (2000). *The emergence of the speech capacity.* Mahwah, NJ: Erlbaum.

Oller, D. K., & Eilers, R. E. (1988). The role of audition in infant babbling. *Child Development, 59,* 441–449.

Oller, D. K., & Pearson, B. Z. (2002). Assessing the effects of bilingualism. In D. K. Oller (Ed.), *Language and literacy in bilingual children.* Clevedon, UK: Multilingual Matters.

Olson, G. M., & Sherman, T. (1983). Attention, learning, and memory in infants. In P. H. Mussen (Series Ed.) & M. M. Haith & J. J. Campos (Vol. Eds.), *Handbook of child psychology: Vol. 2. Infancy and developmental psychobiology* (4th ed.). New York: Wiley.

Olson, H. (1994). The effects of prenatal alcohol exposure on child development. *Infants and Young Children, 6,* 10–25.

Olson, S. L., Bates, J. E., & Kaskie, B. (1992). Caregiver-infant interaction antecedents of children's school-age cognitive ability. *Merrill-Palmer Quarterly, 38,* 309–330.

Olson, S. L., Bates, J. E., Sandy, J. M., & Lanthier, R. (2000). Early developmental precursors of externalizing behavior in middle childhood and adolescence. *Journal of Abnormal Child Psychology, 28,* 119–133.

Olson, S. L., & Kashiwagi, K. (2000). Teacher ratings of behavioral self-regulation in preschool children: A Japanese/U.S. comparison. *Journal of Applied Developmental Psychology, 21,* 609–617.

Olweus, D. (1997). Bully/victim problems in school: Facts and intervention. *European Journal of Psychology of Education, 12,* 495–510.

Olweus, D. (2001). Peer harassment: A critical analysis and some important issues. In J. Juvonen & S. Graham (Eds.), *Peer harassment in school: The plight of the vulnerable and victimized.* New York: Guilford.

Olweus, D., Mattison, A., Schalling, D., & Low, H. (1988). Circulating testosterone levels and aggression in adolescent males: A causal analysis. *Psychosomatic Medicine, 50,* 261–272.

Oosterwegel, A., & Oppenheimer, L. (1993). *The self-system: Developmental changes between and within self-concepts.* Hillsdale, NJ: Erlbaum.

Ornstein, P. A., & Haden, C. A. (2001). Memory development or the development of memory? *Current Directions in Psychological Science, 10,* 202–205.

Ornstein, P. A., Naus, M. J., & Liberty, C. (1975). Rehearsal and organizational processes in children's memory. *Child Development, 56,* 818–830.

Osherson, D. N. (1990). *An invitation to cognitive science.* Cambridge, MA: MIT Press.

Osofsky, J. (1995a). Children who witness domestic violence: The invisible victims. *Social Policy Report: Society for Research in Child Development, 18,* 1–16.

Osofsky, J. (1995b). The effects of exposure to violence on young children. *American Psychologist, 50,* 782–788.

Oster, H., Hegley, D., & Nagel, L. (1992). Adult judgments and fine-grained analysis of infant facial expressions: Testing the validity of a priori coding formulas. *Developmental Psychology, 28,* 1115–1131.

Owen, D. R. (1979). Psychological studies in XYY men. In H. L. Vallet & I. H. Porter (Eds.), *Genetic mechanisms of sexual development.* New York: Academic Press.

Oyama, S. (2000). *Evolution's eye: A systems view of the biology-culture divide.* Durham, NC: Duke University Press.

Oyserman, D., Gant, L., & Ager, J. (1995). A socially contextualized model of African American identity: Possible selves and school persistence. *Journal of Personality and Social Psychology, 69,* 1216–1232.

Oyserman, D., & Markus, H. (1990). Possible selves and delinquency. *Journal of Personality and Social Psychology, 59,* 112–125.

Oyserman, D., & Saltz, E. (1993). Competence, delinquency, and attempts to attain possible selves. *Journal of Personality and Social Psychology, 65,* 360–374.

Oyserman, D., Terry, K., & Bybee, D. (2002). A possible selves intervention to enhance school involvement. *Journal of Adolescence, 25,* 313–326.

Paarlberg, K. M., Vingerhoets, A., Passchier, J., & Dekker, G. A. (1995). Psychosocial factors and pregnancy outcome: A review with emphasis on methodological issues. *Journal of Psychosomatic Research, 39,* 563–595.

Packard, B. W-L., & Nguyen, D. (2003). Science career-related possible selves of adolescent girls: A longitudinal study. *Journal of Career Development, 29,* 251–263.

Paikoff, R. L., & Brooks-Gunn, J. (1990). Physiological processes: What role do they play during the transition to adolescence? In R. Montemayor, G. R. Adams, & T. Gullotta (Eds.), *From childhood to adolescence: Vol. 2. Advances in adolescent development.* London: Sage.

Pajares, F., & Miller, M. D. (1994). Role of self-efficacy and self-concept beliefs in mathematical problem solving: A path analysis. *Journal of Educational Psychology, 86,* 193–203.

Paley, V. G. (1984). *Boys and girls: Superheroes in the doll corner.* Chicago: University of Chicago Press.

Palincsar, A. S., & Brown, A. L. (1984). Reciprocal teaching of comprehension-fostering and comprehension-monitoring activities. *Cognition and Instruction, 1,* 117–175.

Palincsar, A. S., & Herrenkohl, L. R. (1999). Designing collaborative contexts: Lessons from three research programs. In A. M. O'Donnell & A. King (Eds.), *Cognitive perspectives on peer learning.* Mahwah, NJ: Erlbaum.

Pallas, A. M., Entwisle, D. R., Alexander, K. L., & Stluka, M. F. (1994). Ability-group effects: Instructional, social, or institutional? *Sociology of Education, 67,* 27–46.

Paneth, N. S. (1995). The problem of low birth weight. *The future of children* (Vol. 5. No. 1). Los Angeles: Packard Foundation.

Panigrahy, A., Filiano, J. J., Sleeper, L. A., et al. (1997). Decreased kainite binding in the arcuate nucleous of the sudden infant death syndrome. *Journal of Neuropathological Experimental Neurology, 56,* 1253–1261.

Parekh, V. C., Pherwani, A., Udani, P. M., & Mukkerjie, S. (1970). Brain weight and head circumference in fetus, infant, and children of different nutritional and socioeconomic groups. *Indian Pediatrics, 7,* 347–358.

Parikh, B. (1980). Development of moral judgment and its relation to family environment factors in Indian and American families. *Child Development, 51,* 1030–1039.

Paris, S. G. (1975). Integration and inference in children's comprehension and memory. In F. Restle, R. Shiffrin, J. Castellan, H. Lindman, & D. Pisoni (Eds.), *Cognitive theory* (Vol. 1). Mahwah, NJ: Erlbaum.

Paris, S. G. (Ed.). (2002). *Perspectives on object-centered learning in museums.* Mahwah, NJ: Erlbaum.

Paris, S. G., & Lindauer, B. K. (1976). The role of inference in children's comprehension and memory for sentences. *Cognitive Psychology, 8,* 217–227.

Paris, S. G., & Oka, E. R. (1986). Children's reading strategies, meta-cognition, and motivation. *Developmental Review, 6,* 25–56.

Parke, R. D. (1977). Some effects of punishment on children's behavior-revisited. In E. M. Hetherington & R. D. Parke (Eds.), *Contemporary readings in child psychology.* New York: McGraw-Hill.

Parke, R. D. (1978). Parent–infant interaction: Progress, paradigms, and problems. In G. P. Sackett (Ed.), *Observing behavior: Vol. 1. Theory and applications in mental retardation.* Baltimore: University Park Press.

Parke, R. D. (1996). *Fatherhood.* Cambridge, MA: Harvard University Press.

Parke, R. D. (2002). Fathers and families. In M. H. Bornstein (Ed.), *Handbook of parenting* (2nd ed., Vol. 3). Mahwah, NJ: Erlbaum.

Parke, R. D., & Buriel, R. (1998). Socialization in the family: Ethnic and ecological perspectives. In W. Damon (Series Ed.) & N. Eisenberg (Vol. Ed.), *Handbook of child psychology: Vol. 3. Social, emotional, and personality development* (5th ed.). New York: Wiley.

Parke, R. D., & Ladd, G. W. (Eds.). (1992). *Family-peer relationships: Modes of linkage.* Hillsdale, NJ: Erlbaum.

Parke, R. D., Simpkins, S. D., McDowell, D. J., Kim, M., Killian, C., Dennis, J., et al. (2002). Relative contributions of families and peers to children's social development. In P. K. Smith & C. H. Hart (Eds.), *Blackwell handbook of childhood social development.* Madden, MA: Blackwell Publishers.

Parke, R. D., & Slaby, R. G. (1983). The development of aggression. In P. H. Mussen (Series Ed.) & E. M. Hetherington (Vol. Ed.), *Handbook of child psychology: Vol. 4. Socialization, personality, and social development* (4th ed.). New York: Wiley.

Parker, J. G., & Asher, S. R. (1987). Peer relations and later personal adjustment: Are low-accepted children at risk? *Psychological Bulletin, 102,* 357–389.

Parker, J. G., Rubin, K. H., Price, J. M., & DeRosier, M. E. (1995). Peer relationships, child development, and adjustment: A developmental psychopathology perspective. In D. Cicchetti & D. J. Cohen (Eds.), *Developmental psychopathology: Vol. 2. Risk, disorder, and adaptation.* New York: Wiley.

Parmelee, A. H., & Garbanati, J. (1987). Clinical neurobehavioral aspects of state organization in newborn infants. In A. Kobayashi (Ed.), *Neonatal brain and behavior.* Nagoya, Japan: University of Nagoya Press.

Parmelee, A. H., & Sigman, M. D. (1983). Perinatal brain development and behavior. In P. H. Mussen (Series Ed.) & M. M. Haith & J. J. Campos (Vol. Eds.), *Handbook of child psychology: Vol. 2. Infancy and developmental psychobiology* (4th ed.). New York: Wiley.

Parten, M. B. (1932). Social participation among preschool children. *Journal of Abnormal and Social Psychology, 27,* 243–269.

Pascalis, O., De Schonen, S., Morton, J., & Deruelle, C. (1995). Mother's face recognition by neonates: A replication and an extension. *Infant Behavior and Development, 18,* 79–85.

Passarotti, A. M., Paul, B. M., Bussiere, J. R., Buxton, R. B., Wong, E. C., & Stiles, J. (2003). The development of face and location processing: An FMRI study. *Developmental Science, 6,* 100–117.

Pastor, P. N., Makuc, D. M., Reuben, C., & Xia, H. (2002). *Chartbook on trends in the health of Americans, United States, 2002.* Hyattsville, MD: National Center for Health Statistics.

Paterson, S., Brown, J. H., Gsodl, M., Johnson, M. H., & Karmiloff-Smith, A. (1999). Cognitive modularity and genetic disorders. *Science, 286,* 2355–2358.

Patterson, C. J. (1982). Self-control and self-regulation in childhood. In T. M. Field, A. Huston, H. C. Quay, L. Troll, & G. E. Finley (Eds.), *Review of human development.* New York: Wiley.

Patterson, C. J. (1992). Children of lesbian and gay parents. *Child Development, 63,* 1025–1042.

Patterson, C. J. (1995a). Lesbian and gay parenthood. In M. H. Bornstein (Ed.), *Handbook of parenting: Vol. 3. Status and social conditions of parenting.* Mahwah, NJ: Erlbaum.

Patterson, C. J. (1995b). Lesbian mothers, gay fathers, and their children. In A. R. D'Augelli & C. J. Patterson (Eds.), *Lesbian, gay, and bisexual identities across the lifespan: Psychological perspectives.* New York: Oxford University Press.

Patterson, C. J. (2002). Lesbian and gay parenthood. In M. Bornstein (Ed.). *Handbook of parenting* (2nd ed., Vol. 3). Mahwah, NJ: Erlbaum.

Patterson, C. J., & Chan, R. W. (1999). Families headed by lesbian and gay parents. In M. E. Lamb (Ed.), *Parenting and child development in "nontraditional" families.* Mahwah, NJ: Erlbaum.

Patterson, G. R. (1982). *Coercive family process.* Eugene, OR: Castalia.

Patterson, G. R., Littman, R. A., & Bricker, R. W. (1967). Assertive behavior in children: A step toward a theory of aggression. *Monographs of the Society for Research in Child Development, 32(5,* Serial No. 113).

Patterson, G. R., Reid, J. B., & Dishion, T. J. (1992). *Antisocial boys.* Eugene, OR: Castalia.

Patterson, M. L., & Werker, J. F. (2002). Infants' ability to match dynamic phonetic and gender information in the face and voice. *Journal of Experimental Child Psychology, 81,* 93–115.

Pecheux, M., Lepecq, J., & Salzarulo, P. (1988). Oral activity and exploration in 1–2-month-old infants. *British Journal of Developmental Psychology, 6,* 245–256.

Pederson, D. R., & Moran, G. (1995). A categorical description of infant-mother relationships in the home and its relation to Q-sort measures of infant-mother interaction. In E. Waters, B. E. Vaughn, G. Posada, & K. Kondo-Ikemura (Eds.), Caregiving, cultural, and cognitive perspectives on secure-base behavior and working models. *Monographs of the Society for Research in Child Development, 60* (2–3, Serial No. 244).

Pederson, D. R., & Moran, G. (1996). Expressions of the attachment relationship outside of the Strange Situation. *Child Development, 67,* 915–927.

Pederson, D. R., & Ter Vrugt, D. (1973). The influence of amplitude and frequency of vestibular stimulation on the activity of two-month-old infants. *Child Development, 44,* 122–128.

Pedlow, R., Sanson, A., Prior, M., & Oberklaid, F. (1993). Stability of maternally reported temperament from infancy to 8 years. *Developmental Psychology, 29,* 998–1007.

Pegg, J. E., Werker, J. F., & McLeod, P. J. (1992). Preference for infant-directed over adult-directed speech: Evidence from 7-week-old infants. *Infant Behavior and Development, 15,* 325–345.

Peiper, A. (1963). *Cerebral function in infancy and adulthood.* New York: Consultants Bureau.

Peisner-Feinberg, E. S., Burchinal, M. R., Clifford, R. M., Culkin, M. L., Howes, C., Kagan, S. L., et al. (2001). The relation of preschool child-care quality to children's cognitive and social developmental trajectories through second grade. *Child Development, 72,* 1534–1553.

Pelaez-Nogueras, M., Field, T., Cigales, M., Gonzalez, A., & Clasky, S. (1994). Infants of depressed mothers show less "depressed" behavior with their nursery teachers. *Infant Mental Health Journal, 15,* 358–367.

Pelham, W. E., & Hinshaw, S. P. (1992). Behavior intervention for attention-deficit hyperactivity disorder. In S. M. Turner, K. S. Calhoun, & H. E. Adams (Eds.), *Handbook of clinical behavior therapy* (2nd ed.). New York: Wiley.

Pellegrini, A. D., & Bartini, M. (2001). Dominance in early adolescent boys: Affiliative and aggressive dimensions and possible functions. *Merrill-Palmer Quarterly, 47,* 142–163.

Penner, S. G. (1987). Parental responses to grammatical and ungrammatical child utterances. *Child Development, 58,* 376–384.

Pennington, B. F. (2001). Genetic methods. In C. A. Nelson & M. Lucian. (Eds.), *Handbook of developmental cognitive neuroscience.* Cambridge, MA: MIT Press.

Pepler, D. J., King, G., & Byrd, W. (1991). A socialcognitively based social skills training program for aggressive children. In D. J. Pepler & K. H. Rubin (Eds.), *The development and treatment of childhood aggression.* Hillsdale, NJ: Erlbaum.

Perez-Granados, D. R., & Callanan, M. A. (1997). Conversations with mothers and siblings: Young children's semantic and conceptual development. *Developmental Psychology, 33,* 120–134.

Perlmutter, M., Behrend, S. D., Kuo, F., & Muller, A. (1989). Social influences on children's problem solving. *Developmental Psychology, 25,* 744–754

Perner, J., Ruffman, T. K., & Leekam, S. R. (1994). Theory of mind is contagious: You catch it from your sibs. *Child Development, 65,* 1228–1238.

Perret-Clermont, A. (1980). *Social interaction and cognitive development in children.* London: Academic Press.

Perry, D. G., & Bussey, K. (1979). The social learning theory of sex differences: Imitation is alive and well. *Journal of Personality and Social Psychology, 37,* 1699–1712.

Perry, D. G., & Perry, L. C. (1983). Social learning, causal attribution, and moral internalization. In J. Bizanz, G. L. Bizanz, & R. Kail (Eds.), *Learning in children: Progress in cognitive development research.* New York: Springer-Verlag.

Perry, D. G., Perry, L. C., & Weiss, R. J. (1989). Sex differences in the consequences that children anticipate for aggression. *Developmental Psychology, 25,* 312–319.

Perry, M., Church, R. B., & Goldin-Meadow, S. (1988). Transitional knowledge in the acquisition of concepts. *Cognitive Development, 3,* 359–400.

Perry, M., & Elder, A. D. (1997). Knowledge in transition: Adults' developing understanding of a principle of physical causality. *Cognitive Development, 12,* 131–157.

Peters, B. R., Atkins, M. S., & McKay, M. M. (1999). Adopted children's behavior problems: A review of five explanatory models. *Clinical Psychology Review, 19,* 297–328.

Peters, D. P. (1991). The influence of stress and arousal on the child witness. In J. Doris (Ed.), *The suggestibility of children's recollections.* Washington, DC: American Psychological Association.

Petersen, A. C. (1987). The nature of biological-psychosocial interactions: The sample case of early adolescence. In R. M. Lerner & T. L. Foch (Eds.), *Biological-psychosocial interactions in early adolescence.* Hillsdale, NJ: Erlbaum.

Petersen, A. C. (1988). Adolescent development. *Annual Review of Psychology, 39,* 583–607.

Peterson, C. C. (2000). Kindred spirits: Influences on siblings' perspectives on theory of mind. *Cognitive Development, 15,* 435–455.

Peterson, C., & Biggs, M. (2001). "I was really, really, really mad!" Children's use of evaluative devices in narratives about emotional events. *Sex Roles, 45,* 801–825 .

Peterson, L. (1983a). Influence of age, task competence, and responsibility focus on children's altruism. *Developmental Psychology, 19,* 141–148.

Peterson, L. (1983b). Role of donor competence, donor age, and peer presence on helping in an emergency. *Developmental Psychology, 19,* 873–880.

Petitto, L. A., & Marentette, P. F. (1991). Babbling in the manual mode: Evidence for the ontogeny of language. *Science, 251,* 1493–1496.

Pettigrew, T. F., & Tropp, L. R. (2000). Does intergroup contact reduce prejudice: Recent meta-analytic findings. In S. Oskamp (Ed.), *Reducing prejudice and discrimination.* Mahwah, NJ: Erlbaum.

Pettit, G. S., Bakshi, A., Dodge, K. A., & Coie, J. D. (1990). The emergence of social dominance in young boys' play groups: Developmental differences and behavior correlates. *Developmental Psychology, 26,* 1017–1025.

Pettit, G. S., & Dodge, K. A. (2003). Violent children: Bridging development, intervention, and public policy. *Developmental Psychology, 39,* 187–188.

Pettit, G. S., Laird, R. D., Dodge, K.A., Bates, J. E., & Criss, M. M. (2001). Antecedents and behavior-problem outcomes of parental monitoring and psychological control in early adolescence. *Child Development, 72,* 583–598.

Phelps, E., & Damon, W. (1989). Problem solving with equals: Peer collaboration as a context for learning mathematics and spatial concepts. *Journal of Educational Psychology, 4,* 639–646.

Phillips, D. A. (1984). The illusion of incompetence among academically competent children. *Child Development, 55,* 2000–2016.

Phillips, D. A. (1987). Socialization of perceived academic competence among highly competent children. *Child Development, 58,* 1308–1320.

Phillips, D. A., & Zimmerman, M. (1990). The developmental course of perceived competence and incompetence among competent children. In R. J. Sternberg & J. Kolligian (Eds.), *Competence considered.* New Haven, CT: Yale University Press.

Phillips, R. B., Sharma, R., Premachandra, B. R., Vaughn, A. J., & Reyes-Lee, M. (1996). Intrauterine exposure to cocaine: Effect on neurobehavior of neonates. *Infant Behavior and Development, 19,* 71–81.

Phinney, J. S. (1993). A three stage model of ethnic identity development in adolescence. In M. E. Bernal & G. P. Knight (Eds.), *Ethnic identity: Formation and transmission among Hispanics and other minorities.* Albany: SUNY Press.

Phinney, J. S., & Kohatsu, E. L. (1997). Ethnic and racial development and mental health. In J. Schulenberg, J. L. Maggs, & K. Hurrelmann (Eds.), *Health risks and developmental transitions during adolescence.* Cambridge: Cambridge University Press.

Piaget, J. (1926). *The language and thought of the child.* New York: Harcourt Brace.

Piaget, J. (1929). *The child's conception of the world.* London: Routledge & Kegan Paul.

Piaget, J. (1932). *The moral judgment of the child.* London: Routledge and Kegan Paul.

Piaget, J. (1951). *Play, dreams, and imitation in childhood.* New York: Norton.

Piaget, J. (1952). *The origins of intelligence in children.* New York: International Universities Press.

Piaget, J. (1954). *The construction of reality in the child.* New York: Basic Books.

Piaget, J. (1957). Logique et equilibre dans les comportements du sujet. In L. Apostel, B. Mandelbrot, & J. Piaget (Eds.), *Etudes d'epistemologie genetique* (Vol. 2). Paris: Presses Universitaires de France.

Piaget, J. (1964). Development and learning. In R. E. Ripple & V. N. Rockcastle (Eds.), *Piaget rediscovered.* Ithaca, NY: Cornell University Press.

Piaget, J. (1968). *On the development of memory and identity.* Barre, MA: Clark University Press and Barre Publishers.

Piaget, J. (1969). *The child's conception of time.* London: Routledge & Kegan Paul.

Piaget, J. (1970). *The child's conception of movement and speed.* London: Routledge & Kegan Paul.

Piaget, J. (1971). *Science of education and the psychology of the child.* New York: Viking.

Piaget, J. (1972). Intellectual evolution from adolescence to adulthood. *Human Development, 15,* 1–12.

Piaget, J. (1976). *To understand is to invent: The future of education.* New York: Penguin.

Piaget, J. (1977a). Les operations logiques et la vie sociale. In *Etudes Sociologiques.* Geneva, Switzerland: Librairie Droz. (Original work published in 1945.)

Piaget, J. (1977b). *The development of thought: Equilibration of cognitive structures.* New York: Wiley.

Piaget, J. (1979). Correspondence and transformation. In F. B. Murray (Ed.), *The impact of Piagetian theory.* Baltimore: University Park Press.

Piaget, J. (1980). Recent studies in genetic epistemology. *Cahiers Foundation Archives, Jean Piaget,* No. 1.

Piaget, J. (1983). Piaget's theory. In P. H. Mussen (Series Ed.) & W. Kessen (Vol. Ed.), *Handbook of child psychology: Vol. 1. History, theory, and methods* (4th ed.). New York: Wiley.

Piaget, J., & Inhelder, B. (1956). *The child's conception of space.* London: Routledge & Kegan Paul.

Piaget, J., & Inhelder, B. (1973). *Memory and intelligence.* New York: Basic Books.

Piaget, J., & Inhelder, B. (1974). *The child's construction of quantities.* London: Routledge & Kegan Paul.

Piaget, J., Inhelder, B., & Szeminska, A. (1960). *The child's conception of geometry.* New York: Basic Books.

Piaget, J., & Szeminska, A. (1952). *The child's conception of number.* New York: Basic Books.

Pianta, R. C. (1999). *Enhancing relationships between children and teachers.* Washington, DC: American Psychological Association.

Pick, H. L. Jr. (1992). Eleanor J. Gibson: Learning to perceive and perceiving to learn. *Developmental Psychology, 28,* 787–794.

Pillard, R. C. (1990). The Kinsey scale: Is it familial? In D. P. McWhirter, S. A. Sanders, & J. M. Reinsch (Eds.), *Homosexuality/heterosexuality: Concepts of sexual orientation. The Kinsey Institute series, Vol. 2.* New York: Oxford University Press.

Pillemer, D. B., Picariello, M. L., & Pruett, J. C. (1994). Very long-term memories of a salient preschool event. *Applied Cognitive Psychology, 8,* 95–106.

Pine, J. M., Lieven, E. V. M., & Rowland, C. F. (1997). Stylistic variation at the "single-word stage": Relations between maternal speech characteristics and children's vocabulary composition and usage. *Child Development, 68,* 807–819.

Pine, K. J., & Messer, D. J. (1998), Group collaboration effects and the explicitness of children's knowledge. *Cognitive Development, 13,* 109–126.

Pinker, S. (1987). The bootstrapping problem in language acquisition. In B. MacWhinney (Ed.), *Mechanisms of language acquisition.* Hillsdale, NJ: Erlbaum.

Pinker, S. (1994). *The language instinct: How the mind creates language.* New York: William Morrow.

Pinker, S. (1999). *Words and rules.* New York: HarperCollins.

Pinto, A., Folkers, E., & Sines, J. O. (1991). Dimensions of behavior and home environment in school-age children: India and the United States. *Journal of Cross-Cultural Psychology, 22,* 491–508.

Pipp, S. (1990). Sensorimotor and representational internal working models of self, other, and relationship: Mechanisms of connection and separation. In D. Cicchetti & M. Beeghly (Eds.), *The self in transition: Infancy to childhood.* Chicago: University of Chicago Press.

Pipp, S. (1993). Infants' knowledge of self, other, and relationship. In U. Neisser (Ed.), *Ecological and interpersonal knowledge of self.* New York: Cambridge University Press.

Pipp, S., Easterbrooks, M. A., & Harmon, R. J. (1992). The relation between attachment and knowledge of self and mother in one- to three-year-old infants. *Child Development, 63,* 738–750.

Pipp, S., Fischer, K. W., & Jennings, S. (1987). Acquisition of self- and mother knowledge in infancy. *Developmental Psychology, 23,* 86–96.

Pipp-Siegel, S., & Foltz, C. (1997). Toddlers' acquisition of self/other knowledge: Ecological and interpersonal aspects of self and other. *Child Development, 68,* 69–79.

Pleck, J. H. (1997). Paternal involvement: Levels, sources, and consequences. In M. E. Lamb (Ed.), *The role of fathers in child development* (3rd ed.). New York: Wiley.

Plomin, R. (1990). *Nature and nurture.* Belmont, CA: Wadsworth.

Plomin, R. (1994). *Genes and experience: The interplay between nature and nurture.* Thousand Oaks, CA: Sage.

Plomin, R. (1995). Molecular genetics and psychology. *Current Directions in Psychological Science, 4,* 114–117.

Plomin, R. (2000a). Behavioral genetics. In M. Bennett (Ed.), *Developmental psychology: Achievements and prospects.* Philadelphia: Psychology Press.

Plomin, R. (2000b). Behavioral genetics in the 21st century. *International Journal of Behavioral Development, 24,* 30–34.

Plomin, R., DeFries, J. C., McClearn, G. E., & Rutter, M. (1997). *Behavioral genetics* (3rd ed.). New York: W. H. Freeman.

Plomin, R., Emde, R. N., Braungart, J. M., Campos, J., Corley, R., Fulker, D. W., et al. (1993). Genetic change and continuity from fourteen to twenty months: The MacArthur Longitudinal Twin Study. *Child Development, 64,* 1354–1376.

Plomin, R., Fulker, D. W., Corley, R., & DeFries, J. C. (1997b). Nature, nurture, and cognitive development from 1 to 16 years: A parent–offspring adoption study. *Psychological Science, 8,* 442–447.

Plomin, R., Reiss, D., Hetherington, E. M., & Howe, G. W. (1994). Nature and nurture: Genetic contributions to measures of the family environment. *Developmental Psychology, 30,* 32–43.

Plomin, R., & Rutter, M. (1998). Child development, molecular genetics, and what to do with genes once they are found. *Child Development, 69,* 1223–1242.

Plomin, R., & Walker, S. O. (2003). Genetics and educational psychology. *British Journal of Educational Psychology, 73,* 3–14.

Plumert, J. M. (1995). Relations between children's overestimation of their physical abilities and accident proneness. *Developmental Psychology, 31,* 866–876.

Polivy, J., & Herman, C. P. (2002). Causes of eating disorders. *Annual Review of Psychology, 53,* 187–213.

Pollack, W. (1998). *Real boys: Rescuing our sons from the myths of boyhood.* New York: Random House.

Pollitt, E., Golub, M., Gorman, K., Grantham-McGregor, S., Levitsky, D., Schurch, B., et al. (1996). A reconceptualization of the effects of undernutrition on children's biological, psychosocial, and behavioral development. *Social Policy Report: Society for Research in Child Development, 10,* 1–31.

Pollitt, E., Gorman, K., Engle, P., Martorell, R., & Rivera, J. (1993). Early supplementary feeding and cognition: Effects over two decades. *Monographs of the Society for Research in Child Development, 58*(6, Serial No. 235).

Pomerantz, E. M., Ruble, D. N., Frey, K. S., & Greulich, F. (1995). Meeting goals and confronting conflict: Children's changing perceptions of social comparison. *Child Development, 66,* 723–738.

Pomerleau, A., Bolduc, D., Malcuit, G., & Cossette, L. (1990). Pink or blue: Environmental gender stereotypes in the first two years of life. *Sex Roles, 22,* 359–367.

Pomerleau, A., Malcuit, G., & Sabatier, C. (1991). Child-rearing practices and parental beliefs in three cultural groups of Montreal: Québècois, Vietnamese, Haitian. In M. H. Bornstein (Ed.), *Cultural approaches to parenting.* Hillsdale, NJ: Erlbaum.

Poole, D. A., & Lindsay, D. S. (2002). Children's suggestibility in the forensic context. In M. L. Eisen, J. A. Quas, & G. S. Goodman (Eds.), *Memory and suggestibility in the forensic context.* Mahwah, NJ: Erlbaum.

Porter, R. H., Balogh, R. D., & Makin, J. W. (1988). Olfactory influences on mother-infant interaction. In C. Rovee-Collier & L. P. Lipsitt (Eds.), *Advances in infancy research* (Vol. 5). Norwood, NJ: Ablex.

Posada, G., Waters, E., Crowell, J. A., & Lay, K. (1995). Is it easier to use a secure mother as a secure base? Attachment Q-sort correlates of the Adult Attachment Interview. In E. Waters, B. E. Vaughn, G. Posada, & K. Kondo-Ikemura (Eds.), *Caregiving, cultural, and cognitive perspectives on secure-base behavior and working models. Monographs of the Society for Research in Child Development, 60*(2–3, Serial No. 244).

Posner, M. C., Petersen, S. E., Fox, P. T., & Raichley, M. E. (1988). Localization of cognitive operations in the human brain. *Science, 240,* 1627–1631.

Post, S. G., Underwood, L. G., Schoss, J. P., & Hurlbut, W. B. (Eds.). (2002). *Altruism and altruistic love: Science, philosophy, and religion in dialogue.* London: Oxford University Press.

Poulin, F., Cillessen, A. H. N., Hubbard, J. A., Coie, J. D., Dodge, K. A., & Schwartz, D. (1997). Children's friends and behavioral similarity in two social contexts. *Social Development, 6,* 224–236.

Poulin-Dubois, D., Graham, S., & Sippola, L. (1995). Early lexical development: The contribution of parental labeling and infants' categorization abilities. *Journal of Child Language, 22,* 325–343.

Poulin-Dubois, D., Serbin, L. A., Eichstedt, J. A., Sen, M. G., & Beissel, C. F. (2002). Men don't put on make-up: Toddlers' knowledge of the gender stereotyping of household activities. *Social Development, 11,* 166–181.

Poulin-Dubois, D., Serbin, L. A., Ken-Yon, B., & Derbyshire, A. (1994). Infants' intermodal knowledge about gender. *Developmental Psychology, 30,* 436–442.

Poulson, C. L., & Nunes, L. R. P. (1988). The infant vocal-conditioning literature: A theoretical and methodological review. *Journal of Experimental Child Psychology, 46,* 438–450.

Povinelli, D. J. (1995). The unduplicated self. In P. Rochat (Ed.), *The self in infancy. Theory and research.* Amsterdam: Elsevier.

Povinelli, D. J. (2001). The self: Elevated in consciousness and extended in time. In C. Moore & K. Lemmon (Eds.), *The self in time: Developmental perspectives.* Mahwah, NJ: Erlbaum.

Povinelli, D. J., & Bering, J. M. (2002). The mentality of apes revisited. *Current Directions in Psychological Science, 11,* 115–119.

Powell, G. F., Brasel, J. A., & Blizzard, R. M. (1967). Emotional deprivation and growth retardation simulating ideopathic hypopituitarism: I. Clinical evaluation of the syndrome. *New England Journal of Medicine, 276,* 1271–1278.

Power, T. G. (2000). *Play and exploration in children and animals.* Mahwah, NJ: Erlbaum.

Powlishta, K. K. (1995). Intergroup processes in childhood: Social categorization and sex role development. *Developmental Psychology, 31,* 781–788.

Powlishta, K. K., Sen, M. G., Serbin, L. A., Poulin-DuBois, D., & Eichstedt, J. A. (2001). From infancy

through middle childhood: The role of social and cognitive factors in becoming gendered. In R. K. Unger (Ed.), *Handbook of the psychology of women and gender.* New York: Wiley.

Prader, A., Tanner, J. M., & Von Harnack, G. A. (1963). Catch up growth following illness or starvation. *Journal of Pediatrics, 62,* 646–659.

Pratt, M. W., Kerig, P., Cowan, P. A., & Cowan, C. P. (1988). Mothers and fathers teaching 3-year-olds: Authoritative parenting and adult scaffolding of young children's learning. *Developmental Psychology, 24,* 832–839.

Prencipe, A., & Helwig, C. C. (2002). The development of reasoning about the teaching of values in school and family contexts. *Child Development, 73,* 841–856.

Pressley, M. (1992). How *not* to study strategy discovery. *American Psychologist, 47,* 1240–1241.

Pressley, M., Borkowski, J. G., & O'Sullivan, J. (1985). Children's metamemory and the teaching of memory strategies. In D. L. Forrest-Pressley, G. E. MacKinnon, & T. G. Waller (Eds.), *Metacognition, cognition, and human performance: Vol. 1. Theoretical perspectives.* New York: Academic Press.

Pressley, M., Forrest-Pressley, D., & Elliot-Faust, D. J. (1988). What is strategy instructional enrichment and how to study it: Illustrations from research on children's prose memory and comprehension. In F. E. Weinert & M. Perlmutter (Eds.), *Memory development: Universal changes and individual differences.* Hillsdale, NJ: Erlbaum.

Pressley, M., Levin, J. R., & Bryant, S. L. (1983). Memory and strategy instruction during adolescence: When is explicit instruction needed? In M. Pressley & J. R. Levin (Eds.), *Cognitive strategy research: Psychological foundations.* New York: Springer-Verlag.

Price, J. M. (1996). Friendship of maltreated children and adolescents: Contexts for expressing and modifying relationship history. In W. M. Bukowski, A. F. Newcomb, & W. H. Hartup (Eds.), *The company they keep.* New York: Cambridge University Press.

Price-Williams, D., Gordon, W., & Ramirez, M. (1969). Skill and conservation: A study of pottery-making children. *Developmental Psychology, 1,* 769.

Prior, M., Smart, M. A., Sanson, A., & Oberklaid, F. (1993). Sex differences in psychological adjustment from infancy to 8 years. *Journal of the Academy of Child and Adolescent Psychiatry, 32,* 291–304.

Pullybank, J., Bisanz, J., Scott, C., & Champion, M. A. (1985). Developmental invariance in the effects of functional self-knowledge on memory. *Child Development, 56,* 1447–1454.

Putallaz, M., & Wasserman, A. (1990). Children's entry behavior. In S. R. Asher & J. D. Coie (Eds.), *Peer rejection in childhood.* New York: Cambridge University Press.

Putnam, S. P., Sanson, A. V., & Rothbart, M. K. (2002). Child temperament and parenting. In M. H. Bornstein (Ed.), *Handbook of parenting* (2nd ed., Vol. 1). Mahwah, NJ: Erlbaum.

Pynoos, R., Frederick, C., & Nader, K. (1987). Life threat and post-traumatic stress in school-age children. *Archives of General Psychiatry, 44,* 1057–1063.

Pynoos, R., Goenjian, A., Tashjian, M., Krakashian, M., Manjikian, A., Manoukian, G., et al. (1993). Post-traumatic stress reactions in children after the 1988 Armenian earthquake. *British Journal of Psychiatry, 163,* 239–247.

Quas, J. A., Goodman, G. S., Bidrose, S., Pipe, M., Craw, S., & Ablin, D. S. (1999). Emotion and memory: Children's long-term remembering, forgetting, and suggestibility. *Journal of Experimental Child Psychology, 72,* 235–270.

Quiggle, N. L., Garber, J., Panak, W. F., & Dodge, K. A. (1992). Social information processing in aggressive and depressed children. *Child Development, 63,* 1305–1320.

Quinn, P. C. (1999). Development of recognition and categorization of objects and their spatial relations in young

infants. In L. Balter & C. S. Tamis-Monda (Eds.), *Child psychology: A handbook of contemporary issues.* Philadelphia: Psychology Press.

Quinn, P. C., & Eimas, P. D. (1996). Perceptual organization and categorization in young infants. In C. K. Rovee-Collier & L. P. Lipsitt (Eds.), *Advances in infancy research* (Vol. 10). Norwood, NJ: Ablex.

Rabain-Jamin, J. (1984). Language and socialization of the child in African families living in France. In P. M. Greenfield & R. R. Cocking (Eds.), *Cross-cultural roots of minority child development.* Hillsdale, NJ: Erlbaum.

Radford, A. (1990). *Syntactic theory and the acquisition of English syntax: The nature of early child grammars of English.* Oxford, England: Blackwell.

Radke-Yarrow, M., McCann, K., DeMulder, E., & Belmont, B. (1995). Attachment in the context of high-risk conditions. *Development and Psychopathology, 7,* 247–265.

Radke-Yarrow, M., & Zahn-Waxler, C. (1986). The role of familial factors in the development of prosocial behavior: Research findings and questions. In D. Olweus, J. Block, & M. Radke-Yarrow (Eds.), *Development of antisocial and prosocial behavior.* Orlando, FL: Academic Press.

Radziszewska, B., & Rogoff, B. (1991). Children's guided participation in planning imaginary errands with skilled adults or peer partners. *Developmental Psychology, 27,* 381–389.

Rakic, P. (1988). Specifications of cerebral cortical areas. *Science, 241,* 170–176.

Ramey, C. T., Campbell, F. A., Burchinal, M., Skinner, M. L., Gardner, D. M., & Ramey, S. L. (2000). Persistent effects of early childhood education on high-risk children and their mothers. *Applied Developmental Psychology, 4,* 2–14.

Ramey, C. T., & Ramey, S. L. (1998). Early intervention and early experience. *American Psychologist, 53,* 109–120.

Ramey, C. T., Ramey, S. L., & Lanzi, R. G. (2001). Intelligence and experience. In R. J. Sternberg & E. L. Grigorenko (Eds.), *Environmental effects on cognitive abilities.* Mahwah, NJ: Erlbaum.

Ramsay, C., & Lewis, M. (2001). Temperament, stress, and soothing. In T. D. Wachs & G. A. Kohnstamm (Eds.), *Temperament in context.* Mahwah, NJ: Erlbaum.

Ramsey, P. G. (1991). *Making friends in school: Promoting peer relationships in early childhood.* New York: Teachers College Press.

Rapoport, J. L., Buchsbaum, M. S., Zahn, T. P., Weingartner, H., Ludlow, D., & Mikkelson, E. J. (1978). Dextroamphetamine: Cognitive and behavioral effects in normal prepubertal boys. *Science, 199,* 560–563.

Raskin, P. A., & Israel, A. C. (1981). Sex-role imitation in children: Effects of sex of child, sex of model, and sex-role appropriateness of modeled behavior. *Sex Roles, 7,* 1067–1077.

Ratner, N. B. (1988). Patterns of parental vocabulary selection in speech to very young children. *Journal of Child Language, 15,* 481–492.

Raver, C. C. (1996). Relations between social contingency in mother-child interaction and 2-year-olds' social competence. *Developmental Psychology, 32,* 850–859.

Ravn, K. E., & Gelman, S. A. (1984). Rule usage in children's understanding of "big" and "little." *Child Development, 55,* 2141–2150.

Rawlins, W. K. (1992). *Friendship matters: Communication, dialectics, and the life course.* New York: Aldine de Gruyter.

Rayner, K., Foorman, B. R., Perfetti, C. A., Pesetsky, D., & Seidenberg, M. S. (2001). How psychological science informs the teaching of reading. *Psychological Science in the Public Interest, 2,* 31–74.

Recht, D. R., & Leslie, L. (1980). Effect of prior knowledge on good and poor readers' memory of text. *Journal of Educational Psychology, 80,* 16–20.

Reddy, V. (1999). Prelinguistic communication. In M. Barrett (Ed.), *The development of language*. Hove, UK: Psychology Press.

Redlinger, W. E., & Park, T. (1980). Language mixing in young bilinguals. *Journal of Child Language, 7*, 337–352.

Reese, E., & Fivush, R. (1993). Parental styles of talking about the past. *Developmental Psychology, 29*, 596–606.

Reid, J. B. (1993). Prevention of conduct disorder before and after school entry: Relating interventions to developmental findings. *Development and Psychopathology, 5*, 243–262.

Reid, M., Landesman, S., Treder, R., & Jaccard, J. (1989). "My Family and Friends": Six- to twelve-year-old children's perceptions of social support. *Child Development, 60*, 896–910.

Reid, P. T., & Trotter, K. H. (1993). Children's self-presentations with infants: Gender and ethnic comparisons. *Sex Roles, 29*, 171–181.

Reinisch, J. M., & Sanders, S. A. (1992). Prenatal hormonal contributions to sex differences in human cognitive and personality development. In A. A. Gerall & H. Moltz (Eds.), *Sexual differentiation. Handbook of behavioral neurobiology* (Vol. 11). New York: Plenum Press.

Reinisch, J. M., Ziemba-Davis, M., & Sanders, S. A. (1991). Hormonal contributions to sexual dimorphic behavioral development in humans. *Psychoneuroendocrinology, 16*, 213–278.

Reisman, J. E. (1987). Touch, motion and perception. In P. Salapatek & L. Cohen (Eds.), *Handbook of infant perception: Vol. 1. From sensation to perception*. New York: Academic Press.

Reiss, D., Neiderhiser, J. M., Hetherington, E. M., & Plomin, R. (2000). *The relationship code: Deciphering genetic and social patterns in adolescent development*. Cambridge, MA: Harvard University Press.

Reissland, N. (1988). Neonatal imitation in the first hour of life: Observations in rural Nepal. *Developmental Psychology, 24*, 464–469.

Repacholi, B. M. (1998). Infants' use of attentional cues to identify the referent of another person's emotional expression. *Developmental Psychology, 34*, 1017–1025.

Repacholi, B. M., & Gopnik, A. (1997). Early reasoning about desires: Evidence from 14- and 18-month-olds. *Developmental Psychology, 33*, 12–21.

Repetti, R. L. (1996). The effects of perceived daily social and academic failure experiences on school-age children's subsequent interactions with parents. *Child Development, 67*, 1467–1482.

Rescorla, L. A. (1980). Overextension in early language development. *Journal of Child Language, 7*, 321–335.

Rescorla, L. A. (1981). Category development in early language. *Journal of Child Language, 8*, 225–238.

Rest, J., Narvaez, D., Bebeau, M. J., & Thoma, S. J. (1999). *Postconventional moral thinking: A neo-Kohlbergian approach*. Mahwah, NJ: Erlbaum.

Reznick, J. S., Gibbons, J. L., Johnson, M. O., & Mcdonough, P. M. (1989). Behavioral inhibition in a normative sample. In J. S. Reznick (Ed.), *Perspectives on behavioral inhibition*. Chicago: University of Chicago Press.

Reznick, J. S., Kagan, J., Snidman, N., Gersten, M., Baak, K., & Rosenberg, A. (1986). Inhibited and uninhibited behavior: A follow-up study. *Child Development, 51*, 660–680.

Rheingold, H. L. (1982). Little children's participation in the work of adults, a nascent prosocial behavior. *Child Development, 53*, 114–125.

Rheingold, H. L., & Cook, K. V. (1975). The contents of boys' and girls' rooms as an index of parents' behavior. *Child Development, 46*, 459–463.

Rheingold, H. L., Hay, D. F., & West, M. J. (1976). Sharing in the second year of life. *Child Development, 47*, 1148–1156.

Rholes, W. S., & Lane, J. W. (1985). Consistency between cognitions and behavior: Cause and consequence of cognitive moral development. In J. B. Pryor & J. D. Day (Eds.), *The development of social cognition*. New York: Springer-Verlag.

Riccio, C. A., Hynd, G. W., Cohen, M. J., & Gonzalez, J. J. (1993). Neurological basis of attention deficit hyperactivity disorder. *Exceptional Children, 60*, 118–124.

Ricciuti, H. N. (1993). Nutrition and mental development. *Current Directions in Psychological Science, 2*, 43–46.

Rice, M. L., & Woodsmall, L. (1988). Lessons from television: Children's word learning when viewing. *Child Development, 59*, 420–429.

Richards, D. S., Frentzen, B., Gerhardt, K. J., McCann, M. E., & Abrams, R. M. (1992). Sound levels in the human uterus. *Obstetrics and Gynecology, 80*, 186–190.

Rideout, V. J., Foehr, U. G., Roberts, D. F., & Brodie, M. (1999). *Kids and media at the new millenium. Executive summary*. Menlo Park, CA: Kaiser Family Foundation.

Riese, M. L. (1987). Temperament stability between the neonatal period and 24 months. *Developmental Psychology, 23*, 216–222.

Rieser, J., Yonas, A., & Wikner, K. (1976). Radial localization of odors by human newborns. *Child Development, 47*, 856–859.

Riesman, P. (1992). *First find your child a good mother*. New Brunswick, NJ: Rutgers University Press.

Rigby, K., & Slee, P. (1993). Children's attitudes toward victims. In D. Tattum (Ed.), *Understanding and managing bullying*. Oxford: Heinemann School Management.

Ritts, V., Patterson, M. L., & Tubbs, M. E. (1992). Expectations, impressions, and judgments of physically attractive students: A review. *Review of Educational Research, 62*, 413–426.

Rivera, S. M., Wakeley, A., & Langer, J. (1999). The drawbridge phenomenon: Representational reasoning or perceptual preference? *Developmental Psychology, 35*, 427–435.

Robbins, W. J., Brady, S., Hogan, A. G., Jackson, C. M., & Greene, C. W. (1928). *Growth*. New Haven, CT: Yale University Press.

Roberts, D. F., Foehr, U. G., Rideout, V. J., & Brodie, M. (1999*). Kids and media at the new millenium: A comprehensive national analysis of children's media use*. Menlo Park, CA: Kaiser Family Foundation.

Roberts, R. J., Brown, D., Wiebke, S., & Haith, M. M. (1991). A computer-automated laboratory for studying complex perception-action skills. *Behavior Research Methods and Instrumentation, 23*, 493–504.

Robinson, C. C., & Morris, J. T. (1986). The gender-stereotyped nature of Christmas toys received by 36-, 48-, and 60-month old children: A comparison between nonrequested vs. requested toys. *Sex Roles, 15*, 21–32.

Robinson, E. J. (1981). The child's understanding of inadequate messages and communication failure: A problem of ignorance or egocentrism? In W. P. Dickson (Ed.), *Children's oral communication skills*. New York: Academic Press.

Robinson, J. L., Reznick, J. S., Kagan, J., & Corley, R. (1992). The heritability of inhibited and uninhibited behavior: A twin study. *Developmental Psychology, 28*, 1030–1037.

Rochat, P. (1989). Object manipulation and exploration in 2- to 5-month-old infants. *Developmental Psychology, 25*, 871–884.

Rochat, P. (1993). Hand–mouth coordination in the newborn: Morphology, determinants, and early development of a basic act. In G. J. P. Savelsbergh (Ed.), *The development of coordination in infancy*. London: Elsevier.

Rochat, P. (2001). *The infant's world*. Cambridge, MA: Harvard University Press.

Rochat, P., & Morgan, R. (1995). Spatial determinants in the perception of self-produced leg movements by 3- to 5-month-old infants. *Developmental Psychology, 31*, 626–636.

Rochat, P., & Striano, T. (2002). Who's in the mirror? Self-other discrimination in specular images by four- and nine-month-old infants. *Child Development, 73*, 35–46.

Rode, S., Chang, P., Fisch, R., & Sroufe, L. A. (1981). Attachment patterns of infants separated at birth. *Developmental Psychology, 17*, 188–191.

Roeser, R. W., Eccles, J. S., & Sameroff, A. J. (2000). School as a context for early adolescents' academic and social-emotional adjustment: A summary of research findings. *Elementary School Journal, 100*, 443–471.

Roggman, L. A., Langlois, J. H., Hubbs-Tait, L., & Rieser-Danner, L. A. (1994). Infant day-care, attachment, and the "file drawer problem." *Child Development, 65*, 1429–1443.

Rogoff, B. (1981). Schooling and the development of cognitive skills. In H. C. Triandis & A. Heron (Eds.), *Handbook of cross-cultural psychology: Vol. 4. Developmental psychology*. Boston: Allyn & Bacon.

Rogoff, B. (1990). *Apprenticeship in thinking*. New York: Oxford University Press.

Rogoff, B. (1998). Cognition as a collaborative process. In W. Damon (Series Ed.) & D. Kuhn & R. S. Siegler (Vol. Eds.), *Handbook of child psychology: Vol. 2. Cognition, perception, and language* (5th ed.). New York: Wiley.

Rogoff, B. (2003). *The cultural nature of human development*. New York: Oxford University Press.

Rogoff, B., Baker-Sennett, J., Lacasa, P. & Goldsmith, D. (1995). Development through participation in sociocultural activity. In J. J. Goodnow, P. J. Miller, & F. Kessel (Eds.), *New directions for child development: No. 67. Cultural practices as contexts for development*. San Francisco: Jossey-Bass.

Rogoff, B., Baker-Sennett, J., & Matusov, E. (1994). Considering the concept of planning. In M. M. Haith, J. B. Benson, R. J. Roberts Jr., & B. P. Pennington (Eds.), *The development of future-oriented processes*. Chicago: University of Chicago Press.

Rogoff, B., & Chavajay, P. (1995). What's become of research on the cultural basis of cognitive development? *American Psychologist, 50*, 859–887.

Rogoff, B., Ellis, S., & Gardner, W. (1984). Adjustment of adult-child instruction according to child's age and task. *Developmental Psychology, 20*, 193–199.

Rogoff, B., & Gauvain, M. (1986). A method for the analysis of patterns, illustrated with data on mother-child instructional interaction. In J. Valsiner (Ed.), *The role of the individual subject in scientific psychology*. New York: Plenum.

Rogoff, B., Mistry, J., Goncu, A., & Mosier, C. (1993). Guided participation in cultural activity by toddlers and caregivers. *Monographs of the Society for Research in Child Development, 58*(Serial No. 236).

Rogoff, B., Paradise, R., Arauz, R. M., Correa Chavez, M., & Angelillo, C. (2003). Firsthand learning through intent participation. *Annual Review of Psychology, 54*, 175–203.

Rogoff, B., Topping, K., Baker-Sennett, J., & Lacasa, P. (2002). Mutual contributions of individuals, partners, and institutions: Planning to remember in Girl Scout cookie sales. *Social Development, 11*, 266–289.

Rogoff, B., & Waddell, K. (1982). Memory for information organized in a scene by children from two cultures. *Child Development, 53*, 1224–1228.

Rogosch, F. A., Cicchetti, D., Shields, A., & Toth, S. L. (1995). Parenting dysfunction in child maltreatment. In M. H. Bornstein (Ed.), *Handbook of parenting: Vol. 4. Applied and practical parenting*. Mahwah, NJ: Erlbaum.

Roid, G. (2003). *Stanford-Binet Intelligence Scales* (5th ed.). Chicago: Riverside Publishing.

Roisman, G. I., Madsen, S. D., Hennighausen, K. H., & Collins, W. A. (2001). The coherence of dyadic behavior across parent-child and romantic relationships as mediated by the internalized representation of experience. *Attachment and Human Development, 3,* 156–172.

Roland, A. (1988). *In search of self in India and Japan.* Princeton, NJ: Princeton University Press.

Rommetveit, R. (1979). On the architecture of intersubjectivity. In R. Rommetveit & R. M. Blakar (Eds.), *Studies of language, thought, and verbal communication.* New York: Academic Press.

Roopnarine, J. L. (1984). Sex-typed socialization in mixed-age preschool classrooms. *Child Development, 55,* 1078–1084.

Roopnarine, J. L., Hossain, Z., Fill, P., & Brophy, H. (1994). Play in the East Indian context. In J. L. Roopnarine, J. E. Johnson, & F. H. Hooper (Eds.), *Children's play in diverse cultures.* Albany: SUNY Press.

Roopnarine, J. L., Lasker, J., Sacks, M., & Stores, M. (1998). The cultural contexts of children's play. In O. N. Saracho & Spodek (Eds.), *Multiple perspectives on play in early childhood education.* Albany: State University of New York Press.

Rose, S. A. (1994). From hand to eye: Findings and issues in infant cross-modal transfer. In D. J. Lewkowicz & R. Lickliter (Eds.), *The development of intersensory perception: Comparative perspectives.* Hillsdale, NJ: Erlbaum.

Rose, S. A., & Feldman, J. F. (1995). Prediction of IQ and specific cognitive abilities at 11 years from infancy measures. *Developmental Psychology, 31,* 685–696.

Rose, S. A., Gottfried, A. W., & Bridger, W. H. (1981). Cross-modal transfer and information processing by the sense of touch in infancy. *Developmental Psychology, 17,* 90–98.

Rose, S. A., & Orlian, E. K. (1991). Asymmetries in cross-modal transfer. *Child Development, 62,* 706–718.

Rose, S. A., & Ruff, H. A. (1987). Cross-modal abilities in human infants. In J. D. Osofsky (Ed.), *Handbook of infant development* (2nd ed.). New York: Wiley.

Rosen, G. D., Galaburda, A. M., & Sherman, G. F. (1990). The ontogeny of anatomic asymmetry: Constraints derived from basic mechanisms. In A. B. Scheibel & A. F. Wechsler (Eds.), *Neurobiology of higher cognitive function.* New York: Guilford.

Rosen, K. S., & Rothbaum, F. (1993). Quality of parental caregiving and security of attachment. *Developmental Psychology, 29,* 358–367.

Rosen, T. S., & Johnson, H. L. (1988). Drug-addicted mothers, their infants, and SIDS. *Annals of the New York Academy of Sciences, 533,* 89–95.

Rosenbaum, J. F., Biederman, J., Bolduc-Murphy, E. A., & Faraone, S. V. (1993). Behavioral inhibition in childhood: A risk factor for anxiety disorders. *Harvard Review of Psychiatry, 1*(1), 2–16.

Rosenberg, M. (1985). Self-concept and psychological well-being in adolescence. In R. L. Leahy (Ed.), *The development of the self.* Orlando, FL: Academic Press.

Rosenberg, M. (1986a). *Conceiving the self.* Melbourne, FL: Krieger.

Rosenberg, M. (1986b). Self-concept from middle childhood through adolescence. In J. Suls (Ed.), *Psychological perspectives on the self* (Vol. 3). Hillsdale, NJ: Erlbaum.

Rosengren, K. S., & Braswell, G. (2001). Variability in children's reasoning. In H. W. Reese & R. Kail (Eds.), *Advances in child development and behavior* (Vol. 28). San Diego, CA: Academic Press.

Rosengren, K. S., Gelman, S. A., Kalish, C. W., & McCormick, M. (1991). As time goes by: Children's early understanding of growth in animals. *Child Development, 62,* 1302–1320.

Rosenshine, F., & Meister, C. (1994). Reciprocal teaching: A review of the research. *Review of Educational Research, 64,* 479–530.

Rosenstein, D., & Oster, H. (1988). Differential facial responses to four basic tastes in newborns. *Child Development, 59,* 1555–1568.

Rosenthal, R., & DiMatteo, M. R. (2001). Meta-Analysis: Recent developments in quantitative methods in literature reviews. *Annual Review of Psychology, 52,* 59–82.

Ross, D. S. (1972). *G. Stanley Hall: The psychologist as prophet.* Chicago: University of Chicago Press.

Ross, G. (1980). Categorization in 1- to 2-year-olds. *Developmental Psychology, 16,* 391–396.

Ross, H. S., & Lollis, S. P. (1987). Communication within infant social games. *Developmental Psychology, 23,* 241–248.

Ross, H. S., & Lollis, S. P. (1989). A social relations analysis of toddler peer relationships. *Child Development, 60,* 1082–1091.

Ross, J., Zinn, A., & McCauley, E. (2000). Neurodevelopmental and psychosocial aspects of Turner syndrome. *Mental Retardation and Developmental Disabilities Research Review, 6,* 135–141.

Ross, J. B., & McLaughlin, M. M. (Eds.). (1949). *The portable medieval reader.* New York: Viking Press.

Ross, S. A. (1971). A test of the generality of the effects of deviant preschool models. *Developmental Psychology, 4,* 262–267.

Rosso P. (1990). *Nutrition and metabolism in pregnancy.* New York: Oxford University Press.

Rothbart, M. K. (1989). Behavioral approach and inhibition. In J. S. Reznick (Ed.), *Perspectives on behavioral inhibition.* Chicago: The University of Chicago Press.

Rothbart, M. K., Ahadi, S. A., & Evans, D. E. (2000). Temperament and personality: Origins and outcomes. *Journal of Personality and Social Psychology, 78,* 122–135.

Rothbart, M. K., Ahadi, S. A., & Hershey, K. L. (1994). Temperament and social behavior in childhood. *Merrill-Palmer Quarterly, 40,* 21–39.

Rothbart, M. K., & Bates, J. E. (1998). Temperament. In W. Damon (Series Ed.) & N. Eisenberg (Vol. Ed.), *Handbook of child psychology: Vol. 3. Social, emotional, and personality development* (5th ed.). New York: Wiley.

Rothbart, M. K., Derryberry, D., & Hershey, K. (2000). Stability of temperament in childhood: Laboratory infant assessment to parent report at seven years. In V. J. Molfese & D. L. Molfese (Eds.), *Temperament and personality development across the life span.* Mahwah, NJ: Erlbaum.

Rothbart, M. K., & Goldsmith, H. H. (1985). Three approaches to the study of infant temperament. *Developmental Review, 5,* 237–260.

Rothbart, M. K., & Posner, M. I. (1985). Temperament and the development of self-regulation. In L. C. Hartledge & C. F. Telzrow (Eds.), *The neuropsychology of individual differences: A developmental perspective.* New York: Plenum.

Rothbart, M. K., Posner, M. I., & Hershey, K. L. (1995). Temperament, attention, and developmental psychopathology. In D. Cicchetti & D. J. Cohen (Eds.), *Manual of developmental psychopathology* (Vol. 1). New York: Wiley.

Rothbaum F., Pott, M., Azuma, H., Miyake, K., & Weisz, J. (2000). The development of close relationships in Japan and the United States: Paths of symbiotic harmony and generative tension. *Child Development, 71,* 1121–1142.

Rousseau, J. J. (1948). Emile. London: J. M. Dent. (Original work published 1762)

Rovee-Collier, C. K. (1987). Learning and memory in infancy. In J. Osofsky (Ed.), *Handbook of infant development* (2nd ed.). New York: Wiley.

Rovee-Collier, C. K. (1999). The development of infant memory. *Current Directions in Psychological Science, 8,* 80–85.

Rovee-Collier, C. K., Hartshorn, K., & DiRubbo, M. (1999). Long-term maintenance of infant memory. *Developmental Psychobiology, 35,* 91–102.

Rovee-Collier, C. K., & Hayne, H. (1987). Reactivation of infant memory: Implications for cognitive development. In H. W. Reese (Ed.), *Advances in child development and behavior* (Vol. 20). New York: Academic Press.

Rovee-Collier, C. K., & Shyi, G. (1992). A functional and cognitive analysis of infant long-term retention. In M. L. Howe, C. J. Brainerd, & V. F. Reyna (Eds.), *Development of long-term retention.* New York: Springer-Verlag.

Royer, J. M., Tronsky, L. N., Chan, Y., Jackson, S. J., & Marchant, H. III (1999). Math-fact retrieval and the cognitive mechanism underlying gender differences in math test performance. *Contemporary Educational Psychology, 24,* 181–266.

Rubenstein, A. J., Kalakanis, L., & Langlois, J. H. (1999). Infant preferences for attractive faces: A cognitive explanation. *Developmental Psychology, 35,* 848–855.

Rubenstein, J., & Howes, C. (1976). The effect of peers on toddler interaction with mother and toys. *Child Development, 47,* 597–605.

Rubin, J. Z., Provenzano, F. J., & Luria, Z. (1974). The eye of the beholder: Parents' views on sex of newborns. *American Journal of Orthopsychiatry, 44,* 512–519.

Rubin, K. H. (1988). *The social problem-solving test—revised.* Waterloo, Ontario: University of Waterloo Press.

Rubin, K. H. (1989). *The Play Observation Scale (POS).* Unpublished manuscript. University of Waterloo, Waterloo, Ontario.

Rubin, K. H. (1993). The Waterloo Longitudinal Project: Correlates and consequences of social withdrawal from childhood to adolescence. In K. H. Rubin & J. B. Asendorpf (Eds.), *Social withdrawal, inhibition, and shyness in childhood.* Hillsdale, NJ: Erlbaum.

Rubin, K. H., & Asendorpf, J. B. (Eds.). (1993). *Social withdrawal, inhibition, and shyness in childhood.* Hillsdale, NJ: Erlbaum.

Rubin, K. H., Bream, L., & Rose-Krasnor, L. (1991). Social problem solving and aggression in childhood. In D. J. Pepler & K. H. Rubin (Eds.), *The development and treatment of childhood aggression.* Hillsdale, NJ: Erlbaum.

Rubin, K. H., Bukowski, W., & Parker, J. G. (1998). Peer interactions, relationships, and groups. In W. Damon (Series Ed.) & N. Eisenberg (Vol. Ed.), *Handbook of child psychology: Vol. 3. Social, emotional, and personality development* (5th ed.). New York: Wiley.

Rubin, K. H., Burgess, K. B., & Coplan, R. J. (2002). Social withdrawal and shyness. In P. K. Smith & C. H. Hart (Eds.), *Blackwell handbook of childhood social development.* Madden, MA: Blackwell Publishers.

Rubin, K. H., Burgess, K. B., Dwyer, K. M., & Hastings, P. D. (2003). Predicting preschoolers' externalizing behaviors from toddler temperament, conflict, and maternal negativity. *Developmental Psychology, 39,* 164–176.

Rubin, K. H., Fein, G. G., & Vandenberg, B. (1983). Play. In P. H. Mussen (Series Ed.) & E. M. Hetherington (Vol. Ed.), *Handbook of child psychology: Vol. 4. Socialization, personality, and social development* (4th ed.). New York: Wiley.

Rubin, K. H., & Krasnor, L. R. (1986). Social-cognitive and social behavioral perspectives on problem solving. In M. Perlmutter (Ed.), *Minnesota symposia on child psychology: Vol. 19. Cognitive perspectives on children's social and behavioral development.* Hillsdale, NJ: Erlbaum.

Rubin, K. H., LeMare, L. J., & Lollis, S. (1990). Social withdrawal in childhood: Developmental pathways to peer rejection. In S. R. Asher & J. D. Coie (Eds.), *Peer rejection in childhood.* New York: Cambridge University Press.

Rubin, K. H., Lynch, D., Coplan, R., Rose-Krasnor, L., & Booth, C. L. (1994). "Birds of a feather . . .": Behavioral concordances and preferential personal attraction in children. *Child Development, 65,* 1778–1785.

Rubin, K. H., & Maioni, T. L. (1975). Play preference and its relationship to egocentrism, popularity and classification skills in preschoolers. *Merrill-Palmer Quarterly, 21,* 171–179.

Rubin, K. H., & Rose-Krasnor, L. (1992). Interpersonal problem solving and social competence in children. In W. B. Van Hasselt & M. Hersen (Eds.), *Handbook of social development.* New York: Plenum.

Rubin, K. H., Stewart, S. L., & Chen, X. (1995). Parents of aggressive and withdrawn children. In M. H. Bornstein (Ed.), *Handbook of parenting. Vol. 1. Children and parenting.* Mahwah, NJ: Erlbaum.

Rubin, K. H., Watson, K. S., & Jambor, T. W. (1978). Free-play behaviors in preschool and kindergarten children. *Child Development, 49,* 534–536.

Rubin, Z. (1980). *Children's friendships.* Cambridge, MA: Harvard University Press.

Ruble, D. N., & Dweck, C. S. (1995). Self-perceptions, person conceptions, and their development. In N. Eisenberg (Ed.), *Review of personality and social psychology: Vol. 15. Development and social psychology: The interface.* Thousand Oaks, CA: Sage.

Ruble, D. N., & Flett, G. L. (1988). Conflicting goals in self-evaluative information seeking: Developmental and ability level analyses. *Child Development, 59,* 97–106.

Ruble, D. N., & Frey, K. S. (1987). Social comparison and outcome evaluation in group contexts. In J. C. Masters & W. P. Smith (Eds.), *Social comparison, social justice, and relative deprivation.* Hillsdale, NJ: Erlbaum.

Ruble, D. N., & Frey, K. S. (1991). Changing patterns of behavior as skills are acquired: A functional model of self-evaluation. In J. Suls & T. A. Wills (Eds.), *Social comparison: Contemporary theory and research.* Hillsdale, NJ: Erlbaum.

Ruble, D. N., Grosovsky, E. H., Frey, K. S., & Cohen, R. (1990). Developmental changes and competence assessment. In A. K. Boggiano & T. S. Pittman (Eds.), *Achievement motivation.* New York: Cambridge University Press.

Ruble, D. N., & Martin, C. L. (1998). Gender development. In W. Damon (Series Ed.) & N. Eisenberg (Vol. Ed.), *Handbook of child psychology: Vol. 3. Social, emotional, and personality development* (5th ed.). New York: Wiley.

Ruble, D. N., & Stangor, C. (1986). Stalking the elusive schema: Insights from developmental and social-psychological analyses of gender schemas. *Social Cognition, 4,* 227–261.

Ruddy, M. G. (1993). Attention shifting and temperament at 5 months. *Infant Behavior and Development, 16,* 255–259.

Rudolph, K. D., Lambert, S. F., Clark, A. G., & Kurlakowsky, K. D. (2001). Negotiating the transition to middle school: The role of self-regulatory processes. *Child Development, 71,* 929–946.

Ruff, H. A., Capozzoli, M., & Weissberg, R. (1998). Age, individuality, and contexts as factors in sustained visual attention during the preschool years. *Developmental Psychology, 34,* 454–464.

Ruff, H. A., & Kohler, E. C. J. (1978). Tactual-visual transfer in six-month-old infants. *Infant Behavior and Development, 1,* 259–264.

Ruff, H. A., & Rothbart, M. K. (1996). *Attention in early development.* New York: Oxford University Press.

Ruffman, T., Perner, J., Naito, M., Parkin, L., & Clements, W. A. (1998). Older (but not younger) siblings facilitate false belief understanding. *Developmental Psychology, 34,* 161–174.

Rushton, J. P., Fulker, D. W., Neale, M. C., Nias, D. K. B., & Eysenck, H. J. (1986). Altruism and aggression: The heritability of individual differences. *Journal of Personality and Social Psychology, 50,* 1192–1198.

Russell, A., Mize, J., & Bissaker, K. (2002). Parent-child relationships. In P. K. Smith & C. H. Hart (Eds.), *Blackwell handbook of childhood social development.* Madden, MA: Blackwell Publishers.

Russell, A., & Saebel, J. (1997). Mother-son, mother-daughter, father-son, and father-daughter: Are they distinct relationships? *Developmental Review, 17,* 111–147.

Russell, G., & Russell, A. (1987). Mother–child and father–child relationships in middle childhood. *Child Development, 58,* 1573–1585.

Russell, J. (1982). Cognitive conflict, transmission and justification: Conservation attainment through dyadic interaction. *Journal of Genetic Psychology, 142,* 283–297.

Rust, J., Golombok, S., Hines, M., & Johnston, K. (2000). The role of brothers and sisters in the gender development of preschool children. *Journal of Experimental Child Psychology, 77,* 292–303.

Rutter, M. (1976). Maternal deprivation 1972–1978: New findings, new concepts, new approaches. *Child Development, 50,* 283–305.

Rutter, M. (1983). School effects on pupil progress: Research findings and policy implications. *Child Development, 54,* 1–29.

Rutter, M. (1987). Continuities and discontinuities from infancy. In J. D. Osofsky (Ed.), *Handbook of infant development* (2nd ed.). New York: Wiley.

Rutter, M. (2002). Nature, nurture, and development: From evangelism through science toward policy and practice. *Child Development, 73,* 1–21.

Rutter, M., & Caesar, P. (Eds.). (1991). *Biological risk factors for psychosocial disorders.* Cambridge: Cambridge University Press.

Rutter, M., MacDonald, H., Lecouteur, A., Harrington, R., Bolton, P., & Bailey, A. (1990). Genetic factors in child psychiatric disorders: II. Empirical findings. *Journal of Child Psychology and Psychiatry, 31,* 39–84.

Ryan, A. M. (2001). The peer group as a context for the development of young adolescent motivation and achievement. *Child Development, 72,* 1135–1150.

Rymer, R. (1994). *Genie: A scientific tragedy.* New York: Harper Collins.

Saarni, C. (1989). Children's understanding of strategic control of emotional expression in social transactions. In C. Saarni & P. L. Harris (Eds.), *Children's understanding of emotion.* Cambridge: Cambridge University Press.

Saarni, C. (1990). Emotional competence: How emotions and relationships become integrated. In R. A. Thompson (Ed.), *Nebraska symposium on motivation: Vol. 36. Socioemotional development.* Lincoln: University of Nebraska Press.

Saarni, C. (1999). *The development of emotional competence.* Guilford series on social and emotional development. New York: Guilford.

Saarni, C., Mumme, D., & Campos, J. J. (1998). Emotional development: Action, communication, and understanding. In W. Damon (Series Ed.) & N. Eisenberg (Vol. Ed.), *Handbook of child psychology: Vol. 3. Social, emotional, and personality development* (5th ed.). New York: Wiley.

Sachs, J. (2001). Communication development in infancy. In J. B. Gleason (Ed.), *The development of language* (5th ed.). Boston: Allyn and Bacon.

Sachs, J., & Devin, J. (1976). Young children's use of age-appropriate speech styles in social interaction and role-playing. *Journal of Child Language, 3,* 81–98.

Sachs, O. (1993, May 10). A neurologist's notebook: To see and not see. *New Yorker,* pp. 59–73.

Sadker, M., & Sadker, D. (1994). *Failing at fairness : How America's schools cheat girls.* New York: Scribner.

Sage, N. A., & Kindermann, T. A. (1999). Peer networks, behavior contingencies, and children's engagement in the classroom. *Merrill-Palmer Quarterly, 45,* 143–171.

Sagi, A., & Hoffman, M. L. (1976). Empathic distress in the newborn. *Developmental Psychology, 12,* 175–176.

Sagi, A., Lamb, M. E., Shoham, R., Dvir, R., & Lewkowicz, K. S. (1985). Parent–infant interaction in families on Israeli kibbutzim. *International Journal of Behavioral Development, 8,* 273–284.

Sagi, A., van IJzendoorn, M. H., Aviezer, O., Donnell, F., Koren-Karie, N., Joels, T., et al. (1995). Attachments in multiple-caregiver and multiple-infant environments: The case of the Israeli kibbutzim. In E. Waters, B. E. Vaughn, G. Posada, & K. Kondo-Ikemura (Eds.), Caregiving, cultural, and cognitive perspectives on secure-base behavior and working models. *Monographs of the Society for Research in Child Development, 60*(2–3, Serial No. 244).

Saigal, S., Hoult, L. A., Streiner, L. L., Stoskopf, F. L., & Rosenbaum, P. L. (2000). School difficulties in adolescence in a regional cohort of children who were extremely low birth weight. *Pediatrics, 105,* 325–331.

Salmivalli, C. (2001). Group view on victimization: Empirical findings and their implications. In J. Juvonen & S. Graham (Eds.), *Peer harassment in school: The plight of the vulnerable and victimized.* New York: Guilford.

Saltzstein, H. D., Weiner, A. S., Munk, J. J., Supraner, A., Blank, R., & Schwartz, R. P. (1987). Comparison between children's own moral judgments and those they attribute to adults. *Merrill-Palmer Quarterly, 33,* 33–51.

Sameroff, A. J., Seifer, R., Baldwin, A., & Baldwin, C. (1993). Stability of intelligence from preschool to adolescence: The influence of social and family risk factors. *Child Development, 64,* 80–97.

Samuels, C. A. (1986). Bases for the infant's developing self-awareness. *Human Development, 29,* 36–48.

Sandberg, S., Rutter, M., Pickles, A., McGuinness, D., & Angold, A. (2001). Do high-threat life events really provoke the onset of psychiatric disorder in children? *Journal of Child Psychology and Psychiatry, 42,* 523–532.

Sander, L. W., Snyder, P. A., Rosett, H. L., Lee, A., Gould, J. B., & Ouellette, E. (1977). Effects of alcohol intake during pregnancy on newborn state regulation: A progress report. *Alcoholism: Clinical and Experimental Research, 1,* 233–241.

Sanders, J., Koch, J., & Urso, J. (1997). *Gender equity right from the start.* Mahwah, NJ: Erlbaum;

Sanson, A., Hemphill, S. A., & Smart, D. (2002). Temperament in social development. In P. K. Smith & C. H. Hart (Eds.), *Blackwell handbook of childhood social development.* Malden, MA: Blackwell Publishers.

Sanson, A., Prior, M., & Kyrios, M. (1990). Contamination of measures in temperament research. *Merrill-Palmer Quarterly, 36,* 179–192.

Sanson, A., & Rothbart, M. K. (1995). Child temperament and parenting. In M. H. Bornstein (Ed.), *Handbook of parenting: Vol. 4. Applied and practical parenting.* Mahwah, NJ: Erlbaum.

Sanvitale, D., Saltzstein, H. D., & Fish, M. C. (1989). Moral judgments by normal and conduct-disordered preadolescent and adolescent boys. *Merrill-Palmer Quarterly, 35,* 463–481.

Sasanuma, S. (1980). Do Japanese show sex differences in brain asymmetry? Supplementary findings. *Behavioral and Brain Sciences, 3,* 247–248.

Savin-Williams, R. C. (1987). *Adolescence: An ethological perspective.* New York: Springer-Verlag.

Savin-Williams, R. C. (1998). *. . . and then I became gay: Young men's stories.* New York: Routledge.

Saxe, G. B. (1988). The mathematics of child street vendors. *Child Development, 59,* 415–425.

Saxe, G. B. (1991). *Culture and cognitive development: Studies in mathematical understanding.* Hillsdale, NJ: Erlbaum.

Saxe, G. B., & Moylan, T. (1982). The development of measurement operations among the Oksapmin of Papua New Guinea. *Child Development, 53,* 1242–1248.

Sayegh, Y., & Dennis, W. (1965). The effect of supplementary experiences upon the behavioral development of infants in institutions. *Child Development, 36,* 81–90.

Scarborough, H., & Wyckoff, J. (1986). Mother, I'd still rather do it myself: Some further non-effects of "motherese." *Journal of Child Language, 13,* 431–437.

Scarr, S. (1981). *Race, social class, and individual differences in IQ: New studies of old problems.* Hillsdale, NJ: Erlbaum.

Scarr, S. (1992). Developmental theories for the 1990s: Development and individual differences. *Child Development, 63,* 1–19.

Scarr, S. (1993). Biological and cultural diversity: The legacy of Darwin for development. *Child Development, 64,* 1333–1353.

Scarr, S. (1998). American child care today. *American Psychologist, 53,* 95–108.

Scarr, S., & Kidd, K. K. (1983). Developmental behavior genetics. In P. H. Mussen (Series Ed.) & M. M. Haith & J. J. Campos (Vol. Eds.), *Handbook of child psychology: Vol. 2. Infancy and developmental psychobiology* (4th ed.). \New York: Wiley.

Scarr, S., & McCartney, K. (1983). How people make their own environments: A theory of genotype–environment effects. *Child Development, 54,* 424–435.

Scarr, S., Pakstis, A. J., Katz, S. H., & Barker, W. B. (1977). Absence of a relationship between degree of white ancestry and intellectual skills within a black population. *Human Genetics, 39,* 69–86.

Scarr, S., & Weinberg, R. A. (1983). The Minnesota Adoption Studies: Genetic differences and malleability. *Child Development, 54,* 260–267.

Scarr-Salapatek, S. (1975). Genetics and the development of intelligence. In F. Horowitz (Ed.), *Review of child development research* (Vol. 4). Chicago: University of Chicago Press.

Schacter, F. F., Shore, E., Hodapp, R., Chalfin, S., & Bundy, C. (1978). Do girls talk earlier? Mean length of utterance in toddlers. *Developmental Psychology, 14,* 388–392.

Schaffer, C. E., & Blatt, S. J. (1990). Interpersonal relationships and the experience of perceived efficacy. In R. J. Sternberg & J. Kolligian (Eds.), *Competence considered.* New Haven, CT: Yale University Press.

Schaffer, H. R. (1986). Some thoughts of an ordinologist. *Developmental Review, 6,* 115–121.

Schaffer, H. R., & Emerson, P. E. (1964). The development of social attachments in infancy. *Monographs of the Society for Research in Child Development, 29*(3, Serial No. 94).

Schaie, K. W. (1996). *Intellectual development in adulthood: The Seattle Longitudinal Study.* Cambridge: Cambridge University Press.

Schlegel, A. (2001). The global spread of adolescent culture. In L. J. Crockett & R. K. Silbereisen (Eds.), *Negotiating adolescence in times of social change.* New York: Cambridge University Press.

Schlesinger, I. M. (1988). The origin of relational categories. In Y. Levy, I. M. Schlesinger, & M. D. S. Braine (Eds.), *Categories and processes in language acquisition.* Hillsdale, NJ: Erlbaum.

Schmidt, L. A., & Fox, N. A. (1997). The development and outcomes of childhood shyness: A multiple psychophysiologic measure approach. In R. Vasta (Ed.), *Annals of child development* (Vol. 13). London: Kingsley.

Schmidt, L. A., & Fox, N. A. (1998). Fear-potentiated startle responses in temperamentally different human infants. *Developmental Psychobiology, 32,* 113–120.

Schmidt, L. A., Fox, N. A., Rubin, K. H., & Sternberg, E. M. (1997). Behavioral and neuroendocrine responses

in shy children. *Developmental Psychobiology, 30,* 127–140.

Schmidt, L. A., Fox, N. A., Schulkin, J., & Gold, P. W. (1999). Behavioral and psychophysiological correlates of self-presentation in temperamentally shy children. *Developmental Psychobiology, 35,* 119–135.

Schmidt, U. (2000). Eating disorders. In D. Kohen (Ed.), *Women and mental health.* London: Routledge.

Schmuckler, M. A. (1995). Self-knowledge of body position: Integration of perceptual and action system information. In P. Rochat (Ed.), *The self in infancy: Theory and research.* Amsterdam: Elsevier.

Schneider, B. A., & Trehub, S. E. (1985). Behavioral assessment of basic capabilities. In S. E. Trehub & B. A. Schneider (Eds.), *Auditory development in infancy.* New York: Plenum.

Schneider, B. H., Atkinson, L., & Tardif, C. (2001). Child–parent attachment and children's peer relations: A quantitative review. *Developmental Psychology, 37,* 86–100.

Schneider, B. H., & Byrne, B. M. (1985). Children's social skills training: A meta-analysis. In B. H. Schneider, K. H. Rubin, & J. E. Ledingham (Eds.), *Children's peer relations: Issues in assessment and intervention.* New York: Springer-Verlag.

Schneider, B. H., Rubin, K. H., & Ledingham, J. E. (Eds.). (1985). *Children's peer relations: Issues in assessment and intervention.* New York: Springer-Verlag.

Schneider, W. (1999). The development of metamemory in children. In D. Gopher & A. Kuriat (Eds.), *Attention and performance: XVII. Cognitive regulation of performance: Interaction of theory and application.* Cambridge, MA: MIT Press.

Schneider, W., & Bjorklund, D. F. (1998). Memory. In W. Damon (Series Ed.) & D. Kuhn & R. S. Siegler (Vol. Eds.), *Handbook of child psychology: Vol. 2. Cognition, perception, and language* (5th ed.). New York: Wiley.

Schneider, W., Borkowski, J. G., Kurtz, B. E., & Kerwin, K. (1986). Metamemory and motivation: A comparison of strategy use and performance in German and American children. *Journal of Cross-Cultural Psychology, 17,* 315–336.

Schneider, W., Gruber, H., Gold, A., & Opwis, K. (1993). Chess expertise and memory for chess positions in children and adults. *Journal of Experimental Child Psychology, 56,* 328–349.

Schneider, W., Korkel, J., & Weinert, F. E. (1987). *The knowledge base and memory performance: A comparison of academically successful and unsuccessful learners.* Paper presented at the meeting of the American Educational Research Association, Washington, DC.

Schneider, W., & Pressley, M. (1997). *Memory development between 2 and 20* (2nd ed.) Mahwah, NJ: Erlbaum.

Schneider-Rosen, K., & Cicchetti, D. (1984). The relationship between affect and cognition in maltreated infants: Quality of attachment and the development of visual self-recognition. *Child Development, 55,* 648–658.

Schneider-Rosen, K., & Cicchetti, D. (1991). Early self-knowledge and emotional development: Visual self-recognition and affective reactions to mirror self-image in maltreated and nonmaltreated toddlers. *Developmental Psychology, 27,* 471–478.

Schofield, J. W. (1995). *Computers and classroom culture.* New York: Cambridge University Press.

Schonert-Reichl, K. A. (1999). Relations of peer acceptance, friendship adjustment, and social behavior to moral reasoning during early adolescence. *Journal of Early Adolescence, 19,* 249–279.

Schonfeld, A. M., Mattson, S. N., Lang, A., Delis, D. C., & Riley, E. P. (2001). Verbal and nonverbal fluency in children with heavy prenatal alcohol exposure. *Journal of Studies on Alcohol, 62,* 239–246.

Schuengel, C., Bakermans-Kranenburg, M., van IJzendoorn, M. H., & Blom, M. (1999). Unresolved loss and

infant disorganization: Links to frightening maternal behavior. In J. Solomon & C. George (Eds.), *Attachment disorganization.* New York: Guilford.

Schulman, A. H., & Kaplowitz, C. (1977). Mirror-image response during the first two years of life. *Developmental Psychobiology, 10,* 133–142.

Schunk, D. H. (1983). Reward contingencies and the development of children's skills and self-efficacy. *Journal of Educational Psychology, 75,* 511–518.

Schunk, D. H. (1984). Self-efficacy perspective on achievement behavior. *Educational Psychologist, 19,* 48–58.

Schunk, D. H. (1987). Peer models and children's behavioral change. *Review of Educational Research, 57,* 159–174.

Schwartz, C. E., Wright, C. I., Shin, L. M., Kagan, J., & Rauch, S. L. (2003). Inhibited and uninhibited infants "grown up": Adult amygdalar response to novelty. *Science, 300,* 1952–1953.

Schwartz, D., Dodge, K. A., Pettit, G. S., & Bates, J. E. (1997). The early socialization of aggressive victims of bullying. *Child Development, 68,* 665–675.

Schwartz, R. G., & Camarata, S. (1985). Examining relationships between input and language development: Some statistical issues. *Journal of Child Language, 12,* 199–207.

Schwartz, R. G., Leonard, L. B., Frome-Loeb, D. M., & Swanson, L. A. (1987). Attempted sounds are sometimes not: An expanded view of phonological selection and avoidance. *Journal of Child Language, 14,* 411–418.

Schwartzman, H. (1978). *Transformations: The anthropology of children's play.* New York: Plenum. 1978.

Schwebel, D. C., Rosen, C. S., & Singer, J. L. (1999). Preschoolers' pretend play and theory of mind: The role of jointly constructed pretend. *British Journal of Developmental Psychology, 17,* 333–348.

Schweinhart, L. J., & Weikart, D. P. (1991). Response to "Beyond IQ in Preschool Programs?" *Intelligence, 15,* 313–315.

Scott, J. P. (1987). Critical periods in the processes of social organization. In M. H. Bornstein (Ed.), *Sensitive periods in development: Interdisciplinary perspectives.* Hillsdale, NJ: Erlbaum.

Sears, R. R. (1977). Sources of life satisfactions of the Terman gifted men. *American Psychologist, 32,* 119–128.

Seashore, M. J., Leifer, A. D., Barnett, C. R., & Leiderman, P. H. (1973). The effects of denial of early mother–infant interaction on maternal self-confidence. *Journal of Personality and Social Psychology, 26,* 369–378.

Sebald, H. (1989). Adolescent peer orientation: Changes in the support system during the last three decades. *Adolescence, 24,* 937–945.

Segal, L. B., Oster, H., Cohen, M., Caspi, B., Myers, M., & Brown, D. (1995). Smiling and fussing in seven-month-old preterm and full-term Black infants in the still-face situation. *Child Development, 66,* 1829–1843.

Segal, N. L. (1999). *Entwined lives.* New York: Penguin Putnam.

Seginer, R. (1998). Adolescents' perceptions of relationships with older sibling in the context of other close relationships. *Journal of Research on Adolescence, 8,* 287–308.

Seidman, E., Allen, L., Aber, J. L., Mitchell, C., & Feinman, J. (1994). The impact of school transition in early adolescence on the self-system and perceived social context of poor urban youth. *Child Development, 65,* 507–522.

Seifer, R. (2000). Temperament and goodness of fit: Implications for developmental psychopathology. In A. J. Sameroff & M. Lewis, (Eds.), *Handbook of developmental psychopathology* (2nd ed.). Dordrecht, Netherlands: Kluwer Academic Publishers.

Seifer, R., & Schiller, M. (1995). The role of parenting sensitivity, infant temperament, and dyadic interaction in attachment theory and assessment. In E. Waters, B. E.

Vaughn, G. Posada, & K. Kondo-Ikemura (Eds.), Caregiving, cultural, and cognitive perspectives on secure-base behavior and working models. *Monographs of the Society for Research in Child Development, 60* (2–3, Serial No. 244).

Seifer, R., Schiller, M., Sameroff, A. J., Resnick, S., & Riordan, K. (1996). Attachment, maternal sensitivity, and infant temperament during the first year of life. *Developmental Psychology, 32,* 12–25.

Selman, R. L. (1980). *The growth of interpersonal understanding: Development and clinical analyses.* New York: Academic Press.

Semendeferi, K. (1999). The frontal lobes of the great apes with a focus on the gorilla and the orangutan. In S. T. Parker, R. W. Mitchell, & H. L. Miles (Eds.), *The mentalities of gorillas and organgutans.* Cambridge: Cambridge University Press.

Seong, H., Bauer, S. C., & Sullivan, L. M. (1998). Gender differences among top performing elementary school students in mathematical ability. *Journal of Research and Development in Education, 31,* 133–141.

Serbin, L. A., Connor, J. M., Burchardt, C. J., & Citron, C. C. (1979). Effects of peer presence on sex-typing of children's play behavior. *Journal of Experimental Child Psychology, 27,* 303–309.

Serbin, L. A., Poulin-Dubois, D., Colburne, K. A., Sen, M. G., & Eichstedt, J. A. (2001). Gender stereotyping in infancy: Visual preferences for and knowledge of gender-stereotyped toys in the second year. *International Journal of Behavioral Development, 25,* 7–15.

Serbin, L. A., Powlishta, K. K., & Gulko, J. (1993). The development of sex-typing in middle childhood. *Monographs of the Society for Research in Child Development, 58*(Serial No. 232).

Serbin, L. A., & Sprafkin, C. (1986). The salience of gender and the process of sex-typing in three- to seven-year-old children. *Child Development, 57,* 1188–1199.

Serbin, L.A., Stack, D. M., Schwartzman, A. E., Cooperman, J., Bentley, V., Saltaris, C., et al. (2002). A longitudinal study of aggressive and withdrawn children into adulthood: Patterns of parenting and risk to offspring. In R. J. & R. D. Peters (Eds.), *The effects of parental dysfunction on children.* New York: Kluwer Academic/Plenum Publishers.

Serbin, L. A., Zelkowitz, P., Doyle, A., & Gold, D. (1990). The socialization of sex-differentiated skills and academic performance: A mediational model. *Sex Roles, 23,* 613–628.

Sethi, A., Mischel, W., Aber, J. L., Shoda, Y., & Rodriguez, M. L. (2000). The role of strategic attention deployment in development of self-regulation: Predicting preschoolers' delay of gratification from mother-toddler interactions. *Developmental Psychology, 36,* 767–777.

Shantz, C. U. (1983). Social cognition. In P. H. Mussen (Series Ed.) & J. H. Flavell & E. M. Markman (Vol. Eds.), *Handbook of child psychology: Vol. 3. Cognitive development* (4th ed.). New York: Wiley.

Shantz, C. U. (1987). Conflicts between children. *Child Development, 58,* 283–305.

Shantz, C. U., & Hartup, W. W. (Eds.). (1995). *Conflict in child and adolescent development.* New York: Cambridge University Press.

Sharan, S. (1984). *Cooperative learning.* Hillsdale, NJ: Erlbaum.

Sharpe, R. M., & Skakkebaek, N. E. (1993). Are oestrogens involved in falling sperm counts and disorders of the male reproductive tract? *Lancet, 341,* 1392–1395.

Shatz, M. (1983). On transition, continuity, and coupling: An alternative approach to communicative development. In R. M. Golinkoff (Ed.), *The transition from prelinguistic to linguistic communication.* Hillsdale, NJ: Erlbaum.

Shatz, M., & Gelman, R. (1973). The development of communication skills: Modifications in the speech of young children as a function of the listener. *Monographs of the Society for Research in Child Development, 38* (5, Serial No. 152).

Shatz, M., & McCloskey, L. (1984). Answering appropriately: A developmental perspective on conversational knowledge. In S. A. Kuczaj (Ed.), *Discourse development: Progress in cognitive developmental research.* New York: Springer-Verlag.

Shayer, M., Kucheman, D. E., & Wylam, H. (1976). The distribution of Piagetian stages of thinking in British middle and secondary school children. *British Journal of Educational Psychology, 46,* 164–173.

Shayer, M., & Wylam, H. (1978). The distribution of Piagetian stages of thinking in British middle and secondary school children: II. 14 to 16 year old and sex differentials. *British Journal of Educational Psychology, 48,* 62–70.

Shaywitz, B. A., Shaywitz, S. E., Pugh, K. R., Constable, R. T., Skudlarski, P., Fulbright, R. K., et al. (1995). Sex differences in the functional organization of the brain for language. *Nature, 373,* 607–609.

Shaywitz, S. E., Shaywitz, B. A., Pugh, K. R., Fulbright, R. K., Constable, R. T., Mencl, W. E., et al. (1998). Functional disruption in the organization of the brain for reading in dyslexia. *Proceedings of the National Academy of Science USA, 95,* 2636–2641.

She, H-C. (2000). The interplay of a biology teacher's beliefs, teaching practices and gender-based student-teacher classroom interaction *Educational Research, 42,* 100–111.

Shea, D. L., Lubinski, D., & Benbow, C. P. (2001). Importance of assessing spatial ability in intellectually talented young adolescents: A 20-year longitudinal study. *Journal of Educational Psychology, 93,* 604–614.

Sheldon, A. (1990). Pickle fights: Gendered talk in preschool disputes. *Discourse Processes, 13,* 5–31.

Sheldon, A. (1992). Conflict talk: Sociolinguist challenges to self-assertion and how young girls meet them. *Merrill-Palmer Quarterly, 38,* 95–117.

Shepard, T. H. (1986). Human teratogenicity. *Advances in Pediatrics, 33,* 225–268.

Sherif, M., Harvey, O. J., White, B. J., Hood, W. R., & Sherif, C. W. (1961). *Intergroup conflict and cooperation: The Robbers Cave experiment.* Norman: University of Oklahoma Press.

Shigetomi, C. C., Hartmann, D. P., & Gelfand, D. M. (1981). Sex differences in children's altruistic behavior and reputations for helpfulness. *Developmental Psychology, 17,* 434–437.

Shirley, M. M. (1933). *The first two years; a study of twenty-five babies.* Minneapolis: University of Minnesota Press.

Shoda, Y., Mischel, W., & Peake, P. K. (1990). Predicting adolescent cognitive and self-regulatory competencies from preschool delay of gratification: Identifying diagnostic conditions. *Developmental Psychology, 26,* 978–986.

Shonkoff, J. P., & Phillips, D. A. (2000). *From neurons to neighborhoods: The science of early childhood development.* Washington, DC: National Academy Press.

Shore, C. M. (1995). *Individual differences in language development.* Thousand Oaks, CA: Sage.

Shu, S. (1999). *Grandparents, parents, and children: A study of three-generation family structure and intergenerational relationships in contemporary China.* Unpublished doctoral dissertation, University of London.

Shucard, J. L., & Shucard, D. W. (1990). Auditory evoked potentials and hand preference in 6-month-old infants: Possible gender-related differences in cerebral organization. *Developmental Psychology, 26,* 923–930.

Shucard, J. L., Shucard, D. W., Cummins, K. R., & Campos, J. J. (1981). Auditory evoked potentials and sex-related differences in brain development. *Brain and Language, 13,* 91–102.

Shulman, S., & Collins, W. A. (Eds.). (1997). *New directions for child development: No. 78. Romantic relationships in adolescence: Developmental perspectives.* San Francisco: Jossey-Bass.

Shultz, T. R., & Darley, J. M. (1991). An information-processing model of retributive moral judgments based on "legal reasoning." In W. M. Kurtines & J. L. Gewirtz (Eds.), *Handbook of moral behavior and development: Vol. 2. Research.* Hillsdale, NJ: Erlbaum.

Shultz, T. R., & Wright, K. (1985). Concepts of negligence and intention in the assignment of moral responsibility. *Canadian Journal of Behavioural Science, 17,* 97–108.

Shultz, T. R., Wright, K., & Schleifer, M. (1986). Assignment of moral responsibility and punishment. *Child Development, 57,* 177–184.

Shure, M. B. (1989). Interpersonal competence training. In W. Damon (Ed.), *Child development today and tomorrow.* San Francisco: Jossey-Bass.

Shurkin, J. N. (1992). *Terman's kids: The groundbreaking study of how the gifted grow up.* Boston: Little, Brown.

Shwe, H. I., & Markman, E. M. (1997). Young children's appreciation of the mental impact of their communicative signals. *Developmental Psychology, 33,* 630–636.

Shweder, R. A., Goodnow, J., Hatano, G., LeVine, R. A., Markus, H., & Miller, P. (1998). The cultural psychology of development: One mind, many mentalities. In W. Damon (Series Ed.) & R. M. Lerner (Vol. Ed.), *Handbook of child psychology: Vol. 1. Theoretical models of human development* (5th ed.). New York: Wiley.

Shweder, R. A., Jensen, L. A., & Goldstein, W. M. (1995). Who sleeps by whom revisited: A method for extracting the moral goods implicit in practice. In J. J. Goodnow, P. J. Miller, & F. Kessel (Eds.), *New directions for child development: No. 67. Cultural practices as contexts for development.* San Francisco: Jossey-Bass.

Shweder, R. A., Mahapatra, M., & Miller, J. (1987). Culture and moral development. In J. Kagan & S. Lamb (Eds.), *The emergence of morality in young children.* Chicago: University of Chicago Press.

Shweder, R. A., & Much, M. C. (1987). Determinations of meaning: Discourse and moral socialization. In W. M. Kurtines & J. L. Gewirtz (Eds.), *Moral development through social interaction.* New York: Wiley.

Sieber, J. E. (1992). *Planning ethically responsible research: A guide for students and internal review boards.* Newbury Park, CA: Sage.

Siegal, M. (1987). Are sons and daughters treated more differently by fathers than by mothers? *Developmental Review, 7,* 183–209.

Siegal, M., & Peterson, C. C. (Eds.). (1999). *Children's understanding of biology and health.* New York: Cambridge University Press.

Siegal, M., & Share, D. L. (1990). Contamination sensitivity in young children. *Developmental Psychology, 26,* 455–458.

Siegel, L. S. (1984). Home environment influences on cognitive development in preterm and full-term children during the first 5 years. In A. W. Gottfried (Ed.), *Home environment and early cognitive development.* New York: Academic Press.

Siegel, L. S. (1989). A reconceptualization of prediction from infant test scores. In M. H. Bornstein & N. Krasnegor (Eds.), *Stability and continuity in mental development.* Hillsdale, NJ: Erlbaum.

Siegel, L. S. (1992). Infant motor, cognitive, and language behaviors as predictors of achievement at school age. In C. K. Rovee-Collier & L. P. Lipsitt (Eds.), *Advances in infancy research* (Vol. 7). Norwood, NJ: Ablex.

Siegler, R. S. (1976). Three aspects of cognitive development. *Cognitive Psychology, 8,* 481–520.

Siegler, R. S. (1978). The origins of scientific reasoning. In R. S. Siegler (Ed.), *Children's thinking: What develops?* Hillsdale, NJ: Erlbaum.

Siegler, R. S. (1981). Developmental sequences within and between concepts. *Monographs of the Society for Research in Child Development, 46*(2, Serial No. 189).

Siegler, R. S. (1988). Individual differences in strategy choices: Good students, not-so-good students, and perfectionists. *Child Development, 59,* 833–851.

Siegler, R. S. (1991). *Children's thinking* (2nd ed.). Englewood Cliffs, NJ: Prentice Hall.

Siegler, R. S. (1995). How does change occur?: A microgenetic study of number conservation. *Cognitive Psychology, 28,* 225–273.

Siegler, R. S. (1996). *Emerging minds: The process of change in children's thinking.* New York: Oxford University Press.

Siegler, R. S. (1998). *Children's thinking* (3rd ed.). Upper Saddle River, NJ: Prentice Hall.

Siegler, R. S. (2000). The rebirth of children's learning. *Child Development, 71,* 26–35.

Siegler, R. S., & Jenkins, E. (1989). *How children discover new strategies.* Hillsdale, NJ: Erlbaum.

Siegler, R. S., & Shipley, C. (1995). Variation, selection, and cognitive change. In T. J. Simon & G. S. Halford (Eds.), *Developing cognitive competence: New approaches to process modeling.* Hillsdale, NJ: Erlbaum.

Siegler, R. S., & Shrager, J. (1984). Strategy choices in addition and subtraction: How do children know what to do? In C. Sophian (Ed.), *Origins of cognitive skills.* Hillsdale, NJ: Erlbaum.

Siervogel, R. M., Waynard, L. M., Wisemandle, W. A., Roche, A. F., Guo, S. S., Chumlea, W. C., et al. (2000). Annual changes in total body fat and fat-free mass in children from 8 to 18 years in relation to changes in body mass index: The Fels Longitudinal Study. *Annals of the New York Academy of Science, 904,* 420–423.

Sigel, I. E. (1986). Reflections on the belief–behavior connection: Lessons learned from a research program on parental belief systems and teaching strategies. In W. K. Ashmore & D. M. Brodzinsky (Eds.), *Thinking about the family: Views of parents and children.* Hillsdale, NJ: Erlbaum.

Sigel, I. E., & McGillicuddy-De Lisi (2002). Parental beliefs are cognitions: The dynamic belief systems model. In M. H. Bornstein (Ed.), *Handbook of parenting* (2nd ed., Vol. 3). Mahwah, NJ: Erlbaum.

Sigman, M. (1995). Nutrition and child development: More food for thought. *Current Directions in Psychological Science, 4,* 52–55.

Signorella, M. L., Bigler, R. S., & Liben, L. S. (1993). Developmental differences in children's gender schemata about others: A meta-analytic review. *Developmental Review, 13,* 147–183.

Signorella, M., & Liben, L. S. (1984). Recall and reconstruction of gender-related pictures: Effects of attitude, task difficulty, and age. *Child Development, 55,* 393–405.

Signorelli, N. (2001). Television's gender role images and contribution to stereotyping: Past, present, future. In D. G. Singer & J. Singer (Eds.), *Handbook of children and the media.* Thousand Oaks, CA: Sage.

Signorelli, N., & Bacue, A. (1999). Recognition and respect: A content analysis of prime-time television characters across three decades. *Sex Roles, 40,* 527–544.

Silver, L. B. (1999). *Attention-deficit hyperactivity disorder* (2nd ed.). Washington, DC: American Psychiatric Press.

Simmons, R. G., & Blyth, D. A. (1987). *Moving into adolescence: The impact of pubertal change and social context.* Hawthorne, NY: Aldine de Gruyter.

Simmons, R. G., Carlton-Ford, S. L., & Blyth, D. A. (1987). Predicting how a child will cope with the transition to junior high school. In R. M. Lerner & T. M. Foch (Eds.), *Biological-psychosocial interactions in early adolescence.* Hillsdale, NJ: Erlbaum.

Simon, T. J., & Halford, G. S. (Eds.). (1995). *Developing cognitive competence: New approaches to process modeling.* Hillsdale, NJ: Erlbaum.

Simpson, J. M. (2001). Infant stress and sleep deprivation as an actiological basis for sudden infant death syndrome. *Early Human Development, 61,* 1–43.

Skelton, C. (2001). *Schooling the boys: Masculinities and primary education.* Buckingham, UK: Open University Press.

Skinner, B. F. (1953). *Science and human behavior.* New York: Macmillan.

Skinner, B. F. (1957). *Verbal behavior.* New York: Appleton-Century-Crofts.

Skowronski, J. J., Betz, A. L., Thompson, C. P., & Larsen, S. F. (1995). Long-term performance in autobiographical event dating: Patterns of accuracy and error across a two-and-a-half year time span. In A. L. Healy & L. B. Bourne (Eds.), *Acquisition and long-term retention of knowledge and skills: The durability and specificity of cognitive procedures.* Newbury Park, CA: Sage.

Slaby, R. G., & Frey, K. S. (1975). Development of gender constancy and selective attention to same-sex models. *Child Development, 46,* 849–856.

Slade, A. (1987). Quality of attachment and early symbolic play. *Developmental Psychology, 23,* 78–85.

Slade, A. (1987). A longitudinal study of maternal involvement and symbolic play during the toddler period. *Child Development, 58,* 367–375.

Slater, A. (1995). Visual perception and memory at birth. In C. K. Rovee-Collier & L. P. Lipsitt (Eds.), *Advances in infancy research* (Vol. 9). Norwood, NJ: Ablex.

Slater, A., Cooper, R., Rose, D., & Morison, V. (1989). Prediction of cognitive performance from infancy to early childhood. *Human Development, 32,* 137–147.

Slater, A., Johnson, S. P., Brown, E., & Badenoch, M. (1996). Newborn infants' perception of partly occluded objects. *Infant Behavior and Development, 19,* 145–148.

Slater, A., Johnson, S. P., Kellman, P. J., & Spelke, E. S. (1994). The role of three-dimensional depth cues in infants' perception of partly occluded objects. *Early Development and Parenting, 3,* 187–191.

Slater, A., Mattock, A., & Brown, E. (1990). Size constancy at birth: Newborn infant's responses to retinal and real size. *Journal of Experimental Child Psychology, 49,* 314–322.

Slater, A., Mattock, A., Brown, E., & Bremner, J. G. (1991). Form perception at birth: Cohen and Younger (1984) revisited. *Journal of Experimental Child Psychology, 51,* 395–406.

Slater, A., & Morison, V. (1985). Shape constancy and slant perception at birth. *Perception, 14,* 337–344.

Slater, A., von der Schulenburg, C., Brown, E., Badenoch, M., Butterworth, G., Parsons S., et al. (1998). Newborn infants prefer attractive faces. *Infant Behavior and Development, 21,* 345–354.

Slaughter-DeFoe, D. T., Nakagawa, K., Takanishi, R., & Johnson, D. J. (1990). Toward cultural/ecological perspectives on schooling and achievement in African- and Asian-American children. *Child Development, 61,* 363–383.

Slobin, D. I. (1982). Universal and particular in the acquisition of language. In E. Wanner & L. R. Gleitman (Eds.), *Language acquisition: The state of the art.* Cambridge: Cambridge University Press.

Slobin, D. I. (1985a). Crosslinguistic evidence for the language-making capacity. In D. I. Slobin (Ed.), *The crosslinguistic study of language acquisition: Vol. 2. Theoretical issues.* Hillsdale, NJ: Erlbaum.

Slobin, D. I. (Ed.). (1985b). *The crosslinguistic study of language acquisition: Vol. 2. Theoretical issues.* Hillsdale, NJ: Erlbaum.

Slomkowski, C. L., & Dunn, J. (1993, March). *Conflict in close relationships.* Paper presented at the meeting of the Society for Research in Child Development, New Orleans.

Slomkowski, C. L., & Killen, M. (1992). Young children's conceptions of transgressions with friends and nonfriends. *International Journal of Behavioral Development, 15,* 247–258.

Smetana, J. G., & Bitz, B. (1996). Adolescents' conceptions of teachers' authority and their relations to rule violations in school. *Child Development, 67,* 1153–1172.

Smetana, J. G., & Braeges, J. L. (1990). The development of toddlers' moral and conventional judgments. *Merrill-Palmer Quarterly, 36,* 329–346.

Smetana, J. G., Killen, M., & Turiel, E. (1991). Children's reasoning about interpersonal and moral conflicts. *Child Development, 62,* 629–644.

Smetana, J. G., Schlagman, N., & Adams, P. (1993). Preschoolers' judgments about hypothetical and actual transgressions. *Child Development, 64,* 202–214.

Smilansky, S. (1968). *The effects of sociodramatic play on disadvantaged preschool children.* New York: Wiley.

Smiley, P. A., & Dweck, C. S. (1994). Individual differences in achievement goals among young children. *Child Development, 65,* 1723–1743.

Smiley, P., & Huttenlocher, J. (1989). Young children's acquisition of emotion concepts. In C. Saarni & P. L. Harris (Eds.), *Children's understanding of emotion.* Cambridge: Cambridge University Press.

Smith, B. A., & Blass, E. M. (1996). Taste-mediated calming in premature, preterm, and full-term human infants. *Developmental Psychology, 32,* 1084–1089.

Smith, B. A., Stevens, K., Torgerson, W. S., & Kim, J. H. (1992). Diminished reactivity of postmature human infants to sucrose compared with term infants. *Developmental Psychology, 28,* 811–820.

Smith, C. L. (1979). Children's understanding of natural language hierarchies. *Journal of Experimental Child Psychology, 27,* 437–458.

Smith, E., & Udry, J. (1985). Coital and non-coital sexual behaviors of white and black adolescents. *American Journal of Public Health, 75,* 1200–1203.

Smith, P. K. (1978). A longitudinal study of social participation in preschool children: Solitary and parallel play reexamined. *Developmental Psychology, 14,* 517–523.

Smith, P. K., & Drew, L. M. (2002). Grandparenthood. In M. H. Bornstein (Ed.), *Handbook of parenting* (2nd ed., Vol. 3). Mahwah, NJ: Erlbaum.

Snarey, J. R. (1985). Cross-cultural universality of social-moral development: A critical review of Kohlbergian research. *Psychological Bulletin, 97,* 202–232.

Snarey, J. R., & Keljo, K. (1991). In a Gemeinschaft voice: The cross-cultural expansion of moral development theory. In W. M. Kurtines & J. L. Gewirtz (Eds.), *Handbook of moral behavior and development: Vol. 1. Theory.* Hillsdale, NJ: Erlbaum.

Snow, C. E. (1983). Saying it again: The role of expanded and deferred imitations in language acquisition. In K. E. Nelson (Ed.), *Children's language* (Vol. 4). Hillsdale, NJ: Erlbaum.

Snow, C. E. (1999). Social perspectives on the emergence of language. In B. MacWhinney (Ed.), *The emergence of language.* Mahwah, NJ: Erlbaum.

Snow, C.E., Burns, M.S., & Griffin, P. (Eds.). (1998). *Preventing reading difficulties in young children: Committee on the prevention of reading difficulties in young children.* Washington, DC: National Research Council.

Snow, C. E., & Ferguson, C. (1977). *Talking to children: Language input and acquisition.* Cambridge: Cambridge University Press.

Snow, C. E., & Goldfield, B. A. (1983). Turn the page please: Situation-specific language acquisition. *Journal of Child Language, 10,* 551–569.

Snow, C. E., Pan, B. E., Imbens-Bailey, A., & Herman, J. (1996). Learning how to say what one means: A longitudinal study of children's speech act use. *Social Development, 5,* 56–84.

Snow, C. E., Perlman, R., & Nathan, D. (1987). Why routines are different: Toward a multiple-factors model of the relation between input and language acquisition. In K. E. Nelson & A. VanKleeck (Eds.), *Children's language* (Vol. 6). Hillsdale, NJ: Erlbaum.

Snyder, J. J., & Patterson, G. R. (1995). Individual differences in social aggression: A test of a reinforcement model of socialization in the natural environment. *Behavior Therapy, 26,* 371–391.

Snyder, J., West, L., Stockemer, V., & Gibbons, S. (1996). A social learning model of peer choice in the natural environment. *Journal of Applied Developmental Psychology, 17,* 215–237.

Snyder, T. D., & Hoffman, C. M. (2000). Digest of education statistics: 1999. *Education Statistics Quarterly, 2,* 123–126.

Sohlberg, M. E., & Olweus, D. (2003). Prevalence estimation of school bullying with the Olweus bully/victim questionnaire. *Aggressive Behavior, 29,* 239–268.

Sokolov, E. N. (1960). *Perception and the conditioned reflex.* New York: Macmillan.

Solomon, G. E. A., Johnson, S. C., Zaitchik, D., & Carey, S. (1996). Like father, like son: Young children's understanding of how and why offspring resemble their parents. *Child Development, 67,* 151–171.

Solomon, J., & George, C. (Eds.). (1999). *Attachment disorganization.* New York: Guilford.

Somary, K., & Stricker, G. (1998). Becoming a grandparent: A longitudinal study of expectations and early experiences as a function of sex and lineage. *Gerontologist, 38,* 53–61.

Sonnenschein, S. (1988). The development of referential communication: Speaking to different listeners. *Child Development, 59,* 694–702.

Sophian, C. (1995). *Children's numbers.* Madison, WI: Brown & Benchmark.

Sophian, C. (1998). A developmental perspective on children's counting. In C. Donlan (Ed.), *The development of mathematical skills: Studies in developmental psychology.* Hove, UK: Psychology Press.

Sorce, J. F., Emde, R. N., Campos, J. J., & Klinnert, M. D. (1985). Maternal emotional signaling: Its effect on the visual cliff behavior of 1-year-olds. *Developmental Psychology, 21,* 195–200.

Sostek, A. M., Vietze, P., Zaslow, M., Kreiss, L., van de Waals, F., & Rubenstein, D. (1981). Social context in caregiver-infant interaction. A film study of Fais and the United States. In T. M. Field, A. M. Sostek, P. Vietze, & P. H. Leiderman (Eds.), *Culture and early interactions.* Hillsdale, NJ: Erlbaum.

Spangler, G., & Grossmann, K. E. (1993). Biobehavioral organization in securely and insecurely attached infants. *Child Development, 64,* 1439–1450.

Spearman, C. (1927). *The abilities of man.* New York: Macmillan.

Speer, J. R., & Flavell, J. H. (1979). Young children's knowledge of the relative difficulty of recognition and recall memory tasks. *Developmental Psychology, 15,* 214–217.

Spelke, E. S. (1976). Infants' intermodal perception of events. *Cognitive Psychology, 8,* 533–560.

Spelke, E. S. (1985). Perception of unity, persistence, and identity: Thoughts on infants' conceptions of objects. In J. Mehler & R. Fox (Eds.), *Neonate cognition: Beyond the blooming buzzing confusion.* Hillsdale, NJ: Erlbaum

Spelke, E. S. (1988). Where perceiving ends and thinking begins: The apprehension of objects in infancy. In A. Yonas (Ed.), *Minnesota symposia on child psychology: Vol. 20. Perceptual development in infancy.* Hillsdale, NJ: Erlbaum.

Spelke, E. S. (1991). Physical knowledge in infancy: Reflections on Piaget's theory. In S. Carey & R. Gelman (Eds.), *The epigenesis of mind.* Hillsdale, NJ: Erlbaum.

Spelke, E. S., Breinlinger, K., Macomber, J., & Jacobson, K. (1992). Origins of knowledge. *Psychological Review, 99,* 605–632.

Spelke, E. S., & Cortelyou, A. (1981). Perceptual aspects of social learning: Looking and listening in infancy. In M. E. Lamb & L. R. Sherrod (Eds.), *Infant social cognition: Empirical and theoretical considerations.* Hillsdale, NJ: Erlbaum.

Spelke, E. S., & Hermer, L. (1996). Early cognitive development: Objects and space. In R. Gelman & T. Au (Eds.), *Perceptual and cognitive development.* San Diego, CA: Academic Press.

Spelke, E. S., & Newport, E. L. (1998). Nativism, empiricism, and the development of knowledge. In W. Damon (Series Ed.) & R. M. Lerner (Vol. Ed.), *Handbook of child psychology: Vol. 1. Theoretical models of human development* (5th ed.). New York: Wiley.

Spelke, E. S., & Owsley, C. J. (1979). Intermodal exploration and knowledge in infancy. *Infant Behavior and Development, 2,* 13–28.

Spelke, E. S., Phillips, A., & Woodward, A. L. (1995). Infants' knowledge of object motion and human action. In D. Sperber, D. Premack, & A. J. Premack (Eds.), *Causal cognition.* Oxford, England: Clarendon Press.

Spencer, M. B., & Markstrom-Adams, C. (1990). Identity processes among racial and ethnic minority children in America. *Child Development, 61,* 290–310.

Spencer, S. J., Steele, C. M., & Quinn, D. M. (1999). Stereotype threat and women's math performance. *Journal of Experimental Social Psychology, 35,* 4–28.

Sprauve, M. E. (1996). Substance abuse and HIV in pregnancy. *Clinical Obstetrics and Gynecology, 39,* 316–332.

Springer, K. (1996). Young children's understanding of a biological basis for parent-offspring relations. *Child Development, 67,* 2841–2856.

Springer, K., & Belk, A. (1994). The role of physical contact and association in early contamination sensitivity. *Developmental Psychology, 30,* 864–868.

Springer, K., & Keil, F. C. (1991). Early differentiation of causal mechanisms appropriate to biological and nonbiological kinds. *Child Development, 62,* 767–781.

Springer, S. P., & Deutsch, G. (1998). *Left brain, right brain* (5th ed.). San Francisco: Freeman.

Sroufe, L. A. (1986). Bowlby's contribution to psychoanalytic theory and developmental psychology: Attachment, separation, loss. *Journal of Child Psychology and Psychiatry, 27,* 841–849.

Sroufe, L. A. (1990). An organizational perspective on the self. In D. Cicchetti & M. Beeghly (Eds.), *The self in transition: Infancy to childhood.* Chicago: University of Chicago Press.

Sroufe, L. A. (1996). *Emotional development.* New York: Cambridge University Press.

Sroufe, L. A., Bennett, C., Englund, M., Urban, J., & Shulman, S. (1993). The significance of gender boundaries in preadolescence: Contemporary correlates and antecedents of boundary relations and maintenance. *Child Development, 64,* 455–466.

Stack, D. M., & Muir, D. W. (1992). Adult tactile stimulation during face-to-face interactions modulates five-month-olds' affect and attention. *Child Development, 63,* 1509–1525.

Stangor, C., & McMillan, D. (1992). Memory for expectancy-congruent and expectancy-incongruent information: A review of the social and social developmental literatures. *Psychological Bulletin, 111,* 42–61.

Stangor, C., & Ruble, D. N. (1987). Development of gender role knowledge and gender constancy. In L. S. Liben & M. L. Signorella (Eds.), *New directions for child development: No. 38. Children's gender schemata.* San Francisco: Jossey-Bass.

Stanovich, K. E. (1993). Does reading make you smarter? Literacy and the development of verbal intelligence. In H. W. Reese (Ed.), *Advances in child development and behavior* (Vol. 24). San Diego, CA: Academic Press.

Stanovich, K. E. (2000). *Progress in understanding reading: Scientific foundations and new frontiers.* New York: Guilford.

Stanovich, K. E., Cunningham, A. E., & West, R. F. (1998). Literacy experiences and the shaping of cognition. In S. G. Paris & H. M. Wellman (Eds.), *Global prospects for education: Development, culture, and schooling.* Washington, DC: American Psychological Association.

Stanwood, G. D., & Levitt, P. (2001). The effects of cocaine on the developing nervous system. In C. A. Nelson & M. Luciana (Eds.), *Handbook of developmental cognitive neuroscience.* Cambridge, MA: MIT Press.

Starkey, P., & Cooper, R. (1980). Perception of numbers by human infants. *Science, 210,* 1033–1034.

Stattin, H., & Magnusson, D. (1990). *Pubertal maturation in female development.* Hillsdale, NJ: Erlbaum.

Staub, E. (1971). Helping a person in distress: The influence of implicit and explicit rules of conduct on children and adults. *Journal of Personality and Social Psychology, 17,* 137–145.

Steele, C. M. (1997). A threat in the air: How stereotypes shape intellectual identity and performance. *American Psychologist, 52,* 613–629.

Steele, C. M., & Aronson, J. (1995). Stereotype threat and the intellectual test performance of African-Americans. *Journal of Personality and Social Psychology, 69,* 797–811.

Steele, C. M., & Aronson, J. (1998). Stereotype threat and the test performance of academically successful African Americans. In C. Jencks & M. Phillips (Eds.), *The Black-White test score gap.* Washington, DC: Brookings Institution.

Steele, C. M., Spencer, S. J., Hummel, M., Carter, K., Harber, K., Schoem, D., & Nisbett, R. (in press). African-American college achievement: A "wise" intervention. *Harvard Educational Review.*

Steele, H., Steele, M., & Fonagy, P. (1996). Associations among attachment classifications of mothers, fathers, and their infants. *Child Development, 67,* 541–555.

Stein, A.H., Pohly, S. R., & Mueller, E. (1971). The influence of masculine, feminine, and neutral tasks on children's achievement behavior, expectancies of success, and attainment values. *Child Development, 42,* 195–207.

Steinberg, L. (2001). We know some things: Parent–adolescent relationships in retrospect and prospect. *Journal of Research on Adolescence, 11,* 1–19.

Steinberg, L., Mounts, N. S., Lamborn, S. D., & Dornbusch, S. M. (1991). Authoritative parenting and adolescent adjustment across varied ecological niches. *Journal of Research on Adolescence, 1,* 19–36.

Steiner, J. E. (1979). Human facial expressions in response to taste and smell stimulation. In H. W. Reese & L. P. Lipsitt (Eds.), *Advances in child development and behavior* (Vol. 13). New York: Academic Press.

Stenberg, C. R., Campos, J. J., & Emde, R. N. (1983). The facial expression of anger in seven-month-old infants. *Child Development, 54,* 178–184.

Stern, M., & Karraker, K. (1992). Modifying the prematurity stereotype in matters of premature and ill full-term infants. *Journal of Clinical Child Psychology, 21,* 76–82.

Sternberg, R. J. (1985). *Beyond IQ: A triarchic theory of human intelligence.* New York: Cambridge University Press.

Sternberg, R. J. (2000). The concept of intelligence. In R. J. Sternberg (Ed.), *Handbook of intelligence.* New York: Cambridge University Press.

Sternberg, R. J., & Grigorenko, E. J. (2002a). *Dynamic testing: The nature and measurement of learning potential.* New York: Cambridge University Press.

Sternberg, R. J., & Grigorenko, E. J. (Eds.). (2002b). *The general factor of intelligence: How general is it?* Mahwah, NJ: Erlbaum.

Sternberg, R. J., & Lubart, T. I. (1991). An investment theory of creativity and its development. *Human Development, 34,* 1–31.

Sternberg, R. J., & Lubart, T. I. (1995). *Defying the crowd: Cultivating creativity in a culture of conformity.* New York: Free Press.

Sternberg, R. J., & Lubart, T. I. (1996) Investing in creativity. *American Psychologist, 51,* 677–688.

Sternberg, R. J., Grigorenko, E. L., & Bundy, D. A. (2001). The predictive value of IQ. *Merrill-Palmer Quarterly, 47,* 1–41.

Stevens, J. H. Jr. (1984). Black grandmothers' and black adolescent mothers' knowledge about parenting. *Developmental Psychology, 20,* 1017–1025.

Stevens, M., Golombok, S., Beveridge, M., & Study Team, ALSPAC (2002). Does father absence influence children's gender development?: Findings from a general population study of preschool children. *Parenting: Science and Practice, 2,* 47–60

Stevenson, H. W., Chen, C., & Lee, S. Y. (1993). Mathematics achievement of Chinese, Japanese, and American children: Ten years later. *Science, 259,* 53–58.

Stevenson, H. W., Lee, S., Chen, C., Stigler, J. W., Hsu, C., & Kitamura, S. (1990). Contexts of achievement: A study of American, Chinese, and Japanese children. *Monographs of the Society for Research in Child Development, 55* (1–2, Serial No. 221).

Stevenson, H. W., Lee, S. Y., & Stigler, J. W. (1986). Mathematics achievement of Chinese, Japanese, and American children. *Science, 231,* 693–699.

Stevenson, H. W., & Stigler, J. W. (1992). *The learning gap: Why our schools are failing and what we can learn from Japanese and Chinese education.* New York: Summit Books.

Stevenson, H. W., Stigler, J. W., Lee, S., Lucker, G. W., Kitamura, S., & Hsu, C. (1985). Cognitive performance and academic achievement of Japanese, Chinese, and American children. *Child Development, 56,* 718–734.

Stevenson, M. R., & Black, K. N. (1988). Paternal absence and sex-role development: A meta-analysis. *Child Development, 59,* 793–814.

Stevenson-Hinde, J., & Verschueren, K. (2002). Attachment in childhood. In P. K. Smith & C. H. Hart (Eds.), *Blackwell handbook of childhood social development.* Malden, MA: Blackwell Publishers.

Stice, E., Presnell, K., & Bearman, S. K. (2001). Relation of early menarche to depression, eating disorders, substance abuse, and comorbid psychopathology among adolescent girls. *Developmental Psychology, 37,* 608–619.

Stifter, C. A., & Braungart, J. M. (1995). The regulation of negative reactivity in infancy: Function and development. *Developmental Psychology, 31,* 448–455.

Stifter, C. A., Coulehan, C. M., & Fish, M. (1993). Linking employment to attachment: The mediating effects of maternal separation anxiety and interactive behavior. *Child Development, 64,* 1451–1460.

Stifter, C. A., & Fox, N. A. (1990). Infant reactivity: Physiological correlates of newborn and 5-month temperament. *Developmental Psychology, 26,* 582–588.

Stigler, J. W., & Hiebert, J. (1999). *The teaching gap: Best ideas from the world's teachers for improving education in the classroom.* New York: The Free Press.

Stigler, J. W., Fernandez, C., & Yoshida, M. (1996). Traditions of school mathematics in Japanese and American classrooms. In L. P. Steffe & P. Nesher (Eds.), *Theories of mathematical learning.* Mahwah, NJ: Erlbaum.

Stipek, D. J. (1992). The child at school. In M. E. Lamb & M. H. Bornstein (Eds.), *Developmental psychology: An advanced textbook* (3rd ed.). Hillsdale, NJ: Erlbaum.

Stipek, D. J. (2002). *Motivation to learn: Integrating theory and practice* (4th ed.). Boston: Allyn & Bacon.

Stipek, D. J., & Gralinski, J. H. (1991). Gender differences in children's achievement-related beliefs and emotional responses to success and failure in mathematics. *Journal of Educational Psychology, 83,* 361–371.

Stipek, D. J., Gralinski, J. H., & Kopp, C. B. (1990). Self-concept development in the toddler years. *Developmental Psychology, 26,* 972–977.

Stipek, D. J., & MacIver, D. (1989). Developmental change in children's assessment of intellectual competence. *Child Development, 60,* 521–538.

Stipek, D. J., Recchia, S., & McClintic, S. (1992). Self-evaluation in young children. *Monographs of the Society for Research in Child Development, 57*(1, Serial No. 226).

Stipek, D. J., & Tannatt, L. (1984). Children's judgments of their own and their peers' academic competence. *Journal of Educational Psychology, 76,* 75–84.

Stjernfeldt, M., Berglund, K., Lindsten, J., & Ludvigssonf, J. (1986). Maternal smoking during pregnancy and risk of childhood cancer. *Lancet, 1,* 1350–1352.

Stocker, C. M., & Mantz-Simmons, L. M. (1993). *Children's friendship and peer status: Links with family relationships, temperament, and social skills.* Unpublished manuscript.

Stocker, C., & Dunn, J. (1990). Sibling relationships in childhood: Links with friendships and peer relationships. *British Journal of Developmental Psychology, 8,* 227–244.

Stoddart, T., & Turiel, E. (1985). Children's concepts of cross-gender activities. *Child Development, 56,* 1241–1252.

Stoll, C., Dott, B., Alembik, Y., & Roth, M. (1993). Evaluation of routine prenatal ultrasound examination in detecting fetal chromosomal abnormalities in a low risk population. *Human Genetics, 91,* 37–41.

Stone, A., Webb, R., & Mahootian, S. (1991). The generality of gesture-speech mismatch as an index of transitional knowledge: Evidence from a control-of-variables task. *Cognitive Development, 6,* 301–313.

Stone, C. A., & Day, M. C. (1978). Levels of availability of a formal operational strategy. *Child Development, 49,* 1054–1065.

Stormshak, E. A., Bierman, K. L., McMahon, R. J., Lengua, L. J., & Conduct Problems Prevention Research Group (2000). Parenting practices and child disruptive behavior problems in early elementary school. *Journal of Clinical Child Psychology, 29,* 17–29.

Straker, G. (1992). *Faces in the revolution.* Cape Town, South Africa: David Philip.

Strapp, C. M. (1999). Mothers', fathers', and siblings' responses to children's language errors: Comparing sources of negative evidence. *Journal of Child Language, 26,* 373–391.

Straughan, R. (1986). Why act on Kohlberg's moral judgments? (Or how to reach Stage 6 and remain a bastard). In S. Modgil & C. Modgil (Eds.), *Lawrence Kohlberg: Consensus and controversy.* Philadelphia: Falmer.

Strayer, F. F., & Noel, J. M. (1986). The prosocial and antisocial functions of preschool aggression: An ethological study of triadic conflict among young children. In C. Zahn-Waxler, E. M. Cummings, & R. Iannotti (Eds.), *Altruism and aggression: Biological and social origins.* Cambridge: Cambridge University Press.

Strayer, F. F., Verissimo, M., Vaughn, B. E., & Howes, C. (1995). A quantitative approach to the description and classification of primary social relationships. In E. Waters, B. E. Vaughn, G. Posada, & K. Kondo-Ikemura (Eds.), Caregiving, cultural, and cognitive perspectives on secure-base behavior and working models. *Monographs of the Society for Research in Child Development, 60* (2–3, Serial No. 244).

Streissguth, A. P., & Connor, P. D. (2001). Fetal alcohol syndrome and other effects of prenatal alcohol: Developmental cognitive neuroscience implications. In C. A. Nelson & M. Luciana (Eds.), *Handbook of developmental cognitive neuroscience.* Cambridge, MA: MIT Press.

Streri, A., Lhote, M., & Dutilleul, S. (2000). Haptic perception in newborns. *Developmental Science, 3,* 319–327.

Striano, T., & Rochat, P. (2000). Emergence of selective social referencing in infancy. *Infancy 1,* 253–264.

Striano, T., Tomasello, M., & Rochat, P. (2001). Social and object support for early symbolic play. *Developmental Science, 4,* 442–455.

Subrahmanyam, K., & Greenfield, P. M. (1994). Effect of video game practice on spatial skills in girls and boys. *Journal of Applied Developmental Psychology, 15,* 13–32.

Subrahmanyam, K., & Greenfield, P. M. (1998). Computer games for girls: What makes them play? In J. Cassell & H. Jenkins (Eds.), *From Barbie to Mortal Kombat: Gender and computer games.* Cambridge, MA: MIT Press.

Subrahmanyam, K., Greenfield, P. M., Kraut, R., & Gross, E. (2001). The impact of computer use on children's and adolescents' development. *Applied Developmental Psychology, 22,* 7–30.

Sue, S., & Ozaki, S. (1990). Asian-American educational achievements: A phenomenon in search of an explanation. *American Psychologist, 45,* 913–920.

Sullivan, M. W. (1982). Reactivation: Priming forgotten memories in human infants. *Child Development, 53,* 516–523.

Sullivan, M. W., Lewis, M., & Alessandri, S. M. (1992). Cross-age stability in emotional expressions: During learning and extinction. *Developmental Psychology, 28,* 58–63.

Suls, J., & Wills, T. A. (Eds.). (1991). *Social comparison: Contemporary theory and research.* Hillsdale, NJ: Erlbaum.

Super, C. M. (1981). Cross-cultural research on infancy. In H. C. Triandis & A. Heron (Eds.), *Handbook of cross-cultural psychology: Vol. 4. Developmental psychology.* Boston: Allyn & Bacon.

Super, C. M., & Harkness, S. (1986). The developmental niche: A conceptualization at the interface of child and culture. *International Journal of Behavioral Development* (Special Issue: Cross-cultural human development) *9,* 545–569.

Super, C. M., & Harkness, S. (1997). The cultural structuring of child development. In J. W. Berry, P. R. Dasen, & T. S. Saraswathi (Eds.), *Handbook of cross-cultural psychology: Vol. 2. Basic processes and human development.* Boston: Allyn and Bacon.

Super, C. M., & Harkness, S. (2002). Culture structures the environment for development. *Human Development, 45,* 270–274.

Susman-Stillman, A., Kalkose, M., Englund, B., & Waldman, I. (1996). Infant temperament and maternal sensitivity as predictors of attachment security. *Infant Behavior and Development, 19,* 33–47.

Sussman, E. J., Inoff-Germain, G., Nottelmann, E. D., Loriauz, L., Cutler, G. B., & Chrousos, G. P. (1987). Hormones, emotional dispositions, and aggressive attributes in young adolescents. *Child Development, 58,* 1114–1134.

Sussman, N. M. (2000). The dynamic nature of cultural identity throughout cultural transitions: Why home is not as sweet. *Personality and Social Psychology Review, 4,* 355–373.

Sutton-Smith, B., & Roberts, J. M. (1973). The cross-cultural and psychological study of games. In B. Sutton-Smith (Ed.), *The folkgames of children.* Austin: University of Texas Press.

Suzuki, L. A., & Valencia, R. (1997). Race-ethnicity and measured intelligence. *American Psychologist, 52,* 1103–1114.

Svejda, M. J., Pannabecker, B. J., & Emde, R. N. (1982). Parent-to-infant attachment: A critique of the early "bonding" model. In R. N. Emde & R. J. Harmon (Eds.), *The development of attachment and affiliative systems*. New York: Plenum.

Swain, I. U., Zelazo, P. R., & Clifton, R. K. (1993). Newborn infants' memory for speech sounds retained over 24 hours. *Developmental Psychology, 29*, 313–323.

Taddio, A., Katz, J., Bersich, A. L., Goren, K. (1997). Effect of neonatal circumcision on pain response during subsequent routine vaccination. *Lancet, 349*, 599–603.

Taddio, A., Shah, V., Gilbert-MacLeod, C., & Katz, J. (2002). Conditioning and hyperalgesia in newborns exposed to repeated heel lances. *Journal of the American Medical Association, 288*, 857–861.

Tager-Flusberg, H., & Calkins, S. (1990). Does imitation facilitate the acquisition of grammar? Evidence from a study of autistic, Down's syndrome and normal children. *Journal of Child Language, 17*, 591–606.

Takahashi, K. (1986). Examining the Strange Situation procedure with Japanese mothers and 12-month-old infants. *Developmental Psychology, 22*, 265–270.

Takahashi, K. (1990). Are the key assumptions of the "Strange Situation" procedure universal? A view from Japanese research. *Human Development, 33*, 23–30.

Tamis-LeMonda, C. S., & Bornstein, M. H. (1991). Individual variation, correspondence, stability, and change in mother and toddler play. *Infant Behavior and Development, 14*, 143–162.

Tamis-Lemonda, C. S., & Bornstein, M. H. (1994). Specificity in mother–toddler language-play relations across the second year. *Developmental Psychology, 30*, 283–292.

Tamis-LeMonda, C. S., Bornstein, M. H., Cyphers, L., & Toda, S. (1992). Language and play at one year: A comparison of toddlers and mothers in the United States and Japan. *International Journal of Behavioral Development, 15*, 19–42.

Tamis-LeMonda, C. S., Uzgiris, I. C., & Bornstein, M. H. (2002). Play in parent-child interactions. In M. H. Bornstein (Ed.), *Handbook of parenting* (2nd ed., Vol. 5). Mahwah, NJ: Erlbaum.

Tamres, L. K., Janicki, D., & Helgeson, V. S. (2002). Sex differences in coping behavior: A meta-analytic review and an examination of relative coping. *Personality and Social Psychology Review, 6*, 2–30.

Tangney, J., & Fischer, K. (Eds.). (1995). *Self-conscious emotions: The psychology of shame, guilt, embarrassment, and pride*. New York: Guilford.

Tanner, J. M. (1963). The regulation of human growth. *Child Development, 34*, 817–847.

Tanner, J. M. (1987). Issues and advances in adolescent growth and development. *Journal of Adolescent Health Care, 8*, 470–478.

Tanner, J. M. (1990). *Fetus into man: Physical growth from conception to maturity* (2nd ed.). Cambridge, MA: Harvard University Press.

Tanner, J. M., Whitehouse, R. H., & Takaishi, M. (1966). Standards for growth and growth velocities. *Archives of Disease in Childhood, 41*, 467.

Tappan, M. B. (1997) Language, culture, and moral development: A Vygotskian perspective. *Developmental Review, 17*, 78–100.

Tardif, T., Gelman, S. A., & Xu, F. (1999). Putting the "noun bias" in context: A comparison of English and Mandarin. *Child Development, 70*, 620–635.

Tasker, F. L., & Golombok, S. (1997). *Growing up in a lesbian family: Effects on child development*. New York: Guilford.

Taylor, H. G., Klein, N., Minich, N. M., & Hack, M. (2000). Middle-school-age outcomes in children with very low birthweight. *Child Development, 71*, 1495–1511.

Taylor, J., Iacono, W. G., & McGue, M. (2001). Evidence for a genetic etiology of early-onset delinquency. *Journal of Abnormal Beahvior, 109*, 634–643.

Taylor, L., & Ingram, R. E. (1999). Cognitive reactivity and despressotypic information processing in children of depressed mothers. *Journal of Abnormal Psychology, 108*, 202–210.

Taylor, M. G. (1996). The development of children's beliefs about social and biological aspects of gender differences. *Child Development, 67*, 1555–1571.

Taylor, M., Cartwright, B. S., & Bowden, T. (1991). Perspective taking and theory of mind: Do children predict interpretive diversity as a function of differences in observers' knowledge? *Child Development, 62*, 1334–1351.

Taylor, M., Esbensen, B. M., & Bennett, R. T. (1994). Children's understanding of knowledge acquisition: The tendency for children to report that they have always known what they have just learned. *Child Development, 65*, 1581–1604.

Taylor, R. D., Casten, R., & Flickinger, S. M. (1993). Influence of kinship social support on the parenting experiences and psychosocial adjustment of African-American adolescents. *Developmental Psychology, 29*, 382–388.

Teasley, S. (1995). The role of talk in children's peer collaborations. *Developmental Psychology, 31*, 207–220.

Teller, D. Y., & Bornstein, M. H. (1987). Infant color vision and color perception. In P. Salapatek & L. Cohen (Eds.), *Handbook of infant perception: Vol. 1. From sensation to perception*. New York: Academic Press.

Temple, E., Poldrack, R. A., Deutsch, G. K., Miller, S., Tallal, P., Merzenich, M. M., et al. (2003). Neural deficits in children with dyslexia ameliorated by behavioral remediation: Evidence from fMRI. *Proceedings of the National Academy of Sciences, 100*, 2860–2865.

Tenenbaum, H. R., & Leaper, C. (2003). Parent-child conversations about science: The socialization of gender inequities? *Developmental Psychology, 39*, 34–47.

Teo, T., Becker, G., & Edelstein, W. (1995). Variability in structured wholeness: Context factors in L. Kohlberg's data on the development of moral judgment. *Merrill-Palmer Quarterly, 41*, 381–393.

Terman, L. M. (1925). *Genetic studies of genius: Vol. 1. Mental and physical traits of a thousand gifted children*. Stanford, CA: Stanford University Press.

Terwogt, M. M. (2002). Emotional states in self and others as motives for helping in 10-year-old children. *British Journal of Developmental Psychology, 20*, 131–147.

Tesser, A. (1984). Self-evaluation maintenance processes: Implications for relationships and for development. In J. C. Masters & K. Yarkin-Levin (Eds.), *Boundary areas in social and developmental psychology*. New York: Academic Press.

Tessler, M., & Nelson, K. (1994). Making memories: The influence of joint encoding on later recall. *Consciousness and Cognition, 3*, 307–326.

Teti, D. M. (1992). Sibling interaction. In V. B. Van Hasselt & M. Hersen (Eds.), *Handbook of social development*. New York: Plenum.

Thabet, A., & Vostanis, P. (1999). Post-traumatic stress reactions in children of war. Journal of *Child Psychology and Psychiatry and Allied Disciplines, 40*, 385–391.

Tharp, R. G. (1989). Psychocultural variables and constants: Effects on teaching and learning in schools. *American Psychologist, 44*, 349–359.

Thatcher, R. W., Lyon, G. R., Ramsey, J., & Krasneger, J. (1996). *Developmental neuroimaging*. San Diego, CA: Academic Press.

Thelen, E. (1994). Three-month-old infants can learn task-specific patterns of interlimb coordination. *Psychological Science, 5*, 280–285.

Thelen, E. (1995). Motor development: A new synthesis. *American Psychologist, 50*, 79–95.

Thelen, E. (2000). Motor development as foundation and future of developmental psychology. *International Journal of Behavioral Development, 24*, 385–397.

Thelen, E., & Adolph, K. E. (1992). Arnold L. Gesell: The paradox of nature and nurture. *Developmental Psychology, 28*, 368–380.

Thelen, E., Corbetta, D., & Spencer, J. (1996). The development of reaching during the first year: The role of movement speed. *Journal of Experimental Psychology: Human Perception and Performance, 22*, 1059–1076.

Thelen, E., & Fisher, D. M. (1983). The organization of spontaneous leg movements in newborn infants. *Journal of Motor Behavior, 15*, 353–377.

Thelen, E., & Smith, L. B. (1998). Dynamic systems theories. In W. Damon (Series Ed.) & R. M. Lerner (Vol. Ed.), *Handbook of child psychology: Vol. 1. Theoretical models of human development* (5th ed.). New York: Wiley.

Thoman, E. B. (1990). Sleeping and waking states in infants: A functional perspective. *Neuroscience and Behavioral Reviews, 14*, 93–107.

Thoman, E. B. (1993). Obligation and option in the premature nursery. *Developmental Review, 13*, 1–30

Thomas, A., & Chess, S. (1977). *Temperament and development*. New York: Bruner/Mazel.

Thomas, A., & Chess, S. (1984). Genesis and evaluation of behavioral disorder: From infancy to early adult life. *American Journal of Psychiatry, 141*, 1–9.

Thomas, A., & Chess, S. (1986). The New York Longitudinal Study: From infancy to early adult life. In R. Plomin & J. Dunn (Eds.), *The study of temperament: Changes, continuities and challenges*. Hillsdale, NJ: Erlbaum.

Thomas, A., Chess, S., & Birch, H. G. (1968). *Temperament and behavior disorders in children*. New York: New York University Press.

Thompson, R. A. (1990). Vulnerability in research: A developmental perspective on research risk. *Child Development, 61*, 1–16.

Thompson, R. A. (1998). Early sociopersonality development. In W. Damon (Series Ed.) & N. Eisenberg (Vol. Ed.), *Handbook of child psychology: Vol. 3. Social, emotional, and personality development*, (5th ed.). New York: Wiley.

Thompson, R. A. (2000). The legacy of early attachments. *Child Development, 71*, 145–152.

Thompson, R. A., Connell, J. P., & Bridges, L. J. (1988). Temperament, emotion, and social interactive behavior in the Strange Situation: A component process analysis of attachment system functioning. *Child Development, 59*, 1102–1110.

Thompson, R. A., Flood, M. F., & Lundquist, L. (1995). Emotion regulation: Its relations to attachment and developmental psychopathology. In D. Cicchetti & S. L. Toth (Eds.), *Emotion, cognition, and representation. Rochester Symposium on Developmental Psychopathology (Vol. 6)*. Rochester, NY: University of Rochester Press.

Thompson, R. A., Lamb, M. E., & Estes, D. (1982). Stability of infant-mother attachment and its relationship to changing life circumstances in an unselected middle-class sample. *Child Development, 53*, 144–148.

Thompson, R. A., & Limber, S. (1990). "Social anxiety" in infancy: Stranger wariness and separation distress. In H. Leitenberg (Ed.), *Handbook of social and evaluation anxiety*. New York: Plenum.

Thompson, T. L., & Zerbinos, E. (1995). Gender roles in animated cartoons: Has the picture changed in 20 years? *Sex Roles, 32*, 651–674.

Thompson, T. L., & Zerbinos, E. (1997). Television cartoons: Do children notice it's a boy's world? *Sex Roles, 37*, 415–432.

Thomson, J. R., & Chapman, R. S. (1977). Who is "Daddy" revisited: The status of two-year-olds' overextended words in use and comprehension. *Journal of Child Language, 4,* 359–375.

Thorne, B. (1993). *Gender play: Girls and boys in school.* New Brunswick, NJ: Rutgers University Press.

Thurstone, L. L. (1938). *Primary mental abilities.* Chicago: University of Chicago Press.

Thurstone, L. L., & Thurstone, T. G. (1962). *SRA Primary Mental Abilities.* Chicago: Science Research Associates.

Tiedemann, J. (2000). Parents' gender stereotypes and teachers' beliefs as predictors of children's concept of their mathematical ability in elementary school. *Journal of Educational Psychology, 92,* 144–151.

Tieszen, H. R. (1979). Children's social behavior in a Korean preschool. *Journal of Korean Home Economics Association, 17,* 71–84.

Tinbergen, N. (1973). *The animal in its world: Explorations of an ethologist, 1932–1972* (Vols. 1 & 2). Cambridge, MA: Harvard University Press.

Tisak, M. S., & Turiel, E. (1988). Variation in seriousness of transgressions and children's immoral and conventional concepts. *Developmental Psychology, 24,* 352–357.

Tobey, A. E., & Goodman, G. S. (1992). Children's eyewitness memory: Effects of participation and forensic context. *Child Abuse and Neglect, 16,* 779–796.

Toda, S., & Fogel, A. (1993). Infant response to the still-face situation at 3 and 6 months. *Developmental Psychology, 29,* 532–538.

Tolchinsky-Landsmann, L., & Levin, I. (1985). Writing in preschoolers: An age-related analysis. *Applied Psycholinguistics, 6,* 319–339.

Tomasello, M. (1999a). *The cultural origins of human cognition.* Cambridge, MA: Harvard University Press.

Tomasello, M. (1999b). Having intentions, understanding intentions, and understanding communicative intentions. In P. D. Zelazo, J. W. Astington, & D. R. Olson (Eds.), *Developing theories of intention.* Mahwah, NJ: Erlbaum.

Tomasello, M. (2000). Do young children have adult syntactic competence? *Cognition, 74,* 209–253.

Tomasello, M. (2001). Perceiving intentions and learning words in the second year of life. In M. Bowerman & S. C. Levinson (Eds.), *Language acquisition and conceptual development.* New York: Cambridge University Press.

Tomasello, M., Conti-Ramsden, G., & Ewert, B. (1990). Young children's conversations with their mothers and fathers: Differences in breakdown and repair. *Journal of Child Language, 17,* 115–130.

Tomasello, M., & Farrar, M. J. (1986). Joint attention and early language. *Child Development, 57,* 1454–1463.

Tomasello, M., & Merriman, W. E. (Eds.). (1995). *Beyond names for things: Young children's acquisition of verbs.* Hillsdale, NJ: Erlbaum.

Tomasello, M., Savage-Rumbaugh, S., & Kruger, A. C. (1993). Imitative learning of actions on objects by children, chimpanzees, and enculturated chimpanzees. *Child Development, 64,* 1688–1705.

Tongsong, T., Wanapirak, C., Sirivatanapa, P., Piyamongkol, W., Sirichotiyakul, S., & Yampochai, A. (1998). Amniocentesis related to fetal loss: A cohort study. *Obstetrics and Gynecology, 92,* 64–67.

Tooby, J., & Cosmides, L. (1995). Mapping the evolved functional organization of mind and brain. In M. S. Gazzaniga (Ed.), *The cognitive neurosciences.* Cambridge, MA: MIT Press.

Topping, K. (1988). *The peer tutoring handbook: Promoting co-operative learning.* London: Croom Helm.

Touchette, N. (1990). Evolutions: Fertilization. *Journal of NIH Research, 2,* 94–97.

Tout, K., de Haan, M., Campbell, E. K., & Gunnar, M. R. (1998). Social behavior correlates of cortisol activity in child care: Gender differences and time-of-day effects. *Child Development, 69,* 1247–1262.

Tracy, R. L., & Ainsworth, M. D. S. (1981). Maternal affectionate behavior and infant–mother attachment patterns. *Child Development, 52,* 1341–1343.

Trainor, L. J., & Heinmiller, B. M. (1998). The development of evaluative responses to music: Infants prefer to listen to consonance over dissonance. *Infant Behavior and Development, 21,* 77–88.

Trautner, H. M. (1992). The development of sex-typing in children: A longitudinal analysis. *German Journal of Psychology, 16,* 183–199.

Travers, J. R., & Light, R. J. (Eds.). (1982). *Learning from experience: Evaluating early childhood demonstration programs.* Washington, DC: National Academy Press.

Trehub, S. E. (1976). The discrimination of foreign speech contrasts by infants and adults. *Child Development, 47,* 466–472.

Trehub, S. E., & Henderson, J. (1994, July). *Caregivers' songs and their effect on infant listeners.* Proceedings of the Meeting of the International Conference for Music Perception and Cognition. Liege, Belgium.

Trehub, S. E., & Schellenberg, E. G. (1995). Music: Its relevance to infants. In R. Vasta (Ed.), *Annals of child development* (Vol. 11). London: Kingsley.

Trehub, S. E., & Schneider, B. A. (1983). Recent advances in the behavioral study of infant audition. In S. E. Gerber & G. T. Mencher (Eds.), *Development of auditory behavior.* New York: Grune & Stratton.

Trehub, S. E., Schneider, B. A., Morrongiello, B. A., & Thorpe, L. A. (1988). Auditory sensitivity in school-age children. *Journal of Experimental Child Psychology, 46,* 273–285.

Trehub, S. E., Thorpe, L. A., & Cohen, A. J. (1991, April). *Infants' auditory processing of numerical information.* Paper presented at the meeting of the Society for Research in Child Development, Seattle.

Tremblay, R. E., Japel, C., Perusse, D., McDuff, P., Boivin, M., Zoccolillo, M., et al. (1999). The search for the age of 'onset' of physical aggression: Rousseau and Bandura revisited. *Criminal Behaviour and Mental Health, 9,* 8–23.

Tremblay, R. E., Pihl, R. O., Vitaro, F., Dobkin, P. L. (1994). Predicting early onset of male antisocial behavior from preschool behavior. *Archives of General Psychiatry, 51,* 732–739

Trevathen, W. R. (1987). *Human birth: An evolutionary perspective.* New York: Aldine de Gruyter.

Trickett, P. K., & McBride-Chang, C. (1995). The developmental impact of different forms of child abuse and neglect. *Developmental Review, 15,* 311–337.

Trivers, R. L. (1971). The evolution of reciprocal altruism. *Quarterly Review of Biology, 46,* 35–57.

Trivers, R. L. (1972). Parental investment and sexual selection. In B. Campbell (Ed.), *Sexual selection and the descent of man 1871–1971.* New York: Aldine de Gruyter.

Trivers, R. L. (1983). The evolution of cooperation. In D. L. Bridgeman (Ed.), *The nature of prosocial development.* New York: Academic Press.

Tronick, E. Z. (1989). Emotions and emotional communication in infants. *American Psychologist, 44,* 112–119.

Tronick, E. Z., Morelli, G. A. Ivey, P. K. (1992). The Efe forager infant and toddler's pattern of social relationships: Multiple and simultaneous. *Developmental Psychology, 28,* 568–577.

Tu, W. (1994). Embodying in the universe: A note on Confucian self-realization. In R. T. Ames, W. Dissanayake, & T. P. Kasulis (Eds.), *Self as person in Asian theory and practice.* Albany: State University of New York Press.

Tubman, J. G., Lerner, R. M., Lerner, J. V., & Von Eye, A. (1992). Temperament and adjustment in young adulthood: A 15-year longitudinal analysis. *American Journal of Orthopsychiatry, 62,* 564–574.

Tucker, C. J., McHale, S. M., & Crouter, A. C. (2001). Conditions of sibling support in adolescence. *Journal of Family Psychology, 15,* 254–271.

Tudge, J. R. H. (1989). When collaboration leads to regression: Some negative consequences of socio-cognitive conflict. *European Journal of Social Psychology, 19,* 123–138.

Tudge, J. R. H. (1992). Processes and consequences of peer collaboration: A Vygotskian analysis. *Child Development, 63,* 1364–1379.

Tudge, J. R. H., Lee, S., & Putnam, S. (1995, April). *Young children's play in sociocultural context: South Korea and the United States.* Paper presented at the biennial meetings of the Society for Research in Child Development, Indianapolis.

Tudge, J. R. H., & Rogoff, B. (1989). Peer influences on cognitive development: Piagetian and Vygotskian perspectives. In M. H. Bornstein & J. Bruner (Eds.), *Interaction in human development.* Hillsdale, NJ: Erlbaum.

Turiel, E. (1998). The development of morality. In W. Damon (Series Ed.) & N. Eisenberg (Vol. Ed.), *Handbook of child psychology: Vol. 3. Social, emotional, and personality development* (5th ed.). New York: Wiley.

Turiel, E. (2002). *The culture of morality.* New York: Cambridge University Press.

Turiel, E., Killen, M., & Helwig, C. C. (1987). Morality: Its structure, functions, and vagaries. In J. Kagan & S. Lamb (Eds.), *The emergence of moral concepts in young children.* Chicago: University of Chicago Press.

Turiel, E., & Wainryb, C. (1994). Social reasoning and the varieties of social experiences in cultural contexts. In H. W. Reese (Ed.), *Advances in child development and behavior* (Vol. 25). San Diego, CA: Academic Press.

Turkheimer, E. (1991). Individual and group differences in adoption studies of IQ. *Psychological Bulletin, 110,* 392–405.

Turkheimer, E. (2000). Three laws of behavior genetics and what they mean. *Current Directions in Psychological Science, 9,* 160–164.

Turkheimer, E., & Waldron, M. (2000). Nonshared environment: A theoretical, methodological, and quantitative review. *Psychological Bulletin, 126,* 78–108.

Turner, P. J., & Gervai, J. (1995). A multidimensional study of gender typing in preschool children and their parents: Personality, attitudes, preferences, behavior, and cultural differences. *Developmental Psychology, 31,* 759–772.

Twenge, J. M., & Campbell, W. K. (2001). Age and birth cohort differences in self-esteem: A cross-temporal meta-analysis. *Personality and Social Psychology Review, 5,* 321–344.

Tzuriel, D. (2001). *Dynamic assessment of young children.* New York: Kluwer Academic Publishers.

U.S. Bureau of the Census (2001). *Statistical abstract of the United States* (121st ed.). Washington, DC: U.S. Government Printing Office.

U.S. Department of Education (2001). *Digest of education statistics 2000.* Washington, DC: U.S. Government Printing Office.

Underwood, M. K. (2003). *Social aggression among girls.* New York: Guilford.

Underwood, M. K., Coie, J. D., & Herbsman, C. R. (1992). Display rules for anger and aggression in school-age children. *Child Development, 63,* 366–380.

UNICEF. (2002). *The state of the world's children 2002.* New York: United Nation's Children's Fund.

Updegraff, K. A., McHale, S. M., & Crouter, A. C. (2000). Adolescents' sex-typed friendship experiences: Does having a sister versus a brother matter? *Child Development, 71,* 1597–1610.

Urbain, E. S., & Kendell, P. C. (1980). Review of social-cognitive problem-solving interventions with children. *Psychological Bulletin, 88,* 109–143.

Urberg, K. A. (1999). Introduction: Some thoughts about studying the influence of peers on children and adolescents. *Merrill-Palmer Quarterly, 45,* 1–12.

Urberg, K. A., Degirmencioglu, S. M., & Pilgrim, C. (1997). Close friend and group influence on adolescent cigarette smoking and alcohol use. *Developmental Psychology, 33,* 834–844.

Uttal, D. H. (2000). Seeing the big picture: Map use and the development of spatial cognition. *Developmental Science, 3,* 247–286.

Valian, V. (1986). Syntactic categories in the speech of young children. *Developmental Psychology, 22,* 562–579.

Valian, V. (1996). *Parental replies: Linguistic status and didactic role.* Cambridge, MA: MIT Press.

Valian, V. (1999). Input and language acquisition. In W. C. Ritchie & T. K. Bhatia (Eds.), *Handbook of child language acquisition.* San Diego, CA: Academic Press.

Valsiner, J. (1997). *Culture and the development of children's action: A theory of human development.* New York: Wiley.

van Bakel, H. J. A., & Riksen-Walraven, J. M. (2002). Parenting and development of one-year-olds: Links with parental, contextual, and child characteristics. *Child Development, 73,* 256–273.

Van Balen, F. (1998). Development of IVF children. *Developmental Review, 18,* 30–46.

Van Den Bergh, B. R. H. (1992). Maternal emotions during pregnancy and fetal and neonatal behavior. In J. G. Nijhuis (Ed.), *Fetal behavior: Developmental and perinatal aspects.* New York: Oxford University Press.

van den Boom, D. C. (1994). The influence of temperament and mothering on attachment and exploration: An experimental manipulation of sensitive responsiveness among lower-class mothers with irritable infants. *Child Development, 65,* 1457–1477.

van den Boom, D. C. (1995). Do first-year intervention effects endure? Follow-up during toddlerhood of a sample of Dutch irritable infants. *Child Development, 66,* 1798–1816.

van den Boom, D., & Hoeksma, J. B. (1994). The effect of infant irritability on mother-infant interaction: A growth-curve analysis. *Developmental Psychology, 30,* 581–590.

Van der Veer, R., & Valsiner, J. (1988). Lev Vygotsky and Pierre Janet: On the origin of the concept of sociogenesis. *Developmental Review, 8,* 52–65.

Van Giffen, K., & Haith, M. M. (1984). Infant visual response to gestalt geometric forms. *Infant Behavior and Development, 7,* 335–346.

van IJzendoorn, M. H. (1992). Intergenerational transmission of parenting: A review of studies in nonclinical populations. *Developmental Review, 12,* 76–99.

van IJzendoorn, M. H. (1995). Associations between adult attachment representations and parent-child attachment, parent responsiveness, and clinical status: A meta-analysis on the predictive validity of the Adult Attachment Interview. *Psychological Bulletin, 117,* 387–403.

Van IJzendoorn, M. H., & De Wolff, M. S. (1997). In search of the absent father-meta-analyses of infant-father attachment: A rejoinder to our discussants. *Child Development, 68,* 604–609.

van IJzendoorn, M. H., Goldberg, S., Kroonenberg, P. M., & Frenkel, O. J. (1992). The relative effects of maternal and child problems on the quality of attachment: A meta-analysis of attachment in clinical samples. *Child Development, 63,* 840–858.

van IJzendoorn, M. H., Juffer, F., & Duyvesteyn, M. G. C. (1995). Breaking the intergenerational cycle of insecure attachment: A review of the effects of attachment-based interventions on maternal sensitivity and infant security. *Journal of Child Psychology and Psychiatry and Allied Disciplines, 36,* 225–248.

van IJzendoorn, M. H., & Kroonenberg, P. M. (1988). Cross-cultural patterns of attachment: A meta-analysis of the Strange Situation. *Child Development, 59,* 147–156.

Van Loosbroek, E., & Smitsman, A. W. (1990). Visual perception of numerosity in infancy. *Developmental Psychology, 26,* 916–922.

Van Tuinen, I., & Wolfe, S. M. (1993). *Unnecessary cesarean sections: Halting a national epidemic.* Washington, DC: Public Citizens' Health Research Group.

Vandell, D. L. (2000). Parents, peer groups, and other socializing influences. *Developmental Psychology, 36,* 699–710.

Vandell, D. L., Minnet, A. M., Johnson, B. S., & Santrock, J. W. (1990). *Siblings and friends: Experiences of school-aged children.* Unpublished manuscript, University of Texas at Dallas.

Vasta, R. (Ed.). (1982). *Strategies and techniques of child study.* New York: Academic Press.

Vasta, R., Knott, J. A., & Gaze, C. E. (1996). Can spatial training erase the gender differences on the water-level task? *Psychology of Women Quarterly, 20,* 549–567.

Vasta, R., & Liben, L. S. (1996). The water-level task: An intriguing puzzle. *Current Directions in Psychological Science, 5,* 171–177.

Vasta, R., Rosenberg, D., Knott, J. A., & Gaze, C. E. (1997). Experience and the water-level task revisited: Does expertise exact a price? *Psychological Science, 8,* 336–339.

Vaughn, B. E., & Bost, K. K. (1999). Attachment and temperament: Redundant, independent, or interacting influences on interpersonal adaptation and personality development? In J. Cassidy & P. R. Shaver (Eds.), *Handbook of attachment: Theory, research, and clinical applications.* New York: Guilford.

Vaughn, B. E., Bradley, C. F., Joffe, L. S., Seifer, R., & Barglow, P. (1987). Maternal characteristics measured prenatally are predictive of ratings of temperamental "difficulty" on the Carey Infant Temperament Questionnaire. *Developmental Psychology, 23,* 152–161.

Vaughn, B. E., Kopp, C. B., & Krakow, J. B. (1984). The emergence and consolidation of self-control from eighteen to thirty months of age: Normative trends and individual differences. *Child Development, 55,* 990–1004.

Vaughn, B. E., & Waters, E. (1990). Attachment behavior at home and in the laboratory: Q-sort observations and Strange Situation classifications of one-year-olds. *Child Development, 61,* 1965–1990.

Verba, M. (1994). Beginnings of collaboration in peer interactions. *Human Development, 37,* 125–139.

Verbeek, P., Hartup, W. W., & Collins, W. A. (2000). Conflict management in children and adolescents. In F. Aureli & F. B. M. de Waal (Eds.), *Natural conflict resolution.* Berkeley: University of California Press.

Verma, S. A., & Saraswathi, T. S. (2002). Adolescence in India: Street urchins or Silicon Valley millionaires? In B. B. Brown, R. W. Larson, & T. S. Saraswathi (Eds.), *The world's youth: Adolescence in eight regions of the globe.* New York: Cambridge University Press.

Vernon, S. A., & Ferreiro, E. (1999). Writing development: A neglected variable in the consideration of phonological awareness. *Harvard Educational Review, 69,* 395–415.

Verschueren, K., Marcoen, A., & Schoefs, V. (1996). The internal working model of the self, attachment, and competence in five-year-olds. *Child Development, 67,* 2493–2511.

Vierikko, E., Pulkkinen, L., Kaprio, J., Viken, R., & Rose, R. J. (2003). Sex differences in genetic and environmental effects on aggression. *Aggressive Behavior, 29,* 55–68.

Vietze, P. M., & Vaughan, H. G. (1988). *Early identification of infants with developmental disabilities.* Philadelphia: Grune & Stratton.

Vihman, M. M. (1985). Language differentiation by the bilingual infant. *Journal of Child Language, 12,* 297–324.

Vihman, M. M., & Miller, R. (1988). Words and babble at the threshold of language acquisition. In M. D. Smith & J. L. Locke (Eds.), *The emergent lexicon.* Orlando, FL: Academic Press.

Vincent, K. R. (1991). Black/White IQ differences: Does age make the difference? *Journal of Clinical Psychology, 47,* 266–270.

Vinden, P. G. (1999). Children's understanding of mind and emotion: A multi-culture study. *Cognition and Emotion, 13,* 19–48.

Vogel, E. (1963/1991). *Japan's new middle class.* Berkeley: University of California Press.

Volling, B. L., Youngblade, L. M., & Belsky, J. (1997). Young children's social relationships with siblings and friends. *American Journal of Orthopsychiatry, 67,* 102–111.

Volterra, V., & Taeschner, T. (1978). The acquisition and development of language by bilingual children. *Journal of Child Language, 5,* 311–326.

Von Senden, M. (1960). *Space and sight.* New York: Free Press.

Vondra, J. I., Hommerding, K. D., & Shaw, D. S. (1999). Stability and change in infant attachment style in a low-income sample. *Monographs of the Society for Research in Child Development, 64*(3), 119–144.

Voyer, D., Voyer, S., & Bryden, M. P. (1995). Magnitude of sex differences in spatial abilities: A meta-analysis and consideration of critical variables. *Psychological Bulletin, 117,* 250–270.

Vuchinich, S. (1990). The sequential organization of closing in verbal family conflict. In A. D. Grimshaw (Ed.), *Conflict talk: Sociolinguistic investigations of arguments in conversations.* Cambridge: Cambridge University Press.

Vuchinich, S., Bank, L., & Patterson, G. R. (1992). Parenting, peers, and the stability of antisocial behavior in preadolescent boys. *Developmental Psychology, 28,* 510–521.

Vurpillot, E. (1968). The development of scanning strategies and their relation to visual differentiation. *Journal of Experimental Child Psychology, 6,* 632–650.

Vurpillot, E., & Ball, W. A. (1979). The concept of identity and children's selective attention. In G. A. Hale & M. Lewis (Eds.), *Attention and cognitive development.* New York: Plenum.

Vurpillot, E., Castelo, R., & Renard, C. (1975). Extent of visual exploration and number of elements present around the stimulus in a perceptual differentiation task. *Année Psychologique, 75,* 362–363.

Vygotsky, L. S. (1934/1962). *Thought and language.* Cambridge, MA: MIT Press.

Vygotksy, L. S. (1978). *The collected works of L. S. Vygotsky: Vol. 1. Problems of general psychology.* New York: Plenum Press.

Vygotsky, L. S. (1981). The genesis of higher mental functions. In J. V. Wertsch (Ed.), *The concept of activity in Soviet psychology.* Armonk, NY: M. E. Sharpe.

Waas, G. A. (1988). Social attributional biases of peer-rejected and aggressive children. *Child Development, 59,* 969–975.

Wachs, T. D. (1988). Relevance of physical environment influences for toddler temperament. *Infant Behavior and Development, 11,* 431–445.

Wachs, T. D. (1992). *The nature of nurture.* Newbury Park, CA: Sage.

Wachs, T. D. (1994). Fit, context, and the transition between temperament and personality. In C. F. Halverson Jr., G. A. Kohnstamm, & R. P. Martin (Eds.), *The developing structure of temperament and personality from infancy to adulthood.* Hillsdale, NJ: Erlbaum.

Wachs, T. D. (2000). *Necessary but not sufficient: The respective roles of single and multiple influences on individual development.* Washington, DC: American Psychological Association.

Wadsworth, S. J., Corley, R. P., Hewitt, J. K., & DeFries, J. C. (2001). Stability of genetic and environmental influences on reading performance at 7, 12, and 16 years of age in the Colorado Adoption Project. *Behavior Genetics, 31,* 353–359.

Wadsworth, S. J., Corley, R. P., Hewitt, J. K., Plomin, R., & DeFries, J. C. (2002). Parent-offspring resemblance for reading performance at 7, 12 and 16 years of age in the Colorado Adoption Project. *Journal of Child Psychology and Psychiatry and Allied Disciplines, 43,* 769–774.

Wagner, B. M., & Phillips, D. A. (1992). Beyond beliefs: Parent and child behaviors and children's perceived academic competence. *Child Development, 63,* 1380–1391.

Wainryb, C. (1993). The application of moral judgments to other cultures: Relativism and universality. *Child Development, 64,* 924–933.

Wainryb, C. (2000). Values and truths: The making and judging of moral decisions. In M. Laupa (Ed.), *New directions for child and adolescent development: No. 89. Rights and wrongs: How children and young adults evaluate the world.* San Francisco: Jossey-Bass.

Wainryb, C., & Ford, S. (1998). Young children's evaluations of acts based on beliefs different than their own. *Merrill-Palmer Quarterly, 44,* 484–503.

Wainryb, C., Shaw, L., & Maianu, C. (1998). Tolerance and intolerance: Children's and adolescents' judgments of dissenting beliefs, speech, persons, and conduct. *Child Development, 69,* 1541–1555.

Wakely, A., Rivera, S., & Langer, J. (2000). Can young infants add and subtract? *Child Development, 71,* 1525–1534.

Waldman, I. D. (1996). Aggressive boys' hostile perceptual and response biases: The role of attention and impulsivity. *Child Development, 67,* 1015–1033.

Waldman, I. D., Weinberg, R. A., & Scarr, S. (1994). Racial-group differences in IQ in the Minnesota Transracial Adoption Study: A reply to Levin and Lynn. *Intelligence, 19,* 29–44.

Walker, H. M., Colvin, G., & Ramsey, E. (1995). *Anti-social behavior in school: Strategies and best practices.* Pacific Grove, CA: Brooks/Cole.

Walker, L. J. (1989). A longitudinal study of moral reasoning. *Child Development, 60,* 157–166.

Walker, L. J. (1991). Sex differences in moral reasoning. In W. M. Kurtines & J. L. Gewirtz (Eds.), *Handbook of moral behavior and development: Vol. 2. Research.* Hillsdale, NJ: Erlbaum.

Walker, L. J. (1995). Sexism in Kohlberg's moral psychology? In W. M. Kurtines & J. L. Gewirtz (Eds.), *Moral development: An introduction.* Needham Heights, MA: Allyn & Bacon.

Walker, L. J., DeVries, B., & Trevarthen, S. D. (1987). Moral stages and moral orientations in real-life and hypothetical dilemmas. *Child Development, 58,* 842–858.

Walker, L. J., Hennig, K. H., & Krettenauer, T. (2000). Parent and peer contexts for children's moral reasoning development. *Child Development, 71,* 1033–1048

Walker, L. J., & Taylor, J. H. (1991). Family interactions and the development of moral reasoning. *Child Development, 62,* 264–283.

Walker-Andrews, A. S. (1997). Infants' perception of expressive behaviors: Differentiation of multimodal information. *Psychological Bulletin, 121,* 437–456.

Walker-Andrews, A. S., Bahrick, L. E., Raglioni, S. S., & Diaz, I. (1991). Infants' bimodal perception of gender. *Ecological Psychology, 3,* 55–75.

Wallach, M. A., & Kogan, N. (1966). *Modes of thinking in young children.* New York: Holt, Rinehart, and Winston.

Waller, N. G., Kojetin, B. A., Bouchard, T. J. Jr., Lykken, D. T., & Tellegen, A. (1990). Genetic and environmental influences on religious interests, attitudes, and values: A study of twins reared apart and together. *Psychological Science, 1,* 138–142.

Wallerstein, J. S., Lewis, J. M., & Blakeslee, S. (2000). *The unexpected legacy of divorce: A 25 year landmark study.* New York: Hyperion.

Walton, G. E., Bower, N. J., & Bower, T. G. (1992). Recognition of familiar faces by newborns. *Infant Behavior and Development, 15,* 265–269.

Wang, Q. (2001). Culture effects on adults' earliest childhood recollection and self-description: Implications for the relation between memory and the self. *Journal of Personality and Social Psychology, 81,* 220–233.

Wang, Q., Leichtman, M. D., & Davies, K. I. (2000). Sharing memories and telling stories: American and Chinese mothers and their 3-year-olds. *Memory, 8,* 159–177.

Ward, M. J., & Carlson, E. A. (1995). Associations among adult attachment representations, maternal sensitivity, and infant–mother attachment in a sample of adolescent mothers. *Child Development, 66,* 69–79.

Wark, G. R., & Krebs, D. L. (1996). Gender and dilemma differences in real-life moral judgment. *Developmental Psychology, 32,* 220–230.

Warkany, J. (1977). History of teratology. In J. G. Wilson & F. C. Fraser (Eds.), *Handbook of teratology: Vol. 1. General principles and etiology.* New York: Plenum.

Warkany, J. (1981). Prevention of congenital malformations. *Teratology, 23,* 175–189.

Warren, A. R., & McCloskey, L. A. (1997). Language acquisition in social contexts. In J. B. Gleason (Ed.), *The development of language* (4th ed.). Boston: Allyn and Bacon.

Warren, K. R., & Bast, R. J. (1988). Alcohol-related birth defects: An update. *Public Health Reports, 103,* 638–642.

Washington, J., Minde, K., & Goldberg, S. (1986). Temperament in premature infants: Style and stability. *Journal of the American Academy of Child Psychiatry, 25,* 493–502.

Wasserman, G. A., Liu, X., Pine, D. S., & Graziano, J. H. (2000). Contribution of maternal smoking during pregnancy and lead exposure to early child behavior problems. *Neurotoxicology and Teratology, 23,* 13–21.

Wasz-Hockert, O., Michelsson, K., & Lind, J. (1985). Twenty-five years of Scandinavian cry research. In B. M. Lester & C. Z. Boukydis (Eds.), *Infant crying: Theoretical and research perspectives.* New York. Plenum.

Waters, E. (1995). The Attachment Q-Set (Version 3.0) (Appendix A). In E. Waters, B. E. Vaughn, G. Posada, & K. Kondo-Ikemura (Eds.), *Caregiving, cultural, and cognitive perspectives on secure-base behavior and working models. Monographs of the Society for Research in Child Development, 60*(2–3, Serial No. 244).

Waters, E., & Deane, K. E. (1985). Defining and assessing individual differences in attachment relationships: Q-methodology and the organization of behavior in infancy and early childhood. In I. Bretherton & E. Waters (Eds.), Growing points of attachment theory and research. *Monographs of the Society for Research in Child Development, 50*(1–2, Serial No. 209).

Waters, E., Vaughn, B. E., Posada, G., & Kondo-Ikemura, K. (Eds.). (1995). Caregiving, cultural, and cognitive perspectives on secure-base behavior and working models. *Monographs of the Society for Research in Child Development, 60*(2–3, Serial No. 244).

Watson, J. B. (1928). *Psychological care of infant and child.* New York: Norton.

Watson, J. B., & Rayner, R. (1920). Conditioned emotional reactions. *Journal of Experimental Psychology, 3,* 1–14.

Watson, J. D. (1968). *The double helix: A personal account of the discovery of the structure of DNA.* New York: Atheneum.

Watson, J. D. (1990). The Human Genome Project: Past, present, and future. *Science, 248,* 44–49.

Watson, J. D., & Crick, F. H. C. (1953). Molecular structure of nucleic acid: A structure for deoxyribose nucleic acid. *Nature, 171,* 737–738.

Watson, M., & Fischer, K. A. (1977). A developmental sequence of agent use in late infancy. *Child Development, 48,* 828–836.

Waxman, S. R. (1990). Linguistic biases and the establishment of conceptual hierarchies. *Cognitive Development, 5,* 123–150.

Webb, N. M., & Palinscar, A. S. (1996). Group processes in the classroom. In D. C. Berliner & R. C. Calfee (Eds.), *Handbook of educational psychology.* New York: Simon & Schuster Macmillan.

Wechsler, D. (1967). *Manual for the Wechsler Preschool and Primary Scale of Intelligence.* New York: Psychological Corporation.

Wechsler, D. (1989). *Wechsler Preschool and Primary Scale of Intelligence-Revised.* New York: Psychological Corporation.

Wechsler, D. (1991). *Wechsler Intelligence Scale for Children-Third Edition.* New York: Psychological Corporation.

Weinberg, M. K., Tronick, E. Z., Cohn, J. F., & Olson, K. L. (1999). Gender differences in emotional expressivity and self-regulation during early infancy. *Developmental Psychology, 35,* 175–188.

Weine, S., Becker, D., McGlashan, T., Vojvoda, D., Hartman, S., & Robbins, J. (1995). Adolescent survivors of "ethnic cleansing" on the first year in America. *Journal of the American Academy of Child and Adolescent Psychiatry, 34,* 1153–1159.

Weinraub, M., Clemens, L. P., Sockloff, A., Ethridge, T., Gracely, E., & Myers, B. (1984). The development of sex role stereotypes in the third year: Relationships to gender labeling, gender identity, sex-typed toy preference, and family characteristics. *Child Development, 55,* 1493–1503.

Weisner, T. S. (1996). The 5 to 7 transition as an ecocultural project. In A. Sameroff & M. M. Haith (Eds.), *The five to seven year shift: The age of reason and responsibility.* Chicago: University of Chicago Press.

Weisner, T. S., Garnier, H., & Loucky, J. (1994). Domestic tasks, gender egalitarian values and children's gender typing in conventional and nonconventional families. *Sex Roles, 30,* 23–54.

Weisner, T. S., & Wilson-Mitchell, J. E. (1990). Nonconventional family life styles and sex typing in six-year-olds. *Child Development, 61,* 1915–1933.

Weiss, B., Dodge, K. A., Bates, J. E., & Pettit, G. S. (1992). Some consequences of early harsh discipline: Child aggression and a maladaptive social information processing style. *Child Development, 63,* 1321–1335.

Weiss, M. G., & Miller, P. H. (1983). Young children's understanding of displaced aggression. *Journal of Experimental Child Psychology, 35,* 529–539.

Weissberg, R. P. (1985). Designing effective social problem-solving programs for the classroom. In B. H. Schneider, K. H. Rubin, & J. E. Ledingham (Eds.), *Children's peer relations: Issues in assessment and intervention.* New York: Springer-Verlag.

Wekselman, K., Spiering, K., Hetterberg, C., Kenner, C., & Flandermeyer, A. (1995). Fetal alcohol syndrome from infancy to childhood: A review of the literature. *Journal of Pediatric Nursing, 10,* 296–303.

Welch-Ross, M. K. (1995). An inegrative model of the development of autobiogrpahical memory. *Developmental Review, 15,* 338–365.

Welch-Ross, M. K., & Schmidt, C. R. (1996). Gender schema development and children's constructive story memory: Evidence for a developmental model. *Child Development, 67,* 820–835.

Wellman, H. M. (1977). Preschoolers' understanding of memory-relevant variables. *Child Development, 48,* 1720–1723.

Wellman, H. M. (1988). The early development of memory strategies. In F. E. Weinert & M. Perlmutter (Eds.), *Memory development: Universal changes and individual differences.* Hillsdale, NJ: Erlbaum.

Wellman, H. M. (2002). Understanding the psychological world. In U. Goswami (Ed.), *Blackwell handbook of childhood cognitive development.* Malden, MA: Blackwell.

Wellman, H. M., & Gelman, S. A. (1998). Knowledge acquisition in foundational domains. In W. Damon (Series Ed.) & D. Kuhn & R. S. Siegler (Vol. Eds.), *Handbook of child psychology: Vol. 2. Cognition, perception, and language* (5th ed.). New York: Wiley.

Wellman, H. M., Ritter, K., & Flavell, J. H. (1975). Deliberate memory behavior in the delayed reactions of very young children. *Developmental Psychology, 11,* 780–787.

Wender, P. H. (1995). *Attention-deficit hyperactivity disorder in adults.* New York: Oxford University Press.

Wentworth, N., Benson, J. B., & Haith, M. M. (2000). The development of infants' reaches for stationary and moving targets. *Child Development, 71,* 576–601.

Wentworth, N., Haith, M. M., & Hood, R. (2002). Spatiotemporal regularity and interevent contingencies as information for infants' visual expectations. *Infancy, 3,* 303–322.

Wentzel, K. R., & Erdley, C. A. (1993). Strategies for making friends: Relations to social behavior and peer acceptance in early adolescence. *Developmental Psychology, 29,* 819–826.

Werker, J. F., & Tees, R. C. (1999). Influences on infant speech processing: Toward a new synthesis. *Annual Review of Psychology, 50,* 509–535.

Werner, E., & Smith, R. (1982). *Vulnerable but invincible: A study of resilient children.* New York: McGraw Hill.

Werner, L. A., & Bargones, J. Y. (1992). Psychoacoustic development of human infants. In C. Rovee-Collier & L. P. Lipsitt (Eds.), *Advances in infancy research* (Vol. 7). Norwood, NJ: Ablex.

Wertheimer, M. (1961). Psychomotor coordination of auditory-visual space at birth. *Science, 134,* 1692.

Wertheimer, M. (1985). The evolution of the concept of development in the history of psychology. In G. Eckardt, W. G. Bringmann, & L. Sprung (Eds.), *Contributions to a history of developmental psychology.* Berlin: Mouton.

Wertsch, J. V. (1981). *Voices of the mind.* Cambridge, MA: Harvard University Press.

Wertsch, J. V., & Kanner, B. G. (1992). A sociocultural approach to intellectual development. In R. J. Sternberg & C. Berg (Eds.), *Intellectual development.* New York: Cambridge University Press.

Wertsch, J. V., & Tulviste, P. (1992). J. S. Vygotsky and contemporary developmental psychology. *Developmental Psychology, 28,* 548–557.

Westinghouse Learning Center. (1969). *The impact of Head Start: An evaluation of the effects of Head Start on children's cognitive and affective development.* Washington, DC: Clearinghouse for Federal Scientific and Technical Information.

Whelan, T. A., & Kirkby, R. J. (2000). Parent adjustment to a child's hospitalization. *Journal of Family Studies, 6,* 46–64.

White, B. L., Castle, P., & Held, R. (1964). Observations on the development of visually directed reaching. *Child Development, 35,* 349–364.

White, B. L., Kaban, B. T., Attanuccu, J., & Shapiro, B. B. (1978). *Experience and environment: Major influences on the development of the young child* (Vol. 2). Englewood Cliffs, NJ: Prentice Hall.

White, S., & Tharp, R. G. (1988, April). *Questioning and wait-time: A cross-cultural analysis.* Paper presented at the meeting of the American Educational Research Association, New Orleans.

White, T. G. (1982). Naming practices, typicality, and underextension in child language. *Journal of Experimental Child Psychology, 33,* 324–346.

White, T. L., Leichtman, M. D., & Ceci, S. J. (1997). The good, the bad, and the ugly: Accuracy, inaccuracy, and elaboration in preschoolers' reports about a past event. *Applied Cognitive Psychology, 11,* S37–S54.

Whitehurst, G. J., & DeBaryshe, B. D. (1989). Observational learning and language acquisition: Principles of learning, systems, and tasks. In G. E. Speidel & K. E. Nelson (Eds.), *The many faces of imitation in language learning.* New York: Springer-Verlag.

Whitehurst, G. J., & Lonigan, C. J. (2001). Emergent literacy: Development from prereaders to readers. In S. B. Neuman & D. K. Dickinson (Eds.), *Handbook of early literary research.* New York: Guilford.

Whitehurst, G. J., & Novak, G. (1973). Modeling, imitation training, and the acquisition of sentence phrases. *Journal of Experimental Child Psychology, 16,* 332–345.

Whitehurst, G. J., & Sonnenschein, S. (1985). The development of communication: A functional analysis. In G. J. Whitehurst (Ed.), *Annals of child development* (Vol. 2). Greenwich, CT: JAI Press.

Whiteside, M. F., & Becker, B. J. (2000). Parental factors and the young child's post-divorce adjustment: A meta-analysis with implications for parenting arrangements. *Journal of Family Psychology, 14,* 5–26.

Whiting, B. B., & Edwards, C. P. (1988). *Children of different worlds: The formation of social behavior.* Cambridge, MA: Harvard University Press.

Whiting, B. B., & Whiting, J. W. M. (1975). *Children of six cultures: A psycho-cultural analysis.* Cambridge, MA: Harvard University Press.

Whitley, R., & Goldenberg, R. (1990). Infectious disease in the prenatal period and the recommendations for screening. In I. R. Merkatz & J. E. Thompson (Eds.), *New perspectives on prenatal care.* New York: Elsevier.

Whitney, E. N., & Rolfes, S. R. (2002). *Understanding nutrition* (9th ed.). Belmont, CA: Wadsworth Publishing Company.

Wigfield, A., Battle, A., Keller, L. B., & Eccles, J. S. (2002). Sex differences in motivation, self-concept, career aspiration and career choice: Implications for cognitive development. In A. V. McGillicuddy-De Lisi & R. De Lisi (Eds.), *Biology, society, and behavior: The development of sex differences in cognition.* Greenwich, CT: Ablex.

Wigfield, A., Eccles, J. S., MacIver, D., Reuman, D. A., & Midgley, C. (1991). Transitions during early adolescence: Changes in children's domain-specific self-perceptions and general self-esteem across the transition to junior high school. *Developmental Psychology, 27,* 552–565.

Wigfield, A., Eccles, J. S., Yoon, K. S., Harold, R. D., Arbreton, A., Freedman-Doan, K., et al. (1997). Changes in children's competence beliefs and subjective task values across the elementary school years: A three-year-study. *Journal of Educational Psychology, 89,* 451–469.

Wilcox, A. J., Baird, D. D., Weinberg, C. R., Hornsby, P. P., & Herbst, A. L. (1995). Fertility in men exposed prenatally to diethylstilbestrol. *New England Journal of Medicine, 332,* 1411–1416.

Wiley, A. R., Rose, A. J., Burger, L. K., & Miller, P. J. (1998). Constructing autonomous selves through narrative practices: A comparative study of working-class and middle-class families. *Child Development, 69,* 833–847.

Williams, J. (1987). *Psychology of women: Behavior in a biosocial context.* New York: Norton.

Williams, J. E., & Best, D. L. (1990). *Measuring sex stereotypes: A multinational study.* Newbury Park, CA: Sage.

Williams, W. M. (1998). Are we raising smarter children today? School- and home-related influences on IQ. In U. Neisser (Ed.), *The rising curve.* Washington, DC: APA.

Willingham, W. W., & Cole, N. S. (Eds.). (1997). *Gender and fair assessment.* Mahwah, NJ: Erlbaum.

Willingham, W. W., Cole, N. S., Lewis, C., & Leung, S. W. (1997). Test performance. In W. W. Willingham & N. S. Cole (Eds.), *Gender and fair assessment.* Mahwah, NJ: Erlbaum.

Wilson, E. O. (1975). *Sociobiology: The new synthesis.* Cambridge, MA: Harvard University Press.

Wilson, M. (Ed.). (1995). *African American family life: Its structural and ecological aspects.* San Francisco: Jossey-Bass.

Wilson, R. S. (1983). The Louisville Twin Study: Developmental synchronies in behavior. *Child Development, 54,* 298–316.

Wilson, R. S. (1986). Growth and development of human twins. In F. Falkner & J. M. Tanner (Eds.), *Human growth: A comprehensive treatise.* New York: Plenum.

Wilson, S. M., Corley. R. P., Fulker, D. W., & Reznick, S. J. (2001). Experimental assessment of specific cognitive abilities during the second year of life. In R. N. Emde & J. K. Hewitt (Eds.), *Infancy to early childhood.* New York: Oxford University Press.

Windle, M., & Lerner, R. M. (1986). The "goodness-of-fit" model of temperament-context relations: Interaction or correlation? In J. V. Lerner & R. M. Lerner (Eds.), *New directions for child development: No. 31. Temperament and social interaction in infants and children.* San Francisco: Jossey-Bass.

Windsor, J. (1993). The functions of novel word compounds. *Journal of Child Language, 20,* 119–138.

Winner, E. (1996). *Gifted children.* New York: Basic Books.

Winner, E. (2000). The origins and ends of giftedness. *American Psychologist, 55,* 159–169.

Winsler, A., Dias, R. M., McCarthy, E. M., Atencio, D. J., & Chabay, L. (1999). Mother-child interactions, private speech, and task performance in preschool children with behavior problems. *Journal of Child Psychology and Psychiatry, 40,* 891–904.

Winston, R. M. L., & Handyside, A. H. (1993). New challenges in human in vitro fertilization. *Science, 260,* 932–936.

Witelson, S. F. (1976). Sex and the single hemisphere: Specialization of the right hemisphere for spatial processing. *Science, 193,* 425–427.

Wolchik, S. A., Wilcox, K. L., Tein, J., & Sandler, I. N. (2000). Maternal acceptance and consistency of discipline as buffers of divorce stressors on children's psychological adjustment problems. *Journal of Abnormal Child Psychology, 28,* 87–102.

Wolff, P. H. (1959). Observations on newborn infants. *Psychosomatic Medicine, 21,* 110–118.

Wolff, P. H. (1966). The causes, controls and organization of behavior in the neonate. *Psychological Issues, 5*(17).

Wolff, P. H. (1969). The natural history of crying and other vocalizations in early infancy. In B. Foss (Ed.), *Determinants of infant behavior* (Vol. 4). London: Methuen.

Wood, D., Bruner, J., & Ross, G. (1976). The role of tutoring in problem solving. *Journal of Child Psychology and Psychiatry, 17,* 89–100.

Wood, D., Wood, H., Ainsworth, S., & O'Malley, C. (1995). On becoming a tutor: Toward an ontogenetic model. *Cognition and Instruction, 13,* 565–581.

Wood, E., Desmarais, S., & Gugula, S. (2002). The impact of parenting experience on gender stereotyped toy play of children. *Sex Roles, 47,* 39–49.

Wood, W., & Eagly, A. H. (2002). A cross-cultural analysis of the behavior of women and men: Implications for the origins of sex differences. *Psychological Bulletin, 128,* 699–727.

Woodward, A. L., & Markman, E. M. (1998). Early word learning. In W. Damon (Series Ed.) & D. Kuhn & R. S. Siegler (Vol. Eds.), *Handbook of child psychology: Vol. 2. Cognition, perception, and language* (5th ed.). New York: Wiley.

Woody-Dorning, J., & Miller, P. H. (2001). Children's individual differences in capacity: Effects on strategy production and utilization. *British Journal of Developmental Psychology, 19,* 543–557.

Worobey J., & Blajda, V. M. (1989). Temperament ratings at 2 weeks, 2 months, and 1 year: Differential stability of activity and emotionality. *Developmental Psychology, 25,* 257–263.

Wright, J. C., Huston, A. C., Vandewater, E. A., Bickham, D. S., Scantlin, R. M., Kotler, J. A., et al. (2001). American children's use of electronic media in 1997: A national survey. *Applied Developmental Psychology, 22,* 31–47.

Wu, X., Hart, C. H., Draper, T. W., & Olsen, J. A. (2001). Peer and teacher sociometrics for preschool children: Cross-information concordance, temporal stability, and reliability. *Merrill-Palmer Quarterly, 47,* 416–443.

Wynn, K. (1992). Addition and subtraction by human infants. *Nature, 358,* 749–750.

Wynn, K. (1995). Origins of numerical knowledge. *Mathematical Cognition, 1,* 36–60.

Wynn, K. (1998). Numerical competence in infants. In C. Donlan (Ed.), *The development of mathematical skills: Studies in developmental psychology.* Hove, UK: Psychology Press.

Xu, F., & Spelke, E. S. (2000). Large number discrimination in 6-month-old-infants. *Cognition, 74,* B1–B15.

Yang, M. T.-L., & Cobb, P. (1995). A cross-cultural investigation into the development of place value concepts of children in Taiwan and the United States. *Educational Studies in Mathematics, 28,* 1–33.

Yankowitz, J. (1996). Surgical fetal therapy. In J. A. Kuller, N. C. Cheschier, & R. C. Cefalo (Eds.), *Prenatal diagnosis and reproductive genetics.* St. Louis, MO: Mosby.

Yarrow, L. J., McQuiston, S., MacTurk, R. H., McCarthy, M. E., Klein, R. P., & Vietze, P. M. (1983). Assessment of mastery motivation during the first year of life: contemporaneous and cross-age relationships. *Developmental Psychology, 19,* 159–171.

Yarrow, L. J., Rubenstein, J. L., & Pedersen, F. A. (1975). *Infant and environment: Early cognitive and motivational development.* Bethesda, MD: NICHD.

Yates, G. C. R., Yates, S. M., & Beasley, C. J. (1987). Young children's knowledge of strategies in delay of gratification. *Merrill-Palmer Quarterly, 33,* 159–169.

Yates, M., & Youniss, J. (1996). A developmental perspective on community service in adolescence. *Social Development, 5,* 85–111.

Yeates, K. O., Schultz, L. H., & Selman, R. L. (1991). The development of interpersonal negotiation strategies in thought and action: A social-cognitive link to behavioral adjustment and social status. *Merrill-Palmer Quarterly, 37,* 369–406.

Yeung, W. J., Sandberg, J. F., Davis-Kean, P. E., & Hoffert, S. L. (2001). Children's time with fathers in intact families. *Journal of Marriage and the Family, 63,* 136–154.

Yonas, A. (1981). Infants' responses to optical information for collision. In R. N. Aslin, J. R. Alberts, & M. R. Peterson (Eds.), *Development of perception: Psychobiological perspectives: Vol. 2. The visual system.* New York: Academic Press.

Yonas, A., & Granrud, C. E. (1985). Development of visual space perception in young infants. In J. Mehler & R. Fox (Eds.), *Neonate cognition.* Hillsdale, NJ: Erlbaum.

Yonas, A., & Owsley, C. (1987). Development of visual space perception. In P. Salapatek & L. Cohen (Eds.), *Handbook of infant perception: Vol. 2. From perception to cognition.* New York: Academic Press.

Yoon, C. K. (2002). Stephen Jay Gould, 60, is dead; enlivened evolutionary theory. *New York Times,* May 21.

Young, K. T. (1991). What parents and experts think about infants. In F. S. Kessel, M. H. Bornstein, & A. J. Sameroff (Eds.), *Contemporary constructions of the child: Essays in honor of William Kessen.* Hillsdale, NJ: Erlbaum.

Youngblade, L. M., & Belsky, J. (1992). Parent–child antecedents of 5-year-olds' close friendships: A longitudinal analysis. *Developmental Psychology, 28,* 700–713.

Youngblade, L. M., & Dunn, J. (1995). Individual differences in children's play with mother and sibling: Links to relationship and understanding of other people's feelings and beliefs. *Child Development, 66,* 1472–1492.

Younger, A. J., & Piccinin, A. M. (1989). Children's recall of aggressive and withdrawn behaviors: Recognition memory and likability judgments. *Child Development, 60,* 580–590.

Younger, A. J., Schwartzman, A. E., & Ledingham, J. E. (1985). Age-related changes in children's perceptions of aggression and withdrawal in their peers. *Developmental Psychology, 21,* 70–75.

Youniss, J., McLellan, J. A., & Mazer, B. (2001). Voluntary service, peer group orientation, and civic engagement. *Journal of Adolescent Research, 5,* 456–468.

Youniss, J., & Volpe, J. (1978). A relational analysis of children's friendship. In W. Damon (Ed.), *New directions for child development: No. 1. Social cognition.* San Francisco: Jossey-Bass.

Yowell, C. M. (2000). Possible selves and future-orientation: Exploring hopes and fears of Latino boys and girls. *Journal of Early Adolescence, 20,* 245–280.

Yowell, C. M. (2002). Dreams of the future: The pursuit of educational and career possible selves among ninth grade Latino youth. *Applied Developmental Science, 6,* 62–72.

Yussen, S. R., & Levy, Y. M. (1975). Developmental changes in predicting one's own span of short-term memory. *Journal of Experimental Child Psychology, 19,* 502–508.

Zabriski, A. L., & Coie, J. D. (1996). A comparison of aggressive-rejected and nonaggressive-rejected children's interpretations of self-directed and other-directed rejection. *Child Development, 67,* 1048–1070.

Zahn-Waxler, C., Friedman, R. J., Cole, P. M., & Mizuta, I. (1996). Japanese and United States preschool children's responses to conflict and distress. *Child Development, 67,* 2462–2477.

Zahn-Waxler, C., & Radke-Yarrow, M. (1982). The development of altruism: Alternative research strategies. In N. Eisenberg (Ed.), *The development of prosocial behavior.* San Diego, CA: Academic Press.

Zahn-Waxler, C., Radke-Yarrow, M., Wagner, E., & Chapman, M. (1992). Development of concern for others. *Developmental Psychology, 28,* 126–136.

Zahn-Waxler, C., Robinson, J. L., & Emde, R. N. (1992). The development of empathy in twins. *Developmental Psychology, 28,* 1038–1047.

Zahn-Waxler, C., Schiro, K., Robinson, J., Emde, R. N., & Schmitz, S. (2001). Empathy and prosocial patterns in young MZ and DZ twins: Development and genetic and environmental influences. In R. N. Emde & J. K. Hewitt (Eds.), *Infancy to early childhood: Genetic and environmental influences on developmental change.* Oxford: Oxford University Press.

Zametkin, A. J., Nordahl, T. E., Gross, M., King, A. C., Semple, W. E., Rumsey, J., et al. (1990). Cerebral glucose metabolism in adults with hyperactivity of childhood onset. *New England Journal of Medicine, 20,* 1361–1366.

Zarbatany, L., Hartmann, D. P., Elfand, D. M., & Vinciguerra, P. (1985). Gender differences in altruistic reputation: Are they artifactual? *Developmental Psychology, 21,* 97–101.

Zarbatany, L., Hartmann, D. P., & Rankin, D. B. (1990). The psychological functions of preadolescent peer activities. *Child Development, 61,* 1067–1080.

Zeifman, D. M. (2001). An ethological analysis of human infant crying: Answering Tinbergen's four questions. *Developmental Psychobiology, 39,* 265–285 .

Zelazo, N. A., Zelazo, P. R., Cohen, K. M., & Zelazo, P. D. (1993). Specificity of practice effects on elementary neuromotor patterns. *Developmental Psychology, 29,* 686–691.

Zelazo, P. D. (1999). Language, levels of consciousness, and the development of intentional action. In P. D. Zelazo, J. W. Astington, & D. R. Olson (Eds.), *Developing theories of intention.* Mahwah, NJ: Erlbaum.

Zelazo, P. D., & Frye, D. (1998). Cognitive complexity and control: II. The development of executive function in childhood. *Current Directions in Psychological Science, 7,* 121–126.

Zelazo, P. R. (1971). Smiling to social stimuli: Eliciting and conditioning effects. *Developmental Psychology, 4,* 32–42.

Zelazo, P. R., Weiss, M. J. S., & Tarquino, N. (1991). Habituation and recovery of neonatal orienting to auditory stimuli. In M. J. S. Weiss & P. R. Zelazo (Eds.), *Newborn attention: Biological constraints and the influence of experience.* Norwood, NJ: Ablex.

Zentner, M. R., & Kagan, J. (1998). Infants' perception of consonance and dissonance in music. *Infant Behavior and Development, 21,* 483–492.

Zeskind, P. S., & Lester, B. M. (2001). Analysis of infant crying. In L. T. Singer & P. S. Zeskind (Eds.), *Biobehavioral assessment of the infant.* New York: Guilford Press.

Zeskind, P. S., & Marshall, T. R. (1988). The relation between variations in pitch and maternal perceptions of infant crying. *Child Development, 59,* 193–196.

Zeskind, P. S., & Ramey, C. T. (1981). Preventing intellectual and interactional sequelae of fetal malnutrition: A longitudinal, transactional and synergistic approach to development. *Child Development, 52,* 213–218.

Zigler, E. F., & Finn-Stevenson, M. (1999). Applied developmental psychology. In M. H. Bornstein & M. E. Lamb (Eds.), *Developmental psychology: An advanced textbook* (4th ed.). Mahwah, NJ: Erlbaum.

Zigler, E. F., & Muenchow, S. (1992). *Head Start: The inside story of America's most successful educational experiment.* New York: Basic Books.

Zigler, E. F., & Styfco, S. J. (Eds.). (1993). *Head Start and beyond: A national plan for extended childhood intervention.* New Haven, CT: Yale University Press.

Zill, N., Morrison, D. R., & Coiro, M. J. (1993). Long-term effects of parental divorce on parent–child relationships, adjustment, and achievement in young adulthood. *Journal of Family Psychology, 7,* 1–13.

Zimmerman, B. J. (1983). Social learning theory: A contextualist account of cognitive functioning. In C. J. Brainerd (Ed.), *Recent advances in cognitive-developmental theory: Progress in cognitive development research.* New York: Springer-Verlag.

Zimmerman, B. J., & Blom, D. E. (1983). Toward an empirical test of the role of cognitive conflict in learning. *Developmental Review, 3,* 18–38.

Zucker, K. J. (2001). Biological influences on psychosexual differentiation. In R. Unger (Ed.), *Handbook of the psychology of women and gender.* New York: Wiley.

Zucker, K. J., Bradley, S. J., Oliver, G., Blake, J., Fleming, S., & Hood, J. (1996). Psychosexual development of women with congenital adrenal hyperplasia. *Hormones and Behavior, 30,* 300–318.

Zucker, K. J., Wilson-Smith, D. N., Kurita, J. A., & Stern, A. (1995). Children's appraisals of sex-typed behavior in their peers. *Sex Roles, 33,* 703–725.

Zukow-Goldring, P. (1995). Sibling caregiving. In M. H. Bornstein (Ed.), *Handbook of parenting; Vol. 3, Status and social conditions of parenting.* Mahwah, NJ: Erlbaum.

Zukow-Goldring, P. (2002). Sibling caregiving. In M. H. Bornstein (Ed.), *Handbook of parenting* (2nd ed., Vol. 3). Mahwah, NJ: Erlbaum.

Zupan, B. A., Hammen, C., & Jaenicke, C. (1987). The effects of current mood and prior depressive history on self-schematic processing in children. *Journal of Experimental Child Psychology, 43,* 149–158.

Credits

Sources for Chapter-Opening Vignettes

Chapter 1

S. J. Breiner, *Slaughter of the Innocents: Child Abuse through the Ages* (New York: Plenum, 1990).

B. K. Greenleaf, *Children through the Ages: A History of Childhood* (New York: McGraw-Hill, 1978).

S. N. Hart, "From Property to Person Status: Historical Perspective on Children's Rights," *American Psychologist* 46 (1991), pp. 53–59.

W. L. Langer, "Infanticide: A Historical Survey," *History of Childhood Quarterly 1* (1974), pp. 53–365.

C. A. Mounteer, "Roman Childhood, 200 B.C. to A.D. 600," *Journal of Psychohistory 14* (1987), pp. 233–254.

J. Sommerville, *The Rise and Fall of Childhood* (Beverly Hills, Calif.: Sage, 1982).

R. C. Trexler, "The Foundlings of Florence, 1395–1455," *History of Childhood Quarterly 1* (1973), pp. 259–284.

Chapter 2

M. R. Lepper, D. Greene, and R. E. Nisbett, R. E. (1973). Undermining Children's Intrinsic Interest with Extrinsic Reward: A Test of the "Overjustification" Hypothesis. *Journal of Personality and Social Psychology 28* (1973), pp. 129–137.

Chapter 3

Alan Boyle, "Scientists Clone a Calico Kitty," MSNBC Web site, February 14, 2002.

Associated Press, "Texas Researchers Clone a Cat," February 15, 2002.

Graham Jones, "First Human Clone Bid Planned," CNN.com, August 7, 2001.

Texas A&M University, Office of University Relations, "Texas A&M Clones First Cat," Press Release, February 14, 2002.

Chapter 4

David Holmstrom, "U.S. Hospitals Are Flooded with Babies Abandoned by Alcohol and Drug Abusers," *Christian Science Monitor*, September 17, 1992.

Donna O'Neal and Debbie Salamone, "Cocaine Mom's Case Thrown Out," *Orlando Sentinel*, July 24, 1992, p. B1.

Mimi Hall, "Cocaine-Babies Case Appealed," *USA Today*, March 6, 1992, p. 3A.

Andrew Stone, "Prosecutors Focus on Drug Use, Pregnancy," *USA Today*, February 26, 1990, p. 3A.

Catherine Foster, "Fetal Endangerment Cases Increase," *Christian Science Monitor*, October 10, 1989.

Andrea Stone, "It's 'Tip of Iceberg' in Protecting Infants," *USA Today*, August 25, 1989, p. 3A.

Chapter 5

March of Dimes, "March of Dimes Selects Premature Birth Survivor as 2001 National Ambassador," Press Release, January 9, 2001, marchofdimes.com.

March of Dimes, "March of Dimes 2001 National Ambassador Justin Lamar Washington," Press Release, marchofdimes.com.

March of Dimes, "March of Dimes Selects Justin Washington for Second Year as National Ambassador," Press Release, January 19, 2002, marchofdimes.com.

Chapter 8

S. J. Ceci and M. Bruck, *Jeopardy in the Courtroom: A Scientific Analysis of Children's Testimony* (Washington, D.C.: American Psychological Association, 1995).

Chapter 9

"Really Helping Out Around the House," *Washington Post*, March 13, 2001.

Dan Shine, "Boy, 8, Helps Bring Life Into World," *Detroit Free Press*, March 10, 2001.

Dan Shine, "Boy, 8, Helps Mom Deliver Sister at Home," *Milwaukee Journal Sentinel*, March 13, 2001.

"Special Delivery," ABCNews.com.

Chapter 10

James Astill, "Shepherd School," *The Guardian*, April 2, 2002.

"No Swots, Please, We're Masai; Kenya," *The Economist* (U.S.), March 23, 2002.

Jacqueline S. Phillips and Navaz Peshotan Bhavnagri, "The Maasai's education and empowerment: Challenges of a migrant lifestyle," *Childhood Education*, Spring 2002, pp. 140–147.

First quotation from "No Swots, Please, We're Masai; Kenya," *The Economist* (U.S.), March 23, 2002.

Remaining quotations from James Astill, "Shepherd School," *Guardian* (Manchester, England), April 2, 2002.

Chapter 12

Charmagne Helton, "Mom Loses Custody over Day Care," *USA Today*, July 27, 1994, p. 1A.

Elizabeth Kastor, "The Maranda Decision," *Washington Post*, July 30, 1994, p. D1.

Associated Press, "Court Gives Daughter Back to Mom: Ruling Overturned in Day Care Case," November 9, 1995.

Jeanne May, "Parents to Share Maranda Equally: Long Custody Battle Ends with Settlement," *Detroit Free Press*, October 17, 1996, p. 1A.

Chapter 16

M. J. G. Itard, *The Wild Boy of Aveyron* (New York: Appleton-Century-Crofts, 1932/1962).

M. Newton, *Savage Girls and Wild Boys: A History of Feral Children* (New York: Thomas Dunne Books St. Martin's Press, 2003).

J. A. L. Singh and R. Zingg, *Wolf-Children and Feral Man* (New York: Harper & Row, 1942).

Photos

Chapter 1

Opener: SW Productions/Getty Images. Page 4 (top): Peter Byron/Photo Edit. Page 4 (bottom): Courtesy New York Public Library Picture Collection. Page 5: Bettmann/Corbis. Page 6: Courtesy National Library of Medicine. Page 7: Culver Pictures, Inc. Page 9: LIFE Magazine, ©Time Inc. Picture Collection. Page 10: Bob Daemmrich/The Image Works. Page 14: Power Press/Corbis-Sygma. Page 15: Anne Nielsen/Stone/Getty Images. Page 16: Courtesy Jean Piaget Society. Page 17 (left): Elizabeth Crews/The Image Works. Page 17 (right): David Young-Wolff/PhotoEdit. Page 19: Rober Allyn/SUPERSTOCK. Page 21: Courtesy Michael Cole. Page 22: Lawrence Migdale/Photo Researchers. Page 23: Courtesy Cornell University. Page 24 (left): Sean Sprague/The Image Works. Page 24 (right): Kathy McLaughlin/The Image Works. Page 25: Corbis-Bettmann. Page 26: Michael Newman/PhotoEdit. Page 28: Bruce Ayres/Stone/Getty Images. Page 30: Jeff Greenberg/Photo Researchers. Page 31: Courtesy Albert Bandura, Stanford University. Page 36: Nina Leen/Time Inc. Picture Collection.

Chapter 2

Opener: Mark Richards/PhotoEdit. Page 48: Lawrence Migdale/Photo Researchers. Page 56: ©Elizabeth Crews. Page 58: Topham/The Image Works. Page 62: Peter Essick/The Image Works. Page 63 (left): Alan & Sandy Carey/Photo Researchers. Page 63 (right): Eastcutt/Mamatiuk/The Image Works. Page 64: Andrew M. Levine/Photo Researchers.

Chapter 3

Opener: International Stock/Image State. Page 72: Courtesy College of Veterinary Medicine Texas A&M University. Page 75 (left): ©Thaves 2001. Distributed by NEA Inc. Page 75 (right): ©Joel Gordon, 1989. Page 77: Courtesy of the U.S. Department of Energy Genomes to Life Program, http://eogenomestolife.org. Page 78: Culver Pictures, Inc. Page 82: Bill Longcore/Science Photo Source/Photo Researchers. Page 83: Bill Aaron/PhotoEdit. Page 89: Courtesy Dr. Thomas J. Bouchard Jr. Page 92 (left): Larry S. Voight/Photo Researchers. Page 92 (right): Jeff Isaac/Photo Researchers.

Chapter 4

Opener: CNRI/Phototake. Page 101: Petit Format/Photo Researchers. Pages 102 & 104: Images provided by Anatomical Travelogue, www.anatomicaltravel.com. From the book *From Conception to Birth: A Life Unfolds,* authored by Alexander Tsiaras. Page 111: Mark Richards/PhotoEdit. Page 113 (top): ©James W. Hanson. Page 113 (bottom): Courtesy of the New York State Office of Alcoholism and Substance Abuse Services. Page 122: Yoav Levy/Phototake. Page 123: Courtesy Van De Silva.

Chapter 5

Opener: Arthur Tilley/Taxi/Getty Images. Page 132: Jules Perrier/Corbis Images. Page 136: Rick Friedman/Black Star. Page 137: Ansell Horn/Phototake. Page 141: Joanna B. Pinneo/Aurora & Quanta Productions. Page 144 (left): Petit Fromat/Photo Researchers. Page 144 (right): Elizabeth Crews/The Image Works. Page 149: Photo used by permission of Dr. Charles Super, Pennsylvania State University. Page 151 (top): Photo by permission of Dr. Janette Benson, University of Denver. Page 151 (bottom): David Young-Wolff/Stone/Getty Images. Page 155: From: "The Development of Face and Location Processing: An FMRI Study," by A.M. Passarotti, B.M. Paul, J.R. Bussiere, R.B. Buxton, E.C. Wong & J. Stiels, 2003, *Developmental Science,* 6, Blackwell Publishing. Provided by A.M. Passarotti, Michigan State University. Page 157: Bob Daemmrich/Stock, Boston. Page 162: Natalie Behring/Getty Images News and Sport Services. Page 163: Oscar Burriel/Photo Researchers.

Chapter 6

Opener: BrandX Pictures/Getty Images. Page 172: Penny Gentieu/Stone/Getty Images. Page 174: Jeff Greenberg/PhotoEdit. Page 175: From: "Differential Facial Responses to Four Basic Tastes in Newborns," by D. Rosenstein and H. Oster, 1988, *Child Development,* 59, pp. 1561–1563. ©1988 by The Society for Research in Child Development, Inc. Reprinted by permission. Page 180: Michael Newman/PhotoEdit. Page 181: Photo by David Linton. Reproduced with permission of Ann Linton. Page 182: From "The Recognition of Facial Expressions in the First Two Years of Life: Mechanisms of Development," by Charles A. Nelson, *Child Development,* 58, Figure 1, p. 892. ©1987 by The Society for Research in Child Development, Inc. Reprinted by permission. These photos were made available by Martin Banks and Arthur Ginsburg. Page 189: From: "Size Constancy at Birth: Newborn Infants' Responses to Retinal and Real Size," by A. Slater, A. Mattock, and E. Brown, 1990, *Journal of Experimental Child Psychology,* 49, pp. 317 and 318. ©1990 by Academic Press. Reprinted by permission. Page 191: Mark Richard/PhotoEdit. Page 194: Elizabeth Hathon/Corbis Images. Page 198: From *The World of the Newborn* (pp. 128–129) by Daphne Maurer and Charles Maurer. 1988, New York: Basic Books. ©1988 by Charles Maurer and Daphne Maurer.

Chapter 7

Opener: David Young-Wolfe/Stone/Getty Images. Page 211: ©Yves de Braine/Black Star. Page 217 (left): ©Eliza-

beth Crews. Page 217 (right): ©Peter Byron/PhotoEdit. Page 219: ©Myrleen Ferguson Cate/PhotoEdit. Page 223: Reprinted with permission from "Imitation of Social and Manual Gestures by Human Neonates" by A.N. Meltzoff and M.K. Moore, 1977, *Science,* 298, p. 75. ©1977 by the American Association for the Advancement of Science. Reprinted by permission. Page 225: Lon C. Diehls/PhotoEdit. Page 227: From "Constancy of Generic Identity in the Years Three to Six" by R. De Vries, 1969, *Monographs of the Society for Research in Child Development,* 34 (3, Serial No. 127), p. 8. ©1969 by the Society for Research in Child Development. Reprinted by permission. Page 230: ©Elizabeth Crews. Page 231: Mischael Newman/PhotoEdit. Page 238: ©Steve Thomas, The Last Navigator. Page 241: ©Momatiuk/Eascott/Woodfin Camp & Associates. Page 242: ©Bob Daemmrich/The Image Works.

Chapter 8

Opener: Peter Cade/Stone/Getty. Page 259: Bob Schatz/Image State. Page 263: These photos were made available by Dr. C. Rovee-Collier. Page 265: ©Elizabeth Crews. Pages 266, 269 & 275: Micheal Newman/PhotoEdit. Page 277: Bill Aaron/PhotoEdit. Page 281: Lawrence Migdale/Stone/Getty Images.

Chapter 9

Opener: Paul Chesley/Stone/Getty Images. Page 303: David Young-Wolff/PhotoEdit. Page 309: Ronnie Kaufman/Corbis Images. Page 310: Robert Brenner/PhotoEdit. Page 316: From *Apprenticeship in Thinking* (p.49) by B. Rogoff, 1990, New York: Oxford University Press. ©1990 by Barbara Rogoff. Reprinted by permission. Page 318: Gale Zucker/Stock, Boston. Page 320: ©Baby Blues Partnership. Reprinted with Special Permission of King Features Syndicate. Page 329: Ellen Senisi/The Image Works. Page 338: Michael Newman/PhotoEdit. Page 339: Sean Spraguel/Line Air.

Chapter 10

Opener: Bob Daemmrich/The Image Works. Page 348: Culver Pictures Inc. Page 351: R. Rowan/Photo Researchers. Page 355: From "Predictive Validity of the Fagan Test of Infant Intelligence" by J.F. Fagan III, P. Shephard, & C. Knevel, 1991, *Meeting of the Society for Research in Child Development,* ©1993 by J. F. Fagan III. Reprinted by permission. Page 357: Syracuse Newspapers/Peter Chen/The Image Works. Page 363: ©The New Yorker Collection 1998 Mike Twohy from cartoonbank.com. All Rights Reserved. Page 368: Lawrence Migdale/Photo Researchers. Page 374: Ralf-Finn Hestoft/Corbis-SABA. Page 384: From *Frames of Mind: The Theory of Multiple Intelligence* (p.189) by H. Gardner, 1983, New York: Basic Books. ©1983 by Basic Books. Reprinted by permission. Page 385: From *Gifted Children,* by E. Winner, 1996, New York: Basic Books, pp. 84–85. Copyright ©1996 by Basic Books. Reprinted by permission.

Chapter 11

Opener: Chuck Keeler/Corbis Images. Page 396: Courtesy M.I.T. Page 399: Laura Dwight/Corbis Images. Page 402: Novastock/Photo Researchers. Page 404: © LWA-Dann Tardif/Corbis. Page 406: © Elizabeth Crews. Page 410: David J. Sams/Stone/Getty Images. Page 416: © 1997 by NEA, Inc. Page 422: Jonathan Nourok/PhotoEdit. Page 428: Jennie Woodcock/Reflections/Corbis Images. Page 429: © Elizabeth Crews.

Chapter 12

Opener: Elyse Lewin/The Image Bank/Getty Images. Page 437: Camille Tokerud/Photo Researchers. Pages 438 & 447: © Laura Dwight Photography. Page 454: Jeff W. Myers/Stock, Boston. Page 457: Stephanie Maze/Woodfin Camp & Associates. Page 459: Carolyn A. McKeone/Photo Researchers. Page 463: Courtesy Harlow Primate Laboratory, University of Wisconsin. Page 464: John Fortunato/Stone/Getty Images. Page 468: David Young-Wolff/PhotoEdit. Page 471: © AP/Wide World Photos.

Chapter 13

Opener: Jeff Meyers/Taxi/Getty Images. Page 484: Deborah Davis/Photo Edit. Page 487: Joseph Pobereskin/Stone/Getty. Page 491: Andanson James/Sygma/Corbis. Page 496: Michael Newman/Photo Edit. Page 497: LWA-Dan Tandif/Corbis. Page 501 (top): CALVIN AND HOBBES © 1993 Watterson. Reprinted with permission of UNIVERSAL PRESS SYNDICATE. All rights reserved. Page 501 (bottom): Brand X Pictures/Getty. Page 508: Jeneart LTD/The Image Bank/Getty.

Chapter 14

Opener: Tom and Dee McCarthy/Corbis Images. Page 515: Craig Hammell/Corbis. Page 516: PEANUTS reprinted by permission of United Features Syndicate, Inc. Page 529: Charles D. Winters/Photo Researchers. Page 534: Jeff Isaac Greenberg/Photo Researchers. Page 538: P. Davidson/The Image Works. Page 543 (left): Richard Hutchings/Photo Edit. Page 543 (right): Jonathan Nourok/PhotoEdit. Page 547: Etta Hulme/Reprinted by permission of NEA, Inc. Page 548: From "Coping with the Consequences of Living in Danger: The Case of Palestinian Children and Youth" by K. Kostelny & J. Garbarino, 1994, *International Journal of Behavioral Development,* 17, 595-611.

Chapter 15

Opener: Andersen Ross/PhotoDisc, Inc./Getty Images. Page 561: © 2002, Baby Blues Partnership Distributed by King Features Syndicate. Page 563: © Donald Dietz/Stock, Boston. Page 565: Chris Kelly *www.digitalsportsarchive.com.* Page 572: ©2003 ZITS Partnership. Distributed by King Features Syndicate. Page 575: Will & Deni McIntyre/Photo Researchers. Page 581: Spencer Grant/Photo Edit. Page 582: Michael Newman/Photo Edit. Page 586: Photomondo/Photodisc Green/Getty. Page 589: Lawrence Migdale/Photo Researchers.

Chapter 16

Opener: Ariel Skelley/Corbis Images. Page 607: Tony Freedman/Photo Edit. Page 614 (left): Carolyn A. McKeone/Photo Researchers. Page 614 (right): Jeff Greenberg/Photo Researchers. Page 617: Michael Newman/Photo Edit. Page 621: Jennie Woodcock/Reflections P./Corbis. Page 623: Lawrence Migdale/Photo Researchers. Page 624: © Laura Dwight Photography. Page 625: M. Sherif, O.J. Harvey, B. Jack White, William R. Hood, Carolyn W. Sherif, photograph p. 103 from the Robbers Cave Experiment, ©1988 by Muzafer Sherif, Wesleyan University Press reprinted by permission of the University Press of New England. Page 629: Gallant/The Image Bank/Getty Images. Page 632: Richard Hutchings/Photo Researchers.

Author Index

Subject Index